Michigan
Geography
and Geology

Randall Schaetzl
Editor in Chief
Michigan State University

Joe Darden
Associate Editor
Michigan State University

Danita Brandt
Associate Editor
Michigan State University

With assistance from Richard Groop and Mark Finn

Custom Publishing

New York   Boston   San Francisco
London   Toronto   Sydney   Tokyo   Singapore   Madrid
Mexico City   Munich   Paris   Cape Town   Hong Kong   Montreal

**Pearson
Custom Publishing**
is a division of

www.pearsonhighered.com

ISBN 10: 0-536-98716-5
ISBN 13: 978-0-536-98716-7

Contents

iii

4   Paleozoic Environments and Life (S. LoDuca)   **40**

5   The "Lost Interval": Geology from the Permian to the Pliocene (M.A. Velbel)   **60**

List of Authors and Contributors

Randall Schaetzl, Editor in chief and physical geography editor
Department of Geography and Department of Geological Sciences, Michigan State University

Danita Brandt, geology editor
Department of Geological Sciences, Michigan State University

Joe Darden, human geography editor
Department of Geography, Michigan State University

Richard Groop, cartography editor
Department of Geography, Michigan State University

Mark Finn, cartographer, GI Scientist and graphics production
Department of Geography, Michigan State University

John Anderton
Department of Geography, Northern Michigan University

Jeffrey Andresen
State Climatologist and Department of Geography, Michigan State University

Alan Arbogast
Department of Geography, Michigan State University

Ted Batterson
Department of Fisheries and Wildlife, Michigan State University

Jean Battle
US Army Corps of Engineers, Coos Bay, OR

David Beede
Department of Animal Science, Michigan State University

William Blewett
Department of Geography–Earth Science, Shippensburg University of Pennsylvania

Ted Bornhorst
A.E. Seaman Mineralogical Museum, Michigan Tech University

Daniel Brown
School of Natural Resources and Environment, University of Michigan

Donald Christenson
Department of Crop and Soil Sciences, Michigan State University

George Cornell
Native American Institute, Michigan State University

Don Dickman
Department of Forestry, Michigan State University

Kaz Fujita
Department of Geological Sciences, Michigan State University

Joelle Gehring
Michigan Natural Features Inventory, Michigan State University

Reuben Goforth
Department of Forestry and Natural Resources, Purdue University

Jay Harman
Department of Geography, Michigan State University

William Harrison III
Department of Geology, Western Michigan University

Alan Holman
Department of Anthropology, Michigan State University

Jerome Hull
Department of Horticulture, Michigan State University

Christina Hupy
Department of Geography and Anthropology, University of Wisconsin–Eau Claire

Joseph Hupy
Department of Geography and Anthropology, University of Wisconsin–Eau Claire

A.J. Jacobs
Department of Sociology, East Carolina University

Kevin Kincare
US Geological Survey, Reston, VA

Larry Lankton
Department of Social Sciences, Michigan Tech University

Grahame Larson
Department of Geological Sciences, Michigan State University

Larry Leefers
Department of Forestry, Michigan State University

Kenneth Lewis
Department of Anthropology, Michigan State University

Steve LoDuca
Department of Geography and Geology, Eastern Michigan University

William Lovis
Department of Anthropoplogy and the MSU Museum, Michigan State University

David Lusch
Department of Geography, Michigan State University
Remote Sensing and GIS Research and Outreach Services, Michigan State University

Jacob McCarthy
Department of Animal Science, Michigan State University

George Merk
Department of Geological Sciences, Michigan State University

Joseph Messina
Department of Geography, Michigan State University

Sarah Nicholls
Department of Community, Agriculture, Recreation and Resource Studies, Michigan State University
Department of Geography, Michigan State University

Kevin Patrick
Department of Geography and Planning, Indiana University of Pennsylvania

Dale Rozeboom
Department of Animal Science, Michigan State University

Richard Santer
Ferris State University

Norm Sleep
Department of Geophysics, Stanford University

Amanda Sollman
Department of Animal Science, Michigan State University

Lawrence Sommers
Department of Geography, Michigan State University

Morris Thomas
Department of Geography, Michigan State University

Michael Velbel
Department of Geological Sciences, Michigan State University

Igor Vojnovic
Department of Geography, Michigan State University

Darryl Warncke
Department of Crop and Soil Sciences, Michigan State University

William Welsh
Department of Geography and Geology, Eastern Michigan University

Julie Winkler
Department of Geography, Michigan State University

Lois Wolfson
Department of Fisheries and Wildlife, Michigan State University

Catherine Yansa
Department of Geography, Michigan State University

Tom Zabadal
SW Michigan Research and Extension, Michigan State University

Preface and Acknowledgments

The use and application of geographic knowledge is commonplace in workplaces and schools of all kinds—in Michigan and elsewhere. Michigan's geography and geology are subjects taught across the state, and are commonly a focus of elementary education at the fourth grade level. Most Colleges and Universities in Michigan also have a stand-alone course devoted to one or the other, or both.

For many years in the 1970's through the 1990's, Dr. Harold "Duke" Winters taught the Geography of Michigan at Michigan State University (MSU). He used a spiral-bound, mimeographed coursepack as his only text resource, because, even then, the few textbooks available to him were either not suitable, or dated. In the 1990's, after Dr. Winters' retirement, Professor Randall Schaetzl took over the class, and renamed it the Geography of Michigan and the Great Lakes Region (GEO 333). Still faced with the textbook dilemma, he helped create the GEO 333 web site (http://www.msu.edu/geogmich), which has stood as a valuable resource on Michigan for not only the MSU community but for educators and inquisitive people throughout the upper Midwest. Despite the thorough nature of the web site, it is not a book, and nothing can quite compare to a book. Students found it useful, but intimidating. They had a difficult time navigating it. They wanted a book.

Likewise, geology instructors were struggling with the lack of a college-level text devoted to our state. Although a classic text, Dorr and Eschman's (1970) *Geology of Michigan* was getting dated. The wealth of new geologic information amassed in the post-plate tectonics era was lacking from the book, as was information about the major hydrocarbon finds of the late 20th century in the state.

With that in mind, in 2004 Professor Schaetzl formed a team of editors from within the MSU faculty—Professors Joe Darden and Richard Groop from Geography, and Danita Brandt from Geosciences. Together, they developed an outline of what a comprehensive, college-level text on the Geography and Geology of Michigan should contain. The book was divided into logical sections on geology, physical geography and human/historical geography, and assigned to editors Brandt, Schaetzl, and Darden, respectively. Groop became the cartographic consultant, and Schaetzl took on editor-in-chief duties. Dozens of authors were contacted, generally with the notion that the "state's expert" on each chapter topic should be given the right of first refusal. In most cases, it was an easy sell. All recognized the need for such a book. Writing began in earnest in 2004, and by the fall of that year the team was joined by Mark Finn, a Master's student in Geography at MSU, who became our graphics and GIS expert. His tremendous talents were soon recognized; we discovered how fortunate we were to have him on board. By early 2008, most of the work—writing, editing, revising, rewriting, constructing graphics, rewriting, proofing, etc.—was done, and shortly thereafter the manuscript was submitted to the publisher. *Michigan Geography and Geology* was finished.

This book is intended for the college student and those readers seeking current knowledge on Michigan's geography and geology. It is a collection of brief, review essays on a number of systematic and thematic topics on Michigan's physical and cultural resources—typical of a regional geography/geology treatise. Each chapter has a list of selected references, to allow the reader to move beyond what is written here, into a larger literature. Students and readers of the book should be especially pleased with the high quality graphics in the book. Many of the maps within this cover have never been published before, and the updates made to the many previously published maps and graphics were long overdue.

We heartily thank the many authors and reviewers who have contributed to this project. A full list of reviewers and acknowledgments is below. Richard Groop, Chairperson of Geography, diverted a wealth of funds to this project, on behalf of the Department. He also offered tremendous in-kind and unwavering moral support, without which this book might never have been completed. Scholars from most of Michigan's major universities are represented in the author list, which is as it should be.

It has now been nearly three decades since Professor Larry Sommers' classic (1984) text, *Michigan A Geography*, was published, and over 30 years since the publication of *Geology of Michigan*. Professor Sommers, a contributing author in *Michigan Geography and Geology*, began his writing for this book with his usual enthusiasm and drive, and worked for short while on the Introduction. Shortly before the book was finished, however, he passed away on August 3, 2007, at the age of 88. It is fitting that we dedicate this book to him, and hope that it stands a a testament to his lively spirit and love of geographic inquiry.

The following people served as chapter reviewers: Linda Barrett, Scott Beld, Ty Black, Bill Botti, Carlton Brett, Joe Calus, Bill Cambray, Renato Cerdena, Debra Che, Douglas Christensen, Pat Colgan, Tom Coon, Sid Covington, Brian Cronenwett, Paul Daniels, Frank Dennis, Tim Friggins, David Gillette, Steve Gold, Ron Goldy, Norm Grannemann, William Grvelding, Ed Hansen, Jay Harman, Don Holecek, Christina Hupy, Charles Hyde, John Jakle, Louise Jezerski, Paul Karrow, Alan Kehew, Zenia Kotval, Gene LaBerge, Pat LeBeau, Steve LoDuca, Walt Loope, Tom Lowell, John Luczaj, David MacLeod, Tim Maness, Chris Maydfa, Kim Medley, Dave Mickelson, Doreen Mobley, Marshall Mohney, Mike Moore, Chuck Nelson, Fred Nurnberger, Dave Patton, Larry Pedersen, Rolf Peterson, Karen Potter-Witter, Frank Quinn, Karl Raitz, Karen Renner, Bernie Rink, Curtis Roseman, Chris Schumacher, Paul Seelbach, Dick Skaggs, Pat Soranno, Carol Swinehart, Larry Taylor, Kurt Thelen, June Thomas, Richard Thomas, Linda Thomasma, Robert "Rocky" Ward, Kevin Wehrly, Doug Welsch, Keith Widder, Bernie Zandstra.

We also acknowledge the many other, behind the scenes people and organizations who have helped make this book a reality. Although we cannot list their precise contributions here, we greatly appreciate all they have done: Sarah Acmoody, Laura Akright, David Barnes, LeRoy Barnett, Robert Barron, Randy Bleich, Michelle Borkowski, Julie Brixie, Robert Burtch, Karel Bush, Norman Caldwell, F.W. Cambray, Douglas Christensen, Eric Clark, David Cook, Michael Creighton, Aureal Cross, Charles Cusack, John Demler, Lisa Eldred, James Farlow, Trent Faust, Joseph Fenicle, Kazuya Fujita, F. Gehring, Kirk Goldsberry, Mark Harvey, J. Alan Holman, Joyce, Marshall and Lisa Jacobs, Joe Jarecki, John Jaszczak, Matthew Klein, Dave Kleweno, David Kristovich, Neil Laird, Ronnie Lester, Carolyn Lewis, William Lovis, David Lusch, Erin Lynch, Kevin Mackey, Vince Matthews, Julie Meyerle, B. Noel, Jack Owens, Lina Patino, Aaron Pollyea, Jason Price, Robert Regis, Glen Richards, George Robinson, Christy Rybak, Annika, Heidi, and Maddi Schaetzl, Bill Schmidt, Amber Schultz, Duncan Sibley, L.L. Sloss, Seth Stein, Helen Taylor, Corey Teitsma, James Trow, Aric and Paul Velbel, Jean-Marie Vianney, David Westjohn, E.H.T. Whitten, and the folks at Michigan Natural Features Inventory.

Introduction: Defining the State of Michigan

Randall J. Schaetzl, Richard Santer and Lawrence Sommers

What makes Michigan so special may be not only what actually is here—an inventory of what is within its borders (Table 1.1)—so much as the unique and complex ways that the physical and cultural resources *intertwine*. The interwoven patterns that Michigan's cities, farms, lakes, roads, hills, rivers, factories, rocks, animals, and forests make on the landscape are a mosaic that, on first view, defies explanation. But, in fact, explanation is possible and it is an exciting and challenging endeavor. Geographers continually attempt to document and explain this spatial diversity—its patterns, causes and consequences; this book is but a record of one such attempt. In this book, we holistically examine the physical and cultural, modern and historical, natural and human-made resources of the state of Michigan, with its key location within the Great Lakes region. The chapters that follow contain hundreds of generalizations, details, examples, linkages and explanations of what lies within and beyond the state borders, as Michigan is not an isolated political unit. This book is, therefore, an attempt to bring much of what encompasses—literally what *defines*—the state of Michigan together.

■ Importance of the Great Lakes

Michigan's nickname is the *Great Lake State*, and rightfully so. The name Michigan is derived from the Native American (Algonquin) words *Michi* (great, large) and *gama* (lake or waters). The word "Michigan" appeared on a French map as early as 1681 as Lac de Michigani du Illinois, today's Lake Michigan (Karpinski 1931, 99).

Our state borders on the inland waters of four of the world's Great Lakes—Michigan, Huron, Superior, and Erie—each of which has a colorful geologic and maritime history, and which are of great importance to our economy (see Chapter 14). Michigan has over 5,100 km of shoreline on these four Great Lakes—more than any other state except Alaska. We also lay claim to 183 named bays (Table 1.1). Approximately 99,000 km² of Great Lakes' waters lie within Michigan's borders. The commodities we produce flow continually through this inland waterway, and our climate is impacted by these waters daily. We may not see or think about the Great Lakes often, but they impact our lives continually. How the lakes fit into Michigan's geography is a theme that is featured throughout this book.

Since statehood, it has been traditional for publishers, cartographers and graphic artists to illustrate Michigan by only its Lower Peninsula on maps of our state, and recently by its two major peninsulas, placing undue emphasis on the land portion of the state and giving the implication that the Great Lakes shore is the real political "edge" of the state of Michigan. But our borders are not at the shore, but far out, within the Great Lakes. Leaving this water area out, on maps (and in our minds), omits almost 40% of Michigan's total territory of 250,736 km². Recent efforts at illustrating the importance of the Great Lakes to Michigan's peoples and economy have, therefore, been directed toward ensuring that the current maps of Michigan show the state outline as *including* the Great Lakes (Plate 1). Viewing the state map in this way changes the familiar shape of Michigan from two separate land peninsulas to a more water-dominated shape, while retaining the recognition of the "pleasant peninsulas" that is part of our state motto. Such a

TABLE 1.1   The numbers of major physical and political features in Michigan

83 Counties

1245 Civil and Charter Townships (134 duplicate names)

1339 Cities, Towns and Villages (3 duplicate names)

57 Intermediate School Districts

514 Public School Districts

11 named Peninsulas[1] (Keweenaw, Huron/Aura, Moran, DeTour, Stonington, Garden, Leelanau, Old Mission, Thumb, Woodtick, Lost)

183 named Bays on the Great Lakes and connecting waters (11 duplicate names)

348 named Islands in the Great Lakes and connecting waters (see Table 14.2)

1. The state motto (*Si Quaerus Peninsulam Amoemam Circumspice*), literally means, "If you seek a pleasant peninsula, look about you." The peninsulas listed, of course, jut out from Michigan's main peninsulas: the Upper and Lower Peninsulas.

map representation of Michigan emphasizes the importance of water and the Great Lakes themselves to Michigan's population, ecology, climate, agriculture, and image.

With all this water comes a plethora of islands. There are over 350 named islands in the Great Lakes' part of Michigan and its connecting waterways—scattered primarily through the northern parts of the lakes and assigned to 19 counties (Tables 1.1, 14.2). Only a few are permanently inhabited, and many have substantial population and human activity only in the summer. Increases in development pressures will affect both the Detroit River connecting waterway and the northern islands, bringing new governmental and law enforcement challenges.

The best known and historically significant of these islands are Mackinac Island, Beaver Island and Isle Royale. For example, the British built Fort Mackinac on Mackinac Island in northern Lake Huron in 1780 after the French had surrendered the area to the British in 1761. In 1796, the United States gained control of the Island but it was recaptured by the British in 1812, only to be returned to the US in 1815. The fort was abandoned in 1894 and half of the island was then designated by the state of Michigan as Mackinac Island State Park. Today Mackinac Island is a statewide and nationwide tourist mecca. Contrast this picture with that of Isle Royale, an island gem National Park in Lake Superior (Chapter 24). It's distinctively wild, rugged and remote landscapes attract the adventuresome and nature-seekers. It is like nowhere else.

■ Michigan's boundaries

Land and water literally define the state of Michigan (Plates 1, 11). The following discussion, therefore, outlines how Michigan's state land and water boundaries were established (Table 1.2); these sagas constitute an interesting and truly *geographical* way to begin this book.

Michigan's international boundaries

The mid-Great Lakes' boundary with Canada was mainly settled by the 1783 Treaty of Paris, which ended the Revolutionary War and gave the land called New France to the fledgling United States. Details and other sections of the boundary were addressed in the treaties of 1814, 1842 and 1908 (Scheuer 1980, Carroll 2001, 2004). However, there have been several disputes as to the exact location of this boundary, taking several years to resolve.

Boundaries drawn up in the Treaty of Paris were, in large part, based on a map created by John Mitchell, a professional cartographer. His famous map of the region (Fig. 1.1) showed two large islands in Lake Superior: Isle Royale and Isle Phelipeaux (Dunbar and May 1995). Both were given to the US, although Isle Philipeaux was later shown not to exist. However, because both islands were shown centrally located in the Lake, according to the Mitchell Map, it apparently made sense to the negotiators of the time to award them both to the US, even though Isle Royale was later seen to be much closer to Canada (then a colony of Great Britain) than to the US and present-day Minnesota (Fig. 1.2).

TABLE 1.2 The primary documents involved in Michigan's contemporary boundary locations, 1783–1973

1783–1908		International Treaties
	1783	Treaty of Paris
	1814	Treaty of Ghent
	1842	Webster and Ashburton Treaty
	1908	U.S.-Gt. Britian Demarcation Treaty (U.S. and Canada Water/Island borders)
1787		Congress Act under Articles of Confederation. Northwest Ordinance (Border descriptions for future states)
1802–1857		U.S. Congress Statehood Acts
	1802	Ohio (proviso line to include Maumee Bay-Toledo)
	1816	Indiana (10 miles north of NW Ordinance line)
	1818	Illinois (60 miles north of NW Ordinance line)
	1836	Michigan (Toledo strip created)
	1848	Wisconsin (Headwaters of Montreal River and main channels uncertain)
	1857	Minnesota (Pigeon River mouth "turning point" ambiguous)
1805		U.S. Congress Michigan Territorial Act (Describes border as in Northwest Ordinance)
1850 and 1908		Michigan Constitutions (Revised border description with Wisconsin)
1917		Michigan and Ohio legislatures Resolutions: August 10, 1917 Michigan Joint Resolution (Retracement and monumenting OH-MI border)
1926–1936		U.S. Supreme Court Decisions (Wisconsin-Michigan border segments)
1947		Interstate Compact Michigan PA 267–1947; MCL 2.201–208 (Minnesota-Michigan-Wisconsin border)
1973		U.S. Supreme Court—special Masters Report and Decision (Lake Erie boundary)

Two of Michigan's riverine boundaries with Canada—the Detroit and St Marys Rivers—were only vaguely defined by the Treaty of Paris, and finally completed by an Anglo-American Joint Commission, established by the Treaty of Ghent which ended the War of 1812. In the Detroit River lie four islands—Bois Blanc *aka* Boblo, Stony, Sugar and Fox (Carroll 2004; Fig. 1.3). These islands were only a few tens of meters from the much larger and American-controlled Grosse Isle, and were to be assigned to either the US or Canada, based on the Commission's recommendations. Both sides were mainly concerned with the strategic military importance of the islands. The War of 1812, fresh in everyone's minds, had made it clear that Detroit was an important strategic location for any potential US invasion of Canada, or vice versa. Additionally, the British in Canada valued Detroit (and other border locations) because of the contact it provided with Native Americans still in the US, to maintain friendly relations with them and cultivate an anti-American bias (Scheuer 1980). These feelings weighed heavily in the boundary negotiations involving the Detroit River, and the disposition of its islands. Each side assumed that islands would be fortified if they fell into the control of the other nation. Navigation on the Detroit River provided a second incentive to boundary negotiations, as the river had only three clear, navigable channels (Scheuer 1980). If the eastern channel was chosen as the boundary, all of the islands would go to the USA. Use of the western channel would bestow similar advantages to Canada (Great Britain). The middle channel—the deepest of the lot—would have given Bois Blanc Island to Britain and the other three to the US. Deadlock ensued, but rational minds won out, and the middle channel was agreed to as the US-Canadian boundary, providing that "no military works shall be erected on any of the islands." Stony, Fox and Sugar Islands were now officially in US hands and within Michigan's boundaries.

FIGURE 1.1   A portion of the Mitchell map of 1755—one of the first maps of the Great Lakes region, and a main source used for the delineation of Michigan's southern boundary. Source: US Library of Congress, public domain.

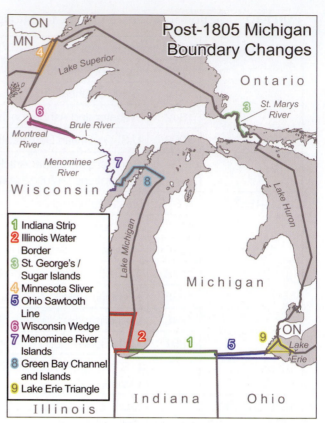

FIGURE 1.2   Changes made to Michigan's boundaries, both state and international, since 1805.

A similar situation existed in the St Marys River in the eastern Upper Peninsula (Fig. 1.4). The US had already taken possession of Drummond Island, near the mouth of the St Marys River. Unable to agree on the ownership of the remaining several large islands in the St Marys River, the matter was left undecided until the Webster-Ashburton Treaty of 1842. The language of this treaty is quite clear. The border "shall run into and along *the ship channel* between Saint Joseph and St. Tammany Islands, to the division of the channel at or near the head of St. Joseph's Island; thence . . . , around the lower end of . . . Sugar Island, and following the middle of the channel which divides (it) from St. Joseph's Island; thence, up the east Neebish channel, nearest to St. George's Island, through the middle of Lake George; thence, west of Jonas' Island, into St. Marys River, to a point in the middle of that river. . . ." The configuration of that boundary, interestingly enough, does not coincide with the current, normal shipping channel.

Michigan also has an international and a state boundary (with Minnesota) at the NW end of Lake Superior. In 1842, the International Boundary was agreed to be placed at the Pigeon River, extending from Lake Superior to the Pigeon River mouth proper (Figs. 1.2, 1.4). However, a long, narrow point of land, i.e., Pigeon Peninsula, juts out from the river mouth on its southern side. Drawing the Michigan-Minnesota boundary directly south from the river mouth, rather than from the end of the Pigeon Peninsula, i.e., Pigeon Point, would have left the eastward end of this peninsula within Michigan, based on its 1836 statehood act which described the Michigan border as the place where International Boundary "last touches Lake Superior." For several years, therefore, the ownership of this land was in doubt. To solve this dilemma, in 1947, an interstate Boundary Compact set the *turning point* of the line farther out, into the Lake, beyond Pigeon Point and away from the river mouth (Santer 2005; Fig. 1.4). This act gave Michigan no further claim to the end of Pigeon Point and a sliver-shaped water area within Lake Superior, relinquishing this area to Minnesota (Table 1.2).

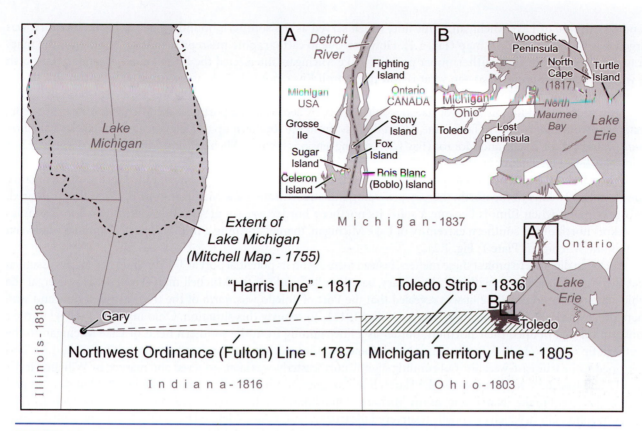

FIGURE 1.3   The southern part of Michigan, illustrating the various lines associated with boundary disputes in this area, and showing the location of the Toledo Strip.

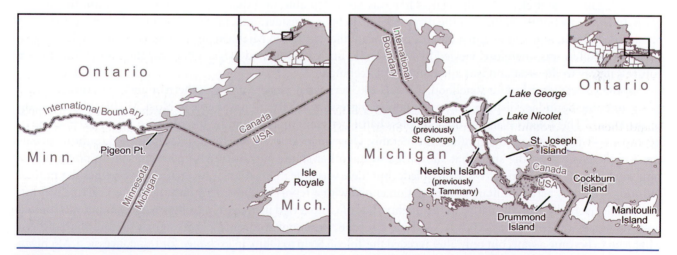

FIGURE 1.4   The international boundary as it currently exists along Pigeon Point and the St Marys River.

Michigan's southern boundary

On the south, Michigan's boundaries form a series of straight line segments (Plate 1). The story behind these boundary lines begins when Congress enacted the Northwest Ordinance of 1787, outlining the Northwest Territories (Chapter 28). This legislation mandated that a new state (or states) would have an east-west boundary running "through the southerly bend or extreme of Lake Michigan." This line, which served as the southern boundary of Michigan Territory, was largely based on the Mitchell map (Fig. 1.1). However, due to cartographic misrepresentation, a line on this map, drawn due east from the southernmost point of Lake Michigan, intersected the International Boundary far north of where it actually should have—in what is now the Detroit River, not Lake Erie as intended. Thus, use of this line as a boundary would have, in theory, given to Ohio all the ports on Lake Erie, especially the important port at Toledo. Similarly, Indiana and Illinois (not yet states) would have been deprived of a port on Lake Michigan. Later, more correct, maps would show that, in fact, a line drawn due east from the southern tip of Lake Michigan intersects Lake Erie *south* of the ports of Toledo and Monroe (Fig. 1.3), creating tensions between Michigan and Ohio. The use of the Mitchell map (Northwest Ordinance line) as a state border was, obviously, fraught with problems and destined to change.

When Indiana presented itself for admission to the union in 1816, Congress moved the Northwest Ordinance line 10 miles (16 km) to the north, thereby providing Indiana with the Lake Michigan port of Gary, that it desired. Two years later, when Illinois became a state, its northern border was set at 42°, 30' N latitude, about 60 miles (96.6 km) north of the southern extremity of Lake Michigan, thereby forming a mid-lake, water boundary between Illinois and Michigan (Plate 1; Fig. 1.2).

Michigan did little to protest these matters, instead focusing on its potential port at Toledo. Ohio had always assumed that the Port of Toledo was within its boundary, based on its "read" of the Mitchell map (Fig. 1.1). However, at the Ohio state convention in 1802, it was revealed that the Port of Toledo was *north* of the true east-west line, and was, therefore, technically in Michigan Territory (Miller 1911). To remedy this situation, Ohio inserted a clause in their constitution that defined their northern border as a line running from the southern bend of Lake Michigan to the southern tip of the Woodtick Peninsula, at North Cape, near Toledo, leaving that key port within Ohio (Fig. 1.3). This line, no longer a true east-west line but running slightly northeasterly, was later surveyed and marked by William Harris in 1817 and has come to be known as the Harris line. Congress admitted Ohio to the union in 1802 but did not give its official consent to the "Harris line" as the Michigan-Ohio boundary. In response, Michigan countered with an 1818 survey by John Fulton, which essentially resurveyed the true east-west line as defined by the 1787 Northwest Ordinance. After measuring the line eastward from Lake Michigan to Lake Erie, Fulton found that the Ohio boundary was, indeed, *south* of the mouth of the Maumee River, theoretically giving Toledo to Michigan. The disputed region between the Harris and Fulton lines, 8–13 km wide and 1,210 km² in area, came to be known as the "Toledo Strip" (Fig. 1.3).

Michigan made it clear that the Harris line was not acceptable, and that it owned the land within the Toledo Strip. Indeed, most of the settlers in the disputed Toledo Strip considered themselves Michiganders. A railroad had already been built, and a large canal had been planned, that started in Michigan and terminated at Toledo. To give this port to Ohio was, therefore, viewed by Michigan as unreasonable and illegal. Ohio saw the port at Toledo as a future gateway to the west and was adamant about keeping it.

In 1833 Michigan asked for statehood, using its 1805 territorial version of the southern boundary. Largely because of the ongoing boundary dispute, however, Ohio's congressional delegation was able to block Michigan's admission to the Union. The Toledo War—as this bloodless battle between Michigan and Ohio over the Toledo Strip came to be known—would heat up the conflict considerably. Over the next few years, both states instituted criminal penalties for citizens within the strip that submitted to the other state's authority. Militias were sent to positions on opposite sides of the Maumee River near Toledo, but there was little interaction between the two sides besides mutual taunting. The only actual military confrontation ended with a report of shots fired into the air, but no one was hit.

Politics, actually, won the battle, as the mighty state of Ohio levied its weight in Congress. Legislation was drafted and Michigan was forced to accept it. On June 15, 1836, President Andrew Jackson signed the bill that allowed Michigan to become a state, but only after it ceded the Toledo Strip to Ohio. In exchange for this concession, Michigan would be granted the western 3/4 of the Upper Peninsula (the portion of the Upper Peninsula east of the northernmost extremity of Lake Michigan had already been included within its territorial boundaries). This act has come to be known as the "Toledo Compromise." At the time, it appeared that Ohio had clearly won the battle, as the UP was considered a worthless, swampy wilderness of "perpetual snow," fit only for bears and Indians. The vast mineral riches of the land, unknown of until the discovery of copper (Chapter 12) and iron (Chapter 11) in the 1850's, would make Michigan the real winner in the end.

But the story was not over. By 1914, North Cape, at the tip of the Woodtick Peninsula in Maumee Bay, and the land terminus for the Harris line (Fig. 1.3), had eroded considerably northward, leaving its monument (set there, earlier, by surveyors) somewhere at the bottom of Lake Erie. To forestall another Toledo War, the Michigan and Ohio governors (Ferris and Willis) agreed to a joint resurvey and monumenting endeavor, from the Indiana border to the Lake Erie shore. The survey party was placed under the field direction of S.S. Gannett, a US Geological Survey geographer and engineer. To "wage peace" in placing the 70 five-foot (1.5 m) tall granite posts a mile (1.6 km) apart, the surveyors varied from a straight line to line segments, based on the understanding of local landowners as to where the border lay (Santer 1990). Thus, today the Michigan-Ohio border is somewhat saw-toothed.

Left for further dispute was the tip of the Lost Peninsula at the southern end of Maumee Bay, and the Lake Erie water border (Michigan Geological and Biological Survey 1916; Fig. 1.3). Thus, in 1973, another prolonged challenge with Ohio resulted in Michigan losing a claim to about 388 km² in Lake Erie (Fig. 1.2). The dispute arose out of the use of the word "northeast" in the 1836 statehood act. Michigan asserted that its border continued to extend *northeasterly* along the Harris line to the International Boundary, out in the Lake. (Recall that the Harris line was not really a due east-west line, but in actuality ran slightly northeasterly.) Ohio claimed that the boundary turned at North Cape, just offshore, and then ran along a true northeast (45°) bearing, through the lighthouse on Turtle Island (Fig. 1.3). In the end, Ohio won this legal battle, on the basis that 19th century dictionaries defined "northeast" as halfway between north and east (Santer 2005). Thus, Michigan lost its rights to a triangle-shaped area of Lake Erie and the bottomland resources and relics therein (Santer 2005). However, Michigan retained its ownership of Point Place at the tip of the Lost Peninsula—within the state of Michigan but the only land connection to it is through Toledo.

Michigan's northern and western boundary

In the 1920's and 1930's Michigan unsuccessfully attended to other boundary issues with Wisconsin. Thinking that a "continuous waterway" existed between Green Bay and Lake Superior, and that this would make a natural boundary between Wisconsin and Michigan, in 1840 surveyors were sent to mark the line. However, surveyors William Burt and Thomas Cram reported that no such waterway existed. Instead, the Menominee and the Montreal Rivers, on the eastern and western ends of this proposed boundary, were found not to meet at all, and that the Montreal River did not even originate in Lac Vieux Desert (Lake of the Desert), as was originally thought (Fig. 1.5). Lac Vieux Desert, the headwaters of the southward-flowing Wisconsin River, would instead become a key axis of the boundary. After some haranguing, when Wisconsin entered the union in 1848, the boundary was drawn up as a line from, "the mouth of the Menominee River; thence up the channel . . . to the Brule River; thence up . . . to Lake Brule; thence along the southern shore of Lake Brule in a direct line to the center of the channel between Middle and South Islands, in the Lake of the Desert; thence in a direct line to the head waters of the Montreal River; thence down the *main channel* of the Montreal River to the middle of Lake Superior" (US Congress 1846; Fig. 1.5).

This would ordinarily have been an ample description, except for an 1847 boundary survey by William Burt, and his interpretation of the nature and location of the Montreal River. The Montreal River has two main branches (Fig. 1.5), and the land between the Montreal River branches, rich in iron ore of the Gogebic Range (Chapter 11), was only one of the many spoils to be awarded the victor of this boundary battle. Burt had chosen the eastern branch of the Montreal River as the "main channel" and in so doing, essentially gave 932 km² of land to its south to Wisconsin (Kellogg 1917; Fig. 1.5). This "mistake" arose because of the vagueness of the term "head waters of the Montreal River" and the actual location of the Lake of the Desert. In 1850, in response to the uncertain survey situation, Michigan revised its new Constitution description to read, ". . . through the middle of the main channel of the said Montreal River to the head waters." After Wisconsin refused to participate in a joint survey in 1907, Michigan, in its 1908 Constitution, again reworded this boundary description to read, ". . . through the head waters thereof, thence in a direct line to the center of the channel between Middle and South Islands in the Lake of the Desert."

The dispute would actually fester so long that it landed both parties in the US Supreme Court as late as 1926 (Martin 1930). Michigan's claim was that the Lake of the Desert was, in fact, Island Lake, the source of the *western* branch of the Montreal River (Fig. 1.5), while Wisconsin claimed that it was Lac Vieux Desert, the French term for "Lake of the Desert." Wisconsin was, of course, correct in this assertion. However, if its claim held in court, Michigan stood to gain a tremendous amount of land (Fig. 1.5). In the end, in a friendly action before the US Supreme Court, it was announced that the boundary would be decided for Wisconsin, giving it the disputed, wedge-shaped piece of land (Fig. 1.2).

There were other disputes, and as with most water boundaries, they centered on islands (Hyde 1912, Santer 2005). First, there was the matter of the islands in the Great Lakes. The islands north of the Door Peninsula (Wisconsin) were to be divided between the two states based on the location of the "centre of the most usual ship channel of the Green Bay" and then to the "middle of Lake Michigan." The location of this boundary also had to eventually be decided in court, as the location of the ship channel had changed over time, as ships became larger (Fig. 1.5).

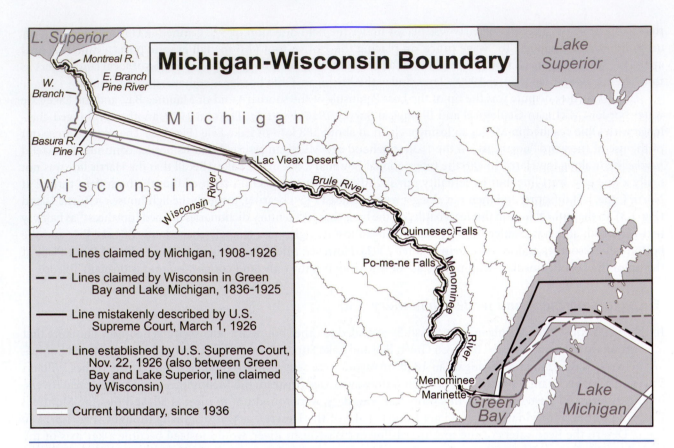

FIGURE 1.5   Key locations along the Wisconsin-Michigan boundary. The part of the map depicting the dispute between Michigan and Wisconsin over some islands in Green Bay, which were to be awarded to the state based on which side of the "most usual ship channel" they lay on, is also shown. After Martin (1930).

Next, the islands in the riverine boundaries had to be legally decreed to one state or the other. The original language of the MI-WI boundary defined it as being in the *middle* of the *main channel* of the Menominee River, but then, where is the main channel and what should be done with the >130 islands in the river? Is the main channel where the river flows widest, deepest or passes the greatest volume of water? As is obvious, there are always contentious issues with any water boundary.

In a series of protracted legal battles before the US Supreme Court (Martin 1930, 1938), Wisconsin largely walked away the victor on almost all of the boundary issues. And in a compromise agreement, Michigan and Wisconsin agreed that the islands in the Menominee River above Quinnesec Falls would go to Michigan, those below to Wisconsin (Miller 1911).

The status of Michigan's boundary description

Amazingly, when Michigan adopted its third Constitution in 1963, it omitted any mention of a state boundary description. It's true—Michigan has no written description incorporating all the post-1908 border changes discussed above! In recent years, attempts have been made by geographers and surveyors to have a modern, comprehensive description of the state's area placed in the Legislature's *Michigan Manual* (SB 1129–2006; SB 1130–2006). To date, this type of description has not materialized.

■ Michigan's land shape

Michigan is a land of peninsulas, largely because it is a land among big waters. Having two large peninsulas, both mitten-shaped, is unique for any interior land mass. These shapes are due largely to bedrock geology and its influence on the scour patterns of the many glaciers that have invaded the state (Chapter 17). In the Lower

Peninsula, weaker shales were scoured away, while resistant limestones and sandstones stood up as ridges and, if jutting into the water, peninsulas (Plate 6). Lakes Michigan, Huron and Erie all owe their shape and location to the underlying shale bedrock, and the scouring work of glaciers. The shape of the Upper Peninsula and Lake Superior is also indebted to glaciers and geology for its shape. Glaciers scoured away weaker sandstones and left the hard, basaltic lava flows, over one billion years old, to stand up as resistant ridges, e.g., the Copper Range atop the thumb-shaped Keweenaw Peninsula, and Isle Royale itself (Plate 6). The smooth, curving, Lake Superior shoreline in the eastern UP, and the Lake Michigan coast from Benton Harbor to Sleeping Bear Dunes National Lakeshore, mirror the strike of the underlying Paleozoic sandstones, shales and limestones (Plate 6). The Niagara dolostone, made famous for the waterfall that pours over it, is the hard, thick rock unit that is also responsible for the prominence of the Garden Peninsula (Michigan) and the Bruce Peninsula (Ontario), and for the existence of Drummond Island, Michigan and Manitoulin Island, Ontario. The Leelanau Peninsula, too, is held up by strong limestones. Even the Thumb signifies its acceptance of geology, for it, too, was formed by glacial scour along the strike of the hard Marshall Sandstone. Yes, geology, both hard rock geology and glacial processes and geomorphology, are key to understanding Michigan's geography. This, too, will be a theme repeated throughout the book.

■ Regional patterns reflecting the human element

Michigan is a state of great unevenness in terms of its economic development and productivity. Geographers study why these patterns have come to exist, and how they may affect other aspects of our state (Chapters 27, 34). The greatest core area of population and economic intensity is found in southeastern Lower Michigan, e.g., Wayne, Oakland and Macomb Counties. These counties contain 40% of the state's population, produce 49% of the value of manufacturing wages, and 38% of the value added. Wayne County alone contains 20% of the state's population. Greater Detroit is still the major core area of Michigan's manufacturing, wholesale and retail trade, and transportation, government and service activities. Lately, however, this core has become increasingly hollow in the center, as sprawl and urban decentralization have led to massive changes in the locations of the homes and workplaces of many of Michigan's inhabitants (Chapter 32). The rapidity and importance of sprawl, and its complexity of consequences, have led geographers to increasingly study the nature and impacts of land use change on our state, nation and world (Chapter 29).

Southern Michigan is quite different from the "up north" areas, and the UP. Where does the northwoods begin, and the agrarian and industrial south end? Many geographers have traditionally drawn this line roughly from Muskegon to Bay City. However, we now realize that such a line may bend northward, through Clare, to Tawas City, following major landform, soil, forest and climate boundaries. South of this line are most of our major cities, universities and especially our best agricultural areas with their fertile soils and nearness to markets (Chapters 36–39). To the north are found woods, hills, waters, clean air, trendy and interesting communities, great golf and water sports, and overall, many more places that we consider "natural" (Chapters 35, 40, 41). For this reason, many people vacation or own second homes in northern Michigan.

Michigan's agricultural product inventory is a long one. We rank first, second or third on many important agricultural commodities, such as cucumbers, tart and sweet cherries, pickles, dark red, cranberry, navy and black turtle beans, fresh market carrots, celery, processed asparagus, blueberries, red potatoes, potato chips, Easter lilies, Christmas trees and apples! Agriculturally, Michigan is the second most diverse state in the US, behind only California. This diversity results from our varied climates, especially our notable lake effect, and soils, all set at a latitudinal location that allows for the growth of commodities with northerly and/or southerly affinities. If one examined no aspect of Michigan's geography other than agriculture, our diversity would still be evident, for agriculture is at the apex of so many other cultural, economic and physical factors (Chapters 36–38).

■ This book, this state

There are few states whose geography is so interesting, diverse and challenging. What a pleasure and privilege it is to not only live amidst our peoples, forests, waters, and weather, but also to be able to study and write about it. In this book we lean and build upon the knowledge of our predecessors, both in published form (Dorr and Eschman 1970,

Sommers 1977, 1984, Eichenlaub et al. 1990, Santer 1977, 1993, Dunbar and May 1995, Dickman and Leefers 2003) and also through years of professional contact. And we embrace the new data at our fingertips—data they did not have. We hope that our meager effort at embracing Michigan's geographic features and diversity will help us all to learn more about Michigan and understand and appreciate it better.

Literature Cited

Carroll, F.M. 2001. A Good and Wise Measure. The Search for the Canadian-American Boundary, 1783–1842. University of Toronto Press, Toronto. 462 pp.

Carroll, F.M. 2004. The search for the Canadian-American boundary along the Michigan frontier—1819–1827. Michigan Historical Review 30:7–104.

Dickman, D.I. and L.A. Leefers. 2003. The Forests of Michigan. University of Michigan Press, Ann Arbor. 297 pp.

Dorr, J.A. Jr. and D.F. Eschman. 1970. Geology of Michigan. Univ. of Michigan Press, Ann Arbor. 476 pp.

Dunbar, W.F. and G.S. May. 1995. Michigan A History of the Wolverine State. Wm. B. Eerdmans Publ. Co., Grand Rapids, MI. 769 pp.

Eichenlaub, V.L., Harman, J.R., Nurnberger, F.V., and H.J. Stolle. 1990. The Climatic Atlas of Michigan. Univ. Notre Dame Press, Notre Dame, IN. 165 pp.

Hyde, C.C. 1912. Notes on rivers as boundaries. The American Journal of International Law 6:901–909.

Karpinski, L.C. 1931. Bibliography of printed maps of Michigan 1804–1880. Michigan Historical Commission, Lansing, MI. 539 pp.

Kellogg, L.P. 1917. The disputed Michigan-Wisconsin boundary. Wisconsin Magazine of History 1:304–307.

Martin, L.W. 1930. The Michigan-Wisconsin boundary case in the supreme court of the United States, 1923–1926. Annals of the Association of American Geographers 20:105–163.

Martin, L.W. 1938. The second Wisconsin-Michigan boundary case in the supreme court of the United States, 1932–1936. Annals of the Association of American Geographers 28:77–126.

Michigan Geological and Biological Survey. 1916. Report of the director and report on retracement and permanent monumenting of the Michigan-Ohio boundary. Publication 22, Geological Series 18. 225 pp.

Miller, G.J. 1911. The establishment of Michigan's boundaries: A study in historical geography. Bulletin of the American Geographical Society 43:339–351.

Santer, R.A. 1977. Michigan Heart of the Great Lakes. Kendall/Hunt, Dubuque, IA. 364 pp.

Santer, R.A. 1990. Waging peace. Michigan History Magazine Nov-Dec: 26–31.

Santer, R.A., 1993. Geography of Michigan and the Great Lakes Basin. Kendall/Hunt, Dubuque, IA. 422 pp.

Santer, R.A. 2005. Michigan border changes since 1837. Chronicle of the Historical Society of Michigan 27(4):26–27, 34.

Scheuer, M.F. 1980. From the St. Lawrence to Lake Superior: Peter Buell Porter, the Anglo-American Joint Commission of 1816–1822 and the Charting of the Canadian-American Boundary. M.A. thesis, Carleton Univ., Ottawa.

Sommers, L.M. 1977. Atlas of Michigan. Michigan State Univ. Press, East Lansing. 242 pp.

Sommers, L.M. 1984. Michigan A Geography. Westview Press, Inc., Boulder, CO. 254 pp.

United States Congress. 1836. Michigan Enabling Act. June 15, 1836.

United States Congress. 1846. Wisconsin Enabling Act. August 6, 1846.

Further Readings

Gilpin, A.R. 1970. The Territory of Michigan, 1805–1837. Michigan State University Press, East Lansing. 234 pp.

Parkins, A.E. 1918. The Historical Geography of Detroit. Michigan Historical Commission, Lansing. 356 pp.

2

Geology: Introduction and Overview

Danita Brandt

■ Introduction

Michigan's geology—its minerals, rocks, structures and landforms—is the foundation upon which many of the major economic and recreational activities of the state rest. We extract water, oil, natural gas and brines from rocks. We mine and quarry them for limestone, salt, gypsum, coal, copper, iron, clay, sand and gravel. The beauty and serenity of our rocky shorelines, waterfalls and lakes inspire and awe us all. Michigan's geology is more than "just underfoot"; every rock tells a story. Therefore, we introduce this book on Michigan's physical and cultural features by starting at the beginning with Michigan's pre-history; a story that begins nearly four billion years ago in what is now the Upper Peninsula.

Soon after Michigan's statehood in 1837, the legislature appointed Douglass Houghton the first state geologist (Fig. 2.1). Houghton's work on the Precambrian rocks of the Upper Peninsula spurred mineral exploration there, such that by the middle of the 19th century copper was being mined from volcanic rocks and conglomerates in the Keweenaw Peninsula (Chapter 12) and iron mines had begun exploiting the banded iron formations of the Upper Peninsula (Chapter 11). In 1845, Houghton even reported finding gold in streams west of Marquette and near Ishpeming. In the Lower Peninsula, brines extracted from salt deposits in the Lower Peninsula stimulated the development of a chemical industry centered at Midland (Chapter 16). Petroleum was discovered in Michigan in 1886. Limestone, gypsum and shale provided the raw materials for Michigan's impressive lime and cement industries. Sand and gravel from glacial deposits made the aggregate business possible. Water—much of it very high quality—is found in abundance both in the surficial glacial deposits and the underlying sedimentary rocks

FIGURE 2.1 Douglass Houghton, Michigan's first state geologist. Courtesy of Bentley Historical Library, University of Michigan.

of Michigan, in addition to the stores of fresh water held in the glacially carved Great Lakes (Chapter 16). The philosopher Will Durant once said, "Civilization exists by geologic consent (subject to change without notice!)" and Michigan is a good illustration of this point. It is not that raw materials create civilizations, but that they make some of the conveniences that we associate with them possible, and provide the energy resources to make use of them.

The study of geology was, and is, conducted by geological surveys, at the national level by the US Geological Survey, and at the local level by the Michigan Geological Survey (now the Office of Geological Survey in the Department of Environmental Quality) and at many of Michigan's state colleges and universities. As with all sciences, service to society has been a major driving force in the development of the geological sciences. One might turn Durant's quotation around and say that "geology exists by society's consent" for no one could imagine spending the amount of time and money that has been expended on understanding of the history of the Earth if it was not also of practical, societal use.

■ Michigan's place in Earth history

The rocks of the geological record have been developed by a variety of processes over a long period of time; to read it one must understand these processes. Many of them can be observed in action at the surface today, e.g., erosion and deposition. Others require the acquisition and interpretation of data collected by indirect geophysical means, to decipher what is happening deep within the Earth. The concept of using observations that can be verified by others and explaining them by observable processes separates the scientific approach from other ways of interpreting the Earth.

Radiometric dates of Moon rocks and meteorites indicate that our solar system, including our home planet, is a mind-bending 4.6 billion years (Ga) old. No rocks of this age are preserved on Earth, however, due to the constant recycling of Earth's crust via plate tectonics. The oldest Earth materials currently known are 4.2 Ga old crystals of the mineral zircon (Zr_2SiO_4), preserved in ancient sedimentary rocks in Australia. These zircon crystals are evidence of an even older igneous *parent rock* from which they were weathered. In the northern hemisphere, the most ancient rock known is a 3.96 Ga metamorphic rock from northwestern Canada (Cloud 1988). Michigan's geologic history reaches back almost as far, about 3.5 Ga, to rocks originally formed from volcanic eruptions and tectonic plate collisions. The subsequent geologic record in Michigan reveals eons of sea-level rise and fall, development of coal swamps, arid uplands and most recently (geologically speaking) the multiple advances of Pleistocene glaciers.

■ Michigan's rocks and minerals

The outermost layer of the solid Earth, the *lithosphere* (Greek *lithos,* rock) is made of hard rock. Rocks are a mixture of different naturally occurring compounds called *minerals*. Only eight elements—oxygen (O), silicon (Si), aluminum (Al), iron (Fe), calcium (Ca), sodium (Na), magnesium (Mg) and potassium (K)—form 99% of the Earth's mass, and a handful of minerals (chief among them the silicates, which include quartz and feldspar) account for the bulk of the lithosphere.

Minerals that occur in economically important deposits in Michigan include iron and copper minerals in the Upper Peninsula, which were formed as the result of igneous and metamorphic processes, gypsum and halite (rock salt) in the Lower Peninsula, formed as the result of sedimentary processes, and quartz-rich sand, deposited over almost all of the state as the result of glacial processes. Michigan's minerals are beautifully cataloged in an encyclopedic monograph by the former curator of the University of Michigan's mineralogy collection (Heinrich 2004). An online listing of these minerals is available through the Michigan Department of Environmental Quality website (www.michigan.gov/deqogs).

All of the three major rock types are found in Michigan. *Igneous rocks*—literally "fire formed" (Latin, *igneus*)—originate as magma (molten rock) in the Earth's interior. They then form either *extrusively*, by cooling quickly at the Earth's surface, e.g., lava flows, or *intrusively*, by cooling slowly, deep within the crust. Extrusive igneous rocks are characterized by microscopic crystals, as the magma cooled so rapidly that the atoms did not have time to organize themselves into large crystals. Granite, a familiar intrusive igneous rock type, formed by slow cooling of magma at depth in the crust, which allows for the growth of crystals large enough to see with the unaided eye. Igneous rocks with a low silica content are referred to as *mafic*—a contraction of the two elements magnesium (Mg) and iron (Fe); they are made up mostly of olivine, pyroxene and plagioclase feldspar minerals and are generally dark in color, e.g., basalt and gabbro. Igneous rocks that are high in silica are referred to as *felsic*—a contraction of the names of the two minerals feldspar and silica; they are mostly made up of quartz, alkali feldspar and mica and are generally light in color, e.g., granite and rhyolite. In general, mafic rocks comprise the crust of the ocean basins whereas continental crust is composed of felsic rocks (Table 2.1).

Sedimentary rocks (Latin *sedimentum*, "to settle") form at the Earth's surface, from weathering and erosion of pre-existing rocks. This material—the sediments—may then be transported by streams, wind or ice and be deposited in a variety of settings where they may be *lithified* (turned into stone)—ultimately becoming sedimentary rocks. An important characteristic of sedimentary rocks is their layering, called *stratification*, that forms during deposition (Fig. 2.2).

TABLE 2.1   Michigan's major igneous rocks[1]

Aphanitic *Fine-grained crystals too small to see;* **Extrusive**	Rhyolite	Andesite	Basalt Example: Portage Lake Lava	
Phaneritic *Mineral crystals clearly visible to unaided eye;* **Intrusive**	**Granite** Example: Archean granites, western Upper Peninsula	**Diorite**	**Gabbro**	**Serpentinite** **Peridotite** **Pyroxenite** Example: Yellow Dog Peridotite

1: Quartz content decreases, and iron and magnesium contents increase, to the right.
After: www.michigan.gov/deqogs

FIGURE 2.2 Laminated (layered) sand near Waters, MI. Photo by R. Schaetzl.

TABLE 2.2 Michigan's major sedimentary rocks

A. Clastic sediments					
	Gravel	**Sand**	**Silt**	**Clay**	
Grain Size	Coarse grained, grains >2 mm diameter	Medium grained, grains 2 mm to 1/16 mm diameter	Fine grained, grains from 1/16 to 1/256 mm diameter—feels gritty	Very fine-grained, grains <1/256 mm diameter—feels smooth	
Rock name	Conglomerate	Sandstone	Siltstone	Shale Mudstone Claystone Clayshale	
Example	Copper Harbor Conglomerate	Marshall Sandstone	Saginaw Formation	Antrim Shale	
B. Physically or biologically precipitated sediments					
Composition	**Halite**	**Gypsum**	**Calcite**	**Dolomite**	**Quartz**
Rock name	Rock Salt	Rock Gypsum	Limestone	Dolostone	Chert
Example	Salina Group	Lucas Formation	Rogers City Limestone	Lucas Formation	Bois Blanc Formation

After: www.michigan.gov/deqogs

The three main types of sedimentary rock—sandstone, shale and carbonate (limestone)—are all found in abundance in Michigan, particularly in the Lower Peninsula and eastern Upper Peninsula (Table 2.2; Plate 5).

During weathering, some minerals do not alter chemically; quartz (SiO_2) is the best example of this. The grains may become smaller and smoother as they collide and abrade with one another, but their chemical composition stays the same. Quartz grains accumulate to form the common sand deposits seen on beaches and sand bars in Michigan streams. When the grains are cemented together, i.e., become *lithified*, the sedimentary rock sandstone is formed.

When the silicate minerals in igneous rocks, particularly feldspars, are affected by weathering at the earth's surface, they break down, chemically, into *clay minerals*. The potassium, sodium and calcium from the feldspars dissolve during weathering and are carried away in solution. Clay particles, being extremely small, tend to separate from sand grains during transportation, so that when a river enters a lake or the sea the larger sand grains drop out first, and the clays are carried further out, into deeper waters. Here, they may settle to form clay layers that, if lithified, become a sedimentary rock called shale.

The common elements that go into solution during weathering, mainly K, Na, Ca and Mg, are precipitated by a variety of processes in lakes and oceans. If the body of water evaporates faster than fresh water is being supplied, its salinity will go up and eventually the elements in solution will precipitate. This is how salt deposits were formed in the Michigan Basin (Chapter 4). Rocks formed in this way are termed *evaporites*. The most common evaporite mineral is sodium chloride—common salt (NaCl)—but chlorides and bromides of other elements can also form. Most of the world's chemical plants, including Dow Chemical Company in Midland, were originally sited near such deposits (Chapter 16), nature having done most of the work in separating the elements for us.

Calcium carbonate ($CaCO_3$) is extracted from seawater by a variety of animals, and some plants. These organisms use $CaCO_3$ in the form of the minerals *calcite* and *aragonite* to construct their shell or skeleton in the same way that we use calcium minerals to construct our bones and teeth. When the creatures die, their soft body parts decay, leaving the carbonate to accumulate into rocks we know as *limestone*. Collectively, limestone, and the related magnesium-bearing carbonate rock *dolostone*, are referred to as carbonate sedimentary rocks (Fig. 2.3).

Metamorphic rocks are those that have been literally "changed," by exposure to deep-seated, high temperatures and/or pressures. These changes occur as the result of (1) exposure to high heat, e.g., exposure to upwardly migrating molten rock can "cook" the rock into which it intrudes, causing *contact metamorphism*, and (2) and through the heat and pressure of plate collision, which deforms rocks over a much larger area and is referred to as *regional metamorphism*. Most metamorphic rocks represent the core of ancient mountains that have been exposed at the surface of the Earth through millennia of weathering, erosion and uplift of the crust as the mountain is worn away (Table 2.3).

Under metamorphism, the grains of quartz in sandstone can become welded together, forming *quartzite*. Clay minerals in shale may become *slates* or *schists*. Slate is finer grained than schist and is formed at lower temperatures. The grains of calcite and dolomite in carbonates become larger and the spaces between the grains obliterated, forming *marble*. When igneous rocks are metamorphosed, they, too develop new textures and minerals. When deformed at high temperatures, granite can develop banding and foliation, i.e., a preferred alignment of minerals, and be transformed into *gneiss*. The olivines and pyroxenes in mafic rocks can alter to amphibole and develop a schist-like appearance. Because these rocks were difficult to differentiate in the field, they were given the name *greenstone*—Michigan's state mineral. Granite gneiss and greenstone form an important part of the geology of the Upper Peninsula (Chapter 3).

FIGURE 2.3 Sugar Loaf, a famous Mackinac Island landmark. This prominent feature is composed of Mackinac breccia, a carbonate rock exposed on Mackinac Island and near St. Ignace. Photo by D. Brandt.

TABLE 2.3 Michigan's major metamorphic rocks

Texture	Rock Name	Diagnostic Features and Michigan Examples
Foliated *Rocks show a preferred orientation or segregation of mineral grains*	**Slate**	Fine-grained; minerals invisible to the naked eye; rock cleaves into thin, smooth-sided slabs Example: Siamo Slate
	Phyllite	Fine grained; mineral grains barely or not visible, soft sheen
	Schist	Medium grained; many minerals visible to the naked eye; high mica content imparts flakey texture (schistosity). Example: Michigamme Schist
	Gneiss	Coarse to medium grained; banded appearance from segregation of like minerals (gneissic banding). Example: Compeau Creek Gneiss
Nonfoliated *Coarsely crystalline, homogeneous texture*	**Quartzite**	Metamorphosed quartz sandstone; may show banding if impurities are present. Examples: Bessemer, Goodrich, Mesnard and Ajibic Quartzites
	Marble	Metamorphosed limestone or dolomite; may show banding if impurities are present. Example: Kona Dolomite

After: www.michigan.gov/deqogs

FIGURE 2.4
Precambrian-aged pillow basalts exposed just west of Marquette, MI. Photo by R. Schaetzl.

The bedrock geology of Michigan

The distribution of the bedrock types in Michigan reflects regional differences in geologic processes and history. The oldest rocks in Michigan are 3.5 Ga igneous and metamorphic rocks in the western Upper Peninsula, referred to as *basement* rock, and they, along with similar rocks in neighboring Ontario, form the ancient core of the North American continent (Chapter 3). These rocks formed through the paroxysms of tectonic plate collisions billions of years ago. For example, pillow basalts along U.S. Highway 41 just west of Marquette record the eruption of underwater volcanoes in what is now Michigan billions of years ago (Fig. 2.4).

Younger sedimentary rocks later accumulated on top of the basement rock in what is now the Lower Peninsula and eastern Upper Peninsula, from 500 Ma (million years ago) to 280 Ma (Chapter 4). These sediments were derived from erosion of ancient landscapes, including the ancestral Appalachian Mountains located hundreds of kilometers to the east (Fig. 4.2), and then transported and deposited in a slowly subsiding geologic basin. Because this geologic basin is centered on the Lower Peninsula of Michigan, it is referred to as the Michigan Basin. A similar structure, centered on a neighboring Midwestern state, is known as the Illinois Basin. The factors responsible for the formation of these basins are the subjects of on-going research.

The bedrock geology maps (Plates 5, 6) show the distribution of the shallowest bedrock in Michigan by their respective ages and lithologies. Most of these rock units are not exposed at the surface, but are covered by unconsolidated sediments, including sand, gravel, silt and clay, deposited during multiple advances and retreats of glaciers (Chapters 6, 17). The best places to find bedrock exposures are in the western Upper Peninsula, as well as along the shores of the Great Lakes, near some rivers, in roadcuts and in quarries. The "bull's eye" pattern that characterizes the bedrock geology maps of the Lower Peninsula (Plates 5, 6) reflects the underlying geologic structure of the bedrock. The layers of sedimentary rock in the Lower Peninsula are gently curved and stacked like nested cereal plates or bowls—this is the Michigan Basin. The distribution of the unconsolidated geologic deposits that overlie and cover most of Michigan's bedrock is shown on surficial geology maps (Plates 9, 10).

Stories encoded in rocks

Earth's geologic record is complex and incomplete, written over a period of 4.6 billion years. Michigan's geologic story is written in its rocks and fossils, and that story is "read" using basic geologic principles (below) that were codified in the 1500's (Fig. 2.5). In an undeformed sequence of sedimentary rocks, the lowest stratum (layer) is the oldest (*principle of superposition*). Rock layers are originally deposited conforming to the land surface (*principle of*

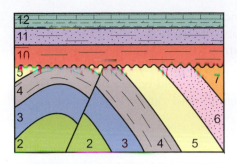

FIGURE 2.5 The principles of super-position, original horizontality and cross-cutting relations, which allow for a reconstruction of the sequences of geologic events. These principles are represented by this diagram as follows:
A. Sedimentary layers 2, 3, 4, 5, 6 and 7 were deposited sequentially (principle of superposition: oldest beds on the bottom). B. Folding of layers 2–7 (principle of original horizontality). C. Faulting of beds 2–7 (principle of cross-cutting relations). D. Erosion of beds 4, 5, 6 and 7 (principle of cross-cutting relations). E. Deposition of beds 10, 11 and 12. After Poort and Carlson (2005).

original horizontality), and will continue laterally until they thin or pinch out (*principle of lateral continuity*). A geologic feature that cuts across another is younger than the feature it cuts (*principle of cross-cutting relationships*), whereas a feature that is incorporated into another is older (*principle of included fragments*). Fossils are found in a definite and determinable order (*principle of faunal succession*).

These principles were the basis for the development of the geological time scale (Plate 3)—a hierarchy of time divisions, starting with dividing all of Earth history into three eons, the Archean and Proterozoic (together, formerly called the Precambrian Eon), and Phanerozoic. Eons are divided into eras, which are further divided into periods and epochs, although only the epochs of the Cenozoic Era are shown on Plate 3. Note that the eons, eras, periods and epochs are not of equal length. The actual ages of the named time periods were not known until the early 20th century, after the discovery of radioactivity and the application of this phenomenon to dating geologic materials. The importance of faunal succession in the construction of the timescale is evident in the names of eons and eras: Proterozoic literally means "before life" (*protero*, before; *zoic*, life) and reflects the lack of obvious fossils with easily preserved exoskeletons. The transition from the Proterozoic to the Phanerozoic (*phaneros*, visible) Eon is marked by the appearance of abundant "shelly" fossils. That the fossils change in a "definite and determinable order" is seen by the era nomenclature. The Paleozoic Era ("ancient life") is characterized by a large proportion of fossils that are extinct and have no direct descendents, e.g., trilobites. The Mesozoic Era ("middle life") is characterized by both fossils of extinct organisms (most famously, the dinosaurs) and groups that are still around today. In the Cenozoic Era, ("new life"), most fossil forms can be linked to a living relative.

The time scale we use today is an historical document reflecting the efforts of generations of geologists, mostly European (Harbaugh 1974). As a result, the period names make more intuitive sense to students of European geology. The Devonian, for example, is named for Devon, England, where rocks of this age are well exposed; the Cretaceous is named for the great chalk deposits (Latin *creta*, chalk) exposed along the White Cliffs of Dover, also in England. In North America, geologists have replaced the Carboniferous Period (named for the carbon, or coal-bearing, strata of that age in England) with the Pennsylvanian (North America's "coal age") and Mississippian Periods. The Mississippian Period is named for the river, not the state, particularly for the abundant limestone beds exposed along the Mississippi River south of St. Louis.

The geologic timescale is a living document and continues to evolve, thanks to the efforts of the International Stratigraphic Commission (ISC), the committee charged with settling questions pertaining to defining geologic units and demonstrating their time-equivalency, i.e., correlation. Most recently, the ISC decided that what most textbooks still call the Quaternary Period—from about 1.8 million years (Ma) ago to the present—did not merit status as a period, because at "only" 2 million years in length, it was by far the shortest period. Therefore, the Quaternary Period has been subsumed into the Neogene Period of the Cenozoic Era (Gradstein and Ogg 2004). In order not to create unnecessary confusion, however, we have elected to retain the Quaternary Period in Plate 3.

The vertical succession of Michigan's geologic units can be represented schematically as a stratigraphic column (Catacosinos et al. 2001; Plate 4). When describing rock units such as these, geologists use the terms *Group, Formation, Member and Bed* to describe a hierarchy of relationships between these units. A *Formation* is the fundamental unit that is mapped in the field; it may contain many different lithologies (rock types) but it is distinct from others above and below. For example, a vertical sequence of alternating sandstone and shale beds could be described as a *Formation* if it can be distinguished from a dominantly limestone unit above it and is thick enough to show up on a map drawn to a standard scale. Formations are given names that reflect their general rock type and the geographic area where the unit was first described, e.g., the Marshall Sandstone is a succession of sandstone beds exposed and initially described near Marshall, MI. Geologic units that contain a mixture of rock types, e.g., interbedded sandstones and shales, are given the designation Formation, as in the Saginaw Formation, which contains various beds of sandstone, siltstone, shale and coal. *Members* are identifiable units of a contrasting rock type within a formation, and a *Bed* describes a single, distinctive layer of rock bound above and below by rocks of another lithology. A succession of several formations that appear to have formed in a similar environment would be described as a *Group*, and a succession of several groups is collective referred to as a *Supergroup*. All these category names are proper nouns, and as such are capitalized.

■ Putting dates on geologic events

The physical relationship between strata and the fossils they contain allow us to construct a relative ordering of geologic events, e.g., sediment deposition, erosion, mountain building, and construct a geologic time scale. We use the term "relative time" scale because, at the time this framework was constructed, there was no way to put

FOCUS BOX: Radiometric dating

Some elements contain naturally occurring radioactive atoms, which are unstable and spontaneously give off atomic particles in order to reach a more stable state. The disintegration of these atoms into other, more stable forms is called radioactive decay. The decay of the uranium into non-radioactive lead is often used to calculate the age of rocks. In isotope terminology, uranium is referred to as the parent isotope and the decay product, lead, is the daughter isotope. The important characteristic about radioactive decay is that half of the parent atoms decay to the daughter atoms in a given period of time, known as the half life, and the half life of an element is constant. Therefore, if we know the half life and can measure the ratio of parent to daughter elements in a mineral, we can determine the age of the mineral. For example, let's say that we know that the half-life of a particular isotope is four million years, and when we analyze a sample of this mineral, we find that it contains 50% parent and 50% daughter isotopes. We would be able to conclude the crystal formed 4 million years ago, i.e., one half-life has gone by. If this mineral was allowed to decay for another half life (4 million years), half of the remain-

ing parent (50% of the original amount) would have decayed to the daughter and the ratio would be 25% parent/75% daughter isotopes.

Radiometric dating is actually more complex than this because of a variety of factors, e.g., the loss of parent or daughter isotopes from the crystal, which would introduce error into the calculations. It also requires careful choice of samples to analyze. Nonetheless, radiometric dating techniques have produced consistent results that have enabled us to put numbers on the geologic time scale (Plate 3).

Radiocarbon (^{14}C) dating is perhaps the most familiar but, as a consequence, possibly the most misunderstood isotope used in radiometric dating (see FOCUS BOX in Chapter 13). Because of its geologically short half-life of 5568 years, ^{14}C dating is useful for up to 70,000 years, which is applicable only to geologically very young material; it is used in dating archaeological sites, but of no use in determining the age of the Earth or dating most rocks. Other, more long-lived radioisotopes are used for these types of geological research.

Radioactive isotopes frequently used in radiometric dating of geologic materials

Radioactive parent	Stable daughter product	Currently accepted half-life values
Rubidium-87	Strontium-87	47.0 billion years
Thorium-232	Lead-208	14.1 billion years
Uranium-238	Lead-206	4.5 billion years
Potassium-40	Argon-40	1.3 billion years
Uranium-235	Lead-207	713 million years

exact numbers/ages on it. Early attempts to determine rock ages did so by estimating the time it would take to deposit thick sequences of sediments recorded in the stratigraphic section, or how long it would take the sea to reach its present salinity, assuming it was freshwater to begin with (Albritton 1984). An attempt was also made to calculate the age of the Earth on the basis of how long it would take to cool to its present temperature, assuming it had once been completely molten. However a truly numerical scale that had to wait for the discovery of radioactivity at the end of the 19th century and the construction of mass spectrometers in the 20th century. The method is simple in principle (see FOCUS BOX on previous page).

■ Driving the story—plate tectonics

Early maps that depicted the coastlines of the Americas and Africa elicited discussion on the similar shapes of the two land masses. This geometry gave rise to suggestions that they might represent a jigsaw pattern of continental edges that had drifted apart. In the early 20th century, the idea of *Continental Drift* as a way of explaining the distribution of the continents on the Earth's surface was brought to the attention of the geological community in two publications, one by Alfred Wegener in 1912, the other by Frank Taylor, who was also responsible for some of the early glacial mapping of Michigan (Taylor 1910). The idea met with much opposition in the geological establishment, because the proponents of continental drift did not have a physically reasonable mechanism by which to explain continental movement. Thus, the idea of continental drift lay moribund until the 1950's, when new technologies, particularly sonar and magnetic profiling of the ocean floor, made possible new discoveries on the topography, magnetic characteristics and age of the ocean crust and led to the development of a plausible mechanism for plate movement—sea-floor spreading (Oreskes 2003). This improved model for continental movement is called *Plate Tectonics* (Greek, *tektonikós* builder).

Plate tectonics theory is based on our understanding that the lithosphere is a relatively rigid shell about 100 km (60 miles) thick that has cooled from hotter material below. The lithosphere is segmented into seven major and several minor *tectonic plates* (Fig. 2.6). These plates diverge along the mid-oceanic ridge to form new ocean crust (Fig. 2.7), and converge by sinking back into the mantle at deep-sea trenches, also known as subduction zones, e.g., in the western Pacific (Fig. 2.8). Production of new lithosphere at divergent margins (also termed rifts or spreading centers) keeps pace with subduction at convergent margins to maintain a constant-radius Earth. A third type of plate margin, called a transform margin, allows one plate to move horizontally past another. The San Andreas fault zone is one of the best known examples of a transform margin.

Plate tectonics theory (see FOCUS BOX on page 21) is the principal geologic paradigm today because it ties together many disparate geological observations and relates them into a coherent whole. The topography of the ocean floor—mid-ocean ridges and deep-ocean trenches—is readily explained by plate tectonic theory as divergent-plate boundaries and convergent boundaries, respectively. Convergent plate boundaries are sites of active volcanism

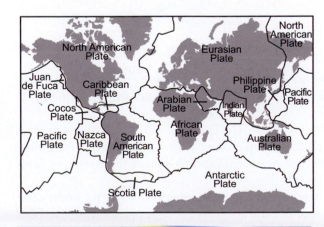

FIGURE 2.6   World map showing tectonic plate boundaries.

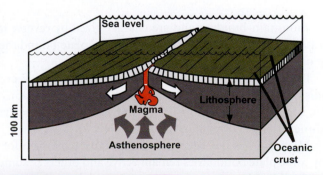

FIGURE 2.7   Diagram of a divergent tectonic plate boundary.

FIGURE 2.8 Diagram of the three different types of convergent tectonic plate boundaries. Source: Tarbuk and Lutgens (1999). Courtesy of Prentice Hall.

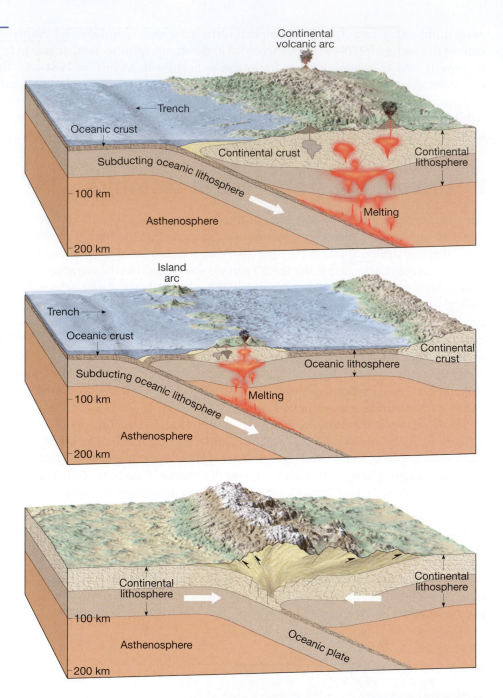

and mountain-building and are characterized by reverse faults related to this compression (Fig. 2.9), and by the formation of igneous intrusions. Divergent plate boundaries are sites of normal faults, related to extension or rifting of the crust, and basalt flows.

Plate tectonics is also the driving force in the rock cycle (Fig. 2.10). The heat and pressure involved in plate collisions produce the magmas that cool to form igneous rock. Deformation at plate margins forms metamorphic rocks and the ensuing uplift (mountain-building) drives the weathering and erosion of these rocks to form sediments and sedimentary rocks.

Michigan has not been the site of active tectonism for over a billion years. Geologists do not yet understand why some plate boundaries remain active and others become inactive, and not every geologic phenomenon has been explained by plate tectonics. Our understanding of plate tectonic theory, as with every scientific theory, will continue to evolve as new technologies make new kinds of observations possible.

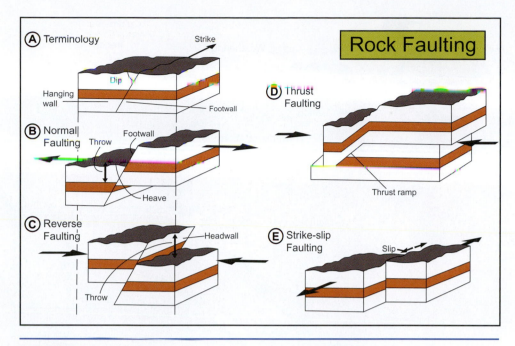

FIGURE 2.9 Major type of faults (reverse, normal, transverse) that occur in rocks. After Tarbuk and Lutgens (1999).

FOCUS BOX: "Just a theory!"

Plate tectonics is a theory, the highest status that a concept is given by scientists. Unfortunately, the common definition of "theory" translates to guess, conjecture or idea, and the use of a phrase that sets scientists' teeth on edge: "it's just a theory." All theories begin with an idea, but an idea evolves into a scientific theory through several stages of development that involve testing the theory's effectiveness in explaining natural phenomena. An idea becomes a possible explanation for understanding some phenomenon if it is supported by observations. At this stage, we refer to the possible explanation as a hypothesis (Greek *hypo*, under; *tithemi*, place). We place our observations under this idea, meaning we try to explain our observations using this idea. The next step in the evolution of idea to theory is to test it to see if our hypothesis holds under different circumstances. The most important thing about such tests is that they should be capable of demonstrating that the idea is wrong! One test for plate tectonics predicted that the age of the ocean floor should be younger at the oceanic ridges and become progressively older towards the continents. If this had turned not to be the case we would have had to rethink the whole idea, i.e., it was a test that could have negated the hypothesis. We say that the age pattern of the ocean floors is a proof of, or supports, the plate tectonic hypothesis—not the same as saying it is true. Scientists rarely if ever use the word "true." The word "prove" means to test; think of the expression "proving ground," where automobiles are tested. Hypotheses are not accepted on the basis of a single test, and the tests have to be repeatable by other scientists. Eventually, if a consistent pattern emerges—one that can be used to explain existing observations and to predict new ones—then the term theory will be applied to the hypothesis.

The plate tectonic concept met these criteria and is now the accepted theory of the way the physical Earth behaves. Science uses many theories to explain observations: atomic theory, electromagnetic theory and evolutionary theory, for example. Each of them have undergone rigorous tests and are now a useful part of scientific thinking.

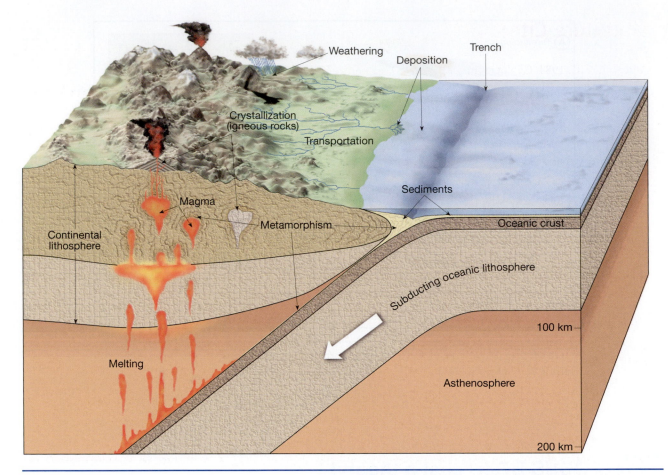

FIGURE 2.10   The rock cycle as it relates to plate tectonics. Plate tectonic processes provide the forces necessary for the transformation of the different rock types into other rocks. Source: Tarbuk and Lutgens (1999). Courtesy of Prentice Hall.

Overview of Michigan's geologic story

The following 11 chapters describe Michigan's geologic history and its importance to the citizens of the state. This history begins nearly 4 Ga, where these old rocks give evidence for a tectonically active Michigan during the Archean and Proterozoic Eons, including volcanic eruptions, mountain-building and an episode during which the proto-North American continent was nearly ripped apart (Chapter 3). By the end of the Proterozoic, tectonic activity in Michigan had ceased, and Michigan was covered by a succession of shallow, tropical seas until the end of the Paleozoic Era. The record of this sea-level rise and fall is left in a thick sequence of sedimentary rocks that were deposited in the slowly subsiding Michigan Basin (Chapter 4). The latest part of the Paleozoic Era, almost the entire Mesozoic Era, and much of the Cenozoic Era did not leave a physical geological record in Michigan; this "lost geologic interval" is the subject of Chapter 5. The most recent geologic deposits in Michigan, and indeed Michigan's modern topography, are a result of the repeated advance and retreat of huge continental ice sheets during the Pleistocene Epoch, better known as the *Ice Age* of the Cenozoic Era. Because of the geologic youth of this interval, the sediments, animals and plants that existed during that time are well-represented and well studied (Chapters 6, 7, 8 and 13). The geologic resources (oil, natural gas, iron and copper) that were critical to Michigan's economic development are the subjects of Chapters 10, 11 and 12. Interspersed with all this is a survey of the record of Michigan earthquakes, and a discussion of the potential for seismic hazards in Michigan (Chapter 9).

Literature Cited

Albritton, C.C. 1984. Geologic time. Journal of Geological Education 32:29–37.

Catacosinos, P.A., Harrison, W.B., III, Reynolds, R.F., Westjohn, D.B. and M.S. Wollensak. 2001. Stratigraphic Lexicon for Michigan. Geological Survey Division, Department of Environmental Quality and Michigan Basin Geological Society: Lansing, MI.

Cloud, P. 1988. Oasis in space. Norton: New York, NY.

Gradstein, F.M. and J.G. Ogg. 2004. Geologic time scale 2004—why, how, and where next! Lethaia 27:175–181.

Harbaugh, J.W. 1974. Stratigraphy and the geologic time scale. W.C. Brown: Dubuque, IA.

Heinrich, E.W. 2004. Mineralogy of Michigan, updated and revised by George W. Robinson. Michigan Technological University: Houghton, MI.

Oreskes, N. 2003. Plate tectonics: An insider's history of the modern theory of the Earth. Westview Press: Boulder, CO.

Tarbuk, E.J. and F.K. Lutgens. 1999. Earth: An Introduction to Physical Geology. Prentice Hall: Upper Saddle River, NJ.

Taylor, F. B. 1910. Bearing of the Tertiary mountain belt on the origin of the Earth's plan. Geological Society of America Bulletin 21:179–226.

Further Readings

Barker, C.F. 2005. Under Michigan: The story of Michigan's rocks and fossils. Wayne State University Press: Detroit.

Bickford, M.E., Van Schmus, W.R. and I. Zietz. 1986. Proterozoic history of the midcontinent region of North America. Geology 14:492–496.

Catacosinos, P.A. and P.A. Daniels (eds.) 1991. Early sedimentary evolution of the Michigan Basin. Geological Society of America Press: Boulder, CO.

Condie, K.C. 1989. Plate tectonics and crustal evolution. Pergamon Press: Oxford.

Dorr, J. A. and D. F. Eschman. 1970. Geology of Michigan. The University of Michigan Press: Ann Arbor.

Gradstein, F.M., Ogg, J.G. and A.G. Smith. (eds). 2005. A geologic time scale 2004. Cambridge University Press: Cambridge.

Holman, J.A. 1995. Ancient life of the Great Lakes Basin. The University of Michigan Press: Ann Arbor.

LaBerge, G.L. 1994. Geology of the Lake Superior Region. Penokean Press: Oshkosh, WI.

Lemon, R.R. 1990. Principles of stratigraphy. Merrill Publishing: Columbus, OH.

McPhee, J. 1980. Basin and Range. Farrar, Straus, and Giroux: New York, NY.

Marvin, U.B. 1973. Continental Drift: The Evolution of a Concept. Smithsonian Institution Press: Washington, DC.

Paull, R.K. and R.A. Paull. 1977. Geology of Wisconsin and Upper Michigan. Kendall-Hunt: Dubuque, IA.

Poort, J.M. and R.J. Carlson. 2005. Historical Geology: Interpretations and Applications. Prentice Hall: Upper Saddle River, NJ.

Press, F. and R. Siever. 1986. Earth. Freeman: New York, NY.

Stanley, S. 1989. Earth and Life Through Time. Freeman: New York, NY.

Van Andel, T.H. 1985. New Views on an Old Planet. Cambridge University Press, Cambridge.

Winchester, S. 2001. The map that changed the world. Harper Collins: New York, NY.

3

Michigan's Earliest Geology: The Precambrian

Theodore J. Bornhorst and Danita Brandt

Introduction

The term Precambrian refers to a *time* in Earth history before the Cambrian Period, and the rocks formed during that time. The Precambrian extends from the origin of the Earth (~4.56 billion years ago), to the base of the Cambrian, at 542 million years ago, spanning over four billion years and representing 88% of Earth's history (Fig. 3.1; Plate 3). Michigan's Precambrian rocks are ~3.6–1.0 billion years old. These igneous, metamorphic and meta-sedimentary rocks are exposed at the surface throughout the western half of the Upper Peninsula (Fig 3.2), but lie buried beneath younger (Paleozoic) sedimentary rocks in the eastern Upper Peninsula, and in the Lower Peninsula (Plate 5, Chapter 4).

Marking time in the Precambrian

Early geologists working on Precambrian rocks did not have the luxury of a rich fossil record—the basis for the divisions of the geologic time scale for younger rocks (Chapters 2, 4)—so their efforts to construct a relative geologic time scale for Precambrian rocks were based entirely on the physical relations between them, especially cross-cutting relations and the principle of superposition (Fig. 2.5, Chapter 2). In addition, the great age of these rocks meant that many had been deformed, weathered and eroded to form the next generation of rocks. The record is complicated and incomplete!

Even before isotope dating made it possible to provide a quantitative or numerical time scale for the Precambrian and its rocks (Robb et al. 2004; Chapter 2), geologists recognized that rocks exposed in the western Upper Peninsula were Precambrian in age (Van Hise and Leith 1909, 1911). As our ability to resolve time in the Precambrian improved, it was subdivided into three great eons (from oldest to youngest): Hadean, Archean and Proterozoic. All geologic ages are determined by isotope dating and are listed in this chapter using standard abbreviations: Ga (giga or billions of years ago) or Ma (millions of years ago).

Earliest Earth history

The Earth formed about 4.5 Ga (Valley 2006), as interstellar gas and dust produced by a supernova started rotating around a new star—our sun. The dust accreted to form planetesimals (small planets), and these in turn collided to form the planets of our solar system (Wood et al. 2006). The Moon formed during this time, as a result of a Mars-sized body colliding with the Earth (Wood and Halliday 2005).

Both the Earth and the Moon continued to be bombarded by fragments left over from the early solar system. The Moon retains evidence of this activity in the form of impact craters, but the combination of plate tectonics

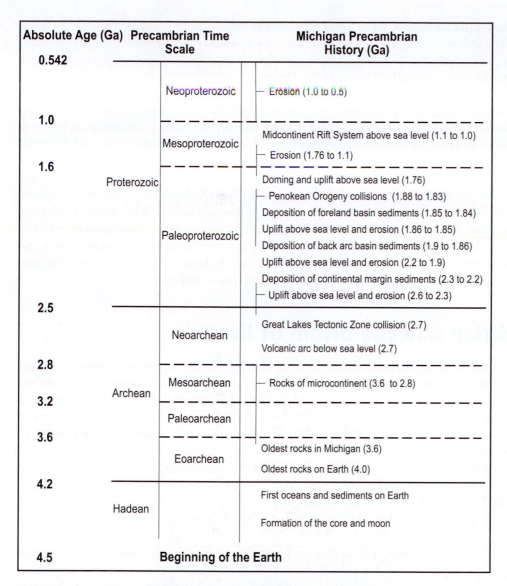

Absolute Age (Ga)	Precambrian Time Scale		Michigan Precambrian History (Ga)
0.542			
		Neoproterozoic	Erosion (1.0 to 0.5)
1.0			
	Proterozoic	Mesoproterozoic	Midcontinent Rift System above sea level (1.1 to 1.0)
1.6			Erosion (1.76 to 1.1)
		Paleoproterozoic	Doming and uplift above sea level (1.76)
			Penokean Orogeny collisions (1.88 to 1.83)
			Deposition of foreland basin sediments (1.85 to 1.84)
			Uplift above sea level and erosion (1.86 to 1.85)
			Deposition of back arc basin sediments (1.9 to 1.86)
			Uplift above sea level and erosion (2.2 to 1.9)
			Deposition of continental margin sediments (2.3 to 2.2)
			Uplift above sea level and erosion (2.6 to 2.3)
2.5			
	Archean	Neoarchean	Great Lakes Tectonic Zone collision (2.7)
			Volcanic arc below sea level (2.7)
2.8			
		Mesoarchean	Rocks of microcontinent (3.6 to 2.8)
3.2			
		Paleoarchean	
3.6			
		Eoarchean	Oldest rocks in Michigan (3.6)
			Oldest rocks on Earth (4.0)
4.2			
	Hadean		First oceans and sediments on Earth
			Formation of the core and moon
4.5	**Beginning of the Earth**		

FIGURE 3.1 Nomenclature and absolute time frame of the Precambrian. Significant Precambrian geologic events are discussed in the text and are shown with respect to the Precambrian time scale. See also Plate 3.

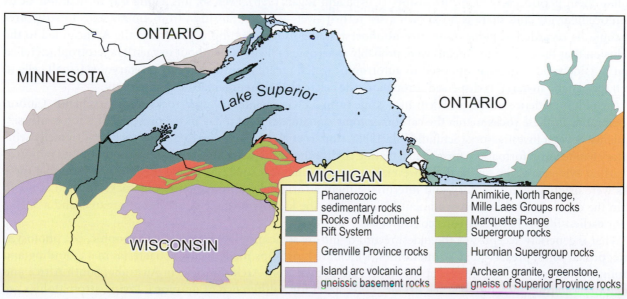

FIGURE 3.2 Generalized geologic map of the northern Great Lakes region. After Schulz and Cannon (2007).

and erosion has reshaped the Earth's surface so many times that most of the evidence for these early impacts has been obliterated. The earliest Earth was hot and barren, punctuated by abundant geothermal springs and volcanoes. This time in Earth's history is referred to as the Hadean Eon, for *Hades*, the Greek god of the underworld. Little physical evidence remains from this earliest time, as the Hadean protocrust (the cooled molten material that formed the outermost layer of the Earth) was recycled back into the underlying mantle by plate tectonic-like processes (Frei et al. 2004, but also see O'neil et al. 2008).

Early Earth's atmosphere was likely toxic to life as we know it today. Initially the Earth was dominated by a hot, CO_2-rich, steamy atmosphere (Zahnle 2006). Eventually, much of this CO_2 got cycled back into the mantle. Removal of CO_2 from the atmosphere eliminated any CO_2 greenhouse effect, which, combined with too little warming from the dim light of the young Sun, resulted in the surface of the Earth becoming very cold (Harland 2007). Slowly, the composition of the Earth's atmosphere changed, so that by the beginning of the Archean (4.2 Ga) the atmosphere and hydrosphere were not much different than today, although the atmosphere still lacked O_2 to sustain aerobic life (Zahnle 2006). The surface was hot, due to the renewed greenhouse effect in the atmosphere. In addition, by ~4.2 Ga, oceans and early continents had formed (Cavosie et al. 2005, Valley 2006). The appearance of oceans and water-laid sediments at 4.2 Ga marked the end of the Hadean and the beginning of the Archean eon (Fig. 3.1). As is obvious, life on Earth was intimately tied to the evolution of the Precambrian atmosphere and hydrosphere.

■ The Precambrian and the origin of life

Life evolved under conditions much different from today, before the development of a protective ozone layer and significant free oxygen in the atmosphere. Volcanic out-gassing supplied carbon dioxide, sulfur dioxide, carbon monoxide, chlorine, nitrogen, hydrogen and water vapor to the early Earth atmosphere; life likely originated from these inorganic precursors. A graduate student at the University of Chicago demonstrated this scenario in a famous laboratory experiment, in 1952. Stanley Miller attempted to simulate conditions of the early Earth, as then understood. He sealed ammonia, methane and hydrogen in an apparatus, applied energy in the form of a spark (simulating lightning), and eight days later the water in the vessel had turned cloudy, due to the formation of amino acids—the building blocks of life. Interestingly, Charles Darwin anticipated this experiment almost a century earlier, when he wrote in a letter to a friend his view of the environment in which life originated, ". . . in some warm little pond, with all sorts of ammonia and phosphoric salts, light, heat, electricity, etc. present" (Letter 7471–Darwin 1871).

Amino acids are relatively easy to make, and because they are present in some meteorites, some have suggested that the Earth may have been salted with the building blocks of life from extraterrestrial sources during the intense bombardment period, early in Earth's history (Chyba and Sagan 1996). Even so, it is a long way from amino acids to multicellular life, and there is no known fossil record—yet—of this transition from amino acids to structures that could be regarded as living. Our current understanding of the conditions present in the Archean led to the conclusion that the earliest organisms were probably anaerobic (able to live without oxygen), heterotrophic (relied on an outside food source, as opposed to autotrophs, which create their own food) prokaryotes (small cells in which the genetic material is dispersed throughout the cell, rather than organized in a nucleus).

The oldest evidence of life on Earth may come from 3.8 Ga metamorphosed rocks from Greenland. Carbon isotope ratios in these rocks match the carbon isotopic signatures found today in the presence of photosynthesizing plants. Several investigators (Schindlowski 1988, Mojzsis et al. 1996) interpreted these rocks as originally sedimentary banded iron formation, formed in a marine environment; they concluded that the carbon isotopes indicated the earliest evidence of life on Earth. However, Fedo and Whitehouse (2002) disputed the interpretation that these rocks were originally sedimentary, and interpreted them as originally ultramafic igneous rocks, formed at depth within the crust—not a likely environment for life. Thus, the identity of these structures as organic, and a 3.8 Ga age for earliest life on Earth, remains controversial.

What *is* generally accepted as the oldest record of life are structures interpreted as autotrophic, i.e., photosynthetic, prokaryotes, preserved as stromatolites, which are build-ups made by cyanobacterial mats, binding and trapping sediment. The oldest fossil stromatolites are known from Archean rocks in Australia, South Africa and Minnesota (Schopf 1992, but also see Braser et al. (2002) for a difference of opinion). Living stromatolites are found in restricted bays in West Australia, making cyanobacteria the longest-surviving group of organisms on Earth.

FIGURE 3.3 Stromatolitic Kona Dolomite, Marquette, Michigan; the oldest evidence of life in Michigan. The fine mound-like layers are fossil cyanobacteria mats. The field of view of the photo is 15.5 by 10.3 cm; US quarter for scale. Photo by G. Robinson of a specimen in the collection of the Mineral Museum of Michigan, Michigan Technological University's A.E. Seaman Mineral Museum.

Michigan's Kona Dolomite contains fossil stromatolites, and although considerably younger (2.25 Ga) than the Archean stromatolites of other localities, they do represent the oldest record of life in Michigan (Fig. 3.3).

By the end of the Archean, at 2.5 Ga, Earth's photosynthesizing organisms were enriching the atmosphere in oxygen. By about 1.9 Ga, eukaryotic cells appeared as fossils, and the Earth's atmosphere was sufficiently enriched in free oxygen to support this more complex life form (Knoll 2003). Eukaryotic cells are 100 times larger than prokaryotic cells, contain more genetic material and this material is organized in a nucleus. Michigan has the distinction of having the oldest known eukaryote fossils—a distinctively spiraled, filamentous alga called *Grypania spiralis*, found in the 1.87 Ga Negaunee Iron Formation, near Ishpeming (Han and Runnegar 1992).

Life on Earth remained at the unicellular microbial level for nearly three billion years—most of Earth history—before soft-bodied, multicellular animals appeared, about 700 Ma. There is no record in Michigan of this next step in the history of life. Once multicellular animals appeared, other evolutionary innovations quickly followed, so quickly that the term "Cambrian explosion" (Runnegar 1982) is used to describe this rapid increase in the diversity of life forms (Chapter 4). Originally, the boundary between the Precambrian and the younger Paleozoic strata was defined by this abrupt appearance of abundant, skeletonized organisms—when it was presumed that there had been no life during the Precambrian. We now know that the record of life on Earth stretches back nearly to the beginning of the geologic record, and new discoveries continue to fill in the gaps in our understanding of the transition from Darwin's "warm little pond" to the first living organism.

Overview of Precambrian geologic events in Michigan

The remainder of this chapter focuses on the Precambrian rock record in Michigan. Michigan's Precambrian rocks are the result of three major episodes of geologic activity (Figs. 3.1, 3.4). The oldest, Archean episode (an episode is a series of more or less continuous geologic events), culminated with a continental collision that created the Great Lakes Tectonic Zone, at ~2.7 Ga. The Archean episode was followed by roughly 300 million years of erosion, in which no known rocks formed in Michigan. The second, Paleoproterozoic, episode began at about 2.3 Ga, with deposition sediments in a shallow sea. It culminated with a multiphase collision event called the Penokean Orogeny at ~1.85 Ga. An orogeny is the process of mountain building that involves folding and faulting. As with

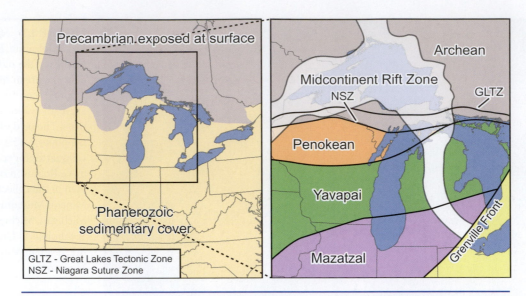

FIGURE 3.4   Highly generalized Precambrian crustal provinces of Michigan and surrounding areas. The inset shows where Precambrian rocks are exposed at the surface. The Archean, Paleoproterozoic, and Mesoproterozoic episodes of Michigan are discussed in the text. In the Lower Peninsula, the Yavapai, Mazatzal and Grenville provinces are buried beneath Phanerozoic sedimentary rocks of the Michigan Basin (Chapter 4). The Yavapai province was formed and accreted to rocks to the north between 1.8 to 1.7 Ga, and the Mazatzal province was formed and accreted between 1.7 to 1.6 Ga (NICE Working Group 2007). The Grenville province was accreted by continental collision at 1.05 Ga that resulted in compression of the Mesoproterozoic Midcontinent Rift System (Chapter 12). After NICE Working Group (2007).

the Archean episode, the Paleoproterozoic episode was followed by ~750 million years of erosion and quiescence. The last, Mesoproterozoic, episode occurred between 1.1 and 1.0 Ga, with the formation of the Midcontinent Rift System (Chapter 12). Subsequently, from about 1.0 Ga to 542 Ma, there was yet another protracted period of erosion and no recorded rock forming events in Michigan. As a result, rocks of Neoproterozoic age are absent from Michigan (Fig. 3.1). In the sections that follow, the details of these Precambrian events are discussed.

▪ The Archean eon in Michigan

The oldest rocks in Michigan (~3.6 Ga) are located just north of the Wisconsin border, near Watersmeet (Fig. 3.5; Sims 1993b). These Archean age rocks form the geologic "basement" of the Upper Peninsula—the foundation upon which all the younger rocks are deposited, or into which they intrude.

Rocks of the Archean eon in Michigan have a complex history, spanning from 3.6 to 2.6 Ga. The oldest recorded event is the formation of gneiss, by high grade metamorphism of sedimentary and volcanic rocks, deep within the crust. This gneiss was part of a micro-continent that eventually moved northward, as a result of north-dipping subduction. As a result of this subduction, an Archean volcanic arc formed below sea level, over the subduction zone, but that volcanism ended upon collision of the microcontinent along the Great Lakes Tectonic Zone (GLTZ).

Micro-continent of gneiss

The rocks that collided with the volcanic arc along the GLTZ from the south consist of 3.6 to 2.8 Ga banded and migmatitic gneiss (Table 3.1). Gneiss is a high-grade metamorphic rock that forms deep in the Earth, e.g., in the cores of mountain ranges. The banded gneiss in Michigan consists of alternating light- and dark-colored layers of differing composition, from centimeters to tens of meters in thickness. The migmatitic gneiss is also banded, but includes a granite (melted) component that cross-cuts layering, and the layering may be quite

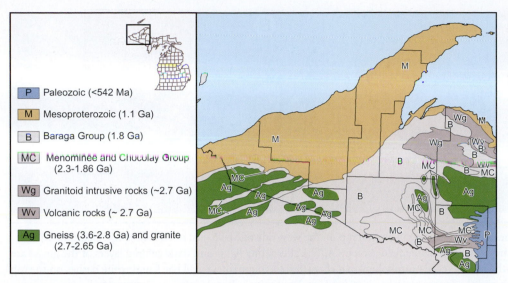

FIGURE 3.5 Generalized geology of the exposed Precambrian rocks in the western Upper Peninsula of Michigan and northern Wisconsin. The rock units are combined to correspond to the sequence of events as described in the text. After Sims (1993) and Schulz and Cannon (2007).

Legend:

- **P** Paleozoic (<542 Ma)
- **M** Mesoproterozoic (1.1 Ga)
- **B** Baraga Group (1.8 Ga)
- **MC** Menominee and Chocolay Group (2.3-1.86 Ga)
- **Wg** Granitoid intrusive rocks (~2.7 Ga)
- **Wv** Volcanic rocks (~ 2.7 Ga)
- **Ag** Gneiss (3.6-2.8 Ga) and granite (2.7-2.65 Ga)

TABLE 3.1   Precambrian rock types and formal unit names, representative of the western Upper Peninsula

Precambrian Episode	Formal unit names	Typical rock types[1]
Mesoproterozoic volcanic and sedimentary rocks of the Keweenawan Supergroup of the Midcontinent Rift System	Group names: Powder Mill, Oronto Selected Formation names: Portage Lake Volcanics, Copper Harbor Conglomerate, Nonesuch Shale, Freda Sandstone, Jacobsville Sandstone	**basalt lava flows,** rhyolite lava and pyroclastic tuffs, andesite lava flows, **sandstone, conglomerate,** siltstone, **shale**
Mesoproterozoic plutonic rocks	These generally small plutonic bodies in Michigan lack formal names	**diabase,** gabbro, peridotite, pyroxenite, diorite
Paleoproterozoic igneous rocks that are interbedded with, and cross-cut, Paleoproterozoic sedimentary rocks	Formation names: Hemlock Formation, Badwater Greenstone, Emperor Volcanic Complex, Peavy Pond Complex	**basalt to andesite lava flows and pyroclastic rocks, diabase dikes and sills,** stocks of granite, granodiorite, tonalite, syenite, gabbro, norite
Paleoproterozoic sedimentary rocks of the Marquette Range Supergroup	Group names: Chocolay, Menominee, Baraga, Paint River Selected Formation names: Mesnard Quartzite, Kona Dolomite, Randville Dolomite, Bad River Dolomite, Wewe Slate, Ajibik Quartzite, Negaunee Iron Formation, Ironwood Iron Formation, Siamo Slate, Goodrich Quartzite, Michigamme Formation	**graywacke, shale, banded iron formation, quartzite, argillite, dolomite,** orthoquartzite, sandstone, siltstone, chert, conglomerate; metamorphic equivalents of some of these rocks include slate, schist, metaconglomerate
Neoarchean plutonic rocks	Generally lacking formal names in Michigan; Bell Creek Granite (south of GLTZ)	**granite, tonalite, granodiorite,** trondjemite, diorite, syenite, hornblendite, peridotite, gabbro
Neoarchean volcanic dominated rocks	Formation names: Mona Formation, Kitchi Formation, Lighthouse Point Basalt	**basalt pillow lava flows, andesite, dacite,** rhyolite, volcanic conglomerate, pyroclastic air-fall and ash-flow tuffs, iron formation; metamorphic equivalents of some of these rocks include amphibolite, schist
Mesoarchean to Eoarchean microcontinent rocks	Lacking consistent formal names in Michigan	**gneiss, migmatitic gneiss, amphibolite,** tonalitic augen gneiss

1. Major lithologies are shown in **bold**.

FIGURE 3.6 Migmatitic gneiss of Archean age in an outcrop on the west side of M-95, just north of the Michigamme River, near Republic, being studied by students learning field geology. A. The alternating light- and dark-colored layers of the gneiss are clearly visible. B. Inset shows the marble-cake morphology that characterizes migmatite. Small black and white dashes on the top of the scale are each 1 cm long and the longer black bar is 10 cm long. Photos by T. Bornhorst.

irregular, reminding one of "marble cake" (Fig. 3.6). The migmatite was likely formed at temperatures and depths where the rock was beginning to be melted. In Minnesota, similar gneisses formed at temperatures of ~700° C and at depths of around 18 km (Moecher et al. 1986). Similar temperatures and depths have been proposed for the gneiss near Republic, Michigan (Attoh and Klasner 1989). This implies that 18 km of covering rock has been removed to expose these rocks at the surface, providing us, today, with a very deep window into Michigan's Archean crust.

Volcanic arc

To the north of the micro-continent, subduction of oceanic crust resulted in a volcanic arc (Fig. 3.7). In the Marquette area, the preserved volcanic rocks resulting from this arc are of Archean age (Fig. 3.5), have a maximum thickness of ~16 km, and erupted at ~2.7 Ga (Bornhorst and Johnson 1998). Up to 10 km of the volcanic rocks consist of pillow basalt lava flows, termed the Mona Formation and Lighthouse Point Basalt (Johnson and Bornhorst 1991, Bornhorst and Johnson 1993). The pillows indicate that these flows were erupted underwater. Visitors to the area may be familiar with the excellent exposure of pillow lavas ~10 km west of Marquette on US Hwy 41 (Fig. 2.4). Explosively erupted tuffs (metamorphic schists) and iron formation are interbedded within the basalt flows (Table 3.1). The iron-formation is interpreted as having been deposited by hot waters (hydrothermal fluids) that were expelled onto the ocean floor ~2.7 Ga. Overlying the pillowed basalt flows are up to 6 km of rock, interpreted as explosively erupted tuffs and lahars (or wet slurries) that flowed down the slopes of nearby volcanoes (termed the Kitchi Formation). This impressive thickness of volcanic rocks was formed in a volcanic arc that grew below sea level.

Archean plate tectonics

Continental crust on the Earth was established by ~4.28 Ga, based on the age of ancient greenstone rocks in Canada (O'neil et al. 2008). Plate tectonic processes, similar to today, began at nearly the same time as the age of the first continental crust (Friend and Nutman 2005). Because of geologic recycling back into the underlying mantle, there are only a few scattered localities, including in Michigan, where rocks older than 3.5 Ga are preserved (Nutman 2006). Because continental crust is less dense and, thus, is rarely subducted back into the mantle, it has slowly grown in size over time. Rocks formed at 2.8 Ga are relatively common on nearly all continents and form large continental cores, or shields, such as the Canadian Shield (Card 1990) which extends into the Upper Peninsula as a physiographic region known as the Superior Bedrock Uplands (Plate 8B).

In Michigan, the earliest evidence for the operation of plate tectonic processes is ~2.7 Ga, with the formation of a volcanic arc. This arc formed as a result of north-directed subduction of oceanic crust (Fig. 3.7). The lack of a spreading center between the subduction zone and the microcontinent of gneiss resulted in the closing of the gap between them. The microcontinent of gneiss discussed above collided into the arc along a geologic structure termed the Great Lakes Tectonic Zone (GLTZ). This 1,200 km long collision zone trends east-west, from Minnesota to the Marquette area to Ontario (Sims et al. 1980, Sims 1993a). Not only did the collision end the volcanism in the arc, but the rocks near the collision were intensely deformed and metamorphosed. During collision there was also intrusion of magmas from about 2,705 to 2,665 Ma (Wilkin and Bornhorst 1992, Bornhorst and Johnson 1998). The largest of these intrusions were huge batholiths of granitoid (granite like) rock that enveloped much of the area of the western Upper Peninsula. Once solidified, these magmas effectively "stitched together" the GLTZ.

The GLTZ collision resulted in the formation of a small to moderately high mountain range—high enough to actually reach above sea level! The mountains were barren rock, as plants or other complex life forms did not yet exist. By 2,585 Ma, the collision was clearly over, mountain building had ended, and erosion had begun (age of post tectonic intrusion in Fig. 3.7; Sims and Peterman 1992). There was a long period (about 300 million years!) of erosion; during this time in Michigan there are no recorded rock forming events (Fig. 3.1). Erosion of the Archean rocks probably left a generally flat platform of dry, barren rock.

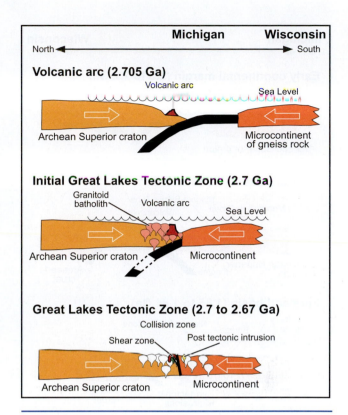

FIGURE 3.7   Generalized diagrams depicting the succession of events that formed the Archean rocks exposed in the western Upper Peninsula of Michigan.

■ The Paleoproterozoic era

Rocks of Paleoproterozoic age (2.3–1.76 Ga) are exposed in the western Upper Peninsula (Fig. 3.4, 3.5). A major erosional unconformity (300 million year time gap) separates the Archean "basement" rocks (discussed above) from the overlying succession of Paleoproterozoic sedimentary rocks. Although the Paleoproterozoic sediments are metamorphosed, they retain enough of their original sedimentary characteristics to allow us to interpret the environments in which they formed.

Paleoproterozoic sedimentary and volcanic rocks were deposited on the newly rifted edge of a continent that, because of rifting, was submerged under an ocean that deepened to the south (Fig. 3.8). Their deposition was influenced by changing sea level and by events to the south (as determined from rocks exposed in northern Wisconsin), including the formation of several volcanic arcs related to subduction, collision of these arcs into the margin of the continent and finally, the end of subduction with continental collision. In Michigan, these Paleoproterozoic rocks are collectively termed the Marquette Range Supergroup (Table 3.1). This supergroup is subdivided into a lower Chocolay Group, a middle Menominee Group, and an upper Baraga Group, each separated by unconformities that represent long periods of erosion. The description (below) of the rocks, environments, and geologic history of Michigan's Paleoproterozoic, will use these Groups as the framework, beginning with the oldest—the Chocolay Group.

The Chocolay Group

The oldest Paleoproterozoic rocks, the lowest units of the Chocolay Group, contain layers of dark-colored, fine-grained sediments that have larger fragments embedded in them. This is characteristic of deposits that form on the ocean floor as icebergs melt and deposit the mixed grain sizes there. These *tillite* rocks are, therefore, evidence of glaciation in or near Michigan, during the Paleoproterozoic.

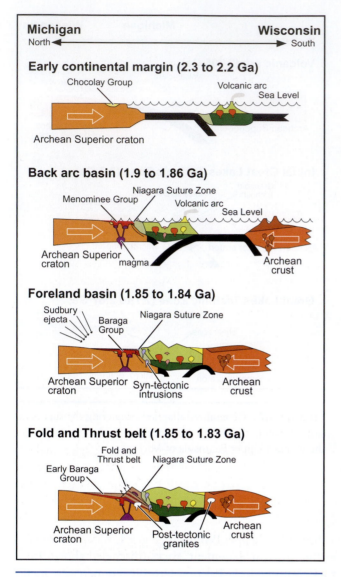

FIGURE 3.8 Generalized diagrams depicting the succession of events that formed the Paleoproterozoic rocks exposed in the western Upper Peninsula. After Schulz and Cannon (2007).

Overlying the tillite is metamorphosed sandstone, the Mesnard Quartzite, which is very quartz-rich with well-preserved ripple marks, indicating that the sand originally was deposited in a nearshore (beach), marine environment (Fig. 3.9). The quartzite is overlain by the Kona Dolomite, a sedimentary carbonate deposit that contains beautiful examples of *stromatolites*, distinctive layered rocks constructed by cyanobacterial mats trapping and binding fine-grained, carbonate muds (Fig. 3.3). The Kona Dolomite contains structures that resemble gypsum crystals. Gypsum, an evaporite mineral, and the stromatolites themselves are characteristic of a shallow marine (ocean) environment. Despite its name, the Kona Dolomite is actually only about 50% dolomite, with the rest of the rocks being interbedded metamorphosed muds (slate) with lesser amounts of metamorphosed, quartz-rich sands (quartzite). (Geologic supergroups, groups and formations can contain a wide variety of lithologies regardless of their formal name.) The interpretation of all the rocks comprising the formation termed the Kona Dolomite indicates that they were first deposited in a restricted lagoonal setting, behind a barrier bar and later in an open, marine tidal flat (Taylor 1972).

Overlying the Kona Dolomite is metamorphosed shale, the Wewe Slate, which suggests a slightly deeper-water environment than the dolomite. A long period of erosion followed the Chocolay depositional episode.

The Menominee Group

The Ajibik Quartzite, which marks the beginning of the Menominee Group, lies unconformably on the underlying Chocolay Group, separated from it by as much as 300 million years of erosion. Like the Mesnard Quartzite, the Ajibik Quartzite consists of metamorphosed quartz-rich sands that were deposited in nearshore (beach), shallow marine environments. This was followed by deposition of alternating layers of thinly bedded shale and thicker (up to a meter thick) poorly-sorted sands, termed the Siamo Slate. The poor sorting—a mix of grain sizes that ranges from mud to sand size—is thought to be due to rapid deposition from a kind of submarine landslide. The term *turbidite* or "mass flow deposit" is used to describe sediments of this type. These turbidites were deposited in deep water, submarine fans.

A thick deposit of iron-rich, siliceous ooze also accumulated in this deep-water environment. This rock is the famed Negaunee Iron Formation, which occurs in the Marquette area. It consists of alternating bands of iron oxides and silica (red chert) and is the source of the iron ore currently being mined at the Tilden and Empire Mines (Chapter 11). It is particularly well exposed at Jasper Knob, in the City of Ishpeming (Fig. 11.3). In the Marquette area, the Negaunee Iron Formation is especially thick, up to 1,150 m, because it was deposited in a fault-bounded, subsiding trough in the same geographic location as the older GLTZ (Scott and Lukey 1999). Banded iron formations are common in the Paleoproterozoic in Michigan and elsewhere. Their sudden and widespread appearance in the Paleoproterozoic is likely related to changes in the Earth's atmosphere, especially the increased presence of oxygen, which also led to more oxygen in ocean water (Chapter 11).

The end of Menominee Group deposition was marked by another long period of non-deposition, resulting in an unconformity between it and the overlying Baraga Group rocks.

FIGURE 3.9   Close-up of ripple marks in the Mesnard Quartzite within the Chocolay Group. Photo from prominent outcrops on the north side of US Hwy 41, on the eastern outskirts of Negaunee. Small black and white dashes on bottom of the scale are each 1 cm long and the longer black bar is 10 cm long. Photo by T. Bornhorst.

FIGURE 3.10   Slate of the Michigamme Formation of the Baraga Group along M-28 north of Crystal Falls. There are many similar outcrops of gray cleaved slate from Crystal Falls north towards US Hwy 41. Photo by R. Schaetzl.

The Baraga Group

The basal unit of the Baraga Group, the Goodrich Quartzite, contains fragments of the Negaunee Iron Formation, formed by erosion of the underlying iron formation and incorporation of clasts in the sand, as the Goodrich was deposited. The Goodrich Quartzite consists of metamorphosed, quartz-rich sands that were deposited in a nearshore marine environment. In Michigan, among the oldest Baraga Group sediments is a 2–4 m thick layer that has anomalous concentrations of platinum group elements and contains clasts, interpreted as shock-metamorphosed quartz, melt spherules and tektites (Pufahl et al. 2007). The physical and chemical characteristics of this layer have led to its interpretation as distal ejecta from the impact of a large meteorite—perhaps the result of impact that produced the Sudbury structure in Ontario (Fig. 3.4) at about 1.85 Ga (Addison et al. 2005).

The Goodrich Quartzite was followed by deposition of muds (metamorphosed into slate) and iron formation that were deposited in a shallow marine environment (Ojakangas et al. 2001). Most of the Baraga Group consists of a very thick (several km thick) succession of metamorphosed shale (slate) termed the Michigamme Formation (Fig. 3.10). The muds of the Michigamme Formation were deposited as turbidites (mass flow deposits) in submarine fans.

■ Plate tectonics during the Paleoproterozoic in Michigan

An early continental margin

Chocolay Group sediments were deposited in a geologic setting that was similar to the Atlantic coast margin at the time when Europe had first separated from North America and formed a narrow version of the Atlantic Ocean (Larue 1981, Ojakangas et al. 2001, Schulz and Cannon 2007). The rift basins in this continental margin correspond to pre-existing zones of weakness, such as the older Archean GLTZ in the Marquette area. Great thicknesses of sediments were deposited in the rift basins. The deposition of the Chocolay Group ended at ~2.2 Ga, 100 million years after it began (Ojakangas et al. 2001). There was a break in time (hiatus) of roughly 300 million years, from the end of Chocolay sedimentation until the beginning of deposition of the Menominee Group rocks (Schulz and Cannon 2007; Fig. 3.1). During this hiatus, Michigan was uplifted above sea level and the barren rock, lacking a protective cover of vegetation, was once again exposed to the forces of erosion by water and wind.

Volcanic arc

Beginning about 1.9 Ga, near the end of the hiatus, there was south-directed subduction and development of a volcanic arc—the remnants of which are now exposed in northern Wisconsin (Fig. 3.8). At ~1.88 Ga, this arc collided with the margin of the continent along the Niagara Suture Zone (NSZ) (Fig. 3.5), thereby beginning a long episode of Paleoproterozoic deformation termed the Penokean Orogeny.

Back-arc basin

The collision mentioned above resulted in a change in the direction of subduction from the south to the north (compare the direction of A and B in Fig. 3.8; Holm et al. 2005). A new volcanic arc developed over the north-directed subduction. Subduction of ocean lithosphere induces convection in the underlying asthenospheric mantle. Mantle convection is a very slow movement, in response to gravitational instability. Buoyant, hot mantle materials rise upward until they near the base of the lithosphere, where they can spread laterally, cool and become denser, and then sink downward (Fig. 12.4). The lateral spreading induces tension in the lithosphere, which causes it to stretch, thin, and break (rift). The stretched and thinned area (landward of the volcanic arc) is termed a back-arc basin. In Michigan, a back-arc basin, below sea level, developed on the stable continent, to the north of the new volcanic arc. Menominee Group sediment was deposited in this back-arc basin, on top of the eroded older Chocolay and Archean rocks, from about 1.88–1.86 Ga (Fig. 3.8). This event was followed by ~10 million years of erosion (1.86–1.85 Ga), when the area was again uplifted to above sea level (Schulz and Cannon 2007, Fig. 3.1).

Foreland basin

Continental collision at 1.85 Ga resulted in an uplifted zone in northern Wisconsin and adjacent Michigan, but the area to the north of the uplift was once again submerged below sea level (foreland basin in Fig. 3.8). Large thicknesses of sediments of the Baraga Group were deposited in this rapidly subsiding basin. The rapid subsidence corresponds to the final docking of the continent with the edge of the craton in Wisconsin at about 1.84 Ga (Schulz and Cannon 2007).

Foreland fold and thrust belt

As the subsidence ended, the rocks of Michigan (in "front" of the collision taking place in northern Wisconsin) were deformed by collision-related forces. In the foreland of Michigan, the Paleoproterozoic rocks were subjected to this Penokean deformation (Klasner 1978) for about 10 million years (1.84–1.83 Ga). The early phase of this deformation was thin-skinned and did not involve the older Archean rocks (Nachatilo and Bauer 1993), i.e., only the Paleoproterozoic rocks were folded and thrust faulted, with the thrusting resulting in a tectonic stacking of these rocks into a pile up to 15 km thick (Attoh and Klasner 1989). As they were buried during stacking, they were metamorphosed. The Archean GLTZ was a zone of weakness during the deposition of the Paleoproterozoic sediments in the basins that developed on top of it, and as a result it was later reactivated during Penokean deformation (Thover et al. 2007). Major fault zones often continue to be reactivated long after their initial formation.

The end of the Penokean Orogeny resulted in a Penokean mountain range (above sea level) that extended laterally for at least 800 km. The bedrock of northern Wisconsin and adjacent western Upper Peninsula are the roots of this Penokean mountain range (Fig. 3.4). The Precambrian roots are all that remain of the Penokean Mountains, however, after millions of years of erosion. The rolling, bedrock-controlled topography of northern Wisconsin and adjacent western Upper Peninsula is actually a result of sculpting from geologically very recent glaciation (Chapter 17). Just east of Sault Ste. Marie, in Ontario, are large bedrock uplands known as the Penokean Highlands; these are also eroded remnants of the Penokean Mountains.

After folding and thrusting

The Paleoproterozoic sedimentary rocks and underlying Archean rocks of the western Upper Peninsula were deformed again at ~1.76 Ga, after a hiatus of about 70 million years (Tinkham and Marshak 2004). This event domed and block-faulted these rocks. The cause of this deformation has not been well determined, but it may have been a result of plate collision (termed Yavapai; Fig. 3.4) to the south (Schulz and Cannon 2007). At the end of this event, the Precambrian rocks of the western Upper Peninsula were again exposed above sea level. In Michigan, there was (again) a protracted period of erosion, with no known deposition, from about 1.76 to ~1.1 Ga. This erosion left a generally flat platform of barren rock in its wake.

The Mesoproterozoic era

The continental platform of Archean and Paleoproterozoic rocks, which was above sea level, began to undergo rifting at ~1.1 Ga. The resultant Midcontinent rift system is a major geologic structure that extends for more than 2,000 km, following the geographic shape of Lake Superior and then southeasterly through the Lower Peninsula (Figs. 12.1, 12.5). A continental rift occurs where the Earth's crust is stretched, thinned and broken, to form a linear depression that may become filled with volcanic and sedimentary rocks. The East African rift is a contemporary continental rift. The Precambrian Midcontinent rift was, however, formed on a landscape of barren rock; vegetation and other complex life forms did not exist during the Mesoproterozoic eon.

The Mesoproterozoic era in Michigan is represented by a thick succession of volcanic and sedimentary rocks, formed within the Midcontinent rift system (Table 3.1; Chapter 12). Evidence for rifting in Precambrian rocks outside of the rift in western Upper Peninsula is especially notable in the form of diabase dikes. These dikes were likely to have been feeders to lava flows on the flanks of the rift, but the lava flows are not present now, i.e., they have been eroded away. Early in the history of the rift, basaltic magmas intruded along faults and fractures, from ~1.109 to 1.106 Ga, producing a dike swarm from Baraga to Marquette (Green et al. 1987, Davis and Green 1997; Fig. 3.3; see FOCUS BOX on the following page).

During and after rifting, the area likely remained above sea level. After rifting ended, between ~1.0 and ~0.54 Ga, the region experienced yet another protracted period of erosion, that once again left the area as a low relief platform. This eroded platform of Precambrian rocks was eventually submerged under a Paleozoic ocean (Chapter 4). Paleozoic sediments were deposited on top of Precambrian rocks throughout all of Michigan, but those in the western Upper Peninsula were removed by erosion due to recent Pleistocene glaciation (Fig. 3.2; Plate 5).

Precambrian mineral resources

The first major mining rush in North America was in search for copper; it began in the 1840s, in the Precambrian rocks of Michigan's Keweenaw Peninsula (Chapter 12). Next, the mining of iron from Paleoproterozoic sedimentary rocks of Michigan began in 1845, and continues today in the Marquette area (Chapter 11). The metals extracted from these mines in the last half of the 19th century played an important economic role, as the new state of Michigan developed and as the nation fought a Civil War. The iron and copper mines have had, and continue to have, a significant impact on the economy of the Upper Peninsula.

Gold in the Marquette area was first mined in the 1880s, and again in the 1980s, from the Ropes gold mine. This gold is in a Precambrian fault zone, in Archean volcanic rocks (Bornhorst et al. 1986). By today's standards, the Ropes gold mine is quite small, having produced only about 125,000 oz of gold and 175,000 oz of silver (Reed 1991).

Other small, generally unprofitable, metallic mines and exploration prospects are scattered throughout exposed Precambrian rocks in the Great Lakes region. Exploration for metallic mineral resources hosted by Precambrian rocks continues today, and with new discoveries the economic importance of Precambrian rocks may be temporarily revived (see FOCUS BOX on the following page).

Although metals are the most notable earth resources hosted by Precambrian rocks of Michigan, other Precambrian rock units have economic uses. Examples include (1) Archean verde antique (a dark green serpentine with white and greenish-white mottling/veins, formed by alteration of rocks adjacent to the Ropes gold mine), which was used as a decorative building stone, (2) slate of the Baraga Group, used for roofing, (3) graphite (metamorphosed organic-rich sediments) from the Michigamme Formation of Baraga Group, used for paint and (4) Mesoproterozoic Jacobsville sandstone, which was used for building stone; in the Houghton area there are multiple buildings built with this beautiful rock (Fig. 3.11). Today, the Kona Dolomite and other Precambrian rocks are quarried for crushed stone. Former

FOCUS BOX: Precambrian rocks: Mineral resources for the future?

Precambrian rocks exposed in the western Upper Peninsula have been exploited for mineral resources for >150 years. Discovery of a mineral resource that can be extracted for a profit requires careful and patient work, over many years. The process of exploration involves the study of rocks exposed at the surface, measurement of geophysical characteristics on the ground or from an airplane, e.g., the magnetic or gravity field and, lastly, drilling of holes into the subsurface to extract core samples. Core drilling is the principal way to test the potential for buried mineral resources.

Kennecott Minerals Company had explored the Precambrian rocks of Michigan for nearly 10 years before announcing, in 2002, the discovery of a valuable nickel and copper deposit, named the Eagle deposit. Since 2002, they have continued to study the deposit via core drilling, while also collecting environmental data. The deposit is small (4 million metric tons), but high grade (3.6 % Ni and 2.9 % Cu). Its sulfide minerals are hosted within a tabular dike ~40 km NW of Marquette—part of the Mesoproterozoic dike swarm from Baraga to Marquette. The deposit (and dike) is covered by about 10 m of unconsolidated glacial sediments. Michigan's hard rock mining law, passed in 2006, sets stringent requirements to ensure that the environment, natural resources and public health and welfare are adequately protected, before mining can begin. Kennecott Minerals' permit application for mining was approved in December 2007 by the Michigan Department of Environmental Quality, after nearly one year of review with public input. The entire project site will cover less than 36 hectares.

A different company began drilling in 2002, and announced in 2003, the discovery of a significant massive sulfide deposit (DeMatties 1989), hosted by Paleoproterozoic volcanic rocks in Michigan. Massive sulfide deposits are formed when metal-bearing hot waters are expelled onto the sea floor; the metals are precipitated when the hot waters mix with cold sea water. This deposit is named the Back Forty deposit (or L-K deposit), and is located near the Michigan-Wisconsin border. It contains zinc, copper and gold. Whether this deposit makes it to the permitting stage is, as of this writing, to be determined.

The mining of nonferrous metallic minerals has the potential to make significant contributions to Michigan's economy, if and when deposits are discovered and the mining company can demonstrate that they meet Michigan's strong mining regulations.

FIGURE 3.11 Jacobsville Sandstone of Mesoproterozoic age (red, red and white banded) is the prominent building stone in this historic building, built in 1893 as the Supply Office for the Quincy Mine. This building is currently the gift shop and ticket office for the Quincy Mine Hoist Association historic site tours. The Quincy Mine location is a Heritage Site of the Keweenaw National Historical Park. The black basalt used in the building is an example of a use of waste rock (Portage Lake Volcanics; Chapter 12) from the native copper mines. Photo by R. Schaetzl.

waste rocks, originally adjacent to ore in abandoned mines and left on the surface at the end of mining, have also been used for crushed rock and building stone. Clearly, both nonmetallic and metallic mineral resources from Precambrian rocks of Michigan have, and are likely to continue to, play a role in Michigan's economy for many years to come.

■ Conclusions

The Precambrian rocks of Michigan formed over a period of about 2.5 billion years. During this time the continents have successively grown in size (Hoffman 1988, Card 1990). In Michigan, volcanism in an Archean arc ended when a microcontinent collided into the volcanic arc along the Great Lakes Tectonic Zone. After this collision, the newly added microcontinent made the original continent larger, extending further to the south. Paleoproterozoic sediments were deposited on this new continental margin (and later became rocks). The continent enlarged once again, with a series of collision events along the Niagara suture zone in northern Wisconsin (Penokean Orogeny). The younger Precambrian rocks that exist as the basement beneath Phanerozoic sedimentary rocks in the Lower Peninsula (Fig. 3.2) were added to the continent, making it larger, by yet another younger Precambrian collision. Finally, Mesoproterozoic rifting stretched the crust, again increasing its size. Rifting eventually ceased or else the continent would have broken apart and this story would have ended much differently!

Literature Cited

Addison, W.D., Brumpton, G.R., Vallini, D.A., McNaughton, N.J., Davis, D.W., Kissin, S.A., Fralick, P.W. and A.L. Hammond. 2005. Discovery of distal ejecta from the 1850 Ma Sudbury impact event. Geology 33:193–196.

Attoh, K. and J.S. Klasner. 1989. Tectonic implications of metamorphism and gravity field in the Penokean orogen of northern Michigan. Tectonics 8:911–933.

Bornhorst, T.J. and R.C. Johnson. 1998. Archean evolution of the southern edge of the Superior Province in Michigan: Geological Society of America Abstracts with Programs 30A:159.

Bornhorst, T.J. and R.C. Johnson. 1993. Geology of volcanic rocks in the southern half of the Ishpeming greenstone belt, Michigan. US Geological Survey Bulletin 1904–P. 13 pp.

Bornhorst, T.J., Shepeck, A.W. and D.M. Rossell. 1986. The Ropes gold mine, Marquette County, Michigan, U.S.A.—an Archean hosted lode gold deposit: In: MacDonald, A.J. (ed), Proceedings of Gold '86, an International Symposium on the Geology of Gold. Toronto. pp. 213–227.

Braiser, M.D., Green O.R., Jephcoat A.P., Kleppe A.K., Van Kranendonk M.J., Lindsay J.F., Steele A. and N.V. Grassineau. 2002. Questioning the evidence for Earth's oldest fossils. Nature 416(6876):76–81.

Card, K.D. 1990. A review of the Superior Province of the Canadian Shield, a product of Archean accretion. Precambrian Research 48:99–156.

Cavosie A.J., Valley J.W. and S.A. Wilde. 2005. Magmatic $\delta^{18}O$ in 4400–3900 Ma detrital zircons: A record of the alteration and recycling of crust in the Early Archean. Earth and Planetary Science Letters 235:663–681.

Chyba, C.F. and C. Sagan. 1996. Comets as a source of prebiotic organic molecules for the early Earth. In: Thomas, P.J., Hicks, R.D., Chyba, C.F. and C.P. McKay (eds), Comets and the Origin and Evolution of Life. Springer, New York. pp. 147–173.

Davis, D.W. and J.C. Green. 1997. Geochronology of the North American Midcontinent rift in western Lake Superior and implications for its geodynamic evolution. Canadian Journal of Earth Sciences 34:476–488.

DeMatties, T.A. 1989. A proposed geologic framework for massive sulfide deposits in the Wisconsin Penokean volcanic belt. Economic Geology 84:946–952.

Fedo, C.M. and M.J. Whitehouse. 2002, Metasomatic origin of quartz-pyroxene rock, Akilia, Greenland, and implications for Earth's earliest life. Science 296:1448–1452.

Friend C.R.L. and A.P. Nutman. 2005. Complex 3670–3500 Ma orogenic episodes superimposed on juvenile crust accreted between 3850 and 3690 Ma, Itsaq Gneiss Complex, southern West Greenland. Journal of Geology 113:375–397.

Frei, R., Polat, A. and A. Meibom. 2004. The Hadean upper mantle conundrum: Evidence for source depletion and enrichment from Sm-Nd, Re-Os, and Pb isotopic compositions in 3.71 Gy boninite-like metabasalts from the Isua Supracrustal Belt, Greenland. Geochimica et Cosmochima Acta 68:1645–1660.

Green, J.C., Bornhorst, T.J., Chandler, V.W., Mudrey, M.G., Myers, P.E., Pesonen, L.J. and J.T. Wilband. 1987. Keweenawan dykes of the Lake Superior region: Evidence for evolution of the Middle Proterozoic Midcontinent rift of North America. In: Halls, H.C. and W.F. Fahrig (eds), Mafic Dyke Swarms, Geological Association of Canada Special Paper 34:289–302.

Han, T.M. and B. Runnegar. 1992. Megascopic eukaryotic algae from the 2.1-billion-year-old Negaunee iron-formation, Michigan. Science 257: 232–235.

Harland, W.B. 2007. Origins and assessment of snowball Earth hypotheses. Geological Magazine 144:633–642.

Hoffman, P.F. 1988. United plates of America, the birth of a craton-Early Proterozoic assembly and growth of Laurentia. Annual Reviews of Earth and Planetary Science 16:543–603.

Holm, D.K., Van Schmus, W.R., MacNeill, L., Boerboom, T., Schweitzer, D. and D. Schneider. 2005. U–Pb zircon geochronology of Paleoproterozoic plutons from the northern mid-continent, USA: evidence for subduction flip and continued convergence after geon 18 Penokean orogenesis. Geological Society of America Bulletin 117:259–275.

Johnson, R.C. and T.J. Bornhorst. 1991. Archean geology of the northern block of the Ishpeming greenstone belt, Marquette County, Michigan. US Geological Survey Bulletin 1904–F. 20 pp.

Klasner, J.S. 1978. Penokean deformation and associated metamorphism in the western Marquette Range, northern Michigan. Geological Society of America Bulletin 89:711–722.

Knoll, A., 2003. Life on a Young Planet: The First Three Billion Years of Evolution on Earth. Princeton University Press, Princeton, NJ.

Larue, D.K. 1981. The Chocolay Group, Lake Superior region: Sedimentological evidence for deposition in basinal and platform settings on an Early Proterozoic craton. Geological Society of America Bulletin 92:417–435.

Letter 7471-Darwin. 1871. Letter 7471-Darwin, C.R. to Hooker, Jo.D., Feb. 1, 1871. www.darwinproject.ac.uk/darwinletters/calendar/entry-7471.html (last accessed March, 2008.)

Moecher, D.P., Perkins, D. III, Leier-Englehardt, P.J. and L.G. Medaris, Jr. 1986. Metamorphic conditions of Late Archean high grade gneisses, Minnesota River Valley, U.S.A. Canadian Journal of Earth Sciences 23:633–645.

Mojzsis, S.J., Arrhenius, G., McKeegan, K.D., Harrison, T.M., Nutman, A.P. and C.R.L. Friend. 1996. Evidence for life on Earth before 3,800 million years ago. Nature 384: 55–59.

Nachatilo, S.A. and R.L. Bauer. 1993. Structural analyses of Archean rocks in the Negaunee area, Michigan—constraints on Archean versus Proterozoic deformation: US Geological Survey Bulletin 1904–0. 29 pp.

NICE Working Group. 2007. Reinterpretation of Paleoproterozoic accretionary boundaries of the north-central United States based on new aeromagnetic-geologic compilation. Precambrian Research 157:71–79.

Nutman, A.P. 2006. Antiquity of the oceans and continents. Elements 2:223–227.

Ojakangas, R.W., Morey, G.B. and D.L. Southwick. 2001. Paleoproterozoic basin development and sedimentation in the Lake Superior region, North America. Sedimentary Geology 141–142:319–341.

O'neil, J., Carlson, R.W., Francis, D. and R.K. Stevenson. 2008. Neodymium–142 evidence for Hadean mafic crust. Science 321:1828–1831.

Pufahl, P.K., Hiatt, E.E., Stanley, C.R., Morrow, J.R., Nelson, G.J. and C.T. Edwards. 2007. Physical and chemical evidence of the 1850 Ma Sudbury impact event in the Baraga Group, Michigan. Geology 35: 827–830.

Reed, R.C. 1991. Economic geology and history of metallic minerals in the Northern Peninsula of Michigan. In Catacosinos P.A. and P.A. Daniels, Jr. (eds), Early sedimentary evolution of the Michigan Basin. Geological Society of America Special Paper 256:13–51.

Robb, L.J., Knoll, A.H., Plumb, K.A., Shields, G.A., Strauss, H. and J. Veizer. 2004. The Precambrian: the Archean and Proterozoic Eons. In: Gradstein, F.M., Ogg, J.G. and A.J. Smith (eds), A Geologic Time Scale 2004. Cambridge University Press, Cambridge. pp. 129–140.

Runnegar, B. 1982. The Cambrian Explosion: Animals or fossils? Australian Journal of Earth Sciences 29: 395–411.

Schindlowski, M. 1988. A 3,800-million-year isotopic record of life from carbon in sedimentary rocks. Nature 333:313–318.

Schopf, J.W. 1992. The oldest fossils and what they mean. In: Schopf, J.W. (ed), Major Events in the History of Life. Jones and Bartlett Publishers, Boston, MA. pp. 29–63.

Schulz, K.J. and W.F. Cannon. 2007. The Penokean orgony in the Lake Superior region. Precambrian Research 157:4–15.

Scott, G.W. and H.M. Lukey. 1999. Geologic field trip to the Tilden Mine. Institute on Lake Superior Geology Proceedings, Volume 45. Field Trip Guidebook. pp. 114–128.

Sims, P.K. 1993a. Great Lakes Tectonic Zone in the Marquette area, Michigan-Implications for Archean tectonics in north-central United States. In: Sims, P.K. (ed), Contributions to Precambrian Geology of the Great Lakes Region. US Geological Survey Professional Paper 1904E.19 pp.

Sims, P.K. 1993b. Minnesota River Valley Subprovince (Archean gneiss terrane). In: Sims, P.K. and L.M.H. Carter (eds), Archean and Proterozoic Geology of the Lake Superior Region, U.S.A. US Geological Survey Professional Paper 1556:14–23.

Sims, P.K., Card, K.D., Morey, G.B. and Z.E. Peterman. 1980. The Great Lakes tectonic zone—A major crustal structure in central North America. Geological Society of America Bulletin 91:690–698.

Sims, P.K. and Z.E. Peterman. 1992. Guide of the geology of the Great Lakes tectonic zone in the Marquette area, Michigan—A late Archean paleosuture: Institute on Lake Superior Geology Proceedings, Volume 83. Field Trip Guidebook. pp. 105–135.

Taylor, G.L. 1972. Stratigraphy, Sedimentology, and Sulphide Mineralization of the Kona Dolomite. Ph.D. Dissertation, Michigan Technological University, Houghton. 112 pp.

Tinkham, D.K. and S. Marshak. 2004. Precambrian dome-and-keel structure in the Penokean orogenic belt of northern Michigan, USA. In: Whitney, D.L., Teyssier, C. and C.S. Siddoway (eds), Gneiss Domes in Orogeny. Geological Society of America Special Paper 380:321–338.

Thover, E., Holm, D.K., van der Pluijm, B.A., Essene, E.J. and F.W. Cambray. 2007. Late Paleoproterozoic (geon 18 and 17) reactivation of the Neoarchean Great Lakes Tectonic Zone, northern Michigan, USA: evidence from kinematic analysis, thermobarometry and ^{40}Ar/^{39}Ar geochronology. Precambrian Research 157:144–168.

Valley, J.W. 2006. Early Earth. Elements 2:201–204.

Van Hise, C.R. and C.K. Leith. 1909. Precambrian geology of North America. US Geological Survey Bulletin 360. 930 pp.

Van Hise, C.R. and C.K. Leith. 1911. The Geology of the Lake Superior Region. US Geological Survey Monograph 57. 641 pp.

Wilkin, R.T. and T.J. Bornhorst. 1992. Geology and geochemistry of granitoid rocks in the Archean Northern complex, Michigan, U.S.A. Canadian Journal of Earth Sciences 29:1674–1685.

Wood, B.J. and A.N. Halliday. 2005. Cooling of the Earth and core formation after the giant impact. Nature 437:1345–1348.

Wood, B.J., Walter, M.J. and J. Wade. 2006. Accretion of the Earth and segregation of its core. Nature 444:825–833.

Zahnle, K.J. 2006. Earth's earliest atmosphere. Elements 2:217–222.

Further Readings

Bowring, S.A. and I.S.P. Williams. 1999. Priscoan (4.00±4.03) orthogneisses from northwestern Canada. Contributions to Mineralogy and Petrology 134:3–16.

LaBerge, G.L. 1994. Geology of the Lake Superior Region. Geoscience Press, Phoenix, AZ.

Nisbet, E.G. and N.H. Sleep. 2001. The habitat and nature of early life. Nature 409:1083–1091.

Orgel, L.E. 1994. The Origin of Life on the Earth. Scientific American (October) pp. 77–83.

Reed, J.C., Jr., Bickford, M.E., Houstone, R.S., Link, P.K., Rankin, D.W., Sims, P.K. and W.R. Van Schmus (eds.). 1993. Precambrian Conterminous U.S. Geological Society of America. The Geology of North America. C-2.

Rollinson, H. 2007. When did plate tectonics begin? Geology Today 23:186–191.

Sims, P.K. and L.M.H. Carter (eds). 1993. Archean and Proterozoic Geology of the Lake Superior Region, U.S.A. U.S. Geological Survey Professional Paper 1556.

Thurston, P.C., Williams, H.R., Sutcliffe, R.H. and G.M. Scott. 1992. Geology of Ontario. Ontario Geological Survey Special Volume 4.

Windley, B.F. 1995. The Evolving Continents. John Wiley and Sons, New York.

Paleozoic Environments and Life

4

Steve LoDuca

■ Introduction

The Paleozoic Era comprises nearly 300 million years of Earth history, from 542 million to 251 million years ago (Ma). A great deal of change can happen over such an enormous expanse of time, even at the relatively slow "average" rates that characterize many Earth processes, and that was certainly the case for Michigan! For the area that would become the Great Lake State, the Paleozoic Era was a time of crustal warping, invasion of inland seas and the literal accumulation of kilometers of sediment, which would later turn to rock. In total, the Paleozoic sedimentary rock sequence beneath Michigan reaches nearly 5 km in thickness. It comprises one of the most complete and thickest successions of Paleozoic rocks in the Midwest, and these rocks provide a detailed account of environmental change during the Paleozoic Era. Although the Paleozoic Era was a very long time ago, much of Michigan's present-day geographic character is a lasting legacy of its Paleozoic past.

In North America, the Paleozoic Era is subdivided into seven periods (Plate 3). From oldest to youngest, they are the Cambrian, Ordovician, Silurian, Devonian, Mississippian, Pennsylvanian and Permian. In Michigan, each is represented by sedimentary rocks and fossils, with the exception of the Permian (Chapter 5). We will begin our exploration of Michigan's Paleozoic environments and life with the Cambrian Period, making our way toward the present and taking stock of the major components of the Earth's system (hydrosphere, geosphere, atmosphere and biosphere) as we go. The major sedimentary rock packages deposited in Michigan during the Paleozoic Era are listed in stratigraphic order—oldest at the bottom, youngest at the top—in Table 4.1 and on Plate 6. These sources are our roadmap through time; it will be helpful to refer to them often.

Keep two things firmly in mind while reading this chapter. First, the geographic features that characterize Michigan today did not yet exist during the Paleozoic. For example, in the Paleozoic, hundreds of millions of years before glaciers carved the Great Lakes basins, there were no Upper and Lower Peninsulas, but these terms are used in the chapter for the sake of locating features and events. Second, although this overview will focus on Michigan, I will occasionally expand the scope to continental and global scales. This is necessary because some events, such as the growth of coral reefs in Michigan, only make sense when viewed in the context of the "big picture."

■ The Cambrian Period (542–488 Ma)

Stretching as far as the eye can see is a barren landscape of rock and sediment. This is Michigan at the dawn of the Paleozoic Era, during the earliest part of the Cambrian Period. Later in the Cambrian, this scene would change dramatically, as the sea slowly invaded. To understand how and why, we must consider the world's ocean basins, which at that time included the Iapetus Ocean, formed when the large continental block known as Laurentia (North America + Greenland) rifted apart from the paleo-European continent, called Baltica, near the end of the Proterozoic

TABLE 4.1   Generalized Paleozoic stratigraphic succession in Michigan

Age	Rock Unit	Rock Type(s)	Thickness (meters)
PENNSYLVANIAN	Grand River Formation	Sandstone	85
PENNSYLVANIAN	Saginaw Formation	Sandstone with coal beds; limestone	170
MISSISSIPPIAN	Bayport Formation	Limestone	60
MISSISSIPPIAN	Michigan Formation	Shale, limestone, gypsum	105
MISSISSIPPIAN	Marshall Formation	Sandstone	75
MISSISSIPPIAN	Coldwater Formation	Shale, some limestone and sandstone	335
MISSISSIPPIAN	Sunbury Formation	Shale	30
DEVONIAN	Ellsworth Formation	Shale	245
DEVONIAN	Antrim Formation	Shale	195
DEVONIAN	Traverse Group	Limestone, shale (coral reefs)	250
DEVONIAN	Rogers City Formation	Limestone	70
DEVONIAN	Dundee Formation	Limestone	75
DEVONIAN	Detroit River Group	Limestone, dolostone; sandstone at base	440
DEVONIAN	Bois Blanc Formation	Dolostone	110
SILURIAN	Bass Islands Group	Dolostone, shale	180
SILURIAN	Salina Group	Salt, dolostone, shale, gypsum	750
SILURIAN	Engadine Group	Dolostone (large coral reefs)	210
SILURIAN	Manistique Group	Dolostone, limestone	60
SILURIAN	Burnt Bluff Group	Dolostone, limestone (coral reefs)	105
SILURIAN	Cataract Group	Dolostone with shale (coral reefs)	40
ORDOVICIAN	Richmond Group	Limestone, shale	275
ORDOVICIAN	Collingwood Formation	Shale	18
ORDOVICIAN	Trenton Formation	Limestone	165
ORDOVICIAN	Black River Formation	Dolostone	150
ORDOVICIAN	St. Peter Formation	Sandstone	365
CAMBRIAN	Au Train Formation	Dolostone	90
CAMBRIAN	Munising Formation	Sandstone; conglomerate at base	75

Shaded intervals indicate significant spans of time without rock representation in Michigan, i.e., major unconformities. In ascending order, the packages of rock between these unconformities correspond to the Sauk, Tippecanoe, Kaskaskia and Absaroka cratonic sequences of North America. The specific names of these unconformities, in ascending order starting with the top of the Au Train Formation, are Knox, Wallbridge and Mississippian-Pennsylvanian. Unit thicknesses are approximate and in most cases represent maximum values for units that vary in thickness across the state. For a more detailed version, see Plate 4. After Catacosinos et al. (2001).

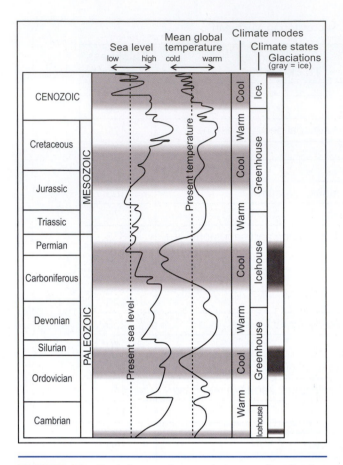

FIGURE 4.1 Earth System changes, in terms of sea level and climate, for the last 550 million years of Earth history. Note that for much of the Paleozoic Era, sea level was considerably higher than at present. After Boggs (2006).

Eon (Plate 3). Then, as now, plate tectonics led to the formation of major seafloor spreading zones and associated mid-ocean ridges, but rates of seafloor spreading during the Cambrian were greater than today. In general, during times of accelerated seafloor spreading, increased heat flow from the mantle below causes the mid-ocean ridges to rise, displacing great volumes of seawater and pushing global sea level upward. The opposite happens during times of slow seafloor spreading—the mid-ocean ridges cool and subside, and global sea level falls. Such fluctuations in plate tectonic activity, together with glacial advances and retreats linked to climate change, explain most episodes of sea level change throughout Earth history. By the latter part of the Cambrian, high rates of seafloor spreading, combined with melting of the glaciers of the late Proterozoic, had resulted in so much sea level rise that much of North America, including most of Michigan, was covered by a vast, shallow inland sea (Fig. 4.1, 4.2A). The northern part of the continent, however, remained above sea level during this time.

As the Cambrian seas encroached onto what is today Michigan, great thicknesses of sand accumulated on the sea bottom and around the shores. Eventually, through compaction and natural cementation, this sand would be transformed into layers of sandstone that comprise the Munising Formation (Table 4.1, Plate 4). The Munising Formation is exposed in many parts of the northern Upper Peninsula, but nowhere more spectacularly than in the cliffs at Pictured Rocks National Lakeshore (PRNL) along the southern shore of Lake Superior (Fig. 4.3). At this location and others in the Upper Peninsula, the lower sandstone layers differ in terms of mineral composition and texture from those of the upper part. On this basis, the Munising Formation is divided into two units. The lower, or older, of the two is the Chapel Rock Member, named for the famous landform in the Pictured Rocks area sculpted into this sandstone by relatively recent erosional activity (Fig. 4.3A; Plate 4). The mineral composition of this unit indicates that the sand was derived from the erosional remnants of the Penokean Mountains (Chapter 3), which by the Cambrian, over a billion years removed from their formation, had eroded into a gently rolling upland called the Northern Michigan Highlands. The mineral composition of the overlying unit, called the Miner's Castle Member (also named for a well-known erosional landform at Pictured Rocks; Fig. 4.3B; Plate 4), is indicative of source areas to the east and NE, in Canada. By this time, the very latest part of the Cambrian Period, the Northern Michigan Highlands were almost completely submerged.

Michigan's climate during this time was very unlike that of today, mainly because the entire continent occupied a different latitudinal position. In the Cambrian, North America straddled the equator; Michigan itself was located just south of the equator and would remain in a low-latitude position throughout the Paleozoic Era (Figs. 4.2A, 4.4). Thus, temperatures were warm year-round. Temperatures globally were also rather warm during the early part of the Paleozoic Era, so that the planet lacked continental glaciers, even at high latitudes (Fig. 4.1). Even Michigan's wind patterns were strange relative to today, since its low-latitude setting placed it within the realm of the easterly trade winds.

Although the Cambrian land surface was essentially barren rock, apart from some bacteria and possibly some algae, the oceans were quite another matter. Indeed, Cambrian seas were the incubator for one of the biosphere's most important episodes of evolutionary activity, an event known as the Cambrian Explosion. This evolutionary "burst" occurred over a relatively brief span of about 15 million years during the middle part of the Cambrian Period,

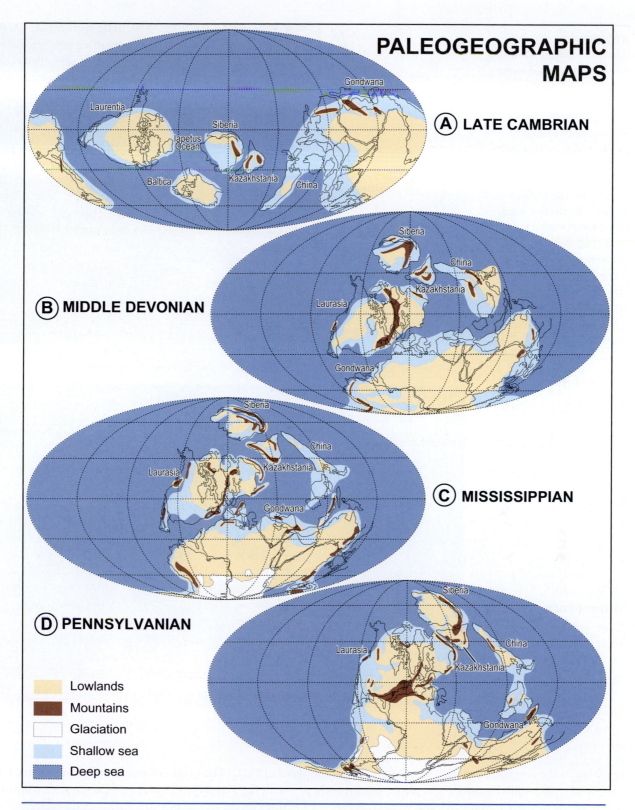

FIGURE 4.2   Global paleogeography during the Paleozoic Era. After Wicander and Monroe (2004). A. Late Cambrian. Note the equatorial position of North America (= Laurentia) and extensive coverage of North America by shallow seas. B. Middle Devonian. Note the continued equatorial position of North America and collision between North America and Europe (= Baltica) to form Laurasia. C. Mississippian. Note that the southern super-continent of Gondwana, composed of Australia, Antarctica, Africa, South America and India, is approaching Laurasia. D. Pennsylvanian. Note the collision of Gondwana and Laurasia to form the bulk of Pangea, and the uplift of the Appalachian Mountains along the eastern margin of North America.

FIGURE 4.3 Cambrian sandstones of the Munising Formation exposed along the shore of Lake Superior at Pictured Rocks National Lakeshore in the Upper Peninsula. (A) Chapel Rock. At this locality only the Chapel Rock Member is exposed. Photo by S. LoDuca. (B) Miner's Castle. The reddish sandstone layers visible in the lower cliff face comprise the upper part of the Chapel Rock Member, above which are the basal layers of the Miner's Castle Member. Photo by R. Schaetzl.

(A)

(B)

resulting in the emergence of the "Cambrian Fauna" (Sepkoski 1981). (The origin of single-celled life forms, and a variety of multi-celled animals and algae, significantly pre-date the Cambrian Explosion; Chapter 3). Important components of the Cambrian Fauna were trilobites—an extinct group in the Phylum Arthropoda related to spiders, insects and crustaceans—and brachiopods, a still-living but now rather uncommon group of marine shellfish superficially similar to clams (Fig. 4.5). Fossils of both groups are known from the Miner's Castle Member of the Munising Formation in Dickinson County. A variety of archaic arthropods, aquatic worms and sponges comprised the other main elements of the Cambrian Fauna.

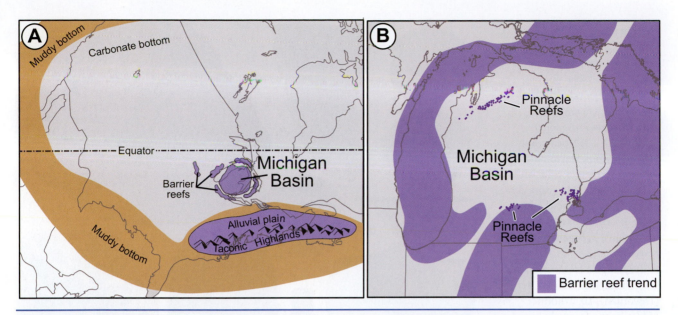

FIGURE 4.4 Silurian paleogeography. A. During the Silurian, North America straddled the equator and was rotated nearly 90° clockwise, relative to its present orientation, so that the modern-day east coast faced south. Note the Taconic Mountains, uplifted during the preceding Ordovician Period, and the presence of extensive reefs around Michigan Basin. The entire continent was covered by a shallow sea. After Wicander and Monroe (2004). B. Detail of the Michigan Basin during the Silurian. Large barrier reefs greatly restricted the flow of water into and out of the basin during this time, contributing to the formation of thick evaporite deposits in the basin center. Note pinnacle reefs positioned inboard of barrier reefs, in slightly deeper water. The sizes and positions of the barrier reefs are approximate.

■ The Ordovician Period (488–444 Ma)

During the early part of the Ordovician Period, Michigan remained covered by a shallow sea, and sediments that comprise the Au Train Formation—a sandy dolostone—were deposited (Plate 4). Similar rocks of this age in the Lower Peninsula comprise the Prairie du Chien Group, but are not exposed because they are deeply buried beneath younger Paleozoic rocks. Today, the resistant Au Train Formation forms a prominent cliff, known as the Cambro-Ordovician Escarpment, where it intersects the surface in the northern part of the eastern Upper Peninsula. As rivers flow northward toward Lake Superior, they fall off the edge of the relatively hard Au Train rocks and erode into the softer, underlying Munising Formation sandstones, forming many picturesque waterfalls. Indeed, many of Michigan's most famous waterfalls, including Tahquamenon, Miner's, Laughing Whitefish, Munising and Au Train, are situated in this distinctive geologic setting (Fig. 4.6).

About 480 million years ago, a major worldwide drop in sea level left most of Michigan high and dry (Fig. 4.1), and the area began to erode. In general, such a reversal from sediment accumulation to sediment erosion results in a "gap" in a sedimentary succession, termed an unconformity. The significant unconformity produced in the Michigan sedimentary rock succession, as a result of this prolonged episode of exposure, is depicted by the shaded interval immediately above the Au Train Formation in Table 4.1 and by the wavy line at this level in the Michigan stratigraphic column (Plate 4). The Michigan landscape at this time must still have looked rather barren and bleak, as land plants and animals had not yet evolved.

After several million years, sea level began to rise, and Michigan was once again submerged beneath a shallow, tropical sea. Sands eroded from the Wisconsin Highlands and other source areas to the west were deposited across Michigan during the early part of this sea level rise, in beach and nearshore marine settings. These sediments comprise the St. Peter Formation, a relatively pure (> 98% quartz) sandstone. In neighboring states, the St. Peter Formation is an important source of silica for the production of glass and molding sand for foundries, but in Michigan the St. Peter Formation is too deeply buried under layers of younger Paleozoic rocks to be economically mined or quarried.

The St. Peter Formation in Michigan is overlain by thick deposits of limestone and dolostone, made up of large numbers of shells from Michigan's Middle Ordovician sea. Some shells are still more or less intact, but most were

FIGURE 4.5 Paleozoic fossils of the Michigan Basin. Photos by S. LoDuca. All fossils are approximately × 1 except 14 (× ½) and 20 (× 2). 1. Gastropod (*Platyceras*, Devonian). 2. Bryozoan (*Prasopora*, Ordovician). 3. Horn coral (*Heliophyllum*, Devonian). 4. Coral (*Favosites*, Silurian). 5. Brachiopod (*Mucrospirifer*, Devonian). 6. Crinoid cup (*Megistocrinus*, basal view, Devonian). 7. Brachiopod (*Paraspirifer*, Devonian). 8. Brachiopod (*Rafinesquina*, Ordovician). 9. Crinoid stem (Devonian). 10. Trilobite (*Eldredgeops*, formerly known as *Phacops*, Devonian). 11. Seed fern (*Neuropteris*, Pennsylvanian). 12. Trilobite (*Flexicalymene*, enrolled specimen, Ordovician). 13. Bivalve (*Nuculopsis*, Mississippian). 14. Bivalve (*Megalomus*, Silurian). 15. Brachiopod (*Platystrophia*, Ordovician). 16. Blastoid (*Hyperoblastus*, Devonian). 17. Sponge (stromatoporoid, Devonian). 18. Horn coral (*Streptelasma*, Ordovician). 19. Trilobite (*Dechenella*, top and side views of enrolled specimen, Devonian). 20. Crinoid (*Eutaxocrinus*, complete crown, Devonian).

broken down on the sea floor, forming fine carbonate (lime) mud. Over time, this shell and lime mud material compacted and hardened to form layers of limestone ($CaCO_3$). In places, some of the calcium in the limestone was later replaced by magnesium, forming the mineral dolomite [$(CaMg)(CO_3)_2$] and converting the limestone into the sedimentary rock called dolostone. Today, limestones and dolostones (collectively called *carbonates*) of Middle Ordovician age (Black River and Trenton formations, Table 4.1) are quarried extensively in the Upper Peninsula, especially around Escanaba (Fig. 4.5).

Along the eastern margin of Laurentia during the Middle Ordovician, an important geosphere event was underway. Subduction of one tectonic plate beneath another, along a newly-formed plate boundary, produced major volcanoes and forced up a mountain belt called the Taconic Mountains, in the New England area (Fig. 4.4A). Thin layers of clay (bentonite) within the Trenton Formation (Table 4.1, Plate 4), which may be observed in outcrops of this

FIGURE 4.6 Waterfalls of the Upper Peninsula and the location of the Cambro-Ordovician Escarpment. A. Map of the major waterfalls in Michigan. Note that many are positioned along the Cambro-Ordovician Escarpment, formed where the resistant rocks of the Au Train Formation intersect the surface. This escarpment runs along the Lake Superior shoreline in Alger County, forming the high cliffs at Pictured Rocks National Lakeshore. B. Some of the typical, larger waterfalls in Michigan, all of which are on the Cambro-Ordovician Escarpment. Clockwise from lower left: Sable Falls, in Pictured Rocks National Lakeshore, a few km west of Grand Marais. Upper Tahquamenon Falls, in Tahquamenon Falls State Park, near Paradise. Laughing Whitefish Falls, in western Alger County. Photos by R. Schaetzl.

FIGURE 4.7 Marine fauna of the Ordovician Period. Fossils of all of these groups are common in the Ordovician-age rocks of Michigan. After Lutgens and Tarbuk (2000). 1. A large straight-shelled nautiloid, the dominant predator of the Ordovician seas. 2. trilobite 3. tabulate coral 4. rugose ("horn") coral 5. brachiopod. 6. bryozoa.

unit in the Upper Peninsula (Delta County), are composed of altered ash from these volcanoes. Sediment derived from erosion of the Taconic Mountains was transported west into the shallow sea that covered the interior of the continent, the finest-grained material (silt and clay) contributing to the formation of Late Ordovician siltstones and shales in Michigan (Collingwood Formation, Richmond Group, Table 4.1).

Like the Cambrian, the Ordovician was an important time in the history of the marine biosphere. During the Early Ordovician, a second relatively rapid burst of evolutionary activity, called the Ordovician Radiation, resulted in the establishment of many new groups of marine life, and the emergence of the Paleozoic Fauna (Sepkoski 1981). In the Paleozoic Fauna, like the Cambrian Fauna, trilobites and brachiopods were major elements, but joining these groups in importance were crinoids (sea lilies), bryozoa (moss animals), a variety of mollusks, including straight-shelled nautiloids (related to modern squid but with a conical shell on the outside) and reef-building stony corals (Fig. 4.7). Well-preserved fossils of all of these groups are abundant in Ordovician-age carbonates that crop out in many places in the Upper Peninsula, especially near Escanaba (Fig. 4.5, 2, 8, 12, 15, 18). Primitive jawless fish, known as ostracoderms, with eel-like bodies and heads clad in bony armor, were another important component of the Ordovician biosphere.

At the end of the Ordovician, a devastating episode of extinction eliminated many species from across all of the major groups of the Paleozoic Fauna within a relatively short span of time. This was the first of five *mass extinction events* in Earth history. The cause of this event is not known with certainty, but it may be related to an episode of global cooling known to have occurred at this time (Fig. 4.1). During this relatively brief cooling event, large continental glaciers formed on the southern super-continent of Gondwana (Fig. 4.2), resulting in a global drop in sea level (Fig. 4.1). In Michigan, withdrawal of the sea led to the formation of a minor unconformity (Plate 4).

■ The Silurian Period (444–416 Ma)

During the Early Silurian, global climate warmed. Glaciers in Gondwana melted, sea level rose and Michigan was once again beneath a shallow sea. In addition, an important geosphere event was in full swing: the development of the Michigan Basin (see FOCUS BOX on the following page). The Michigan Basin is a classic example of an intracratonic

FOCUS BOX: The Michigan Basin

The roughly circular Michigan Basin encompasses most of Michigan and parts of neighboring states. Covering some 207,000 km² (Catacosinos et al. 1991; Plate 5), it is slightly larger than the Illinois Basin and somewhat smaller than the Williston Basin (Montana-North Dakota-Saskatchewan area)—two other significant North American intracratonic basins of Paleozoic age. Along its western margin, the basin is bounded by broad crustal upwarps—the Kankakee and Wisconsin Arches. The eastern margin is bounded by the Findlay and Algonquin Arches (see Figure below).

Within the basin, rock layers dip toward the basin center, near Midland, at a very gentle slope that averages about 11 m/km (Heinrich 1976; Plate 5). Because of this architecture, and because the basin was later eroded flat across the top, different geologic units intersect the surface at different places, giving the geologic map of Michigan its distinctive "bull's-eye" appearance (Plates 5, 6). Note that Lakes Michigan and Huron wrap around the western and eastern sides of the basin, respectively. The positions and shapes of these two Great Lakes basins, formed much later in Earth history (Chapters 13, 17), reflect the composition and arrangement of rock units across the basin surface. In profile, the body of sedi-

mentary rock within the basin, estimated at 450,000 km³ (Cohee 1965), is lens-shaped, reaching a maximum thickness of approximately 4,800 m at the basin center (Catacosinos et al. 1991), but thinning considerably out toward the edges (see Figure below, and Plate 5). The shape of this rock body is a direct consequence of basin subsidence—as the basin subsided, more "room" was available for sediment to accumulate, especially in the middle.

The cause behind the formation of the Michigan Basin is uncertain, but may be related to an earlier, mid-Proterozoic rifting episode that weakened the crust in this area and emplaced large bodies of relatively dense igneous rock (Chapters 3, 12). Later, during the early Paleozoic Era, changes in deep-seated thermal activity beneath this area, or perhaps crustal stresses from tectonic collisions along the eastern margin of Laurentia, may have caused this relatively dense portion of crust to begin to subside (Howell and van der Pluijm 1990, Kaminski and Jaupart 2000). Whatever the cause, it is clear that basin subsidence was particularly active during the Silurian and into the later Paleozoic, because sedimentary rock units deposited during these times markedly increase in thickness as they approach the middle of the basin.

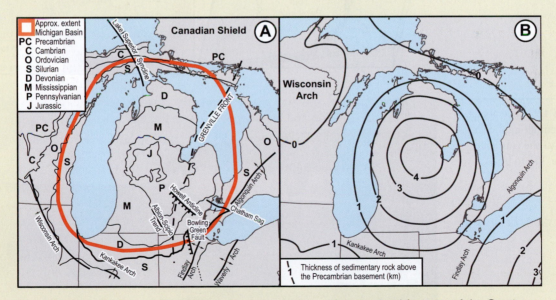

The Michigan Basin. A. The Michigan Basin and other major structural features of the Great Lakes region. See Plate 5A for a cross-section view of the basin. B. Total thickness of Paleozoic sedimentary rocks in the Michigan Basin. Note pronounced increase in thickness toward the center of the basin. After Howell and van der Pluijm (1990).

basin, formed when a region of the Earth's crust in the interior of a continent gradually sags downward (subsides) over a long interval of time. Some subsidence of the Michigan Basin had occurred during the Ordovician, but the main phase of subsidence began during the Silurian and would continue into the latter part of the Paleozoic.

Coral reefs flourished during the Silurian, and around the margin of the Michigan Basin a significant barrier reef complex began to take shape during the middle part of this period, its length rivaling that of the modern-day Great Barrier Reef of Australia (Fig. 4.4). In slightly deeper water, closer to the basin center, grew towering pinnacle reefs, up to 100 m high. The great height of these reefs is a direct reflection of local geosphere dynamics: as the basin subsided, reef growth kept pace so that the reef tops remained near sea level, resulting in their tall but relatively narrow shapes. The calcium carbonate skeletons of the corals and other marine organisms in the reefs contributed to the formation of thick deposits of limestone and dolostone (Burnt Bluff Group, Manistique Group, Engadine Group; Plate 4). Today, in the deep subsurface of the Michigan Basin in the Lower Peninsula, Silurian reefs host enormous quantities of hydrocarbons, which filled the myriad nooks and crannies within the reefs later in Earth history (Chapter 10).

Where Silurian rocks intersect the surface along the northern part of the present-day Michigan Basin (Plate 5), the carbonate units in the middle part of the succession, because they are more resistant to erosion and weathering than rock units immediately below (Cataract Group) and above (Salina Group), form a distinctive ridge called the Niagara escarpment (Fig. 4.8). Moving from west to east, the Niagara escarpment forms the Door Peninsula of Wisconsin, the Garden Peninsula (home to Fayette State Park) of the Upper Peninsula (Fig. 4.9), the core of

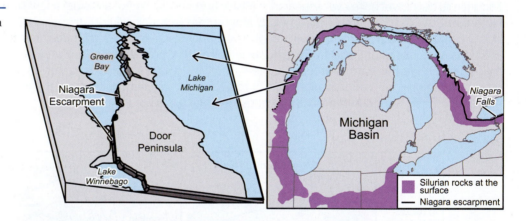

FIGURE 4.8 Distribution of Silurian bedrock in the Michigan Basin, and the location of the Niagara escarpment. After Milstein (1987).

FIGURE 4.9 The Niagara Escarpment along the western edge of the Garden Peninsula. Photo by R. Schaetzl.

Drummond Island, much of Manitoulin Island and the Bruce Peninsula of Ontario, and the major "step" over which the Niagara River plunges to form Niagara Falls. Excellent examples of Silurian reef corals can be viewed in the Niagara escarpment on state-owned land near Raber, in Chippewa County (Milstein 1987; Fig. 4.5, 4). Economically important quarries are developed in Silurian carbonate rocks at many places along the escarpment in the Upper Peninsula, especially on Drummond Island (Fig. 4.10).

By the latter part of the Silurian, reefs had dramatically altered the local environment of the Michigan Basin by largely cutting off the marine water within it, from the open ocean (Fig. 4.4). In this setting, high rates of evaporation driven by the warm, dry climate increased the concentration of dissolved salts so much that they began to precipitate. This extremely saline sea was maintained for long periods of time in the Michigan Basin by a delicate balance between water removal by evaporation, and replacement from the open ocean. This, combined with steady subsidence of the basin, resulted in evaporite deposits many hundreds of meters thick that comprise the Salina Group rocks (Plate 4). Most of the evaporite material of the Salina Group is rock salt (halite), but significant amounts of anhydrite (which is converted to gypsum in near-surface settings through the addition of water) and sylvite are present as well. In total, the Michigan Basin is estimated to contain over 60 trillion metric tons of Silurian-age salt deposits (Cohee 1965). Today, this rock salt is mined in the Detroit and Windsor areas (Fig. 4.11).

Carbonate rocks of the Bass Islands Group (Table 4.1; Plate 4) cap the Silurian sedimentary rock succession in Michigan. These dolostones are quarried for aggregate in Monroe County (Fig. 4.10), and contain an abundance of cavities, known as vugs, some of which bear outstanding crystals of the mineral celestine (Heinrich, 1976). Recently, because of its high porosity, the Bass Islands Group was selected as the target of a CO_2 injection well in Otsego County. Strata of the overlying Bois Blanc Formation and Detroit River Group (see below) serve as a "cap," preventing the injected CO_2 from migrating back to the surface.

During the Silurian, the marine Paleozoic Fauna rebounded from the Ordovician extinction event. Apart from more vigorous reef building, the overall look of the marine biosphere during the Silurian was much the same as the Ordovician, although trilobite diversity was greatly diminished relative to earlier times. Other important members

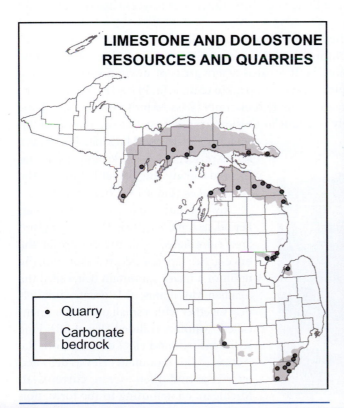

FIGURE 4.10 Principal areas of carbonate bedrock in Michigan, and the locations of major limestone and dolostone quarries.

FIGURE 4.11 Silurian rock salt (Salina Group), Detroit Salt Company mine, Detroit, Michigan. Note the well-developed layering and crystalline texture. All of the salt currently excavated from the Detroit Salt Company mine is used for road deicing. Photo by R. Schaetzl.

of the Silurian biosphere were early jawed fishes, the acanthodians, most of which were small (typically 15 cm in length) and all of which had unusual fins supported along their leading edges by stout spines of bone. On land, communities of plants and animals were just becoming established. Silurian land plants were typically 5–20 cm tall and of very simple form, consisting of clusters of branches without true leaves. Early land animals, too, were rather diminutive, primarily scorpions and millipedes. Fossils of Silurian land plants and animals are well known from New York State, but do not occur in Michigan because the entire area was submerged during this time.

The Devonian Period (416–359 Ma)

A major drop in sea level occurred during the early part of the Devonian Period, leaving most of Michigan high and dry (as it was previously, during the Early Ordovician) for an interval of several million years (Fig. 4.1). Only the northwestern part of the Michigan Basin remained submerged, allowing for deposition of carbonate muds in that area (Garden Island Formation). In the dry parts of the basin, a major erosional surface developed, visible in Table 4.1 and Plate 4, above the Bass Islands Group.

The Early Devonian drop in sea level was followed by yet another sea level rise that reestablished a shallow sea across Michigan (Figs. 4.1, 4.2B). Carbonate muds and sands that accumulated along the bottom and around the shores of the Middle Devonian sea during the initial part of this sea level rise comprise the Bois Blanc and Sylvania formations, respectively (Table 4.1; Plate 4). During the remainder of the Middle Devonian, thick packages of carbonate sediment were deposited in the Michigan Basin that comprise, in ascending order, the Detroit River Group, Dundee Formation, Rogers City Formation and Traverse Group (Table 4.1; Plate 4). The Detroit River Group contains significant halite deposits near the basin center, indicating a brief episode of evaporite conditions in the Michigan Basin during the early part of the Middle Devonian. Today, this halite is extracted using solution mining techniques near Midland (Chapter 16). Where Middle Devonian-age carbonate rocks intersect the surface in Michigan, in the northern and southeastern parts of the Lower Peninsula (Plate 5), they are quarried extensively (Fig. 4.10). Indeed, the Carmeuse Lime and Stone Quarry at Rogers City is the world's largest limestone quarry (Fig. 4.12).

Starting in the latest Silurian and continuing into the Middle Devonian, localized pockets of Silurian salt in the shallow subsurface were removed by groundwater solution. In the Mackinac Straits region, this led to the formation of a distinctive type of rock, called a collapse breccia. It formed where areas of unsupported overlying rock material broke and fell into the underlying salt-solution cavities (Mackinac Breccia, Plate 4). The Mackinac Breccia includes fragments of Late Silurian and Devonian carbonate rock units (Bass Islands Group, Bois Blanc Formation, Detroit River Group). Because it is relatively resistant to erosion, it is exposed in the region today, including places on Mackinac Island, as a series of scenic sea stacks and sea arches formed during the glacial history of the Great Lakes (Fig 4.13; Chapter 13).

By the latter part of the Devonian Period, tectonic activity in the New England area culminated with the closure of the once-great Iapetus ocean basin and the uplift of a major mountain belt, called the Acadian Mountains, as Laurentia and Baltica, together with a small micro-continent called Avalonia, collided (Fig. 4.2B). Fine sediment (silt and clay) derived from the erosion of this mountain belt was delivered by rivers and then ocean currents to Michigan, contributing to the formation of thick intervals of shale (Antrim and Ellsworth formations; Plate 4). Thick deposits of black, fossil-poor shale are

FIGURE 4.12   Layers of Devonian limestone (Rogers City Formation) in the Carmeuse Lime and Stone Quarry (formerly the O.N. Calcite Quarry), near Rogers City, Michigan. Photo by S. LoDuca.

characteristic of Late Devonian sedimentary rock successions across North America, including Michigan, and appear to reflect prolonged periods of seafloor and near-bottom anoxia, perhaps related to episodes of high organic productivity combined with poor circulation (Brown and Kenig 2004). In the Michigan Basin, these black shales are important source rocks for hydrocarbons, especially natural gas (Chapter 10).

Marine invertebrates of the Paleozoic Fauna flourished in Michigan's Devonian sea, outstanding fossils of which can be observed in scattered outcrops along the Lake Huron and Lake Michigan shorelines, including Fisherman's Island State Park near Charlevoix (Fig. 4.5, 1, 3, 5, 6, 7, 9, 10, 16, 17). As was the case during the Silurian, coral reefs still thrived in the Michigan Basin, but now were restricted to the northern margin (see FOCUS BOX below).

The top predators in the Devonian seas were fish called placoderms, the heads of which were encased in bony, helmet-like armor (Fig 4.14). Some placoderms were small (30–60 cm), but the largest of these "armored sharks" exceeded 10 m in length! Fragments of the bony armor of this extinct group of fish are occasionally found in the Devonian rocks of Michigan, mainly in Monroe and Presque Isle Counties. Other major groups of fish in the Devonian seas were the primitive, armored, jawless ostracoderms, the spiny acanthodians, early sharks and rays, and early members of the group of fish that would eventually come to dominate the seas—the

FIGURE 4.13 Castle Rock. This distinctive erosional landform, located just north of the Mackinac Bridge in the Upper Peninsula, is formed of resistant Mackinac Breccia. Photo by R. Schaetzl.

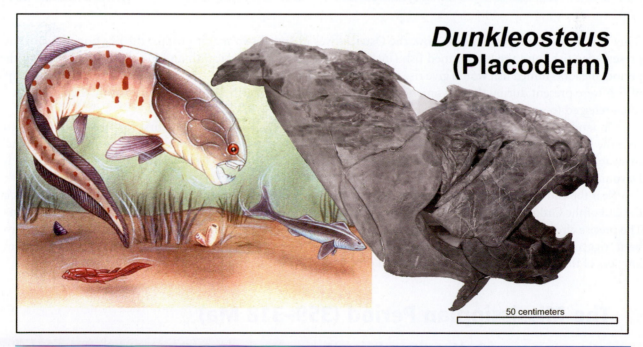

FIGURE 4.14 Fish of the Devonian Period. In image at left: Clockwise from lower right: early shark; small, bottom-living placoderm ("armored shark"); large predatory placoderm. After Wicander and Monroe (2004). Image at right shows the external armor plating, made of bone, that covered the head region of a giant Devonian placoderm called *Dunkleosteus*. Photo by S. LoDuca.

FOCUS BOX: Michigan's state stone

Along the Lake Michigan shore, near Petoskey, are found curious objects that have come to be known as "Petoskey stones" (see Figure B below). These smooth pebbles, with their distinctive and regular geometric patterns of hexagons, grace the shelves of nearly every gift shop from Traverse City to Charlevoix, and are prized by rock hounds and beachcombers alike. The origin of Petoskey stones is as fascinating as their appearance. Petoskey stones are actually corals belonging to the extinct genera *Hexagonaria* and *Prismatophyllum*. Fossils of both of these coral genera are abundant in Middle Devonian limestones of the Traverse Group (Table 4.1; Plate 4), which crop out along the Lake Michigan shoreline. As the waves erode the limestone, coral heads are released from their rock tomb and are gradually abraded and polished by the waves. Each hexagon of the Petoskey Stone is a coral chamber, and the distinctive "rays" within are the internal walls of the chamber, known in coral terminology as *septa*. Occasionally, "rough" Petoskey stones, i.e., fossil corals that have yet to be smoothed by the waves, are encountered along the beach as well (see Figure A below). In 1965, through an act of the State Legislature, the Petoskey stone became the official State Stone of Michigan

A. The Devonian coral *Hexagonaria* "in the rough." B. A Petoskey Stone—a polished specimen of the coral *Hexagonaria*. Photos by D. Brandt.

bony fish or Osteichthyes. Then as now, the Osteichthyes included two major groups: the ray-finned fish (most present-day fish) and the lobe-finned fish (includes the present-day coelacanth and lungfish). By the end of the period, the lobe-finned fish would give rise to the first land-living vertebrates—the amphibians. More major groups of fish were present during the Devonian than at any other time in Earth history. For this reason, the Devonian is often referred to as the "Age of Fish."

On land, a number of large plant species evolved during the Devonian, and the first forests were established. (For the first 90% of Earth history, forests were entirely absent from the biosphere, despite the continuous presence of sizable land areas.) The fossilized remains of primitive trees (*Callixylon*) from these early forests are found in Devonian shales near Alpena.

Near the end of the Devonian, a mass extinction once again decimated the biosphere. This extinction, like that at the end of the Ordovician, eliminated many species from all of the major groups that comprised the Paleozoic Fauna. The precise circumstances behind this mass extinction event are unknown, but like the Ordovician event it may have been triggered by a relatively brief episode of global cooling (McGee 1996). Widespread episodes of anoxia in the shallow seas of this time, discussed above in connection with black shale deposition, may also have played a role as well.

■ The Mississippian Period (359–318 Ma)

During the earliest part of the Mississippian Period, Michigan remained beneath a tropical sea (Fig. 4.2C). Clay and silt derived from the Acadian Mountains to the east continued to accumulate on the sea floor (Sunbury and Coldwater formations [shales]; Table 4.1). Toward the close of Early Mississippian time, however, vast amounts of

FIGURE 4.15   Layers of Mississippian sandstone (Marshall Formation) in Jude's Quarry, Napoleon, Michigan. Note sandstone slabs stacked on pallets for shipment. Photo by S. LoDuca.

sand were deposited across large parts of the Michigan Basin (Marshall Formation, Table 4.1). Today, the Marshall Formation is quarried near Napoleon, in Jackson County, as an important source of stone for the landscaping industry (Fig. 4.15). In the past, near Grindstone City, sandstones from the Marshall Formation were mined and used as grindstones in corn and wheat gristmills, and for sharpening stones. In the subsurface, the Marshall Formation forms an important aquifer for much of the southern Lower Peninsula; nearer the basin center, this unit contains salty brines that are commercially extracted for the chemical industry (Chapter 16).

During the Late Mississippian, alternating layers of carbonate mud and evaporite minerals were deposited in the Michigan Basin; these comprise the Michigan Formation (Table 4.1; Plate 4). Apparently, conditions in the basin at this time were somewhat similar to those of the Late Silurian, with evaporating seawater in the basin being largely cut-off from the open ocean for extended lengths of time. In this case, however, reefs were not present and the precipitated mineral was primarily anhydrite, not halite, indicating that a slightly different balance was maintained between the rate of water loss by evaporation and the rate (and perhaps character) of water exchange with the open ocean. Anhydrite deposits of the Michigan Formation were later converted to gypsum in places where these deposits were brought close to the surface by erosion of overlying rocks. For decades, gypsum mines have commercially extracted this material, used in the manufacture of Plaster of Paris and wallboard, from shallow shafts in the Michigan Formation in western Michigan (Grand Rapids area) and from open-pit strip mines in the eastern part of the state, near Alabaster and Tawas. In 2004 alone, nearly 500,000 metric tons of gypsum were mined in Michigan, with a value of about $5.6 million.

By the latter part of the Mississippian, rising global sea level resulted in better connectivity between the waters of the Michigan Basin and the open ocean, and thick deposits of lime mud accumulated (Table 4.1). These Late Mississippian-age, Bayport Formation limestones are quarried in Eaton County in the Lower Peninsula (Fig. 4.10). At the end of the Mississippian, conditions changed once again, as Earth's climate cooled (Fig. 4.1). A build-up of enormous continental glaciers on Gondwana, associated with yet another episode of global cooling, resulted in a pronounced lowering of global sea level (Fig. 4.1). This, combined with uplift of the basin, led to the removal of the sea from Michigan, and the subsequent formation of a major unconformity, visible above the Bayport Formation in Table 4.1 (Plate 4).

Within the Mississippian biosphere, the Paleozoic Fauna continued to thrive in the sea. Reefs, however, were substantially less abundant than they had been during the Devonian and Silurian periods; this was but one long-lasting consequence of the devastating Late Devonian mass extinction event (see above). Crinoids—relatives of starfish and sea urchins that superficially look like flowers (hence their common name "sea lilies")—thrived in the Mississippian seas. Much of the limestone of Mississippian age in Michigan and elsewhere is formed largely of the fragmented skeletal remains of crinoids, including their distinctive cylindrical "stems" (Fig. 4.5 9). Indeed, the Mississippian Period is often referred to as the "Age of Crinoids." Fossils from the Mississippian-age Marshall Formation in the south central part of the State are well known to fossil collectors, and include brachiopods, bivalves, straight-shelled nautiloids, shark teeth and even driftwood (Dorr and Moser 1964; Fig. 4.5M). Elsewhere in the Mississippian, amphibians and the earliest reptiles were gaining ground in terrestrial environments. The latter were small, only about 15 cm or so in length, but the former included species that reached lengths of 2 m! These large amphibians looked somewhat like giant salamanders, but were covered in bony scales.

■ The Pennsylvanian Period (318–299 Ma)

During the Early Pennsylvanian, extensive coastal swamps and deltas formed around a small body of marine water that occupied the central part of the Michigan Basin. Numerous small-scale fluctuations in sea level at this time resulted in alternating deposits of sand, silt and clay, together with coal, around the shore of this sea (Saginaw Formation, Table 4.1; Fig. 4.16; Plate 4). These sea-level fluctuations were global, the rises and falls linked to retreats and advances, respectively, of massive continental glaciers on Gondwana that formed during this prolonged cool period in Earth history (Figs. 4.1, 4.2D). Temperatures in Michigan remained relatively warm, however, as a consequence of its equatorial position. Today, this particular part of the Michigan sedimentary sequence, including coal beds, can be seen in abandoned clay pits at Fitzgerald Park in Grand Ledge, just west of Lansing (Fig. 4.17). Coal was mined

FIGURE 4.16   A Pennsylvanian coal swamp. The large tree on the far right (only part of which is visible) is a relative of the common horsetail. The two trees on the far left are scale trees, giant relatives of present-day club moss. Fossils of these extinct plants are known from Pennsylvanian-age rocks in Michigan. After Lutgens and Tarbuk (2000). Courtesy of the Field Museum, Chicago.

from the Saginaw Formation during the late 1800s and early 1900s; the last commercial coal mine in Michigan ceased operations in 1952. The coal reserves of Michigan, all of which are within the Saginaw Formation, have been estimated at 220 million tons (Cohee et al. 1950). The sandstone layers of the Saginaw Formation form an important aquifer (Chapter 16), and the shales have been mined as an important source of clay for the manufacture of bricks and tile.

Plant life flourished in the Pennsylvanian-age coastal swamps of Michigan. The particular kinds of plants that formed the forests then, however, were very unlike those of today; they included tree-sized relatives of horsetails and club mosses (Fig. 4.16). In this swampy setting, plant remains accumulated in abundance, to form coal deposits—a common theme throughout the world during the Pennsylvanian Period. For this reason, in places outside of North America, this time interval (together with the time encompassed by the Mississippian Period) is referred to as the Carboniferous Period—carbon for coal. It is worth noting that coal formation is an important way that the biosphere directly contributes to the formation of geosphere materials. (A further case involves the formation of carbonate rocks from the shells of marine invertebrates.) The animals of the Pennsylvanian coal swamps included large insects such as dragonflies, with nearly one meter wingspans, and cockroaches the size of large dinner plates. The only backboned, land-living animals (tetrapods) of this time were amphibians and reptiles. At this stage in the history of life, reptiles were beginning to challenge amphibians for dominance of the land, but evolution of the first dinosaurs was still a long way off.

The youngest known Paleozoic sediments in Michigan were deposited during the Late Pennsylvanian. These sandy sediments, apparently deposited by streams, comprise the Grand River Formation—today a thick package of sandstone. At Fitzgerald Park, near Grand Ledge, the Grand River has cut deeply into this material in relatively recent times, forming sheer cliffs that attract rock-climbing enthusiasts.

Along the eastern margin of North America during the Late Pennsylvanian, uplift of the Appalachian Mountains began as the southern super-continent of Gondwana approached, and eventually collided with, the

FIGURE 4.17   Layers of Pennsylvanian sandstone and coal (Saginaw Formation) in an abandoned clay pit, Fitzgerald Park, Grand Ledge, Michigan. Photo by S. LoDuca.

northern super-continent of Laurasia, forming the great super-continent known as Pangaea (Fig. 4.2D). As a consequence of this colossal episode of mountain building, and the broader, regional-scale uplift it produced, Michigan became an upland environment—a setting that is not conducive to the accumulation and preservation of sediment. For this reason, rocks from the last chapter of the Paleozoic, the Permian Period, are not present in the state (Chapter 5).

■ Conclusions

From dry land to shallow seas, from trilobites to towering horsetails, the environments and life forms of Michigan changed repeatedly and dramatically during the long span of time known as the Paleozoic Era. As recorded by a thick succession of sedimentary rock layers beneath the state, the Paleozoic history of Michigan includes numerous prolonged inundations by the sea, the rise of one major marine fauna and its replacement by another, the initial development of forests on the land, two mass extinction events, radical changes in local seawater chemistry, several episodes of climate change and the formation and infilling of a major geologic basin. And these are just the highlights! Then, as now, change was the rule, not the exception, in the Earth System.

Literature Cited

Boggs, S. 2006. Principles of Sedimentology and Stratigraphy. Prentice Hall, Upper Saddle River, NJ.

Brown, T.C. and F. Kenig. 2004. Water column structure during deposition of Middle Devonian—Lower Mississippian black and green/gray shales of the Illinois and Michigan basins: a biomarker approach. Palaeogeography Palaeoclimatology Palaeoecology 215:59–85.

Catacosinos, P.A., Daniels, P.A., Jr., and W.B. Harrison, III. 1991. Structure, stratigraphy, and petroleum geology of the Michigan basin. In: Leighton, M.W., Kolata, D.R., Oltz, D.F. and J.J. Eidel (eds.), Interior Cratonic Basins. American Association of Petroleum Geologists Memoir 51. pp. 561–601.

Catacosinos, P.A., Westjohn, D.B., Harrison, III, W.B., Wollensak, M.S. and R.F. Reynolds. 2001. Stratigraphic Lexicon for Michigan. Michigan Department of Environmental Quality Geological Survey Division, Bulletin 8.

Cohee, G.V. 1965. Geologic history of the Michigan Basin. Washington Academy of Sciences Journal 55:211–223.

Cohee, G.V., Burns, R.N., Brown, R.A. and D. Wright. 1950. Coal resources of Michigan. U.S. Geological Survey Circular 77.

Dorr, J.A. and F. Moser. 1964. Ctenacanth sharks from the mid-Mississippian of Michigan. Papers of the Michigan Academy of Science, Arts, and Letters 49:105–113.

Heinrich, E.W. 1976. The Mineralogy of Michigan. Michigan Geological Survey, Bulletin 6. 225 pp.

Howell, P.D. and B.A. van der Pluijm. 1990. Early history of the Michigan basin: subsidence and Appalachian tectonics. Geology 18:1195–1198.

Kaminski, E. and C. Jaupart. 2000. Lithosphere structure beneath the Phanerozoic intracratonic basins of North America. Earth and Planetary Science Letters 178:139–149.

Lutgens, F.K. and E.J. Tarbuk. 2000. Essentials of Geology. Prentice-Hall: Upper Saddle River, NJ.

McGee, G. R. 1996. The Late Devonian Mass Extinction: The Frasnian/Famennian Crisis. Columbia Univ. Press: New York, NY.

Milstein, R.L. 1987. Middle Silurian paleoecology; The Raber Fossil Beds, Chippewa County, Michigan. In: D.L. Biggs (ed.), Centennial Field Guide Volume 3, North Central Section. Geological Society of America, Boulder: CO. pp. 281–284.

Sepkoski, J. 1981. A factor analytic description of the Phanerozoic marine fossil record. Paleobiology 7:36–53.

Wicander, R. and J.S. Monroe. 2004. Historical Geology. Brooks/Cole-Thomson Learning: Belmont, CA.

Further Readings

Dorr, J.A. and D.F. Eschman. 1970. Geology of Michigan. The Univ. of Michigan Press: Ann Arbor.

Fisher, J.H., Barratt, M.W., Droste, J.B. and R.H. Shaver. 1988. Michigan basin. In: L.L. Sloss (ed.), Sedimentary Cover—North American Craton: U.S., The Geology of North America. Geological Society of America: Boulder, CO. pp. 361–382.

Kesling, R.V. and R.B. Chilman. 1975. Strata and Megafossils of the Middle Devonian Silica Formation. University of Michigan Museum of Paleontology, Papers on Paleontology. No. 8.

Kinch, J. 1987. Jackson's coal mines. Michigan History 71(Jul-Aug):32–37.

LaBerge, G.L. 1994. Geology of the Lake Superior Region. Geoscience Press, Phoenix, AZ.

Lilienthal, R.T. 1978. Stratigraphic cross-sections of the Michigan Basin. Michigan Geological Survey Report of Investigations 19.

Martin, H.M. 1964. The first four billion years. In: C.M. Davis (ed.), Readings in the Geography of Michigan. Ann Arbor Publishers: Ann Arbor, MI. pp. 7–28.

Middlewood, E.A. 1981. Salt. Michigan History 65(Jan-Feb): 16–19.

Paull, R.K. and R.A. Paull. 1977. Geology of Wisconsin and Upper Michigan: Including Parts of Adjacent States. Kendall/Hunt Publishing Company: Dubuque, IA.

Paull, R.K. and R.A. Paull. 1980. Wisconsin and Upper Michigan, Including Parts of Adjacent States: Highway Guide. Kendall/Hunt Publishing Company: Dubuque, IA.

Schultz, G.M. 2004. Wisconsin's Foundations. The Univ. of Wisconsin Press: Madison.

5

The "Lost Interval": Geology from the Permian to the Pliocene

Michael A. Velbel

From the Appalachian to the Rocky Mountains, most of the geologic record of the Paleozoic, Mesozoic and Cenozoic Eras in North America is preserved in sedimentary rocks. Sedimentary rocks of a given age are generally present if (1) conditions during that time favored deposition of sediment, and (2) those sediments survived subsequent erosion. If either of those conditions was not met, sedimentary rocks of that age are absent.

For a considerable interval of time, between the Coal Age (Carboniferous; Plate 3) and the Ice Age (Pleistocene Epoch; Chapter 6), geologic evidence is available outside of Michigan, but there is little direct geological evidence in Michigan itself. Dorr and Eschman (1970) referred to this as the "Lost Interval" of Michigan's geology. Throughout the Great Lakes region, Paleozoic sedimentary rocks are well-represented in Michigan (Chapter 4) and are directly overlain by glacial drift of Pleistocene age (Chapter 6). Mesozoic and Cenozoic rocks are, however, uncommon throughout most of the Great Lakes region, and Michigan is not unique in having a poor geologic record of this time interval. In Michigan, the "Lost Interval" includes the latest Pennsylvanian and Permian Periods, almost all of the Mesozoic Era and all of the Cenozoic Era up to the Pleistocene. With the exception of the Middle Jurassic redbeds and the Pleistocene glacial deposits, most of the last 290 million years of geologic time left no rocks to record the geologic processes that operated here, or the conditions that existed during that time (Dorr and Eschman 1970, Fisher et al. 1988).

The absence of sedimentary strata for most of the "Lost Interval" makes scientific understanding of what was happening in Michigan during this time challenging, but not impossible. The geologic processes that operated in Michigan during this time left several kinds of evidence, including a sparse record of sedimentary deposits of Middle Jurassic age, and a record of post-Pennsylvanian thermal modification of older rocks in and around the Michigan Basin. Four categories of evidence for the "Lost Interval" are reviewed in this chapter: (1) rocks in Michigan that formed between the Pennsylvanian and the Pleistocene, (2) observable and/or measurable features in older rocks in Michigan that modified those rocks after they formed, (3) hard-to-find rock materials, that occur only locally in Michigan or that formed under less-common circumstances, and (4) rocks of "Lost Interval" age found elsewhere in the Great Lakes regions. The "Lost Interval" is not entirely lost.

◾ Rocks that formed during the "Lost Interval"

There are no exposures of "Lost Interval" rocks in Michigan, as they are all deeply buried beneath glacial drift (Plate 5). However, in the west-central part of the Lower Peninsula, rocks from this interval were recovered in the late 19th and early 20th centuries via subsurface drilling for oil, gas and groundwater, and by quarrying for building stone (Fig. 5.1). These "Lost Interval" redbeds (sandstones and shales, stained red by iron oxides), limestone, and gypsum occur in depressions cut into Mississippian and Pennsylvanian sedimentary rocks (Kelly 1936, Cohee 1965, Dorr and Eschman 1970, Ells 1979, Fisher et al. 1988, Westjohn and Weaver 1998; Plates 5, 6). Fossilized plant spores and pollen from the redbeds, most recently interpreted as Middle Jurassic in age (Fisher et al. 1988, Cross 1998, Catacosinos et al. 2001), have been studied since the late 1960s by Aureal Cross and his students at Michigan State University. The maximum preserved thickness of the redbeds is ~130 m (400 ft; Cohee 1965, Dorr and Eschman 1970, Fisher et al. 1988). Detailed study of the thickness variations suggests that these sediments were deposited in stream-eroded valleys cut into the underlying Pennsylvanian rocks (Ells 1979, Fisher et al. 1988) and surrounded by low hills of Pennsylvanian sedimentary rocks, mostly shales (Fig. 5.2). Sedimentary gypsum layers usually indicate evaporation of standing water; therefore, the occurrence of gypsum coexisting with redbed sandstones and shales suggests semiarid or arid conditions in what is now Michigan during the Middle Jurassic (Cohee 1965, Dorr and Eschman 1970).

During the Jurassic, the area that is now Michigan was near the interior of a large supercontinent, probably with an arid climate. This supercontinent—Pangea—assembled during the Carboniferous and included ancestral North America (Fig. 4.2D). During the Pennsylvanian, erosion of the mountains (just formed during the assembly of Pangea) produced the sediments that became the Pennsylvanian sandstones and shales that are now preserved in the eastern US, including Michigan. Between Pennsylvanian and Jurassic time, Pangea drifted north, but by the Jurassic it was still largely astride the equator. The mountains had long since eroded away, and Pangea was a large continental land mass, mostly desert, as the region that is now Michigan was far inland and away from oceanic sources of moisture.

Macrofossils, e.g., shells or trace fossils, are usually recovered from outcrops, not from small, broken-up subsurface rock samples from wells. Therefore, we are unlikely to find Mesozoic animal fossils in Michigan. A thin (< 20 m) sequence of redbeds, evaporites and limestones of Late Jurassic age is also present in north-central Iowa (Shaffer 1969, Ells 1979, Richardson and Hansen 1991, Cody et al. 1996), and parts of northwestern Minnesota, North Dakota, Manitoba and Ontario (Mossler 1978, Dutch, 1981, Setterholm and Morey, 1995, Cross 1998).

FIGURE 5.1 Michigan redbed sandstone, used as building material. Photo by M. Velbel.

FIGURE 5.2 Erosional landscape on shale bedrock in semiarid American west; this may be what Michigan's landscape looked like during the Middle Jurassic. Photo by M. Velbel.

As in Michigan, these mid-continent Jurassic rocks are unfossiliferous. Dinosaurs, like those that left a fossil record in Mesozoic sedimentary rocks elsewhere in North America, may have lived in what is now Michigan as well, but their fossil remains were not preserved here.

The section below discusses the various lines of evidence that exist regarding the nature and age of the redbeds in Michigan.

■ Post-Pennsylvanian modification of Paleozoic and older rocks

Thermal maturation of organic material

Coal occurs in the Pennsylvanian strata of Michigan (Chapter 4). It forms from the preservation and burial of thick accumulations of plant remains, e.g., as peat in swamps. Because oil and natural gas form through processes that are also driven by increased temperature, petroleum geologists have studied the thermal history of the Michigan Basin, including its coal deposits. With prolonged exposure of the plant remains to increased pressure (and especially temperature) during burial, peat "matures" into coal. The eventual grade of coal that results from thermal maturation ranges from *lignite* ("brown coal") through *bituminous* coal up to *anthracite* (Fig. 5.3; Monroe and Wicander 2006).

One important finding that is potentially relevant to the question of the "Lost Interval" is that Michigan's Pennsylvanian coal was heated to an extent that either (1) required a post-depositional heating event, e.g., exposure to circulation of hot, dense brines in the subsurface after its deposition (Luczaj et al. 2006), or (2) the coal was buried beneath 300–2000 m (1000–6540 ft) of post-Pennsylvanian sediment (Sleep et al. 1980, Cercone 1984, Nunn et al. 1984, Vugrinovich 1988, Fisher et al. 1988, Cercone and Pollack 1991, Pollack and Cercone 1994). With regard to (2), because overlying rocks are now absent, their former thickness and physical properties must be inferred from other evidence, adding controversy to the interpretations.

The sediment required to account for the observed thermal maturity of the coal and other fossil-fuel organic matter in the Michigan Basin would have to have been both deposited on top of (and therefore after) the Pennsylvanian coal-bearing strata, and subsequently removed during "Lost Interval" time (Vugrinovich 1988). The ancestral Appalachian Mountains would have been the likely source of this sediment. There is abundant geological evidence in the Appalachian region that the late Paleozoic (Alleghanian) mountain belt (the erosion of which supplied the sand and mud which became the Carboniferous sandstones and shales of eastern North America) remained tectonically active, and therefore was a source of clastic sediment until at least the Permian (Beaumont et al. 1987, Crowley 1991).

Researchers (Cercone 1984, Vugrinovich 1989) have concluded that the event that produced the thermal maturation in Michigan Basin sedimentary organic matter was over by the Middle Jurassic. Fossil

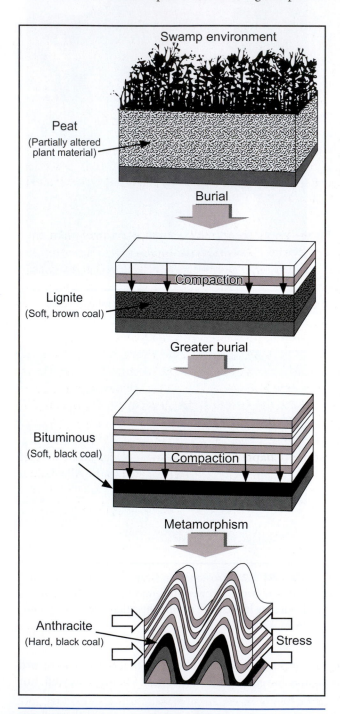

FIGURE 5.3   Successive stages in the formation of coal. Michigan coal reached bituminous grade sometime during the Lost Interval. After Tarbuck and Lutgens (1998).

pollen and spores change color when heated. The fossil pollen that establishes a Middle Jurassic age for Michigan's "Lost Interval" redbeds show no color change, providing evidence that subsurface heating in the Michigan Basin was over by the Middle Jurassic. The thermally altered Paleozoic coal and the unaltered Middle Jurassic pollen both bracket the thermal event, and provide direct evidence that, if there actually was sediment deposited during the early "Lost Interval," it was eroded by Middle Jurassic time, and that this sediment had thicknesses somewhat greater than what is now present in the Middle Jurassic redbeds.

Presence of hydrothermal minerals

Carbonate minerals, including dolomite, and pyrite (FeS_2), an iron sulfide mineral, occur in fracture-filling veins and vugs (cavities) in Paleozoic sedimentary rocks of Michigan (Fig. 5.4).

FIGURE 5.4   Fenestral dolomite, Dundee Limestone, Fork Field, Mecosta County, MI. Note fractures and white hydrothermal dolomite cement in some of the vugs. Scale in cm. Photo by W. Harrison, III.

Using the principle of cross-cutting relations (Fig. 2.5), we know that these veins are younger than their host rock. Therefore, the formation of these veins occurred after deposition of the Paleozoic limestones of Michigan. The pore fluid responsible for vein mineralization and other post-depositional (diagenetic) mineralogical changes in sedimentary rocks is sometimes preserved as small fluid inclusions in the hydrothermal or diagenetic minerals. Microthermometric analysis of these fluid inclusions can reveal the temperature at which the solutions were trapped (Barker and Reynolds 1984, Goldstein and Reynolds 1994). Luczaj et al. (2006) interpreted data from fluid inclusions in the Devonian-aged Dundee Formation (Plate 4) to suggest that hydrothermal activity with fluid temperatures up to at least 140°C modified the Dundee Formation limestones after they were deposited, lithified and fractured. Such hot fluids may have entered the Michigan Basin by long-distance hydrologic flow from the region of the Appalachian Mountain belt. A similar scenario was proposed for the Illinois Basin by Garven et al. (1993). While it is possible that such modification was already over before the Pennsylvanian coals and other sedimentary rocks of Michigan were deposited, the fluid inclusion evidence indicates that post-Middle Devonian hydrothermal fluids *were* present in the Michigan Basin. If the pyrite-carbonate veins in the younger Mississippian Bayport Limestone (Chapter 4) near Bellevue (Dorr and Eschman 1970, Blaske 2003, Heinrich 2004, Luczaj et al. 2006) have similar origins, they are likely related to the Alleghanian (Late Paleozoic) mountain building episode in Eastern North America. Such subsurface flow of hot fluids may have continued long enough to influence the Pennsylvanian shales and coals, but direct evidence of this is presently lacking.

Preservation of geologic deposits under uncommon circumstances

Examples from Michigan

Another line of evidence that might shed light on the "Lost Interval" includes unusual geologic deposits that occur only locally or that were formed and/or preserved under less-common circumstances. Unfortunately, glacial deposits cover much of this evidence in Michigan. However, continued drilling for water, oil and natural gas, quarrying for rocks and the exploration of caves may uncover new information. A few examples of this sort of evidence are known from Michigan and are described below; other examples occur only in neighboring states and provinces and are described in the next section.

FIGURE 5.5 Mackinaw Breccia, a collapse breccia formed by Devonian-age collapse of caves in Silurian limestones. Some of the largest breccia fragments have been removed by weathering and erosion, making it easier to see the variety of sizes and shapes of the breccia fragments. This photo is from an outcrop on Mackinac Island. Photo by M. Velbel.

Breccias are deposits of broken angular rock fragments (clasts). Some breccias form by the collapse of caves. Caves form in easily-dissolved rocks like limestone in response to groundwater activity; large landscapes pockmarked by collapsed caves are called karst landscapes (Chapter 16). Ancient limestones experienced similar cave formation and collapse, forming paleocaves and paleokarst. A well-known example from Michigan, the Mackinaw Breccia (Fig. 5.5), preserves fragments of Devonian limestone in an area otherwise dominated by older Silurian carbonates, showing that the Devonian limestones were deposited over a larger area than their present distribution suggests (Dorr and Eschman 1970). Pennsylvanian sandstones also occur in paleocaves in Devonian limestones at the western edge of the Illinois Basin, near Rock Island County, Illinois (Hammer et al. 1985). This finding shows that Pennsylvanian sediments covered more of Illinois and Iowa during the Pennsylvanian than their present distribution would indicate. Further exploration of Michigan's caves and karst for ancient cave fills and collapse features may turn up additional evidence relevant to Michigan's "Lost Interval."

Cryptoexplosion structures may have several origins, including fracturing and displacement beneath meteorite/bolide craters, and subsurface explosions driven by as-yet-poorly-understood internal processes (Snyder and Gerdemann 1965, Nicolaysen and Ferguson 1990). Luczaj (1998, 1999) described a number of cryptoexplosion structures in the Great Lakes region. In some, blocks of rock have moved differentially along vertical faults, as when one holds a fistful of pencils and allows some of them to slide lengthwise relative to others. Individual fault blocks in cryptoexplosion structures might be moved upward or downward relative to the surrounding undisturbed rock. In some of these structures, displacement is upward in the center of the structure and downward farther out. Where blocks are displaced downward, younger strata are displaced downward a similar vertical distance, pushing them to the same depths as older rocks in the surrounding undisturbed area. Subsequent widespread erosion may remove the younger layers, eliminating from the undisturbed area the evidence that the younger strata were ever present in the region. However, local masses of the younger rock are preserved in the down-dropped blocks in cryptoexplosion structures.

One cryptoexplosion structure is known from Michigan's Lower Peninsula (Milstein 1988), but it is Ordovician in age and therefore preserves only slightly younger strata already well-known from the immediate surroundings. Experience in neighboring states suggests that some cryptoexplosion structures exist directly beneath the glacial sediments. The Des Plaines Disturbance in the suburbs of Chicago, IL preserves Mississippian-Pennsylvanian strata in an area of northeastern Illinois otherwise devoid of strata of those ages (Emrich and Bergstrom 1962). The Des Plaines Disturbance was recognized by careful study of water well logs. A post-Pennsylvanian cryptoexplosion structure in Michigan might locally preserve specific post-Pennsylvanian strata not otherwise preserved here. This would be a significant scientific find, and would confirm that coal-bearing Pennsylvania strata were once overlain by younger rock.

Some breccias occur in association with various natural explosions such as volcanic eruptions; these are called diatreme breccias. Among the clasts in some diatreme breccias are fragments of rock that fell into the fracture during the explosion and became incorporated into the breccia.

Both cryptoexplosion structures and kimberlites occur in the western Upper Peninsula. *Kimberlites* are roughly cylindrical masses of usually broken-up (brecciated) rock, explosively emplaced into shallower crust from below (Fig. 5.6). Consisting of rocks derived from greater depths and higher-pressure regions of Earth's crust, they often contain high-pressure minerals such as diamonds, and are therefore often known as "diamond pipes." Luczaj (2001) noted that, "at least 27 post-Ordovician kimberlites have been identified along the Wisconsin/Upper Michigan border" (Memmi and Pride 1997). Kimberlites in the Precambrian rocks of the western Upper Peninsula contain fragments of Ordovician limestone, in an area that is presently many kms from the nearest outcrop of Ordovician strata (Cannon and Mudrey, 1981). The igneous host material of the clasts is 150–210 Ma in age (Jurassic; Jarvis and Kalliokoski 1988). Projecting Ordovician rock layers from their present outcrops to the kimberlite location suggests that Ordovician strata were at least 200 m (660 ft) above the now-exposed kimberlite when it was intruded (Cannon and Mudrey, 1981).

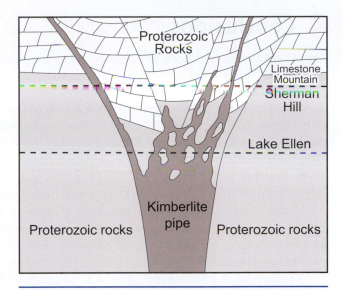

FIGURE 5.6 Idealized cross section of a kimberlite pipe and its overlying, disturbed strata. Dashed lines suggest the stages of erosion of various small kimberlites and cryptoexplosion structures of the western Upper Peninsula of Michigan and nearby Wisconsin. After Cannon and Mudrey (1981).

At other localities in the western Upper Peninsula, locally deformed strata associated with possible cryptoexplosion structures are as young as Late Ordovician or Early Devonian (Cannon and Mudrey, 1981). If the Upper Peninsula's cryptoexplosion structures are related to the nearby kimberlite, as suggested by Cannon and Mudrey (1981), and were active over similar ranges of time, then (1) whatever process formed them was still operating after Ordovician and Devonian sediments had been deposited and lithified, and at least as long as the Jurassic, and (2) Ordovician and Devonian strata formerly extended farther to the NW than their present distribution would suggest (Plate 5), and were not yet eroded away during the Jurassic.

Examples from neighboring states

Faults can create basins into which sediments can be deposited and preserved. In Iowa, Pennsylvanian strata are preserved in small, fault-bounded basins (the Plum River Fault Zone) contained in older Devonian limestone, a considerable distance from the main Pennsylvanian outcrop area of the Illinois Basin (Ludvigson and Bunker 1988). Unfortunately, the glacial deposits in Michigan are much thicker than in Iowa and obscure structures in the underlying bedrock. However, Michigan has numerous fault zones in its Paleozoic rocks. Therefore, it is possible that additional "Lost Interval" strata are concealed beneath the Michigan's glacial sediments.

Examples from Michigan and neighboring states and provinces suggest that preservation of rocks from some part of the "Lost Interval" is possible in cryptoexplosion structures, diatreme or kimberlite breccias, small fault-bounded basins and/or paleocave-collapse/paleokarst breccias. In each example, rocks of a local "Lost Interval" may be preserved, providing direct evidence of these younger rocks.

A recent discovery illustrates how profound the scientific impact of new discoveries might be. A collapse sinkhole was recently discovered during expansion of a limestone quarry in east-central Indiana (Farlow et al. 2001). The sediment discovered in the Pipe Creek Sinkhole has produced Early Pliocene vertebrate fossils, the first Tertiary continental biota known from the interior of eastern North America (Farlow et al. 2001). For the first time, geologists have direct evidence of what kinds of plants and animals (including extinct peccaries, camelids, large rhinoceros-like mammals and dog-like carnivores) lived in the southern Great Lakes region during the Pliocene. The Pliocene of Michigan was likely quite similar to the Pliocene of northern Indiana.

■ Conclusions

The "Lost Interval" in Michigan's geologic history represents the time between the Coal Age (Pennsylvanian) and the Ice Age (Pleistocene), a long time interval lacking an easily accessible rock record. The geologic processes that operated in Michigan during the "Lost Interval" left several kinds of evidence, including a sparse record of sedimentary deposits of Middle Jurassic age, and a record of post-Pennsylvanian thermal modification of older rocks in and around the Michigan Basin. Deposition of sedimentary rocks (almost certainly dominated by sandstones and shales derived from the ancestral Appalachians and deposited in coastal and continental sedimentary environments) likely continued for some time after the time represented by the youngest Paleozoic sedimentary rocks of the Michigan Basin. Evidence suggests that hundreds of meters of sediment were deposited in the Lower Peninsula during the Permian and/or Triassic. If these rocks were present, they were eroded completely away by the Middle Jurassic. During the Middle Jurassic, redbed sands and muds, along with limestones and evaporites, were deposited in valleys in a hilly landscape (Fig. 5.2) on Pennsylvanian sedimentary rocks of Michigan's Lower Peninsula. The similarity of Middle Jurassic redbeds of Michigan and mid-Mesozoic redbed sequences elsewhere in North America indicate that paleoenvironmental conditions in Michigan were similar to those better documented elsewhere during the Age of Dinosaurs.

The thermal-maturation indicators of Michigan Basin Paleozoic sedimentary organic matter and Middle Jurassic pollen and spores are direct evidence that there was some sort of heating event after the Pennsylvanian, but before the Middle Jurassic. The heat source was most likely hot fluids. Late Jurassic, Cretaceous and/or Cenozoic sedimentary rocks were probably also deposited, and might have been thick enough to insulate the buried rocks enough to allow temperatures slightly higher than the present, but at no time after the Middle Jurassic did sediments accumulate to great enough thicknesses for paleotemperatures at depth to thermally modify fossil pollen and spores in the Middle Jurassic sedimentary rocks.

Plant and animal life in Michigan throughout the "Lost Interval" was almost certainly similar to that elsewhere in neighboring parts of North America, which was a continental environment throughout almost the entire time (Monroe and Wicander 2006). Dinosaurs most likely lived in what is now Michigan during the Mesozoic portion of the "Lost Interval."

The Pipe Creek Sinkhole of Indiana provides direct evidence of numerous aspects of Pliocene environments in the Great Lakes region. It is also a testimonial to observers (quarry operators and scientists) with open eyes and minds, who recognized the unusual sediment among the locally ordinary rock and thereby found an important part of the "Lost Interval." Professional geologists will eventually find out more about what Michigan was like between the Pennsylvanian and the Pleistocene. Alert professional and amateur observers, e.g., quarry operators, well drillers, construction workers and rock-hounds, may continue to discover additional informative geologic features that will add to our scientific understanding of Michigan during the "Lost Interval." The "Lost Interval" is not really lost— it is just waiting to be discovered.

Literature Cited

Barker, C.E. and T.J. Reynolds. 1984. Preparing doubly polished sections of temperature sensitive sedimentary rocks. Journal of Sedimentary Petrology 54:635–636.

Beaumont, C., Quinlan, G. and J. Hamilton. 1987. The Alleghanian Orogeny and its relationship to the evolution of the eastern interior, North America. In: Beaumont, C. and A. Tankard (eds), Sedimentary Basins and Basin-Forming Mechanisms. Canadian Society of Petroleum Geologists Memoir 12:425–445.

Blaske, A.R. 2003. Geology of the Mississippi Valley type mineralization at Bellevue, Michigan. Institute on Lake Superior Geology, Part I—Proceedings and Abstracts 49:5–6.

Cannon, W.F., and M.G. Mudrey Jr. 1981. The potential for diamond-bearing kimberlite in northern Michigan and Wisconsin. U.S. Geological Survey Circular 482.

Catacosinos, P.A., Westjohn, D.B., Harrison, III, W.B., Wollensak, M.S. and R.F. Reynolds. 2001. Stratigraphic Lexicon for Michigan. Michigan Department of Environmental Quality Geological Survey Division, Bulletin 8.

Cercone, K.R. 1984. Thermal history of Michigan Basin. American Association of Petroleum Geologists Bulletin 68:130–136.

Cercone, K.R. and H.N. Pollack. 1991. Thermal maturity of the Michigan Basin. In: Catacasinos, P.A. and P.A. Daniels Jr. (eds.), Early Sedimentary Evolution of the Michigan Basin. Geological Society of America Special Paper 256:1–11.

Cody, R.R., Anderson, R.R., and R.M. McKay, 1996. Geology of the Fort Dodge Formation. In: Cody, R., Anderson, R. and R. McKay (eds), Geology of the Fort Dodge Formation (Upper Jurassic) Webster County, Iowa. Iowa Geological Survey Bureau, Guidebook Series 19:3–24.

Cohee, G.V. 1965. Geologic history of the Michigan Basin. Journal of the Washington Academy of Sciences 55:211–223.

Cross, A.T. 1998. The Ionia Formation: New designation for the Mid-Jurassic age "Red Beds" of the Michigan Basin. American Association of Petroleum Geologists Bulletin 82:1766.

Crowley, K.D. 1991. Thermal history of Michigan Basin and southern Canadian Shield from apatite fission track analysis. Journal of Geophysical Research 96:B697–711.

Dorr, J.A. Jr., and D.F. Eschman. 1970. Geology of Michigan. University of Michigan Press: Ann Arbor.

Dutch, S.I. 1981. Post-Cretaceous vertical motions in the eastern midcontinent, U.S.A. Zeitschrift für Geomorphologie Supplementband 40:13–25.

Ells, G D. 1979. The Mississippian and Pennsylvanian (Carboniferous) systems in the United States—Michigan. U.S. Geological Survey Professional Paper 1110:J1–J17.

Emrich, G.H. and R.E. Bergstrom. 1962. Des Plaines disturbance, northeastern Illinois. Geological Society of America Bulletin 73:959–968.

Farlow, J.O., Sunderman, J.A., Havens, J.J., Swinehart, A.L., Holman, J.A., Richards, R.L., Miller, N.G., Martin, R.A., Hunt, R.M., Jr., Storrs, G.W., Curry, B.B., Fluegeman, R.H., Dawson, M.R., and M.E.T. Flint. 2001. The Pipe Creek sinkhole biota, a diverse Late Tertiary continental assemblage from Grant County, Indiana. American Midlands Naturalist 145:367–378.

Fisher, J.H., Barratt, M.W., Droste, J.B. and R.H. Shaver. 1988. Michigan Basin. In: Sloss, L.L. (ed.) Sedimentary Cover—North American Craton. Geological Society of America, The Geology of North America D-2:361–382.

Garven, G., Ge, S., Person, M. A. and D.A. Sverjensky. 1993. Genesis of stratabound ore deposits in the midcontinent basins of North America. 1. The role of regional groundwater flow. American Journal of Science 293:497–568.

Goldstein, R.H. and T.J. Reynolds. 1994. Systematics of fluid inclusions in diagenic minerals. Society for Sedimentary Geology (SEPM) Short Course 31. 199 pp.

Hammer, W.R., Anderson, R.C. and D.A. Schroeder. 1985. Devonian and Pennsylvanian stratigraphy of the Quad-Cities regions, Illinois-Iowa. Great Lakes Section, Society of Economic Paleontologists and Mineralogists 15th Annual Field Conference. Guidebook.

Heinrich, E.W. 2004. Mineralogy of Michigan. Michigan Technological University: Houghton, MI. 252 pp.

Jarvis, W. and J. Kalliokoski. 1988. Michigan kimberlite province. Abstract, 31st Annual Meeting of the Institute on Lake Superior Geology 34:46–48.

Kelly, W.A. 1936. The Pennsylvanian system of Michigan. Occasional Papers on the Geology of Michigan, Michigan Geological Survey Publication 40, Geological Series 34, Part 2, pp. 149–226.

Luczaj, J. 1998. Argument supporting explosive igneous activity for the origin of "cryptoexplosion" structures in the midcontinent, United States. Geology 26:295–298.

Luczaj, J. 1999. Argument supporting explosive igneous activity for the origin of "cryptoexplosion" structures in the midcontinent, United States: Reply. Geology 27:279–285.

Luczaj, J.A. 2001. A mineralized breccia pipe near Racine, Wisconsin: Evidence for post-Silurian igneous activity. In, R.D. Hagni (ed.), Studies on Ore Deposits, Mineral Economics, and Applied Mineralogy: With Emphasis on Mississippi Valley-type Base Metal and Carbonatite-related Ore Deposits: University of Missouri-Rolla Press, Rolla. pp. 31–43.

Luczaj, J.A., Harrison, W.B. III, and N.S. Williams. 2006. Fractured hydrothermal dolomite reservoirs in the Devonian Dundee Formation of the central Michigan Basin. American Association of Petroleum Geologists Bulletin 90:1787–1801.

Ludvigson, G.A. and B.J. Bunker. (eds.) 1988. New Perspectives on the Paleozoic History of the Upper Mississippi Valley: An Examination of the Plum River Fault Zone. Iowa Department of Natural Resources, Geological Survey Bureau, Guidebook No. 8.

Memmi, J.M. and D.E. Pride. 1997. The application of Diamond Exploration Geoscientific Information System (DEGIS) technology for integrated diamond exploration in the north-central United States of America. International Journal of Remote Sensing 18:1439–1464.

Milstein, R.L. 1988. Impact origin of a cryptoexplosive disturbance, Cass County, Michigan. Michigan Department of Environmental Quality, Geological Survey Division, Report of Investigations 28.

Monroe, J.S. and R. Wicander. 2006. The Changing Earth: Exploring Geology and Evolution. Thompson Brooks/Cole Publishers, Pacific Grove, CA.

Mossler, J.H. 1978. Results of subsurface investigations in north-western Minnesota, 1972. Minnesota Geological Survey Report of Investigations 19. 18 pp.

Nicolaysen, L.O. and J. Ferguson. 1990. Cryptoexplosion structures, shock deformation and siderophile concentration related to explosive venting of fluids associated with alkaline ultramafic magmas. Tectonophysics 171:303–335.

Nunn, J.A., Sleep, N.H. and W.E. Moore. 1984. Thermal subsidence and generation of hydrocarbons in Michigan Basin. American Association of Petroleum Geologists Bulletin 68:296–315.

Pollack, H.N. and K.R. Cercone. 1994. Anomalous thermal maturities caused by carbonaceous sediments. Basin Research 6:47–51.

Richardson, S.M. and K.S. Hansen. 1991. Stable isotopes in the sulfate evaporites from southeastern Iowa, U.S.A.: Indications of postdepositional change. Chemical Geology 90:79–90.

Setterholm, D.R. and G.B. Morey. 1995. An extensive pre-Cretaceous weathering profile in east-central and southwestern Minnesota. U.S. Geological Survey Bulletin 1989:H1-H29.

Shaffer, B.L. 1969. Palynology of the Michigan "Red Beds." Ph.D. Dissertation, Dept. of Geosciences, Michigan State University, East Lansing.

Sleep, N.H., Nunn, J.A. and L. Chou. 1980. Platform basins. Annual Reviews of Earth and Planetary Science 8:17–34.

Snyder, F.G. and P.E. Gerdemann. 1965. Explosive igneous activity along an Illinois-Missouri-Kansas axis. American Journal of Science 263:465–493.

Tarbuck, E.J. and F.K. Lutgens. 1998. The Earth: An Introduction to Physical Geology. 6th ed. Prentice Hall, Upper Saddle River, NJ.

Vugrinovich, R. 1988. Shale compaction in the Michigan Basin: Estimates of former depth of burial and implications for paleogeothermal gradients. Bulletin of Canadian Petroleum Geology 36:1–8.

Vugrinovich, R. 1989. Subsurface temperatures and surface heat flow in the Michigan Basin and their relationships to regional subsurface fluid movement. Marine and Petroleum Geology 6:60–70.

Westjohn, D.B. and T.L. Weaver. 1998. Hydrogeologic framework of the Michigan Basin regional aquifer system. U.S. Geological Survey Professional Paper 1418.

Further Readings

Barker, C.E. and R.H. Goldstein. 1990. Fluid inclusion technique for determining the maximum temperature and its comparison to the vitrinite reflectance geothermometer. Geology 18:1003–1006.

Fisher, J.H. and M.W. Barratt. 1985. Exploration in Ordovician of central Michigan Basin. American Association of Petroleum Geologists Bulletin 69:2065–2076.

Luczaj, J.A. 2006. Evidence against the Dorag (mixing-zone) model for dolomitization along the Wisconsin arch—A case for hydrothermal diagenesis. American Association of Petroleum Geologists Bulletin 90:1719–1738.

Rampino, M.R., Glikson, A., Koeberl, C., Reimold, W.U. and J. Luczaj. 1999. Argument supporting explosive igneous activity for the origin of "cryptoexplosion" structures in the midcontinent, United States: Comments and Reply. Geology 27:279–285.

Velbel, M.A., Price, J.R. and D.S. Brandt. 1994. Sedimentology, paleogeography, and geochemical weathering of the Pennsylvanian strata of Grand Ledge, Michigan. Eastern Section—American Association of Petroleum Geologists Annual Meeting Field Trip Guidebook; Great Lakes Section—SEPM 24th Annual Fall Field Conference Guidebook; and Michigan Basin Geological Society Field Trip Guidebook. 58 pp.

6

Late Quaternary History of the Eastern Mid-Continent Region, USA

Grahame J. Larson and Kevin Kincare

Introduction

Ever since T.C. Chamberlin (1883) published the first map of the drift (glacial deposits) in the mid-continent region of North America, glacial geologists have attempted to divide and subdivide the drift, in order to unravel the glacial history of the region. This work has lead to several time-stratigraphic classifications of the last (Wisconsin) glaciation, most of which apply only to specific areas. For example, Willman and Frye (1970) developed a widely accepted classification for the Lake Michigan-Illinois area (Table 6.1) based on the time-sequence stratigraphy of drift units, buried soils and [14]C (radiocarbon) age determinations (chronostratigraphy). In their classification, the last glacial *stage* is divided into five *substages*, some representing glacial, and some named for nonglacial conditions. Another widely accepted classification (Table 6.1; Dreimanis and Karrow 1972), applies to the eastern-northern Great Lakes area; it is also based on time-sequence stratigraphy of drift units and ^{14}C age determinations, but not buried soils. In this classification the last glacial *stage* is divided into three *substages*, that are further subdivided into *stadials* representing glacial conditions and *interstadials* representing nonglacial conditions.

A difficulty inherent with the above classifications is that time intervals (*stages*, *substages*, *stadials*, and *interstadials*) have time-parallel boundaries that do not correspond to the timing of events across the larger region. For example, a glacial advance in the eastern Great Lakes area during the Port Bruce Stadial may have resulted in a ~1500 year interval of ice cover in southern

TABLE 6.1 Illinois and Ontario chronostratigraphic classifications[1]

Illinois (Willman and Frye 1970)	Ontario (Dreimanis and Karrow 1972)
Wisconsin Stage	**Wisconsin(an) Stage**
Valderan Substage[2]	Late Wisconsin(an) Substage
	Driftwood Stadial
	North Bay Interstadial
	Valders Stadial
Twocreekan Substage	Two Creeks Interstadial
Woodfordian Substage	Port Huron Stadial
	Mackinaw Interstadial
	Port Bruce Stadial
	Erie Interstadial
	Nissouri Stadial
Farmdalian Substage	Middle Wisconsin(an) Substage
	Plum Point Interstadial
Altonian Substage	Cherrytree Stadial
	Port Talbot Interstadial
	Early Wisconsin(an) Substage
	Guildwood Stadial
	St. Pierre Interstadial
	Nicolet Stadial

1: After Karrow et al. (2000)
2: Renamed Greatlakean Substage by Evenson et al. (1976)

Ontario, but the same advance may have resulted in only ~500 years of ice cover in northern Ohio. Likewise, a temporary retreat of the glacier margin in the Lake Michigan-Illinois area during the Farmdalian Substage may have resulted in a soil-forming interval in northern Illinois lasting several thousand years, but this same interval may have lasted <1000 years in eastern Wisconsin. To overcome this problem, Johnson et al. (1997) and Karrow et al. (2000) proposed a time-stratigraphic classification system for the last glaciations. This system includes diachronic (through time) time divisions, and better represents the timing of events associated with what we know was a dynamic ice margin. In this chapter, we have built on this diachronic-time classification system, to frame and review the history of glaciation for the eastern part of the mid-continent, with emphasis on ice-margin fluctuations during the last glaciation. We also present, in several Focus Boxes, descriptions of some of the more important stratigraphic sections used to construct that history.

■ The eastern mid-continent, prior to glaciation

Little is known about climate in the eastern part of the mid-continent prior to Late Quaternary glaciations, because much of the geologic record has been removed by glacial erosion, or is now deeply buried beneath glacial sediments. However, some clues remain. For example, in northern Indiana remnants of Pliocene (5.3–1.8 Ma) frogs, pond turtles, fishes, birds, snakes and mammals have been found in sinkholes buried beneath glacial deposits (Holman 1998, Farlow et al. 2001). Collectively, these remnants indicate a dry, open, prairie-like or savanna environment. In other areas, analyses of the bedrock topography buried beneath glacial deposits indicate that, during the Pliocene, major rivers flowed where the Great Lakes are today (Fig. 13.1; Horberg and Anderson 1956).

■ Age and extent of the glacial deposits

It is not known when the eastern part of the mid-continent was first glaciated. However, evidence from Ohio, Indiana and Illinois suggests that sometime, prior to 780,000 years ago, glacier ice extended over much of the Great Lakes area and dammed several northward-draining valleys in Illinois, Indiana, and Ohio, forming lakes (Fullerton 1986, Johnson 1986). Paleomagnetic data from some of the sediments deposited in these lakes are magnetically reversed and therefore must predate 780,000 years ago (Matuyama-Brunhes boundary)—when the Earth's magnetic field was last reversed. Also, oxygen isotope records from deep ocean cores (Fig. 6.1) suggest that glaciations large enough to extend into the mid-continent occurred many times over the last 800,000 years (Ruddiman and Raymo 1988, Shackleton et al. 1988). The ocean core records also reveal that the penultimate (second to last) glaciation occurred sometime between about 202,000 and 132,000 years ago, and that the last glaciation occurred between about 79,000 and 10,000 years ago (Ruddiman and Raymo 1988, Shackleton et al. 1988).

The penultimate (Illinois) glaciation in the eastern part of the mid-continent (Chamberlin 1896, Leverett 1899) corresponds to Marine Isotope Stage (MIS) 6 of the oxygen isotope record (Follmer 1983, Curry and Pavich 1996; Fig. 6.1). It probably reached its maximum extent about 150,000 years ago and is represented by an extensive drift sheet, in places exceeding tens of meters in thickness (Fig. 6.2). Because glacial ice is usually channeled through lowlands and major river valleys, the southern margin of the drift sheet is generally lobate, except where uplands of the Appalachian Mountains obstructed ice flow. Where exposed, the Illinois drift sheet is highly weathered, with soil development up to several meters in thickness. In many places to the north, the weathered surface and associated soil lies buried beneath drift of the last glaciation (Follmer 1978, 1983, Curry and Pavich 1996) and marks an especially warm interval known as the Sangamon interglaciation (Leverett 1898) that corresponds approximately to MIS 5 (Follmer 1983, Curry and Pavich 1996).

The last (Wisconsin) glaciation (Chamberlin 1894) corresponds to MIS 2–4. In the eastern-northern Great Lakes area, it also may correspond to all or part of Michigan's substages 5a–5d (Karrow et al. 2000). The Wisconsin glaciation reached its maximum extent about 23,900 years ago[1] (Fullerton 1986) and, like the Illinois glaciation,

---

[1] Time reported in this text is in calendar years ago; dates reported in parentheses are in radiocarbon years BP (Before Present). Conversion of radiocarbon dates from the last 47,000 radiocarbon years, to calendar years, was achieved using a calibration curve published by Fairbanks et al. (2005). Conversion from 47,000 to 50,000 radiocarbon years to calendar years was achieved by visual extrapolation of the Fairbanks et al. (2005) curve.

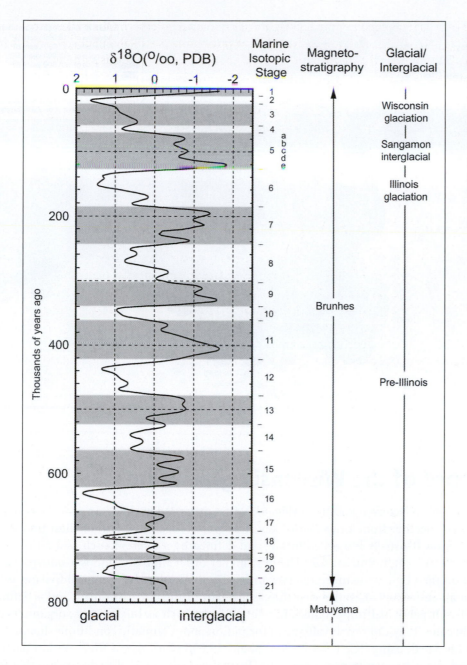

FIGURE 6.1 Stacked and smoothed record of δ18O in deep, seafloor cores, which corresponds with both global ice volume fluctuations and global climate fluctuations. Also shown are marine isotope stages (MIS), magnetostratigraphy, and glacial and interglacial events recognized in the terrestrial record of the mid-continent of North America. After Imbrie et al. (1984).

is represented by a thick, extensive drift sheet (Fig. 6.2) with a lobate margin. With the exception of southern Minnesota, eastern Wisconsin, eastern Ohio, New York, and places in Pennsylvania, the drift sheet does not extend as far south as the drift sheet associated with the Illinois glaciation. It also is not as weathered, with soil development usually >1 m thick.

Drift sheets older than those associated with Wisconsin and Illinois glaciations also occur in the eastern part of the mid-continent (Fig. 6.2). However, their number and ages are uncertain (Hallberg 1986); therefore they are not attributed to particular glaciations, but collectively referred to as Pre-Illinoian. In parts of Kansas, Nebraska, Wisconsin, Iowa, and Missouri (and locally in southwestern Ohio), one or more Pre-Illinoi(an) drift sheets extend beyond the limits of the Wisconsin and Illinois glaciations. This drift is characterized by a very high degree of weathering (Willman and Frye 1970). In Pennsylvania, this drift is generally very thin and patchy, and often consists of only a few scattered, erratic boulders on bedrock. Highly weathered erratic boulders also have been reported in northern Kentucky; their presence suggests that one or more Pre-Illinoian glaciations must have extended into northern Kentucky (Teller and Goldthwait 1991).

FIGURE 6.2 Extent of drift sheets in the eastern part of the mid-continent of North America. Sites corresponding to locations of sections described in text boxes are shown as dots, and labelled. After Ehlers and Gibbard (2004).

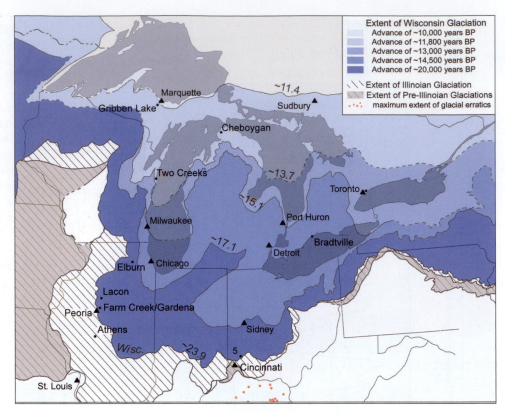

Temporal record of the Wisconsin glaciation

The diachronic classification of the Wisconsin glaciation (Fig. 6.3), first proposed by Johnson et al. (1997) and Karrow et al. (2000), was pieced together from a number of key stratigraphic sections. The smallest time division in the classification is a *phase*. It usually is applied locally and defined by a referent such as a unit of till, outwash, lacustrine sediment, loess, peat, or buried soil. The next higher order time division is a *subespisode*— applied more regionally and defined by one or more referent units. The highest order time subdivision is an *episode*. It applies throughout an entire region, in this case the eastern part of the mid-continent, and is defined by one or more referent units. Of particular importance are referent units such as buried soils, organic beds, and fossiliferous sediments, because they can reveal valuable information about climatic conditions during ice-free intervals. Also, they can be dated, using ^{14}C, as far back as about 53,000 years ago, if they contain datable organic materials such as wood, plant fragments, peat, and shells (Fairbanks et al. 2005). The discussion that follows highlights the important events of each of the major time units in the eastern part of the mid-continent, as shown in Figure 6.3.

The Sangamon episode

The Don Formation, exposed near the city of Toronto, Ontario (see FOCUS BOX on the following page), serves as the referent for the Sangamon Episode, i.e., the last interglacial, in the eastern-northern Great Lakes area. It probably represents a time span limited to MIS 5e—about 130,000–115,000 years ago (Karrow et al. 2000). The Don Formation consists of fluvio-lacustrine sediments, and includes fossils that indicate a climate as warm or warmer than present (Terasmae 1960, Eyles and Williams 1992). In the Lake Michigan-Illinois area, on the other hand, the Sangamon Geosol (buried soil) exposed near the city of Athens, in central Illinois (see FOCUS BOX on page 74),

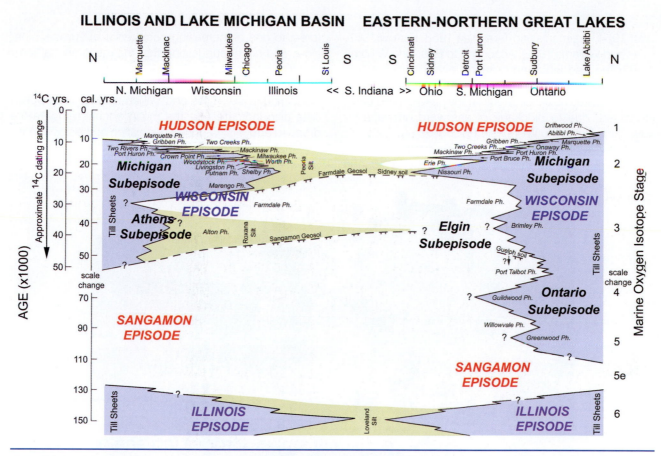

FIGURE 6.3 Comparison of time-distance diagrams for Illinois, the Lake Michigan basin, and the eastern and northern Great Lakes. After Karrow et al. (2000) and Johnson et al. (1997).

serves as the referent for the Sangamon Episode (Johnson et al. 1997). It probably represents a time span including all of MIS 5—about 130,000–75,000 years ago (Follmer 1983). Soil analyses of the geosol also suggest that the climate in the Lake Michigan-Illinois area during the early part of the Sangamon Episode was warmer than present (Follmer 1983). The lateral extent of the geosol is considerable, and correlative buried soils have been reported throughout much of the upper Mississippi River basin (Curry and Follmer 1992, Hall and Anderson 2000), including northern Illinois (see FOCUS BOX below). Recently, [10]Be data suggested that a correlative buried soil in northern Illinois developed from at least 155,000 to 55,000 years ago (Curry and Pavich 1996).

FOCUS BOX: A fossiliferous lake deposit from the last interglacial

A section formally exposed at the abandoned Don Valley (Taylors) Brickyard in Toronto, Ontario, provides a unique insight into climate of ~125,000 years ago, during the Sangamon Episode (last interglacial). First described by Coleman (1894), it has since been the object of much study.

At the top of the section are silty rhythmites (Scarborough Formation). Below these is bedded sand (Don Formation) with layers of muddy strata. Found within the bedded sand are pelecypods and gastropods (Coleman 1933), molluscs (Baker 1931), pollen and plant remains (Terasmae 1960, Richard et al. 1999), diatoms

(Duthie and Mannada Rani 1967), caddisflies (Williams and Morgan 1977), ostracods (Poplawski and Karrow 1981), and vertebrates (Harington 1990). Beneath the bedded sand is a bouldery diamicton (York Till) that rests on bedrock.

According to Terasmae (1960) and Karrow (1967, 1974) the diamicton is the wave-washed remnant of a till probably deposited during the Illinois Episode (Table 6.1). The bedded sand (Don Formation), on the other hand, is believed to be deltaic and deposited in relatively shallow water during the Sangamon Episode (Wright 1914,

Watt 1954, Dreimanis and Terasmae 1958, Karrow 1967, Eyles and Williams 1992). According to Eyles and Williams (1992) the bedded sand grades upward into the silty rhythmites (Scarborough Formation), which may have been deposited as water depths in the Lake Ontario basin increased, due to blockage of eastward drainage by advancing ice of the Wisconsin Episode.

Analysis of the pollen from the bedded sand (Don Formation) show a transition from a diverse deciduous forest to one of increasing occurrence of spruce, pine, alder, and birch, suggesting that the mean annual temperature was probably 2° C warmer than present, during the deposition of the lower part of the bedded sand. (Terasmae 1960, Eyles and Williams 1992). The pollen data also indicate that the mean annual temperature dropped about 3° C during deposition of the upper part, and that cooling continued during the deposition of the overlying Scarborough Formation.

Fossiliferous Don Formation, Toronto, Ontario. Photo from Coleman (1933).

FOCUS BOX: A record of the last interglacial-glacial transition in central Illinois

A quarry near Athens, IL provides one of the best records of the last interglacial-glacial transition in eastern North America (Follmer 1978, 1979, Curry and Follmer 1992). The section includes Sangamon and Farmdale Geosols, both of which are excellent regional stratigraphic markers. The quarry is the type locality of the Sangamon Geosol (Follmer 1983), which also serves as the referent for the Sangamon Episode (Table 6.1; Figure 6.3; Johnson et al. 1997).

At the top of the section is silt (Peoria Silt), the upper part of which is dolomitic while the lower part is organic rich and contains well-preserved spruce wood, needles, and other plant debris. Below the silt is a stratified, leached, organic silt (Robein Tongue of Peoria Silt) that has a thin soil developed in it (the Farmdale Geosol). The soil has a ~20 cm thick A horizon, which is a leached, black, silt loam, and has a ~60 cm thick B horizon. It also shows signs of cryoturbation—mixing by frost action.

Samples of organic material and wood from this soil have been dated to 30,300 and 26,700 years ago (Follmer 1979), while pollen found in silt immediately above the soil indicate a forested landscape, dominated by mostly pine and spruce, with a grass and herb understory (King 1979). Below the stratified, leached, organic-rich silt loam is a pedogenically altered silt (Roxana Silt) containing common biopores. Beneath it is a clay (Berry Clay), followed by a diamicton (Glasford Formation) resting on limestone. Developed in the clay and diamicton is a locally gleyed soil—the Sangamon Geosol—characterized by a ~2 m thick, clay-rich Bt horizon and a loamy C horizon extending to a depth of at least 4.9 m.

Curry and Follmer (1992) interpreted the pedogenically modified clay (Berry Clay) as colluvial material deposited during the Sangamon Episode, and argued that pedogenic modification (soil formation) of the clay continued until about 75,000–50,000 years ago, when climatic conditions shifted from interglacial to periglacial. They also argued that the pedogenically altered silt (Roxana Silt) burying the clay is loess, deposited as climatic conditions continued to deteriorate, and that the overlying organic-rich silt loam (Robein Tongue of Peoria Silt) is derived from reworking of the older silt. The soil (Farmdale Geosol) developed in the organic silt loam (Robein Silt) is believed to have formed ~30,000 to 26,500 years ago, during a short period of warmer climate (MIS 3; Fig. 6.1). The massive silt loam (Peoria Silt) unit above the soil, on the other hand, is believed to be loess—deposited sometime after 26,500 years ago, when areas to the north were under full glacial conditions.

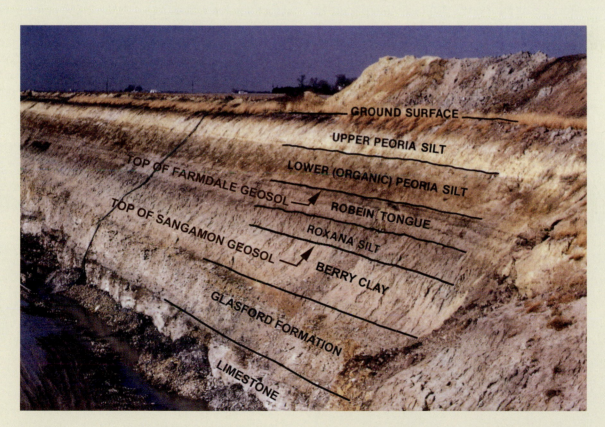

Sangamon and Farmdale Geosols at the Athens North Quarry, central Illinois. Modified from a photo by B. Curry, Illinois State Geological Survey.

FOCUS BOX: Well preserved Sangamon and Farmdale Geosols in western and northern Illinois

At the Sister's Section, located NE of Lacon, IL, is a remarkably well preserved Sangamon Geosol. It was first described by McKay et al. (2005) and includes a dark, silt loam A horizon ~30 cm thick, that overlies a light colored, loamy E horizon ~20 cm thick, and a clay-rich Bt horizon ~2.2 m thick. The geosol is developed in stratified sand and gravel, and diamicton (Pearl Formation) of probable fluvial/alluvial and/or slopewash origin. Beneath the stratified sand and gravel and diamicton is a weathered, weakly stratified diamicton (Radnor Member of the Glasford Formation), believed to be till deposited during the Illinois Episode. Conformably overlying the Sangamon Geosol is reddish brown to dark brown silt (Roxana Silt) interpreted as loess, deposited during the Wisconsin Episode. Above that is light gray to yellow brown silt (Morton Tongue of the Peoria Silt), also interpreted as loess. According to McKay et al. (2005), the A horizon of the Sangamon Geosol has incorporated within it a significant amount of loess (Roxana Silt) associated with the last glaciation.

Additionally, at the Felts Section, south of Elburn, IL, are exceptionally well persevered Sangamon and Farmdale Geosols (Curry et al. 1999). Here, the Sangamon Geosol includes a brown, sandy silt to clay loam A/B horizon ~90 cm thick and a brown, loam C horizon ~40 cm thick. The soil is developed mainly in cobbly, boulder, sand and gravel (Pearl Formation), interpreted as being proximal outwash deposited during the Illinois Episode. Overlying the geosol are silt and organic-rich silt (Robein Member of Roxana Silt), interpreted as colluviated loess. Curry et al. (1999) believed that the geosol probably developed under several climatic regimes during the Sangamon Episode, with vegetation types ranging from prairie to deciduous forest. The Farmdale Geosol consists of gray silt loam ~80 cm thick; it is developed in organic, leached silt (Robein Member of Roxana Silt). The soil contains wood fragments in its upper part, as well as rare, *in situ* spruce stumps dated at ~29,600 years ago (Curry et al. 1999). Burying the geosol is laminated silty clay (Peddicord Tongue of Equality Formation), interpreted as lacustrine sediment, and capping the section is silty diamicton (Tiskilwa Formation) interpreted as subglacial till deposited during the Wisconsin Episode.

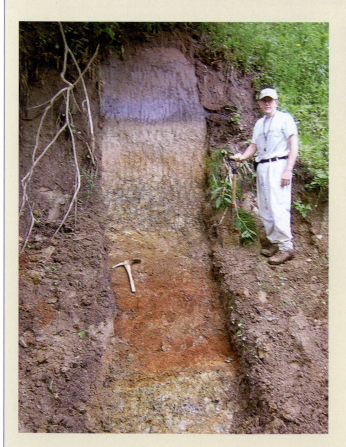

Left: The Sangamon Geosol at the Sister's Section, western Illinois. Photo by R. Berg, Illinois State Geological Survey. Right: Farmdale Geosol (waist level) at the Felts Section, northern Illinois. Note wood fragment at bottom left. Photo by B. Curry, Illinois State Geological Survey.

The Wisconsin episode

Eastern-Northern Great Lakes area

In the eastern-northern Great Lakes area, the Wisconsin Episode (last glaciation) is divided into three subepisodes: Ontario, Elgin, and Michigan (Fig. 6.3). The Ontario is the oldest—named after the province of Ontario where the best stratigraphic evidence for the subepisode is located (Karrow et al. 2000). It includes three phases with material referents in the Toronto area, mainly tills and glaciolacustrine sediments. Representing a time of cold climate and extensive ice cover, the Ontario Subepisode probably corresponds to MIS 4, and perhaps part or all of sustages 5a–5d (Karrow et al. 2000; Fig. 6.3). During the Greenwood Phase, ice extended well into the Ontario basin, but during the Willowvale Phase it withdrew, probably into the eastern end of the basin (Karrow et al. 2000). During the Guildwood Phase, the ice margin readvanced westward across the Ontario basin and possibly into the north-central part of the Erie basin (Dreimanis 1992). Little is known about where the ice margin stood in the Huron basin during the early part of the Greenwood and Willowvale phases, but during the Guildwood Phase it probably extended into part or all of Georgian Bay.

To date, no Ontario Subepisode sediments have been reported in Michigan. However, there are reports of buried organic material that have yielded infinite (generally >40–45,000 years ago) ^{14}C dates (Eschman 1980, Winters et al. 1986). Some of this material may have accumulated during the Ontario Subepisode, when parts of southern Ontario were covered by glacier ice, or earlier, e.g., during the Sangamon Eposide.

The Elgin Subepisode (Fig. 6.3) is named after Elgin County, on the north shore of Lake Erie. Here, the best evidence for the episode occurs, mainly in the form of lacustrine and organic sediments (Karrow et al. 2000). The Elgin Subepisode includes the Port Talbot, Brimley, and Farmdale phases; it represents a time of moderated (warmer) climate and significant ice contraction. Of particular significance is the Port Talbot Phase, defined by pollen- and macrofossil-bearing lacustrine sediments located near Port Talbot, along the north shore of Lake Erie (see FOCUS BOX below). Pollen from this site indicates initially warm and dry climatic conditions (but cooler than an interglacial), followed by climatic cooling and possibly a forest-tundra environment (Berti 1975). Dates on the peat and wood found within the sediments range from ~51,200 to 47,300 years ago (Dreimanis et al. 1966, Dreimanis and Karrow 1972). Ages of >49,000 years also have been obtained from a buried soil and overlying fossiliferous sediments in the city of Guelph (Karrow et al. 1982). Analyses of the fossils indicate a cooler and dryer climate than present; it is possible that the buried soil and sediment is associated with the Elgin Subepisode, or alternatively the Ontario Subepisode or some earlier time (Karrow et al. 1982).

FOCUS BOX: Evidence for cooling climatic conditions in southern Ontario

A section in and below the bluffs along the north shore of Lake Erie, between Plum Point and Bradtville, Ontario, provides unique insights into the changing climatic conditions there, as glacial ice invaded the area during the Wisconsin Episode (MIS-4; Fig. 6.1). First described by Dreimanis (1957, 1958), this section contains the referent (Member C of Tyrconnell Formation) for the Port Talbot Phase, as well as the referent (Catfish Creek Till) for the Nissouri Phase (Karrow et al. 2000).

At the top of the section is a sandy diamicton (Catfish Creek till), beneath which is clay and silt (Member D of Tyrconnell Formation; formally glaciolacustrine unit II), followed by silt and fine sand (Member C of Tyrconnell Formation; formally Port Talbot II) containing spruce and tamarack, as well as thin layers and lenses of peat, gyttja, and coarse sands containing shells. Below the silt and fine sand are varved clay and silt (Member B of Tyrconnell Formation; formally glaciolacustrine unit I), and below that is a greenish-colored, carbonate-poor clay (Member A of Tyrconnell Formation; formally Port Talbot I). Under the green clay is another diamicton (Upper Bradtville till of Bradtville Drift), underlain by bedded clay and silt, followed by a third diamicton (Lower Bradtville till of Bradtville Drift), underlain by bedded clay and silt. At the base of the section and resting on bedrock is a fourth diamicton (Lowermost Bradtville till of Bradtville Drift).

According to Dreimanis (1987), the diamictons beneath the green clay (Member A of Tyrconnell Formation) are tills; the clay and silt between the diamictons are glaciolacustrine sediments. Initially, Dreimanis (1966) and Dreimanis and Karrow (1972) thought that the diamictons and bedded clays and silts were deposited early during the Wisconsin Episode, as ice invaded the region from the NE, but later Dreimanis (1992) argued that they were deposited during the Illinois Episode. The green clay (Member A of Tyrconnell Formation) is believed to be a soil (Quigly and Dreimanis 1972). Dreimanis (1992) argued that the soil developed during the Sangamon Episode, when ancestral Lake Erie was at a low level and draining via the now-buried Erigan channel. Analyses by Berti (1975) of pollen from the green clay indicate that the soil developed under relatively warm, dry conditions. The varved clay and silt (Member B of Tyrconnell Formation) directly above the green clay are believed to be glaciolacustrine sediments, deposited during the Wisconsin Episode, as ice advanced into the region from

the north. The silt and fine sand above (Member C of Tyrconnell Formation) are believed to be paludal (swampy, marshy) sediments, deposited as the ice margin temporarily withdrew (Dreimanis et al. 1966). Berti (1975) found that the pollen within the varved clay and silt (Members B), and the silt and fine sand, (Member C) were mostly spruce and pine, suggesting a moist and cool forest-tundra environment. Also, samples of the gyttja and peat found within the silt and fine sand (Member C) have yielded ages of ~51,200 to 38,400 years ago (Dreimanis et al. 1966). The clay and silt (Member D) near the top of the section is believed to be glaciolacustine sediment deposited as the ice margin again advanced into the region, whereas the diamicton (Catfish Creek till) at the top of the section is believed to be till, deposited as the ice margin advanced over the region (Dreimanis 1966).

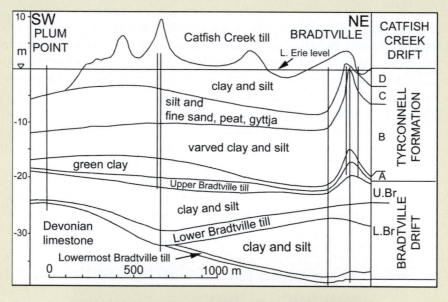

Top: Stratigraphic section of the Catfish Creek Drift, Tyrconnel Formation, and Bradtville Drift. After Dreimanis (1992). Bottom: Gyttja and peat layers in Member C of the Tyrconnell Formation near Bradtville, Ontario. Truncating the gyttja and peat layers is Catfish Creek Drift. Photo by A. Dreimanis.

In Michigan, buried organic materials—wood, muck, and marl—have yielded ages ranging from ~51,900 to 42,300 years ago (Eschman 1980, Winters et al. 1986). Of particular interest is material reported near Kalkaska in the northwestern Lower Peninsula (Winters et al. 1986). This material includes a pollen record that shows vegetation evolving from a cold, open forest into a closed boreal forest ~40,300 years ago, and suggests that the climate near Kalkaska at this time was possibly influenced by an ice margin in southern Ontario (Winters et al. 1986). Also of interest is organic material exposed in the banks of the Black River in the southeastern Lower Peninsula, which has been dated at ~51,900 years ago (Eschman 1980). It contains a mixed terrestrial and aquatic fauna that clearly have boreal affinities (Karrow et al. 1997). These buried organic materials confirm that the Lower Peninsula was not covered by ice during the Elgin Subepisode (Port Talbot phase), although an ice margin to the north, or even within the Upper Great Lakes' basins, appears likely.

The Michigan Subepisode (Fig. 6.3) is the last subepisode of the Wisconsin Episode. It is so named because the landscape of Michigan is dominated by glacial sediments deposited at this time—near the end of the Wisconsin glaciation (Johnson et al. 1997, Karrow et al. 2000). The Michigan Subepisode includes 11 phases, defined mainly by till units found in Michigan, Ohio and Ontario. It marks a period of cold climate and maximum expansion of ice, followed by warming and ice-margin retreat. The Nissouri Phase at the beginning of the subepisode is of particular significance, because it was during this phase that the ice margin advanced rapidly out of the Erie and Huron basins, to cover all of Ontario and Michigan, as well as much of Indiana and Ohio. Upon reaching its most southerly position near Cincinnati, the margin overrode and buried a forest (see FOCUS BOX below) that has been dated at ~23,700 years ago (Lowell et al. 1990).

Following the Nissouri Phase ice advance, the ice margin retreated northward, towards the Erie and Huron basins, only to periodically readvance. The exact timing of these readvances is not well known, mainly because of the paucity of *in situ* datable organic material, especially wood, during this cold climatic interval. A notable exception, however, is the readvance associated with the Onaway Phase. It buried a bryophyte (moss) bed near Cheboygan, Michigan (see FOCUS BOX on page 81) that has been dated at ~13,600 years ago (Larson et al. 1994).

FOCUS BOX: A buried organic mat near Cincinnati, Ohio

The Sharonville section records when glacial ice reached its terminal position near Cincinnati, OH, during the Wisconsin Episode. The section, located near the town of Sharonville, has been extensively described by Lowell et al. (1990). It includes a 2–3 cm thick organic mat that consists chiefly of decimated plant remains and bryophytes (mosses), dated from ~25,900 to 25,300 years ago. Locally, upright stumps of larch are rooted in the mat and have yielded ages that average ~23,500 years old. Beneath the mat is a pedologically altered, organic-rich silt; samples of disseminated organic material from this silt have been dated at ~31,800 to 29,300 years ago. Beneath the organic silt is clay-rich diamicton, which overlies Ordovician shale and limestone. Above the organic mat is a massive calcareous clay, that grades upward into compact silt-rich diamicton.

According to Lowell et al. (1990), the clay-rich diamicton near the base of the section is till. They assign no age to it but, on the basis of ^{14}C dates associated with disseminated organic material found in the organic silt (loess?), they argued that the diamicton must have been deposited sometime prior to 32,300 years ago. From ^{14}C dates associated with the stumps rooted in the organic silt, and the upright positions of the stumps, they also argued that the trees were killed by overriding glacier ice ~23,500 years ago (Nissouri Phase). They interpreted the compact, silt-rich diamicton capping the section as till, deposited when the ice margin advanced towards its terminal position near Cincinnati (Fig. 6.2).

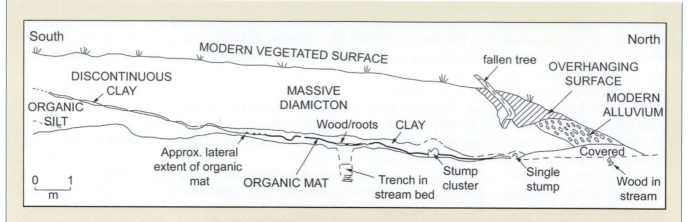

Upper: Stratigraphic section associated with the Sharonville buried organic mat. After Lowell et al. (1990). Middle: Sharonville buried organic mat. Photo by T. Lowell. Lower: Sharonville buried log. Photo by T. Lowell.

FOCUS BOX: A buried bryophyte bed in the northern Lower Peninsula of Michigan

The Cheboyan bryophyte bed section records a retreat of the ice margin from the Lower Peninsula ~15,100 to 14,500 years ago, followed by a significant readvance. The section is located several km west of Choboygan. It was first described by Farrand et al. (1969) and later by Larson et al. (1994). It includes a 5 mm thick bryophyte (moss) bed that contains plant debris, mainly willow, as well as snails, pollen, and vole fecal pellets. This material has been dated at ~14,600 to 11,500 years ago (Farrand et al. 1969; Larson et al. 1994). The bed is underlain by sand and gravel, and is buried by laminated silt and fine sand, above which is a red-pink, clayey diamicton. Capping the section is stratified sand and gravel.

Farrand et al. (1969) interpreted the sand and gravel below the bryophyte bed to be glacial outwash, deposited as the ice margin retreated during the end of the Wisconsin Episode, and the laminated silt and fine sand above the bed to be lacustrine materials, deposited in a glacial lake. Based on four new, narrowly-ranging, ^{14}C ages, Larson et al. (1994) assigned an age of about 13,600 years (Two Creeks Phase) to the bed and suggested that it is generally contemporaneous with the Two Creeks Forest bed in eastern Wisconsin. Larson et al. (1994) also suggested that the red diamicton (Munro Lake till) above the bed is till, deposited by the same ice advance that blocked off eastward drainage from the Lake Michigan basin and buried the Two Creeks forest bed. Schaetzl (2001) suggested that this advance was probably from the NW. The stratified sand and gravel capping the section is most likely associated with glacial Lake Algonquin (Farrand et al. 1969; Larson et al. 1994).

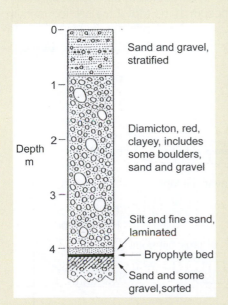

Left: The stratigraphic section associated with Cheboygan bryophyte bed. After Larson et al. (1994). Right: Sample of the Cheboygan bryophyte bed, capped by laminated silt and fine sand. Also shown in the foreground are bryophyte fragments, *Salix* twigs, snails, and vole fecal pellets retrieved from the bryophyte bed. Photos by G. Larson.

Lake Michigan-Illinois area

In Lake Michigan-Illinois area, the Wisconsin Episode is subdivided into the Athens and Michigan Subepisodes (Fig. 6.3). The Athens Subepisode includes the Alton and Farmdale phases, based on a record of loess and buried soils exposed near the city of Athens in central Illinois (Johnson et al. 1997). The Michigan Subepisode has nine phases, based mainly on till units found in Illinois, Wisconsin, and northern Michigan (Hansel and Johnson

1992). In general, the phases of the Michigan Subepisode are generally concurrent with those in the eastern-northern Great Lakes area (Karrow et al. 2000).

The Alton Phase was a time of transition from interglacial to periglacial conditions in central Illinois, and its referent material is the Roxana Silt (Johnson et al. 1997). Little is known about the ice margin position during the Alton Phase, but it may have extended as far south as north-central Wisconsin and central Minnesota, where it contributed massive quantities of silt into the upper Mississippi drainage system (Grimley 2000). The following Farmdale Phase was a time of significant reduction in loess supply, probably because of ice margin retreat from the upper Mississippi basin and a concurrent return to a milder climate. The Farmdale Geosol and Robein Silt (see FOCUS BOX below), exposed along the banks of Farm Creek, near Peoria, Illinois (Frye and Willman 1960), serve as the referent for the Farmdale Phase. Based on radiocarbon dates at and near the exposure, the Farmdale Geosol is believed to have developed from ~33,400 to 26,500 years ago (Willman and Frye 1970, Johnson 1976). The geosol also is found at other localities in Illinois and western Indiana (Curry and Follmer 1992, Hall and Anderson 2000); in eastern Indiana and Ohio it is referred to as the Sidney Soil (Hall and Anderson 2000).

FOCUS BOX: A buried soil in central Illinois

The Farm Creek section, located just east of Peoria, is a classic Pleistocene exposure, and the type section for the Farmdale Geosol (Leverett 1899, Leighton 1926, 1931, Willman and Frye 1970, Follmer et al. 1979). According to Follmer et al. (1979) a weathered silt (Peoria Silt), interpreted as loess, occurs at the top of the section, and is

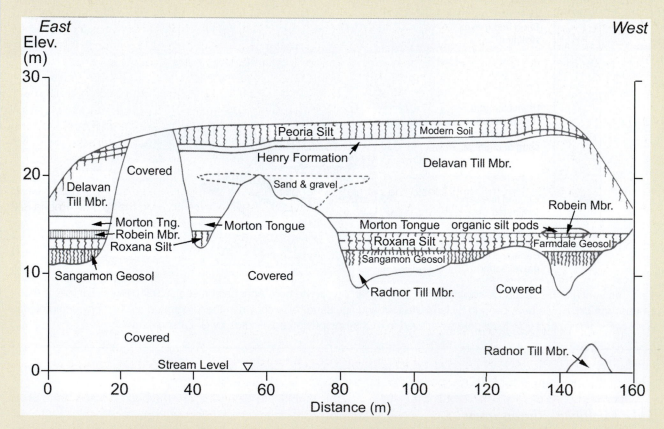

Above: The stratigraphic section at Farm Creek, central IL. After Follmer et al. (1979). Facing Page: The Farmdale Geosol developed in Robein Silt Member of the Roxana Silt at Farm Creek. Wd—Delavan Till Member of the Wedron Formation, Pm—Morton Tongue of the Peoria Silt, Rr—Robein Member of the Roxana Silt, R—Roxana Silt. Photo and annotation by D. McKay, Illinois State Geological Survey.

in color, and leached. Locally separating the two silt units is leached, organic rich-silt or silty, peaty muck (Robein Member of the Roxana Silt), interpreted as an organic-rich soil. Beneath the lower silt unit is a leached, weathered, massive diamicton (Radnor Till Member of Glasford Formation), containing the Sangamon Geosol in its the upper part.

According to Willman and Frye (1970), the diamicton at the base of the section (Radnor Till) was deposited during the Illinois Episode, and was later leached and weathered during the Sangamon Episode. They also believe the silt unit (Roxana Silt) burying the diamicton was deposited during the early part of the Athens Subepisode of the Wisconsin Episode, when ice advanced into the upper Mississippi River basin, and that the peaty muck (Robein Member) above it accumulated during a prolonged retreat of the ice margin (Farmdale Phase). The muck represents the O horizon of the Farmdale Geosol (Follmer et al. 1979) and probably formed by accumulation of organic debris and silt from sheetwash and eolian deposition (Willman and Frye 1970). This soil (two dates) has been dated at ~32,000 and 33,000 years ago (Follmer et al. 1979). The silt unit (Morton Tongue) burying the muck was deposited during the Michigan Subepisode of the Wisconsin Episode as the ice margin advanced to its terminal position, just south of Peoria. It is equivalent to the lower part of the Peoria loess, beyond the terminal position (Willman and Frye 1970) and includes organic material that has been dated at ~24,200 and 24,200 years ago (Willman and Frye 1970). According to Willman and Frye (1970), the diamicton (Delavan Till) overlying the silt unit was deposited as the ice margin advanced to its terminal position, while the sandy gravel (Henry Formation) was deposited as the ice margin retreated from that position. They also believe the silt capping the section (Peoria Silt) was deposited following retreat of the ice margin. It, too, is equivalent to the upper part of the Peoria Silt beyond the terminal position (Willman and Frye 1970).

underlain by a sandy gravel (Henry Formation), interpreted as outwash. Beneath the sandy gravel is a compact, massive diamicton (Delavan Till Member of Wedron Formation), believed to be till, and beneath the diamicton are two silt units interpreted as loess. The upper silt unit (Morton Tongue) is dolomitic and contains streaks of plant debris, humus, moss, wood, and fossil snail shells, while the lower silt unit (Roxana Silt) is massive, darker

At a number of localities in the Lower Peninsula of Michigan, buried organic materials, in places meters thick, have been dated, yielding ages from 51,000 to 28,700 years ago (Eschman 1980; Winters et al. 1986). The presence of this material indicates that much of the Lower Peninsula was cool but ice free during the Alton and Farmdale phases, and that climate at that time was probably wetter than in central Illinois.

As in the eastern-northern Great Lakes area, the Michigan Subepisode in the Lake Michigan-Illinois area marks a period of cooling and expansion of the ice, eventually followed by general warming and retreat. Maximum glacier expansion occurred early in the Michigan Subepisode, during the Shelby Phase. At that time, the ice margin advanced out of the Lake Michigan basin, south to as far as Peoria, where it overrode and buried a moss layer (see FOCUS BOX on the following page) that has been dated at ~23,500 years ago (Follmer 1979).

FOCUS BOX: A buried bryophyte bed near Peoria, Illinois

The Gardena section reveals when advancing glacier ice reached its terminal position in central Illinois, during the Wisconsin Episode. Located a few km east of Peoria, IL, it was first described by Follmer et al. (1979) and Miller (1979). The section includes a bryophyte (moss) bed about 3 cm thick that has been dated at ~23,500 years ago. The bed is developed on silt loam and silty clay (Morton Tongue of the Peoria Silt), believed to be equivalent to the lower part of the Peoria loess beyond the terminal position of the last glaciation (Follmer et al. 1979). The bryophyte bed is buried by finely laminated, gray silt loam and silty clay, interpreted as lacustrine sediment (Miller 1979). Above the clay is brown-to-gray sandy diamicton (Delavan Till Member of the Wedron Formation), interpreted as till deposited when the glacier margin advanced to its terminal position (Shelby Phase) near Peoria (Follmer et al. 1979).

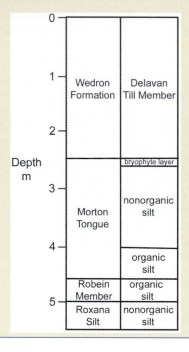

Left: Stratigraphic section associated with Gardena bryophyte bed. After Follmer et al. (1979). Right: The Gardena bryophyte bed, North-Central Illinois. Photo by L. Follmer, Illinois State Geological Survey.

After advancing to Peoria, the ice margin began to slowly retreat northward, punctuated by a few, brief readvances. The exact timing of each readvance is uncertain, because of the paucity of *in situ*, datable organic materials. However, the timing of the readvance associated with the Two Rivers Phase is well documented, because advancing ice overrode and buried a forest near Two Creeks, Wisconsin (see FOCUS BOX below). Wood from this forest bed has been dated at ~13,600 years ago (Broecker and Farrand 1963, Leavitt and Kalin 1992, Kaiser 1994).

FOCUS BOX: A buried forest bed in east-central Wisconsin

The Two Creeks section is well-known because it provides clear evidence for a major retreat of the ice margin in east-central Wisconsin near the end of the Wisconsin Episode, followed by a readvance about 13,600 years ago. The section is located along the western shore of Lake Michigan near the village of Two Creeks, WI. It was first described by Goldthwait (1906) and subsequently by Thwaites and Bertrand (1957), Black (1970), Evenson et al. (1973) and Kaiser (1994). Within the section is a 5–50 mm thick, buried forest bed that includes logs of spruce and pine, needles, cones, twigs, bark, and bryophytes (Wilson 1932). It is underlain by bedded silt and clay, and gray diamicton. It is buried by bedded sand and reddish-brown diamicton. Locally, lenses of gravel occur between the forest bed and the underlying bedded silt and clay. The forest bed serves as the referent for the Two Creeks Phase (Johnson et al. 1997). Logs and wood from it have yielded multiple ^{14}C dates that average ~13,600 years ago (Kaiser 1994). Analyses of tree rings also indicate some of the trees were >200 years old (Kaiser 1994).

According to recent work by Mickelson and Socha (in review), the gray diamicton beneath the forest bed is till (Ozaukee Till), deposited as the ice margin of the Lake Michigan lobe readvanced (Port Huron Phase) southward ~15,100 years ago, to a position just south of Milwaukee. They interpret the bedded silt and clay above the gray diamicton as lacustrine sediment, deposited within an ice-marginal lake—glacial Lake Chicago. Development of the Two Creeks forest is believed by Broecker and Farrand (1963) to record a drop in the level of the ice-marginal lake just prior to 13,600 years ago, and emergence of dry land near Two Creeks. They also attribute the drop in lake level to continued northward retreat of the ice margin and uncovering of lower drainage outlets near the Straits of Mackinac. The rhythmically bedded sand above the forest bed is believed by Acomb et al. (1982) to be lacustrine sediment deposited as lake level rose to flood the forest bed, induced by a readvance of the ice margin (Two Rivers Phase) and blockage of the outlets near the Straits by ice. They also interpret the reddish-brown diamict (Two Rivers Till) capping the rhythmically bedded sand as till, deposited as the ice margin advanced south to a position near Two Rivers, WI.

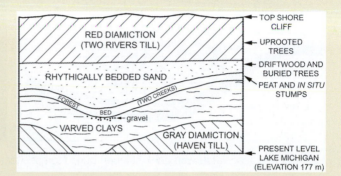

A stratigraphic section associated with the Two Creeks forest bed, east-central Wisconsin. After Broecker and Farrand (1963).

The timing of the readvance associated with the Marquette Phase is well established, because glacial sediments associated with that readvance buried a forest near Marquette (see FOCUS BOX below). Wood buried by this readvance has been dated at ~11,500 years ago (Lowell et al. 1999, Pregitzer et al. 2000). The latest known readvance was the Cochrane readvance, in northern Ontario, ~9,400 years ago. After this, the ice sheet split into two large remnants east and west of Hudson's Bay, and was entirely gone by about 6,800 years ago (Dyke and Prest 1987).

FOCUS BOX: A buried forest in northern Michigan

The Lake Gribben section provides evidence for a significant retreat of the ice margin in northern Michigan, near the end of the Wisconsin Episode, followed by a readvance ~11,500 years ago. The section, located SW of Marquette, was first described by Hughes and Merry (1978), and later by Lowell et al. (1999) and Pregitzer et al. (2000). A buried forest within the section, consisting mainly of spruce with some larch, serves as the referent for the Gribben Phase (Karrow et al. 2000). The trees here are rooted in a thin paleosol, developed on pebbly sand, and overlain by horizontally bedded clay, silt, and fine sand. Capping the section is cross-bedded sand and gravel. The buried forest has yielded nine, narrowly-ranging calibrated ^{14}C ages (Lowell et al. 1999). Tree ring analyses indicate that some of the spruce trees were >150 years old when buried (Pregitzer et al. 2000).

According to Lowell et al. (1999), the pebbly sand beneath the buried forest is outwash, deposited as the margin of the Superior ice lobe retreated northward into the Superior basin prior to 11,500 years ago. They also interpret the horizontally bedded clay silt and fine sand overlying the forest as lacustrine or extreme distal outwash, deposited in a deepening ice-marginal lake contained by advancing ice of the Superior lobe (Marquette Phase). The trough cross-bedded, sandy gravel, overlying the horizontally bedded clay, silt, and fine sand, is probably outwash, deposited as the ice margin advanced just after about 11,500 years ago, to a position beyond the south shore of Lake Superior and north of Lake Gribben.

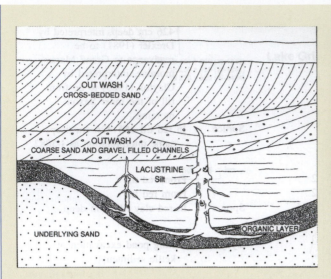 

Left: Section associated with Lake Gribben buried forest. After Lowell et al. (1999). Right: Lake Gribben buried forest, northern Michigan. Photo by T. Bornhorst.

◼ Hudson episode

Post-glacial time is represented by the Hudson Episode (Fig. 6.3), named so because Hudson Bay is dominated by marine, fluvial, and paludal sediments, deposited since deglaciation (Johnson et al. 1997, Karrow et al. 2000). As yet, there is no particular referent for the Hudson Episode, but a possible candidate is marine sediment associated with the Tyrrell Sea that occupied Hudson Bay after retreat and breakup of the ice sheet (Shilts 1984, Dredge and Cowan 1989). In the eastern part of the mid-continent, deposits associated with the Hudson Episode include lacustrine sediments deposited in the Great Lakes since deglaciation (Colman et al. 1994, Rae et al. 1994), as well as within smaller inland lakes. Other deposits include loess, dune sand, fluvial deposits, and organic accumulations in swamps and bogs.

◼ Conclusions

The number of times the mid-continent was glaciated during last 900,000 years is not definitively known, but it appears that glaciation has occurred in this area about every 100,000 years. The last two glaciations—the Illinois and Wisconsin—occurred between 202,000 to 132,000 and 79,000 to 10,000 years ago, respectively. Separating them was a warm interval known as the Sangamon interglaciation, which peaked around 130,000–115,000 years ago.

The record of the Wisconsin glaciation in the eastern part of the mid-continent is well represented by glacial and nonglacial sediments, buried soils, and organic deposits. It shows that glacial ice initially advanced southward and southwestward over southern Ontario, and extended into the western part of the Ontario basin, the eastern part of the Erie basin, and probably into the northern part of the Huron and Superior basins by about 70,000 years ago. It also shows that the ice margin remained and oscillated there for several tens of thousands of years, until about 31,200 years ago, after which it advanced over the rest of the Great Lake basins as far south as Illinois, Indiana, Ohio, and Pennsylvania. After reaching its southern limit near the Ohio River, about 23,500 years ago, the ice margin retreat northward. The retreat however was interrupted by a number of major readvances. Not until just after about 11,500 years ago did the ice margin finally retreat north of the Great Lakes.

Literature Cited

Acomb, L.J., Mickelson, D.M. and E.B. Evenson. 1982. Till stratigraphy and late glacial events in the Lake Michigan Lobe of eastern Wisconsin. Geological Society of America Bulletin 93:289–296.

Baker, F.C. 1931. A restudy of the interglacial molluscan fauna of Toronto, Canada. Illinois Academy of Science Transactions 23:358–366.

Berti, A.A. 1975. Paleobotany of Wisconsinan interstadials, eastern Great Lake region, North America. Quaternary Research 5:591–619.

Black, R.F. 1970. Glacial geology of the Two Creeks forest bed, Valderan type-locality, and Northern Kettle Moraine State Forest. Wisconsin Geological and Natural History Survey Informational Circular 13. 40 pp.

Broecker, W.S. and W.R. Farrand. 1963. Radiocarbon age of the Two Creeks forest bed, Wisconsin. Geological Society of America Bulletin 280:795–802.

Chamberlin, T.C. 1883. Preliminary paper on the terminal moraines of the second glacial epoch. U.S. Geological Survey 34th Annual Report, pp. 291–402.

Chamberlin, T.C. 1894. Glacial phenomena of North America. In: J. Geikie, The Great Ice Age, 3rd Edition, Stanford: London. pp. 724–775.

Chamberlin, T.C. 1896. Nomenclature of glacier formations. Journal of Geology 4:872–876.

Coleman, A.P. 1894. Interglacial fossils from the Don Valley. American Geologist 13:85–95.

Coleman, A.P. 1933. The Pleistocene of the Toronto region. Ontario Department of Mines Annual Report 41. Pt. 7.

Colman, S.M., Forester, R.M., Reynolds, R.L., Sweetkind, D.S., King, J.W., Gangemi, P., Jones, G.A., Keigwin, L.D. and D.S. Foster. 1994. Lake-level history of Lake Michigan for the past 12,000 years: the record from deep lacustrine sediments. Journal of Great Lakes Research 20:73–92.

Curry, B.B., Grimley, D.A. and J.A. Stravers. 1999, Quaternary geology, geomorphology, and climatic history of Kane County, Illinois. Illinois Geological Survey Guidebook 28. 40 pp.

Curry, B.B. and L.R. Follmer. 1992. Last interglacial-glacial transition in Illinois: 135–25 ka. In: P.U. Clark and P.D. Lea (eds.), The Last Interglacial-Glacial Transition in North America, Geological Society of America Special Paper 270:71–88.

Curry, B.B. and M. Pavich. 1996. Absence of glaciation in Illinois during marine isotope stages 3 through 5. Quaternary Research 46:19–26.

Dredge, L.A. and W.R. Cowan. 1989. Quaternary geology of the south-western Canadian Shield. In: R.J. Fulton (ed.), Quaternary Geology of Canada and Greenland, Geological Survey of Canada No. 1 and Geological Society of America, Geology of North America v. K-1. pp. 214–249.

Dreimanis, A. 1957. Stratigraphy of the Wisconsin glacial stage along the northwestern shore of Lake Erie. Science 126:166–168.

Dreimanis, A. 1958. Wisconsin stratigraphy at Port Talbot on the north shore of Lake Erie, Ontario. Ohio Journal of Science 58:65–84.

Dreimanis, A. 1987. The Port Talbot interstadial site, southwestern Ontario. In: D.C. Roy (ed.), Northeastern section of the Geological Society of America Centennial Field Guide, 5:345–348.

Dreimanis, A. 1992. Early Wisconsinan in the north-central part of the Lake Erie basin: A new interpretation. Geological Society of America Special Paper 270:109118.

Dreimanis, A. and P.F. Karrow. 1972. Glacial history of the Great Lakes-St. Lawrence region, the classification of the Wisconsin(an) stage, and its correlatives. 24th International Geological Congress, Sect. 12. pp. 5–15.

Dreimanis, A. and J. Terasmae. 1958. Stratigraphy of Wisconsin glacial deposits of Toronto area, Ontario. Geological Association of Canada Proceedings 10:119–135.

Dreimanis, A., Terasmae, J. and G.D. McKenzie. 1966. The Port Talbot Interstade of the Wisconsin Glaciation. Canadian Journal of Earth Sciences 3:305–325.

Duthie, H.C. and R.G. Mannada Rani. 1967. Diatom assemblages from Pleistocene interglacial beds at Toronto, Ontario. Canadian Journal of Botany 45:2249–2261.

Dyke, A.S. and V.K. Prest, 1987. Late Wisconsinan and Holocene History of the Laurentide Ice Sheet. Geographie Physique et Quaternaire 41:237–264.

Ehlers, J. and P.L. Gibbard (eds.). 2004. Quaternary Glaciations—Extent and Chronology, Part II: North America. Elsevier: Amsterdam. 440 pp.

Eschman, D.F. 1980. Some evidence of Mid-Wisconsinan events in Michigan. Michigan Academician 12:423–436.

Evenson, E.B., Eschman, D.F. and W.R. Farrand. 1973. The "Valderan" problem, Lake Michigan basin. 22nd annual field conference, Midwest Friends of the Pleistocene, June 1–3, 1973. pp. 1–59.

Evenson, E.B., Farrand, W.R., Eschman, D.F., Mickelson, D.M. and L.J. Maher. 1976. Greatlakean Substage: a replacement for the Valderan Substage in the Lake Michigan basin. Quaternary Research 6:411–424.

Eyles, N. and N.S. Williams. 1992. The sedimentary and biological record of the last interglacial-glacial transition at Toronto, Canada. In: P.U. Clark and P.D. Lea (eds.), The Last Interglacial-Glacial Transition in North America, Geological Society of America Special Paper 270:119–128.

Fairbanks, R.G., Mortlock, R.A., Chiu, T.-C., Cao, L., Kaplan, A., Guilderson, T.P., Fairbanks, T.W. and A.L. Bloom. 2005. Marine radiocarbon calibration curve spanning 10,000 to 50,000 years B.P. based on paired ^{230}Th/^{234}U/^{238}U and ^{14}C dates on pristine corals. Quaternary Science Reviews 24:1781–1796.

Farlow, J.O., Sunderman, J.A., Havens, J.J., Swinehart, A.L., Holman, J.A., Richards, R.L., Miller, N.G., Martin, R.A., Hunt, Jr., R.M., Storrs, G.W., Curry, B.B., Fluegeman, R.H., Dawson, M.R. and M.E.T. Flint. 2001. The Pipe Creek sinkhole biota, a diverse late Tertiary continental fossil assemblage from Grant County, Indiana. American Midlands Naturalist 145:367–378.

Farrand, W.R., Zahner, R. and W.S. Benninghoff. 1969. Cary-Port Huron interstade: Evidence from a buried bryophyte bed, Cheboygan, Michigan. Geological Society of America Special Paper 123:249–262.

Follmer, L.R. 1978. The Sangamon Soil in its type area—A review, In: Quaternary soils, Geo Abstracts, Norwich. pp. 125–165.

Follmer, L.R. 1979. A historical review of the Sangamon Soil, In: Wisconsinan, Sangamonian and Illinois stratigraphy in central Illinois. Illinois State Geological Survey Guidebook 13:79–91.

Follmer, L.R. 1983. Sangamonian and Wisconsinan petrogenesis in the midwestern United States. In: S.C. Porter (ed.), Late Quaternary Environments of the United States, Vol. 1, The Late Pleistocene. University of Minnesota Press, Minneapolis. pp. 138–144.

Follmer, L.R., McKay, E.D., Lineback, J.A. and D.L. Gross. 1979. Wisconsinan, Sangamonian and Illinois stratigraphy in central Illinois. Illinois State Geological Survey Guidebook 13:1–68.

Frye, J.C. and H.B. Willman. 1960. Classification of the Wisconsinan Stage in the Lake Michigan glacial lobe. Illinois State Geological Survey Circular 285. 16 pp.

Fullerton, D.S. 1986. Stratigraphy and correlation of glacial deposits from Indiana to New York and New Jersey. In: V. Sibrava, D.Q. Bowen, and G.M. Richmond (eds.), Quaternary Glaciations in the Northern Hemisphere, Quaternary Science Reviews 5:23–36.

Goldthwait, J.W. 1906. Correlation of the raised beaches on the west side of Lake Michigan. Journal of Geology 14:411–424.

Grimley, D.A. 2000. Glacial and nonglacial sediment contributions to Wisconsin Episode loess in the central United States. Geological Society of America Bulletin 112:1475–1495.

Hall, R.D. and A.K. Anderson. 2000. Comparative soil development of Quaternary paleosols of the central United States. Palaeogeography, Palaeoclimatology, Palaeoecology 158:109–145.

Hallberg, G.R. 1986. Pre-Wisconsin glacial stratigraphy of the Central Plains region in Iowa, Nebraska, Kansas, and Missouri. Quaternary Science Reviews 5:11–15.

Hansel, A.K. and W.H. Johnson. 1992. Fluctuations of the Lake Michigan lobe during the late Wisconsin Subepisode. Sveriges Geologiska Unfersöking, Series Ca, 81:133–144.

Harington, C.R. 1990. Vertebrates of the last interglaciation in Canada: a review with new data. Géographie physique et Quaternaire 44:375–387.

Holman, J.A. 1998. Pre-Wisconsinan amphibian and reptile remains from northeastern Indiana. Michigan Academician 30:358–359.

Horberg, C.L. and R.C. Anderson. 1956. Bedrock topography and Pleistocene glacial lobes in central United States. Journal of Geology 64:101–106.

Hughes, J.D. and W.J. Merry. 1978. Marquette buried forest 9,850 years old. American Association for Advancement of Science, Abstract for Annual Meeting. 12–14 February, 1978.

Imbrie, J., Hays, J.D., Martinson, D.G., MacIntyre, A., Mix, A.C., Morley, J.J., Pisias, N.G., Prell, W.L. and N.J. Schackelton. 1984. The orbital theory of Pleistocene climate: support from a revised chronology of the marine $\delta^{18}O$ record. In: A. Berger, J. Imbrie, L. Hays, G. Kukla, and B. Saltzman (eds.), Milankovitch and Climate, 269–305, Dorfrecht, Reidel.

Johnson, W.II. 1976. Quaternary Stratigraphy in Illinois, Status and Current Problems. In: W.C. Mahaney (ed.), Quaternary Stratigraphy of North America. Dowen, Hutchinson and Ross: Stroudsburg, PA. pp. 161–196.

Johnson, W.H. 1986. Stratigraphy and correlation of the glacial deposits of the Lake Michigan Lobe prior to 14 ka BP. In: V. Sibrava, D.Q. Bowen and G.M. Richmond (eds.), Quaternary Glaciations in the Northern Hemisphere. Quaternary Science Reviews 5:17–22.

Johnson, W.H., Hansel, A.K, Bettis III, E.A., Karrow, P.F., Larson, G.J., Lowell, T.V. and A.F. Schneider. 1997. Late Quaternary temporal and event classifications, Great Lakes Region, North America. Quaternary Research 47:1–12.

Kaiser, K.F. 1994. Two Creeks interstadial dated through dendrochronology and AMS. Quaternary Research 42:288–298.

Karrow, P.F. 1967. Pleistocene geology of the Scarborough area. Ontario Department of Mines Geological Report 46. 108 pp.

Karrow, P.F. 1974. Till stratigraphy in parts of southwestern Ontario. Geological Society of America Bulletin 85:761–768.

Karrow, P.F., Dreimanis, A. and P.J. Barnett. 2000. A proposed diachronic revision of Late Quaternary time-stratigraphic classification in the eastern and northern Great Lakes area. Quaternary Research 54:1–12.

Karrow, P.F., Hebda, R.J., Presant, E.W. and G.J. Ross. 1982. Late Quaternary inter-till paleosol and biota at Guelph, Ontario. Canadian Journal of Earth Sciences 19:1857–1872.

Karrow, P.F., Seymoure, K.L., Miller, B.B. and J.E. Mirecki. 1997. Pre-Late Wisconsinan Pleistocene biota from southeastern Michigan, U.S.A. Palaeogeography, Palaeoclimatology, Palaeoecology 133:81–101.

King, F.B. 1979. Plant macrofossils from the Athens North Quarry. In: Wisconsinan, Sangamonian and Illinois stratigraphy in central Illinois: Illinois State Geological Survey Guidebook 13:114–115.

Larson, G.J., Lowell, T.V. and N.E. Ostrom. 1994. Evidence for the Two Creeks interstade in the Lake Huron basin. Canadian of Journal Earth Sciences 31:793–797.

Leighton, M.M. 1926. A notable type Pleistocene section; The Farm Creek exposure mear Peoria, Illinois. Journal of Geology 34:167–174.

Leighton, M.M. 1931. The Peorian Loess and classification of the glacial drift sheets of the Mississippi Valley. Journal of Geology 39:45–53.

Leavitt, S.T. and R.M. Kalin. 1992. A new tree-ring width, $\delta^{13}C$, ^{14}C inestigation of the Two Creeks Site. Radiocarbon 34:792–797.

Leverett, F. 1898. The weathered zone (Sangamon) between the Iowan loess and the Illinoian till sheet. Jounal of Geology 6:171–181.

Leverett, F. 1899. The Illinois glacier lobe: U.S. Geological Survey Monograph 38. 817 pp.

Lowell, T.V., Savage, K.M., Brockman, C.S. and R. Struckenrath. 1990. Radiocarbon analyses from Cincinnati, Ohio, and their implications for glacial stratigraphic interpretations. Quaternary Research 34:1–11.

Lowell, T.V., Larson, G.J., Hughes, J.D. and G.H. Denton. 1999. Age verification of the Lake Gribben forest bed and the Younger Dryas advance of the Laurentide ice sheet. Canadian Journal of Earth Sciences 36:383–393.

McKay, E.D., Berg, R.C., Hansel, A.K., Kemmis, T.J. and A.J. Stumpf. 2005. Quaternary deposits and history of the ancient Mississippi River Valley, north-central Illinois. Illinois Open File Series 2005–7. 77 pp.

Mickelson, D.M. and B.J. Socha, , in press. Quaternary geology of Manitowoc and Calumet Counties. Wisconsin Geological and Natural History Survey Bulletin.

Miller, N.G. 1979. Paleoecological comments on fossil mosses in a buried organic bed near Peoria, Tazewell County, Illinois. Illinois State Geological Survey Guidebook 13:116.

Poplawski, S. and P.F. Karrow. 1981. Ostracods and paleoenvironments of the late Quaternary Don and Scarborough formations, Toronto, Ontario. Canadian Journal of Earth Sciences 18:1497–1505.

Pregitzer, K. S., Reed, D.D., Bornhorst, T.J., Foster, D.R., Mroz, G.D., Mclachlan, J.S., Laks, P.E., Stokke, D.D., Martin, P.E. and S.E. Brown. 2000. A buried spruce forest provides evidence at the stand and landscape scale for the effects of environment on vegetation at the Pleistocene/Holocene boundary. Journal of Ecology 88:45–53.

Quigley, R.M. and A. Dreimanis. 1972. Weathered interstadial green clay at Port Talbot, Ontario. Canadian Journal of Earth Sciences 9:991–1000.

Rae, D.K., Moore, Jr. T.C., Lewis, C.F.M., Mayer, L.A., Dettman, D.L., Smith, A.J. and D.M. Dobson. 1994. Stratigraphy and paleolimnology of the lower Holocene sediments in northern Lake Huron and Georgian Bay. Canadian Journal of Earth Sciences 31:1586–1605.

Richard, P.J.H., Occhietti, S., Clet, M. and A.C. Larouche. 1999. Paléophytogéographie de la formation de Scarborough: nouvelles données et implications. Canadian Journal of Earth Sciences 36:1589–1602.

Ruddiman, W.F. and M.E. Raymo. 1988. Northern Hemisphere climate regimes during the past 3 Ma; possible tectonic connections, In: N.J. Shackleton, R.G. West, and D.Q. Bowen (eds.), The past three million years; evolution of climatic variability in the North Atlantic region: A discussion. Philosophical Transactions of the Royal Society of London, Series B 318:411–430.

Schaetzl, R.J. 2001. Late Pleistocene ice flow directions and the age of glacial landscapes in northern lower Michigan. Physical Geography 22:28–41.

Shackleton, N.J., Imbrie, J., and N.G. Pisias. 1988. The evolution of oceanic oxygen-isotope variability in the North Atlantic over the past three million years. In: Shackleton, N.J., R.G. West, and D.Q. Bowen (eds.), The past three million years; evolution of climatic variability in the North Atlantic region: A discussion. Philosophical Transactions of the Royal Society of London, Series B 318:679–699.

Shilts, W.W. 1984. Quaternary events, Hudson Bay lowland and southern district of Keewatin. In: Quaternary Stratigraphy of Canada—A Canadian Contribution to IGCP Project 24. Geological Survey of Canada Paper 84–10:117–126.

Terasmae, J. 1960. A palynological study of Pleistocene interglacial beds at Toronto, Ontario. Geological Survey of Canada Bulletin 56:24–40.

Teller, J.T. and R.P. Goldthwait. 1991. The Old Kentucky River, a major tributary to the Teays River. In: W.N. Melhorn and J.P. Kempton, Geology and Hydrogeology of the Teays-Mahomet Bedrock Valley System. Geological Society of America Special Paper 258:29–41.

Thwaites, F.T. and K. Bertrand. 1957. Pleistocene geology of the Door Peninsula, Wisconsin. Geological Society of America Bulletin 68:831–879.

Watt. A.K. 1954. Correlation of the Pleistocene geology as seen in the subway with that of the Toronto region, Canada. Geological Association of Canada Proceedings 6:69–81.

Williams, N.E. and A.V. Morgan. 1977. Fossil caddisflies (Insecta: Trichoptera) from the Don Formation, Toronto, Ontario, and their use in paleoecology. Canadian Journal of Zoology 55:519–527.

Willman, H.B. and J.C. Frye. 1970. Pleistocene stratigraphy of Illinois. Illinois State Geological Survey Bulletin 94.

Wilson, L.R. 1932. The Two Creeks forest bed, Manitowoc County, Wisconsin. Transactions of the Wisconsin Academy of Sciences, Arts and Letters 27:31–46.

Winters, H.A., Rieck, R.L. and R.O. Kapp. 1986. Significance and ages of mid-Wisconsinan organic deposits in southern Michigan. Physical Geography 7:292–305.

Wright, G.F. 1914. Age of the glacial deposits in the Don Valley, Toronto, Ontario. Geological Society of America Bulletin 25:205–214.

7

The Last 17,000 Years of Vegetation History

Christina M. Hupy and Catherine H. Yansa

■ Introduction

The return of plant life to Michigan after final recession of the glaciers encompasses a complex and fascinating sequence of events. Plant species migrated in from various places and at different times. Once established on the landscape, their distributions and abundances were in constant fluctuation in response to variations in climate and ecological processes. This chapter is the story of the in-migration and redistribution of plants during post-glacial times. Only by knowing the forces and factors that have affected plants in Michigan's past can we understand their current distribution (Chapter 21). Moreover, insights gained from investigations of past biodynamics can be used to predict future changes in the species composition and distribution of Michigan's ecosystems in response to global warming and other future environmental changes that may occur.

The current landscapes of Michigan hold the keys to unraveling the complex history of plant occupation in our state. Plant fossils preserved in the sediments of lakes and bogs record the details and sequences of vegetation shifts and climate changes in the state since the last glaciation. By retrieving these sediments and examining the fossils they contain, we can obtain a better understanding of the dynamics of current forest systems in Michigan. Specifically, the analysis of past vegetation (paleoecology) provides a long-term (prehistoric) perspective on the plant geography and forest ecology of Michigan.

■ Paleoecological proxies and research methods

The vegetation history of Michigan can be largely reconstructed through the study of plant fossils, such as seeds, leaves, stems, cones, and pollen grains, most of which are recovered from aquatic sediments. These fossils can be identified to taxa (species, genus or family levels) based on their morphology, i.e., shape and size. Once the fossils are identified, they are correlated to their modern living representatives, which have specific tolerance ranges for temperature, precipitation, and soil type—a concept known as the "modern analog" principle (Overpeck et al. 1985). Fossils of different plants found together, a fossil assemblage, are indicative of a particular vegetation assemblage that may have existed for a time interval in the past. Based on the modern analog principal, shifts in the dominance of different taxa from assemblage to assemblage indicate vegetation change through time, and can be used to infer past climate and landscape changes.

Fossils are preserved when plant remains (pollen, seeds, etc.) are washed or blown into lakes and bogs, accumulate at the bottoms of these basins, and become buried by sediments (Fig. 7.1). Persistent moisture in aquatic sediments, as well as acidic conditions, inhibit decay and allow for the preservation of these plant fossils. The

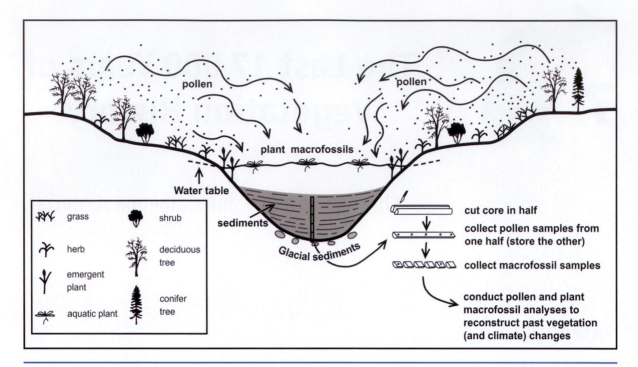

FIGURE 7.1   Schematic illustration (not to scale) of pollen and macrofossil deposition in and around a typical lake basin.

deposition and preservation of plant fossils may, however, be episodic in bogs and peatlands, because they often undergo periodic drying. Consequently, lakes and ponds are preferred as sites for paleoecological study (Bennett and Willis 2001).

Pollen production rates vary among plant species. Wind-pollinated plants, such as oaks (*Quercus*) and pines (*Pinus*), produce large quantities of pollen, which are mixed together by air currents and fall into aquatic environments as "pollen rain" (Davis 1967). Insect-pollinated plants, such as many species of maple (*Acer*), produce significantly less pollen and thus are under-represented in the pollen rain.

Sediments from the bottoms of lakes and bogs, which contain these plant fossils, are retrieved using a coring device (Figs. 7.1, 7.2). The coring device, operated from the water surface using either a raft or the ice as a platform, collects sediment cores from the bottom of the lake (or pond) basin. Sediment samples are collected at regularly spaced intervals from the cores, and later analyzed for pollen and plant macrofossils (Fig. 7.1). Fossil seeds and other plant macrofossils from certain stratigraphic levels can also be sampled, and their ages assessed using radiocarbon dating. The resulting radiocarbon ages can then be converted to calendar "dates" (Stuiver et al. 1998; Chapter 13).

Pollen samples from the cores are first prepared by removing any sediments (sand, silt, and clay) from the sample to concentrate the pollen, using a series of standard chemical treatments (Faegri and Iverson 1975). A sub-sample of each prepared pollen sample is then viewed under a microscope and individual pollen grains are identified and counted (Bennett and Willis 2001). The resulting pollen data are plotted as abundance in standard pollen diagrams. The pollen diagram shown in Figure 7.3 is based on data obtained from the North American Pollen Database (www.ncdc.noaa.gov/paleo/napd.html)—a repository for pollen data collected by different scientists from sites all over North America. Note that the X (horizontal) axis of these diagrams shows the percentage of total pollen for each taxa (pollen type) and the Y (vertical) axis displays the age of the sediments and their depth of the sediment core. Pollen diagrams are read from the bottom upwards with an eye toward dramatic shifts in the relative abundance of key pollen types or taxa. A shift in the relative abundance of a key pollen type may indicate a change in the surrounding forest, in response to a warming or cooling of

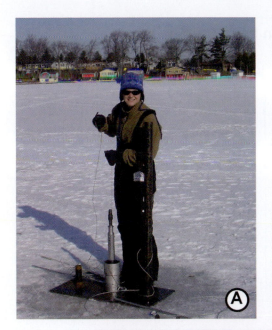

FIGURE 7.2   Photographs of lake sediment core extraction for fossil pollen and plant macrofossil analyses, using a Livingston coring device. Photos by R. Schaetzl. A. The piston driven component of the Livingston coring device is lowered below ice surface in order to retrieve sediment core. B. The sediment core is being extruded from Livingston coring device. C. A one-meter long extruded sediment core, on top of a plastic sled.

the regional climate, or some other environmental change, e.g., fire or precipitation regime. Pollen diagrams may be divided into pollen zones, which are considered to represent fossil assemblages, and hence plant communities, of the past. Shifts in the dominance of different taxa between pollen assemblages indicate large vegetation shifts, and, by inference, are proxies for paleoclimate change. Maps displaying isopolls, lines representing equal pollen percentages for individual taxa, are also useful in interpreting past vegetation shifts through time (Fig. 7.4).

FIGURE 7.3 Summary of pollen data from Wintergreen Lake, Kalamazoo County. The study was originally conducted by Manny et al. (1978). Pollen data were downloaded from NAPD (2005).

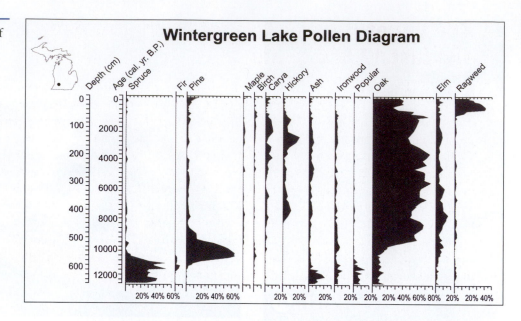

FIGURE 7.4 Maps of selected species isochrones, for multiple time periods in Michigan's past: 13,000, 11,000, 10,000, 7,000, 3,000, and 500 years ago. The isochrones represent lines of equal pollen percentage for each taxa in the pollen record at a variety of sites, for spruce (20%), pine (20%), hemlock (3%), birch (10%), elm (10%), ash (5%), maple (2%), beech (2%), and oak (20%). The percentages represent the amount of pollen for each species in a particular lake's record. After Webb et al. (1983).

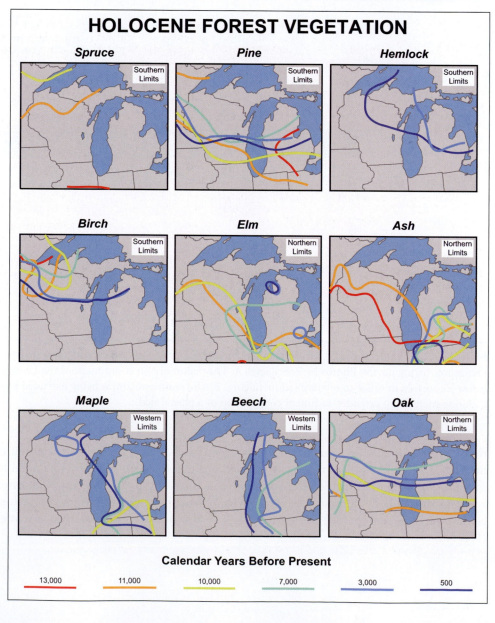

The vegetation history of Michigan over the last 17,000 years

In this chapter, we focus on the broad changes in the species composition and distribution of plant communities in Michigan over the past 17,000 years, primarily using data from studies of fossil pollen, augmented by analyses of seeds and other plant macrofossils. The last 17,000 years are referenced in calendar years before present. For a discussion of calendar vs radiocarbon years, see the Focus Box in Chapter 13.

Vegetation changes through time are discussed below in five different intervals of relative forest stability. This reconstruction focuses on the arrival, establishment, and range (distributional) shifts of important tree species and associated forest communities. We also examine the inferred paleoclimate changes that are largely responsible for these vegetation shifts. The paleovegetation changes are summarized in the isopoll maps and charts for important species (Fig. 7.4, and, as reconstructed plant communities, Fig. 7.5). Also, two pollen diagrams from Michigan, one from Wintergreen Lake, which is representative of the southern Lower Peninsula (Fig. 7.3; NAPD 2005) and the other, from Kitchner Lake, which is typical for the Upper Peninsula (Fig. 7.6; NAPD 2005), are provided to illustrate the major paleovegetation changes in the state.

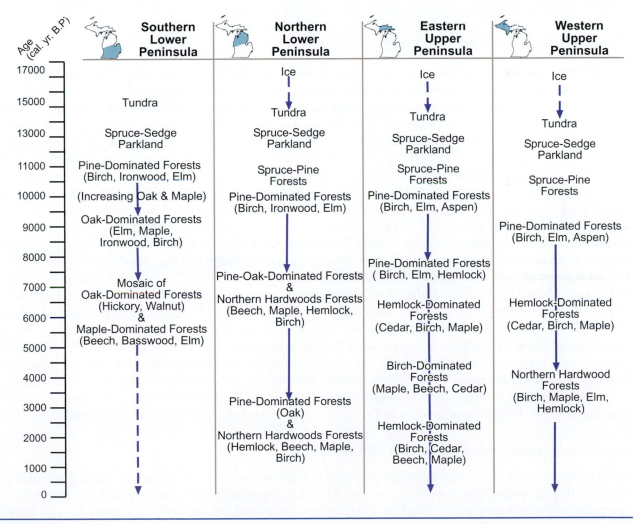

FIGURE 7.5   Summary of the major vegetation changes in Michigan (by sub-region) from 17,000 years ago to present. Solid arrows indicate the persistence of a forest type and dashed arrows indicate fluctuations between types.

FIGURE 7.6 Summary of pollen data from Kitchner Lake, Menominee County. The study was originally conducted by Woods and Davis (1989). Pollen data were downloaded from NAPD (2005).

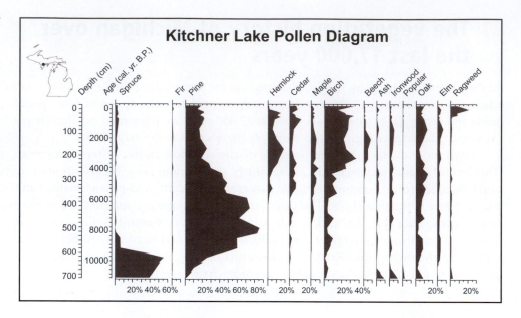

Plant colonization: 17,000 to 13,000 years ago

The first plant communities to colonize eastern North America after the recession of the glaciers were mainly comprised of species that exist today in cold, Arctic environments. These and all subsequent plants migrated northward from areas south of the maximum glacial limit after the ice sheet melted. The first of these plants arrived in the southern Lower Peninsula about 17,000 years ago. They did not shift northwards as biomes—where entire collections of tree species migrate together—but rather, they moved in an individualistic manner dependent upon species-specific rates of seed production, dispersal and the availability of suitable micro-sites (Davis 1981, Jackson et al. 2000). The plants colonized an unstable landscape that was undergoing periglacial (intermittently frozen) processes and which had variable amounts of inundation by glacial lakes and meltwater streams (Wright 1976; Chapters 6, 8, 13). Glacial readvances also affected the timing and pattern of plant colonization and succession. Because the landscapes of Michigan were unstable at this time and some lakes were not yet formed or remained filled with ice blocks, only a few of the plant fossil sites record this initial colonization of arctic plants. For example, this pioneering period of vegetation is not represented in the pollen record of Wintergreen Lake (Fig. 7.3).

Available plant fossil data indicate that this early, colonizing vegetation was "tundra-like," being comprised of mainly non-arboreal (herb) plants, including sedges (species of Cyperaceae), wormwood (*Artemisia*), and shrubs such as willow (*Salix*) (Kerfoot 1974). Leaves of arctic tundra plants, such as arctic dryad (*Dryas integrifolia*) and snowbed willow (*Salix herbacea*), were recovered along with willow stems that date to 13,950 years ago at the Cheboygan bryophyte bed site in the northern Lower Peninsula (Larson et al. 1994; Chapter 6). This tundra-like phase occurred earlier in areas to the south, e.g., from 20,600 and 18,900 years ago, in northeastern Illinois (Curry and Yansa 2004). Based on the temperature ranges of these arctic-adapted plant species, Baker et al. (1986) estimated that the average summertime temperature in the upper Midwest was about 10°C cooler during at this time than it is today. Soon thereafter, however, the climate began to warm and spruce vegetation invaded, replacing the arctic-adapted plants.

Spruce-sedge parkland: 13,000 to 11,000 years ago

Pollen and plant macrofossil records throughout central and eastern North America all report spruce-dominated vegetation during this period—the transition from the Late Pleistocene to early Holocene. Originally, this vegetation was interpreted as that of a spruce-dominated, or boreal *forest* (Delcourt and Delcourt 1991). But more recently, this vegetation has been considered to have a more open character, resembling more of a spruce-sedge parkland (Yansa 2006). Ample habitat for sedges and other marsh plants was provided by the high water tables—a result of melting ice blocks and permafrost (Webb et al. 2004). The dominant tree species of this community was white spruce (*Picea glauca*);

however, black spruce (*P. mariana*) occupied swampy locales (Pregitzer et al. 2000, Webb et al. 2004). Subdominant (secondary) trees included black ash (*Fraxinus nigra*), poplar or aspen (*Populus* spp.) and balsam fir (*Abies balsamea*) (Kapp 1999).

There are numerous reports of now-extinct Pleistocene megafauna associated with the spruce fossils of the Upper Midwest. In Michigan, finds of mastodon (*Mammut americanum*) and less commonly mammoth (*Mammuthus jeffersoni*) skeletons are associated with the spruce phase (Oltz and Kapp 1963, Kapp 1986; see Focus Box below; Chapter 8).

The onset of the spruce phase in Michigan occurred earliest in the southern part of this state and later towards the north. This pattern is expected, because the glaciers retreated in a northwards direction, resulting in a temperature gradient (cooling) from south to north. In the southwestern Lower Peninsula, the spruce phase persisted from about 15,300 to 11,400 years ago in the vicinity of Wintergreen Lake (Fig. 7.3). During the latter part of the spruce phase in this area, deciduous trees, such as poplar, black ash, and ironwood (*Ostrya virginiana*) or bluebeech (*Carpinus caroliniana*), appeared in greater numbers (Kapp 1999).

Meanwhile, to the north, local climatic conditions were affected by cold, dense winds blowing off of the ice sheet (Barnosky et al. 1987, Krist and Schaetzl 2001), accounting for the presence of tundra and boreal species in the pioneering vegetation of northern Michigan (Lawrenz 1975, Pregitzer et al. 2000). Over time, due to the warming climate, the cold-tolerant tundra plants decreased in abundance and eventually died off, while boreal ones remained.

FOCUS BOX: Mastodon habitat in the Lower Peninsula

Numerous pollen and plant macrofossil studies conducted by the late Ronald Kapp and his students of Alma College have documented that a spruce-sedge parkland occupied Lower Michigan during the Late Pleistocene (17,000–10,000 years ago). These studies identified an open environment with some trees, mainly white spruce (*Picea glauca*) and ash (*Fraxinus*), and abundant herbs, such as wormwood (*Artemisia*), grasses (*Poaceae*), and sedges (*Cyperaceae*). Several of these studies involved the analysis of plant fossils in direct association with mastodon (*Mammut americanum*) skeletons, e.g., Oltz and Kapp (1963), Held and Kapp (1969), Kapp (1986), Bears and Kapp (1987), and Kapp et al. (1990) (Chapter 8).

For example, at the Heisler Mastodon site in Calhoun County, wood in contact with mastodon bones dates to 13,080 years ago (Bears and Kapp 1987). A few of the mastodon skeletons show signs of butchery and post-date the local arrival of Paleoindians (Fisher 1984). The Eldridge Mastodon specimen, for example, has deep cut marks, which indicate the presence of Paleoindians in Montcalm County sometime between 14,120 and 12,000 years ago, based on radiocarbon dates on wood that bracket the skeleton (Kapp et al. 1990). The mastodon habitat reconstructed from these pollen and plant macrofossil studies is depicted in the figure. Refer to the legend of Figure 7.1 to interpret the plant icons.

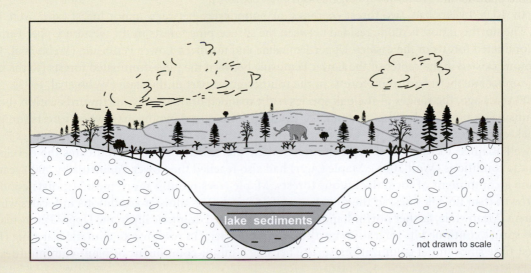

The boreal spruce phase in the Kitchner Lake area of the Upper Peninsula (Delta County) occurred from 13,000 to 10,300 years ago (Fig. 7.6). Birch (*Betula*) and pine (*Pinus*) were present in low abundances in certain areas of the Upper Peninsula during this time, but they became more common after the boreal (spruce) phase (Pregitzer et al. 2000).

The climate changed, warming quickly, during the spruce phase, driven mainly by shifting orbital cycles (variations in the orbit of the earth around the sun) that affected the amount of solar radiation (insolation) received at the earth's surface (COHMAP 1988). Astronomical calculations and models suggest that, from 12,000 to 9000 years ago, 7% more insolation was received during summers and 7% less during winters, compared to today (COHMAP 1988, Kutzbach et al. 1998). Climate model data also suggest that by about 11,000 years ago, summer temperatures were comparable to or slightly warmer (ca. +1° C) than modern (pre-industrial levels, ca. A.D. 1800), whereas winters were still several degrees cooler (Kutzbach et al. 1998). In response to this warming, several species of pine and birch as well as other deciduous trees became more common, and closed-canopy forests developed (Kapp 1999).

Early Holocene species diversification: 11,000 to 6800 years ago

The early Holocene was marked by rapid northward plant migration in response to climate changes, resulting in increased species diversity in the forests of both the Upper and Lower Peninsulas. By this time, the ice front was positioned farther north, primarily in Ontario, and was retreating rapidly, and the waterlogged landscapes of Michigan were starting to dry out. Summers were now slightly warmer (ca. +1°C) than they are today, but winters were still several degrees cooler (Webb et al. 2004).

As summers in Michigan became warmer, more temperate types of conifers and pines displaced spruce northwards. Pine first appeared in the southwestern Lower Peninsula during the spruce phase at 13,000 years ago (Fig. 7.3), and by 11,000 years ago several species of pine dominated many of the forests of the southern Lower Peninsula (Manny et al. 1978, Kapp 1999). Jack and/or red (*Pinus banksiana/resinosa*) pine arrived first, followed by white pine (*Pinus strobus*). During this period of pine expansion, several deciduous taxa also increased in abundance, including birch (most likely *Betula papyrifera*), ironwood (*Ostrya* or *Carpinus*), and elm (*Ulmus*), in response to the warming summers. These trees became significant components of these pine-dominated forests. The resulting community, a mixed conifer-northern hardwood forest, dominated primarily by pine, occupied most of the southern Lower Peninsula. Other deciduous trees, such as oak, walnut (*Juglans*), hickory (*Carya*), and basswood (*Tilia*), also expanded their ranges into the Lower Peninsula after 11,000 years ago, but were probably limited to favorable micro-habitats (Kapp 1999).

Meanwhile, in the northern Lower Peninsula and most of the Upper Peninsula, spruce persisted as the dominant tree until about 10,000 years ago. At this time, the spruce-pine forests in the central Upper Peninsula transitioned to pine-dominated forests that included (as sub-dominants) birch, aspen, hornbeam, juniper/cedar (probably *Thuja occidentalis*), and elm (Fig. 7.6). The spruce-pine forests in the western Upper Peninsula persisted for several more centuries, until about 10,500 years ago (Booth et al. 2002).

Thus, by 10,000 years ago, two forest ecotones, or boundaries, between major forest types were present in Michigan. The northernmost ecotone resided between the spruce-pine forests in the western Upper Peninsula and the pine-dominated forests in the eastern Upper Peninsula and northern Lower Peninsula (Webb et al. 1983). The second ecotone existed in the center of the Lower Peninsula between the pine-dominated forests (to the north) and the mixed conifer-northern hardwood forests in the southernmost part of the state (Webb et al. 1983).

By 9000 years ago, the ranges of the oak species had expanded dramatically northwards within the southern Lower Peninsula, as pines declined in abundance. The shift from mixed conifer-hardwood forests (dominated by pine) to oak-dominated forests in the southern Lower Peninsula at this time is evident in Figures 7.3 and 7.5. Oaks are well adapted to warm and dry conditions; their increased abundance indicates the development of these climatic conditions (Wolf 2004). Maple (*Acer*) had also reached the Lower Peninsula by 9000 years ago and had become a component of local deciduous forests. Maple trees require more mesic (moist) conditions for optimal growth than do oak trees, so the presence of maple indicates moister conditions in locales where maple was dominant. Meanwhile, farther north, stands of spruce decreased dramatically in the Upper Peninsula (replaced by pine) as spruce continued its migration northward into Ontario, in response to climatic warming (Liu 1990). For the first time since initial colonization, spruce became a minor component of plant communities throughout Michigan (spruce pollen abundances are <20% after 9000 years ago; Figs. 7.3, 7.6). Michigan had become a warm environment.

The trend of plant species diversification in local floras, evident in the isopolls from 11,000 to 10,000 years ago (Fig. 7.4), slowed considerably after 9000 years ago. After 9000 years ago, two more species of note, hemlock (*Tsuga canadensis*) and beech (*Fagus grandifolia*) migrated into the state. Their late arrival has been mainly attributed lags in the development of a suitable microclimate for hemlock, and the slow dispersal rate of beech seeds (Davis et al. 1986).

Hemlock, a characteristic species of northern mesic forests, prefers moist, acidic soils, and is relatively shade tolerant. It reached Michigan relatively late, compared to most other northern species such as spruce and pine, entering Michigan from its eastern refugia and arriving in the northern part of the state about 7800 years ago (Davis et al. 1986; Fig. 7.6). It then spread slowly across the northeastern Upper Peninsula and did not become a significant component of the forests there and in the northern Lower Peninsula for at least a thousand years (Davis et al. 1986).

Beech initially reached the Lower Peninsula about 7800 years ago from its refugia in the south, and continued to migrate slowly northward (Figs. 7.3, 7.4; Woods and Davis 1989). Beech, along with other mesic species such as basswood, elm, and ironwood, became a subdominant in the newly formed, maple-dominated forests. These forests most likely occupied moist, fertile sites in the Lower Peninsula (Kapp 1999). Small pockets of swamp hardwood forests, comprised of species of ash, basswood, maple, and elm, existed in the wettest areas (Bailey and Ahearn 1981).

At this time, the oak- and maple-dominated forests co-existed as a mosaic that covered most of the southern Lower Peninsula. Hickory (*Carya* spp.) and walnut (*Juglans nigra*) were components of the oak-dominated forests present on the dry (xeric) sandy sites (Kapp 1999). The prevalence of oak, hickory, and walnut correlates with the climate at the time—with its slightly warmer summers than today (because summertime insolation was still higher than at present), and greater aridity beginning at 8800 years ago, which lasted into the mid-Holocene (Webb et al. 1983, Bartlein et al. 1998, Kutzbach et al. 1998, Booth et al. 2002, Calcote 2003).

Mid-Holocene climate and vegetation shifts: 6800 to 3200 years ago

The mid-Holocene is marked by continued variations in climate and corresponding shifts in the distribution and dominance of several tree species. Pollen records from eastern North America document peak warmth and aridity beginning around 6800 years ago; this period is referred to as the Hypsithermal, Altithermal, or mid-Holocene warming (Kutzbach et al. 1998). In some other areas of North America, this warming occurred earlier (Barnosky et al. 1987, Webb et al. 1993, Yansa 2006). By about 6000 years ago, summertime insolation was about 5% greater than it is today; causing temperatures from June to August to be 0.5 to 2°C warmer than at present (Kutzbach et al. 1998). This period of Michigan's past was not only warm, but also dry. Compared to modern levels, precipitation was approximately 20% less at ca. 6000 years ago, and for a few millennia thereafter (Bartlein et al. 1984, Webb et al. 1993).

In the Upper Peninsula, the mid-Holocene warm/dry interval began at 8800 years ago and lasted until around 6600 years ago (Fig. 7.5). This interval is marked by increase in the abundance of pine species, which are well adapted to this type of climate (Kapp 1999; Booth et al 2002). Thereafter, the climate in the Upper Peninsula shifted. Beginning at about 6600 years ago, there was a slight increase in precipitation and winter temperatures, coupled with a slight decrease in summer temperatures (Booth et al. 2002, Calcote 2003). This slightly cooler/moister trend accounts for the decline of pine populations and the corresponding abundance increase in hemlock (Fig. 7.6). By 6000 years ago, hemlock had spread from the eastern Upper Peninsula in both a westward direction across the Upper Peninsula and in a southwesterly direction into the Lower Peninsula (Davis et al. 1986, Calcote 2003). Other mesic taxa, such as cedar, birch, and maple, likewise expanded their ranges in the Upper Peninsula at this time (Booth et al 2002, Calcote 2003).

As the climate was becoming slightly cooler and moister in the Upper Peninsula by about 6000 years ago, the southern Lower Peninsula, along with much of the southern Great Lakes region, were experiencing peak aridity and warmth. Patches of prairie and oak savanna, driven by fire, were developing on the driest sites in the southwestern Lower Peninsula (Ahearn and Kapp 1990, Kapp 1999). Mixed oak forests (with hickory) dominated much of the rest of the Lower Peninsula. Correspondingly, there were slight decreases in the pollen abundances of the mesic deciduous trees (beech, maple, basswood, and elm), due to the warmth and aridity (Fig. 7.3). The mesic beech-maple forests were most likely limited to moist, loamy soils on areas of ground moraine (Kapp 1999). Hardwood swamp forests comprised of elm and ash were probably restricted to wet low-lying sites near lakes, such as the area around Saginaw Bay, and near rivers (Kapp 1999).

The forest tension zone, an ecotone between the deciduous forests (mixed-oak forests and beech-maple forests) of the southern Lower Peninsula and the mixed coniferous-deciduous forests (dominated by pine) of the northern Lower Peninsula, which had formed during the early Holocene, shifted northward during this mid-Holocene interval. The northward shift of the forest tension zone (Curtis 1959; Chapter 21) within the central part of the Lower Peninsula is assumed to have been a vegetative response to the warmer/drier climatic regime (Fig. 7.4). This ecotone reached its furthest northern extent during the entire Holocene, about 6000 years ago (Webb et al. 1983).

Several other vegetation changes are evident during the mid-Holocene. These include a dramatic decrease in hemlock pollen abundances at several sites in the Upper Peninsula and elsewhere in the Great Lakes Region between 5500 and 4000 years ago—attributed primarily to an insect/pathogen outbreak (Davis et al. 1986, Calcote 2003). The range of yellow birch (*Betula alleghaniensis*), a species with similar habitat characteristics as hemlock, expanded significantly, as did its abundance in the Upper Peninsula after 5000 years ago, during the population decline of hemlock (Jackson and Booth 2002). Beech trees reached the Upper Peninsula by 4400 years ago but became only a minor component of local forests (Fig. 7.6). By about 4000 years ago, insolation (sunlight and heat) values throughout the year attained modern levels and thereafter other mechanisms exclusively determined climatic and vegetation patterns (COHMAP 1988).

Late Holocene vegetation dynamics: 3200 years ago to 150 years ago

Climatic reconstructions for much of eastern North America, including the Lower Peninsula, indicate a marked increase in precipitation and an associated temperature decrease starting at about 3200 years ago (Webb et al. 2004). Interestingly, this cool/moist trend began earlier in the Upper Peninsula. Embedded within this overall cool/moist pattern were alternating wet and dry intervals and temperature variations, which caused shifts in the range distributions of various plant communities in Michigan during the late Holocene (Jackson and Booth 2002, Webb et al. 2004).

Of these climatic perturbations, the most significant is the transition from the mid-Holocene warmth and aridity to a cooler and moister regional climate at about 3200 years ago, and persistence of this climate until ~1000 years ago (Bernabo 1981, Jackson and Booth 2002). During this time, extensive bogs, marshes and peatlands formed in much of the central and eastern Upper Peninsula in response to the increased moisture (Kapp 1999) and the rebound of the land mass, which caused many northwardly-draining rivers to flow more sluggishly. Correspondingly, there were expansions in the ranges of several key, mesic species, e.g., beech, birch, and hemlock, within the Upper Peninsula from 3200 to 1000 years ago (Davis et al. 1986, Woods and Davis 1989, Jackson and Booth 2002).

Species diversity also increased in the forests of the Upper Peninsula during the late Holocene. Newly formed hemlock-dominated forests, containing birch, maple, ash, and beech as subdominants, occupied moist, fertile soils throughout the eastern Upper Peninsula (Calcote 2003). Pine forests and mixed pine forests (containing some hardwoods) inhabited the drier, sandier sites (Kapp 1999). In the western Upper Peninsula at this time, northern hardwood forests, comprised of birch, maple, and elm, were more common than pine forests. This trend is evident in the pollen diagram for Kitchner Lake (Fig. 7.6), while at 3200 years ago the pollen abundance of birch is much greater than that of pine, which had reached its lowest level since initial colonization.

Meanwhile, in the Lower Peninsula, the beech-maple forests expanded from their limited locations after 3200 years ago as a result of increased moisture. Correspondingly, the oak-dominated forests, and the prairie/oak savannas in southwestern Lower Michigan, contracted in areal extent (Kapp 1999). In the central Lower Peninsula, the cooling climate encouraged the range expansion of white pine and the mixed pine-hardwood forests.

In response to the cool and wet climate, the tension zone in the Lower Peninsula had shifted south by 3000 years ago. South of the tension zone, expansion of the beech-maple forests is clearly evident in the pollen record (Fig. 7.3), where beech pollen percentages increase dramatically just after 3200 and oak pollen percentages decline slightly. Throughout much of the southern Lower Peninsula, oak forests became less common at this time, but they remained a significant forest type in the mosaic dominated by beech-maple forests and, to a lesser extent, by swamp hardwood forests (Kapp 1999; Chapter 21).

Relatively little is known about climate and associated vegetation changes in the Upper Peninsula after 3200 years ago. Available pollen data from the eastern Upper Peninsula indicate the continued expansion of the cool mesic northern hardwood forests (dominated by birch, cedar, hemlock, and beech), after 3000 years ago (Delcourt et al. 2002).

More detailed pollen data are available for the Lower Peninsula (Bernabo 1981, Hupy 2006). Studies have detected vegetation changes in association with two climatic episodes in the late Holocene—the Medieval Warm Period (MWP), from 1000 to 800 years ago, and the Little Ice Age (LIA), from 600 to 150 years ago. Both of these climatic intervals have been recognized throughout much of northern North America, northwestern Europe and at other locales in the middle and high latitudes (Bradley 1999). Compared to today's climate, the average summertime temperature was probably 0.5 to 0.8°C warmer during the MWP and about 1°C cooler during the LIA (Bradley 1999). Bernabo's (1981) study of four lakes situated along a 75-km transect in the northern Lower Peninsula (from Charlevoix to Crawford County) detected increases in the pollen abundances of pine and oak, associated with the MWP temperature increases beginning around about 1000 years ago. Pollen data collected from three lakes spanning the forest tension zone in the central Lower Peninsula also detected vegetation responses to climatic variations over the past 2000 years (Hupy 2006). Three major ecotonal shifts were detected, including the range expansion of oak forests northward during the MWP as well as the expansions of both the beech-maple forests and the mixed pine forests during the LIA (see FOCUS BOX below).

Vegetation disturbance caused directly by Native American land use has not yet been identified in the pollen records of Michigan, but undoubtedly occurred, given the archaeological record (Chapter 25). In contrast, pollen records throughout eastern North America and the Midwest indicate dramatic changes in the forest communities associated with Euro-American logging, fire and agriculture (Kapp 1999). The activities of Euro-American settlers are evident in many pollen records for Michigan. For example, the pollen records of both Wintergreen (Fig. 7.3) and Kitchner Lakes (Fig. 7.6) clearly indicate the historic period by the dramatic decline in forest species and concurrent increase in the pollen of ragweed (*Ambrosia*-type) and Eurasian crop weeds. Pollen records also document the mid- and late-20th century reforestation of Michigan and confirm that the species composition and age structure of these young forests differed significantly from the pre-settlement forests (Scull and Harman 2004, Hupy and WinklerPrins 2005) Discussions of the pre-settlement forests and subsequent changes associated with Euro-American land use are provided in Chapters 21 and 40.

FOCUS BOX: Ecotone dynamics: The last 2,000 years of vegetation change

Fossil pollen data collected from Cowden Lake, Montcalm County, located within the floristic tension zone of the central Lower Peninsula, have documented significant shifts in the dominance of different tree species over the last 2000 years (Hupy 2006). In sum, these data demonstrated that the tension zone—a major vegetation boundary in the state—is dynamic in nature and responds to small-scale oscillations in climate over short time periods. Three separate ecotone shifts, and four different pollen assemblages, were identified, for this time period.

From 2100 to 1650 years ago, oak-dominated forests were prevalent near Cowden Lake, indicating a relatively mild (warm) and dry climate. At about 1700 years ago,

the climate became cooler and moister, which caused a substantial decline in populations of oak species and the expansion of beech-maple forests. Oak-dominated forests expanded once again after 1300 years ago, in response to the warmer temperatures associated with the MWP. Forests surrounding Cowden Lake also responded to the LIA, when regional temperatures fell by about 1° C (Bernabo 1981). After about 800 years ago, during the LIA, oak abundance in the local vegetation declined and pine became more common. Beech-Maple forests also expanded at this time, not only in the Cowden Lake area but also at other locales in Michigan (Bernabo 1981, Davis et al 1986).

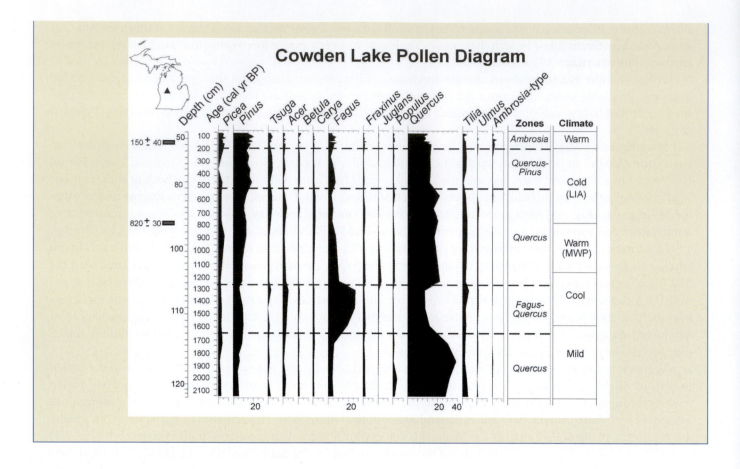

■ Conclusions

Fossil pollen records indicate that the composition and distribution of Michigan's vegetation have been in slow and constant flux since the last glacial recession. Species migrated northward from refugia to the south and east of the ice sheet, as changing climatic and substrate (soils) conditions allowed. The first arrivals were pioneering arctic tundra-adapted plants that quickly colonized the barren landscape, south to north, between 17,000 and 13,000 years ago. This vegetation was succeeded by a spruce parkland that lasted until about 11,000 years ago. Pine and the majority of deciduous trees arrived in Michigan thereafter. At this point, competition between different species in response to climate changes began in earnest, which resulted in the expansion and contraction of the distribution of different species, each according to their climatic tolerances.

Climatic changes during the Holocene varied across the state, which helps explain why the species composition of forests in the Upper Peninsula differed from those of the Lower Peninsula. Pine forests were dominant in most of the Upper Peninsula for much of the early and mid-Holocene, in response to the prevailing warm/dry climate and the sandy soils that prevail there. Starting at about 6600 years ago, the climate of the Upper Peninsula became cool and moist, which caused greater abundance and range expansion of several mesic taxa. Northern hardwoods forests, dominated by mesic birch, maple, hemlock, and beech trees, occupied the moist fertile sites (only in the eastern half of the Upper Peninsula), while pine-dominated forests were present on the drier sites. In contrast, the mid-Holocene warm/dry interval occurred later, from 6000 to 3200 years ago, in much of the Lower Peninsula, during which oak forests were more dominant. With the onset of a cool and moist climate after 3200 years ago in the Lower Peninsula, oak forests declined in areal extent as the more mesic beech-maple forests expanded. Meanwhile in the Upper Peninsula, the mesic taxa, especially hemlock, continued to increase in abundance.

Detailed vegetation-climate reconstructions based on fossil pollen analyses demonstrate that plants respond to climate changes of varying degrees. Forests respond to long-term (millennial-scale) climate changes associated with variations in insolation. At the same time these plant communities also react to smaller-scale shifts in temperature and precipitation, such as during the Medieval Warm Period and Little Ice Age. Indeed, the vegetation encountered by the first Euro-Americans in Michigan was a not the long-term norm, but may have represented a relatively new arrangement of species and forest communities, the geographic ranges of which had only been stable for the past few hundred years.

Literature Cited

Ahearn, P., and R.O. Kapp. 1990. Pollen analysis and vegetational history associated with archaeological sites in Berrien County, Michigan. In: E.B. Garland (ed.), Late Archaic and Early Woodland Adaptation in the Lower St. Joseph River Valley, Berrien County, Michigan. Michigan Cultural Resource Investigation Series, Volume 2. State of Michigan, Department of Transportation, Kalamazoo. pp. 113–123.

Bailey, R.B. and P.J. Ahearn. 1981. A late and postglacial pollen record from Chippewa Bog, Lapeer Co. Michigan: further examination of white pine and beech immigration into the central Great Lakes Region. In: R.C. Romans (ed.), Geobotany II. Plenum Publishing Company., New York. pp. 53–74.

Baker, R.G., Rhodes, R.S. II, Schwert, D.S., Ashworth, A.C., Frest, T.J., Hallberg, G.R., and J.A. Janssens. 1986. A full-glacial biota from southeastern Iowa, USA. Journal of Quaternary Science 1:91–107.

Barnosky, C.W., Grimm, E.C. and H.E. Wright Jr. 1987. Towards a postglacial history of the northern Great Plains: A review of the paleoecologic problems. Annals of the Carnegie Museum 56:259–273.

Bartlein, P.J., Webb, I.T. and E. Fleri. 1984. Holocene climatic change in the northern Midwest: pollen-derived estimates. Quaternary Research 22:361–374.

Bartlein, P.J., Anderson, K.H., Anderson, P.M., Edwards, M.E., Mock, C.J., Thompson, R.S., Webb, R.S., Webb, T., III and C. Whitlock. 1998. Paleoclimate simulations for North America over the past 21,000 years: Features of the simulated climate and comparisons with paleoenvironmental data. Quaternary Science Reviews 17:549–585.

Bears, R.E. and R.O. Kapp. 1987. Vegetation associated with the Heisler Mastodon Site, Calhoun County, Michigan. Michigan Academician 19:133–140.

Bennett, K.D. and K.J. Willis. 2001. Pollen. In: Smol, J.P., Birks, H.J.B. and W.M. Last (eds), Tracking environmental change with lake sediments. Kluwer Academic Press., Dordrecht: The Netherlands. pp. 5–32.

Bernabo, J.C. 1981. Quantitative estimates of temperature changes over the last 2700 years in Michigan, based on pollen data. Quaternary Research 15:143–159.

Bradley, R.S. 1999. Paleoclimatology: Reconstructing Climates of the Quaternary. Harcourt Academic Press. San Diego, CA.

Calcote, R. 2003. Mid-Holocene climate and the hemlock decline: the range limit of *Tsuga canadensis* in the western Great Lakes region, USA. The Holocene 13:215–224.

COHMAP. 1988. Climatic Changes of the Last 18,000 Years: Observations and Model Simulations. Science 241:1043–1052.

Curry, B.B. and C.H. Yansa. 2004 Stagnation of the Harvard sublobe (Lake Michigan lobe) in northeastern Illinois, USA, from 24,000 to 17,600 BP and subsequent tundra-like ice-marginal paleoenvironments from 17,600 to 15,700 BP. Géographie Physique et Quaternaire 58:305–321.

Curtis, J.T. 1959. The Vegetation of Wisconsin. University of Wisconsin Press: Madison.

Davis, M.G. 1967. Pollen deposition in lakes as measured by sediment traps. Geological Society of America Bulletin 78:849–858.

Davis, M.B. 1981. Quaternary history and the stability of deciduous forests. In: West, D.C., Shugart, H.H. and D. B. Botkin (eds), Forest succession: concepts and applications. Springer-Verlag: New York. pp. 132–153.

Davis, M.B., Woods, K.D., Webb, S.L. and R.P. Futyma. 1986. Dispersal versus climate: expansion of Fagus and Tsuga into the Upper Great Lakes region. Vegetatio 67:93–103.

Delcourt, H.R. and P.A. Delcourt. 1991. Quaternary ecology: a paleoecological perspective. Chapman and Hall, New York, NY.

Delocourt, P.A., Nester, P.L., Delcourt, H.R., Mora, C. I. and K. Orvis. 2002. Holocene lake-effect precipitation in northern Michigan. Quaternary Research 57:225–233.

Faegri, K. and J. Iverson. 1975. Textbook of Pollen Analysis. Munksgaard: Copenhagen, Denmark.

Fisher, D.C. 1984. Mastodon butchery by North American Paleo-Indians. Nature 308:271–272.

Held, E.R. and R.O. Kapp. 1969. Pollen analysis at the Thaller Mastodon site, Gratiot County, Michigan. Michigan Botanist 8:3–10.

Hupy, C.M. 2006. The dynamics of the forest transition zone in central Lower Michigan, U.S.A.: Two millennia of change. Ph.D. Diss. Michigan State Univ., East Lansing.

Hupy, C.M. and A.M.G.A. WinklerPrins. 2005. A political ecology of forest exploitation in the Lower Peninsula of Michigan: 1800–1950. The Great Lakes Geographer 12:26–42.

Jackson, S.T., Overpeck, J.T., Webb, I.T., Williams, J.W., Hansen, B.C.S., Webb, R.S. and K.H. Anderson. 2000. Vegetation and environment in eastern North America during the Last Glacial Maximum. Quaternary Science Reviews 19:489–508.

Jackson, S.T. and R.K. Booth. 2002. The role of late Holocene climate variability in the expansion of yellow birch in the western Great Lakes region. Diversity and Distributions 8:275–284.

Kapp, R.O. 1986. Late-Glacial Pollen and Macrofossils Associated with the Rappuhn Mastodont Lapeer County Michigan USA. American Midlands Naturalist 116:368–377.

Kapp, R.O., Cleary, D.L., Snyder, G.G. and D.C. Fisher. 1990. Vegetational and climatic history of the Crystal Lake area and the Eldridge Mastodont site, Montcalm County, Michigan. American Midlands Naturalist 123:47–63.

Kapp, R.O. 1999. Michigan Late Pleistocene, Holocene and Presettlement Vegetation and Climate. In: J.R. Halsley and M.D. Stafford (eds), Retrieving Michigan's Buried Past: The Archaeology of the Great Lakes State. Cranbrook Institute of Science., Bloomfield Hills: MI. pp. 30–58.

Kerfoot, W.C. 1974. Net accumulation rates and the history of cladoceran communities. Ecology 55: 51–61.

Krist, F. and R.J. Schaetzl. 2001. Paleowind (11,000 BP) directions derived from lake spits in northern Michigan. Geomorphology 38:1–18.

Kutzbach, J.E., Gallimore, R., Harrison, S.P., Behling, P., Selin, R. and F. Larrif. 1998. Climate and biome simulations for the past 21,000 years. Quaternary Science Reviews 17:473–506.

Larson, G.J., Lowell, T.V. and N.E. Ostrom. 1994. Evidence for the Two Creeks interstade in the Lake Huron Basin. Canadian Journal of Earth Sciences 31:793–797.

Lawrenz, R. 1975. Biostratigraphic study of Green Lake Michigan. Masters Thesis. Central Michigan University. Mt. Pleasant.

Liu K.-B. 1990. Holocene paleoecology of the boreal forest and Great Lakes-St. Lawrence forest in northern Ontario. Ecological Monographs 60:179–212.

Manny, B.A., Wetzel, R.G. and R.B. Bailey. 1978. Paleolimnological sedimentation of organic carbon, nitrogen, phosphorus, fossil pigments, pollen and diatoms in a hypereutrophic, hardwater lake: A case history of eutrophication. Polskie Archiwum Hydrobiologii 25:243–267.

North American Pollen Database (NAPD). 2005. http://www.ncdc.noaa.gov/paleo/napd.html. Accessed November 2005.

Oltz, D.F. and R.O. Kapp 1963. Plant remains associated with mastodon and mammoth remains in central Michigan. American Midlands Naturalist 70:339–346.

Overpeck, J.T., Webb, T., and I.C. Prentice. 1985. Quantitative interpretation of fossil pollen spectra—Dissimilarity coefficients and the method of modern analogs. Quaternary Research 23:87–108.

Pregitzer, K.S., Reed, D.D., Bornhorst, T.J., Foster, D.R., Mroz, G.D., McLachlan, J.S., Laks, P.E., Stokke, D.D., Martin, P.E. and S.E. Brown. 2000. A buried spruce forest provides evidence at the stand and landscape scale for the effects of environment on vegetation at the Pleistocene/Holocene boundary. Journal of Ecology 88:45–53.

Scull, P.R. and J.R. Harman. 2004. Forest distribution and site quality in southern Lower Michigan, USA. Journal of Biogeography 31:1503–1514.

Stuiver, M., Reimer, P.J., Bard, E., Beck, J.W., Burr, G.S., Hughen, K.A., Kromer, B., Mccormac, F.G., Van der Plicht, J. and M. Spurk. 1998. INTCAL98 Radiocarbon age calibration, 24,000–0 cal BP. Radiocarbon 40:1041–1083.

Webb, I.T., Cushing, E.J. and H.E. Wright. 1983. Holocene changes in the vegetation of the Midwest. In: H.E. Wright (ed), Late Quaternary Environments of the United States. University of Minnesota Press, Minneapolis. pp. 142–165.

Webb, I.T., Bartlein, P.J., Harrison, S.P. and K. H. Anderson. 1993. Vegetation, lake levels, and climate in Eastern North America for the past 18,000 years. In: Wright, H.E., Kutzbach, J.E., Webb, T., Ruddiman, W.F., Street-Perrott, F.A. and P.J. Bartlein (eds), Global Climates since the Last Glacial Maximum. University of Minnesota Press., Minneapolis. pp. 415–467.

Webb, I.T., Shuman, B. and J.W. Williams. 2004. Climatically forced vegetation dynamics in eastern North America during the Late Quaternary Period. In: Gillespie, A.R., Porter, S.C. and B.F. Atwater (eds), The Quaternary Period in the United States. Elsevier: Amsterdam, The Netherlands. pp. 459–478.

Wolf, J. 2004 A 200-year fire history in a remnant oak savanna in southeastern Wisconsin. American Midlands Naturalist 152:201–213.

Woods, K.D. and M.B. Davis. 1989. Paleoecology of range limits: beech in the Upper Peninsula of Michigan. Ecology 70:681–696.

Wright, H.E. Jr. 1976. The dynamic nature of Holocene vegetation: A problem in paleoclimatology, biogeography, and stratigraphic nomenclature. Quaternary Research 6:581–596.

Yansa, C.H. 2006. The timing and nature of Late Quaternary vegetation changes in the northern Great Plains, USA and Canada: a re-assessment of the spruce phase. Quaternary Science Reviews 25:263–281.

Further Readings

Alley, R.B., Mayewski, P.A., Sowers, T., Stuiver, M., Taylor, K.C. and P.U. Clark. 1997. Holocene climatic instability: A prominent, widespread event 8200 yr ago. Geology 25:483–486.

Baker, R.G., Maher, L.J., Chumbley, C.A. and K.L. Van Zant. 1992. Patterns of Holocene environmental change in the Midwestern United States. Quaternary Research 37:379–389.

Booth, R.K. and S.T. Jackson. 2003. A high-resolution record of late-Holocene moisture variability from a Michigan raised bog, USA. The Holocene 13:863–876.

Booth, R.K., Jackson, S.T. and T.A. Thompson. 2004. Paleoecology of a northern Michigan Lake and the relationships among climate, vegetation, and the Great Lakes water levels. Quaternary Research 57:120–130.

Bradley, R.S., Huges, M.K. and H.F. Diaz. 2003. Climate in Medieval time. Science 302:404–405.

Bradshaw, R.H.W. and I.T. Webb. 1985. Relationships between contemporary pollen and vegetation data from Wisconsin and Michigan, USA. Ecology 66:721–737.

Brubaker, L.B. 1975. Postglacial forest patterns associated with till and outwash in north central Upper Michigan. Quaternary Research 5:499–527.

Flakne, R. 2003. The Holocene vegetation history of Isle Royale National Park, Michigan, USA. Canadian Journal of Forest Research 33:1144–1166.

Gajewski, K. 1987. Climatic impacts on the vegetation in Eastern North America during the past 2,000 years. Vegetatio 68:179–190.

McMurray, M., Kloos, G., Kapp, R.O. and K. Sullivan. 1978. Paleoecology of Crystal Marsh, Montcalm County, based on macrofossil and pollen analysis. Michigan Academician 10:403–417.

Shuman, B., Bartlein, P.J., Logar, N., Newby, P. and T. Webb. 2002. Parallel vegetation and climate responses to the early-Holocene collapse of the Laurentide Ice Sheet. Quaternary Science Reviews 21:1793–1805.

Pleistocene Fauna

8

J. Alan Holman and Danita Brandt

■ Introduction

Michigan's fossil record extends back to the Archean Eon (Chapter 3), and is especially rich during the Paleozoic Era (Chapter 4). That record was interrupted by the "Lost Interval" of missing Mesozoic Era strata (Chapter 5), and as a consequence, there is little prospect of finding dinosaur fossils in Michigan. There are also no significant post-Paleozoic fossil deposits until about 50,000 years ago, during the Pleistocene Epoch of the Cenozoic Period (Plate 4). The reason for the lack of fossils from the Late Pennsylvanian Period to the Early Pleistocene was the absence, during that interval, of suitable environments for burial and preservation of sediments and entombed organic material. During the Pleistocene, however, numerous bogs that formed after the retreat of the glaciers provided suitable conditions for trapping and preserving fossil remains, including aquatic invertebrates and aquatic and terrestrial vertebrates. Thus, we begin there.

■ Invertebrate Pleistocene fauna

The Pleistocene invertebrate fossil record in Michigan comprises members of only two major taxonomic groups (phyla): molluscs and arthropods. The fossils all belong to extant genera, i.e., alive today, and represent fresh water and terrestrial niches. Among the molluscs, fossil gastropods (snails) include the genera *Physa*, *Helix* and *Planorbis* (Fig. 8.1A). Pelecypods (clams) are quite abundant in Michigan Pleistocene deposits, and include the freshwater genera *Anodonta* and *Piscidium* (Fig. 8.1B). Among the aquatic arthropods, microscopic ostracodes are most abundant as fossils (Fig. 8.1C), and among terrestrial arthropods, insects, especially beetles, dominate the arthropod fossil record. Bits and pieces of insects are more common as fossils than entire organisms, and the hardened front wings (elytra) are the most commonly found beetle fossils (Fig. 8.1D).

Although undoubtedly an important component of Michigan's Pleistocene ecosystems and food-webs, invertebrates are not as well known as are Michigan's Pleistocene vertebrates, which include members of five classes: Osteichthyes (bony fish), Amphibia, Reptilia, Aves (birds) and Mammalia. These are discussed below.

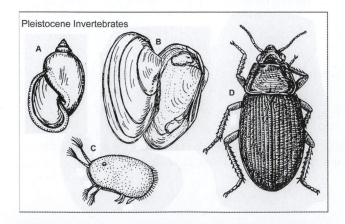

FIGURE 8.1 Some of Michigan's Pleistocene invertebrates. A. The gastropod *Physa*. B. The clam *Anodonta*. C. An Ostracod. D. A Pleistocene beetle.

Vertebrate Pleistocene fauna

Michigan's Pleistocene vertebrates are remarkably restricted in time and space. The most ancient ones consist of fishes and small mammals known from a single site that existed about 55,000 years ago. The next oldest vertebrates consist of a duck and a mammoth, each from separate sites and dated about 30,000 years ago. The remainder of the Michigan Pleistocene vertebrates are known from a plethora of sites that range from about 14,500 to 11,000 years ago, the end of the Pleistocene. All of the verified Pleistocene vertebrates of Michigan (Holman 2001, Seymour 2004) have been found in the southern half of the Lower Peninsula, south of a boundary marked by the Mason-Quimby Line (Holman 1991, Fig. 8.2), a line originally drawn to indicate the distribution of American Mastodonts and most Paleo-Indian fluted spear points (Cleland et al. 1998).

Michigan's known Pleistocene vertebrate fauna is composed of at least 39 taxa, including seven fishes, three amphibians, two reptiles, two birds and 25 mammals. Of these, 33 were either identified positively or at least tentatively to the species level (Table 8.1). Mastodonts, giant browsing megaherbivores, have yielded by far the most abundant vertebrate remains in the Pleistocene of Michigan.

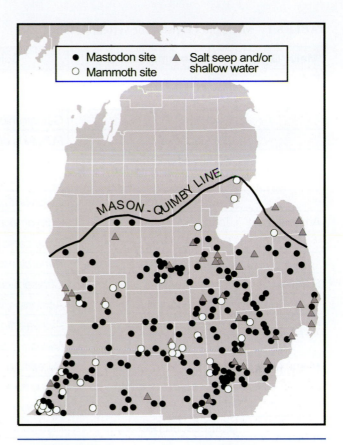

FIGURE 8.2   Locations of known Mastodon and Mammoth sites in Michigan, in relation to the Mason-Quimby Line. There is no undisputed evidence of Pleistocene vertebrates and very little evidence of Paleo-Indian activity north of this line in Michigan.

Michigan's fossil giants: mammoths and mastodonts

People are often confused by the terms mastodont and mammoth, thinking that both names refer to a single Ice Age mammal that looks like a long-haired elephant. Actually, these huge mammals have a long and separate evolutionary history and are as different from one another as horses are from rhinos! That is, they are members of different major groups; mastodonts belong to the Family Mammutidae, whereas mammoths are members of the Family Elephantidae (which also includes the modern elephants). Mastodonts and mammoths also differ in a number of skeletal characteristics, e.g., the shape of the skull and tusks, but are most easily distinguished based on the structure of their teeth. Mastodont teeth (Fig. 8.3A) have chewing surfaces composed of large knobs, the individual knobs usually with worn-down central portions. The knobs are arranged in two rows. The name mastodont comes from the structure of these teeth, which technically means "nipple tooth." Mammoths have teeth (Fig. 8.8B), with chewing surfaces that are composed of a single row of thin enamel plates. The jaw muscles and teeth of mastodonts and mammoths work differently to produce two kinds of chewing motions. In mastodonts, the lower jaw moves up and down against the upper jaw producing a crunching type of chewing motion. In mammoths, the lower jaw moves backward and forward, causing a grinding type of chewing.

The differences in jaws, muscles, and teeth are associated with the feeding habits of these two animals. Mastodonts ate and chewed *mast* and other types of *browse* between the upper and lower teeth, whereas mammoths ground up grass between the transverse enamel ridges of their teeth. In the Pleistocene, mastodonts were most abundant in eastern woodlands; mammoths were abundant in the prairie states. Thus, mastodont fossils are much more abundant in Michigan than those of mammoths.

TABLE 8.1   Michigan's Pleistocene vertebrate fauna

Major Group	Common name	Scientific name	Reference
Fish	Northern pike	*Esox lucius*	Shoshani et al. (1989)
	Minnows	Cyprinidae	Seymour (2004)
	Suckers	Catostomidae	Seymour (2004)
	Sticklebacks	*Pungitius cf. P. pungitius*	Seymour (2004)
	Sunfishes and basses	*Pomoxis*	Holman (1979)
	Perch	*Perca flavescens*	Shoshani et al. (1989)
	Drums and Croakers	*Aplodinotus cf. A. grunniens*	Seymour (2004)
Amphibians	Toads	*Bufo americanus*	Holman (1988)
	Bullfrog	*Rana catesbeiana*	DeFauw and Shoshani (1991)
	Green frog	*Rana clamitans*	DeFauw and Shoshani (1991)
Reptiles	Painted turtle	*Chrysemys picta*	Holman and Fisher (1993)
	Softshell turtles	*Apalone spinifera*	Holman and Fisher (1993)
Birds	Lesser Scaup duck	*Aythya affinis*	Holman (1976)
	Wild turkey	*Meleagris gallopavo*	Shoshani et al. (1989)
Mammals	Pygmy shrew	*Sorex hoyi*	Seymour (2004)
	Black bear	*Ursus americanus*	Eshelman (1974)
	Ermine	*Mustela erminea*	Seymour (2004)
	Flat-headed peccary[1]	*Platygonus compressus*	Wilson (1967)
	Moose	*Alces alces*	Shoshani et al. (1989)
	Scotts moose[1]	*Cervalces scotti*	Garland and Cogswell (1985)
	Wapiti (elk)	*Cervus elaphus*	Hay (1923)
	White-tailed deer	*Odocoileus virginianus*	Holman et al. (1986)
	Caribou	*Rangifer tarandus*	Hibbard (1952)
	Woodland muskox[1]	*Bootherium bombifrons*	Holman (1990)
	American beaver	*Castor canadensis*	Shoshani et al. (1989)
	Giant beaver[1]	*Castoroides ohioensis*	Holman (1991)
	Deer mouse	*Peromyscus maniculatus*	Seymour (2004)
	Collared lemming	*Dicrostonyx groenlandicus*	Seymour (2004)
	Northern bog lemming	*Synaptomys borealis*	Seymour (2004)
	Brown lemming	*Lemmus cf. L. trimuronatus*	Seymour (2004)
	Southern Red-backed vole	*Clethrionomys cf. C. gapperi*	Seymour (2004)
	Meadow vole	*Microtus pennsylvanicus*	Holman (1979)
	Yellow-cheeked vole	*Microtus xanthognathus*	Seymour (2004)
	Muskrat	*Ondatra zibethicus*	Shoshani et al. (1989)
	Meadow jumping mouse	*Zapus cf. Z. hudsonius*	Seymour (2004)
	Rabbit	Unidentified	Seymour (2004)
	American Mastodont[1]	*Mammut americanum*	Garland and Cogswell (1985)
	Jefferson Mammoth[1]	*Mammuthus jeffersoni*	Abraczinskas (1993)
	Woolly Mammoth[1]	*Mammuthus primigenius*	Case et al. (1935)

1. Extinct

The abbreviation "cf." Indicates that the genus or species is tentatively identified.

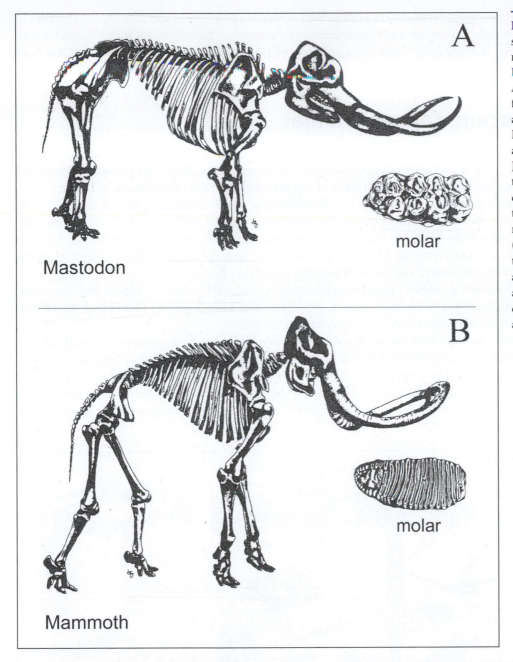

A

molar

Mastodon

B

molar

Mammoth

FIGURE 8.3 A comparison of mastodonts and mammoths from the Pleistocene of Michigan. A. Skeleton (left) and surface view of tooth (right) of an American Mastodont. B. Surface view of tooth (left) and a skeleton (right) of a Jefferson Mammoth. Note: the name "mastodont" comes from a Greek word that, translated to English, requires a "t" at the end (Haynes 1991). However, the terminal "t" has largely disappeared in common usage, and both spellings, "mastodont" and "mastodon," appear in the literature.

In Michigan, mastodonts are thought to have preferred open spruce woodlands, as well as open pine and spruce forests. Food remains found inside the rib cages of mastodonts showed the presence of twigs, conifer cones, leaves, tough grasses and marsh and swamp plants. Only one species of mastodont actually occurred in the Pleistocene in Michigan. It ranged from about 2.5 to 3 m high at the shoulders and weighed from about four to six tons. There are at least 61 mastodont sites in Ontario, 211 in Michigan, 136 in Ohio, 23 in Indiana, 40 in Illinois and 20 in Wisconsin, all associated with the last glaciation.

At least 27 mammoth sites are known in Ontario, 49 in Michigan, 57 in Ohio, 13 in Indiana, 11 in Illinois and 28 in Wisconsin. Each site may contain either one or two different species of mammoth. Two species of mammoths are recognized in Michigan, the Jefferson Mammoth and the Woolly Mammoth (Table 8.1); the latter species is very rare in the state. The Jefferson Mammoth is usually identified on the basis of being larger and having less complicated teeth than the Woolly Mammoth. The Jefferson Mammoth is thought to have become extinct almost 13,000 years ago in the Great Lakes region. It preferred grasslands (in Michigan) and was only about one-fourth as abundant as Mastodonts in the state.

Because of cave paintings and engravings in Eurasia, as well as thousands of bones and even frozen carcasses in Siberia, we know that the Woolly Mammoth had the general appearance of a relatively small, shaggy elephant with small ears and a short trunk. It entered the Great Lakes region from time to time, and besides Michigan, has been reported from Ontario and Ohio. A complete skull has even been found in southeastern Ohio.

■ Post-Pleistocene faunal changes

Of the 33 vertebrates identified to species in Table 8.1, seven became extinct by the end of the Pleistocene, and others occupy a much-reduced geographic range today in Michigan than they did then. Still other groups have vanished entirely from Michigan since the Pleistocene. At least some of this faunal change can be attributed to changes in climate and subsequent shifts in habitats. For example, the distribution of fossil lemmings indicates that they were more widely dispersed during the Pleistocene, ranging as far south as Virginia, Tennessee and Arkansas. The three Pleistocene species found as fossils in Michigan do not live here today, but are found only much farther north, in the tundra of Alaska, Canada and Greenland. This shift in their range may correspond with the waning of the Pleistocene ice sheets and northern shift of the cooler habitats in which they lived.

Likewise during the Pleistocene, caribou ranged across Michigan and as far south as Virginia and Tennessee. Today the nearest caribou to Michigan are found along the north shore of Lake Superior. This shift in range mirrors the climate/habitat changes associated with the final retreat of the ice.

Some Pleistocene vertebrates may have succumbed to other ecologic pressures in combination with climate change. The Giant Beaver (*Castoroides ohioensi*; Fig. 8.4) is a spectacular, extinct rodent that was as large as a medium-sized Black Bear. Fossils of this animal have been found in at least 10 sites in Michigan. The incisor teeth (Fig. 8.4B) of the Giant Beaver appear to be a combination of a gouge and a chisel that could cut wood and strip bark as well as allowing the animals to root for aquatic plants. Its molars, however, were adapted for eating succulent aquatic plants.

FIGURE 8.4 Drawings of the extinct Giant Beaver. A. Giant Beavers near a pond. B. A Giant Beaver skull (in side view); 1= incisor teeth, 2= molar teeth.

Stag Moose

FIGURE 8.5 A drawing of a Scott's Moose (Stag Moose) in an open coniferous forest.

It is thought that the Giant Beaver became extinct because of its competition with the more resourceful modern beaver and because of the reduction of typical Giant Beaver habitat at the end of the Pleistocene.

The extinct Scotts (Stag) Moose (*Cervalces scotti*; Fig. 8.5) differs from the true Moose (*Alces alces*) in having narrower antlers with a more complicated branching pattern, and a different enamel pattern on the teeth. Despite these differences, it is thought that both may have occupied similar habitats. Therefore, competition for food under fluctuating climate conditions may have contributed to the extinction of Scott's Moose.

Explaining the reduction in numbers of individuals of other Michigan Pleistocene vertebrates is complicated by the appearance during the Pleistocene of a new group of predatory mammals—*Homo sapiens*. Humans must have impacted the Pleistocene fauna in the same way we impact ecosystems today—through hunting and habitat destruction. The effect of human hunting on several large game animals, including wild turkey, black bear and moose, is documented over historic timescales in Michigan. Today moose occur only in Michigan's Upper Peninsula and are the subject of intensive wildlife-management efforts. Wapiti (elk) were extirpated from Michigan by 1880, but have since been reintroduced in the central part of northern Lower Michigan. Wild turkey hybrids have been re-introduced successfully in many parts of the Lower Peninsula.

■ Extinction of the megaherbivores

All of Michigan's extinct Pleistocene vertebrates were large mammals, including the peccary (Fig. 8.6), Scott's Moose (Fig. 8.5), Woodland Muskox (Fig. 8.7), Giant Beaver and the three elephant-like giant herbivores (megaherbivores), the American Mastodont, Jefferson Mammoth and Wooly Mammoth. Michigan's mastodonts and mammoths were the dominant vertebrates in the Pleistocene ecosystems of Michigan, and in many other Pleistocene ecosystems in the New World. Like the present elephants and rhinos of Africa, they kept the vertebrate community in equilibrium by means of their feeding and other activities (Owen-Smith 1987). No such megaherbivores (giant herbivores) now exist in the New World, and, obviously, when the mastodonts and mammoths suddenly became extinct at the end of the Pleistocene, most of the ecosystems in this half of the globe changed forever. It has been documented in Africa that when the megaherbivores become extinct, other large mammals also become extinct—almost a domino effect. This certainly must have happened in North America (Holman 2001).

FIGURE 8.6   Pleistocene Peccaries. A. A group of Flat-headed Peccaries in an open situation. B. A Flat-headed Peccary skull (in side view).

FIGURE 8.7   Woodland Muskoxen. A. A group of Woodland (Helmeted) Muskoxen in sparse cover. B. A skull (in top view) of a Woodland Muskox (upper). Same skull in side view (lower).

The possible role of Paleo-Indians as hunters of mammoths and mastodonts is a topic of current research, e.g., Fisher (1984a, b). Another topic of interest regarding these megaherbivores, independent of possible human intervention, is the suggestion that mastodonts and mammoths were dependant on the sodium that was found in the surficial salt deposits in Michigan (Fig. 8.2), in the same way that elephants are dependant on a salt supply today in Africa (Owen-Smith 1987, Holman et al. 1998). The abundance of mastodonts and mammoths in Michigan, relative to surrounding states, may be the result of yearly treks to Michigan to procure this essential element of their diet.

■ Epilogue

Small bands of Late Pleistocene hunters occasionally came upon mastodonts drinking from small, glacially derived ponds. Some may have tried to kill these megaherbivores with spears armed with fluted points. Others gathered turtles and smaller prey.

After the Pleistocene, humans became agriculturalists, then industrialists and finally technologists. Fields of grain replaced the natural grasslands and woodlands of the Pleistocene and domestic herbivores (cows, sheep, and goats) replaced the extinct Pleistocene ones. The intrepid turtles persisted through these myriad climate, habitat, and cultural changes to survive to the present day, whereas their megaherbivore brethren did not (Holman and Fisher 1993). Certainly there is more to learn about the underlying explanations for the distribution and evolutionary history of Michigan's Pleistocene fauna.

Literature Cited

Abraczinskas, L.M. 1993. Pleistocene proboscidian sites in Michigan: New records and an update on published sites. Michigan Academician 25:443–490.

Case, E.C., Scott, I.D., Badenoch, B.M. and T.E. White. 1935. Discovery of *Elaphas primigenius americanus* in the bed of Glacial Lake Mogodore, in Cass County, Michigan. Papers of the Michigan Academy of Science, Arts, and Letters 20:449–454.

Cleland, C.E., Holman, M.B. and J.A. Holman. 1998. The Mason-Quimby Line revisited. Wisconsin Archeologist 79:8–27.

DeFauw, S.L. and J. Shoshani. 1991. *Rana catesbeiana* and *R. clamitans* from the Late Pleistocene of Michigan. Journal of Herpetology 25:95–99.

Eshelman, R.E. 1974. Black Bear from Quaternary deposits in Michigan. Michigan Academician 6:291–298.

Fisher, D.C. 1984a. Mastodon butchery by North American Paleo-Indians. Nature 308:71–272.

Fisher, D.C. 1984b. Taphonomic analysis of Late Pleistocene mastodon occurrences: Evidence of butchery by North American Paleo-Indians. Paleobiology 10:338–357.

Garland, E.B. and J.W. Cogswell. 1985. The Powers Mastodont Site, Van Buren County, Michigan. Michigan Archaeologist 31:3–39.

Hay, O.P. 1923. The Pleistocene of North America and its vertebrated animals from the states east of the Mississippi River and from the Canadian provinces east of Longitude 95. Carnegie Institution, Washington, DC.

Hayes, G. 1991. Mammoths, Mastodonts, and Elephants. Cambridge University Press, Cambridge.

Hibbard, C.W. 1952. Remains of barren ground caribou in Pleistocene deposits of Michigan. Papers of the Michigan Academy of Science, Arts, and Letters 37:235–237.

Holman, J.A. 1976. A 25,000-year-old duck: More evidence for a Michigan Wisconsinan interstadial. American Midlands Naturalist 96:501–503.

Holman, J.A. 1979. New fossil vertebrate remains from Michigan. Michigan Academician 11:391–397.

Holman, J.A. 1988. The status of Michigan's Pleistocene herpetofauna. Michigan Academician 20:125–132.

Holman, J.A. 1990. A Late Wisconsinan woodland musk ox, *Bootherium bombifrons*, from Montcalm County, Michigan, with remarks on Michigan musk oxen. Michigan Academician 2:1–10.

Holman, J.A. 1991. New records of Michigan Pleistocene vertebrates with comments on the Mason-Quimby Line. Michigan Academician 23:273–283.

Holman, J.A. 2001. In Quest of Great Lakes Ice Age Vertebrates. Michigan State Univ. Press: East Lansing.

Holman, J.A., Abraczinskas, L.M. and D.B. Westjohn. 1998. Pleistocene proboscidians and Michigan salt deposits. National Geographic Research 4:4–5.

Holman, J.A. and D.C. Fisher. 1993. Late Pleistocene turtle remains (Reptilia: Testudines) from southern Michigan. Michigan Academician 25:491–499.

Holman, J.A., Fisher, D.C. and R.O. Kapp. 1986. Recent discoveries of fossil vertebrates in the Lower Peninsula of Michigan. Michigan Academician 18:431–463.

Owen-Smith, N. 1987. Pleistocene extinctions: The pivotal role of megaherbivores . Paleobiology 13:351–362.

Seymour, K.L. 2004. Pleistocene vertebrates from the Pre-Late Wisconsinan Mill Creek Site, St. Clair County, Michigan. Michigan Academician 36:191–211.

Shoshani, J., Fisher, D.C., Zawiskie, J.M., Thurlow, S.J., Shoshani, S.L., Benninghoff, W.S. and F.H. Zoch. 1989. The Shelton Mastodon Site: Multidisciplinary Study of a Late Pleistocene (Twocreekan) Locality in Southeastern Michigan. University of Michigan Museum of Paleontology Contributions 27:393–436.

Wilson, R.L. 1967. The Pleistocene vertebrates of Michigan. Papers of the Michigan Academy of Science, Arts, and Letters 52:197–234.

Further Readings

Barondess, M.M. 1996. Backhoes, bulldozers and behemoths. Michigan History Magazine (Jan/Feb) 80:29–32.

Dorr, J.A. and D.F. Eschman, 1970. Geology of Michigan. Univ. of Michigan Press, Ann Arbor.

Fisher, D.C. 1996. How to date a mastodon. Michigan History Magazine (Jan/Feb) 80:33.

Hibbard, C.W. 1951. Animal life in Michigan during the Ice Age. Michigan Alumnus Quarterly Review 57:200–208.

Hibbard, C.W. and F.J. Hinds. 1960. A radio-carbon date for a woodland musk ox in Michigan. Papers of the Michigan Academy of Science, Arts, and Letters 45:103–108.

Hibbard, E.A. 1958. Occurrence of the extinct moose, Cervalces, in the Pleistocene of Michigan. Papers of the Michigan Academy of Science, Arts, and Letters 43:33–37.

Holman, J.A. 1975. Michigan's fossil vertebrates. Publications of the Museum, Michigan State University, Educational Bulletin 2:1–54.

Holman, J.A. 1995a. Ancient life of the Great Lakes basin. University of Michigan Press: Ann Arbor.

Holman, J.A. 1995b. Issues and innovations in Pleistocene vertebrate paleontology in

Michigan—the last fifty-five years. Michigan Academician 27:409–424.

Holman, J.A. (ed). 2002, Michigan's Ice Age behemoths. Michigan Academician 34:221–392.

Holman, J.A. and M.B. Holman. 2003. The Michigan Roadside Naturalist. University of Michigan Press, Ann Arbor.

Kapp, R.O. 1970. A 24,000-year-old Jefferson mammoth from Midland County, Michigan. Michigan Academician 3:95–99.

Karrow, P.F., Seymour, K.L., Miller, B.B. and J.E. Mirecki. 1997. Pre-Late Wisconsinan biota from southeastern Michigan, U.S.A. Palaeogeography Palaeoclimatology Palaeoecology 33:81–101.

Kurta, A. 1995. Mammals of the Great Lakes Region. University of Michigan Press, Ann Arbor.

MacAlpin, A. 1940. A census of mastodon remains in Michigan. Papers of the Michigan Academy of Science, Arts, and Letters 25:481–490.

Skeels, M.A. 1962. The mastodons and mammoths of Michigan. Papers of the Michigan Academy of Science, Arts, and Letters 47:101–133.

9

Earthquakes

Kazuya Fujita and Norman H. Sleep

Introduction

One of the most disquieting feelings we can experience is the movement of what we believe to be solid, stable ground under our feet—an earthquake. Additionally, earthquakes in many parts of the world have resulted in liquefaction (where the ground behaves as if it were a fluid), resulting in frightening tales of the ground opening up and swallowing cities whole. Fortunately, the eastern US in general, and Michigan in particular, is not a region of frequent earthquake activity. Despite this, >150 "seismic events" have been reported in Michigan in the past 200 years (plus a large number of tiny events associated with the intentional collapse and filling of a mine in 1995). In this chapter, we use the term "earthquake" for an event caused by natural processes at depth within the Earth. In contrast, a "seismic event" is anything that causes shaking of the ground, including earthquakes. Seismic events that are not earthquakes include man-made events such as explosions, mine and building collapses, sonic booms that shake the ground and natural surficial phenomena such as cryoseismisms ("ice quakes") and landslides. Of the 150 seismic events in Michigan's recent past, about 50 were explosions associated with scientific studies conducted in Lake Superior from 1964 to 1966, and another 50 were associated with a 1906 mine collapse. Most of the rest are also associated with mining or various kinds of explosions. A few, small (but legitimate) earthquakes, however, have occurred within Michigan, and about 40 earthquakes (some quite large) have occurred in nearby states and have been clearly felt within the state.

In the distant geologic past, earthquake activity was probably more significant in Michigan, especially during its three major episodes of tectonic activity: the Penokean orogeny, the formation of the Keweenaw age mid-continent rift system (Chapter 12), and during their subsequent closure. All of these events were, however, in the Precambrian Eon, at least a billion years ago.

Causes and formation of earthquakes

Most natural earthquakes occur along faults, which are fractures in the Earth where one side moves with respect to the other; volcanoes are responsible for most of the rest. When earthquakes occur, there is a sudden release of energy that radiates out from the source in the form of seismic waves (Fig. 9.1). Although we generally think of earthquakes as instantaneous occurrences at a point, really large earthquakes, such as the 2004 Sumatra earthquake (Lay et al. 2005, Stein and Okal 2005), have very large source regions (hundreds of km long by tens of km wide) and can last up to several minutes. The point of initial rupture of an earthquake is known as the *hypocenter*, and can be located up to hundreds of km under the surface. The projection of the hypocenter, vertically upward and onto the Earth's surface, is called the *epicenter*.

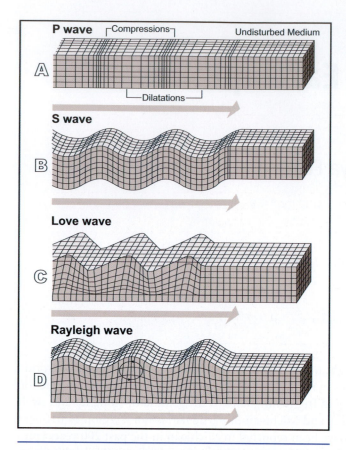

FIGURE 9.1   Types of seismic waves. After Bolt (2004).
A. P (primary, pressure) waves. B. S (secondary, shear) waves.
C. Love waves. D. Rayleigh waves. P- and S-waves are body
waves, whereas Love and Rayleigh waves are surface waves.
The displacement of the ground is shown as the wave passes
through from left to right.

Fault motion can occur under horizontal compression (creating reverse or thrust faults), horizontal extension (creating normal faults), or under shearing (both compression and extension, acting horizontally, creating strike-slip faults). In real-world situations, especially away from the Earth's surface, the compressional and extensional stresses are not in the horizontal plane. Therefore, there also are *transpressional* or *transtensional* earthquakes, a mix of strike-slip and reverse or normal faulting. In the context of plate motions, most large earthquakes on divergent plate boundaries, e.g., Mid-Atlantic Ridge, are associated with normal faults, whereas most large convergent boundary earthquakes are associated with thrust or reverse faults, e.g., in the Himalayas and in subduction zones. Transform boundary earthquakes are within strike-slip faults, e.g., the San Andreas.

Earthquakes radiate energy as four kinds of waves (Fig. 9.1; Bolt 2004). Two of them, P- (Primary) and S- (Secondary) waves, travel through the interior earth and are called *body waves*. P-waves are like sound waves and compress or expand the earth (hence sometimes referred to as "push" or pressure waves). S-waves represent shearing motion (hence sometimes referred to as "shake" or shear waves), and travel considerably more slowly. The other two kinds of waves travel along the surface of the Earth and are therefore collectively called *surface waves*. Love waves shake the ground sideways and can cause considerable damage, while Rayleigh waves are like big rolls that travel along the surface.

Earthquake waves are recorded on seismometers, which convert the ground motion into an electric current, which is then recorded digitally on a computer (or using a pen and ink on a piece of paper). The resulting record is called a seismogram.

■ Quantification of earthquake intensity and magnitude

Quantification, or estimating the size and shaking magnitude of earthquakes, is important in hazard assessment, including such policy decisions as how much reinforcement to require of structures. A significant fraction of the earthquakes in Michigan is reported based on macroseismic (or "felt report") data, i.e., they were reported as being felt by individuals, with no instrumental recordings. Determining the occurrence, location and size of these events requires the use of written accounts.

Earthquakes can be quantified by their intensity and/or magnitude. Intensity is a subjective measure of the effects of earthquakes, primarily on humans. The most commonly used intensity scale in the US is the Modified Mercalli (MM) scale of 1931 (Willmore 1979, Bolt 2004). Intensities are stated in terms of how people perceived the earthquake (felt, felt strongly, sleeping people awakened; Table 9.1) and how it affected things (objects moved, windows rattled, buildings destroyed, etc.). Based on these observations, the amount of ground shaking can be estimated. For events prior to the early part of the 20th century, this is often the only way that an earthquake can be quantified. The observed intensities estimated at various localities are then plotted on a map, producing a map of the variation of intensity with location. Isolines of equal intensity, called isoseismals, can then be drawn. Higher accelerations (usually measured as a fraction of the gravitational attraction of the Earth) yield greater damage.

TABLE 9.1   Modified (simplified) Mercalli Scale for earthquake intensity[1]

I	Felt only by a few people in extremely favorable conditions.
II	Felt by persons at rest or on upper floors of buildings.
III	Felt clearly indoors, hanging objects swing. Vibration like a light truck passing by.
IV	Vibrations like a heavy truck passing by, or heavy objects striking the walls. Windows, dishes, doors rattle. Cars rock, walls creak.
V	Felt outdoors, sleeping people woken up. Small objects knocked over, doors swing open and closed. Shutters and wall hangings move. Plaster may crack. Tall objects may sway.
VI	Felt by all; many are frightened, people run outdoors. Windows, glass, dishes broken, items knocked off walls and shelves. Furniture may be moved. Bells ring, trees and bushes shake.
VII	Difficult to stand, noticeable by drivers. Furniture broken, adobe cracked, weak chimneys broken, plaster and loose bricks fall. Cracks in unreinforced buildings. Waves on ponds, water becomes turbid. Small landslides occur.
VIII	Adobe buildings may collapse, considerable damage to unreinforced buildings. Chimneys, smokestacks, monuments fall. Loose paneling in walls knocked out; heavy furniture overturned. Branches broken from trees.
IX	General panic. Adobe buildings destroyed, normal buildings severely damaged, reinforced structures unaffected. Foundations damaged, reservoir dams damaged, underground pipes broken, cracks observed in the ground. Some liquefaction.
X	Most masonry and frame structures destroyed. Some bridges destroyed, serious damage to dams, dikes and embankments. Large landslides. Rails bent.
XI	Few structures remain undamaged. Bridges collapse. Railroad tracks greatly bent, underground pipelines severed.
XII	Damage nearly total. Large objects thrown into the air.

1. Adapted from Willmore (1979) and Bolt (2004)

Magnitude is a measure of the size of an earthquake, estimated from the amount of ground motion, objectively measured using a seismometer. The original magnitude scale was developed in southern California in the 1930s by C.F. Richter and was based on the logarithm of the distance-corrected amplitude, as recorded by a seismometer. Today, this is known as a local magnitude (M_L). In the 1940s, Richter and his colleague Beno Gutenberg used P-waves recorded at greater distances to develop the body wave magnitude (m_b) scale. They later used lower frequency surface waves to develop the surface wave magnitude (M_S), a better measure for larger earthquakes. Finally, in the 1980s, it became apparent that the very largest earthquakes would not be accurately measured even using M_S. Thus, moment magnitude (Mw) was developed, based on the seismic moment (a measure of earthquake energy) of the earthquake. Commonly, earthquake magnitude is referred to as being on the "Richter scale," but this strictly applies only to M_L. Bolt (2004) provided a summary of waves, faulting and quantification.

■ Examples of earthquakes in Michigan

Seismic events have been reported from all over Michigan (Fig. 9.2). However, many things can generate vibrations of the ground—and not many of the events reported in Michigan are naturally occurring (tectonic) earthquakes, i.e., those created by stresses within the Earth. Unless otherwise specified, the examples of seismic events reported below, from various parts of Michigan, are taken from Fujita and Sleep (1991; see therein for references). Because Michigan is a generally aseismic (stable) region, residents who are not accustomed to earthquakes have reported a variety of non-earthquake events as being earthquakes.

Seismicity Map of Michigan

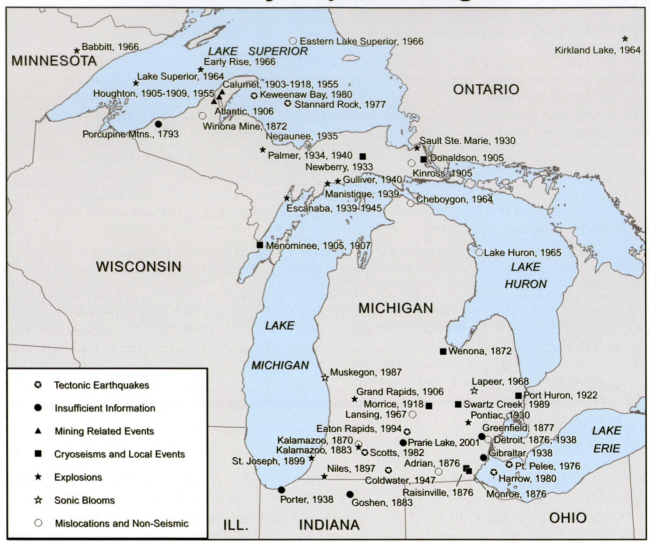

FIGURE 9.2 Seismicity map of Michigan, showing all known and reported events. Only those solid circles with inscribed stars are confirmed natural events. After Fujita and Sleep (1991).

Mining-related, seismic events

Most of the seismic events reported from the Upper Peninsula are associated with mining. The Keweenaw Peninsula was the focus of copper mining in Michigan during the late 19th and early 20th centuries (Chapter 12). The copper deposits (and hence, the mining activity) outcrop along and near the Keweenaw Fault (Fig. 12.9), and thus many seismic events were initially associated with movement along that fault (Docekal 1970). Closer examination indicates that most of the events occurred during the peak mining period (1905–1918), including the two largest events, the Calumet earthquake of 1905 and the Atlantic Mine event in 1906. Other smaller events are probably large rock bursts (Crane 1929) which were felt in the towns.

The Calumet earthquake of July 27, 1905, had a maximum intensity of VII (Table 9.1); it toppled chimneys and broke windows in the Calumet area. A loud explosion, which was heard within the copper mines, was associated with the earthquake. The event was felt to about 80 km north and south of Calumet. It was also felt at Marquette, although not at the sparsely populated points in between. Although no specific incidents were reported in any of the mines, the felt area of this event is very tiny compared to its intensity, an indicator of a very shallow source. In addition, the detached felt area at Marquette may be a result of a shock wave in the atmosphere, possibly resulting from a large "air burst" (Crane 1929) due to a mine collapse; it is located approximately at the right distance for an atmospheric refraction (see below, under "explosions"). This event is likely the result of mining-induced stresses (Hasegawa et al. 1989), although some accumulated tectonic stress may have been released.

The strongest event in the Upper Peninsula (intensity VIII) occurred at Atlantic Mine on May 26, 1906. This event was a mine collapse which resulted in the closure of the Atlantic Mine; railroad tracks were deformed over the mine and there was considerable caving that created a series of pits (Kilpela 1995). Most of the destruction (which yielded the high intensity) occurred directly over the collapsed area. The event was only felt as far away as Houghton (10 km), and over only a ~300 km² area—very small for an event of this intensity, suggestive of a very shallow source. Two additional events in 1955, and a long sequence in 1995, are also associated with settling in underground copper mines.

Mislocated events

Events can be mislocated with either felt reports or even with instrumental data. In the 19th century, many events were simply located to the nearest town with a newspaper from where the event was reported. In addition, poor communications resulted in some earthquakes being considered local when they actually occurred far away. A typical example is the October 20, 1870, event reported in Kalamazoo. This event caused minor chimney damage and cracked plaster (intensity VI). The time of occurrence, however, is the same as the maximum intensity IX event that occurred in La Malbaie, Quebec, which was also felt in Sault Ste. Marie and possibly as far away as Iowa (Fujita and Sleep 1991).

In more recent times, instrument-recorded events have also been mislocated. An example is the Cheboygan event of August 15, 1964, which the International Seismological Center located "by inspection." Relocation of this event with additional data placed it in the Kirkland Lake, Ontario mining district—a conclusion supported by the extremely high frequency signal generated by this event. A 1965 event, initially located below Lake Huron based on incomplete data, turned out, instead, to be an earthquake in Missouri.

Cryoseisms

An interesting class of seismic events is called cryoseisms—"ice quakes" which commonly occur in water-saturated ground. They are especially well documented in New England (Lacroix 1980). The expansion of water when it freezes to ice causes stresses in the ground. The ground breaks much like a bottle left in a freezer. They often generate very strong vibrations over a very small region and sometimes create fractures in the ground. The best example of a cryoseism in Michigan is the February 22, 1918, event in Morrice. A 45-meter long, one-meter deep crack, with numerous diverging cracks, opened on a farm. The ground shook and sounds were heard. Other probable cryoseisms are the 1876 Raisinville and Monroe events. One particularly enigmatic event was reported from Wenona on February 6, 1872. Because no locality named Wenona exists today, this event has been assigned to two localities: the Winona Mine in the Upper Peninsula (which had not yet been established in 1872), and Bay City, which merged with the town of Wenona in the late 19th century. A report in the Detroit Free Press stated that the shock, with slight ground motion, lasted 10 seconds and the sound from it traveled from the N-NE. In a report to the American Journal of Science, a Mr. Cowles stated that there were three shocks lasting 30 seconds, accompanied by a rumbling noise (Rockwood 1872). He then indicated that the vibrations traveled from the N-NE and "were plainly observable by persons out of doors," a highly unusual occurrence for a small earthquake. The event was not reported in Bay City, across the river from Wenona. The similarity in wording between the Free Press report and the American Journal of Science article suggests they were written by the same person, most likely Ed Cowles, who can be shown to be an editor resident in Wenona. It would appear that he exaggerated the size of the event in his second report. Temperatures were very cold at the time, and it is possible this was a cryoseism.

Explosions

Underground explosions can produce seismic waves, just as earthquakes do. The monitoring of underground nuclear tests during the "cold war" was the major impetus for the development of well-calibrated global seismic networks in the 1960s. Monitoring of clandestine nuclear tests by rogue nations continues to be a focus of research today. Less apparent, but equally important to the earthquake history of Michigan, are surface explosions. In many cases, it can be difficult for an observer to determine whether vibrations are traveling through the ground or through the air—especially if you are located in a frame house. Both earthquakes and shock waves cause walls and windows to vibrate, create noise and cause objects to shake. The analysis of explosions is further complicated by the fact that the temperature decrease in the troposphere (the lowest layer of the atmosphere), coupled with a temperature increase in the stratosphere (the layer above the troposphere), results in the refraction of shock wave energy and, significantly, the creation of a *shadow zone* where no sound is heard (Gutenberg 1951). In the atmosphere, this *cone of silence* extends from about 50 to 100 km from an explosion, although the distance is seasonally variable.

One of the largest "earthquakes" attributed to Michigan is the February 4, 1883 Kalamazoo event (Fig. 9.2). In some sources, this event is assigned a felt area of 400,000 km² because of confusion with an earthquake in southern Illinois that occurred 12 hours previously. The Kalamazoo event is reported from Kankakee, from other parts of Illinois and from Kalamazoo, Berrien Springs and Dowagiac; however, it is not reported from Three Rivers, MI, or from northern Indiana. The event turned out to be a shock wave from a head-on collision of two freight trains on the Lake Shore Railway near LaPorte, Indiana. The train was carrying both oil and dynamite, and the various explosions of the canisters explain the multiple shocks reported. Residents of northern Indiana were aware of the accident and did not report an earthquake; the localities farther away reported this as an earthquake since they were unaware of the accident and there was a zone of silence due to the atmospheric refraction that included intervening areas like Three Oaks, MI, and Gary, IN.

Other explosions which have been mistaken for earthquakes include the St. Joseph event of October 10, 1899, and the Grand Rapids event (actually felt throughout the western Lower Peninsula) of May 19, 1906. The first is the result of a powder mill explosion in Miller, IN, while the latter is due to a powder mill explosion in Pleasant Prairie, WI. In both cases, clear regions of silence are observed 50–100 km from the explosion and the "earthquake" is reported from beyond that zone.

Small local explosions can also shake windows and be initially reported as an earthquake. An example occurred on November 19, 1930, when 24 kg of dynamite were stolen and detonated on the shores of Commerce Lake, near Pontiac.

Natural earthquakes

The largest natural earthquake in Michigan occurred near Coldwater on August 9, 1947 (Fig. 9.2). The earthquake was widely felt throughout southern Michigan, Ohio, Indiana and even in the Chicago area. It was felt with a maximum intensity of VI near Coldwater, where several chimneys were damaged. The earthquake was also felt with intensity IV–V along the Grand River from Lansing to Grand Rapids, probably as a result of the unconsolidated sediment in the river valley that amplified vibrations (Fig. 9.3). If these are excluded, the zone of highest intensities is highly elongated in a NW-SE direction; in California and elsewhere, isoseismals are usually elongated along the direction of strike-slip faults. This elongation also follows a discontinuity in the magnetic field produced by subsurface rocks. The combination suggests that the Coldwater event may have been a strike-slip earthquake along a NW-oriented fault. A second, small earthquake, on November 26, 1982, near Scotts (Kalamazoo area) may also have occurred on this fault; it was not felt.

A second, modest earthquake occurred just south of Lansing, on September 4, 1994. Initially the epicenter was reported as being north of Lansing. However, detailed study of the macroseismic data (Faust et al. 1997; Fig. 9.4) and analysis of the seismogram recorded at the University of Michigan indicated that the earthquake occurred near Eaton Rapids, in Eaton County. As with the Coldwater event, elevated intensities were associated with river valleys and glacial moraines. The most interesting effect of this event, however, was that it was perceived at least one intensity unit less within the

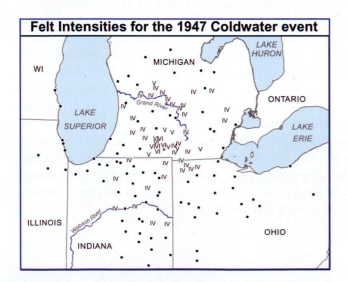

FIGURE 9.3   Isoseismals for the 1947 Coldwater earthquake event. Intensities are given by Roman numerals, dots represent felt localities with intensity of III or less. After Fujita and Sleep (1991).

Metropolitan Lansing area, due to the presence of cultural noise—traffic and other noise-generating activities made the earthquake "less prominent." The event was widely perceived as a loud sound and modest shaking—no physical damage was observed. Based on the distribution of the isoseismals, the event was likely shallow (~10 km); Faust et al. (1997) suggested that it may have occurred along a NW-oriented fault.

A number of small events also have occurred in western Lake Erie, just beyond the Michigan state line. The first, on February 2, 1976, occurred off Pt. Pelee, Ontario, and was felt with intensity IV along the shores of Lake Erie, while the second occurred off Colchester, Ontario, and was felt from Detroit to Toledo (maximum intensity V).

Problematic events

A pair of events was reported from Gibralter and Downriver Detroit in 1938. It is unclear whether these were real tectonic earthquakes; they were only felt right along the river, indicating they were very shallow. Although these events cannot be documented to be explosions, their oddly shaped, highly elongate and concentrated felt areas leave open the possibility that these may be anthropogenic in origin.

An event was also reported from the Livonia area on August 17, 1877, where windows rattled and horses were frightened. There is insufficient data to confirm whether this was a real earthquake. However, if it was, the intensity was about III–IV. In some reports, the intensity of this earthquake has been cited as high as VII (significant damage), which is not supported by documents of the time. Finally, another small event, whose cause is unknown, was reported from the Prairie Lake area (north of Jackson) in 2001.

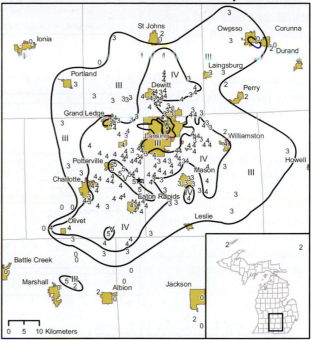

Isoseismals for the 1994 Eaton Rapids event

FIGURE 9.4 Isoseismals for the 1994 Eaton Rapids (Lansing) event. Intensities denoted by numbers. Note the low intensities in Lansing metropolitan area. After Faust et al. (1997).

■ Underlying causes of Michigan earthquakes

While glaciers covered northern North America (Chapter 6), the lithosphere was depressed due to the weight of the ice. When the ice sheet melted, the lithosphere "rebounded," creating crustal stresses (Fig. 9.5a). This mechanism has been cited as the cause of earthquakes along the Atlantic margin of Canada (Stein et al. 1989), where the edge of the ice sheet persisted. Although post-glacial (isostatic) rebound has also been ascribed as the cause of earthquakes in Michigan, and elsewhere in the immediate region, the location of the edge of the ice sheet varied with time and a large-scale unloading event, triggering high stresses, never occurred. In addition, the maximum horizontal stress in the lithosphere is triggered where the rebound causes maximum curvature in the lithosphere, either in space or time. Southern Michigan has been fairly stable, based on shorelines, for the past 8,000 years (Clark et al. 1990), undergoing only very slow tilting today (subsidence in the south, uplift in the north; Fig. 9.5b) at rates of <0.5 mm/yr (Chapter 13). These two facts suggest that stresses associated with deglaciation are by themselves too small to be a significant trigger for earthquakes. In addition, deglaciation stresses south of the ice sheet should be compressional and oriented perpendicularly to the ice front. As noted below, our region has E-NE–W-SW oriented compression (Zoback 1992), approximately parallel to the edge of the ice sheet.

A more likely cause of earthquakes, based on this orientation of the maximum compressive stress, are intraplate stresses resulting from spreading at the Mid-Atlantic ridge. Since the early 1970s, it has been apparent that the plates are an integral part of the driving mechanism for plate tectonics, rather than passive passengers on a convecting mantle. At subduction zones, plates are pulled into the mantle; at ridges, plates slide off of thermally elevated mid-ocean ridges, "pushing" the plate in front of them (Forsyth and Uyeda 1975). Models of intraplate

FIGURE 9.5 Glacial unloading affects crustal stress and causes surface uplift. Left: Lithospheric stress model for a melting glacier. A glacier of constant thickness melts on left side (top), producing shallow tension beneath the load, and shallow compression on the right (center). The stress changes are large on each side of the edge of the glacier. Uplift occurs within the deglaciated region (bottom). After Stein et al. (1989). Right: Observed present uplift rates in units of mm/yr in Michigan. After Clark et al. (1991).

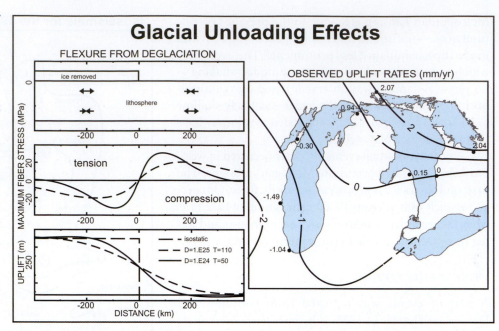

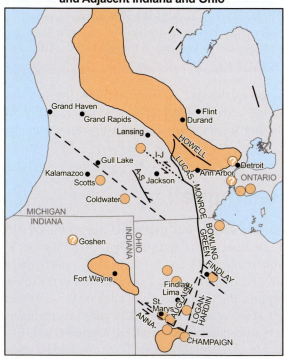

FIGURE 9.6 Fault and gravity high map of southern Michigan, northeastern Indiana, and northwestern Ohio. Color dots represent earthquakes, with "?" symbols used where it is uncertain whether they were natural or not. Solid lines denote mapped faults. Dashed lines denote faults suspected from geophysical data. Color fields represent gravity highs. After Faust et al. (1997), with additional data from Lyons (1970) and Ruff et al. (1994).

stresses (Richardson 1992), and most of the stress determinations from earthquakes and other indicators in the eastern United States, are consistent with the plate boundary stress model (Zoback 1992) and yield NE-SW oriented compression in the eastern US and southern Canada; the orientation of stresses appears unchanged on either side of the deglaciation line.

Deglaciation may play a limited role, however, by enhancing (or decreasing) the ambient plate tectonic stresses. Increased stress could increase the potential for a given fault orientation to slip and affect the orientation of slip when it does. Deglaciation stresses may change the dominant mechanism over state-sized regions from strike-slip to thrust, as in the St. Lawrence River area (Zoback 1992).

Plate boundary stresses are thought to reactivate pre-existing zones of weakness (old faults). In southern Michigan, one major zone of pre-existing faults is the mid-Michigan gravity high, interpreted as being part of a Keweenawan age rift system that extends north-south across the northern Lower Peninsula and then bends, just north of Lansing, and strikes towards Detroit (Fig. 12.1). Natural earthquakes in Michigan, however, all lie well to the south of the gravity high (Fig. 9.6). All mapped faults in southern Michigan, however, do have NW-SE orientations (Faust et al. 1997) and may represent a series of fractures in the Precambrian basement rocks, which formed adjacent to the primary rift system. Alternatively, the Keweenawan rift may have exploited a pre-existing network or faults. In either event, most of the natural seismicity in southern Michigan appears to occur along these faults. The events in western Lake Erie may either be associated with the continuation of the Keweenawan rift, the edge of the Grenville Front, or the St. Lawrence-New Madrid rift system discussed in the next section (Fig. 12.1).

Out of state earthquakes

Although no large earthquakes have occurred within the state, a number of significant earthquakes occurring outside the state have been felt, some quite strongly, in Michigan (Fig. 9.7). Most out-state earthquakes felt in Michigan occur on old rift structures either along the St. Lawrence River, and its extensions into the Canadian Shield and into the New Madrid seismic zone of Missouri and Tennessee (Adams and Basham 1991, Johnston and Schweig 1996).

A number of events have occurred along the lower St. Lawrence River valley, including some of the strongest events in eastern Canada. The majority of the larger events are associated with the St. Lawrence rift system, and are presumed to represent the reactivation of old rift structures under the present-day stress regime (Adams and Basham 1991). To the SW, this zone extends through Lake Erie, western Ohio and to either northern Kentucky or directly to the New Madrid zone. The Anna region in Ohio has also seen significant seismicity, including magnitude 4–5 events. The largest of these occurred in 1937 and was felt in southeastern Michigan. These earthquakes have been postulated to be associated with a continuation of the Mid-Michigan gravity anomaly (Lyons 1970, Ruff et al. 1994; Fig. 12.1). Three additional, out-of-state earthquakes of note have been felt in Michigan—the 1886 Charleston, SC event, the 1936 Timiskaming, Canada, event (the most widely felt event in Michigan, on a branch of the St. Lawrence rift system) and the 1909 northeastern Illinois earthquake.

The New Madrid zone is the source of the largest earthquakes to have struck the eastern and central US, e.g., Johnston and Schweig (1996). In the winter of 1811–1812, three Mw ~7.0–7.5 events and hundreds of smaller aftershocks occurred along the Mississippi River near New Madrid, Missouri. These earthquakes sent energy radiating out through the generally "solid" crust of the eastern US, ringing church bells in South Carolina and shaking the Detroit area enough to loosen trapped gasses from the bottoms of lakes. The uplift due to one of the earthquakes created waterfalls and presumably resulted in the story that the Mississippi River ran backwards for a period of time. Although these events were once thought to be as large as M ~8, reanalysis of the intensity data, taking the local geology into account (settlements mainly in river valleys), suggests that they were smaller (Hough et al. 2000). Subsequent events in the New Madrid area have been felt in southwestern Michigan, most notably the Charleston, MO, earthquake of October 31, 1895. This event was felt sufficiently strongly in the Benton Harbor–St. Joseph area that people ran out of doors in fright.

The New Madrid earthquakes all occur within a Paleozoic structure known as the Reelfoot rift and associated tectonic elements (Johnston and Schweig 1996). This rift is generally thought to have formed when the Iapetus Ocean (the predecessor to the Atlantic) opened, in Late Proterozoic to Early Cambrian time. As late as the Cretaceous Period, igneous intrusions were emplaced and a general zone of weakness formed in the crust. The New Madrid region has, therefore, remained seismically active at the M ~4 level over the past 200 years, and intensive geologic and geophysical work has been conducted to study the crustal structure and the stress and deformation fields in the region. This work has led to two conflicting opinions about the seismic hazard in the region (Atkinson et al. 2000). Studies of liquefaction, the "fluid" behavior of water-saturated ground when shaken by seismic waves (the shaking increases water pressure in intergrain pores in the sediments and makes them lose cohesion, hence the soil "flows"), suggest that large M ~7–8 events have occurred multiple times in the past, most notably around 1500 and 900 AD. These studies suggest a recurrence interval (time between earthquakes) of around 400–500 years. On the

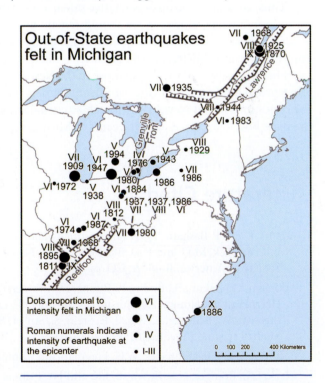

FIGURE 9.7 Out of state earthquakes felt in Michigan. Dots are proportional the intensity with which the event was felt in Michigan and the Roman numerals denote the maximum intensity at the epicenter. Rifts are shown by toothed lines and are named. The dashed line represents the Grenville Front. After Fujita and Sleep (1991).

other hand, global positioning system studies of the deformation of the New Madrid region today point to recurrence intervals of 1,000–1,500 years (Newman et al. 2001).

The stress directions observed in recent New Madrid events are consistent with the plate driving forces from the Mid-Atlantic ridge. However, it is clear that the intense seismic activity in the New Madrid area has not been going on for a long time, or otherwise mountains and other topographic features would be observed. Grollimund and Zoback (2001) suggested that deglaciation stresses were amplified by a zone of weakness in the crust, leading to a triggering of earthquakes. This seismicity is then suggested to continue for geologically short, but societally long, time of several thousands of years.

Expected earthquake hazards

Seismic hazard assessment depends on the estimation of where and how often earthquakes will occur, how large they will be, and how long the resultant shaking will last. In addition, natural events must be discriminated from anthropogenic ones. The "occurrence" of many events, both real and anthropogenic, has been used to argue against the siting of various forms of facilities, e.g., hazardous waste storage, nuclear power plants, etc., although, as documented in this chapter, Michigan is relatively free of seismic hazard. Based on historical data, Michigan is susceptible to feeling several naturally occurring events every century, mainly from outside the state. The expected maximum intensity is up to about III north of a line between Muskegon and Port Huron, and up to VI south of that line. In addition, about once every 50 years, a magnitude 3–4 event occurs within the state, south of a line between Grand Rapids and Pontiac. For the southern part of the state, such events mean cracked plaster, collapse of weakly constructed chimneys, shaking of items off of shelves and vibrating windows. It is unlikely that any significant liquefaction events will occur within the state, and there should be no danger to well-constructed buildings and structures, even without special reinforcement.

Thus, although Michigan is relative safe from seismic activity, we should not be surprised to be slightly shaken up once in a while. However, we should remain aware that not too far to our south, the New Madrid zone could generate another M ~7–8 earthquake, which could cause minor damage in the upper Midwest, including Chicago and southwestern Michigan. The intensity is likely to be less than V, based on the 1811–1812 events.

Finally, an event of the size of those in the New Madrid sequence on the St. Lawrence-New Madrid zone beneath Ohio or Lake Erie would cause significant damage in southeastern Michigan. However, there is no evidence that the conditions like at New Madrid, such as crustal weak zones or heightened stresses above the background due to the plate boundary forces, occur nearer to Michigan.

Literature Cited

Adams, J. and P. Basham. 1991. The seismicity and seismotectonics of eastern Canada. In: Slemmons, D.B., Engdahl, E.R., Zoback, M.D. and D.D. Blackwell (eds.), Neotectonics of North America, Decade Map, vol. 1. Geological Society of America, Boulder, CO. pp. 261–276.

Atkinson, G., Bakun, B., Bodin, P., Boone, D., Cramer, C., Frankel, A., Gasperini, P., Gomberg, J., Hanks, T., Herrmann, B., Hough, S., Johnston, A., Kenner, S., Langston, C., Linker, M., Mayne, P., Petersen, M., Powell, C., Prescott, W., Schweig, E., Segall, P., Stein, S., Stuart, B., Tuttle, M. and R. VanArsdale. 2000. Reassessing the New Madrid seismic zone. Eos 81:397, 402–403.

Bolt, B.A. 2004. Earthquakes. W.H. Freeman and Company, New York.

Clark, J.A., Pranger, H.S. II, Walsh, J.K. and J.A. Primus. 1990. A numerical model of glacial isostasy in the Lake Michigan basin. Geological Society of America, Special Paper 251:111–123.

Crane, W.R. 1929. Rock bursts in the Lake Superior copper mines, Keweenaw Point, Mich. U.S. Department of Commerce, Bureau of Mines, Bulletin 309.

Docekal, J. 1970. Earthquakes of the stable interior, with emphasis on the midcontinent. Ph.D. Dissertation, University of Nebraska, Lincoln. (Diss. Abstr. 71–2880. Diss. Abstr. Intl. 31:4777B).

Faust, T.H., Fujita, K., Mackey, K.G., Ruff, L.J. and R.C. Ensign. 1997. The September 2, 1994 Central Michigan earthquake. Seismological Research Letters 68:460–464.

Forsyth, D. and S. Uyeda. 1975. On the relative importance of the driving forces of plate motion. Geophysical Journal of the Royal Astronomical Society 43:163–200.

Fujita, K. and N.H. Sleep. 1991. A re-examination of the seismicity of Michigan. Tectonophysics 186:75–106.

Grollimund, B. and M.D. Zoback. 2001. Did deglaciation trigger intraplate seismicity in the New Madrid seismic zone? Geology 29:175–178.

Gutenberg, B. 1951. Sound propagation in the atmosphere. In: T.F. Malone (ed.), Compendium of Meteorology. American Meteorological Society, Boston, MA. pp. 266–375.

Hasegawa, H.S., Wetmiller, R.J. and D.J. Gendzwill. 1989. Induced seismicity in mines in Canada—an overview. Pure and Applied Geophysics 129:423–454.

Hough, S.E., Armbruster, J.G., Seeber, L. and J.F. Hough. 2000. Modified Mercalli intensities and magnitudes of the 1811–1812 New Madrid earthquakes. Journal of Geophysical Research 105:23839–23864.

Johnston, A.C. and E.S. Schweig. 1996. The enigma of the New Madrid earthquakes of 1811–1812. Annual Reviews of Earth and Planetary Science 24:339–384.

Kilpela, T. 1995. The Hard Rock Mining Era in the Copper Country. Published by the author.

Lacroix, A.V. 1980. A short note on cryoseisms. Earthquake Notes 51:15–20.

Lay, T., Kanamori, H., Ammon, C.J., Nettles, M., Ward, S.N., Aster, R.C., Beck, S.L., Bilek, S.L., Brudzinski, M.R., Butler, R., DeShon, H.R., Ekström, G., Satake, K. and S. Sipkin. 2005. The Great Sumatra-Andaman earthquake of 26 December, 2004. Science 309:1127–1133.

Lyons, P.L. 1970. Continental and oceanic geophysics. In: H. Johnson and B.L. Smith (eds.) The Megatectonics of Continents and Oceans. Rutgers University Press, New Brunswick, NJ. pp. 147–166.

Newman, A., Schneider, J., Stein, S. and A. Mendez. 2001. Uncertainties in seismic hazard maps for the New Madrid seismic zone and implications for seismic hazard communication. Seismological Research Letters 72:647–663.

Richardson, R.M. 1992. Ridge forces, absolute plate motions, and the intraplate stress field. Journal of Geophysical Research 97:11739–11748.

Rockwood, C.G. 1872. Notices of recent American earthquakes. American Journal of Science, Series 3, 4:1–4.

Ruff, L.J., LaForge, R., Thorson, R., Wagner, T. and F. Goudaen. 1994. Geophysical Investigations of the Western Ohio-Indiana Region. U.S. Nuclear Regulatory Commission, CR-3145, vol. 10.

Stein, S. and E. Okal. 2005. Size and speed of the Sumatra earthquake. Nature 434:581–582.

Stein, S., Cloetingh, S., Sleep, N.H. and R. Wortel. 1989. Passive margin earthquakes, stresses and rheology. In: S. Gregersen and P.W. Basham (eds.), Earthquakes at North-Atlantic Passive Margins: Neotectonics and Postglacial Rebound. D. Reidel Publishing, Dordrecht, Netherlands. pp. 231–259.

Willmore, P.L. (ed.) 1979. Manual of Seismological Observatory Practice (World Data Center A for Solid Earth Geophysics, Report SE-20). U.S. Department of Commerce, Boulder, CO.

Zoback, M.L. 1992. Stress field constraints on intraplate seismicity in eastern North America. Journal of Geophysical Research 97:11761–11782.

Further Readings

Fuller, M.L. 1912 (reprinted 1992). The New Madrid Earthquake. U.S. Geological Survey Bulletin 494.

Hough, S.E. 2002. Earthshaking Science. Princeton University Press, Princeton, NJ.

Page, J. and C. Officer 2004. The Big One. Houghton-Mifflin, New York, NY.

Penick, J.L., Jr. 1981. The New Madrid Earthquakes. University of Missouri Press, Columbia, MO.

Stein, S. and S. Mazzotti (eds). 2007. Continental Intraplate Earthquakes: Science, Hazard, and Policy Issues. Geological Society of America Special Paper 425.

10

Hydrocarbon Resources

William Harrison III

■ Introduction

At the beginning of the 21st century, the focus of much national attention is on our country's dependence on foreign oil. In 2006, the US was the world's leading consumer of oil. At nearly 20.6 million barrels per day, the US then consumed as much oil as the 2nd through 6th place countries (China, Japan, Russia, Germany and India) combined. With 2006 US oil production at around 8.4 million barrels per day, we needed to import over 12 million barrels per day—2.5 times the second place importing country, Japan.

Unknown to many, however, is the fact that the US is also the world's third largest *producer* of oil, behind only Saudi Arabia and Russia (US Energy Information Administration 2007a). Michigan has notable hydrocarbon resources that contribute to this national production total. As of 2004, Michigan ranked 18th among the 50 states in oil production and 12th in production of natural gas. Although Michigan produced and used coal as an important energy resource from the late 19th into the early 20th century, commercial coal production ceased in the 1950s. In 2005, Michigan's annual hydrocarbon production supplied about 29% of the state's needs for natural gas and 3% of its crude oil needs (Westbrook 2005, US Energy Information Administration 2007b). In 2004, oil and natural gas accounted for nearly 50% of the total economic value of mineral natural resources produced in the state, which includes such commodities as glass and foundry sand, construction sand and gravel, crushed stone, iron ore, gypsum and various salt compounds derived from solution salt mining. Since the start of commercial production of oil and natural gas in Michigan in 1925, there have been more than 1.25 billion barrels of oil and 6.5 trillion cubic feet of natural gas produced from more than 26,500 wells in 64 of the 68 counties of Michigan's Lower Peninsula (Fig. 10.1). Although a few exploratory wells have been drilled in Michigan's Upper Peninsula, there has never been any commercial production in the Upper Peninsula.

As of 2006, >52,000 oil and gas wells had been drilled throughout the Lower Peninsula, including 14,794 oil wells, 13,081 gas wells, 21,173 dry holes and 3,039 facility wells (Fig. 10.1). The most densely drilled areas are in and around established oil and gas fields, which generally occur in localized geographic areas, controlled by the reservoir formation and the surrounding rock layers. Key characteristics of a conventional oil or gas reservoir are the presence of a porous and permeable rock formation (the *reservoir*), encased by impermeable layers and some geological structures that prohibit the migration of the hydrocarbons (the *seal* and *trap*), which is connected to an underlying rock formation that has generated large quantities of oil or gas due to heat and pressure of burial acting on organic matter in that rock (the *source rock*). The concentration of wells in fields shows the occurrence of specific zones of porous intervals in certain formations, or the presence of good hydrocarbon traps, e.g., faults and folds. Different parts of the state have oil and gas fields in different geological formations, at different depths and in different rock types with different trap types.

Although Michigan's oil and gas history began primarily with the search for oil, the exploration and production emphasis has shifted in the last 30 years toward natural gas. When compared to oil reservoirs, natural gas

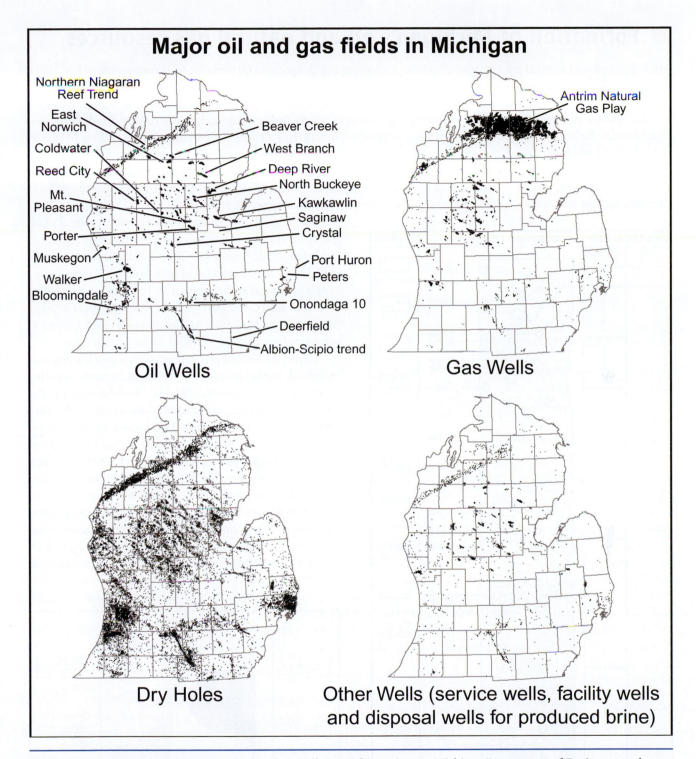

FIGURE 10.1 Locations of oil, gas and other deep wells in Michigan. Source: Michigan Department of Environmental Quality, Geological Survey Division.

reservoirs typically have much higher initial recovery of original natural gas, although enhanced recovery operations do yield additional natural gas reserves, as well. A particularly valuable use of depleted natural gas (and some oil) reservoirs is their conversion for use as underground natural gas storage reservoirs. Michigan currently leads the nation in underground natural gas storage with a capacity that exceeds one trillion cubic feet—almost 1/7 of the underground storage capacity for the entire US.

■ Formation of Michigan's oil and natural gas resources

Michigan's oil and natural gas are produced from rocks ranging in age from Ordovician to Pennsylvanian (Fig. 10.2). Small quantities of natural gas are also produced in the glacial deposits overlying the subcrop of Antrim Shale bedrock, and may occur in localized areas, where buried, Pleistocene-age, organic matter exists (Rieck and Winters 1980).

Oil and natural gas started out as plankton—microscopic plants and animals such as diatoms and radiolarians—that form the base of the food chain in aquatic ecosystems. During the Paleozoic Era, tremendous numbers of plankton and other organisms died and settled to the bottom of the shallow sea that covered much of the Lower Peninsula (Chapter 4). Burial, compaction, heat and the passage of time combined to transform these organisms into their chief chemical components—carbon and hydrogen, or *hydrocarbons*. This transformation occurred over millions of years, and for this reason oil and natural gas are considered non-renewable resources.

The organic matter that forms the raw material of oil and natural gas was largely concentrated in fine-grained mud that, under more burial and compaction, became shale. Oil geologists refer to the rock from which the organic matter is derived as the *source rock*. In the Michigan Basin, the Ordovician Collingwood Shale, Devonian Detroit River Group and the Devonian Antrim Shale (Fig. 10.2, Plate 4) are examples of source rocks for oil and natural gas.

As more sediment gets deposited on top of the organic-rich mud, temperatures and pressures increase. At temperatures >65° C (corresponding to a burial depth of about 2.1–5.5 km), the organic matter is converted to complex mixtures of hydrocarbon molecules—crude oil. Natural gas (methane), a much simpler molecule of one carbon atom and four hydrogen atoms, can be formed at the same time as crude oil, or generated later by much higher heat and pressure that breaks down the crude oil compounds into simpler molecules like methane. The latter process is called cracking, which is similar to the refining process we use on crude oil to make substances like, gasoline, diesel fuel, jet fuel, kerosene and a wide array of other petrochemicals (Fig. 10.3).

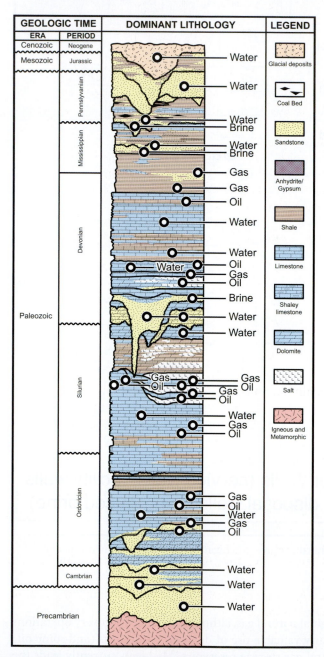

FIGURE 10.2   Locations of oil-, gas-, brine- and fresh water-producing strata within Michigan rocks, with emphasis on the Lower Peninsula. Modified from Plate 4.

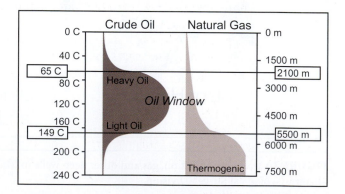

FIGURE 10.3   Diagram showing how organic materials are "cooked" into hydrocarbons. As the temperature of the buried material reaches 65° C, chemical reactions begin to transform it into forms of hydrocarbon chemicals, one of which is crude oil. The depths of burial that control this reaction are generally between 2,100 and 5,500 m (65° and 149 °C). At burial temperatures >149 °C, chemical reactions convert the crude oil to natural gas.

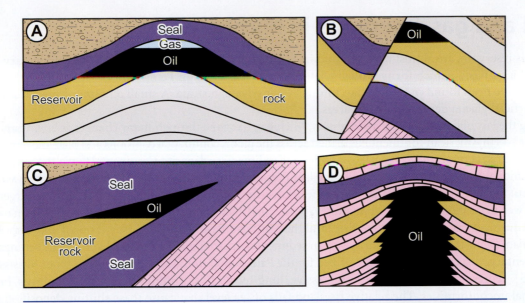

FIGURE 10.4 Idealized geological cross-sections of four types of oil and gas traps that may be found in the Michigan basin. After Boggs (2006). A. A conventional structural anticlinal trap, formed as geological forces warp rock layers upward. Because oil and gas are more buoyant than trapped water, they migrate through the porous and permeable reservoir rock to the highest part of the structure, where their vertical migration is stopped by the sealing rock layer. B. A fault trap, created by processes similar to those in A, except the rock layers break and are displaced along the plane of the fault. Vertical migration is still stopped by a seal, but a portion of the seal in a lateral direction is formed by the fault or the juxtaposition of a different sealing rock layer. C. A stratigraphic trap, formed when the reservoir layer pinches out updip into a sealing layer. D. A reef trap, common in Michigan, formed when a coral reef, with its complex community of corals or other skeleton-building creatures, construct a mound of porous sedimentary rock (Chapter 4). Layers deposited over and around the reef structure must be seals for oil and gas to accumulate in the reef reservoir.

Hydrocarbons are less dense than the water that originally occupied the pore space in sediments and rocks. Thus, they migrate upward through the pore spaces in the rock layers, because of buoyancy forces. The hydrocarbons, perhaps along with some water, continue to migrate until they encounter a layer of impermeable or non-porous rock strata, the *seal* or *trap-rock*. Shale and evaporites, e.g., rock salt, are especially common seal rocks in Michigan. The seal rock traps the oil and natural gas beneath it, in a zone of porous rock called the *reservoir* (Fig. 10.4).

All our oil production, and much of the state's natural gas production, is found in geological structures such as anticlines or faults (Figs. 2.9, 10.4). In these geologic structures, the seal layer is an inverted bowl shape that traps the hydrocarbons from migrating in any direction except down—which they cannot do because of buoyancy forces. A hydrocarbon trap may be formed in different ways, but it always involves a zone of porous rocks surrounded by, in all up-dip directions, a seal. Oil and natural gas can remain in a trap for millions of years, until a drill bit and pipe penetrate it like a giant straw, to extract the energy resources.

Although most traps for oil and gas are formed by geological structures, there is one important trap type in Michigan that forms in a completely different way. Pinnacle reef traps (Fig. 10.4D) have produced nearly 1,200 separate oil and gas fields in Michigan. They form as coral/stromatoporoid reefs grow up from the sea floor, reaching up to 200 m in height (Chapter 4). The reefs grow by the sediment trapping and binding processes associated with corals, sponges, algae and early marine mineral cementation. They form large mounds that are the reservoir; subsequent draping deposits of salt or anhydrite cover the reef and comprise the seal.

■ Oil and gas reservoirs in Michigan

Oil and gas reservoirs are almost always found in sedimentary rocks. Great thicknesses of sedimentary rocks exist in the Michigan Basin, which formed during late Precambrian through Pennsylvanian time (Chapter 4). To date, oil and gas have been found in Ordovician through Pennsylvanian strata. A small amount of gas has also migrated into the surficial glacial deposits in a few areas.

During the last billion years of Earth's history, Michigan has gone through many changes in environment and climate. As the North American continent has drifted across the globe, continental collisions and plate movements resulted in greatly varied structural and geological conditions and sedimentary deposits. Continental fluvial, terrestrial and lacustrian depositional environments occurred in the late Precambrian of central Michigan, as seen in core samples from the bottom of the state's deepest well that reached 5,324 m—the McClure Oil Company—Sparks, Eckelberger, Whightsil # 1–8 deep well in Gratiot County. Carbonates, evaporites and a few sandstones that formed in shallow marine settings dominated during most of the Paleozoic Era, until the Michigan Basin became mostly exposed above sea level in the Pennsylvanian. Deposition of these Pennsylvanian sediments occurred mainly in fluvial and deltaic settings.

Sedimentary Megasequences, first described for the Paleozoic cratonic sediments in the Upper Mississippi Valley (Sloss 1963), represent transgressive and regressive, long-term (10's of millions of years), deposits, bounded by interregional unconformities. The relative rises and falls of sea level that cause these shifting depositional environments are thought to be controlled by global tectonics and sea floor spreading that change the volume of ocean ridges, and therefore the volume of ocean basins that hold the global oceans. The typical pattern of sedimentary deposits in a Megasequence begins with a transgressive, nearshore and shelf sandstone deposited on top the previous unconformity. As transgression continues, offshore sediments of outer shelf and deeper water are deposited. The Megasequence is capped by carbonates from shelf environments. Sloss divided the Paleozoic into four Megasequences; Sauk (Cambian to Lower Ordovician), Tippecanoe (Lower Ordovician to Lower Devonian), Kaskaskia (Lower Devonian to Lower Pennsylvanian) and Absaroka (Lower Pennsylvanian to Permian).

The Mt. Simon Sandstone (Middle Cambrian) represents the beginning of Paleozoic deposition and the Sauk sequence in the Lower Peninsula (Plate 4). These coastal and shallow marine deposits mark the beginning of a thick transgressive interval of sandstone, siltstone and shale that continues into the upper Cambrian. There have been a few oil and gas shows in this clastic rock interval, but no commercial production has yet been established. These clastic strata are overlain by a thick, dolomitic, carbonate interval of the Trempealeau and Prairie du Chien (Plate 4). This carbonate interval has not demonstrated significant hydrocarbon potential to date, although there is a small amount of oil production from the upper Prairie du Chien from one field in Arenac County, and some gas from a sandstone stringer in the upper Prairie du Chien (Foster Fm.).

Major quantities of oil and gas in Michigan begin to appear in the Tippecanoe Megasequence (Sloss 1963) rocks, starting with the marine shelf St. Peter Sandstone (Middle Ordovician; Plate 4). The Tippecanoe sequence continues upward to the base of the Devonian. Major reservoir intervals in the Tippecanoe sequence also include the Ordovician Trenton-Black River open shelf deposits and the Silurian Niagaran reefs (Plate 4).

The Kaskaskia Megasequence includes most of the rest of Michigan's hydrocarbon-bearing strata. Rocks ranging from lower-Middle Devonian to the top of the Mississippian, restricted carbonates and interbedded evaporites of the Lucas, open marine carbonates of the Dundee and Traverse Formations, the black, deeper water, anoxic, Antrim shales, the fine-grained fluvial and deltaic sandstones and shales of the Berea Sandstone and the marine shelf sandstones of the Michigan Formation are all included in the Kaskaskia sequence (Plate 4). Sparse hydrocarbon production from Pennsylvanian, Saginaw Formation sandstones in the Absaroka Megasequence and the Pleistocene glacial drift occur above the Kaskaskia sequence boundary.

■ History of oil and natural gas exploration and development in Michigan

Oil and natural gas exploration and development usually follow a predictable pattern (Fig. 10.5)—initial discovery of a new 'play,' followed by frenzied development to maturity of the field and eventual decline as the reservoir is played out. In Michigan, the decline of one formation "play" was often shortly followed by the exciting development of a new one.

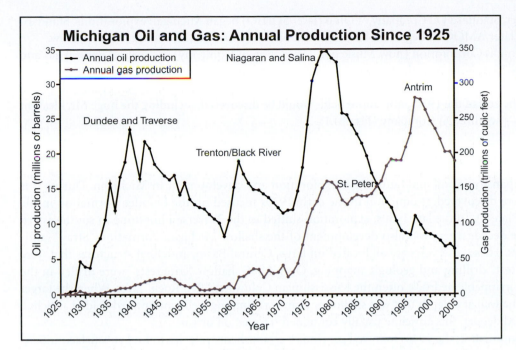

FIGURE 10.5 Annual production of oil and gas in Michigan since 1925. Major oil and gas plays are indicated at various peaks of production. Compiled from various sources.

Early discoveries

Oil Springs, Ontario, was the site of the world's first commercial oil well in 1858. A few years later, independent "wildcat" explorers from Canada drilled some test wells in several locations in St. Clair County, trying to expand on the discoveries near Oil Springs and Petrolia, Ontario. Although records for this time are scant and mostly by word of mouth, some of this exploration may have been as early as 1861 (Westbrook 1991). Michigan's State Geologist R.A. Smith (1912) reported on several wells drilled near Port Huron, in 1886 and 1887, that found "showings" of natural gas in the Traverse Limestone and oil in the Dundee Formation. By 1910, there were at least 21 wells in the Port Huron field—each producing about 10 barrels of oil per day from around 150 m depth.

Many other wells drilled in southeastern Michigan for salt brine production, or as water supply wells, also encountered oil or natural gas—usually to the detriment of the well's original purpose (Chapter 16). Numerous accounts of explosions and fires in domestic water wells (Westbrook 1991) also attested to the abundance of hydrocarbons in southeastern Michigan, especially St. Clair, Macomb, Oakland and Wayne Counties. Most of these "inadvertent discoveries" were in the Berea Sandstone, Traverse Limestone and the Antrim Shale (Plate 4). More than 100 of these types of wells were known by 1912 (Smith 1912). Often the natural gas from these wells was used for local domestic heating. Westbrook (1991, 2005) and Smith (1912, 1914) reported numerous other accounts of hydrocarbon discoveries in wells in Monroe, Lenawee, Livingston, Muskegon, Allegan and Alcona Counties between 1899 and 1920. The Deerfield Field, discovered in Monroe County in 1920, produced oil in five wells from the Trenton Formation and represented exploration expanded from the large Trenton fields just across the state line in northern Ohio (Fig. 10.1).

The beginnings of commercial exploitation of oil and natural gas in Michigan are generally credited to the discovery of the Saginaw Field in 1925 (Carlson 1927, Catacosinos et al. 1991, Westbrook 1991, 2005; Fig. 10.1). Located on the north side of the city of Saginaw, this field produced oil and minor amounts of natural gas from the Mississippian-aged Berea Sandstone at a depth of about 550 m. Development of the Saginaw Field occurred rapidly; by the end of 1927 the Saginaw Field had produced well over half a million barrels of oil. More than 300 wells were drilled in the field, with initial average production of 22 barrels per day. Although the wells gradually declined in production volume, the field has produced more than 1.7 million barrels of oil.

Most of the exploration in the Saginaw Field and throughout Michigan was done by small local companies organized by local businessmen and investors. Sun Oil Company was the first "major" oil company to operate in Michigan. Sun Oil had been previously very successful in developing a large oil field in northwestern Ohio and had a refinery in Toledo. Shortly thereafter, Standard Oil Company of Ohio (later SOHIO) began Michigan explorations. Standard Oil Company of Indiana (later AMOCO) began explorations and built a refinery at Zilwaukee, near Saginaw.

In 1927, the Muskegon Oil Corporation (now Muskegon Development Company) discovered natural gas and oil at 520 m in the Traverse Limestone near the town of North Muskegon. Initial average oil production from individual wells in the Muskegon Field was hundreds of barrels per day, dwarfing the average per well production from the Saginaw Field. Before the end of the 1920s, nine more fields would be discovered, including the huge Mt. Pleasant field, by another "major"—the Pure Oil Company (Fig. 10.1).

Rapid expansion of discoveries

The 1930s saw a major expansion of oil and natural gas exploration and development in Michigan. During this time period, >65 fields were discovered. Production in the early 1930s focused on the Dundee Formation in the Central Michigan Basin (Plate 4). In the late 1930s, exploration shifted to the Traverse Limestone in southwestern Michigan. Throughout the decade, there was also development of the shallow Michigan Formation "Stray" sandstone natural gas reservoirs. These reservoirs are all located on large, Central Basin, anticlinal structures that were discovered through "core test" drilling and geologic mapping. Over 4,000 shallow "core tests" were drilled in the 1930s and early 1940s to a mappable bedrock, often the Mississippian Coldwater "Red Rock" layer. When the target layer was encountered in the well at a depth that was shallower than surrounding wells, an upward-folded anticline was identified. When drilled deeper, this anticline usually contained trapped oil or gas.

Exploration and development in the 1940s followed previously established strategies to find subsurface anticlinal structures with hydrocarbon accumulations. Over 8,600 wells were drilled throughout the Lower Peninsula during this decade, and the resulting structural contour maps showed the locations of many anticlinal features that would be eventually drilled and produce hydrocarbons. One of the largest of these structures is the Reed City field in western Osceola and Lake Counties (Fig. 10.1). It was the single largest field discovered during the 1940s, and produced natural gas from four horizons (Table 10.1). Another significant discovery during that decade was the Deep River field, in Arenac County, in the Dundee Limestone. Unlike most productive oil fields up to this point, the Deep River is not developed on top of a structural anticline. Instead it is a long, narrow, linear zone of dolomitized/altered limestone surrounded by dense, non-porous limestone, thought to be related to hydrothermal dolomitization along a fault (Wylie and Wood 2005).

During the 1950s, new technology made huge impacts on hydrocarbon exploration. Gravimeters—instruments that can measure minute differences in the Earth's gravity—offered new images of subsurface strata, allowing geophysicists to locate buried Silurian pinnacle reefs, which are often natural hydrocarbon reservoirs (Chapter 4; Fig. 4.4B). The first discoveries in the Middle Silurian reef reservoirs of St. Clair County established the potential for stratigraphic-style hydrocarbon traps (Fig. 10.4) that would dominate Michigan's exploration activities throughout most of the 1970s and 1980s.

Michigan's pinnacle reefs occur in a belt that nearly encircles the Michigan Basin (Figs. 4.4, 10.6). Typically, each reef field represents a mass of carbonate rock that was deposited by skeletal-producing marine organisms (corals, sponges, stromatoporoids) in reef communities. Because the reefs grew much more rapidly than the adjacent non-reef areas, thousands of mounds, ranging from 15 to >150 m in height, developed. During the Silurian, the reef barrier caused significant restriction of the interior of the Michigan Basin, such that during periods of sea level drop, abundant evaporite deposits formed, to overlay and eventually bury/seal the reefs (Chapter 4), most commonly the Salina Group evaporates, i.e., halite and/or anhydrite. The evaporate seals kept the hydrocarbons, which had migrated into the porous reef structure from underlying shale beds, trapped in the reef. About 40 such fields were found in southeastern Michigan from the mid-1950s through the 1960s. Each Niagaran reef field is a geographically and laterally isolated carbonate buildup. Most are single reef developments. A few of the largest reefs, however, are actually several individual reefs that had coalesced into one reef complex before growth terminated. Reef fields range in area from a few, to several hundred, hectares.

The other notable event during this decade was the 1957 chance discovery, on the advice of a fortuneteller, of the Albion-Scipio field that spans Hillsdale, Jackson and Calhoun Counties (Fig. 10.1; Table 10.1). The Albion-Scipio field reservoir is a fractured, hydrothermally dolomitized portion of the Middle Ordovician Trenton and Black River Formations (Plate 4). It is the state's only *giant field*—defined as those that have produced >100 milion barrels of oil. Over 700 wells have been completed into this reservoir that has produced around 125 million barrels of oil and

TABLE 10.1   The largest producing oil and gas fields in Michigan, as of 1986

Field Name	Producing rock unit	Year of Disc	County	Depth (m)	Cum Oil 1986 (BBLS)	Cum Gas 1986 (MCF)	Barrel of oil equivalent (BOE) 1986	Rank oil	Rank gas	Rank BOE
Albion-Pulaski-Scipio Trend	Trenton-Black River (dolomite)	1957	Hillsdale	1090	132,130,227	220,260,151	168,840,252	1	1	1
Reed City	Reed City (dolomite)	1941	Oseola	1093	49,212,857	13,262,556	51,423,283	3	9	2
Porter	Dundee (limestone)	1931	Midland	1041	50,546,816	4,965,878	51,374,462	2	20	3
Mount Pleasant	Dundee (limestone)	1927	Midland	1081	29,190,203	7,965,509	30,517,788	4	15	4
Deep River	Dundee (dolomite)	1943	Arenac	852	27,281,203	0	27,281,203	5	29	5
Coldwater	Dundee (limestone)	1944	Isabella	1125	22,312,167	6,277,030	23,358,339	6	16	6
Buckeye North	Dundee (limestone)	1936	Gladwin	1102	20,909,734	9,781	20,911,364	7	28	7
Beaver Creek Unit	Richfield (dolomite)	1947	Crawford	1268	16,418,262	21,020,025	19,921,600	10	4	8
East Norwich	Richfield (dolomite)	1942	Missaukee	1338	15,951,039	15,718,982	18,570,869	13	6	9
Walker	Traverse (limestone)	1940	Kent	342	17,784,287	3,658,751	18,394,079	8	25	10
Freeman Redding	Dundee (limestone)	1938	Clare	1184	16,981,158	1,945,432	17,305,397	9	26	11
Kawkawlin	Dundee (dolomite)	1939	Bay	1071	16,269,991	0	16,269,991	11	29	12
West Branch	Dundee (limestone)	1934	Ogemaw	808	16,113,322	78,936	16,126,478	12	27	13
Chester 18 - 30N - 02W	Niagaran (dolomite)	1971	Otsego	1845	13,001,360	9,416,003	14,570,694	14	13	14
Headquarters	Richfield (dolomite)	1952	Roscommon	1569	11,274,640	4,248,560	11,982,733	15	24	15
St. Helen	Richfield (dolomite)	1941	Roscommon	1274	8,742,534	14,656,999	11,185,367	20	7	16
Rose City	Richfield (dolomite)	1942	Ogemaw	1257	9,295,996	9,908,970	10,947,491	19	12	17
Bloomingdale	Traverse (limestone)	1938	Van Buren	379	10,071,247	0	10,071,247	16	29	18
Peters	Niagaran (dolomite)	1955	St. Clair	727	5,953,689	23,234,018	9,826,025	29	3	19
Onondaga 10 - 01N - 02W	Niagaran (dolomite)	1971	Ingham	1153	7,908,077	10,527,645	9,662,685	22	11	20
Adams North	Dundee (dolomite)	1940	Arenac	885	9,591,484	0	9,591,484	17	29	21

(continued)

TABLE 10.1   The largest producing oil and gas fields in Michigan, as of 1986 (continued)

Field Name	Producing rock unit	Year of Disc	County	Depth (m)	Cum Oil 1986 (BBLS)	Cum Gas 1986 (MCF)	Barrel of oil equivalent (BOE) 1986	Rank oil	Rank gas	Rank BOE
Salem	Traverse (limestone)	1937	Allegan	482	9,504,515	0	9,504,515	18	29	22
Kalkaska 21 - 27N - 08W	Niagaran (dolomite)	1971	Kalkaska	2000	6,802,956	10,751,849	8,594,931	27	10	23
Hamilton	Richfield (dolomite)	1952	Clare	1568	7,221,133	4,445,484	7,962,047	25	23	24
Crystal	Dundee (dolomite)	1935	Montcalm	971	7,934,350	0	7,934,350	21	29	25
Fork	Dundee (limestone)	1942	Mecosta	1172	7,777,026	0	7,777,026	23	29	26
Columbus Sec 03	Niagaran (dolomite)	1971	St. Clair	853	6,797,581	4,979,326	7,627,469	28	19	27
Stoney Lake	Traverse (limestone)	1946	Oceana	497	7,604,154	0	7,604,154	24	29	28
Muskegon	Traverse and Dundee (limestone)	1928	Muskegon	518	7,056,391	0	7,056,391	26	29	29
Rapid River 24 - 28N - 07W	Niagaran (dolomite)	1970	Kalkaska	2063	1,894,917	27,592,662	6,493,694	34	2	30
Boyd	Niagaran (dolomite)	1961	St. Clair	749	2,242,567	19,989,573	5,574,163	33	5	31
Bear Lake 22 - 23N - 15W	Niagaran (dolomite)	1974	Manistee	1384	3,471,073	8,258,832	4,847,545	30	14	32
Frederic 10 - 28N - 04W	Niagaran (dolomite)	1971	Cradford	2123	3,088,006	4,504,803	3,838,807	31	22	33
Rapid River 32 - 28N - 07W	Niagaran (dolomite)	1973	Kalkaska	1955	2,640,384	5,498,100	3,556,734	32	18	34
Northville	Trenton-Black River (dolomite)	1954	Washtenaw	1340	1,150,593	14,332,358	3,539,319	37	8	35
Grant 29 - 25N - 12W	Niagaran (dolomite)	1973	Grand Traverse	1743	1,646,237	6,011,022	2,648,074	36	17	36
Onondaga 21 A - 01N - 02W	Niagaran (dolomite)	1971	Ingham	1106	1,827,463	4,845,940	2,635,120	35	21	37

250 billion cubic feet of natural gas (Table 10.1). Production here has doubled the oil production of the state's next largest field, Porter Field (Fig. 10.1). The entire trend is over 56 km long and up to 2.4 km wide. This type of stratigraphic/diagenetic trap field results from the local dolomitization (recrystallization of limestone) around faults and fractures within otherwise dense and non-porous limestone.

The modern era

The 1970s began with Albion-Scipio drilling winding down. Extension of the field to the NW, however, accidentally crossed the belt of Silurian reefs that nearly encircles the basin (Fig. 10.6). As a result, discoveries in the next two decades would confirm that the Michigan basin was almost entirely encircled by these reefs.

Several wells also penetrated productive reefs on the way down to the Ordovician Trenton-Black River target in Calhoun County (Fig. 10.1). These discoveries suggested that there existed a broad fairway of potential reef targets across southern Michigan. Expansion of exploration for Silurian reefs throughout the southern Lower Peninsula continued, therefore, through the 1970s, 1980s, and 1990s, in Oakland, Livingston, Ingham, Eaton and Calhoun Counties. More than 330 individual reefs are now known in the counties of southern Michigan. However, most are not nearly as large in area or as productive of oil or gas as the initial ones discovered in St. Clair County. Many of the newer fields are only one-well fields, but they may nonethe-

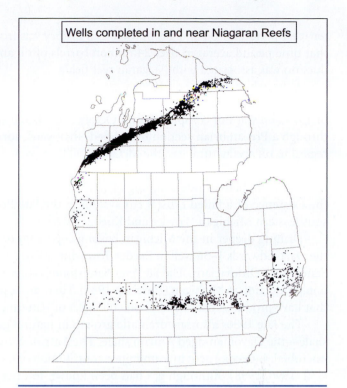

FIGURE 10.6 Locations of wells completed into and next to Silurian Niagaran Pinnacle Reefs. Note that the well locations outline the Northern and Southern Reef Trends. Wells in the Albion-Scipio and Stoney Point oil fields (Fig. 10.1) also are shown in the south central part of the state, because those wells drilled through the Niagaran on the way down to the Trenton-Black River. Source: D. Barnes, Western Michigan University.

less eventually produce hundreds of thousands of barrels of oil and some associated natural gas. The Southern Niagaran Reef Trend covers eight counties from St. Clair to Calhoun (Fig. 10.6). Cumulative production from this Trend exceeds 100 million barrels of oil and 400 billion cubic feet of natural gas. Porous reservoir rock in these reefs is mostly controlled by the original depositional facies, but may be overprinted by diagenetic alteration of fracturing and dolomitization. Due to the mixed patterns of sediment types and their diagenesis, some reefs produce throughout their entire volume. Other reefs only produce around their perimeter, and still others only produce in the central core of the reef feature.

A few discoveries of Silurian reefs in the northern and western Lower Peninsula in the early 1950s, and again in 1969, confirmed that reefs could also be found in other parts of the basin (Fig. 10.6). Development of the northern part of the basin for Silurian reefs then began in earnest in 1970, with discoveries in Grand Traverse, Kalkaska and Otsego Counties. Drilling in these counties, along with Manistee County discoveries in the mid-1970s, would dominate the Michigan exploration scene for the next 20 years. Hydrocarbon production in the northern and western portions of the Silurian reef trend would far surpass that in the southern part. There are nearly 800 known reefs in parts of 13 counties, from Presque Isle in the NE to Ottawa on the west side of the Michigan Basin. Cumulative production from the Northern Reef Trend has exceeded 325 million barrels of oil and nearly two trillion cubic feet of natural gas.

In the 1970s, rapid expansion of drilling and field discovery occurred on Northern Lower Peninsula Silurian reefs, with nearly 500 new fields discovered. About 130 new fields were also discovered in the Southern Reef Trend in the 1970s. The decade of the 1970s produced around 225 million barrels of oil and almost 874 billion cubic feet of natural gas, and most of this production was from the Niagaran reefs. Niagaran reef exploration and development continued at a strong pace through the 1980s, with more than 360 additional fields discovered in the Northern and Southern Trends. The 1980s hold the decadal record for total hydrocarbon production in the state, with more than 238 million barrels of oil production and an additional 1.4 trillion cubic feet of natural gas. The most productive ten-year period for oil and gas in Michigan history was from 1975 to 1984; annual hydrocarbon production during that time period averaged over 24 million barrels of oil and 136 billion cubic feet of natural gas. Most of this production was associated with Niagaran reef fields.

Although the 1970s and 1980s were dominated by the Niagaran reef play, several other noteworthy events also occurred. The deepest hole ever drilled in Michigan spudded in North Star Township of Gratiot County in spring of 1974 and was not completed until October of 1975. It reached a total depth of 5,324 m, in a basalt dike that cut through a Precambrian section of red beds that were more than 1,500 m thick. Although declared a dry hole with regard to oil and natural gas, the McClure Oil Company-Sparks, Eckelberger, Whightsil, #1–8 well proved to be an important scientific test. Information derived from well data, and associated seismic, gravity and magnetic surveys, led to a much better understanding of central Michigan Basin deep structure. Analysis of these data demonstrated the existence of a failed crustal rift system in the late Precambrian that extended from the Upper Peninsula to southeastern Michigan (Fowler and Kuenzi 1978).

Drilling deeper in the Michigan basin gained a lot of additional momentum in 1980, with the completion of the Dart-Edwards 1–36 well in Reeder Township, Missaukee County, and its discovery of natural gas in the St. Peter Sandstone (Ordovician). The St. Peter Sandstone is currently the geologically oldest and deepest zone of hydrocarbon production in Michigan (Harrison 1987). There are approximately 75 fields in the St. Peter Sandstone in Michigan that have produced over 800 billion cubic feet of natural gas.

The late 1980s also saw dramatic growth in natural gas production from the shallow, restricted marine, black shale—the Devonian-aged Antrim shale. The Antrim natural gas has been determined to be primarily the result of microbial (biogenic) activity with minor contribution of thermogenic natural gas from deeper into the basin (Martini et al. 1996, 1998). Although gas had been known to exist in the Antrim Shale was known for decades, it was not considered a serious zone of commercial production. During the 1970s and 1980s, thousands of wells were drilled in the northern Lower Peninsula for Niagaran reefs. In each of these wells, strong natural gas shows were always encountered when drilling through the Antrim Shale. Most operators considered these "nuisance shows," until the Niagaran reef production began significant declines and a few operators began novel completion and processing of the Antrim Shale natural gas reserves. Two major problems in Antrim natural gas production had kept most operators from trying this play. First, a considerable amount of formation water is produced initially with the gas. It was not uncommon to see a barrel of water produced for every thousand cubic feet of natural gas (1 MCF). Second, the maximum rate of natural gas production was often less than 100 MCF per day. Michigan operators were used to having natural gas wells that produced thousands or even tens of thousands of MCF of natural gas per day. The high cost of water disposal and low volume of natural gas production seemed to make the Antrim Shale a marginal or even uneconomic natural gas play. As a result, a few operators decided on a different approach to producing the Antrim Shale natural gas. Instead of completing and producing individual wells, as had previously been common practice, Antrim operators decided to drill multiple wells in an area and connect them to a central processing facility to process the natural gas. A single water disposal well was then drilled to a deeper, often Traverse or Dundee, formation and all the water from all the wells in that project was disposed of, down one well. Dozens of Antrim natural gas wells could now be handled by a single disposal well. The produced natural gas was then piped to another processing facility to remove CO_2 and other impurities. Natural gas from hundreds, sometimes thousands, of wells was treated at the natural gas processing facilities that were actually owned by Michigan natural gas utilities that purchased the natural gas. This economy of scale proved profitable for the operators, allowing rapid and extensive developmental drilling for Antrim gas.

Another factor in the rapid development of Antrim shale natural gas was the federal Section 29-unconventional fuels tax credit in place in the late 1980s and early 1990s. This law encouraged capital investment in drilling and infrastructure for Antrim natural gas and provided an opportunity for research and experimentation that brought much new technology to the play. One example is the development of high volume, electric, submersible pumps that rapidly dewatered the near-borehole environment and allowed for increasingly higher rates of natural gas production. As water production declined in the Antrim reservoir, natural gas production dramatically increased. Standard well completion practices now include using a post-drilling fluid and sand mixture that is injected into the producing zone under high pressure so as to fracture the formation and place sand in the fractures to allow better flow of natural gas and water out of the formation.

Throughout the 1990s and into the 2000s, the drilling and production of Antrim shale wells has dominated the Michigan oil and natural gas scene. From 75–90% of the wells drilled in Michigan during this 15-year period have been Antrim wells. During this time of Antrim peak production, over 9,000 commercial wells were drilled in nine counties in the northern Lower Peninsula. The play area extends from Alpena to Manistee Counties (Fig. 10.1B) and has produced over 2.5 trillion cubic feet of natural gas, making it the most prolific natural gas zone in the Michigan Basin. Antrim exploration and expansion continues in every direction from the core area (Fig. 10.1B), but mainly to the north and west, as well as filling in some areas in the heart of the trend that might have been overlooked before.

As of 2007, many of the historical plays and explorations trends have dramatically declined in productivity. Many of the fields discovered in the 1920s through 1950s are now abandoned or contain only a few stripper wells that produce one or two barrels per day. Even the giant Albion-Scipio field that once had over 700 producing wells is now down to less than a dozen, each only producing a few barrels per day. New fields are, however, still being discovered in the Niagaran Reef trend and the St. Peter Sandstone. Infill and horizontal drilling in known fields has also been able to recover some of the undrained reserves. New wells continue to be drilled for Antrim Shale gas, as the area of production continues to expand across the northern Lower Peninsula. The use of high resolution three-dimensional seismic techniques for exploration has found new traps in the Ordovician Trenton/Black River formations, outside of the Albion-Scipio field. Use of 3-D seismic has also fostered discoveries in the Devonian Traverse Limestone and Silurian Burnt Bluff Group. As can be seen, new technologies show that continued exploration throughout the Michigan Basin will lead to discoveries of new fields that will provide additional energy resources from Michigan's geological formations well into the 21st century.

■ Conclusions

The Michigan Basin is a rich, hydrocarbon-bearing region that has generated in excess of a billion of barrels of oil and trillions of cubic feet of natural gas. The number of oil and natural gas wells drilled in the Basin approached 60,000 by the late 2000s. The challenge for future explorers is to find reservoirs where these natural resources still lay buried. Throughout hydrocarbon exploration and development history in Michigan, wildcat drilling, innovative ideas and new technologies have combined to provide new opportunities that resulted in significant additional energy resources. Each hydrocarbon play or formation has had a development trend documenting rapid growth, due to expanding exploration and development after initial discovery, to an inevitable decline (Fig. 10.5). Numerous plays in Michigan have been through this cycle. The most recent is the Antrim Shale that saw great growth in the 1990s and is now experiencing decline. Whether it will be drilling deeper, as was the case with the St. Peter Sandstone in the 1980s, or re-evaluating bypassed shallower zones, as with the Antrim Shale in the 1990s, Michigan operators will continue to seek the next producing zone.

New technologies are continually being developed to access the remaining large reserves of unrecovered or bypassed oil remaining in the basin. Horizontal drilling, three dimensional seismic exploration, water, and chemical or CO_2 flooding to enhance oil recovery, have all been tried with success. It is likely that these and many other types of secondary and tertiary efforts will be tried in the future to recover valuable energy resources. Additional applications of fundamental geological knowledge and the development of new and innovative technologies will continue to allow recovery of precious hydrocarbon resources in cost-effective and environmentally safe ways to energize our future.

Literature Cited

Boggs, S. Jr. 2006. Principles of Sedimentology and Stratigraphy. Pearson/Prentice Hall, Upper Saddle River, NJ.

Carlson, C.G. 1927. Geology of the Saginaw oil field, Michigan, and discussion of Michigan's oil prospects. Bulletin of the American Association of Petroleum Geologists 11:959–965.

Catacosinos, P.A., Daniels, P.A. and W.B. Harrison III. 1991. Structure, stratigraphy and petroleum geology of the Michigan Basin. American Association of Petroleum Geologists, Petroleum Basins Series: Interior Cratonic Basins. pp. 561–601.

Fowler, J.H. and W.D. Kuenzi. 1978. Keweenawan turbidites in Michigan. Journal of Geophysical Research 83:5833–5843.

Harrison, W.B. III. 1987. Michigan's "deep" St. Peter gas play continues to expand. World Oil Magazine (April):56–61.

Martini, A.M., Budai, J.M., Walter, L.M. and M. Schoell. 1996. Microbial generation of economic accumulations of methane within a shallow organic-rich shale. Nature 383:155–158.

Martini, A.M., Walter, L.M., Budai, J.M., Ku, T.C.W., Kaiser, C. and M. Schoell. 1998. Genetic and temporal relations between formation waters and biogenic methane: Upper Devonian Antrim Shale, Michigan Basin, USA. Geochimica et Cosmochimica Acta 62:1699–1720.

Rieck, R.L. and H.A. Winters. 1980. Distribution and significance of glacially buried organic matter in Michigan's southern peninsula. Physical Geography 1:74–89.

Smith, R.A. 1912. Oil and Natural Gas in Michigan. Annual Report of the Board of the Geological and Biological Survey for 1911, Michigan Geological and Biological Survey, Publication 8, Geological Series 6. 6 pp.

Smith, R.A. 1914. The occurrence of oil and natural gas in Michigan. Annual Report of the Board of the Geological and Biological Survey for 1912, Michigan Geological and Biological Survey, Publication 14, Geological Series 11. 47 pp.

Sloss, L.L. 1963. Sequences in the cratonic interior of North America. Geological Society of America Bulletin 74:93–114.

U.S. Energy Information Administration. 2007a. http://www.eia.doe.gov/emeu/cabs/topworldtables1_2.htm

U.S. Energy Information Administration. 2007b. http://tonto.eia.doe.gov/state/state_energy_profiles.cfm?sid=MI

Westbrook, J.R. 1991. Michigan oil and natural gas story: county by county. Michigan Oil and Natural Gas News, Mt. Pleasant. 208 pp.

Westbrook, J.R. 2005. A history of Michigan oil and natural gas—exploration and production. Clarke Historical Library, Central Michigan University, Mt. Pleasant. 84 pp.

Wylie, A.S., Jr. and J.R. Wood. 2005. Historical production trends suggest remaining upside for E & D in Michigan. Oil and Natural Gas Journal 103: 38–46.

Further Readings

Catacosinos, P.A., Harrison, W.B. III, Reynolds, R.F., Westjohn, D.B. and M.S. Wollensack. 2001. Stratigraphic Lexicon for Michigan. Michigan Geological Survey Bulletin 8. Department of Environmental Quality and Michigan Basin Geological Society. 56 pp. http://www.deq.state.mi.us/documents/deq-ogs-gimdl-BU08.PDF. Accessed December, 2007.

Dorr, J.A. and D.F. Eschman. 1970. Geology of Michigan. University of Michigan Press. Ann Arbor. 476 pp.

Fisher, J.H., Barratt, M.W., Droste, J.B. and R.H. Shaver. 1988. Michigan Basin. In: Sloss, L.L., (ed), Sedimentary Cover—North American Craton: U.S., The Geology of North America., Vol. D-2, Geological Society of America, Boulder, CO. pp. 361–382.

Hake, B.F. 1938. Geologic occurrence of oil and natural gas in Michigan. Bulletin of the American Association of Petroleum Geologists 22:393–415.

Huh, J.M., Briggs, L.I. and D. Gill. 1977. Depositional environments of Pinnacle reefs, Niagara and Salina Groups, Northern shelf, Michigan Basin. In: Fisher, J.H. (ed.), Reefs and Evaporites-Concepts and Depositional Models, American Association of Petroleum Geologists, Studies in Geology 5:1–22.

Iron Ores
and Iron Mining

George P. Merk

■ Introduction

In the early 1800's the Upper Peninsula was viewed as a "barren waste." However, since the first iron ore shipment of 90 kg in 1846, mines here have produced well over a billion tons of iron ore. Some barren waste!

Iron ore has really only one use—as a raw material for iron and steel manufacturing (Chapter 30). Thus, iron ore was the foundation of the American industrial revolution, providing the framework of modern life, skyscrapers, autos, appliances and more. And Michigan's iron ore from the "barren waste" played a central role.

■ Discovery of the ore

The history of Michigan's iron mining is one of continuing education and adjustment. By its nature, iron mining is a process of depletion. To endure, a mining company must learn all the ways that the iron ore deposits can occur, then discover and develop new deposits as the old ones are exhausted. To remain competitive, a mining company must continually streamline its operation, trim costs and restructure to meet the changing needs of its customers.

Favorable attention was first drawn to the Upper Peninsula through an 1841 report by Douglass Houghton, Michigan's first state geologist, describing the presence of copper on the Keweenaw Peninsula (Wallin 1977; Fig. 2.1). This announcement brought a rush of copper-seeking prospectors to the region. But to insure that all mining locations were properly located and recorded, a federal survey of the area was first required (Chapter 28). Consequently, the natives were induced to give up their claims to the Upper Peninsula lands in 1842 with the Treaty of La Pointe (Fig. 26.2).

Houghton had the vision to combine a geological survey with the linear survey of the Upper Peninsula, and to put surveyor William Austin Burt in charge (Fig. 11.1). Burt, a pioneer surveyor known for his accuracy, had invented a solar compass to determine true north (Fig. 28.13), independent of the Earth's magnetic field (whose magnetic north is offset from geographic or "true" north). In September 1844, while running a section line near present day Negaunee, in Marquette County, Burt and his crew noted remarkable variation in the direction indicated by their magnetic compass; the north end of the needle was pointing almost due west (Burt 1994). They found that the compass needle's deflection was due to nearby outcrops of iron ore. The survey crew had accidentally discovered one of the richest iron ore districts in the world (Fig. 11.2). Houghton's choice of Burt and his solar compass had paid off.

FIGURE 11.1   William Austin Burt, surveyor. Burt discovered iron in the subsurface of rocks in the Upper Peninsula because of deflection of his compass needle, while mapping near Negaunee. Photo from Burt (1985). Courtesy of the Karl Mark Pall Collection.

■ The geology of iron formations

Iron is the 4th most abundant element in the earth's crust, comprising about 5% of its total mass. Because iron is chemically reactive, it combines readily with other elements to form a variety of iron-bearing minerals, such as hematite, magnetite and goethite. Rocks with large amounts of iron minerals are referred to as iron formations. One particularly interesting and common type of iron formation in Michigan contains iron-rich minerals in layers, alternating with silica-rich layers of chert; these rocks are our famous *banded iron formations*, commonly abbreviated as BIF (Goldich 1973; Fig. 11.3). Also present are fossil stromatolites, consisting of filament-like cyanobacteria, and spore-like *Eosphaera spiralis*, a probable photosynthetic algae (Han and Runnegar 1992).

The origin of iron formations has been somewhat of a puzzle, because of their apparent confinement to the earliest eons of Earth history, the Archean and Proterozoic, and because iron and silica show different chemical behaviors today. Iron tends to be transported under acidic conditions, and precipitated under alkaline conditions, whereas silica reacts in the opposite manner. The association of iron with silica in the BIFs, therefore, appears not to be related to pH, but to oxygen content of the water that the minerals formed in.

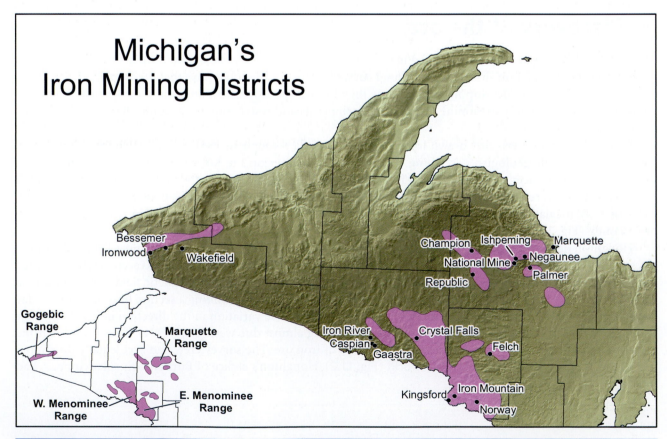

FIGURE 11.2   Generalized map of the major iron ranges and mining districts of the Upper Peninsula.

FIGURE 11.3   Two photos of banded iron formation (BIF) rock, which consists of thin, uniform layers of red hematitic chert alternating with gray bands of specularite, from Jasper Knob, Negaunee. Photos by R. Schaetzl.

Ancient, Precambrian seas were very oxygen-poor, while the atmosphere was rich in CO_2. The abundance of carbon dioxide would have caused acidic rain and acidic ground water, which would have dissolved iron from the rocks on the (then barren) land. The low oxygen content of the waters would have allowed this iron to be transported in its soluble, reduced, ferrous (Fe^{++}), form into the Early Proterozoic seas. And, with a greater carbon dioxide content, the less-alkaline sea water could have carried large amounts of dissolved iron and calcium as well. In such an oxygen-poor environment as these oceans were, iron oxide minerals could form only locally where the ferrous iron could be oxidized to ferric (Fe^{+++}) iron. But what would have caused the seas to suddenly (geologically speaking) become oxygen-rich, if only locally? It has been suggested that colonies of photosynthetic bacteria and algae created such local, oxygen-rich oases, around stromatolites living beneath the wind-mixed surface layer of a stratified Early Proterozoic sea (Kappler et al. 2005). Where the depositional environment was oxidizing, iron oxide and iron silicate minerals could have formed, while under anaerobic conditions iron carbonate, iron sulfide and silica minerals would form. Once free oxygen became more generally abundant in the oceans, most iron minerals were deposited in oxide form, and the association of iron with silica ceased, ending the age of the banded iron formations.

   After the iron formations were deposited, the Great Lakes region was involved in intense crustal deformation and mountain building (Chapter 3). The iron formations were so complexly folded and broken by faults that in places they now extend to depths of more than 1,200 m beneath the surface (LaBerge 1994). Magmas (molten rock) intruded into the iron formations, cooling to form cross-cutting dikes of igneous rocks. The great heat and pressure resulting from deep burial, crustal compression and igneous intrusions subjected the iron formation to varying degrees of metamorphism. In those parts of the iron formation that were most strongly metamorphosed, the iron oxide minerals became the hard iron ores magnetite and specularite. The soft iron ores, mainly hematite, occur in the less strongly metamorphosed iron formations. Most of the iron formations are located in three distinct areas, each now known as an *iron range*—the Marquette, Menominee and Gogebic Iron Ranges (Fig. 11.2).

◼ Discovery and early mining operations in Michigan's three iron ranges

The first iron mines in the Marquette Range were opened in 1847, and then only in the surface exposures of the hard magnetite and specularite ores, the first ore to be discovered (Van Hise et al. 1897). These mines were small open pits, where mining was primarily by hand. A few dozen men worked in the pit, prying lose the exposed ore with picks and breaking it into manageable pieces with hammers, then loading it into wagons, to be hauled away by mules (Fig. 11.4). Later, as the pits got deeper and the rocks harder, miners hammered holes into the ore with hand drills, tamped in a charge of black blasting powder (they began using nitroglycerine in 1873 and the less-volatile

FIGURE 11.4 An 1860 photo from an historic open-pit mining operation, the Jackson Mine, pit No. 1. From May (1967, 184). Courtesy of Eerdmans Publishing Company.

dynamite soon after), so as to blast the ore loose. Before the railroads came to the mines, the ore was stockpiled, to be hauled by sleigh to Lake Superior in winter when the ground froze (Cummings 1909).

Development of the Marquette district began slowly, but was hastened by the building of railroads from the mines to Lake Superior ore docks in the late 1850s, the opening of the Soo locks in 1855, expansion of the New England manufacturing plants and the increased demands for iron caused by the Civil War. All of these developments added to the need for iron in the nation (Merritt 1914, Boyum 1983a, b). As a result, the Marquette District was soon covered with test pits by prospectors seeking iron ore. In 1861, when the Civil War began, there were three mines in operation. By 1865 there were seven (Beeson and Lemmer 1966). By 1873, the 40 pits carved into the Marquette Range iron formations had yielded an annual iron ore production of one million tons.

Some 80 km south of the Marquette District are the three segments of the Menominee Range, or District—the second great iron-producing area to be discovered in the Upper Peninsula (Buell 1905; Fig. 11.2). The iron formations here were first reported by William Burt when he crossed a low, iron-rich ridge near Crystal Falls, during his survey of the area in 1845. Then, beds of specularite were noted near present-day Iron Mountain by federal geologists Foster and Whitney in 1848. The western part of the district was discovered when an "outcrop of iron six feet high" was noted near present-day Iron River by Federal surveyor Harvey Mellen in his 1851 report.

Exploratory work in the Menominee Range did not begin until the 1870s, having been impeded by the lack of cheap and ready transportation for the iron ore and the dominance of soft hematite ore in the district. Only when a rail line was built in 1877 to transport the ore from the mines to the Lake Michigan docks at Escanaba, could the ore in this area be mined profitably. At that time, the soft hematite ore, which later came to comprise the bulk of the ore shipped from the Lake Superior area, was contemptuously called Lake Superior mud, and ignored as worthless. The reason: in the 1870s, the Marquette District's hard ores were so abundant, and mining and furnace methods so crude, that only the hard specularite and magnetite ores were considered valuable. However, by 1874, with the development of more sophisticated smelting procedures, some furnace operators began using the more abundant hematite ores. But it would still be a decade before the soft ores were universally accepted.

The Gogebic Range, at the western end of the Upper Peninsula, was Michigan's third iron ore district to be discovered (Winchell 1904; Fig. 11.2). Its magnetic iron ore (dominated by the mineral magnetite) was first noted in

Wisconsin in 1848 by Dr. A. Randall, a government geologist. In 1872, the Gogebic's buried iron ore belt was mapped indirectly by using an instrument called a dip needle (the operation of which is described below) by Raphael Pumpelly and Thomas Brooks of the Michigan Geological Survey. The first to actually see the buried iron ore was Richard Langford, a hunter and trapper, who saw it in 1873 beneath the roots of an uprooted tree. Initial production of ore from the Gogebic District was delayed until 1884, once again because of a lack of ready transportation and the general disdain for soft hematite ores that were also present there.

Methods of iron ore exploration and development

The development of mining districts usually followed a predictable pattern. Although the first ore deposits were found mostly by accident, later discoveries were achieved by systematic explorations. These were initiated by companies or individuals to determine if land suspected of containing ore deposits was worth buying at the stated government price. Such evaluations were conducted by prospectors and geologists.

When prospecting for iron ore, attention was first paid to outcropping rocks to determine whether a region contained iron formations. However, because the bedrock in the Upper Peninsula was often buried beneath thick glacial debris, the prospector would habitually examine the banks and beds of streams, and the cavities under overturned trees, for bedrock exposures or any loose fragments of it. Once in proximity to the iron formation, the prospector looked for an outcrop of iron ore or for signs that the iron ore might be nearby, such as (1) the presence of a large boulder containing ore, (2) red, hematite-rich soil in the roots of fallen trees, or (3) the deflection of the compass needle by local magnetic attraction.

The first ores discovered were usually the hard magnetite and specularite ores (Cannon 1973). These dense ores were more readily found because of their resistance to erosion, causing them to more commonly form ridges and outcrops, as well as their ability to magnetically deflect compass needles. However, most of the iron ore mined in the Michigan districts had been the soft hematite ores. Although more abundant, this earthy ore was not as likely to deflect a magnetic needle, and was more susceptible to erosion, therefore tending to be found in lower areas and not form rock outcrops. As a result, it was much harder to find. The location of subsurface iron ores was also difficult to predict; folds, faults and igneous intrusions caused the ore to appear capriciously in pockets within the iron formation.

Knowing that the soft hematite ores never outcrop (pure, hard ores rarely do), it became evident to prospectors that something more than looking over the surface was necessary. After the few ore outcrops were found and their characteristics noted, exploration for buried iron ore was conducted by digging test pits, by dip-needle surveys (introduced in the 1860s), and by diamond drilling (in the 1870s). The diamond drill was particularly helpful; it cut out a neat core that could be lifted up intact and laid out on the surface. This core sample of the strata under the surface revealed accurately the location and depth of the ore body, and the nature and quantity of the overburden above it. The great Cliffs Shaft Mine, which had no outcrop, was discovered by diamond drilling in 1877–1878. Before it closed in 1967, this mine had produced 30 million tons of high grade, hard ore!

When an ore deposit was found, careful work was necessary to determine the quantity of marketable ore present, as defined by the volume of the deposit and its quality. The majority of mining company failures occurred because their ore deposits were not rich enough to be mined profitably. A smaller number of failures happened because the ore deposit was too small, even though the ore was of high quality.

To determine an ore deposit's boundaries, the area was first roughly mapped, noting all outcrops, then traversed with the dip needle to trace its underground outline. The dip needle works as follows. It is counterpoised, resting horizontally when there is no local attraction but dipping in a vertical plane when magnetically attracted. The direction in which the dip needle points is due to the combined magnetic effect from both the Earth and the local ore deposit. The intensity of local attraction depends upon the amount of magnetite in the rock. Dip needle exploration was generally successful in locating and tracing the boundaries of iron ore deposits because most iron ore contained enough magnetite to produce an appreciable deflection in an ordinary compass bearing.

Usually, the only iron ore rich enough to be mined at a profit occurred in small pockets within a larger area of iron formation. While most of the iron formation contained only 25–35% iron, the iron contents in some of the small ore pockets reached 50%. These rich iron ore pockets were rare, probably <6% of the iron formations.

When found, each of these pockets became a new mine; in time the iron ore districts were dotted with them. A few miners would first come in, clear the forest, build a cluster of houses near the mine, and settle another village, generally taking the name of the mine. Conditions were primitive. In the 1800s, to maintain its work force, the mining companies began providing employees with houses, general stores, hospitals and schools, a practice called *paternalism.*

By 1875, as the easily accessible, open-pit exposures became exhausted, some of the ore pockets were followed underground. Others could not, however, because they sloped downward too steeply or because the deposit was too irregular in outline. Thus, the change to underground mining began tentatively. At first, it became an operation in an underground quarry or cave. The miners simply left the overburden and drove under the capping to follow the ore. To move the ore out to the surface, inclined skiproads were built back to the ore face. If there was danger of the roof caving in, pillars of ore were left to support it.

To gain more knowledge of the buried, "pockety" ore deposits, exposed deposits were reexamined. Maps were made by following the outcrops, by charting the pits and by dip needle surveys. Nevertheless, failure to locate any additional ore deposits was common; iron ore discoveries still occurred more by happenstance than by science. Hampering all this effort was the fact that the various ways that iron ores could occur, i.e., their geologic modes of formation, were neither known nor understood. This knowledge accumulated and evolved as the dip needle, the diamond drill and the microscopic analysis of rock thin-sections (introduced in the 1870s) permitted more detailed study. Thus, it became apparent to some geologists in the 1870s that a breakthrough was needed to answer a basic question: Why were the iron ore minerals more concentrated in some places in the iron formations than others?

Roland Irving and Charles Van Hise, geologists with the US Geological Survey, theorized that the sequential increase of iron minerals, leading to the ore deposits, was the result of some sort of alteration that the geochemical iron formation had undergone (Vance 1960). But how could they prove it? Before the 1870s it was almost impossible to determine the minerals making up the finer grained rocks. But then, microscopic analysis of rock thin sections was introduced. When a rock slice is ground down into a thin section several tenths of a mm thick, the rock becomes semi-transparent. Viewed through a microscope, its minerals can then be seen side-by-side in a natural state, allowing deductions to be made about the rock's composition and, perhaps, geological history.

In their thin-section analyses during the 1880s, Irving and Van Hise were able to trace the sequence of mineralogical changes resulting from the alteration of the various iron formations into high-grade iron ores. Their data suggested that the iron ore bodies were simply extremely weathered versions of the original iron formations. The ore bodies had formed wherever locally concentrated underground water, as it flowed through the structural rock troughs, gradually oxidized the iron carbonate and iron silicate minerals, converting then to iron oxide. More importantly, these same waters also dissolved the silica from the chert and iron silicates and removed it from the iron formation. The end result was iron ores that were essentially localized concentrations of the enriched residues left behind by weathering (Fig. 11.5). The leaching of the silica amounted to a removal of nearly 50% of the original rock volume, thus allowing the iron content to increase form the 25–35% range in the original iron formation, to the 55–60% commonly observed in an ore body. The enriched residues occurred wherever downward trickling groundwater was channeled and concentrated, explaining why the iron minerals were richer in low, localized pockets. Thus, the best places to prospect for iron ore deposits in the iron formations were along the bottoms of downfolded rocks and at the intersections of faults, folds and dikes, for these naturally weaker areas in the bedrock allowed water to move through more readily. Subsequently, exploration for buried iron ores was conducted by digging test pits, diamond drilling and sinking shafts in strategic places, as suggested by the models. The accumulated knowledge from these focused explorations served as an invaluable, but never infallible, guide to the mining operations.

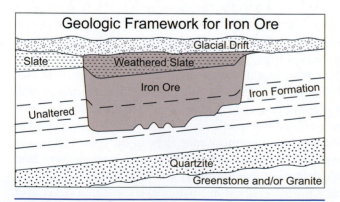

FIGURE 11.5 Diagram showing the main way that iron-bearing rocks become enriched in iron minerals via weathering and leaching.

■ The onset of underground mining operations

Once a buried ore deposit was found and a profile of its boundaries determined by diamond drilling, a vertical mine shaft was opened into the ore body. To facilitate the removal of ore, main tunnels were then cut laterally from the shaft at various levels (like the floors in a tall building) into the ore body. In some cases, the ore bodies were followed to depths ultimately as great as 1,000 m.

To produce more iron ore, the mining companies became committed to larger-scale, deep underground mines. But as the mining went deeper it became increasingly difficult, and costs rose sharply. More efficient mining methods and more powerful machinery were needed. In the late 1870s, a compressed air system was implemented to run the drilling machines and hoisting drums, to improve ventilation, and to keep the mines free from water (with pumps). Compressed-air power was then replaced in the 1880s by electric power—generated by steam from coal-fired plants. Although coal had to be imported to run these plants, electric power transformed the working conditions underground, leading to greater efficiency, ore production and mine safety (Fig. 11.6). The candles formerly used in the miners' caps (Fig. 11.7) gave way to brighter carbide lamps, and these in turn gave way to brilliant lamps powered by batteries. In 1892, electric trams, which could pull as many as 10 cars of ore at once to the surface, advanced production. Further modernization occurred in 1910 when electricity generated by hydro-electric generators at local waterfalls became available, eliminating the need for coal to run the coal-fired electric generators.

From 1890 to 1900, Michigan led nation in iron ore production. Michigan's iron mining industry had become a big business, vital to a growing nation whose steel mills had become dependent upon regular shipments of high quality iron ore. To maintain its production schedule, Michigan iron mines were committed to maintain expensive exploration programs to find and develop new ore deposits as the old ones were depleted. And to meet its growing financial demands, in this period of alternating boom and bust economic cycles, the mining companies continually had to strive to reduce their operational costs and to maintain cash reserves for periods of unexpected expenses. A popular method for Michigan's mining companies to meet these production and financial demands was through company mergers. The pooling of resources permitted greater operating efficiencies,

FIGURE 11.6 An 1894 view of the Chapin Mine's D shaft complex in Iron Mountain, looking east. The Millie Mine, originally the Hewitt Mine, can faintly be seen above and to the left of the shaft housing near the crest of Millie Hill. Pewabic Hill rises in the background. From the collection of the Menominee Range Historical Museum.

FIGURE 11.7 Photograph of eleven of the twelve men who were entombed while working on the fourth level of the Pewabic Mine, when a room above them collapsed in 1894. These eleven were rescued after over 40 hours; the 12th man was crushed to death. From the collection of the Menominee Range Historical Museum. Public domain.

lower production costs, increased capital resources and greater ease in meeting production quotas. The mergers resulted in Michigan's iron districts being controlled ultimately by a few large, successful companies, e.g., Cleveland-Cliffs Co., Pickands, Mather and Co., Oliver Iron Mining Co., and Oglebay, Norton and Co. (Havighurst 1958).

■ The era of iron ore enrichment

By the 1940s, Michigan's iron mines had removed some 650 million tons of iron ore, and it was apparent that the high-grade, direct shipping ores, mined since 1847, were becoming exhausted. Although the Marquette region still had millions of tons of banded iron formations remaining, enclosing the high-grade ore, this low-grade iron source was not acceptable for blast furnaces. As early as 1881, therefore, attempts had been made to separate the iron bands from the cherty bands in the BIF, but no practical way had been found to yield a marketable product. Unless a new source of high-grade iron ore could be found, Michigan's days as an iron ore producer appeared to be numbered.

The crisis was averted in the 1950s by the introduction of methods to concentrate low-grade ore into a form acceptable to the iron and steel makers (Chapter 30). In short, a method had been developed to enrich, or concentrate, the low-grade ores into a higher quality end product; this process came to be known as benification. The concentration process occurs at the mines themselves, so that only the finished product needs to be shipped, thereby minimizing transportation costs.

In this concentration process, the iron ore is first crushed and ground to face-powder consistency. This is usually accomplished by simply rolling it over and over in large cylindrical drums—the ore simply grinds and crushes itself. Then, when concentrating magnetite-rich rock, a mixture of the finely ground rock and water enters tanks where stainless steel drums with powerful internal magnets collect the magnetic iron particles, while the nonmagnetic silica is washed away in the waste water. When concentrating hematite-rich rock, the finally ground rock-water mixture is conditioned by adding caustic soda and a dispersant. Cooked corn starch is then introduced to selectively gather together the fine iron particles. Separation occurs in long tanks where the flocculated iron particles settle and are recovered in the underflow, while the fine silica is carried away in the frothy overflow.

FIGURE 11.8   Iron ore (taconite) pellets. Photo by R. Schaetzl.

The collected iron mineral concentrates are then mixed with water and bentonite clay, heated and rolled about in a huge drum to produce marble-like pellets, which are then kiln-fired to make them hard. These iron ore pellets are the end product of the benification process and are the raw product for the iron-making blast furnaces (Fig. 11.8). They are about 65% iron. Steel mills prefer the pellets over traditional ores. Not only are they richer and more uniform in iron content, but they reduce more readily in the blast furnace, and produce more iron with less fuel than did the direct-shipping ores (Kakela 1994). The iron ore concentrate powder can also be mixed with a fluxing agent, such as ground limestone, exactly to the specifications of the blast furnace production crew, thereby eliminating the need to add flux at the blast furnace (Chapter 30).

■ Modern challenges

Since the American Revolution, US iron mines had been the sole supplier or iron ore for American furnaces and steel mills. This monopoly was broken in the 1980s when American steel mills began importing iron ore and steel from China, Russia, Canada, South America, Africa and Australia. Not only was the demand for American iron ore declining, but the importation of less expensive foreign steel and steel products had increased substantially.

FIGURE 11.9 The Tilden open pit iron mine near Negaunee, in Marquette County. Photo by R. Schaetzl.

Michigan's mining industry confronted this challenge by phasing out its costly and now obsolescent underground mines. Mining ended in the Gogebic district in 1966, and in the Menominee in 1981. Replacing these operations were large, capital-intensive, open pit mining and pelletizing operations, and only in the Marquette Range. As of 2007, the remaining two open-pit mining operations, the Empire and Tilden Mines (Fig. 11.9), had a combined annual pellet capacity of 13.5 million tons—a total almost equal to the combined annual production from the Marquette, Menominee and Gogebic districts in their heyday! The future looks bright for these two mines, for ores are plentiful at the mining locations; the main concerns center on imported iron and steel that drive US prices down and reduce the competitiveness of local iron ore mines (Chapter 30).

■ Conclusions

For over 140 years, a steady stream of ships has carried Michigan's iron ore to the iron and steel mills of America (Fig. 11.10). This complex, interlocking operation—from open pit and mine shaft to the blast furnace—is the product of years of experience and vision. Many difficulties have been taken on—and surmounted. To endure and stay competitive, Michigan's iron mining companies have had to be innovative and nimbly evolve with the changing times. Indeed, the history of Michigan iron mining is one of continuing education and adjustment—a tribute to the generations of people who brought this great resource from an unexplored wilderness to its central place in shaping America.

FIGURE 11.10 On the top (deck) of the iron ore docks at Marquette, Michigan. Photo by R. Schaetzl.

Literature Cited

Beeson, L. and V.F. Lemmer. 1966. The effects of the Civil War on mining in Michigan. Michigan Civil War Centennial Observance Commission. 33 pp.

Boyum, B.H. 1983a. The Marquette mineral district of Michigan. Cleveland-Cliffs Iron Co, Ishpeming, MI. 62 pp.

Boyum, B.H. 1983b. The saga of iron mining in Michigan's Upper Peninsula. John M. Longyear Research Library, Marquette, MI. 48 pp.

Buell, J.L. 1905. Menominee Range: Proceedings, Lake Superior Mining Institute 11:38–49.

Burt, J.S. 1985. They Left Their Mark. Landmark Enterprises, Rancho Cordova, CA.

Burt, J.S. 1994. "Boys, look around and see what you can find." Michigan History Magazine 78 (Nov-Dec):11–15.

Cannon, W.F. 1973. High grade magnetite deposits at Republic, Michigan: their bearing on the genesis of Marquette Range hard ore. 19th Annual Institute on Lake Superior Geology, Madison WI.

Cummings, G.P. 1909. Reminiscences of the early days on the Marquette Range. Proceedings of the Lake Superior Mining Institute 14:212–215.

Goldich, S.S. 1973. Age of Precambrian banded iron formation. Economic Geology 68:1126–1134.

Han, T.T. and B. Runnegar. 1992. Megascopic eukaryotic algae from the 2.1 billion-year-old Negaunee iron formation, Michigan. Science 257:232–235.

Havighurst, W. 1958. Vein of iron, the Pickands Mather story. World Publishing Company, New York. 232 pp.

Kakela, P.J. 1994. The shift to taconite pellets. Michigan History Magazine 78(Nov-Dec):70–75.

Kappler, A., Pasquero, C., Konhauser, K. and D.K. Newman. 2005. Deposition of banded iron formations by anoxygenic phototropic Fe (II) bacteria. Geology 33:865–868.

LaBerge, G.L. 1994. Geology of the Lake Superior Region. Geoscience Press, Tuscon, AZ.

May, G.S. 1967. Pictorial History of Michigan: The Early Years. Wm. Eeerdmans Publishing Co., Grand Rapids, MI.

Merritt, D.H. 1914. History of Marquette ore docks. Proceedings of the Lake Superior Mining Institute 24:297–304.

Vance, M.M. 1960. Charles Richard Van Hise: scientist progressive. State Historical Society of Wisconsin, Madison.

Van Hise, C.R., Bayley, W.S. and H.L. Smyth. 1897. The Marquette iron-bearing district of Michigan. United States Geological Survey Monograph 28. 608 pp.

Wallin, H.M. 1977. Douglass Houghton, Michigan's first state geologist, 1837–1845. Miscelleneous Publication, Michigan Department of Natural Resources, Lansing.

Winchell, H.V. 1904. The Gogebic Range. Proceedings of the Lake Superior Mining Institute 10:158–162.

Further Readings

Allen, R.C. and H.M. Martin. 1922. A brief history of the geological and biological survey of Michigan: 1837 to 1920. Michigan History Magazine 6:675–735.

Bickford, M.D., Van Schmus, W.R. and I. Zietz. 1986. Proterozoic history of the mid-continent region of North America. Geology 14:492–496.

Boyum, B.H. 1994. William Gwinn Mather. Michigan History Magazine 78(Nov-Dec):77–79.

Dorr, J.A. Jr. and D.F. Eschman. 1970. Geology of Michigan. University of Michigan Press, Ann Arbor. 476 pp.

Evans, H.O. 1942. Iron pioneer: Henry W. Oliver, 1840–1904. E.P. Dutton and Company, Inc., New York. 370 pp.

Foster, J.W. and J.D. Whitney. 1851. Report on the geology of the Lake Superior land district. Part 2: The iron region together with the general geology. U.S. 32nd Congress Special Session, Senate Executive Document, Vol. 3, no. 4. 406 pp.

James, H.L. 1954. Sedimentary facies of iron formation. Economic Geology 49:235–293.

Jenson, M.L. and A.M. Bateman. 1979. Economic mineral deposits. Wiley and Sons, New York. 593 pp.

LaFayette, K.D. 1977. Flaming brands, fifty years of iron making in the Upper Peninsula of Michigan, 1848–1898. Northern Michigan University Press, Marquette. 48 pp.

Leith, A., Leith, C.K. and R.J. Lund. 1935. Precambrian rocks of the Lake Superior region. United States Geological SurveyProfessional Paper 184. 34 pp.

Mather, W.G. 1903. Charcoal iron industry of the Upper Peninsula of Michigan. Proceedings of the, Lake Superior Mining Institute 9:63–69.

May, G.S. and V.F. Lemmer. 1969. Thomas Edison's experimental work with Michigan iron ore. Michigan History Magazine 3(Mar-Apr):108–130.

Merk, G.P. 1994. From surveyors to scientists. Michigan History Magazine 78(Nov-Dec):16–22.

Van Hise, C.R. and C.D. Leith. 1911. The geology of the Lake Superior region. United States Geological Survey Monograph 51. 641 pp.

Winchell, H.V. 1894. Historical sketch of the discovery of mineral deposits in the Lake Superior region. Proceedings of the Lake Superior Mining Institute 2:33–78.

12

Copper Mining: A Billion Years of Geologic and Human History

Theodore J. Bornhorst and Larry D. Lankton

■ Introduction

The western Upper Peninsula has a rich geologic and human history. The area was part of an old Precambrian continent, extending into Canada, that rifted (extended) apart 1.1 Ga (billion years ago; Fig. 12.1). Thick successions of volcanic and sedimentary rocks were deposited in this rift. After the rift was filled with these rocks, hot waters moving through them filled the open pore spaces with native copper and other minerals. These copper deposits were exposed at the surface after retreat of the last continental glaciers (Chapter 6). Some 7,000 years ago, native peoples first discovered this copper, and then, later, Europeans became interested in it, spurring the first major mining rush in North America—on Michigan's Keweenaw Peninsula in the mid-1840s (Fig. 12.2). Over the next four decades, people flocked to the Keweenaw, as this modern mining district developed. By 1880, native copper mines there were producing 80% of the new copper for the US. Record production of copper occurred in 1916, but by then the situation had inverted, with less than 20% of the nation's new copper coming from the Keweenaw.

The Keweenaw is a "melting pot" of peoples from all over the globe, all with the common bond—the mining of native copper. In 1908, there were children from over 30 countries being taught in public schools there. In 1992, in recognition of the historical importance of Keweenaw copper, Congress created the Keweenaw National Historical Park. The Keweenaw Peninsula is a now dormant, world-class mining district. No other place on the planet has had such an abundance of mineable native copper.

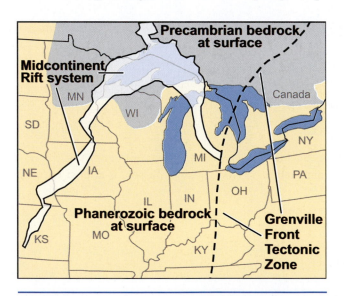

FIGURE 12.1 Location of the 1.1 billion year old Midcontinent rift system of North America. The rift system ends abruptly against the younger Grenville front tectonic zone. The rocks of the rift system are buried beneath younger Phanerozoic rocks, except in vicinity of Lake Superior. Gray areas consist of older (greater than 1.1 billion years old) Precambrian continental basement.

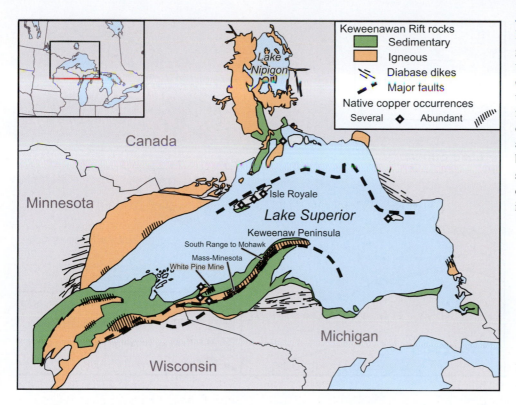

FIGURE 12.2 Generalized geology of the exposed portion of the 1.1 billion year old Midcontinent rift system in the Lake Superior region. Gray areas consist of older Precambrian bedrock and younger Phanerozoic bedrock. The map demonstrates the widespread occurrence of native copper in the rift rocks.

■ The Midcontinent rift system, ca. 1.1 to 1.0 billion years ago

Copper in Michigan's Upper Peninsula is hosted by rocks filling the 1.1 to 1.0 Ga (Keweenawan age) Midcontinent rift system. The rift system is a major geologic feature in the North American continent that extends more than 2,000 km from eastern Kansas to western Lake Superior, and then southeasterly through southern Michigan (Fig. 12.1). A continental rift is a linear zone where the Earth's crust is pulled apart, or rifted. During rifting, the crust is stretched, thinned and broken, often forming a down-dropped linear depression, or graben. As rifting proceeds, this depression often becomes filled with volcanic and sedimentary materials. The Keweenaw Peninsula is almost entirely composed of these rift-related rocks (Fig. 12.3).

Volcanic materials, mainly lava, began filling the rift about 1.1 Ga when a rising mantle plume impinged on the base of the crust. The plume consisted of hot mantle material (solid or partially melted) that rose upward until it spread laterally at the base of the crust (Fig. 12.4). The lateral movement of this "mushrooming" plume caused the crust to extend or pull apart, forming a rift bounded by inwardly dipping, normal faults (Fig. 12.5). As the hot mantle rose, it also depressurized and melted, to produce basaltic magma. Some magma seeped upward along faults, fractures and linear fissure vents, erupting onto the surface as lava flows. The basaltic lava flows erupted onto the land surface of the rifting continent (Fig. 12.7). The rocks that formed from these eruptions are today called the Portage Lake Volcanics. In the western Upper Peninsula, the thickness of erupted volcanic rocks is approximately 13 km (Fig. 12.6). In the Keweenaw Peninsula proper, the Portage Lake Volcanics consist of over 200 individual lava flows, with a total thickness of about 5 km. This lava was erupted over a geologically short span of time—2–3 million years (Fig. 12.6; Davis and Paces 1990). The center of the rift, now beneath Lake Superior, is filled with more than 25 km of volcanic rocks (Cannon et al. 1993; Fig. 12.5). Subaerial (on land) eruption of these lava flows facilitated degassing of volatiles, particularly SO_2. This degassing formed sulfur-deficient rocks, which later favored the generation of native copper, rather than copper sulfide minerals.

FIGURE 12.3
Generalized geology of the Keweenaw Peninsula, showing some place names used in the text. See Figure 12.2 for overall setting of the Keweenaw Peninsula and Figure 12.8 for the locations of the major native copper deposits, and additional place names.

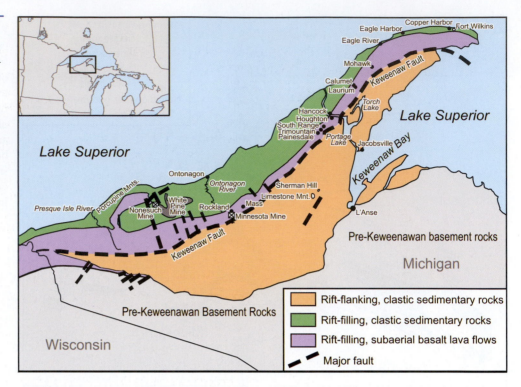

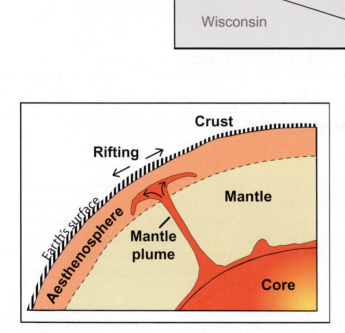

FIGURE 12.4   Cross-section of the Earth's interior, showing a plume consisting of hot rising mantle anchored at the core-mantle boundary. The hot mantle impinges on the base of the lithosphere and mushrooms outward causing extension (rifting). As the hot mantle depressurizes, it melts, generating abundant mafic magmas which rise upward and are either erupted as lava flows within the subsiding rift, or solidify beneath the surface as gabbro.

Typical lava flows in the rift have thicknesses of about 10–20 m and consist of a massive (vesicle-free) interior, capped by a vesicular (holes left behind by gases trapped in the solid lava) and/or brecciated (rubbly/broken vesicular lava) flow top. Because vesicles in rocks are commonly filled with secondary minerals (termed amygdules), vesicular flow tops are called amygdaloids, and brecciated flow tops are called fragmental amygdaloids (Butler and Burbank 1929). A few of the thicker flows can be traced laterally along strike as far as 90 km. One lava flow, the Greenstone flow, is particularly noteworthy. It is exposed from near Allouez to the tip of the Keweenaw Peninsula and on Isle Royale some 80 km to the NW of the peninsula. This flow is up to 400 m thick and, based on areal extent, contains 800–1500 km³ of magma, making it one of the largest know lava flows on Earth.

During intervals of volcanic quiescence, red-brown, pebble-to-boulder sized gravels, with lesser amounts of interbedded sand, silt, and mud, were transported from the edges of the rift by streams, toward the center, and deposited on top of the essentially flat-lying lava flows (Fig. 12.7B). These sediments would eventually lithify into rocks that are today conglomerates, sandstones, siltstones and shales. Individual layers of these clastic sediments have thicknesses from a few cm up to about 40 m. As volcanism renewed, these clastic sediments were buried by more lava flows (Fig. 12.7C). While they constitute volumetrically less than 5% of the total the rift-filling volcanic section, these sedimentary beds are important marker horizons.

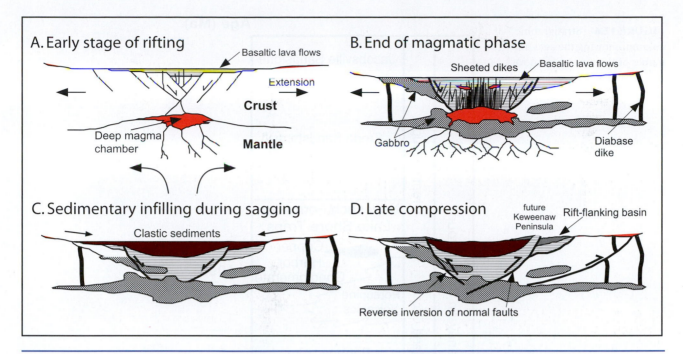

FIGURE 12.5   Cross-sections showing progressive development of the Midcontinent rift system. A. Rifting (extension) begins as a result of the impinging mantle plume. Early magmatism consists of widespread basalt lava flows from melting of mantle rocks and less common rhyolite from melting of crustal rocks. B. The rift subsides along normal faults as the crust continues to thin by extension. Basalt lava flows with occasional interflow gravels, sands and silts (clastic sedimentary rocks) fill the subsiding rift (Fig. 12.6). Gabbro underplates and intrudes the crust. Mafic magma is intruded along linear fractures to form diabase dikes. By the end of the magmatic phase of the rift, the crust is beginning to separate. As a result of movement of the crustal plate and dying of the plume, the magmatic phase ends. C. The rift continues to sag and the resulting basin is filled with clastic sediments, deposited in alluvial fans, shallow lakes, and rivers. D. Late in the history of the rift, compression as a result of continental collision along the Grenville Front tectonic zone (Fig. 12.1) inverts originally down- dropped normal faults into reverse faults and uplifts the once buried rift-filling rocks. Adjacent to the uplifts, rift-flanking basins form and are filled with clastic sediments, mainly sands. Compression also produces low angle thrust faults that cut older basement rocks and displace diabase dikes.

The rift eruptions ended rather abruptly, probably because of the dying of the hot mantle plume and the drifting of crust off of the center of the plume. As magmatic activity waned, the rift continued to sag, because the dense, thick basalts that filled the rift rested on a warm and relatively plastic crust below. Clastic sediments (gravels, sands, silts and muds) had also filled the sagging rift (Fig. 12.7C). Today, a total thickness of up to eight km of rift-filling sedimentary rocks exists beneath the center of Lake Superior (Cannon et al. 1993), with a maximum thickness of about six km exposed on the Keweenaw Peninsula (Figs. 12.3, 12.6).

The oldest rift-filling sedimentary rocks are red-brown conglomerates and sandstones (lithified gravels and sands) of the Copper Harbor Conglomerate (Fig. 12.6), deposited in alluvial fans in the rift (Elmore 1984). Alluvial fans formed near the edge of the rift, as rivers carried gravel and sand into the rift. Today, these conglomerates and sandstones are nearly continuously exposed along the Lake Superior shoreline from Eagle River to the tip of the peninsula (Fig. 12.3).

In the middle portion of the rift-filling alluvial fan unit there exists a succession of subaerial lava flows—the Lake Shore Traps (Fig. 12.6). These flows, with a maximum thickness of 600 m, represent some of the last significant magmatic activity of the rift system. The massive interiors of these lava flows are more resistant to erosion than the underlying and overlying conglomerates and sandstones. As a result, harbors at Eagle Harbor and Copper Harbor are maintained by the massive interior of these lava flows at their mouths. Remains of one of the earliest forms of life on Earth, algal stromatolites, are interlayered with the conglomerates and sandstones on the Keweenaw Peninsula (Elmore 1983). These algal mats formed in shallow lakes on the surfaces of the alluvial fans.

FIGURE 12.6 Stratigraphic column, showing the ages and names of the Keweenawan rocks in the western Upper Peninsula.

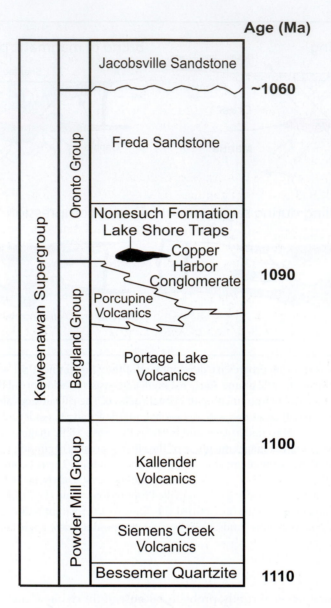

Age (Ma)

		Jacobsville Sandstone	~1060
	Oronto Group	Freda Sandstone	
		Nonesuch Formation	
		Lake Shore Traps	
	Bergland Group	Copper Harbor Conglomerate	1090
		Porcupine Volcanics	
Keweenawan Supergroup		Portage Lake Volcanics	
	Powder Mill Group	Kallender Volcanics	1100
		Siemens Creek Volcanics	
		Bessemer Quartzite	1110

FIGURE 12.7 Cross-sections, showing progressive filling of the rift with lava flows and occasional interflow clastic sediments. A. Basaltic lava flows are erupted from fissure vents within the center of the rift. B. Erosion of rocks on the flanks of the rift during periods of waning volcanism results in the deposition of widespread, but volumetrically minor, clastic sediments. C. Continued eruption of lava flows results in subsequent burial of the clastic sediments.

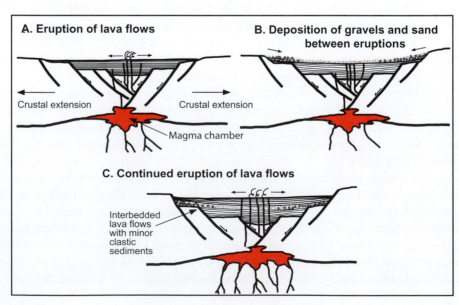

A. Eruption of lava flows

Crustal extension   Crustal extension

Magma chamber

B. Deposition of gravels and sand between eruptions

C. Continued eruption of lava flows

Interbedded lava flows with minor clastic sediments

The red-brown Copper Harbor Conglomerate is overlain by up to 215 m of rocks of the Nonesuch Formation, which is characteristically composed of grey-to-black siltstones, shales, carbonate laminates and minor sandstones, with low-to-moderate amounts of total organic carbon and pyrite (FeS_2; Fig. 12.6). These largely grey-to-black shales were deposited in lakes with bottom conditions from anoxic (low oxygen) to oxic (rich in oxygen) (Elmore et al. 1989). The anoxic conditions allowed for the preservation of the organic carbon and pyrite. Precambrian hydrocarbons seep from this unit at the now closed White Pine mine (Mauk 1992).

The last rift-filling sediments were sands, silts and muds, deposited by shallow rivers; these sediments formed the rock that today is called the Freda Sandstone (Fig. 12.6). This succession of red-brown sedimentary rocks, >3,700 m thick, almost completely filled the rift (Fig. 12.5D).

The last phase of the Midcontinent rift system was characterized by compression, probably caused by a continental collision along the Grenville front about 1.06 Ga (Cannon 1994; Fig. 12.1). The Keweenaw Fault, originally formed during rift extension, was a normal fault with the rocks towards the center of the rift dropping downward to form a graben (Fig. 12.5). Compression then caused the rift-filling rocks to be squeezed and forced upward. The originally normal Keweenaw Fault was therefore inverted into a high-angle reverse fault with many km of reverse displacement (Fig. 12.5). Other secondary compressional faults are also common in the area of native copper deposits (Fig. 12.8).

The Keweenawan rock strata dip moderately northwesterly toward the center of the rift (in what is now Lake Superior), and their dip angles increase toward the base of the section (Fig. 12.8). Some of this dip was the result of sagging during deposition of these rocks within the extending rift system. The remaining dip was the result of tilting of the beds during rift compression.

Upward motion along the Keweenaw Fault resulted in a rift-flanking basin. Over three km of red-colored, shallowly dipping sand, later to become the Jacobsville Sandstone, was deposited by rivers in this basin, during and after active reverse movement along the Keweenaw Fault (Figs. 12.3, 12.6). Although the age of the sandstone is not

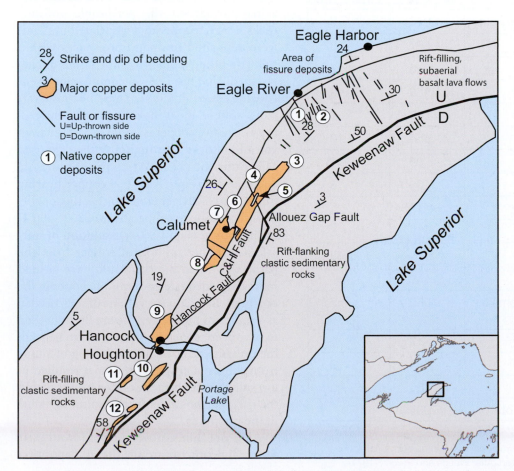

FIGURE 12.8 Locations of the major native copper deposits and generalized geologic structure of the Keweenaw Peninsula. The strike and dip of bedding indicate that the beds are steeply dipping NW of the Keweenaw fault, and shallowing towards Lake Superior. Beds to the SE are nearly flat lying, except very near the fault (for a cross-section see Figure 12.9D). Faults are closely associated with the native copper deposits and played a major role in their genesis. The names of the numbered deposits are given in Table 12.1.

well known, it seems likely it was deposited over 50 million years from the beginning of compression: between 1.06 and 1.0 Ga. The Jacobsville sandstone is a beautiful red, white and brown rock, commonly used for building stone in the region (Fig. 3.11).

Rocks of the Keweenaw Peninsula native copper mining district

The volcanic rocks that fill the Midcontinent rift system are well known for hosting widespread and locally abundant, native copper deposits (Fig. 12.2, Table 12.1). Native copper represents over 99% of the metallic minerals in the mined ore bodies of the Keweenaw Peninsula—the largest accumulation of native copper on Earth. Although native copper occurs in small amounts in subaerially erupted basalts elsewhere in the world, the Keweenaw Peninsula is the only place with so much native copper as to result in a world-class mining district. Copper elsewhere usually occurs as a sulfide mineral (copper with sulfur), but in the Keweenaw region much of the copper is in metallic form. There are also >100 different hydrothermal minerals in the Keweenaw Peninsula (Table 12.2). The major copper ore-producing rocks are geographically restricted to a 45 km-long belt from South Range to Mohawk (Fig. 12.2) within the Portage Lake Volcanics. A smaller, satellite district occurs to the SW (Mass-Minesota, Fig. 12.2). Together, these deposits of native copper fueled the 19th and 20th century mining industry.

A close relationship in time exists between native copper mineralization and the other hydrothermal minerals that filled vesicles and veins throughout the permeable volcanic rocks. Native copper and associated minerals were deposited in open pore spaces within the rift-filling rocks by hot mineralizing waters during the 1.06 Ga compression event (Bornhorst et al. 1988). These hot mineralizing waters must have been widespread, because native copper is found in Keweenawan volcanic rocks throughout the exposed Midcontinent rift in Wisconsin, Minnesota and Ontario (Fig. 12.2). The copper-bearing fluids were likely generated by heating of rift-filling basalts up to temperatures of 300°–500° C during burial (Fig. 12.9). Dissolution of only a few parts per million of copper from the basalt that filled the rift would have yielded more than adequate amounts of copper in the ore fluids. Based on the volume of rock needed as a source of the copper, the ore fluids needed to have been tapped only some 10 km beneath the present ore horizons. Degassing of sulfur from subaerial erupted lava flows resulted in low sulfur contents in the buried basalts within the rift, and subsequently low sulfur contents in the ore fluids.

The ore fluids moved upward from their source at depth, toward the sites of deposition

TABLE 12.1 Production of refined copper from selected native copper deposits: 1845–1968

Name of Deposit	Refined copper produced (kg x 10^6)	Number on Figure 12.8
Calumet & Hecla Conglomerate	1,920	7
Kearsarge flow top	1,027	3
Baltic flow top	838	12
Pewabic flow top	489	9
Osceola flow top	262	8
Isle Royale flow top	155	10
Atlantic Ashbed	65	11
Allouez Conglomerate	33	5
Houghton Conglomerate	17	4
Kingston Conglomerate	12	6
Evergreen Series	33	na
Other flow top and conglomerate deposits	62	na
Cliff Fissure	17	1
Central Fissure	24	2
Other fissure deposits	56	na
Native Copper District Total	5,007	

Names used in the text and their associated deposit: Quincy, Franklin-Pewabic flow top; Huron-Isle Royale flow top; Trimountain, Champion, South Range Mines-Baltic flow top. After Weege and Pollock (1971).

TABLE 12.2   Common minerals associated with native copper deposits of the Keweenaw Peninsula

Primary Hydrothermal Minerals	Secondary (Supergene) Minerals
analcime: $Na[AlSi_2O_6] \cdot H_2O$	chrysocolla: $(Cu^{2+},Al)_2H_2Si_2O_5(OH)_4 \cdot nH_2O$
anhydrite: $CaSO_4$	cuprite: Cu_2O
barite: $BaSO_4$	malachite: $Cu^{2+}_2(CO_3)(OH)_2$
calcite: $CaCO_3$	tenorite: $Cu^{2+}O$
celadonite: $KFe^{3+}(Mg,Fe^{2+}) \cdot Si_4O_{10}(OH)_2$	
chalcocite: Cu_2S	
chlorite: $(Mg,Fe^{2+},Al,Fe^{3+})_{4-6}(Si,AlFe^{3+})_4O_{10}(OH,O)_8$	
copper (native): Cu	
datolite: $Ca_2B_2Si_2O_8(OH)_2$	
dolomite (ferroan): $Ca(Mg,Fe^{2+})(CO_3)_2$	
epidote: $Ca_2(Fe^{3+},Al)_3(SiO_4)_3(OH)$	
feldspar (microcline, adularia): $KAlSi_3O_8$	
gypsum: $CaSO_4 \cdot 2H_2O$	
hematite: Fe_2O_3	
laumontite: $Ca_4[Al_8Si_{16}O4_8] \cdot 18H_2O$	
mohawkite: a mixture of algodonite (Cu_6As) and domeykite (Cu_3As)	
prehnite: $Ca_2Al_2Si_3O_{10}(OH)_2$	
pumpellyite: $Ca_2(Mg,Al)Al_2Si_3(O,OH)_{14}$	
quartz: SiO_2	
silver (native): Ag	

nearer the surface. The fundamental control on the movement of ore fluids to sites of deposition is permeability; the more permeable pathways were the brecciated and vesicular lava flow tops, interflow sedimentary rocks and fractures/faults. The major compressional event late (1.06 Ga) in the history of the Midcontinent rift system distinguishes it from other flood basalt provinces in the world. Perhaps this was critical to the generation of these native copper deposits, as it may have provided a network of faults/fractures that integrated the plumbing system and allowed for easier and more rapid upward movement of the ore fluids (Bornhorst 1997). Major faults also helped focus the ore fluids to areas where they intersected locally thick, permeable and porous strata (Fig. 12.9). A combination of mixing of the ore fluids with cooler and more dilute resident fluids, and the chemical reactions between the ore fluids and host rocks, likely caused the precipitation of native copper and associated minerals at about 225° C. Without sulfur in the rift-filling volcanic host rocks, copper was precipitated as native copper instead of copper sulfide minerals such as chalcocite (Table 12.2).

The copper ores

In this region, native copper ore occurs in brecciated and amygdaloidal flow tops (58.5% of production), interflow conglomerate beds (39.5% of production) and cross vein systems (about 2% of production). Small quantities of native silver (<1% of the metal recovered) accompany the native copper. The native copper ore had sufficient permeability (ability to transmit fluids) to allow the movement of hot ore fluids (hydrothermal fluids) and high

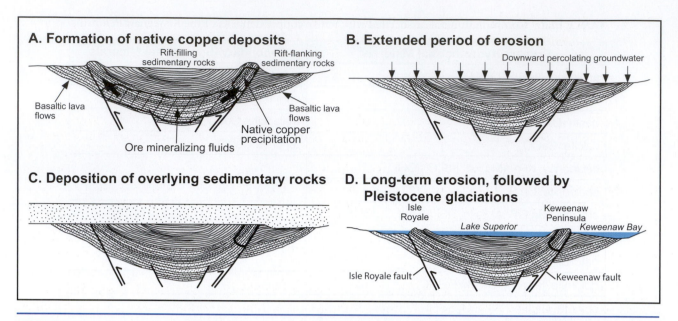

FIGURE 12.9   Cross-sections showing evolution of the Lake Superior region from the time of native copper mineralization to the present. A. Formation of native copper deposits from hot ore mineralizing fluids generated within rift-filling basaltic rocks. These fluids moved upward within the rocks and precipitated as native copper. B. After the end of regional compression and deposition of the native copper deposits, the rift rocks underwent an extended period of erosion, removing sufficient amounts of overlying rock to expose the native copper deposits at the surface. Once exposed at the surface, the native copper deposits were subjected to downward percolating groundwater. C. The exposed rift rocks were buried beneath Phanerozoic sedimentary rocks. D. Multiple glaciations in the past two million years stripped away the Phanerozoic sedimentary rocks and the softer clastic sedimentary rocks filling the center of the rift, once again exposing the native copper deposits at the surface and resulting in the present day topography.

enough porosity to have resulted in precipitation of large amounts of native copper and associated hydrothermal minerals. Native copper and other hydrothermal minerals occur as fine disseminations, as vesicle fillings (up to a few cm across) and as small-to-moderate sized masses weighing up to several tons. Brecciated flow tops (fragmental amygdaloids) are the most common hosts for native copper deposits and are "sandwiched" between underlying, barren, massive basalt of the same flow and overlying barren, massive basalt of the succeeding flow. In general, these tabular lodes are 3–5 m thick, with lateral (strike) extent of 1.5 to 11 km, and from 1.5 to 2.6 km down dip (Butler and Burbank 1929). Although interflow conglomerate beds make up less than 5% of the rift-filling volcanic succession, they host comparatively large amounts of native copper (~40% of district production). Conglomerate deposits were "sandwiched" between overlying massive basalts and underlying lava flow tops which commonly contained sand and silt in pores.

Between 1845 and 1968, the mines of the Keweenaw Peninsula produced about five billion kg of refined copper, derived from 380 million tons of ore (Table 12.1). Early mines in the district, such as the Cliff and Central mines, exploited ore veins (Fig. 12.8). Native copper veins are tabular open space fillings that occur along faults and open fractures that cut the adjacent lava flows and sedimentary layers at high angles. Veins were of slight economic importance, however, yielding only 2% of the mined native copper. Native copper in veins can occur as finely disseminated (fine particles spread through rock or other minerals) with other hydrothermal minerals, and as masses weighing many tons. The average thickness of the Cliff vein is 15 m (Butler and Burbank 1929).

Large copper masses were proportionately more common in veins than in other deposits. These large masses created problems for miners as they could not be broken by blasting. Instead, they had to be cut by hand, which was labor intensive and expensive (Broderick 1931).

Most native copper occurs within the tabular and dipping tops of lava flows and sedimentary layers. The total mass of economically mineable, native copper in these amygdaloidal or conglomerate lode deposits was many times greater than in the veins. Native copper in the lode deposits also occurs in finely disseminated forms, and as masses weighing many tons. The Calumet and Hecla (C&H) Conglomerate, the largest single native copper lode in the district, yielded 1.9 billion kg of copper over a strike length of 4.9 km and 2.8 km down-dip with a thickness of between 1.5 to over 20 m, typically five m.

The White Pine deposit

The White Pine mine (Fig. 12.3), which closed in 1996, is a well known example of a copper deposit hosted by the shale and sandstone of the Nonesuch Formation (Fig. 12.6). Unlike the mines of the Keweenaw Peninsula, at the White Pine mine about 80% of the copper occurs as chalcocite (Cu_2S), with the remainder being native copper. The White Pine deposit is nonetheless grouped as part of the Keweenaw Peninsula mining district. The White Pine deposit is a world-class ore deposit, yielding roughly 2.0 billion kg of copper and 1.4 million kg of silver from 198 million tons of ore from 1953 to 1996 (a mean grade of 11.4 kg of copper and 7.0 g of silver per ton; Johnson et al. 1995).

Most of the chalcocite is submicroscopic in size and is found in the lower five m of the Nonesuch shale (Fig. 12.6). Black-to-dark gray shales and siltstones contain the highest amount of organic matter and also the highest copper grades (Mauk 1992). The chalcocite ore grades upward into a pyrite (FeS_2)-bearing shale that lacks copper. Chalcocite mineralization is interpreted by Mauk (1992) to be a result of warm mineralizing fluids (about 100° C) expelled during shallow burial and lithification of the rift-filling sedimentary rocks. These low temperature, mineralizing fluids first flowed through the oxidized beds of the underlying Copper Harbor Conglomerate. Upon entering the reduced pyrite-bearing shales and siltstones, the copper from the fluids replaced iron in the pyrite, precipitating the chalcocite (Brown 1971). This chalcocite origin follows a sequence of events common to shale-hosted copper deposits elsewhere in the world. Unique to the White Pine deposit, however, is a second-stage of native copper mineralization that was deposited after, yet spatially coincident with, the initial chalcocite mineralization. This second-stage of native copper occurs as sheets along faults and adjacent beds, and as local disseminations in the top three m of the underlying sandstone (top of the Copper Harbor Conglomerate; Fig. 12.6). Faults (high angle normal and reverse faults and low angle thrust faults) and folds in the rocks at the White Pine mine are mostly related to late rift compression. A major fault, the White Pine fault, bisects the deposit. The close temporal association of the younger second-stage of native copper mineralization with faults generated during late compression of the rift supports the hypothesis that the second-stage mineralizing fluids were likely of the same origin as those related to native copper in the Keweenaw Peninsula. Without the superposition of the later native copper (20% of the deposit) onto the earlier chalcocite (80% of the deposit), the White Pine deposit may not have been economically feasible to mine.

■ Regional history from rifting to glaciation, ca. 1.0 billion to 2 million years ago

Following the formation of the copper deposits, the Keweenaw Peninsula was subjected to a 500 million year period of erosion, from about 1.0 Ga (end of rift related events) to 500 Ma. During this period, many km of rock were eroded, exposing the native copper deposits at the surface (Fig. 12.9). Downwardly percolating groundwater interacted with, and selectively altered, the native copper ores and produced a suite of colorful supergene minerals such as cuprite (Cu_2O), tenorite (CuO), malachite $Cu_2(CO_3)(OH)_2$, and chrysocolla $(Cu,Al)_2H_2Si_2O_5(OH)_4 \cdot nH_2O$ (Table 12.2). Today, these supergene minerals are found near the surface (<300 m) and are likely near the same position beneath the surface as they were 500 Ma.

In Michigan, the rocks and copper ores of the Midcontinent rift system were buried by Phanerozoic sediments (Fig. 12.9) associated with the deposition in the Michigan basin; this sedimentation event started in the late Cambrian (~500 Ma) and ended in the middle Jurassic (~175 Ma) (Catacosinos et al. 2001; Chapter 4). Evidence of the presence of these overlying rocks occurs as isolated outliers of Ordovician limestone, e.g., Limestone Mountain and Sherman Hill, about 35 km south of Houghton (Fig. 12.3). These Phanerozoic geologic processes were largely non-tectonic and lacked major faulting. Another period of long-term erosion then followed, from the middle Jurassic to the Pleistocene glacial period.

■ Regional history: Pleistocene glaciation and float copper, ca. 2 million to 10,000 years ago

Many of the overlying Phanerozoic rocks in the Copper Range were eroded by Pleistocene glaciers. The current bedrock topography, therefore, reflects the cumulative effect of these glacial episodes. Harder rocks, like the Portage Lake Volcanics, stood up as ridges, such as the Copper Range (Figs. A.1, A.2), while the weaker, less competent, nearly flat-lying sandstones, and the siltstones, shales and sandstones in the center of the rift, were eroded into lowlands. By preferentially eroding out the less competent rocks, the glaciers formed the western arm of Lake Superior, which follows the horseshoe shape of the rift (Fig. 12.1). The high ridge making up the "backbone" of the Keweenaw Peninsula—the Copper Range—may only have been eroded slightly. As a result, by the end of the most recent glacial retreat, native copper ores once again were exposed at the surface.

As the last glaciers retreated, about 11,000 years ago (Chapter 6), they left deposits of gravel, sand and mud, which blanketed much of the bedrock, partly or completely filled in bedrock valleys and formed ridges of their own. By removing most of the Phanerozoic rocks, the glaciers once again exposed the native copper deposits in the Keweenaw, and in so doing eroded and entrained masses of native copper. These masses of malleable native copper "floating" in the glacial ice were often smoothed and flattened. Therefore, the gravels and sands left behind by the retreating glacier contain small (cm across) to very large (25 tons) native copper masses, locally termed "float copper." The most famous example of float copper was the Ontonagon boulder, a 1,678 kg specimen visited by numerous explorers and finally transported from the Keweenaw to the Smithsonian Institution in Washington, DC, in 1843 (Krause 1992).

Water filled the scoured out Lake Superior basin as the glaciers melted. The water levels and areal expanses of the various lakes that post-dated the glaciers depended on the position of the ice front and the elevations of their outlets, all of which were affected, in turn, by isostatic crustal rebound (a result of removing the weight of the ice; Chapter 24). Glacial Lake Duluth was the largest of these glacial lakes; only locations above roughly 396 m in elevation, e.g., Brockway Mountain and Mt. Bohemia, were emergent islands in it. In all, 15 different lake stages are recognized in the Lake Superior basin (Farrand 1960). As the lake levels receded to the current level of Lake Superior, more and more of the Keweenaw Peninsula and Isle Royale emerged. The high areas could have been explored by native peoples while still islands.

As these lakes receded, native peoples began to get ready access to the Peninsula. The float copper within the surface gravels and sands had, by now, been weathered by surface waters and took on a distinct green coating from the mineral malachite. These green rocks stood out against the surrounding white, brown and gray rocks, making float copper readily discovered and collected by native peoples. Native copper, still bound within its host rock, was also exposed at the surface and marked by the same green coloration. This native copper was still attached to bedrock and it required effort for extraction, but it was also a target of the earliest mining.

FOCUS BOX: Keweenaw National Historical Park

Mining districts have finite lives, and the towns and cities within those districts typically have single-industry economies. When mines shut down, the local communities suffer contraction. People leave, shops, schools and churches close, and entire neighborhoods of worker houses can disappear.

On the Keweenaw, the long decline and final shutdown of the Calumet & Hecla mine devastated the village and township of Calumet, once the most bustling and populated spot along the mineral range. In the late 1980s, the idea was born in Calumet that maybe its future resided in its past, that maybe its history could be "sold" to revitalize the community, boost tourism and stimulate economic development. In the East, a National Historical Park

had recently been sited in Lowell, Massachusetts, a 19th century industrial city devoted to textile production. The idea gained currency in Calumet that perhaps it, too, because of its history as a key mining center, could become a unit within the National Park Service. The Park Service conducted studies of Calumet's mining core, its housing, and its commercial district, and also evaluated the Quincy mine's physical remains, about 16 km to the south. Calumet and Quincy both passed muster as National Historic Landmarks in 1988, which cleared the way for their consideration as a park. Over the next several years, local boosters, supported by Michigan congressmen and senators, politicked for a National Park, and the Park Service responded by drawing up various plans. The process of launching a new park culminated on October 27, 1992, when the US Congress passed Public Law 102–543, which created the Keweenaw National Historical Park (KNHP). The legislation stated that the Keweenaw was nationally significant because of (1) its unique geology, (2) the prehistoric use of its copper by Native Americans, (3) the importance of the region as a leading copper producer and developer of new technologies, (4) its long history of corporate paternalism and (5) because it became home to so many European ethnic groups that migrated to the US. The KNHP's Quincy unit of 485 hectares includes the mine site on the hill above Hancock—dominated by a 48 m tall shaft-rockhouse, attended by a massive steam-powered hoist—as well as the dormant Quincy smelter on the north shore of Portage Lake. The Calumet unit of 303 hectares includes the village of Calumet with its late 19th early 20th century streetscapes, and much of Calumet Township. The structures within the Calumet unit reflect a great diversity of structural types and cultural uses: mine structures, private and company-built houses, office buildings, shops, stores, schools, churches, clubs, a fire station and a major theatre and village hall. Year by year, the KNHP's reputation grows, as its attractions are further restored.

■ Regional history: Initial copper mining, ca. 7,000 yrs ago

About 7,000 years ago, humans first exploited copper on the Keweenaw Peninsula and Isle Royale (Martin 1999). Little is known about these peoples, but they did leave behind evidence of where and how they took the copper. They picked up pieces of float copper and freed the copper still bound up in rock by bashing it with hard hammer stones. When done, they abandoned their stone tools and pits, some of which reached depths of up to eight meters.

The first copper-gatherers hammered the soft metal into different shapes. Cold-working the copper made it brittle, so they heated semi-completed artifacts in a fire to anneal it, allowing them to perform more work on it. Besides hammering the copper flat, artisans hammered it around or inside forms, to give it different shapes. They used sandstone, sand and wood ashes to grind or polish the metal as the fashioned hooks, knives, chisels, awls, axes, scrapers, beads and other decorative items and tools. As they traded these copper objects, Lake Superior copper diffused across much of eastern North America (Martin 1999).

■ Regional history: Early European and American explorers, ca. 1610 to 1845

In the 17th century, European metals arrived in the New World, making the continued taking of Keweenaw copper unnecessary. Although Native Americans stopped "mining" it at this time, Europeans became interested in it. In the 17th and 18th centuries, French and British expeditions sought Lake Superior copper, but they arrived with too few men and tools to succeed. Beginning in 1820, a chain of American expeditions led to the first major mine rush of North America in the 1840s.

In 1820, Lewis Cass, governor of the Michigan Territory, and John Calhoun, the US Secretary of War, supported a 40 man expedition to Lake Superior that included the famed geographer, geologist and ethnologist Henry Rowe Schoolcraft. The expedition sought to discover what in the Lake Superior region could help open up the west and make it more attractive to future settlement—and it included an exploration of the Keweenaw. Schoolcraft subsequently led two more explorations to the copper region in 1831 and 1832, accompanied by Douglass Houghton (Fig. 2.1), who, in 1837, became Michigan's first state geologist. In 1840, Houghton explored the Keweenaw's geology again, and in 1841 reported his findings to Michigan's legislature (Krause 1991). Houghton's report stimulated great interest among geologists, miners and entrepreneurs.

In 1826 and 1842, the US government signed cession treaties with the Chippewa Indians, which gave the US mineral and property rights to the copper-rich lands. Then, in 1843, a mineral land agency was opened in Copper Harbor, which first leased and later sold property along the mineral range. Thousands traveled to seek copper in the Keweenaw, many in small boats guided across Lake Superior by colorful, French voyageurs. To get to the area, however, explorers and settlers had to cope with beautiful yet dangerous Lake Superior, with thick, tangled woods

FIGURE 12.10 Winter interrupted transport over the Great Lakes, but sometimes made travel easier on the Keweenaw itself. This early 20th century photo shows an "ice bridge" over Portage Lake, connecting Houghton with Ripley. Smelters stand alongside the Ripley shoreline on both the left and right, and the Quincy mine and its railroad occupy the top of the hill. Photo courtesy Michigan Technological University Archives and Copper Country Historical Collections.

and swamps that thwarted travel while hiding the tops of copper lodes, with black flies and mosquitoes that made summer in the woods a miserable experience, and with snow and a winter (Fig. 12.10) that lasted half the year and froze them out from the "world below" from November until early May (Lankton 1997).

■ Regional history: Opening of a modern mining district, ca. 1845 to 1890

Paying lodes of copper proved elusive in the first half-decade of mining. The earliest companies had to employ at least 200 men and sink $100,000 or more into a mine in order to first test the ground and then move into production. Because the capital requirements of copper mining were so high, while the chances of success so low, incorporated mining companies became the preferred means of opening new mines (Gates 1951). They tapped many investors, instead of just a few, so each investor had a limited stake in this risky venture.

The first mining companies searched for mass copper in fissure veins and failed to produce any bonanzas. Then the Pittsburgh and Boston Mining Company turned the fortunes of the district around. On the northern end of the Keweenaw, not far from Eagle River, the company struck it rich at the Cliff mine and in 1849 started paying out millions of dollars in dividends (Chaput 1971). Soon the Minesota [sic] mine, on the Keweenaw's southern end, uncovered a second mass copper bonanza. With profitable mass copper mines near the base and tip of the peninsula, a clutch of other mines sought riches in the middle of the Copper Range. In the late 1850s and early 1860s, the Quincy, Pewabic, Franklin and Huron mines opened not on fissure veins, but on amygdaloid lodes (Lankton and Hyde 1982). A bit later, about 20 km north of Portage Lake, Edwin Hulbert discovered the richest native copper lode, the C&H Conglomerate. By the early 1870s, the Calumet and Hecla Mining Company, working that lode, became one of the world's largest and richest copper mines (Benedict 1952).

The early mass copper mines tended to run rich in copper and then peter out fast. Nonetheless, they provided the district with its first successes. Amygdaloid and conglomerate lodes, however, produced more sustained wealth (Butler and Burbank 1929).

During the 1840s–1860s period, companies devised better mining, milling and smelting technologies to extract and process the native copper (Egleston 1879). Underground, men had first performed all work by hand. Miners

FIGURE 12.11 In the 1920s, a miner standing on rudimentary scaffolding runs a one-man drilling machine powered by compressed air. Of the 1,900 men killed underground in the copper mines, 16% of the victims fell to their deaths from precarious positions like the one shown here. Photo courtesy Michigan Technological University Archives and Copper Country Historical Collections.

used hand-held drill steels and sledgehammers to produce the shot holes that they then charged with explosives to blast the rock apart. Trammers loaded broken rock into cars and pushed them to the shafts for hoisting. For a brief time, men lifted the copper rock (ore) out of the mine by turning windlasses, which drew up bucketsful of rock at a time. Companies next turned hoisting over to horses, harnessed to sweeps that rotated a winding drum. Finally they used steam engines to lift the heavy rock and copper ore from the mine (Lankton 1991). The mechanization of mining occurred more rapidly on the surface than underground. The first important machines used underground did not arrive until 1880, when power rock drills driven by compressed air replaced hand drills (Fig. 12.11). At the same time, dynamite replaced blasting powder. Machine drills and high explosives had ushered in an era of modern mining (Lankton 1983).

The copper ore hoisted to the surface contained much more waste rock than copper; the ore averaged only 1–2% copper. Companies could not smelt their mine product without first concentrating it at a mill, where rise-and-fall crushers, called stamps, broke the rock into pieces the size of peas. Flowing water carried the heavier copper and lighter rock from the stamps to series of washing and separating machines that captured the copper, while letting the waste byproduct, the rock, tail off. The captured copper, now called "mineral," ran from 60–80% copper (Benedict 1955).

Because stamp mills used up to 30 tons of water for each ton of ore stamped, companies located them alongside rivers or lakes, such as Portage Lake, Torch Lake and Lake Superior. The lakes provided water and served as dumps for the waste stamp sands. Troughs spilled mill tailings into the water, redrawing shorelines and creating flat beaches of coarse, grey-black sand, upon which nothing grew (Fig. 12.12). The mines had a waste byproduct, too—poor rock, which they often piled up alongside shafts, used to fill ravines, or crushed to serve as railroad ballast or concrete aggregate. But nothing rivaled stamp sands in terms of how they altered the environment. Such despoliation, however, was not an issue in the 19th century. The industrial society on the Keweenaw had no environmental ethic, and the unfettered mining companies hewed to no regulations. Fortunately, the industrial waste contained almost no acid-generating copper sulfide minerals, limiting their environmental damage.

FIGURE 12.12 The Calumet and Hecla stamp mills used troughs or launders, like that shown on the right, to wash tailings or sands into Torch Lake. Later, companies would dredge up these sands and reprocess them, to get out additional copper passed over in earlier times. Photo courtesy Michigan Technological University Archives and Copper Country Historical Collections.

Throughout the 1850s, the mining companies shipped their mineral and mass to Baltimore, Boston, Pittsburgh, Cleveland and Detroit for smelting. Eventually, a smelter opened on Portage Lake in 1860, and subsequently, several large mines, starting with Calumet and Hecla, built their own smelters that used reverberatory furnaces. At one end of the furnace, coal burned in a fire box. A low bridge wall separated the fuel from the furnace charge, which rested in a shallow hearth. Heat and flame swept over the bridge wall and reverberated along the hearth, melting the copper and rock (Cooper 1901, Conant 1931). When all was molten, furnacemen skimmed off the molten slag. Using a paddle-like tool, a "rabble," they splashed the copper around, mixing air into the melt to oxidize trace impurities. Then they plunged green, hardwood poles into the melt. The poles rapidly combusted and the wood's carbon combined with excess oxygen to produce gases that went up the stack. Furnacemen then ladled the copper into molds to produce ingots and cakes of various sizes and shapes.

This finished copper had many uses. It was easily alloyed with tin to make bronze, and with zinc to make brass. Copper is a good conductor of heat and is corrosion resistant. In its pure and alloyed forms, it is an attractive metal that is easily machined or formed. In the mid-19th century, fabricators used copper to sheath the hulls of wooden ships, to make pots and pans, roofing and gutters, buttons, machine bearings, hardware, candlesticks and cannons.

As soon as the Lake mines opened, they dominated American copper production (Hyde 1998). Through the late 1880s, Michigan accounted for at least half of the nation's output, and sometimes for as much as 90%. The C&H mine alone often produced two-thirds of Michigan's production, and Houghton County became home to the region's biggest mines, mills and smelters (Gates 1951).

The mining companies built communities to attract and house workers. They called these settlements mine "locations," because they were less than full-fledged towns (Fig. 12.13). At locations, the companies owned the land and served as paternal overseers. They built housing (boarding houses first, then single-family dwellings), provided gardens, let employees erect churches, controlled schools and set up medical programs and hospitals. In early days, they operated farms and maybe a store or two (Lankton 1991). But they never developed a complete town with a main street full of shops, restaurants, bars and hotels. To find a full range of goods and services, a working family had to go to a nearby commercial village, often a waterfront settlement such as Copper Harbor, Eagle Harbor, Eagle River, Houghton or Hancock (Mason 1991, Lankton 1997). Inland commercial villages developed, too. Rockland serviced the population of the Minesota mine, and Calumet and Laurium traded with workers at the Calumet and Hecla, Osceola and Tamarack mines (Fig. 12.14).

Americans from New England, New York and the Lower Peninsula migrated to Lake Superior, but not to work underground or as menial laborers. They managed, kept books, served as engineers, mechanics, surveyors, geologists or store keepers. The Native American population on the Keweenaw was small and clustered at the bottom of Keweenaw Bay and the mouth of the Ontonagon River. They sometimes served as guides and packers, helped

FIGURE 12.13 At the Quincy mine location, the small T-shaped houses in the foreground, built during the Civil War, were still occupied by employees and their families 50–60 years later. The location included only a few shops and stores, so residents often went down to Hancock for provisions and entertainment. Photo courtesy Michigan Technological University Archives and Copper Country Historical Collections.

FIGURE 12.14 All the shop and store-keepers in Red Jacket village (now known as Calumet) were no doubt anxious every year for the break-up and removal of winter snow and ice. Photo courtesy Michigan Technological University Archives and Copper Country Historical Collections.

unload ships and sold fish and berries to new settlers. But they, too, were not miners. Instead, immigrants carried the copper industry on their backs in the 19th century, especially Cornishmen from the copper and tin mines of Cornwall, England, joined by Germans and Irishmen (Rowe 1974, Thurner 1994). These ethnic groups put many men underground. Meanwhile, French Canadians eschewed the mines proper and worked at stamp mills or in forests, where they cut mine timbers and thousands of cords of wood to fuel steam boilers and family cook stoves (Fig. 12.15).

FIGURE 12.15 Two mines in the district, the Tamarack (shown here) and Calumet and Hecla, had weak hanging walls—the rock that was overhead after miners had hollowed out some ground. To prop up the hanging and protect the men working underground, these two companies had to plant "a forest of trees" in their mines each year. Despite this effort, 45% of all the men killed in the mines died from rock falls from the hanging walls. Photo courtesy Michigan Technological University Archives and Copper Country Historical Collections.

■ Regional history: Peak of mining, ca. 1890–1915

Open pit mines in Butte, MT, surpassed Lake Superior's copper production in the late 1880s, and Michigan's share of national production declined steadily into the 20th century. The Lake mines accounted for 80% of the nation's new copper in 1880 but only 40% in 1890, 25% in 1900, 20% in 1910 and 15% in 1920 (Gates 1951, Hyde 1998). The region's diminishing percentage did not necessarily signify decline. On the contrary, the mines expanded greatly in the late 19th and early 20th centuries to meet the demand for copper wire, due to the rise of the electrical industry. Established companies such as C&H and Quincy pushed production to new peaks; mining revived in Keweenaw and Ontonagon counties. In Houghton Country, along the Baltic lode, the new Baltic, Trimountain and Champion mines opened, all run by the Copper Range Consolidated Mining Company (Fields 1997; Fig. 12.16). By 1900, the mines were producing about 68 million kg of copper annually, up from 23 million kg in 1880 and 45 million kg in 1890. In 1910 the mines, mills and smelters produced 102 million kg of refined copper and employed 18,000 people (Gates 1951).

Local society shared in this boom time. Houghton County's population swelled to 88,000 by 1910, as immigrants from Finland, Italy and Eastern Europe came to take jobs in the industry. Towns like Calumet, Houghton and Hancock modernized and made themselves over. They added new utility services, a street car line and paved streets (Fig. 12.17). Impressive new masonry structures of brick or sandstone lined downtown streets: fire halls, banks, churches, theatres, fraternal organizations and department stores (Eckert 2000).

But trouble underlay the veneer of modernity and industrial wealth. Around 1910, about 60 men died in the mines each year, most often under falls of rock (Lankton and Martin 1987). The Finns and southern and eastern Europeans arriving on Lake Superior confronted more social discrimination than earlier arrivals (Karni et al. 1975). The mining companies needed these new immigrants but treated them with little respect, because they did not come from mining traditions and were not versed in the rigors of industrial work. The new men, in turn, found mine work hard, disagreeable and unsafe (Fig. 12.18). They complained about working conditions and wages. The mining companies had other problems, besides growing labor unrest. They ran some of the oldest and deepest hardrock mines in the country and suffered the highest production costs.

FIGURE 12.16   The Copper Range company, early in the 20th century, occupied much of the Portage Lake shoreline, just west of Houghton. A large dock (center) received coal from lake freighters; other freighters (far right) left Copper Range docks, loaded with ingots and cakes of smelted copper. The Copper Range railroad, whose roundhouse is in the foreground, connected the company's mines, mills and smelter and moved vast tonnages of stamp rock, copper mineral, copper ingot and coal. Photo courtesy Michigan Technological University Archives and Copper Country Historical Collections.

FIGURE 12.17   By 1910, the Houghton Country Traction Company had 43 km of track, and its street cars ran from Houghton through Hancock and Calumet and on to Mohawk, with a spur running over to Lake Linden and Hubbell. Photo courtesy Michigan Technological University Archives and Copper Country Historical Collections.

FIGURE 12.18 The newest immigrants to the Keweenaw often got stuck into the worst jobs, such as tramming rock to the shafts for hoisting. Filling and pushing tram cars was the hardest underground work, and poorly paid trammers often led the way in protesting working conditions and wages. Photo courtesy Michigan Technological University Archives and Copper Country Historical Collections.

To extend their working lives, the mining companies brought in new efficiency experts and engineers. They pushed their men harder and adopted new technologies, such as rock drilling machines that could be run by one man instead of two. This last change, because it threatened the employment of so many miners, triggered the worst strike in the history of the mines. This conflict, with the Western Federation of Miners (WFM), dragged on from July 1913 to April 1914, before the badly beaten union called it off (Thurner 1984, Lankton 1991). During the strike, both the WFM and the companies perpetrated acts of violence, and on Christmas Eve, 1913, the worst tragedy in Copper Country history occurred at Italian Hall in Calumet. Strikers' families were celebrating Christmas on the second floor, when panic suddenly broke out (perhaps because of an erroneous cry of "Fire!"). Adults and children rushed down the stairs, failed to get out the doors and in the log-jam of people at the bottom, 74 persons died, 50 of them children. The Italian Hall disaster was the hardest event in the region's hardest of times.

◼ Regional history: Onset of decline, ca. 1920

The mines hit record peaks of annual production (121 million kg in 1916) and dividends ($24 million in 1917) during the WW I era, when high copper prices gave the mines a great boost. Shortly after the war, the American economy slumped, and the copper market collapsed (Gates 1951, Hyde 1998). In 1920–1921, many mines on the Keweenaw shut down, either temporarily or permanently. These years marked the onset of their permanent decline. To stave off financial loss and closure, mining firms consolidated, with bigger firms taking control of several smaller ones (Benedict 1952). In the 1920s, C&H operated a string of contiguous mines from Calumet northward, and it assessed their operations, shaft by shaft, mill by mill, rail line by rail line, to determine which facilities to keep and which to close. C&H also conducted geologic explorations along the mineral range, looking for new copper (Butler and Burbank 1929).

When they could afford it, the companies spent money on new technologies: drills and explosives, power shovels and electric haulage locomotives underground (Crane 1929). On the surface, they installed larger smelters with semi-automatic casting machines. Calumet and Hecla, Copper Range and Quincy opened new shallow "mines" at their stamp mills—reclamation marking a new, bright spot for the companies. The stamp sands washed out of mills always contained some copper, but in flecks too small to recover using gravity separation techniques. Calumet and Hecla had run assay tests of its tailings; it knew that one-fourth of the copper raised out of its mine now rested on the bottom of Torch Lake, in stamp sands. C&H pioneered in dredging up these stamp sands, regrinding them, and using new separating machines, chemicals and oils to capture the fine copper fragments. The company started reclaiming tailings in 1915 and before shutting down its reclamation facilities in 1951, C&H had reworked 38 million tons of tailings and reclaimed 192 million kg of copper. In the troubled 1920s and 1930s, this reclaimed copper accounted for 60% of C&H's dividends (Benedict 1952, 1955).

After 1920–21, companies' fortunes sometimes rose a bit, but the mines never reached their previous production levels. They were shadows of their former selves, especially during the Great Depression, when the few surviving companies trimmed or suspended operations. The Quincy mine, after mining almost continuously from the 1850s until the Depression, closed all its shafts from 1931 until 1937 (Lankton and Hyde 1982). In 1939, C&H stopped mining on its once fabulously rich conglomerate lode. By 1940, the mines produced only 41 million kg of copper, accounting for just 5% of the total US production. Mine employment had plummeted to only 3,500 workers. Local communities, businesses, churches and institutions of all kinds felt the pinch. About 14,500 workers lost their jobs and were left to find work elsewhere. Houghton County lost 40,000 residents between 1910 and 1940, and another 8,000 during World War II. And although 88,000 resided in the county in 1910, only 40,000 still lived there in 1945 (Gates 1951).

During the labor-friendly era of Franklin D. Roosevelt's presidency, the copper miners finally unionized and entered into collective bargaining agreements with Calumet and Hecla, Copper Range, Quincy and Isle Royale. Shortly after World War II, Quincy and Isle Royale shuttered their shafts, leaving only two companies to continue mining. Every three years, one union contract expired and C&H and Copper Range tried to hammer out a new one, often leading to strikes. The workers, rightfully, wanted better wages and benefits, while the companies, rightfully, argued they were marginal producers, struggling to stay in business.

To improve their economic situations, the two companies diversified. C&H acquired a copper tubing company, formed a chemical company, used its machine shop and foundry to produce castings and equipment for outside firms, started fledgling mining operations in Illinois, Wisconsin and Nevada, sold timber off its more than 97,000 hectares in Michigan and sold waterfront property to vacationers (Lankton 1991). Copper Range did about the same: it ran a timber sales operation, a copper/brass fabricating company in Pittsburgh, a railroad, a motor-bus line and a water-supply plant that served not only its locations, but Houghton and Hancock. Most importantly, however, Copper Range opened the White Pine mine on mineral lands C&H had once worked, but abandoned. Copper Range had acquired this Ontonagon County property for $165,000 in 1929, and then waited for the right time to exploit it (Fields 1997). Copper in and around this property had been discovered and mined in the 1860s and C&H had mined native copper there only from 1914 to 1921.

Regional history: The opening of White Pine mine, early 1950s

The Korean War caused the US government to seek to boost domestic copper production. Copper Range received a $57 million construction loan from the government, plus a contract for nearly 245,000 tons of copper from the company's new White Pine mine. Located 120 km SW of the historic native copper district, White Pine, put into production in 1953, was an entirely different type of copper mine. Its host rock was neither a basalt nor a conglomerate, but the Nonesuch Shale (Fig. 12.6). The 200-million-ton ore body contained little native (metallic) copper, but much chalcocite, or copper sulfide (Table 12.2), in grains so small as to be practically invisible. By 1946, tests showed the chalcocite could be economically recovered despite the fine size.

To open and operate White Pine, Copper Range built a mid-20th century version of a mine location (Chabot 2000). In the age of post-war suburbanization, it laid out curvilinear streets (all named after trees) and built inexpensive versions of the modern ranch house with attached garages. The settlement had schools, three churches, a small store—and off to the side, a trailer park. The mine proper used mining, milling and smelting technologies unlike those of the native copper mines, because its deposit was so different. Shortly after opening, the White Pine mine was out-producing the surviving native copper mines in Houghton and Keweenaw counties.

■ Regional history: The end of copper mining, 1968 and 1996

The last native copper mines did a good job of maximizing their return from the capital invested in their mine plants. Copper Range operated its Champion mine in Painesdale until 1967, and a new owner of Calumet & Hecla's mining division, Universal Oil Products, brought the curtain down on C&H's operations in 1968, while in the midst of a strike. From the mid-1840s to the late 1960s, the native copper mines on the Keweenaw produced a total of five billion kg of copper (Table 12.1).

After C&H's closure, for a quarter century, the White Pine mine alone carried on copper production in the Upper Peninsula. Production peaked in 1975 at 83 million kg. The mine closed in 1981 and reopened in 1986 as an employee-owned company with financial support from the State of Michigan (Chabot 2000). In 1989, the employee-owned company was sold to Metall Mining Company of Canada. Economic, environmental and labor problems buffeted White Pine before it, too, closed in 1996. Over its four decades, White Pine produced two billion kg of copper.

■ Copper mining in the future

The future of copper mining in the western Upper Peninsula depends on economics. In order to open a mine, copper has to be at a sufficient concentration (grade) in the ore, with a sufficient mass (tonnage) available for mining, and the price of copper has to be high enough to make it all profitable. In building a mine there are other considerations, including stability of rock underground and environmental impact.

Much copper remains in the old mines. When the native copper mines of the Keweenaw Peninsula closed in 1968, they left in the old mines proven and possible mineral resources of roughly 200 million tons containing 2.3 billion kg of copper. When the White Pine Mine closed, they left in the ground 150 million tons of ore containing 1.4 billion kg of copper (Johnson et al. 1995). But can it be economically extracted today? In 2008, the costs of exploration, permitting and environmental controls to reopen a mine—and then the costs of mining, processing and transporting the copper—make reopening the old mines difficult. There are several known copper prospects that have not been mined. Near the mouth of the Presque Isle River, as it enters Lake Superior, there is another deposit like the one at the White Pine Mine, with about 95 million tons of ore containing about 2.4 billion kg of copper (Cannon 1985). This deposit is higher grade, yet was not mined because of difficult mining conditions. In the 1970s, the last serious exploration in the Keweenaw Peninsula resulted in the discovery of several small high grade deposits of chalcocite in the tops of lava flows that contain about 136 million kg of copper. These remain to be mined. And it is certainly possible there are deposits yet to be discovered. So while today we may not envision copper mining in the western Upper Peninsula, the situation could change, bringing copper mining back to Michigan.

■ Conclusions

The landscape of the Copper Country still shows evidence of a century and a half of copper mining. Much of the land—once clearcut to provide wood for mine supports, building construction and fuel—is now reforested; it looks more like it did before the mining era, rather than during. Hillocks of poor rock still dot the landscape where mines operated, but they too are disappearing as they are crushed for construction use. Flat, stamp sand beaches line the lakefronts that were home to stamp mills and reclamation plants. Traces of the dead mining industry can be found in the cities and villages that look like time has stood still since about 1910, the peak of native copper mining, or since about 1960, in the case of White Pine. Company-built houses still line streets or lanes at mine locations and mill towns (Fig. 12.19). And the ruins of mines, mills and smelters—from tall smoke stacks to shaft-rockhouses to the massive concrete foundations for steam stamps—mark the rise and fall of an industry that provided great riches to some, and employment for tens of thousands, as it wrested wealth out of rock.

FIGURE 12.19   In the 19th and early 20th centuries, Calumet & Hecla built rows of identical company houses for workers to rent. When the company sold them off, new owners individualized them by changing colors, siding, windows and doors, and by adding porches and garages. Many of these houses still occur in the Keweenaw, as exemplified by these hones in Calumet. Photo by R. Schaetzl.

Literature Cited

Benedict, C.H. 1955. Lake Superior Milling Practice. Michigan College of Mining and Technology Press, Houghton, MI.

Benedict, C.H. 1952. Red Metal: The Calumet & Heclas Story. University of Michigan Press, Ann Arbor.

Bornhorst, T.J. 1997. Tectonic context of native copper deposits of the North American Midcontinent Rift System. Geological Society of America Special Paper 312:127–136.

Bornhorst, T.J., Paces, J.B., Grant, N.K., Obradovich, J.D. and N.K Huber. 1988. Age of native copper mineralization, Keweenaw Peninsula, Michigan. Economic Geology 83:619–625.

Broderick, T.M. 1931. Fissure vein and lode relations in Michigan copper deposits. Economic Geology 26:840–856.

Brown, A.C. 1971. Zoning in the White Pine Copper deposit, Ontonagon County, Michigan. Economic Geology 66:543–573.

Butler, B.S. and W.S. Burbank. 1929. The Copper Deposits of Michigan. U.S. Geological Survey Professional Paper 144. Washington, DC.

Cannon, W.F. 1994. Closing of the Midcontinent Rift—A far field effect of Grenvillian contraction. Geology 22:155–158.

Cannon, W.F. 1985. Mineral resources map of the Iron River 1 x 2 degree quadrangle, Michigan and Wisconsin. U.S. Geological Survey Miscellaneous Investigation Series Map I-1360-A.

Cannon, W.F., Peterman, Z.E. and P.K. Sims. 1993. Crustal-scale thrusting and origin of the Montreal River monocline—A 35-km-thick cross section of the Midcontinent Rift in northern Michigan and Wisconsin. Tectonics 12:728–744.

Catacosinos, P.A., Harrison, W.B., Reynolds, R.F., Westjohn, D.B. and M.S Wollensak. 2001. Stratigraphic Lexicon for Michigan. Michigan Department of Environmental Quality, Geologic Survey Division Bulletin 8. Lansing, MI.

Chabot, L. 2000. "I'll eat every pound of copper from that mine." Michigan History 84(Jan–Feb):10–17.

Chaput, D. 1971. The Cliff: America's First Great Copper Mine. Sequoia Press, Kalamazoo, MI.

Conant, H.D. 1931. The Historical Development of Smelting and Refining Native Copper. Mining Congress Journal 17:531–532.

Cooper, J.B. 1901. Historical Sketch of Smelting and Refining Lake Copper. Lake Superior Mining Institute Proceedings 7:44–49.

Crane, W.R. 1929. Mining Methods and Practice in the Michigan Copper Mines. US Bureau of Mines Bulletin 306. Washington, DC.

Davis, D.W. and J.B. Paces. 1990. Time resolution of geologic events on the Keweenaw Peninsula and implications for development of the Midcontinent rift system. Earth and Planetary Science Letters 97:54–64.

Eckert, K.B. 2000. The Sandstone Architecture of the Lake Superior Region. Wayne State University Press, Detroit, MI.

Egleston, T. 1879. Copper Mining on Lake Superior. American Institute of Mining Engineers 6:275–312.

Elmore, R.D. 1983. Precambrian non-marine stromatolites in alluvial fan deposits, the Copper Harbor Conglomerate, upper Michigan. Sedimentology 30:829–842.

Elmore, R.D. 1984. The Copper Harbor Conglomerate: A late Precambrian fining-upward alluvial fan sequence in northern Michigan. Geological Society of America Bulletin 95:610–617.

Elmore, R.D., Milavec, G.J., Imbus, S.W. and M.H. Engel. 1989. The Precambrian Nonesuch Formation of the North American Mid-Continent Rift, Sedimentology and organic geochemical aspects of lacustrine deposition. Precambrian Research 43:191–213.

Farrand, W.R. 1960. Former shorelines in western and northern Lake Superior Basin. Ph.D. Dissertation 5366. University of Michigan, Ann Arbor.

Fields, R.A. 1997. Range of Opportunity: An Historic Study of the Copper Range Company. Quincy Mine Hoist Association, Hancock, MI.

Gates, W.B. 1951. Michigan Copper and Boston Dollars: An Economic History of the Michigan Copper Mining Industry. Harvard University Press, Cambridge, MA.

Hyde, C.K. 1998. Copper for America: The United States Copper Industry from Colonial Times to the 1990s. University of Arizona Press, Tucson, AZ.

Johnson, R.C., Andrews, R.A., Nelson, W.S., Suszek, T. and K. Sikkila. 1995. Geology and mineralization of the White Pine copper deposits. Unpublished Copper Range Company Report.

Karni, M.G., Kaups, M.E. and D.J. Ollila (eds). 1975. The Finnish Experience in the Western Great Lakes Region: New Perspectives. Institute for Migration, Turku, Finland.

Krause, D. 1992. The Making of a Mining District: Keweenaw Native Copper. Wayne State University Press, Detroit, MI.

Lankton, L.D. 1983. The machine under the garden: Rock drills arrive at the Lake Superior copper mines, 1868–1883. Technology and Culture 24:1–37.

Lankton, L. 1991. Cradle to Grave: Life, Work, and Death at the Lake Superior Copper Mines. Oxford University Press, New York.

Lankton, L. 1997. Beyond the Boundaries: Life and Landscape at the Lake Superior Copper Mines, 1840–1875. Oxford University Press, New York.

Lankton, L.D. and C.K. Hyde. 1982. Old Reliable: An Illustrated History of the Quincy Mining Company. Quincy Mine Hoist Association, Hancock, MI.

Lankton, L.D. and J.K. Martin. 1987. Technological advance, organizational structure, and underground facilities in the Upper Michigan copper mines. Technology and Culture 28:42–66.

Martin, S.R. 1999. Wonderful Power: The Story of Ancient Copper Working in the Lake Superior Basin. Wayne State University Press, Detroit, MI.

Mason, P.P. (ed). 1991. Copper Country Journal: The Diary of Schoolmaster Henry Hobart, 1863–1864. Wayne State University Press, Detroit, MI.

Mauk, J.L. 1992. Geology and stable isotope and organic geochemistry of the White Pine sediment-hosted stratiform copper deposit. Society of Economic Geologists Guidebook Series 13:63–98.

Rowe, J. 1974. The Hard-Rock Men: Cornish Immigrants and the North American Mining Frontier. Liverpool University Press, Liverpool, England.

Thurner, A.W. 1984. Rebels on the Range: The Michigan Copper Miners' Strike of 1913–1914. Houghton County Historical Society, Lake Linden, MI.

Thurner, A.W. 1994. Strangers and Sojourners: A History of Michigan's Keweenaw Peninsula. Wayne State University Press, Detroit, MI.

Further Readings

Bornhorst, T.J. (ed). 1992. Keweenawan Copper Deposits of Western Upper Michigan. Society of Economic Geologists Guidebook Series 13.

Bornhorst, T.J. and W.I. Rose Jr. 1994. Self-guided geological field trip to the Keweenaw Peninsula, Michigan. Great Lakes Geoscience LLC, Ontonagon, MI.

Forster, J.H. 1884. Early settlement of the copper regions of Lake Superior. Michigan Pioneer Collections 7:181–193.

Foster, J.W. and J.D. Whitney. 1850. Report on the Geology and Topography of a Portion of the Lake Superior Land District in the State of Michigan, Part 1, Copper Lands. U.S. House, Exec. Doc. 69 (31st Cong., 1st Sess.).

LaBerge, G.L. 1994. Geology of the Lake Superior Region. Penokean Press, Oshkosh, WI.

White, W.S. 1968. The native-copper deposits of northern Michigan. In: Ridge, J.D. (ed.), Ore Deposits of the United States, 1933–1967 (the Graton Sales volume). American Institute of Mining, Metallurgical, and Petroleum Engineering, New York. pp. 303–325.

13

Evolution of the Great Lakes

Kevin Kincare and Grahame J. Larson

■ Introduction

The Great Lakes are one of Michigan's most distinctive geographic features. The familiar shape of the Great Lakes is however, a recent phenomenon. Their present form is the result of a number of geologic factors, such as glacial erosion and deposition, isostatic depression and subsequent rebound due to glacial-ice load (see FOCUS BOX on page 177), distribution of glacial meltwater, and changing lake outlets. In this chapter, we will examine the formation of the Great Lakes, as well as the many changes they went through before becoming the familiar features we know today.

■ Origin and development of lake basins

The shape and location of each Great Lake has been largely determined by its underlying geology. Most of the bedrock beneath each lake basin is easily-eroded Paleozoic sedimentary deposits (Plate 6), with the exception of Lake Superior, which is a structural basin underlain by complex Middle Proterozoic rocks (Chapter 12). Therefore, prior to Late Cenozoic Ice Age, each lake basin was probably already a river valley draining to an ancestral St. Lawrence River (Fig. 13.1). The structural bedrock highs of the Kankakee arch south of Chicago, and the Findley arch on the west side of Lake Erie (see FOCUS BOX, Chapter 4), would have effectively prevented the pre-glacial rivers in the Great Lakes region sea-floor from draining to the Mississippi River.

Recent climatic evidence from cores of sea-floor sediment and ice caps indicate that at least 40 separate glaciations occurred during the last 2.75 million years (Fig. 6.1). Each glaciation that was extensive enough to reach Michigan probably further eroded the lake basins and altered the Great Lakes. Most of the glacial deposits in Michigan are from the last two of these glaciations (the early and late Wisconsin advances, both <80,000 years ago) and the majority of these deposits are from the final phase of deglaciation (<20,000 years ago). Older glacial deposits, found to the south of Michigan, in Illinois, Indiana, and Ohio (Fig. 6.2), show that earlier glaciations advanced well to the south of Michigan. However, we have not found any evidence yet for older glacial deposits in Michigan, although this may change with advances in dating techniques and additional field research. Although the glaciers were agents of erosion each time they covered Michigan, our state still has some of the thickest glacial deposits in North America, up to 365 m thick in northern Lower Michigan (Rieck and Winters 1993, Soller 1998; Fig. 17.8). Given this fact, our discussion will center on deposits of the late Wisconsin glaciation.

■ Glaciers and lakes

The Laurentide ice sheet is a term used for the continental glacier whose center was in the Hudson Bay area and spread out, to eventually cover much of Canada and the northern United States. A second ice sheet, the Cordilleran

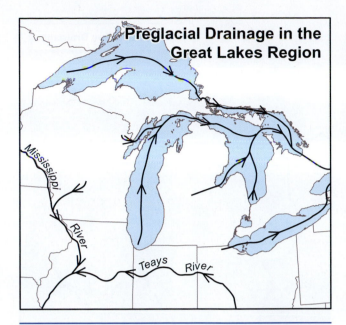

FIGURE 13.1   Preglacial drainage in the Great Lakes region during the Late Cenozoic, prior to glaciation. Probable river patterns are based on known bedrock structures and geophysical reconnaissance of buried valleys. After Hough (1958) and Flint (1971).

FIGURE 13.2   Farthest extent of Late Wisconsin ice advance, which occurred about 23,000 yrs ago in Illinois and Ohio, but later at other points along the ice margin.

ice, formed in the northern Rocky Mountains and, in places, merged with the Laurentide ice sheet. Three major lobes of the Laurentide ice sheet moved across and covered Michigan from out of the overdeepened lake basins and are named after those basins, the Lake Michigan, Saginaw, and Huron/Erie lobes (Figs. 17.4, 17.12). The farthest extent occurred during the Last Glacial Maximum (LGM) and was well to the south in Indiana and Ohio (Fig. 13.2).

The ice at the LGM began to retreat around 21,500 years ago. Evidence from the cross-cutting relationships of former ice margins and their related outwash shows that the lobes did not move synchronously (Mickelson et al. 1983, Kehew et al. 1999). The thinner, weaker Saginaw lobe probably retreated from south-central Michigan first, leaving fine-grained deposits in the St. Joseph River valley, from a lake that was trapped by the Lake Michigan and Huron/Erie lobes which were still much farther south (Fig. 13.3). At this time, before the Great Lake basins opened up, meltwater drainage was down the Wabash and Kankakee Rivers (Fig. 13.4).

The pull-back of the ice from the LGM did not proceed as a long, steady retreat, but was uneven and punctuated by a series of rapid retreats and readvances (Chapters 6, 17). This complicated (and sometimes confusing) series of events led to numerous proglacial and post-glacial lakes within each Great Lake basin. At times, these lakes were separate, while at other times they were confluent or connected by river channels.

Lakes are often associated with glaciation, particularly during glacial retreat, because drainage can easily become blocked by ice on one side and by landforms of a previous ice advance on the other. Therefore, knowing the record of glacial retreat (Chapter 6) is important for understanding the sequence of glacial lake levels. Leverett and Taylor (1915) produced the most detailed compilation of field data on glacial lake phases in the Great Lakes basin— almost 100 years ago!

Lakes can produce a definitive set of features based on particular types of depositional and erosional patterns. The low-energy environments of lakes generally lead to fine-grained deposits, e.g., silt and clay, on their beds. Two major exceptions to this are sandier shoreline areas (high energy due to wave action) and river mouths (where deltas are typically built).

A lake, by definition, has the same surface elevation at all points. On this basis, shorelines from ancient lakes can be traced from place to place, even if intervening parts of the shoreline no longer exist due to erosion or burial. Deltas can also show a former lake-surface elevation where a river entered a lake, as well as showing the off-shore connection to sediments of deeper, quiet-water deposits. Lakes have the power to erode as well. Many shorelines are not traced by beach deposits, but by wave-cut bluffs (strandlines) eroded into adjoining headlands, as well as spits, which may contain the eroded material, transported into the spit (Fig. 13.5). River channels that are now dry

FIGURE 13.3   Map of the ice margin about 19,000 years ago, showing the Saginaw lobe reentrant.

FIGURE 13.4   Map of the ice margin about 18,000 years ago, showing meltwater drainage overflowing to the Wabash and Kankakee Rivers.

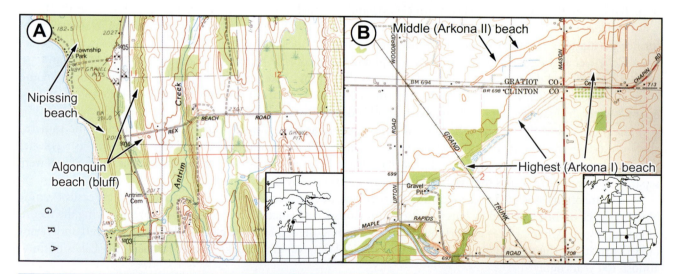

FIGURE 13.5   Topographic maps showing strandlines and/or beach ridges of some former glacial lakes in Michigan. A. Well-developed shorelines inferred from wave-cut bluffs. Two shorelines are visible on this map, as long, steep banks that were cut by prolonged wave action. The lower bluff is from the Nipissing phase; the higher one is from Glacial Lake Algonquin. The bluff east of Antrim Creek in not a shoreline, its base rises upstream and it lacks a flat platform on its shoreward side. Note the prominent drumlins on the east edge of this map. Source: Atwood 1:25,000 quadrangle, 5 m contour interval. B. Shorelines inferred from more subtle beach ridges. Two beaches (highest and middle Lake Arkona) are seen here as linear ridges, often with interconnected, closed contours, on the topographic map. These features are accumulations of sand, formed due to wave action and longshore transport at the former shoreline. Sandy beach ridges are preferred building locations, due to better drainage than adjacent clayey lake bottom sediments. In this case, the beaches are being used for a cemetery (a high, dry, sandy location on the otherwise wet lake plain) and, in places, it is being mined for sand and gravel. Source: Ovid West 1:24,000 quadrangle, 5 ft contour interval.

FOCUS BOX: Radiocarbon years vs. calendar years

In the scientific literature, one may encounter ages for events given in radiocarbon years BP (before present), as well as in calendar years ago. To make things more confusing, these two methods seemingly express different ages for the same geologic event. To make sense of this, a little history and explanation are needed.

The discovery in the early 20th century of a radioactive isotope of carbon (^{14}C) was important for the study of recent deposits because its relatively short half-life (5730 yrs) made it ideal for determining the ages of organic material younger than about 40,000–50,000 years old. It forms as a result of cosmic rays interacting with nitrogen in the atmosphere. Most importantly, because ^{14}C is in the atmosphere, all living things have ^{14}C incorporated into their tissues. When an organism dies, it no longer assimilates ^{14}C, so its ^{14}C mass begins to decrease by radioactive decay. Determining the radioactivity that remains in a dead organism allows us to approximate the elapsed time since it died.

The study of *dendrochrononlogy* also allowed scientists to determine the age of trees, and ancient wooden materials, like beams and logs, by matching patterns of their annual growth rings. Unfortunately, the tree-ring chronology, which goes back around 8000 yrs (Stuiver 1978), did not match the ^{14}C chronology because the ^{14}C chronology was based on the assumption that the initial concentration of ^{14}C in the atmosphere has always been constant. Not only has the concentration of ^{14}C in the atmosphere changed over time, but more ^{14}C is produced at higher latitudes, and there are biological and chemical energy pathways that favor uptake of lighter isotopes (^{12}C and ^{13}C) over ^{14}C (Faure 1986). Therefore, a calendar year is constant, but a "radiocarbon year" can vary over time (see Figure). Study of these problems has led to the development of radiocarbon year corrections (or calibrations), not only by using tree ring data but also with corals, ice cores, and marine-sediment cores that are applied to ^{14}C ages to calibrate them to calendar years. Ages reported in the literature now specify which is being used. Radiocarbon ages are typically reported in years BP. The "present" is assumed to be 1950—before the open-air testing of atomic weapons, which sent the ^{14}C content of the atmosphere off the scale. Currently, all but the oldest ^{14}C dates can be readily calibrated to calendar years. All radiocarbon dates mentioned in this chapter have been converted from radiocarbon years BP to calendar years ago, using the calibration curve of Fairbanks et al. (2005).

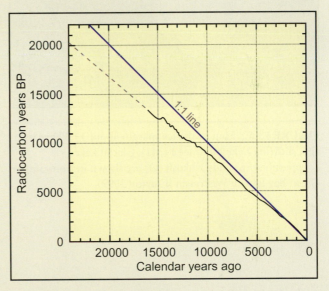

Graph of calendar years vs. radiocarbon years. By reading the graph one can see, for example, that a sample from a tree that died 12,500 radiocarbon years BP is approximately 15,000 calendar years old. After: Quaternary Isotope Lab, Univ. of Washington.

or have rivers too small to have cut its channel provide evidence of old glacial lake outlets. Each bit of evidence, separately or in combination, is used to map ancient lake margins, and their cross-cutting relationships tells us the order in which they occurred.

■ Early lakes of the Lake Erie/Huron basin

The history of the lakes in the Erie and Huron basins are so closely tied together that they must be discussed together. Retreat of the Huron/Erie lobe from the Fort Wayne moraine around 17,400 years ago formed the first important proglacial lake of the Great Lakes basin—Glacial Lake Maumee (Fig. 13.6, Table 13.1). There were three phases of Lake Maumee (I, II, and III) which initially filled the lowland west of Lake Erie and spilled over the drainage divide

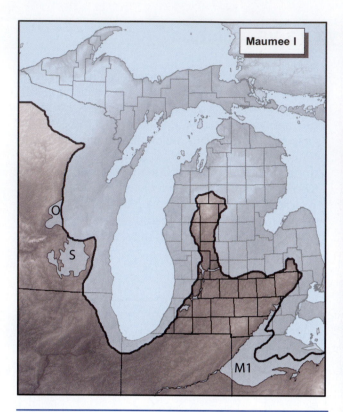

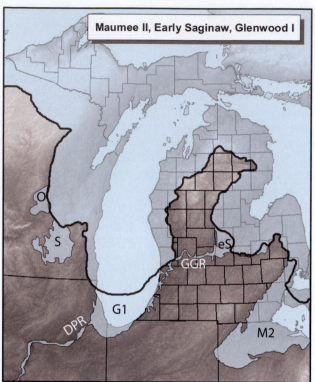

FIGURE 13.6 Map of the ice margin about 17,500 years ago, showing Lake Maumee I (M1). Glacial Lakes Scuppernong (S) and Oshkosh (O) are shown in front of the Green Bay lobe in Wisconsin (Clayton 1997).

FIGURE 13.7 Map of the ice margin about 17,100 years ago, showing Lake Maumee II (M2), Early Lake Saginaw (eS), and the Glenwood I phase of Lake Chicago (G1). At this time, the Glacial Grand River (GGR) drained Early Lake Saginaw into Lake Chicago, and the Des Plaines River drained Lake Chicago to the Mississippi River drainage basin (via the Illinois River). Glacial Lakes Scuppernong (S) and Oshkosh (O) are shown in front of the Green Bay lobe in Wisconsin (Clayton 1997).

to the Wabash River near present day Fort Wayne, Indiana (Calkin and Feenstra 1985). The Maumee I shoreline (the elevation of the outlet and associated beaches) was at 244 m above sea level and, as the Huron/Erie lobe continued its retreat, extended from Fort Wayne into Michigan through Lenawee County to Macomb County. After the Huron/Erie lobe ice readvanced to the Defiance moraine, Lake Maumee was present only in northeastern Ohio. Ice retreat again allowed expansion of Lake Maumee into southeastern Michigan. But the retreat also uncovered a lower outlet, lowering Maumee I to the Maumee II elevation of 232 m (Fig. 13.7). Shoreline features of Maumee II are not well developed in Michigan and are known mostly from Ohio (Calkin and Feenstra 1985). There is no outlet at 232 m elevation across the Defiance moraine, so it is thought that the ice advance ending Maumee II (and building the Flint moraine) buried the outlet channel (Leverett and Taylor 1915). With the lower outlet buried, the previous and higher (244 m) outlet was used again. Ice retreat from the Flint moraine opened up an impressive channel near Imlay City (Lapeer County) allowing Maumee III to stabilize at 238 m and drain eastward into the Saginaw lowlands. This well-developed channel is clearly visible on a topographic map of Lapeer County, extending from the Lake Maumee plain to the Flint River.

Retreat of the Saginaw lobe margin from the Flint moraine also started opening up the Saginaw lowlands in central Michigan, forming Early Lake Saginaw (Fig. 13.7). This lake drained westward via the Glacial Grand River, through the Maple River valley at the village of Maple Rapids, to eventually empty into Glacial Lake Chicago, Glenwood I phase. The Allendale delta, just east of Grand Rapids, marks the location of the mouth of the Glacial Grand River at this time (Bretz 1953). Strandlines of Early Lake Saginaw exist at 225 m and 222 m in northern Shiawassee County. After the Huron lobe retreated out of Michigan's thumb, Maumee III merged with Early Lake Saginaw into

TABLE 13.1   Post-glacial lakes and levels from 17,000–2000 years ago in the Lakes Superior, Michigan, Huron, and Erie basins[1]

Years ago	Superior basin	Michigan basin	Huron basin	Erie basin
				Maumee I (244)
17000		Glenwood I (195)	Early Saginaw (225)	Maumee II (232)
				Maumee III (237)
			Arkona (216–212)	
		Mackinaw (170?)	post-Arkona low (?)	Ypsilanti (<166)
16000		Glenwood II (195)	Saginaw (212)	Whittlesey (225)
15000			Warren I & II -Wayne (210-199)	
			Warren III (206-203)	
			Grassmere-Lundy (195-189)	
14000		Calumet? (189)	Early Algonquin (184)	Early Erie (<159)
		Two Creeks (170?)	Kirkfield (173?)	
		Calumet (189)	Huron Algonquin (184)	
		Toleston? (184)		
13000	Duluth (331)	Main Algonquin (184)		
	Duluth (331)	Algonquin (184)		
		Algonquin (descending)		
12000	Duluth (331)/Minong (220)	Algonquin (descending)		
		Chippewa (75)	Stanley (66)	
11000	Minong (220)			
		Mattawa flood		
10000		Mattawa flood		
		-closed basins?-		
9000		Olson forest bed (153)		
8000	-Superior basin confluent with Huron basin-			
			Sanilac forest bed (165)	
7000				
6000		Nipissing (184)		
		-coastal dune building begins-		
5000				
4000				
3000		Algoma (181)		
2000	-Superior basin outlet rebounds above Huron Basin, present configuration of lakes achieved- -lake levels continue to fluctuate due to climate and rebound-			

1. Compiled from Fullerton (1980), Calkin and Feenstra (1985), Eschman and Karrow (1985), Farrand and Drexler (1985), Hansel et al. (1985), Larsen (1987), Lewis and Anderson (1989), Schneider and Hansel (1990), Colman et al. (1994), Larson et al. (1994), Baedke and Thompson (2000), and Lewis at al. (2007).

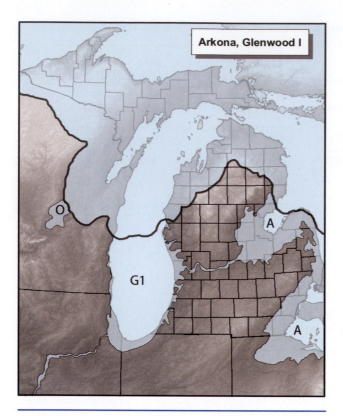

FIGURE 13.8 Map of the ice margin about 16,500 years, ago showing Lake Arkona (A), the Glenwood I phase of Lake Chicago (G1) and Glacial Lake Oshkosh (O) in Wisconsin.

Lake Arkona, at an initial elevation of 216 m (Fig. 13.8). Based on shoreline data, Lake Arkona subsequently declined to 213 m and then to 212 m. The reason for the decline in Lake Arkona's level has been variously attributed to decreases in meltwater production during a glacial readvance, outlet downcutting, climate, and the ability of a single outlet to drain a lake at several elevations (Calkin and Feenstra 1985). Well-developed Arkona beaches exist on the lake plain east of Maple Rapids in southeastern Gratiot County, northeastern Clinton County, and along the Shiawassee-Saginaw County line.

Lake Arkona expanded to the north and east as the ice margin retreated, during a period known as the Mackinaw interstade (Eschman and Karrow 1985). Eventually, the ice margin retreated far enough into southern Ontario that it opened isostatically-depressed outlets (see FOCUS BOX below) in southeastern Georgian Bay, thereby draining the Saginaw lowlands. This event left the Lake Erie basin with no meltwater source (the St. Clair River was dry at the time), as well as an isostatically-depressed outlet in the vicinity of the Niagara River. As a result, a very low level lake named Lake Ypsilanti existed for a short time in the Erie basin, which only had drainage from local rivers (Calkin and Feenstra 1985) and probably occupied about half the area that Lake Erie does today.

FOCUS BOX: Isostatic rebound

Obviously, the water level of a lake is the same elevation all around its shoreline, making a perfect horizontal "trace" of the water line. Today, however, ancient shorelines of glacial and post-glacial Great Lake phases are often not at the same elevation as which they formed. Instead, they commonly "rise" as they are traced to the north and northeast (Stanley 1936, Deane 1950, Schaetzl et al. 2002). What would cause these shorelines to rise, when they were originally horizontal?

The answer is a concept called *isostasy*. The rigid lithosphere (crust) of the earth "floats" on top of a viscous asthenosphere. Any change in the load placed upon the crust causes the asthenosphere to flow—either toward an area where the load has decreased or away from an area with an increased load. In the case of glacial isostasy, adding *glacial* mass depresses the lithosphere into the softer asthenosphere. Conversely, melting the glacier removes the load and the land bounces back, or rebounds—a process called isostatic rebound (see Figure). Greater amounts of rebound in northern Michigan illustrate that the glacier was thicker, and had more mass

there, than in the south (Martini et al. 2001). Glacial Lake Algonquin exhibits the best preserved paleolake shoreline in Michigan (Fig. 13.5) and shows remarkable amounts of rebound. At Manistee, its shoreline elevation is 184 m, while at Sault St. Marie it has been uplifted to nearly 305 m. Other paleo-lakes show similar patterns of uplift (Calkin and Feenstra 1985, Fraser et al. 1990).

The asthenosphere does not react quickly to glacial loading and unloading; it lags behind due to its high viscosity. In fact, Michigan is still very slowly "rebounding" from the ice load that has been gone for almost 11,000 years. Southwestern Lake Michigan and southwestern Lake Superior appear to actually be sinking, i.e., shorezones here are very slowly being drowned, because their outlets (at Port Huron and Sault Ste. Marie, respectively) are rising!

When glacial rebound was first being studied, it was thought that there were structurally-controlled "hinge lines," south of which there was no uplift, on the assumption that the underlying bedrock moves like a door on a hinge. Leverett and Taylor (1915), Hough (1958), and Dorr and Eschman (1970) all developed maps showing hinge lines in different places for each major glacial lake (see Figure below). However, the mapped hinge lines do not align with either the underlying bedrock (Plate 6) or any known fault systems. Rebound measurements of shorelines from different times, e.g., Algonquin and Nipissing, show that the rate of rebound is initially fast and decreases over time. Isostasy is a better explanation of these observed responses of the earth's surface rather than the old idea of hinge lines.

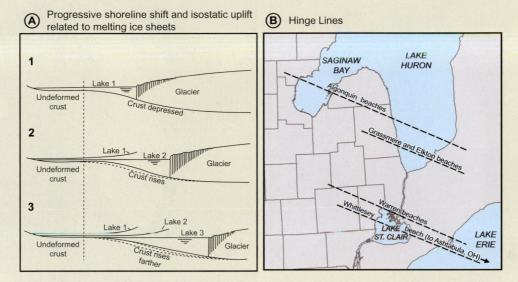

Illustrations of concepts of isostatic rebound. A. Figure showing how the mass of a glacier causes isostatic depression, whereas the removal of the glacial mass allows for isostatic rebound. Also shown are preglacial shorelines, initially formed horizontally, but now rising as the glacial load decreases and rebound proceeds. After Martini et al. (2001). B. Map showing four separate hinge lines, once proposed as a mechanism for rebound in southeastern Michigan and southwestern Ontario. After Leverett and Taylor (1915, 505).

The Port Huron glacial advance about 16,000 years ago (Blewett and Winters 1995; Chapters 6, 17) ended the Mackinaw interstade and not only closed the outlet in Ontario but also separated the Saginaw lowlands from southeastern Michigan (Fig. 13.9). The Port Huron moraine cuts off Lake Arkona beaches in southeastern Michigan from Lake Arkona beaches in the Saginaw lowlands, illustrating that they preceded the Port Huron glacial advance. Thus separated from the Saginaw Valley, a large lake with well-developed beach ridges at 225 m called Lake Whittlesey formed in the Lake Erie basin (Leverett and Taylor 1915). Lake Whittlesey drained across the Thumb through a channel near Ubly, in Huron County. The Ubly channel ends at a delta (now cut by the Cass River, 4 km upstream of Caro, in Tuscola County), where it emptied into Lake Saginaw at 212 m, which itself overflowed into the Glacial Grand River and eventually into the Glenwood II phase of Lake Chicago (contributing more sediment to the Allendale delta). Lake Whittlesey shorelines in Michigan appear along the eastern edge of the Defiance moraine from Lenawee County through to Sanilac County.

Retreat from the Port Huron maximum exposed lower outlets and reconnected the proglacial lakes of southeastern Michigan with the Saginaw lowland, ending Lake Whittlesey and forming Lakes Warren I and II at 210–205 m, respectively. These Warren lakes drained through the Glacial Grand River to Lake Chicago; there is debate as to whether Glenwood II or Calumet existed at the time. The Warren lakes were followed by Lake Wayne at 201–199 m, when ice retreat exposed a lower outlet to the east through New York state (Fullerton 1980). Closure of the eastern outlet returned drainage to the Glacial Grand River for Lake Warren III at 206–203 m, based on evidence in north-central New York and incision of the Allendale delta (Muller 1977, Fullerton 1980).

The eastern outlet apparently reopened during the ensuing ice retreat, allowing the lower Lake Grassmere (195 m) to follow Warren III (Calkin and Feenstra 1985). Two other drops in lake level stabilized briefly, forming stages known as Lakes Lundy (189 m) and Elkton (187 m). After this event, around 14,400 years ago, the Lake Erie basin was separated from direct meltwater input and dropped to the low, Early Lake Erie level. Isostatic uplift

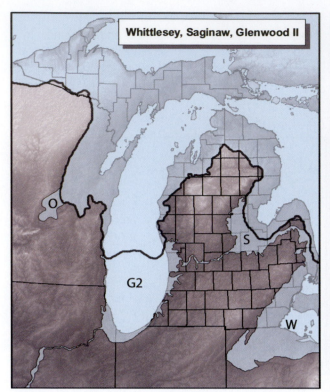

FIGURE 13.9   Map of the ice margin about 15,900 years ago, showing Lake Whittlesey (W), Lake Saginaw (S), the Glenwood II phase of Lake Chicago (G2) and Glacial Lake Oshkosh in Wisconsin.

FIGURE 13.10   Map of the ice margin about 14,000 years ago, showing the low lake levels associated with the Twocreekan interstadial (Two Rivers Phase).

caused the outlet at Niagara River to slowly rise, and as a result the level of Lake Erie also rose over the ensuing 14,000 years, to its present level.

The lake in Lake Huron basin, still in contact with the retreating Port Huron ice margin, probably dropped to the 184 m level of Early Lake Algonquin, most likely draining south via an outlet at Port Huron (Deane 1950). Direct evidence for this lake has not been found, because subsequent lake stages at the same elevation obscured its beaches (Eschman and Karrow 1985). Continued ice retreat past the Straits of Mackinac however, resulted in extension of Early Lake Algonquin into the Lake Michigan basin, eventually leading to the Two Creeks low phase (Fig. 13.10; Hansel et al. 1985). When the retreating ice margin opened a lower outlet near Fenelon Falls, SE of Georgian Bay, Early Lake Algonquin dropped an even lower phase—the Kirkfield Phase. The Kirkfield Phase ended and returned to the Algonquin level when its outlet either rebounded or was covered by a glacial advance. The latter seems more likely, since the timing appears to coincide with the Two Rivers Phase advance (Chapter 6). This glacial readvance also separated the Lakes Michigan and Huron basins again.

■ Early lakes of the Lake Michigan basin

Whenever the Straits of Mackinac were covered by ice, lake-level fluctuations in the Lake Huron basin did not affect events occurring in the Lake Michigan basin, except for some drainage down the Glacial Grand River. Recall that the Saginaw lobe retreated into south-central Michigan long before the Lake Michigan lobe retreated into the Lake Michigan basin. Meltwater from south-central Michigan, therefore, initially overflowed down the Wabash River, along with over-flow from Lake Maumee. Ice retreat to the Valparaiso moraine allowed much of the drainage from south-central Michigan to be redirected to the SW, via the Kankakee River, toward Illinois, and also formed several ice-marginal lakes between the ice margin and the Kalamazoo moraine (Figs. 13.4, 13.6). Only after ice retreated from the Valparaiso position, toward the Lake Border moraine, probably after 17,500 years ago (Farrand and Eschman 1974), did meltwater finally form a lake within the Lake Michigan basin. Known as the Glenwood I phase of Lake Chicago (Fig. 13.7), it stood at 195 m, based on an extensive spit in the Chicago area—about 18 m above current lake level. Lake Chicago drained to the south into the Des Plaines and Illinois Rivers (known as the Chicago outlet), to the Mississippi River.

Prolonged ice recession from the Lake Border moraine during the Mackinaw Interstade eventually formed a lower level Mackinaw phase lake (also referred to as the intra-Glenwood low phase) in the Lake Michigan basin. This lake drained eastward into the Huron basin via an outlet at or near the Straits of Mackinac (Monaghan and Hansel 1990). The elevation of this lake is not known, but Hansel et al. (1985) cited a lack of shore-feature evidence as reason to believe that the Mackinaw Phase water level was lower than present. Monaghan and Hansel (1990) reported a 16,400 year age from wood at the base of a spit near present lake elevation in Berrien County. The rising lake level, which formed the spit, was caused by closure of the Mackinac Straits by the Port Huron ice advance; this marks the end of the Mackinaw Phase. Isolation of the Lake Michigan basin returned drainage to the Chicago outlet, beginning the Glenwood II phase lake level at 195 m (Fig. 13.9). The Glenwood II phase lasted until at least 15,150 years ago (Karrow et al. 1975). Hough (1963) believed that erosion of the Chicago outlet initiated two later lake phases at lower levels. The first was the Calumet phase at 189.0 m; the second was the Toleston at 184.5 m. Both of these phases were initially based on beaches, spits and wave-cuts near the original Glenwood phase spit. Calumet beaches have been traced into southwestern Michigan. The St. Joseph River also built a large delta in Berrien County during the Calumet phase (Kincare 2007). Tracing Toleston phase

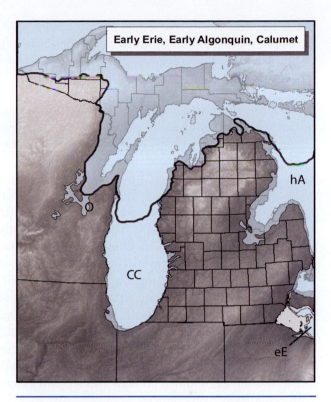

FIGURE 13.11 Map of the ice margin about 13,700 years ago, showing Early Lake Erie (eE), Huron Lake Algonquin (hA), the Calumet phase of Lake Chicago (CC) and Glacial Lake Oshkosh in Wisconsin.

beaches is difficult, because two subsequent lake phases were at the same elevation. There exists debate as to when the Calumet phase was initiated, with some researchers arguing it was prior to development of the Two Creeks Forest bed found in eastern Wisconsin that has been dated at 13,760 years ago (Bretz 1951, 1959, Eschman and Farrand 1970, Kaiser 1994). Others have argued that it was later (Hough 1958) and possibly related to the amount of discharge entering the lake (Hansel and Mickelson 1988). Hansel et al. (1985) doubted the existence of a Toleston phase entirely.

Retreat of the Lake Michigan lobe ice margin from the Port Huron moraine, and the opening of the Straits of Mackinac, eventually allowed Lake Chicago to drop to the level of Early Lake Algonquin in the Huron basin, and then to the level of the Kirkfield phase. During the Kirkfield phase, lake level in the Lake Michigan basin must have been lower than present to allow for the growth of the Two Creeks forest, near present lake level.

A glacial readvance then covered the Straits of Mackinac outlet again, during the Two Rivers Phase, burying the Two Creeks forest bed beneath glacial till (Chapter 6). The advance again isolated the Lake Michigan basin from the Huron basin, causing lake level in the Lake Michigan basin to rise to 189 m, the level of the Calumet phase of Lake Chicago, and returning drainage to the Chicago outlet (Fig. 13.11). The ice advance, during the Two Rivers Phase in Michigan, is assumed to have been at about 13,700 years ago by radiocarbon dates on the Cheboygan bryophyte bed in Cheboygan County (Larson et al. 1994; Chapter 6). This was the last oscillation of ice into the Lower Peninsula of Michigan. Its departure across the Straits of Mackinac ended Lake Chicago, allowing free drainage through the Straits of Mackinac and forming Main Lake Algonquin at about 13,000 years ago (Hansel et al. 1985). However, glaciers would enter the Upper Peninsula at least two more times and continue to influence the levels of the Great Lakes.

■ Main Lake Algonquin to Lakes Chippewa and Stanley

Main Lake Algonquin, the most extensive of the proglacial Great Lakes, probably drained through both the Chicago and Port Huron (St. Clair River) outlets (Leverett and Taylor 1915, Hough 1958). Hansel et al. (1985) and Larsen (1987), however, contended that outlets uncovered in Georgian Bay, Ontario by glacial retreat, also may have been drainage paths. Regardless, this lake left an indelible mark upon Michigan (Fig. 13.12); its shorelines are marked by well-developed wave-cut bluffs (Schaetzl et al. 2002), beaches (Futyma 1981), and extensive spits (Krist and Schaetzl 2001). As the ice retreated, Lake Algonquin expanded northward, covering much of the eastern half of the isostatically depressed Upper Peninsula, with many islands protruding above the water surface (Schaetzl et al. 2002). The Lake Algonquin shoreline eventually reached at least as far as 65 km north of Sault Ste. Marie (Farrand and Drexler 1985).

Continued ice retreat eventually began uncovering a series of lower outlets east of Georgian Bay—similar to outlets used during the earlier Kirkfield Phase. These outlets were isostatically depressed by the weight of the ice, allowing for drainage across the divide through Ontario. Thus, several post-Main Lake Algonquin phases temporarily stabilized at successively lower elevations as each new outlet was opened. Some of these lower beaches are easily visible on Mackinac Island (Stanley 1945) and many other places near the coast along the northern sections of Lakes Michigan and Huron and in the eastern Upper Peninsula (Schaetzl et al. 2002).

The lowest (by far!) lake level began when the North Bay, Ontario outlet opened around 11,200 years ago, allowing most of the volume of Lake Algonquin to suddenly drain eastward, through Canada (Fig. 13.13). As a result, two very low, small lakes formed in the Lake Michigan and Huron basins. Lake Chippewa (in the Lake Michigan basin) may have been as low as 70 m (Larsen 1987) while Lake Stanley (in the Huron Basin) was even lower—about 45 m (Eschman and Karrow 1985). The level of Lake Chippewa was controlled by a river channel eroded into soft bedrock at the bottom of the Straits of Mackinac, where it flowed eastward into Lake Stanley (Hough 1958). Today, we refer to this valley as the Mackinac Gorge. Only about 800 years separated the Main Algonquin high level from the Chippewa low level. Recently, Lewis et al. (2007) suggested Lake Stanley may have only dropped to 127 m, basing their argument on the elevation of seismic reflections and an erosion surface seen in offshore cores. They also have suggested that, by 9000 years ago, Lakes Chippewa and Stanley were temporarily closed basins, i.e. had no outward drainage, and that an early Holocene dry climate played a part in the inability of lake levels to keep pace with isostatically rising outlets.

FIGURE 13.12   Map of the ice margin about 12,900 years ago, showing Main Lake Algonquin (mA), Early Lake Erie (eE), and Lake Ontonagon (O).

FIGURE 13.13   Map of the ice margin about 11,600 years ago, during the Marquette glacial readvance (Gribben Phase), showing Early Lake Erie (eE), Lake Stanley (S), Lake Chippewa (C), and Lake Minong (M).

Opening the Lake Superior basin

In some ways, the development of Lake Superior is simpler than the other Great Lakes, because the Superior basin was the last to be deglaciated. However, complicating its development are the facts that the basin twice had separate eastern and western lakes, and was subjected to inflows from Lake Agassiz—the largest North American glacial lake, covering a large area in Manitoba and western Ontario, Canada, at the time of the inflows. The Lake Superior basin also experienced the largest amount of isostatic depression (and hence, rebound) of the Great Lake basins, and its outlet at Sault Ste. Marie, being on the eastern edge of the basin, is rebounding more than its western margins.

The oldest existing shorelines in the Superior basin were formed during the retreat of the Two Rivers Phase ice, roughly 12,900 years ago (Fig. 6.3). At this time, Lake Duluth formed at the western end of the basin, as well as the much smaller Lake Ontonagon in Gogebic, Ontonagon, and Houghton Counties (Fig. 13.12). Lake Ontonagon's outlet was at 403 m, draining to the SW through Wisconsin (Leverett 1929). Lake Duluth overflowed to the south, through outlets in Minnesota and Wisconsin, at an elevation of ~331 m. As Lake Duluth was expanding northward along the western shore (and extinguishing Lake Ontonagon), Lake Algonquin was also expanding northward across the eastern Upper Peninsula. Once the retreating ice margin cleared the Keweenaw Peninsula and the Huron Mountains, Lake Duluth merged with Lake Algonquin—which was at a lower level. It is not known how far north Lake Algonquin eventually extended, because the subsequent Marquette phase ice readvance wiped away its northern shorelines as far south as Alona Bay, Ontario (Farrand and Drexler 1985). Following the merger of these two lakes, the level of Lake Algonquin did not remain stable, but slowly fell due to the progressive opening of lower outlets to the east (see above). A bedrock drainage divide at Sault St. Marie, however, prevented the water level in the Superior basin from falling to the level of Lake Stanley in the Huron basin, establishing a new lake in the Superior basin named Lake Minong. It was around this time that a pathway also may have opened for water from Lake Agassiz (Moorhead phase) to escape east into the Superior basin and drain into the North Atlantic (Fisher 2003). Farrand and Drexler (1985) pointed out that Minong shorelines are 40 m above the present outlet at Sault Ste. Marie. A barrier to drainage, perhaps a moraine across Whitefish Bay (Saarnisto 1974), must therefore have existed during Lake Minong, to hold this water up. During the peak of the Marquette Phase ice readvance (Chapter 6), Lake Minong was quite small, pinned into the SE corner of the Superior basin. But as the ice retreated, Lake Minong expanded to the north and west. When the ice cleared the Keweenaw Peninsula, Lake Duluth in the west merged with Lake Minong in the east. Shorelines from Lake Minong are found on Isle Royale, and are the highest shorelines along the north shore of Lake Superior.

During the Marquette Phase ice readvance around 11,580 years ago (Fig. 13.13), the advancing ice margin once again separated the eastern and western portions of the Lake Superior basin, leaving a much diminished Lake Minong in the east and reestablishing Lake Duluth in the west. The advance even briefly squeezed Lake Duluth out of Michigan, leaving a renewed Lake Ontonagon in the western corner of the Upper Peninsula. As the ice margin subsequently retreated, Lake Duluth began expanding northward again, subsuming Lake Ontonagon (Fig. 13.14). When the ice margin pulled back from the Huron Mountains in Marquette County, eastern outlets opened up and again allowed the level of Lake Duluth to fall (Farrand and Drexler 1985). Discharge from Lake Duluth initially went south from Munising via the AuTrain-Whitefish channel, and then found a lower outlet on the north side of the Marquette phase moraines in Marquette and Alger Counties toward Lake Minong (Leverett 1929, Blewett 1994).

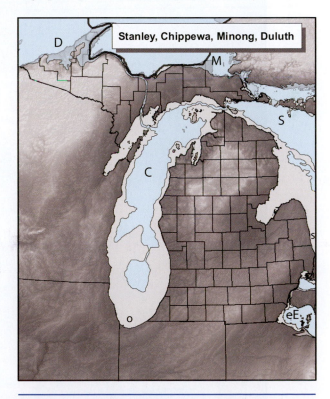

FIGURE 13.14 Map of the ice margin about 11,200 years ago, during retreat of the Marquette ice, showing the rising Lakes Stanley (S) and Chippewa (C), and Lakes Duluth (D) and Minong (M). The locations of the Olson (o) and Sanilac (s) drowned forest beds are also shown.

■ The Nipissing transgression

As soon as the North Bay, Ontario outlet was uncovered by glacial retreat (about 11,200 years ago), leading to the rapid draining of Lake Algonquin and forming the low-level Lakes Chippewa and Stanley, the outlet started to rebound. The slow but steady rise of the outlet caused the level of these low lakes to rise as well. Without any other influences, the rising lake level should have been a long, uninterrupted asymptotic curve—rapid lake level rises at first, and slowing down over time. However, brief spikes of high lake level interrupted this pattern, because the Marquette Phase ice retreat had opened outlets from Lake Agassiz into the Lake Superior basin, allowing Lake Agassiz floodwaters to discharge into the Superior basin, raising lake levels briefly but markedly each time. The high levels quickly overwhelmed Lake Minong, which was at the time overflowing into the Lake Michigan and Huron basins. At least two floods from Lake Agassiz tore through the Lake Superior basin, the first raising the lake level by as much as 35 m in a very short time period, and in so doing downcutting the Lake Minong outlet and lowering the Minong lake level (Safarudin and Moore 1999). These floods caused a series of temporary rises in levels of Lakes Chippewa and Stanley called the Mattawa highstands (Lewis and Anderson 1989, Lewis et al. 2007), which peaked between 10,600 and 9,300 years ago, before dropping back down to the rising post-Chippewa/Stanley level (Fig. 13.14). Recall that the Chippewa-Stanley lake level was already gradually rising due to the slow isostatic rebound of the North Bay outlet, before flood inflows from the Mattawa highstands occurred. It is likely that the Agassiz floods also eroded the St. Marys River down to bedrock, allowing the rising Chippewa-Stanley Lakes to merge with the a post-Minong lake in the Superior basin.

The results of these floods are observable in the bathymetry of Lake Michigan—between the Garden Peninsula of Delta County and the Door Peninsula of Wisconsin (Fig. 13.15). A distinct channel ending in a delta can be seen

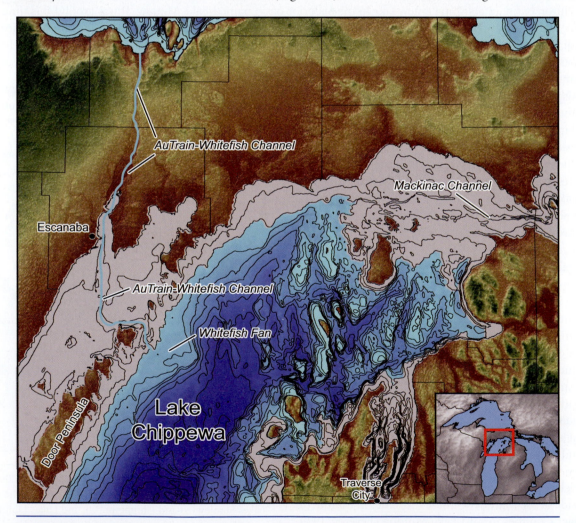

FIGURE 13.15   Digital elevation model (DEM) of the northwest edge of Lake Michigan, showing the Au Train-Whitefish channel descending from onshore to offshore and connecting with the submerged Whitefish fan. DEM data courtesy of the Michigan Center for Geographic Information (www.michigan.gov/cgi).

along the lake bottom. The channel and delta clearly extend directly from the onshore AuTrain-Whitefish Channel, which is a major topographic feature of the Upper Peninsula today. The delta (called the Whitefish fan) is at an elevation of about 126 m and represents the water surface at the time of its formation.

Several drowned forests have been found under the present day upper Great Lakes, attesting to the once low Chippewa-Stanley levels in the Michigan and Huron basins (Fig. 13.14). Wood samples from the Olson drowned forest site, 25 m under Lake Michigan near Chicago, have yielded an average age of 9,155 years (Schneider and Popadic 1994), and samples from the Sanilac drowned forest dated to about 7,350 years ago in 12.5 m water depth (Hunter et al. 2006).

By 6,300 years ago, the North Bay outlet had rebounded to 184 m, roughly the same elevation as the Chicago and Port Huron outlets, allowing all three outlets to be active simultaneously. This point marks the beginning of the Nipissing phase of the upper Great Lake basins (Fig. 13.16). The North Bay outlet continued to rebound, however, and therefore soon all drainage was via the two southern outlets (Chicago and Port Huron) only. Reoccupation of the Port Huron outlet also reestablished drainage from the upper Great Lakes into the lower Great Lakes (Erie and Ontario) after thousands of years of hydrologic separation.

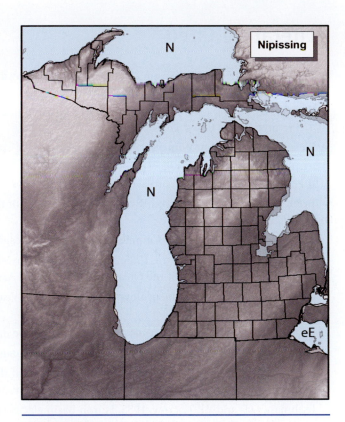

FIGURE 13.16 Map of the Nipissing phase (N) highstand about 6,000 years ago.

Studies by Fraser et al. (1990) indicate that the Nipissing phase high level (as well as the subsequent fall in lake level) was also strongly influenced by climate as well as by rebound.

Nipissing phase shorelines appear in many places all around the coasts of Lakes Superior, Michigan and Huron, and are often the first prominent shoreline above present lake level (Hough 1958; Fig. 13.5). They are second only to Algonquin shorelines in strength of development and have a more widespread geographic occurrence. Nipissing shorelines appear within a few meters of 184 m as far north as Traverse City and then gradually increase to 197 m at Sault Ste. Marie.

■ The modern Great Lakes

Because the glacial sediments of the Port Huron outlet were more susceptible to erosion than the bedrock at the Chicago outlet, the Port Huron outlet was gradually lowered by discharge from the Huron basin, allowing it to eventually take all the waters from the upper Great Lakes. The slowly falling Nipissing lake level did, however, stabilize long enough for a poorly-developed beach system to form around 3,400 years ago. Known as Lake Algoma, its elevation was 181.4 m. This event probably represents a temporary shift to a cooler and/or wetter paleoclimate and a subsequent rise in lake level (Fraser et al. 1990). Lake Algoma ended around 2,300 years ago (Baedke and Thompson 2000).

Lastly, rebound of the St. Marys River outlet caused the Lake Superior basin to separate from Lake Huron around 2,280 years ago (Farrand and Drexler 1985). At this time, the modern Great Lakes achieved their present configuration. Studies of beach ridges in embayments around Michigan and Indiana suggest that lake levels have fluctuated on both a 160 year and a 30 year cycle since the end of Lake Algoma (Baedke and Thompson 2000; Chapter 14). Historical records show lake level has varied by about 1.2 m since 1880 A.D. (Fraser et al. 1990).

Literature Cited

Baedke, S.J. and T.A. Thompson. 2000. A 4,700-year record of lake level and isostasy for Lake Michigan. Journal of Great Lakes Research 26:416–426.

Blewett, W.L. 1994. Late Wisconsin history of Pictured Rocks National Lakeshore and vicinity. National Park Service, Pictured Rocks Resource Report 94–01.

Blewett, W.L. and H.A. Winters. 1995. The importance of glaciofluvial features within Michigan's Port Huron moraine. Annals of the Association of American Geographers 85:306–319.

Bretz, J.H. 1951. The stages of Lake Chicago: Their causes and correlations. American Journal of Science 249:401–429.

Bretz, J.H. 1953. Glacial Grand River, Michigan. Papers of the Michigan Academy of Sciences, Arts and Letters 38:359–382.

Bretz, J.H. 1959. The double Calumet stage of Lake Chicago. Journal of Geology 67:675–684.

Calkin, P.E. and B.H. Feenstra. 1985. Evolution of the Erie-basin Great Lakes. In: Karrow P.F. and P.E. Calkin (eds), Quaternary Evolution of the Great Lakes. Geological Association of Canada Special Paper 30. pp. 149–170.

Clayton, L. 1997. Pleistocene geology of Dane County, Wisconsin. Wisconsin Geological and Natural History Survey Bulletin 95.

Deane, R.E. 1950. Pleistocene geology of the Lake Simcoe district, Ontario. Geological Survey of Canada Memoir 256.

Dorr, Jr. J.A. and D.F. Eschman. 1970. Geology of Michigan. Univ. of Michigan Press, Ann Arbor.

Eschman, D.F. and W.R. Farrand. 1970. Glacial history of the Glacial Grand valley. In: Guidebook to Field Trips, Geological Society of America, North-Central Section Annual Meeting, East Lansing, MI. pp. 131–157.

Eschman, D.F. and P.F. Karrow. 1985. Huron Basin glacial lakes. In: P.F. Karrow and P.E. Calkin (eds), Quaternary Evolution of the Great Lakes, Geological Association of Canada Special Paper 30. pp. 79–94.

Fairbanks, R.G., Mortlock, R.A., Chiu, T.-C., Cao, L., Kaplan, A., Guilderson, T.P., Fairbanks, T.W. and A.L. Bloom. 2005. Marine radiocarbon calibration curve spanning 0 to 50,000 years B.P. based on paired ^{230}Th/^{234}U and ^{14}C dates on pristine corals. Quaternary Science Reviews 24:1781–1796.

Farrand, W.R. and C.D. Drexler. 1985. Late Wisconsinan and Holocene history of the Lake Superior basin. In: P.F. Karrow and P.E. Calkin (eds), Quaternary Evolution of the Great Lakes, Geological Association of Canada Special Paper 30. pp. 17–32.

Farrand, W.R. and D.F. Eschman. 1974. Glaciation of the southern Peninsula of Michigan: A review. Michigan Academician 7:31–56.

Faure, G. 1986. Principles of Isotope Geology. John Wiley and Sons, New York.

Fisher, T.G. 2003. Chronology of glacial Lake Agassiz meltwater routed to the Gulf of Mexico. Quaternary Research 59:271–276.

Flint, R.F. 1971. Glacial and Quaternary Geology. John Wiley and Sons, New York.

Fraser, G.S., Larsen, C.E. and N.C. Hester. 1990. Climatic control of lake levels in the Lake Michigan and Lake Huron basins. In: Schneider A.F. and G.S. Fraser (eds), Late Quaternary History of the Lake Michigan Basin, Geological Society of America Special Paper 251. pp. 75–90.

Fullerton, D.S. 1980. Preliminary correlation of Post-Erie interstadial events (16,000–10,000 radiocarbon years before present), central and eastern Great Lakes region, and Hudson, Champlain and St. Lawrence lowlands, United States and Canada. US Geological Survey Professional Paper 1089.

Futyma, R.P. 1981. The northern limits of glacial Lake Algonquin in Upper Michigan. Quaternary Research 15:291–310.

Hansel, A.K. and D.M. Mickelson. 1988. A reevaluation of the timing and causes of high lake phases in the Lake Michigan Basin. Quaternary Research 29:113–128.

Hansel, A.K., Mickelson, D.M., Schneider, A.F. and C.E. Larsen. 1985. Late Wisconsinan and Holocene history of the Lake Michigan basin. In: P.F. Karrow and P.E. Calkin (eds), Quaternary Evolution of the Great Lakes. Geological Association of Canada Special Paper 30. pp. 39–54.

Hough, J.L. 1958. Geology of the Great Lakes. Univ. of Illinois Press, Urbana.

Hough, J.L. 1963. The prehistoric Great Lakes of North America. American Scientist 54:84–109.

Hunter, R.D., Panyushkina, I.P., Leavitt, S.W., Wiedenhoeft, A.C. and J. Zawiskie. 2006. A multiproxy environmental investigation of Holocene wood from a submerged conifer forest in Lake Huron, USA. Quaternary Research 66:67–77.

Karrow, P.F., Anderson, T.W., Clarke, A.H., Delorme, L.D. and M.R. Sreenivasa. 1975. Stratigraphy, paleontology and the age of Lake Algonquin sediments in southwestern Ontario, Canada. Quaternary Research 5:49–87.

Kaiser, K.F. 1994. Two Creeks Interstade dated through dendrochronology and AMS. Quaternary Research 42:288–298.

Kehew, A.E., Nicks, L.P. and W.T. Straw. 1999. Palimpsest tunnel valleys: evidence for relative timing of advances in an interlobate area of the Laurentide Ice Sheet. Annals of Glaciology 28:47–52.

Kincare, K.A. 2007. Response of the St. Joseph River to lake-level changes during the last 12,000 years in the Lake Michigan basin. Journal of Paleolimnology 37:383–394.

Krist, F. and R.J. Schaetzl. 2001. Paleowind (11,000 BP) directions derived from lake spits in northern Michigan. Geomorphology 38:1–18.

Larsen, C.E. 1987. Geological history of Glacial Lake Algonquin and the Upper Great Lakes. US Geological Survey Bulletin 1801.

Larson, G.J., Lowell, T.V. and N.E. Ostrom. 1994. Evidence for the Two Creeks interstade in the Lake Huron basin. Canadian Journal of Earth Sciences 31:793–797.

Leverett, F. 1929. Moraines and shore lines of the Lake Superior region. US Geological Survey Professional Paper 154–A.

Leverett, F. and F.B. Taylor. 1915. Pleistocene of Michigan and Indiana and the History of the Great Lakes. United States Geological Survey Monograph 53.

Lewis, C.F.M. and T.W. Anderson. 1989. Oscillations of levels and cool phases of the Laurentian Great Lakes caused by inflows from glacial Lakes Agassiz and Barlow-Ojibway. Journal of Paleolimnology 33:445–461.

Lewis, C.F.M., Heil, C.W., Hubeny, J.B., King, J.W., Moore, T.C. and D.K. Rea. 2007. The Stanley unconformity in Lake Huron basin: evidence for a climate-driven closed lowstand about 7900 14C BP, with similar implications for the Chippewa lowstand in Lake Michigan basin. Journal of Paleolimnology 37:435–452.

Martini, I.P., Brookfield, M.E. and S. Sadura. 2001. Principles of Glacial Geomorphology and Geology. Prentice Hall, Upper Saddle River, NJ.

Mickelson, D.M., Clayton, L., Fullerton, D.S. and H.W. Borns Jr. 1983. Late glacial record of the Laurentide Ice Sheet in the United States, In: Late Quaternary Environments of the United States, Wright, H.E., Jr. (ed), Volume 1: The Late Pleistocene (S.C. Porter, editor), University of Minnesota Press, Minneapolis. pp. 3–37.

Monaghan, G.W. and A.K Hansel. 1990. Evidence for the intra-Glenwood (Mackinaw) low-water phase of glacial Lake Chicago. Canadian Journal of Earth Sciences 27:1236–1241.

Muller, E.H. 1977. Late glacial and early postglacial environments in western New York. Annals of the New York Academy of Sciences 288:223–233.

Rieck, R.L. and H.A. Winters. 1993. Drift volume in the southern peninsula of Michigan—a prodigious Pleistocene endowment. Physical Geography 14:478–493.

Saarnisto, M. 1974. The deglaciation history of the Lake Superior region and its climatic implications. Quaternary Research 4:316–339.

Safarudin and T.C. Moore. 1999. The history and architecture of lacustrine depositional systems in the northern Lake Michigan Basin. Journal of Paleolimnology 22:475–496.

Schaetzl, R.J., Drzyzga, S.A., Weisenborn, B.N., Kincare, K.A., Lepczyk, X.C., Shein, K.A., Dowd, C.M. and J. Linker. 2002. Measurement, correlation, and mapping of Glacial Lake Algonquin shorelines in northern Michigan. Annals of the Association of American Geographers 92:399–415.

Schneider, A.F. and T.H. Popadic. 1994. The Nipissing transgression in the Lake Michigan Basin: Summary and speculation. Geological Society of America, North Central Section 28th Annual Meeting Abstract 26(4):27.

Soller, D.R. 1998. Map showing the thickness and character of Quaternary sediments in the glaciated United States east of the Rocky Mountains; northern Great Lakes states and central Mississippi Valley states, the Great Lakes, and southern Ontario (80 degrees 31' to 93 degrees west longitude). US Geological Survey IMAP 1970–B.

Stanley, G.M. 1936. Lower Algonquin beaches of Penetanguishene Peninsula. Geological Society of America Bulletin 47:1933–1960.

Stanley, G.M. 1945. Prehistoric Mackinac Island. Michigan Geological Survey Publication 43.

Stuiver, M. 1978. Atmospheric carbon dioxide and carbon reservoir changes. Science 199:253–258.

Further Readings

Alley, R.B. 2000. The two-mile time machine: ice cores, abrupt climate change, and our future. Princeton Univ. Press, Princeton, NJ.

Schneider, A.F. and G.S. Fraser (eds). 1990. Late Quaternary history of the Lake Michigan Basin. Geological Society of America Special Paper 251.

Teller, J.T. 1987. Proglacial lakes and the southern margin of the Laurentide ice sheet. In: Ruddiman, W.F. and H.E. Wright Jr. North America and adjacent oceans during the last deglaciation. Geological Society of America Geology of North America K-3:39–69.

14

The Modern Great Lakes

Ted R. Batterson

■ Introduction

The Great Lakes are a prominent physical feature of North America that have tremendous economic, cultural, and environmental importance. The Great Lakes ecosystem includes Lakes Superior, Michigan, Huron, Erie and Ontario as well as their connecting channels and watersheds (Fig. 14.1). This vast freshwater ecosystem is highly dynamic—physically, chemically, and biologically. It is impacted not only from activities within the watershed but also from those outside of the boundaries of the basins, due to such things as long-range, airborne transport. With the exception of Lake Michigan, the only Great Lake wholly contained within the United States, the lakes are a shared international resource, providing a variety of ecosystem services and functions, including climate regulation, water supply, transportation, fish production, and recreation. Costanza et al. (1997) placed an annual value on the ecosystem services of the Great Lakes at $8,498/ha. With a total surface area of 245,280 km^2 this estimate would make the Great Lakes worth $208.4 billion/year, or $84.4 billion/year for the waters controlled by Michigan.

The Great Lakes have also been vital to the development of Michigan as a state—first as a means of conveyance, serving as highways to the exploration of the interior of North America (Chapter 27), and then as a pathway to move goods, the first of which was furs. The oldest permanently occupied settlement in Michigan, Sault Ste. Marie, was established in 1667 at the rapids (Sault) of the St. Marys River, where a portage took voyageurs up to Lake Superior (Catton 1976). Other important early Michigan settlements were also along the Great Lakes—at the Straits of Mackinac as well as at Detroit. Later, the lakes became important for many other goods and services provided to Michigan citizens.

Michigan's land mass borders on four of the five Great Lakes (Superior, Michigan, Huron and Erie; Plate 1) and Michigan's true boundaries (mostly to the middle of the lakes; Chapter 1) contain 40.5% of the surface area of the lake ecosystem—far more than any other state (Figs. 14.1, 14.2). The Canadian province of Ontario is second to Michigan in ownership of the Great Lakes with 35.9% under its control, whereas the other seven states (Wisconsin, New York, Ohio, Minnesota, Illinois, Pennsylvania, and Indiana in rank order from most to least) combined only own 23.6% (Fig. 14.2). With the exception of two small portions of Gogebic and Berrien Counties, the entire land mass of Michigan lies within the Great Lakes basin.

■ The Great Lakes: by the numbers

In surface area, the Great Lakes constitute the largest freshwater lake system in the world. All five of the lakes rank, globally, in the top 20 by either surface area or volume. Lake Baikal, in Siberia, is the largest freshwater lake in the world by volume, holding slightly more fresh water than all five of the Great Lakes combined, because of its great

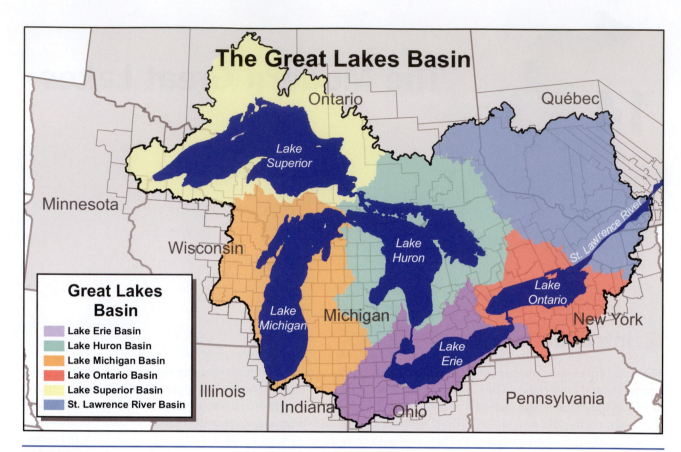

The Great Lakes Basin

FIGURE 14.1 The Great Lakes watershed, showing the watershed for each lake as well as counties within the basin both in the US and Canada. After the Great Lakes Commission, Ann Arbor, MI.

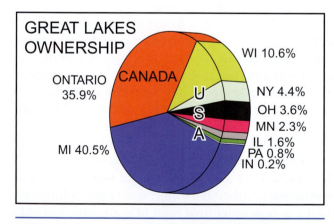

FIGURE 14.2 Ownership of the Great Lakes by the eight states and the province of Ontario, Canada.

depth (Table 14.1). Together, Lake Baikal and the Great Lakes hold approximately 36% of the total surface freshwater found in world's lakes, rivers and streams (van der Leeden et al. 1990). If spread out evenly, the water in the Great Lakes would cover the entire continental US to a depth of approximately 3.3 m. Lake Superior, the largest of the Great Lakes, holds more water than all four other Great Lakes combined. In surface area, the Great Lakes would cover all of the land mass of New England, as well as almost 67% of the land mass of New York. Any way you measure it, they are like an inland ocean—a very large hydrologic system!

Hydrologically, the Great Lakes are an interconnected, stair-step waterway that stretches almost 2,011 km from the western tip of Lake Superior, east to the St. Lawrence River (Fig. 14.3). Water continually flows from Lake Superior, at the highest surface elevation, through the St. Marys River, into Lake Huron. Although separate geographically, Lakes Michigan and Huron are hydrologically one water mass, both at the same surface elevation and connected by the 7 km-wide Straits of Mackinac. Water flows from Lake Huron through the St. Clair River, then into the very shallow Lake St. Clair, and then via the Detroit River into Lake Erie. Before the completion of the Erie and Welland Canals, in 1825 and 1829, respectively, all water leaving Lake Erie flowed through the Niagara River over Niagara Falls and then on to Lake Ontario. Water leaves the eastern end of Lake Ontario via the St. Lawrence

TABLE 14.1   The Earth's largest lakes[1]

Area			Volume		
Rank	**Name**	**Area (km²)**	**Rank**	**Name**	**Volume (km³)**
1	Caspian Sea[2]	374,000	1	Caspian Sea[2]	78,200
2	Lake Superior[3]	82,680	2	Lake Baikal	23,000
3	Lake Victoria	69,000	3	Lake Tanganyika	18,900
4	Aral Sea[2]	64,100	4	Lake Superior[3]	11,600
5	Lake Huron[3]	59,800	5	Lake Nyasa	7,725
6	Lake Michigan[3]	58,100	6	Lake Michigan[3]	4,680
7	Lake Tanganyika	32,900	7	Lake Huron[3]	3,580
8	Lake Baikal	31,500	8	Lake Victoria	2,700
9	Lake Nyasa	30,900	9	Lake Issyk-Kul'	1,730
10	Great Bear Lake	30,200	10	Lake Ontario[3]	1,710
11	Great Slave Lake	27,200	11	Great Slave Lake	1,070
12	Lake Erie[3]	25,700	12	Aral Sea[2]	1,020
13	Lake Winnipeg	24,600	13	Great Bear Lake	1,010
14	Lake Ontario[3]	19,000	16	Lake Erie[3]	545
	Great Lakes Total =	245,280		Great Lakes Total =	22,115

1. After van der Leeden et al. (1990).
2. Salt lake
3. These values do not exactly match those contained in other sources, e.g., Swinehart (2000).

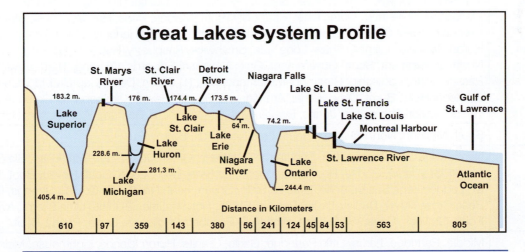

FIGURE 14.3   Great Lakes system profile. After Gauthier et al. (1999).

River which flows approximately 869 km into the Atlantic Ocean's Gulf of St. Lawrence. Together, this inland waterway, with all its interconnecting passageways, canals, locks and dams, is called the St. Lawrence Seaway; it is a major passageway for commodities to travel from the heartland of the US and Canada to the Atlantic Ocean. The lakes also contain an amazing number of islands, from the large Isle Royale, a US National Park (Chapter 24), to some so small as to not even be named (Table 14.2).

TABLE 14.2   Named Michigan Islands within the Great Lakes[1]

County	Islands
Alcona	Black River
Alger	*Grand, Lost,* Wood, Williams, Au Train
Alpena	Bird, Scarecrow, Sulphur, Grass, Thunder Bay, Sugar, Gull, Crooked, Middle, Round
Arenac	Charity, Little Charity, Gull
Bay	Gull, Channel, Shelter
Charlevoix	*Beaver, High, Garden, Hog,* Gull, Trout, Whiskey, Squaw, Pismire, Grape, Horseshoe, Shoe, Hat, Tims
Chippewa	Albany, Saddlebag, *Drummond, Frying Pan, Crab, Arnold, Surgeon, Fisher, Bird, Garden, Bellevue, Long, Espanore, Gravel, Canoe, Meade, Shelter, Lime, Burnt, Harbor,* Twin, Round, Bass Reef, Love, Edward, Hart, Little Lime, Sweets, Squaw, Pipe, Pipe Twins, Little Cass, Cass, Macomb, Andrews, Big Trout, Maple, Butterfield, Bow, Little Trout, Surveyors, Arrow, Adelaide, Fairbank, Cove, Young, Picnic, Willoughby, Sam, Wreck, Boulnger, Gull, Saltonstall, Mare, Long, Standerson, Twin Sisters, Spence, Norris, Claw, Harris, Wilson, Cedar, Cherry, Propeller, Rogg, Howard, Bald, Little Rogg, Quarry, LaPointe, Bay, Fire, Grape, Ashman, Round, Iroquois, Rose, Tahquamanon, James, Jim, Rutland, Peck, *Neebish, Sugar,* Pilot, Pine, Steamboot, (1) Sand, (2) Sand, the Moon Group, Rains, Hen, Chicken, Duck, Advance, Rock, Gem, Cook, Hog, No. 1, No. 2, No. 3, Mouse, Whitehead
Delta	*St. Martin, Summer, Little Summer,* Poverty, Gull, Little Gull, Gravelly, Rocky, (1) Round, (2) Round, St. Vitals, Snake
Emmet	Ile Aux Galets, Waugoshonce, Temperance
Grand Traverse	Marion
Houghton	Traverse
Huron	*Heisterman/Stony (the " / " implies that the island has two names), Defoe, Duck, Hog, Lone Tree, Middle Ground,* North, Maisou, North Mineshas, South Mineshas
Keweenaw	*Manitou, Isle Royale.* Little Siskiwit, Siskiwit, Redfin, Paul, Castle, (1) Long, Stone House, Menagerie, Shiverette, Outer, Inner, Channel, Wright, Malone, Ross, Hat, Schooner, Middle, Cemetery, West Caribou, East Caribou, Rabbit, Mott, Outer Hill, Inner Hill, Mad, Star, Davidson, Heron, Tookers, Tallman, Shaw, Lone Tree, Smithwick, Raspberry, Bat, Minong, Flag, Smith, North Government, South Government, Gale, Newman, Edwards, (2) Long, Third, Boys, Merritt, Passge. Pete, Battleship, Steamboat, Diamond, Net, (1) Green, Dean, Captain Kidd, Cork, Johnson, Belle, Burnt, Clay, Horner, Amygdaloid, Round, Hawk, Kamloops, (2) Green, Arch, Wilson, Taylor, Thompson, Johns, Beaver, Salt, Grace, Booth, Barnum, Washington, Bottle
Leelanau	South Manitou, North Manitou, South Fox, North Fox, Bellow/Gull
Mackinac	Naubinway, Gravel, Little Hog, Epoufette, St. Helena, Green, *Bois Blanc, Mackinac, Big St. Martin, St. Martin,* Goose, Round, *Marquette, La Salle,* Birch, Long, Goat, Haven, Boot Jack, St. Ledger, Lone Susan, Echo, Little La Salle, Government, No. 8, Hill, Coryell, Strongs, Gravelly, Bear, Crow, Rover, Dudley, Dollar, Rogers, Booth, Dot, (1) Little, (2) Little, Little Ellen's, Avery Point, Grover's, Cove, White Loon, Whitefish, Raspberry, Polleck's, Eagle, Penny, Boot
Marquette	Middle, Partridge, Larus, Little Partridge, Garlic, Granite, Huron Islands, Lighthouse, McIntrye, Gull, and three unnamed
Monroe	Guard, Indian, Turtle (NW half only)
St. Clair	*Dickinson, Harsens,* Strawberry, Green, Middle, North, Sand, Gull, Russell
Wayne	*Grosse Ile, Belle Isle,* Sturgeon, Bar, Celeron, Round, Horse, Hickory, Swan, Calf, Sugar, Meso, Fox, Grassy, Elba, Stony, Mud, Zug

1: Islands over 2.6 km[2] in area are italicized. After Santer (2003).

■ Water levels and water balance of the Great Lakes

During, and since, the retreat of the last glaciers, water levels and outflows of the Great Lakes have varied dramatically. These extremes were caused by various factors, including changing climate, natural openings and closings of channel outlets as the ice retreated or readvanced, as well as the isostatic (crustal) rebound that has been occurring after the weight of the glaciers was removed (Chapter 13). Within the last 1,000 years, evidence suggests that lake level variability has exceeded the range of levels recorded by human instrumentation by 1.5 m on Lakes Michigan and Huron (Gauthier et al. 1999). As a consequence of these fluctuations, shoreline position, and the structures placed on the shore, have varied dramatically. River mouths, embayments, baymouth barriers, and coastal dunes all have been impacted by the changing lake levels (Chapter 18).

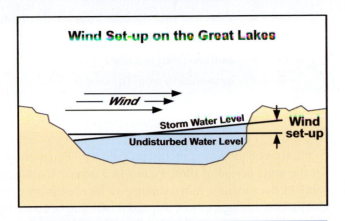

FIGURE 14.4   Wind set-up on the Great Lakes. After Gauthier et al. (1999).

Great Lakes water levels vary on many temporal scales, on hourly, daily, interannual and millennial frequencies. At any point on the Great Lakes, daily and hourly fluctuations in lake levels occur, ranging from a few cm to several meters. These small water level perturbations are largely independent of the volume of water in the lake. Instead, they are typically caused by meteorological forces, such as winds or changing barometric pressure. Examples of meteorologically induced water level disturbances are storm surges, wind tides and seiches. In addition to these meteorological phenomena, there are also astronomical (or true) tides on the Great Lakes. True tides on the Great Lakes have a mean range of about 3 mm (Liu et al. 1976)—small, compared to the more pronounced lake level fluctuations resulting from meteorological forces.

Storm surges—sudden and usually unexpected rises in lake level—also generate water level changes that can have disastrous impacts on shoreline structures, as well as humans. One example occurred in Lake Michigan on June 26, 1954, when a fast-moving storm raised water levels as much as 3 m along the Chicago shoreline and killed at least seven people (Ewing et al. 1954). Another example of a more dramatic change in water level due to a storm surge occurred on Lake Erie on April 6, 1979 (Hamblin 1979). During that storm, the change in water level between one end of Lake Erie and the other—from Toledo, OH to Buffalo, NY—was 4.5 m.

Wind tides differ from storm surges because the former have longer wavelengths and durations of build-up time. A wind tide typically takes hours to reach equilibrium, whereas a storm surge might only take minutes. The amount of rise in water level produced during a wind tide is known as wind set-up (Fig. 14.4). Lake Erie is particularly vulnerable to wind tides because of its WSW-ENE orientation, which parallels the prevailing winds. The largest recorded wind set-up on Lake Erie was 4.2 m (Liu et al. 1976). It has been estimated that wind set-ups on Lakes Michigan and Huron would be only 25% of the magnitude of that on Lake Erie and only 17% for Lakes Superior and Ontario (Bajorunas 1960, as cited in Liu et al. 1976).

Seiches are free lake surface oscillations that continue after external forces that caused the initial oscillation have ceased. Therefore, they follow either storm surges or wind tides. Great Lakes water level fluctuations caused by seiches have been as great as 0.3 m (Schertzer 1982).

Fortunately, all of these types of water level changes are transient, and the resulting impacts are localized and short term. Potentially more problematic are lake level changes due to changing water volumes within the basins. They involve time periods that are long enough to absorb any local short-period variations, so that the entire surface can be assumed to be level. Lake levels rise with increasing water volume and decline with decreasing water volume, a change that can be expressed mathematically as:

$$\Delta V \sim (I + R + P + D_i + G_i) - (Q + E + D_o + G_o)$$

where:

ΔV =   change in lake volume due to rise or fall in level

I =   inflow from the lake above (upstream)

R = runoff from drainage basin, into the lake

P = precipitation onto the lake

D_i = diversion into the lake from another basin (omitted for Lake Huron)

G_i = ground water inflow

Q = outflow from the lake

E = evaporation from the lake

D_o = diversion from the lake into another basin (omitted for Lake Huron)

G_o = seepage into the lake substrate

In the above equation, sometimes called the "Equation of Hydrologic Balance," all terms are in the same units and for the same period of time. Figure 14.5 depicts the various components of the Great Lakes water cycle. Although some of the medium-range changes in lake levels are due to human-mediated alterations, such as diversions and channel deepenings, as well as crustal rebound or scouring of river outlets, these effects are comparatively small in comparison to changes due to meteorological factors.

The Great Lakes undergo an annual cycle of lake level change, with lows in the winter and highs in mid-summer (Fig. 14.6). Of course, the amplitudes of the cycles change from year to year and from lake to lake. Richards (1967) offered a clear and concise description of this phenomenon: Rising water levels occur in the spring and early summer, (1) after snow-melt and spring floods, and when (2) precipitation is at its greatest, (3) groundwater levels are highest, and (4) evaporation rates are low (due to the low water temperatures). Conversely, falling water levels occur in the fall and winter, when (1) evaporation rates are high, (2) groundwater levels are lowest, (3) precipitation is at its lightest, and (4) most of the winter's precipitation on the watershed is locked up as snow.

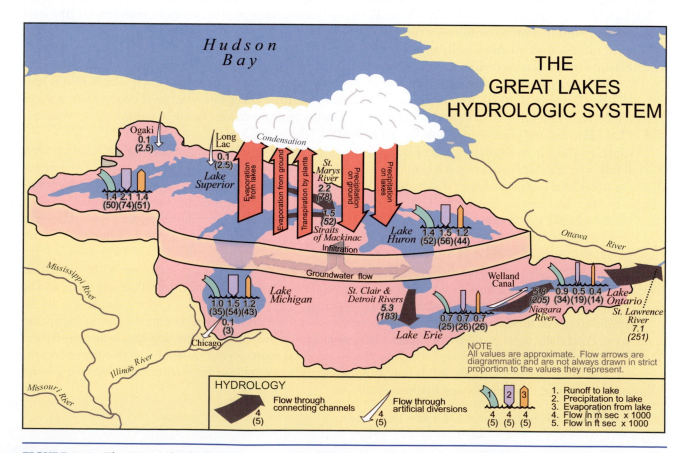

FIGURE 14.5   The Great Lakes hydrologic system. After Fuller et al. (1995).

Various data on Great Lakes water levels from the US Army Corps of Engineers indicate that the average annual variation in lake levels on Lakes Superior, Michigan, Huron and Erie is about 0.3 m, whereas for Lake Ontario it is slightly over 0.5 m. Their data also show that, for the period 1918–2003, the range in mean monthly water levels from extreme high to extreme low has been 1.19 m for Lake Superior, 1.92 m for Lakes Michigan and Huron, 1.86 m for Lake Erie, and 2.02 m for Lake Ontario (Fig. 14.7). The time intervals between successive high water periods, or between successive low water periods, are highly irregular. Rises and falls may be gradual or abrupt.

Exceptionally low levels on the Great Lakes were experienced in the mid-1920s, mid-1930s, and early 1960s. High levels occurred in 1929–30, 1952, 1973–74, 1985–86, and 1997–98. Record highs for all Great Lakes, except Lake Ontario, were reached in 1986; record lows in 1964. One unresolved question about Great Lakes' water levels is whether long-term periodicities exist. For years, efforts have been made to identify a pattern of long-term variations. Cycles of 7, 11, and 90 years have been postulated, but their validity is still in doubt.

In addition to these natural changes in water level fluctuations (largely due to meteorological conditions), human alterations have also had an impact. For example, outflows from the Great Lakes have changed over time, due to human intervention. Flow from Lake Superior has changed as humans have altered the St. Marys River, beginning with the locks that were put in place at Sault Ste. Marie, as well as with the comple-

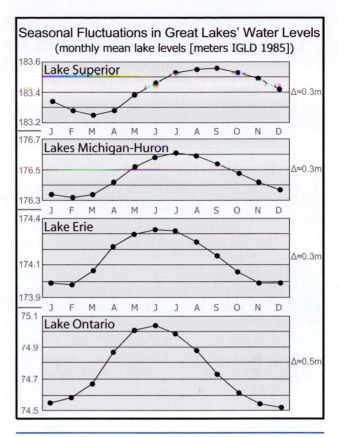

FIGURE 14.6 Seasonal fluctuations in Great Lakes' water levels. Source: U.S. Army Corps of Engineers Detroit District Web site: http://www.lre.usace.army.mil/greatlakes/hh/greatlakeswaterlevels/historicdata/greatlakeshydrographs/, Accessed January, 2006.

tion of the Compensating Works at the head of the St. Marys Rapids in 1921. Outflows from Lake Superior are adjusted at the Compensating Works (a gated dam) to help maintain a relative balance between water levels on Lake Superior and on Lakes Huron and Michigan. The Compensating Works functions by the opening or closing any of the 16, 16 m-wide gates, eight of which are in Canada. At a minimum, one gate is kept half open to maintain sufficient water flow for fish ecology within the St. Marys Rapids, immediately below the Compensating Works. This regulation of flow from Lake Superior is determined on, and carried out, on a monthly basis by the International Lake Superior Board of Control, in accordance with conditions specified by the International Joint Commission (IJC), a binational organization between the US and Canada (Clites and Quinn 2003). Additionally, since 1960, outflow from Lake Ontario has been regulated on a weekly basis, to meet the riparian, hydropower and navigational needs along the St. Lawrence River. Beginning in the 1930s and continuing through the 1950s, the navigation channels in the St. Clair-Detroit system (St. Clair River, Lake St. Clair and Detroit River) were deepened to accommodate deeper drafts of commercial vessels on the Great Lakes. These dredging activities increased the flows of the St. Clair and Detroit Rivers, and as a result have permanently lowered the levels of Lakes Michigan and Huron by an estimated 38 cm (Gauthier et al. 1999).

Other human alterations, termed "diversions," have also changed the natural amount of water in the Great Lakes. A diversion is defined as water that is conveyed by canal, pipeline, modified channel or any other similar means, from its basin of origin for use in another drainage basin (International Joint Commission 2000). Diversions are further classified as being either interbasin, meaning into or out of the Great Lakes basin, or intrabasin, where water is diverted from one sub-basin to another. There are currently 14 existing diversions on the Great Lakes (International Joint Commission 2000; Table 14.3).

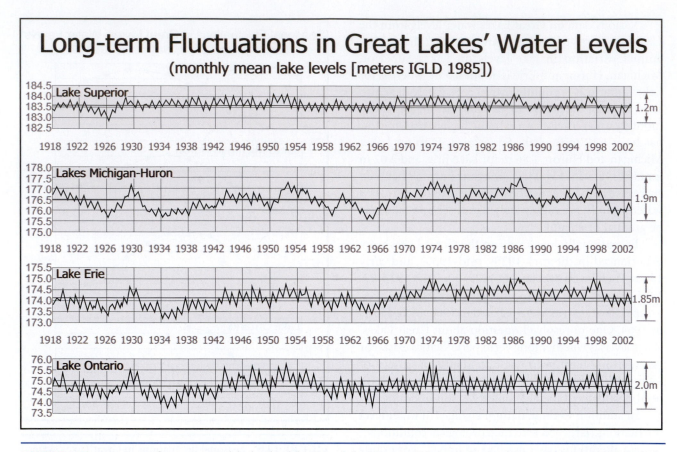

FIGURE 14.7   Long-term fluctuations in lake levels of the Great Lakes. Source: U.S. Army Corps of Engineers Detroit District Web site: http://www.lre.usace.army.mil/greatlakes/hh/greatlakeswaterlevels/historicdata/greatlakeshydrographs/, Accessed January, 2006.

TABLE 14.3   Existing diversions into and out of the Great Lakes Basin[1]

Interbasin	Operational date (original project)	Average annual discharge (m³/s)
Long Lac (into Lake Superior basin)	1939	45
Ogoki (into Lake Superior basin)	1943	113
Chicago (out of Lake Michigan basin)	1900 (1848)	91
Forestport (out of Lake Michigan basin)	1825	1.4
Portage Canal (into Lake Michigan basin)	1860	1
Ohio & Erie Canal (into Lake Erie basin)	1847	0.3
Pleasant Prairie (out of Lake Michigan basin)	1990	0.1
Akron (out of and into Lake Erie basin)	1998	0.01
Intrabasin		
Welland Canal	1932 (1829)	260
New York State Barge Canal (Erie Canal)	1918 (1825)	20
Detroit	1975	4
London, Ontario	1967	3
Raisin River, Ontario	1968	0.7
Haldimand, Ontario	1997	0.1

1. After International Joint Commission (2000).

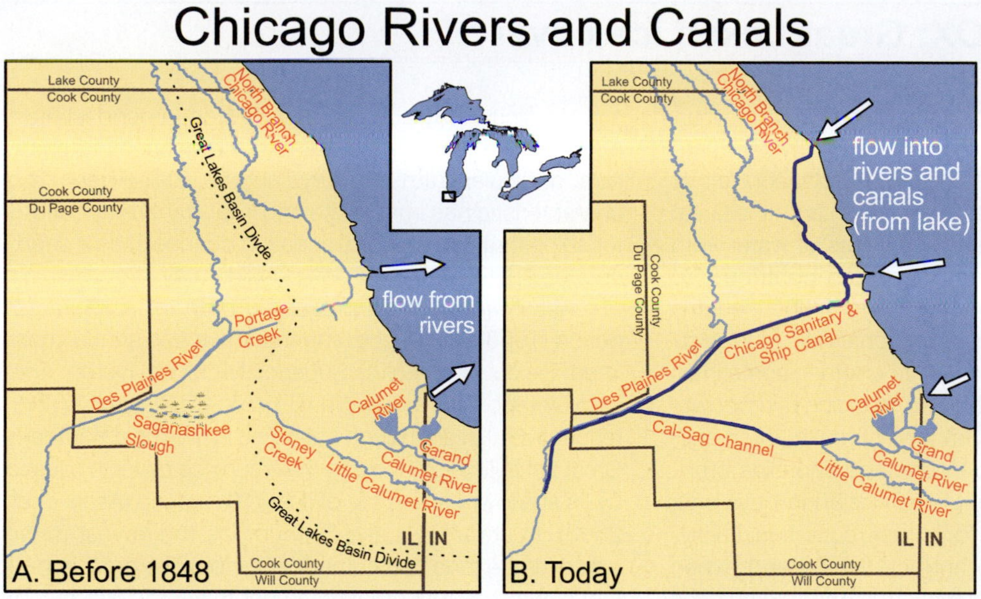

Chicago Rivers and Canals

FIGURE 14.8 Rivers and canals in the vicinity of Chicago, before 1848 and at present.

One important, and controversial, Great Lakes' diversion is in Chicago (Table 14.3). Prior to 1848, the Chicago and Calumet Rivers flowed south and eastward, into the southern end of Lake Michigan. This portion of Lake Michigan served as the source for the drinking water supply for the city of Chicago, as well as being a sink for the city's sewage. Unfortunately, discharge of raw sewage into Lake Michigan led to repeated outbreaks of water-borne diseases in the city, such as cholera and typhoid fever. Additionally, many had long recognized in these rivers an opportunity—for they could help bridge a possible waterway connection between the Great Lakes and the Mississippi River, and then on to the Gulf of Mexico. To alleviate the problem of water-borne disease, as well as to allow for river transportation between the Great Lakes and the Mississippi River, canals were constructed and the flows of the lower Chicago and Calumet Rivers reversed, beginning in 1848 (Fig. 14.8). Thus, the natural watershed of the Great Lakes was compromised—water began flowing out of Lake Michigan, into the Chicago and Calumet Rivers, and thence into the Des Plaines River, to the Illinois and Mississippi Rivers, and ultimately into the Gulf of Mexico. Despite this dramatic and history-steeped example, the overall impact of human alterations on Great Lakes water levels is small compared to natural meteorological variations.

The US Army Corps of Engineers' Detroit District, in conjunction with the Great Lakes Commission and the University of Wisconsin Sea Grant, have developed several documents that help explain changing Great Lakes water levels and help Great Lakes basin residents adapt to these dynamic processes (Gauthier et al. 1999, Keillor 2003).

■ Effects on climate

Due to their enormous size and the high specific heat of water, the Great Lakes have significant influence on the region's climate (Chapters 19, 38). This is especially true for Michigan, which is virtually surrounded by the lakes and is downwind from two of the largest ones—Superior and Michigan. Because water's specific heat is so great, a lake must absorb vast quantities of heat in order for the water temperature to increase (Chapter 38). This explains why lake temperatures rise so slowly in the spring—the lake is acting like a heat sink. Likewise, the slowly cooling water temperatures in autumn are due to the large amounts of heat that must be released. Thus, the lakes help to moderate air temperatures in nearby locations—cooling the summers and warming the winters, delaying the onset of spring and prolonging warm, fall weather.

The lakes also act like giant humidifiers, increasing atmospheric moisture content in nearby air masses throughout the year—as long as they don't freeze over (which rarely happens). In the winter, when moist air from the

FOCUS BOX: Great Lakes ice cover

Ice cover on the Great Lakes is highly variable from year-to-year, and is exceedingly important to both water quantity and quality, as well as to shipping and transportation. Widespread ice cover reduces evaporation from the Great Lakes and, therefore, moderates the loss of water from them during the winter. This in turn can contribute to higher water levels the following spring. Huge ice jams can form in Great Lakes connecting channels, constricting the flow of water from one lake to another, sometimes creating flooding above the jam and reducing hydropower downstream. When the ice jam finally breaks, the resulting surge of water and ice can damage shoreline properties and structures. Stable ice formation in bays can, however, provide a platform for winter recreational activities such as snowmobiling and ice fishing and, when along shorelines, can protect wetlands and shore zones from erosion.

A simple sequence of ice formation on the Great Lakes rarely occurs because of variable prevailing weather conditions during the winter months. Typically, however, ice first forms along the shores, shallow embayments, e.g., Saginaw Bay and Big Bay de Noc, around islands, e.g., Apostle and Manitoulin, and the connecting channels, particularly the St. Marys and St. Clair Rivers. This characteristic has immediate and important ramifications for ships that use these connecting channels, as it shortens their navigation seasons considerably.

Assel et al. (2003) presented data for a 39-winter period (1963–2001), showing that the mean annual maximum ice cover on Lakes Superior, Michigan, Huron, Erie, and Ontario was 68.3, 39.6, 64.3, 87.3, and 27.8%, respectively. Even though Lake Erie is the most southerly Great Lake, its high average maximum ice cover is caused by its shallowness; ≈21% of it is ≤10 m deep (Assel et al. 2003). In contrast, Lake Ontario has the lowest mean ice coverage, due to a number of factors, the most important of which are its great mean depth (86 m), depth configuration, and relatively mild winter air temperature regime. Interestingly, only Lakes Superior and Erie have been entirely frozen between 1963–2001; only once for Lake Superior in 1996 and five times for Lake Erie in 1977, 1978, 1979, 1996, and 1997.

lakes reaches land and cools, it condenses into snow, creating snowfall in some downwind nearshore areas known as "snowbelts." "Lake effect" snow is a signature part of Michigan's winter weather (Chapter 19). Some of the most significant "snowbelts" in the Great Lakes occur in Michigan—on the Keweenaw Peninsula and further to the east, around Marquette, as well as in the Gaylord area (Fig. 19.9).

Michigan is one of the nation's major fruit producing states, largely because of Lake Michigan's "lake effect" on the state's western areas (Michigan Agricultural Statistics 2004). In those areas the "lake effect" helps delay blossoming of fruit trees in the spring, which reduces the possibility of freeze damage (Chapter 38). In addition, "lake-effect" snow provides extra moisture for the trees and insulates their roots from deep soil frost (Isard and Schaetzl 1995).

■ Other human perturbations of the Lakes

Native Americans had little actual impact on the Great Lakes. However, with the settlement and development of lands along the shoreline and within the basin by Europeans, the Great Lakes ecosystem began to be physically, chemically, and biologically altered. Some of the physical alterations have already been mentioned; the focus here is on chemical changes in the Great Lakes. Due to their vast size, the impacts of expanding human populations within the basin (Chapter 34) on the lakes' chemical characteristics went virtually unnoticed by the public until the 1960s. However, during that decade, the public became keenly aware of chemical changes that were occurring in most of the lakes. These changes resulted in eutrophication, or nutrient enrichment, of parts of the lakes. Lake Superior, with less human activity within its watershed, its greater volume, and the lowest levels of natural nutrient concentrations, experienced almost no eutrophication. Conversely, Lake Erie, the smallest lake with some of the densest human population surrounding it, had it the worst.

The eutrophication of the Great Lakes has been largely the result of increasing phosphorus (P) concentrations from sewage effluents and surface runoff (Beeton 1965, 1969, Burns 1985, McGucken 2000). Fortunately, the lakes

FOCUS BOX: Lake Erie

Lake Erie was in such bad shape, ecologically, that, in an August 20, 1905 article, Time magazine stated, "the lake has been brought to its deathbed by the citizens and industries that surround it; only a massive transfusion of money and effort can save it from becoming a North American Dead Sea." Four years later, on August 1, 1969, Time published another story, again decrying the plight of Lake Erie, saying it was "in danger of dying by suffocation" and showing a photograph of the Cuyohoga River in downtown Cleveland, Ohio—on fire. They credited the Cleveland Plain Dealer newspaper for the photo. That image of the "river that caught fire" became a rallying point for environmentalists in their ongoing fight for cleaner water. However, that image of the burning Cuyohoga River was not of the fire of June 22, 1969, but of an earlier fire that had occurred in December 1952, when an oil slick had caught on fire, destroying three tugs, several buildings, and a ship repairyard. The 1952 fire caused nearly 30 times the damage of the 1969 fire, but it was the latter that got all of the national attention.

There is good news here. Lake Erie underwent a dramatic recovery, as documented in a book entitled "Erie: The Lake that Survived" (Burns 1985). Unfortunately, the lake has suffered more recent human-caused disturbances, such as zebra mussels that have disrupted the ecology of the lake once again.

---

have had a dramatic recovery from the 1960s' eutrophication, largely because of reduced P loadings and the relatively rapid flushing of most of the lakes (Table 14.4). However, some have contended that we might have done too good of job in reducing P concentrations in Lake Erie, and that the lake is now undergoing oligotrophication, the opposite of eutrophication (Parker et al. 2000).

Recently, concerns about chemical changes in the Great Lakes (resulting from human activities) have focused on toxic chemical substances, e.g., heavy metals such as mercury and numerous synthetic organic compounds such as DDT, PCBs, and dioxins. These substances have wide-ranging implications for the lakes' biota, as well as for human health. Much has been written about the issue, including untold numbers of scientific articles, reports, newspaper and magazine stories and numerous books (or portions thereof), the latter of which from various viewpoints, e.g., Ashworth (1986), Colborn et al. (1990), and Weller (1990). Dempsey (2001, 2004) has dealt with this subject from a Michigan perspective.

TABLE 14.4   Flushing rates of the Great Lakes[1]

Lake	Time (years)
Superior	173
Michigan	62
Huron	21
Ontario	7.5
Erie	2.7

1. Also known as residence time or turnover time. After Quinn (1992).

Toxic contaminants in the Great Lakes have had, and will continue to have, wide-ranging and long-lasting impacts on humans and the biota of the lakes for decades to come. Fortunately, due to the concerted efforts of many (governments, non-government organizations, and private citizens), the concentrations of many contaminants within the Great Lakes have declined over the past 20 years. Examples of recovery by fish and wildlife, e.g., lake trout and bald eagles, due to these declining concentrations of toxins, can be found in Giesy et al. (2002).

Great Lakes biological communities, particularly the fisheries, have also been subjected to human-mediated change. The Great Lakes have a relatively low fish diversity, compared to other aquatic environments. Coon (1999) lists 179 existing fish species: 157 native species and 22 that were introduced from outside of the basin, many of which were purposefully introduced, such as the common carp, brown trout, rainbow (steelhead) trout, as well as the Chinook and coho salmon (Chapter 23). Although low in species diversity, the fishery has been an invaluable resource to people within and outside the basin for centuries. Fish first served as food for native peoples, then for those who immigrated to the basin, as well as to markets outside the basin through commercial fishing operations. Commercial fishing, along with logging, trapping and mining, was a key natural resource extraction industry that generated economic wealth and stimulated settlement and development of many Great Lakes' ports (Brown et al. 1999).

Unfortunately, the commercial fishery on most of the Great Lakes, including Michigan operations, was in great peril by the late 1950s to early 1960s. Declining stocks of native species, particularly lake trout, were mostly due to

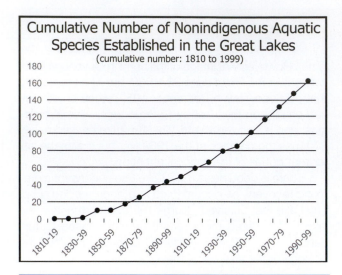

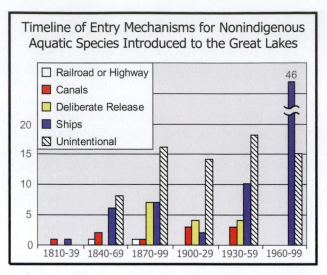

FIGURE 14.9 Cumulative number of nonindigenous, aquatic species established in the Great Lakes, by decade, from 1810 to 1999. After Mills et al. (1993) and Ricciardi (2001).

FIGURE 14.10 Timeline of entry mechanisms for non-indigenous aquatic species introduced to the Great Lakes, from 1810 to 1999. After Mills et al. (1993) and Ricciardi (2001).

overexploitation, as well as losses resulting from sea lamprey predation (Hansen 1999). The demise of the lake trout, the main top predator in most of the Great Lakes, led to a significant food-web disruption and massive increases in alewife, a non-native fish, which had been a prey item of lake trout. On numerous occasions throughout the early 1960s, km and km of Michigan's Great Lakes shoreline were littered with rotting and decaying alewife carcasses. Conditions were so bad that along some shorelines beaches were closed and communities used bulldozers to clear away the dead alewife. At this time, Michigan took the lead in introducing two, non-native Pacific salmon to the Great Lakes: coho in 1966 and Chinook in 1967 (Tanner and Tody 2002). The introductions (actually re-introductions, because both species had been introduced earlier, Chinook in 1873 and coho in 1933) heralded the beginning of an economically important recreational fishery that continues to this day. Soon, other states followed Michigan's lead and planted these non-native fish, which continue to support a billion dollar recreational fishery (Kocik and Jones 1999).

Other nonindigenous, aquatic species have also been introduced to the Great Lakes by human activities. Over 180 nonindigenous aquatic species have been identified in the Great Lakes, but the actual number of invaders is probably much greater because microscopic or otherwise inconspicuous species have likely gone undetected. NOAA's Great Lakes Environmental Research Laboratory in Ann Arbor has maintained a list of known aquatic nonindigenous species introduced into the Great Lakes that, until recently, listed 162 species (based on Mills et al. [1993] and Ricciardi [2001]). In 2008, they updated the list, to include 186 species. Figure 14.9 shows the cumulative number of known aquatic invaders to the Great Lakes, which led Ricciardi (2001) to wonder if an "invasional meltdown" was happening within the basin. Non-native organisms gain entry to the Great Lakes through a variety of mechanisms, including deliberate release, e.g., Chinook and coho salmon, and commercial ships (Fig. 14.10). Since 1959, most non-native aquatic species have gained entry to the Great Lakes via shipping, coinciding with the opening of the St. Lawrence Seaway (Mills et al. 1993). Shipping has always been an important industry on the Great Lakes. Historic demands for moving goods on the Great Lakes led to the opening of the Erie and Welland Canals in the early 1800s. The latter bypasses Niagara Falls, a natural barrier to the upstream migration of many aquatic organisms. With the opening of the St. Lawrence Seaway in 1959, foreign ships could now ply the waters of the Great Lakes, often bringing with them unwanted organisms such as zebra mussels, one of the most well-known foreign invaders in recent history.

The zebra mussel is a small, extremely prolific, bivalve mollusk, native to the Black, Caspian and Azov Seas. It was first discovered in North America in June 1988 in Lake St. Clair (Hebert et al. 1989), having arrived in the ballast water of transoceanic ships from Europe. Size-distribution of individuals collected from Lake St. Clair in 1988 indicated that it was possibly first introduced there in either the fall of 1985 or the spring of 1986. The zebra mussel

spread rapidly throughout the basin, due to the ready movement of its veliger life stage, when it is microscopic and free-floating. It has now reached many other watersheds, including the Mississippi, Hudson and Susquehanna Rivers.

The zebra mussel is a biofouler, having up to 200 byssal threads that allow it to attach firmly to any solid surface. Densities of $114,000/m^2$ have been reported in Europe (Wiktor 1963). Ludyanskiy et al. (1993) mention a report of densities as great as $750,000/m^2$ in the Great Lakes. These densities result from their ability to form layers. In one massive colony, the mussels exceeded 1.5 m in thickness (Gary Longton, DTE Energy, personal communication). These high densities and overall numbers can exert large and far-reaching impacts on freshwater ecosystems, through biofouling and filter-feeding. Biofouling has led to a number of problems in the Great Lakes, including clogged water intake pipes at manufacturing operations, municipal drinking sources, and power plants. Pimentel (2005) estimated that it costs $500 million/year to control and combat zebra mussels and their close cousin, the quagga mussel. In addition, the mussels have been implicated in the decline, and in some cases the almost complete disappearance, from all four lower lakes, of a small, shrimp-like organism *Diporeia* spp., an important native prey item of many Great Lakes fish (Dermott and Kerec 1997, Nalepa et al. 1998, Lozano et al. 2001, Nalepa et al. 2005).

Many other changes in the biota of the Great Lakes have happened as the result of non-native aquatic species, causing great costs, with losses estimated to be about $5.7 billion/year (Pimentel 2005).

Conclusions

Michigan is surrounded by one of the world's greatest natural resources—the Great Lakes. These complex and ever-changing lakes constitute one of the largest surface freshwater systems in the world. Over time, the Great Lakes have been subjected to many human-induced stresses, including hydrologic modifications, nutrient loadings, toxic contaminants, and invasive species. Many of these stresses have been impacting the lakes for over a century, appearing gradually over time, often in nearshore areas or in shallower portions of the basin. The vast size of the lakes, temporary recoveries from some of the stressors, time delays between the introduction of stress and subsequent impacts and the failure to understand some ecosystem-disruptions, have led to the false assumption that the Great Lakes ecosystem is healthy and resilient (Bails et al. 2005). Fortunately, Bails et al. (2005) have proposed a prescription for the protection and restoration of the Great Lakes ecosystem, which we must follow if we want to retain this true resource treasure.

Literature Cited

Ashworth, W. 1986. The Late, Great Lakes. Alfred A. Knopf, New York.

Assel, R., Cronk, K. and D. Norton. 2003. Recent trends in Laurentian Great Lakes ice cover. Climatic Change 57:185–204.

Bails, J., Beeton, A., Bulkley, J., DePhilip, M., Gannon, J., Murray, M., Regier, H. and D. Scavia. 2005. Prescription for Great Lakes ecosystem protection and restoration (avoiding the tipping point of irreversible change). Available on-line at http://sitemaker.umich.edu/scavia/files/prescription_for_great_lakes_08_30_2006.pdf. Accessed October, 2008.

Beeton, A.M. 1965. Eutrophication of the St. Lawrence Great Lakes. Limnology and Oceanography 10:240–254.

Beeton, A.M. 1969. Changes in the environment and biota of the Great Lakes. In: Proceedings of a Symposium, Eutrophication: Causes, Consequences, Correctives. National Academy of Sciences: Washington, DC. pp. 150–187.

Brown, R.W., Ebener, M. and T. Gorenflo. 1999. Great Lakes Commercial Fisheries: Historical Overview and Prognosis for the Future. In: W.W. Taylor and C.P. Ferreri (eds), Great Lakes Fisheries Policy and Management: A Binational Perspective. Michigan State University Press, East Lansing. pp. 307–354.

Burns, N.M. 1985. Erie: The Lake that Survived. Rowan and Allanheld, Totowa, NJ.

Catton, B. 1976. Michigan: A Bicentennial History. W.W. Norton and Company, Inc., New York.

Clites, A.H. and F.H. Quinn. 2003. The history of Lake Superior regulation: implications for the future. Journal of Great Lakes Research 29:157–171.

Colborn, T.E., Davidson, A., Green, S.N., Hodge, R.A., Jackson, C.I. and R.A. Liroff. 1990. The Great Lakes, Great Legacy? The Conservation Foundation: Washington, DC and The Institute for Research on Public Policy, Ottawa, Ontario.

Coon, T.C. 1999. Ichthyofauna of the Great Lakes Basin. In: W.W. Taylor and C.P. Ferreri (eds), Great Lakes Fisheries Policy and Management: A Binational Perspective. Michigan State University Press, East Lansing. pp. 55–71.

Costanza, R., d'Arge, R., de Groot, R., Farber, S., Grasso, M., Hannon, B., Limburg, K., Naeem, S., O'Neill, R.V., Paruelo, J., Raskin, R.G., Sutton, P. and M. van den Belt. 1997. The value of the world's ecosystem services and natural capital. Nature 387:253–260.

Dempsey, D. 2001. Ruin and Recovery: Michigan's Rise as a Conservation Leader. University of Michigan Press, Ann Arbor.

Dempsey, D. 2004. On the Brink: The Great Lakes in the 21st Century. Michigan State University Press, East Lansing.

Dermott, R. and D. Kerec. 1997. Changes in the deepwater benthos of eastern Lake Erie since the invasion of *Dreissena*: 1979–1993. Canadian Journal of Fisheries and Aquatic Sciences 54:922–930.

Ewing, M., Press, F. and W.L. Donn. 1954. An explanation of the Lake Michigan wave of 26 June 1954. Science 120:684–686.

Fuller, K., Shear, H. and J. Wittig (eds.). 1995. The Great Lakes: An Environmental Atlas and Resource Book. US Environmental Protection Agency and Government of Canada. Great Lakes National Program Office, USEPA, Chicago, IL. Publication No. EPA-905-B-95-001.

Gauthier, R., Donahue, M.J., Wagemakers, J. and T. Crane (eds.). 1999. Living with the lakes. US Army Corps of Engineers and Great Lakes Commission, Ann Arbor, MI.

Giesy, J.P., Jones, P.D., Kannan, K. and A.L. Blankenship. 2002. Persistent Organic Pollutant Residues and Their Effects on Fish and Wildlife of the Great Lakes. In: United States Environmental Protection Agency, The Foundation for Global Action on Persistent Organic Pollutants: A United States Perspective, Office of Research and Development, Report EPA/600/P-01/003F NCEA-I-1200, Washington, DC.

Hamblin, P.F. 1979. Great Lakes storm surge of April 6, 1979. Journal of Great Lakes Research 5:312–315.

Hansen, M.J. 1999. Lake Trout in the Great Lakes: Basinwide Stock Collapse and Binational Restoration. In: W.W. Taylor and C.P. Ferreri (eds), Great Lakes Fisheries Policy and Management: A Binational Perspective. Michigan State University Press, East Lansing. pp. 417–453.

Hebert, P.D.N., Muncaster, B.W. and G.L. Mackie. 1989. Ecological and genetic studies on *Dreissena polymorpha* (Pallas): a new mollusc in the Great Lakes. Canadian Journal of Fisheries and Aquatic Sciences 46:1587–1591.

International Joint Commission. 2000. Protection of the Waters of the Great Lakes: Final Report to the Governments of Canada and the United States. International Joint Commission: Ottawa, Ontario and Washington, DC.

Isard, S.A. and R.J. Schaetzl. 1995. Estimating soil temperatures and frost in the lake effect snowbelt region, Michigan, USA. Cold Regions Science and Technology 23:317–332.

Keillor, P. (ed.) 2003. Living on the Coast: Protecting Investments in Shore Property on the Great Lakes. US Army Corps of Engineers, Detroit, MI, and University of Wisconsin-Madison.

Kocik, J.F. and M.L. Jones. 1999. Pacific Salmonines in the Great Lakes Basin. In: W.W. Taylor and C.P. Ferreri (eds), Great Lakes Fisheries Policy and Management: A Binational Perspective. Michigan State University Press, East Lansing. pp. 455–488.

Liu, P.C., Miller, G.S. and J.H. Saylor. 1976. Water Motion. In: Great Lakes Basin Commission, Great Lakes Basin Framework Study, Appendix 4: Limnology of Lakes and Embayments. Great Lakes Basin Commission, Ann Arbor, MI. pp. 119–149.

Lozano, S.J., Scharold, J.V. and T.F. Nalepa. 2001. Recent declines in benthic macroinvertebrate densities in Lake Ontario. Canadian Journal of Fisheries and Aquatic Sciences 58:518–529.

Ludyanskiy, M.L., McDonald, D. and D. MacNeill. 1993. Impact of the zebra mussel, a bivalve invader. BioScience 43:533–544.

McGucken, W. 2000. Lake Erie Rehabilitated: Controlling Cultural Eutrophication, 1960s–1990s. University of Akron Press, Akron, OH.

Michigan Agricultural Statistics. 2004. Michigan rotational survey: fruit inventory 2003–2004. Michigan Department of Agriculture: Lansing, MI.

Mills, E.L., Leach, J.H., Carlton, J.T. and C.L. Secor. 1993. Exotic species in the Great Lakes: a history of biotic crises and anthropogenic introductions. Journal of Great Lakes Research 19:1–54.

Nalepa, T.F., Harston, D.J., Fanslow, D.L., Lang, G.A. and S.J. Lozano. 1998. Declines in benthic macroinvertebrate populations in southern Lake Michigan, 1980–1993. Canadian Journal of Fisheries and Aquatic Sciences 55:2402–2413.

Nalepa, T.F., Fanslow, D.L. and A.J. Foley, III. 2005. Spatial patterns in population trends of the amphipod *Diporeia* spp. and *Dreissena* mussels in Lake Michigan. Verhandlungen Internationale Vereinigung fuer Theoretische und Angewandte Limnologie 29:426–431.

Parker, S.L., Mills, E.L., Rudstam, L.G. and D.W. Einhouse. 2000. The effect of oligotrophication and dreissenid invasions on eastern Lake Erie and its primary forage species, the rainbow smelt (*Osmerus mordax*). Great Lakes Research Review 5:13–17.

Pimentel, D. 2005. Aquatic nuisance species in the New York State Canal and Hudson River Systems and the Great Lakes Basin: an economic and environmental assessment. Environmental Management 35:692–701.

Quinn, F.H. 1992. Hydraulic residence times for the Laurentian Great Lakes. Journal of Great Lakes Research 18:22–28.

Ricciardi, A. 2001. Facilitative interactions among aquatic invaders: is an "invasional meltdown" occurring in the Great Lakes? Canadian Journal of Fisheries and Aquatic Sciences 58:2513–2525.

Richards, T.L. 1967. Meteorological problems on the Great Lakes. In: C.E. Dolman (ed), Water Resources of Canada: Symposia presented to the Royal Society of Canada. University of Toronto Press, Toronto, Canada. pp. 96–107.

Santer, R.A. 2003. Allured amazed awestruck: my favorite island. Michigan History Magazine 87 (Nov-Dec): 46–47.

Schertzer, W.M. 1982. How Great Lakes Waters Move. In: A.D. Misener and G. Daniels (eds), Decisions for the Great Lakes. Great Lakes Tomorrow and the Purdue Foundation, P.O. Box 1935, Hiram, OH. pp. 51–64.

Swinehart, C. 2000. Great Lakes basin facts package. Michigan State University Extension Bulletin E2744, East Lansing, MI.

Tanner, H.A. and W.H. Tody. 2002. History of the Great Lakes Salmon Fishery: A Michigan Perspective. In: Lynch, K.D. Jones, M.L. and W.W. Taylor (eds), Sustaining North American Salmon: Perspectives Across Regions and Disciplines. American Fisheries Society, Bethesda, MD. pp. 139–153.

van der Leeden, F., Troise, F.L. and D.K. Todd. 1990. The Water Encyclopedia. Lewis Publishers, Inc., Chelsea, MI.

Weller, P. 1990. Fresh Water Seas: Saving the Great Lakes. Between the Lines, Toronto, Ontario.

Wiktor, J. 1963. Research on the ecology of *Dreissena polymorpha* Pall. in Szczecin lagoon (Zalew Szczecinski). Ekologia Polska-Seria A. 11:275–280.

Further Readings

Annin, P. 2006. The Great Lakes Water Wars. Island Press, Washington, DC.

Bogue, M.B. 2000. Fishing the Great Lakes: an environmental history 1783–1933. University of Wisconsin Press, Madison.

Dann, S.L. and B.C. Schroeder. 2003. The Life of the Lakes: A Guide to the Great Lakes Fishery. Michigan Sea Grant College Program MICHU #03–400 and MSU Extension Bulletin E-2440, 8–2003, Ann Arbor and East Lansing, MI.

Dennis, J. 2003. The Living Great Lakes: Searching for the Heart of the Inland Seas. Thomas Dunne Books, New York.

Eichenlaub, V.L. 1979. Weather and Climate of the Great Lakes Region. University of Notre Dame Press, Notre Dame, IN.

Grady, W. 2007. The Great Lakes: The Natural History of a Changing Region. Greystone Books, Vancouver, British Columbia.

Surface Water Resources

Lois Wolfson

■ Introduction

Michigan's state motto, "If you seek a pleasant peninsula, look about you," and its nicknames, "The Great Lake State" and "The Water Wonderland," remind us that the state is surrounded and dominated by water. Even the name "Michigan" is derived from the Native American word "Michi-gama" meaning "large lake" or "place of great waters." No place in Michigan is further than 137 km from a Great Lake shore, and 40 of Michigan's 83 counties touch at least one of the Great Lakes. Michigan truly is a water-dominated state.

Michigan's land base is divided into an Upper and Lower Peninsula by the Straits of Mackinac, which link Lakes Michigan and Huron (Plates 1, 11). The Mackinac Bridge, one of the longest suspension bridges in the world, spans eight km to connect the Upper and Lower Peninsulas. The total area of the state consists of 150,778 km² of land, 99,909 km² of Great Lakes water, and 3,092 km² of inland waters (MDOT 2006). In addition, with approximately 5,292 km of Great Lakes shoreline, Michigan has more length of freshwater coastline than any country, and more total shoreline than any other state except Alaska (Plate 1).

■ Michigan waters

Michigan has more than 11,000 inland lakes >2 ha in size, with nearly 1000 lakes larger than 40 ha. The largest inland lake is Houghton Lake in Roscommon County, with an area >8,100 ha. The Upper Peninsula's largest lake is Gogebic Lake in Gogebic and Ontonagon County, with an area of 5,415 ha (Table 15.1). Torch Lake, in Antrim and Kalkaska Counties, is the deepest inland lake in the state, with a maximum depth of 91 m and an average depth of 34 m. Elk Lake, in Antrim and Grand Traverse Counties, places second, with a maximum depth of 59 m. Although Houghton Lake is the largest inland lake in surface area, it is a very shallow lake, with a maximum depth of only 6.1 m and an average depth of approximately two meters. Because of its depth, Torch Lake contains more than 20 times the water volume of Houghton Lake. The highest density of lakes occurs in Roscommon and Cheboygan Counties, with over 11% of each covered by lakes (Fig. 15.1A). Iron, Marquette and Oakland Counties have the highest actual number of lakes (Fig. 15.1B).

Michigan has over 300 named rivers, totaling approximately 87,389 km in length (Plate 11). Some rivers share the same name. There are eight different Pine Rivers and seven different Black Rivers, for example. Michigan's longest river, the Grand River, flows 418 km through the cities of Jackson, Lansing, Ionia and Grand Rapids, emptying into Lake Michigan at Grand Haven (Michigan in Brief 2006). Perennial streams and rivers that flow all year long as a result of constant inputs of groundwater make up 62% of the total. The remaining streams have only intermittent flow regimes (MDEQ 2004a). In addition, Michigan has 19,312 km of streams designated by the Michigan Department of Natural Resources (MDNR) as cold water trout streams (Fig. 15.2).

TABLE 15.1 The top 20 inland lakes in Michigan, by surface area[1]

	Lake	Size (hectares)	Maximum depth (m)	County
1	Houghton	8,111	6.1	Roscommon
2	Torch	7,596	86.9	Antrim and Kalkaska
3	Charlevoix	6,985	37.1	Charlevoix
4	Burt	6,928	22.2	Cheboygan
5	Mullett	6,730	45.1	Cheboygan
6	Gogebic	5,415	10.7	Gogebic and Ontonagon
7	Manistique	4,099	6.0	Luce and Mackinac
8	Black	4,099	15.2	Cheboygan and Presque Isle
9	Crystal	3,930	53.3	Benzie
10	Portage	3,901	16.4	Houghton
11	Higgins	3,885	41.1	Crawford and Roscommon
12	Fletcher Pond	3,630	3.0 (estimate)	Alpena and Montmorency
13	Hubbard	3,581	25.9	Alcona
14	Leelanau	3,367	36.9	Leelanau
15	Indian	3,237	4.6	Schoolcraft
16	Elk	3,128	58.5	Antrim and Grand Traverse
17	Michigamme Reservoir	2,913	12.8 (estimate)	Iron
18	Glen	2,535	39.6	Leelanau
19	Grand	2,290	7.6	Presque Isle
20	Long	2,287	7.6	Alpena and Presque Isle

1: Source: Institute for Fisheries Research (http://www.michigan.gov/documents/dnr/MI20LargestInlandLakes_183503_7.pdf). Accessed February, 2008.

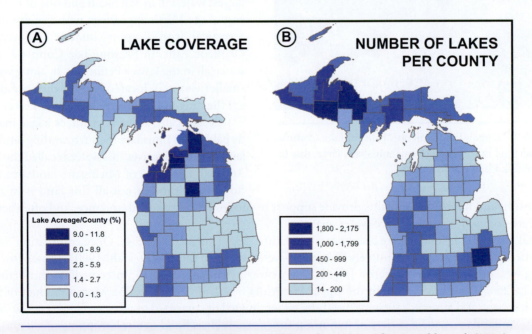

FIGURE 15.1 Distribution of inland lakes in Michigan, by county. After Annable et al. (1991). A. Percent of lake area within each county. B. Total number of Michigan lakes within individual counties.

FIGURE 15.2 Augusta Creek, in Kalamazoo and Calhoun Counties, is a pristine, cold water trout stream that is over 60 km long. Photo by L. Wolfson.

FIGURE 15.3 Upper Tahquamenon Falls, in Luce County. The summertime flow shown here is unusually large, due to a recent rainfall. Photo by R. Schaetzl.

Associated with some of these rivers and streams are the 200 waterfalls in Michigan, with the vast majority located in the Upper Peninsula (Fig. 4.6). Waterfalls are only found where bedrock is close to the surface. Because most of the Lower Peninsula's bedrock is overlain with glacial deposits, few waterfalls are found there. The Upper Tahquamenon Falls, in Luce County, is the largest waterfall in Michigan and one of the largest falls east of the Mississippi River, with a width of 61 m and a vertical drop of approximately 15.2 m (Fig. 15.3). Ocqueoc Falls, in Presque Isle County is the largest waterfall in the Lower Peninsula. It, along with another smaller waterfall located a short distance down-river, are the only notable waterfalls in the Lower Peninsula.

Periodically, a river, stream, or a lake may overflow its banks and inundate the surrounding landscape. The land area that receives this water is called the floodplain. Approximately 6% of Michigan's land area is prone to flooding, although not all this land is in floodplain; some is swamp and marsh. Floodplains provide support to species diversity and abundance, and often act as buffers to reduce erosion and protect surface water quality.

Coastal and inland wetlands are also key water features in Michigan (Fig. 15.4). Once comprising over 4.5 million ha, Michigan has lost approximately 50% of its wetlands since the 1980s (Dahl 1990). Losses from draining and filling wetlands have been greatest in southern Lower Michigan (> 40%), intermediate in northern Lower Michigan (> 25%), and least severe in the Upper Peninsula (< 20%) (Comer 2003). More than half of Michigan's cedar, black spruce, and tamarack swamps have been either drained or converted to other wetland types since European settlement. Wetlands provide a variety of important functions, such as flood control, trapping of silt and other sediment, and retaining nutrients and pesticides. They also provide breeding and nesting areas for fish and wildlife and are vital to numerous threatened and endangered species.

FIGURE 15.4 A sphagnum peat-dominated bog in the western Upper Peninsula. These acidic environments are very important ecologically and are often associated with wet forests of black spruce and tamarack. Photo by R. Schaetzl.

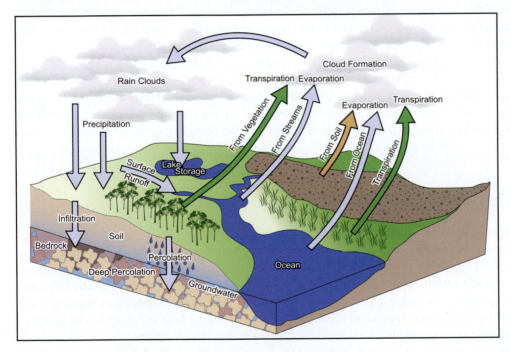

FIGURE 15.5 The hydrologic cycle, shown here, depicts the constant movement of water on, above, and below the Earth's surface. Source: Dept. of Natural Resource Ecology and Management, Iowa State Univ., Ames, Iowa. T. Schultz, illustrator.

The hydrologic cycle

The amount of water on earth today is nearly the same as it was hundreds of millions of years ago—about 1.36 billion km³. Neither increasing nor diminishing, the earth's water has been cycled over and over again as it changes form and constantly moves among the Earth's oceans, inland waters, atmosphere, and rocks. This natural process is known as the hydrologic cycle (Fig. 15.5). Water that is evaporated or sublimated from the Earth's surface soon undergoes condensation and falls back to the earth as precipitation in the form of rain, snow, sleet, hail, etc. Precipitation may be intercepted or taken up by plants, returned to the atmosphere as water vapor through evaporation or transpiration, stored in surface water bodies, infiltrate into the soil and move downward to groundwater, or flow over the land surface until it reaches a stream, lake, or other body of water. Surface water moves by gravity and can either run off the land or infiltrate into the soil. Water that enters the soil percolates until a depth is reached wherein all the pore spaces are completely filled with water; the water within this area is called groundwater (Chapter 16). If precipitation reaches the soil surface faster than it can infiltrate, the water may pool on the surface, become stored in lakes and wetlands, or move by overland flow or surface runoff to a nearby stream or lake (Cech 2003).

■ Watersheds

A watershed (or drainage basin) is the total land area that contributes water to an area, such as a stream or lake. The boundary of a watershed is referred to as the drainage divide (or topographic divide) and is delineated by the highest points of land that drain to the receiving body of water. Every stream, tributary or lake has an associated watershed; small watersheds are embedded within larger watersheds. Watersheds can be as small as a few hectares, draining to a small lake, or as large as the Great Lakes basin, which encompasses all five Great Lakes and drains approximately 521,779 km^2 (USEPA 1995; Chapter 14). Michigan has 62 major watersheds, 26 of which drain to Lake Michigan, 15 to Lake Huron, 13 to Lake Superior, and 8 to Lakes Erie and St. Clair (National Rivers 1999; Fig. 15.6).

Michigan has only two small areas of land that lie outside the Great Lakes watershed—one in the western Upper Peninsula and one along the Indiana border (Annable et al. 1991); both areas eventually drain to the Mississippi River. All other parts of the state drain to one of the Great Lakes (Fig. 15.6). Eventually, water flows out of each of the Great Lakes through each lake's connecting channel to the St. Lawrence River and finally to the Atlantic Ocean (Chapter 14). Within the state, the Saginaw Bay watershed is the largest, covering more than 22,533 km^2, all or part of 22 counties, and draining approximately 15% of Michigan's total land area (USEPA 2001).

Any activity on land can have an impact within its watershed and may affect the quality of the receiving water body. Pollutants found in surface runoff from parking lots, agricultural fields and urban lawns, or from failing on-site wastewater treatment systems, can eventually enter streams and lakes and have adverse effects on the water and its biota. Forested lands, however, along lakes and streams often provide benefits to the receiving water body by stabilizing stream banks, shading stream channels, and intercepting and reducing surface runoff (Zorn and Sendek 2001).

■ Surface water distribution: rivers and streams

Rivers and streams consist of a main channel and its tributaries. The headwaters mark the beginning of the stream and the mouth denotes the point where the water flows into another river, stream, lake or the ocean. Stream flow, also known as discharge, is the volume of water passing a given stream cross section over a designated period of time (USGS 2002). It is measured in volume per unit time, e.g., cubic meters per second (m^3/sec) or km^3/year, and is often designated as Q in equations. Hydrologic properties, including precipitation, evaporation, transpiration, infiltration, overland flow and groundwater flow, are crucial components of stream flow and are intricately linked with a river's geomorphic, chemical and biological characteristics (Wiley and Seelbach 1997).

Water flowing in a stream can be divided into two components: base flow and overland flow. Base flow results from that part of precipitation that infiltrates into the soil, moves into the groundwater and then discharges to the stream (Chapter 16). Overland flow results from precipitation moving overland to a stream, without first percolating into the ground (Grannemann et al. 2000). Most rivers and streams receive water from a combination of these sources (Wiley and Seelbach 1997). Groundwater, as well as subsurface water, provide the base flow to a stream through discharge and sustain stream flow when precipitation is low or nonexistent. Overall, about 80% of the annual stream flow in the Lower Peninsula comes from base flow (GCAC 2006), and rivers such as the Au Sable, Manistee, Muskegon, Sturgeon and Kalamazoo receive the majority of their water from base flow (Fig. 15.7). In the thumb area, base flow is low due to (1) the clay-rich character of the glacial deposits in this area, which promote runoff rather than infiltration, and (2) the shallow limestone bedrock, which allows the little water that actually does percolate to bypass the river and flow underground, directly to Lake Huron (Annable et al. 1991).

FIGURE 15.6   The major watersheds of Michigan; all but two of them flow to one of the Great Lakes. After Annable et al. (1991).

In areas where streams receive the majority of their water from groundwater (base flow), stream flow is fairly uniform throughout the year. Similarly, since groundwater temperatures vary little, groundwater dominated streams have more stable temperatures throughout the year than do streams receiving the majority of their water from runoff. The geology of the drainage area through which rivers flow also influences the amount and composition of water that streams and rivers receive. Rivers that drain through glacial deposits of sand and coarse textured glacial till, such as in the High Plains region of northern Lower Michigan (Plate 8A, Chapter 17), generally have exceptionally large groundwater inputs and, as a consequence, very stable flow regimes. The Au Sable River may have the most stable stream flow regime of any large stream in the United States (Zorn and Sendek 2001). Rivers in Michigan that drain

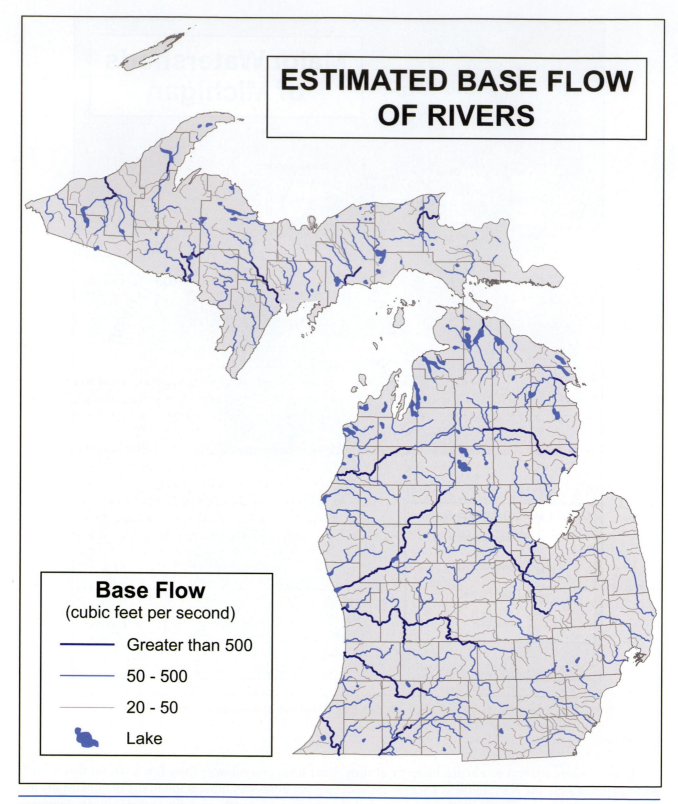

FIGURE 15.7   Base flow provides a significant portion of the total flow to many rivers in Michigan. This map illustrates the estimated base flow for Michigan's major rivers. After Groundwater Inventory and Mapping Project (2005).

FIGURE 15.8 The Au Sable River, a predominantly groundwater-fed river, flows over 320 km, until it empties into Lake Huron near the city of Oscoda. Photo by R. Schaetzl.

these types of geologic areas are typically cold, clear trout streams, e.g., the Sturgeon, Manistee, Boardman and AuSable Rivers (Wiley et al. 1998; Fig. 15.8) and are dominant in the Upper Peninsula, and northern and north central portions of the state. The watersheds of these streams are relatively small, and inputs of groundwater are high (MDEQ 2004a).

Streams receiving the majority of their input from overland flow or storm flow, i.e., runoff, often have more variable annual flow and may flood more often than streams fed mainly by groundwater. Although rainfall may be high during the summer months, much of this water is lost through evapotranspiration, which, in turn, reduces stream flow. Water temperatures in these types of streams are strongly influenced by air temperatures and are typically warm during the day but cool at night (Wiley and Seelbach 1997). Watersheds in the southeastern part of the state are usually dominated by glacial deposits with low permeabilities (Chapter 16) that reduce the groundwater discharge to rivers. As a consequence, these rivers receive the majority of their water from overland flow, and their discharge fluctuates markedly throughout the year. More than half of the rivers along the eastern Lower Peninsula, from about Iosco County to the southern border, are largely dependent on surface runoff and thus tend to flow intermittently, depending on climatic conditions (MDEQ 2004a).

In general, rivers in northwestern and northern Michigan tend to maintain their flow through the dry months, whereas rivers in southern Michigan and the thumb area have lower and more variable discharges (Annable et al. 1991). Other processes, such as evapotranspiration, topography, infiltration, and landscape characteristics all contribute to spatial and temporal patterns in stream flow (Wiley and Seelbach 1997; Cech 2003).

In wet months, during times of snowmelt, or when ice jams form and back up water, water can overflow its stream banks, resulting in flooding. Frequent flooding occurs in the southern two-thirds of the Lower Peninsula, particularly along Saginaw Bay, Lake St. Clair and Lake Erie. These flood-prone areas typically have minimal land-surface relief and less permeable soils (USGS 1991).

■ Surface water formation and distribution: inland lakes

Like most lakes of the world, the majority of Michigan's natural lakes were formed directly by glacial processes (Chapters 6, 13, 17). Glaciers scoured and gouged the land, forming large depressions that were later filled with water, or left blocks of ice partially or wholly buried in the glacial drift (the rocks and debris left by the glacier); as these ice blocks melted they formed lakes called kettles. Kettle lakes tend to be deep, with irregularly shaped outlines and bathymetry (Kalff 2002); many have only very small drainage basins, e.g., Higgins, Cadillac and

Black Lakes. Lakes are not common in Michigan on former proglacial lake plains, where the land is flat and less permeable (Plates 9, 10, 11).

In Michigan, lakes also formed through other processes not directly linked to glacial retreat. Riverine lakes, for example, developed in wide floodplain areas as a section of river channel was cutoff from the main channel through sediment deposition or erosion. Scientists refer to these horseshoe-shaped lakes as oxbow lakes. Other riverine lakes, such as drowned river mouth lakes along the Great Lakes, were formed by erosion of tributary river channels during extremely low lake levels, followed by rises in water level, e.g., Muskegon and Spring Lakes. Another type of lake found in the southern portion of the Upper Peninsula, as well as a few areas in the Lower Peninsula, particularly in the counties of Presque Isle, Alpena, Cheboygan, Iosco and Monroe, is a karst lake (Chapter 16). These lakes generally lie in basins of highly soluble limestone rock, where an underground cavern in the limestone has collapsed, leaving a water-filled depression. Karst lakes, or dolines, are often distinguished by their very steep underwater slopes and bedrock shorelines (Kalff 2002). Lastly, some lakes now occur in scour-valleys, known by geologists as tunnel channels. These lakes formed when subglacial water, under tremendous pressure, scoured out long, deep valleys beneath the glacier, later to be filled with water as long, deep, narrow lakes (Plate 11). Torch, Leelanau, Charlevoix and Elk Lakes are examples of "tunnel channel lakes."

■ Surface water quality

To help protect the state's waters, Michigan has developed water quality standards that are defined within Part 31 of the Natural Resources and Environmental Protection Act (NREPA), P.A. 451 (1994). These standards provide legal narrative and numerical details on the amount of pollutants that can enter water from various sources, or that may be present in the water. Additionally, all surface waters of the state have been designated for specific uses which include agriculture, industrial water supply, public water supply, navigation, warm water fishery, aquatic life and wildlife and partial and total body contact recreation. Both the standards and designated uses were established to protect, enhance and maintain water quality and natural resources, and meet the requirements of the federal Clean Water Act as well as the US-Canada Great Lakes Water Quality Agreement for all surface waters within Michigan jurisdiction.

Overall, the quality of Michigan's surface waters varies from pristine to poor, reflecting the characteristics of the watershed, including the basin geology, soils, landscape, land uses and human population centers and their related activities. Inland waters of the Upper Peninsula and the northern Lower Peninsula generally have very good to excellent quality. These waters typically support diverse communities of aquatic organisms, including cold water fisheries, and often are in predominantly forested watersheds. Waters in southern Michigan generally have good water quality, tend to support warm water fish communities and typically are in watersheds dominated by agricultural and urban land uses (MDEQ 2004a; Fig. 15.9). Major urban centers in the southern portion of the state contribute to the runoff of toxic materials and nutrients from impervious (roof or paved) surfaces that can degrade water quality and subsequently affect biological communities.

Rivers and streams

Of the total river lengths assessed by the Michigan Department of Environmental Quality (MDEQ) since 1997, approximately 74% support designated uses and water quality standards. Of all designated uses, the one most commonly impaired is aquatic life and wildlife, followed by total body contact recreation. Many of the sites not meeting designated uses are located in the southern half of the Lower Peninsula, which has the greatest densities of population, construction, housing development, industries, municipalities, roads, expressways and agricultural activity (MDEQ 2004a). Many of these waters, however, are generally of good quality in their upper reaches or headwaters, and some, such as the Dowagiac, Rogue and Pere Marquette Rivers, support cold water fishes in these reaches (Bedford 2005). Larger rivers supporting warm water fishes include the Grand, Tittabawassee, Cass and Flint (GCAC 2006).

Since 1970, 3,365 km of 16 rivers and streams have been designated as state Natural Rivers under the Natural Rivers Program. The goal of the program is to protect rivers that are currently in good to excellent condition and, under the authority of Part 305, Natural Rivers of PA 451 (1994), create development guidelines to preserve, protect and enhance the state's natural river systems. Michigan's Natural Rivers include the Jordan, Betsie, Rogue, Two Hearted, White, Boardman, Huron, Pere Marquette, Flat, Rifle, Lower Kalamazoo, Pigeon, AuSable, Fox, Pine and Upper Manistee (MDNR 2004; Fig. 15.10).

FIGURE 15.9 The Red Cedar River, a tributary to the Grand River, is typical of many warm water streams that freeze under winter conditions. The river runs through the campus of Michigan State University. Photo by R. Schaetzl.

Designated Natural Rivers in Michigan

Two Hearted
Fox
Pigeon
Jordan
Boardman
Betsie
Au Sable
Upper Manistee
Pine
Rifle
Pere Marquette
White
Rogue
Flat
Lower Kalamazoo
Huron

— Natural Rivers
— Other Rivers

FIGURE 15.10 Map of the 16 rivers and streams in Michigan, portions of which have been designated as state Natural Rivers under the Natural Rivers Program. After: DNR Natural Rivers Program (2008).

FIGURE 15.11   Lime Lake, in Leelanau County, is a clear, nutrient-poor oligotrophic lake. Photo by R. Schaetzl.

FIGURE 15.12   Yellow water lily (*Nuphar sp.*) and water shield (*Brasenia sp.*) plants dominate eutrophic Duck Lake, a shallow lake in Kalamazoo County. Photo by L. Wolfson.

Inland lakes

Lakes are often classified into trophic states, which indicate their biological productivity and nutrient content. Lakes low in nutrients, with high water clarity, high dissolved oxygen levels and few aquatic plants, are referred to as oligotrophic (Fig. 15.11); those with high amounts of nutrients, low water clarity, low dissolved oxygen levels in the bottom waters and thick growths of aquatic plants are classified as eutrophic (Fig. 15.12). Mesotrophic lakes have moderate amounts of nutrients and fall between oligotrophic and eutrophic lakes. Oligotrophic waters are generally more suitable for cold water fish, such as salmon and trout, while eutrophic systems support warm water fish,

TABLE 15.2   Summary of the trophic status of Michigan's public access lakes[1]

Trophic status	Number of lakes	Hectares
Oligotrophic (low nutrients)	118 (16%)	66,609 (33%)
Mesotrophic (moderate nutrients)	386 (53%)	81,200 (40%)
Eutrophic (high nutrients)	196 (27%)	48,986 (24%)
Hypereutrophic (excessive nutrients)	30 (4%)	6,757 (3%)
Total Assessed	730	203,552 (100%)

1: Source: MDEQ (2006).

including largemouth bass and sunfish. If too many nutrients, particularly phosphorous and nitrogen, are added to lakes, plant growth can increase and degrade the water quality (Vollenweider 1968). When this condition, known as cultural eutrophication, occurs, lakes can become unsuitable for fish, other aquatic life, and recreational activities. Nutrient inputs to lakes are usually associated with the activities of people within the surrounding watershed. Major contributors include fertilization from farm fields, lawns, and golf courses, septic system leakages, animal wastes, stormwater runoff and illicit wastewater discharges. Controlling point source nutrients from entering the water has reversed eutrophication in some cases (Edmondson 1970); however, internal nutrient cycling, nonpoint source pollution, and newly recognized stresses such as climate change and global nitrogen cycles will continue to be challenges in reducing cultural eutrophication.

In Michigan, 730 lakes with public access sites have been assessed by the MDEQ, by measuring parameters such as transparency, P content and chlorophyll *a*. These 730 lakes represent approximately 57% of the 360,008 ha of lakes in the state (MDEQ 2006). The majority are considered oligotrophic or mesotrophic (Table 15.2). Approximately 27.5% are classified as eutrophic, with only 4% having excessive nutrients.

Impacts on water quality

The quality of surface water is greatly influenced by surrounding land uses and activities. As water moves through the hydrologic cycle, it readily dissolves and carries many minerals and other substances with which it comes into contact. With increasing development and suburbanization (Chapter 32), much of the landscape is being converted from permeable soils and vegetative cover to impermeable surfaces, increasing the potential for surface runoff and erosion. Roads and parking lots, which inhibit infiltration and increase surface runoff, are replacing natural soils, forested areas and wetlands. These changes not only affect the volume of surface runoff and the hydrology of water bodies, but also increase the potential for pollutants, such as oils, grease, salt, antifreeze and other materials, to move into receiving waters.

Pollutants affecting water and its quality may be derived from point and/or nonpoint sources. Point source pollution can be readily identified and often is easier to control since it comes from a distinct source, such as wastewater discharge from a pipe. Nonpoint sources of pollution are more diffuse and generally more difficult to isolate or identify, e.g., stormwater and surface runoff. Pollutants associated with these sources include sediment nutrients, heavy metals, pathogens, and other contaminants.

Stormwater

Stormwater can move chemicals, soil, and other pollutants into a storm sewer system or directly to a lake, river or stream. Some storm sewers are combined with sanitary sewer systems—designed to convey both sewage and stormwater (combined in one pipe) to a wastewater treatment plant. During excessive rain events, these combined sewers often receive more water than the treatment plant can handle. When this occurs, the water from the combined sewer overflows, resulting in the movement of untreated or partially treated human and industrial waste, toxic materials, debris and pathogens directly into lakes and streams. In Michigan, over 50 cities still have combined systems; however, over the last 10 years, many cities with combined sewer systems have installed treatment facilities for overflows, designed to capture the combined sewage and rain water long enough to provide initial treatment and disinfection. The treatment significantly reduces the amount of pollutants discharged and the associated public health risk (MDEQ 2004b, Public Sector Consultants 2002).

Fertilizers and manure

In agricultural areas, the use of fertilizers, chemicals and manure can also have significant impacts on water quality. Fertilizers, particularly P and N, stimulate plant growth, and chemicals, such as pesticides and fungicides, may be toxic to aquatic organisms. The growing number of animal feeding operations (AFOs), and the consolidation of animals into small lots, have increased the amount of manure output per unit area. When these animal wastes are applied to land, and exceed crop needs or the land base to which they are applied, they can be carried in surface runoff to streams. Bacteria and pathogens present in the manure can present health hazards to the receiving waters. In 1999, it was estimated that Michigan had approximately 250 large confined animal feeding operations (CAFOs; MDEQ and EPA 2004). However, almost all animal farms in Michigan are considered to be AFOs, where animals are confined for more than 45 days during the year, and no vegetation is present in the confined area during the normal growing season (Bolinger and Bickert 2006).

Sediment runoff

Sediment/siltation runoff, derived mainly from soil erosion from both urban and agricultural lands, is the leading pollutant to Michigan's rivers and streams (Table 15.3). Increased siltation to streams and lakes can decrease water clarity and make it difficult for aquatic plants to grow, or for fish to see their prey. These sediments can cover bottom dwellers and fish eggs, and clog fish gills. Many of these sediments also carry P, a nutrient that can cause excessive plant growth in both streams and lakes. Through programs such as Michigan's Section 319 Nonpoint Source Management program, the Great Lakes Basin program for Soil Erosion and Sediment Control, and Conservation Planning, many areas across the state have put in place a variety of best management practices to reduce soil loss and stream bank erosion.

Mercury

Mercury leads the list of pollutants impairing Michigan lakes, ponds, and reservoirs (Table 15.4). Due to widespread atmospheric deposition of mercury into Michigan's surface waters, and its ability to convert to the organic and more toxic form through natural processes, Michigan has enacted a generic, statewide, mercury-based fish consumption advisory that applies to all of Michigan's inland lakes (MDCH 2003). However, if fish contamination issues with polychlorinated biphenyl (PCB) and mercury are excluded, nearly 98% of the public lakes that have been assessed meet the state's water quality standards. That percentage drops to approximately 36% when mercury and PCBs are included (MDEQ 2004a).

The toxic form of mercury, called methylmercury, is hazardous to wildlife and human health. According to the Michigan Environmental Council, the worst mercury-polluted lake in the state, based on fish tissue analysis, is Deer Lake in Marquette County, followed by Chaney Lake in Gogebic County (MEC 2004). Although mercury levels in Deer Lake fish decreased after remedial action plans were set in place, they have since leveled off to concentrations still above the "trigger level" for fish consumption advisories. Within the fish tissue, the highest concentrations of mercury are found in older northern pike (USEPA 2006b).

Non-native invasive species

A more recent, and perhaps more long-lasting, concern to Michigan waters is the introduction of invasive exotic species—non-native organisms that enter lakes and disrupt the ecosystem (Chapter 14). These "biological pollutants" are having a large impact on inland waters, and include plants such as Eurasian water milfoil, curly-leaf pondweed and purple loosestrife. Animal species of concern are the zebra mussel, river ruffe, rusty crayfish, round goby and the spiny water flea, among others (Great Lakes Commission 1996). Invasive species generally have fewer competitors in their new environment, giving them a competitive advantage over native species, allowing them to

TABLE 15.3 Main causes of impairments for river and streams in Michigan[1]

Rank	Cause of Impairment	Total km² impaired
1	Sedimentation/siltation	3,953.6
2	Priority organic compounds	2,921.7
3	Habitat alterations	2,427.5
4	Nutrients	2,015.8
5	Flow alterations	1,877.1
6	Mercury	1,198.1
7	Pathogens	1,180.6
8	Filling and draining	811.1
9	Organic enrichment/low dissolved oxygen	579.2
10	Non-native aquatic plants	321.5

1: Source: USEPA (2002).

TABLE 15.4 Main causes of impairments for lakes, ponds and reservoirs in Michigan[1]

Rank	Cause of impairment	Total hectares impaired
1	Mercury	90,735.9
2	Priority organic compound(s)	49,718.1
3	Pesticides	9,564.7
4	Organic enrichment/low dissolved oxygen	4,688.3
5	Phosphorus	1,749.0
6	Pathogens	1,600.9
7	Copper	1,076.0
8	Nutrients	868.0
9	pH	374.7
10	Non-native aquatic plants	319.7

1: Source: USEPA (2002).

out-compete the natives for food and habitat (Mills et al. 1993). They also interfere with commercial and recreational activities. The zebra mussel, first discovered in Lake St. Clair in 1988, has now been found in over 200 inland lakes in 47 counties across Michigan (Michigan Sea Grant 2005; Chapter 14). Research has also linked the presence of zebra mussels with an increase in the blue-green algal species, *Microcystis* (Sarnelle et al. 2005). This species produces microcystin, a toxin that can be harmful to humans and animals.

The spread of non-natives may occur through a variety of mechanisms, including ballast water exchange from large freighters, overland transport, transport on boat hulls, motors, or trailers, bait bucket transfer or through the aquarium trade. In 1996, Michigan implemented the Nonindigenous Aquatic Nuisance Species State Management Plan, to develop strategies to confront the spread of aquatic nuisance species. Additional task forces, public education programs, and inspection programs have been initiated to deal with the spread of these species and prevent new species from entering Michigan waters.

Areas of concern and TMDLs

Within the Great Lakes, 43 specific locations have been identified as having serious water quality problems that are causing known impairments. Known as Areas of Concern (AOCs), the 14 that affect Michigan's water include Deer and Torch Lakes and the Manistique, Menominee and St. Mary's Rivers in the Upper Peninsula, and Muskegon and White Lakes, and the Clinton, Detroit, Kalamazoo, Raisin, Rouge, Saginaw River/Bay and St. Clair Rivers in the Lower Peninsula (MDEQ 2004b). Water quality problems in these areas include heavy metals, organic compounds, contaminated sediment and the necessity for fish-consumption and wading/swimming advisories.

Under section 303(d) of the Clean Water Act, states are required to develop lists of waters that are impaired and do not meet prescribed standards. TMDLs, or total maximum daily loads, which specify the maximum amount of a pollutant that a body of water can receive and still meet water quality standards, are then developed and approved by the state. In Michigan, two rivers, the south branch of the River Raisin and Blakely drain/Marsh Creek, within the St. Clair River basin are impaired due to sediments; TMDLs are being developed for these rivers. Since 1996, 13 other rivers and creeks in the state have approved TMDLs, including the Grand, Bass, Belle, Coldwater, Ecorse and Portage Rivers, and Black, Carrier and Malletts Creeks (USEPA 2006a). Other TMDLs have been or are being developed for mercury, PCBs, pathogens, nutrients, pesticides and a variety of other pollutants (USEPA 2006a). The Lower Grand, Clinton, Huron and Kalamazoo Rivers lead the list, respectively, with the number of water bodies within their watershed with impaired waters.

Water use conflicts and management

The connection between surface water and groundwater is an obvious feature of the hydrologic cycle (Fig. 15.5). However, it is often neglected in the management and use of water resources. Because groundwater is a major part of the flow to most of Michigan's surface water, pumping or withdrawing it from shallow groundwater can reduce stream flow or lower lake levels of those lakes and streams receiving that groundwater (see Focus Box below). Similarly, groundwater withdrawal may also have an indirect impact on surface water quality. For example, a decrease in river flow because of diminishing inputs from groundwater may result in a rise in stream temperatures, or it may concentrate pollutants. These situations can lead to water use conflicts, particularly when precipitation is low and groundwater recharge is minimal.

Under Michigan's Water Use Reporting Program, thermoelectric power plants, self-supplied industrial facilities, public water supply and non-agricultural irrigators are required to annually report their water use to the MDEQ. The majority of these water withdrawals are from the Great Lakes (Chapter 16). However, Michigan also recently enacted legislation to resolve conflicts between water users, expand water use registration and reporting requirements to major water users, and protect Michigan's water resources against diversions to other regions. The passage of P.A. 148 (2003), which became Part 327 of Act 451 (NREPA), also specifies that agricultural water users, with the capacity to withdraw surface or groundwater that exceeds 454,609 liters (100,000 gallons) per day, report actual water withdrawals annually. Amendments to Part 327 in 2006 and new legislation passed in 2008 require reporting and registration for new or increased large capacity withdrawals.

With multiple uses of water and the need to ensure water quantity and quality, these reporting systems, laws and regulations, and water quality standards provide a means for managing the water resources of Michigan and help promote a better understanding of the interactions among the Great Lakes, inland lakes, streams and groundwater. They assist in identifying existing water needs, safeguarding water supplies for the multitude of activities that Michigan citizens depend upon and enjoy, and help project water demands for today and the future.

FOCUS BOX: Riparian vs. groundwater rights: a case study

Water rights in Michigan are subject to the reasonable use doctrine, which permits a landowner to use water on their property as long as it does not unreasonably interfere with the rights of adjacent or neighboring landowners, decrease the value of the neighboring land or unreasonably impair the quality of the water leaving their property. In times of water shortage, use must be prorated and be equitable among users.

This doctrine was the subject of contention when local residents and property owners in Mecosta County sued Ice Mountain's parent company, Nestle Waters North America, over the withdrawal of groundwater in 2001, to be used as bottled water. The group, Michigan Citizens for Water Conservation, argued that the groundwater withdrawals were bad for the environment because they dropped water levels and flows in neighboring lakes, streams and wetlands. Four wells owned by Nestle, on a site referred to as the Sanctuary Springs, had been given permission to extract groundwater at 400 gallons per minute (gpm) from an aquifer that was a source of "spring water" and thus hydrologically connected to surface water in the vicinity. After 19 days of testimony, the Mecosta County Circuit Court Judge ruled in the citizens' favor and ordered Nestle to stop withdrawing water from the wells, citing that the withdrawals caused a "material diminishment" of water flows and levels.

That 2003 decision, however, was put on hold during Nestle's appeal, allowing the company to continue to pump 250 gpm from the aquifer. The Michigan Court of Appeals in 2005 found that the Circuit Court Judge had applied the wrong law in his decision and that people who use groundwater, regardless of its destination, have legal standing equal to riparian owners. Although the Circuit Court had correctly determined that Ice Mountain's withdrawals interfered with the plaintiffs' riparian rights, the Appellate court panel stated that Ice Mountain should not be completely barred from using the wells. The defendant is "entitled to make reasonable use of the available water resources, and plaintiffs may properly be compelled to endure some measure of loss, as long as an adequate supply of water remains for their own water uses" according to the opinion of the Appellate Court Judge.

Following the decision by the Michigan Court of Appeals, the company and the citizens group tentatively reached an agreement on the amount of water the bottler can withdraw from the Sanctuary Springs source. Although the court reduced the interim pumping level to 200 gpm, the final rate will be determined under a balancing test to be applied by a trial court in upcoming proceedings.

Literature Cited

Annable, M.D., Kubitz, J.A. and P.M. Ryan. 1991. An Introduction to Michigan's Water Resources. Michigan State University, Institute of Water Research, East Lansing, MI. 64 pp.

Bedford, J. 2005. Our Finest Trout Fishing. Michigan Sportsman. Michigan Sportsman Magazine 4 (April):24–26, 52.

Bolinger, D. and B. Bickert. 2006. I'm not a CAFO. Michigan Agricultural Environmental Assurance Program. Michigan State University, Department of Biosystems and Agricultural Engineering, East Lansing, MI. 1 p.

Cech, T.V. 2003. Principles of Water Resources: History, Development, Management, and Policy. John Wiley and Sons, Inc., New York. 446 pp.

Comer, P. 2003. Michigan's Vegetation circa 1800. Michigan Department of Natural Resources, Michigan Natural Features Inventory, Lansing, MI. Accessed at: http://www.michigan.gov/dnr/0,1607,7-153-10370_22664-70465--,00.html

Dahl, T.E. 1990. Wetland Losses in the United States 1780 to 1980s. US Department of the Interior, US Fish and Wildlife Service, Washington, DC. 13 pp.

DNR Natural Rivers Program. no date. Michigan Department of Natural Resources, Lansing, MI.

Edmondson, W.T. 1970. Phosphorus, nitrogen, and algae in Lake Washington after diversion of sewage. Science 169: 690–691.

GCAC. 2006. Final Report to the Michigan Legislature in Response to Public Act 148 of 2003. Michigan Department of Environmental Quality, Groundwater Conservation Advisory Council, Lansing, MI. 54 pp.

Grannemann, R.J., Nicholas, J.R., Reilly, T.E. and T.C. Winter. 2000. The Importance of Ground Water in the Great Lakes Region. Water Resources Investigations Report 00–4008. Lansing, MI. US Geological Survey, Lansing, MI. 14 pp.

Great Lakes Commission. 1996. Annual Report of the Great Lakes Panel on Aquatic Nuisance Species. Great Lakes Commission, Ann Arbor, MI.

Groundwater Inventory and Mapping Project. 2005. Michigan State University, Remote Sensing and GIS Research and Outreach Services, Michigan State University, East Lansing, MI.

Kalff, J. 2002. Limnology. Prentice Hall, Upper Saddle River, NJ. 592 pp.

MDCH. 2003. Michigan 2003 Fish Advisory. Michigan Department of Community Health, Lansing, MI.

MDEQ. 2004a. Water Quality and Pollution Control in Michigan: 2004 Sections 303(D) and 305(B) Integrated Report. Michigan Department of Environmental Quality, Lansing, MI. 60 pp.

MDEQ. 2004b. Combined Sewer Overflow (CSO) & Sanitary Sewer Overflow (SSO). 2004 Annual Report. Michigan Department of Environmental Quality, Lansing, MI. 260 pp.

MDEQ. 2006. Water Quality and Pollution Control in Michigan. 2006 Sections 303(D) and 305(A) Integrated Report. MDEQ, Water Bureau, Lansing, MI. 108 pp.

MDEQ and EPA. 2004. Alternative Permitting Approach for Concentrated Animal Feeding Operations (CAFOs) Project. 2003 Annual Report. Michigan Department of Environmental Quality, Lansing, MI.

MDNR. 2004. The Natural Rivers Program. Fisheries Division, Michigan Department of Natural Resources, Lansing, MI.

MEC. 2004. Mercury Pollution of Fish in Michigan Lakes: A Ranking of Detailed Fish Tissue Analysis. A briefing report from the State Environmental Leadership Program and Michigan Environmental Council. Accessed at: http://www.mecprotects.org/10MercLakes.pdf

MDOT. 2006. Michigan's State Facts. Michigan Department of Transportation, Lansing, MI.

Michigan in Brief. 2006. Michigan in Brief, Information about the State of Michigan. History, Arts and Library, Library of Michigan, Lansing, MI. 6 pp.

Michigan Sea Grant. 2005. Zebra Mussel Infestation Michigan Inland Lakes 1992–2005. University of Michigan, Ann Arbor, MI.

Mills, E.L., Leach, J.H., Carlton, J.T. and C.L. Secor. 1993. Exotic species in the Great Lakes: A history of biotic crises and anthropogenic introductions. Journal of Great Lakes Research 19: 1–54.

National Rivers. 1999. Overview of Rivers of Michigan. National Organization for Rivers, Colorado Springs, CO.

Public Sector Consultants. 2002. Michigan in Brief. Michigan Nonprofit Association and the Council of Michigan Foundations. Lansing, MI. 290 pp.

Sarnelle, O., Wilson, A.E., Hamilton, S.K., Knoll, L.B. and D.E. Raikow. 2005. Complex interactions between the Zebra Mussel, *Dreissena polymorpha*, and the harmful phytoplankter, *Microcystis aeruginosa*. Limnology and Oceanography 50: 896–904.

USEPA. 1995. The Great Lakes: An Environmental Atlas and Resource Book. K. Fuller, H. Shear and J. Wittig (eds). EPA-905-B-95-001. US Environmental Protection Agency, Great Lakes National Program Office, Chicago, IL.

USEPA. 2001. Saginaw River/Bay Area of Concern. US Environmental Protection Agency, Great Lakes National Program Office, Chicago, IL.

USEPA. 2002. Assessment Data for the State of Michigan Year 2002. National Assessment Database. US Environmental Protection Agency, Washington, DC.

USEPA. 2006a. Total Maximum Daily Loads, 2006 Section 303(d) List Fact Sheet for Michigan. U.S. Environmental Protection Agency, Office of Wetlands, Oceans, and Watersheds, Washington, DC.

USEPA. 2006b. Deer Lake Area of Concern. US Environmental Protection Agency, Great Lakes National Program Office, Chicago, IL.

USGS. 2002. Monitoring our Rivers and Streams. U.S. Geological Survey, Fact Sheet 077-02. Denver, CO. 4 pp.

USGS. 1991. National Water Summary 1988–89-Hydrologic Events and Floods and Droughts. US Geological Survey, Water Supply Paper 2375. Washington, DC.

Vollenweider, R.A. 1968. Scientific fundamentals of the eutrophication of lakes and flowing waters, with particular reference to nitrogen and phosphorus as factors in eutrophication. Organization for Economic Cooperation and Development (OECD), Technical Report DA 515C1168 27. Paris. 250 pp.

Wiley, M.J. and P.W. Seelbach. 1997. An Introduction to Rivers—the Conceptual Basis for the Michigan Rivers Inventory (MRI) Project. Michigan Department of Natural Resources, Fisheries Division, Special Report #20, Ann Arbor, MI.

Wiley, M.J., Seelbach, P.W. and S.P. Bowler. 1998. Ecological Targets for Rehabilitation of the Rouge River, Final Report. School of Natural Resources and Environment, University of Michigan, Ann Arbor.

Zorn, T.G. and S.P. Sendek. 2001. AuSable River Assessment. Michigan Department of Natural Resources, Fisheries Special Report #26, Ann Arbor, MI.

Further Readings

Davenport, T.E. 2003. The Watershed Project Management Guide. Lewis Publishers, Boca Raton, Florida. 271 pp.

National Research Council. 1999. New Strategies for America's Watersheds. National Academy Press, Washington, DC. 311 pp.

Wetzel, R.G. 2001. Limnology: Lake and River Ecosystems. Elsevier Academic Press, San Diego, CA. 985 pp.

16 Groundwater and Karst

David P. Lusch

■ Importance of groundwater in Michigan

We all need water to live, and in Michigan much of that water comes from groundwater resources. The 1990 US Census reported that, for household water supplies in Michigan, 29.5% of the households relied on a private water supply (virtually all were water wells), while the remaining 70.5% depended on public water. Michigan ranked first in the nation in total number of private water wells (~1.25 million wells) and 7th for proportion of the state's household water supply needs provided by private wells. About 2.6 million Michigan citizens obtain their drinking water from private wells, withdrawing about 734,370 cubic meters (194 million gallons) of groundwater per day.

Michigan has more than 12,000 public water supply systems (Fig. 16.1). Of these, approximately 10,650 are non-community public water supplies, with groundwater as their source. There are 1,132 community water supply systems in the state that rely on groundwater sources to serve the drinking water needs of about 1.7 million citizens. During 2006, the community public water supply systems in the state withdrew 342.7 million cubic meters (90.5 billion gallons) of groundwater (MDEQ 2006). Michigan has 9% of the nation's public groundwater supply systems—the highest share of any state. Additionally, groundwater supplies about 4.8% of the combined water needs of Michigan's thermoelectric power plants, self-supplied industries, irrigators, and public water supplies.

Groundwater is also critical to the maintenance of many ecosystems in Michigan, because it provides a steady flow of cool, high-quality water to streams, lakes, and wetlands. This "base flow" is especially important during periods of low precipitation, when surface runoff is minimal (Grannemann et al. 2000; Chapter 15). Groundwater is also the source of most of the water stored in the Great Lakes, e.g., groundwater contributes about 80% of the water flowing into Lake Michigan (Grannemann et al. 2000, Coon and Sheets 2006). Coon and Sheets (2006) estimated that there are 4,101.5 cubic kilometers (984 cubic miles) of fresh groundwater stored in the various aquifers within the Great Lakes Basin—equivalent to about 83.4% of the volume of Lake Michigan. Clearly, groundwater is an underappreciated resource in our state!

■ The basics of groundwater

Groundwater (Fig. 16.2) exists wherever a porous geologic media is saturated, i.e., all the pore spaces are filled with water. The upper surface of the saturated zone, i.e., the water table, is smoothly undulating and generally mimics the land surface—it has a higher elevation under uplands and is found at lower elevations beneath valleys (Fig. 16.3). In areas of hummocky topography, however, closed depressions often contain flow-through lakes or wetlands. In these situations, the water table may slope in the direction of groundwater flow, rather than being sub-parallel to the land surface (Kehew et al. 1998). Throughout most of Michigan, the water table is within three m of

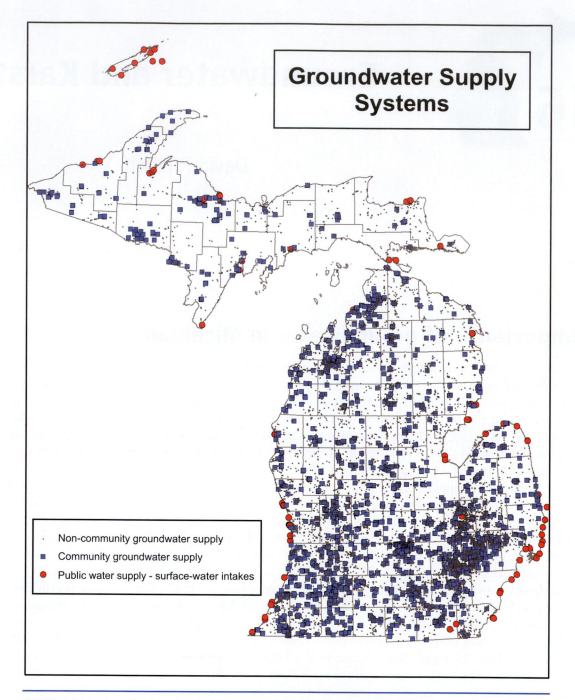

FIGURE 16.1   Distribution of public water supply systems in Michigan. Source: State of Michigan (2005).

the surface (Fig. 16.4). Beneath the highlands of southwestern and northern Lower Michigan and the Upper Peninsula, however, the water table is deeper, sometimes >30 m below ground.

Any geologic material that is capable of storing and transmitting groundwater is called an aquifer (Latin *aqua*: water, and *ferre*: to bear). In Michigan, aquifers are differentiated based on the type of geologic material that stores the groundwater. In *glacial* aquifers, the saturated, porous media is composed of the unconsolidated glacial deposits, like those that blanket most of the state. These sediments exhibit varying amounts of primary porosity—the proportion of void space that is native to the deposit. *Bedrock* aquifers occur in some of the

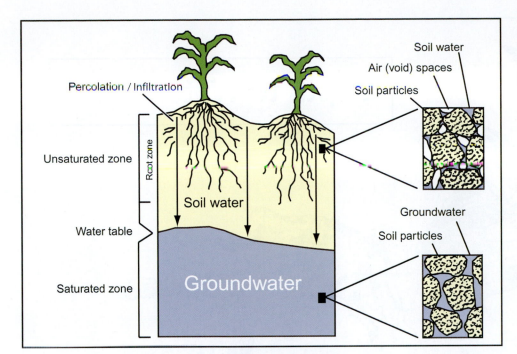

FIGURE 16.2 Soil water in the unsaturated zone compared to groundwater in the saturated zone.

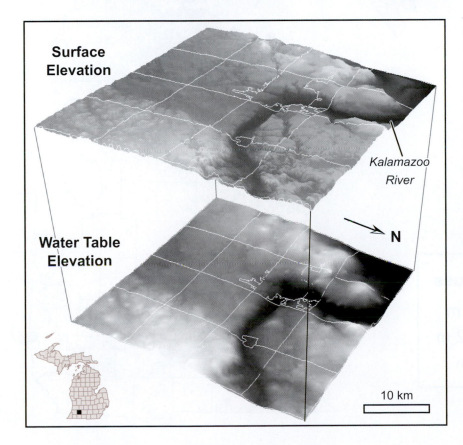

FIGURE 16.3 As these maps of Kalamazoo County show, the water table surface is smoothly undulating and generally mimics the land surface. The water table has a higher elevation under surface highlands, and is found at lower elevations beneath surface lowlands. These maps were created by D. Lusch, using the US Geological Survey National Elevation Dataset (surface map), and digital water well logs, obtained from MDEQ.

more permeable consolidated rock types that underlie the glacial deposits. They exhibit varying amounts of both primary and secondary porosity—the void space created by post-depositional geologic processes, including fracturing and solution widening of joints. Fracture porosity can occur in any rock type, but solution porosity is restricted to the carbonate-rich limestone (calcium carbonate, $CaCO_3$) and dolostone (calcium magnesium carbonate, $CaMg(CO_3)_2$) rocks.

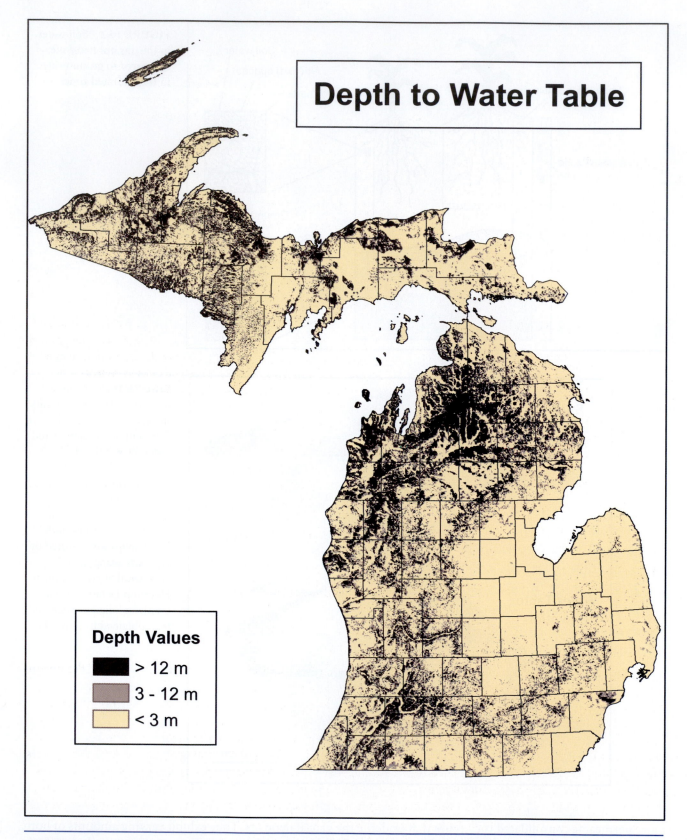

FIGURE 16.4   Depth to the water table in Michigan, compiled from digital surface hydrography, topography, soils and wetland data, in addition to digital records from wells screened in unconfined glacial aquifers. After State of Michigan (2005) and MDEQ (2006a).

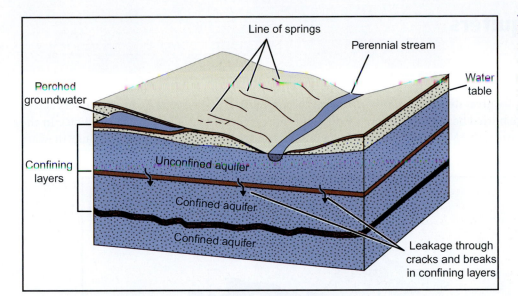

FIGURE 16.5 A generalized diagram showing the distinctions between, and characteristics of, unconfined versus confined aquifers.

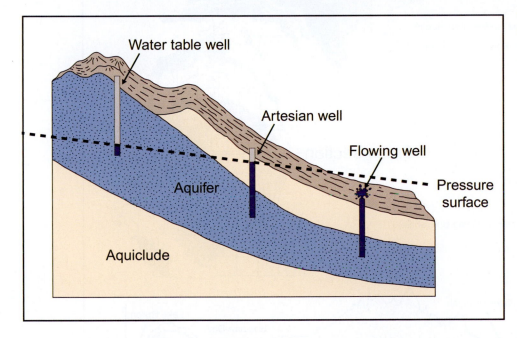

FIGURE 16.6 Diagram of wells in unconfined and confined aquifers. After Fetter (2001).

Aquifers also vary by their position in the subsurface. The first aquifer that occurs below ground is the unconfined, or *water table* aquifer (Fig. 16.5). The upper surface of the unconfined aquifer is the water table. It receives recharge from water infiltrating through the unsaturated zone, and it stores groundwater at the prevailing atmospheric pressure, i.e., it is "open" to the atmosphere through the unsaturated zone. Most lakes and wetlands in Michigan, and all perennial streams, are the surface expression of this aquifer. Almost everywhere within glacial deposits, however, there are textural differences that are significant enough to envelop one or more confined aquifers. *Confined* aquifers are partially protected from surface or near-surface contaminants by their outward pressure gradient, and the lower hydraulic conductivity of an upper confining layer, or aquiclude. Most of the glacial aquifers, and many of the bedrock aquifers, in Michigan are only partially confined—by "leaky" or discontinuous confining layers, called aquitards. As a result, no aquifer is perfectly protected, making the use of a variety of best management practices by people a necessity to prevent groundwater contamination.

Groundwater in confined aquifers (also known as *artesian* aquifers) is held at pressures above atmospheric. As such, the standing water level in a well that penetrates a confined or artesian aquifer rises *above* the top of the aquifer. Note that such an artesian well does not necessarily flow at the surface (Fig. 16.6). Most flowing wells tap artesian groundwater, but not every artesian well flows.

Bedrock aquifers

Bedrock geology

Many of the carbonate rocks, and most of the sandstones, in the Michigan Basin (Plate 5; Chapter 4) are potential aquifers (Fig. 16.7). There are great differences in the economic accessibility of the various bedrock aquifers across Michigan, because they are buried beneath considerably different thicknesses of glacial deposits (Fig. 17.8). In the northwestern Lower Peninsula, the Marshall and Saginaw aquifers (sandstone) are not utilized, because they are

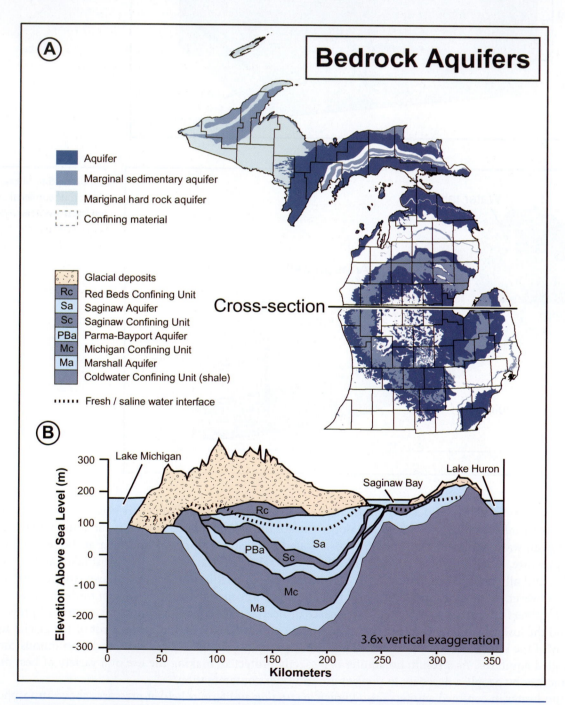

FIGURE 16.7   The bedrock aquifers of Michigan. Source: State of Michigan (2005). A. Map view. B. Cross-section view of the Lower Peninsula. After Hoaglund et al. (2002).

deeply buried beneath >180 m of glacial deposits, which contain several aquifers that meet the local water supply needs. In south-central Michigan, these same aquifers are more shallowly buried and, therefore, more widely utilized. These variable conditions result in a very uneven distribution of bedrock water wells in Michigan (Fig. 16.8). Some of the shallowly buried bedrock aquifers, especially in the NE and SE parts of the Lower Peninsula, are carbonate-rich rocks that have developed notable solution porosity (see page 225).

Water yields from bedrock aquifers

As mentioned above, the primary and secondary porosities of the bedrock aquifers beneath Michigan vary widely. As a result, their water yields also vary considerably (Fig. 16.9). The highest estimated yields from bedrock aquifers occur in the central and southern Lower Peninsula, especially in Jackson, Calhoun and Barry Counties, where high yields are associated with the Marshall sandstone. Lower yields are typical from the sandstone and carbonate aquifers in the Upper Peninsula, and from the predominately carbonate strata that underlie both the northern swath of the Lower Peninsula and the SE corner of the state.

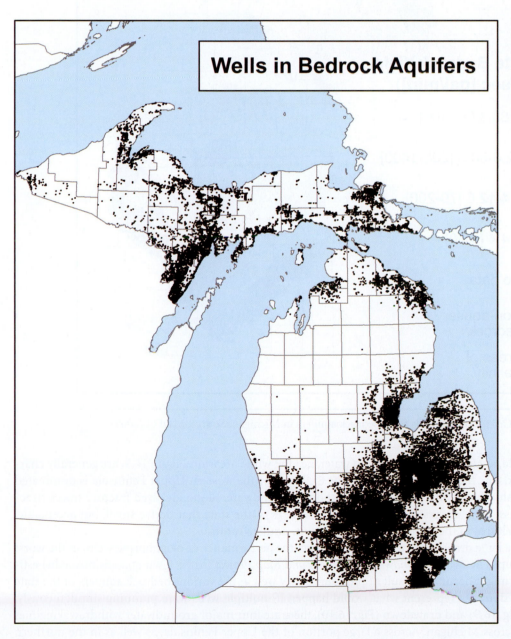

FIGURE 16.8 Locations of water wells in bedrock aquifers in Michigan. All other water wells in Michigan tap the unconsolidated glacial deposits that overlie the bedrock. Source: State of Michigan (2005).

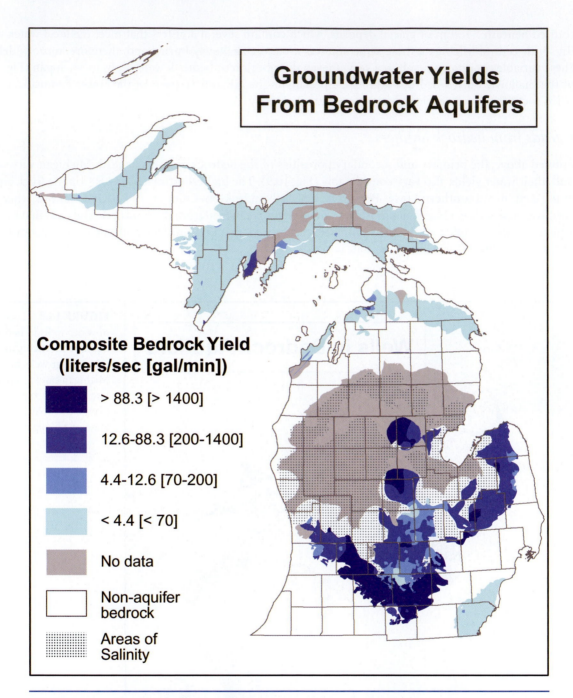

FIGURE 16.9   Groundwater yields from bedrock aquifers in Michigan. Source: MDEQ (2005).

In the Lower Peninsula, areas that yield almost no water, i.e., the white areas on Figure 16.9, are generally characterized by shale bedrock, e.g., the Coldwater shale (Plate 6). Much of the western Upper Peninsula is dominated by igneous and metamorphic rocks (Plate 6), that only produce groundwater along localized fracture traces (fracture porosity). Nevertheless, there are residential wells in these areas of the state that derive small, but acceptable, volumes of water from fractures in the upper parts of these "non-aquifer" units.

Pumpage that creates a large drawdown can adversely impact the performance of neighboring wells, in the worst case causing them to dry up. The 2005 *Groundwater Inventory and Map Project* (http://gwmap.rsgis.msu.edu) estimated the drawdown that might occur as a result of pumping a new well in the various bedrock aquifers of the state (Fig. 16.10). This analysis does not represent what would happen if multiple wells were pumping simultaneously. Considering both yield (Fig. 16.9) and drawdown (Fig. 16.10), there are four major groundwater withdrawal regimes for the bedrock aquifers across Michigan. Across a large portion of the Upper Peninsula, as well as in the northern

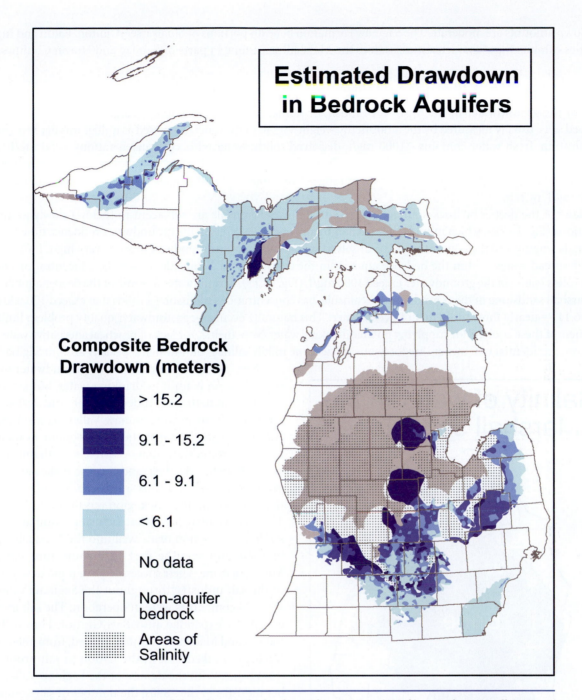

FIGURE 16.10 Estimated drawdown in bedrock aquifers 152.4 m (500 ft) away from a well, as a result of pumping it at the estimated yield shown in Figure 16.9 for 100 days continuously, assuming a storativity of 0.004. After MDEQ (2005).

and southeastern portions of the Lower Peninsula, the estimated yields are so small that groundwater withdrawal will not cause a significant drawdown 150 m away. In other locales, the aquifer characteristics permit large yields, but such pumpage creates a large drawdown. Such conditions occur in the central and north-central portions of the Lower Peninsula, and in four restricted areas in Barry, northeastern Jackson, northern Ingham and northwestern Lapeer Counties. All these areas are associated with the Saginaw Formation or the Marshall sandstone. In a few areas, the aquifer properties promote the optimal circumstance—minimal drawdown even at high rates of withdrawal. These groundwater conditions are common in a narrow band across northeastern Calhoun, southern Jackson and northern Hillsdale counties—all associated with the southernmost margin of the Marshall sandstone. Lastly, the hydraulic properties of some bedrock aquifers in Michigan are such that both the estimated yields and the associated drawdown amounts are moderate. The Saginaw Formation beneath portions of Shiawassee, Clinton, Eaton and Ingham Counties exhibits these characteristics, as does the Marshall sandstone in parts of Sanilac and Huron Counties.

Groundwater quality in bedrock aquifers

Much of the groundwater in Michigan is brackish, or saline. Saline water contains a significant concentration of dissolved salts, usually measured by the amount (by weight) of salt in the water, expressed as milligrams per liter (mg/L). By definition, fresh water contains <1000 mg/L dissolved solids; water with salt concentrations >250 mg/L, however, usually tastes salty. The US Environmental Protection Agency's (USEPA) recommended drinking water limit for salts is 500 mg/L. By definition, saline water ranges from 1000 to 35,000 mg/L, and ocean water contains about 35,000 mg/L of salt.

Many of the deeper bedrock aquifers in the central Lower Peninsula are subjacent to (below) slowly permeable formations (Fig. 16.7B), which impede their recharge from above. As a result, the groundwater residence time for these aquifers is lengthy and the concentration of dissolved solids (salts) in the groundwater can be very high. Indeed, there are widespread zones, within the bedrock aquifers in the central Lower Peninsula, where the concentrations of dissolved solids (salts) in the groundwater exceed 1000 mg/L (Fig. 16.11). Groundwater in some of the deeper aquifers, e.g., the Marshall sandstone in the central Lower Peninsula, has concentrations of dissolved solids that exceed 100,000 mg/L (Fig. 16.11)—nearly three times that of ocean water! This naturally occurring groundwater quality problem limits the usefulness of these aquifers for supplying potable drinking water. Nonetheless, for lack of practical alternative water supplies, some residential well owners are forced to utilize some mildly saline groundwater, especially around Saginaw Bay.

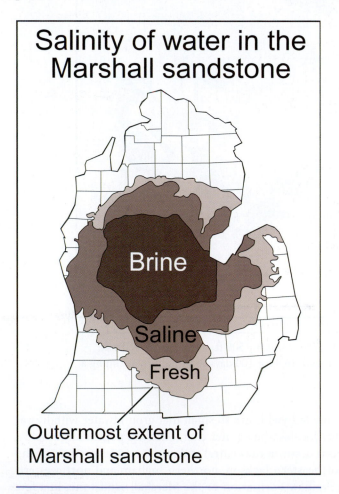

Non-potable, saline and brine groundwater in central Michigan is unfit as drinking water, but is a useful resource, nonetheless. Indeed, in the mid-1800s a salt industry began in the Saginaw Valley, as a synergistic enterprise associated with the lumber boom. Evaporating the brine groundwater that occurred beneath much of the area (within the Marshall sandstone) to make salt was only profitable, however, if fuel was cheap. Wood waste from the many sawmills in the region was the perfect solution. The East Saginaw Salt Manufacturing Company drilled the first production brine well into the Marshall aquifer in 1860, and was the first to manufacture salt from Michigan brine. Their success led to a rapid development of the salt industry throughout the Saginaw Valley. By 1862, 23 companies were in operation. The salt industry eventually expanded into Bay, Gratiot, Huron, Iosco, Isabella and Macomb Counties. Indeed, from 1880–1892, Michigan ranked first in the nation in salt production from brine. With the demise of the Saginaw Valley lumber industry in the 1890s, the number of salt companies in the Saginaw Bay area also declined rapidly, as the cheap fuel source for evaporating the water was lost. The last salt produced from these *natural brine* sources in Michigan was made in 1943, in Saginaw.

Michigan's petroleum industry is another interesting legacy of these Saginaw brine wells. In 1925, the Saginaw oil field became the first commercial petroleum success in the state (Chapter 10). Its discovery was based on the mapping of an anticlinal structure in the bedrock, with information from brine well drilling records.

In 1881, *solution mining* for salt began in Manistee. Using this technique, *artificial* brine is produced by

FIGURE 16.11   Distribution of freshwater (<1000 mg/L), saline water (1000–100,000 mg/L) and brine (>100,000 mg/L) in the Marshall sandstone aquifer. After Westjohn and Weaver (1998).

pumping fresh water down an injection well, into rock salt beds. After dissolving some of the salt, the injected water is pumped back to the surface through a production well located near the injection site. Salt is then extracted from this artificial brine by evaporation. Solution mining has been used to produce salt at Algonac, Ludington, Manistee, Marine City, St. Clair, Whitehall and Wyandotte.

The Dow Chemical Company, one of the world's primary producers of chemical products, is headquartered in Midland, not coincidentally because of the vast amounts of non-potable groundwater there. In the late 1800s, numerous brine wells in the Midland-Saginaw area were producing salt (sodium chloride). However, the groundwater also contained bromine and magnesium, in high concentrations. Extracting these other compounds inexpensively was the problem that Herbert Dow solved.

FOCUS BOX: Herbert Dow and Dow Chemical

Herbert Dow came to Midland in 1890. As a college student, he had developed an electrolytic process to extract bromine from brine groundwater. Using borrowed money, a homemade, steam-powered electric generator, and a reactivated brine well, Dow perfected his production methods and pioneered the manufacture of commercial quantities of bromine by electrolysis (see Figure below). In 1895, Dow built an electrolytic plant for extracting chlorine from brine groundwater. Two years later, he founded the Dow Chemical Company.

Dow also perfected the extraction of sodium, magnesium and calcium salts from the brine, producing carbon tetrachloride, chloroform and lead arsenate. These chemicals were the forerunners of an extensive line of agricultural chemicals that Dow Chemical eventually produced. In 1916, Dow scientists pioneered a method to make magnesium metal from the electrolysis of magnesium chloride, another product of the Midland brines. During WW II, Dow Chemical produced 84% of the nation's magnesium, which was critical to the war effort, because it was used in aircraft wheels, engines, and frames, in a variety of ordnance equipment, in incendiary bombs, flares and tracer powder and in a variety of alloys with aluminum.

Cheaper energy costs have since led to the migration of chlorine production to Texas and Louisiana. Other brine well sites, e.g., in Arkansas, have since been found to contain higher concentrations of bromine. Both of these factors led to the closure of the Midland brine wells in the 1980s.

The old mill Herbert Dow used as a laboratory and bromine processing facility when he came to Midland in 1890. Used with permission of the Post Street Archives, Midland.

Arsenic in Michigan's bedrock aquifers

Arsenic, the 20th most common element in the Earth's crust, is abundant in the soils and rocks of Michigan. Arsenic in groundwater is usually the result of arsenic-bearing minerals dissolving naturally over time. Long known as a poison, arsenic has more recently also been identified as a cancer-causing agent. While some foods contain arsenic, human exposure to arsenic is also possible by consuming contaminated drinking water.

For many years, the maximum contaminant level for arsenic in drinking water was 50 µg/L for community water supplies. But in January 2001, the USEPA established a new maximum level of 10 µg/L. Although public water supplies had to comply with this new regulation by January 23, 2006, the Michigan Department of Environmental Quality (MDEQ) required all new facilities in Michigan to meet the 10 µg/L standard by 2004.

In Michigan, arsenic concentrations in groundwater are often elevated for wells completed in the Marshall sandstone, but groundwater in other bedrock aquifers, e.g., the Michigan and Saginaw Formations, also show elevated arsenic levels (Fig. 16.12). In a study of arsenic concentrations in >3000 wells in the Thumb (Haack and Rachol

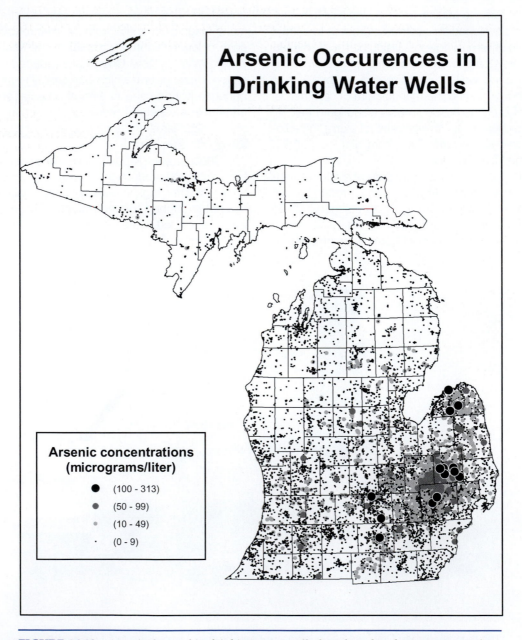

FIGURE 16.12 Arsenic detected in drinking water wells, based on data from water samples submitted to the State of Michigan laboratory for analysis, between 1983 and 2003. Source: MDEQ (2003).

2000), the highest arsenic concentration (220 μg/L) occurred in a well completed in the Marshall sandstone. However, arsenic concentrations exceeding the previous USEPA standard of 50 μg/L were measured in water from all aquifer units, except those in sand and gravel deposits.

USEPA data indicate that as many as 367,000 Michigan citizens in 176 communities may be drinking water with arsenic levels that exceed 10 μg/L (US House of Representatives 2001), and as many as 169,000 Michigan citizens in 76 communities may be drinking water with arsenic concentrations exceeding 20 μg/L. Overall, 12% of Michigan public water systems are estimated to contain arsenic at levels that exceed 10 μg/L. Only Arizona and Nevada have a higher percentage of public water systems affected by high arsenic levels, and only California, Arizona, New York and Washington are estimated to have more citizens exposed to arsenic at levels >10 μg/L.

Flowing wells

Flowing artesian wells occur where the pressure in an aquifer forces groundwater above the ground surface, so that the well will flow without a pump. Flowing well conditions can be created either geologically (Fig. 16.13A) or topographically (Fig. 16.13B). In the more common (geologic) scenario, wells tap an artesian aquifer that is confined by

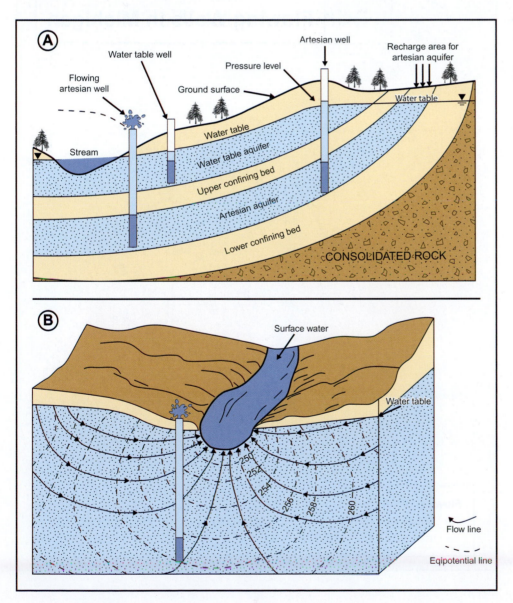

FIGURE 16.13 Examples of groundwater conditions leading to artesian aquifers, wells and flowing wells. A. Geologically controlled artesian conditions. B. Non-artesian flowing wells.

an overlying layer of geologic material that has a lower hydraulic conductivity (or permeability). A recharge area at an elevation higher than the wells creates the hydraulic head that pressurizes the water within the confined aquifer. Any well that penetrates through the confining unit releases this pressure, allowing the artesian groundwater to rise within the well casing to its equilibrium level—the elevation of the water table in the recharge zone. Topographic conditions can also result in non-artesian wells that flow. In unconfined aquifers, flowing wells can occur wherever the well intake (screen) is deep enough in the water table aquifer to intercept groundwater, whose hydraulic pressure is higher than the land surface.

Flowing wells are found throughout Michigan, in either glacial deposits or bedrock (Fig. 16.14). More than 200 flowing well districts have been identified in Michigan (Leverett et al. 1906, 1907, Allen 1977). About 3% (450 wells) of all the new water wells drilled between June 2001 and June 2002 flowed (Gaber 2005). Many Michigan towns and villages are known for their flowing wells: Indian River in Cheboygan County, Rapid River in Delta County, Norway in Dickinson County, Alanson, Conway, Harbor Springs and Oden in Emmet County, Cedar in Leelanau County, Naubinway in Mackinaw County, Onekama in Manistee County, Ortonville in Oakland County, West Branch

FIGURE 16.14 Locations of flowing wells—both freshwater and saline—in Michigan. After Allen (1977).

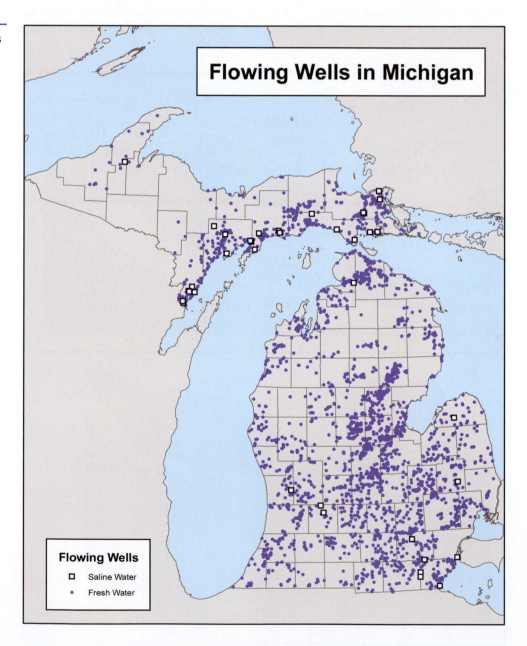

Flowing Wells in Michigan

Flowing Wells
□ Saline Water
• Fresh Water

FIGURE 16.15 This flowing artesian well is located in a roadside park along US Hwy 2, just west of the Norway, in Dickinson County. The spring emerged in 1903, when an exploratory boring was drilled to a depth of 333.5 m (1094 ft.) by an iron mining company. This artesian flow has continued for >100 years. Photo by R. Schaetzl.

and Rose City in Ogemaw County and Marion in Osceola County (Fig. 16.15). In the late 19th and early 20th centuries, flowing wells attracted visitors to many Michigan hotels and resorts that advertised the therapeutic benefits of their "artesian mineral waters."

Some of the largest artesian flow rates reported by Leverett et al. (1907) were from wells in Rose City, that reportedly flowed at about 17.0 L/s (270 gpm). In 1907, the total flow from 20 artesian wells in Rose City was 144.5 L/s (2290 gpm). In 1986, several high-pressure flowing wells were encountered in the village of Cedar in Leelanau County. The fountains from these wells reached nearly 21 m above the surface! Allen (1977) reported an artesian head of 25 m above the ground surface from a bedrock well near Naubinway. According to Gaber (2005), this is the highest reported artesian head in the state.

FOCUS BOX: Water, water everywhere—flowing well problems

In 1989, an abandoned flowing well on vacant property in Rose City abruptly began to discharge a large volume of groundwater from around the *outside* of the casing, which quickly eroded a large and expanding hole around the well. The initial flow rate was measured at 75.7 L/s (1200 gpm), but a week later the flow was still 50.5 L/s (800 gpm). An oversized pipe was driven 12 m down, around the existing well casing, but the flow broke out of it. Attempts were made to seal this new annular flow, using bentonite grout, but it washed out each time. Next, a high-capacity pump was used to continually dewater the site, while a 3.1 m deep by 4.6 m wide hole was excavated around the well. A layer of bentonite grout 31 cm thick was poured over the bottom of the hole, to form a seal, and a circular steel plate "donut" was installed on top of the bentonite. A tractor tire was used as an O-ring seal between the plate and the well casing. Next,

cement grout was pumped down three pipes that penetrated the plate, while concrete was poured on top of the steel donut to provide down-pressure. Dewatering continued for 62 hours after the concrete was poured to ensure that it properly hardened. In the end, all of these elaborate engineering efforts failed. When a cap was installed on the top of the riser pipe in the center of the steel donut (thereby confining the artesian flow), and the dewatering pump was shut off, groundwater immediately gushed up, around the perimeter of the concrete. In frustration, the landowner constructed a clay berm around the run-away well in order to form a pond, with a water level about 1.2 m higher than the original grade. The water head of the pond reduced the flow rate from the well to about 37.9 L/s (600 gpm), but to this day, the well continues to discharge into the pond, and the pond discharges continuously into a nearby creek.

■ Karst—areas of special concern

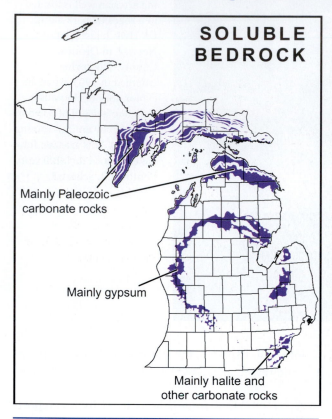

FIGURE 16.16 Locations of soluble bedrock units (limestone, dolostone, gypsum, and halite) in Michigan. See Plate 6 for more detail.

The term karst refers to a set of bedrock attributes and related landforms, usually in areas shallowly underlain by soluble bedrock (Ralston 2000). Precipitation infiltrating into secondary porosity features is made weakly acidic by its chemical reaction with CO_2 in the atmosphere and soil. Once it becomes part of the groundwater, this weak carbonic acid (H_2CO_3) slowly dissolves the soluble bedrock along the surfaces of joints, fractures and bedding planes, creating additional solution porosity. These solution cavities can become large enough to form caves. When the roof of a near-surface cave collapses, it forms surface features called sinkholes, or dolines.

In the Michigan Basin, limestone and dolostone are the most common karst-prone, bedrock formations. Gypsum (calcium sulfate) and halite (sodium chloride), two of the evaporite rock types found beneath Michigan, are also prone to solution (Fig. 16.16). In the Lower Peninsula, most of the extensive carbonate rocks are deeply buried beneath glacial deposits (Plate 6) and, thus, do not support karst terrain. Between roughly Alpena and Rogers City, however, karst-prone rocks are near the surface; several large sinkholes, some up to 1.6 km long and 60 m deep, occur in this area, in part due to deep, evaporite karst collapse (USGS 2005). Many of these sinkholes occur along an extensive, subsurface fissure system. Some are filled with water, but occasionally the sediment plugs in the fissure systems fail and the sinkhole lakes drain through the subterranean openings (see FOCUS BOX below).

Large, active subsidence features are rare in the Lower Peninsula, but one has been reported in Presque Isle County. One night, in the mid-1930s, a large sinkhole, 4.6 m deep and 9.1 m across, developed in Grand Lake Road, about 4 km west of Hwy M-65. The Road Commission set logs across the bottom of the hole and filled it with gravel. A noticeable depression still develops in the road every few years, however, requiring more gravel to fill it (Black 1983, 23). Small, active sinkholes, locally referred to as soil swallows, are also common in Monroe County.

FOCUS BOX: Who pulled the plug on Rainy Lake?

Rainy Lake, a 2 km long lake in southwestern Presque Isle County, is underlain by five sinkholes, the deepest of which has up to 30.5 m of water in it. In the past, Rainy Lake has had significant water level fluctuations, caused by catastrophic drainage through these swallow holes. Drainage occurs when the sediment "plugs" that seal the swallow holes give way. After each drain event, the sinkhole walls of lake clay become unstable, slump and mud seals/plugs the active swallow. As a result, the lake gradually fills. Rainy Lake drained in 1894, 1925, 1950 and 1980. The last event actually occurred between 1979 and 1982. By February 1982, the water level in the lake had declined by more than 12 m (Black 1983; see Figures below). Measurements taken in September 1982 documented that the rate of water loss in Rainy Lake was 37.9 L/sec (Stewart 1981)! After beginning to drain through its bottom sinkholes in 1979, Rainy Lake reached its lowest level in 1982. A low, but not lowest, level was captured on an aerial photograph taken in May, 1981 (bottom photograph in the figure below). By the spring of 1983, after the sinkholes once again became naturally plugged, the lake had refilled to its normal level (middle photograph).

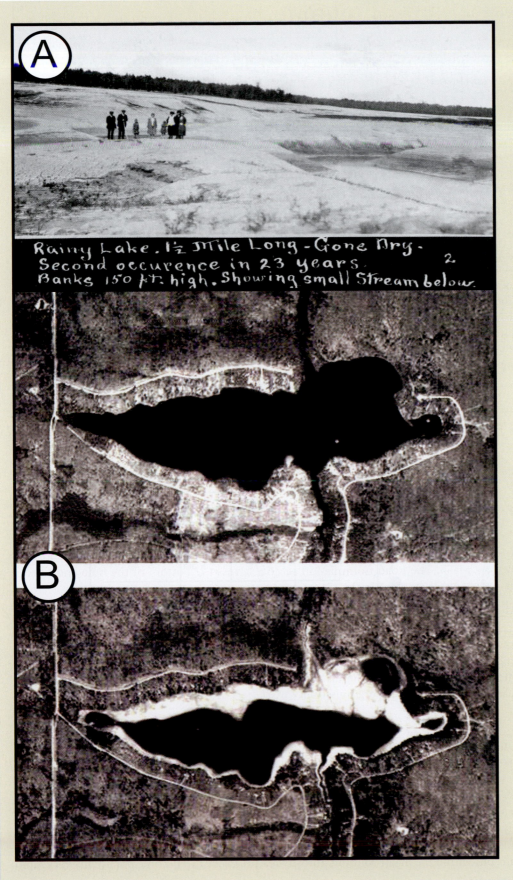

Rainy Lake. 1½ Mile Long - Gone Dry.
Second occurence in 23 years.   2.
Banks 150 ft. high. Showing small Stream below.

Photos of Rainy Lake, in Presque Isle County.
A. People walking on the bottom of Rainy Lake, after the 1925 drainage event. Photo by W. Gregg.
B. Aerial photograph comparisons of the 1981 drainage event. Middle: the lake at its normal, full state (April 20, 1983). Bottom: The lake during the May, 1981 drainage event. Photos courtesy of the Michigan State University RS&GIS Aerial Image Archive.

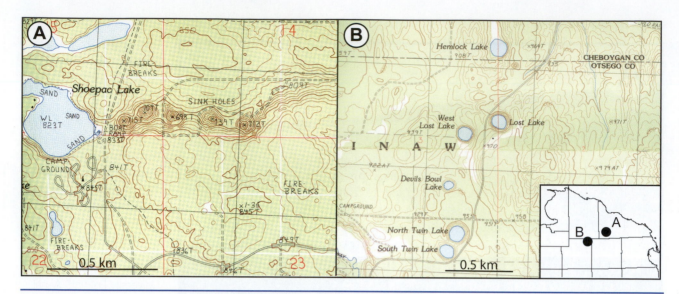

FIGURE 16.17   Examples of some well-formed sinkholes in the northeastern Lower Peninsula, taken from 1:24,000 scale topographic maps, with 10-foot contour intervals. A. Sinkholes near Shoepac Lake, Allis Township, Presque Isle County. Shoepac Lake has not drained, yet, but has had portions of the shoreline slump into the lake due to unstable plugs in this sinkhole lake. Slumping occurred in appoximately 1954, 1969 and 1994 on the east, northeast and southern shorelines (Black 1995). From the Lake Geneva quadrangle. B. Sinkholes in sections 3 and 10, Corwith Township, Otsego County. From the Hardwood Lake quadrangle.

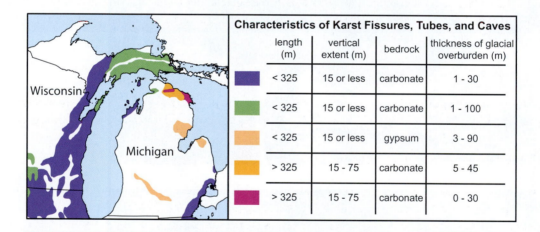

FIGURE 16.18   Types and characteristics of karst features in Michigan and parts of Wisconsin. Although the figure describes numerous caves, only a handful of *accessible* caves have been documented in Michigan, one in the Lower Peninsula and a few in the Upper Peninsula. After USGS (2005). See also http://www.caves.org/conservancy/mkc/

Most large, deep, well-formed sinkholes, however, occur in the northeastern Lower Peninsula (Fig. 16.17). Karst-prone, carbonate rocks also underlie the eastern half of the Upper Peninsula and extend into eastern Wisconsin. Karst features are poorly developed in these formations, however, consisting mostly of small caves, each with <300 m of known passageways and <15 m of vertical extent (USGS 2005). Fissures developed along joint lines in this part of Michigan are about the same size as the caves (Fig. 16.18).

Karst aquifers, typically in limestone and dolostone, tend to be notably heterogeneous and anisotropic, making the flow rates and directions in a mature karst region extremely complex. Flow rates within the secondary porosity features tend to be moderate, but within the major solution porosity features, they can become potentially very rapid

(Ralston 2000). Typical groundwater flow velocities in bedrock aquifers range from a few m/yr to a few tens of m/yr. In karst aquifers, however, groundwater flow rates may reach many cm/sec within large solution conduits.

The rapid infiltration rates of surface and soil water into karstic drinking water aquifers, coupled with the rapid and unpredictable lateral flow regime within them, can lead to water quality concerns. In 1991, 30 cases of gastroenteritis occurred at a resort on Drummond Island, an area underlain by shallowly buried, fractured carbonate bedrock. The cause was traced to a leaking septic tank. Dye injected into the failed septic tank appeared in the drinking water well within two days (Institute of Water Research 1992).

Evaporite karst occurs in the Kent and Iosco County areas, where groundwater has dissolved gypsum bedrock of the Michigan Formation, causing a widespread collapse breccia to form (Black 2003). These evaporites have been dissolved to a depth of at least 275 m. Surface expressions of this dissolution include soil and stream swallows, mantled and exposed extension fractures, subsidence features, and sinkholes. Major sinkholes occur along collapse faults. The glacial mantle in the collapse areas is thin, usually from 2–24 m thick. Dozens of collapses have also occurred in Kent County over the past 60 years. The greatest impact has been in the town of Grandville, where numerous street, sidewalk, foundation, and underground utility collapses have occurred (Black 2003). A second major evaporite sequence, the Detroit River Group, has also produced areally extensive collapse breccias in and around the Straits of Mackinac.

■ Glacial aquifers

Michigan and the Great Lakes Region are in the core of the most extensive and complex areas of continental glaciation in the nation (Chapters 6, 17; Plate 9). In order to visualize this complexity better, a new glacial landsystems map of Michigan (Plate 10) was recently compiled (MDEQ 2006b) by combining Quaternary geology features (Farrand and Bell 1982) with soil texture data. These complex glacial deposits also contain tremendous volumes of high quality groundwater; Coon and Sheets (2006) estimated that 2,144.5 km³ of fresh groundwater is stored in the glacial aquifers of the Lower Peninsula alone.

Lithology of the glacial deposits

Because of their inherent complexity, most individual glacial aquifer units have not been mapped. Nonetheless, we do know that the glacial deposits of Michigan are generally configured in a discontinuous, layered system, with multiple, coarser-textured aquifers of varying thickness, separated by typically leaky, finer-textured aquitards. Fortunately, the aquifer status of the upper portion of the glacial deposits can be characterized by interpreting water well records.

The Michigan DEQ maintains an electronic database, which classifies the various lithologies reported on water well drilling logs into four groups: (1) aquifer (AQ), (2) marginal aquifer (MAQ), (3) partially confining material (PCM), and (4) confining material (CM). This classification uses both the primary lithology and any secondary modifiers. For example, "sand with clay" would be categorized as a marginal aquifer, rather than an aquifer. A fifth class (NA) is assigned to lithology entries that could not be classified. An aquifer index (AI) was later developed by the Groundwater Inventory and Mapping Project (MDEQ 2006b) to quantify the percent of aquifer material reported on the digital well records, based on this lithology classification. The AI was only computed for wells where ≤25% of the logged interval was classified as NA. An aquifer index map (Fig. 16.19) was compiled by interpolating the values computed from the digital well records (point data) onto a 1km² grid. The patterns of AI values nicely match the overall arrangement of the glacial landsystems (Plate 10). Regions with very low AI values (claydominated) are associated with the lacustrine landsystems. A notable exception to this covariation occurs in the vicinity of Menominee County, where low AI values are associated with dense lodgement tills.

The moderate and high AI values in Figure 16.19 are generally associated with the outwash landsystems (Plate 10). The High Plains and moraines of north-central Lower Michigan are the largest and thickest area of coarse sediments. The southeastern Michigan interlobate region (Plate 8) is particularly well defined by the local extent of moderate AI values. The lodgement till, or fine superglacial drift landsystems, in the south-central Lower Peninsula and in the western Upper Peninsula, are dominated by moderately low AI values.

FIGURE 16.19
Interpolated aquifer index values for glacial deposits used for groundwater supplies. Values near zero indicate clay- and silt-dominated deposits that are likely to be poor aquifers, partially confining materials, or confining units. Values near 3.0 indicate that sand and gravel aquifer materials dominate the well depth. Source: MDEQ (2006b).

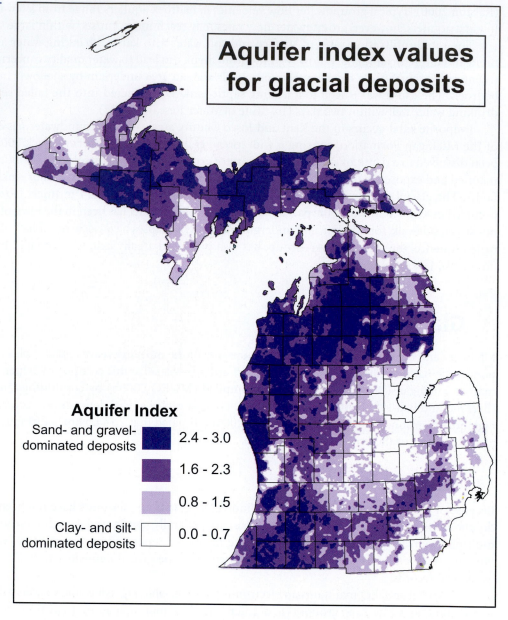

Thicknesses of the various glacial landsystems can be assessed by comparing the aquifer index values for the 0–6 m depth range with the index values for the 6–12 m depth increment. Only a few areas of the state exhibit textural homogeneneity, i.e., near-zero difference values, across the entire 0–12 m depth range. In several areas of the state, aquifer materials dominate the near-surface portion of the glacial sediments, but overlay finer-textured glacial units at a depth of 6–12 m, e.g., outwash over either till or lacustrine deposits (Fig. 16.20). Lacustrine landsystems, in which the upper 6 m of the glacial deposits are dominated by coarse-textured sediments, while the subjacent 6 m are finer-textured, occur in the southeastern Lower Peninsula (particularly in Monroe County). This area is mantled by thin sand sheets and small inland dunes. The prevalence of the large AI differences in the south-central Lower Peninsula shows that this area is composed of finer-textured sediments in the upper 6 m, overlying coarse-textured deposits at depth.

When Frank Leverett first studied the deposits of Oakland County (Leverett 1900), he used the term "great gravel plain" to describe the interlobate outwash plain that trends NE-SW across the county. In places, the surface of this outwash deposit exhibits considerable local relief, due to the presence of kames, older moraine fragments partially

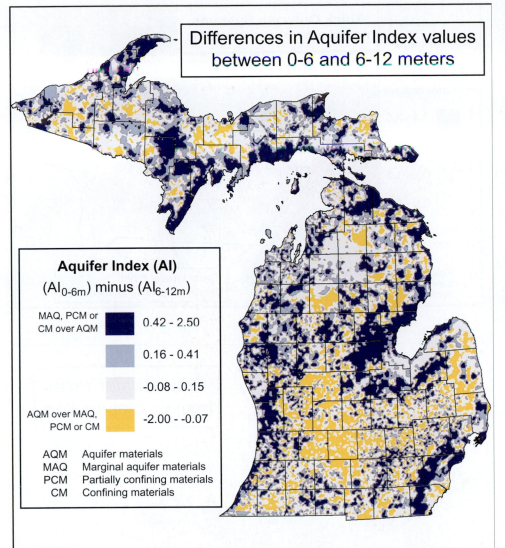

FIGURE 16.20
Differences in aquifer index values between the 0–6 m and 6–12 m depth increments. Areas with similar aquifer indexes (textures) in the upper and lower depth zones are shown in gray. Regions with finer-textured sediments (MAQ, PCM and CM) overlaying coarser-textured deposits (AQ) are shown in yellow. The blue areas depict coarser-textured materials (AQ) in the upper 6 m overlaying finer-textured sediments (MAQ, PCM and CM) in the 6–12 m zone. Darker blues indicate more contrasting AI values. Source: MDEQ (2006b).

buried in the outwash, and the numerous kettles. So much glaciofluvial sediment was deposited in contact with stagnant ice blocks in Oakland County that no other large area in the Lower Peninsula has more lakes (Winters et al. 1985). Figure 16.21 depicts Leverett's "great gravel plain" on top of the AI map for the upper 12 m of glacial sediments. The spatial correspondence between these two maps is striking. This thick body of outwash sediments is clearly depicted by the lithology data recovered from water well records, which show the upper 12 m of the glacial deposits in this area are dominated by aquifer materials (sand and gravel). The Defiance spillway, a broad, shallow valley that once carried outwash discharges southwesterly along the Defiance Moraine, also shows up as a narrow, but thick, accumulation of coarse-textured glacial sediments, especially near Tecumseh.

Water yields from glacial aquifers

In many areas of Michigan, the glacial deposits, and therefore the aquifers within them, are extremely heterogeneous. As a result, well water yields from glacial deposits also exhibit a high degree of spatial variability (Fig. 16.22). The industry-standard, minimum well yield for a residential home is 0.63–0.95 L/sec (10–15 gpm). Several regions of minimal yield (<0.63 L/sec) occur in Michigan, notably in the areas northwest, south and southeast of Saginaw Bay, the tip of the Thumb and in the southeastern Lower Peninsula. Many areas in Delta and Menominee Counties also exhibit poor water well yields.

FIGURE 16.21 Thick outwash systems (at least 12 m of sand and gravel) in a portion of the southeastern Lower Peninsula, as shown by the Aquifer Index. The proglacial and ice-contact outwash landsystems (Plate 10) are shown in yellow. Source: MDEQ (2006b).

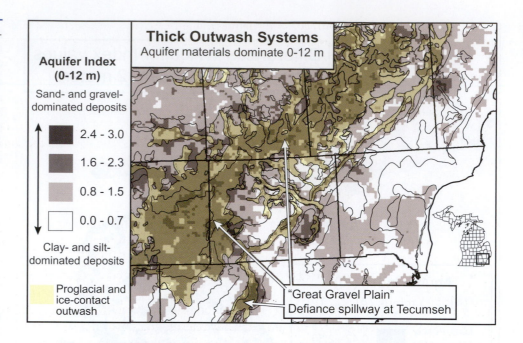

FIGURE 16.22 Generalized, estimated yield of groundwater from wells developed in the glacial aquifers of Michigan. Source: MDEQ (2006b).

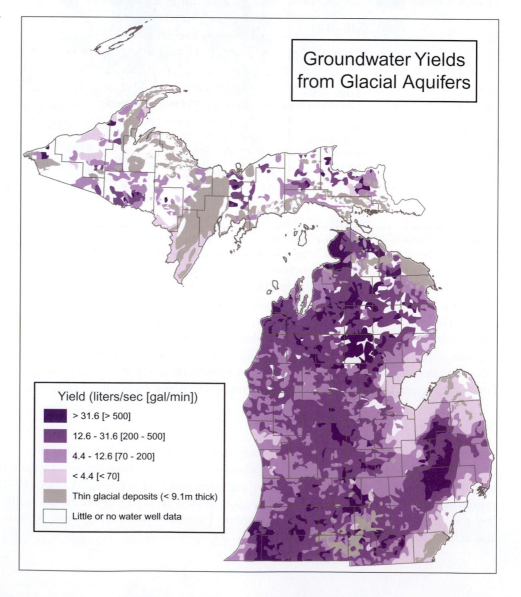

A yield of 4.42 L/sec (70 gpm) currently defines a "high-capacity" well. Such wells are routinely possible throughout much of the Lower Peninsula (Fig. 16.22). Zones of very high yield potential are located in the southwestern and south-central Lower Peninsula, in the core of the Thumb (Oakland, Lapeer and southeastern Tuscola Counties), in the Houghton-Higgins lakes district and across the northern Lower Peninsula.

Areas of thin glacial deposits (<9.1 m) make legally constructed water wells screened in the glacial deposits unlikely in the central and southeastern portions of the Upper Peninsula, in the Thumb and in the northeastern, southeastern and south-central Lower Peninsula (Fig. 16.22). As discussed above, the thin glacial deposits that dominate large areas of the northeastern and southeastern Lower Peninsula, and the southern coastal fringe of the eastern Upper Peninsula, are karst-prone areas.

Groundwater quality in glacial aquifers

Nitrate contamination   One of the major contaminants found in the glacial aquifers of Michigan is nitrate (NO_3). Nitrate can enter the groundwater system through improperly constructed or poorly maintained wells that are located near major NO_3 sources, e.g., livestock waste, septic drain field effluent, crop and lawn fertilizers or land-applied septage. Shallow water wells in coarse-textured, unconfined aquifers are the most vulnerable to nitrate contamination.

Large concentrations of nitrite (NO_2^-) in the blood stream (converted from NO_3) reduce the ability of the red blood cells (hemoglobin) to carry oxygen, a malady referred to as methemoglobenemia. Acutely poisoned persons exhibit a characteristic blue discoloration of the skin, due to the reduction of oxygen in their blood. This condition can be fatal to infants under six months of age, if medical treatment is not provided.

The USEPA established a maximum contaminant level for nitrate in drinking water at 10 mg/L of N, and 1 mg/L of nitrite. Based on random sampling, the Michigan Department of Agriculture (MDA) estimated that <1.9% of all rural domestic wells in the state exceed this limit (Pigg 2001). MDA estimated that 3.9% of farm wells in Michigan have nitrate-N levels ≥10 mg/L. Several areas of the state suffer from widespread nitrate contamination of groundwater, especially in the west-central and southwestern Lower Peninsula (Fig. 16.23). On a positive note, the MDA study concluded that the majority (90.5%) of the state's domestic wells have nitrate-N levels <2 mg/L.

Arsenic contamination   As discussed above, naturally-occurring arsenic contamination in Michigan's groundwater is usually associated with bedrock aquifers, especially the Marshall, Saginaw and Michigan formations (Fig. 16.12). However, arsenic concentrations of ≥40 µg/L—four times the new drinking water standard—have also been detected in wells completed in glacial deposits in three southeastern Michigan counties (Haack and Rachol 2000). In Sanilac County, the second highest arsenic concentration from any groundwater source (49 µg/L) was recorded from a well completed in a glacial aquifer. In Shiawassee County, the two highest arsenic concentrations in the county (31 and 40 µg/L) were recorded for wells completed in glacial materials.

Agricultural chemicals   Based on samples from 303 wells in 12 Midwestern states, Kolpin et al. (1998) documented relatively widespread, low-level concentrations of herbicides in some shallow glacial aquifers. The most frequently detected compounds were the transformation products of herbicides. Unterreiner and Kehew (2005) also documented herbicides and herbicide degradates in some shallow glacial aquifers in the southwestern Lower Peninsula. In an MDA study of domestic well water quality between 1997 and 2000 (Pigg 2001), samples from 391 randomly selected wells were tested for 75 different pesticides. Only one pesticide, atrazine, was detected in one farm well. This report estimated that <2.4% of farm wells and <1.7% of rural non-farm wells in Michigan contain one or more pesticides.

◼ Conclusions

Overall, Michigan is blessed with a huge volume of potable groundwater to supply the drinking water, irrigation, and industrial needs of our citizens. Many of the inland lakes, and all of the prodigious streams, of our "Water Wonderland" owe their existence to plentiful groundwater. Although perennial, our potable groundwater is a finite resource, whose sustainability can be threatened by both overuse and by widespread land uses that impede

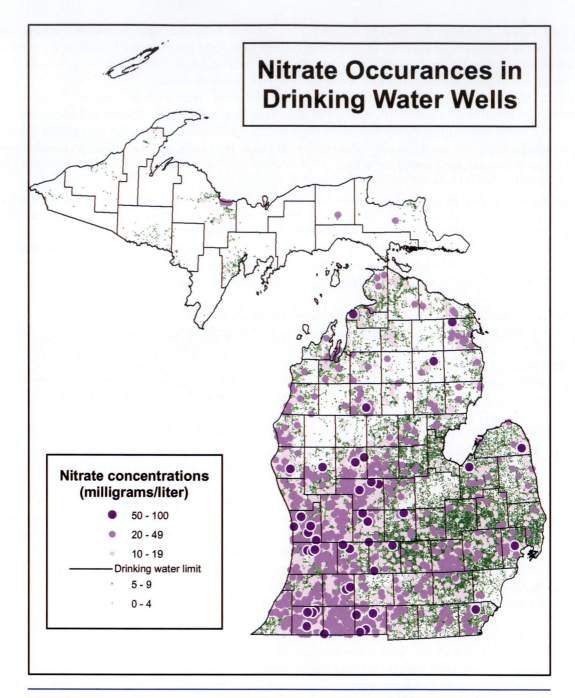

FIGURE 16.23 Nitrate concentrations in groundwater samples from Michigan water wells, submitted to local health departments from 1983 to 2003. Source: MDEQ WaterChem Database (http://www.deq. state.mi.us/documents/deq-wd-gws-ciu-no3.htm)

natural recharge. Given the unconfined or leaky confined nature of most of Michigan's groundwater, there is no such thing as natural protection from contamination by hazardous substances at the surface and near-surface. Of the 70 Superfund sites in Michigan, 54 (77%) involve groundwater contamination. Unfortunately, there are nearly 9200 sites on the 2007 list of *uncorrected* leaking underground storage tanks. Once contaminated, practical groundwater remediation is very difficult (in some circumstances, impossible), and always very expensive. Only Michigan's citizens, through their land management practices and policies, can protect this vital resource.

Literature Cited

Allen, W.B. 1977. Flowing wells in Michigan. US Geological Survey, Water Information Series Report 2. 27 pp.

Black, T.J. 1983. Selected views of the tectonics, structure and karst in Northern Lower Michigan. In: Kimmel R.A. (ed), Tectonics, Structure and Karst in Northern Lower Michigan. Michigan Basin Geological Society Field Conference Proceedings. Michigan Basin Geological Society: East Lansing. pp. 11–35.

Black, TJ. 1995. Karst Geology of the Northeast Lower Peninsula, Michigan. Field Conference sponsored by the Michigan Basin Geological Society, the American Institute of Professional Geologists, and the Michigan Karst Conservancy. Michigan Basin Geological Society. p. 6.

Black, T.J. 2003. Evaporite karst in Michigan. In: B.F. Beck (ed), Sinkholes and the Engineering and Environmental Impacts of Karst. Geotechnical Special Publication No. 122. ASCE/National Ground Water Association/GEO Institute: Reston, VA. pp. 141–149.

Coon, W.F. and R.A. Sheets. 2006. Estimate of ground water in storage in the Great Lakes Basin, United States, 2006. US Geological Survey Scientific Investigations Report 2006–5180. 19 pp.

Gaber, M.S. 2005. Flowing Well Handbook. Michigan Department of Environmental Quality, Water Bureau, Drinking Water and Environmental Health Section. http://www.deq.state.mi.us/documents/deq-wb-dwehs-wcu-flowwellhandbook.pdf (last accessed January, 2007).

Grannemann, N.G., Hunt, R.J., Nicholas, J.R., Reilly, T.E. and T.C. Winter. 2000. The Importance of Ground Water in the Great Lakes Region. US Geological Survey Water-Resources Investigations Report 00–4008. 13 pp.

Haack, S.K. and C.M. Rachol. 2000. USGS Fact sheets on arsenic in ground water: Genesee, Huron, Lapeer, Livingston, Sanilac, Shiawassee, Tuscola, Washtenaw counties. Department of the Interior, US Geological Survey. FS-127-00 through FS-134-00.

Hoaglund, J.R. III, Huffman G.C. and N.G. Grannemann. 2002. Michigan Basin regional ground water flow discharge to three Great Lakes. Ground Water 40:390–406.

Institute of Water Research. 1992. "A vacation that's enough to make you sick." Gem Notes: The Groundwater Education in Michigan (GEM) Program. Vol 4, No.1. Institute of Water Research, Michigan State University, East Lansing.

Farrand, W.R. and D.L. Bell. 1982. Quaternary Geology (map) of Southern Michigan with surface water drainage divides. Quaternary Geology of Northern Michigan 1:500,000 scale maps. Department of Natural Resources, Geological Survey Division, Lansing, MI.

Fetter, C.W. 2001. Applied Hydrogeology. Prentice-Hall, Upper Saddle River, NJ.

Kehew, A.E., Passero, R.N., Krishnamurthy, R.V., Lovett, C.K., Betts, M.A. and B.A. Dayharsh. 1998. Hydrogeochemical interaction between a wetland and an unconfined glacial drift aquifer, southwestern Michigan. Ground Water 36:849–856.

Kolpin, D.W., Stamer, J.K. and D.A. Goolsby. 1998. Herbicides in Ground Water of the Midwest: A Regional Study of Shallow Aquifers, 1991–94. US Geological Survey Fact Sheet 076–98.

Leverett, F. 1900. US Geological Survey Field Notebook 159. US Geological Survey Field Notebook Library, Denver, CO.

Leverett, F., Fuller, M.L., Sherzer, W.H., Bowman, I., Lane, A.C. and J.A. Udder. 1906. Flowing wells and municipal water supplies in the southern portion of the southern peninsula of Michigan. US Geological Survey Water-Supply Paper 182. 292 pp.

Leverett, F., McLouth, C.D., Fuller, M.L., Gregory, W.M., Cooper, W.F. and C.A. Davis. 1907. Flowing wells and municipal water supplies in the middle and northern portions of the southern peninsula of Michigan. US Geological Survey Water-Supply Paper 183. 393 pp.

MDEQ. 2003. Arsenic in Well Water: Health Information for Water Well Users. Michigan Department of Environmental Quality Information Pamphlet EQC 2106.

MDEQ. 2006a. Water Withdrawals for Public Water Supply in Michigan: 2006. 10 pp. http://www.michigan.gov/documents/deq/deq-wb-wurp-PublicReport06_212347_7.pdf (last accessed December, 2007).

MDEQ. 2006b. Technical Report—Groundwater Inventory and Mapping Project. 257 pp. http://gwmap.rsgis.msu.edu (last accessed January, 2007).

Pigg, R.W. 2001. Michigan Department of Agriculture, Domestic Supply Well Baseline Study Report. 56 pp. http://www.michigan.gov/documents/MDA_FullBaselineStudyReport_98224_7.pdf (last accessed July, 2007).

Ralston, M.R. 2000. Groundwater management in karst terrain. Groundwater Symposium 2000, Pennsylvania Department of Environmental Protection. State of Pennsylvania, Harrisburg, PA.

State of Michigan. 2005. Center for Geographic Information, Michigan Geographic Data Library. Wellogic Statewide Wells Database.

Stewart, D.C. 1981. Water-loss Problem at Rainy Lake, Presque Isle County, Michigan. Department of Geology, Bowling Green University. Study done for the Rainy Lake Property Owners Association. 8 pp.

Unterreiner, G.A. and A.E. Kehew. 2005. Spatial and temporal distribution of herbicides and herbicide degradates in a shallow glacial drift aquifer/surface water system, southwestern Michigan. Groundwater Monitoring and Remediation 25:1–10.

US Census Bureau. 1990. Summary Tape File 3 (STF 3)—Sample data. H023, Source of Water—Universe: Housing units.

USGS. 2005. Engineering Aspects of Karst. National Atlas of the United States. http://nationalatlas.gov/mld/karst0m.html (last accessed February, 2006).

US House of Representatives. 2001. Public Exposure to Arsenic in Drinking Water in Michigan. Prepared for Rep. David E. Bonior by the Minority Staff, Special Investigations Division, Committee on Government Reform. March 30, 2001. 7 p. http://oversight.house.gov/documents/20040607132512-45841.pdf (last accessed July, 2007).

Westjohn, D.B. and T.L Weaver. 1998. Hydrogeologic Framework of the Michigan Basin Regional Aquifer System. US Geological Survey Professional Paper 1418. 47 pp.

Winters, H.A., Rieck, R.L. and D.P. Lusch. 1985. Quaternary geomorphology of southeastern Michigan. Field Trip Guide for AAG Annual Meeting, Detroit, MI. Department of Geography, Michigan State University, East Lansing.

Further Readings

Alley, W.M., Reilly, T.E. and O.L. Franke. 1999. Sustainability of Ground-Water Resources. US Geological Survey Circular 1186. 79 pp.

Heath, R.C. 1983. Basic Ground-water Hydrology. US Geological Survey Water Supply Paper 2220. 84 pp.

Winter, T.C., Harvey, J.W., Franke, O.L. and W.M. Alley. 1998. Ground Water and Surface Water: A Single Resource. US Geological Survey Circular 1139. 79 pp.

17

The Physical Landscape: A Glacial Legacy

William L. Blewett, David P. Lusch and Randall J. Schaetzl

■ Introduction

Michigan's location at the confluence of six major glacial lobes has produced one of the most complicated and picturesque physical landscapes in the Midwest (Fig. 17.1). Chapter 6 provides a review of the glacial chronology associated with this terrain, and Chapter 13 discusses the sequence of lakes that formed as these glaciers retreated from the state. In this chapter, we examine the sediments that remained after the ice left, and discuss the processes that were involved in creating the landforms we see today. We focus on areas of the state where recent research has markedly improved our understanding of landscape genesis, and review the state's glacial legacy in terms of economics and land use.

Geographers traditionally divide Michigan into two physiographic regions: (1) the Superior Bedrock Uplands, encompassing the crystalline rocks of the western Upper Peninsula (Plate 8, Chapter 3) and (2) the Central Lowlands, covering the remainder of the state (Thornbury 1965). These regions are further subdivided based on topography, surficial geology, soils, and sediment type (Plates 7, 8, 9, 12). The Sandy High Plains and Interlobate Uplands on Plate 8, for example, define part of the Lower Peninsula's vast interlobate region, where a sort of glaciological train wreck among the Michigan, Saginaw and Huron-Erie glacial lobes left a tangled mass of sandy, glacial debris, blanketing nearly 50,000 km², that in places is many tens of meters in thickness. This tract dominates the physical landscape of southern Michigan like no other, and is unique among Midwestern states (Rieck and Winters 1993). In the Upper Peninsula, the different bedrock geology and thinner glacial deposits left a more complicated regional landform pattern. The western Upper Peninsula generally displays thin, discontinuous *drift* (a general term encompassing all glacial sediments) mantling the bedrock-controlled topography of moderate relief, whereas the eastern Upper Peninsula contains somewhat thicker drift, mantling bedrock escarpments developed on Paleozoic sedimentary rocks (Chapter 4). Finally, many of these deposits were significantly modified by the actions of large glacial lakes, which occupied the basins of the Great Lakes, as the glaciers withdrew. As reviewed in Chapter 13, these lakes and their spillways flooded large parts of the state, especially in the coastal margins of the Lower Peninsula and across vast tracts of the eastern Upper Peninsula.

■ Preglacial and bedrock topography

The eastern Upper Peninsula and all of the Lower Peninsula are developed upon the Michigan structural basin, centered on Gladwin County (Chapter 4, Plate 5). The carbonate and sandstone rocks of the Michigan Basin are generally resistant to physical erosion, compared to the much weaker shale, gypsum and rock salt units. This differential resistance to physical erosion, coupled with the subcropping pattern of the various rock units in the basin (Plates 4, 5; Fig. 17.2) probably led to a pre-glacial landscape in which broad lowlands had developed in

FIGURE 17.1 The Grand Sable Banks, near Grand Marais, in the Upper Peninsula. The Banks consist of nearly 100 m of stratified sediment, mostly sand and gravel, capped by the Grand Sable Dunes (Chapter 18). Photo by R. Schaetzl.

FIGURE 17.2 Resistance to physical erosion, of the various bedrocks types in the Michigan Basin. Compiled by D. Lusch from Ontario Ministry of Northern Development and Mines (2004), Cannon et al. (1999), Milstein (1987), Reed and Daniels (1987) and Wold (1980).

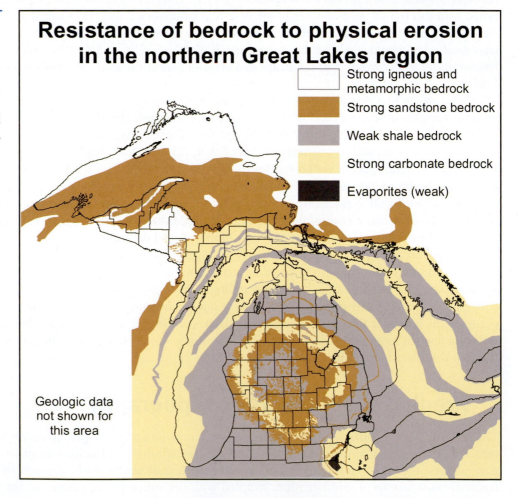

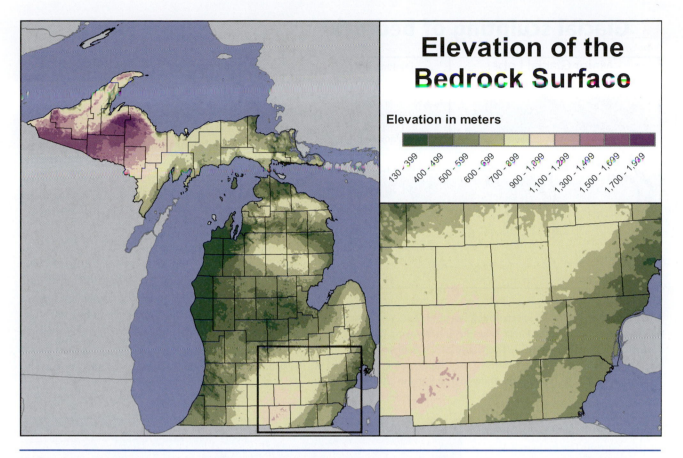

FIGURE 17.3   Elevation of the bedrock surface in Michigan, with detail on the elevations for a portion of southeastern Michigan. The highest elevations on the bedrock surface beneath the Lower Peninsula occur in Hillsdale County. This map was created using the US Geological Survey National Elevation Dataset, digital water well and oil/gas logs, obtained from MDEQ, and SSURGO soils data, from the Natural Resources Conservation Service.

shale-dominated areas, while uplands developed on the more-resistant sandstone or carbonate rocks. Indeed, as early as the 19th century, some scientists (Spencer 1881, 1890) had postulated that, prior to the glacial episodes, the Great Lakes Region was drained by north- and east-flowing rivers, whose valleys had eroded into the weaker shales (Fig. 13.1).

Michigan's buried bedrock surface has four notable highlands (Fig. 17.3; Plate 7). The Superior Bedrock Uplands in the western Upper Peninsula are supported primarily by igneous and metamorphic rocks that are very resistant to physical erosion (Plate 6). The three bedrock highlands in the Lower Peninsula are composed of resistant sandstone or carbonate formations. The northernmost, sweeping in an arc from Alpena County on the east to Antrim and Leelanau Counties on the west, is underlain by resistant Traverse Group limestones. These formations also form the foundation of many of the islands in the northern Lake Michigan archipelago (Plate 8). The dominant bedrock feature of the northern Lower Peninsula, however, is centered beneath Crawford, Oscoda, Roscommon and Ogemaw Counties—underlain by the resistant Marshall and Michigan Formations. These same units support the largest and highest bedrock feature in Lower Michigan, which trends SW from the tip of the Thumb, to Hillsdale, Branch and St. Joseph Counties (Plate 6). The bedrock surface beneath the Lower Peninsula actually reaches its highest elevation (>335 m) in Hillsdale County—an area known as the Irish Hills (Fig. 17.3, Plate 8). Bedrock lowlands in the state are usually underlain by weak shales (Antrim, Bedford, Coldwater, Ellsworth, and Point Aux Chenes formations) and easily dissolved evaporite rocks, e.g., Detroit River Group (Plates 3, 6).

■ Glacial sculpting of bedrock

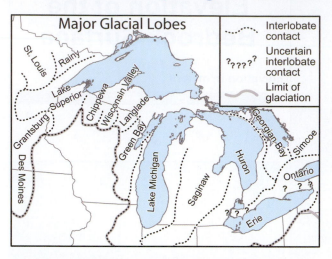

FIGURE 17.4 Lobes and selected sublobes of the Late Wisconsin Laurentide ice sheet in the Great Lakes Region, showing the location of major interlobate areas. The Chippewa, Wisconsin Valley and Langlade lobes are subdivisions of the Chippewa lobe. After Mickelson et al. (1983) and Krzyszkowski and Karrow (2001).

The patterns of these bedrock units in the Michigan Basin, and of the pre-glacial valleys that developed on them (Fig. 13.1), had a profound influence on the flow direction of the ice sheets that invaded Michigan from the north and east. The preglacial topography guided the ice, producing lobes of thicker, more strongly flowing ice along the axes of lowlands, which in turn led to increased erosion and bedrock scour of the softer rocks that laid beneath (Fig. 17.4). An outstanding example of both this differential resistance to erosion and the glacial scouring effect can be observed in the bottom topography of Lake Huron (Fig. 17.5). Here, the weak shale units were deeply scoured by the glaciers, leaving the stronger sandstone and carbonate units standing as distinct bedrock ridges, or cuestas (Fig. 17.2). Figure 17.5 illustrates that concept. The resistant Traverse Group limestones form the lakeshores and headlands from Thunder Bay at Alpena, northward to Presque Isle. Southeastward from Thunder Bay, an

FIGURE 17.5   Bottom topography of Lake Huron. The bathymetric map, from NOAA, National Geophysical Data Center, clearly shows the Alpena-Amberley Ridge. The NE face of the ridge is very steep—the lake bottom descends to a depth of more than 200 m, while the ridge crest is generally only 30 to 60 m below the lake surface. SW of the ridge crest, the lake bottom descends more gradually to depths of 70–100 m. Data from http://www.ngdc.noaa.gov/mgg/greatlakes/greatlakes.html

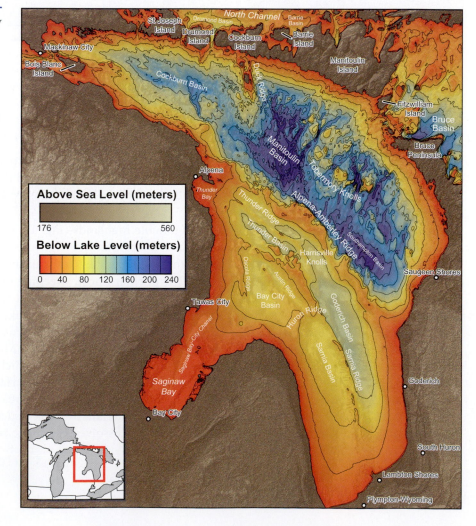

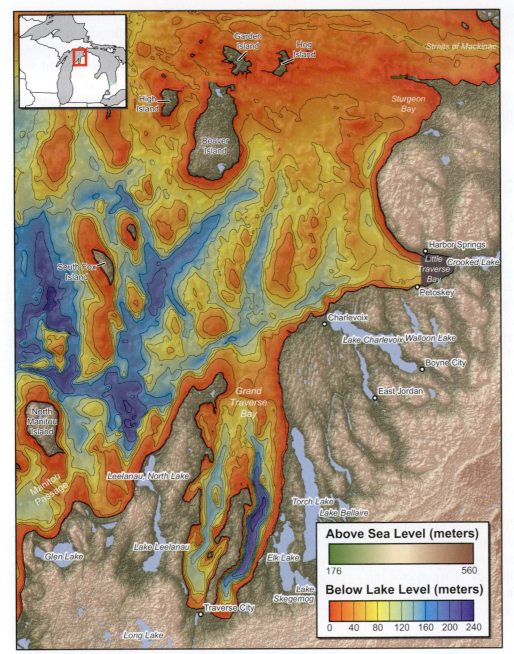

FIGURE 17.6 Tunnel valleys in NW Lower Michigan occur offshore, in and around Grand Traverse Bay. Bathymetric map from NOAA, National Geophysical Data Center http://www.ngdc.noaa.gov /mgg/greatlakes/lakemich_ cdrom/html/area6.htm.

underwater continuation of this resistant rock formation forms the most important bathymetric feature of the Lake Huron basin: the Alpena-Amberley Ridge, which extends across the lake bottom, to Clark Point on the Canadian shore (Fig. 17.5). This ridge rises to within 11 m of the lake surface near the middle of Lake Huron, at Six Fathom Bank (Edsall et al. 1992).

Although scouring by glacial ice was undoubtedly an important geomorphic agent in sculpting the Great Lakes region, other subglacial erosional processes were dominant in localized areas. Near Grand Traverse Bay, in the northwestern Lower Peninsula, both onshore and underwater, the terrain is notable for a complex network of long valleys, presumably carved by high-pressure, subglacial meltwater (Fig. 17.6). Because they were presumably formed under the ice, geomorphologists refer to these features as tunnel valleys (Kehew et al. 1999). On the mainland, portions of these tunnel valleys are occupied by deep, elongated lakes, e.g., Elk, Intermediate and Torch Lakes, as well as Lakes Leelanau and Charlevoix, and extensive linear wetlands (Fig. A9). Similar features are present, but less pronounced, in the northeastern Lower Peninsula, in Otsego and Montmorency Counties (Plate 7), and in south-central Michigan (Fisher and Taylor 2002). Offshore, the same tunnel valleys form a chaotic knot of underwater valleys between the Grand Traverse mainland and the northern Lake Michigan archipelago (Fig. 17.6). Indeed, even the two massive arms of Grand Traverse Bay were likely sculpted by this subglacial process. On the mainland, some tunnel valleys terminate abruptly at major moraines, where they grade into large, ice-contact, outwash fans (Fig. A9). The surfaces of these sand and gravel fans may be up to 100 m above the floors of the adjacent tunnel valleys—additional evidence that high-pressure meltwater was involved (Benn and Evans 1998, Sugden and John 1988).

Thickness of the glacial sediments

Michigan's glacial deposits, of which there are several kinds, e.g. till and lacustrine sediment (Fig. 17.7), vary in thickness across the state. The thickness of the glacial deposits in Michigan is perhaps best understood in the context of ice dynamics. In effect, the continental ice sheet behaved like a giant bulldozer, scraping sediments from source regions in east-central Canada and depositing them throughout the Great Lakes region. This process left a northern, bedrock-dominated realm, swept mostly clean of unconsolidated sediments, flanked by a southern depositional belt of thick glacial debris. Lake Superior marks the general boundary between these two regions. North of the lake, glacial drift is thin or absent, and bedrock exposures are common. Conversely, the Lower Peninsula lies wholly within the depositional zone of the glaciers, and in places exhibits some of the thickest drift in the US (Rieck and Winters 1993; Fig. 17.8). The Upper Peninsula, located in the transition zone between these two realms, shows characteristics of both.

Superimposed upon this general framework, the lobation of the ice sheet also influenced the amount of glacial deposition that occurred from place to place. Thinner amounts of glacial drift were deposited in the northeastern and southeastern corners of the Lower Peninsula, and generally throughout the Upper Peninsula (Fig. 17.8). Most of the thick glacial sediments were deposited along the *margins* of actively flowing ice lobes or within stagnant marginal zones, sometimes tens of kilometers wide. Prolific sediment production was also especially concentrated in interlobate zones (Rieck and Winters 1993).

The southeastern Michigan interlobate region (Plate 8A) is a good example of how a regional bedrock highland can influence drift thickness, and determine the location and trend of the suture between two ice lobes. As both the Saginaw and Huron-Erie lobes (Fig. 17.4) melted, during the waning phases of the last glacial episode, their thicknesses (and therefore their ability to flow) was especially diminished along the crest of the bedrock high that trends from the tip of the Thumb, SW to Hillsdale County (Fig. 17.3). Within each lobe, the ice flow directions were toward the local margin, creating a splayed flow pattern (Fig. 17.9). As melting proceeded, a V-shaped reentrant developed between the two lobes, open to the SW (Fig. 17.10). Outwash streams, choked with coarse-textured sediment, flowed into and across this reentrant, building a "great gravel plain" (Leverett

FIGURE 17.7 Examples of two common types of glacigenic sediments. Photos by R. Schaetzl. A. Glacial till. Note that this sediment is unstratified and unsorted. B. Glaciolacustrine sediment. Note the fine layering that is typical of lake sediment.

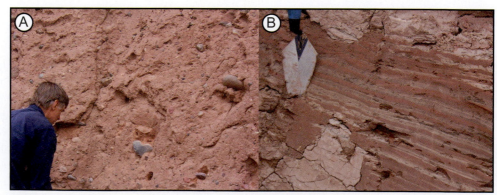

1900) that spans central Oakland County diagonally, from NE-SW (Fig. 16.21). So much of this outwash was deposited in contact with stagnant ice blocks here, that no other area in the Lower Peninsula has more kettle (ice block) lakes.

The southeastern Michigan interlobate zone is also "palimpsest" atop the underlying bedrock ridge, making it higher than it would be otherwise (Fig. 17.3, Plates 7, 8). The term palimpsest refers to a manuscript page that was written on, scraped off or erased, and used again. Geomorphologists have adopted the term to refer to a landscape in which the topographic features are broadly inherited from a buried surface (Kehew et al. 1999, Indiana Geological Survey 2007). The "High Plains" of the north-central Lower Peninsula (Schaetzl and Weisenborn 2004), a broad, sandy upland dominated by coarse-textured glacial sediments, is also palimpsest, forming a glacial veneer on top of the bedrock high beneath Crawford, Oscoda, Roscommon, and Ogemaw Counties (Fig. 17.3).

Not all high elevation landscapes in Michigan are palimpsest. Grove Hill, the highest point in the Lower Peninsula (522 m), is located in north-central Osceola County (Waite 2003; Plate 7). In this vicinity, the bedrock surface only reaches elevations of 160–170 m, meaning that the thickness of the glacial deposits here must be >350 m. To the NW, the bedrock surface declines in elevation, while the topographic surface remains high (Plate 7, Fig. 17.3),

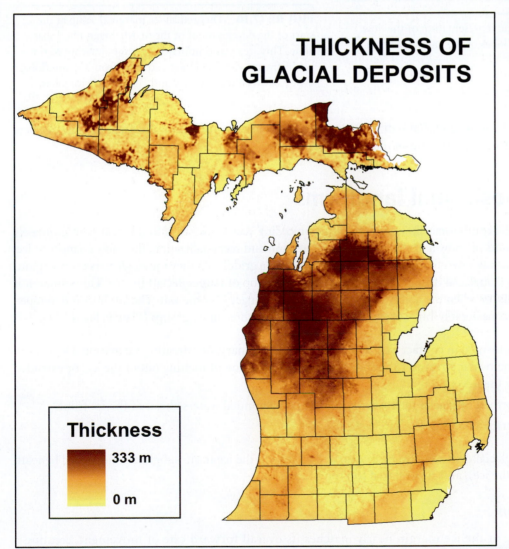

THICKNESS OF GLACIAL DEPOSITS

Thickness

333 m

0 m

FIGURE 17.8 Thickness of glacial deposits in Michigan. Source: RS and GIS, Michigan State University. Compiled from US Geological Survey National Elevation Dataset, and digital water well and oil/gas logs, obtained from MDEQ.

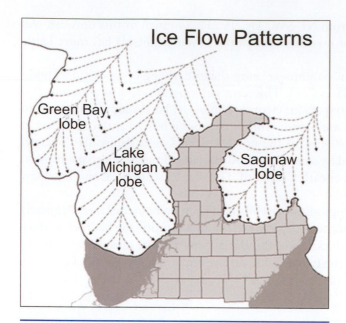

FIGURE 17.9   Diagrammatic representation of the flow pattern within the retreating lobes of the Late Wisconsin ice sheet.

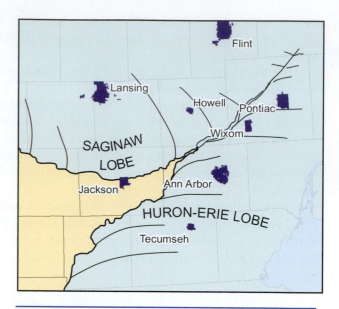

FIGURE 17.10   Theoretical ice marginal setup at the start of the development of the SE Michigan interlobate zone. This area was dominated by sediment-choked outwash streams, flowing along and away from the interlobate crease between the Saginaw and Huron-Erie ice lobes.

resulting in the greatest thickness of glacial sediments in the state—over 365 m! Again, the great thicknesses here can be attributed to the general interlobate setting of this region (Fig. 17.4).

■ Glacial depositional landforms

Glaciers form where climatic conditions allow snow from the preceding year to persist into the next year, ultimately leading to thick accumulations of snow and ice. Through compression and recrystallization, the snow changes to ice, and begins to move under its own weight, much like pancake batter on a griddle. As they move, glaciers carry copious amounts of debris beneath (subglacial drift), within (englacial), and on top of (superglacial) the ice. This sediment is deposited when the ice melts, or when the ability of the ice to carry it changes in some way. The landforms developed upon these sediments vary considerably, but can generally be divided into three main groups (Plate 9, Fig. 17.11):

1. *ice-marginal landforms*, formed in contact with a slowly moving, stationary, or retreating ice margin. Deposition is associated with (1) meltwater streams, (2) ponded waters, or (3) sediment melting out of the ice, or extruded and pushed forward by the ice.
2. *proglacial landforms*, formed by glacial meltwater streams, and by ponded waters ahead of the ice front.
3. *subglacial landforms*, formed beneath the ice sheet.

As mentioned above, glacial drift can also be categorized relative to the ice itself: subglacial (deposited beneath the ice), englacial (within the ice), and superglacial (on top of the ice).

Ice-marginal landforms

Often, the rate of melting at the ice margin nearly matches its overall forward rate of movement, creating a quasi-stationary ice margin for long periods of time, perhaps years. Then, although the ice margin is stationary, internal ice movement still brings drift to the ice margin (much like a conveyor belt) and forms end moraines (Plate 9, Figs. 17.11A, 17.12, 17.13)—hummocky ridges of glacial till that mark former ice margins. "Till" is defined

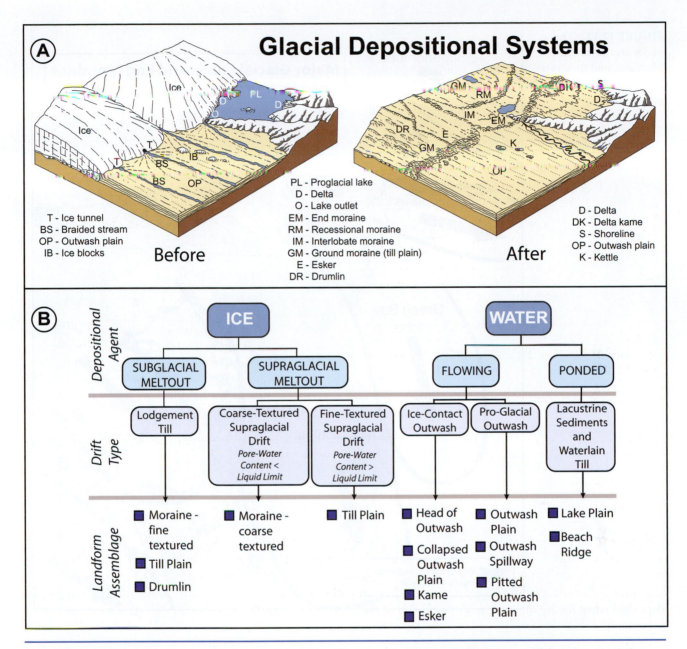

FIGURE 17.11   Classifications/nomenclature of glacial landforms and sediments. A. Landforms and their genesis. Before and After diagrams, showing the formation of common glacial landforms found in Michigan and elsewhere. After Strahler and Strahler (1992). B. A classification of the various types of glacial and related depositional systems, and the types of sediments and landforms that typically result. After Brown et al. (1998).

as unconsolidated, unstratified and unsorted material, containing rock fragments of varying sizes and having been deposited directly by the ice as it melts or sublimates. In Michigan, most end moraines are between 1.5 and 12 km in width, and have 20–110 m of local relief. Although most end moraines form along stationary ice margins (by the "conveyor belt effect," and with other debris arriving at the margin via internal ice-shear), some small push moraines can form by the "bulldozer effect," as the ice margin makes a short, but strong surge forward, piling up small amounts of drift in front of the ice margin. Most of Michigan's end moraines are at least partially forested today, as the steep slopes lead to erosion problems if intensively farmed. However, on the flat, wet lake plains of the Thumb, some of the better farmland is actually on the higher, drier moraines. All of Michigan's end moraines can also be considered recessional moraines, as they lie behind the terminal (farthest out) moraine in Ohio and Indiana (Fig. 17.4).

FIGURE 17.12   The major end moraines in Michigan, and their relationship to the principal glacial lobes.

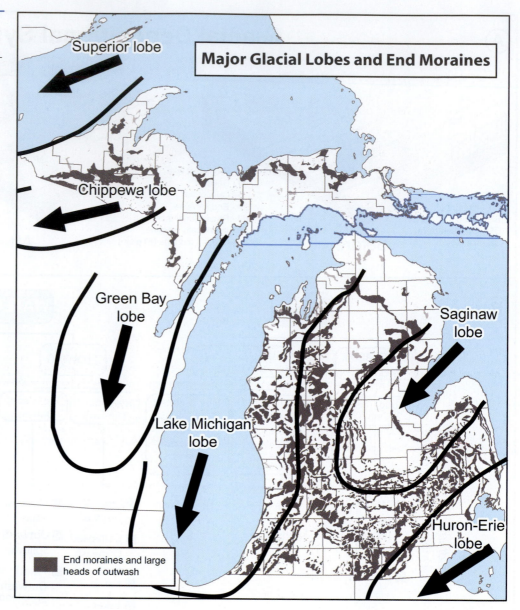

The intersection of two glacial lobes is often a locus of *outwash* deposition by superglacial meltwater, because it is lower than the ice surfaces on either side (Fig. 17.11A). These interlobate zones are home to hummocky, interlobate moraines, kettles and kettle lakes and small, often perched, outwash plains. Sand and gravel resources are abundant within interlobate zones because of the tremendous sorting power of glacial meltwater, which deposits coarse-textured sediments near the ice margin, but carries silt and clay particles great distances away. Where meltwater outlets are blocked by ice, proglacial lakes can form and back up against the ice margin; fine (silt and clay) sediments can be deposited within these lakes, as ice-contact lake or deltaic sediments. Commonly, outwash deposits in the interlobate region tend to wholly or partially bury blocks of ice, which later melt to form isolated depressions called kettles (or kettle lakes, if filled with water). Many of Michigan's 11,000 inland lakes are associated with interlobate zones (Scott 1925). Detroit's northwestern suburbs are built on the large, hilly, interlobate moraines and outwash plains that formed between the Saginaw and Huron-Erie ice lobes (Plate 8). Other interlobate regions in Lower Michigan are centered on Barry County, and the area near Cadillac (Plate 8A).

Major end moraines in Michigan generally follow looping patterns, associated with the margins of the principal glacial lobes (Figs. 17.12, 17.13). Tracing individual moraines on a glacial landform map is often quite difficult,

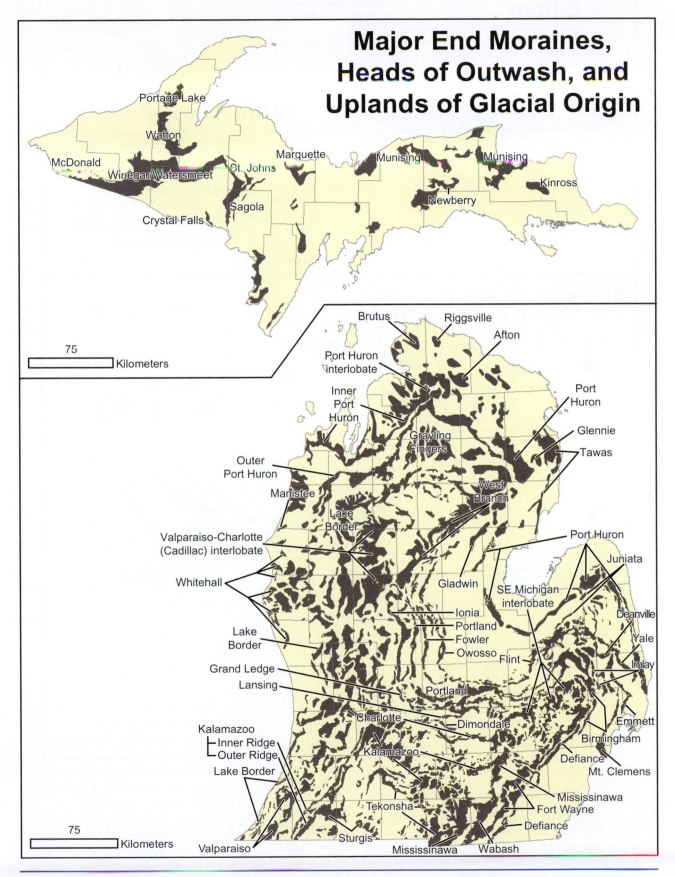

Major End Moraines, Heads of Outwash, and Uplands of Glacial Origin

75 ⊢————⊣ Kilometers

75 ⊢————⊣ Kilometers

FIGURE 17.13   A map of the major end moraines, heads of outwash and other uplands of glacial origin, with names, in Michigan. Compiled by the authors from various sources.

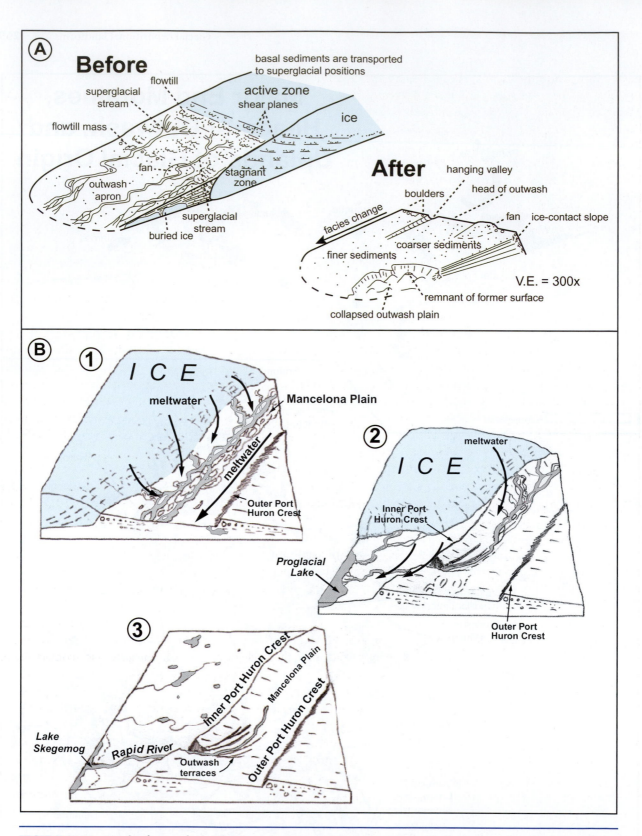

FIGURE 17.14 Heads of outwash. A. Their genesis. One possible mechanism for the formation of heads of outwash (or morphosequences). These landforms are widespread in northern Michigan and in interlobate regions. After Koteff and Pessl (1981). B. The Inner and Outer Port Huron moraines, in the northwestern Lower Peninsula—both heads of outwash—and the drainage reversal of the Rapid River, associated with them. During final deglaciation (1), meltwater drained the ice margin along a series of braided streams, oriented parallel to the glacial margin. As the Inner Port Huron moraine was abandoned farther south (2), ice remained at this same position farther north. The proto-Rapid River, taking advantage of a low spot within the moraine, cut a lower, shorter channel, across the moraine (head of outwash), to proglacial lakes to the west (3), abandoning the Mancelona Plain, and establishing its present course. After Blewett (1991).

however, owing to the complexity of the patterns, and the tendency for geologists to designate moraines based on the lobe that formed them. Thus, moraines often change names as they loop from one lobe to another (Leverett and Taylor 1915); many even change names at state borders (Flint et al. 1959)! The two most conspicuous end moraines in the Lower Peninsula are the West Branch, and the Inner and Outer Port Huron moraines (Fig. 17.13). The West Branch moraine represents a significant ice-marginal position that formed during the initial deglaciation of the Lower Peninsula, ~16,300 years ago. The Saginaw lobe portion of this moraine is named West Branch, whereas the Lake Michigan Lobe portion is known as the Lake Border. The younger (15,200 years ago, Chapter 6) Port Huron moraine is located "inside" (north) of the West Branch moraine, and can be traced from the city of Port Huron northwestward, across the Thumb and around Saginaw Bay, to its interlobate apex at Gaylord (Fig. 17.13; Plate 8). The Port Huron to Gaylord section of this ice-marginal landform is primarily a typical end moraine. To the SW of Gaylord, the moraine splits into two ridges, the Inner and Outer Port Huron moraines, the terms "inner" and "outer" referring only to their positions relative to the Lake Michigan glacial lobe. Much of the Inner and Outer Port Huron moraines are actually *heads of outwash*—not true end moraines (see below). The Inner moraine eventually merges with the Manistee moraine in Grand Traverse County. The Outer Port Huron moraine can be traced southwestward to Whitehall, from where it continues westward, across the floor of Lake Michigan and along the eastern margins of Wisconsin.

Moraine patterns are less continuous in the Upper Peninsula (Plate 8B, Fig. 17.13). The eastern Upper Peninsula is dominated by two, large, east-west trending moraine ridges. The more northerly is called the Munising moraine (Plate 8), the more southerly the Newberry moraine (Fig. 17.13). Farther west, the Munising moraine aligns with the Marquette moraine and, together, they delimit the southern edge of the Marquette or Gribben advance, an important glacial readvance that reached its maximum approximately 11,500 years ago (Lowell et al. 1999; Chapter 6). K.I. Sawyer International Airport in Marquette County is built on the outwash plain associated with the Marquette moraine. In the western Upper Peninsula, moraines are more difficult to identify due to thin drift and high-relief bedrock. The Watersmeet moraine of Iron, Gogebic and Ontonagon Counties is an important exception.

Based on a study of the Inner and Outer Port Huron moraines between Elmira and Kalkaska, Blewett and Winters (1995) concluded that many of the larger, higher-relief "moraines" found throughout northern Michigan are better interpreted as complex, ice-marginal landforms consisting of stratified, sandy drift; they called these features heads of outwash. Although the genesis of these landforms is still a matter of debate, Koteff and Pessl (1981) defined similar features in New England, using a stagnation-zone model (Fig. 17.14A), in which a thin belt of stagnant or "dead" ice forms along the margin of the glacier. Shear planes develop between the upstream (active) ice and the stagnant marginal zone, facilitating the delivery of drift from the base of the glacier to supraglacial locations across the stagnant zone. Meltwater and mass wasting then transport these sediments beyond the ice margin, forming individual or coalescing outwash aprons (heads of outwash), deltas and fans. Proglacial sediments associated with a head of outwash often grade from coarse to fine textures, with increasing distance from the ice margin, with boulders deposited near the glacier's edge. The area along the ice margin serves as the apron's head of outwash. With final melting of the glacier, the inner margins of these ice-contact, stratified deposits collapse to the angle of repose, forming a steep ice-contact slope. The result is an asymmetrically shaped landform in profile, steepest on the up-ice side (Fig. 17.14). As the active ice zone retreats, a series of heads of outwash may be left in the landscape, each delimiting a former ice-marginal position. Heads of outwash form sandy, dry landscapes, although many have numerous kettles and kettle lakes. Heads of outwash and related landforms are common throughout northern Michigan and the interlobate regions farther south; some are mapped as "ice-contact outwash" on Plate 10. The most conspicuous example, forming one of the most impressive viewpoints in the Lower Peninsula, is associated with the Inner Port Huron ice-contact slope at the Deadman's Hill overlook (just off US-131), in Antrim County. Other examples include the Munising moraine between Munising and Grand Marais (Blewett and Rieck 1987; Plate 8B), the Kalamazoo moraine SW of Kalamazoo, the Kalalmazoo-Mississenewa moraine near Chelsea (Rieck 1976, 1979) and sections of the Manistee moraine west of Traverse City (Fig. 17.13). Collectively, the widespread occurrence of heads of outwash in Michigan affirms the importance of ice-marginal stagnation and meltwater deposition in developing some of the high-relief portions of Michigan's landscape.

Proglacial landforms

Meltwater draining from the ice margin is often choked with sediment. In situations where the land slopes away from the ice front, braided meltwater streams deposit much of this sediment beyond the ice margin, as an outwash plain (Figs. 17.11, 17.15, 17.16; Plate 9). In response to a general flattening of their gradients, these meltwater streams

FIGURE 17.15 Stratified, sandy and gravelly, glacial outwash sediments from a borrow pit near Waters. Photos by R. Schaetzl. A. The pit face, showing the layered (stratified), and coarse-textured nature of outwash sediment. B. Closeup of stratified, sandy and gravelly outwash sediment. The cross bedding that is observed in some of the layers is associated with the slow, downstream growth of sand bars within the meltwater stream.

FIGURE 17.16 A broad, flat, outwash plain near Schoolcraft, in Kalamazoo County. This outwash plain was home to vast expanses of prairie grasses in presettlement times (Chapter 21). Moraine-like landforms can be seen on the horizon. Photo by R. Schaetzl.

flow more slowly in the distant, proglacial landscape. As a result, coarse-textured sediments are deposited nearer the ice margin, while silt- and clay-sized sediments are transported for longer distances, and may only settle out when they reach lakes or the ocean. Kettles develop in outwash plains if the sediment buries ice blocks, which later melt. The volume of buried ice, compared to the volume of outwash sediments, determines whether a pitted outwash plain (sediment dominant) or a collapsed outwash plain (ice dominant) will form (Fig. 17.11B).

Flat, sandy, and gravelly outwash plains are among the most common glacial features in Michigan (Figs. 17.11A, 17.16, Plate 10), often predominating in the tracts between moraines, and across interlobate regions. Important examples include the Mancelona Plain in Antrim, Kalkaska and Grand Traverse Counties, which lies between the Inner and Outer Port Huron moraines (Blewett and Winters 1995; Plate 8A; Fig. 17.14B), the Kingston Plains south and east of Pictured Rocks National Lakeshore in Alger, Schoolcraft and Luce Counties (Blewett and Rieck 1987), the Baraga Plains in Baraga County (Arbogast and Packman 2004, Plate 8), and the broad outwash plains of Cass, Kalamazoo and St. Joseph Counties (Fig. 17.16). Many are too dry to farm, due to the sandy soils, and have remained forested, but some are successfully irrigated for row crop agriculture. The outwash plains of Cass and St. Joseph Counties were once home to tallgrass prairies and thus have highly productive soils (Chapters 20, 21; Fig. 17.16). For this reason, and because of the plentiful groundwater here which can be used for irrigation, a large and economically lucrative seed corn industry has developed. Outwash is also an excellent source of aggregate (sand and gravel).

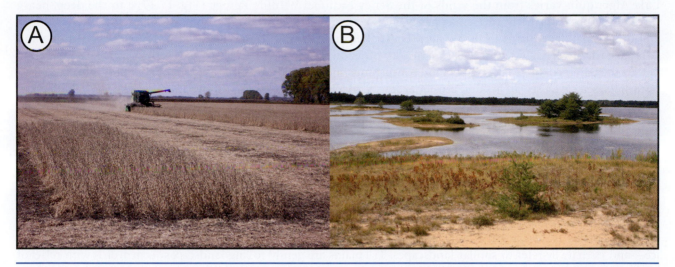

FIGURE 17.17   Images of typical glacial lake plains in Michigan. A. The flat plain of Glacial Lake Saginaw in Saginaw County, which in largely underlain by loamy and silty sediments. The soils that have developed on these sediments, when drained, have fostered some of the most productive agriculture in the state. Photo by R. Schaetzl. B. The flat plain of Glacial Lake Algonquin in Schoolcraft County. The lake bed sediments here are sandy, and are dotted with small dunes that may have formed soon after the lake drained, but before vegetation could be established (Chapter 18). Most of this lake plain is forested, providing excellent habitat for wildlife and waterfowl. Photo by S. Harding.

As the ice began to recede into the Great Lakes basins, in some areas the exposed proglacial land surface sloped back, toward the ice margin. This led to the formation of numerous proglacial lakes (Chapter 13). As deglaciation proceeded, the deepest offshore areas of these lakes became filled with fine-textured, stratified deposits (Fig. 17.7B). The littoral zones of most of these lakes in Michigan were quite shallow, facilitating subaqueous, i.e., under water, erosion by waves. This wave beveling, coupled with deposition of lake sediment in deep-water areas, especially during the over-winter freeze-up, caused many lake bottoms to become exceedingly flat (Plates 7, 10; Fig. 17.17). After these glacial lakes drained, the lake floors were exposed as broad, flat plains with fine-textured soils. Where the lake plain sediments are loamy, silty or clayey, agriculture has flourished, but only after the normally flat, wet landscapes have been artificially drained by perforated underground pipes called tiles, which drain the groundwater into deep drainage ditches at the fields' edges (Chapter 36). Some of Michigan's best farmland, e.g., parts of the Thumb, as well as Monroe and Chippewa Counties, are associated with this type of lake plain (Fig. 17.17A). Where the lake plain sediments are sandy, such as the eastern Upper Peninsula, forests are common, as there is little to be gained economically by draining these wet sands. Today, many of these wet, sandy lake beds are in the public domain as National Wildlife Refuges, State Game Areas or State Forests (Fig. 17.17B).

Most lake plains in Michigan border the Great Lakes, but some extend far inland (Taylor 1990, Chapter 13; Plates 8, 10). The most extensive lake plain in the Lower Peninsula, which borders Saginaw Bay and covers parts of the Thumb, formed beneath Glacial Lake Saginaw and its higher- and lower-level phases (Bretz 1951, Eschman and Karrow 1985). These lakes formed in front of the retreating Saginaw Lobe, and drained westward, through the Maple River and into the Grand River valley (Fig. 13.8). Much of the city of Detroit, and many of its inner suburbs, are situated on the Lake Maumee plain, which formed beneath the Erie lobe lakes that inundated southeastern Michigan (Fig. 13.7). On the west side of the Lower Peninsula, a small lake plain centered on Allegan, Ottawa and Muskegon Counties is associated with a high-level lake in the Michigan basin—Glacial Lake Chicago (Plate 8). This lake plain is quite sandy and much of it is currently forested. Another expansive lake plain, formed beneath Glacial Lake Algonquin (Schaetzl et al. 2002), spans much of the eastern Upper Peninsula and even extends a few tens of kms into the northern Lower Peninsula (Fig. 13.12). Lake Algonquin is unusual for Michigan, in that it contained numerous islands, such as the bedrock-cored Munuscong Islands in eastern Mackinac County, many of which were quite large and persisted through all of the various stages (Fig. 13.12; Larsen 1987, Schaetzl et al. 2002). Krist and Schaetzl (2001) mapped the long, gravelly spits that extend from many of these islands, which formed in response to the strong southeasterly winds of the time. Just south of Mackinac City, Interstate Highway 75 follows one of these spits, using it as a high, dry pathway across the otherwise wet lake plain. The floor of

Lake Algonquin varies from the sands of the Seney National Wildlife Refuge (Fig. 17.17B) to the deep, heavy clays of Chippewa County, where hay has been grown, since the pine lumbering days (Plate 8B). There are several other small lake plains in the western Upper Peninsula associated with Glacial Lakes Duluth, Minong and Baraga, each of which has an interesting history of its own.

As they drained, these lakes left behind conspicuous shorezone features, in the form of abandoned beach ridges, sand spits, sea caves, sea arches and erosional scarps, many of which are high above modern lake level. Skull Cave, Arch Rock and the prominent slopes associated with the Grand Hotel and Fort Mackinac on Mackinac Island are well-known examples of these ancient landforms (Chapter 13).

Subglacial landforms

Glaciers also form subglacial landforms, and they do it in two ways: (1) by erosion of pre-existing sediment or bedrock, and (2) by deposition and sculpting of new sediment. Often, it is difficult to determine which process was dominant. Subglacial landforms are common in Michigan, and are variously called till plains, ground moraines or drift plains (Fig. 17.11A, Plate 9). All three of these terms imply the same genesis—they formed mainly *under* the ice—and essentially refer to similar landscapes. Till plains are gently rolling landscapes, commonly with relief of less than 10 m km^{-2}, with wetter areas in low depressions (Fig. 17.18). Till plain sediments can be highly variable—sands can abut clays, silts may overlie sand and gravel, and muck often fills the wet depressions. Smaller subglacial landforms often associated with till plains include drumlins and eskers (Fig. 17.11A).

Drumlins are elongate, spoon-shaped hills that are typically 500–1500 m long and 200–600 m wide (Fig. 17.19; Plate 8). Few states have as many excellent examples of these interesting glacial landforms as does Michigan (Bergquist 1941, 1942). Drumlins tend to occur on till plains in groups of 50–500, called "swarms." They form subglacially, as the ice is advancing, although their exact genesis is still debated (Fig. 17.11A). The long axes of the drumlins always parallel the direction of ice flow, with their steepest slope facing up-ice, making them excellent indicators of past ice movement. Many researchers have found that drumlins tend to form best where ice is advancing out of a deep basin and on to an upland, as in upstate New York (Francek 1991) or southeastern Wisconsin (Borowiecka and Erickson 1985). This same situation exists for several of Michigan's larger drumlin fields—the Antrim-Charlevoix field and several small fields in the northeastern Lower Peninsula (Schaetzl 2001; Fig. 17.20; Plate 8A). Other drumlin swarms, such as the Union City field in St. Joseph County or the Menominee field, which covers much of Menominee County, formed on relatively flat ground moraines in interior Michigan.

Eskers are sand and gravel ridges that originally formed as meltwater channel deposits on top of the glaciers, or in tunnels beneath or within them (Fig. 17.11A). With the melting of the ice sheet, these sediments were left as meandering, often segmented, ridges. Eskers are typically aligned at right angles to the major end moraines, and sometimes

FIGURE 17.18   Typical till plain, or ground moraine, in southern Michigan. This view, in Ingham County, shows the rolling nature of till plains, and that many till plains in Michigan have productive, loamy soils. Photo by R. Schaetzl.

display small outwash fans at their downstream ends, where they exited the ice tunnel. Because the superglacial and subglacial streams that formed eskers had their headwaters far up-ice, many eskers can be traced for tens of km across the landscape. Eskers can only be well preserved where the ice is stagnant and melting. Actively flowing ice will collapse meltwater channels and tunnels and incorporate the stream sediments into the entrained drift. As a result, conspicuous eskers in Michigan are commonly associated with ice lobes that have undergone widespread stagnation—especially the Saginaw lobe marginal zones in south-central and northeastern Lower Michigan (Fig. 17.21). Eskers are important sources of sand and gravel, and for this reason many have been completely removed by mining.

The Mason esker is Michigan's longest and most famous esker (Figs. 17.21, 17.22). Trending from near Mason, in central Ingham County, to DeWitt in southern Clinton County, the Mason Esker was initially >30 km long. Along

FIGURE 17.19 Drumlins typical of the Antrim-Charlevoix drumlin field in the northwestern Lower Peninsula. Photo by R. Schaetzl.

FIGURE 17.20 Map of the major drumlin fields in Michigan.

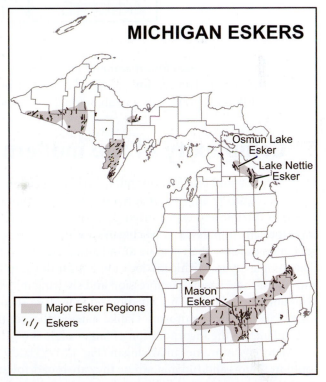

FIGURE 17.21 Map of the esker regions of Michigan, and the names and locations of major eskers within those regions. After Rieck (1972) and Farrand and Bell (1972).

FIGURE 17.22
Topographic map of a section of the Mason esker, near Holt. Note that, where the esker is absent, in its place are long, narrow gravel-pit lakes.

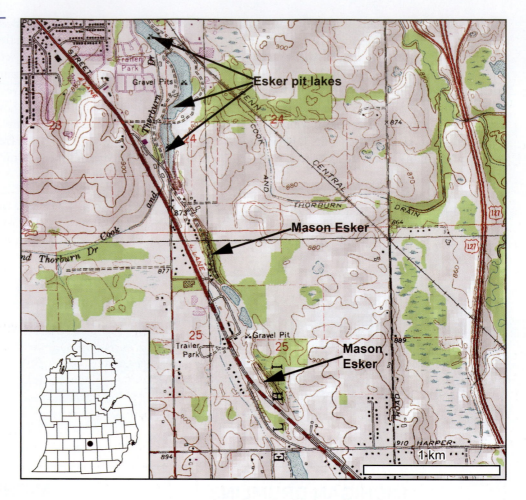

its route, the esker crosses four major end moraines. As a reliable source of construction aggregate and railroad ballast in a heavily populated region, nearly all of the Mason Esker has been removed, and today can be traced as a linear series of flooded gravel pits and abandoned excavations.

■ Complexity of the modern landscape

Frank Leverett and Frank Taylor published Michigan's first glacial geology maps (Leverett and Taylor 1915; Leverett 1929), recognizing an intricate assemblage of end moraines associated with the various glacial lobes (Figs. 17.12, 17.13). A capable and experienced geologist who mapped landforms across much of the northeastern US, Leverett was especially impressed by Michigan's surficial geology, noting that "the Wisconsin drift in Michigan has perhaps greater complexity than is to be found anywhere else in the United States" (Leverett 1904, 102). Today we attribute that complexity to Michigan's location amidst the deep basins of the Great Lakes. Where ice was forced to ride up and out of these basins, compression and shearing in the ice were maximized, leading to the deposition of voluminous amounts of drift. This situation often leads to stagnation of the underlying ice and formation of a distinctive suite of ice-wastage landforms. Unlike states farther south, the ice in Michigan may have been partially frozen to its bed, enhancing the incorporation of large volumes of drift into the ice (Mickelson et al. 1983).

Many end moraines in Michigan (Fig. 17.13; Plate 9) do not resemble the classical end moraines found further south in Illinois and Indiana, where they are broad, low-relief features, composed of till, that formed along actively moving ice margins. In Michigan, the moraines are often narrower, exhibit greater relief, contain more sand and gravel, show evidence of at least partial ice stagnation and many are better interpreted as heads of outwash and related features (Fig. 17.14A). When Leverett and Taylor first mapped the glacial landforms of Michigan, they were aware of these differences, but followed the standard practices of the time, by mapping all of these features as end moraines.

Today, we know that the true nature of ice marginal deposition in Michigan is more complicated than Leverett and Taylor's reconnaissance mapping of end moraines (Plate 9) might suggest.

■ Nature of drainage in Michigan

Michigan lies at the heart of the Great Lakes-St. Lawrence drainage basin, one of the largest and most economically important watersheds in North America (Chapter 14). The Detroit, St. Clair and St. Marys Rivers (Michigan's 1st, 2nd and 3rd largest, by volume) are significant links in this vast system, and exhibit impressive mean annual discharges. In contrast, streams draining Michigan's interior have relatively small discharges, and are of limited extent (Plate 11, Figs. 15.6, 15.7). Their size is restricted by the relatively short distance to their outlets—typical of rivers on peninsulas—and by the presence of extensive lake and wetland districts, where conditions for drainage initiation (at least in the short term) are unfavorable. Here, lakes and wetlands serve as localized traps for surface water, and along with the highly permeable sandy drift, typical of these areas, reduce the potential for surface runoff and stream formation.

Initiation of drainage

Michigan's postglacial drainage history is complex. Many rivers, e.g., the Manistee, Au Sable, Muskegon, Kalamazoo, St. Joseph and Cass (Plate 11), began as braided meltwater streams, associated with the rapidly retreating glacial margin. Choked with massive volumes of sediment-laden meltwater in the summer (but dry in winter), these rivers drained toward the ice-filled Lake Huron or Michigan basins, but often never made it—being blocked by the ice sheet that was occupying the basins. During times of high levels in the glacial lakes (base level for the streams), these meltwater streams often filled their valleys with thick sequences of sandy alluvium. During the waning phases of the glacial era, particularly at times of lower base level, the streams began to incise (cut down) their over-filled valleys, leaving behind a series of terraces, or steps, within the broader valley. The terraces that are so common in many of Michigan's river valleys attest to their long and complex history. The Manistee River valley is an excellent example of a stream system that was filled with glacial outwash while it carried meltwater, but has since incised into this sediment, to form up to eight separate terraces (Fig. 17.23).

Other rivers, such as the Grand, Indian, AuTrain, Whitefish, St. Marys, St. Clair and Detroit, served as important links among the series of ancient proglacial lakes that formerly occupied the Great Lakes basins (Karrow

FIGURE 17.23 An image of the Manistee River, south of Mesick, showing its current floodplain and three terraces (step-like treads), relics of former, higher floodplain levels. Photo by R. Schaetzl.

FIGURE 17.24   A map of the valley of the Grand River, near Ionia, and the surrounding landscape.

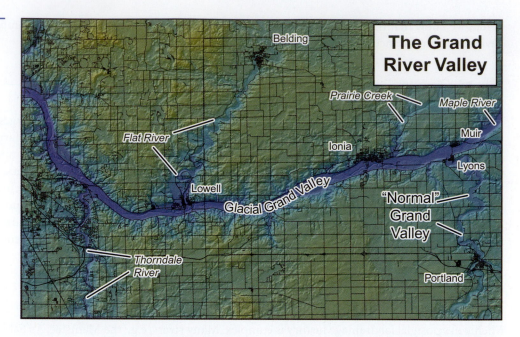

and Calkin, 1985; Chapter 13). Particularly noteworthy here is the Maple-Grand valley, which drained Glacial Lake Saginaw for several centuries (Fig. 13.8), and today exhibits an unusually wide valley for such a small river (Fig. 17.24). The valley of the Grand River downstream from Muir and Lyons, is an excellent example of an "underfit" stream valley (Kehew 1993). Here, the modern Grand River meanders across a floodplain that is typically >1 km wide, having been carved by glacial meltwater spilling out of several proglacial lakes that occupied the Saginaw Lowlands (Chapter 13). This valley is typical of many that drained proglacial lakes—wide valleys that today are occupied by comparatively narrow streams. Indeed, because meltwater streams exhibited discharges far greater than their modern precipitation-groundwater dominated descendants, many Michigan rivers are underfit.

Postglacial times were often characterized by stream flow *reversals* as the ice withdrew, especially in the Lower Peninsula. Prior to final deglaciation, ice still overflowed from the Great Lakes basins, forcing meltwater to flow toward the center of the peninsula or along the glacial margin (Fig. 17.25A). With further melting, however, the much lower basins of the Great Lakes were uncovered, and many streams reversed their courses (Fig. 17.25B). Drainage reversal is nicely illustrated in the northern Lower Peninsula, along the headwaters of the Rapid River near Kalkaska (Blewett 1991). Here, as the ice margin held a position along the Inner Port Huron Moraine, meltwater discharged from the ice, onto the adjacent outwash plain, where it flowed to the SW, parallel to the ice margin (Fig. 17.14B1). As the ice margin retreated and pivoted in a northwesterly direction, away from the head of outwash, areas along the margin to the south became ice free, while ice still remained in contact with the head of outwash farther north (Fig. 17.14B2). This setup allowed meltwater streams that formerly had drained parallel to the ice margin to find steeper gradients and lower outlets back, through the head of outwash (Fig. 17.14B3). Although documented in detail for the Rapid River, this model can be applied to nearly every major river system in the northern Lower Peninsula, including the Manistee, Betsie, Boardman, Cedar, Jordan and Boyne Rivers. The Au Sable, Rifle and Thunder Bay Rivers followed a similar pattern, except here the ice margin was pivoting to the NE, as it abandoned the Port Huron moraine in the northeastern Lower Peninsula (Burgis 1977).

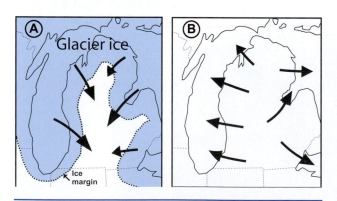

FIGURE 17.25   Drainage reversals in Michigan. During the Late Pleistocene (A), meltwater streams flowed away from the Great Lakes basins toward the center of the Lower Peninsula, which was ice-free. After the glaciers melted (B), streams reversed their courses, toward the much lower lake basins.

FOCUS BOX: The Huron River water gap at Ann Arbor

The concept of *palimpsest landscapes* helps to explain a major geomorphic "curiosity" found in Michigan—every major stream in southern Michigan cuts across at least two moraines and flows toward (not away from) these former ice margins. This cross-cutting relationship between a stream valley and the major topographic ridges of the area (the moraines)—another type of drainage reversal—is best shown by the Huron River, as it bisects the Fort Wayne and Defiance moraines near Ann Arbor. Originating in west-central Oakland County, the Huron River flows to the SW, across Livingston County (Plate 11). But near the border of Washtenaw County, the Huron River abruptly turns 120° left, to flow southeasterly—directly toward and through the massive Fort Wayne moraine at Ann Arbor. Here, the river is actually flowing *toward* the ice margin,

i.e., the moraine, indicating that the lower reach of the river was established after the ice margin retreated from this position.

How can this be explained? Winters and Rieck (1982) discovered that, where rivers traverse moraines in southern Michigan, a bedrock valley commonly exists in the subsurface; that is the case here. A large, deep bedrock valley lies directly beneath the section of the Huron River valley, where it traverses these moraines. This water gap—through the moraine—is not primarily the result of fluvial (river) erosion. Rather, the stream was established within a palimpsest gap in the moraine—a topographic sag in the moraine above the buried bedrock valley. With continued retreat of the ice margin, this early Huron River drained eastward, undoubtedly deepening the water gap.

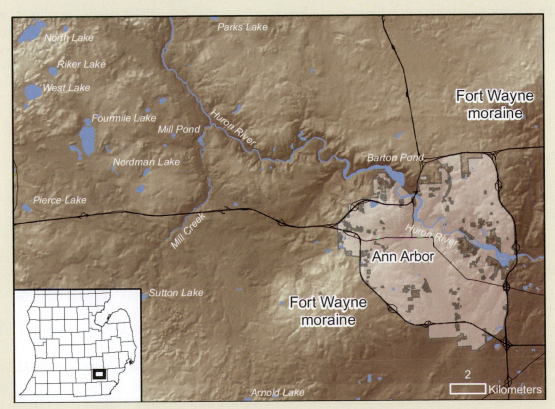

The Huron River water gap, through the Fort Wayne moraine, in the vicinity of Ann Arbor. Topography is shown by color shading.

Streams in coastal zones of the Great Lakes often began simply as short-distance drainages, oriented nearly perpendicular to the lakeshore. Called "parallel drainage," this situation is best observed along the Lake Superior coastline, from Freda west toward the Porcupine Mountains (Hack 1965), on the eastern shore of the Thumb along Lake Huron (Plate 8A), and farther south along the coasts of Lake St. Clair, the Detroit River and Lake Erie. Michigan has some of the best examples of parallel drainage patterns anywhere.

All of the earliest ancestral Great Lakes once stood at higher levels than today. Streams that flowed into these higher lakes formed deltas, indicating the position of the ancient coastline. Today, these deltas stand high above the modern levels of the Great Lakes, attesting to those higher lake levels. A particularly prominent delta exists where the Au Sable River entered a high-level glacial lake in the Huron basin (Plate 8A). A similar delta exists near Allendale, at the mouth of the Glacial Grand River.

■ Conclusions

Michigan's physical landscape mainly reflects the actions of the major glacial lobes that retreated from the state between about 18,000 and 11,000 years ago, acting upon a complex assortment of bedrock lithologies. This situation produced an intricate and tangled pattern of glacial landforms and sediments that surpass all other Midwestern states in their complexity, and form the basis for the state's important agricultural, timber, recreational and aggregate (sand and gravel) economies. Michigan's northern latitude placed it within an important transition zone within the continental ice sheet, where ice was frozen to the bed, producing intensive shearing within the glacier that led to the formation of high-relief, hummocky, ice-wastage terrain. These formations make up the now highly-prized lake districts of Michigan's northwoods, as well as those in the southeastern and southwestern parts of the Lower Peninsula. Even the automobile industry, for which Michigan is so famous, owes its success in part to the cheap transportation provided by the Great Lakes system.

Our economic success has come, however, at a high environmental price. Highly permeable drift and extensive lakes and wetlands make the state very susceptible to surface and groundwater contamination, a situation that was largely ignored until the 1960s (Chapter 16). Since then, Michigan has made enormous progress in this regard, but in many cases, irreparable damage has been done. Michigan's environmental challenge is to continue to protect and enhance its glacial resources at a time of diminishing state appropriations. In this light, it is vital that we understand our glacial legacy, so that we can become better stewards of our land and water resources.

Literature Cited

Arbogast, A.F. and S.G. Packman. 2004. Middle Holocene mobilization of aeolian sand in western upper Michigan and the probable relationship with climate and fire. The Holocene 14:464–471.

Benn, D.I. and D.J. Evans. 1998. Glaciers and Glaciation. Oxford University Press, New York.

Bergquist, S.G. 1941. The distribution of drumlins in Michigan. Papers of the Michigan Academy of Sciences, Arts and Letters 27:451–464.

Bergquist, S.G. 1942. New drumlin areas in Cheboygan and Presque Isle Counties, Michigan. Papers of the Michigan Academy of Sciences, Arts and Letters 28:481–485.

Blewett, W.L. 1991. The Glacial Geomorphology of the Port Huron Complex in Northwestern Southern Michigan. Ph.D. Dissertation, Michigan State University, East Lansing.

Blewett, W.L. and R.L. Rieck. 1987. Reinterpretation of a portion of the Munising Moraine in northern Michigan. Geological Society of America Bulletin 98:169–175.

Blewett, W.L. and H.A.Winters. 1995. The importance of glaciofluvial features within Michigan's Port Huron moraine. Annals of the Association of American Geographers 85:306–319.

Borowiecka, B.Z. and R.H. Erickson. 1985. Wisconsin drumlin field and its origin. Zeitschrift fur Geomorphologie 29:417–438.

Bretz, J.H. 1951. Causes of the glacial lake stages in Saginaw Basin. Journal of Geology 59:244–258.

Brown, D.G., Lusch, D.P. and K.A. Duda. 1998. Supervised classification of types of glaciated landscapes using digital elevation data. Geomorphology 21:233–250.

Burgis, W.A. 1977. Late Wisconsinan history of northeastern Lower Michigan. Ph.D. Dissertation, University of Michigan, Ann Arbor.

Cannon, W.F., Kress, T.H. Sutphin, D.M., Morey, G.B., Meints, J. and R. Barber-Delach. 1999. Digital geologic map and mineral deposits of the Lake Superior region. US Geological Survey Open-File Report 97–0455.

Edsall, T.A., Brown, C.L., Kennedy, G.W. and T.P. Poe. 1992. Lake trout spawning habitat in the Six Fathom Bank-Yankee Reef lake trout sanctuary, Lake Huron. Journal of Great Lakes Research 18:70–90.

Eschman, D.F. and P.F. Karrow. 1985. Huron Basin Glacial Lakes: A Review. In: P.F. Karrow and P.E. Calkin (eds), Quaternary Evolution of the Great Lakes. Geological Society of Canada Special Paper 30:79–93.

Farrand, W.R. and D.L. Bell. 1982. Quaternary Geology (map) of Southern Michigan with surface water drainage divides. 1:500,000 scale. Department of Natural Resources, Geological Survey Division, Lansing, MI.

Fisher, T.G. and L.D. Taylor. 2002. Sedimentary and stratigraphic evidence for subglacial flooding, south-central Michigan. Quaternary International 90:87–115.

Flint, R.F., Colton, R.B., Goldthwait, R.P. and H.B. Wilman. 1959. Glacial Map of the United States east of the Rocky Mountains. Geological Society of America, Denver, CO.

Francek, M.A. 1991. A spatial perspective on the New York drumlin field. Physical Geography 12:1–18.

Hack, J.T. 1965. Postglacial drainage evolution and stream geometry in the Ontonagon area, Michigan. US Geological Survey Professional Paper B1–B40.

Indiana Geological Survey. 2007. Indiana Geology Glossary. http://igs.indiana.edu/Geology/glossary/listEntireGlossary.cfm

Karrow, P. and P. Calkin (eds). 1985. Quaternary Evolution of the Great Lakes. Geological Association of Canada Paper 30.

Kehew, A.E. 1993. Glacial-lake outburst erosion of the Grand Valley, Michigan, and its impacts on glacial lakes in the Lake Michigan basin. Quaternary Research 39:36–44.

Kehew, A.E., Nicks, L.P. and W.T. Straw. 1999. Palimpsest tunnel valleys: evidence for relative timing of advances in an interlobate area of the Laurentide ice sheet. Annals of Glaciology 28:47–52.

Koteff, C. and F. Pessl. 1981. Systematic ice retreat in New England. US Geological Survey Professional Paper 1179.

Krist, F. and R.J. Schaetzl. 2001. Paleowind (11,000 BP) directions derived from lake spits in northern Michigan. Geomorphology 38:1–18.

Krzyszkowski, D. and P.F. Karrow. 2001. Wisconsinan inter-lobal stratigraphy in three quarries near Woodstock, Ontario. Géographie Physique et Quaternaire 55:3–22.

Larsen, C.E. 1987. Geological history of glacial Lake Algonquin and the upper Great Lakes. US Geological Survey Bulletin 1801.

Leverett, F. 1900. US Geological Survey Field Notebook 159. US Geological Survey Field Notebook Library, Denver, CO.

Leverett, F. 1904. Review of the glacial geology of the Southern Peninsula of Michigan. Report of the Michigan Academy of Sciences 6:100–110.

Leverett, F. 1929. Moraines and shorelines of the Lake Superior Region. US Geological Survey Professional Paper 154–A.

Leverett, F. and F. B. Taylor. 1915. The Pleistocene of Indiana and Michigan and the History of the Great Lakes. US Geological Survey Monograph 53. Washington, DC.

Lowell, T.V., Larson, G.L., Hughes, J.D. and G.H. Denton. 1999. Age verification of the Lake Gribben forest bed and the Younger Dryas Advance of the Laurentide ice sheet. Canadian Journal of Earth Science 36:383–393.

Mickelson, D.M., Clayton, L., Fullerton, D.S. and H.W. Borns, Jr. 1983. The Late Wisconsinan Glacial Record of the Laurentide Ice Sheet in the United States. In: H.E. Wright, Jr. (ed), Late-Quaternary Environments of the United States. University of Minnesota Press, Minneapolis. pp. 3–37.

Milstein, R.L. 1987. Bedrock geology of southern Michigan. 1:500,000 map. Michigan Department of Natural Resources, Lansing.

Ontario Ministry of Northern Development and Mines. 2004. Resident Geologist Program, Geology of the Southwestern District. http://www.mndm.gov.on.ca/mndm/mines/resgeol/southern/southwestern/geo_e.asp (last accessed March, 2008).

Rieck, R.L. 1972. Morphology, structure and formation of eskers with illustrations from Michigan and a bibliographical index to esker literature. M.A. Thesis, Wayne State University, Detroit, MI.

Rieck, R.L. 1976. The glacial geomorphology of an interlobate area in southeastern Michigan: Relationships between landforms, sediments, and bedrock. Ph.D. Dissertation, Michigan State University, East Lansing.

Rieck, R.L. 1979. Ice stagnation and paleodrainage in and near an interlobate area. Michigan Academician 11:219–235.

Rieck, R.L. and H.A. Winters. 1993. Drift volume in Michigan; a prodigious Pleistocene endowment. Physical Geography 14:478–493.

Schaetzl, R.J. 2001. Late Pleistocene ice flow directions and the age of glacial landscapes in northern lower Michigan. Physical Geography 22:28–41.

Schaetzl, R.J., Drzyzga, S.A., Weisenborn, B.N., Kincare, K.A., Lepczyk, X.C., Shein, K.A., Dowd, C.M. and J. Linker. 2002. Measurement, correlation, and mapping of Glacial Lake Algonquin shorelines in northern Michigan. Annals of the Association of American Geographers 92:399–415.

Schaetzl, R.J. and B.N. Weisenborn. 2004. The Grayling Fingers region of Michigan: soils, sedimentology, stratigraphy and geomorphic development. Geomorphology 61:251–274.

Scott, I.D. 1921. Inland Lakes of Michigan. Michigan Geological and Biological Survey Publication 30. Geological Series 25.

Spencer, J.W. 1881. Discovery of the preglacial outlet of the basin of Lake Erie into that of Lake Ontario. American Philosophical Society Proceedings 19:300–337.

Spencer, J.W. 1890. Origin of the basins of the Great Lakes of America. American Geologist 7: 86–97.

Sugden, D.E. and B.S. John. 1988. Glaciers and Landscape. Edward Arnold, London.

Reed, R.C. and J. Daniels. 1987. Bedrock geology of northern Michigan. 1:500,000 map Michigan Department of Natural Resources, Lansing.

Taylor, L.D. 1990. Evidence for high glacial-lake levels in the northeastern Lake Michigan basin and their relationship to the Glenwood and Calumet phases of Glacial Lake Chicago. In: A.F. Schneider and G.S. Fraser (eds), Late Quaternary History of the Lake Michigan Basin. Geological Society of America, Special Paper 251. pp. 91–109.

Thornbury, W.D. 1965. Regional Geomorphology of the United States. John Wiley and Sons, New York.

Waite, C. 2003. Forest Land Surveyor, Huron-Manistee National Forests. Personal communication.

Winters, H.A. and R.L. Rieck. 1982. Drainage reversals and transverse relationships of rivers to moraines in southern Michigan. Physical Geography 3:70–82.

Wold, R.J. 1980. Review of Lake Michigan seismic reflection data. US Geological Survey Open File Report 80–902.

Further Readings

Andrews, J.T. 1987. The Late Wisconsin glaciation and deglaciation of the Laurentide ice sheet. In: W.F. Ruddiman and H.E. Wright, Jr. (eds), North America and adjacent oceans during the last deglaciation. Geological Society of America K-3:13–37.

Blewett, W.L. 1994. Late Wisconsin history of Pictured Rocks National Lakeshore and vicinity. Pictured Rocks Resource Report 94–01. 8 pp.

Bretz, J.H. 1953. Glacial Grand River, Michigan. Michigan Academy of Sciences, Arts and Letters 38:359–382.

Dodson, R.L. 1993. Reinterpretation of the northern portion of the Tekonsha Moraine, south-central Michigan. Physical Geography 14:139–153.

Dredge, L.A. and L.H. Thorleifson. 1987. The middle Wisconsinan history of the Laurentide ice sheet. Geographie Physique et Quaternaire 41:215–235.

Dreimanis, A. 1977. Late Wisconsin glacial retreat in the Great Lakes region, North America. Annals of the New York Academy of Science 288:70–89.

Dyke, A.S. and V.K. Prest. 1987. Late Wisconsinan and Holocene history of the Laurentide ice sheet. Geographie Physique et Quaternaire 41:237–263.

Farrand, W.R. and D.F. Eschman. 1974. Glaciation of the southern peninsula of Michigan: a review. Michigan Academician 7:31–56.

Flint, R.F. 1971. Glacial and Quaternary Geology. John Wiley and Sons, New York.

Horberg, C.L. and R.C. Anderson. 1956. Bedrock topography and Pleistocene glacial lobes in central United States. Journal of Geology 64:101–116.

Karrow, P.F. 1987. Glacial and glaciolacustrine events in northwestern Lake Huron, Michigan and Ontario. Geological Society of America Bulletin 98:113–120.

Meek, N. and H.A. Winters. 1989. Method for recognizing local bedrock influence on drift plains. Professional Geographer 41:465–470.

Peterson, W.L. 1986. Late Wisconsinan glacial history of northeastern Wisconsin and western upper Michigan. US Geological Survey Bulletin 1652.

Richmond, G.M. and D.S. Fullerton. 1986. Introduction to Quaternary glaciations in the United States of America. Quaternary Science Reviews 5:3–10.

Schaetzl, R.J., Krist, F., Rindfleisch, P., Liebens, J. and T. Williams. 2000. Postglacial landscape evolution of northeastern lower Michigan, interpreted from soils and sediments. Annals of the Association of American Geographers 90:443–466.

Strahler, A.H. and Strahler, A.N. 1992. Modern Physical Geography. John Wiley and Sons, New York.

Winters, H.A. and R.L. Rieck. 1980. Significance of landforms in southeast Michigan. Annals of the Association of American Geographers 70:413–424.

Wright, H.E. Jr. 1971. Retreat of the Laurentide ice sheet from 14,000 to 9,000 years ago. Quaternary Research 1:316–330.

18

Sand Dunes

Alan F. Arbogast

■ Introduction

One of the most distinctive aspects of Michigan's physical geography is the widespread occurrence of sand dunes. Sand dunes are usually associated with hot and dry environments, where persistent winds blow across a desolate and barren landscape. However, sand dunes can form anywhere—as long as a significant source of sand exists, vegetation cover is minimal and strong winds periodically blow. Such conditions have existed at various times and places throughout Michigan's past, since glacial ice finally retreated from the region about 11,000 years ago (Chapter 6). As a result, sand dunes occur today in many places in the state (Farrand and Bell 1982, Plates 9, 10). This chapter focuses on the geography of the many sand dunes in Michigan and briefly describes what is known about their age and evolution.

■ Why sand dunes in Michigan?

When considering the presence of sand dunes in Michigan, it is important to remember that the large, melting glaciers described in Chapters 6 and 17 deposited a tremendous amount of sandy sediment. The glaciers eroded and ground up rocks from the Canadian Shield into a vast number of sand-sized particles, many of which were eventually deposited in Michigan in a variety of settings, including outwash plains, proglacial lake beds, kames and moraines (Leverett and Taylor 1915, Blewett and Winters 1995, Schaetzl and Weisenborn 2004; Chapters 13, 17).

After these sands were deposited, they could potentially be moved again by a variety of processes, including the wind. For this kind of reworking to occur on a large scale, extensive deposits of sparsely vegetated sand have to be present, because dense vegetation tends to protect and stabilize the sand. This protection occurs because (1) plants form a "dead air" barrier that shields the surface from the direct force of the wind, and (2) root networks hold sand deposits together.

Although it is difficult to imagine areas of sparsely vegetated sand in Michigan's dense pre-settlement forest, such landscapes did occur throughout much of the state. In the past, bare sandy surfaces must have been common for short periods immediately following ice retreat, and after proglacial lakes drained and exposed their lake beds (Chapter 13). Yet another way that sandy sediments could have been made susceptible to wind transport was by a dramatic environmental change—one that reduced vegetation cover, such as a drier climate, e.g., Davis et al. (2000), or perhaps frequent fires (Booth et al. 2002). Any and all of the above scenarios could have and probably did occur in Michigan's geologic past.

One place where significant deposits of unvegetated sand currently exist is the lakeshore. Sandy beaches abound in the Great Lakes region and are particularly plentiful in Michigan. After these sands were deposited in glacial landforms, they made their way into the lakes via coastal erosion, and by rivers flowing from the interior. These sand deposits were later carried by lake currents (Chrzastowski and Thompson 1992), before being washed up on to the beach, where they could then be blown into coastal dunes.

In summary, environmental conditions have been favorable for the formation of sand dunes throughout much of the state in the past, and continue to be so along many coastlines today. The bulk of this chapter will focus on coastal dunes, with an additional emphasis on dunes scattered throughout the state's interior.

Coastal sand dunes

When most people think about sand dunes in Michigan, they usually picture the magnificent coastal dunes along the shore of Lake Michigan. This body of dunes may collectively form the largest complex of freshwater coastal sand dunes in the world (Peterson and Dersch 1981). A variety of additional coastal dune fields occur in the state, however, including isolated dune fields along both coasts of the Upper Peninsula, and along much of the Lake Huron coast (Plate 9).

Michigan's coastal dunes fall into two main categories: foredunes and transgressive dunes (Olson 1958a, b, c, Loope and Arbogast 2000, Arbogast et al. 2002a). Foredunes are very common along much of the Lakes Huron and Michigan coasts. They consist of sub-linear dune ridges that generally parallel the shoreline, just inland of the normal high water line (Fig. 18.1). Although most foredunes are small (~5 m high), a somewhat higher foredune ridge, e.g., Hesp (2002), exists in some places, such as at Warren Dunes and Hoffmaster State Parks. Olson (1958a, b, c) demonstrated that foredunes form along the Lake Michigan shore during low lake stages when beaches expand (widen) and sand supply increases. In this model, wind blows across the beach and moves sand inland a few meters, where it is deposited, either because sand grains become trapped by beach grass or because they fall behind a small mound that protects them from the wind. If lake level remains low, the cover of beach grass gradually expands and progressively more sand is trapped, resulting in foredune growth. Van Dijk (2004) showed that most sand is supplied to foredune systems along Lake Michigan between October and April when winds are strongest. Foredunes are usually temporary features on the landscape, because they are very susceptible to erosion when a period of high lake level inevitably returns. In some protected embayments, e.g.,

FIGURE 18.1 A small foredune near Charlevoix, Michigan. Note the relatively small size of this dune and that it parallels the coastline. Photo by A. Arbogast.

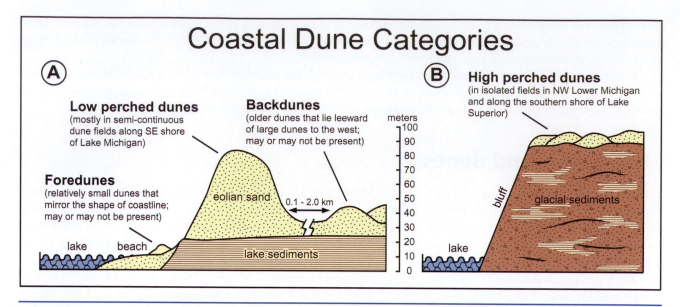

FIGURE 18.2 Generalized diagram of some of the major dune categories. Foredunes occur on the beach above the high water line. High perched dunes mantle high bluffs underlain by glacial sediments. Low perched dunes, in contrast, are larger dunes that bury lower surfaces formed by lake deposition.

Sturgeon Bay, however, parallel sets of foredune ridges occur, with those farthest inland being the oldest and those progressively closer to the lake decreasing in relative age. Such foredune sequences may have formed in response to gradual drops in lake level following the Nipissing high stand, several thousand years ago (Chapter 13), and have been used in the reconstruction of lake levels since that time (Thompson and Baedke 1997, Baedke and Thompson 2000).

In contrast to foredunes, which form on the highest part of the beach proper, transgressive dunes are eolian (wind-formed) landforms that develop as sand migrates further inland from the beach area, over vegetated or semi-vegetated surfaces, e.g., Hesp and Thom (1990). In Michigan, these older surfaces typically consist of forests and wetlands that are overrun and buried by eolian sand (Arbogast et al. 2002a). In many places, these transgressive dunes are now stable and covered by forest. In other places, they are active and exhibit large areas of bare sand. Generally speaking, transgressive dunes are much larger than foredunes—up to 60 m tall (Figs. 18.2, 18.3). One of the distinctive aspects of Michigan's transgressive dunefields is that they mantle geomorphic surfaces that are elevated *above* the beach. Thus, transgressive dunes in Michigan can also be referred to as *perched dunes,* to reflect the fact that they sit atop relatively high surfaces (Dow 1937, Snyder 1985, Anderton and Loope 1995). Perched dunes can be further subdivided into *high perched dunes* and *low perched dunes,* based on their relative position above the lakeshore (Fig. 18.2).

As the name implies, high perched dunes are elevated well above the lake, whereas the base of low perched dunes is only a few meters above the water line (Fig. 18.2). High perched dunes are commonly found in northwestern Lower Michigan and along the southern shore of Lake Superior. These dunes are distinctive because they occur in isolated fields that mantle high (up to 90 m high) bluffs that are typically composed of glacial sediments (Dow 1937, Snyder 1985, Anderton and Loope 1995, Loope and Arbogast 2000). Although several high perched dune fields occur in northwestern Lower Michigan, the best known is in Sleeping Bear Dunes National Lakeshore (Snyder 1985). Another prominent high perched dune field is the Grand Sable dune field (Figs. 17.1, 18.4A, B), which lies along the southern shore of Lake Superior in Pictured Rocks National Lakeshore (Anderton and Loope 1995). In contrast to these two perched dune fields that are currently active, high perched dunes at Nodaway Point along the southeastern shore of Lake Superior are entirely forested and stable (Arbogast 2000).

Research at Sleeping Bear Dunes National Lakeshore (Snyder 1985), Grand Sable Dunes (Anderton and Loope 1995) and Nodaway Point (Arbogast 2000) indicates that, like foredunes, the evolution of high perched dunes is tied directly to lake level fluctuations that, in turn, govern the amount of sand that is available for wind transport. In contrast to foredunes, which derive their sands from enlarged beaches during low lake stages, the sand in high

Dune Movement

FIGURE 18.3 Looking north at forested, transgressive dunes near Holland. Transgressive dunes migrate inland and bury older surfaces as they grow. In contrast to foredunes, these dunes are up to 60 m tall. Photo by A. Arbogast.

FIGURE 18.4 Images of the Grand Sable Dune Field, Alger County, Michigan. A. The dune field is perched about 90 m above Lake Superior. The source for these eolian sands is the lake-facing bluff, which is composed of sandy glacial sediments. Photo by R. Schaetzl. B. The topography of the dune field is very irregular, with patches of bare (active) sand interspersed with vegetated areas that are more stable. Photo by A. Arbogast.

perched dune systems is derived from erosion of the high lakeward bluff that lies below the base of the dunes (Marsh and Marsh 1987; Fig. 18.2B). Sand is delivered to high perched dunes when lake level is high (Anderton and Loope 1995). During these periods, waves crash against the base of the bluff and undercut it through erosion, causing the entire bluff to destabilize. When this happens, vegetation slides into the lake by gravity and large bare patches of sediment develop on the bluff face. When strong winds strike these bare areas, as they tend to do near the lakeshore, particularly during the winter months (Marsh and Marsh 1987), sand is then transported up and over the bluff edge to form dunes (Fig. 18.5A). As more and more sand is blown inland, over the bluff edge, the dunes grow. When lake level subsequently drops, the high perched dunes tend to stabilize because waves can no longer directly erode the bluff base (Fig. 18.5B). As a result, vegetation expands across the bluff face, sealing off the source of sand

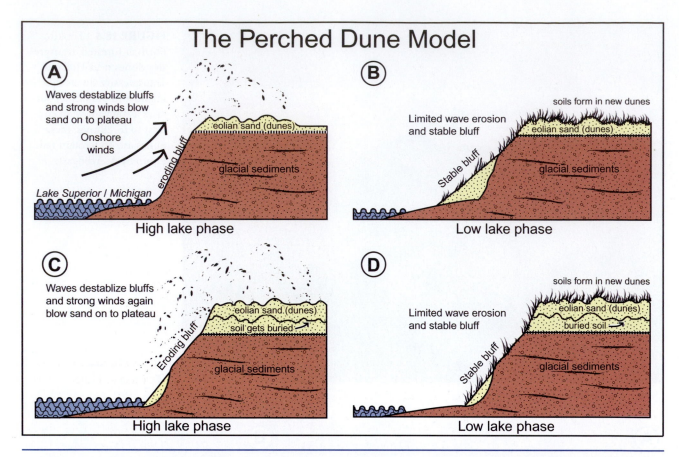

The Perched Dune Model

A Waves destablize bluffs and strong winds blow sand on to plateau

Onshore winds

Lake Superior / Michigan

eolian sand (dunes)

Eroding bluff

glacial sediments

High lake phase

B Limited wave erosion and stable bluff

soils form in new dunes

eolian sand (dunes)

Stable bluff

glacial sediments

Low lake phase

C Waves destablize bluffs and strong winds again blow sand on to plateau

Eroding bluff

eolian sand (dunes)

soil gets buried

glacial sediments

High lake phase

D Limited wave erosion and stable bluff

soils form in new dunes

eolian sand (dunes)

buried soil

Stable bluff

glacial sediments

Low lake phase

FIGURE 18.5   The Perched Dune Model. After Anderton and Loope (1995). A. Bluffs destabilize when lake level rises because waves erode cliff bases. This process allows sand to be transported from the upper bluff to the nearby dune field. Soils that had formed on the dunes above get buried by additions of new sand, leaving behind buried paleosols. B. When lake level is low, dunes are stable because the bluff is protected from wave erosion and becomes vegetated, cutting off any sand supply to the dunes above. New soils form on the stable sand dunes. C. As lake level subsequently rises, bluffs are destabilized and additional deposits of sand blow into the dunes, burying soils once again, as buried paleosols. D. When lake level drops again, the bluff stabilizes, vegetation spreads across dunes, and new soils again form. Radiocarbon dating of organic matter contained within paleosols enables the history of dune evolution to be reconstructed.

within the bluff itself to the dune field. Because sand is no longer supplied to the dunes above, the cover of vegetation in the dune field also expands, further stabilizing the dunes and resulting in the formation of soils in the dune sediments. The cycle of dune growth begins anew when lake level rises and waves begin to erode the bluff base once more (Fig. 18.5C). Soils that had developed on the dunes while they were stable (when lake levels were low; Fig. 18.5B) are buried when fresh deposits of sand are blown onto them, from the exposed bluff face. Soils then form in these fresh eolian deposits when the lake once again falls, the bluff stabilizes, and sand is no longer delivered to the dunes (Fig. 18.5D). Given this distinct cyclic pattern, perched dunes preserve within them a record of lake level fluctuation and eolian activity that has been reconstructed by radiocarbon dating the organic residue contained within the buried soils (paleosols) that formed at different times (Anderton and Loope 1995).

Research at Sleeping Bear Dunes National Lakeshore (Snyder 1985), Grand Sable Dunes (Anderton and Loope 1995, Loope et al. 2004) and Nodaway Point (Arbogast 2000) indicates that sand was first supplied to these high perched dune fields about 5000 years ago during the Nipissing stage of the Great Lakes (Larsen and Schaetzl 2001; Chapter 13). At this point in time, waves from this relatively high lake vigorously eroded the bluffs, exposing sands that were then blown onto the adjacent plateaus. Since then, the high perched dunes at Grand Sable Dunes and Sleeping Bear Dunes National Lakeshore have gone through several cycles of stability and growth in response to fluctuating lake levels (Snyder 1985, Anderton and Loope 1995). The dunes at Nodaway Point stabilized shortly after the drop from the Nipissing high stand because waves could no longer reach the bluff base (Arbogast 2000).

FIGURE 18.6 A typical example of low perched dunes along Lake Michigan. Dunes like these are very common along the south-eastern shore of Lake Michigan. Similar dunes also occur in isolated fields in northwestern Lower Michigan and along the southern coast of Upper Michigan. Photo by A. Arbogast.

Although Michigan's high perched dune fields are spectacular, perhaps the most impressive dunes in the state are the low perched dunes that semi-continuously line the shore of Lake Michigan south of Manistee (Plate 9). These low, perched dunes mantle old, glacial lake plains that lie very close (<10 m) to the elevation of the current Great Lakes; many of the dunes are up to 60 m in height (Figs. 18.2A, 18.6). This complex of dunes occurs because (1) the western side of Lower Michigan has an abundant supply of sand, (2) prevailing winds in the Great Lake region are westerly, i.e., the dominant airflow is west to east, and (3) the fetch across Lake Michigan is long; wind blows freely over the water until it encounters the sandy deposits on the west coast of Lower Michigan. Given that some of these low perched dune fields are many km long, they contain an incredible amount of sand.

The first scientist to seriously consider the age and evolution of the low perched dunes was Tague (1946), who investigated a cluster of coastal dunes in southwestern Lower Michigan. This study was conducted before the advent of reliable dating techniques such as radiocarbon dating, so Tague (1946) could not accurately determine the age of the dunes. Given that they mantle proglacial lake surfaces, he hypothesized that the dunes on the east side of the complex were associated with the Glenwood/Calumet stages of ancestral Lake Michigan (Chapter 13). Tague (1946) further believed that lake-fronting dunes mostly formed during the (later) Nipissing lake stage (Chapter 13), with perhaps a less significant period of dune growth during the (still later) Algoma lake stage.

In the years following Tague's (1946) work, no systematic studies were conducted on the age and evolution of Lake Michigan coastal dunes until the latter part of the 1990s. During this lengthy interval, the apparent default assumption of most researchers was that most of the coastal dunes probably formed during the high Nipissing lake stage, e.g., Dorr and Eschman (1970), Buckler (1979) as per the Tague (1946) model. As a result, investigations of the dunes were qualitative in nature and associated with the processes that modify the dunes locally.

These descriptive studies actually began with Scott (1942), who studied dunes that had been modified through the formation of blowouts, which are localized areas of extensive wind erosion that create broad, bowl-like features in dunes (Fig. 18.7A, B). In areas where blowouts are prominent, the dunes have a well-developed parabolic (U-shape) form when viewed from the above. This form of dune develops when vegetation anchors the limbs of the dune while the nose migrates downwind as the blowout enlarges. Along Lake Michigan, most parabolic dunes have a pair of limbs that open to the west, along with a nose that points to the east (Fig. 18.7A), indicating that prevailing winds were westerly when the most recent blowouts formed. Some of the older, backdunes have limbs that open to the southwest (Fig. 18.7A), however, reflecting prevailing southwesterly winds. Scott (1942) proposed that dunes modified in this fashion be called *secondary dunes* because they usually show evidence of at least two periods of activity.

Following Scott's (1942) study, the next significant work on large coastal dunes along Lake Michigan was conducted by Olson (1958a, b, c). A major contribution of this work was that stabilized dunes undergo a distinct series of plant successional stage, in which dunes are first vegetated by beach grass that ultimately evolves into a cover of

FIGURE 18.7   Low perched dunes along the Lake Michigan shore. A. A shaded relief, digital elevation model of parabolic dunes near Holland. Dunes in this area can be subdivided into backdunes, which are about 10 m high, and larger dunes (at the coast) that are up to 60 m high. Backdunes at this location formed between 5000 and 3500 years ago, when prevailing winds were southwesterly. Sand has been supplied episodically to the larger dunes for the past 5000 years. The orientation of blowouts in these larger dunes indicates that the most recent sand-moving winds have been westerly. B. Westerly view of a blowout axis near Holland. Photo by A. Arbogast.

trees (Olson 1958a). Olson (1958c) also noted that many large dunes were modified by waves that eroded their bases; Olson (1958c) used the term *cliffed dunes* to describe dunes shaped in this way.

In the 1970s, two very general descriptions of the dunes were published, beginning with Dorr and Eschman (1970), who focused on dunes in a chapter of their book *Geology of Michigan*. They assumed a Nipissing age for the dunes along the southeastern shore of Lake Michigan and used the term *high dunes* to portray their immense size. In 1979, Buckler conducted an inventory of the dune areas along the coast of Lake Michigan, in association with the recently enacted Sand Dune Protection and Management Act (Michigan Legislature 1976; see FOCUS BOX below). He used the term *barrier dunes* for these features because they often form a distinct physical boundary between the interior and the lakeshore. Fig. 18.7A provides some sense of this physical barrier.

In the late 1990s, research refocused on the age and evolution of the low perched dunes along Lake Michigan (Arbogast and Loope 1999, Loope and Arbogast 2000, Van Oort et al. 2001, Arbogast et al. 2002a, 2004, Fisher and Loope 2005). This shift occurred in large part because dating techniques now exist that can accurately estimate the

FOCUS BOX: Human interactions with coastal dunes

Michigan's coastal dunes are heavily utilized for recreation, industrial purposes, and home/condominium development. From a recreational standpoint, they are a popular outdoor destination for thousands of people at places such as Pictured Rocks National Lakeshore, Sleeping Bear Dunes National Lakeshore and in numerous state and local parks. Coastal dunes, however, have another important use—the sand is mined for industrial purposes. Most of this sand is used for metal casts (see Figure on facing page) in the automobile industry; many automobile parts are made from forge-cast steel. Coastal dune sand is well suited for this purpose because it (1) has the preferred sub-angular to sub-rounded grain shape, (2) is largely of the correct size (0.15–0.6 microns dia.) and the grains are all about the same size, (3) can withstand the high temperatures (from 1,300° to 1,700° C) of the molten metal, (4) has the proper chemical attributes,

(5) is porous enough to allow gases to escape, and (6) is easy to mine and transport by lake barge and rail to foundries near Detroit.

Sand mining has been controversial, however, because a number of large dunes have been destroyed over the years. In response to public outcry, the Sand Dune Protection and Management Act was passed in 1976 by the Michigan Legislature (Michigan State Legislature 1976). With this statute, the state began regulating the sand mining industry by requiring (1) specific plans for sand removal prior to mining, and (2) reclamation of the pit after the mining operations are complete.

Dunes face additional pressures from home and condominium construction (see Figure on facing page). In response to these growing impacts, the previous legislation was amended in 1989 and again in 1994 (Michigan Legislature 1994) to include the designation *critical dunes* to provide further protection of 32,784 hectares (80,000 acres) where the highest and most spectacular coastal dunes occur. These laws (1) prohibit development on dune slopes steeper than 33% slope, unless granted via a variance, (2) prohibit structures on the first lakeward-facing slope in a critical dune area, and (3) require environmental impact assessments for special use projects, such as subdivisions and condominium complexes. The State of Michigan continues to seek a balance among the various demands placed upon the dune landscape.

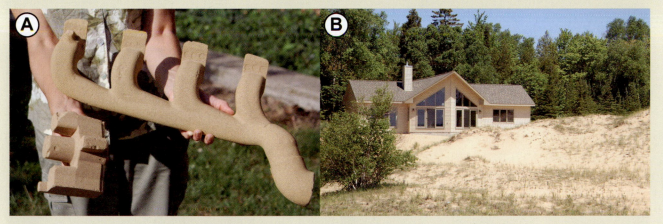

A. Photograph of foundry casts made with dune sand. Due to its physical and chemical nature, coastal dune sand is ideal for the production of casts such as these. B. Example of home construction in coastal sand dunes along the shore of Lake Michigan. Given their scenic nature, coastal sand dunes are a favored location for development. Photos by R. Schaetzl.

age of the dunes. One method frequently employed is radiocarbon dating, which calculates the amount of radioactive decay of the ^{14}C isotope in ancient carbon samples (see FOCUS BOX, Chapter 13). Another method commonly used for this application is optical stimulated luminescence (OSL) dating, which estimates the last time sand grains within dunes were exposed to sunlight (Murray and Wintle 2000).

One reason why research refocused on the age and evolution of the dunes was the discovery that many of the lake-fronting dunes contain a variety of buried soils (paleosols). This finding alone was significant, because it meant that the dunes did not form during a single period of time, or as a result of one event, as perhaps was previously assumed, e.g., Tague (1946), Dorr and Eschman (1970). Instead, they formed in distinct stages, punctuated by periods of stability and soil formation. These soils are beautifully preserved in many exposures along the coast and can be easily seen as dark, organic-rich bands that can be traced horizontally (Fig. 18.8A). Most of these soils are weakly developed (Fig. 18.8B), indicating only brief periods of landscape (dune) stability. A few soils, however, are well developed and represent much longer periods of dune stability (Fig. 18.8C). Organic residue from these soils has been collected at many places and numerous radiocarbon dates have been obtained (Arbogast and Loope 1999, Loope and Arbogast 2000, Arbogast et al. 2002a, 2004). The dates obtained from the organic matter in a paleosol provide an estimate of when that soil was buried by an influx of eolian sand. Given that numerous ages have been obtained from a variety of sites, it has been possible to reconstruct the evolution of dune activity along the lakeshore.

Radiocarbon dating of buried soils in the dunes has demonstrated that the evolution of the low-perched dune fields along Lake Michigan is much more complex than previously thought (Tague 1946, Buckler 1979) and that sand is generally supplied to them in accordance with the perched dune model (Snyder 1985, Anderton and Loope 1995, Loope and Arbogast 2000; Fig. 18.5). A compilation of data from several exposures at Van Buren State Park (Fig. 18.9) is representative for this portion of the lakeshore, and are used here as an example. In most cases, the lower sediments along the beach front consist of lake sands that probably accumulated during the Nipissing Great Lakes, or perhaps before. After this ancestral high lake stage occurred, this portion of the lakeshore was a marsh—between 6000 and 5000 years ago. Between about 5000 and 2000 years ago, the dunes in the Van Buren area grew rapidly. During the early part of this interval, eolian sand spread up to 1 km inland and accumulated in distinct parabolic *backdunes* that are themselves up to 10 m high (Fig. 18.7A). OSL dating of these backdunes indicates that they quickly stabilized, because their supply of sand was cut off by the dunes at the beach edge (Hansen et al. 2003). Although the dunes rapidly grew at the beach edge, several periods of stability nevertheless occurred in which vegetation expanded

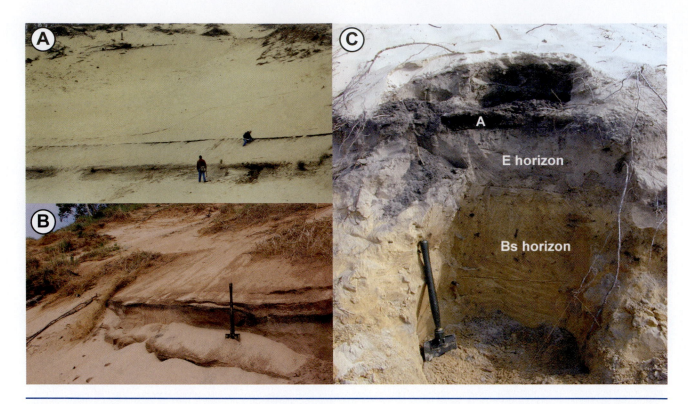

FIGURE 18.8   Buried soils in coastal dunes. A. Cross-section of a series of buried soils in a coastal sand dune at Van Buren State Park, near South Haven. The dark lines—buried soils—mark the former ground level at different times in the past. Photo by E. Hansen. B. A weakly developed buried soil in a coastal sand dune. This soil formed in about 150 years and consists mainly of an organic-rich A horizon. Photo by A. Arbogast. C. A well developed buried soil in coastal sand dune. This soil formed in about 1500 years—a long enough period of time that incipient E and Bs horizons could form. See Arbogast et al. (2004) for more information about this buried soil. Photo by A. Arbogast.

FIGURE 18.9   Composite stratigraphic sequence in the coastal dunes at Van Buren State Park. Thick eolian sands mantle marsh sands rich in organic matter which, in turn, overlie sandy lake sediments. The ^{14}C dates shown are from organic materials contained within buried soils, exposed along about 200 m of shoreline, and are interpreted to represent the time intervals within which soil burial probably occurred. Photo by A. Arbogast.

across the dunes. Many of these episodes appear to have lasted about 150 years (Loope and Arbogast 2000), and are marked by the existence of weakly developed, but now buried, soils similar to that shown in Figure 18.8B. As with the high perched dunes, these periods of stability appear to have occurred during lower lake stages. Time after time, the soils on the tops of the dunes became buried during the next high lake stage. As a result, the dunes grew in distinct and episodic stages (Fig. 18.9).

Following this period of rapid dune growth, which ended about 2000 years ago at Van Buren State Park, many of the low perched dunes stabilized for about 1500 years (Van Oort et al. 2001, Arbogast et al. 2002a, 2004). This extended period of stability—longer than any of the previous stable periods—resulted in the formation of a well developed soil on the dunes (Fig. 18.8C). The reason for this extended period of dune stability is unclear, because it appears to have occurred during a period of fluctuating lake levels. It ended between about 500 and 300 years ago, when eolian sand began to accumulate again on the tops of the dunes (Arbogast et al. 2004; Fig. 18.9). Since that time, many of the dunes have experienced at least two additional (but small) periods of growth, both of which appear to have occurred during high lake stages (Van Oort et al. 2001, Arbogast et al. 2002a) in accordance with the perched dune model.

■ Interior sand dunes

In addition to Michigan's famous coastal dunes, a variety of other dune fields are scattered throughout the interiors of both peninsulas (Farrand and Bell 1982, Plate 9). These interior dunes tend to be forested (Fig. 18.10) and,

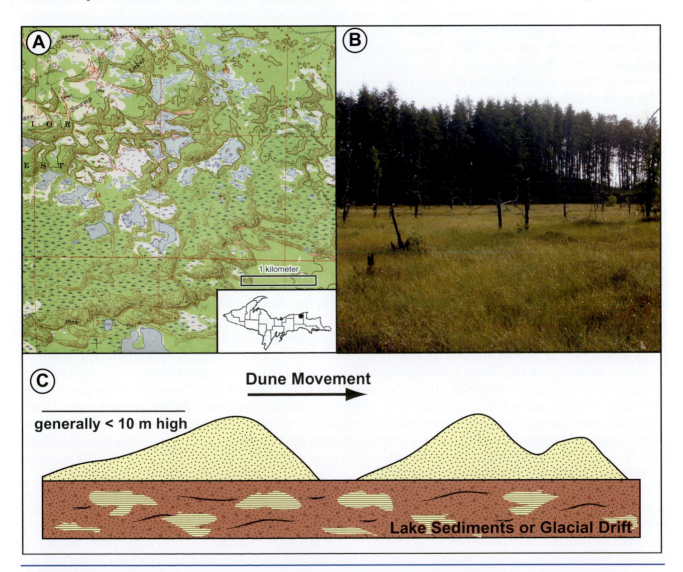

FIGURE 18.10 Interior dunes in Michigan. A. Part of the Betsy Lake 7.5 minute topographic map, showing some interior dunes in the Upper Peninsula. Note the northwest orientation of the limbs of these parabolic dunes, suggesting that northwesterly winds prevailed at the time the dunes formed. B. A typical interior dune in Michigan's Upper Peninsula, a few km northeast of Newberry, Luce County. The small hill is a sand dune that formed thousands of years ago. It has probably been covered with trees since that time. Dunes similar to this one occur in the interior of both peninsulas wherever sandy sediments were mobilized by the wind. Photo by A. Arbogast. C. Typical cross-section through a lake plain in Michigan with its small, parabolic dunes.

thus, inactive. They formed by the same processes that shaped the coastal dunes. In fact, some of these interior dunes apparently formed along the shorelines of some of the proglacial lakes described in Chapter 13. As noted earlier, Tague (1946) argued that the most easterly dunes of the coastal dune complex in Berrien County formed during the Glenwood/Calumet stages of ancestral Lake Michigan (Figs. 13.7, 13.9). In this context, Hansen (personal communication) has identified at least one dune ridge in this area that appears to be this old.

Although some interior dunes apparently formed on the coasts and broad deltas of glacial lakes, a variety of other dune fields clearly developed in different environmental settings. In contrast to coastal dunes, which depend on beaches and exposed bluffs as sand sources, e.g., Olson (1958a), Anderton and Loope (1995), Arbogast et al. (2002a), the apparent sand sources for interior dunes in Michigan were old lake beds and sandy outwash plains and deltas that had remained unvegetated for sufficiently long periods of time for wind to erode and transport sediment into dunes.

Although non-coastal, interior dunes are randomly scattered throughout much of the state (Plate 9), the best examples are in the central and east-central parts of the Lower Peninsula—the Houghton and Saginaw dune fields, respectively. The Saginaw dune field is generally located in and around the Saginaw Lowlands; it is the largest interior dune field in Lower Michigan. Although most of these dunes occur on the bed of Glacial Lake Saginaw (Chapter 13), a few, such as those in Arenac County, are associated with an outwash plain that flanks the Port Huron moraine (Arbogast et al. 1997). Dunes in the Houghton dune field mantle a sandy plain that lies east of the headwaters of the Muskegon River.

Interior dunes generally range in height from between a few meters to about 20 m. Most are parabolic in shape, with limbs pointing to the west-northwest (Arbogast et al. 1997; Fig. 18.10A). This orientation means that the prevailing winds were west-northwesterly when the dunes formed. Currently, winds in south-central Michigan are dominantly from the southwest, implying that the climate and winds were slightly different at the time these dunes formed. OSL dating indicates that dunes in the Houghton and Saginaw dune fields were last active about 9000 years ago (Arbogast et al. 2003).

A variety of non-coastal dunes also occur in the Upper Peninsula (Plate 9, Fig. 18.10). The majority of these dunes occur in the eastern part of the Upper Peninsula and mantle the lake bed of proglacial Lake Algonquin, which drained about 11,200 years ago (Larsen 1987, Schaetzl et al. 2002; Fig. 13.12, Chapters 13, 17). The largest suite of dunes is the Newberry dune field, which generally ranges from Trout Lake on the southeastern margin to about 20 km NW of Seney (Arbogast et al. 2002b; Plate 9, Fig. 18.10). Another set of dunes occurs near Crisp Point; this field is centered about 25 km SW of Whitefish Point (Plate 9). Lastly, another set of interior dunes, the Baraga dunes, occur in the western part of the Upper Peninsula, on a sandy plain known and the Baraga Plains (Arbogast and Packman 2004). The source of sand for this dune field is the underlying outwash and glaciolacustrine sands. Consistent with the interior dunes in Lower Michigan, the vast majority of these interior dunes are parabolic, with west to northwesterly limb orientations (Arbogast et al. 2002b, Arbogast and Packman 2004; Fig. 18.10A).

The first study of interior dunes in the Upper Peninsula was conducted by Bergquist (1936) who speculated on the age of the dunes on the Glacial Lake Algonquin plain. Without the aid of dating techniques, he assumed that they probably formed immediately after the lake drained. Recent OSL dating of the eolian sands indicates that dunes near Crisp Point, as well as at scattered sites in the Newberry dune field, apparently formed between about 10,000 and 8,500 years ago and therefore generally fit the Bergquist (1936) model (W. Loope, personal communication 2006). OSL dating at other localities within the Newberry dune field, however, suggests that some dunes here (and elsewhere in the Upper Peninsula) were last active much later in time—between about 7000 and 5500 years ago (Arbogast and Packman 2004, Arbogast et al. 2002b).

These ages, all of which post-date the initial exposure of these surfaces by thousands of years, pose interesting and unresolved questions about the environment of northern Michigan, because they imply that the many sandy surfaces were sparsely vegetated at a various times, several thousand years after deglaciation and after lake drainage. These sandy surfaces may have been bare and erodable because the climate was slightly warmer and drier during that time than it is now (Davis et al. 2000, Booth et al. 2002), which may have reduced vegetation cover sufficiently for dunes to form. Another potential explanation is that the dunes began to form earlier, shortly after deglaciation, e.g., Bergquist (1936), and the dunes remained active for several thousand years, perhaps because regional water tables were probably low in association with much lower water levels in the Great Lakes at that time (Chapter 13). Still another potential cause for reduced vegetation and dune formation is fire, which reduces vegetation cover and may have been more common during the time that the dunes formed (Delcourt at al. 2002). Clearly, questions remain unresolved as to why dune activity occurred (or continued for) so long after deglaciation in much of Michigan's Upper Peninsula.

■ Conclusions

One of the most notable aspects of Michigan's physical geography is the presence of numerous sand dunes. Magnificent coastal dunes line the western shoreline of Lake Michigan, and to a lesser extent, Lakes Superior and Huron. These dunes have evolved over the past 5000 years and have grown in distinct stages that are closely related to lake level fluctuations. The coastal dunes are heavily utilized for recreation, economic development, and for foundry sand. The coastal environment continues to be favorable for the development of dunes and will continue to be so for the foreseeable future.

In addition to the coastal dunes, numerous smaller dunes occur in the interior of the state. Some of these dunes are probably old coastal dunes that formed in association with proglacial lakes. Other interior dunes formed as wind eroded sands from outwash plains, river floodplains and old lake beds, as late as 9000 years ago. In Michigan's Upper Peninsula, some interior dunes last formed between 7000 and 5500 years ago. Given the lengthy interval of time since the interior dunes formed, they will most likely remain stable unless some kind of major environmental disturbance occurs.

Literature Cited

Anderton, J.B. and W.L. Loope. 1995. Buried soils in a perched dunefield as indicators of Late Holocene lake-level change in the Lake Superior basin. Quaternary Research 44:190–199.

Arbogast, A.F. 2000. Estimating the time since final stabilization of a perched dunefield along Lake Superior. Professional Geographer 52:594–606.

Arbogast, A.F. Schaetzl, R.J. Hupy, J.P. and E.C. Hansen. 2004. The Holland Paleosol: An informal pedostratigraphic unit in the coastal dunes of southeastern Lake Michigan. Canadian Journal of Earth Sciences 14:1385–1400.

Arbogast, A.F., Scull, P., Schaetzl, R.J., Harrison, J., Jameson, T.P. and S. Crozier. 1997. Concurrent stabilization of some interior dune fields in Michigan. Physical Geography 18:63–79.

Arbogast, A.F. and W.L. Loope. 1999. Maximum-limiting ages of Lake-Michigan coastal dunes: their correlation with Holocene lake level history. Journal of Great Lakes Research 29:372–382.

Arbogast, A.F. Hansen, E.C. and M.D. Van Oort. 2002a. Reconstructing the geomorphic evolution of large coastal dunes along the southeastern shore of Lake Michigan. Geomorphology 46: 241–255.

Arbogast, A.F. and S.G. Packman. 2004. Middle Holocene mobilization of aeolian sand in western upper Michigan and the probable relationship with climate and fire. The Holocene 14:464–471.

Arbogast, A.F. Wintle, A.G. and S.C. Packman. 2002b. Widespread middle Holocene dune formation in the eastern upper peninsula of Michigan and the relationship to climate outlet-controlled lake level. Geology 30:55–58.

Arbogast, A.F. Wintle, A.G. and S.C. Packman. 2003. Early Holocene mobilization of eolian sand in eastern lower Michigan. International Quaternary Association Bi-annual meeting, Reno, NV. Programs with Abstracts. p. 165.

Baedke, S.J., and T.A. Thompson. 2000. A 4,700 year record of lake level and isostasy for Lake Michigan. Journal of Great Lakes Research 26:416–426.

Bergquist, S.G. 1936. The Pleistocene history of the Tahquamenon and Manistique drainage region of the northern peninsula of Michigan. Annual Report of the Michigan Geological Survey Division, Department of Conservation for 1936.

Blewett, W.L. and H.A. Winters 1995. The importance of glaciofluvial features within Michigan's Port Huron moraine. Annals of the Association of American Geographers 85:306–319.

Booth, R.K. Jackson, S.T. and T.A. Thompson. 2002. Paleoecology of a northern Michigan lake and the relationship among climate, vegetation, and Great Lakes water levels. Quaternary Research 57:120–130.

Buckler, R.W. 1979. Dune Inventory and Barrier Dune Classification Study of Michigan's Lake Michigan shore. Michigan Dept. of Natural Resources, Geological. Survey Division Investigation 23. Lansing, MI.

Chrzastowski, M.J. and T.A. Thompson. 1992. Late Wisconsinan and Holocene coastal evolution of the southern shore of Lake Michigan. In: Quaternary Coasts of the United States: Marine and Lacustrine Systems, SEPM Special Publication 48:397–413.

Davis, M. Winkler, M.G. Flakne, R. Douglas, C. Calcote, R. and K.L. Cole. 2000. Holocene climate in the western Great Lakes National Parks and Lakeshores: Implications for future climate change. Conservation Biology14: 968–983.

Delcourt, P.A. Nester, P.L. Delcourt, H.R. Mora, C.I. and K.H. Roves. 2002. Holocene lake-effect precipitation in northern Michigan. Quaternary Research 57:225–233.

Dorr, J.A. Jr. and D.F. Eschman. 1970. Geology of Michigan. University of Michigan Press, Ann Arbor.

Dow, K.W. 1937. The origin of perched dunes on the Manistee moraine, Michigan. Michigan Academician 23:427–440.

Farrand, W.R. and D.L. Bell. 1982. Quaternary geology (map) of southern Michigan with surface water drainage divides. 1:500,000. Department of Geological Sciences, University of Michigan, Ann Arbor.

Fisher, T.G. and W.L. Loope. 2005. Aeolian sand preserved in Silver Lake: A reliable signal of Holocene high stands of Lake Michigan. The Holocene 15:1072–1078.

Hansen, E.C., Arbogast, A.F., Packman, S.C., and B. Hansen. 2003. Post-Nipissing origin of a backdune complex along the southeastern shore of Lake Michigan. Physical Geography 23:233–244.

Hesp, P.A. and B.G. Thom. 1990. Geomorphology and evolution of active transgressive dunefields. In: K. Nordstrom and N. Psuty (eds), Coastal Dunes: Form and Process. John Wiley and Sons, New York. pp. 253–288.

Hesp, P. 2002. Foredunes and blowouts: Initiation, geomorphology, and dynamics. Geomorphology 48:245–268.

Larsen, C.E. 1987. Geological History of Glacial Lake Algonquin and the Upper Great Lakes. U.S. Geological Survey Bulletin 1801. 34 pp.

Leverett, F. and F.B. Taylor. 1915. The Pleistocene of Indiana and Michigan and the history of the Great Lakes. U.S. Geological Survey Monograph 53. 529 pp.

Loope, W.L. and A.F. Arbogast. 2000. Dominance of a ~150-year cycle of sand-supply change in late Holocene dune building along the eastern shore of Lake Michigan. Quaternary Research 54:414–422.

Loope, W.L. Fisher, T.G. Jol, H.M. Goble, R.J. Anderton, J.B. and W. L. Blewett. 2004. A Holocene history of dune-mediated landscape change along the southeastern shore of Lake Superior. Geomorphology 61:303–322.

Michigan State Legislature. 1976. Sand Dune Protection and Management Act: Act No. 222, Public Acts of 1976. Lansing, MI.

Michigan State Legislature. 1994. Natural Resources and Environmental Protection Act, Parts 353 and 637: Act No. 451, Public Acts of 1994. Lansing, MI.

Murray, A.S. and A.G. Wintle. 2000. Luminescence dating of quartz using an improved single-aliquot regenerative-dose protocol. Radiation Measurements 32:57–73.

Olson, J.S. 1958a. Lake Michigan dune development 1: Wind velocity profiles. Journal of Geology 66:254–263.

Olson, J.S. 1958b. Lake Michigan dune development 2: Lake level, beach and dune oscillations. Journal of Geology 66:345–351.

Olson, J.S. 1958c. Lake Michigan dune development 3: Lake-level, beach, and dune oscillations. Journal of Geology 66:473–483.

Peterson, J.M. and E. Dersch. 1981. A guide to sand dune and coastal ecosystem functional relationships. Extension Bulletin E-1529, MICHU-SG-81-501. 18 pp.

Schaetzl, R.J., Drzyzga, S.A., Weisenborn, B.N., Kincare, K.A., Lepczyk, X.C., Shein, K.A., Dowd, C.M. and J. Linker. 2002. Measurement, correlation, and mapping of Glacial Lake Algonquin shorelines in northern Michigan. Annals of the Association of American Geographers 92:399–415.

Schaetzl, R.J. and B.N. Weisenborn. 2004. The Grayling Fingers geomorphic region of Michigan: Soils, sedimentology, stratigraphy and geomorphic development. Geomorphology 61:251–274.

Scott, I.D. 1942. The dunes of Lake Michigan and correlated problems. Michigan Academician 44: 53–61.

Snyder, F.S. 1985. A spatial and temporal analysis of the Sleeping Bear Dunes complex, Michigan. Ph.D. Dissertation, University of Pittsburgh, Pittsburgh.

Tague, G.C. 1946. The post-glacial geology of the Grand Marais Embayment, Berrien County, Michigan. Michigan Department of Conservation Publication 45, Geological Series 38 Part 1. 80 pp.

Thompson, T.A. and S.J. Baedke. 1997. Strand-plain evidence for late Holocene lake-level variations in Lake Michigan. Geological Society of America Bulletin 109:666–682.

Van Dijk, D. 2004. Contemporary geomorphic processes and change on Lake Michigan coastal dunes: an example from Hoffmaster State Park, Michigan. Michigan Academician 35:425–453.

Van Oort, M. Arbogast, A.F. Hansen, E.C. and B. Hansen. 2001. Geomorphological history of massive parabolic dunes, Van Buren State Park, Van Buren County, Michigan. Michigan Academician 33:175–188.

Further Readings

Ahlbrandt, T.S. and M.E. Brookfield (eds). 1983. Eolian Sediments and Processes. Elsevier Science, Amsterdam.

Albert, D.A. 2000. Borne of the Wind: An Introduction to the Ecology of Michigan Sand Dunes. Michigan Natural Features Inventory. Lansing, MI.

Bagnold, R. 1941. The Physics of Blown Sand and Desert Dunes. Dover Publications, Mineola, NY.

Nordstrom, K.F. Psuty, N. and B. Carters (eds). 1990. Coastal Dunes: Form and Process. John Wiley and Sons, New York.

Weather and Climate

Jeffrey A. Andresen and Julie A. Winkler

■ Introduction

Weather is defined as the short-term variations in the earth's atmosphere; climate refers to the slowly varying characteristics of the atmosphere over longer periods of time (American Meteorological Society 2000). The climate of a location reflects the complex interactions of atmospheric circulation with regional and local topography and land cover. This chapter introduces the primary circulation features and systems influencing Michigan's weather and climate, and describes the climate patterns across the state. In addition, past and potential future climate variability and change are examined.

■ Atmospheric circulation and Michigan's weather and climate

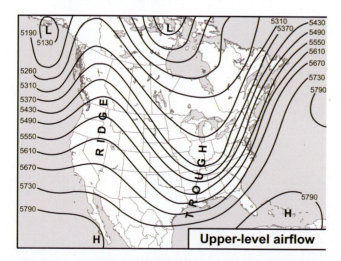

Upper-level airflow

FIGURE 19.1 Waves and airflow in the midlatitude westerlies. This map is for the 500 hectopascal (hPa) surface, meaning that everywhere on the map the air pressure is 500 hPa. The isolines give the height in meters of the 500 hPa pressure surface, above sea level. Note that the 500 hPa pressure surface is located closer to the earth's surface in the vicinity of a trough, and higher above the earth's surface in the vicinity of a ridge. After Lutgens and Tarbuck (2004).

Atmospheric circulation spans a range of spatial and temporal scales, all of which are important for understanding weather and climate. Systems that cover large portions of a hemisphere and persist for several weeks or even months, e.g., jet streams, are referred to as "macroscale" or "planetary" features (Orlanski 1975). Those systems that extend over only portions of a continent, and have a lifespan on the order of a week, are called "synoptic-scale" features. Features that are regional and local in scale, and persist for a few hours or even minutes, are known as "mesoscale" or "microscale" features.

Longwaves and jet streams

For all mid-latitude locations, including Michigan, the winds aloft generally blow from west to east, in a wavy pattern. The westerly flow is the result of the hemispheric temperature gradient (warm at the equator and cold at the poles), and the deflection of airflow due to the Coriolis Effect (Rossby 1939). Atmospheric waves are a series of ridges (crests) and troughs (valleys) (Fig. 19.1). Ridges represent tall, warmer columns of air, whereas troughs represent shorter, colder air columns. Atmospheric waves transport warm air poleward and cold air equatorward (Peixoto and Oort 2002).

Longwaves in upper-air flow, also called planetary waves, are slow moving macroscale features (American Meteorological Society 2000). Longwave troughs typically form downstream of large mountain ranges, such as the Rockies (Holton 1992). In winter, longwave troughs can also form over the cold eastern portion of continents (Holton 1992), whereas in summer, longwave ridges are often found over warm continental interiors. In addition, the formation of longwaves is related to atmospheric teleconnections (see FOCUS BOX below).

The location and strength of longwaves help explain the variability in Michigan's weather at weekly to seasonal scales. For example, if Michigan is located to the east of a longwave trough axis, upper-level winds are generally southwesterly and warm. On the other hand, cold conditions are likely when Michigan is located east of a ridge axis, in an area of northwesterly airflow. An extended warm period of several weeks can be replaced in a matter of a few days with a cold spell (or vice versa), simply by a rearrangement of the longwaves across the Northern Hemisphere.

Currents of faster moving air, known as jet streams, are often observed within the upper-level westerly airflow. The jet stream of most importance to Michigan is known as the "polar front" jet stream. In summer, as the North American continent warms, this jet stream moves northward and is positioned close to Michigan (Fig. 19.2). In winter, the jet is located south of Michigan, in the area of greatest temperature contrast. The jet stream is generally weaker in summer compared to winter, as the temperature differences across North America are relatively small in summer.

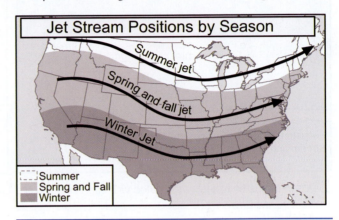

FIGURE 19.2   Mean positions of the polar front jet stream over the United States, by season. After Oliver and Hidore (2002).

FOCUS BOX: Atmospheric teleconnections and long-range forecasting

Atmospheric teleconnections are linkages between weather conditions in distant regions of the globe (American Meteorological Society 2000). Teleconnection patterns partially explain the interannual variability in the location and strength of atmospheric longwaves and jet streams. Perhaps the best known atmospheric teleconnection is ENSO (El Niño/Southern Oscillation), often is simply referred to as El Niño. During ENSO warm phase, i.e., El Niño, warm sea surface temperatures are found over the eastern Pacific, and surface air pressures are higher than normal in the western Pacific and lower than normal in the eastern Pacific (McPhaden et al. 2006). During ENSO cold phase, i.e., La Niña, colder than normal sea surface temperatures are found in the eastern Pacific, and surface pressure anomalies are reversed.

These temperature and pressure anomalies can cause downstream changes in longwave and jet stream patterns. During the winter when an El Niño is occurring, the jet stream is usually strongest over the south-

ern US (see Figure on following page). The northern US, including Michigan, experiences weaker winds aloft, fewer storms and warmer than average conditions, although the strength of the signal is weaker for Michigan compared to locations farther west. Wintertime airflow during La Niña events is more "wavy" than usual, producing colder and wetter conditions over the western US, warmer and drier than average conditions over the southern US, and wetter than average conditions in the Ohio Valley (Climate Prediction Center 2005a). In Michigan, little systematic deviation of temperature and precipitation from normal is observed during La Niña events. These general patterns need to be interpreted cautiously, however, as the strength, onset and duration of ENSO events vary substantially from one event to the next.

Many other teleconnection patterns also exist. One that has some significance for Michigan is called the North Atlantic Oscillation (NAO). A positive NAO phase represents a deeper than normal low pressure system over

Iceland and a stronger high pressure system near the Azores; these systems are weaker than normal during a negative NAO phase (Rogers 1984). Michigan tends to have above average temperatures in winter and spring during the positive NAO phase, although again the signal is not particularly strong (Climate Prediction Center 2005b).

Teleconnection patterns are an important consideration for long range forecasts (several weeks to a year or more). The relatively weak association between Michigan's weather and important teleconnection patterns, such as ENSO and NAO, make long range forecasting for Michigan challenging.

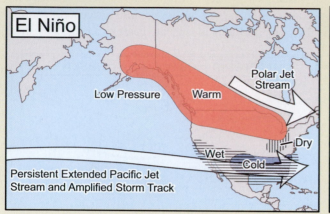
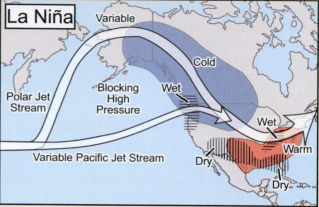

Weather anomalies typically associated with strong El Nino and La Nina events. After Climate Prediction Center (2005a).

Airflow source regions

The locations of longwaves and jet streams influence the sources of the air that reaches Michigan. Michigan's variable weather is a reflection of four primary, but very different, airflow source regions: (1) northwestern Canada, (2) Gulf of Mexico/southern US, (3) Hudson Bay/northeastern Canada and (4) northern Rockies/Pacific Northwest (Shadbolt et al. 2006). Less frequently, airflow originates from the East Coast and western Atlantic, and on occasion from the southwestern US and northern Mexico.

The relative importance of the different airflow source regions varies with season (Fig. 19.3). In winter, a longwave ridge is typically present over western North America (Lahey et al. 1958), and as a result, airflow reaching Michigan primarily originates from northwestern Canada, bringing cold air into the state. Not all winter days are dominated by cold, Canadian air, however. Michigan experiences milder wintertime temperatures when the airflow originates from the northern Rockies/Pacific Northwest, or from the Gulf of Mexico/southern US source regions. In spring, the western longwave ridge weakens (Lahey et al. 1958), and airflow from northwestern Canada is less frequent. The two, principal, springtime airflow source regions are Hudson Bay/northeastern Canada and Gulf of Mexico/southern US. The former source region is active when a longwave ridge forms over central Canada, whereas the Gulf of Mexico/southern US region is active when a upper-level trough is located over the western or central US, and/or when a longwave ridge is located over the eastern states. These source regions are also important in summer, although summertime airflow is more frequently from the Gulf of Mexico/Southern US; the opposite is true in spring. The frequent flow of cool, dry air from Hudson Bay, northeastern Canada is one of the reasons that the freeze hazard in Michigan can often extend into late spring and early summer. Airflow from this region also is responsible for refreshing, relatively cool, summer days. On the other hand, airflow originating from the Gulf of Mexico/southern US is warm and humid, and can contribute to uncomfortable, muggy summer days and thunderstorms. In fall, a longwave ridge begins to reform over western North America (Lahey et al. 1958), causing airflow from the northwestern Canada source region to once again increase in frequency. The Hudson Bay/northeastern Canada and Gulf of Mexico/southern US source regions are also active in fall.

Shortwaves, anticyclones, and cyclones

Synoptic-scale features, including atmospheric shortwaves, surface anticyclones and surface cyclones, are also important for understanding the day-to-day variability in Michigan's weather. Atmospheric shortwaves have wavelengths of ~1500 km, and are fast-moving, traversing the US in only a few days (Holton 1992). Shortwaves and longwaves

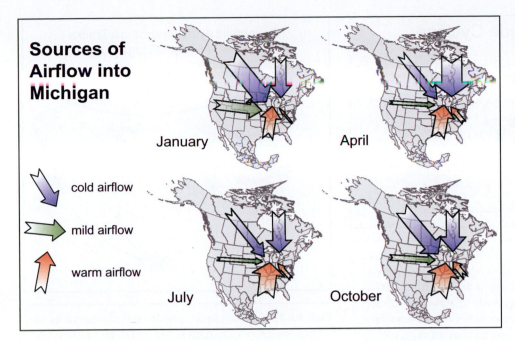

Sources of Airflow into Michigan

January

April

cold airflow

mild airflow

warm airflow

July

October

FIGURE 19.3 Airflow source regions for Michigan, by season. The size of the arrows indicates the relative frequency of airflow from the different source regions. After Shadbolt et al. (2006).

are interrelated, as shortwaves move through the long-wave pattern and are, in essence, "steered" by the long-waves. Shortwaves are important because they provide the necessary rising and sinking motion for the formation of surface pressure systems (Fig. 19.4). Low pressure systems, or cyclones, form east of the axis of a shortwave trough, in an area of rising motion (Carlson 1991). On the other hand, high pressure systems, or anticyclones, are usually found to the east of a ridge axis, in an area of sinking motion.

Anticyclones, also known as high pressure cells, rotate in a clockwise direction in the Northern Hemisphere, and are usually composed of a single, relatively uniform, air mass. Because of the generally sinking motion associated with anticyclones, they often bring clear to partly cloudy conditions and weak winds. Many of the anticyclones that affect Michigan initially form in Canada, and are associated with cooler than normal temperatures (Klein 1957, Zishka and Smith 1980).

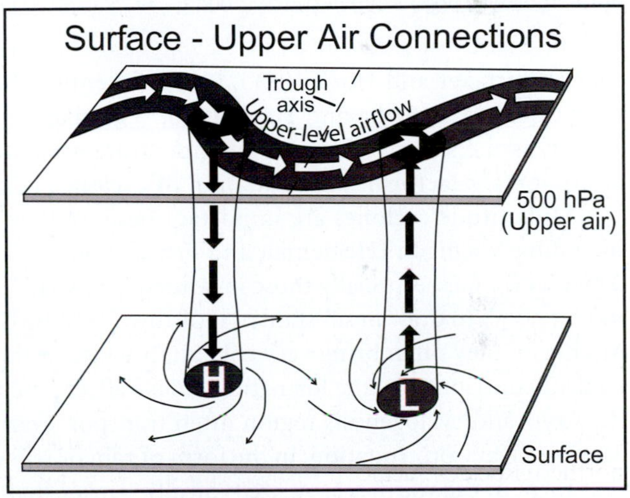

Midlatitude cyclones, or low pressure cells, are

Surface - Upper Air Connections

Trough axis

Upper-level airflow

500 hPa (Upper air)

H

L

Surface

FIGURE 19.4 Relationships between surface high and low pressure systems, rising and sinking motion, and shortwave troughs and ridges. After Aguado and Burt (2004).

more complex. They rotate counterclockwise in the Northern Hemisphere, and are composed of two or more air masses with different temperature and humidity characteristics (Fig. 19.5). The transition zones between these air masses are called "fronts" (Bjerknes and Solberg 1922). Lifting of air parcels along frontal boundaries often produces clouds and precipitation.

Although cyclones can form anywhere, there are several principal areas of cyclogenesis in North America (Whittaker and Horn 1981). Of particular importance for Michigan are the Alberta and Colorado cyclogenesis regions (Fig. 19.6). Both areas are located on the leeward (downwind) side of the Rocky Mountains, where stretching of air columns, due to the sloping topography, causes the air to become unstable (Holton 1992). Cyclogenesis is enhanced when a shortwave trough is present and the jet stream is strong (Hovanec and Horn 1975, Carlson 1991). Consequently, the Colorado cyclogenesis region is most active during the cold season (Hovanec and Horn 1975, Whittaker and Horn 1981), when the polar front jet tends to be located over the southern and central US (see FOCUS BOX below). The Alberta cyclogenesis region is active throughout the

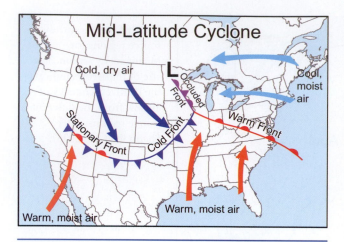

FIGURE 19.5 Idealized structure of a midlatitude cyclone. Along the warm front, warm air is advancing into regions previously occupied by cooler air. At the cold front, colder air is advancing into areas previously occupied by warmer air. The occluded front marks a complex frontal boundary, with cold air near the surface and warmer air aloft; it often forms when cyclones have reached a mature stage of development. After Lutgens and Tarbuck (2004).

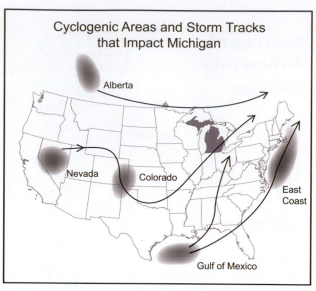

FIGURE 19.6 Cyclogenesis regions and storms tracks for surface low pressure systems in the central and eastern US. After Trewartha and Horn (1980).

year (Whittaker and Horn 1981). Less frequently, Michigan experiences cyclones that form along the western Gulf Coast (Trewartha and Horn 1980, Whittaker and Horn 1981). This cyclogenesis region is only active in winter, as the strong wintertime temperature gradient between the continental US and the Gulf of Mexico is an important factor in the formation of cyclones in this area.

Midlatitude cyclones are important because they produce over half of the precipitation in the eastern US, including Michigan (Heideman and Fritsch 1988). Much of this precipitation occurs along frontal boundaries. Alberta cyclones, especially those in winter, are usually associated with only light precipitation. These storms track too far north to draw in substantial moisture from the Gulf of Mexico. As wintertime Alberta cyclones pass through Michigan, they often bring very cold air, because of the northerly surface airflow west of the cyclone center. This cold air contributes to the formation of lake effect precipitation (see below). In contrast, cyclones originating from the Colorado cyclogenesis region often transport warm air and copious amounts of moisture from the Gulf of Mexico. Heavy precipitation, in the form of rain or snow, is fairly common with these storms. Midlatitude cyclones that form in the warm season are typically weaker than those that form in the cool season, because of the smaller temperature contrast, and the weaker jet stream. This does not mean, however, that warm season cyclones do not produce significant weather. These systems tap into abundant heat and moisture, which makes the air unstable, and as a result strong thunderstorms and heavy precipitation are frequently associated with them.

FOCUS BOX: A strong midlatitude cyclone: The "*Edmund Fitzgerald* storm"

The fate of the ore freighter *Edmund Fitzgerald* is immortalized in the 1976 folk song, "The Wreck of the Edmund Fitzgerald," by Gordon Lightfoot. As the song's lyrics "the gales of November" suggest, strong midlatitude cyclones are frequent in northern Michigan in late autumn. These storms typically form in or near the "Colorado" cyclogenesis region, when the temperature contrast across the central and southern US is large. They are steered northeasterly, toward Michigan, by southwesterly upper-level winds in the eastern arm of a longwave trough. The storms are closely linked to a shortwave trough, which provides the necessary rising motion for the storms to intensify. The relatively warm waters of the Great Lakes also contribute to the strength of these storms.

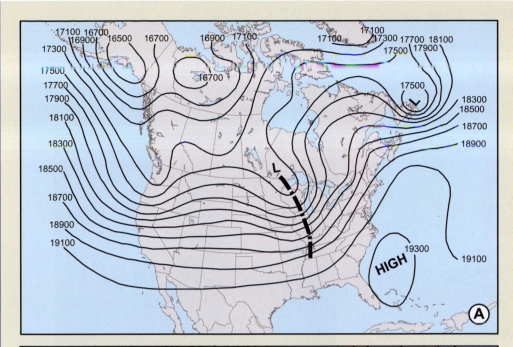

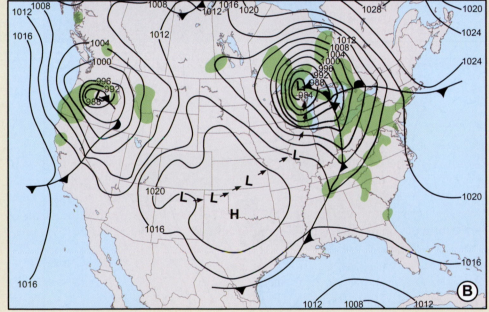

National Weather Service weather maps for November 10, 1975. After NOAA (2007). A. The 500 hPa map. This upper-level map shows the shortwave trough (indicated by a dashed line) over the Great Lakes region. The trough supported the development of the *Edmund Fitzgerald* storm. The surface low pressure system is located to the east the trough axis. B. The surface weather map. The lines on the map are isobars—lines of equal pressure. Wind speeds are large where isobars are closely packed together. The series of "L's" connected by arrows depict the track of the low pressure system. Green-shaded areas were experiencing precipitation.

The midlatitude cyclone responsible for the tragic sinking of the *Edmund Fitzgerald* in Lake Superior is a classic example of one of these fall storms. The storm originated on November 8, 1975 in northern New Mexico (see Figure above). By November 9, the storm was located in central Kansas. Over the next 36 hours, it intensified, as it moved northeasterly, toward James Bay, Canada. As the storm moved over Lake Superior, the winds over the lake switched direction from northeasterly to north-westerly (keep in mind the cyclonic circulation around low pressure systems) and strengthened. Wind speeds in excess of 50 knots were recorded in the eastern portion of Lake Superior. The *Edmund Fitzgerald* sank on the evening of November 10, off Whitefish Point, Michigan. The reasons for the sinking are still not fully known, but at the time the freighter sank, wave heights in eastern Lake Superior were as high as 5 m (National Weather Service Marquette, MI Forecast Office 2005).

FOCUS BOX: Why didn't it snow?

Local meteorologists forecasted five inches of snow overnight, but the total accumulation in the morning was only an inch. What happened? Give the meteorologists a break! Forecasting the location and amount of heavy snow is extremely challenging. One reason that snowfall forecasts fail is that the heaviest snowfall generally occurs in a very narrow band, to the NW of a surface low pressure system (Goree and Younkin 1966; see Figure below).

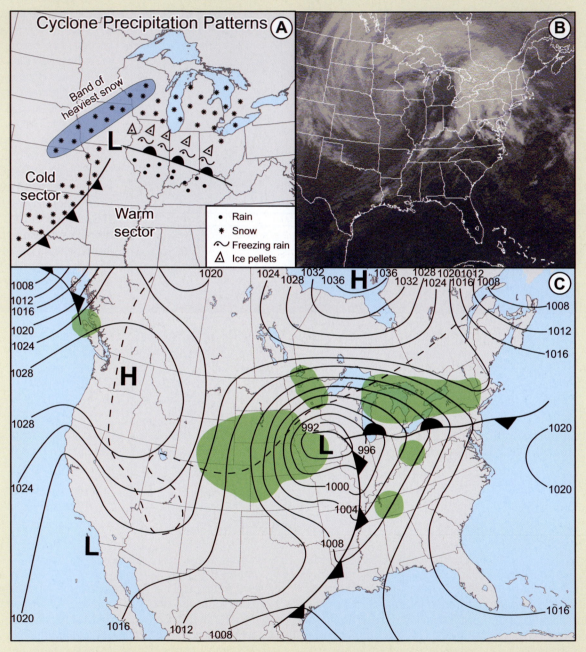

Typical precipitation patterns associated with a cool season midlatitude cyclones, especially those that originate from the Colorado cyclogenesis region. A. Generalized Low pressure system, and its wintertime precipitation pattern. After Grenci and Nese (2001). B. Satellite image (visible light) of the weather of the morning of April 11, 2008, during which a surface Low pressure system with a well-defined dry slot was present in the Midwest. Lansing received no precipitation from this storm, as it was in the dry slot. C. Surface weather map from two hours previous, April 11, 2008.

A slight shift in the track of the storm means that this narrow area of heaviest snowfall will be displaced from where it was originally forecasted.

Another complication in weather forecasting is the development of a "dry slot." Midlatitude cyclones are composed of three-dimensional airstreams that tilt either upwards or downwards with height (Carlson 1980, Bierly and Winkler 2001). The airstreams are especially well developed when cyclones are at a mature stage of development, which is often the case by the time they reach Michigan. The "comma-shaped" cloud patterns seen on satellite images (see Figure) are a reflection of these airstreams. The "dry stream" descends from higher elevations and flows toward the center of the low pressure system from the south and SW; it can be seen as a dark, usually cloudless, area, on the satellite image below, known as the dry slot. Precipitation decreases as the dry slot forms and expands toward the cyclone center. It probably snowed a lot less than predicted if your area "got dry slotted!"

Mesoscale convective systems

Mesoscale circulation features also influence Michigan's weather and climate. One such feature is a "mesoscale convective system" (MCS)—an organized complex of thunderstorms (American Meteorological Society 2000). The lifetime of a MCS is longer than that of the thunderstorms that comprise the complex itself (Houze 1993), and MCSs typically persist for several hours or longer. The causes of MCSs are complex, but include topography, shortwave troughs, frontal boundaries, and the interaction of individual thunderstorms (Houze 1993). Although MCSs are more frequent in the central US, they are, nonetheless, a common feature in Michigan, where they are estimated to produce ~10% of the warm season precipitation (Fritsch et al. 1986). In addition, the strong updrafts and downdrafts within MCSs can produce high winds, tornadoes, hail, lightning and heavy precipitation/flash flooding.

Influence of the Great Lakes

Michigan's proximity to the Great Lakes has a profound influence on its weather and climate (Scott and Huff 1996). Overall, these "lake effect" influences result in a cloudier, wetter and more moderate climate, than in areas less influenced by the lakes. Lake effect influences are related to three major physical differences between water and nearby land surfaces:

1. *Changes in friction/surface drag* As winds pass across the open waters of the lake, onto the downwind lakeshore land surface, friction increases. As a result, the winds slow down and (potentially) some vertical lifting motion is initiated, which can lead to the formation of clouds and precipitation downwind of the lakes.

2. *Changes in heat content* The amount of heat needed to increase the temperature of liquid water is at least four times greater than that needed to heat up adjacent soil surfaces. This results in a significant differences in the Great lakes' water temperatures vs that of the air that passes over, as well that of as nearby land surfaces (Chapters 38, 39). Maximum and minimum water temperatures are so delayed that, each year, they typically peak approximately 4–6 weeks after air temperatures do (Eichenlaub et al. 1990). For example, maximum surface water temperatures generally occur in late August or September, and minima in March.

3. *Changes in moisture content* As winds pass across the open water of the Great Lakes, changes in the air's humidity may take place. If the air is relatively colder than the water, e.g. in fall and winter, rapid evaporation from the relatively warmer water may markedly increases the humidity of the air. If the air is warmer than the water, e.g. in spring and summer, some condensation of water vapor may take place near the cooler water surface, possibly resulting in fog, and ultimately to a loss of atmospheric water vapor into the lakes.

It is important to note that these modifications typically act in combination. For example, relatively cold, dry air passing across the warmer lakes in the fall or early winter typically picks up both heat and water vapor, which in turn lead to atmospheric instability, clouds and precipitation in downwind areas. As the modified air reaches the shoreline, downwind, the increased friction with the land surface causes localized convergence, further enhancing atmospheric instability and cloudiness (Fig. 19.7).

FIGURE 19.7 Conceptual diagram of influence of the Great Lakes on weather and precipitation, especially snowfall.

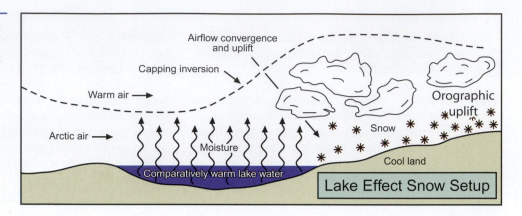

Air modification, resulting from the proximity of the lakes, tends to be greatest in downwind areas. The Great Lakes lie within the Northern Hemisphere's band of westerly winds, which results in dominant west-to-east winds in the region. There are seasonal variations; during the warm season, mean winds tend to be relatively weaker and move from the SW, while during the winter, they tend to stronger and more northwesterly. Collectively, however, these patterns lead to most significant lake effect influences downwind of Lakes Superior and Michigan in western and northern sections of the Lower Peninsula and the Upper Peninsula, especially during the cold season.

Michigan's weather and climate are influenced by lake effect in many ways, and across large areas. Arguably, the spatially most widespread impact is on cloudiness, which in turn directly impacts insolation (incoming solar radiation) rates and air temperatures. Clouds associated with the lake effect are typically of the stratocumulus or cumulus variety, form within 10–40 km of the upwind lakeshore (Kristovich and Laird 1998), and flow in bands or streams parallel to winds just above ground surface (Fig. 19.8). Because Michigan's source regions for relatively cold, continental air masses are in the interior sections of northern North America and the Arctic (Fig. 19.3), a majority of lake-related cloudiness is associated with northwesterly winds during fall and winter. Enhanced cloudiness results in mean daily insolation rates in Michigan and across much of the Great Lakes Region that are <75% of rates in areas upwind of the lakes, ranking the region statistically among the cloudiest areas in the US. In December, when passage of cold air across the relatively warm lakes is most common, the impact and spatial pattern are even more striking, with mean insolation rates in some cases <50% of rates just outside the region (NREL 2004). During the late spring and summer seasons, when lake water temperatures are relatively cooler than air and adjacent land surfaces, the impact on cloudiness is symmetrically the opposite, as the cooler water leads to relatively greater atmospheric stability, general low-level sinking motion, and fewer clouds over and immediately downwind of the lakes. Overall, however, reductions in warm season cloudiness are more than offset by enhanced cloudiness of the late fall and winter season (Changnon and Jones 1972).

Air temperatures in Michigan are directly impacted by the direct moderating effects of air flow across the Great Lakes, with cooler temperatures in downwind areas during spring and summer, and warmer temperatures during fall and winter. Combined with the enhanced cloudiness, daily and annual temperature ranges are also reduced downwind. For example, Changnon and Jones (1972) estimated that mean winter maximum and minimum temperatures in areas just east of the lakes are 6% and 15%, respectively, warmer than locations upwind of the lakes, while mean summer maximum and minimum temperatures on the downwind side are 3% and 2% lower than those upwind, respectively. Extreme minimum temperatures in areas within 20 km of the shores of the Great Lakes are as much as 11°C warmer than those at inland locations at the same latitude, a condition that is especially beneficial to the fruit industry (Chapter 38). The impact is somewhat less in the summer season, with extreme maximum temperatures in coastal areas being as much as 8°C cooler than those at inland locations (Eichenlaub et al. 1990).

Given enough atmospheric lift and moisture, lake effect clouds may produce precipitation. Altered precipitation patterns are among the most significant lake influences on regional climate. Lake effect snowfall greatly enhances the seasonal snowfall totals of areas generally within 100 km downwind of the lakeshore (Norton and Bolsenga 1993). Braham and Dungey (1984) estimated that 25–50% of the yearly snowfall on the eastern shores

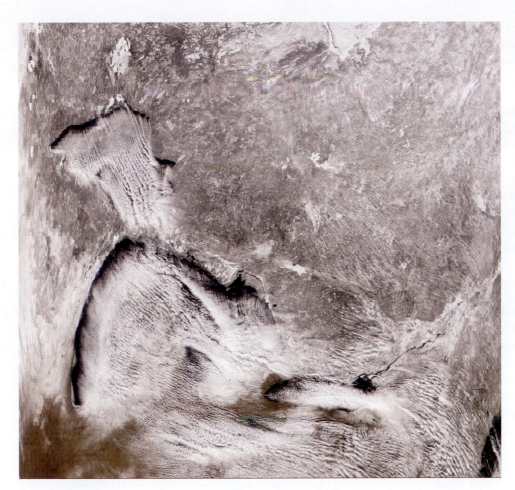

FIGURE 19.8   Satellite image (visible light) of a major lake effect outbreak on January 20, 2008. Note the strong lake effect cloud "banding" pattern, downwind from the open waters of the Great Lakes, and the lack of lake effect clouds downwind of the frozen Lake Nipigon, Ontario. Photo courtesy of the Aqua Modis program: http://rapidfire.sci.gsfc.nasa.gov/

of Lake Michigan could be attributed to lake effect. A more general increase of 25–30% for downwind areas of the region was noted by Changnon and Jones (1972). Meteorological conditions associated with lake effect snowfall events include (1) a difference in temperature between the lake surface and air at the 850 mb level $\geq 13°C$, (2) an inversion layer (temperatures increasing with height) at least 1000 m above the surface, (3) a wind fetch of ≥ 80 km over open water, (4) geostrophic wind speeds >5 m/s, and (5) rising surface pressure (Rothrock 1969; Fig. 19.7).

Lake effect snowfall typically occurs as one of four major types: (1) broad areas of parallel bands (Fig. 19.8), (2) shoreline bands, with a line of convection roughly parallel to the lee shore, (3) singular midlake bands, with convergence centered over the lake, and (4) mesoscale cyclonic disturbances moving across the lakes (Hjelmfelt 1990). Of these types, the parallel bands are the most common in Michigan (Fig. 19.8), accounting for as much as half of the total events (Kelly 1986). One precipitation type often associated with lake effect precipitation is soft hail or graupel, which is a result of the specialized cloud environments found in compact and intense convection. While typically less than a few mm in diameter and non-destructive, soft hail has traditionally been counted as regular "hail," which misleadingly increases the overall frequency of hail in areas downwind of the lakes (Changnon 2002). Finally, it is important to note that the presence of the lakes also acts to suppress convection and precipitation during spring and summer, when the lakes are relatively cooler than the air above. Changnon and Jones (1972) found precipitation decreases of 20–30% over the eastern half of Lake Michigan, when compared with upwind areas.

Physical differences between lake water and adjacent land surface temperatures frequently result in the formation of localized winds. During the spring and summer, when lake temperatures are relatively cool and regional winds are weaker, solar heating of adjacent land areas during daytime hours leads to the relative upward motion of the atmosphere over the land, and the establishment of a local circulation setup, with surface winds turning from the lake towards the land. These cool, "lake breezes" may move as far as 65 km inland, but usually remain within 20 km of the shoreline (Estoque and Gross 1981). In the fall and winter seasons, or during nighttime hours, when the water/land temperature pattern is opposite that of the warm season, a reverse air flow pattern is possible. Then, "land breezes" blow from the lakeshore out, onto the lake.

The combined impacts of temperature differences between land and lake surfaces also influences evapotranspiration—evaporation from water and land surfaces. Winter evapotranspiration values in areas downwind of the lakes are 15–50% greater than in upwind locations (Changnon and Jones 1972). Free water evaporation rates on the lakes are estimated to range from approximately 500 mm/yr over Lake Superior, to 900 mm/yr over Lake Erie (Richards and Irbe 1969). With relatively high evaporation rates on the lakes, dew point temperatures and humidity values on the adjoining land mass tend to be greater, especially on the eastern shores. On a larger spatial scale, Bates et al. (1993) simulated the hydrology of the Great Lakes region with a regional climate model during a 10-day early winter period in 1985–1986. They concluded that approximately 60% of the evaporation from the lakes was recycled, in the form of precipitation, and that the lakes contributed 23% of the water in the Great Lakes' basin's precipitation. Meteorologically, the collective addition of moisture and heat from the Great Lakes has also been shown to increase the strength of weak low pressure systems moving across the region (Sousounis and Fritsch 1994).

Influence of microclimate

Microclimate refers to weather conditions averaged over time for spatial scales of <1000 m, which includes agricultural fields, woodlots, residential neighborhoods and similar settings. The endless combinations of environmental characteristics such as topography, plant canopy structure, and soil type in a particular area may result in a large variety unique microclimatic conditions. The most important physical factors determining the extent of the microclimatic influence are aspect (direction with respect to the sun), topography and soil and surface cover. Each of these factors may influence the rates of energy transfer at the surface, which may in turn control localized rates of heating, cooling, evapotranspiration, etc.

During daylight hours, differences in the absorption of incident solar radiation and its dissipation may lead to significant differences in surface or near-surface air temperatures at microclimatic scales. Reflectivities of natural surfaces generally range from <10% for some water bodies, to 10–25% for most vegetation, to as high as 95% for fresh snow, which results in a wide range of potential rates of heating. In addition, the more direct the angle of the sun on the surface, the greater the potential rate of heating. Thus, south-facing slopes tend to be warmer during daylight hours than north-facing slopes, sometimes by several degrees or more (Andresen et al. 2001).

Besides differential rates of heating of a particular surface, one must also consider the rates of heat dissipation and the amount of water present on or near the surface. A potentially large fraction of the daytime net radiation available above a surface may be consumed in evapotranspiration. Thus, well-watered, vegetation-covered surfaces tend to be relatively cooler than bare, dry surfaces. Soil type is also an important consideration, with coarse-textured soils with lower water-holding capacities generally warmer than moister, fine-textured soils. It is not coincidental that the all-time extreme maximum temperature recorded in Michigan (112°F at Mio, on July 13, 1936) occurred above a sandy soil, following an extended drought. Finally, the presence of wind above a surface acts to move or advect heat energy to or from the surface. Surfaces exposed to the prevailing winds are thus somewhat cooler during the daytime than sheltered surfaces.

During twilight or nighttime hours, without incoming solar radiation and under mostly clear skies and light winds, the ground surface will cool, as it emits longwave radiation back to the atmosphere. Because air itself is an effective thermal insulator, the surface and any vegetation quickly become cooler than the air above it. The surface cooling results in the formation of a surface inversion layer, in which air temperatures increase with height, i.e., are coolest at the surface. The inversion layer may slowly grow in thickness during the nighttime hours. When inversions like this occur, ground surface temperatures may be several degrees cooler than air that is 1–2 m above the surface. For this reason, frost is commonly observed on the ground, while the official observation temperature, taken 1.5 m above the ground surface, remains a few degrees above freezing. Within the inversion layer, atmospheric stability is strong so that any movement of the air (wind) is typically weak.

Since cool air is denser than warm air, the air cooled near the surface may flow downhill like a liquid, due to the force of gravity—movement of air known as cold air drainage (Chapter 38). Drainage of cold air beneath an inversion creates pronounced microclimates as it quickly leaves some areas and pools in others, potentially leading to temperature differences of several degrees in only a short horizontal distance. Topography is, therefore, strongly linked to patterns of cold air drainage. Hilltops, ridges, hillsides, and other topographical features, where relatively cooler air can drain away, are likely to experience relatively milder minimum nighttime temperatures. In contrast, low-lying areas, especially depressions where cold air can literally collect or pond, typically experience lower minimum temperatures (Chapters 38, 39).

Soil type and moisture also affect how easily frost forms. One factor influencing the rate at which the ground surface cools is the movement of heat energy upwards, out of the soil profile, termed "ground heat flux." The greater this upwards flux is during the nighttime, the less the rate of surface cooling. In Michigan, observable effects of microclimate are found most frequently in western sections of Lower Michigan and across the Upper Peninsula where hilly topography, e.g., deep canyons or ravines, immediate proximity to large lakes, and highly variable soil types and vegetation occur (Hunckler and Schaetzl 1997).

■ Michigan's current climate

Michigan's "normal" climate, based on international agreement, is defined as weather conditions averaged over three consecutive decades, i.e., a 30 year period (WMO 1989). Some climate normals for Michigan, based on the 1971–2000 period, are given in Figure 19.9. Mean January temperatures in Michigan generally decrease from south to north as expected, but there are also important west to east patterns, resulting from the proximity of the Great Lakes and prevailing winds, especially in winter when coldest overall temperatures tend to be observed in interior areas of the northern Lower and Upper Peninsulas, far from the lakeshore. A somewhat similar, but less amplified, pattern is noticeable in July, when warmest mean temperatures are found in southeastern sections of the Lower Peninsula, due to the relatively lower frequency of wind flow across the cooler lakes, and to the warmer, developed land cover surface associated with the Detroit metro area.

Total annual precipitation generally increases from minimum values just under 740 mm/yr in the northeastern Lower Peninsula (climatologically the driest region in the US, east of the Mississippi River) to maximum levels of 950 mm/yr or more in the southwestern Lower Peninsula (Fig. 19.9).

Total annual snowfall in the state is highly variable, but generally increases from minimum values of about 90 cm/yr in the extreme southeastern Lower Peninsula, to maximum values in the northwestern Lower and northern Upper Peninsulas, where annual mean totals in some locations are >550 cm (Fig. 19.9). Seasonal snowfall totals and seasonal duration of snow cover in the Upper Peninsula are climatologically among the greatest of any location in the US east of the Rocky Mountains. In these major snowbelt areas, e.g., highland areas of the interior northern Lower Peninsula, a major portion of the snowfall is associated with lake effect processes (Changnon and Jones 1972, Norton and Bolsenga 1993), while over the remainder of the state, the majority of snowfall is due to midlatitude cyclones moving through the region. Snowfall in some of the snowbelt areas is given an additional boost from topography, e.g., the elevation difference between the spine of the Keweenaw Peninsula and the surface of Lake Superior is over 300 m (Hjelmfelt 1992; Fig. 19.7). A minor snowfall maximum in the eastern sections of the Thumb is associated with cold, northerly or northeasterly winds, which bring lake effect snow off of Lake Huron. Finally, a connection between total annual precipitation and snowfall is somewhat evident, with the additional lake effect snowfall in western and northern sections of the state during the winter resulting in relatively higher annual precipitation totals in those sections of the state.

Annual patterns

As noted earlier in this chapter, annual weather and climate cycles in Michigan are linked directly to changes in the location of the jet stream, which in turn are linked to the annual cycle of solar insolation (incoming solar radiation). Climatologically, the solar insolation cycle in Michigan is closely related to the seasons, with some modifications associated with lake effect cloudiness. Solar insolation values tend reach maximum levels in late June, with annual minimum values occurring from late December into early January.

Air temperatures during the year tend to lag behind the solar insolation cycle by several weeks. Mean daily and extreme daily temperatures at six locations across the state for the 1971–2000 period are given in Figure 19.10. The daily temperature series shown in Figure 19.10 all follow a roughly sinusoidal annual pattern, typical of all midlatitude locations. The range of mean temperatures between warmest areas of the state (in the southern Lower

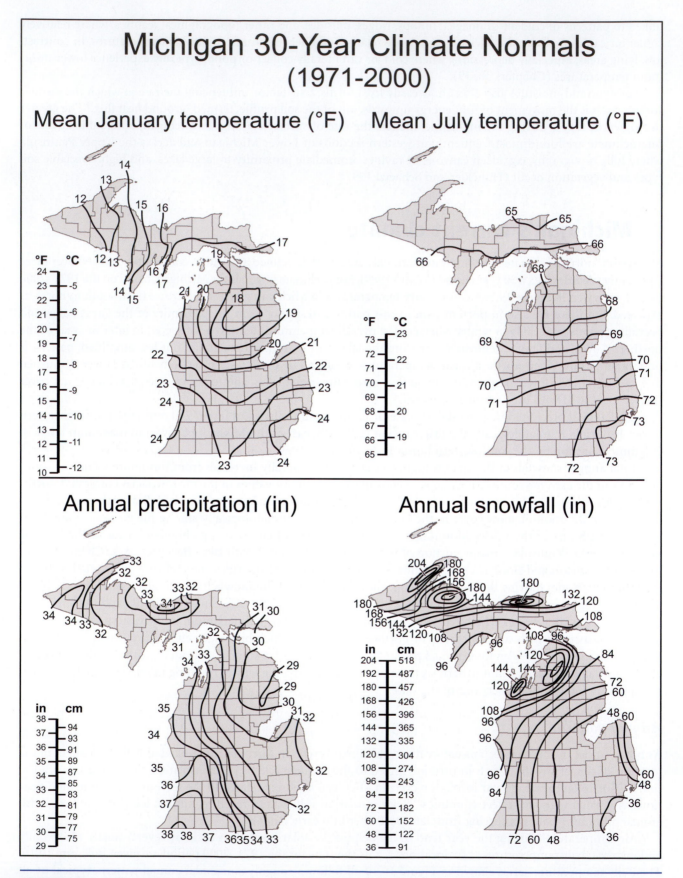

FIGURE 19.9   Mapped climatic data for Michigan, for the period 1971–2000. Mean air temperatures in (A) January and (B) July. Mean annual (C) precipitation and (D) seasonal snowfall. Source: Michigan State Climatologist's Office, East Lansing.

Mean Daily Temperatures: 1971 - 2000

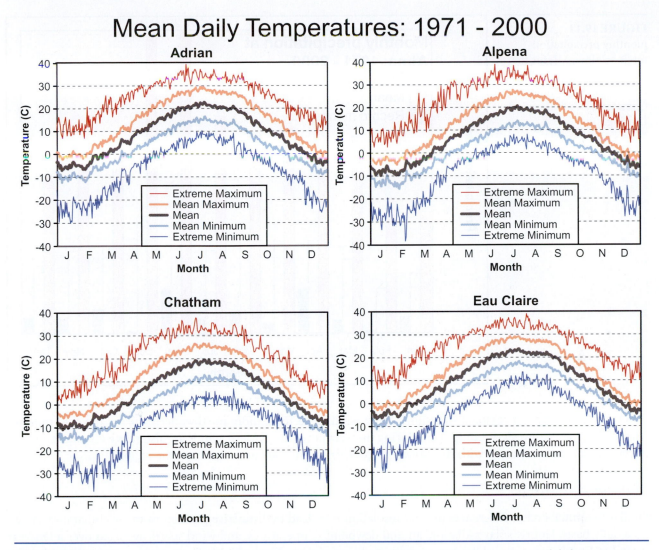

FIGURE 19.10   Climographs showing the average maximum, mean, and minimum daily temperatures, and daily temperature extremes, at four locations in Michigan, for the period 1971–2000. Source: Michigan State Climatologist's Office, East Lansing.

Peninsula: Eau Claire and Adrian) and the cooler Upper Peninsula (Chatham) tends to increase from approximately 5°C during the mid-summer to about 8°C during the winter. Mean and extreme temperatures reach annual maxima during the last two weeks of July, into the first week of August. Annual minima tend to occur during the last half of January, into the first week of February. Minimum temperatures tend to more variable over time than maximum temperatures. This variability is due to relatively greater frequency and influence of microclimate effects, e.g., radiational cooling under clear, calm conditions, during the early morning hours in which the minimum temperatures tend to occur. Daily temperatures also tend to be most variable during the winter months, with the least variability during the summer.

Although precipitation occurs relatively evenly during the year across Michigan, the highest monthly totals tend to occur during the summer or early fall months, while the driest month over nearly all of the state is February (Fig. 19.11). Completely dry months have occurred in the state, but are rare. This overall, annual precipitation pattern is the result of warmer temperatures, higher specific humidity values (the "raw material" of precipitation), and more frequent, synoptic-scale flow of low-level atmospheric moisture northward, from the Gulf of Mexico, during the summer months.

Wind speeds in Michigan also follow a seasonal pattern, with highest mean wind speeds occurring during the winter, closely followed by the fall and spring seasons. Overall, the mean wind direction in Michigan is westerly, with

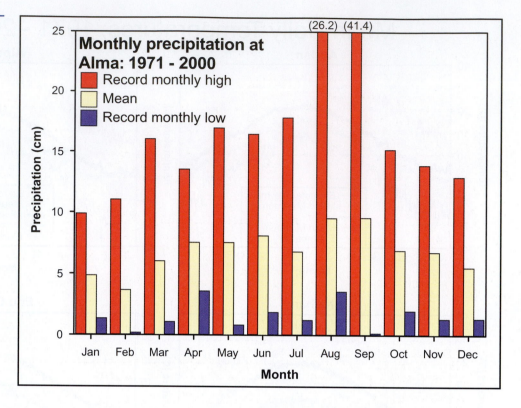

some subtle but distinct seasonal variations. Mean winds tend to be more northwesterly during the cold months, with more of a southwesterly component during the warm months. Easterly winds are also relatively common during the spring, in association with the passage of cool, dry, Canadian air masses into the region.

Diurnal patterns

Similar to annual cycles, differences in solar insolation rates lead to distinctive patterns of many climatic variables, on a daily basis. Hourly solar radiation, air and dewpoint temperatures, and wind speed, averaged over a ten-year period at East Lansing, are plotted as a function of local time in Figure 19.12. These representative diurnal cycles are driven primarily by the energy balance of the surface, which is dominated by incoming solar radiation during the daytime hours and outgoing longwave energy at night. Wind speed (Fig. 19.12) increases quickly, along with solar radiation, just after sunrise, peaks just after solar noon at approximately 13:30, and then falls back to relatively low values again during the overnight hours. Air temperatures have a similar pattern, but lag farther behind solar radiation values, with the mean daily maximum occurring closer to 16:00 and almost 2.5 hours behind the solar peak. Likewise, the mean daily minimum temperature coincides with the end of the period of overnight net longwave cooling, near sunrise. Differences associated with the rates of surface heating or cooling can also be observed on Figure 19.12. During the morning hours, just after sunrise, when net radiation rates are increasingly positive, the air temperature rises relatively rapidly; after sunset, when net radiation values turn weakly negative, the diurnal drop in temperature is slower and more grad-

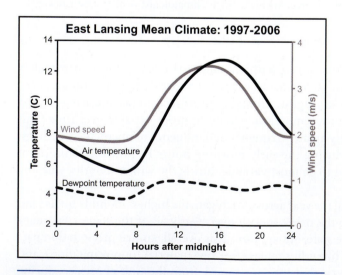

FIGURE 19.12 Mean climatic data for East Lansing, MI, for the period 1997–2006. Source: Michigan State Climatologist's Office, East Lansing.

TABLE 19.1   A select list of Michigan climate extremes

Variable	Value	Location (MI)	Date
Temperatures			
Extreme maximum temperature	112° F	Mio	July 13, 1936
Maximum mean monthly temperature	79.1° F	Coldwater	July, 1934
Extreme minimum temperature	–51° F	Vanderbilt	Feb. 9, 1934
Minimum mean monthly temperature	–1.1° F	Bergland	January, 1977
Precipitation			
Greatest 5-minute total	1.52"	Fowlerville	July 6, 1994
Greatest 30-minute total	3.60"	Detroit	July 24, 1969
Greatest 60-minute total	4.55"	Royal Oak	July 18, 1967
Greatest daily total	9.78"	Bloomingdale	Sep. 1, 1914
Greatest yearly total	56.38"	Niles	1954
Lowest yearly total	15.86"	Mt. Clemens	1958
Snowfall			
Greatest 1-day total	30"	Herman	Dec. 19, 1996
Greatest 2-day total	35"	Herman	Feb. 11–12, 1969
Greatest 3-day total	44.2"	Copper Harbor	Jan. 22–24, 1982
Greatest monthly total	129.5"	Copper Harbor	Jan. 1982
Greatest seasonal total	391.9"	Delaware	Sep. 1978–May, 1979
Greatest snow depth	80"	Marquette	Feb. 16, 1971
Maximum # consecutive snowdays	59	Houghton	Dec. 17, 1993–Feb. 13, 1994

Source: Michigan State Climatologist's Office.

ual. The diurnal pattern of dew point temperatures, a measure of atmospheric humidity, is different, but still directly linked to the other variables. After sunrise, incoming solar radiation evaporates dew or frost on the surface, which results in an increase in water vapor and dew point. The gradual drop in humidity during the afternoon hours is associated with increasing turbulence, and growth of the planetary boundary layer, which mixes some of the water vapor with drier air above. Similarly, the minor increase of humidity between about 19:00 and 22:00 is due to the collapse of the planetary boundary layer and the formation of a surface inversion layer, which acts to trap water vapor close to the surface. Finally, another drop off in humidity begins about 23:00 and continues until sunrise, in association with the formation of dew or frost on the surface.

Climate extremes

Climate extremes are an important part of a region's climatology; they represent historical limits of weather conditions and are frequently associated with major impacts on human and natural ecosystems (Table 19.1). Climate extremes in Michigan are similar in magnitude to surrounding areas. Maximum and minimum temperature extremes are a few degrees cooler and warmer, respectively, than nearby areas west of Michigan not influenced by lake effect. Heavy precipitation extreme totals in the central US tend to decrease from south to north, as the distance from the Gulf of Mexico water vapor source region increases. Not surprisingly, many extreme events in Michigan have occurred in southern sections of the state. Extreme snowfall events are concentrated in the lake effect snowbelt regions, especially in the Keweenaw Peninsula, and near Herman, on the Peshekee Highlands (Plate 8B). In terms of the frequency of weather-related natural disasters, e.g., hurricanes and severe drought, Michigan ranked lowest in the continental US, with an average of 1–3 events per year (Lott and Ross 2006).

■ Severe weather, storms, and hazards

Severe thunderstorms and tornadoes

A severe thunderstorm is defined by the National Weather Service (NWS) as, a storm producing hail ≥20 mm in diameter, and/or wind gusts ≥26 m/s, and/or a tornado. Fortunately, very few of the approximately 25–40 thunderstorms that occur at any one site in Michigan, in a typical year, meet these criteria. Severe thunderstorms and tornadoes are generally associated with cases of extreme atmospheric instability (especially in the lowest 10 km of the atmosphere) and/or rapid changes in wind speeds and directions, vertically. Climatologically, these conditions occur less frequently in Michigan than in neighboring states.

Some severe thunderstorms produce hail, which forms as a frozen raindrop or graupel pellet in a cumulonimbus cloud, and grows by the accretion of supercooled water. Hailstones in Michigan are typically marble-size or smaller. Hail is most frequently observed in the spring and early summer months. A higher frequency of hail is noted in the fall months over the northwestern Lower Peninsula, and in the northern Upper Peninsula. This occurs is because soft hail (or graupel), while non-destructive, is also counted generically as hail and is commonly associated with the lake effect precipitation that occurs in these areas during that season (see above).

Whereas severe thunderstorms and associated violent weather phenomena do occur on a regular basis in Michigan, they are not as common as in states further south and west. Tornado occurrences in Michigan average about five per year, with ~90% of confirmed tornadoes occurring in the southern half of the Lower Peninsula (Fig. 19.13). Tornadoes in the state travel mostly from SW to NE, following the motion of the parent thunderstorm. It is interesting to note an area from Saginaw to Monroe Counties, where the frequency of severe weather is relatively higher than in other areas of the state. Reasons for this pattern are not clear, but likely involve the tendency of organized convection to be suppressed as it crosses the open and relatively cooler waters of the Great Lakes (especially Lake Michigan, in this case). Farther inland, away from the lakes, these storms can more easily form (or reorganize and become stronger).

As is the case in much of the Upper Midwest, the greatest numbers of tornadoes in Michigan occur during the month of June, while the most severe tornadoes and greatest loss of life and property have tended to occur earlier in the spring, most typically during April (Nurnberger and Meyer 1988, Changnon and Kunkel 2006). The potential severity of tornadoes tends to be greater during the spring than in summer, because jet stream winds and regional differences in air temperature and humidity (key factors in severe thunderstorm and tornado formation) tend to be relatively greater then. Tornadoes occur at all hours of the day, but are most common between the hours of 3–6 pm local time (NOAA/SPC 2007).

Arguably the most destructive tornado in the state's history occurred in the Beecher/Flint area on

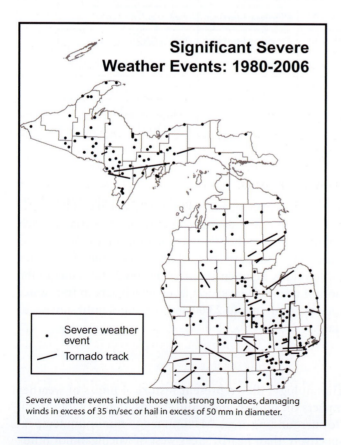

Severe weather events include those with strong tornadoes, damaging winds in excess of 35 m/sec or hail in excess of 50 mm in diameter.

FIGURE 19.13 Occurrences of severe thunderstorms, for the period 1980–2005. Source: NOAA Storms Prediction Center, Norman, OK.

June 8th, 1953, when 116 people lost their lives in an F5 intensity tornado. Other major tornado outbreaks during the past century include the Palm Sunday tornado outbreak of April 11, 1965, which caused >$51 million in damage across the southern Lower Peninsula, the outbreak of April 3, 1956 across the southwestern Lower Peninsula, which included two separate F5 intensity tornadoes, and the Kalamazoo tornado of May 13, 1980, which moved through downtown, leading to five fatalities and >$50 million in damage.

Lightning

Surprisingly, Michigan ranks second after Florida in terms of lightning deaths and injuries (Ferrett and Ojala 1992), in spite of relatively infrequent occurrence of cloud-to-ground lightning flashes compared to other areas of the US. From 1959 to 2004, 401 people in Michigan either lost their lives or were injured by lightning (NCDC 2005). Reasons that have been proposed for the large number of lightning fatalities in Michigan are the popularity of water sports and outdoor games, e.g., golf, in the state.

Severe winter weather

Snowstorms and blizzards may cause major disruptions to transportation and normal daily activities. Changnon and Kunkel (2006) found an average of 17 fatalities and mean annual losses of $125 million in the Midwest, associated with heavy snowfall and blizzard events between 1949 and 2000. While the number of overall regional events examined in the study was found to have peaked in the late 1970s, associated economic losses had increased over time, which the authors attribute to increasing societal vulnerability and possibly to increasing storm strength.

Technically, snowstorms refer only to the actual event of heavy snow falling, regardless of wind speed. The NWS characterizes heavy snowfall as a ≥15 cm in a period of 12 hours, or ≥20 cm during a 24-hour period. Blizzard conditions are characterized by considerable falling and/or blowing snow, reducing visibility frequently to <400 m, *and* sustained wind or frequent gusts to 16 m/s or greater, over a period of ≥3 hours. Thus, blizzard conditions can technically occur either during or after heavy snow has fallen. Strong winds associated with blizzard conditions cause extensive blowing and drifting snow, which makes snow removal difficult or impossible, and may lead to hazardous and even life-threatening conditions, with low visibilities and dangerous wind chill temperatures.

Major snowstorms in Michigan are most frequent in northern and western sections of the state, where lake effect snow is most common (Fig. 19.9D). Across the lake effect belts of the northern Upper Peninsula, the annual mean of ≥8 snowfall events of ≥15cm, and a maximum annual snowstorm frequency of >20 events per year, are the highest totals in the continental US east of the Rockies (Changnon et al. 2006). Within the state, the snowfall in a 10-year event (an event so large that it that occurs only once every 10 years, on average) ranges from ~30 cm in the extreme southeastern Lower Peninsula, to ~40 cm in the northwestern Lower Peninsula, to >55 cm in the Upper Peninsula, from the Keweenaw Peninsula eastward to near the Pictured Rocks National Lakeshore (Changnon 2006). Statistically, snowstorms have occurred in the state from September through May, but tend to be most common in the month of December across northern sections of the state, and in January across the south.

Drought

Drought is a prolonged period of abnormally low precipitation, that may adversely affects growing or living conditions. The true meaning and use of the term, however, is much broader, and depends greatly on the type of impact and region affected. The American Meteorological Society (2003) groups drought into four different categories: (1) Meteorological or climatological, which refers only to the magnitude of the precipitation shortfall and duration, (2) Agricultural, which links the impacts of precipitation and soil moisture deficit to agricultural impacts, (3) Hydrological, which pertains to surpluses or deficits of surface or subsurface water (usually over relatively long periods), and (4) Socioeconomic, which describes the combined impact of water deficits on supply and demand of some economic good.

Thus, drought conditions, while completely valid and descriptive in one of the categories, may or may not be consistent across all four. It is possible, for example, for a hydrological drought to have little if any agricultural impact, e.g., in irrigated areas.

Of all types of major natural disasters, drought is among the most costly and extensive from a spatial perspective, and its impacts are frequently intensified by concurrent high air temperatures. Prior to Hurricane Katrina in 2005, the drought of 1988 (which led to widespread and serious impacts in Michigan) was the most costly natural disaster in US history, with 5,000–10,000 associated fatalities (mostly from heat stress) and >$60 billion dollars in economic losses across the central and eastern US (Lott and Ross 2006).

The formation and persistence of drought is associated with both large scale synoptic factors, such as jet stream configuration and sea surface temperature patterns, as well as regional or local factors linked with soil/vegetation/ atmosphere feedback mechanisms. Mild drought conditions are relatively common in Michigan, but severe drought conditions over large areas with below normal precipitation over several consecutive month periods are not (Eichenlaub 1990).

■ Climate variability and climate change

Climate variability and climate change are topics of considerable interest for Michigan's citizens. Recent concerns and debate about anthropogenic influences on climate, such as the impact of increasing greenhouse gases, have further highlighted the importance of climate to human habitation.

Historical climate variability and change

Detecting and depicting past climate variations is hindered by the short period for which climate observations are available (Lamb 1977). In Michigan, the observational record for temperature and precipitation extends as far back as the mid to late 1800s at only few stations. Meteorological station location/density is another concern, especially in the vicinity of the Great Lakes, where dense networks are needed to detect climate gradients near the lakeshore. Also, only a few buoy observations are available over the Great Lakes. Another problem encountered when studying climate variability and change is that time series of climate observations often contain "inhomogeneities" caused by changes in instrumentation, observation time, the location of the observing station and the character of the area immediately surrounding the station. These inhomogeneities can cause artificial trends and discontinuities in the time series, which are often difficult to distinguish from "real" features.

Global and regional temperature trends

Through careful and thorough analysis of observations, climatologists have been able to detect important climate variations and trends. At the *global* scale, an important feature is the unprecedented warmth at the end of the 20th century and beginning of the 21st century (Brohan et al. 2006; Fig. 19.14). Temperature trends at the *regional* scale are considerably more complicated. For example, the eastern US (including Michigan) experienced much less warming from 1901–2000, as compared to other areas in the Northern Hemisphere, e.g., west-

FIGURE 19.14 Global temperature anomalies from 1850 to 2005. After Brohan et al. (2006).

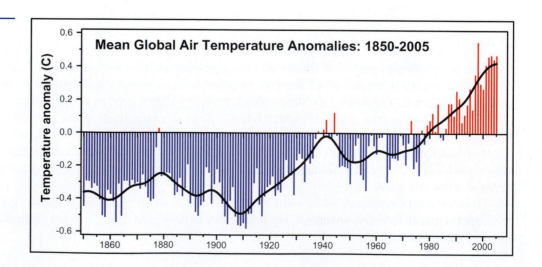

Mean Global Air Temperature Anomalies: 1850-2005

ern Canada or central Eurasia (IPCC 2001). An even more complex picture emerges when the last century is divided into subperiods. From 1910–1945, Michigan and the eastern US experienced only moderate warming, compared to other locations (IPCC 2001). This was followed by a period of substantial regional cooling from 1946–1975, and then more recently (1976–2000), by a warming trend that is equal in magnitude to that for most other areas of the world. A further complication is that the most recent warming trend in Michigan and the eastern US is not uniform across all seasons. Rather, the warming has primarily been a wintertime phenomenon (IPCC 2001).

Climate trends in Michigan

The trend in Michigan's mean temperature for 1894–2006 is similar to temperature trends seen at the global scale—cooling from approximately 1940 through the 1970s, followed by warming from the early 1980s that continues to present (Fig. 19.15A). Considerable year-to-year variation exists, however, indicating that even during periods of general warming, some years with cooler than average temperatures can be expected. Thus, one must be careful to not attribute a particularly warm month, season or year to "global warming" or, alternatively, to argue that a colder than normal year is evidence that long-term warming is not occurring.

When only daily minimum temperatures are considered, a strong temporal trend is observed, as illustrated by the time series of mean winter (December, January and February) minimum temperatures for Ironwood (Fig. 19.16). A substantial increase, on the order of 4° C, in mean winter minimum temperatures is evident, beginning in the mid-1980s and continuing through present. In contrast, changes in daily maximum temperatures (not shown) have been relatively modest. Thus, Michigan's increase in average temperature in the latter part of the 20th century may be primarily due to increasing minimum temperatures.

State mean precipitation has generally increased over the period of record, although distinct drought periods are evident, particularly the 1930s and 1960s (Fig. 19.15B). Even more notable is the increase in the number of wet days (with measureable precipitation), and the frequency of a wet day followed by a second wet day (Fig. 19.17). The increased frequency of wet days is associated with more cloudiness and, hence, less incoming solar radiation, as seen at Lansing (Fig. 19.18).

One of the more striking changes in Michigan's climate is the decrease in the amount of ice cover on the Great Lakes (Fig. 19.19). The number of days with

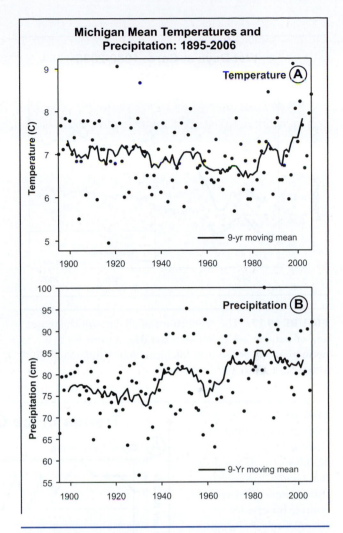

FIGURE 19.15 Mean, statewide temperature and precipitation data, for the period 1895–2006. Source: Michigan State Climatologist's Office, East Lansing.

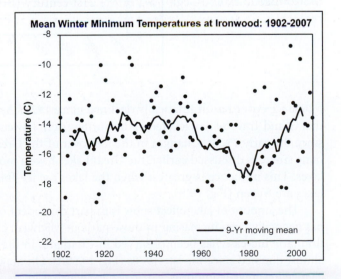

FIGURE 19.16 Mean winter minimum temperature, 1961–2004, at Ironwood. Source: Michigan State Climatologist's Office, East Lansing.

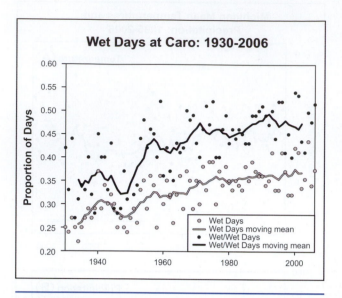

FIGURE 19.17   The proportions of all days which are wet, and of wet days which follow a wet day, at Caro, for the period 1930–2006. Source: Michigan State Climatologist's Office, East Lansing.

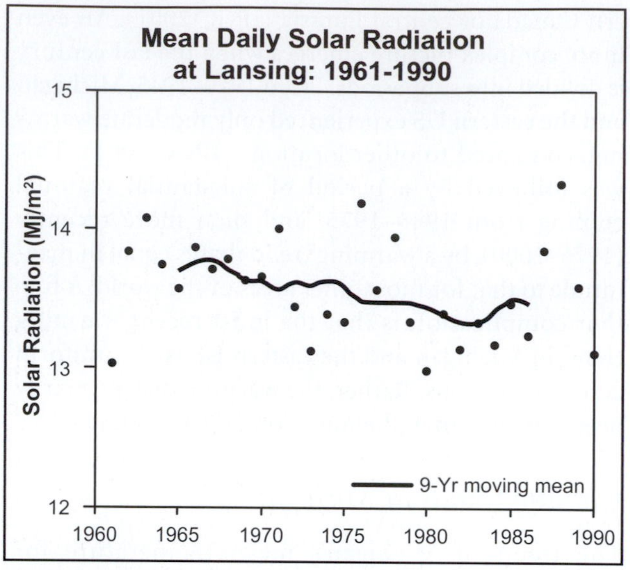

FIGURE 19.18   Mean daily solar radiation, for the period 1961–1990, at Lansing. Source: Michigan State Climatologist's Office, East Lansing.

FIGURE 19.19   Ice cover changes at two different Great Lakes' locations. A. Number of years per decade that Grand Traverse Bay froze completely over. Source: Traverse City Record-Eagle. B. Percentage of days per year from 1973–2003 with >20% ice cover on the Great Lakes. Source: Assel (2003).

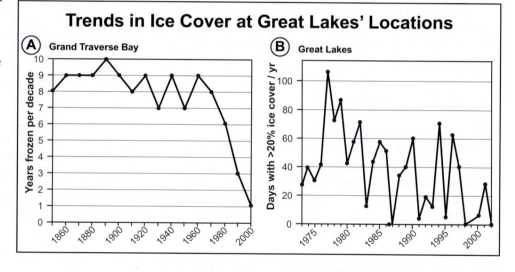

>20% ice cover has dramatically declined since 1972 (Assel 2003). Furthermore, the number of years per decade that Grand Traverse Bay, located in the northwestern Lower Peninsula, has been frozen over has dramatically decreased since the early 1970s. Changes in the ice cover of the Great Lakes have significant implications for Michigan's climate since, as discussed earlier, the Great Lakes have a moderating influence on the local climate downwind of the lakes. This influence is greatest when the lakes are ice-free and considerably reduced, if not eliminated, when the lakes are frozen (Fig. 19.8).

The amount of lake-effect snow is in part dependent on the length of time the Great Lakes are ice-free. Snowfall has generally been increasing in those parts of Michigan close to, and downwind of, the Great Lakes. A particularly dramatic increase has been observed in Chatham, in the central Upper Peninsula, where snowfall amounts have almost doubled since the late 1970s (Fig. 19.20A). On the other hand, locations father from the lakes have seen little change in snowfall amounts, e.g., Bay City, which is located near Saginaw Bay, and hence, is upwind of the water surfaces (Fig. 19.20B). Recent data have shown that Michigan's generally warmer winters are leading to thinner snowpacks overall, and, therefore, colder wintertime soil temperatures, especially in lake effect areas (Isard et al. 2007).

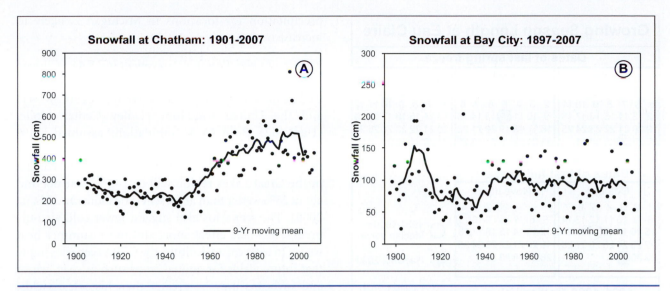

FIGURE 19.20   Historical variations in snowfall at Chatham and Bay City. Source: Michigan State Climatologist's Office, East Lansing.

■ Future climate change

In addition to natural causes (such as variations in solar radiation), anthropogenic influences can cause climate to change. The two anthropogenic influences that have received the most attention are increasing greenhouse gases and land use/land cover change. Greenhouse gases, such as CO_2, absorb longwave radiation emitted by the earth's surface, effectively "trapping" it in the lower atmosphere. Changes in land use and land cover, such as deforestation and urbanization, impact the earth's climate by modifying the albedo (reflectivity) of the earth's surface, with consequent changes to the surface energy and moisture balances.

Climate scenarios

The primary tools for projecting and understanding Earth's future climate are Global Climate Models (GCMs). GCMs have been developed by a number of atmospheric modeling centers worldwide. The majority of the GCMs suggest that global temperatures over the next century will increase on the order of 1.1–6.4° C (IPCC 2007). GCM simulations have a coarse horizontal scale (typically 100–300 km) and rarely are directly suitable for climate impact assessments, as most impacts are likely to be felt at the local and/or regional scales. Therefore, GCM simulations need to be "downscaled" to a finer spatial resolution (Winkler et al. 1997). The output from the downscaling procedures is one or more climate scenarios, where a "scenario" is defined simply as a plausible future climate (IPCC 2001). Climate scenarios are shrouded in uncertainty that must be considered when interpreting and using them. Major sources of uncertainty include (1) uncertainty on how greenhouse gas emissions will change in the future, (2) the limited understanding of how the Earth's carbon cycle will respond to changes in greenhouse gases, (3) an incomplete understanding of the sensitivity of the Earth's climate to changes in greenhouse gases, (4) error introduced during the downscaling process, and (5) the range of possible responses of natural and human systems to climate change.

Climate scenarios for Michigan

Three assessments of potential impacts of climate change on Michigan are highlighted below: (1) the 1997–2000 Great Lakes Regional Assessment (GLRA), (2) the Union of Concerned Scientists/Ecological Society of America (UCS/ESA) report on "Confronting Climate Change in the Great Lakes Region," published in 2003 and updated in 2005, and (3) the *Pileus Project: Climate Science for Decision Making* conducted by researchers from Michigan State University from 2002–2007. In general, these assessments suggest that Michigan's temperatures during the 21st century may increase substantially, with consequent increases in heat accumulation and the length of the frost-free season. Precipitation changes are surrounded by much more uncertainty; there is little consensus on whether the amount of

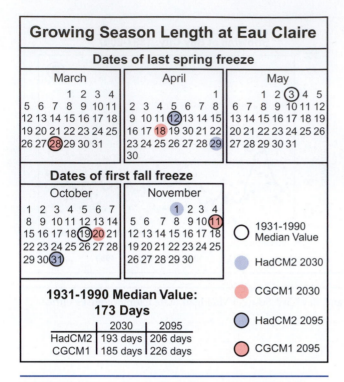

FIGURE 19.21 Median values of temperature threshold parameters for Eau Claire, for the assessment decades of 2025–2034 and 2090–2099. Differences were calculated between the two assessment decades and a control period of 1994–2003. These differences were then compared to observed median values for 1931–1990. Growing season length was calculated for each year separately, and the median value was determined from the values for each year. Consequently, the change in the growing season length does not necessarily equal the sum of the change in the dates of last spring freeze and first fall freeze. After Winkler et al. (2000).

precipitation for locations in Michigan is likely to increase or decrease.

The Great Lakes Regional Assessment (GLRA) Climate scenarios for this assessment were developed from two GCMs: the Canadian Climate Center Model (CGCM1) and the United Kingdom Hadley Center Model (HadCM2). Both GCM simulations assumed a 1% increase in CO_2 per year. The GLRA climate scenarios suggest that, by the end of the 21st century, the climate of the Great Lakes region will be 2–4° C warmer and about 25% wetter than at present (Sousounis and Bisanz 2000). The scenarios also suggest fewer cold air outbreaks, less lake effect snow and more summer heat waves. In terms of agriculture, the GLRA scenarios imply that future yields for annual crops such as corn, wheat and soybeans may be greater than historical yields, through the middle of the 21st century (approximately 2050), and then may decrease in the latter half of the century. Michigan's agriculture also will likely need to adjust to increases in growing season length, an earlier date of last spring freeze and a later date of first fall freeze (Fig. 19.21). Changes in heat accumulation will cause important growth stages for perennial plants, including fruit trees, to occur earlier. However, it is not clear from the GLRA analyses whether these plants will be more or less sensitive than at present to damaging springtime cold temperatures, that occur after the plants have reached sensitive growth stages (see Chapter 38).

Assessment by the Union of Concerned Scientists/ Ecological Society of America (UCS/ESA) The UCS/ESA also based their analyses on only two scenarios (Kling et al. 2003). One scenario was derived from an updated version of the Hadley Center model (HadCM3), and the other from the Parallel Climate Model developed by the National Center for Atmospheric Research in the United States. Similar to the GLRA, these scenarios assumed a 1% increase in CO_2 per year. The UCS/ESA scenarios suggested that, by the end of the 21st century, temperatures in Michigan will rise by 3–6° C in winter and 4–7° C in summer. Precipitation is projected to increase in winter, but decrease in summer. The authors of the UCS/ESA report speculated that, by 2030, Michigan's climate will feel like that currently experienced in Ohio, and that by the end of the 21st century, Michigan's climate will be similar to Arkansas' current climate. In terms of impacts, the UCS/ESA report inferred that groundwater supplies will decrease, lake levels will decline and that optimal weather conditions for agriculture are likely to shift northward. They also speculated that, while winter cold-related morbidity or mortality likely will decrease, summer heat-related morbidity or mortality will increase. The areal extent of the boreal forests in Michigan may shrink in response to warmer temperatures. Other possible impacts based on these scenarios include a decline in cold-water fish species and a northward expansion of warm-water fish species, along with less wetland habitat. Winter recreation, such as downhill skiing and ice fishing, also was hypothesized to suffer from warmer temperatures.

The Pileus Project The climate scenarios for the Pileus Project were downscaled from simulations from GCMs developed by the Canadian Climatic Center, the Hadley Center (Great Britain), the National Center for Atmospheric Research (US) and the Max Planck Institute (Germany). Two greenhouse gas emission scenarios, popularly known as A2 and B2 (SRES 2000), were used in the simulations. Pileus Project results support the GLRA results—the length of the growing season and the amount of heat accumulation are likely to increase (Fig. 19.22). For the period

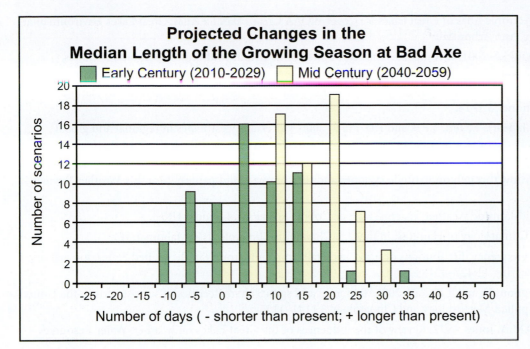

FIGURE 19.22
Projected changes in the median length of the growing season at Bad Axe, for 2010–2029 and 2040–2059. An ensemble of scenarios was created using four GCMs, two greenhouse gas estimates for the future, and multiple downscaling methodologies. Source: *Pileus Project* web site www.pileus.msu.edu.

2010–2029, the majority of the scenarios suggest an increase in the median length of the growing season. When averaged across all the scenarios, a six-day increase in the median growing season length is projected. Additionally, almost all the scenarios for the period 2040–2059 suggest an increase in the median length of the growing season, by an average of 16 days. Similar to the previous GLRA assessment, Pileus Project results indicate that, at this point in time, it is not possible to speculate on whether the frequency of plant-damaging cold temperatures will increase or decrease. The scenarios suggest that there will be a larger shift in the date of the last spring freeze, compared to the time of the first fall freeze. Also, and in contrast to the results of the UCS/EPA study, Pileus Project scenarios project only a modest increase in the number of "hot" days (maximum temperatures ≥35°C). The frequency of wet days is expected to decline during the 21st century, and the frequency of extended dry spells is projected to increase.

Conclusions

Michigan's weather and climate are varied and fascinating. Day-to-day weather variations are caused by atmospheric circulation features at a wide range of spatial scales. Michigan's current climate is a reflection of the frequency of these different circulation features and their interaction with the local and regional topography, including the Great Lakes. Analysis of the historical climate record for Michigan points to interesting temporal variations in the state's climate. Both natural and anthropogenically induced changes in Michigan's climate are expected in the future.

Literature Cited

Aguado, E. and J.E. Burt. 2004. Understanding Weather and Climate. Pearson/Prentice Hall, Upper Saddle River, NJ.

American Meteorological Society. 2000. Glossary of Meteorology. American Meteorological Society, Boston, MA.

Andresen, J.A., Potter, B.E., McCullough, D.G., Kohler, N., Lusch, D.P., Bauer, L. and C. Ramm. 2001. Effects of winter temperatures on Gypsy Moth egg masses in the Great Lakes region of the United States. Agricultural and Forest Meteorology 110:85–100.

Assel, R.A. 2003. An Electronic Atlas of Great Lakes Ice Cover. NOAA Great Lakes Ice Atlas, Great Lakes Environmental Research Laboratory, Ann Arbor, MI.

Bierly, G.D. and J.A. Winkler. 2001. A composite analysis of airstreams within cold-season Colorado cyclones. Weather and Forecasting 16:57–80.

Bjerknes, J. and H. Solberg. 1922. Life cycle of cyclones and the polar front theory of atmospheric circulation. Geofysiske Publikationer 3:1–18.

Brohan, P., Kennedy, J.J., Haris I., Tett, S.F.B. and P.D. Jones. 2006. Uncertainty estimates in regional and global observed temperature changes: a new dataset from 1850. Journal of Geophysical Research 111:D12106, doi:10.1029/2005JD006548

Carlson, T.N. 1980. Airflow through midlatitude cyclones and the comma cloud pattern. Monthly Weather Review 108:1498–1509.

Carlson, T.N. 1991. Mid-latitude Weather Systems. Harper-Collins Academic, London, UK.

Changnon, S.A. 2002. Climatology of Hail Risk in the U.S. Changnon Climatologists, Mahomet, IL.

Changnon, S.A. 2006. Frequency distributions of heavy snowfall from snowstorms in the United States. Journal of Hydrological Engineering 11:427–431.

Changnon, S.A., Changnon, D. and T.R. Karl. 2006. Temporal and spatial characteristics of snowstorms in the United States. Journal of Applied Meteorology and Climatology 8:1141–1155.

Changnon, S.A. and D.M.A. Jones. 1972. Review of the influences of the Great Lakes on weather. Water Resources Research 8:360–371.

Changnon, S.A. and K.E. Kunkel. 2001. Causes of record high flood losses in the central United States. Water International 26:223–230.

Climate Prediction Center. 2005a. El Nino/Southern Oscillation (ENSO). http://www.cpc.noaa.gov/products/precip/CWlink/MJO/enso.shtml (last accessed August, 2007).

Climate Prediction Center. 2005b. North Atlantic Oscillation. http://www.cpc.noaa.gov/products/precip/CWlink/pna/nao.shtml (last accessed August, 2007).

Eichenlaub, V.L., Harman, J.R., Nurnberger, F.V. and H.J. Stolle. 1990. The Climatic Atlas of Michigan. University of Notre Dame Press, South Bend, IN.

Ferrett, R.L. and C.F. Ojala. 1992. The lightning hazard in Michigan. Michigan Academician 24:427–441.

Fritsch, J.M., Kane, R.J. and C.R. Chelius. 1986. The contribution of mesoscale convective weather systems to the warm-season precipitation in the United States. Journal of Climate and Applied Meteorology 25:1333–1345.

Goree, P.A. and R.J. Younkin. 1966. Synoptic climatology of heavy snowfall over the central and eastern United States. Monthly Weather Review 94:663–668.

Grenci, L.M. and J.M. Nese. 2001. A World of Weather: Fundamentals of Meteorology. Kendall/Hunt Publishing Company, Dubuque, IA.

Heideman, K.F. and J.M. Fritsch. 1988. Forcing mechanisms and other characteristics of significant summertime precipitation. Weather and Forecasting 3:115–130.

Hjelmfelt, M.R. 1992. Orographic effects in simulated lake-effect snowstorms over Lake Michigan. Monthly Weather Review 120:373–377.

Holton, J.R. 1992. Introduction to Dynamic Meteorology. Elsevier, New York.

Houze, R.A. 1993. Cloud Dynamics. Academic Press, New York.

Hovenec, R.D. and L.H. Horn. 1975. Static stability and the 300 mb isotach field in the Colorado cyclogenetic area. Monthly Weather Review 103:628–638.

Hunckler, R.V. and R.J. Schaetzl. 1997. Spodosol development as affected by geomorphic aspect, Baraga County, Michigan. Soil Science Society of America Journal 61:1105–1115.

Intergovernmental Panel on Climate Change (IPCC). 2001. Observed Climate Variability and Change. C.K. Folland, and T.R. Karl, co-ordinating lead authors. In: Houghton, J.T., Ding, Y., Griggs, D.J., Noguer, M., van der Linden, P.J., Dia, X., Maskell, K. and C.A. Johnson (eds), Climate Change 2001: The Scientific Basis. Cambridge University Press, Cambridge, UK. pp. 99–181.

Intergovernmental Panel on Climate Change (IPCC). 2007. Summary for Policymakers. In: Solomon, S., Quin, Q., Manning, M., Chen, Z., Marquis, M., Averyt, K.B., Tignor, M. and H.L. Miller (eds), Climate Change 2007: The Physical Science Basis. Contribution of Working Group I to the Fourth Assessment Report of the Intergovermental Panel on Climate Change. Cambridge University Press, Cambridge, UK. pp. 1–18.

Isard, S.A., Schaetzl, R.J. and J.A. Andresen. 2007. Soils cool as climate warms in Great Lakes Region, USA. Annals of the Association of American Geographers 97:467–476.

Kelly, R.D. 1986. Mesoscale frequencies and seasonal snowfalls for different types of Lake Michigan snowstorms. Journal of Climatology and Applied Meteorology 25:308–321.

Klein, W.H. 1957. Principal tracks and mean frequencies of cyclones and anticyclones in the Northern Hemisphere. Weather Bureau Research Paper 40. US Department of Commerce, Washington, DC.

Kling, G.W., Hayhoe, K., Johnson, L.B., Magnuson, J.J., Polasky, S., Robinson, S.K., Shuter, B.J., Wander, M.M., Wuebbles, D.J. and D.R. Zak. 2003. Confronting climate change in the Great Lakes region. Report of the Union of Concerned Scientists and the Ecological Society of America. UCS Publications, Cambridge, MA.

Kristovich, D.A.R. and N.F. Laird. 1998. Observations of widespread lake-effect cloudiness: Influences of lake surface temperature and upwind conditions. Weather and Forecasting 13:811–821.

Lahey, J.F., Bryson, R.A., Reid, A., Wahl, E.W., Horn, L.H. and V.D. Henderson. 1958. Atlas of 500 mb Wind Characteristics for the Northern Hemisphere. Science Report 1. University of Wisconsin Press, Madison.

Lamb, H.H. 1977. Climatic History and the Future. Princeton University Press, Princeton, NJ.

Lott, N. and T. Ross, 2006. Tracking and evaluating U.S. billion dollar weather disasters, 1980–2005. National Climatic Data Center Research Report, Asheville, NC.

Lutgens, F.K. and E.J. Tarbuck. 2004. The Atmosphere: An Introduction to Meteorology. Prentice Hall, Upper Saddle River, NJ.

McPhaden, M.J., Zebiak, S.E. and M.H. Glantz. 2006. ENSO as an integrating concept in earth science. Science 314:1740–1745.

National Renewable Energy Laboratories. 2004. NREL Solar Atlas for Photovoltaic Panels. National Renewable Energy Laboratory, Golden, CO.

National Climatic Data Center, 2005. Storm Data: 2004 Annual Summaries. National Oceanic and Atmospheric Administration, National Environmental Satellite Data Information Service, National Climatic Data Center, Asheville, NC.

National Oceanic and Atmospheric Administration (NOAA). 2007. Daily Weather Map Series. http://docs.lib.noaa.gov/rescue/dwm/data_rescue_daily_weather_maps.html (last accessed August, 2007.)

National Weather Service Marquette, Michigan, Weather Forecast Office. 2005. Storm Warning: Advances in Marine Communications and Forecasting. http://www.crh.noaa.gov/mqt/fitzgerald/ (last accessed November, 2007.)

Norton, D.C. and S.J. Bolsenga. 1993. Spatiotemporal trends in lake effect and continental snowfall in the Laurentian Great Lakes, 1951–1980. Journal of Climate 6:1943–1956.

Nurnberger, F.V. and D.E. Meyer. 1988. Michigan Tornado Statistics, 1918–1987. Michigan Department of Agriculture Report, Lansing, MI.

Oliver, J.E. and J.J. Hidore. 2002. Climatology: An Atmospheric Science. Prentice Hall, Upper Saddle River, NJ.

Orlanski, I. 1975. A rationale subdivision of scales for atmospheric processes. Bulletin of the American Meteorological Society 56:527–530.

Peixoto, J.P. and A.H. Oort. 2002. Physics of Climate. Springer, New York.

Richards, T.L. and J.G. Irbe. 1969. Estimates of monthly evaporation losses from the Great Lakes, 1950–1968, based on the mass transfer technique. Proceedings of the 12th Conference on Great Lakes Research, International Association for Great Lakes Research 18:469–487, May 5–7, 1969. Ann Arbor, MI.

Rogers, J.C. 1984. The association between the North Atlantic Oscillation and the Southern Oscillation in the Northern Hemisphere. Monthly Weather Review 112:1999–2015.

Rossby, C.G. 1939. Relations between variations in the intensity of the zonal circulation and the displacement of the semi-permanent centers of action. Journal of Marine Research 2:38–54.

Rothrock, H.J. 1969. An aid to forecasting significant lake effect snows. Technical memo WBTM CR-30, National Weather Service, Central Region, Kansas City, MO.

Scott, R.W. and F.A. Huff. 1996. Impacts of the Great Lakes on regional climate conditions. Journal of Great Lakes Research 22:845–863.

Shadbolt, R.P., Waller, E.A., Messina, J.P. and J.A. Winkler, 2006. Source regions of lower-tropospheric airflow trajectories for the lower peninsula of Michigan: A 40-year air mass climatology. Journal of Geophysical Research 111: D21117, doi:10.1029/2005JD006657.

Sousounis, P.J. and J.M. Bisanz (eds). 2000. Preparing for a Changing Climate: The Potential Consequences of Climate Variability and Change. University of Michigan, Ann Arbor. http://www.geo.msu.edu/glra/ (last accessed August, 2007).

Sousounis, P.J. and J.M. Fritsch. 1994. Lake-aggregate mesoscale disturbances. Part II. A case study of the effects on regional and synoptic-scale weather systems. Bulletin of the American Meteorological Society 75:1793–1811.

Special Report on Emission Scenarios. 2000. Summary for Policymakers. A Special Report of Working Group III of the Intergovernmental Panel on Climate Change. Cambridge University Press, Cambridge, UK. (Available online at http://www.grida.no/climate/ipcc/emission/index.htm. Accessed August 2007.)

Trewartha, G.T. and L.H. Horn. 1980. An Introduction to Climate. McGraw-Hill, New York.

Whittaker, L.M. and L.H. Horn. 1981. Geographical and seasonal distribution of North American cyclogenesis, 1958–1977. Monthly Weather Review 109:2312–2322.

Winkler, J.A., Andresen, J.A., Guentchev, G., Picardy, J.A. and E.A. Waller. 2000. Climate Change and Fruit Prediction: An Exercise in Downscaling. In: P.J. Sousounis, and J.M. Bisanz (eds), Preparing for a Changing Climate: The Potential Consequences of Climate Variability and Change. University of Michigan: Ann Arbor. (Also available online at http://www.geo.msu.edu/glra/ (last accessed August, 2007).

Winkler, J.A., Palutikof, J.P., Andresen, J.A. and C.M. Goodess. 1997. The simulation of daily time series from GCM output. Part 2: A sensitivity analysis of empirical transfer functions for downscaling GCM simulations. Journal of Climate 10:2514–2532.

World Meteorological Organization. 1989. Calculation of Monthly and Annual 30-Year Standard Normals. WCDP-No. 10, WMO-TD/No. 341. World Meteorological Organization, Geneva.

Zishka, K.M. and P.J. Smith. 1980. The climatology of cyclones and anticyclones over North America and surrounding ocean environs for January and July, 1950–77. Monthly Weather Review 108:387–401.

Further Readings

Bradford, F.C. and H.A. Cardinell, 1952. Eighty Winters in Michigan Orchards. Michigan State College Agricultural Experiment Station Bulletin 149, East Lansing.

Briggs, W.G. and M.E. Graves. 1962. A lake breeze index. Journal of Applied Meteorology 1:474–480.

Cortinas, J. 2000. A climatology of freezing rain in the Great Lakes region of North America. Monthly Weather Review 128:3574–3588.

Eichenlaub, V.L. 1970. Lake effect snowfall to the lee of the Great Lakes: it's role in Michigan. Bulletin of the American Meteorological Society 51:403–412.

McGuffie, K. and A. Henderson-Sellers. 2005. A Climate Modelling Primer. John Wiley and Sons, Hoboken, NJ.

Muller, R.A. 1966. Snowbelts of the Great Lakes. Weatherwise 14:248–255.

Sousounis, P.J. (ed). 2002. Special Section on "The Potential Impacts of Climate Change in the Great Lakes Region." Journal of Great Lakes Research 28:493–642.

Walters, C.K. and J.A. Winkler. 1999. Diurnal variations in the characteristics of cloud-to-ground lightning activity in the Great Lakes region of the United States. Professional Geographer 51:349–366.

20

Soils

Randall J. Schaetzl

■ Introduction

Any discussion of the soils of a region should involve not only *what* soils are there but *why* the distribution of those soils exists the way that it does. That is my purpose here—to introduce and discuss the major soils and soil landscapes of Michigan are, and to explain their distribution.

Soils are vitally important to society—nearly everything we consume (and much of what we wear) ultimately has come from some soil, somewhere. Soils are natural bodies, with layers (horizons) that have formed over long periods of time, via the interaction of various environmental factors (see below). Soils are not dirt—they are wonderfully interesting and complex natural entities that we can use for our good. They can also be destroyed and mismanaged. Most importantly, soils harbor and support myriad forms of life.

To appreciate the full richness and splendor of an automobile no one would question that you would need to open the doors and hood, and maybe even take 'er apart a bit. It's the same with soils. To appreciate and know them we need to dig, open up their dark mystery and explore "the root domain of lively darkness and silence," as once stated by Francis Hole, a soil geographer at the University of Wisconsin. When we look at a soil in a vertical exposure, such as in a roadcut, newly dug drainage ditch or a grave, we see a soil profile with its horizons. This profile may extend all the way down to "not soil" material (or bedrock) below. Most soil profiles in Michigan are 1–3 m thick, and have formed in various kinds of glacial drift, although some are found on sand dunes or lake clay, in the moss and decaying vegetation of swamps and even on weathered bedrock. Everyone who longs to know more about Michigan must know her varied and exquisite soils, and this chapter will, hopefully, start you on that journey.

■ The complex soil landscape of Michigan

There are few states that can boast of the complexity of their soil landscapes (*soilscapes*) as Michigan can. Detailed, county-based mapping of the soils of many of Michigan's counties, by the USDA's Natural Resources Conservation Service (NRCS), has required nothing short of a Herculean effort because the soils vary so markedly (and often unpredictably) from place to place (Plate 12). This complexity exists because of (1) the young age of the Michigan soilscape and (2) the wide variety of soil parent materials (the rocks, sediments, etc. that soils form in) in our state.

Landscapes in Michigan are very young, by geologic standards. On older landscapes, such as in the southeastern US or the tropics, soil-forming processes have had such long periods of time to act on the parent materials that large parts of the landscape have evolved into generally similar soils. That is, there is a kind of equifinality to soil development—different starting points can end up with similar soils—as long as we have had enough (read: LOTS of) time to do it. However, in Michigan, we have not had nearly enough time (in most places, less than 16,000 years) to reach that point, and so our soils strongly reflect the geologic materials in which they were formed. For example, sandy glacial sediment has, today, developed into sandy soils (Fig. 20.1). Loamy sediment has evolved

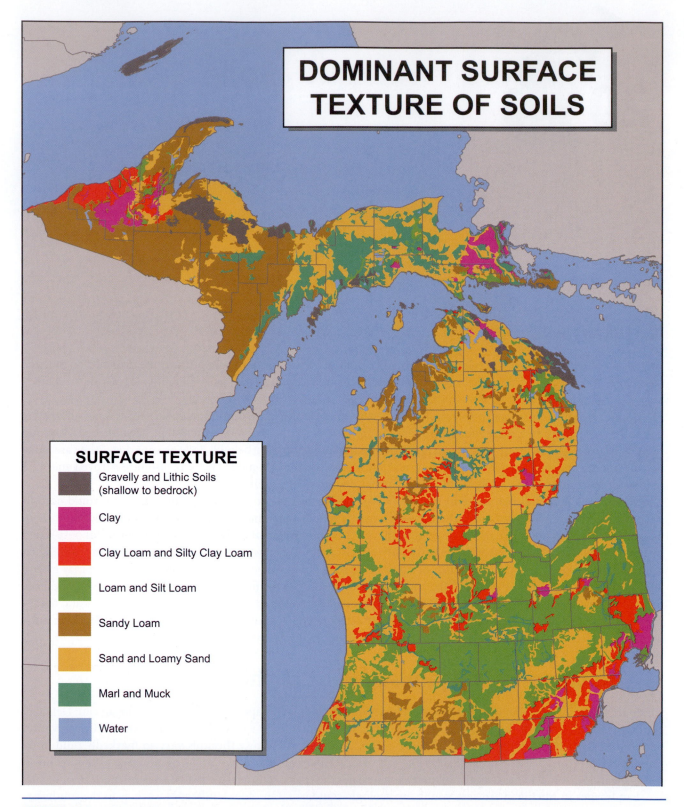

FIGURE 20.1   Map of the soil parent material types in Michigan, arranged by major surface textural groupings. Source: USDA-NRCS STATSGO soils data, Lincoln, NE.

into loamy soils. Additionally, because soils develop from the surface downward, into fresh parent material, our young soils are not very thick. One does not usually need to dig more than a meter or two to find unaltered parent material (the C horizon). In short, Michigan's soils still reflect very closely their parent materials.

This finding brings us to the second reason for our complex soilscapes—the glacial legacy left to us was one of extreme complexity (Plate 9). Glacial sediments (parent materials) typically vary greatly over even short distances, and in Michigan, with its many overlapping lakes, hills and dunes, that is all the more true. Thus, the complex sedimentology that we inherited from the ice sheets has not yet been "spatially simplified" by soil-forming processes.

Another glacial legacy that has directly led to our complex soilscapes involves topography and relief. Many of our landscapes are rolling and hilly, having been little changed from when the ice deposited the sediments in seemingly random assemblages of hills and swales (Plate 8). Post-glacial erosion by streams has incised deep ravines and valleys in places, forming even more relief than what was inherited. In other places, eolian (wind) processes have heaped sand onto an already complex landscape, adding more relief and increasing the complexity of the parent material assemblage (Chapter 18). To be sure, many landscapes have been "leveled" by water and waves, as glacial lakes inundated them (Chapter 13, Plate 8), but even these young landscapes can still have complex soil patterns.

Soils on the tops, sides and bottoms of hills are generally quite different, due to the impact of different water table depths, slope inclinations and aspects, runoff regimes, etc. Thus, even on a landscape where the ice left behind rolling hills of uniform parent material, relief itself has led to a variety of soils, each reflecting its position on the landscape. Well-drained soils with deep water tables tend to form on ridge tops, while soils of other (wetter) drainage classes form lower on the landscape. Over long periods of time, the relief of Michigan's soilscapes will probably decrease, lessening their complexity. But you'll need to check back in 50,000 years to see it.

Other factors, also important in forming the complexity of Michigan's soil landscape, but not as much as those mentioned above, are the influence of snowbelts (Fig. 19.9D) and the fact that Michigan sits at the confluence of three major vegetation biomes: tallgrass prairie, deciduous forest and mixed coniferous-deciduous forest (Chapter 21). These factors all add to the complex spatial pattern of soil development.

■ Factors that affect soil development and distribution

Many decades ago, it was realized that soils form because of the interaction of five major environmental factors. Each factor is meant to define the state and history of the soil system (Wilding 1994), and are thus referred to as a *state factor*. They are not forces or causes, but rather, factors—independent variables that define the soil system. Hans Jenny, a soil scientist at the University of California, formulated this idea, often referred to as the "clorpt" model, as:

$$S = f (cl, o, r, p, t, ...)$$

where S is the soil or a soil property, *cl* is the climate factor, *o* is the organisms factor, *r* is the relief factor, *p* is the parent material factor, *t* is the time factor. The string of dots represents other, unspecified factors that may be important locally but not universally, such as inputs of eolian dust, sulfate deposition in acid rain, or fire history. Climate and organisms are considered to be the "active" factors, while relief, parent material and time are more often "passive," i.e., they are being "impacted" by the active factors and various pedogenic processes. The parent material factor should be viewed as the initial state of the system, including its physical, chemical and mineralogical characteristics, as well as all other inorganic and organic components. As noted above, the *p* factor is particularly important in Michigan.

The state factor approach is particularly useful in understanding soil spatial variability because the factors/controls are generally observable, measurable and most importantly, they often vary spatially. Thus, this model is a favorite of soil mappers and geographers, and has perhaps its most utility at intermediate scales, e.g., in soil mapping. Soil mappers are often be able to explain and predict soil variation as a function of the five factors (Jenny 1946, Johnson and Hole 1994). Indeed, soil mapping may be viewed as a field solution to the state-factor equation.

In this chapter, I will use the state factor model (Jenny 1941) to explain soil variability across the state of Michigan, for as the factors vary from north-to-south, across hillslopes or from one major landform area to another, so do the soils.

FIGURE 20.2   A sandy soil (Entisol) that is about 10,000 years old, from western Baraga County. Note that the soil strongly resembles its parent material (outwash sand), because of the young age of the landscape as well as the lack of clay and weatherable minerals in the sand. Photo by R. Schaetzl.

Time

All of Michigan's soils are younger than about 16,000 years, which is when the glaciers began to expose sediment to soil-forming processes (Chapter 6). Southwestern Michigan was the first area to be deglaciated (Fig. 13.3), while the last area to be deglaciated, at about 11,000 years ago, was the northern fringes of the western Upper Peninsula. Younger soils exist, most notably those on coastal sand dunes that may be no older than 3,000–4,000 years old (Chapter 18). Areas covered by proglacial lakes (Chapter 13) became free of water as the lakes drained, and as soon as these lake floors became subaerially exposed, soils began to form. Most of Michigan's proglacial lakes drained between 12,000 and 9,000 years ago.

The importance of the time factor in soil development in Michigan cannot be overestimated. Young soils strongly resemble their parent materials (Fig. 20.2), and as stated above, our parent material heritage is one of great complexity. Young soils such as ours tend to be only minimally leached of nutrients; pH values are generally quite high in parts of the state where the parent materials are calcareous (chocked full of glacially ground up $CaCO_3$ from limestone bedrock). Young soils (Entisols) tend to be only minimally weathered, implying that they retain large storehouses of primary minerals; as these slowly weather, they release valuable nutrients for plant growth.

Parent material

In young soils, parent material characteristics overwhelmingly impact what the soil is like, and this is the case in Michigan (Bailey et al. 1957; Fig. 20.2). Our soils strongly resemble their parent materials. Most parent materials in Michigan's soils have been transported in by glaciers, wind or water; very few are residual (formed in place from weathered bedrock). The main areas of residual parent materials are in the western Upper Peninsula, where bedrock is close to the surface, although even here the residuum is thin due to glacial scour. Glacial parent materials were transported here from northern source regions, rich in sandstones and limestones, as well as the Canadian Shield with its hard, igneous and metamorphic rocks. Thus, most of the glacial parent materials are sandy, calcareous and rich in weatherable minerals. Most have abundant clasts of granite, basalt, limestone and other rocks as admixtures.

Most of the glacial drift in Michigan is calcareous and has a pH >8.0 because the ice incorporated ground up limestone and dolomite into it. On the Superior Bedrock Uplands of the western Upper Peninsula (Plate 8B), however, these types of bedrock generally do not exist, giving rise to acidic drift with pH values <6.0. Many soil-forming processes, especially podzolization and processes associated with translocation of clay, cannot begin until the parent material has been leached of Ca and Mg cations, i.e., until it has been rendered "non-calcareous" via weathering and leaching. On the acidic soils of the western Upper Peninsula, this "preliminary" leaching has not been not necessary, giving these soils a developmental head-start over all others in the state. Leaching of calcareous materials and their "base cations" (Ca, Mg, Na and K) may take millenia, and occurs from the top of the soil downward. For this reason, many Michigan soils are considered to be only as "thick" as the leached zone; the top of the C horizon is assumed to begin at the bottom of the depth of leaching. In coarse-textured, sandy soils, leaching occurs quickly; many Michigan

FIGURE 20.3 The Chippewa County Clay Plains, an important forage/hay growing area. Broad expanses of moist, clayey soils (Inceptisols) on this Lake Algonquin bed support the growth of hay crops. The growing season is too short here for most "downstate" cash crops such as corn or soybeans, but hay crops thrive here on the moist soils and under the long summer days. Photo by R. Schaetzl.

sands, even though originally calcareous, have been leached to several meters or more. But in loamy and clayey soils leaching is slower, and many of these soils have calcareous C horizons as shallow as 50–75 cm below the surface.

Sediment transported by rivers (alluvium) is often sorted and stratified, i.e., in layers, and much like the glacial drift which the river flows across. Eolian (wind-transported) sand is common not only along the shore of Lake Michigan, but also inland, where small dunes dot many of the interior glacial lake plains (Chapter 18). Because both of these parent materials originated as glacial drift and were later remobilized by water or wind, the soils that developed in them are younger and often less developed than their glacial drift counterparts.

One way that soil parent materials can be categorized is by texture (Fig. 20.1). Most of the "heavy" clay soils in Michigan occur in small, contiguous areas, usually corresponding to proglacial lake plains (Chapter 13). A large area of clayey soils centered on Chippewa County is associated with Glacial Lake Algonquin (Fig. 13.12), while a similar area in the far western Upper Peninsula developed in association with Glacial Lake Duluth (Figs. 13.14, 20.3; Plate 8B). Scattered areas of clay in the interior Lower Peninsula are also usually associated with minor lakes or places where a river was temporarily impounded by ice, depositing clay on the lake bottom. Loamy soils (loam is a texture of intermediate character, containing some silt, clay and sand, but dominated by none of them) are common on Saginaw lobe drift, and the lakes associated with that lobe (Figs. 17.12, 20.1). There are also many loamy soils in the western Upper Peninsula, where they are quite acidic. Sands dominate all other textures of soil parent materials in Michigan. Sandy soils are common on outwash plains, eskers and kames, in dunes and on many sandy moraines and other glacial landforms (Chapter 17). The largest area of sandy soils occurs in the north-central Lower Peninsula, in a roughly rectangular area known as the "High Plains" (Plate 8A). This area was marked by stagnant ice margins at various times in the past, allowing it to fill with sandy sediment carried there by glacial meltwater (Schaetzl and Weisenborn 2004, Schaetzl and Forman 2008; Chapter 17).

The last soil parent material, one which covers nearly 1/8 of the state, is not a mineral material, but instead is the organic plant remains that accumulate and slowly decay in wet areas like bogs and marshes (Fig. 20.4). In water-logged locations, plant matter cannot decay as rapidly as it does on drier, upland sites. Thus, it accumulates in the oxygen-poor water, sometimes to depths exceeding tens of meters. These organic soils, Histosols, have many unique characteristics that will be discussed below.

Climate

The humid continental climate of Michigan (Chapter 19) is *wet enough* for water to move through the soils in ample amounts to leach from them the salts, bases and carbonates that, in desert soils, accumulate due to lack of precipitation (Schaetzl et al. 1996). Our soils are, therefore, "leached"—most to a meter or more. The depth of carbonate leaching is usually associated with the top of the C horizon (for those soils whose parent materials are calcareous).

FIGURE 20.4 A cold, frosty morning in a swampy area in Luce County where consistently high waters tables have led to the accumulation of thick mats of organic matter, dominated by *Sphagnum* moss. Roughly 1/8 of Michigan contains these types of organic soils - Histosols. Photo by R. Schaetzl.

Our soils are also *warm enough* for ample amounts of weathering to proceed, and for freeze-thaw activity to be mainly restricted to areas where winter snowpacks are thin (Isard and Schaetzl 1995, Schaetzl and Tomczak 2002, Isard et al. 2007). Indeed, the impact of snowfall and snowpacks on the distribution of soils in Michigan is very important (Schaetzl and Isard 1991, 1996). Soils are better leached and more strongly developed in snowbelt areas (Fig. 19.9D), because more water moves through them in spring—a time of year when plant uptake of water is minimal (Henne et al. 2007).

Vegetation

Soils form under the direct and indirect influence of flora and fauna. Vegetation impacts soils directly by its production of litter (leaves, stems, seeds, roots, etc.) and by influencing the way that water and cations cycle through the soil. In Michigan, most soils have formed under the influence of forest; a few sandy, flat areas in southwestern Michigan, however, have formed under prairie grasses (Veatch 1927; Chapter 21, Plate 15) and some others have formed in association with wetland grasses, sedges and reeds. Grassland soils have thick, dark A horizons because of the continual growth and in-situ decay of roots (Fig. 20.5). Grasses also cycle base cations more than do trees, keeping their pH and fertility high. Some of Michigan's most productive soils are those that formed under grasses (Mollisols), such as the large area of Mollisols associated with Prairie Ronde and Schoolcraft Prairies (Fig. 20.5; Plate 15).

Forest soils usually have thick mats of litter (O horizons) on the surface, which in cool, northern Michigan decay slower than they accumulate. As the O horizon material decomposes, it forms a substance called humus, which gets translocated into the mineral soil, but only to a shallow depth; thin A horizons form. Root turnover is also slow in forests, so that these soils do not get the constant "below ground" additions of organic materials that grassland soils do. Lastly, most trees (with some notable exceptions, such as sugar maple and basswood) do not cycle base cations as grasses do, leaving them to be leached as water percolates through the soil. In sum, Michigan's forest soils tend to (1) have thinner A horizons, (2) be less naturally fertile, and (3) be more acidic than their grassland counterparts (Fig. 20.6).

Soils develop differently under coniferous forest than they do under broadleaf trees. Needle-leaf litter is more acidic and less prone to decay. Soils in northern Michigan, where many forests have a significant coniferous component (Chapter 21; Plate 15), are more acidic and have thicker O horizons. A major type of soils—Spodosols—are common in northern Michigan, having developed under the influence of coniferous trees (Isard and Schaetzl 1991). These soils are often coarse-textured, acidic and have B horizons enriched in soluble compounds such as Fe and Al. In southern Michigan and where deciduous trees dominate, soils do not get as acidic because the more

FIGURE 20.5 The dark (and thick) surface (A horizon) of soils formed under grassland vegetation in St. Joseph County. Many of these soils (Mollisols) are quite sandy, and when irrigated are very productive. Photo by R. Schaetzl.

FIGURE 20.6 A forest soil (Alfisol), exposed in a ditch in Isabella County. Note the thin A horizon (topsoil) and the light-colored E horizon below. Photo by R. Schaetzl.

base-rich litter recycles back to the mineral soil more quickly. The higher pH that results keeps Fe and Al generally insoluble, and the main component that gets translocated is clay, resulting in soils under deciduous forest with clay-rich B horizons. A second reason that soils under deciduous forest tend to have clay-rich B horizons is that, in sandy soils with minimal clay, coniferous forest is more common (at least in northern Michigan). Thus, to sum it up, on sandy, cool landscapes the soils tend to be acidic Spodosols with thick O horizons and with B horizons enriched in Fe and Al. On loamier parent materials, deciduous forest is more common, and the soils here tend to have higher pH values and more clay-rich B horizons. The latter situation is more common in southern Michigan mainly because this area has more loamy parent materials (Fig. 20.1), i.e., it is a parent material reason, not a climatic one.

Fire is a factor in soil development, and of course it is linked to vegetation. In areas where fires are common, as in some of the many the jack pine and oak forests of northern Michigan, the litter is thin and soil development is

FIGURE 20.7 Drainage ditch on the Saginaw lake plain. The underground drain "tiles" (not entirely visible here) do not allow the water table to rise beyond the depth to which they are buried, allowing these naturally wet soils (Inceptisols) to be farmed. Photo by R. Schaetzl.

minimal (Mokma and Vance 1989, Schaetzl 2002, Henne et al. 2007). Conversely, in areas less prone to fire, thick litter (O horizon) layers promote strong soil development, which in turn aids in forest growth. This positive feedback mechanism leads to productive forests on well-developed soils, as occurs in the northwestern Lower Peninsula.

Relief/topography

Factors like climate and vegetation can be used to explain *regional* patterns of soils and soil properties, because they often change gradually across the state (exceptions, of course, do occur) (Plate 12). The passive state factors relief and parent material, however, can change abruptly on the landscape, and thus are more useful in explaining local-scale and small-scale soil patterns.

Soils often change remarkably along even short hillslopes; this is the effect of relief. In low-lying locations where water tables are high, soils are wetter and display grayish (gleyed) colors, due to the presence of reduced Fe. Translocation processes (to the B horizon) are inhibited in these saturated soils. If the water table overtops the soil surface for extended periods of time, organic matter will begin to accumulate, and Histosols (organic soils) may even form. Many landscapes in Michigan are dominated by wetlands; some do not normally have standing water above the soil surface, and thus have developed into poorly-drained, gray-colored, mineral soils. Many of these soils classify as Inceptisols—mineral soils with weakly developed B horizons. To find vast acreages of wet Inceptisols go to any of Michigan's proglacial lake plains, such as in the Saginaw Bay area (Figs. 20.7, 20.8).

Soils on uplands are generally free from the inhibiting effects of high water tables (unless the upland is flat and broad). Here, soils exhibit shades of red and brown (the Fe is in an oxidized state) and translocation from upper to lower soil horizons occurs freely. On sloping portions of the landscape, soils may be thinner, due to runoff, which slowly and steadily erodes the upper horizons, and also limits the amount of water that infiltrates.

■ Major soil regions of Michigan

Spodosols/Entisols/Histosols on dry, sandy uplands

Throughout the northern Lower Peninsula and large parts of the Upper Peninsula are broad tracts of dry, sandy uplands that support mixed coniferous-deciduous forest (Plate 15). On most of these landscapes, Spodosols are the dominant soil order (Fig. 20.8, Plate 12), although the wettest sites contain deep Histosols.

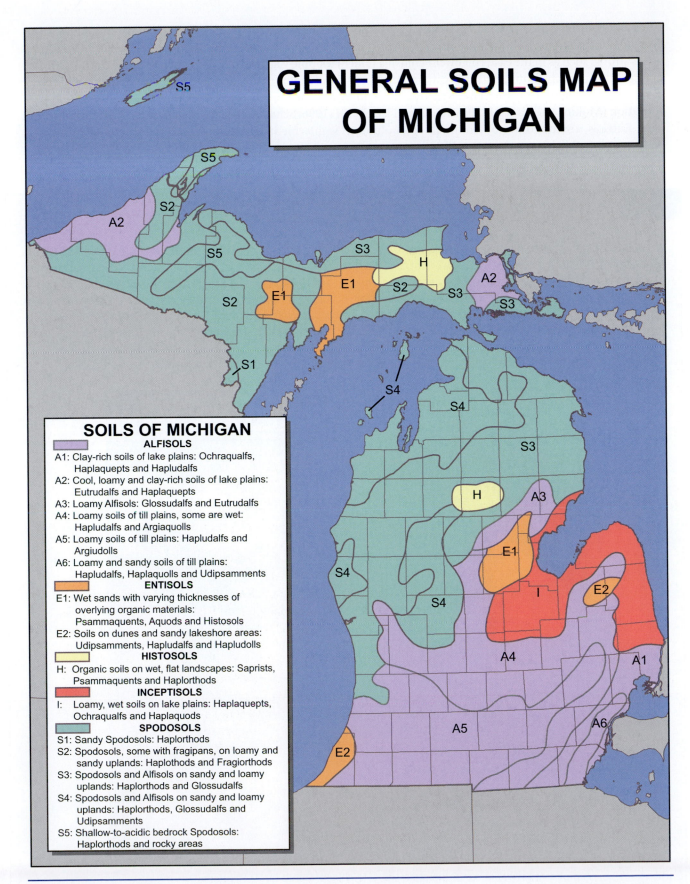

FIGURE 20.8 Map of the major soil types in Michigan, as grouped taxonomically. Source: USDA-NRCS STATSGO soils data, Lincoln, NE.

Three soil series are particularly common here. Kalkaska sand is a strongly-developed Spodosol, and its weaker-developed counterpart is Rubicon. Both are formed in "clean" quartz-rich sand. In areas where soil formation is not as strong, such as in the eastern Lower Peninsula under jack pine vegetation, a still weaker developed soil, Grayling (an Entisol) is widely found. Kalkaska can be viewed as an end member of a Spodosol development sequence, with the weak Grayling on the other end. Kalkaska is found in snowbelt areas, where conditions set up for strong podzolization (Mokma and Vance 1989, Schaetzl and Isard 1991, 1996, Schaetzl 2002). Grayling and Graycalm soils, both weak Entisols, are found in non-snowbelt areas; Rubicon is intermediate in many respects. Most sandy Spodosols and Entisols in Michigan are retained for forestry and recreation-related applications.

FOCUS BOX: Kalkaska sand—Michigan's state soil

In 1990, Michigan passed legislation making the Kalkaska sand Michigan's state soil. Why Kalkaska? First of all, it is a widespread soil that characterizes many parts of northern Michigan. Estimates have placed the extent of Kalkaska sand in Michigan at well over 400,000 hectares. Second, unlike many other official state soils, Kalkaska sand is found almost exclusively in Michigan. Lastly, the Kalkaska profile is striking , with a white E horizon overlying a deep red/brown B horizon. At depth is the tan-colored, sand-textured C horizon—the soil's parent material. Despite its acid, sandy character, Kalkaska sand supports some of the best hardwood forest in northern Michigan, because the B horizon has accumulated so much Fe, Al and humus that it is a nutrient and water storehouse, making Kalkaska perhaps the most fertile of the generally "non-fertile sand soils" in northern Michigan. What a striking state representative!

A profile of Kalkaska sand, the state soil of Michigan. Photo by R. Schaetzl.

Inceptisols on wet, loamy or clayey, lake plains

Broad lake plains in Michigan—in the Saginaw Bay area, in the far SE, in the eastern Upper Peninsula and the northern Lower Peninsula—all were inundated by proglacial lakes as the glaciers retreated (Chapter 13; Plate 10). These landscapes are dominated wave-bevelled till and lacustrine clay; some are also dotted with small dunes (Chapter 18). Soils on these wet, flat landscapes are usually fine-textured and are influenced by high water tables (Fig. 20.9). Most

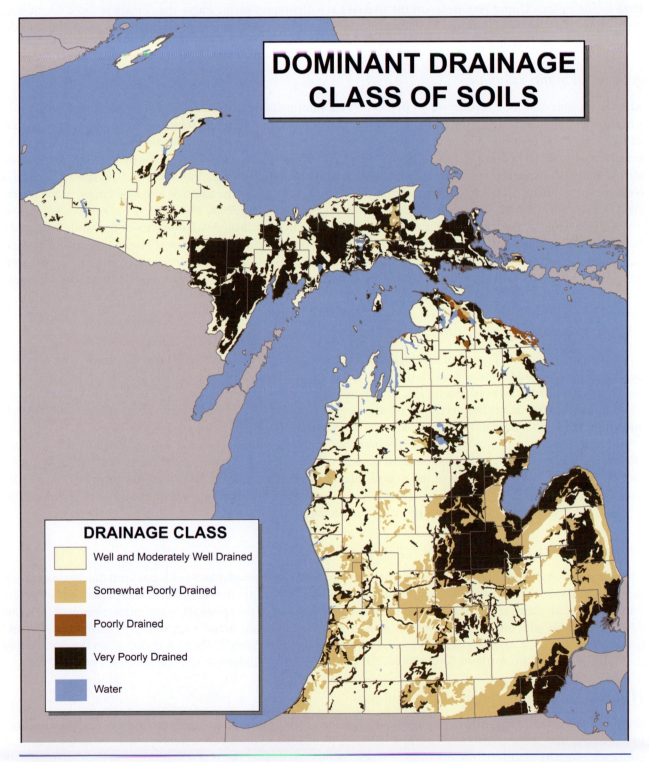

FIGURE 20.9   Map of the major soil types in Michigan, as grouped by drainage class. Source: USDA-NRCS STATSGO soils data, Lincoln, NE.

are thin, wet Inceptisols (Aquepts) that have not been well-leached due to the high water table (Fig. 20.8). Most have long been drained by perforated, plastic underground tubes (referred to as "tile drains" because they were originally made from clay pipes, or tiles), which prevent the water table from rising too close to the surface (Fig. 20.7).

Loamy textures, control of the water table by underground tile drains and broad, flat expanses of uniform soils have facilitated large scale agriculture on these soils. Many of the lake plains (except the wettest parts, the sandy areas, and those in the far north) are the most productive agricultural regions in Michigan (Chapter 36). Even in the eastern Upper Peninsula, on the Glacial Lake Algonquin plain, where the climate is too cold for cash grain crops, the Chippewa County Clay Plains have long been an important hay-growing region, dating back to the heyday of lumbering (Fig. 20.3).

Alfisols on loamy till plains

Alfisols are soils that have medium-high pH values, are minimally weathered and, most importantly, have a sub-surface accumulation of clay in the B horizon (Fig. 20.6). Alfisols do not form, therefore, on clean sands. In Michigan, Alfisols occur wherever the parent material has some clay and the water table is deep enough to allow clay to be translocated to the B horizon. This situation is very common in Michigan, and thus Alfisols are a frequent associate on many landscapes; they dominate landscapes where loamy till is the parent material. The latter situation is common in southern Michigan, for example on the ground moraines of the Saginaw and Erie Lobes, in the northern Lower Peninsula, and on many uplands in the Upper Peninsula (Fig. 20.8, Plate 12).

Alfisols are generally very good agricultural soils, for they lack the droughty tendencies of the sandy Spodosols, have high nutrient contents and generally occur on rolling but not rugged landscapes. The rolling nature of these landscapes has led to a variety of Alfisols of different drainage classes, and perhaps even some Histosols in the low-lying areas. Many of the finer-textured Alfisols are so slowly permeable that they drain slowly; these soils have generally been drained with subsurface tiles.

Mollisols on sandy, former prairies

As discussed in Chapter 21, parts of southwestern Michigan were once covered with tallgrass prairie. The soils that developed here are sandy Mollisols, with thick, dark A horizons. These Mollisols are well-drained and occur on flat, sandy uplands (former outwash plains; Fig. 20.5; Plate 12). When irrigated, these soils are highly productive. Indeed, a vibrant seed corn industry has developed on these soils, because the soils are excellent, occur on broad, flat uplands and, given the abundant shallow groundwater resources, can be readily irrigated.

Mollisols also occur on wet landscapes, where they represent an intermediate form of development between Histosols (which accumulate large amounts of organic matter due to persistent high water tables) and upland soils (which are dry enough that much of the organic matter is quickly oxidized and lost). Thus, many of the poorly-drained soils on lake plains are Mollisols, while the somewhat poorly and moderately drained soils are Inceptisols (Plate 12). These wetter Mollisols are also highly productive, when drained.

Entisols on dunes and dry outwash plains

On clean (little clay) sand parent materials, e.g., sand dunes and many outwash plains, soils can form quickly, but remain droughty and erodable. In areas of thick snowpacks and mixed forest, Spodosols will eventually form, but on young dunes or outwash plains under pines, the soils may not yet have reached the Spodosol "stage" of development (Schaetzl 2002). Weak soils with only A-C profiles (no, or only a weak, B horizon) occur. Such soils are called Entisols ("ent" from "recent") (Fig. 20.2). Many of Michigan's sandy Entisols remain in forest. They are common on the dry sands of the "High Plains" of the northern Lower Peninsula, and on coastal and inland dunes (Chapter 17, Plates 8A, 12).

Histosols in swamps, marshes and wetlands

Bumper stickers tell us that Michigan's informal "state insect" is the mosquito. There are, indeed, many mosquitoes in Michigan, due to the plethora of swamps, marshes, wetlands and bodies of standing water. In young, glaciated landscapes such as Michigan, the drainage network (rivers) has not yet become integrated, and thus, there remain many of these undrained areas. With time, these wetlands will decrease in size and abundance. In the meantime,

FIGURE 20.10 A field of young celery plants on a Histosol (muck) soil in Barry County. These soils are highly productive but first must be drained to lower the water table. Draining the soils, however, makes them susceptible to wind erosion, necessitating the line of trees (wind-break) in the background.

areas with water at and above the surface for months of the year continue to accumulate organic materials, which only very slowly decompose (Fig. 20.4). Thick accumulations of organic materials, regardless of their state of decomposition, are soils called Histosols. If the organic materials are well decomposed and black in color, they are colloquially called mucks; those composed of more "raw" organic materials are less common, and are called "peats." In Michigan, Histosols cover about 1/8 of the land surface; the largest tracts are in the Upper Peninsula, usually on proglacial lake plains (Fig. 20.9, Plates 10, 12). However, any landscape with low, wet areas will probably have some Histosols on it, in the wettest sites where the water table is frequently above the surface. These soils are very important for biodiversity and hydrologic reasons, and they are huge storehouses of carbon.

Most Histosols in Michigan have never been cleared for agriculture and remain in or near their native condition. However, some important areas have been cleared and now support a thriving vegetable (primarily leafy and root-crop vegetables, such as lettuce, onions, carrots, radishes, etc) industry (Fig. 20.10; Chapter 37). Mint is also a crop that thrives on mucks. Turfgrass farms generally are developed on mucks, which provide excellent growing conditions and large, flat expanses of fertile, wet soils.

FOCUS BOX: The NRCS soil mapping effort in Michigan

The branch of the US government that is responsible for inventorying and mapping the soils of the United States is the Natural Resources Conservation Service (formerly the Soil Conservation Service), within the US Department of Agriculture. As of 2005, the soils of every county in Michigan had been mapped in detail by field mappers of the NRCS, who walked most of the land, probing holes, digging pits and generally observing the lay of the land and it flora, to determine and document the character of the soils that blanket our state. By 2007, soil map data were freely available both in paper form (as county soil survey reports) and as digital GIS files. Although 100% accuracy on a soil map is impossible to accomplish, even with unlimited resources, the quality of the NRCS products is very good and highly useful. Many agencies and individuals use soil map data in their planning decisions, and rightfully so. It is difficult to think of a land use decision that could not benefit from accurate and detailed soil knowledge. The soil data are there—use them!

■ Conclusions

Michigan's soil resources are some of the most variable and diverse of any state. Our knowledge of Michigan's soils—both their distribution, as well as their formation and proper management—has increased by orders of magnitude in the past three decades. Soils data are freely available via the internet and other sources. It is our obligation to better "know our soils," so as to incorporate them into our land use decisions and wisely use the soil resources given to us.

Literature Cited

Bailey, H.H., Whiteside, E.P. and A.E. Erickson. 1957. Mineralogical composition of glacial materials as a factor in the morphology and genesis of some Podzols, Grey Wooded, Gray-Brown Podzolic, and Humic-Gley soils in Michigan. Soil Science Society of America Proceedings 21:433–441.

Henne, P.D., Hu, F.S. and D.T. Cleland. 2007. Lake-effect snow as the dominant control of mesic-forest distribution in Michigan. Journal of Ecology 95:517–529.

Isard, S.A. and R.J. Schaetzl. 1995. Estimating soil temperatures and frost in the lake effect snowbelt region, Michigan, USA. Cold Regions Science and Technology 23:317–332.

Isard, S.A., Schaetzl, R.J. and J.A. Andresen. 2007. Soils cool as climate warms in Great Lakes region, USA. Annals of the Association of American Geographers 97:467–476.

Jenny, H. 1941. Factors of Soil Formation. McGraw-Hill, New York. 281 pp.

Jenny, H. 1946. Arrangement of soil series and types according to functions of soil-forming factors. Soil Science 61:375–391.

Johnson, D.L. and F.D. Hole. 1994. Soil formation theory: A summary of its principal impacts on Geography, Geomorphology, Soil-Geomorphology, Quaternary Geology and Paleopedology. In: Factors of Soil Formation: A Fiftieth Anniversary Retrospective. Soil Science Society of America Special Publication 33:111–126.

Mokma, D.L. and G.F. Vance. 1989. Forest vegetation and origin of some spodic horizons, Michigan. Geoderma 43:311–324.

Schaetzl, R.J. 2002. A Spodosol-Entisol transition in northern Michigan: climate or vegetation? Soil Science Society of America Journal 66:1272–1284.

Schaetzl, R.J., Frederick, W.E. and L. Tornes. 1996. Secondary carbonates in three fine and fine-loamy Alfisols in Michigan. Soil Science Society of America Journal 60:1862–1870.

Schaetzl, R.J. and S.A. Isard. 1991. The distribution of Spodosol soils in southern Michigan: a climatic interpretation. Annals of the Association of American Geographers 81:425–442.

Schaetzl, R.J. and S.A. Isard. 1996. Regional-scale relationships between climate and strength of podzolization in the Great Lakes region, North America. Catena 28:47–69.

Schaetzl, R.J. and S.L. Forman. 2008. OSL ages on glacioflurial sediment in northern Lower Michigan constrain expansion of the Laurentide Ice Sheet. Quaternary Research 70:81–90.

Schaetzl, R.J. and D.M. Tomczak. 2002. Wintertime soil temperatures in the fine-textured soils of the Saginaw Valley, Michigan. Great Lakes Geographer 8:87–99.

Schaetzl, R.J. and B.N. Weisenborn. 2004. The Grayling Fingers geomorphic region of Michigan: Soils, sedimentology, stratigraphy and geomorphic development. Geomorphology 61:251–274.

Veatch, J.O. 1927. The dry prairies of Michigan. Michigan Academician 8:269–278.

Wilding, L.P. 1994. Factors of soil formation: Contributions to pedology. In: Factors of Soil Formation: A Fiftieth Anniversary Retrospective. Soil Science Society of America Special Publication 33:15–30.

Further Readings

Asady, G.H. and E.P. Whiteside. 1982. Composition of a Conover-Brookston map unit in southeastern Michigan. Soil Science Society of America Journal 46:1043–1047.

Barrett, L.R. 2001. A strand plain soil development sequence in Northern Michigan, USA. Catena 44:163–186.

Barrett, L.R. and R.J. Schaetzl. 1993. Soil development and spatial variability on geomorphic surfaces of different age. Physical Geography 14:39–55.

Barrett, L.R. and R.J. Schaetzl. 1998. Regressive pedogenesis following a century of deforestation: Evidence for depodzolization. Soil Science 163:482–497.

Franzmeier, D.P. and E.P. Whiteside. 1963. A chronosequence of Podzols in northern Michigan. I. Ecology and description of pedons. Michigan State University Agricultural Experiment Station Quarterly Bulletin 46:2–20.

Franzmeier, D.P. and E.P. Whiteside. 1963. A chronosequence of Podzols in northern Michigan. II. Physical and chemical properties. Michigan State University Agricultural Experiment Station Quarterly Bulletin 46:21–36.

Haile-Mariam, S. and D.L. Mokma. 1995. Mineralogy of two fine-loamy hydrosequences in south-central Michigan. Soil Survey Horizons 37:65–74.

Hole, F.D. 1976. Soils of Wisconsin. University of Wisconsin Press, Madison. 223 pp.

Hunckler, R.V. and R.J. Schaetzl. 1997. Spodosol development as affected by geomorphic aspect, Baraga County, Michigan. Soil Science Society of America Journal 61:1105–1115.

Isard, S.A. and R.J. Schaetzl. 1998. Effects of winter weather conditions on soil freezing in southern Michigan. Physical Geography 19:71–94.

Lichter, J. 1998. Rates of weathering and chemical depletion in soils across a chronosequence of Lake Michigan sand dunes. Geoderma 85:255–282.

Medley, K.E. and J.R. Harman. 1987. Relationships between the vegetation tension zone and soils distribution across central lower Michigan. Michigan Botanist 26:78–87.

Messenger, A.S., Whiteside, E.P. and A.R. Wolcott. 1972. Climate, time, and organisms in relation to Podzol development in Michigan sands: I. Site descriptions and microbiological observations. Soil Science Society of America Proceedings 36:633–638.

Millar, C.E. 1948. Soils of Michigan. Michigan State College, Cooperative Extension Service, Extension Bull. 290. 31 pp.

Mokma, D.L. 1991. Genesis of Spodosols in Michigan, USA. Trends in Soil Science 1:25–32.

Mokma, D.L., Doolittle, J.A. and L.A. Tornes. 1994. Continuity of ortstein in sandy Spodosols, Michigan. Soil Survey Horizons 35:6–10.

Schaetzl, R.J. 1990. Effects of treethrow microtopography on the characteristics and genesis of Spodosols, Michigan, USA. Catena 17:111–126.

Schaetzl, R.J. 1994. Changes in O horizon mass, thickness and carbon content following fire in northern hardwood stands. Vegetatio 115:41–50.

Schaetzl, R.J. and S.N. Anderson. 2005. Soils: Genesis and Geomorphology. Cambridge University Press. 832 pp.

Veatch, J.O. 1931. Natural geographic divisions of land. Papers of the Michigan Academy of Sciences, Arts, and Letters 14:417–432.

Veatch, J.O. 1934. Some characteristics of mature soils in Michigan. American Soil Survey Association Bulletin 15:42–44.

Weisenborn, B.N. and R.J. Schaetzl. 2005. Range of fragipan expression in some Michigan soils: II. A model for fragipan evolution. Soil Science Society of America Journal 69:178–187.

21

Plant Geography

Jay R. Harman

■ Introduction

Michigan resides within one of the great forested regions of North America. Sitting at the northernmost reach of the Eastern Deciduous Forest that covers much of the eastern US, and in contact with the great Boreal Forest to the north across much of central Canada, it lies astride two of the most extensive forests on the continent. In its transitional position between the two, Michigan is a mosaic of communities typical of both regions, presenting a variety of assemblages and species. This variety is further enhanced by the state's large size and complex glacial and post-glacial climatic history (Chapters 6, 7). With each climatic fluctuation, came an infusion of different species into the local flora; at various times biota from the Boreal Forest, Atlantic coastal plain, interior eastern North America, and the prairies of the Great Plains invaded, or for a time even became dominant. In addition, glacial processes within the state left a wide assortment of topographic and textural environments (Chapters 6, 20, Plates 8, 10) that, in local cases, allowed elements of these past floras to persist right into the present. Furthermore, with the arrival of European settlers, the prehistoric disturbance regime was altered, in some places profoundly. Forests were cut and fire frequencies increased, favoring some species over others and sometimes creating entirely new assemblages (Chapter 40). All told, this combined history has resulted in considerable habitat and ecological variety (Whitney 1987).

The focus in this chapter is on the *presettlement* plant geography of Michigan (Plate 15) because post-settlement disturbances have left substantial parts of the landscape in agriculture, and the composition of the remaining forests often heavily altered from their original condition (Chapter 40). These disturbances have complicated the relationship between contemporary forest composition and their broad environmental controls. Inasmuch as a primary aim of this chapter is to explain, as well as describe, Michigan's vegetation, a focus on the presettlement landscape permits a clearer analysis of this relationship. This discussion, consequently, pertains specifically to the vegetative cover as European settlers found it, unless otherwise noted.

■ Environmental factors reflected in plant geography

With the exception of small enclaves of true Prairie and a somewhat greater extent of Savanna Grassland (mixed prairie and open woodland), mostly in the southern and southwestern portions of the Lower Peninsula and some non-forest wetlands adjacent to the Great Lakes, Michigan's presettlement vegetation consisted predominantly of forest (Plate 15). Indeed, the land cover in much of northern Michigan is forested today (Fig. 21.1). Forest dominance results because our climate is sufficiently moist to support the growth of tree cover everywhere in the state (except where local factors or history intervene to permit the persistence of prairie). Determining the presettlement vegetation composition is complicated, obviously, by post-settlement logging and other disturbances. Most of today's forests

FIGURE 21.1   Like other areas of northern Wisconsin and Minnesota, much of the northern half of the Lower Peninsula and the Upper Peninsula remains largely forested today despite having been heavily logged over a century ago (Chapters 29, 41). Seen here is a portion of the uplands of Iron County. Photo by R. Schaetzl.

FIGURE 21.2   Seen here is an open area with many isolated, old white pine stumps, south of Kingston Lake in Alger County. Even though logging in the state reached a peak before 1900, many formerly forested sites such as this one in the Upper Peninsula are still littered with stumps. These types of landscapes have been referred to as stump prairies by Barrett (1998). Photo by R. Schaetzl.

are second, third and even fourth generation regrowth, and the degree to which they resemble their presettlement counterparts varies from place to place as a result; in some cases, reforestation has been painfully slow (Fig. 21.2). Fortunately, scattered remnant stands shed light on the early forest make-up, and extensive notes made by General Land Office surveyors (Chapter 28) provide a useful early picture of these early forests (Comer et al. 1995).

Composition of the plant cover at any one place/time is a result of vegetation dynamics, past history and current environmental constraints, all operating at a number of scales. When one is attempting to understand the *pattern* of plant distributions, however, climate is generally regarded as being the most important large-scale environmental constraint (Daubenmire 1978, Denton and Barnes 1987, Harrington and Harman 1991). Although Michigan is characterized by a generally uniform climate, regional and local differences do have a subtle impact on its overall plant geography. Meanwhile, topography and elevation, while potentially able to affect environmental factors (such as heat and moisture) that shape biotic distributions, are insufficient within Michigan to do so (maximum local relief across the state seldom exceeds 100 m). Consequently, other local factors such as soils and wetness emerge as strong influences on plant geography within the state. As a result, this discussion will be limited to the influences of climate, soils and wetness/drainage.

Climate

Gradients of heat and moisture across Michigan (Fig. 19.9) were (and still are) reflected in the state's vegetation pattern. Heat is an important ecological constraint for several reasons, and one of its climatic expressions is *heat accumulation*—variously characterized as the "length of the growing season" or the accumulation of "growing degree days." Heat is important because plants have genetically set requirements for exposure to heat that need to be met in order for them to pass through their phenological (life-stage) thresholds. For example, although specific requirements differ by species, each will need a minimum amount of accumulated heat for its fruit to mature, and thus for it to successfully reproduce. Heat is also related to evaporative losses of moisture from plant and soil surfaces; greater seasonal totals of such losses are directly related to greater heat accumulation totals. Not all species are equally tolerant of such moisture loss and stress (Oechel and Lawrence 1985). Furthermore, extreme heat and cold creates short term stresses that may lie beyond the tolerance levels of certain species, limiting their distributions. Unusually early autumn freezes may prevent fruit maturity, and late spring frosts may interfere with flowering, thereby affecting a species' ability to reproduce. Furthermore, diseases and insects that threaten forest species are similarly limited (or favored) by unusual heat and cold, because heat is such an important limiting factor.

In Michigan, heat accumulation and length of the growing season (usually measured as the mean number of days between last spring and first autumn freezes) both decline northward, a pattern that impacts plant geography in at least two ways. First, temperate species that require fairly long summers to reproduce are increasingly restricted northward (Fig. 21.3B). Some species native to the forest of the southern Lower Peninsula (and which are characteristic of the Eastern Deciduous Forest south of the state) that drop out northward include tuliptree (*Liriodendron tulipifera*), black gum (*Nyssa sylvatica*), black walnut (*Juglans nigra*), and Ohio buckeye (*Aesculus glabra*) and several species of hickory (*Carya cordiformis, C. glabra,* and *C. ovata*). A number of oak species, such as pin oak (*Quercus palustris*), swamp white oak (*Q. bicolor*) and chinquapin oak (*Q. muhlenbergii*) are distributed similarly. The result of this pattern is that the broadleaved forests of the southern Lower Peninsula, especially in far southwestern and southeastern counties, are compositionally richer than forests farther north. The disappearance of these species northward probably reflects a complex interplay of environmental and competitive factors that are not easily disentangled. Whereas some species are environmentally restricted northward, others are competitively excluded because they have less vigor and cannot compete with other forest species better adapted to the northern environment.

Declining temperatures northward also reduce moisture losses from evapotranspiration, or ET, a term that includes moisture loss from plants (transpiration) as well as from non-transpiring surfaces (evaporation). Lower evaporation rates allow a higher percentage of a given amount of precipitation to remain for plant use, and at the same time are associated with less tissue water loss by transpiration. Lower ET values allow some species, which are limited southward by summer warmth and dryness, to become more common in the north. Several, such as balsam fir (*Abies balsamea*), white spruce (*Picea glauca*) and jack pine (*Pinus banksiana*) are boreal species that reach their southern limits in the state (Fig. 21.3B). They are rare or absent from uplands in the southern Lower Peninsula, where summertime heat and dryness take their toll. Across North America, boreal species in general are limited southward by thermal attributes of the environment, and Michigan is but a microcosm in that regard (Elliott-Fisk 1988).

The geographic limits of a disproportionately large number of tree species are reached in a rather narrow strip across central portions of the Lower Peninsula referred to as the Floristic Tension Zone (Fig. 21.3A). On Plate 15, the tension zone is clearly delineated by the abrupt changeover from "Beech-Sugar Maple Forest" to "Northern Hardwood-Conifer Forest" that stretches from Saginaw Bay to about Ottawa County in west Michigan. In many respects, the Tension Zone in Michigan resembles a transition that stretches NW-SE through central Wisconsin and Minnesota, separating the "Conifer-Hardwood Forest" to the north from other types to the SW (Curtis 1959).

The factors responsible for the Tension Zone have been much debated in the literature; among those proposed are climatic influences (Medley and Harman 1988). Unfortunately, attempts to link gradients of temperature or evaporation with the tension zone are complicated by questions about the representativeness of weather data collected at stations in the central Lower Peninsula, because the landscape is topographically rougher north of the Tension Zone than south of it. Historically, settlements were more likely to be located along rivers—that permitted early

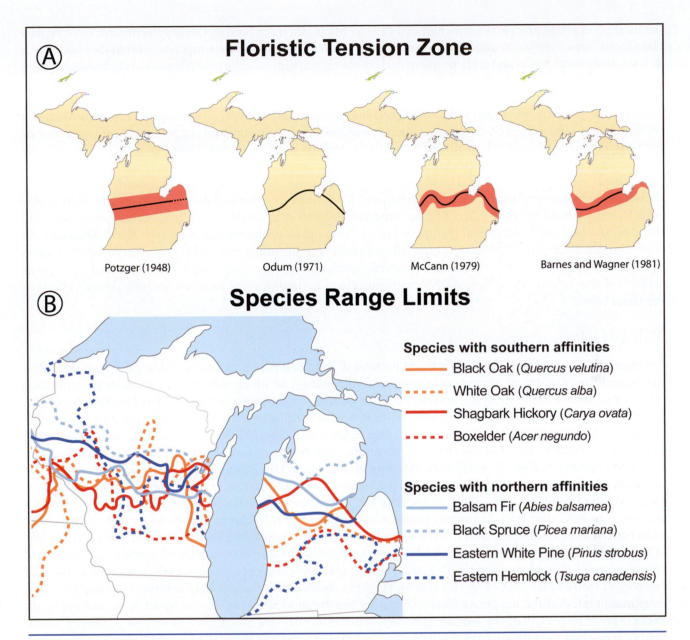

FIGURE 21.3 The floristic tension zone in Michigan. A. Locations of the tension zone, based on research by various authors. B. Range limits of some tree species with northern and southern affinities. These data show that many range limits are reached in and near the tension zone. After Burns and Honkala (1990a, b).

transportation—than they were on ridges, biasing townsites toward lower spots in the landscape. Because weather data have customarily been collected where people live (and most people live in these lower sites), data from these sites may be biased to colder values because of the drainage of cold air into these depressions during calm nights, giving perhaps a false impression that a climatic gradient exists at the Tension Zone. Also note the remarks under "Soils and Drainage" about a possible further soils influence on the location of the Tension Zone.

Another gradient of moisture that appears relevant to Michigan's plant geography is observed downwind from the Great Lakes. With both lake enhancement of winter precipitation, and mitigated summertime heat along and just inland from the eastern shore of Lake Michigan and the southeast shore of Lake Superior, areas immediately east of the Lakes have a longer growing season and more mesic climate than do other areas (Harman 1970). This augmented moisture budget—what Kenoyer (1933) originally referred to as a "marine effect"—seems expressed in the local plant geography particularly well east of Lake Michigan, from Berrien County northward. Here exists a "lake forest" type that has an unusually rich mixture of species from both more temperate areas to the south (such as *Liriodendron* and *Nyssa*) and more northern parts of the region, such as white pine (*Pinus strobus*), hemlock (*Tsuga canadensis*) and yellow birch (*Betula alleghaniensis*) (Kenoyer 1933). In the northern Lower Peninsula, this moisture gradient results in mesic hardwood forests, dominated by beech (*Fagus grandifolia*), sugar maple (*Acer saccharum*), red oak (*Quercus rubra*) and yellow birch, becoming increasingly widespread westward toward Lake Michigan (as in Antrim County) even on sandy soils, whereas such soils on interior uplands support more xeric jack pine or even oak-dominated forests (Harman and Nutter 1973, Mokma and Vance 1989, Henne et al. 2007; Plate 15). An even stronger reflection of this influence is observable on the snowbelt of the Keweenaw Peninsula, as well as on some islands within Lake Michigan (Harman and Plough 1986). Not only does snow fall abundantly here in the winter, but soil moisture supplies are "stretched" by reduced ET during even otherwise dry summers because of its peninsular location amidst the cold waters of Lake Superior (Schaetzl et al. 2005). As a result, boreal species are more common on these sites, and several plants common to moist parts of mountainous western North America have been stranded as "disjuncts" or become especially common here, including thimbleberry (*Rubus parviflorus*) and a *Vaccinium* locally referred to as "bilberry" (probably species *membranaceum*). As a result, they stand not only as artifacts of late- or post-Pleistocene distributions, but also as testimony to the local ameliorating climatic effects of the Great Lakes.

Soils and wetness/drainage

Michigan's plant geography also reflects broad patterns of soils. Soil parent materials within the state overwhelmingly consist of glacial drift, the nature (texture and mineralogy) of which reflects both its mode of deposition (whether deposited primarily by ice or water) and the geologic composition of the underlying rocks (Chapter 20, Plate 12). Extensive portions of the northern Lower Peninsula are characterized by coarse-textured outwash materials and sandy soils (Fig. 20.1). Whereas the change in geology westward across the Upper Peninsula from sedimentary to crystalline composition (Plate 6) has only a subdued expression in the region's soils, the northward increase in the extent of sandy parent materials through the central Lower Peninsula has a clear impact on the distribution of soils and vegetation. Furthermore, the location of the soil texture gradient corresponds closely to the location of the Tension Zone (Figs. 20.1, 21.3A, Plate 12). This correspondence raises obvious questions about whether the two are related. The sandy sediments common in northern Lower Michigan have developed into porous, acid soils, preferred (or at least well-tolerated) by many northern plant species (Medley and Harman 1987; Chapter 20). When combined with the local climate, they became nearly ideal sites for some coniferous species, particularly red (*P. resinosa*) and white pine, which locally formed nearly pure stands in the presettlement forest (note the widespread category of "Mixed Pine Forests" in this area on Plate 15). South of this transition, in contrast, oaks and hickories, trees more typical of the temperate forests of eastern North America, commonly occupied such sandy uplands. Because sandy soils south of the Tension Zone supported mostly dry-site broadleaved forests, while soils of similar texture supported pine stands farther north, a general climatic gradient in central Lower Michigan is implicated (or else soils of similar texture would all have supported similar stands, all things considered). On the other hand, the *sharpness* of the Tension Zone appears to reflect a similarly abrupt northward increase of sandy soils associated with pine-dominated forests in that area.

A more gradual change in vegetation that may also be soil-related occurs westward across the Upper Peninsula. East of the Marquette-to-Green Bay line, soils are generally developed in coarse-textured outwash or lacustrine materials, wetlands are extensive, and the landscape strongly resembles parts of the northern Lower Peninsula. (Fig. 21.4; Heinselman 1965). Westward, however, where crystalline rocks of the Laurentian shield are at or near the surface, upland soils are generally more loamy, poorly drained sites are less extensive (note the greater abundance of "Conifer Swamp" in the eastern Upper Peninsula than in the western parts, on Plate 15), and more forest cover is of the upland variety (Brubaker 1975).

Beyond these large-scale influences, smaller-scale habitats associated with unique soils or site conditions add additional complexity to the state's plant geography. Perhaps most important are the innumerable small wetlands that dot the Michigan landscape. Especially where the wetland soils are acidic, such sites are frequently home to species common to more northern regions. The most acidic of such wetlands are known as *bogs* ("Conifer Swamp" on Plate 15; see also Figure 21.4) and harbor plants more typical of the Boreal Forest (Fig. 21.5). Characteristic

FIGURE 21.4 Shown here is an expansive boreal stand on a very poorly drained site in Crawford County. Many poorly drained sites in the northern Lower Peninsula and eastern Upper Peninsula harbor large expanses of these "Conifer Swamp or Muskeg/Bog" communities. Photo by R. Schaetzl.

FIGURE 21.5 This photo shows an acidic bog in Mackinac County, MI. All across Michigan, but especially in the northern parts of the state, small non-alluvial acidic wetlands called *bogs* harbor remnant boreal communities. Sometimes, these even include such insectivorous species as sundew (*Drosera* spp.) and pitcher plant (*Sarracenia purpurea*). Photo by R. Schaetzl.

trees such as larch (*Larix laricina*) and black spruce (*Picea mariana*) are generally restricted to such sites in the Lower Peninsula, although in the cooler Upper Peninsula they are somewhat more widespread. Other shrubby boreal species restricted to bogs include two native cranberries (*Vaccinuim marcrocarpon* and *V. Oxycoccos*), Labrador tea (*Ledum groenlandicum*), leatherleaf (*Chamaedaphne calyculata*) and andromeda (*Andromeda glaucophylla*). The geographical significance of these and similar bog species is that they are relics of former distributions and provide field evidence that boreal conditions (and biota) once persisted in the southern parts of the state (Chapter 7). Although conditions have obviously warmed since the Pleistocene, flora associated with ice-age environments still persist in these cold, acidic bogs.

Meanwhile, on coarse-textured upland sites, e.g., on sand dunes, plant species tolerant of dry conditions survive. Some of these are typical prairie plants that invaded from western (Great Plains) sources during dry episodes in the middle Holocene (roughly 8,000–4,000 years ago; Chapter 7). At the time of European settlement, Michigan had perhaps 400 km² of prairie (Plate 15), mostly in the southern and southwestern Lower Peninsula, and considerably

FIGURE 21.6 A small prairie relic near Middleville, in Barry County, is shown here. Prairie communities were a part of the original vegetation most commonly in the southwestern part of the Lower Peninsula and today persist mainly on isolated and unplowed sites such as cemeteries and railroad rights-of-way. Photo by R. Schaetzl.

more "Savanna Grassland"—where prairie plants were intermixed with open forest. Today, remnants of these prairie communities persist on unplowed sites such as cemeteries or railroad rights-of-way; otherwise, most are now farmed (Fig. 21.6). Like the boreal bog communities, these prairie remnants provide evidence of past climates (and disturbance regimes) different from the present. They allowed species of now-remote environments to invade the state, and persist only on "compensated" sites that replicate their larger physical environment. Associated prairie species include little and big bluestem grass (*Andropogon scoparius* and *A. gerardii*, respectively), both of which have spread widely from their prairie remnants to other habitats within the state, rattlesnake-master (*Eryngium yuccifolium*) and prairie compass plant (*Silphium* species).

Finally, several habitats, especially sandy lakeshore areas or areas of peat soils (Histosols), are host to some plants that are otherwise found on the Atlantic coastal plain. This distribution has puzzled plant geographers for some time, and several scenarios have been suggested to explain them. Most likely, they are relic populations traceable back to the last glacial advance when plant ranges were rearranged by changing climate. At some point during this time, coastal habitat extended from the Atlantic shoreline westward along parts of the St. Lawrence Valley and into the Great Lakes, permitting an intermingling of species. Included among these plants is the low-growing shrub, beach-heather (*Hudsonia tomentosa*).

■ General vegetation patterns

Lower Peninsula

South of the Tension Zone (Fig. 21.3), early forests consisted of several different community types, depending on overall drainage and, to a lesser extent, history (all forest types cited in this discussion are shown on Plate 15). "Oak-Hickory Forest" was characteristic of well-drained uplands (Fig. 21.7). Characteristic species included some mixture of shagbark hickory (*Carya ovata*), pignut hickory (*C. glabra*), black oak (*Quercus velutina*), scarlet oak (*Q. coccinea*), white oak (*Q. alba*) and red oak (*Q. rubra*). Woods bordering on prairies or savannas ("Savanna Grassland") were sometimes dominated by bur oak (*Q. macrocarpa*), the thick bark on mature specimens of which afforded protection against prairie fires. These oak-hickory woods must have had a relatively bright and open aspect and were probably more prone to small ground fires than were nearby moister sites, which suppressed fire-sensitive species such as red maple (*Acer rubrum*) and black cherry (*Prunus serotina*). However, in the prolonged absence of fires, these species sometimes became co-dominants on these sites (Dodge and Harman 1985, Abrams 1998).

FIGURE 21.7 An oak forest on a coarse-textured (sandy) site in the southwestern Lower Peninsula is depicted here. Forests dominated by species of oak (in the north) and oak and hickory (mostly in the south) were, and remain, common on well-drained uplands throughout the Lower Peninsula. Here, in Barry County, black oak dominates, with lesser amounts of white oak. Photo by R. Schaetzl.

FIGURE 21.8 Shown here is a beech-sugar maple stand in northern Michigan. Forests comprised principally of beech and sugar maple are common on moist but permeable upland soils across the northwestern Lower and eastern Upper Peninsulas. Abundant spring wildflower displays are especially characteristic of such forests. Photo by R. Schaetzl.

   Moister uplands (those with loamier soils) usually supported more mesic "Beech-Sugar Maple" forests. In these stands, beech (*Fagus grandifolia*) and sugar maple (*A. saccharum*) were mixed with lesser amounts of other species such as white ash (*Fraxinus americana*), basswood (*Tilia americana*), black cherry, black walnut (*Juglans nigra*), slippery elm (*Ulmus rubra*) and red oak (*Quercus rubra*). The exact proportions of each species depended largely on site wetness, soil fertility and site history. In general, the less frequent fires and denser overstory characteristic of these forests permitted shade-tolerant species such as sugar maple and beech to succeed themselves and form stable communities (Fig. 21.8). Occasionally, however, tree-falls opened gaps in the canopy that allowed seedlings of less shade-tolerant associates like basswood, ash, red oak and black cherry temporary opportunity to reach the canopy before it closed again, thereby helping to maintain species richness on these sites that otherwise would have almost exclusively been occupied by beech and sugar maple.

FIGURE 21.9 On low permeability or impermeable soils, where water collects during wet weather, various hardwood swamp forest communities, such as this one, are common across much of the Lower Peninsula. This late spring image is from the Muskegon River floodplain, in Clare County. Photo by R. Schaetzl.

Meanwhile, wet-mesic to hydric sites (those in which water stood for some period in wet weather) were in general occupied by "Hardwood Swamp" communities. These usually consisted of some kind of an American elm-ash-red maple assemblage whose exact composition depended on their degree of wetness and recent history (Fig. 21.9). Sometimes, pin oak (*Q. palustris*) or box elder (*Acer negundo*) were dominant; in others, red maple, American elm (*Ulmus americana*), red ash (*Fraxinus pennsylvanica*), and, locally, black ash (*F. nigra*, a species esteemed early on for basket-making) were more common. The wettest sites were often host to species of willow, especially black willow (*Salix nigra*), along with silver maple (*A. saccharinum*), and eastern cottonwood (*Populus deltoides*). The most extensive such wetlands were found on lacustrine sites adjacent to the Great Lakes, especially around Saginaw Bay and in the southeastern Lower Peninsula.

North of the Tension Zone (Fig. 21.3), the prevailing upland forests had a greater evergreen component and consisted of a mosaic of pine-dominated communities alternating with mixed communities of mesic broadleaved/needle-leaved species. This forest type is commonly referred to as "Northern Hardwood Conifer Forest." Sometimes, nearly pure stands of "Mixed Pine Forests" of white or mixed white and red pine were found here as well (Fig. 21.10). They reached their best development on the mesic sandy sites, with Spodosol soils. Higher, well-drained and weakly developed Entisols supported more drought-tolerant "Pine Oak Forests," consisting of pine and either/both black oak and Hill's oak (*Q. ellipsoidalis*); the driest sites were sometimes too dry even for pine (Fig. 21.11). Jack pine possesses serotinous cones that open and disperse their seeds in the presence of heat, associated with low-grade fires, and for that reason it frequently came to dominate dry sites that burned periodically (Simard and Blank 1982). Most of the white pine stands were/are even-aged and probably also owed their existence to infrequent, large fires that had removed hardwood competition (Whitney 1986). However, an accelerated burn or disturbance regime associated with post-settlement logging sometimes eradicated even fire-dependent species such as jack pine from the forest, if the fires occurred at intervals shorter than the time needed for the species to reach sexual maturity (Mokma and Vance 1989). In such cases, the forests became dominated by successional broadleaved species such as aspen that reproduce vegetatively (Fig. 21.12).

Elsewhere, on moister sites with less frequent fires, needleleaf species such balsam fir, white spruce and eastern hemlock (*Tsuga canadensis*) occurred, along with broadleaved species that included red oak, basswood, black cherry, red maple, rock elm (*Ulmus thomasii*), American elm and yellow birch (locally). This type of forest is known as the

FIGURE 21.10 White pine occurred in nearly pure stands or was mixed with red pine (as in this picture) or hardwoods, on sandy soils of intermediate moisture status across both the northern Lower Peninsula and all of the Upper Peninsula. Photo by R. Schaetzl.

FIGURE 21.11 Shown here is a young, oak-dominated forest on the sandy, well-drained soils of Crawford County. On the best-drained uplands in the Northern Lower Peninsula, especially where fires have been frequent, oaks sometimes displace even jack pine as the dominant species. The dense bracken fern (*Pteridium* spp.) understory attests to the dry, sandy soils. Photo by R. Schaetzl.

classic "Northern Hardwood-Conifer Forest" mixture. In the absence of large scale disturbance, the hardwood component in this forest eventually asserted itself, and they became dominated by sugar maple and beech, to the near exclusion of the more shade intolerant boreal conifers and pine species. Following large scale disturbance (such as fire) here, as well, white birch (*Betula papyrifera*), quaking aspen (*Populus tremuloides*) and bigtooth aspen (*P. grandidentata*) were often dominant, but seldom self-succeeding, as they are unable to reproduce in their own shade (Fig. 21.13). Meanwhile, poorly-drained "Conifer Swamp" sites hosted the now familiar assemblages of boreal species. In addition, streamside communities were (and still are) so thickly dominated by speckled alder (*Alnus rugosa*) as to make access to the water difficult for anglers.

FIGURE 21.12 A recently-burned forest site in eastern Crawford County, with aggressive post-fire quaking aspen reproduction is shown here. Note the group of even-aged aspen saplings in the middle of the picture. Through such vegetative regeneration, quaking aspen has become one of the most important post-disturbance species in the forests of Michigan. Photo by R. Schaetzl.

FIGURE 21.13 This image shows a successional, nearly even-aged, stand of white birch in northwestern Lower Michigan. Both quaking aspen and white birch are post-disturbance species and now occupy large tracts of formerly-logged landscape in northern Michigan and adjoining states. Photo by R. Schaetzl.

Upper Peninsula

Upper Peninsula forests were/are a patchwork of the now familiar wetland boreal communities, alternating on uplands with mixed broadleaved-needleleaved stands of Northern Hardwood-Conifer forest. Some differences with the Lower Peninsula forests are, however, notable. First, owing apparently to its somewhat cooler summers, much of the Upper Peninsula supported more stands with boreal affinities than did the Lower Peninsula. The upland boreal elements (balsam fir, white spruce), and associated northern understory trees such as striped maple (*Acer pennsylvanicum*), mountain maple (*A. spicatum*) and yellow birch, are all more prevalent in the Northern Hardwood-Conifer stands than in the Lower Peninsula (Braun 1964, 353–354). Second, level, poorly drained sites with boreal communities are considerably more extensive, especially in the eastern Upper Peninsula than in the Lower Peninsula, fur-

FIGURE 21.14   As seen here, northern white cedar is common on calcareous, sedimentary rock outcrops, e.g., limestone. However, it is also dominant in some northern Michigan wetlands, in the same region. Photo by R. Schaetzl.

ther adding a decidedly more boreal appearance in general to the Upper Peninsula forests. These "Conifer Swamp" or "Muskeg/Bog" wetlands supported stands of larch, black spruce, balsam poplar (*Populus balsamifera*), northern white cedar (*Thuja occidentalis*) and sometimes even jack pine (which is much more common on well-drained sites). White cedar was (and still is) distributed on both poorly drained sites with peat or muck soils, as well as drier limestone-based soils. It is particularly prominent today along the south shore of the Upper Peninsula near the Mackinac Bridge (Fig. 21.14).

On some "Muskeg/Bog" sites, the densities of trees were quite variable, with some sites being so wet that only dwarf, scattered trees, or none at all, occurred. Even today, these sites continue to lend a strong boreal flavor to the overall landscape, e.g., as in the Seney National Wildlife Refuge. The boreal fraction in wetland shrub communities was and is particularly striking. Aside from the common evergreen shrubs (leatherleaf, Labrador tea, swamp laurel and andromeda) typical of such sites, wetlands and lake borders also supported stands of such northern species as alder (*Alnus crispa*; *A. rugosa*), dwarf arctic birch (*Betula pumila var. glandulifera*), sweet gale (*Myrica gale*) and creeping juniper (*Juniperus horizontalis*). Sweetfern (*Comptonia peregrina*) was widespread on drier sandy pinelands and has retained dominance there today. Several species of blueberry (*Vaccinium* spp.) inhabited both dry sandy sites and wetter lowlands; they have become more abundant after logging.

Uplands across the Upper Peninsula were all cloaked in various mixtures of broadleaf/needleleaf species depending on subtleties of soil drainage, texture and site history (Fig. 21.15). Many of the patterns and species relationships found on these uplands were the same as in the northern Lower Peninsula. What is notable is the extensive character of the "Northern Hardwood Conifer Forest" type on these uplands across much of the Upper Peninsula. Small differences in composition occurred from stand to stand depending, as before, on site and history, but, overall, the extensive monotony of these stands was an earmark of the western Upper Peninsula.

One broad pattern of note in these upland forests is the absence of beech from the western Upper Peninsula, west of a Marquette-to-Green Bay line (Chapter 7). West of this line it is replaced by basswood, red and sugar maple, red oak, hemlock, yellow birch and white and red pine. White spruce and balsam fir were originally minor associates in these forests on account of their limited tolerance to shade, but following disturbance (such as logging) they, along with aspen and white birch, became much more common. In fact, across large expanses of the Upper Peninsula, some mixture of balsam fir and white spruce (with aspen) may be one of the most common forest communities today. This forest type appears not to have had any general analogue on the presettlement landscape.

FIGURE 21.15 A second-growth, mixed aspen-birch-balsam fir stand in Mackinac County is shown here. Throughout the northern Great Lakes region, including Michigan, the removal of large expanses of forest permitted the development of widespread successional stands dominated by aspen and white birch. With balsam fir as a shade-intolerant, boreal associate, this aspen-fir assemblage is today perhaps the most extensive and common forest type in the region. Photo by R. Schaetzl.

■ Forest disturbance and succession

All biological communities undergo occasional disturbance. Terrestrial communities sometimes suffer catastrophic disturbances from natural hazards like fire, storms or insect outbreaks, or less disruptive ones associated with the normal death of individual members of the community, such as a single tree. Because disturbances—large and small—alter the micro-environment within the community, they often affect the growth and reproductive rates of the surviving members, and thereby influence its future composition. In a forest stand, for example, future composition is predicted by present rates of growth and mortality in the youngest generation of trees (the seedlings and saplings), which will grow up to become the future overstory. Survival and mortality rates, however, are heavily affected by conditions beneath the overstory—in the shade—and depend directly on the degree to which the seedlings/saplings of each species can tolerate these conditions. Some species, e.g., sugar maple, beech and hemlock, can grow in the shade of the canopy, whereas others such as black cherry and aspen, cannot. Shade-intolerant species are therefore either restricted to brighter sites, or require that disturbance open up the canopy long enough to permit them to grow to canopy height. Often, such an opening is formed by the death and fall of a large tree in the stand—a process called "gap-phase reproduction" (White et al. 1985).

The arrival of European settlers in Michigan initiated an era of both massive forest removal as well as subsequent fires, at frequencies probably quite different from the presettlement disturbance regime. While a few stands escaped altogether, some were cut selectively and many others were logged and then burned several times; such local differences in history probably had a strong influence in determining just what species subsequently came to dominate each stand. Mostly, however, heavy disturbance was the rule across the state, which greatly reduced in frequency (or even eliminated) disturbance-sensitive species, while promoting those that require it. As a result, shade-intolerant species, particularly aspen and white birch, greatly increased in importance (Fig. 21.13), achieving levels of coverage not apparent in presettlement forests.

What is the *geographical* significance of disturbance across Michigan? When an historic event affects large swaths of forest at the same time, it becomes significant if the present-day composition has inherited its influence. A large fire burning across one or more counties, for example, could subsequently lead to relatively homogeneous composition all across the affected area. Mostly, however, the intricacies of site history are small scale and their impact on modern composition, as a result, is most discernible at that scale—the stand level. That is, small scale disturbances *complicate* the gross distributional relationship between broad environmental controls and broad patterns of forest composition, and as such they have limited, large scale, geographic importance. At smaller scales, in contrast, understanding the history of each forest stand is absolutely essential to explaining its current composition and structure. Unfortunately, many of these details come down to which tree fell when, or which particular seedling survived (and which did not), questions for which we have little or no information. In many cases as a result, inferring the histories of some stands becomes a matter of scientific generalization based on the histories of other stands of similar composition for which we might have better records.

Figure 21.16 summarizes many of the site/history/forest composition relationships discussed above. For example, as time since disturbance increases (from right to left across the diagram), fire-sensitive broadleaved species, e.g., beech, sugar maple and hemlock, become more dominant, especially on the more mesic sites such as level plains of fine-to-medium fine lacustrine (lake plain) materials. Overall, the wettest habitats (lower left) are lowlands on peat or muck characterized by boreal "Conifer Swamp" communities. Hardwood ("Beech-Sugar Maple") stands occupy the medium textured, level-to-rolling uplands toward the center of the diagram along the bottom or top of the diagram, but they avoid the highest topography or coarsest outwash soils. The most xeric, disturbed habitat shown on this figure (middle right side) is the red pine-jack pine assemblage, which is limited to coarse soils on disturbed sites, although even more extreme sites exist on which pine is largely absent, usually because of exceptionally severe or frequent disturbance.

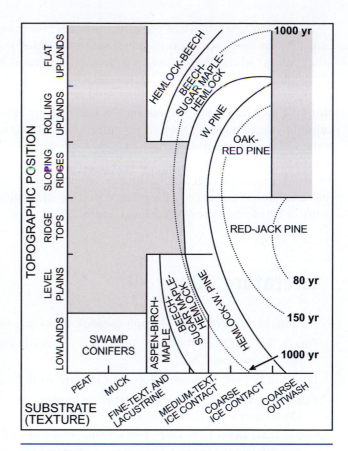

FIGURE 21.16   Vegetation diagram illustrating the distribution of forest types in northern lower Michigan as a function of soils, topographic position and disturbance frequency. Shaded areas reflect those conditions that are not normally found in nature. After Whitney (1986).

■ Michigan forests in a broader perspective

Prior to logging associated with European settlement, "Northern Hardwood-Conifer Forest" covered over half of the Lower Peninsula and most of the Upper Peninsula, easily making it the most important type of forest in Michigan. Actually, this forest region was part of an expanse that originally stretched from northeastern Minnesota eastward through northern Wisconsin, southern Ontario and far southern Quebec, upstate New York and into New England and Atlantic Canada. Everywhere it was dominated by roughly the same sets of species: an admixture of pines in combination with other species from the Boreal Forest to the north and the Eastern Deciduous Forest to the south.

Generally, forest types are named after their dominant trees, but in the case of this region, doing so raises the rather technical question of whether it is a legitimate forest association in the first place. The problem is that most of the dominant species in this forest type are also dominants in adjoining regions. The spruces, fir, larch and jack pine, for example, are characteristic of the Boreal Forest to the north, whereas the constituent species of the mesic hardwood stands, e.g., sugar maple, beech, basswood, red oak, red maple, white ash and black cherry, are more characteristic of forests to the south. In the Northern Hardwood-Conifer Forest stands in Michigan, all these different forest communities manage to co-exist on locally "compensated" sites that re-create their more general habitat requirements, with boreal stands of larch and black spruce and others of beech, maple and basswood interspersed. Typically, boreal species occupy the extreme sites on the moisture continuum where soil pH is most likely to be lowest—on either sandy soils or depressions (bogs). In between, on the intermediate (and less acid) sites, are typically found representatives from the Eastern Deciduous Forest.

With so many important constituent species "borrowed" from adjoining forest regions, might we not want to consider this forest region as merely transitional rather than a stand-alone entity? Despite the many species from other regions whose ranges overlap with it, a strong case can be made for its own status as a distinct region because of the presence of several distinctive species more or less limited to the Northern Hardwood-Conifer Forest, e.g., white and red pine, eastern hemlock, yellow birch, northern white cedar and, in New England, red spruce (Nichols 1935). Not only are the ranges of these species generally coincident with this forest type (although some are shared by adjoining forest regions), they are common and characteristic within it. In Michigan, in fact, the official "state tree" is the white pine, attesting to both its early importance in the forests as well as the esteem with which it is still held today (Whitney 1987). Without doubt, the Northern Hardwood-Conifer Forest plays a transitional role in the forest geography of Eastern North America, lying as it does between two great forest formations on the continent, but the conspicuous presence of the pines, especially white pine, in the state's forests is a bold testament of the individuality of this forest type (Wendel and Smith 1990).

Literature Cited

Abrams, M. D. 1998. The red maple paradox. Bioscience 48:355–364.

Barnes, B.V. and W.H. Wagner Jr. 1981. Trees. A guide to the Trees of Michigan and the Great Lakes Region. University of Michigan Press, Ann Arbor.

Braun, E. L. 1964. Deciduous Forests of Eastern North America. Hafner, New York.

Brubaker, L.B. 1975. Postglacial forest patterns associated with till and outwash in northcentral upper Michigan. Quaternary Research 5:499–527.

Burns, R.M. and B.H. Honkala (eds). 1990a. Silvics of North America. Volume 1: Conifers. Agriculture Handbook 654. US Forest Service, US Government Printing Office, Washington, DC. 675 pp.

Burns, R.M. and B.H. Honkala (eds). 1990b. Silvics of North America. Volume 2: Hardwoods. Agriculture Handbook 654. US Forest Service, US Government Printing Office, Washington, DC. 877 pp.

Comer, P.J., Albert, D.A., Wells, H.A., Hart, B.L., Raab, J.B., Price, D.L., Kashian, D.M., Corner, R.A. and D.W. Schuen. 1995. Michigan's native landscape, as interpreted from the General Land Office Surveys 1816–1856. In: Report to the US EPA Water Division and Wildlife Division, Michigan Department of Natural Resources, Michigan Natural Features Inventory, Lansing. 76 pp.

Curtis, J. T. 1959. The Vegetation of Wisconsin. The University of Wisconsin Press, Madison.

Daubenmire, R. 1978. Plant geography, with special reference to North America. Academic Press, New York.

Denton, S.R., and B.V. Barnes. 1987. Tree species distributions related to climatic patterns in Michigan. Canadian Journal of Forest Research 17:613–629.

Eliott-Fisk, D.L.1988. The boreal forest. In: Barbour, M.G. and W.D. Billings (eds). North American Terrestrial Vegetation. Cambridge University Press, New York. pp. 33–62.

Harman, J.R. 1970. Forest and climatic gradients along the southeast shoreline of Lake Michigan. Annals of the Association of American Geographers 60:456–465.

Harman J.R. and M.D. Nutter. 1973. Soil and forest patterns in northern Lower Michigan. The East Lakes Geographer 8:1–12.

Harman, J.R. and J. Plough. 1986. Asymmetric distribution of coniferous trees on northern Lake Michigan islands. The East Lakes Geographer 21:24–33.

Harrington, J.A. and J.R. Harman. 1991. Climate and vegetation in central North America. Great Plains Quarterly 11:103–112.

Heinselman, M.L. 1965. String bogs and other patterned organic terrain near Seney, Upper Michigan. Ecology 46:185–188.

Henne, P.D., Hu, F.S. and D.T. Cleland. 2007. Lake-effect snow as the dominant control of mesic-forest distribution in Michigan. Journal of Ecology 95:517–529.

Kenoyer, L.A. 1933. Forest distribution in south-west Michigan as interpreted from the original survey. Proceedings of the Michigan Academy of Science, Arts, and Letters 19:107–111.

McCann, M.T. 1979. The plant tension zone in Michigan. M.A. thesis, Western Michigan University, Kalamazoo.

Medley, K.E. and J.R. Harman. 1987. Relationship between the vegetation tension zone and soils distribution across central Lower Michigan. The Michigan Botanist 26:78–87.

Medley, K.E. and J.R. Harman. 1988. Growing season temperature and a Midwestern vegetation transition. The East Lakes Geographer 23:130–136.

Mokma, D.L. and G.F. Vance. 1989. Forest vegetation and origin of some spodic horizons, Michigan. Geoderma 43:311–324.

Nichols, G.E. 1935. The hemlock-white pine-northern hardwood region of Eastern North America. Ecology 16:403–422.

Oechel, W.C. and W.T Lawrence. 1985. Taiga. In: Chabot, B.F. and H.A. Mooney. Physiological Ecology of North American Plant Communities. Chapman and Hall, New York. pp. 66–94.

Schaetzl, R.J., Knapp, B.D., and S.A. Isard. 2005. Modeling soil temperatures and the mesic-frigid boundary in the Great Lakes region, 1951–2000. Soil Science Society of America Journal 69:2033–2040.

Wendel, G.W. and H.C. Smith. Eastern white pine. 1990. In: Burns, R.M. and B.H. Honkala (eds). Silvics of North America. Volume 1: Conifers. Agriculture Handbook 654. US Forest Service, US Government Printing Office, Washington, DC. pp. 476–488.

White, P.S., MacKenzie, M.D. and R.T. Busing. 1985. Natural disturbance and gap phase dynamics in southern Appalachian spruce-fir forests. Canadian Journal of Forest Research 15:233–240.

Whitney, G.G. 1986. Relation of Michigan's presettlement pine forests to substrate and disturbance history. Ecology 67:1548–1559.

Whitney, G.G. 1987. An ecological history of the Great Lakes forest of Michigan. Journal of Ecology 75:667–684.

Further Readings

Albert, D.A. 1995. Regional landscape ecosystems of Michigan, Minnesota, and Wisconsin: A working map and classification. US Department of Agriculture, US Forest Service General Technical Report NC-178. 250 pp.

Barrett, L.R. 1998. Origin and history of stump prairies in northern Michigan: forest composition and logging practices. Great Lakes Geographer 5:105–123.

Cain, S.A. 1935. Studies on virgin hardwood forest, III. Warren's Woods, a beech-maple climax forest in Berrien County, Michigan. Ecology 16:500–513.

Cleland, D.T., Crow, T.R., Saunders, S.C., Dickmann, D.I., Maclean, A.L., Jordan, J.K., Watson, R.L., Sloan, A.M. and K.D. Brosofske. 2004. Characterizing historical and modern fire regimes in Michigan (USA): a landscape ecosystem approach. Landscape Ecology 19:311–325.

Fujinuma, R., Bockheim, J. and N. Balster. 2005. Base-cation cycling by individual tree species in old-growth forests of Upper Michigan, USA. Biogeochemistry 74:357–376.

Host, G.E. and K.S. Pregitzer. 1992. Geomorphic influences on ground-flora and overstory composition in upland forests of northwestern lower Michigan. Canadian Journal of Forest Research 22:1547–1555.

Kapp, R.O. 1978. Presettlement forest patterns of the Pine River Watershed (Central Michigan). Michigan Botanist 17:3–15.

Leahy, M.J. and K.S. Pregitzer. 2003. A comparison of presettlement and present-day forests in northeastern lower Michigan. American Midlands Naturalist 149:71–89.

Maycock, P.F. 1961. The spruce-fir forests of Keweenaw Peninsula, northern Michigan. Ecology 42: 357–365.

Maycock, P.F. and J.T. Curtis. 1960. The phytosociology of boreal conifer hardwood forest of the Great Lakes region. Ecological Monographs 30:1–35.

22

Terrestrial Game and Nongame Fauna

Joelle Gehring

Introduction

Michigan is a state with many diverse ecological communities (Albert 1994). Most have been altered in both quantity and quality from their historical condition by habitat fragmentation induced by agricultural practices, urbanization and timber harvesting, as well as by the interruption of natural processes, e.g., fire. However, due to its wide array of habitats, Michigan still possesses a diversity of mammals, birds, amphibians, reptiles and invertebrate species. The diversity of species changes throughout the seasons, with many bird and bat species temporarily leaving Michigan for warmer climates, other bird species migrating through the state, and yet other bird species, from more northern latitudes, over-wintering in Michigan.

In this chapter, I discuss the fauna currently inhabiting Michigan, separating them into six ecological community (habitat) types, as well as discussing those generalist species which inhabit most, if not all, communities in Michigan. This approach hopefully provides clarity on the interactions and connections among the faunal species, as well connections to their habitats. Several sources, including Harding (1997), Baker (1983), Wood (1951) and Nielsen (1999) provide detailed descriptions of the identification and life history of each species of herpetological fauna, mammal, bird and butterfly, respectively, found in Michigan. The Michigan Natural Features Inventory (MNFI 2007a) provides current information on the status of Michigan's species, i.e., those Federally Endangered, Threatened, etc.

Habitat generalists

Although most Michigan species are habitat specialists and are only or mainly found in specific habitats, others are more ubiquitous and found throughout most of the state, e.g., white-tailed deer, raccoon, blue jay, American crow and mosquito (Table 22.1). These flexible, "generalist" species are found to some extent in all six of the ecological communities discussed below. Generalists tend to be more mobile and do not require highly specific, rare resources for any part of their life history. Because amphibians and reptiles generally require aquatic environments and have lower mobility than birds, mammals and many flying invertebrates, they are generally not habitat generalists.

Despite their current flexibility in habitat use, some generalist species were temporarily impacted by large-scale, significant habitat alterations, resulting in decreased population sizes. However, over time they adapted, evolved and expanded their ranges to utilize a diversity of habitats, including human-altered sites. For example, white-tailed deer were historically limited to the southern portions of Michigan and were rarely found in the more coniferous, heavily forested areas of the Northern Lower and Upper Peninsula (Michigan Department of Natural Resources 2007; see FOCUS BOX below). By the 1870s, they had been almost eliminated from southern Michigan due to unlimited harvest and heavy logging. It was not until the 1930s that white-tailed deer were considered more common again—likely as a result of harvest regulations, some regrowth of cover and adaptation to novel agricultural environments and the heavily forested areas such as the Northern Lower and Upper Peninsula. The history of many generalist species in Michigan parallels that of the white-tailed deer. Thus, when compared to specialist species, populations of generalists are typically better able to withstand habitat alterations or habitat loss over time without becoming rare.

TABLE 22.1   Examples of generalist terrestrial game and non-game fauna found in Michigan

Common name	Scientific name
Invertebrates	
house fly	*Musca domestica*
mosquito	varies (family Culicidae)
Birds	
American crow	*Corvus brachyrhynchos*
American robin	*Turdus migratorius*
blue jay	*Cyanocitta cristata*
mourning dove	*Zenaida macroura*
Mammals	
coyote	*Canis latrans*
Virginia opossum	*Didelphis virginiana*
raccoon	*Procyon lotor*
white-tailed deer	*Odocoileus virginianus*
Reptiles	
common garter snake	*Thamnophis sirtalis*

FOCUS BOX: White-tailed deer in Michigan

White-tailed deer can be found throughout Michigan, in all habitat types. In some areas of the state, deer densities are high enough to adversely affect vegetation and ecosystems via over-browsing (Frelich and Lorimer 1985). High deer densities frequently come into conflict with human societies in urban and agricultural settings as a result of their foraging activities on ornamental landscaping plants and agricultural crops. Livestock in Michigan are also at risk of contracting bovine tuberculosis (TB) from close contact with white-tailed deer carrying the disease, which had originally spread into white-tailed deer populations from cattle. Bovine TB is predominantly a problem in the northeastern Lower Peninsula, and since 1998, 41 herds of cattle have tested positive for it and have subsequently been destroyed. Beef from this area is not allowed to be sold at an interstate level, resulting in local economic impacts. Between 1998 and 2006, the Michigan Department of Agriculture spent $50.5 million preventing the spread of the disease, helping the Upper Peninsula regain TB free status, and helping the Lower Peninsula regain accredited advanced status. Overall, the proportion of deer testing positive for the disease is decreasing; however, in 2006, 41 of 7924 animals tested positive for TB.

Another source of negative economic impact is the prevalence of vehicle-deer collisions. Overall increasing in frequency, 60,875 collisions were reported in 2006, with each costing an average of $2000.

Despite the ecological and societal challenges of high deer densities, white-tailed deer are an important part of the economy and culture of Michigan. Not only does the general public enjoy viewing deer, but in addition, approximately 415,000 deer are harvested annually, by about 725,000 hunters. Michigan businesses, such as lodging, restaurants and outfitter shops benefit greatly from the large influx of hunters every fall. A 2002 report estimated that deer hunters annually spent $281,774,267 on retail items in Michigan (International Association of Fish and Wildlife Agencies 2002). Hunting also provides an opportunity for individuals to spend time out-of-doors, share time with family and friends, and, if fortunate, acquire some venison and good hunting stories.

■ Oak savanna and pine barren ecosystems

Oak savannas and pine barrens are unique Michigan ecosystems that provide habitat for several specialist fauna. These fire-dependent ecosystems are characterized by having qualities of both forests and grasslands (Fig. 22.1). Oak savannas typically have oak trees and shrubs with 5–60% canopy closure and graminoid (grass) groundcover. Pine barrens are similar in structure, with jack pine in the overstory. Oak savannas are one of the most endangered ecosystems in the world, and the status of Michigan's oak savannas is no exception. Historically, the southern portion of the Lower Peninsula had more savanna area than anywhere in the remainder of the state (Chapter 21; Plate 15). These areas were easier to clear than forested areas, which made them early targets for conversion to agriculture and urban development. Savannas are also dependent on regular burning regimes, which were halted after human settlement. Without regular fires, oak savannas are subject to the invasion of woody shrubs and trees, thereby succeeding to a closed canopy oak forest (Fig. 21.7). Similarly, jack pine barrens (Plate 15), found mainly in the northern Lower Peninsula, require regular burning for the maintenance of ecosystem functions. Many plants in pine barrens require fire for germination, including jack pine.

The red-headed woodpecker is one of several species that are specialists in the oak savanna community (Table 22.2). Species typically found in the pine barrens include the prairie warbler, and several butterflies: the hoary elfin, pine elfin and Canadian tiger swallowtail (Table 22.2). The most well-known specialist species of Michigan's pine barrens, however, is the Kirtland's warbler (Fig. 22.2, FOCUS BOX in Chapter 41). This endangered species breeds only in large expanses of jack pine barrens that are 5–7 years old. Their need for large areas of even-aged jack pines is consistent with the historic fire regimes of the area, as large fires would burn hundreds of hectares of land at a time. Jack pine reseeding (stimulated by fire) and subsequent regrowth would then occur simultaneously within the recently burned area. Currently, the US Forest Service, US Fish and Wildlife Service (USFWS), Michigan Department of Natural Resources (MDNR), and other resource management agencies collaborate to harvest and replant jack pine trees in a manner that simulates the natural fire regime, thereby providing nesting sites for the Kirtland's warbler, as well as wood products for the timber industry. Kirtland's warbler populations have continued to grow since this management effort was initiated (Chapter 41). In 2007, the MDNR reported an all-time known population high of 1697 singing males. Local communities and Audubon groups benefit from this rare species by hosting regular festivals, e.g., the Kirtland's Warbler Festival, and tours of its habitat.

FIGURE 22.1 A typical oak savanna, which has characteristics of both Michigan forests and grasslands, is shown here.

TABLE 22.2 Examples of terrestrial game and non-game fauna found in oak savanna and pine barren ecosystems of Michigan

Common name	Scientific name
Invertebrates	
Canadian tiger swallowtail butterfly	*Papilio canadensis*
hoary elfin butterfly	*Callophrys polios*
eastern pine elfin butterfly	*Callophrys niphon*
Karner blue butterfly	*Lycaeides melissa samuelis*
Persius duskywing butterfly	*Erynnis persius*
Amphibians and Reptiles	
racer	*Coluber constrictor*
eastern box turtle	*Terrapene carolina carolina*
Birds	
barn swallow	*Hirundo rustica*
blue-winged warbler	*Vermivora pinus*
eastern bluebird	*Sialia sialis*
golden-winged warbler	*Vermivora chrysoptera*
indigo bunting	*Passerina cyanea*
Kirtland's warbler	*Dendroica kirtlandii*
northern flicker	*Colaptes auratus*
prairie warbler	*Dendroica discolor*
red-headed woodpecker	*Melanerpes erythrocephalus*
tree swallow	*Tachycineta bicolor*
Nashville warbler	*Vermivora ruficapilla*
Mammals	
eastern fox squirrel	*Sciurus niger*

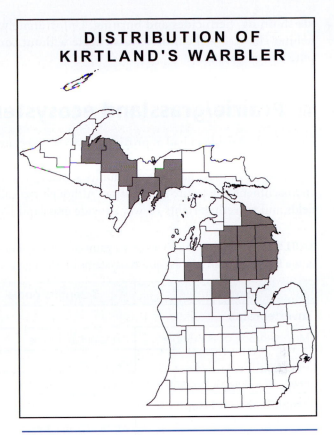

FIGURE 22.2 Range (2007) of the Kirtland's warbler in Michigan. After MNFI (2007a).

With the possible exception of the prairie areas in southern Michigan, the brown-headed cowbird is believed to be a relatively recent, but common, addition to Michigan's fauna (Brewer et al. 1991). Given the brown-headed cowbird's requirement for at least a small amount of open habitat, savannas, pine barrens and fragmented forest edges are optimal habitat for the cowbird. This species evolved on the Great Plains of the US, where it followed the highly mobile bison herds, foraging on the seeds and insects left in their wake. Because it did not remain sedentary long enough to raise young, brown-headed cowbirds evolved to parasitize the nests of other bird species, leaving several eggs for the host bird to incubate, hatch and raise to fledging age. This practice frequently occurred at the expense of the host bird's genetic offspring. After the herds of bison were reduced in the west, and herds of cattle increased in the eastern US, brown-headed cowbirds were able to expand eastward into the fragmented forests, savannas and pine barrens. The brown-headed cowbird now utilizes grain storage areas and agricultural crops, and is a common nest parasite of nesting songbirds in Michigan. Brown-headed cowbird chicks are typically larger than the chicks of the host species. The host chicks are, therefore, frequently suffocated, pushed out of the nest or out-competed for food by the brown-headed cowbird nestlings. Due to the likely detrimental effects of this nest parasite on host bird reproduction, the Kirtland's warbler recovery efforts have included efforts to trap and remove brown-headed cowbirds from the range of the Kirtland's warbler.

Although some oak savanna restoration is underway in Michigan, most of the areas historically covered by this unique habitat are now urban areas or, because of their fertile soils, cropland. Some land management agencies, such as the MDNR, have targeted oak savannas as a priority for conservation and restoration. The MDNR Landowner Incentive Program (LIP) builds collaborations among land managers and private land owners to educate citizens about the uniqueness and value of this ecosystem, to protect existing savannas and to restore them via thinning, herbicides and burning. Unfortunately, populations of those faunal species unable to adapt to habitat changes will continue to struggle without continued efforts to protect and restore these savanna and pine barren habitats.

Prairie/grassland ecosystems

Historically, Michigan had approximately 95,000 hectares of grassland habitat, located mainly in the southern portion of the state and in limited areas along the shorelines of the Great Lakes (Plate 15). However, the state has lost the majority of these natural communities, mainly as a result of urban sprawl, agricultural development and forest encroachment due to fire suppression. Although typically not vegetated with native plants, fallow farm fields, hayfields and powerline rights-of-way provide grassland-like habitat for wildlife today.

TABLE 22.3   Examples of terrestrial game and non-game fauna found in prairie/grassland ecosystems of Michigan

Common name	Scientific name
Invertebrates	
Michigan bog grasshopper	*Appalachia arcane*
regal fritillary butterfly	*Speyeria idalia*
Leonard's skipper butterfly	*Hesperia leonardus*
Amphibians and Reptiles	
tiger salamander	*Ambystoma tigrinum*
six-lined racerunner	*Aspidoscelis sexlineatus*
Birds	
barn owl	*Tyto alba*
bobolink	*Dolichonyx oryzivorus*
dickcissel	*Spiza Americana*
eastern meadowlark	*Sturnella magna*
grasshopper sparrow	*Ammodramus savannarum*
horned lark	*Eremophila alpestris*
northern harrier	*Circus cyaneus*
ring-necked pheasant	*Phasianus colchicus*
savannah sparrow	*Passerculus sandwichensis*
sharp-tailed grouse	*Tympanuchus phasianellus*
short-eared owl	*Asio flammeus*
western meadowlark	*Sturnella neglecta*
Mammals	
meadow vole	*Microtus pennsylvanicus*
thirteen-lined ground squirrel	*Citellus tridecemlineatus*
least weasel	*Mustela nivalis*
American badger	*Taxidea taxus*

Two of the more common species that utilize grassland habitats in Michigan are the thirteen-lined ground squirrel and vesper sparrow. Rare species that are found in these environments include Henslow's sparrow, Kirtland's snake, the Karner blue butterfly and prairie vole (Table 22.3).

The Karner blue butterfly (Fig. 22.3), a Federally Endangered and Michigan Threatened species, evolved with the fire disturbance typical of prairie ecosystems. Depending on the fire-dependent plant, wild lupine, for feeding and egg laying, this butterfly is very limited in its range. It is currently found in areas managed specifically for wild lupine and butterflies, as well as in areas maintained in an early stage of succession, e.g., powerline rights-of-way and highway roadsides. Given the sensitivity of the larva and eggs to crushing, resource managers collaborate with State Game Areas, private landowners, utility companies and the Michigan Department of Transportation to protect the species, while still managing their habitat (Rabe 2001).

Many grassland areas are frequently mowed for hay production. Unfortunately mowing coincides with the nesting season of grassland birds; thereby, forming an ecological trap, as birds are attracted to the grassland area for nesting opportunities but do not successfully reproduce when their nests are destroyed. A common mid-summer site in Michigan is a farmer mowing his or her fields with many birds diving at the tractor as their nests are destroyed. Resource managers have been encouraging private landowners to mow hay only after songbird nesting is completed; however, enforcement is commonly not possible.

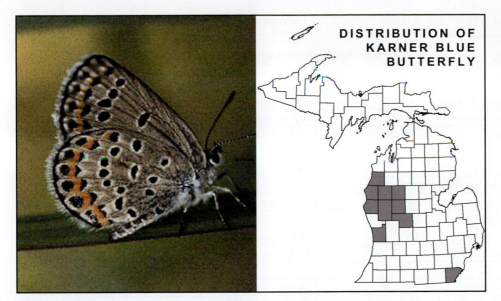

FIGURE 22.3 Image and range (2001) of the Karner blue butterfly in Michigan. Photo by M. Rabe. After Rabe (2001).

In addition to the challenges of balancing agriculture with wildlife habitat, human intolerance of the natural fire regimes of grassland ecosystems allows woody vegetation to encroach, and natural succession to progress to a shrubby or forested community in non-farmed grasslands. Similar to the savanna and pine barrens ecosystems, the MDNR's LIP efforts focus on protecting and managing grassland habitats by providing incentives to promote good farming practices and habitat restoration.

Forest ecosystems

Historically, 14.6 million hectares of Michigan were extensively forested (Plate 15). Mainly in the northern Lower Peninsula and Upper Peninsula, many of these lands have since been cleared for commercial logging, agriculture and urban land uses. In addition to timber harvest, some forested areas in Michigan have been converted to pine plantations for the production of pulp (Chapter 41). Many of the natural processes of a forest are lost after this conversion, and species diversity drops. Historic fire regimes have also been altered or halted in most of Michigan's forest ecosystems, which has resulted in additional changes to some of the forested environments, such as increased understory growth. There are many forest community types in Michigan (Albert 1994, Chapter 21; Plate 15) that vary by species composition, disturbance regime and soil type, among other variables. Michigan Natural Features Inventory has provided detailed information on the forest community types in Michigan (MNFI 2007b; Chapter 21). In this chapter, I focus on the faunal species inhabiting the following broad forest types: deciduous forest, mixed forest and boreal forest. It is important to note that not only does the forest community type affect the faunal species using an area, but the time since the last disturbance and the type of disturbance that occurred is also important. For example, the availability of coarse woody debris, dead trees, i.e., snags, and forest understory can be dramatically affected by the type of disturbance, and can greatly affect both the faunal density and faunal species diversity.

Although some animal species are specific to certain forest types, others are more general in their forest habitat use. For example, the downy woodpecker, big brown bat and white-tailed deer are habitat generalists and use forests throughout Michigan (Table 22.4). Michigan's forests also provide habitat for a large diversity of nesting, Neotropical, migrating warbler species and vireos, such as the black-throated green warbler, American redstart and red-eyed vireo. The moist, nutrient-rich soils of some Michigan forests also provide habitat for several species of salamanders, e.g., the blue-spotted and red-backed salamanders. Deciduous forests harbor several specialists, including the least shrew, cerulean warbler, eastern box turtle, northern ring-necked snake and the hickory hairstreak

TABLE 22.4 Examples of terrestrial game and non-game fauna found in forest ecosystems of Michigan

Common name	Scientific name
Invertebrates	
early hairstreak butterfly	*Erora laeta*
emerald ash borer	*Agrilus planipennis*
gypsy moth	*Lymantria dispar*
hickory hairstreak butterfly	*Satyrium caryaevorum*
mourning cloak butterfly	*Nymphalis antiopa*
Amphibians and Reptiles	
blue-spotted salamander	*Ambystoma laterale*
eastern box turtle	*Terrapene carolina carolina*
northern ring-necked snake	*Diadophis punctatus*
red-backed salamander	*Plethodon cinereus*
Birds	
American redstart	*Setophaga ruticilla*
black-backed woodpecker	*Picoides arcticus*
black-throated green warbler	*Dendroica virens*
boreal chickadee	*Poecile hudsonica*
cerulean warbler	*Dendroica cerulean*
common raven	*Corvus corax*
downy woodpecker	*Picoides pubescens*
gray jay	*Perisoreus canadensis*
hairy woodpecker	*Picoides villosus*
magnolia warbler	*Dendroica magnolia*
northern goshawk	*Accipiter gentilis*
northern parula	*Parula americanai*
ovenbird	*Seiurus aurocapillus*
pileated woodpecker	*Dryocopus pileatus*
prothonotary warbler	*Protonotaria citrea*
red-eyed vireo	*Vireo olivaceus*
red-shouldered hawk	*Buteo lineatus*
ruffed grouse	*Bonasa umbellus*
scarlet tanager	*Piranga olivacea*
spruce grouse	*Falcipennis canadensis*
Mammals	
American marten	*Martes Americana*
arctic shrew	*Sorex arcticus*
big brown bat	*Eptesicus fuscus*
bobcat	*Lynx rufus*
eastern mole	*Scalopus aquaticus*
elk	*Cervus canadensis*
fisher	*Martes pennanti*
gray wolf	*Canis lupus*
least shrew	*Cryptotis parva*
moose	*Alces alces*
northern flying squirrel	*Glaucomys sabrinus*
porcupine	*Erethizon dorsatum*
southern red-backed vole	*Clethrionomys gapperi*
water shrew	*Sorex palustris*
woodland vole	*Microtus pinetorum*
white-tailed deer	*Odocoileus virginianus*

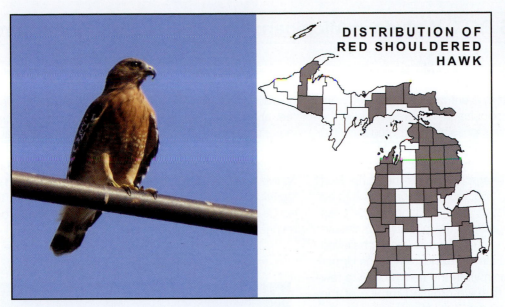

FIGURE 22.4 Image and range (2007) of the red-shouldered hawk in Michigan. Photo by J. Gehring. After MNFI (2007).

butterfly (Table 22.4). Species such as the porcupine and ruffed grouse tend to inhabit mixed forests - with coniferous and deciduous components (Table 22.4). In 1918, Michigan reintroduced elk to the mixed forest areas of the northern Lower Peninsula and their population has grown to a level that now allows a sustainable annual harvest. The arctic shrew, lynx and black-backed woodpecker are found almost exclusively in the boreal forests of Michigan (Table 22.4). During the pre-settlement era, the forests of Michigan supported populations of woodland bison, woodland caribou and several other species now extirpated from the state. Despite the loss of these species, Michigan still maintains a diverse forest fauna.

Timber harvesting is an important part of the economy in many areas of Michigan, and can affect (positively or negatively) the species that use those forested environments (Chapter 41). The red-shouldered hawk (Cooper 1999a; Fig. 22.4) and Northern goshawk (Cooper 1999b) are species that depend on forested areas for nesting. Although these species require large areas of forest, they can tolerate some habitat fragmentation from timber harvest. Both may possibly benefit from low levels of timber harvest, given the propensity of the red-shouldered hawk to hunt along forest edges, and the Northern goshawk's adaptation to hunting ruffed grouse, a species that requires forests of different ages for its life cycle. Ruffed grouse habitat is typically managed by harvesting 2–4 hectares of forest in 10–40 year rotations. Many forest managers in Michigan follow Best Management Practices, with guidelines specific to protecting the nesting areas of these two raptor species, while harvesting timber in the surrounding areas.

In recent decades, Michigan's forests have been challenged by the introduction of exotic pests, such as the gypsy moth (Michigan State University Extension 2007) and the emerald ash borer (Michigan State University 2007). Despite control efforts, these species have spread to many parts of Michigan and threaten the habitat of Michigan wildlife. Resource managers are currently very concerned about the loss of ash trees to the emerald ash borer. Ash trees are an important tree for wildlife; they provide nesting sites and foraging sites, and are the predominant tree species in some lowland deciduous forest ecosystems. Current control efforts include minimizing the transport of firewood, where the emerald ash borer can reside, and the removal and disposal of infected ash trees.

Many of the forested areas of Michigan are very important to the tourism/recreation industry (Chapter 35). In addition to the hunting of wildlife, ecotourism and wildlife viewing are important in some of the forested areas of Michigan, e.g., the Keweenaw Peninsula. Elk viewing is popular in the northern Lower Peninsula. There is no doubt that the potential to observe such charismatic wildlife as wolves, black bear, moose and bald eagles increases the draw of nationwide outdoor enthusiasts/tourists to Michigan.

FOCUS BOX: Wolves in Michigan: the past, present and future

Wolves occurred throughout all of Michigan until 1840, when human populations increased rapidly and high-levels of hunting occurred; eventually wolf bounties were put in place. The wolf population, believed to be in the thousands pre-1800, was possibly extirpated by 1960 (Stebler 1951, Arnold and Schofield 1956). Much of this decimation was based on society's general dislike of predators, frequently characterized as the "Little Red Riding Hood factor." In 1965, the wolf became protected in Michigan and was listed as an Endangered Species in 1973. Although progress in the population's recovery was initially slow, the current population is believed to exceed 500, located almost exclusively in the Upper Peninsula (see figure below). In the early 2000s, a few wolves were thought to have crossed the ice of the Mackinaw Straits and taken up residence in the northern Lower Peninsula; however, this population does not appear to be growing.

The gray wolf was considered recovered and, therefore, delisted in the Great Lakes by the USFWS in 2007. Although no hunting or trapping season has been opened for the species, many stakeholders are anxious about the possibility. Gray wolf populations are very sensitive to anthropogenic take and, although illegal, many wolves are still poached. Researchers have determined that wolf populations are limited more by road density than any other variable, i.e., the more access people have to wolf territories, the more likely poaching is to occur (Mladenoff et al. 1995). Despite increasing wolf popula-

tions, livestock losses to wolves remains relatively low. Researchers are currently studying the use of livestock guarding dogs and fladry, i.e., red flags spaced several feet apart and used in association with livestock fencing to protect livestock from wolf encounters (see figure below). Societal attitudes toward wolves are slowly shifting to increased tolerance, and even reverence. Many Native American tribes living in Michigan have taken an increased role in wolf management. In these cultures, the wolf is commonly considered a brother, and it is awarded respect and appreciation.

Fladry placed around livestock pastures in the Upper Peninsula to prevent wolves from entering. Photo by S. Davidson.

Wolf populations in Michigan's Upper Peninsula, excluding Isle Royale: 1989–2007. After MDNR (2007).

■ Inland lakes and wetland ecosystems

Michigan has more than 11,000 inland lakes and a large diversity of wetlands, e.g., bogs, swamps, coastal marshes, fens and forested wetlands (Chapter 15). Wetlands are among the most reduced land cover in Michigan (Dahl and Allord 1997). Indeed, some of the many habitats commonly included in categories such as "inland lakes and wetland ecosystems" are extremely unique and rare. Before wetland regulations went into effect, these areas were viewed as wastelands and routinely drained, filled or polluted. The inland lakes of Michigan, although widespread, are also frequently subject to intense residential development on the shorelines and recreational use.

Some wetland and inland lake species, e.g., the muskrat, red-winged blackbird, painted turtle and mosquito, have generally tolerated slight changes in land use, as long as wetland areas are not completely drained. Occasionally, wetland species such as the mink, great blue heron, green frog and bog fritillary butterfly are found in close proximity to human development. Some species that have not adapted as well to human-induced habitat alterations include the spotted turtle, Kirtland's snake, Mitchell's satyr butterfly and Duke's skipper butterfly (Table 22.5).

For centuries, the beaver has been an important part of the wetland ecosystems in Michigan. Historically, it was also a very important part of the economy, as the large populations were harvested for their pelts which contributed to the fur trade (Chapter 27). As a result, approximately 200 years ago, beaver populations in the Great Lakes were dramatically reduced by over-trapping (Mahr 1989). Beaver populations have since recovered in some areas. Nonetheless, their recovery is currently at the heart of a resource management challenge, because when beavers construct dams and slow the flow of water, several negative results accrue. Timber managers become concerned that the flooded trees may die if soils are saturated for more than one growing season. Fisheries managers dislike the resulting increase in water temperature, as it is detrimental to trout (Avery 1992, Hill 1982). In many areas, beavers are trapped from priority trout fisheries to prevent their negative impacts to cold-water streams. Alternatively, the beaver is a keystone species, in that many wildlife species benefit from beaver-created wetlands, including waterfowl, reptiles, amphibians, the red-shouldered hawk and other riparian associated plant and animal species. The USFWS estimated that 43% of Endangered and Threatened species rely on

TABLE 22.5   Examples of terrestrial game and non-game fauna found in inland lakes and wetland ecosystems of Michigan

Common name	Scientific name
Invertebrates	
bog fritillary butterfly	Boloria eunomia dawsoni
Dukes' skipper butterfly	Euphyes dukesi
Hine's emerald dragonfly	Somatochlora hineana
Mitchell's satyr butterfly	Neonympha mitchellii
mosquito	varies (family Culicidae)
Amphibians and Reptiles	
Blanchard's cricket frog	Acris crepitans blanchardi
eastern American toad	Bufo americanus
eastern massasauga	Sistrurus catenatus catenatus
green frog	Rana clamitans
Kirtland's snake	Clonophis kirtlandii
mudpuppy	Necturus maculosus
common snapping turtle	Chelydra serpentine
spotted turtle	Clemmys guttata
Birds	
American woodcock	Scolopax minor
American bittern	Botaurus lentiginosus
bald eagle	Haliaeetus leucocephalus
black tern	Chlidonias niger
Canada goose	Branta canadensis
common grackle	Quiscalus quiscula
common loon	Gavia immer
common yellowthroat	Geothlypis trichas
belted kingfisher	Ceryle alcyon
great blue heron	Ardea herodias
green heron	Butorides virescens
least bittern	Ixobrychus exilis
mallard	Anas platyrhynchos
marsh wren	Cistothorus palustris
mute swan	Cygnus olor
osprey	Pandion haliaetus
prothonotary warbler	Protonotaria citrea
red-winged blackbird	Agelaius phoeniceus
sandhill crane	Grus canadensis
Mammals	
American beaver	Castor canadensis
mink	Mustela vison
muskrat	Ondatra zibethicus
river otter	Lutra canadensis

FIGURE 22.5 Image and range (2000) of the eastern massasauga rattlesnake in Michigan. Photo by M. Kost. After Lee and Legge (2000).

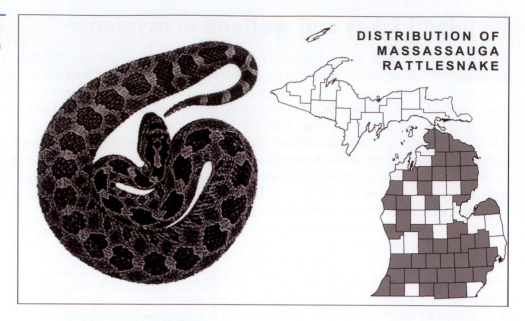

DISTRIBUTION OF MASSASSAUGA RATTLESNAKE

beaver impoundments (Environmental Protection Agency 1995). Additionally, areas flooded by beaver may exhibit improved soil and water quality, because of the more stable water table, and reducing runoff and related stream sedimentation (Arner and Hepp 1989). Although waterfowl hunting provides economic value to beaver impoundments, there is also an economic value afforded to angling and timber production that occur in its absence.

Many wetland habitats are naturally isolated and disjoint. However, the loss of these habitats has increased their fragmentation and created difficulties for genetic exchange among wetland sites. This can be problematic for the many wetland specialists with low mobility, e.g., Mitchell's satyr and Blanchard's cricket frog. Wetland isolation and habitat fragmentation may be part of the reason for the decline in populations of the eastern massasauga rattlesnake (Fig. 22.5). As Michigan's only venomous snake, it has been persecuted by humans as well. Despite these challenges, Michigan currently has a larger population of this species than any other state. The MDNR, the USFWS, and Michigan Natural Features Inventory (MNFI) collaborate on research and educational efforts, to not only learn more about the species, but also to educate the public about its rarity, uniqueness, importance in the ecosystem and, of course, its relative harmlessness (Lee and Legge 2000).

Inland lakes continue to see increased pressure from residential development and recreational uses. While the Canada goose, a wetland species, has been able to utilize the grass lawns of residential areas and golf courses, many species are not able to tolerate the habitat alteration. Lakefront residential areas often pollute inland lakes via septic systems and lawn chemicals/fertilizers. Many aquatic faunal species are sensitive to these types of pollution. Recreational use of inland lakes, particularly by motorized boats and jet skis, not only further pollute the ecosystem with chemicals and noise, but also disturb wildlife using the lake, cause wakes and create wave action that can flood the nests of birds. Having evolved nesting in wetlands with little wave action, the common loon and black tern build nests of mud and vegetation very close to the water surface. A common cause of nest failure for these species is anthropogenically caused wave action.

Wetland regulations have helped to slow the loss of these important ecosystems and their associated wildlife species. In addition, some wetland restoration projects are designed to improve wetlands that have been degraded by direct human activities, such as draining and other, less direct human activities.

■ Dune/shorezone ecosystems

Michigan has more freshwater dunes and shoreline than anywhere in the world (Evers 1994; Chapter 18). Located along the shores of the Great Lakes, these unique areas are prime targets for residential development and recreational use, such as swimming beaches, and breakwaters for mariners. The species that utilize these ecosystems are typically associated with early successional stages and fluctuating habitats. Beach areas and the nearby dunes are commonly used by the ring-billed gull, herring gull, and migrating monarch butterflies. Several less common species associated with Michigan shorelines include the prairie warbler, piping plover, Lake Huron locust and olympia marble butterfly (Table 22.6).

The Great Lakes piping plover is an endangered species that had only about 63 breeding pairs remaining, as of 2007. The plover nests in beach areas covered with cobbles and pebbles, within several hundred meters of the waterline. It migrates to the southern US and beyond for the winter (Fig. 22.6; Hyde 1999). Although this species was once quite common, increased human activity on beaches, hunting, habitat loss to residential development and possibly increased predation have caused their populations to decline. Efforts by the USFWS, MDNR, National Park Service and other stakeholders have educated many shoreline users to avoid disturbing the nesting plovers, roped off piping plover nesting areas to discourage human intrusion and even organized piping plover observers to guard nests and nestlings during periods critical to their survival. Since 1986, the piping plover population has slowly increased; however, careful monitoring and management will likely be required for many years to come.

The double-crested cormorant population is another example of one undergoing ongoing management, and of successful species recovery. By the 1970s, it had decreased to levels warranting the concern of resource managers. It was believed that pollutants in the Great Lakes had caused the decline of this fish-eating bird species. However, with improved regulation of the industrial release of pollutants, cormorant populations have rebounded dramatically, and many

TABLE 22.6   Examples of terrestrial game and non-game fauna found in dune/shoreline ecosystems of Michigan

Common name	Scientific name
Invertebrates	
Lake Huron locust	*Trimerotropis huroniana*
monarch butterfly	*Danaus plexippus*
olympia marble butterfly	*Euchloe olympia*
Birds	
caspian tern	*Sterna caspia*
common tern	*Sterna hirundo*
double-crested cormorant	*Phalacrocorax auritus*
herring gull	*Larus argentatus*
piping plover	*Charadrius melodus*
prairie warbler	*Dendroica discolor*
ring-billed gull	*Larus delawarensis*
spotted sandpiper	*Actitis macularia*
Reptiles	
Fowler's toad	*Bufo woodhousii fowleri*

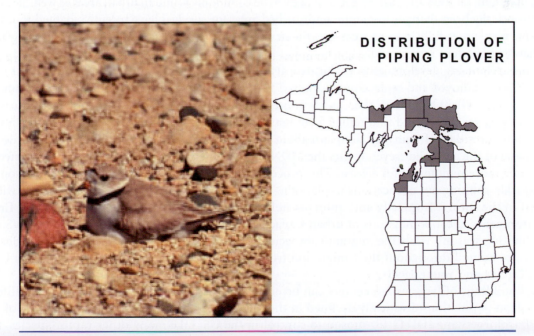

FIGURE 22.6   Image and range (2007) of the piping plover in Michigan. Photo by J. Gehring. After MNFI (2007).

anglers have actually blamed the double-crested cormorant for decreases in fish populations. No scientific research, however, has linked the double-crested cormorant to decreases in sport fisheries in Lake Michigan (Seefelt and Gillingham 2004, Seefelt 2005). Despite the lack of scientific evidence, government agencies such as USDA-APHIS Wildlife Services are killing double-crested cormorants and destroying nests, especially in areas where citizens have complained about low fishing success. These cormorant control polices are likely driven more by social carrying capacity issues and less by scientific management of a once rare species (Wires and Cuthbert 2006).

Not only are the Great Lakes shorelines important for nesting birds, they are also important stopover sites for migrating songbirds. Ornithologists have used NEXRAD Doppler Radar to observe night-migrating songbirds concentrated along some areas of the Great Lakes shorelines in the evenings, as the birds took flight after spending their days at stopover sites. Diehl et al. (2003) observed migrating birds flying over the Great Lakes during the night, but then flying to the nearest shoreline upon sunrise. Given the physical challenges of migration, stopover sites are critical for songbird refueling and resting, and thereby, critical to the survival of Neotropical migratory birds.

Resource managers have become more aware of the values and sensitivity of Michigan's shorelines and the species associated with these sensitive ecosystems. Michigan has embarked on regulatory efforts to protect particularly unique sites and to prevent some shoreline development.

■ Urban ecosystems

Although not considered pristine habitat for Michigan wildlife, several species thrive in environments heavily altered by humans, e.g., cities (Table 22.7). Although most of the native vegetation is no longer present, urban environments frequently provide food in the forms of bird and deer feeders, restaurant garbage and ornamental landscaping and garden plants. Shelter, in the form of abandoned buildings is also readily found. With the exception of household pets and automotive traffic, many wildlife species actually find refuge from some of the daily sources of risk and predation in urban areas, i.e., some predators are unable to adapt to urban areas. For example, urban white-tailed deer are not regulated by their natural predators, such as wolves, or by human hunting, and are a common nuisance species in cities.

Species typically found in urban areas include those generalists listed in Table 22.1, as well as species not native to Michigan, e.g., starling, rock pigeon, house sparrow and cabbage butterfly. The gray and fox squirrels, little brown bat, opossum, raccoon and eastern garter snake can be commonly found in urban areas as well. Several species that have historically been thought to require undisturbed areas for survival have recently adapted to using urban environments very successfully in some areas, e.g., the striped skunk, red-shouldered hawk, coyote, peregrine falcon, Cooper's hawk and eastern screech owl.

Some urban housing developments are located near golf courses and ponds, where the natural vegetation has typically been removed and replaced with mowed turf. While aesthetically pleasing to some humans, these sites also provide excellent habitat for the Canada goose, who forage on the mowed grass, swim in the water, nest in the landscaping vegetation and find refuge from many predators and hunters typical of a more natural environment. Human residents frequently complain about excess goose droppings on their lawns, but do not support euthanasia of the geese. For several years the MDNR has trapped "nuisance geese" and transported them in large cages to a more remote site for release. This process is expensive and time-consuming, and resource managers are quickly running out of locations to place the "nuisance geese." Thus, alternative solutions will need to be explored in the future. Ironically and unfortunately, due to regulations preventing the use of firearms in urban environments, most populations of urban Canada geese are not hunted as part of the USFWS regulated waterfowl hunting seasons, while the migrant subspecies of Canada geese which typically are not considered to be nuisance are hunted throughout their migration from northern North America to the southern US (Rusch et al. 1994, Ogilvie and Young 1998).

The tall buildings of large urban centers can be either beneficial or detrimental to some wildlife species. Peregrine falcon populations drastically declined in the middle of the 20th century due to the use of Dichloro Diphenyl Trichloroethane (DDT) for mosquito control in the US. Like many other raptor species, the peregrine falcon suffered from low nest productivity and thin egg shells, because DDT prevented the proper functioning of calcium in the hawk's body. After DDT applications were drastically reduced in the US, the residual, long-lived DDT still present in the ecosystem became less detrimental to the food chain, as it accumulated and became buried in the sediment of water bodies. Peregrine falcon reintroductions were then initiated, with many chicks originating from captive falconry populations. Peregrine falcon numbers are therefore increasing in Michigan. But now, instead of using cliffs as their nesting sites, they occasionally use tall buildings and bridges. Nesting peregrine falcons are typically a source of pride for communities; many enjoy observing their beauty and dramatic aerial hunting skills. Unfortunately, tall buildings can be detrimental to the migratory songbirds traveling through Michigan on their way to Central and South America. It is not uncommon for night-migrating birds to be attracted to the lights of tall buildings, resulting in collisions with the structures. The USFWS estimates that between 98 and 980 million birds collide with tall buildings in the US every year. The Detroit Audubon Society recently initiated a "lights-out" program, which follows in the footsteps of some other major cities, in which the lights in tall buildings are turned out during the migration seasons. Tall building managers not only benefit financially from reduced energy costs, but also benefit from a positive public image, while they significantly reduce the numbers of birds colliding with their building.

Urbanization of natural sites results in a significant loss of habitat for most native species. As Michigan experiences ever-increasing pressures for development, communities and regions are starting to develop land use policies and plans to address these issues (Chapter 32). These plans prioritize areas (farmland and natural areas) to be protected from urban sprawl, connect those protected areas with habitat corridors for wildlife, and attempt to focus development in other areas.

TABLE 22.7 Examples of terrestrial game and non-game fauna found in urban ecosystems of Michigan

Common name	Scientific name
Invertebrates	
cabbage white butterfly	*Pieris rapae*
eastern tiger swallowtail butterfly	*Papilio glaucus*
Amphibians and Reptiles	
brown snake	*Storeria dekayi dekayi*
eastern garter snake	*Thamnophis sirtalis sirtalis*
Birds	
American robin	*Turdus migratorius*
Canada goose	*Branta canadensis*
Cooper's hawk	*Accipiter cooperii*
eastern screech owl	*Otus asio*
European starling	*Sturnus vulgaris*
house finch	*Carpodacus mexicanus*
house sparrow	*Passer domesticus*
peregrine falcon	*Falco peregrinus*
red-shouldered hawk	*Buteo lineatus*
rock dove	*Columba livia*
Mammals	
eastern fox squirrel	*Sciurus niger*
eastern gray squirrel	*Sciurus carolinensis*
little brown bat	*Myotis lucifugus*
opossum	*Didelphis virginiana*
raccoon	*Procyon lotor*
striped skunk	*Mephitis mephitis*

■ Conclusions

Michigan is fortunate to possess a high diversity of ecosystems and fauna. Despite the challenges presented to this biota by anthropogenic changes and pressures, the people of Michigan are entwined with their natural resources. This relationship generally goes beyond the need for food, clean air and clean water; hunting, trapping and fishing are traditions common to Michigan. Recreational activities such as bird watching, hiking, biking and canoeing have been growing in popularity in more recent generations, and must be balanced against other interests. The importance of Michigan's ecosystems to people is further made evident by the large number of local-based land conservancies and land trusts, and the popularity of natural resource based festivals and gatherings. Given this valuation of the environment in Michigan, it is likely that needed conservation efforts will continue and grow.

Literature Cited

Albert, D.A. 1994. Regional Landscape Ecosystems of Michigan, Minnesota, and Wisconsin: a Working Map and Classification. General Technical Report NC-178. United States Department of Agriculture, North Central Forest Experimental Station, St. Paul, MN.

Arner, D. and G. Hepp. 1989. Beaver pond wetlands: a southern perspective. In: Smith, L.M., Pederson, R.L. and R.M. Kaminski (eds). Habitat Management for Migrating and Wintering Waterfowl in North America. Texas Tech University Press, Lubbock, TX. pp. 117–128.

Arnold, D. and R. Schofield. 1956. Status of Michigan timber wolves, 1954–1956. Michigan Department of Conservation, Game Division Report. No. 2079.

Avery, E. 1992. Effects of removing beaver dams upon a northern Wisconsin trout stream. Final Report. Wisconsin Department of Natural Resources, Madison.

Baker, R.H. 1983. Michigan Mammals. Michigan State University Press, East Lansing.

Brewer, R., McPeek, G. and R. Adams. 1991. The Atlas of the Breeding Birds of Michigan. Michigan State University Press, East Lansing.

Cooper, J. 1999a. Special animal abstract for *Buteo lineatus* (red-shouldered hawk). Michigan Natural Features Inventory, Lansing, MI.

Cooper, J. 1999b. Special animal abstract for *Accipiter gentilis* (northern goshawk). Michigan Natural Features Inventory, Lansing, MI.

Dahl, T. and G. Allord. 1997. History of wetlands in the conterminous United States. United States Geological Survey Water Supply Paper 2425.

Diehl, R., Larkin R. and J. Black. 2003. Radar observations of bird migration over the Great Lakes. Auk 120:278–290.

Environmental Protection Agency. 1995. Facts about wetlands. Office of water, Office of wetlands, oceans, and watersheds (4502F). EPA 843-F-95-001e.

Evers, D.C. 1994. Endangered and Threatened Wildlife of Michigan. University of Michigan Press, Ann Arbor.

Frelich, L. and C. Lorimer. 1985. Current and predicted long-term effects of deer browsing in Michigan, USA. Biological Conservation 34:99–120.

Harding, J. 1997. Amphibians and reptiles of the Great Lakes Region. University of Michigan Press, Ann Arbor.

Hill, E. 1982. Beaver. In: J.A. Chapman and G.A. Feldhammer (eds). Wild Mammals of North America. John Hopkins University Press, Baltimore, MD. pp. 256–281.

Hyde, D. 1999. Special animal abstract for *Charadrius melodus* (piping plover). Michigan Natural Features Inventory, Lansing, MI.

International Association of Fish and Wildlife Agencies. 2002. Economic Importance of Hunting in America. Washington DC. Report available at http://georgiawildlife.dnr.state.ga.us/assets/documents/Hunting%20 Economic%20Impact%202001.pdf (last accessed March, 2008.)

Lee, Y. and J. Legge. 2000. Special animal abstract for *Sistrurus catenatus catenatus* (Eastern Massasauga). Michigan Natural Features Inventory, Lansing, MI.

Mahr, A. 1989. A Chapter of Early Ohio Natural History. The Ohio State University Press, Columbus.

Michigan State University. 2007. Emerald Ash Borer. http://www.emeraldashborer.info/index.cfm (last accessed March, 2008.)

Michigan State University Extension. 2007. Gypsy Moth and Exotic Forest Pests Education Program. http://www.ent. msu.edu/gypsyed/index.html (last accessed September, 2007.)

MNFI - Michigan Natural Features Inventory. 2007a. Michigan's Special Animals. http://web4.msue.msu.edu/ mnfi/data/specialanimals.cfm (last accessed March, 2008.)

MNFI - Michigan Natural Features Inventory. 2007b. Michigan's Natural Communities. http://web4.msue. msu.edu/mnfi/communities/index.cfm (last accessed March, 2008.)

Mladenoff, D., Sickley, T., Haight, R. and A. Wydeven. 1995. A regional landscape analysis and prediction of favorable gray wolf habitat in the Northern Great Lakes region. Conservation Biology 9:279–294.

Nielsen, M. 1999. Michigan Butterflies and Skippers. Michigan State University Press, East Lansing.

Ogilvie, M. and S. Young. 1998. Photographic Handbook of the Wildfowl of the World. New Holland, London, UK.

Rabe, M. 2001. Special animal abstract for *Lycaeides melissa samuelis* (Karner blue). Michigan Natural Features Inventory, Lansing, MI.

Rusch, D., Humburg, D., Samuel, M. and B. Sullivan. (eds). 1994. Biology and management of Canada geese. Proceedings of the 1991 International Canada Goose Symposium.

Seefelt, N. and J. Gillingham. 2004. The double-crested cormorant in Lake Michigan: a review of population trends, ecology, and current management. In: T. Edsall and M. Munawar (eds). Of the State of Lake Michigan: Ecology, Health, and Management. Ecovision World Monograph Series. pp. 315–361.

Seefelt, N. 2005. Foraging ecology, bioenergetics, and predatory impact of breeding double-crested cormorants (*Phalacrocorax auritus*) in the Beaver archipelago, northern Lake Michigan. Ph.D. Dissertation, Department of Zoology, Michigan State University, East Lansing.

Stebler, A. 1951. The ecology of Michigan coyotes and wolves. Ph.D. Dissertation, Department of Zoology, University of Michigan, Ann Arbor.

Wires, L. and F. Cuthbert. 2006. Historic populations of the Double-crested Cormorant (*Phalacrocorax auritus*): implications for conservation and management in the 21st Century. Waterbirds 29:9–37.

Wood, N.A. 1951. The Birds of Michigan. University of Michigan Press, Ann Arbor.

Further Readings

Barrows, W.B. 1912. Michigan Bird Life. Michigan Agricultural College, Lansing, MI.

Burt, W.H. 1946. The Mammals of Michigan. University of Michigan Press, Ann Arbor.

Burt, W.H. 1957. Mammals of the Great Lakes Region. University of Michigan Press, Ann Arbor.

Chartier, A. and J. Ziarno. 2004. A birder's guide to Michigan. American Birding Association, Inc., Colorado Springs, CO.

Erlich, P., Dobkin, D. and D. Wheye. 1988. The Birder's Handbook. Simon and Schuster, Inc., New York.

Harding, J. and J. Holman. 1990. Michigan turtles and lizards: a field guide and pocket reference. Michigan State University Press, East Lansing.

Harding, J. and J. Holman. 1992. Michigan frogs, toads, and salamanders: a field guide and pocket reference. Michigan State University Press, East Lansing.

Kurta, A. 1995. Mammals of the Great Lakes Region. University of Michigan Press, Ann Arbor.

23

Aquatic Fauna

Reuben Goforth

■ Introduction

The Great Lakes basin, within which Michigan is a central feature (Fig. 14.1), encompasses a wide range of aquatic ecosystems and habitats, such as small headwater streams (Fig. 23.1A), mid- to large-sized rivers, e.g., the Grand, Kalamazoo, Huron and Muskegon (Fig. 23.1B), extensive wetlands and marshes, more than 11,000 inland lakes (Fig. 23.1C) and Great Lakes nearshore (Fig. 23.1D) and offshore areas. Within these ecosystems, aquatic habitats range from shallow and fast-flowing (Fig. 23.1E), to slow-moving or still (Fig. 23.1F), to extremely deep and cold, e.g., Lake Superior. River and lake bottom types span many substrate sizes, including clay, sand, organic rich muck, gravels, cobbles and bedrock. It is within the context of these diverse ecosystems and habitats that Michigan's aquatic fauna has become established.

Michigan's most widely recognizable aquatic organisms are fish, freshwater bivalves, aquatic insects and crustaceans, although there are also many other aquatic biota that are equally important to Michigan's aquatic ecosystems, e.g., snails, freshwater sponges. This chapter focuses on the ecology, life history, status, distributions and anthropogenic importance of fish, bivalves, aquatic insects and crustaceans. The scientific names of all organisms referred to by common name in this chapter are found in Tables 23.1 and 23.2.

■ Historical viewpoint

Michigan's aquatic fauna has a very limited biogeographic history, due to the recent glaciation of the Great Lakes region (Johnson 1980, Underhill 1986; Chapter 13). This time period has been insufficient to support the evolutionary development of more than a few endemic species—those that are only found within a particular geographic area (Coon 1999). Thus, Michigan's aquatic fauna is largely comprised of species from adjacent areas—those not covered by the ice.

During continental glaciation, many aquatic organisms retreated through drainage networks to warmer climatic refugia, primarily to the south. When these same glaciers retreated northward, they left behind newly formed aquatic habitats, ripe for invasion (Moyle and Cech 2004). Large quantities of glacial meltwater also created extensive waterway connections between what was to become the Great Lakes basin and other, more interior drainage basins. These connections permitted aquatic organisms from southern and eastern refugia to migrate into the recently deglaciated landscape and become established in these new aquatic habitats. Once the glaciers receded completely, about 11,000 years ago, the water levels in the Great lakes fell dramatically (Chapter 13), effectively isolating the Great Lakes basin from further aquatic introductions due to physical barriers. The greatest contribution to

FIGURE 23.1   Examples of aquatic ecosystems in Michigan. Photos by R. Goforth. A. A small headwater tributary stream of the Ontonogan River, B. A mainstem reach of the Grand River, C. A small inland lake (Rocking Chair Lake), D. A nearshore reach of northern Lake Michigan, E. A shallow, rocky reach of the Presque Isle River, and F. A deep, slow-moving reach of Sucker Creek.

TABLE 23.1   Common and scientific names for aquatic organisms discussed in this chapter

Common name	Scientific name	Common name	Scientific name
Asian carp	*Hypophthalmichthys spp.*	lake trout	*Salvelinus namaycush*
Asiatic clam	*Corbicula fluminea*	bargemouth bass	*Micropterus salmoides*
black bullhead	*Ameiurus melas*	logperch	*Percina caprodes*
black crappie	*Pomoxis nigromaculatus*	longnose sucker	*Catostomus catostomus*
blackside darter	*Percina maculata*	pumpkinseed	*Lepomis gibbosus*
bluegill	*Lepomis macrochirus*	quagga mussel	*Dreissena bugensis*
brook trout	*Salvelinus fontinalis*	rainbow trout	*Oncorhynchus mykiss*
brown bullhead	*Ameiurus nebulosus*	rusty crayfish	*Orconectes rusticus*
brown trout	*Salmo trutta*	smallmouth bass	*Micropterus dolomieu*
channel catfish	*Ictalurus punctatus*	snakehead	*Channa spp.*
Chinook salmon	*Oncorhynchus tshawytscha*	walleye	*Sander vitreus*
coho salmon	*Oncorhynchus kisutch*	white sucker	*Catostomus commersoni*
creek chub	*Semotilus atromaculatus*	yellow bullhead	*Ameiurus natalis*
fathead minnow	*Pimephales promelas*	yellow perch	*Perca flavescens*
Iowa darter	*Etheostoma exile*	zebra mussel	*Dreissena polymorpha*
Johnny darter	*Etheostoma nigrum*		

TABLE 23.2   Fish species that are considered of special interest in Michigan[1]

Family	Common name	Scientific name	Origin	MI status
Petromyzontidae (lampreys)	sea lamprey	*Petromyzon marinus*	I	NL
Acipenseridae (sturgeons)	lake sturgeon	*Acipenser fulvescens*	N	LT
Polyodontidae (paddlefishes)	paddlefish	*Polyodon spathula*	N	X
Lepisosteidae (gars)	spotted gar	*Lepisosteus oculatus*	N	SC
Hiodontidae (mooneyes)	mooneye	*Hiodon tergisus*	N	LT
Anguillidae (eels)	American eel	*Anguilla rostrata*	I	NL
Clupeidae (herrings and shads)	alewife	*Alosa pseudoharengus*	I	NL
	redside dace	*Clinostomus elongatus*	N	LE
	common carp	*Cyprinus carpio*	I	NL
	silver chub	*Macrhybopsis storeriana*	N	SC
Cyprinidae (shiners, minnows, chubs and dace)	bigeye chub	*Hybopsis amblops*	N	X
	pugnose shiner	*Notropis anogenus*	N	SC
	ironcolor shiner	*Notropis chalybaeus*	N	X
	silver shiner	*Notropis photogenis*	N	LE
	weed shiner	*Notropis texanus*	N	X
	pugnose minnow	*Opsopoeodus emiliae*	N	LE
	suckermouth minnow	*Phenacobius mirabilis*	I	NL
	southern redbelly dace	*Phoxinus erythrogaster*	N	LE

(continued)

TABLE 23.2   (continued)

Family	Common name	Scientific name	Origin	MI status
Cobitidae (loaches)	Japanese weatherfish	*Misgurnus anguillicaudatus*	I	NL
	W. Creek chubsucker	*Erimyzon claviformis*	N	LE
Catostomidae (suckers)	bigmouth buffalo	*Ictiobus cyprinellus*	I	NL
	black buffalo	*Ictiobus niger*	I	NL
	river redhorse	*Moxostoma carinatum*	N	LT
Ictaluridae (bullhead catfishes)	margined madtom	*Noturus insignis*	I	NL
	brindled madtom	*Noturus miurus*	N	SC
	northern madtom	*Noturus stigmosus*	N	LE
Cottidae (sculpins)	spoonhead sculpin	*Cottus ricei*	N	SC
Fundulidae (topminnows)	starhead topminnow	*Fundulus dispar*	N	SC
Centrarchidae (sunfishes and black basses)	orange-spotted sunfish	*Lepomis humilis*	I	NA
	redear sunfish	*Lepomis microlophus*	I	NA
Clupeidae (herrings and shads)	alewife	*Alosa pseudoharengus*	I	NA
Gobiidae (gobies)	round goby	*Neogobius melanostomus*	I	NA
	tubenose goby	*Proterorhinus marmoratus*	I	NA
Percidae (perches and darters)	eastern sand darter	*Ammocrypta pellucida*	N	LT
	banded darter	*Etheostoma zonale*	N	SC
	ruffe	*Gymnocephalus cernuus*	I	NA
	channel darter	*Percina copelandi*	N	LE
	river darter	*Percina shumardi*	N	LE
	sauger	*Sander canadensis*	N	LT
	blue pike	*Sander glaucus*	N	X
Salmonidae (salmon and trout)	cisco/lake herring	*Coregonus artedi*	N	LT
	Ives Lake cisco	*Coregonus hubbsi*	N	SC
	deepwater cisco	*Coregonus johannae*	N	X
	kiyi	*Coregonus kiyi*	N	SC
	blackfin cisco	*Coregonus nigripinnis*	N	X
	shortnose cisco	*Coregonus reighardi*	N	X
	shortjaw cisco	*Coregonus zenithicus*	N	LT
	siskiwit Lake cisco	*C. zenithicus bartletti*	N	SC
	Arctic grayling	*Thymallus arcticus*	N	X
Osmeridae (smelts)	rainbow smelt	*Osmerus mordax*	I	NA

1: This list includes both native (N) species of conservation concern and introduced (I) species. The listing status of each species includes introduced species that are not listed (NL) and native species that are state-listed as endangered (LE), state-listed as threatened (LT), of special concern (SC), and extirpated (X).

Michigan's native aquatic fauna came from the historic connections with the Mississippi River basin (Bailey and Smith 1981, Graf 1997), although some species were also introduced from the Atlantic Ocean through the St. Lawrence River and the Great Lakes, as well as from arctic and subarctic waters impounded by continental ice sheets.

■ Michigan fishes

Michigan's fish fauna spans 24 native and four introduced families, and includes a wide variety of species. Determining the exact number of fish species that occur in Michigan at any one time is complicated. Improved genetic analysis techniques have resulted in taxonomic changes that can either add to or decrease the number of accepted species. Twenty six fish species been introduced from outside the state and are now established in Michigan waters, including intentionally stocked salmon and trout species and accidentally introduced species, e.g., the round goby (Fig. 23.2). Continued threats of new introductions from transoceanic ballast water exchange, pet trade releases, e.g., the snakehead, and movements of introduced species through man-made connecting channels, e.g., Asian carp, are somber reminders that Michigan may count additional introduced species as part of its overall fish fauna in the near future.

FIGURE 23.2   The round goby, *Apollonia melanostomus*, a fish species introduced to Michigan waters via transoceanic ballast water exchange. This relatively small (<20 cm), bottom-dwelling fish is very aggressive and capable of displacing native species. They are often a nuisance for perch anglers in the Great Lakes. Photo by R. Goforth.

Species that have been extirpated, or are no longer present in the state but continue to exist in other parts of their native distribution, e.g., paddlefish and Arctic grayling, also affect the number of fish species included in Michigan's fauna. Other fish species are in danger of becoming extirpated in the future. Finally, several species, including the deepwater cisco and shortnose cisco, are considered to be extinct.

Given the considerations above, the following numbers reflect reasonable estimates of Michigan's fish fauna as of 2006. Of the 172 extant, or surviving, Great Lakes fish species reported by Coon in 1999, 147 presently occur in Michigan waters (Table 23.2). Michigan's extant fish fauna is dominated by six of the 24 native families found here, including the Cyprinidae, Catostomidae, Ictaluridae, Salmonidae, Centrarchidae, and Percidae.

Cyprinidae: minnows, shiners, and dace

The family Cyprinidae is the largest family of fishes worldwide (Moyle and Cech 2004); 34 native and four introduced species are currently found in Michigan. Most cyprinids are considered to be warmwater fish—found in waters that routinely exceed 20° C during part of the year. About half of Michigan's cyprinids have moderate to highly limited distributions (Bailey et al. 2004). For example, several cyprinid species reach the northern edge of their distributions in Michigan, and only occur in a few streams and rivers in the southernmost portion of the state. Other cyprinids are principally found south of Grayling, while a few species only occur north of Lansing. The remaining 18 species are generally distributed widely throughout the state.

Cyprinids are generally small in size, i.e., 5–15 cm, and have relatively large eyes, a single dorsal fin and no fin spines (Fig. 23.3A). Despite the common observation that they "all look alike," cyprinids exhibit high levels of adaptation that allow them to occupy a wide range of aquatic habitats (Winfield and Nelson 1991). Most of Michigan's cyprinids feed on small invertebrates, such as zooplankton and aquatic insects. Many species exhibit some level of parental care for the eggs and young; nests of small pebbles arranged in circular piles by breeding males can often be seen in shallow streams in the spring.

From an ecosystem perspective, cyprinids bridge food web connections between invertebrate prey and larger predators. The role of cyprinids as prey for many sport fish in Michigan has made some of them economically impor-

FIGURE 23.3 Examples of species representing some of the more common fish families in Michigan. A. Blackchin shiner (*Notropis heterodon*, Cyprinidae), B. Western Creek Chubsucker (*Erimyzon claviformis*, Catostomidae), C. Brindled madtom (*Noturus miurus*, Ictaluridae), D. Lake trout (*Salvelinus namaycush*, Salmonidae), E. Warmouth (*Lepomis gulosus*, Centrarchidae), F. Rainbow darter (*Etheostoma caeruleum*, Percidae). Photos by R. Goforth.

tant as baitfish, including fathead minnows and creek chubs. These species, among others, are routinely collected and sold as bait for use by anglers. Cyprinids also have aesthetic value, serving as objects of natural fascination for net-wielding children (and some adults!) wading in streams and shallow areas of lakes.

Catostomidae: suckers, redhorses, and jumprock

The family Catostomidae is small (68 total species), and Michigan's fish fauna includes only 15 native and two introduced species from this family. Only one catostomid species, the white sucker, has a truly statewide distribution. It can be found in habitats from small streams to the Great Lakes. Six other sucker species have moderately extensive distributions in Michigan, with most occurring in the Lower Peninsula. The remaining eight sucker species have very limited to highly localized distributions in Michigan, and several of these are known only from 10 or fewer occurrences (Bailey et al. 2004).

Suckers are considered to be warmwater fish and are closely related to cyprinids, sharing many morphological characteristics with this group (Fig. 23.3B). However, catostomids are generally larger, i.e., 30–50 cm, and are distinguished by having a subterminal mouth (located on the lower surface of the head) with fleshy lips. The shape of their mouths allows suckers to probe for benthic, or bottom-dwelling, invertebrate prey. Most catostomids are associated with lotic, or moving water, ecosystems, i.e., streams and rivers. However, some suckers, such as the white sucker and the longnose sucker, also live in lentic (lake) ecosystems. Historically, Native Americans and European settlers in Michigan used suckers for both food and fertilizer. Although suckers are generally not targeted by Michigan anglers today, some southern states still have active sucker fisheries where wading anglers gig for suckers in shallow streams.

Ictaluridae: bullhead catfish

The family Ictaluridae is the largest fish family endemic to North America; Michigan's fish fauna includes nine native and one introduced species. Most of Michigan's catfish species are found only in the Southern Peninsula, although the brown and black bullheads both occur in streams, rivers, and lakes throughout Michigan.

Ictalurids are warmwater fish with barbels around their mouths, scaleless bodies, large heads, an adipose fin (a small, fleshy fin between the dorsal fin and tail fin) and stout pectoral and dorsal fin spines (Fig. 23.3C). There are two types of ictalurids in Michigan: species that are typically sought by anglers (five native species, generally 20–50 cm in length) and madtoms (four native and one introduced species, generally 8–15 cm in length) (Fig. 23.3C). Sport fish such as the channel catfish, brown bullhead and yellow bullhead are actively sought by anglers and can be found in a wide variety of mid- to large-size rivers and inland lakes. In fact, channel catfish are even raised in hatcheries and stocked in some Michigan lakes to meet recreational demands.

The smaller madtoms are more secretive, being found primarily in rivers of the southern Lower Peninsula. Madtoms are notable because they have poison glands associated with their pectoral fin spines that can cause careless handlers to receive a painful, but non-life-threatening, puncture wounds. Unlike the bullhead catfish, madtoms have no direct economic value; they are nonetheless important components of Lower Michigan lotic ecosystems.

Salmonidae: salmon, trout, and whitefish

The family Salmonidae includes approximately 70 species worldwide; Michigan's fish fauna includes 12 native and six introduced salmonid species. Most of Michigan's salmonid species occur either primarily or exclusively in Great Lakes waters (Bailey et al. 2004). For example, introduced Chinook and coho salmon remain in the Great Lakes throughout much of the year, although they migrate into tributary rivers during the breeding season. Additionally, some whitefish inhabit deep waters exclusively, with some species occurring at depths >200 m (Hubbs and Lagler 2004). However, a few species, such as the native brook trout and the introduced rainbow and brown trout, can be found throughout the western and northern portions of the state in shallow streams and rivers with high groundwater inputs.

Distinguishing characteristics of salmonids include: fusiform (torpedo-like) body shape, single dorsal fin, forked tail fin, adipose fin, axillary process (a triangular-shaped, fleshy projection from the base of each pelvic fin) and lack of fin spines (Fig. 23.3D). Unlike most other Michigan fish, salmonids are considered coldwater fish; they inhabit waters that generally remain below about 15° C. They are also unique in that several species have evolved as Great Lakes endemic species (see FOCUS BOX on the following page).

Salmonids have played a large role in Michigan fisheries historically, and they continue to be important today, although for different reasons. Whitefish and lake trout were extremely important for the commercial fishing industry in Michigan, beginning in the mid 1800s. The seemingly endless salmonid resources of the Great Lakes figured significantly in the settlement of Michigan and continued to support an important commercial fishery until the mid-1900s. However, heavy commercial fishing pressures and the accidental introduction of the sea lamprey reduced salmonid stocks to unsustainable levels, and in some cases, endemic whitefish species became extirpated from Michigan, or completely extinct. The widespread establishment of the alewife throughout the Great Lakes, coupled with the loss of most of the Great Lakes top predators, due to overfishing and sea lamprey predation, led to overpopulation and periodic, massive die-offs of alewives. In 1966, Pacific Chinook and coho salmon were introduced to the Great Lakes to both help control alewife populations and to provide recreational fishing opportunities. These species, along with the introduced steelhead and brown trout and the native lake trout, continue to be raised in hatcheries and stocked in Michigan waters, where they support a vigorous recreational fishing industry. These fish can grow to be quite large, as evidenced by the following Michigan state records (as of 2006): lake trout (27.9 kg, 124.5 cm), Chinook salmon (20.9 kg, 110.5 cm) and coho salmon (13.9 kg, 101.6 cm).

Centrarchidae: sunfish and black bass

The family Centrarchidae includes 29 species that are endemic to North America; Michigan's fauna includes 10 native and two introduced species. Members of this family are highly visible in lakes and rivers, and are often the first fish caught by new anglers—especially bluegills. Most of Michigan's centrarchids are distributed widely throughout the state, with only the two introduced species, redear sunfish and orange-spotted sunfish (*Lepomis humilis*), exhibiting highly restricted distributions in southern Michigan (Bailey et al. 2004).

Centrarchids are distinguished by their deeply shaped bodies (tall from top to bottom), thoracic pelvic fins (located towards the front of the body), two broadly-joined dorsal fins and spines in their first dorsal fins and anal fins (Fig. 23.3E). They are warmwater fish, commonly found in shallow waters of slow-moving streams and lakes, where they feed primarily on small invertebrates and other fish. The most commonly encountered Michigan centrarchids are largemouth and smallmouth bass, bluegill, pumpkinseed and black crappie. These species, like other

FOCUS BOX: Endemic Michigan fish

Because Michigan was only recently deglaciated, there has been little time for the development of endemic fish species (Coon 1999). However, several members of the salmonid genus *Coregonus* (more commonly referred to as whitefish, ciscoes or chubs) are endemic to the Great Lakes and Michigan. The four widely recognized endemic whitefish species include the extant kiyi and shortjaw cisco and the extinct deepwater cisco and shortnose cisco. Additional endemic species whose status continues to be disputed are the extant Ives Lake cisco and the extinct blackfin cisco (Bailey and Smith 1981, Coon 1999). It is probable that these endemic coregonines evolved from as few as two ancestral species that entered the Great Lakes from southern refugia after the last glacial retreat (Smith and Todd 1984, Todd and Smith 1992, Coon 1999). The resulting emergence of endemic coregonine species in the Great Lakes was most likely facilitated by the strong philopatry and developmental plasticity exhibited by these fish (Coon 1999). Philopatry refers to the tendency of an organism to return to a specific location, such as a rocky reef or deepwater area, to spawn. Developmental plasticity refers to the ability of cells and tissues of some species to develop in different ways in response to surrounding environmental conditions, thereby allowing individuals to become better suited to using available resources. Thus, the combined tendencies for groups of coregonines to become reproductively isolated and morphologically adaptable allowed them to evolve new species in the Great Lakes, despite the limited timeframe.

centrarchids, spawn in the spring in shallow water depressional nests, constructed and guarded by the males. Most Michigan centrarchids are highly sought after by anglers, especially in inland lakes. Largemouth and smallmouth bass are primarily targeted as catch-and-release sport fish; the state record largemouth bass is 5.4 kg, 68.6 cm. Sunfish, including bluegill, pumpkinseed and black crappie, are widely fished for consumptive uses or just for fun.

Percidae: perches and darters

The family Percidae is comprised of approximately 190 species that occur primarily in eastern North America (Moyle and Cech 2004). Michigan's fish fauna includes 18 native and one introduced species. Percids are considered cool-water fish. Yellow perch and walleye are widely distributed throughout Michigan. In contrast, most of Michigan's darters exhibit very limited geographic distributions, and several are limited to only one or two watersheds. However, Johnny darters, Iowa darters, blackside darters and logperch, like perch and walleye, are distributed throughout most of Michigan (Bailey et al. 2004).

Percids share many morphological traits with centrarchids, including two dorsal fins, thoracic pelvic fins and fin spines. However, perches and darters have two distinctly separated dorsal fins, and they have more fusiform (perches) or elongated (darters) body shapes (Fig. 23.3F). The larger (20–50 cm) yellow perch and walleye are principally piscivorous and are actively sought by anglers in slow-moving rivers, inland lakes, and the Great Lakes. Indeed, fried perch and walleye are popular offerings in many Michigan restaurants, and recreational fishing for these percids is a significant source of tourism revenue.

Darters are much smaller (3–10 cm) and can tolerate faster moving streams and rivers, in addition to having some species that occur in inland lakes and Great Lakes' nearshore areas. Michigan's complement of 15 darter species is small, although some are quite colorful, especially males in breeding coloration (Fig. 23.3F). Darters are too small to be economically important; however, they do have great significance as benthic insectivores in Michigan aquatic ecosystems.

◼ Freshwater bivalves

Bivalve mollusks are among the most readily recognized invertebrates in Michigan waters. More commonly known as clams and mussels, they have two hard valves (shells) that are composed of crystalline calcium carbonate ($CaCO_3$), embedded in a protein matrix. Basic shell structures include the beak (umbo), lateral and pseudocardinal teeth and muscle scars where their adductor muscles attach to the shell (Fig. 23.4). The shells have an outer layer that varies greatly in color; it can be characterized by vividly colored rays and spots in some species of unionaceans (Fig. 23.5).

FIGURE 23.4 Interior and exterior anatomy of a unionacean bivalve mollusk (freshwater clam). Used with permission of the Illinois Natural History Survey, Urbana.

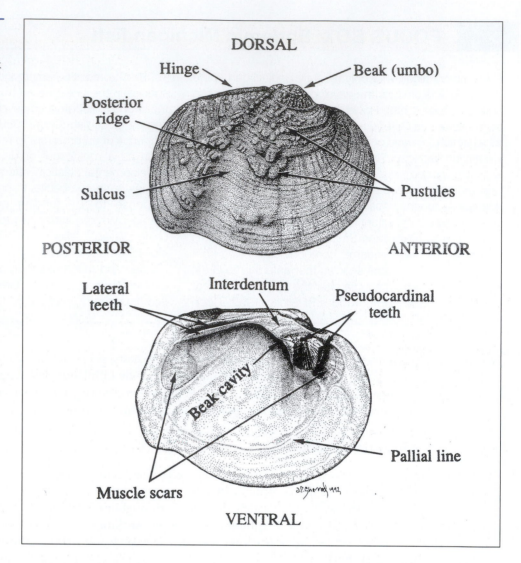

FIGURE 23.5 The plain pocketbook, *Lampsilis cardium,* a native Michigan unionacean that exhibits striking green bands on its periostracum, or outer shell covering. Photo by D. Stagliano.

The inner shell layer can also vary widely in coloration, but is generally white or purple. The shells serve as protection for the delicate body tissues, particularly the gills that are used for both gas exchange and filtering food materials from the water. Bivalve shells are very durable and can persist for long periods of time after the animal dies, which is why they can often be found along the shores of streams, rivers and lakes throughout Michigan.

Four types of bivalves are currently found in Michigan, including members of the superfamily Unionacea, and the families Sphaeriidae, Corbiculidae, and Dreissenidae. The unionaceans are commonly referred to as freshwater mussels or clams (Fig. 23.5). Sphaeriids (fingernail clams or pea clams) are considerably smaller than unionaceans, and like the unionaceans, most sphaeriids found in Michigan are native. The Asiatic clam (family Corbiculidae) was introduced to North America from southeastern Asia in the early 1900s (McMahon 1982). Finally, two dreissenid mussel species, the zebra mussel and the quagga mussel, have been introduced to the Great Lakes region from the Ponto-Caspian region via international shipping ballast water. Although the influences of Asiatic clams remain unclear, the zebra and quagga mussels have significantly altered food webs and biotic community structure in many of Michigan's aquatic ecosystems, especially Great Lakes nearshore areas (Herbert et al. 1991, Leach 1993, Fahnenstiel et al. 1995; Chapter 14). Dreissenid mussels have also had significant economic consequences for Michigan and other Great Lakes states, due to industrial fouling and indirect ecological effects on commercial and recreational fisheries and other activities.

Of the nearly 300 unionacean species known worldwide, 260 are native to North America and 42 are native to Michigan waters (Burch 1975). Unionaceans typically inhabit benthic habitats of streams and rivers, although some species are also lake-dwelling. Their unique life cycle involves a larval stage during which they parasitize fish hosts (see FOCUS BOX below). In Michigan, unionaceans are particularly numerous in southern rivers with well-washed sandy-gravel substrates. Worldwide, this group is considered to be among the most imperiled of all freshwater organisms (Lydeard et al. 2004). This imperilment is exemplified in Michigan, where 13 of the 42 species have been given state and/or federal legal protection. However, no unionaceans known to occur in Michigan have yet become extirpated.

Native Americans may have eaten freshwater clams, although European settlers have generally chosen to use them for purposes other than food. Despite the fact that they are undoubtedly a good source of protein, think about what the bottom of the Grand River would taste like, and you'll probably have a good idea of just how palatable they are! Unionacean clams in Michigan were also once harvested commercially for the pearl button industry. Thick-shelled species were collected from rivers, such as the Grand River (Fig. 23.1B), in the late 1800s and early 1900s. Disks cut from the harvested shells were then drilled and polished to make buttons for clothing (Fig. 23.6). However, the development of plastics made pearl buttons obsolete by the mid-1900s, at which time Michigan clam populations became closed to harvest. Unionacean populations remain closed to harvest in Michigan, although they are still harvested in other states to provide seed material for the Japanese cultured pearl industry. Declining populations in states with open harvests have resulted in some poaching of clams in Michigan.

FIGURE 23.6   A "button blank" three-ridge mussel, *Amblema plicata*, shell. The commercial button industry once relied on harvests of thick-shelled freshwater mussels, from which small disks were removed and refined to produce buttons—before petroleum-based plastics became widely available.

FOCUS BOX: Unionacean life history

Unionaceans are distinguished from other bivalves by their life cycle. Unlike other bivalves, most unionaceans have a larval life stage during which they must successfully parasitize fish (see Figure at top of next page). These larvae, referred to as glochidia, are held in brood pouches of the females until they are ready to be released. Upon release, glochidia must come into contact with the gills or fins of a fish host in order to continue their development. In most cases, the glochidia from individual unionacean species can only successfully parasitize specific fish hosts (Haag and Warren 1997). Some unionacean species have "lures" to help increase the probability that their glochidia will successfully parasitize an appropriate fish host.

Most unionaceans must release many thousands of glochidia in order to have just one glochidium successfully parasitize an appropriate fish, mature into a juvenile clam and drop from the fish into a suitable habitat, where it can develop into an adult. This low reproductive success rate, coupled with the great length of time necessary for most unionaceans to reach reproductive maturity, makes recovery of populations that have been reduced very slow. Further, the loss of suitable fish hosts will have serious consequences for unionaceans that cannot successfully complete their life cycles without these hosts. It is this combination of factors that has led to the high imperilment of unionaceans as a group (Lydeard et al. 2004).

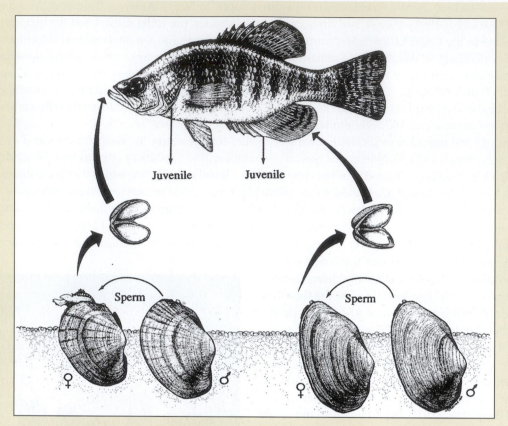

The life cycle of unionacean clams. These freshwater bivalves require a fish host to complete their life cycle. Used with permission of the Illinois Natural History Survey, Champaign, Illinois.

■ Aquatic insects

Michigan's aquatic insect fauna spend all or a portion of their lives on or below the water's surface. They are particularly important for a number of reasons, but mainly because they provide a vital link between lower trophic, or feeding, levels and fish predators—that then serve as important food sources for Michigan's wildlife and human populations. As an example, many serious anglers recognize the importance of using artificial "flies" to mimic aquatic insect larvae and newly emerged adults, so as to catch trout and sunfish. These anglers, along with others who enjoy the outdoors, also experience bites from the many terrestrial adults of species that develop first as aquatic larvae, e.g., mosquitoes, black flies, sand flies or midges, deer flies and horse flies (Merritt and Newson 1978, Kim and Merritt 1987). Besides being a pest to outdoor enthusiasts, mosquitoes can also transmit diseases such as West Nile virus that can be life-threatening to humans. More recently, aquatic insects have become important indicators of the biological and ecological integrity of freshwaters, due to the intolerance of some aquatic insects to degraded environmental conditions (Hilsenhoff 1988, Kerans and Karr 1994). Aquatic insects have even been used as compelling evidence in criminal investigations (Merritt and Wallace 2001).

Most of Michigan's aquatic insects belong to the following orders: Ephemeroptera, Odonata, Plecoptera, Trichoptera, Megaloptera, Hemiptera, Coleoptera and Diptera. The first four of these are almost exclusively comprised of species that have aquatic larvae, while the remaining orders are primarily terrestrial, with some species and/or families that have at least one aquatic life stage. Ephemeroptera (mayflies) larvae exhibit the greatest diversity in streams, where they are algal grazers or collectors of detritus (Edmunds and Waltz 1996). Odonata (dragonflies and damselflies) are common in slow-moving streams and small lakes, where they act as ambush predators among aquatic plants, root wads and organic debris (Westfall and Tennessen 1996). Plecoptera (stoneflies) larvae are largely associated with small, fast-flowing, cool streams, where most are shredders that tear apart leaves that fall into the water (Stewart and Harper 1996). Trichoptera (caddisflies) inhabit a very wide range of aquatic ecosystem types, ranging from small streams to lakes and marshes, where they are best known for their construction of elaborate nets, retreats and portable cases (Wiggins 1996). Megalopterans are found in both lotic and lentic habitats, where they are voracious predators on small aquatic insects, worms and crustaceans (Evans and Neunzig 1996). The Order Hemiptera (true bugs) includes a variety of species that either live on or below the water's surface, where they are primarily predators (Polhemus 1996). Although members of the Order Coleoptera (beetles) are extremely diverse in form and occur in a wide range of aquatic habitats, they rarely occur in numbers equivalent to other aquatic insect orders (White and Brigham 1996). Finally, the Order Diptera (true flies) includes a very wide range of taxa that have successfully colonized nearly every type of aquatic habitat on Earth (Courtney et al. 1996). With some exceptions, the aquatic larvae of dipterans are primarily detrital collectors and predators. Dipterans include numerous species that are considered to be a nuisance to humans and other animals, including mosquitoes (family Culicidae) and blackflies (family Simuliidae).

■ Crustaceans

As a group, crustaceans have a long evolutionary history, over which they have become adapted to a wide variety of aquatic ecosystems (Abele 1982, Covich and Thorpe 1991). Only 10% of all extant crustacean species live in freshwater (Bowman and Abele 1982). However, these freshwater crustaceans often comprise a very high percentage of the overall biomass in aquatic ecosystems, serving as a vital trophic link between photosynthetic primary producers and the prey of top predators. Crustaceans in Michigan range from near-microscopic cladocerans and copepods, to small (0.5–1.0 cm), shrimp-like amphipods and isopods, to the considerably larger (2.0–12.0 cm) crayfish.

Cladocerans and copepods are generically referred to as zooplankton—small invertebrates that typically inhabit lakes and large rivers. Zooplankton serve as a critical trophic link, from photosynthetic phytoplankton to multiple fish life stages, including larvae, juveniles and even the adults of some planktivorous species.

Amphipods and isopods are benthic crustaceans that feed on a range of organic materials, from decaying plants to live algae. The great importance of these benthic crustaceans in Great Lakes food webs is illustrated by the relatively recent disappearance of *Diaporeia* in the lower lakes. *Diaporeia* once comprised up to 70% of the total benthic biomass in these lakes, providing extensive forage for whitefish and preyfish eaten by salmon and trout. However, severe declines in *Diaporeia* have led to reduced fish populations, comprised of emaciated fish. As a result, the quantities and qualities of both commercial and recreational fish catches are declining—with significant economic consequences.

Crayfish are benthic crustaceans that resemble miniature lobsters, and they are readily collected in streams, rivers and inland lakes for use as bait, or just for fun (Fig. 23.7). There are eight crayfish

FIGURE 23.7 Crayfish, such as this small rusty crayfish, *Orconectes rusticus*, are often collected for use as fish bait and, in the case of this individual, as aquarium inhabitants. Photo by R. Goforth.

species in Michigan, including the highly invasive rusty crayfish. This species is of great concern because it readily outcompetes and displaces native crayfish in Michigan and other areas of the Great Lakes. Crayfish are generally considered to be largely opportunistic omnivores, eating everything from scavenged dead and decaying plant material to captured live fish. While some southern species are raised in aquaculture facilities for human consumption, the use of Michigan crayfish is largely restricted to fish bait and occasional aquarium pets.

Conclusions

Michigan's streams, rivers and lakes support a highly diverse aquatic fauna, largely the result of migrating aquatic organisms that entered the Great Lakes basin after the glaciers receded. With few exceptions, Michigan's aquatic fauna have remained largely intact, even though factors related to human activities, e.g., overfishing, habitat loss, introductions of non-native species, declining water quality, etc., have strongly influenced most ecosystems of the state.

The future of Michigan's aquatic fauna remains uncertain in the face of continued landscape transformations and potential new introductions of non-native species. Intensive management of aquatic ecosystems and both listed, i.e., threatened and endangered (Table 23.2), and more common species that help to maintain ecosystem health will undoubtedly be needed to maintain this impressive fauna into the foreseeable future. Given the importance of Michigan's aquatic fauna in supporting ecosystem services, such as supplying clean, potable water sources, as well as providing extensive recreational opportunities, proper management must remain a priority.

Literature Cited

Abele, L.G. 1982. Biogeography. In: L.G. Abele (ed), The Biology of Crustacea. Volume 1. Systematics, the Fossil Record and Biogeography. Academic Press, New York. pp. 242–304.

Bailey, R.M., Latta, W.C. and G.R. Smith. 2004. An Atlas of Michigan Fishes with Keys and Illustrations for their Identification. Miscellaneous Publication Number 192, Museum of Zoology, University of Michigan, Ann Arbor.

Bailey, R.M. and G.R. Smith. 1981. Origin and geography of the fish fauna of the Laurentian Great Lakes Basin. Canadian Journal of Fisheries and Aquatic Sciences 38:1539–1561.

Bowman, T.E. and L.G. Abele. 1982. Classification of the Recent Crustacea. In: L.G. Abele (ed), The Biology of Crustacea. Volume 1. Systematics, the Fossil Record and Biogeography. Academic Press, New York. pp. 1–27.

Burch, J.B. 1975. Freshwater unionacean clams (Mollusca: Pelecypoda) of North America. Malacological Publications, Hamburg, MI.

Coon, T.G. 1999. Ichthyofauna of the Great Lakes Basin. In: W.W. Taylor and C.P. Ferreri (eds), Great Lakes Fisheries and Management: a Binational Perspective. Michigan State University Press, East Lansing. pp. 55–71.

Courtney, G.W., Teskey, H.J., Merritt, R.W. and B.A. Foote. 1996. Aquatic Diptera. In: R.W. Merritt and K.W. Cummins (eds), An Introduction to the Aquatic Insects of North America. Kendall/Hunt Publishing Company, Dubuque, IA. pp. 484–548.

Covich, A.P. and J.H. Thorpe. 1991. Crustacea: Introduction and Peracardia. In: J.H. Thorpe and A.P. Covich (eds), Ecology and Classification of North American Freshwater Invertebrates. Academic Press, Inc., San Diego, CA. pp. 665–689.

Edmunds, G.F., Jr. and R.D. Waltz. 1996. Ephemeroptera. In: R.W. Merritt and K.W. Cummins (eds), An Introduction to the Aquatic Insects of North America. Kendall/Hunt Publishing Company, Dubuque, IA. pp. 126–163.

Evans, E.D. and H.H. Neunzig. 1996. Megaloptera and Aquatic Neuroptera. In: R.W. Merritt and K.W. Cummins (eds), An Introduction to the Aquatic Insects of North America. Kendall/Hunt Publishing Company, Dubuque, IA. pp. 298–308.

Fahnenstiel, G.L., Bridgeman, T.B., Lang, G.A., McCormick, M.J. and T.F. Nalepa. 1995. Phytoplankton productivity in Saginaw Bay, Lake Huron: effects of zebra mussel (Dreissena polymorpha) colonization. Journal of Great Lakes Research 21:465–475.

Graf, D.L. 1997. Northern redistribution of freshwater pearly mussels (Bivalvia: Unionoidea) during Wisconsin deglaciation in the southern glacial Lake Agassiz region: a review. American Midlands Naturalist 138:37–47.

Haag, W.R. and M.L. Warren. 1997. Host fishes and reproductive biology of six freshwater mussel species from the Mobile Basin. Journal of the North American Benthological Society 16:576–585.

Herbert, P.D.N., Wilson, C.C., Murdoch, M.H. and R. Lazar. 1991. Demography and ecological impacts of the invading mollusk Dreissena polymorpha. Canadian Journal of Zoology 69:405–409.

Hilsenhoff, W.L. 1988. Rapid field assessment of organic pollution with a family-level biotic index. Journal of the North American Benthological Society 7:65–68.

Hubbs, C.L. and K.F. Lagler. 2004. Fishes of the Great Lakes Region. University of Michigan Press, Ann Arbor.

Johnson, R.I. 1980. Zoogeography of the North American Unionacea (Mollusca: Bivalvia) north of maximum Pleistocene glaciation. Bulletin of the Museum of Comparative Zoology 149:77–189.

Kerans, B.L. and J.R. Karr.1994. A benthic index of biotic integrity (B-IBI) for rivers of the Tennessee Valley. Ecological Applications 4:768–785.

Kim, K.C. and R.W. Merritt. 1987. Black Flies: Ecology, Population Management, and Annotated World List. Pennsylvania State University Press, University Park, PA.

Leach, J.H. 1993. Impacts of the zebra mussel (Dreissena polymorpha) on water quality and fish spawning reefs in western Lake Erie. In: T.F. Nalepa and D.W. Schloesser (eds), Zebra Mussels: Biology Impact, and Control. Lewis Publishers/CRC Press, Boca Raton, FL. pp. 381–397.

Lydeard, C., Cowie, R.H., Ponder, W.F., Bogan, A.E., Bouchet, P., Clark, S.A., Cummings, K.S., Frest, T.J., Gargominy, O., Herbert, D.G., Hershler, R., Perez, K.E., Roth, B., Seddon, M., Strong, E.E. and F.G. Thompson. 2004. The global decline of nonmarine mollusks. BioScience 54: 321–330.

McMahon, R.F. 1982. The occurrence and spread of the Asiatic freshwater clam, Corbicula fluminea (Müller), in North America: 1924–1982. Nautilus 96:134–141.

Merritt, R.W. and H.D. Newson. 1978. Ecology and management of arthropod populations in recreational lands. In: G.W. Frankie and C.S. Koehler (eds), Perspectives in Urban Entomology. Academic Press, New York. pp. 125–162.

Merritt, R.W. and J.R. Wallace. 2001. The role of aquatic insects in forensic Investigations. In: J.H. Byrd and J.L. Castner (eds), Forensic entomology: The utility of arthropods in legal investigations. CRC Press, Boca Raton, FL. pp. 177–221.

Moyle, P.B. and J.J. Cech, Jr. 2004. Fishes: An Introduction to Ichthyology. Prentice Hall, Upper Saddle River, NJ.

Polhemus, J.T. 1996. Aquatic and Semiaquatic Hemiptera. In: R.W. Merritt and K.W. Cummins (eds), An Introduction to the Aquatic Insects of North America. Kendall/Hunt Publishing Company, Dubuque, IA. pp. 267–297.

Smith, G.R. and T.N. Todd. 1984. Evolution of species flocks of fishes in north temperate lakes. In: A.A. Echelle and I. Kornfield (eds), Evolution of Species Flocks. University of Maine Press, Orono, ME. pp. 45–68.

Stewart, K.W. and P.P. Harper. 1996. Plecoptera. In: R.W. Merritt and K.W. Cummins (eds), An Introduction to the Aquatic Insects of North America. Kendall/Hunt Publishing Company, Dubuque, IA. pp. 217–266.

Todd, T.N. and G.R. Smith. 1992. A review of differentiation in Great Lakes ciscoes. Polskie Archiwum Hydrobiologii 39: 261–267.

Underhill, J.C. 1986. The fish fauna of the Laurentian Great Lakes, the St. Lawrence lowlands, Newfoundland and Labrador. In: C.H. Hocutt and E.O. Wiley (eds), The Zoogeography of North American Freshwater Fishes. John Wiley and Sons, New York. pp. 105–136.

Westfall, M.J., Jr. and K.J. Tennessen. 1996. Odonata. In: R.W. Merritt and K.W. Cummins (eds), An Introduction to the Aquatic Insects of North America. Kendall/Hunt Publishing Company, Dubuque, IA. pp. 164–211.

White, D.S. and W.U. Brigham. 1996. Aquatic Coleoptera. In: R.W. Merritt and K.W. Cummins (eds), An Introduction to the Aquatic Insects of North America. Kendall/Hunt Publishing Company, Dubuque, IA. pp. 399–473.

Wiggins, G.B. 1996. Trichoptera. In: R.W. Merritt and K.W. Cummins (eds), An Introduction to the Aquatic Insects of North America. Kendall/Hunt Publishing Company, Dubuque, IA. pp. 309–386.

Winfield, I.J. and J.S. Nelson. 1991. Cyprinid Fishes: Systematics, Biology, and Exploitation. Chapman and Hall, New York.

Further Readings

Cummings, K.S. and C.A. Mayer. 1992. Field Guide to Freshwater Mussels of the Midwest. Illinois Natural History Survey, Champaign, IL.

Scott, W.B. and E.J. Crossman. 1998. Freshwater Fishes of Canada. Galt House Publications, Ltd., Oakville, ON, Canada.

Smith, D.G. 2001. Pennak's Freshwater Invertebrates of the United States, John Wiley and Sons, New York.

Thorpe, J.H. and A.P. Covich. 1991. Ecology and Classification of North American Freshwater Invertebrates. Academic Press, San Diego, CA.

Trautman, M.B. 1981. The Fishes of Ohio. Ohio State University Press, Columbus, OH.

24

Isle Royale

Jean Battle, John Anderton and Randall Schaetzl

Introduction

Isle Royale, over 535 km² in area, is the largest island in Lake Superior (Fig. A1). It is part of a large archipelago surrounded by over 200 smaller islands. Isle Royale lies 22 km SE of Ontario, Canada, 32 km from Minnesota, and 72 km from the Upper Peninsula of Michigan (Plate 1). Historically, people reached the island via canoes and other watercraft. Today, the island is accessible by boat and by seaplane. Isle Royale has seen many changes in its cultural and natural history, despite its relatively isolated location in the largest freshwater lake in the world. This chapter provides an overview of the many attributes and systems of Isle Royale, while highlighting its unique nature.

Bedrock geology

Bedrock outcrops dominate much of the landscape of Isle Royale, forming a seemingly endless series of ridges and valleys, peninsulas and offshore islands (Fig. 24.1). The rocks of the island primarily consist of 1.0 Ga-old, Precambrian and Middle Proterozoic lava flows and conglomerates. The two main bedrock formations are the Portage Lake Volcanics, which lie below the older, Copper Harbor Conglomerate (Fig. 12.6). Both of these rock units are sources of native copper. The Portage Lake Volcanics are essentially the upper portions of an incredibly thick sequence of lavas that erupted from an ancient rift system, thought to have extended from the western Great Lakes south as far south as Kansas (Fig. 12.1).

The rock sequence forming the Portage Lake Volcanics and the Copper Harbor Conglomerate sedimentary package generally strikes along a NE-SW trend, and dips to the SE, into Lake Superior. The sequence is part of the Lake Superior Syncline, a major structural feature consisting of down-folded rock layers (Fig. 24.2). Isle Royale lies at the NW end of the Lake Superior Syncline, and the Keweenaw Peninsula, with similar geology; lies at the SE end of the syncline (Chapter 12). Synclines are zones of down-folded rock, with strata dipping inward towards a central axis that contains the younger rocks. The Lake Superior Syncline formed as lava flows and sedimentary layers slowly down-warped, filling a large trough (Fig. 12.5). Later in its evolution, streams and rivers flowed in toward the axis of the syncline, depositing pebbles and cobbles, which later formed the Copper Harbor Conglomerate. Continued eruptions of lava filled the rift, causing it to subside from the weight of lava and sediments, as well as from the removal of the supporting magma below. This down-warping continued even after the eruption of lava ceased, and as the sediment that would become the overlying Copper Harbor Conglomerate was being deposited.

The result today is a trough-shaped geologic structure called a syncline (Fig. 24.2), with the upturned beds cropping out on the Keweenaw Peninsula to the SE (where the rock beds dip to the NW) and on Isle Royale (with rock

FIGURE 24.1   View along Stoll Trail, showing rock outcrops. Photo by J. Anderton.

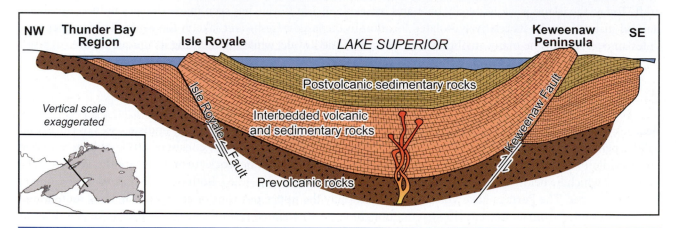

FIGURE 24.2   Structural cross-section through the Lake Superior Syncline. After Huber (1975).

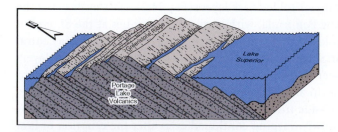

FIGURE 24.3   Block diagram of typical rock sequence on Isle Royale. After Huber (1975).

layers dipping SE). The rocks on Isle Royale dip to the SE at angles ranging from 10° to 50°, steeper on the NW side of the island. The NE-SW strike of the Portage Lake Volcanics and the Copper Harbor Conglomerate parallel the trend of the island. The sedimentary rocks interbedded between lava flows are less resistant than the lavas; they form valleys, while the more resistant lavas form ridges (Figs. A1, 24.3). This arrangement forms the island's distinctive pattern of linear ridges and valleys, along with its many narrow peninsulas and small islands. Jointing and minor faulting have resulted in a few cross-cutting ravines and drainages.

Quaternary geology

Glaciers likely covered Isle Royale several times during the Quaternary Period (Chapter 6), sculpting the bedrock and depositing glacial drift, mainly till and outwash. Consequently, much of the exposed bedrock is striated, scratched, broken and plucked. Glacial ice likely retreated from Isle Royale sometime between 12,900 and 11,500 years ago. The retreating Marquette (Gribben Phase) ice appears to have stabilized for a short time over the SW end of Isle Royale about 11,500 years ago, building a small moraine and associated outwash plain to the SW.

Several high shorelines, each associated with an ancient glacial lake in the Superior basin (Duluth and Post-Duluth glacial lakes), are thought to have been cut at this time (Chapter 13). Of these, the Beaver Bay shoreline at approximately 330 m (1085 ft) above sea level is most prominent on the SW end of the island. Following this, at about 10,800 years ago, Glacial Lake Minong formed along the margin of the retreating Marquette ice. Lake Minong's very prominent shoreline is traceable as a wave-cut bluff or cliff around much of the island, between about 207 to 235 m (680 to 770 ft) in elevation. Indeed, Isle Royale is where the Minong shoreline was first identified by George Stanley in the 1930s (Stanley 1941). Notably, a large bay barrier and lagoon were formed on the SW end of the island during this lake phase. Feldtman Lake is a remnant of that lagoon. Monument Rock, on the NE end of the island, is also a possible Minong stack, formed by wave action that isolates a pillar of resistant rock, usually on a headland.

Following Lake Minong, a series of outburst floods from Glacial Lake Agassiz, located in central Canada, occurred as the retreat of Marquette ice eventually uncovered low outlets to the NW of Isle Royale (Drexler et al. 1983, Phillips and Fralik 1994; Chapter 13). Massive amounts of water streaming out of Glacial Lake Aggasiz entered the Lake Superior basin through these channels. Although it is unclear what effect the catastrophic discharge of waters from Glacial Lake Agassiz had on Isle Royale, the flood waters did breach a large barrier at Nodaway Point at the far SE end of Lake Superior, allowing for a dramatic decline in lake level (Chapter 13). Following this, due to isostatic depression of lake outlets, lake level dropped, forming Lake Houghton, the lowest lake phase in the Superior basin. The Houghton shoreline may be submerged offshore from Isle Royale.

As isostatic rebound (uplift) of the Lake's outlet at Sault Ste. Marie occurred, lake levels also began to rise, culminating in the Nipissing Maximum at about 5,400 years ago (Fig. 13.16). At this time, the waters in the basins of Lakes Superior, Michigan and Huron were confluent, and the lake level was controlled by one or more outlets to the south. The Nipissing Phase is notable in that its waters were above the current shoreline, forming a second prominent paleoshoreline on Isle Royale at about 195 m (640 ft). Like the Minong shoreline, the Nipissing shoreline is traceable around much of the island. It forms several small embayments with bay barriers and lagoons that are now located inland from the modern shoreline. Lake Halloran is good example of a remnant Nipissing Phase lagoon. Suzy's Cave and Amygdaloid Island Arch are probably Nipissing-related coastal features.

Lake levels continued to fluctuate in the Superior basin following the Nipissing Maximum, although the general trend since has been one of declining lake levels, punctuated by brief high phases. One of these high lake levels, which occurred at about 3200 years ago, is known as the Algoma Phase; at least three Post-Algoma highs followed (Farrand and Drexler 1985). Lake Superior became an autonomous lake shortly afterwards, when the rock sill at Sault Ste. Marie became the controlling outlet for the basin (Chapter 13). Evidence of these Late Holocene lake level fluctuations are difficult to identify on Isle Royale; however, the uplift trend has likely created a regressive sequence of coastal deposits, as the island continues to rise slowly from Lake Superior. The modern shoreline is about 183 m (600 ft) in elevation.

Human history and use of the island

The earliest human artifacts indicate that Isle Royale was inhabited since Archaic times (3000 BC), when aboriginal copper miners dug shallow pits to extract the exceptionally pure, metallic copper from veins in the rocks of the island. More than 1000 mining pits from the Archaic and Woodland periods are known to exist on the island. Native peoples also used the island for hunting, fishing and collection of medicinal and edible plants and berries. Inland lake shorelines and ancient beach ridges show evidence of successional aboriginal encampments, which correspond with the gradual emergence of the land mass (Clark 1995).

During the 1600s–1700s, while Native American Ojibway Indians were still present on the island, European trappers and traders also began to exploit the island for its furbearers—mainly beaver, otter and lynx. As time went on, resource extraction by European immigrants began shifting towards larger-scale copper mining and the harvest of whitefish (*Coregonus clupeaformis*), lake trout (*Salvelinus namaycush*) and lake herring or cisco (*Coregonus artedii*) in the surrounding waters (Shelton 1997). While most of the copper mining that occurred later (1850s–1890s) slowed, due to the high cost of extraction and transport, commercial fishing grew, until it peaked at about 100 fishermen working in Isle Royale waters in the early 1900s (Isle Royale National Park 2005).

As Isle Royale transitioned into a commercial fishing-based economy in the late 19th and early 20th centuries, and lake travel via bulk commodity and passenger vessels increased, it became a desirable vacation destination for wealthy residents from cities in the Great Lakes region. People began building seasonal houses on some of the smaller islands surrounding Isle Royale, and lodges and resorts opened at both ends of the main island.

With increased commercial shipping and passenger travel around Isle Royale came the inevitable shipwrecks on the surrounding reefs and shoals that extend waterward from many of the islands of the archipelago (Fig. A1). As a consequence, four lighthouses were constructed in the 1800s to aid navigation and warn sailors of shallow water—Isle Royale Lighthouse, Passage Island Lighthouse, Rock Harbor Lighthouse and Rock of Ages Lighthouse. Although these lights played an important part in aiding ships through and around Isle Royale waters, the area also has an impressive collection of shipwrecks within its waters that are a testament to the risks to property and lives during western Lake Superior voyages.

In 1931, the federal government established Isle Royale National Park. It was officially dedicated in 1940, when land acquisition by the federal government was complete. Isle Royale National Park encompasses the island known as Isle Royale, all of its surrounding islands in the archipelago, and the waters of Lake Superior extending 7.25 km offshore, including to the north, where the boundary abuts the international US-Canadian border (Fig. 1.4). Visitation occurs from May through October, and access has continued via Park Service and private ferry, seaplane or private boat. There are no roads nor private in-holdings within the park.

In 1976, 98% of the park's land mass was designated as wilderness, and with later additions, over 99% of park lands became officially designated as such. In 1980, the US Man and Biosphere Program (USMBP), part of the United Nations Educational, Scientific and Cultural Organization (UNESCO), designated Isle Royale as an International Biosphere Reserve, one of 47 such sites in the United States. Biosphere Reserves exemplify specific ecological systems, and foster long-term study of natural systems and exploration of sustainable human co-existence within these systems (US Man and Biosphere 2006).

Designating Isle Royale as a national park, and later as wilderness, has had a large impact on the nature and extent of human use on the island. All hunting, as well as harvest of plants, ended when the park was established. The majority of commercial fishing in park's Lake Superior waters ceased in the 1960s, with the exception of two remnant fisheries used to monitor sport fish stocks. In 2000, the park banned the collection of greenstones (chlorastrolite, Michigan's state gem) from its shorelines. Park uses have since focused on recreation—boating, sport fishing, hiking and backpacking. Wilderness designation carries a strong mandate to protect the park as "an area where the earth and its community of life is untrammeled by man . . ." (Wilderness Act of 1964). The National Park Service has followed that guidance, and except for primitive campgrounds and a system of rustic trails, Isle Royale wilderness remains largely undisturbed.

■ Natural history

Soils

The soils of Isle Royale primarily reflect the cool, humid climate of the island and the relative youthfulness of the landscape. The glaciers that covered Isle Royale scoured much of the island down to the hard, crystalline bedrock, leaving behind only thin and patchy deposits of glacial drift. The thickest glacial deposits are located on the western part of the island, mainly west of Lake Desor, usually in the valleys between the basalt ridges. Many of the upland areas that have a thick drift cover are located on gentle, SE-facing slopes. Some of the soils that have formed in these glacial materials contain a dense, subsurface pan called a fragipan, that inhibits rooting and often causes water to perch in the upper soil profile, making them abnormally wet, even though they are on uplands. Because of the shallow bedrock and the fragipans, the soils on the island tend to be slightly wetter than one might expect. The soils on the most of the upland ridges of Isle Royale are, nonetheless, mostly well-drained, loamy and shallow or moderately deep to bedrock. Very shallow and shallow soils are found on the steeper, north-facing slopes (Fig. 24.3). Soils formed in talus (rock rubble) are also found mainly on the footslopes below the ridge tops.

Ridges close to Lake Superior tend to be narrow and contain many rock outcrops. Many of these bedrock areas were eroded by high postglacial lake waters which removed much of the glacial deposits (see above). Soils on the ridge tops are usually shallow (<1 m) to hard bedrock; many of these soils are organic soils (Folists)—composed entirely of a thin organic (O) horizon resting directly on the bedrock. The forest litter that comprises the O horizon has only partially decomposed because the soils lack the macroinvertebrates that would otherwise assist in the breakdown of the leaves and litter. Additionally, the cool, moist climate of the island retards the decomposition of the forest debris that falls onto the rock surfaces, allowing it to accumulate. Much of the litter that comprises these sensitive soils burned off in forest fires that swept across the island early in the 1930s. In some areas, a thin (<40 cm) mantle of eolian (wind-deposited) silt is also present above the glacial deposits or bedrock.

In lowland areas, such as in the valleys between the bedrock ridges, the soils are often very poorly drained and have developed in decaying, woody and/or herbaceous vegetation. Most of these wet, organic soils (Saprists and Hemists) contain well over one meter of organic materials. Decomposition here is inhibited by the high water table.

Earthworm activity has also influenced soil development on Isle Royale, especially on the thicker soils. There is almost a complete absence of a light-colored eluvial (E) horizon in these mineral soils because of constant mixing by non-native earthworms. Most of these soils also have dark, red-brown B horizons, reflecting the ongoing, soil-forming process of podzolization.

Vegetation

Boreal forest and northern hardwood forest systems meet on Isle Royale. Arctic temperatures create a "tension zone" between the two forest types, with Lake Superior acting as a background, moderating force (Isle Royale National Park 2005).

The boreal forests are generally located at the NE end of the island, and along the Lake Superior shores. In mature stands, the dominant boreal tree species are balsam fir (*Abies balsamea*) and white spruce (*Picea glauca*), with remnant pockets of paper birch (*Betula papyrifera*). Younger stages are dominated by quaking aspen (*Populus tremuloides*) and paper birch. Common ground cover species include thimbleberry (*Rubus parviflorus*), large leaf aster (*Aster macrophyllus*), wild sarsaparilla (*Aralia nudicaulis*), bunchberry (*Cornus canadensis*), bluebead lily (*Clintonia borealis*), twinflower (*Linnaea borealis*) and a lycopodium (*Lycopodium annotinum*).

The northern hardwood forest community is located in the SW portion of the island, where slightly drier, warmer conditions exist. Sugar maple (*Acer saccharum*) and yellow birch (*Betula alleghaniensis*) dominate, and ground cover consists mostly of maple seedlings. Small stands of northern red oak (*Quercus rubra*), white pine (*Pinus strobus*), jack pine (*P. banksiana*), spruce (*Picea* sp.) or red maple (*Acer rubrum*) occur along dry interior ridges. Black spruce (*Picea mariana*) and white cedar (*Thuja occidentalis*) are common in island swamps and forested wetlands (Isle Royale National Park 2005).

FOCUS BOX: Island biogeography

The theory of island biogeography was developed by ecologists Robert MacArthur and E.O. Wilson in the 1960s (MacArthur and Wilson 2001). In its most basic form, the theory holds that an island will be populated by a subset of species from the mainland, and that factors such as distance from the mainland, island size and number of species already present on the island, all influence immigration of new species and extinction rates for existing species. For example, consider a newly-formed volcanic island. Some species would emigrate from the nearest mainland and establish populations there. The rate of new immigrant species would decline over time, since the number of species established would rise, therefore there would be fewer "new" species from the mainland available. Likewise, the rate of extinction of island species would rise, as the number of species present increases. When an island has only a few species, the extinction rate would be low (only a few species are available to become extinct), but when the number of resident species increases on an island, resources become more limited, and distinct populations become smaller and more prone to collapse (Ehrlich et al. 1988).

According to island biogeography theory, these two forces, immigration and extinction, eventually reach an equilibrium, at which time the number of species remains constant—as long as all factors affecting the species remain the same. The establishment of a new species can only occur at the expense (extinction) of a resident island species. Therefore, the number of species on the island will remain the same, but the species themselves may change, as some species invade and some become extinct (Ehrlich et al. 1988).

Island biogeography helps provide a "jumping off point" for much of the research that occurs in isolated ecosystems such as Isle Royale. At Isle Royale, the theory can be applied both in terms of comparing speciation to the mainland, and investigating inter-island speciation within the island system. Isle Royale has only 18 species of mammals—about 1/3 the number present on the nearby mainland. It has also undergone extinction of species and replacement by others, most notably the shift in its large mammal assemblage from lynx, woodland caribou and coyote, to eastern grey wolf and moose. Human habitation has also played a large role in the extirpation of the pre-settlement large mammal populations (Isle Royale National Park 2005).

Two kinds of bogs can be found on the island. Sphagnous bogs (Fig. 24.4) have no hydrologic outlet and contain species such as mud sedge (*Carex limosa*), sphagnum moss (*Sphagnum sp.*), Labrador tea (*Ledum groenlandicum*), black spruce and tamarack (*Larix laricina*). Cyperaceous bogs usually have a hydrologic connection. Woollyfruit sedge (*C. lasiocarpa*) dominates the vegetation, often with tamarack and white cedar as an overstory (Isle Royale National Park 2005).

The boundaries of Isle Royale's forest community types generally correspond to those present in the General Land Office survey in 1847, but significant changes have occurred within the communities. In 1936, human-caused fires burned approximately 20% of the forest on Isle Royale. Aging paper birch and aspen forests (the first tree species to colonize after the burn) now dominate these areas. Widespread paper birch and white spruce mortality now exist in these older stands, due to drought, insects and disease. The effects of moose browsing are evident on balsam fir, white birch and aspen. Canada yew (*Taxus canadensis*), a slow-growing understory shrub species depleted by moose, has almost vanished from the main island. Moose have most heavily impacted balsam fir on the SW end of the island, where extensive browsing has resulted in severe stunting, affecting the age structure and distribution of the fir, as well as the quality of moose browse (Isle Royale National Park 2005).

FIGURE 24.4 A sphagnous bog at Isle Royale. Photo by J. Dahl.

FOCUS BOX: Effects of moose on the island's flora

The "spruce-moose-savanna effect" is used by researchers to describe the effect that intense browsing pressure by moose has on the flora of Isle Royale. Heavy browsing suppresses the growth of young trees, especially balsam fir (the main winter tree browse species), which opens the forest canopy. This impact, combined with the replacement by thimbleberry of an understory once dominated by more flammable Canada yew, may have resulted in a less fire-prone forest since the arrival of moose on the island (Isle Royale National Park 2005).

In contrast, Passage Island, located 6 km NE of Isle Royale, contains examples of island forest composition prior to the arrival of moose. Moose have never colonized Passage Island, and as a result favorite browse species such as Canada yew and mountain ash (Sorbus decora) are common forest components there (Isle Royale National Park 2005). Passage Island also epitomizes the balsam fir height and age classes and distribution in a forest, sans moose browsing.

The rocky shorelines of Isle Royale, Passage Island and many other nearby islands in the archipelago support unique arctic and alpine plant communities. Species in these communities became established and persisted either prior to or during glacial events. Further expansion of their ranges may have been interrupted by climate change, competition by other species, or both (Marquis and Voss 1981, Slavick and Janke 1983). The result is that the islands support 22 arctic and alpine species, including downy oat grass (*Trisetum spicatum*), alpine bistort (*Polygonum viviparum*), Eastern paintbrush (*Castilleja septentrionalis*) and prickly saxifrage (*Saxifraga tricuspidata*). A dozen Western disjunct species also exist at the park, including devil's club (*Oplopanax horridus*), and blue lips (*Collinsia parviflora*).

Aquatic communities

Isle Royale has two generally distinct aquatic communities (1) inland aquatic systems (inland lakes, streams and wetlands), and (2) Lake Superior aquatic communities. Isle Royale has 162 inland lakes larger than 0.4 ha scattered across it, and some of the surrounding islands also contain small water bodies.

Lake Superior waters can be divided into nearshore and deep water communities. Isle Royale has approximately 480 km of Lake Superior shoreline, most of it abrupt and rocky, with small pockets of shallow emergent shoreline wetlands occurring in some of the more sheltered bays. Nearshore waters have generally been defined as ending at a 10 m depth in Lake Superior (Bennett 1978, Edsall and Charlton 1997). Nearshore waters are warmer than deep water zones, and fill critical habitat needs for invertebrates, fish (for feeding, breeding, and cover), shorebirds, waterfowl and aquatic mammals. At Isle Royale, these waters provide important habitat for forage fish, which, in turn, support larger species, including lake trout, northern pike (*Esox lucius*) and yellow perch (*Perca flavescens*) (National Park Service 2006).

Isle Royale's nearshore waters are probably best known for their lake-run brook trout, known as coasters (*Salvelinus fontinalis*; Fig. 24.5). Coasters have historically been extremely popular sport fish wherever they have been found in Lake Superior; overfishing has contributed to their extirpation from historic locations. Currently, Isle Royale is home to some of the last known viable populations of coaster brook trout, and its populations are protected by the State of Michigan (US Fish and Wildlife Service 2000).

Isle Royale's nearshore waters also support healthy populations of native unionid mussel species (Chapter 23).

FIGURE 24.5   Coaster brook trout. Photo by H. Quinlan.

Over 71% of the 297 native mussel taxa in North America are endangered or imperiled, arguably the most threatened faunal group on earth. Native Great Lakes mussels have disappeared from most of their historic range, as a result of habitat alteration and competition with non-native filter feeders such as zebra mussels (Williams et al. 1993).

Within deeper Lake Superior waters surrounding Isle Royale are extensive reefs that support one of the largest and healthiest remaining lake trout populations in Lake Superior. Up to 12 morphological variants of the three major phenotypes (lean, siscowet and humper) have been historically identified (Goodier 1981). Lake trout remain the most popular sport fish in Isle Royale waters.

Isle Royale's inland lakes vary in size, trophic state and species assemblage. One recent study (Kallemeyn 2000) identified 28 fish species in 32 island lakes, including yellow perch, walleye (*Stizostedion vitreum*), northern pike, white sucker (*Catostomus commersoni*) and several dace and shiner species (family Cyprinidae). In addition, 10 of the 11 lakes sampled in 1999–2000 had native mussel populations, and four had extensive native freshwater sponge populations (Nichols 2001). These sponge colonies are unique, possibly because they have been largely protected from anthropogenic disturbances. Inland lakes of Isle Royale contain sponges over 50 cm in height, with multiple branching, and intricate three-dimensional development rarely found elsewhere.

The rocky shoreline of Isle Royale creates numerous rock pools, which in turn facilitate the development of biotic communities. The hydrology of the pools is driven by wave action, precipitation and runoff. Most of them are ephemeral. They host a limited number of invertebrate species such as non-biting midges (family Chironomidae), water boatmen (Corixidae), darners (Aeshnidae) and small crustaceans or ostracods (class Ostracoda). Boreal chorus frogs (*Pseudacris triseriata maculata*), spring peepers (*Pseudacris crucifer crucifer*) and blue-spotted salamanders (*Ambystoma laterale*) are the vertebrate species most commonly found in these pools. While rock pools are common on the island, very little is known about their distribution across other similar Lake Superior shorelines, or how vital their role is in the lake's splash zone ecology (National Park Service 2006).

Isle Royale has several species of mammals and birds that depend heavily on its aquatic systems. Water-associated bird species that nest on the island include the bald eagle (*Haliaeetus leucocephalus*), osprey (*Pandion haliaetus*), double-crested cormorant (*Phalacrocorax auritus*), herring gull (*Larus argentatus*), great blue heron (*Ardea herodias*) and common loon (*Gavia immer*). Isle Royale is home to approximately 100 breeding pairs of common loons, and is the only documented location where common loons nest on a shoreline of one of the Great Lakes (National Park Service 2006).

Aquatic or semi-aquatic mammals on the island include otter (*Lutra canadensis*), beaver (*Castor canadensis*) and moose (*Alces alces*). Otters inhabit the inland lakes and streams on the main island, and also swim to and from the outer islands. They opportunistically feed on fish, crustaceans, amphibians, reptiles, birds and insects, all of which are plentiful on the island.

FIGURE 24.6   A moose cow feeding on aquatic vegetation, with calf. Photo by W. Route.

Beaver numbers have steadily decreased since the mid-1980s at Isle Royale, probably because they have begun to exhaust sources of aspen near suitable lodge areas. The result is less food for the beavers, forcing them to travel longer distances from the safety of their lodges to access aspen, putting them at greater risk for wolf predation. Much of their current food supply was created as a result of aspen colonization across the portion of the island that burned during the 1936 fire. As natural forest succession continues, the beavers' preferred food supplies will become increasingly scarce, and their population may decline further (National Park Service 2006).

Upland fauna

Isle Royale is located in the southern extent of the geographic range of moose in the Great Lakes region (Fig. 24.6). Since the arrival of moose on Isle Royale in the early 1900s, their history has been one of population booms and crashes. In the late 1920s, the population climbed to as high as 2000–3000 animals. A subsequent crash left the 1935 population at about 500. Why did these large population swings occur? Prior to the arrival of wolves in the 1950s, moose had no major predators on the island, and their population peaked as a result of abundant food supply and then crashed because of eventual overbrowsing. Other factors influencing the health of the moose population include annual snow depths, high summer temperatures and outbreaks of winter ticks (*Dermacentor albipictus*), which can result in significant blood loss, and subsequent hypothermia due to hair loss from scratching. As of 2007, moose numbers were at approximately 385, their lowest since monitoring began in 1959 (Peterson 2007, Peterson and Vucetich 2007).

Grey wolves, also known as timber wolves (*Canis lupus*), arrived via an ice bridge from Ontario, around 1950. In 1959, the first wolf-moose studies began on the island, and have continued to the present. Isle Royale has provided an invaluable study site for predator-prey relationships and population dynamics, due to its isolation, relatively simple community structure, relatively few species and reduced number of research variables, as would be encountered with mainland populations. As a result, the Isle Royale wolf-moose study is the longest-running predator-prey research project in the history of wildlife ecology (Peterson and Vucetich 2006).

Grey wolves had virtually disappeared across their entire range in the lower 48 states, with the exception of Minnesota, prior to the eastern timber wolf being listed as "endangered" in 1967. In 1974, the wolf received protection under the new Federal Endangered Species Act of 1973 in the Great Lakes Region, including at Isle Royale. Because of its importance for the grey wolf, and because of its status as a National Park, the US Fish and Wildlife Service designated Isle Royale as Critical Habitat in 1978 (US Fish and Wildlife Service 1978). In 2007, the grey wolf was delisted in the western Great Lakes portion of its range, where recovery efforts have been deemed successful.

Since 2000, three wolf packs have divided the main island into their territories. Each pack fiercely defends its territorial boundaries, and inter-pack skirmishes can lead to boundary shifts, which in turn affect the percentage of moose habitat that each pack has control over. Isle Royale wolves depend almost entirely on moose for their diet (Fig. 24.7), but occasionally supplement it with snowshoe hare and beaver in the non-winter seasons. Like the moose population, the number of wolves on the island has varied greatly since their arrival (Fig. 24.8). It hit an all-time high of 50 animals in 1980, then crashed to just 14 in 1982, when canine parvovirus was inadvertently introduced to the population by a visitor's dog. In the 1980s and 1990s, wolf numbers remained low, and the National Park Service authorized the use of radio collars and blood collection from a few individuals to better track the health and size of the island population. As of 2007, the wolf population numbered 21 individuals (Peterson 2007, Peterson and Vucetich 2007).

Invasive species

Perhaps the biggest threat to maintaining biological integrity and species diversity of Isle Royale comes from the potential introduction of exotic species. Of its approximately 700 recorded vascular plant species, 100 are exotics. Because of its isolation from mainland sources, Isle Royale is relatively free of the most aggressive and largely uncontrolled non-native plant species currently found on the mainland. The National Park Service has active programs to map and to control non-native plants, including spotted knapweed (*Centaurea maculosa*), mountain bluette (*Centaurea montana*), creeping belle flower (*Campanula rapunculoides*), common burdock (*Arctium minus*) and garlic mustard (*Alliaria petiolata*). Resource management staff combine mapping and surveillance techniques to find new outbreaks, in an attempt to limit the introduction of new exotics. An active visitor education initiative also helps limit the introduction of invasive species (Isle Royale National Park 2005).

FIGURE 24.7   An Isle Royale wolf pack captures and consumes a moose. Photo by J. Vucetich.

FIGURE 24.8   Wolf and
moose population fluctua-
tions on Isle Royale,
1959–2007. After Peterson
and Vucetich (2007).

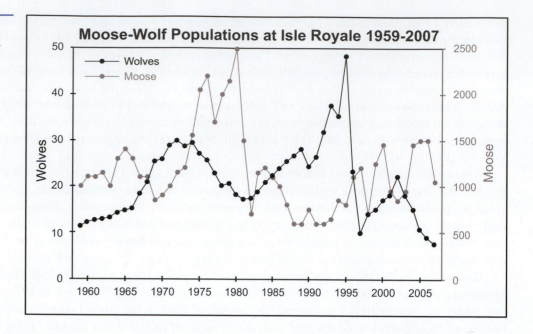

Aquatic exotic species do not lend themselves to control efforts the way that plants do. Lake Superior is a source for new exotics, as a result of the ongoing problem of inadvertent transport of non-native species in ballast water of freighters, in cargo and attached to the hulls of ships (Chapter 14). Exotic fish species, such as round goby (*Neogobius melanostomus*), sea lamprey (*Petromyzon marinus*) and Eurasian ruffe (*Gymnocephalus cernuus*), are all found in Lake Superior, and pose a threat to native fish species in and around park waters. Park staff have been monitoring the inlets and harbors of Isle Royale for the presence of zebra mussels (*Dreissena polymorpha*) and quagga mussels (*Dreissena rostriformis bugensis*), and to date, no island populations have been documented. Spiny water flea (*Bythotrephes longimanus*), another exotic invertebrate filter feeder, is commonly found in Lake Superior waters but has not yet been detected in the island's inland waters (National Park Service 2006).

■ Contaminants

Isle Royale has also been impacted by the long-range drift of airborne pollutants, including mercury. The island has a federal designation as a Class 1 airshed, but unfortunately this designation does not protect it entirely from deposition of atmospheric pollutants from other areas. Mercury concentrations in some of the park's inland lake sport fish have exceeded the consumption advisory issued by the State of Michigan (Kallemeyn 2000). Inland lakes also show varying concentrations of pollutants, such as polychlorinated byphenils (PCBs), toxaphene, lead and polycyclic aromatic hydrocarbons (National Park Service 2006). These findings underscore the need to focus on and address the global impacts of pollutants far from the point of generation.

■ Conclusions

Isle Royale is a fascinating place, both from a cultural and natural history perspective, and with its wilderness and National Park status, it should continue to indefinitely serve as a relatively undisturbed example of island biogeography and of the northern hardwood-boreal forest transition. Potential large scale anthropogenic agents of change are external to the park, however, and it is doubtful that the island's relative isolation alone will adequately protect it from these.

Literature Cited

Bennett, E.B. 1978. Characteristics of the thermal regime of Lake Superior. Journal of Great Lakes Research 4:310–319.

Clark, C.P. 1995. Archeological Survey and Testing at Isle Royale National Park, 1987–1990. NPS Midwest Archeological Center, Occasional Studies in Anthropology. No. 32.

Drexler, C.W., Farrand, W.R. and J.D. Hughes. 1983. Correlation of glacial lakes in the Superior basin with eastward discharge events from Lake Agassiz. In: J.T. Teller and L. Clayton (eds), Glacial Lake Agassiz. Geological Association of Canada Special Paper 26:261–290.

Edsall, T.A. and M.N. Charlton. 1997. Nearshore waters of the Great Lakes. State of the Lakes Ecosystem Conference 1996, Environmental Protection Agency (EPA 905-R-97-015A; Catalogue No. En40-11/35-1-1-1997E).

Ehrlich, P., Dobkin, D.S. and D. Wheye. 1988. Island Biogeography. http://www.stanford.edu/group/stanfordbirds/text/essays/Island_Biogeography.html Accessed September, 2007.

Farrand, W.R. and C.W. Drexler. 1985. Late Wisconsinan and Holocene history of the Lake Superior Basin. In: P.F. Karrow and P.E. Calkin (eds), Quaternary Evolution of the Great Lakes. Geological Association of Canada Special Paper 30:18–32.

Goodier, J.L. 1981. Native lake trout stocks in the Canadian waters of Lake Superior prior to 1955. Canadian Journal of Fisheries and Aquatic Sciences 38:1724–1727.

Huber, N.K. 1975. The geologic story of Isle Royale National Park. US Geological Survey Bulletin B1309. 66 pp.

Isle Royale National Park. 2005. Draft Wilderness and Backcountry Management Plan/Environmental Impact Statement. National Park Service. 241 pp.

Kallemeyn, L.W. 2000. A Comparison of Fish Communities from 32 Inland Lakes in Isle Royale National Park, 1929 and 1995–1997. US Geological Survey, Biological Science Report 00004.

MacArthur, R.H. and E.O. Wilson. 2001. The Theory of Island Biogeography. Princeton University Press, Princeton, NJ.

Marquis, R.J. and E.G. Voss. 1981. Distributions of some western North American plants disjunct in the Great Lakes region. Michigan Botanist 20:53–82.

National Park Service. 2006. Isle Royale National Park, Michigan - Water Resources Management Plan. National Park Service, Fort Collins, CO.

Peterson, R.O. 2007. The Wolves of Isle Royale—A Broken Balance. University of Michigan Press, Ann Arbor.

Peterson, R. and J. Vucetich. 2007. The Wolves and Moose of Isle Royale. http://www.isleroyalewolf.org/ Accessed May, 2007.

Peterson, R. and J. Vucetich. 2006. Ecological Studies of Wolves on Isle Royale, 2005–2006. http://www.isleroyalewolf.org/ Accessed January, 2007.

Phillips, B.A.M. and P.W. Fralik. 1994. A post-Lake-Minong transgressive event on the north shore of Lake Superior, Ontario - Possible evidence of Lake Agassiz inflow. Canadian Journal of Earth Sciences 31:1638–1641.

Shelton, N. 1997. Superior Wilderness—Isle Royale National Park. Isle Royale Natural History Association, Houghton, MI.

Stanley, G.M. 1941. Minong beaches and water plane in Lake Superior. Geological Society of America Bulletin 52:1935.

US Fish and Wildlife Service. 2000. Coaster Brook Trout Broodstock Development Plan, Region 3. Unpublished report to National Park Service, Ashland, WI.

US Fish and Wildlife Service. 1978. Recovery Plan for the Eastern Timber Wolf. Washington, DC.

US Fish and Wildlife Service. 2006. Species Profile for Grey Wolf. http://ecos.fws.gov/species_profile/SpeciesProfile?spcode=A00D#status Accessed March, 2007.

Williams, J., Warren Jr., M., Cummings, K., Harris, J. and R. Neves. 1993. Conservation status of freshwater mussels of the United States and Canada. American Fisheries Society 18:6–22.

Further Readings

Cochrane, T. and H. Tolson. 2002. A Good Boat Speaks For Itself—Isle Royale Fishermen and Their Boats. University of Minnesota Press, Minneapolis.

Glime, J.M. 1993. The Elfin World of Mosses and Liverworts of Michigan's Upper Peninsula and Isle Royale. Isle Royale Natural History Association, Houghton, MI.

Janke, R. 1996. The Wildflowers of Isle Royale. Isle Royale Natural History Association, Houghton, MI.

Kohl, J.G. 1985. Kitchi-Gami: Life Among the Lake Superior Ojibway. Minnesota Historical Society Press, St. Paul, MN.

LaBerge, G.L. 1994. Geology of the Lake Superior Region. Penokean Press, Oshkosh, WI.

Lagler, K.F. and C.R. Goldman. 1959. Fishes of Isle Royale. Isle Royale Natural History Association, Houghton, MI.

Mech, L.D. 1970. The Wolf: The Ecology and Behavior of an Endangered Species. University of Minnesota Press, Minneapolis.

Vucetich, J.A. and R. Peterson. 2004. Grey Wolves—Isle Royale. In: D.W. Macdonald (ed), The Biology and Conservation of Wild Canids. Oxford University Press, New York. pp. 285–296.

25

Between the Glaciers and Europeans: People from 12,000 to 400 Years Ago

William A. Lovis

■ Imagining the past

What must it have been like for Michigan's first inhabitants 12,000+ years ago, with fog-covered, multi-kilometer high glacial ice masses on the northern horizon, and now extinct giants such as mastodont and mammoth, giant beaver and moose, and herds of migrating caribou, colonizing a newly opened landscape? Was anyone standing on the shore of what is now Lake Superior ~11,000 years ago when glacial Lake Agassiz catastrophically burst from its basin in Canada, and, tsunami-like, increased the water volume of the basin by almost 25%? What was it like for the people who lived here 7000 years ago, during the peak of the Hypsithermal warmth, when temperatures were up to ~2° C warmer than today, the Michigan and Huron lake basins were 120 m (400 feet!) below their present level, and the Lower Peninsula was twice its present size and connected directly with Wisconsin and Ontario? How did people react, 3000+ years ago, to novel, strange looking, squash plants, with their ancestral roots in Mexico and which, with minimal effort and the right tactics, could be grown on demand? Can we imagine the many revelations resulting in plant domestication, musical rattles, net floats and food containers, that must have occupied their thoughts?

Archaeologists, who study Michigan's past before Europeans set foot in what is now the western Great Lakes, develop and pursue these types of questions. Presented here is a highly generalized assessment of our current state of knowledge, drawn heavily from several recent syntheses as well as an array of current research (Brashler et al. 2000, Lovis 2008). The overarching time frame for the following discussion is presented in Figure 25.1; significant pre-contact archaeological sites are shown in Figure 25.2.

■ First colonization: the Paleoindians (12,000–10,000 years ago)

It took over 4000 years for the Upper and Lower Peninsulas of Michigan to become free of glacial ice (Chapter 6). This long and dynamic process was accompanied by substantial changes in climate (Chapter 7), animal life (Chapter 8), vegetation (Chapter 7) and the configuration and levels of waters in the Michigan, Huron and Superior lake basins (Chapter 13). Michigan's first colonizers, the Paleoindians (Shott and Wright 1999), were small bands of hunters and gatherers who relied on hunting gregarious herbivores such as caribou, the scavenging of now extinct animals such as mastodont, mammoth and giant moose (Chapter 8), as well as fishing and plant food gathering. The tundra and boreal forest communities of the time would have been less productive than those of modern environments. This postglacial environment was also very wet,

Michigan Prehistory: Time Periods, Ages and Key Events

Cultural Periods		Inception of Cultural Phases Calendar Years ago	Key Cultural Events	Key Geological Events and Time Stratigraphy	
European Contact		AD 1640 360 yrs BP	Europeans arrive in Michigan	High levels of Great Lakes; "premodern" flood phase (800 yrs BP - Little Ice Age)	Holocene
Upper Mississippian/ Late Woodland		AD 1200 800 yrs BP	Upper Mississippian in southwest Michigan	Low levels of Great Lakes; few floods (800-1000 yrs BP - "Medieval Warm Period")	
Woodland	Late	AD 500 1500 yrs BP	Complex, egalitarian social systems		
	Middle	0 AD/BC 2000 yrs BP	Complex mound burial; use of tropical and indigenous cultigens	High levels of Great Lakes; Post-Algoma flood phase (1500-2000 yrs BP)	
	Early	550 BC 2550 yrs BP	Initial mound/earthwork construction First ceramics introduced	Low levels of Great Lakes; "Low" flood interval (2000-3000 yrs BP)	
Archaic	Late	3000 BC 5000 yrs BP	First cultigens (squash)	Nipissing-Algoma high water phase; flooding common (3500-5000 yrs BP)	
	Middle	5-6000 BC 7-800 yrs BP	First extensive regional exchange	Nipissing transgression Chippewa-Stanley phase initiated	
	Early	8000 BC 10,000 yrs BP	Early and Middle Archaic occupations (now submerged under Great Lakes)	Michigan-Huron basins ice-free	
Paleo-Indian		10-9000 BC 12-11,000 yrs BP	Earliest Paleo-Indian penetration in Michigan	Algonquin phase initiated Greatlakean Advance High-level lake in Lake Michigan basin Early Lake Algonquin in Lake Huron basin	Late Wisconsinan (Pleistocene)
Glaciated		11,000 BC 13,000 yrs BP	Port Huron glacial advance; much of southern Lower Michigan is ice-free High-level glacial lakes in all basins (low-level lakes 13,000-13,500 yrs BP)		

FIGURE 25.1   Precontact chronology of Michigan. After Monaghan and Lovis (2005): Table 4.1.

FIGURE 25.2   Key, precontact period, archaeological sites in Michigan, by region. After Monaghan and Lovis (2005). <u>Northern Lake Michigan</u>: Bergquist, Winter, Reindle, Riverside I/II, Sack Bay, Spider Shelter, Summer Island, Little Cedar River. <u>Northern Upper Peninsula</u>: Naomikong Point, Gorto. <u>Sault Ste. Marie and Straits of Mackinac</u>: Fort Brady, Gyftakis, Nelson, Juntunen, Fort Michilimackinac, Arrowhead Drive, Ekdahl-Goudreau, McGregor. <u>Northwestern Lower Peninsula</u>: Columbus Beach, Samel's Field, Sawdust Pile, Screaming Loon,. Skegemog Point, Wycamp Creek, Portage/L'Arbre Croche, Piwangoning Quarry, Johnson, McNeal, O'Neil. <u>Northeastern Lower Peninsula</u>: Goodwin-Gresham, Gaging Station, Hampsher, Mikado. <u>West-Central Lower Peninsula</u>: Carrigan Mounds, Dumaw Creek, Point Arcadia, Croton Dam, 20LU22. <u>Saginaw Bay and Valley</u>: Andrews, Barnes, Bear Creek, Bridgeport, Bussinger, Ebenhoff, Feeheley, Fletcher, Gainey, Hodges, Kantzler, Naugle, Pomranky, Satchell, 20LP98, Birch Run Road, Conservation Park. <u>Grand River and Southwestern Lower Peninsula</u>: Eidson, Elam, Hi-Lo, Leavitt, Schwerdt, Stover, Moccasin Bluff, Rock Hearth. <u>Southeastern Lower Peninsula</u>: Williams, Younge, 20OK394, Holcombe, Paint Creek, Riviere au Vase, Fort Wayne Mound.

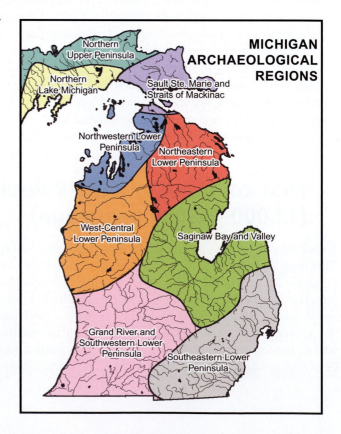

MICHIGAN ARCHAEOLOGICAL REGIONS

with lingering lakes, wetlands, runoff and outwash channels, and other water features. As my late colleague Earl Prahl was fond of observing, "Paleoindians were ridge runners!"

Depending on the specific time period during deglaciation, southern Michigan would have been bisected by the Glacial Grand River valley in what is now the lower Grand River and the upper Maple River drainages (Fig. 13.9), and a vast archipelago existed north of where the city of Indian River is today (Fig. 13.12). The northernmost parts of the Lower Peninsula provide little evidence of Paleoindian colonization at this time. That which is present clearly comes from the south, based on the presence of distinctively fluted spear point styles—a point with parallel edges, a concave base and characteristic flake called a "flute" struck from the base to thin the point (Fig. 25.3A). The Upper Peninsula was colonized later, and from a different direction—northern Wisconsin. Not until ~10,000–9000 years ago, did late Paleoindian groups begin to use northern Michigan for large game hunting—probably targeting migratory herds of caribou. The style affinities of their hunting weapons are clearly with the Plano tradition of the west; spear points with distinctive parallel edges, stemmed hafts for mounting on spears and foreshafts and uniquely refined parallel flaking patterns (Fig. 25.3B). Thus, Michigan's first postglacial colonizers do not synchronize well in either time, or points of origin.

FIGURE 25.3 Paleoindian projectile points. Photos by W. Lovis, from the MSU Museum Collections. A. Fluted point from southern Michigan. B. Plano point from northern Michigan.

Modern forests, changing environment, and mobile hunter-gatherers: the Archaic Period (10,000–2500 years ago)

The distinctive megafauna that inhabited Michigan when it first became ice free were either extinct or had migrated out of the area by ca. 10,000 years ago (Chapter 8), coeval with some major vegetation changes in the southern part of the region (Chapter 7). There are several rather significant points to be made about this long interval that bear directly on how Archaic period populations made their economic livelihood (Robertson et al. 1999, Lovis et al. 2005, Lovis 2008). First, during the early Archaic, broadleaf deciduous (nut and acorn producing) trees began to dominate the vegetation of southern Michigan (Fig. 7.5), and coniferous forests became established north of about the latitude of Saginaw. Second, the bodies of water that occupied the Michigan, Huron and Superior basins had both dropped well below, and subsequently rose substantially above, their modern elevations, before eventually stabilizing at approximately modern levels (Larsen 1999, Larson and Schaetzl 2001, Chapter 13). Thus, the available land area that could be exploited and occupied changed dramatically during the Archaic period. Third, the midpoint of this interval is characterized by warming temperatures, which resulted in the southern Lower Peninsula being invaded by dispersed pockets of grassland (Chapters 7, 21). Finally, and of debatable importance, is the arrival of the first domestic plants into southern Michigan. Perhaps the lesson that can be learned from the preceding litany is that, to properly understand the human past, one must understand well the dynamic and changing physical and biogeographic contexts of the landscape, because people interact with, foster and respond to such changes.

The Archaic time period in Michigan and elsewhere in eastern North America can be subdivided into Early, Middle and Late segments—organizational devices based largely on sequences of changing stone projectile point, knife and other artifact styles, as well as economics and sociopolitical organization (Robertson et al. 1999, Shott 1999,

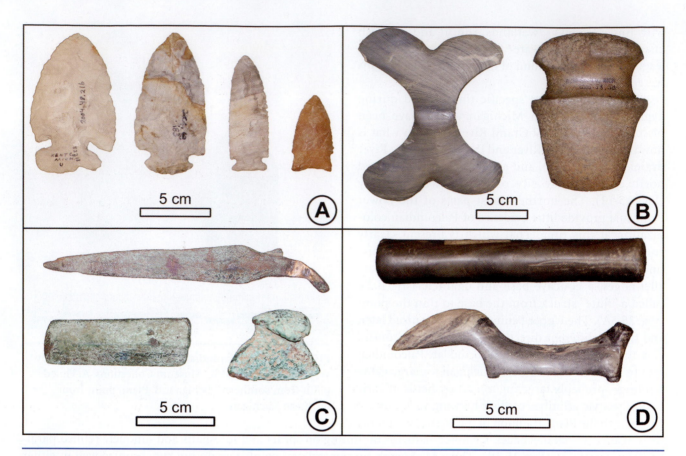

FIGURE 25.4   Examples of Archaic period tools. Photos by W. Lovis, from the MSU Museum Collections. A. Chipped stone projectile points and knives. B. Ground stone atlatl weight and grooved axe. C. Native copper wedge, adze, and knife. D. Ground stone bar amulet and bird stone.

Lovis 2008). Ceramics had not yet been invented; storage and cooking containers were likely manufactured of perishable plant and animal materials, such as bark and hide. Among the most important technological changes are the advent of the spear thrower or atlatl, the active procurement and processing of copper (Martin 1999, Chapter 12) and the labor intensive production of ground and polished stone axes, ornaments and other tools (Fig. 25.4A–D).

Archaic populations were adapted to modern forest conditions. Mobile hunter-gatherer bands engaged in the hunting of large, medium and small game, individualized fishing and intensive seasonal plant collection, including several nut varieties (Robertson et al. 1999). The presence of wild and domestic squash (*Cucurbita pepo*) in the Saginaw Valley by ~4200 and 3000 years ago, respectively, and the later introduction of the common sunflower (*Helianthus annuus*) in southwestern Michigan, apparently had little impact on the economic habits of local populations until much later (Parker 1996, Monaghan et al. 2006).

Available data on the Archaic period are highly variable, in part due to demographic differences resulting in greater or fewer sites, in part due to site formation processes and preservation issues resulting in sites of certain ages being more susceptible to preservation than others and in part due to the variable capability of discovering sites that may be deeply buried, masked by mature forests or which might now lie below the waters of Lakes Huron and Michigan. Southern Michigan has more archaeological sites than other parts of the state (and hence more information exists from there), mainly due to a higher relative carrying capacity, and consequent differences in population density (but see the effects of changing land area in Lovis et al. (2005)). During the Early and Middle Archaic, cultural affinities of southern Michigan are clearly to the south (Fig. 25.4A). But by the Late Archaic, more spatially discrete regional traditions developed, at least as attested by distinctive tool styles and raw material origins. A clear division of the western and eastern Upper Peninsula emerges ~3000 years ago; the former with ties to Wisconsin, and the latter with the Straits of Mackinac, parts of adjacent Ontario and the northern Lower Peninsula. The southern Lower Peninsula, on the other hand, had ties to present day Ontario, Illinois, Indiana, Wisconsin and northern Ohio. Social ties within and between regions were maintained through extensive exchange networks between neigh-

FIGURE 25.5 Archaic and Early Woodland artifacts. Photos by W. Lovis, from the MSU Museum Collections. A. Terminal Archaic Turkey Tail cache from Bay City Michigan manufactured on Wyandotte Chert. B. Adena and Kramer Early Woodland points on exotic or non-local flint. Major units are in cm.

boring groups, evidenced by locally unusual commodities such as copper, marine shell, ochre pigments and desirable varieties of exotic (not locally available) flint from Ontario, Indiana, Ohio and Kentucky (Fig. 25.5A–B). Often these materials occur in ritual contexts, such as burials, or were deposited in groups for future sacred or secular use—a process known as *caching*. Depending on the proportional representation and types of these exotic materials as grave goods, as well as whether they occur in prominent natural features such as glacial kames (perhaps a precursor to burial mounds), burials are categorized as one of three larger regional groups known as Old Copper, Glacial Kame and Red Ochre (Robertson et al. 1999). These are older terms not in common use today, but nonetheless retain general utility as indicators of regional interaction. As population densities increased and regional expressions of identity emerged during the Archaic, the evidence for such socially integrative behavior likewise increased.

◼ Ceramics, horticulture, and fishing: Woodland period economic intensification and the changing social landscape (2500–400 years ago)

Ceramics

The Woodland period in Michigan is signaled by the invention or adoption of fired ceramic containers (see FOCUS BOX on the next page). The 500-year long lag in ceramic introduction between the southern and northern parts of Michigan has resulted in different nomenclatures (Fig. 25.1). Caution—whereas the invention of ceramics, the introduction of plant cultigens and other associated behaviors are often viewed as the hallmark signs of the Woodland period (below), they must be viewed warily. Interpreting the past is not easy. Ceramics are introduced in the southern Lower Peninsula by ~2600 years ago, but are not present in the northern Lower Peninsula or the Upper Peninsula until five centuries later. The introduction of ceramics appears to have had little impact on subsistence, economy, or group organization, particularly in the north. In southern Michigan, the introduction of domestic plants during the Late Archaic apparently does almost nothing to change local hunting-gathering lifeways. Thus, the Archaic to Woodland transition is not as clear cut as it may otherwise seem.

FOCUS BOX: Woodland ceramics

The invention of fired clay pottery is important to Michigan's early occupants because ceramics not only changed their technology, but because they also occupy a unique position in archaeological analysis. Ceramics express a variety of characteristics that assist archaeologists in organizing them in time and space, including (1) their methods of manufacture, (2) the composition of their raw material and firing techniques, (3) their shapes and sizes and (4) their decoration. Michigan's early pottery was not painted, but rather was decorated with finger impressions, pieces of wood, shell, and bone, sometimes with purposefully carved or modified edges, and with a broad range of cord and fabric materials combined in a bewildering array of design combinations (see Figure below).

Examples of Woodland ceramics. A. Laurel Initial Woodland ceramics from the Portage site near Petoskey. Photo by W. Lovis, from the MSU Museum Collections. B. Laurel Initial Woodland rimsherd from the Gyftakis site. Photo by M. Fournier. C. Reproduction Hopewell MiddleWoodland ceramic vessel. Photo by W. Lovis, from the MSU Museum Collections. D. Early Late Woodland vessel from Lapeer County. Photo by W. Lovis, from the MSU Museum Collections. E. Elaborately decorated Late Woodland vessel from near Charlevoix. Photo by W. Lovis, from the MSU Museum Collections.

These decorative combinations changed over time, will only occur in certain areas and are often given descriptive names. Studies of contemporary pottery manufacture suggest that such decoration signals important aspects of group identity—they have a grammar and meaning much like spoken or written language.

Cooking in ceramic containers results in the accumulation of burned food on the interiors and the exteriors of the pottery, thereby providing archaeologists with abundant evidence through which to assess various aspects of the past. Very small (mg-size) residue samples can be subjected to radiocarbon dating, providing important information about when the vessel was used, and when specific styles of pottery were popular (Lovis 1990). Residues can also be subjected to various isotopic analyses, most often those associated with the signatures for maize, i.e., corn *Zea mays* (Morton and Schwartz 2004). The timing of concerted maize use in Michigan and other parts of North America remains an important research question (Hart et al. 2003). Finally, residues can be ana-

lyzed for the presence of plant opal phytoliths—variably shaped silicates formed in plant roots that can be identified to genus, and which give important clues about the composition of the foods. Such information can be matched against the animal bones, plant seeds and nut hulls that are often found in archaeological sites, to gain a more refined view of early economic behaviors. Last, but not least, the pottery fabric itself can be petrographically analyzed to determine the sources of the clays, and the "recipes" used for their production (Stoltman 1989). Ceramics can include various clay minerals, as well as different stone types, or even shell, as an aplastic. The pieces of information that can be gleaned from such nuances of manufacture provide important clues about ceramic origins, and even social ties.

Surprising as it may seem, the advent of ceramics in Michigan starting ~2600 years ago may be as important, or even more important, for modern archaeologists as it was to the people that made and used the first ceramic containers!

In the north, associated with a broad E-W trending zone of similarly adapted peoples known as Laurel, the Initial Woodland period lasts 500 years, followed by an 1100 year long Terminal (sometimes also called Late) Woodland period. In southern Michigan, the Woodland sequence begins with the Early Woodland, beginning 2600 years ago, a Middle Woodland period beginning 2000 years ago, and a Late Woodland period from 1500–400 years ago (European contact). In the southwestern Lower Peninsula and the western Upper Peninsula, between about 800 and 400 years ago, the Late Woodland overlaps with Upper Mississippian, more common to the south and west. Some believe the latter is a product of changing climate; southern populations shift northward during warmer periods, and then retract southward during cooler intervals (Larsen 1999).

Horticulture

One of the most persistent questions in eastern North American archaeology is the timing and economic impact of plant domestication (Smith 1992). Most of us are familiar with the standing triad of domesticated native crops observed by early Europeans when they first encountered Indians in the western Great Lakes region; maize, beans and squash. What we are not generally aware of, however, is that parts of Michigan or the Great Lakes region are not suited to domestic crop production, particularly for those plants that were native to and domesticated in Mexico. With the exception of some warmer pockets around the Straits of Mackinac and the Keweenaw Peninsula, the 120 day growing season necessary for indigenous maize (corn) agriculture is generally confined to the area south of a line from Manistee to Saginaw Bay. North of this line, there is little evidence for prehistoric Woodland period horticulture, but abundant evidence of hunting, gathering and fishing, with the latter ultimately dominating the economy much in the way that horticulture does in the south (Cleland 1982, Smith 2004).

Each of these plants was introduced into Michigan at different times. Wild squash (*Cucurbita* sp.) makes an appearance by 4200 years ago in the Saginaw Valley, and domestic squash by 3000 years ago, but does not appear to be widespread until late in the Woodland period. Maize (*Zea mays*) in Michigan is dated as early as 1400 years ago in southeastern Michigan, but does not become ubiquitous until about 1000 years ago. Beans (*Phaseolus vulgaris*) do not appear in Michigan until 900 to 1000 years ago in the Saginaw Valley, and are rarely recovered thereafter, perhaps due to their fragility and consequent inability to preserve.

The final chapter in this tale is that, even before the introduction of maize and beans, the indigenous populations of eastern North America intensively collected (and for the most part, domesticated) a variety of native plants, including the sunflower (*Helianthus annuus*), goosefoot/lambsquarter (*Chenopodium* sp.), maygrass (*Iva annua*) and knotweed (*Polygonum erectum*); these are known as the Eastern Agricultural Complex (Smith 1987). Changes in seed characteristics, including their size, shape, texture and overall thickness, as well as the thickness of their seed coats, by comparison with wild populations, attest to intensive human selection and use. In Michigan, these same seed plants were collected, sometimes intensively, throughout the Woodland period, but there is limited evidence to argue for their local domestication (Parker 1996). Although sunflower is present as early as the Archaic it, too, does not appear in abundance until later Woodland time periods.

The Early Woodland in southern Michigan is characterized by an essentially Archaic hunting and gathering economy, including larger mammals and nuts, with ceramics superimposed on it. It is not until the Middle Woodland that economic intensification appears to occur, in the form of increasing reliance on the starchy and oily seeded plants enumerated above, as well as a range of aquatic plants including tubers and wild rice (*Zizania aquatica*), aquatic mammals including beaver and muskrat, large, shallow water, riverine and lacustrine fish, as well as migratory aquatic birds, e.g., ducks and geese. Importantly, both the terrestrial and aquatic plants were processed for storage, including the use of large subterranean pits prepared to inhibit spoilage (Holman and Krist 2001), or perhaps even in ceramic containers. Large scale processing and storage of seeds, tubers and nuts at this time is a significant preadaptation for the storage of domestic crops (Lovis et al. 2001). The significance of wetlands to Woodland economies is demonstrated by the location of the largest later Middle Woodland and early Late Woodland sites adjacent to highly productive wetlands. These were probably points of aggregation for highly mobile groups of foragers during productive seasons of the year. By the onset of the Late Woodland, the mixed strategy of reliance on a variety of seasonally available wild foods, coupled with indigenous and imported domestic plants, supported a number of social groups, associated with particular drainage basins through which they moved seasonally (Holman and Kingsley 1996).

About 1000 years ago, during the early Late Woodland period, a significant change takes place across southern Michigan (Brashler et al. 2000). In the Saginaw Valley and southeastern Michigan, several transformations can be documented in the local economy and the fashion in which people interacted with the landscape. A broad range of domestic plants are being produced, processed and stored. These include indigenous cultigens such as wild and domesticated chenopodium, but more importantly including eight and 12 row varieties of maize, tobacco (*Nicotiana rustica*), sunflower and squash (Egan 1990, Lovis et al. 1996, 2001, Parker 1996). Interestingly, nut frequencies diminished in abundance as cultigens increased (Parker 1996). Clearly, the economy had undergone a marked transformation toward horticulture, although wild plants and animals continued to be exploited, the latter with bows and arrows tipped with small triangular points (Fig. 25.6). Moreover, the locations and functions of Late Woodland sites change during this period (Brashler et al. 2000, Lovis et al. 2001). Whereas most late Middle Woodland and early Late Woodland locations are adjacent to wetlands, in both the Saginaw Valley and southeastern Michigan there is a locational shift toward more agriculturally suited soils (Krakker 1983, Lovis et al. 2001). Some areas, particularly southwestern Michigan and the western Upper Peninsula, also have evidence for the construction of ridged fields or garden beds (Buckmaster 2004). By 1000 years ago, the economy of southern Michigan was quite similar to that observed by Europeans when they arrived in the region during the 1600s.

Fishing

In the north, beyond the area where horticulture is a secure adaptation, the Initial Woodland peoples of Michigan were hunters and fishers, but they also gathered wild plant foods in a mobile seasonal cycle. They occupied a vast region of the upper Great Lakes, including the northern parts of the Lower Peninsula, the environs around northern Lake Michigan, and most of the Lake Superior basin. Much like their Archaic forebears, the majority of their fishing was done with technology more appropriate to individualized fishing—harpoons,

FIGURE 25.6   Triangular projectile points from various Michigan Late Woodland sites. Photo by W. Lovis.

including a specific toggle headed type, leisters, spears, fish gorges, hooks and other technologies. Most of this technology is best applied in shallow water, e.g., coastal locations, creeks and river mouths. Importantly, most shallow water fish species spawn or run in the spring, and site locations from the Initial Woodland and throughout the Late Woodland were attuned to this fact (Martin 1989, Smith 2004). Occasionally they were able to catch deep-water fish, but this was the exception. Most of the larger Initial Woodland sites were repeatedly reoccupied because they were good spring fishing locations.

Fishing nets were the technological catalyst for the economic transformation of the Woodland Period in northern Michigan. Netsinkers, notched pebbles of varying size but always with opposing

FIGURE 25.7   An Indian sugar camp. Illustration by S. Eastman, US Army. Reproduced from Drake (1884, 198).

indentations for attachment with line, start to appear in the Initial Woodland, but this was probably related to shallow water, hand seines. Several archaeologists (Martin 1989, Smith 2004) have evaluated the subsequent timing and impact of deep water gill net fishing, initially proposed by Cleland (1982). It is only with the technological shift to deep water net technology that the abundant fall fishery of the Great Lakes could be accessed, specifically whitefish and lake trout, both of which spawn in deep, cold water in the late fall. The importance of this innovation should not be underestimated. By capturing large quantities of fall spawning fish, the products can be dried, smoked, frozen and stored for later consumption, much in the same fashion that domestic plant foods were processed for storage (Cleland 1982). Whitefish and lake trout fulfilled the same economic function as corn, squash and beans; they were abundant and reliable. Indeed, Europeans marveled at the fishing activities of the Indians when they first came into contact with them.

This shallow-to-deep water fishing transformation, about 1200 years ago, did not signal the abandonment of spring fishing. Good spring fishing locations were still occupied, but it was the fall fishing locations in the Straits of Mackinac, along the St. Marys River, and elsewhere, that displayed tremendous increases in size and use. The seasonal cycle, therefore, might have included spring fishing, fowling, maple sap processing (Fig. 25.7), and berry collection, summer hunting and plant collection, fall fishing and hunting, and winter consumption of stored foods, along with hunting and trapping. Stored fall fish provided usable food for the lean seasons of winter and early spring. Because of lower food availability during the winter and early spring, small mobile groups moved into the interior of the Lower and Upper Peninsulas, placing less stress on the available resources.

The changing social landscape

Among the more overt indicators of changing social relationships during the Woodland Period were the presence of constructions such as burial mounds (Fig. 25.8) and circular earthwork enclosures at prominent locations (see FOCUS BOX on the following page). These earthen features were viewed as social markers; they partitioned space in a systematic and understandable fashion. Contrary to past belief, there is no overarching group known as the "moundbuilders"—mounds and earthworks span >1500 years, multiple precontact time periods, and many past cultural groups. Most mounds in Michigan were constructed between about 2500 and 800 years ago. Circular earthworks have their inception as early as 2500 years ago (Garland and Beld 1999), but are most common between about 700 and 1000 years ago. Mound burial essentially ceased, following the transformation to horticulture and intensive fishing, being supplanted by cemetery burial, indicative of changing social and economic relationships suggesting increasing complexity and perhaps altered social identity (O'Shea 1988). At one time, burial mounds and other earthen and stone features were common across Michigan, although few remain today, due to destruction by agriculture and urbanization.

FIGURE 25.8   The Norton Mound Group near Grand Rapids. A. Winter view of the Norton Mound Group. Photo by Dr. Richard Flanders. B. Norton Mound M, the largest mound of the group. Photo by Anonymous. Photos on file at and courtesy of the Archaeological Research Laboratory, Grand Valley State University.

FOCUS BOX: Late Woodland earthworks

Michigan's Late Woodland, doughnut-shaped earthworks have long been the subject of archaeological scrutiny. Their precise function, however, has remained an enigma. The fact that they were large (some >100 m in diameter), circular, earthen embankments (or ridges) with surrounding ditches, with little evidence for household habitation, resulted in interpretations that they were fortifications designed as protection from competing groups. Alternatively, the fact that they began to occur during the transition to intensive horticulture in the region suggested that they might also have functioned as territorial markers, or places where adjacent groups might convene to undertake cooperative exchange, social and ritual activities within a bounded space (O'Shea and Milner 2002). The fact that they often occur in pairs has not been readily explainable.

Recently, evidence has been presented suggesting an alternative view, one that can be coupled with historically documented Algonquin (including the Ottawa/Odawa, Chippewa/Ojibwa and Potawatami) Midewiwin (Grand Medicine Society) ceremonies. This evidence greatly extends the time depth of such ceremonies by half a mil-

lenium, connecting the pre-contact past with the ethnohistoric present. It further suggests that Late Woodland societies were reproducing their cosmological and ritual spaces on a grand, even monumental scale (Howey and O'Shea 2006). By viewing the paired earthworks as intentionally oriented and juxtaposed with one another, as well as with specific spaces for food storage, water sources, mounds, inferred sweat lodges and other features, Howey and O'Shea (2006) made a strong case for planned monument construction and landscape use, replicating Bear's Journey (Bear being a central figure in the origin story of the Midewiwin). Replication of Bear's Journey at this scale (>700 m) would have allowed for active participation of Late Woodland ritual practitioners within a large and intentionally constructed ritual landscape. If one accepts their interpretation, it would mean that the historically documented Midewiwin ceremonies and organization have greater antiquity than had been previously attributed to them, and that Late Woodland societies were actively modifying the landscape at a scale heretofore not adequately explored by archaeologists.

The rise of earthen construction during the Early Woodland period ~2500 years ago, or the Initial Woodland period of ~2000 years ago in the north, appears to be in response to increasing partitioning of space, perhaps due to competing regional identities or exploitation territories (Holman and Kingsley 1996, Brose and Hambacher 1999, Garland and Beld 1999, Brashler et al. 2000). The earliest known earthwork is at the boundary between the Grand River and Saginaw River drainages—areas believed to be more closely integrated with Illinois and Ohio, based on the types of thick Early Woodland ceramics and the flint varieties from each area. It is suggested that this circular earthwork, high on Arthurburg Hill, is a point of socially integrating ritual activity between east and west (Garland and Beld 1999). Although there are few Early Woodland burial mounds known in Michigan, there are a number of

Middle Woodland mounds that reflect this same apportioning of space, and which also act as visible landscape markers. These mounds have been associated with the so-called Hopewell culture of Illinois. Whether in the north or south of Michigan, such mound(s) are found on prominent bluff top locations adjacent to rivers, at important transportation and fishing points such as rapids and portages, and at the confluences of major rivers and streams, or where such water features empty into lakes (Fig. 25.8).

Thus, mounds and mound burial act at a variety of different social scales. They reflect individual social status based on the position, and quantity and types of funerary offerings, that a person is buried with. They reflect group membership in a communal burial setting. They act to integrate the larger group in a collective ritual and ceremonial context. And, lastly, they act to mark group territories to outsiders with prominent features associated with ancestral generations. Repetitive use of these special locations can result in multiple mounds, and mound groups, reflecting great tenure of place.

By the Late Woodland, Michigan had been carved into several social territories with varying regional affinities (Brashler et al. 2000). In part, this was a consequence of both environmental resource potential and the specifics of local economic adaptation, keyed to the variability of Michigan's environments. The western Upper Peninsula had social ties with both Late Woodland and Upper Mississippian groups, across northern Wisconsin. The eastern Upper Peninsula and Straits of Mackinac area, and parts of the northern Lake Huron area, appear to have coalesced into an integrated social unit. Southwestern Michigan experienced increasing interaction with a broad southern Lake Michigan tradition of Late Woodland and Upper Mississippian. The Saginaw Valley appears to have periodically acted in concert with the western Lake Erie basin, or southern Ontario.

The juxtaposition of Late Woodland social groups apparently forged a variety of inter-group mechanisms designed to buffer against potential economic risks and shortfalls. For example, one could speculate on the impact of the cool climatic interval called the Little Ice Age (AD ~1300–1850) on domestic crop production in the more marginal areas of southern Michigan (Holman and Kingsley 1996, Brashler et al. 2000), or how climatically induced changes in biogeography and resource potential resulted in the N-S readjustment of social boundaries (Larsen 1985). Regardless, it is likely that there were cooperative, competitive and hostile types of interactions during the Late Woodland Period (Holman and Kingsley 1996). These interactions may well have fostered symbiotic relationships between groups with different adaptations (Garland 1986, Garland and Beld 1999), including regularized economic and social interactions between coastal and interior populations (O'Shea 2003). Earthworks could serve as points of social integration to periodically reaffirm inter-group relationships through ritual and exchange, as well as to ameliorate conflict or competition (McHale-Milner and O'Shea 1998).

The Late Woodland social landscape of Michigan was complex, dynamic, and highly variable, and it was these Late Woodland groups who ultimately bore the impact of 17th century European expansion (Chapter 27). It is during this extended episode of intensive culture contact that they become historically known in the literature by a variety of translations of their tribal names, applied by missionaries, soldiers, explorers and traders—a story continued in Chapter 26.

Literature Cited

Brashler, J.G., Garland, E.B., Holman, M.B., Lovis, W.A. and S.R. Martin. 2000. Adaptive Strategies and Socioeconomic Systems in Northern Great Lakes Riverine Environments: The Late Woodland of Michigan. In: Emerson, T.E., McElrath, D.L. and A.C. Fortier (eds), Late Woodland Societies: Tradition and Transformation Across the Midcontinent, University of Nebraska Press, Lincoln. pp. 543–579.

Brose, D.S. and M.J. Hambacher. 1999. The Middle Woodland in Northern Michigan. In: J. Halsey (ed), Retrieving Michigan's Buried Past: The Archaeology of the Great Lakes State. Bulletin 64, Cranbrook Institute of Science, Bloomfield Hills, MI. pp. 59–70.

Buckmaster, M.M. 2004. The Northern Limits of Ridge Field Agriculture. In: W.A. Lovis (ed), An Upper Great Lakes Archaeological Odyssey: Essays in Honor of Charles E. Cleland. Cranbrook Institute of Science, Bloomfield Hills, MI. pp. 30–42.

Cleland, C.E. 1982. The inland shore fishery of the northern Great Lakes: Its development and importance in prehistory. American Antiquity 47:761–784.

Drake, F.S. (ed) 1884. The Indian Tribes of the United States: Their History, Antiquities, Customs, Religion, Arts, Language, Traditions, Oral Legends, and Myths. J.P. Lippincott and Company, Philadelphia, PA.

Egan, K.C. 1990. Archaeobotanical Remains from 20SA620. In: J.M. O'Shea and M. Shott (eds), The Bridgeport Township Site, Archaeological Investigation at 20SA620, Saginaw County, Michigan. Anthropological Paper 81, Museum of Anthropology, University of Michigan, Ann Arbor. pp. 203–232.

Garland, E.B. 1986. Early Woodland Occupations in Michigan: A Lower St. Joseph Valley Perspective. In: K.B. Farnsworth and T.E. Emerson (eds), Early Woodland Archaeology. Kampsville Seminars in Archeology, Volume 2. Center for American Archaeology, Kampsville, IL. pp. 47–83.

Garland, E.B. and S.G. Beld. 1999. The Early Woodland: Ceramics, Domesticated Plants, and Burial Mounds Foretell the Shape of the Future. In: J. Halsey (ed), Retrieving Michigan's Buried Past: The Archaeology of the Great Lakes State. Bulletin 64, Cranbrook Institute of Science, Bloomfield Hills, MI. pp. 125–146.

Hart, J.P., Thompson, R.G. and H.J. Brumbach. 2003. Phytolith evidence for early maize (*Zea mays*) in the northern Finger Lakes Region of New York. American Antiquity 68:619–640.

Holman, M.B. and R.G. Kingsley. 1996. Territoriality and Societal Interaction During the Early Late Woodland Period in Southern Michigan. In: Holman, M.B., Brashler, J.G. and K.E. Parker (eds), Investigating the Archaeological Record of the Great Lakes State: Essays in Honor of Elizabeth Baldwin Garland. New Issues Press, Kalamazoo, MI. pp. 341–382.

Holman, M.B. and F.J. Krist, Jr. 2001. Late Woodland Storage and Mobility in Western Lower Michigan. In Pleger, T.C., Birmingham, R.A. and C.I. Mason (eds), Papers in Honor of Carol I. Mason. Wisconsin Archeologist 82:7–32.

Howey, M.C.L. and J.M. O'Shea. 2006. Bear's journey and the study of ritual in archaeology. American Antiquity 71:261–282.

Krakker, J. 1983. Changing Sociocultural Systems during the Late Prehistoric Period in Southeast Michigan. Ph.D. Dissertation, University of Michigan, Ann Arbor.

Larsen, C.E. 1999. A Century of Great Lakes Levels Research: Finished or Just Beginning? In: J. Halsey (ed), Retrieving Michigan's Buried Past: The Archaeology of the Great Lakes State. Bulletin 64, Cranbrook Institute of Science, Bloomfield Hills, MI. pp. 1–30.

Larson, G. and R.J. Schaetzl. 2001. Origin and Evolution of the Great Lakes. Journal of Great Lakes Research 27:518–546.

Lovis, W.A. 1990. Curatorial considerations for systematic research collections: AMS dating a curated ceramic assemblage. American Antiquity 55:382–387.

Lovis, W.A. 2008. Alternative Perspectives on the Michigan Archaic: Research Problems in Context. In: Emerson, T., McElrath, D. and A. Fortier (eds), The Archaic Societies of the Midcontinent. State University of New York Press, Albany, NY. pp. 725–754.

Lovis, W.A., Donahue, R.E. and M.B. Holman. 2005. Long distance logistic mobility as an organizing principle among northern hunter-gatherers: A Great Lakes middle Holocene settlement system. American Antiquity 70:668–692.

Lovis, W.A., Egan, K.C., Monaghan, G.W., Smith, B.A. and E.J. Prahl. 1996. Environment and Subsistence at the Marquette Viaduct Locale of the Fletcher Site. In: Holman, M.B., Brashler, J.G., and K.E. Parker (eds), Investigating the Archaeological Record of the Great Lakes State: Essays in Honor of Elizabeth Baldwin Garland. New Issues Press, Kalamazoo, MI. pp. 251–306.

Lovis, W.A., Egan, K.C., Smith, B.A. and G.W. Monaghan. 2001. Wetlands and emergent horticultural economies in the upper Great Lakes: A new perspective from the Schultz Site. American Antiquity 66:615–632.

Martin, S.R. 1989. A reconsideration of aboriginal fishing strategies in the northern Great Lakes region. American Antiquity 54:594–604.

Martin, S.R. 1999. Wonderful Power, The Story of Ancient Copper Working in the Lake Superior Basin. Wayne State University Press, Detroit, MI.

McHale M.C. and J.M. O'Shea. 1998. The Socioeconomic Role of Late Woodland Enclosures in Northern Lower Michigan. In: R.C. Mainfort and L.P. Sullivan (eds), Ancient Earthen Enclosures of the Eastern Woodlands. University of Florida Press, Gainesville. pp. 181–201.

Monaghan, G.W. and W.A. Lovis. 2005. The Archaeological Perspective and Background: A Problem Oriented Archaeological Perspective on Michigan Prior to European Contact. In: Modeling Archaeological Site Burial in Southern Michigan: A Geoarchaeological Synthesis. Environmental Research Series No. 1, Chapter 4, Michigan Department of Transportation. Michigan State University Press, East Lansing. pp. 69–96.

Monaghan, G.W., Lovis, W.A. and K.C. Egan-Bruhy. 2006. Earliest *Cucurbita* from the Great Lakes USA. Quaternary Research 65:216–222.

Morton, J.D. and H.P. Schwarz. 2004. Palaeodietary implications from stable isotopic analysis of residues on prehistoric Ontario ceramics. Journal of Archaeological Science 31:503–517.

O'Shea, J.M. 1988. Social Organization and Mortuary Behavior in the Late Woodland Period in Michigan. In: R. Yerkes (ed), Interpretations of Culture Change in the Eastern Woodlands during the Late Woodland Period. Occasional Papers in Anthropology, No. 3, Department of Anthropology, The Ohio State University, Columbus. pp. 68–85.

O'Shea, J.M. 2003. Inland foragers and the adoption of maize agriculture in the upper Great Lakes of North America. Before Farming 1:1–21.

O'Shea, J.M. and C. McHale Milner. 2002. Material Indicators of Territory, Identity, and Interaction in a Prehistoric Tribal System. In: W. Parkinson (ed), The Archaeology of Tribal Societies. International Monographs in Prehistory, Ann Arbor, MI. pp. 220–226.

Parker, K.E. 1996. Three Corn Kernels and a Hill of Beans: The Evidence for Prehistoric Horticulture in Michigan. In: Holman, M.B., Brashler, J.G., and K.E. Parker (eds), Investigating the Archaeological Record of the Great Lakes State: Essays in Honor of Elizabeth Baldwin Garland. New Issues Press, Kalamazoo, MI. pp. 307–340.

Robertson, J.A., Lovis, W.A. and J.R. Halsey. 1999. The Late Archaic: Hunter-Gatherers in an Uncertain Environment. In J. R. Halsey (ed.), *Retrieving Michigan's Buried Past: The Archaeology of the Great Lakes State*. Bulletin 64, Cranbrook Institute of Science: Bloomfield Hills, MI. pp. 95–124.

Shott, M. J. 1999. The Early Archaic: Life after the Glaciers. In: J. Halsey (ed), Retrieving Michigan's Buried Past: The Archaeology of the Great Lakes State. Bulletin 64, Cranbrook Institute of Science, Bloomfield Hills, MI. pp. 71–82.

Shott, M.J. and H.T. Wright. 1999. The Paleo-Indians: Michigan's First People. In: J. Halsey (ed), Retrieving Michigan's Buried Past: The Archaeology of the Great Lakes State. Bulletin 64, Cranbrook Institute of Science, Bloomfield Hills, MI. pp. 59–70.

Smith, B.A. 2004. The Gill Net's "Native Country": The Inland Shore Fishery in the Northern Lake Michigan Basin. In: W.A. Lovis (ed), An Upper Great Lakes Archaeological Odyssey: Essays in Honor of Charles E. Cleland. Cranbrook Institute of Science, Bloomfield Hills, MI. pp. 64–84.

Smith, B.D. 1987. The Independent Domestication of Indigenous Seed-Bearing Plants in Eastern North America. In: W. Keegan (ed), Emergent Horticultural Economies of the Eastern Woodlands. Center for Archaeological Investigations, Occasional Paper 7, Southern Illinois University, Carbondale. pp. 3–47.

Smith, B.D. 1992. Prehistoric Plant Husbandry in Eastern North America. In: Rivers of Change: Essays on Early Agriculture in Eastern North America. Smithsonian Institution Press, Washington, DC.

Stoltman, J. 1989. A quantitative approach to the petrographic analysis of ceramic thin sections. American Antiquity 54:147–160.

Further Readings

Cleland, C.E. 1992. Rites of Conquest: The History and Culture of Michigan's Native Americans. University of Michigan Press, Ann Arbor.

Fitting, J.E. 1975. The Archaeology of Michigan. Cranbrook Institute of Science, Bloomfield Hills, MI.

Halsey, J.R. (ed) 1999. Retrieving Michigan's Buried Past: The Archaeology of the Great Lakes State. Bull. 64, Cranbrook Institute of Science, Bloomfield Hills, MI.

Mason, R.J. 2002. Great Lakes Archaeology. Blackburn Press, Caldwell, NJ.

Native Americans

George L. Cornell

■ Introduction

For literally thousands of years, indigenous peoples have resided in what we now call Michigan. The earliest evidence of human habitation in the region suggests that Native peoples were hunting large and small game animals, fishing and gathering plants during the Early Archaic Period (10,000–8000 years ago; Chapter 25), and that there has been continuous occupation of the region ever since. Subsistence patterns were dependent on the numerous plant and animal resources of the region, as well as the fish that were abundant in the region. An environmental analysis of the historical Great Lakes Region supports the notion that indigenous populations had access to ample food supplies and materials with which to construct dwellings and canoes (Halsey 2003).

Kinship played an important role in facilitating cooperation in subsistence and social activities. Indigenous populations were organized in extended families. Small family settlements eventually evolved into larger villages as Native peoples successfully adapted to the local environment. The indigenous peoples of the Upper Great Lakes are included in what are referred to as Woodland Indian cultures today. Obviously, the material culture that the people produced was dependent on what was present on the land. These early cultures lacked metal technology, although they did use copper at various points. Early people used the spear, atlatl (a spear throwing device), and bows and arrows as hunting tools and weapons. These weapons, when fitted with fluted points made of flint (Fig. 25.3), enabled them to kill animals for food and self-defense. Additionally, indigenous peoples were expert at fashioning traps and using snares to procure animals for food. The technology was efficient, although not as durable as goods made of steel (Cornell 2003). As an example, consider that indigenous peoples had to fashion watertight birch bark containers in which to boil foods. This was accomplished by heating stones and placing them in the water-filled containers (stone boiling), and then adding foods to be cooked. Eventually, the container wore out and a new one had to be constructed. Certainly, even though the technique was efficient, it required more time and labor than placing a metal pot over the fire. These differences in cultural patterns and material culture would be exacerbated when Native peoples eventually came in contact with European nations, who were set on colonizing North America in the 16th and 17th centuries.

■ Indigenous peoples and European contact

Indigenous peoples in the Upper Great Lakes region were able to sustain themselves for thousands of years before contact with expanding colonial empires from Europe. The lands that would become known as Michigan in the historical period were primarily occupied in 16th and 17th century by an indigenous confederation of the Ojibway (Chippewa), Odawa (Ottawa) and Potawatomi (Fig. 26.1). Collectively, these groups were organized in a loose knit confederacy, referring to themselves as the "People of the Three Fires." The confederacy was organized along kinship lines, with the Ojibway being the elder brother, the Odawa being the middle sibling and the Potawatomi being the youngest brother and the keeper of the fire. In their own language, Algonquin, they called each other "Anishnabeg" which means "original people." The area was also home to the Miami, Sauk and Fox, Mascouten, Kickapoo and Wyandot tribes (Cornell 2003; Fig. 26.1). These indigenous groups have been mentioned time and time again in the early history of the region, but since the middle of the 18th century the "People of the Three Fires" have come to dominate regional history (White 1991, Tanner 1987).

Over the centuries, Native peoples had raised their children and taught them a specialized world view that was not steeped in "Western Civilization." They understood the world through experience, perceptions of nature and spiritual dictates. The reality of Native peoples was unique and dependent on their environment. Their life-ways would eventually be challenged, how-

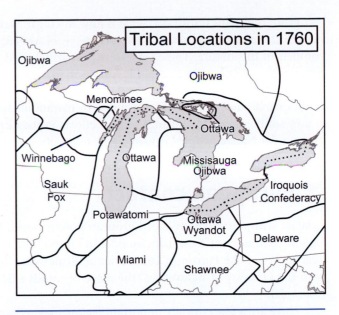

FIGURE 26.1 Locations of the major Indian tribes in the Great Lakes region circa 1760. After Cleland (1992).

ever, as European colonial empires sought new lands and wealth in North America (Cornell 1989).

At this time, the Ojibway, Ottawa and Potawatomi people who primarily occupied Michigan were living well on the abundance of game animals and fish that were common in the Upper Great Lakes region, relying heavily on lake trout, sturgeon, brook trout, suckers, pike, walleye, bass and assorted other small fish. They fished using gorges, fish traps and nets, and constructed weirs. Many of the larger species of fish were speared. Additionally, they hunted moose, elk, whitetail deer, woodland caribou, bear, beaver, muskrat, rabbit, partridge, turkey, duck and other migrating waterfall, along with small game like squirrel. Many of these mammals were captured by using traps and snares, but they were also hunted with bow and arrow and throwing sticks. Clearly, there was an abundance of fish and mammals to support human habitation. Native peoples also planted small gardens in the spring, in which they grew corn, sunflowers, tobacco, squash, pumpkins and beans (Chapter 25). Native peoples also seasonally harvested plants like wild rice. Wild rice was very important in the region, since it could be stored for long periods of time. Great Lakes Indian populations also gathered nuts, blueberries, blackberries and strawberries, and made sugar from the sap of maple trees. All of these natural resources provided the basis for a nutritious diet. In preparation to hunt or gather plants, Great Lakes Indian populations would commonly pray or fast and offer ritualized gifts to the land and spirits. These practices reinforced the bond between "the people" and the earth and were central to the spiritual beliefs of the "Anishnabeg" (Cornell 1986).

The tribal groups that composed the Anishnabeg were incredibly similar in many ways. They shared the same language (with dialectical differences), and they shared many elements of common culture. Their lifestyles did, however, differ a bit, because of the natural resources that were readily available to them. As an example, the growing season in the southern areas for the Potawatomis was much longer than that for the Ojibway in the north; consequently, peoples in the southern areas relied more heavily on gardening and produce than did their northern kinsmen. In contrast, the Ojibway relied more on fish and the bounty of the inland seas, as they inhabited coastline areas and settled on the major watercourses in the upper Great Lakes.

Historically, Anishnabeg villages were located along rivers and large bodies of water. They used both dug-out and birch bark canoes to navigate the waters of the Great Lakes. These vessels also allowed them to transport and trade furs, corn and other commodities. Occupation of village sites was often seasonal, with the spring and summer months generally supporting larger populations at village sites, as fish were abundant and gardens needed to be tended. Winter usually caused the groups to break up into smaller family units that would trap and hunt during the late months of the fall and throughout the winter. This seasonal utilization of resources and the nature of subsistence work were the basis for these fluctuations in village residents.

From the 1640s until 1701, what is now Michigan was ravaged by a series of wars with the Iroquois. The Lower Peninsula was sparsely settled during those years, as Native peoples fled the chaos and hardships that accompany conflicts of this nature. These wars were primarily fueled by the demand for furs, which the Iroquois traded to the English; the Ojibway, Ottawa and Potawatomi primarily traded with the French. It was during the context of these trade wars that the Huron, or Wyandot, came to live near the present site of Detroit. They were pushed out of their traditional homelands east of Lake Huron by marauding bands of Iroquois, and eventually took up residence in what is now southeastern Michigan. Colonial efforts in the Great Lakes region would have additional disastrous consequences for Native peoples, causing large relocations of populations.

■ European contact

Contact with representatives of European powers began for Native peoples in the 16th century, when the French explorer Samuel de Champlain, founder of Quebec and Governor of New France, met with a group of Mascoutens near present Lake Huron in 1616. Etienne Brule—the first European to set foot on Michigan soil—would meet with the Ojibway at Bahweting (the place of rapids—Sault Ste. Marie) in 1622, while serving in the employ of Champlain.

There are a few critically important factors to consider, when one begins to examine early colonial efforts in the "New World," as the Americas became known. First and foremost, colonialism had proven to be an effective strategy for acquiring and maintaining power in Western Europe during the 15th century. Portugal was one of the most powerful nations in the world at the time, based on trade and colonial enterprise in West Africa. Spain would usurp that role after the "discovery" of the "New World" and Columbus' initial voyages, and remained the most powerful nation in Western Europe until 1588, when the Spanish Armada was defeated by weather and the alliance of European nations.

Spain's pre-eminence as a world power was fueled by extractive policies and activities that stripped indigenous nations of wealth and enslaved literally millions of Native peoples. Wealth, in the form of precious metals that Spain collected as tribute and taxes, grew capitalism in Western Europe and provided the funds for military build-ups and the consolidation of power (Weatherford 1988). This acquisition of capital did not go unnoticed by Great Britain, France or the Netherlands. Spain's success in colonial enterprise set a major precedent for other European nations, who were desirous to replicate the production of wealth through colonialism. However, it was not until the Spanish Armada was disabled that representatives of these diverse European nations could safely venture to the new lands, seeking fortune and, sometimes, fame.

The earliest contacts between citizens of European nations and indigenous peoples resulted in the introduction of unknown diseases to North America. The spread of smallpox, measles and yellow fever, to which Native peoples had no immunological protection, caused large numbers of indigenous peoples to die. This phenomenon is commonly labeled a "Virgin Soil Epidemic" and the results, over time, were catastrophic (Crosby 1976). It is estimated that Virgin Soil Epidemics can kill 80–85% of a population into which a new disease is introduced, over a 100 year period of time. Additionally, populations exposed to the diseases also experience decreasing birth rates. The results of the Virgin Soil Epidemics were incredibly devastating to Native communities across North America. The new diseases literally destroyed the fabric of family and community life; they left regions of the continent sparsely populated in relation to earlier population densities. In essence, it was the reality of the epidemics that paved the way for colonialism. European colonies would simply take control of lands that were formerly possessed by indigenous peoples, as these peoples died in large numbers.

Native nations were also easy prey for colonial militias that were armed with superior weapons. Colonial governments soon exerted hegemony over Native peoples, and the history of North America was altered to favor European expansionism (Philbrick 2006).

Conflict arose when European nations contested for empires in North America. After a series of international wars, the British, French and Spanish each carved out a region of occupation and domination. This was especially true in the Great Lakes region, which is rich in natural resources. It had been well settled by Ojibway (Chippewa), Odawa (Ottawa), Potawatomie and other tribal groups. During the 17th and 18th centuries, these groups were closely allied to the French, who sought wealth and influence through participation in the fur trade. Trade with Native peoples was a very lucrative economic activity during this time, and served to aid in the formation of military alliances that were beneficial in the context of wars between competing European powers.

In North America, the British eventually defeated French interests during the French and Indian Wars (1754–1763) and took possession of most of North America. The 13 British Colonies soon rebelled and formed the United States of America shortly thereafter. During this time, Native peoples struggled to retain elements of sovereignty and control of ancestral lands. It was a very difficult period of time for Great Lakes Indian populations, because their former French allies had been supplanted by British agents, and the new trade policies penalized Native peoples. After a very short period of time, British influence was ceded to the fledgling United States, and a whole new set of trade issues was ushered in. This political situation was compounded by the fact that the fur trade had pretty much run its course in the Great Lakes by 1800. These many transitions were very difficult for Native peoples residing in the Great Lakes region, as diseases continued to plague them and the population growth of "New" American citizens was increasing rapidly. As an example, it is estimated that there were, minimally, 60,000 American Indians of differing tribal affiliations in the Great Lakes region in 1768 (Tanner 1987). By 1810, the white population of United States and British citizens within the region had reached 345,000 (Tanner 1987).

Even though it has been very difficult to accurately surmise the historic population estimates for native peoples in the Great Lakes region, it is clear that the large increase in Americans and British citizens caused problems for indigenous peoples, as the newcomers relied on plant and animal resources of the region for subsistence and economic purposes. The United States, still in its infancy, functioned very much like a colonial empire. Land and resources that were possessed by Native nations were procured through treaties with the United States. One must remember that Indian Treaties were initiated by the Executive Office and authorized by Congress, particularly the US Senate, which has the power to ratify treaties, and treaties are protected by the provisions of the US Constitution. Indian lands that were obtained by treaties provided access to natural resources that were the basis for the development of regional economies within the expanding United States. As the federal government continued to acquire land through treaties, many of which were fraudulently negotiated and weakly enforced, Native peoples became pauperized in their own country.

The pattern is a familiar part of American History. Indian nations signed treaties with the United States; the treaties are protected under the provisions of the US Constitution. What Indian nations did not cede to the Federal Government they "reserved" for themselves, hence the name "reservations" for Indian land holdings. The Federal Government, however, had little interest in protecting the rights and guarantees (through treaties) to American Indians. Rather, the United States was primarily interested in converting Indian lands into money to fund government and solidify its place as a world power. Without question, this historic period of federal paternalism and neglect was a very difficult period for American Indians.

◼ The establishment of the state of Michigan

The Northwest Ordinance of 1787 was passed by the Federal Government under the provisions of the Continental Congress (Chapter 28). The lands that would eventually become the State of Michigan were included in the "old Northwest." The creation of the Northwest Ordinance was the handiwork of "Massachusetts veterans of the Revolution, who had formed an organization called the Ohio Company at a meeting held at the Bunch of Grapes tavern in Boston on March 1, 1786" (Dunbar 1970, 164). The Company's plan was to use depreciated paper money to buy land in the "West" for investment purposes. The deal was constructed by Reverend Manasseh Cutler and Colonel William Duer, who handled land negotiations for the Continental Congress (Dunbar 1970, 164). Interestingly, while the land deal on behalf of the Ohio Company was being finalized, Reverend Cutler "insisted that Congress take action to provide for the government of the region in which the tract was located" (Dunbar 1970, 164).

The Northwest Ordinance of 1787 was the outgrowth of this demand. One of the most significant documents in American history, it appears to have been drafted and passed principally to facilitate the deal made by Cutler and Duer. A committee was formed on July 9, 1787, which reported its recommendations two days later. On July 13, Congress passed the Ordinance. That policy decisions of such magnitude and of such importance to the future development of the United States were made so hastily is an amazing fact in American history (Dunbar 1970, 164).

Large tracts of land existed in the "Old Northwest" that had not yet been ceded by Indians in the "Territories" that were being delineated. Clearly, political interests and private entrepreneurs were conspiring to profit from the eventual acquisition of Indian lands in the newly defined and created territories. Consider how this played out for Michigan's Indians. The Treaty at Washington in 1836 ceded lands to the United States that made statehood

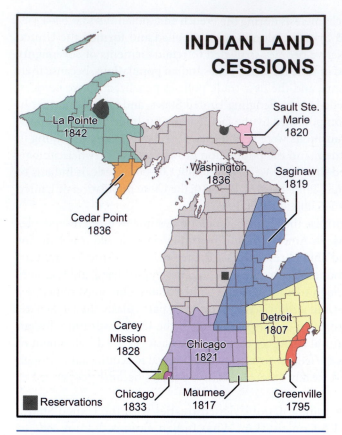

FIGURE 26.2 Major American Indian land cessions, made by treaty, in Michigan. After LeBeau (2005).

possible for Michigan Territory in January of 1837 (LeBeau 2005). The Chippewa and Ottawa, by that Treaty, ceded the vast majority of the Northern Lower Peninsula and the Eastern end of the Upper Peninsula to the US (Fig. 26.2).

The United States then proceeded to sell the lands, or re-grant them, to Michigan by congressional action. Obviously, the lands and resources (timber, minerals and game animals) that were transferred from Indian possession to the US provided the economic basis for regional growth and economic prosperity for the citizens of Michigan (Cornell 1989). This all occurred while Indian people were suffering a declining quality of life, as they no longer had access to historic resources and territories. During this same time period, the Federal Government tried to remake Indians into Christian farmers, but failed miserably. During the 19th century, Congress passed law after law that were intended to assimilate American Indians into the mainstream of American life. Unfortunately, there was a great deal of racism as a part of American culture, and Indians were dehumanized in the popular mind. They were thought of as "savages" and "heathens." Few prominent Americans protested the wrongs that were being perpetrated against American Indians (Pearce 1965). This trend continued well into the 20th century and wasn't reversed until after the conclusion of World War II.

The concentration of Native peoples on reservations

During this period of time, Native peoples in the US were trying to maintain some quality of life for their communities, families and children. This task was difficult, particularly in the 19th and 20th centuries, when American Indians were being concentrated on reservations with little work and very limited access to quality education. Indians protested the harsh treatment and loss of lands, but all too often, these protestations to Congress went unanswered or ignored. Throughout this period of time, American Indians clung tenaciously to their remaining land bases— their "reservations" (Fig. 26.2). These land holdings were their remaining seats of governance and culture, and served as the focal point for the continuation of tribal cultures and languages. The quality of life and opportunities did not begin to radically change on reservations until after World War II (Cornell 1989).

The economic crisis known as the Great Depression in the United States, which lasted from the late 1920s until 1945, was difficult for many. The WW II years began to pull the nation out of this economic tailspin and set it on the road to prosperity for many Americans. Indians were no exception.

The Post-War migration to cities

The post-WW II years witnessed mass movements of Native peoples, seeking employment, to urban areas. Federal programs such as the Relocation Program of the 1950s and 1960s supported Indian movements to cities. Detroit and Grand Rapids became major centers for Upper Great Lakes Indians to find work and establish new residences. Eventually, Indians began to organize and lobby for their collective rights. It wasn't until the 1960s that domestic government and society began to change, to accommodate Indian political action. Much of this change was accomplished through federal courts and federal programs that were developed to wage war on poverty. Since the 1960s, there has been a rapid and upward trend in the restoration of tribal governments in Michigan.

■ Surviving native Tribes and communities

Michigan has always enjoyed a large Native Indian population; for years, Michigan has been home to one of the largest Indian populations east of the Mississippi River. The unique geography of Michigan was primarily responsible for the large number of surviving Indian Tribes and communities. The peninsulas of the state required a "special" trip to travel to the northern regions of the Lower Peninsula; the Upper Peninsula was even more difficult to visit, since car ferries were required before the completion of the Mackinac Bridge in 1957. Thus, the natural features of the land and Great Lakes allowed Indian communities to survive with comparatively little interference for many generations. Of course, missionaries and traders were historically present on the land, but they had little influence in undermining the physical continuity of predominately Native communities and residential settlement patterns. This pattern of historic isolation was primarily responsible for the reintegration, restoration and survival of many of Michigan's Indian Tribes.

■ Fishing rights

In the 1960s, another issue surfaced that would aid the recognition, revitalization and survival of Michigan's Indian tribes. Commercial fishing rights became a very contentious public issue, as Indian tribes in the state exercised their treaty rights to fish in the Great Lakes. These rights were opposed by several non-Native residents of Michigan who, with State support, challenged them in court. The collective action of tribal governments in Michigan during the years that the fishing rights controversy was brewing served to promote recognition efforts, and to revitalize Michigan Indians in their opposition to state allegations that Native fishing rights should be ended. Eventually, the issue had to be settled via litigation.

On April 9, 1973, the United States, on its own behalf and on behalf of the Bay Mills Indian Community, initiated this litigation in order to protect the tribe's rights to fish in certain waters of the Great Lakes, vested in the tribe by virtue of Aboriginal occupation and use, the Treaty of Ghent of 1814 and the Treaty with the Ottawa and Chippewa nation of 1836. In its complaint, the United States asked that the state be enjoined from interfering with the Indians' treaty-confirmed rights to fish in the Great Lakes. The Bay Mills Indian Community, joined by the Sault Ste. Marie tribe of Chippewa Indians, a tribe organized in 1975 under the Indian Reorganization Act 25 U.S.C., section 476, intervened in this action and filed a complaint against the defendants that alleged that a treaty protected and reserved their exclusive right to fish in the waters reserved to the Indians in the Treaty of 1836, and their right to fish in the ceded waters of the Great Lakes, free from state regulation. The United States did not allege that there existed "ceded waters" under the 1836 treaty, but instead alleged that the Indians had an Aboriginal right to fish in the waters adjacent to the lands ceded under the 1836 treaty and adjacent to the lands reserved in that treaty. Also, the United States did not ask for a declaratory judgment that the tribes have exclusive fishing rights in all the waters adjacent to land reservations contained in the 1836 treaty, but instead asked the court to determine whether the State had jurisdiction to regulate fishing within the Bay Mills Indian Community reservation, which it alleged included Whitefish Bay. In effect, the United States' complaint excluded the Chippewa tribe's allegation that it has exclusive fishing rights in certain waters of the Great Lakes, adjacent to 1836 treaty reservation areas, in addition to Whitefish Bay.

The State of Michigan, in its answer, disputed the interpretation given the Treaty of 1836 by the plaintiffs, questioned the continued existence of the tribes which were signatories to the Treaty, and alleged as defenses: (1) that the treaty was a removal treaty, and therefore the Indians intended to relinquish any Aboriginal fishing rights they may have held in 1836; (2) that a subsequent treaty in 1855 discharged all prior rights under the 1836 treaty; (3) that the 1855 treaty was an accord and satisfaction extinguishing all prior rights; (4) that the Indians did not have any Aboriginal rights over the Great Lakes; (5) that Article 13 of the 1836 treaty, which granted the Indians the right to use the fruits of the land until the land is required for settlement, acted as a reservation upon a subsequent condition, and that condition having occurred, the use is extinguished; (6) that the land reservations made in the 1836 treaty have expired by the terms of the treaty; (7) that even though there may be a treaty-protected right to fish, the State of Michigan may still regulate this right in the interest of conservation or under other state police powers; (8) that the expansion of the Sault Ste. Marie Chippewa reservation may be done only with the consent of the state; and (9) that the Chippewa Tribe was dissolved by the 1855 treaty, and the Chippewa tribe from Sault Ste. Marie is not in privy with the original signatories to the treaty (United States of America vs. State of Michigan 1979).

The final determination was that, because the right of the plaintiff tribes to fish in ceded waters of the Great Lakes is protected by US treaties of the Ottawa and Chippewa Indians, that right is preserved and protected under the supreme law of the land, does not depend on State law, is distinct from the rights and privileges held by non-Indians and may not be qualified by any action of the state or its agents, nor regulated by the state or its agents, except as authorized by Congress. Congress has not authorized the state or its agents to regulate the exercise of the treaty fishing rights of the Indians of Michigan. To the extent that any laws or regulations of Michigan are inconsistent with the treaty rights of the Michigan Indians, such laws and regulations are void and of no force and effect as to the plaintiff tribes and their members (United States of America v. State of Michigan 1979). By winning the case in federal courts, Michigan Indian Tribes protected their legal rights to control resources which had been guaranteed as a part of the 1836 Treaty at Washington to the Chippewa and Ottawa (Cornell 1989).

■ Federally recognized Indian tribes in Michigan

During the 1960s and 1970s, there was a renewed effort to seek and secure federal recognition for many of Michigan's Indian Tribes. The resulting efforts were necessitated because the Commissioner of Indian Affairs, John Collier, had ordered that no further efforts be taken to reorganize Michigan Indians under the provisions of the Indian Reorganization Act, which Collier spearheaded and Congress passed in 1934. Collier's official position on behalf of the Bureau of Indian Affairs denied Michigan Indians access to an important federal distinction, and made the recognition process much more difficult. Eventually, seven Michigan Indian Tribes would secure federal recognition during the 1970s and 1980s, bringing the total number of federally recognized tribes in Michigan to 12 (Le Beau 2005; Fig. 26.3, Table 26.1). Many of these are gaming tribes, having secured the legal right to engage in "Las Vegas style entertainment" in 1987 (Fig. 26.4). The following is a brief historical treatment of the tribes.

The Bay Mills Indian Community is a historic Anishnabeg (Chippewa) community. Its residents have a long history in the region. In 1937, the community organized their tribal government, as it exists today, under the provisions of the 1934 Indian Reorganization Act. The Bay Mills Reservation is home to Bay Mills Community College, one of Michigan's two 1994 Tribal Land Grant Colleges. The tribe is a historic fishing community and

FIGURE 26.3 Federally recognized American Indian tribes in Michigan, as of 2000. After LeBeau (2005).

FEDERALLY RECOGNIZED AMERICAN INDIAN TRIBES

1   Keweenaw Bay Indian Community
2   Bay Mills Indian Community
3   Sault Ste. Marie Band of Chippewa Indians
4   Lac Vieux Desert Band of Lake Superior Chippewa Indians
5   Hannahville Indian Community
6   Little Traverse Bay Bands of Odawa Indians
7   Grand Traverse Band of Ottawa and Chippewa Indians
8   Little River Band of Ottawa Indians
9   Saginaw Chippewa Indian Community
10 Match-e-be-nash-she-wish Band of Pottawatomi Indians
11 Nottawaseppi Huron Band of Potawatomi Indians
12 Pokagon Band of Potawatomi Indians

TABLE 26.1   Michigan's current, federally recognized Indian tribes

Tribe name	Location[1]	Tribal enrollment as of 2007	Federally recognized (year)
Bay Mills Indian Community	40 km west of Sault Ste. Marie	1372	1860
Grand Traverse Band of Ottawa and Chippewa Indians	23 km north of Traverse City	3606	1980
Hannahville Potawatomi Indian Community	32 km west of Escanaba, MI	703	1913
Keweenaw Bay Indian Community of Lake Superior Chippewa Indians	105 km NW of Marquette	3159	1936
Lac Vieux Desert Band of Lake Superior Chippewa Indians	Near Watersmeet	>400	1988
Little River Band of Ottawa Indians	Manistee	>3000	1994
Little Traverse Bay Band of Odawa Indians	Petoskey	>3200	1994
Match-E-Be-Nash-She-Wish Band of Pottawatomi Indians (Gun Lake Tribe)	32 km south of Grand Rapids	305	1999
Nottawaseppi Huron Band of Potawatomi Indians	Athens	<500	1995
Pokagon Band of Potawatomi	Dowagiac	2600	1994
Saginaw Isabella Chippewa Tribe	Mt. Pleasant	3400	1864
Sault Ste. Marie Tribe of Chippewa Indians	Salt Ste. Marie	36,000	1972

1: See also Figure 26.3 for a map of these reservation locations.

enjoys a wonderful location on the St. Mary's River and Whitefish Bay.

The Grand Traverse Band of Ottawa and Chippewa Indians was the first tribal group to receive that status under the provisions of the Tribal Federal Acknowledgement Process, adopted by the Bureau of Indian Affairs in 1978. The tribe has a beautiful location adjacent to Grand Traverse Bay, and recently purchased the Grand Traverse Resort in Acme.

The Match-E-Be-Nash-She-Wish Band of Pottawatomi Indians (Gun Lake Tribe) has a history that is linked to the Indian Mission Church at Bradley, in Allegan County. The community had existed in that region long before the establishment of the mission.

The Hannahville Potawatomi Indian Community has been residing in the Menominee County area since at least 1853. The threat of removal caused the movement of some Potawatomi to the Upper Peninsula; the reservation was established by an Act of Congress in 1913. The tribe runs its own school system. Its reservation encompasses 1628 hectares, with 1295 in federal trust. The Hannahville Community received federal recognition in 1937 under the provisions of the 1934 Indian Reorganization Act.

The Keweenaw Bay Indian Community of Lake Superior Chippewa Indians has a land base of almost 22,000 hectares. Approximately 2/3 of that land is tribally

FIGURE 26.4   American Indian and other casinos in Michigan, as of 2000. After LeBeau (2005).

owned, with the remainder owned by members in fee simple, restricted fee or allotted land status. Keweenaw Bay (Fig. 26.3) is the largest reservation in Michigan, having been established by the terms of the Treaty of 1842 at LaPointe, and the tribe reorganized under the provisions of the Indian Reorganization Act. The tribe adopted its constitution, by-laws and corporate charter on November 7, 1936. The importance of retaining such a large land base cannot be understated, as it may be linked to tribal opportunities and options in future years.

The Lac Vieux Desert Band of Lake Superior Chippewa Indians was recognized as a part of the Keweenaw Bay Indian Community until 1988, when it became its own tribal entity. The tribe operates a successful casino and motel, and the community has made significant economic gains over the last 18 years. Much of its economic success is tied to local tourism and seasonal outdoor recreational activities that are prevalent in the region.

The Little River Band of Ottawa Indians has done an excellent job in providing an income stream based on gaming, and is currently the largest employer in Manistee County. The tribe has acquired some lands over the last decade, and has a very active Natural Resources Department as a part of tribal operations. They are headquartered in downtown Manistee.

The Little Traverse Bay Band of Odawa Indians was a signatory to the 1836 Treaty at Washington and the 1855 Treaty at Detroit, yet was not federally recognized until 1994, when it obtained that status, along with the Little River Band and the Pokagon Potawatomi. The Little Traverse Bay Band has been very progressive in its involvement with water quality issues and environmental concerns, and has a small reservation just north of Harbor Springs (Fig. 26.3). The primary economic activity for the tribe, like so many others, is gaming. It is interested in diversifying the tribal economy to provide long term meaningful jobs for its membership.

The Nottawaseppi Huron Band of Potawatomi Indians has had a long history in southwestern Michigan, and initially possessed a 49 hectare State Reservation outside of Athens. The tribe is actively working to provide services to their membership in the areas of health, education and housing.

The Pokagon Band of Potawatomi is also known as the Potawatomi Indian Nation of Michigan and Indiana. Like the Nottawaseppi Huron Band, they were threatened with removal to Indian Territory in the 1830s and 1840s. It was a signatory to the Treaty at Chicago in 1833, yet was not federally recognized as an Indian tribe until 1994. Since then, the tribe has expanded services to tribal members and worked to establish an economic base for tribal operations. The Pokagon Potawatomi have always been well known for their basket-making and progressive attitudes.

The Saginaw Isabella Chippewa Tribe has been a leader in the development of gaming operations that are owned and operated by tribal governments. It currently operates one of the largest casinos between Atlantic City and Las Vegas on its mid-Michigan reservation. The entire Mt. Pleasant region has prospered from the development of the Isabella Reservation community; the tribe is the largest employer in the region. It has also built and operates an excellent tribal museum—the Ziibiwing Cultural Center—located near the casino.

The Sault Ste. Marie Tribe of Chippewa Indians has administrative offices across the Eastern Upper Peninsula. Although federally recognized in 1972, the tribal constitution and by-laws were not adopted until 1975. The tribe has enjoyed enormous growth since that period, and has extensive gaming interests in the Upper Peninsula; it also owns the Greektown Casino in Detroit. They have been leaders in providing health care to tribal members and developing recreational programs and facilities for members and the community. The Sault Ste. Marie tribe has been a signatory to many treaties with the United States, and has exhibited leadership in the areas of economic development and educational services to tribal members.

Two other tribal groups in Michigan are currently pursuing federal recognition: the Grand River Ottawas and the Burt Lake Band of Ottawa and Chippewa Indians.

Michigan Indian tribes make an enormous contribution to regional economies in the state. They employ thousands of members and non-members in their gaming operations, which constitute one of the largest recreational/entertainment industries in Michigan.

■ Conclusions

This chapter has examined the struggle and settlement of Native peoples in Michigan since the early Archaic period. They had more than adequate food supplies and materials to build dwellings for living, and canoes for travel. They were organized in extended families and kinship. Their technology was effective, but not as durable as tools made of steel. The material culture of Native peoples differed from that of Europeans, and played a role in the colonizing process in the 16th and 17th centuries. The land occupied by the Chippewa and Ottawa Indians, and the struggle to keep it, was critical in the European-nature conflict that led to many cession treaties. It was the Treaty at Washington in 1836 which ceded land to the United States, making statehood possible for Michigan Territory in 1837. The ensuing land grab and the concentration of Indians on reservations resulted in a declining quality of life for Native peoples in the 19th and 20th centuries. The post-WWII years witnessed mass movements of Native peoples to urban areas, in search of employment. It was not until the 1960s that Native peoples began to organize for political action; commercial fishing rights, revitalization and survival became major issues. By winning a federal court case, Michigan Indian tribes protected their legal rights to control resources. This was followed by renewed efforts to secure federal recognition of many Indian tribes.

Michigan Indian tribes and communities have made significant gains in recent years. The revitalization of Michigan's Native communities has been a long and difficult struggle. The leadership of tribal governments in the state should be commended for their hard work and diligence. Today, Michigan Indian tribes are major contributors to regional economies in Michigan and work cooperatively with many cities and municipalities in the interests of continuing that trend.

Literature Cited

Cleland, C.E. 1992. Rites of Conquest. The History and Culture of Michigan's Native Americans. University of Michigan Press, Ann Arbor.

Cornell, G.L. 1989. Unconquered Nations: The Native Peoples of Michigan. In: R.J. Hathaway (ed), Michigan: Visions of our Past. Michigan State University Press, East Lansing. pp. 29–31.

Cornell, G.L. 2003. American Indians at Waawiatanong. In: J.H. Hartig (ed), Honoring Our Detroit River. Cranbrook Institute of Science: Bloomfield Hills, MI. pp. 13–14.

Crosby, A.W. 1976. Virgin Soil Epidemics as a factor in the Aboriginal Depopulation in America. William and Mary Quarterly, 3rd Series 32:289–290.

Dunbar, W.F. 1970. Michigan: A History of the Wolverine State. Wm. B. Eerdmans Publishing, Grand Rapids, MI.

LeBeau, P. 2005. Rethinking Michigan History. Michigan State University Press, East Lansing.

Pearce, R.H. 1965. The Savages of America. The John Hopkins Press, Baltimore, MD.

Philbrick, N. 2006. Mayflower: A Story of Courage, Community, and War. Viking Penguin Books, New York.

Tanner, H. 1987. Atlas of Great Lakes Indian History. University of Oklahoma Press, Norman.

Weatherford, J.M. 1988. Indian Givers: How the Indians of the Americas Transformed the World. Fawcett Columbine Books, New York.

United States v State of Michigan. 1979. 471 Supplement 192.

White, R. 1991. The Middle Ground. Cambridge University Press, Cambridge, UK.

Further Readings

Cronin, W. 1983. Changes in the Land: Indians, Colonists, and the Ecology of New England. Hill and Wang, New York, NY.

Debo, A. 1970. A History of the Indians of the United States. University of Oklahoma Press, Norman, OK.

Deloria, V. Jr. and C.M. Lytle. 1983. American Indians, American Justice. University of Texas Press, Austin.

Drinnon, R. 1980. Facing West: The Metaphysics of Indian-Hating and Empire Building. Meridian Books, New York.

Jennings, F. 1975. The Invasion of America: Indians, Colonialism, and the Cant of Conquest. W.W. Norton and Company, Inc., New York.

Wrone, D.R. and R.S. Nelson, Jr. 1973. Who's The Savage? Fawcett Publications, New York.

27

The Settlement Experience

Kenneth E. Lewis

■ Introduction

The settlement of Michigan was part of the larger Euro-American continental expansion of the 19th century. Its settlement history had much in common with other farming regions of the eastern US woodlands. Settled to provide foodstuffs and other products for outside markets, such areas underwent a dramatic process of change, in which immigrants occupied the land, created farms and towns, built transportation facilities and developed social, political, and religious institutions capable of integrating their activities. These areas all started as frontiers, in many ways isolated from the pioneers' homelands. The success of the colonization effort depended on the establishment of a viable economic base in an area where Native peoples had previously subsisted by very different means (Chapter 26). It required creating new communities that first attained self-sufficiency through regional exchange, and later became exporters to outside markets.

What we see as Michigan today is the result of events that occurred over 150 years earlier. Between 1815 and 1860, American settlers transformed a region formerly occupied by Native peoples into the larger national economy. By the time of the Civil War (1861–1865), most of the southern Lower Peninsula was farmed. Wheat, corn, livestock and other agricultural products from Michigan were reaching eastern and international markets, and manufacturing had already emerged in many of its growing urban centers. Thus, a familiar pattern of settlement was already in place, well before Michigan's emergence as an industrial giant at the end of the 19th century. Indeed, this early arrangement set the stage for the state's later development. Farther north in the state, settlement took a different direction. Here, exploitive industries, concentrated on specific natural resources, dominated an extractive economy whose instability produced few permanent settlements and low population densities.

The nature of agricultural colonization helps explain *how* settlement occurred in the southern Lower Peninsula, and why it shifted from a frontier to a commercial society, but it cannot account for the *form* that settlement took. To understand why settlements arose where they did and why they took on their particular roles, we must also examine the circumstances particular to the time and place of this colonization. Immigrants from the East poured into the region from 1815 to the time of the Civil War. The way they occupied the land and built cities and towns reflected both the requirements of antebellum farming, but also the influence of the environment and the political and economic constraints that shaped the conditions in which settlement took place. Examining the colonization of the southern Lower Peninsula as a product of both a larger process, and the context in which it occurred, can help us answer the question of why the landscape they created looked the way it did.

The process of agricultural colonization had especially important implications for the settlement of the southern Lower Peninsula. Farming on the frontier scattered immigrants over a wide area. A pre-existing infrastructure that would have allowed them to process and exchange crops, or to supply farmers with finished goods, did not yet exist. Money and credit were scarce, labor was always in short supply, transportation remained primitive and inadequate and residents lacked most government services. These conditions dispersed and limited the size of immigrant settlements, curtailed markets and restricted the scope of the activities present. But agricultural colonists did not immigrate to escape the world they left behind. As soon as they were able to overcome these obstacles, they turned to large-scale production of commodities, which they processed and marketed locally and shipped over improved transportation, then used the credit they received to invest in their communities and in the institutions that held them together.

The point is clear: understanding how Michigan was settled, and the forces that drove that settlement, are crucial to explaining how it looks today. That is the focus of this chapter—how did early settlement conditions and its geography influence how the state developed, and work to create the geographic patterns that exist today?

■ Early colonization and the rise of the port of Detroit

When settlers came to Michigan following the War of 1812, they entered a land that had a deep past. Native peoples had lived there for millennia, and for the previous 150 years they had been enmeshed by contact and conflict at the periphery of European expansion. French and British colonization had preceded the American appearance—in the 1790s—but had left only a minimal presence. Although the Indian trade had penetrated the interior of Michigan, European settlement had not. Throughout this time, the acquisition and transport of furs remained largely in the hands of Native peoples. European trading posts, forts and missions, were confined to the lakeshores. Small numbers of French farmers were situated near Detroit and the River Raisin to support these settlements, but, by and large, Europeans had made no attempt to extend their presence into the interior of the state.

Despite its ephemeral nature, early European colonization influenced later development by establishing an entrepôt at Detroit. Situated on the Detroit River between Lakes Erie and Huron, Detroit offered easy water access to the northeastern US, and to ports along the Lake Erie shore. In those days, rivers and lakes offered the most efficient means of long-distance transportation, especially for heavy goods, and Detroit's location situated it ideally as a link to lands surrounding the Great Lakes. As the focus of Indian trade, it also lay at the hub of a network of trails that became routes into the interior.

At this time, Michigan's Native inhabitants retained their traditional lands, but incessant warfare and epidemic disease had weakened them severely (Chapter 26). By the time the United States formally established the Territory of Michigan in 1805, Native peoples could no longer resist encroachment by settlers, and thus began to cede their lands, a process that culminated in 1836 (Fig. 26.2). In summary, the initial colonial experience in the Great Lakes did not result in a European occupation of Michigan, but the conditions it produced set in motion a process that established a pattern for future settlement (Tanner 1974, White 1991).

■ Michigan's place in the larger economy

In the early 19th century, Michigan lay well beyond the limits of the European settlements on the eastern seaboard. What, then, brought Americans west to this far territory? To answer this question we must first look at the roles that places like Michigan played in the economy of the larger world.

Since the 16th century, certain European nations had begun to extend their influence beyond their boundaries, in order to incorporate foreign lands within their sphere of influence and trade. In doing so, they sought to create an economic system designed to exploit the low cost of labor and resources in distant lands, which in turn became markets for European goods. That is, their motivations were not for political empires in the traditional sense. This geographical division of production promoted competition among rival nations, and led to continual emigration to new regions. The growth of the world economy propelled colonization in North America, where Great Britain's eventual political control over territory, routes of trade and communication, provided the security necessary to protect settlers and nurture colonial development (Wallerstein 1980, Wolf 1982, Braudel 1984).

British colonization took two forms. The first, called *cosmopolitan frontiers*, arose to directly exploit resources; it had the closest ties to the homeland. These types of activities—fishing, lumbering, ranching and trading—were subordinate to outside markets, managed by homeland interests and resulted in little indigenous development. Their specialized focus also made them inherently impermanent, and thus, these frontiers often experienced boom and bust cycles (Steffen 1980). The fur trade in the Great Lakes was just such a cosmopolitan frontier; it resulted in only a marginal European presence. The episodic industrial colonization in northern Michigan in the 19th century also left a distinctive form of settlement, to which we will return later.

Colonization in southern Michigan was different. Characterized by agricultural settlement by small farmers who sought to become permanent residents and producers, this *insular frontier* did not attract large-scale outside investment directed at a narrow range of resources. Instead, the economy centered around commodities that could be grown efficiently on small-scale, family farms. These conditions made immigration inviting to residents in the eastern states and Europe, who sought to improve their fortunes. In the new country, they engaged in diversified agriculture and reinvested the proceeds in local development and expansion. Colonists' greater tendency toward self-reliance increased the region's insularity and also promoted the growth of indigenous political and social institutions (Steffen 1980).

Settlement commenced in southern Michigan in 1815 and set the pattern for the subsequent development here (Lewis 2002). As in other agricultural frontiers, immigrants came here with the intention of participating in the commercial economy of the United States. The West offered them inexpensive land as a resource, so that they could do that more effectively, and nearly all immigrants shared the hope of eventually improving their lot and that of their children, as producers for an export market.

■ Settlement by small farmers

At the close of the War of 1812, the American presence was confined to the earlier European settlements along its eastern shore. Little was known of the land west of Detroit and Monroe, a country still in the hands of its original inhabitants. Yet, within the next 50 years, agricultural immigration had spread into the interior of the Lower Peninsula and penetrated as far north as a line drawn the between the present-day cities of Saginaw and Muskegon.

In order to explain the origin and development of this commercial farming region, we must first examine the elements that brought it into being. Certainly, the broader desire to incorporate new lands and resources that drove the larger world economy led to expansion in Michigan, and its settlement by small farmers directed its emergence as an insular frontier. But other factors—unique to the time and place of its colonization—produced its distinctive form. What were these? How did they shape Michigan's human landscape?

Motivations for colonization

Underlying all colonization is a desire by people to leave their former homes and emigrate to a new land. Although emigrants have expectations of a better life in the new land, financial gain was not their sole motivation. In addition to the monetary costs of travel and farm-making, emigration also involves the social costs of leaving kin, churches, established communities and familiar environs. Both conditions at home and those they anticipated in the West motivated people to resettle.

Perhaps one of the major reasons that eastern US farmers chose to relocate was the rapid population growth there. Traditional farming in New York and New England was becoming increasingly unprofitable because of higher costs and competition for land, leading younger farmers to look westward for available (and better) land, and causing established farmers to seek opportunities to expand smaller operations. Abundant and inexpensive land also lured immigrants from Europe, where land reform and industrialization had displaced farmers, and intermittent crop failures and the resulting famines drove many in Germany, Great Britain and the Netherlands to seek their fortunes elsewhere. Others in Holland and Germany fled religious persecution, and the fragmentation of older churches in the United States during the Second Great Awakening (1800–1830s) prompted dissidents to relocate. Political uprisings in Europe and Upper Canada brought additional refugees to Michigan (Hansen 1940, Jones 1973, Lucas 1989, Stewart 1992). Americans of African descent, both free and enslaved, also migrated to the state to leave an increasingly marginal status in the South, or to escape bondage by traveling to Canada (Hesslink 1968). In summary, numerous historical factors left no shortage of prospective immigrants.

Perceptions of the land

Agricultural settlers judged the land based on its suitability for growing crops; therefore, perceptions of Michigan's environment were key factors in attracting immigrants. Their evaluation of the potential of, and risks inherent in, its soils, vegetation, climate and disease tempered pioneer images of the region, and helped determine which areas were occupied and the order that they were colonized. Although the environment of the interior of the Lower Peninsula was largely

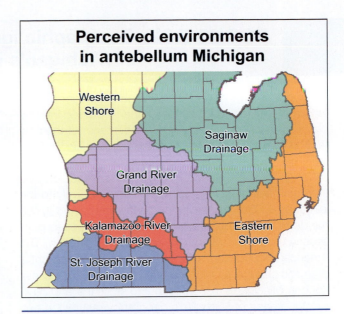

FIGURE 27.1   Environmental zones perceived by settlers in the southern Lower Peninsula. After Lewis (2002).

unknown to Americans in 1815, exploration soon revealed several land types to which settlers ascribed agricultural suitability. Heavily timbered lands, familiar to the residents of the Eastern Seaboard, offered rich soils but required much time and effort to clear/deforest. Oak openings (oak savannas), of which there were many in the southern Lower Peninsula (Plate 15), presented a more open environment of scattered trees and grasses. Immigrants familiar with similar vegetation in the Genesee County in western New York recognized that oak openings were also good farmlands and could be placed in production with less effort. The prairies of southwestern Michigan presented wide areas of open grassland with almost no trees. Although less familiar with the characteristics of prairies and their soils, settlers from the East quickly discerned the richness of prairie soils (Chapter 20) and the relative ease with which they, too, could be converted to arable land. Michigan's interior possessed less desirable lands; these the settlers avoided. Marsh and swamp lands could not be farmed, and pioneer farmers (correctly) considered pine lands, which marked the transition to the coniferous forests to the north, to be associated with inferior soils (Comer et al. 1995, Lewis 2002).

Immigrants identified six distinct land quality zones in southern Michigan, on the basis of past experience in the East (Fig. 27.1). The eastern shore contained low-lying, wet, heavily timbered lands that deterred extensive settlement along the lakeshore. The higher, well-drained oak openings farther inland seemed to offer great potential for farming, whereas, to the north, the Saginaw lowlands presented a mixed image. Immigrants to what would become Shiawassee and Lapeer Counties found inviting open and timbered lands, but the wet and pine lands closer to Saginaw Bay, and the perception of the area as disease-ridden, discouraged settlement in this zone. Southwestern Michigan appeared desirable. Here the prairie lands of the St. Joseph River valley and the oak openings of the Kalamazoo area attracted settlers. These open lands, in turn, led them up the Thornapple River into the vast Grand River basin, whose hardwood forests and oak openings dominated the center of the peninsula. When the settlers reached Michigan's western shore, they encountered sandy soils and coniferous forests that set this region apart and led to its initial rejection as a farming area.

Perceptions of Michigan's lands dramatically affected immigrant preferences for settlement. As farmers, they sought the best soils for crops, but ease of cultivation favored settlement on more open lands, e.g., the Kalamazoo and St. Joseph River basins, as well as the upper Saginaw River valley. Only later did they enter the timbered lands of the central Grand River drainage. Low, wet lands (swamps) and pine forests delayed settlement on both Great Lakes' shores, as well as in the Saginaw lowlands, and effectively established a perceptual boundary that retarded agricultural colonization farther northward (Lewis 2002).

FOCUS BOX: Geographic ignorance and misperceptions of Michigan's interior

Although the area now called Michigan had been known to Europeans for over 150 years when it passed into the possession of the United States, the interior of the new territory was still a mystery. Missionaries, traders and soldiers had long been familiar with the Great Lakes themselves, but the British and French colonists had confined their activities and exploration almost exclusively to the lakeshores. The fur trade had always remained in the hands of Native people, and outside authorities possessed only limited knowledge of the interior. The American occupation, which began in 1796, brought a dramatic change, as newcomers now sought to possess not only Michigan's resources, but to settle the land itself.

Ignorance of Michigan's geography resulted in two major misperceptions about the interior. The first was the myth of a high ridge, sometimes portrayed as a mountain range, that divided the Lower Peninsula and separated the eastward and westward following rivers, e.g., the Kalamazoo and Grand vs the Raisin. This ridge first appeared on maps in 1718 and was not removed until actual surveys in the 1820s showed that it did not exist.

A second image of Michigan's geography centered on the presence of a great swamp that extended across the eastern part of the territory. It arose from the account of a survey of ceded lands in southeastern Michigan, intended for distribution as bounty lands to War of 1812 veterans. This land description, which was publicized in the report of Surveyor General Edward Tiffin, portrayed the whole region as impassible, consisting of low, wet ground, containing marshes, swamps and lakes, interspersed with barren, sandy hills (Chapter 28). In fact, only the southeastern part—the plain of Glacial Lake Maumee (Fig. 13.7), containing the infamous Black Swamp—was like this. Nonetheless, the negative impression conveyed by the Tiffin report jeopardized immigration to the new Michigan territory, forcing its governor, Lewis Cass, to immediately challenge the accuracy of its conclusions (Chapter 28). Fortunately for Michigan, additional surveys revealed that the interior was far different from the southeastern lakeshore, and after these surveys were publicized American immigrants soon began pouring across the Lower Peninsula.

Michigan's Native inhabitants and the fate of their domain

Although environmental conditions clearly shaped pioneer perceptions of the land, other factors also influenced the manner in which it was occupied. Recall that American settlers took possession of a country inhabited by Native peoples, and before immigrants could occupy these territories, the federal government had to terminate their legal rights to possession by treaty. Then, the lands had to be prepared for resale. Both of these processes took time and affected the order in which lands became available for settlement. The United States acquired Indian lands through a series of treaties between 1795 and 1836 (Fig. 26.2), and attempted to deal with the inhabitants by first restricting them to reservations, and later by relocating them to the West (Prucha 1984). Both policies ultimately failed to remove all of Michigan's Native peoples, but the order of the treaty cessions permitted those groups impacted later to adapt more successfully to the threat of dispossession. Memories of recent Indian wars, and the presence of reserve populations of Saginaw-Chippewas and other groups, whom many believed hostile, deterred settlement in the north. In southwestern Michigan, however, a different image of the Native peoples emerged. Here the Potawatomis assumed a crucial role as suppliers of foodstuffs to immigrants, and became an integral part of the frontier economy. Faced with the threat of removal to the West, they adopted a strategy of assimilation. Some managed to purchase land and became settlers on their own territory, while others chose to change their behavior to become invisible in American society. Farther north, the Ottawas chose a similar strategy to avoid removal. By successfully pursuing assimilation while expanding a network of friends and allies among the newcomers, the Ottawas remained in Michigan—on lands permanently granted to them as state residents (Clifton 1984, McClurken 1986, Montfort 1990).

The order in which land actually passed into the hands of settlers was conditioned by the sequence of its sale by the federal government. The United States systematically cataloged all land, following its acquisition, by means of the comprehensive US Public Land survey system (Chapter 28). The survey permitted the General Land Office (GLO) to manage settlement, by controlling how and when particular tracts were alienated. As a result, not all Michigan lands became available for sale at once. Rather, large tracts were placed on the market by federal authorities as the surveys were completed, and the order in which this occurred helped shape the spread of settlement across the region (Fig. 27.2). The GLO encouraged pioneers to occupy the eastern and southern portions of the state, before opening lands farther to the north and west (Barnett 1999). Offering land, however, did not always guarantee its sale, if other factors intervened. Government lands often found no takers, and some immigrants, called preemptors, settled on unsurveyed lands with the intent of purchasing it later.

Pioneer settlement strategies

Settling on the frontier involved more than simply moving to a new place. For agricultural immigrants, the process of farm-making was a costly and arduous endeavor that required not only a long and often difficult journey to a strange land, but also involved clearing the land to raise crops, as well as constructing houses, barns and other structures. Their success depended on overcoming numerous obstacles in the absence of familiar social institutions and ties of kinship, ethnicity and religion. Lack of such support, coupled with perceptions of greater opportunities elsewhere, insured a high rate of turnover among prospective settlers. To surmount these difficulties, many immigrants formed covenanted communities, whose members organized themselves around a set of rules and expectations that formed the basis for central institutions that offered them economic support and social benefits in the new country (Smith 1966). Communities whose members were bound by ties of religion, ethnicity and language came to Michigan for a variety of reasons, both economic and social, but all sought contiguous lands on which to settle. To obtain such large tracts, they often chose lands bypassed by others, thereby promoting the settlement of less desirable areas. Covenanted communities included the German colonies in the Saginaw valley, the Dutch settlements on the western shore and Westphalia, Olivet and Vermontville in the woodlands of the upper Grand River basin (DeForth 1970, Johnson 1972, Lucas 1989, Lewis 2002; see FOCUS BOX below).

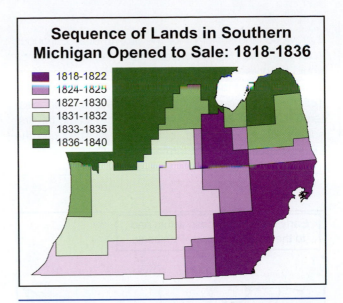

FIGURE 27.2 Sequence of lands in the southern Lower Peninsula opened to sale, 1818–1836. After Barnett (1999) and Lewis (2002).

FOCUS BOX: Overcoming adversity on the frontier: the Westphalia experience

The German colonists in western Clinton County employed a strategy that permitted them to overcome the difficulties of settling on the Michigan frontier. Emigrating from the Prussian provinces of Westphalia and the Rhineland in the 1830s to escape declining economic conditions, they sought to farm the newly-opened lands of central Michigan. But resettlement was not without hardship and risk, and as many as 70% of newly-arrived pioneers failed in their initial attempts at farming. In order to persist where others had not, they formed a covenanted community in which kinship, shared background, ethnicity, place of origin and religion combined to help them establish permanent settlements. Their

community centered around membership in the Catholic Church, whose traditional position of leadership in German villages made it a key institution for social and economic integration, and gave the priest status as a community leader. This closely-knit organization provided the wherewithal to conduct trans-Atlantic immigration and support the formation of new communities in America.

Arriving in Michigan in 1836, immigrants under the leadership of Rev. Anton Kopp became the nucleus of a growing Catholic community in southern Michigan. The Reverend Kopp chose a large, unoccupied, forested tract north of the Grand River upon which to settle. Although difficult to clear, it provided land sufficient for the growth of a contiguous colony, in which traditional patterns of partible inheritance could be preserved, even as the population expanded. Appointed priest to Westphalia by the Bishop of Detroit in 1837, he initially oversaw the distribution of land, administered the parish church and school and became the first supervisor of Westphalia Township in 1839. During the colony's crucial years of formation, the Church played a central role in the success of the Westphalia settlement, by providing its residents the support to help them weather the adversities of reestablishing themselves in the new world. Over the years, the Westphalia community and its members have persisted; the common surnames of Droste, Fedewa, Platte, Rademacher, Thelen, Koenigsknecht and those of other pioneer families attest to their longstanding presence, even today, in this part of the state.

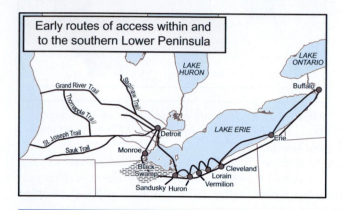

FIGURE 27.3   Early routes of access within and to the southern Lower Peninsula and nearby areas. After Lewis (2002).

Access to the newly opened lands also affected the direction of settlement of Michigan's interior. Prior to American settlement, Detroit had been a gateway to southern Michigan. Later, American pioneers from the East migrated there by land routes along the southern shore of Lake Erie, and arrived by water from ports like Buffalo. The Erie Canal opened an all water route from New York City to the western lakes in 1825, increasing the flow of traffic to Michigan's entrepot and facilitating the export of commerce from Michigan to the East. Detroit had also served as a center of trade, and the focus of a network of trails used by Native peoples from all parts of southern Michigan. Under the United States' administration, these trails became the primary immigration routes to newly-opened lands (Fig. 27.3). Roads built upon the older trails served as the major system of trade and communication on the frontier. Inexpensive to construct, a dendritic network of roads linked the region's settlements to each other, as well as to its administrative center. A maze of regional roads also arose to facilitate regional exchange. By the mid-1820s, Michigan's road network extended across the eastern part of the Lower Peninsula, into the Saginaw area, and, with the opening of the Potawatomi lands in the SW, soon spread across the entire peninsula. During the following decade, roads tied Detroit with the upper Grand River basin and stretched into the recently ceded Ottawa lands to the north. As the network expanded, secondary roads began to link the major thoroughfares, and by mid-century, the state's interior was interconnected by a web of overland routes. These roads helped shape movement into Michigan, as well as facilitating communication and exchange among its new residents, thereby playing a crucial role in the state's development (Lewis 2002).

■ The rise of frontier towns

Settlement in southern Michigan followed the opening of lands and the routes leading to them. Nowhere is the form of this spread more evident than in the distribution of frontier post offices (Ellis 1993, Lewis 2004). Establishing postal service to newly-settled areas was essential to integrating these areas into the social and economic fabric of the expanding nation. The federal government sited post offices in central locations, convenient to those they served. On an agricultural frontier, post offices appeared almost immediately after lands were settled; they commonly occupied space in stores, taverns or the home of the local postmaster (Fuller 1972). The growth of post offices reveals the earliest expansion of interior settlement west of Detroit before 1825, followed by a rapid movement into the St. Joseph valley by 1830. During the following decade, immigrants moved northward into the Kalamazoo, Grand and Saginaw valleys, where several covenanted communities situated themselves on large vacant tracts. By mid-century, settlement had occupied much of southern Michigan and continued to move northward (Fig. 27.4).

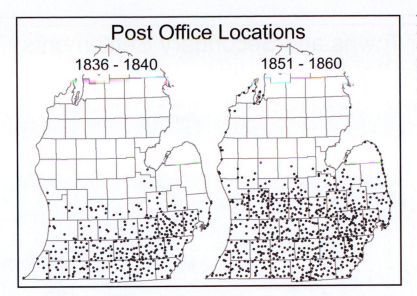

FIGURE 27.4 Distribution of settlement, as epitomized by post office sites, in the Lower Peninsula of Michigan, during the mid-1800s. After Lewis (2002).

The distribution of Michigan's settlements, and the form of its frontier road system, reflected the economic organization of the region and provides clues to the extent of its growth during the frontier period. Like other areas undergoing agricultural colonization, the Michigan countryside gave rise to different types of settlements, whose size and content were tied to their economic function. These settlements arose to support an economy whose operation was restricted largely to internal markets. Although roads allowed immigrants to reach their lands and communicate with one another, they were as yet inadequate to ship bulk commodities out of the region. This lack of efficient transportation effectively isolated Michigan producers from larger eastern markets, and until this obstacle was overcome, settlers were obliged to restrict the extent of their crops. Michigan residents raised corn for both human and animal consumption, as well as potatoes, turnips, squash, gourds, pumpkins, melons and other garden crops. They developed systems of regional exchange in which pioneer farmers, Native Americans, and remnant French settlers traded hunted and foraged wild foods, field and orchard crops, and locally-made goods and labor, through a series of internal markets. These markets became the basis for an economic infrastructure capable of supporting settlers until conditions improved. Although most agriculturists who immigrated to Michigan intended to raise crops, livestock and other products for outside commercial markets, they first had to survive and persist until they could enter the national economy (Lewis 2002).

Michigan's settlements took on a distinctive pattern that is common to frontier regions. The small size of its settlements accommodated Michigan's scattered immigrant population and the limitations of regional trade. Apart from the entrepôt of Detroit, frontier towns were the largest and most important settlements of the time. These central places were focal points of regular social, administrative and religious activity. They contained stores, warehouses, mills, banks, land offices, repair facilities, churches, schools and other important services. These *frontier towns* served as jumping off points for immigrants. Each was a principal terminus in the regional transportation network. As the most important centers of activity, these settlements acquired the largest number of links to other points, and attracted the largest populations. In addition to frontier towns, *secondary centers* also existed; they contained stores, mills and other processing facilities, but occurred more sporadically and were smaller. These settlements served as subsidiary centers of trade linked directly to frontier towns. Most of Michigan's frontier population was dispersed across the interior on *farms* or *semi-nucleated settlements* which were largely devoted to the production of agricultural produce (Casagrande et al. 1964). As colonization spread across the peninsula, the appearance and distribution of these settlements testified to the form this process manifested, as well as the structure of the frontier economy.

The rise of frontier towns mirrored the expansion of frontier Michigan's regional economy. In the first decade of expansion, major centers arose at the eastern shore ports of **Monroe** and **Mt. Clemens**, while major inland milling sites appeared at **Ann Arbor** and **Pontiac**, both on major interior immigration routes. As settlement spread across the Lower Peninsula, **Adrian** appeared on the road leading inland from **Monroe**, and **Niles** became the principal point on the lower St. Joseph River. Later **Marshall**, **Kalamazoo** and **Ionia** attained importance, as settlement shifted

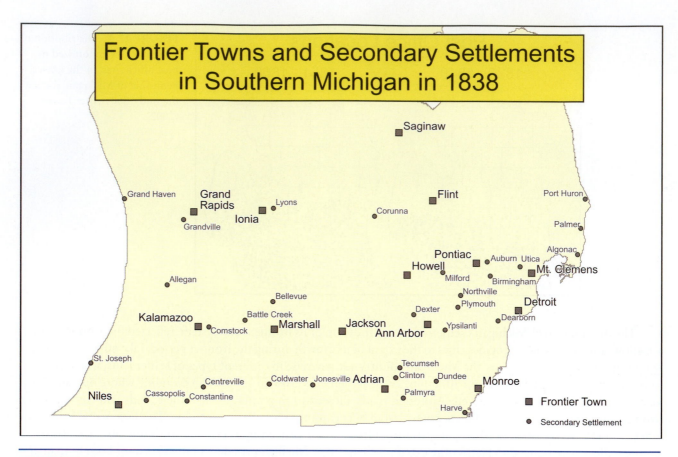

FIGURE 27.5   Michigan's frontier towns and secondary centers, in 1838. After Lewis (2002).

northward, followed by **Grand Rapids,** as immigrants' attention turned to the lower Grand River. **Flint** gained prominence with belated colonization in the Saginaw Valley, and the rise of **Jackson** and **Howell** accompanied settlement in the upper Grand River basin. In the north, **Saginaw** dominated the lower Saginaw basin and linked recent settlements near Saginaw Bay with those farther south. By 1845, pioneer settlement had covered most of southern Michigan that was suitable for agriculture.

Each frontier town lay at the center of a trading area, linked by roads to smaller secondary centers (Fig. 27.5). Their arrangement maximized accessibility between central settlements and those of secondary importance—a pattern usually found in regions organized around internal markets. But like most developing areas, southern Michigan at mid-century was in transition; it was about to emerge from its status as a frontier, as a result of several dramatic innovations that directed its destiny and altered its landscape.

■ The role of railroads and grain elevators

Michigan's incorporation within the national economy depended on the capability of its producers (farmers) to efficiently ship agricultural commodities to distant markets in the East, and on the ability of frontier merchants to buy and sell their goods on credit. Although Michigan possessed many lake ports that provided direct access to the outside world, an absence of canals made it necessary to ship merchandise into and out of its interior by overland routes instead—a slow and expensive journey. Winter weather and ice closed waterways, while summer rains frequently made dirt roads impassable. On the frontier, therefore, infrequent shipping and receiving of goods tied up merchants' capital, and limited long-distance trade. A chronic shortage of capital made merchants reluctant to extend long-term credit to farmers who, in turn, were hesitant to expand production because of the uncertain market for western produce. Two innovations overcame these obstacles, however, and almost immediately the course of Michigan's growth was altered.

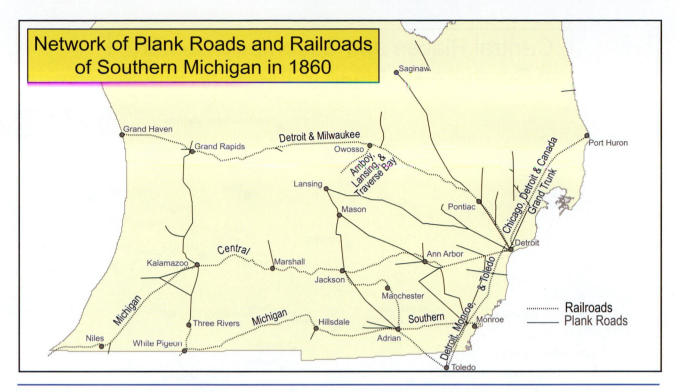

FIGURE 27.6   The network of railroads and major roads in the southern Lower Peninsula, in 1860. After Meints (1992) and Lewis (2002).

The first change involved the coming of railroads, which completely altered the nature of internal trade and connected Michigan with the outside world. Railroads provided cheap, rapid, all-weather, overland transportation. Their efficiency allowed merchants to ship and receive goods at any time of the year, dramatically reducing the amount of their capital tied up in investment. In the 1830s, private investors, and later the State of Michigan, attempted to build a rail network to connect the interior to Lake Erie ports. However, inadequate funding caused these projects to languish, and the lines were only completed in the early 1850s with the backing of eastern and British capital (Fig. 27.6). By the time of the Civil War, railroads had crossed the interior of southern Michigan, joined major settlements on the eastern shore and provided outlets to eastern cities as well as to the emerging western entrepôt of Chicago (Meints 1992).

Although railroads provided the means to move goods within, to and from Michigan cheaply and efficiently, their impact was enhanced by another innovation that further facilitated the shipment of wheat and lowered production costs—the grain elevator. Elevators employed steam-driven machinery to weigh, sort and move grain into and out of storage bins; their use expedited the processing and storage of grain for export. Because elevators mixed and graded grain from different owners on the spot, grain that formerly belonged to the producer, until shipped and sold in the East, was now purchased right at the elevator. Receipts were issued directly to farmers by elevator operators, becoming collateral for loans and advances. Farmers, merchants and businessmen used them as credit to buy goods, expand farms or make other investments. Thus, the appearance of grain elevators in Michigan during the 1850s restructured the nature of frontier marketing by allowing frontier farmers to participate directly in external exchange. As a result, cultivation began to shift toward wheat as an export crop. Indeed, Michigan became a major wheat producer, as farmers expanded their production in the pre-Civil War period. Together with the technological advances brought by railroads, elevators dramatically altered Michigan's regional economy and rapidly reshaped the nature of its settlements (Cronon 1991).

The economic changes brought about by the expansion of export trade from Michigan also modified its frontier landscape. The rail network formed the basis for a system of feeder routes, consisting of plank roads and other improved roads that linked settlements in the interior and created an effective system for shipping goods and produce into and out of the state. As a result of their entry into the national economy, Michigan's urban settlements also expanded rapidly. Those located centrally within the new transportation network became magnets for economic

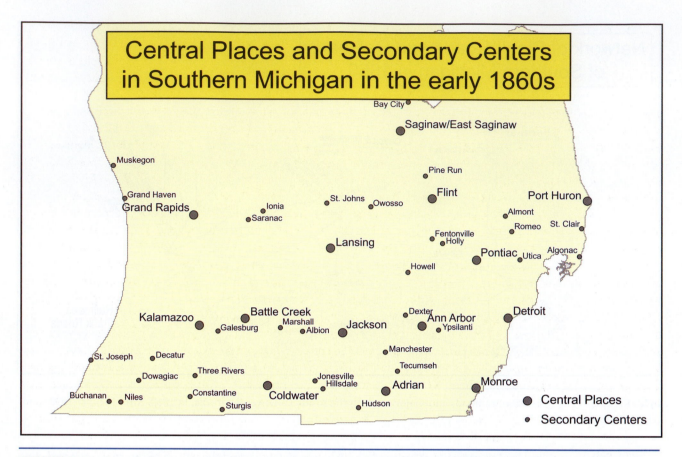

FIGURE 27.7   Central places and secondary centers in the southern Lower Peninsula, in the 1860s. After Lewis (2002).

and social activities essential to the emerging region, e.g., retailing and wholesaling, processing and storage, manufacturing and repair, banking, courts, churches, public accommodation and professional services. Such activities attracted new immigrants, and towns that had been frontier centers grew into cities. **Detroit** claimed more than 70,000 residents in 1860, and 13 other cities could be listed among Michigan's central places, including old frontier towns such as **Adrian, Ann Arbor, Flint, Grand Rapids, Kalamazoo, Jackson, Monroe, Pontiac** and **Saginaw**, as well as newly important places such as **Battle Creek, Coldwater, Port Huron** and the new capital at **Lansing**. The appearance of a large number of secondary centers accompanied the rise of these central places. Many, including Niles, Marshall and Howell, had formerly been frontier towns, although others, such as St. Johns, Lapeer, Three Rivers and Hastings, were new towns or had previously played much smaller roles in the regional economy. Secondary settlements were situated along major routes that connected them to the new central places, providing the secondary centers with access to the outside world (Fig. 27.7). This pattern is characteristic of regions whose trade is oriented toward external markets, and its form testifies to the organizational change that occurred in southern Michigan by this time (Lewis 2002).

Export-based economy, and the settlement landscape of modern Michigan

The shift to an export-based economy produced the settlement landscape of modern Michigan. By 1860, a number of cities had come to dominate the southern Lower Peninsula, where settlers had already placed much of the land perceived to be arable in production (Fig. 27.4). Those towns and cities that became central places continued to play important roles, and the state's economy matured in the second half of the 19th century.

The port of Detroit continued to dominate Michigan's economy as its principal center of export trade. The city's position at the hub of rail and water transport in Michigan allowed it to grow as a manufacturing center (Farmer 1969).

The towns of Adrian, Ann Arbor and Pontiac all used available water power to become important manufacturing centers. Their foundries, factories and machine shops turned out steam engines, agricultural implements, stoves and other finished products, and flour milling remained an important business. Ann Arbor's role as a diversified center was enhanced by the establishment of the University of Michigan and the state medical college, and railroads made Adrian a transportation node in southeastern Michigan (McLaughlin 1995, Lindquist 2004). On the eastern shore, Monroe continued to be an important grain port, linked by rail to the interior as well as to Detroit and the port of Toledo (Chandler 1999). Farther west, Coldwater and Jackson remained central markets and transportation hubs, and began to emerge as manufacturing centers. Chosen as the site of the Southern Michigan Prison, Jackson's entrepreneurs took advantage of cheap, contract prison labor and locally available raw materials to develop industries (Santer 1970). Battle Creek arose as an industrial and commercial center on the Kalamazoo River. Heavily influenced by the Seventh Day Adventist church and its dietary preferences, Battle Creek became a center of cereal and food manufacturing (Straw 1938). Kalamazoo arose as the agricultural market, commercial center and manufacturing hub for southwestern Michigan. Already an industrial settlement that contained foundries, tanneries, mills and a blast furnace, it attracted additional institutions including Kalamazoo College and the state mental hospital (Dunbar 1966). Grand Rapids dominated trade and manufacturing in western Michigan. Already a sawmill hub in the lower Grand River valley, the industrial potential afforded by its location became a focus of furniture making. And, linked by rail to Detroit, it became a marketing center for a wide portion of western Michigan. By 1860, Grand Rapids had become the state's second largest city (Bradshaw 1968). Situated in the center of the southern part of the state, Lansing was a rapidly growing center of trade and manufacturing. As the site of the state government and the agricultural college, Lansing drew immigrants to this recently settled portion of the state (Kestenbaum 1981). In the Saginaw valley, earlier settlements expanded with the growth of commercial lumbering. Flint and Saginaw flourished with the increasing demand for wood products, and emerged as centers of manufacturing and trade, as well as markets for the growing agricultural settlement in the region (Cooper and Stilgenbauer 1934). Finally, Port Huron's strategic position at the head of the St. Clair River helped make it a central place for Michigan's Thumb region. A major port of entry from Canada, its rail links supported its growth as a lumber milling center and made it the principal market for this region (Lewis 2002).

These urban centers and the secondary settlements that supported them established a pattern of settlement that formed the basis for the state's development in the 19th and 20th centuries. Agriculture continued to dominate the region, coupled with manufacturing and trade in the larger urban centers. When the auto industry came to Michigan, it developed in existing industrial cities (Chapter 31). The state is still known for its furniture and cereals. Lansing is still the capital, and most of the early public institutions still operate at their original locations.

■ Colonization in northern Michigan

Because it has served the needs of our modern state well, the pattern described above has persisted. But this pattern did not extend over the remainder of the state; southern and northern Michigan have always remained distinctive regions (Chapter 1). Why is this? Although the population of southern Michigan continued to grow after the Civil War, with few exceptions the bulk of intensive agricultural settlement did not move farther north. Environmental conditions—mainly related to soils and climate—restricted the range of grain farming that characterized agriculture in the south, and its absence obviated the need for a high density farming population and the processing, marketing and transportation services associated with grain production. Without grain farming and the complex settlement infrastructure that accompanied it, northern Michigan's development took another direction.

Immigrant colonization in the northern Lower Peninsula and the Upper Peninsula occurred for different reasons than it did in the south. Cosmopolitan colonization in the northwoods created a different pattern of settlement. Because the environment of the region led to the perception that the area was unsuitable for agriculture, expansion here was driven by other factors. Extractive industries such as lumbering and mining dominated the region. To be successful, these activities had to be organized on a broad scale, requiring infrastructure far different from that associated with farming. Both lumbering and mining were intended to gather specialized products for outside markets, an endeavor that commonly necessitated a large, up front investment of capital. Consequently, extractive industries were funded and controlled largely by nonresidents with little interest in developing the land, or reinvesting their returns in its development.

Industrial frontiers in Michigan were tied closely to export demands from the beginning, and their organization reflected the needs of production. Settlement was structured to facilitate the gathering, processing and transportation of ore and timber. Towns, camps and mills arose quickly where needed, and were just as quickly abandoned when production ceased or moved elsewhere. The built landscape of the northern Lower Peninsula and the Upper Peninsula was, therefore, shaped by the specialized nature of commercial industry and its settlement requirements.

Lumbering

Although settlers in the southern Lower Peninsula had long engaged in sawing and milling of lumber to serve local needs, industrial lumbering began only in the 1840s, centering on the production of pine for construction-grade lumber (Chapter 40). As the forests in Maine became exhausted, the lumber industry moved west to fill the needs still being generated in the East, as well as the growing market in Chicago and the settlements on the treeless prairies. Coniferous forests dominated the sandier soils of northern Michigan (Chapter 21; Plate 15) and mills in the Saginaw basin first began exploiting this resource, shipping lumber to the Albany, NY market, via Lake Erie. On the Lake Michigan shore, other mills at the mouths of the Muskegon and the Grand Rivers arose to serve Chicago and the west. Following the Civil War, the lumber market in northern Michigan exploded. Settlements, i.e., "lumber towns" of various sorts, grew at **Muskegon**, **Manistee**, **Petoskey**, **Ludington**, **Boyne City**, **East Jordan** and **Traverse City** on Lake Michigan, **Oscoda**, **Alpena**, **Tawas City** and **Cheboygan** on Lake Huron, and **Menominee**, **Escanaba**, **Gladstone** and **Manistique** in the Upper Peninsula. The 1855 opening of the Sault Ste. Marie Canal, linking Lakes Superior and Huron, opened navigation to and from Lake Superior; lumber ports opened at **Ontonogan**, **Grand Marais**, **Munising** and **Sault Ste. Marie** (Figs. 27.8–27.10).

Numerous technological advances in milling also increased the efficiency of lumbering. The expansion of the state's rail network following the Civil War introduced efficient overland transportation to the northern Lower Peninsula. Railroads were employed to transport logs from forest to the mills, as well as to ship finished lumber to points in southern Michigan, and greatly assisted the logging industry in extending its exploitation of the state's forest resources (Maybee 1959, Meints 1992; Chapter 40).

FIGURE 27.8 The network of railroads and principal settlements in the northern Lower Peninsula, in the 1880s. After Meints (1992) and Michigan Railway Commission (1919).

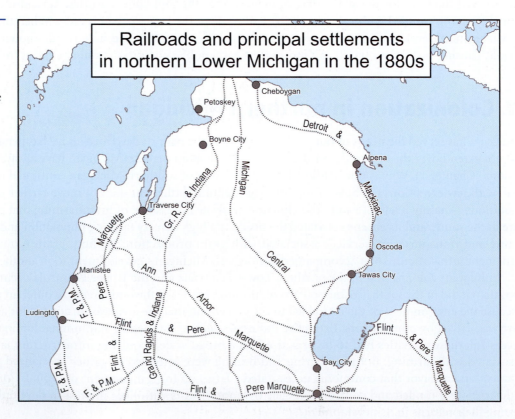

Railroads and principal settlements in northern Lower Michigan in the 1880s

The nature of lumbering determined the content and distribution of the settlements it created. Most of the population was concentrated in mill towns situated at ports or along rail lines. These towns were sited at locations central for processing and transportation, and they grew rapidly as the industry thrived. The settlements of northern Michigan needed large numbers of workers quickly, drawing on French Canadian immigrants, as well as others from Sweden and Norway. Larger mill towns also attracted people associated with supporting the businesses, professions, central services, and civic institutions necessary to maintain metropolitan centers. Linked directly with the metropolitan areas of the East, they acquired the trappings of urban life, and became cosmopolitan centers on the frontier.

In addition to the larger cities, the exhaustive nature of commercial lumbering produced many smaller settlements scattered over large areas. Logging camps and mill towns were foci of specialized activity, and their appearance followed the expansion of timber cutting into the interior, as well as the growth of the rail network. Because of their specialized nature, lumbering and mining settlements in northern Michigan and the Upper Peninsula provided a lucrative market for foodstuffs and forage, drawing farmers to this region. Situated near population centers, they provided hay (for the horses) and potatoes (for the people), as well as livestock and livestock products to support the communities of this industrial frontier (Chase 1936). Michigan's lumber boom reached its peak in the late 1880s. and the distribution of settlements reveals a pattern characterized by key urban processing centers along the lake shores and a linear pattern of settlements along the rail lines of the interior (Fig. 27.9).

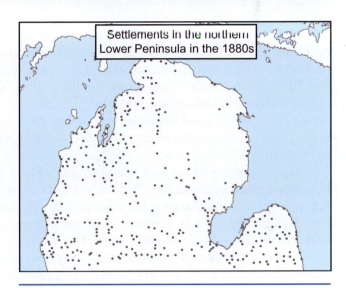

FIGURE 27.9   Distribution of settlements in the northern Lower Peninsula, in the 1880s. After Ellis (1993).

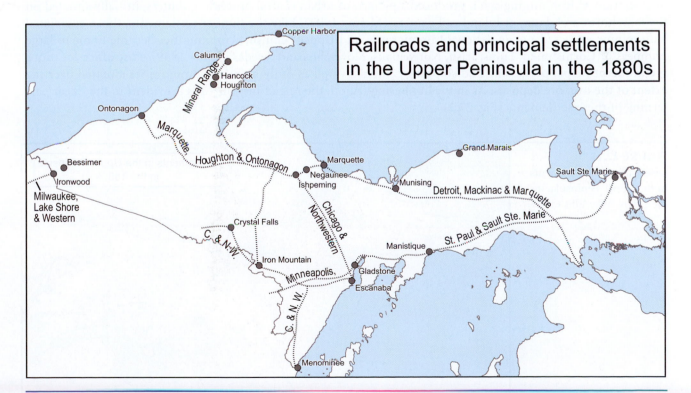

FIGURE 27.10   The network of railroads and principal settlements in the Upper Peninsula, in the 1880s. After Meints (1992) and Michigan Railway Commission (1919).

Mining

Large scale mining in the state was based on copper and iron deposits in the Upper Peninsula (Chapters 11, 12). Their presence attracted the attention of commercial interests as early as the 1840s.

Copper mines were first opened on the Keweenaw Peninsula and later, to the west, around Ontonagon. But by the 1870s, the industry centered on the great deposits around Portage Lake. Upper Peninsula mines were largely financed by Pittsburgh and Boston investors who oversaw their development. Although the mines drew ethnically diverse immigrants to Michigan and supported settlement here, the profits went to the corporate operators and not into the development of the region. As on other industrial frontiers, settlement was concentrated around the principal resource, and the locations of the key towns of **Copper Harbor** in the northern Keweenaw Peninsula, **Hancock** and **Houghton** on Portage Lake, and **Ontonagon** to the west, were reflective of the distribution of ore (Fig. 27.10). Situated along Lake Superior, all of the copper ports had access to water transportation, linking them to the East. Like the lumber milling centers, those associated with the copper industry grew rapidly and acquired urban functions. Houghton became the site of the Michigan School of Mines in 1885; neighboring Hancock attracted foundries and factories. But their dependence on a single industry made settlements in the copper country vulnerable to change, such that, when the mines played out later, many declined (Fuller 1939; Chapter 12).

Increasing demand for iron by American industry also drew commercial mining interests to Michigan's Upper Peninsula in the 1840s (Chapter 11). Here, iron mines were opened in the Marquette Range on Lake Superior, the Gogebic Range at the peninsula's southwestern extreme, and the Menominee Range on northern Lake Michigan (Fig. 11.2). Unlike copper, the iron ore deposits extended over wide areas and the mines were widely distributed. Exploiting this resource at these far-interior locations required transportation capable of moving the heavy ore to the lakeside processing centers. As early as 1857, rails connected iron mines to the port of **Marquette**, and the following decade saw similar lines constructed to **Escanaba**. By the 1870s, Wisconsin railroads connected the Menominee Range, and the mines of the Gogebic district at the western end of the Upper Peninsula, directly with iron mills at Chicago via **Menominee** and **Ironwood**, respectively (White 1886). Railroads also connected the port of Hancock to copper mines in the Keweenaw Peninsula (Fig. 27.10). The industrial organization of iron mining again produced a pattern of urban central processing centers, initially situated on the lakeshores and, later, at inland rail centers (Meints 1992). Like the lumber settlements, those associated with mining attracted a wide variety of immigrants, and Upper Peninsula communities became home to large numbers of Cornishmen, Finns, Irish, Norwegians, Slovenians and Swedes (Fuller 1939). Post office locations reveal the principal processing and shipping centers, as well as outlying mine communities situated over the extent of the iron ore deposits. As in the lumbering region, the role of the railroads is evident in the linear patterning of these settlements (Fig. 27.11).

FIGURE 27.11
Distribution of settlements in the Upper Peninsula, in the 1880s. After Ellis (1993).

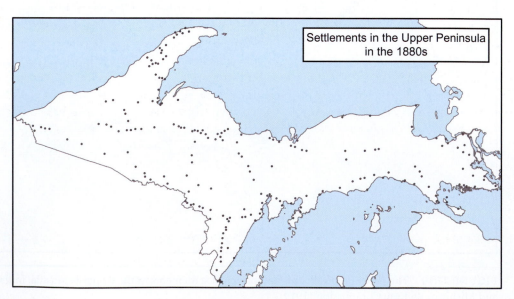

Settlements in the Upper Peninsula in the 1880s

■ The emergence of the fruit industry

The unique environment along the northwestern shore of the Lower Peninsula led to the development of fruit production in the Grand Traverse Bay region, and encouraged its settlement after the Civil War (Chapter 38). Subject to the ameliorating affects of the lake, this narrow strip of land along Lake Michigan lies in a climatic zone where long, cool springs, mild summers and delayed fall cooling provide an ideal setting for the cultivation of grapes and orchard crops.

Lumbering first brought substantial immigration to the Grand Traverse region in the 1850s; agricultural settlement soon followed. The northward expansion of Michigan's railroad network in the 1870s linked the region to larger markets in southern Michigan, and opened the door to commercial production of grain crops. But it was the growth of the Chicago market that encouraged fruit growing. Apple and peach orchards appeared in the 1870s, followed by plums and grapes in the 1880s and, later, cherries. With the decline of lumbering and grain agriculture at the close of the century, fruit growing began to dominate agriculture on Michigan's western shore.

As in other agricultural regions, settlement here remained largely rural. Trade focused on the ports, rail centers and the numerous secondary settlements originally founded for the lumber industry (Haswell and Alanen 1994). Their presence is evident in the distribution of post offices in the later 19th century (Fig. 27.9).

■ Conclusions

Michigan as we know it today is the result of processes largely associated with its settlement in the 19th century. Colonization was complicated by the state's varied environments, and the perceptions of the same by the settlers. Possessing climate and soils deemed suitable for agriculture, southern Michigan attracted frontier farmers and merchants who eventually replicated a regional landscape similar to those they left in the East. Its relatively dense population distribution, permanent settlements and complex transportation infrastructure formed the basis for urban development, diverse economic expansion and industrial growth. Northern Michigan, on the other hand, was a creation of specialized, extractive, industrial activities. Commercial exploitation of lumber, copper, iron and other resources immediately tied settlement to outside markets. Key urban centers, focused on processing and shipping, dominated the built landscape, served by transitory settlements, e.g., mine towns, whose existence depended on resource availability. Consequently the northern Lower Peninsula and the Upper Peninsula were much less densely settled than southern Michigan and took a much different historical trajectory.

It has been nearly a century since Euro-American settlement in Michigan ceased. Pioneer farmers, merchants, loggers, miners and capitalists are all gone. But, in contemplating where we are going, we must understand where we have been and how we came to be where we are. The manner in which Michigan was settled reflects the goals of those who came, as well as the circumstances they encountered in the new country.

Colonization did not take place in a vacuum. All of the immigrants to Michigan were part of a larger world, and their choice to relocate and, subsequently, to pursue particular strategies must also be seen in light of the larger American experience. The nature of settlement in southern Michigan, together with access to capital and raw materials, provided the flexibility that permitted entrepreneurs to participate in the industrial expansion of the last century. The colonization of northern Michigan produced a very different legacy, as the region's fortunes have always depended on its residents' ability to exploit shifting resources. In a sense, it is a frontier that never closed. The nature of each region's development was conditioned by the settlement processes that accompanied its occupation. These patterns remain today and will influence the future. The past is still with us.

■ Literature Cited

Barnett, L. 1999. Mapping Michigan's first land sales. Michigan Out-of-Doors 53(2):44–47.

Bradshaw, J.S. 1968. Grand Rapids furniture beginnings. Michigan History 52:279–298.

Braudel, F. 1984. The Perspective of the World, Vol. 3: Civilization and Capitalism, 15th–18th Century. Harper and Row, New York.

Casagrande, J.B., Thompson, S.I. and P.D. Young. 1964. Colonization as a research frontier: The Ecuadorian case. In: R.A. Manners (ed), Process and Pattern in Culture: Essays in Honor of Julian H. Steward. Aldine, Chicago, IL. pp. 281–325.

Chandler, W.J. 1999. The Antebellum grain trade in Monroe, Michigan. M.A. Thesis. Wayne State University, Detroit.

Chase, L.W. 1936. Michigan's Upper Peninsula. Michigan History 20:313–350.

Clifton, J.A. 1984. The Pokagans, 1683–1983: Catholic Potawatomi Indians of the St. Joseph Valley. University Press of America, Lanham, MD.

Comer, J.C., Albert, D.A., Wells, H.A., Hart, B.L., Raab, J.B., Price, D.L., Kashian, D.M., Comer, R.A. and D.W. Schuen 1995. Michigan=s Native Landscape: As Interpreted from the General Land Office Surveys, 1816–1856. Michigan Department of Natural Resources/Nature Conservancy, Michigan Natural Resources Features Inventory, Lansing, MI.

Cooper, D.G. and F.A. Stilgenbauer. 1934. The urban geography of Saginaw, Michigan. Papers of the Michigan Academy of Science, Arts, and Letters 20:297–311.

Cronon, W. 1991. Nature's Metropolis: Chicago and the Great West. W.W. Norton and Company, New York.

DeForth, P.W. 1970. The spatial evolution of the German-American culture region in Clinton and Ionia Counties, Michigan. M.A. Thesis. Michigan State University, East Lansing.

Dunbar, W.F. 1966. Kalamazoo and How It Grew. Western Michigan University Press, Kalamazoo.

Ellis, D.M. 1993. Michigan Postal History: The Post Offices, 1805–1986. The Depot, Oak Grove, OR.

Farmer, S. 1969. History of Detroit and Wayne County and Early Michigan. Gale Research, Detroit, MI.

Fuller, G.N. 1939. Michigan: A Centennial History of the State and its People. Lewis Publishing Company, Chicago, IL.

Fuller, W.E. 1972. The American Mail: Enlarger of the Common Life. University Of Chicago Press, Chicago.

Hansen, M.L. 1940. The Atlantic Migration, 1607–1860: A History of the Continuing Settlement of the United States. Harvard University Press, Cambridge, MA.

Haswell, S.O. and A.R. Alanen. 1994. A Garden Apart: An Agricultural and Settlement History of Michigan's Sleeping Bear Dunes National Lakeshore Region. Midwest Regional Office, National Park Service and State Historic Preservation Office, Michigan Bureau of History, Lansing, MI.

Hesslink, G.K. 1968. Black Neighbors: Negroes in a Rural Northern Community. Bobbs-Merrill, Indianapolis, IN.

Johnson, H.G. 1972. The Franconian colonies of the Saginaw Valley, Michigan: A study in historical geography. Ph.D. Dissertation, Michigan State University, East Lansing. DAI-B 33/09, ATT 7305410.

Jones, M.A. 1973. The background of emigration from Great Britain in the nineteenth century. Perspectives in American History 7:3–92.

Kestenbaum, J.L. 1981. Out of a Wilderness: An Illustrated History of Greater Lansing. Windsor Publishers, Woodland Hills, CA.

Lewis, K.E. 2002. West to Far Michigan: Settling the Lower Peninsula, 1815–1860. Michigan State University Press, East Lansing.

Lewis, K.E. 2004. Mapping antebellum Euro-American settlement spread in south Lower Michigan. Michigan Historical Review 30:105–134.

Lindquist, C.N. 2004. Adrian: The City that Worked: A History of Adrian Michigan, 1825–2000. Lenewee County Historical Society, Adrian, MI.

Lucas, H.S. 1989. Netherlanders in America. William B Eerdmans, Grand Rapids, MI.

McClurken, J.A. 1986. Ottawa adaptive strategies to Indian removal. Michigan Historical Review 12:29–55.

McLaughlin, M.S. 1995. Ann Arbor, Michigan: A Pictorial History. G. Bradley Publishers, St. Louis, MO.

Maybee, R.H. 1959. Michigan's white pine era, 1840–1900. Michigan History Magazine 43:385–432.

Meints, G.M. 1992. Michigan Railroads and Railroad Companies. Michigan State University Press, East Lansing.

Montfort, M.M. 1990. Ethnic and tribal identity among the Saginaw Chippewa of nineteenth century Michigan. M.A. Thesis. Michigan State University, East Lansing. MAI 28/04, ATT 1340401.

Prucha, F.P. 1984. The Great Father: The United States Government and the American Indians. University of Nebraska Press, Lincoln.

Santer, R.A. 1970. A historical geography of Jackson, Michigan: A study on the changing character of an American city, 1829–1969. Ph.D. Dissertation, Michigan State University, East Lansing. DAI-B 31.05, ATT 7020525.

Smith, P. 1966. As a City upon a Hill: The Town in American History. Alfred A. Knopf, New York.

Stewart, G. 1992. The American Response to Canada since 1776. Michigan State University Press, East Lansing.

Steffen, J.O. 1980. Comparative Frontiers: A Proposal for Studying the American West. University of Oklahoma Press, Norman.

Straw, H.T. 1938. Battle Creek: A study in urban geography, Part II: Origins and development, and functional interpretation. Papers of the Michigan Academy of Science, Arts, and Letters 24:71–92.

Tanner, H.H. (ed.) 1974. Atlas of Great Lakes Indian History. University of Oklahoma Press, Norman.

Wallerstein, I. 1980. The Modern World System II: Mercantilism and the Consolidation of the European World Economy. Academic Press, New York.

White, P. 1886. The iron range of Lake Superior. Michigan Pioneer and Historical Collections 8:145–161.

White, R. 1991. The Middle Ground: Indians, Empires, and Republics in the Great Lakes Region, 1650–1815. Cambridge University Press, Cambridge, UK.

Wolf, E.R. 1982. Europe and the Peoples without History. University of California Press, Berkeley.

Further Readings

Barnett, L. 1987. Building on Michigan's salt springs. Michigan History 71(Jul–Aug):21–23.

Chase, L.W. 1922. Rural Michigan. Macmillan, New York.

Dunbar, W.F. 1969. All Aboard! A History of Railroads in Michigan. William B. Eerdmans, Grand Rapids, MI.

Dunbar, W.F. and G.S. May. 1995. Michigan A History of the Wolverine State. Wm. B. Eerdmans Publishing Company, Grand Rapids, MI.

Fuller, G.N. 1916. Economic and Social Beginnings of Michigan: A Study of the Settlement of the Lower Peninsula during the Territorial Period, 1805–1837. Wynkoop Hallenbeck Crawford, Lansing, MI.

Gray, S.E. 1996. The Yankee West: Community Life on the Michigan Frontier. University of North Carolina Press, Chapel Hill.

May, G.S. and J. Vinyard. 2005. Michigan, the Great Lakes State: An Illustrated History. American Historical Press, Sun Valley, CA.

28

The United States Public Land Survey System

Morris O. Thomas

■ Introduction

Michigan had its cultural landscape altered forever by the implementation of the United States Public Land Survey (USPLS) system, conducted in the 1800's by the General Land Office (GLO). This method of surveying the state was based upon the recommendations a federal committee, set up to determine the best way to survey the land ahead of initial settlement, as well as to facilitate its subsequent sale to the public (Thrower 1961). The chairman of this committee was Thomas Jefferson, who envisioned a system that would divide the land into rectangles based upon a decimal system. The goal of the survey was to accurately describe the size and location of specific rectangular land parcels, so that there would be no irregular pieces of land left behind—a problem common to the metes and bounds land surveys of the time (see FOCUS BOX below).

Before Jefferson could present his plan to Congress, however, he was appointed the United States envoy to France in 1784. Jefferson's recommendations for a grid system remained, but the decimal aspect of it was set aside, in favor of feet and acre units (Linklater 2002). On May 20, 1785, "An Ordinance for Ascertaining the Mode of Disposing of the Lands in the Western Territories" (commonly known as the Land Ordinance of 1785) was passed by the Continental Congress. This act called for the land lying to the NW of the Ohio River, known as the Northwest Territory (Fig. 28.1), to be surveyed in a systematic, rectangular format of land units called townships. Given that the ordinance was allowed to lapse in 1789, the Land Act of 1796 was passed to reestablish most of the essential provisions of the Land Ordinance of 1785, and the survey started (Johnson 1976).

FOCUS BOX: The Metes and Bounds system

Metes and bounds is the name of a method, used for many centuries prior to the 1800's, for describing a parcel of land by starting at a given point and then measuring clockwise around the perimeter of the tract of land. Essentially, the perimeter of a land parcel is described, using local features and compass bearings, but the shape of the land parcel is not restricted, and as a result the parcels were often many-sided, irregularly shaped polygons. The term metes referred to measuring a line between two points at a specific bearing. An example would be "thence northwest for 690 feet." Bounds usually referred to a physical feature that describes the perimeter of the parcel. An example would be "along Mill Creek" or "to the top of the large gray boulder." Together, these terms were used to describe land platted in the United States before 1785. Changes in the locations of the bounds—creeks, trees, bridges and rocks—or the inability to find them at a later point in time, often led to

---

boundary disputes, making this land survey system inferior to the orderly and systematic US Public Land Survey. The field patterns in rural areas that use the metes and bounds method, and the roads that commonly outline their edges, show a distinctly irregular pattern, as opposed to the rectangular shapes of the USPLS (see Figure below).

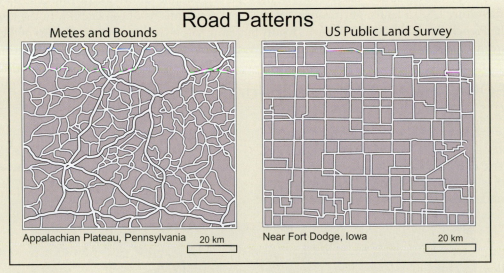

Road Patterns

Metes and Bounds

Appalachian Plateau, Pennsylvania   20 km

US Public Land Survey

Near Fort Dodge, Iowa   20 km

Road networks in areas of the United States, surveyed by the metes and bounds vs USPLS systems.

■ Beginning point of the USPLS

After the established eastern states had relinquished their claims to lands in the Northwest Territory, the survey could begin. The survey of the Northwest Territory (Fig. 28.1) began in 1785, in Ohio, near the present day city of East Liverpool. The existing Ohio-Pennsylvania border served as a north-south meridian, and a base line was extended westward from there. This base line is often referred to as "the Geographers Line." After much of Ohio was surveyed and put up for sale, the survey of other lands, including the new Michigan Territory, began.

The impetus for the survey was many-faceted. First of all, there was pressure for land to be made available for sale to the general public, and lands were needed to compensate war veterans. To meet the latter need, six million acres of military bounty lands were to be set aside, divided equally between the present day states of Illinois, Michigan and Missouri. These lands would be referred to as Military Districts. The Bounty Land Act of January 11, 1812 provided 160 acres (64.7 hectares) of land to each soldier who served in the military during the Revolutionary War, and thus served as an additional inducement to generate enlistments for the impending War of 1812.

The Northwest Territory 1787 - 1803
(The territory north and west of the Ohio River)

FIGURE 28.1 The Northwest Territory from 1787–1803, with contemporary state boundaries shown.

■ Private claims

In Michigan, surveys were needed to document the prior land grants given to settlers and Native Americans by the French and English governments. Most of these tracts were in present day Monroe, Wayne, Macomb, St. Clair and Mackinac Counties. Totaling about 55,000 hectares, these parcels became known as "private claims," to distinguish them from the future USPLS lands. The majority of these private claims had been laid out in the long lot pattern, favored by the French (see FOCUS BOX below). Deputy Surveyor Aaron Greeley completed most of the private claim surveys between 1808 and 1811 and delivered them to Washington, DC.

FOCUS BOX: The French long lot system

Long lots, or ribbon farms, are found on the landscape of North America in areas of French influence. In this system, long, narrow land parcels were laid out, usually perpendicular to, and joining, a major river. This arrangement gave each landowner access to the river, and kept the homesteads close together along it. Parts of the city of Detroit and the Grosse Pointe communities still exhibit this pattern, as do lands along the Raisin River in Monroe County (see Figure below).

Long lots along the River Raisin in Monroe County, and USPLS section lines.

Cession treaties

The next step in the survey process was to acquire title of the lands from the Native Americans; this occurred via cession treaties (Fig. 26.2). Several treaties were negotiated between 1795 and 1842 to transfer the land in the Michigan Territory from the Native Americans to the federal government. The first of these treaties—the Greenville Treaty of 1795—set aside land in a region that began at the River Raisin in Monroe County and extended six miles (9.7 km) inland from Lake Erie, then northward, staying six miles from the Detroit River until Lake St. Clair was reached. It was within this area that the majority of the private claims occurred. The ensuing 1807 Treaty of Detroit greatly expanded the area to be made available to government surveys (Fig. 26.2). This land cession began at Fort Defiance in Ohio, where the Auglaize River meets the Maumee River. From there, a line was extended due north across the Maumee River to a point at the latitude of the outlet of Lake Huron (Port Huron), then northeasterly to White Rock on the shore of Lake Huron (Fig. 28.2). There was subsequent disagreement with the Native Americans, who believed that the line should go from Fort Defiance directly to White Rock. After this matter was resolved, preparations began for the survey of Military District lands within the Michigan Territory.

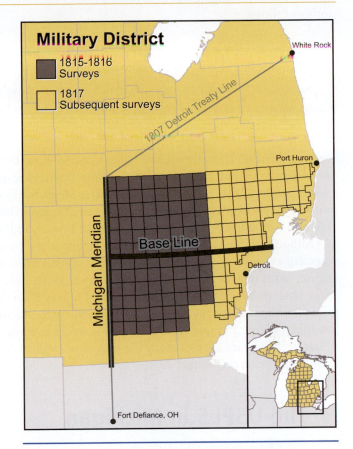

FIGURE 28.2   The 1815–16 Military District surveys, and subsequent township surveys east of the military lands.

The point of beginning for the USPLS in Michigan

Michigan's Public Land Survey actually began at Fort Defiance, Ohio on September 29, 1815. Deputy Surveyors Benjamin Hough and Alexander Holmes, with at least two other crews, began running a meridian northward, following the western boundary of the territory formed by the 1807 Treaty of Detroit (also the western boundary of the Military District). The plan was to survey both lines at the same time. Surveyor contracts stipulated that they would receive $3.00 per mile for the meridian and base line, and $2.50 for each mile of the 92 exterior township boundary lines. The surveys were to be completed by January 1, 1816. The late start created a situation where 1,344 miles (2163 km) of exterior lines needed to be surveyed in about three months (White 1996)!

As D.S. Hough was surveying northward into Michigan Territory, during an unusually cool, wet period, he encountered many lakes and swamps. Therefore, in his letter of October 23, 1815, to Edward Tiffin, the US Surveyor General, he reported that, "The land is for the most part poor and brushy." He also complained about the number of lakes, which were slowing his progress. Deputy Surveyor Thomas Evans also wrote to Tiffin in October of 1815, stating that, "This part of the military district is very swampy and tedious to survey." Deputy Surveyor Alexander Holmes, who was working on a portion of the base line, also wrote to Tiffin. In his letter, dated November 23, 1815, he stated that, "We have suffered almost every hardship and encountered almost every difficulty that could be expected of mortals to endure." From his field notes of November 18, 1815: "We have been wading in ice and water for three days and are completely worn out. Quit and went to Detroit which is situated a little East of South . . ." (Caldwell 2001). Knowing of the these reports and hardships, Tiffin wrote to Josiah Meigs, the General Land Office Commissioner, on November 30, 1815. In this letter, which temporarily stopped the surveys in Michigan and generated a poor impression of Michigan's lands, he described some of the conditions as follows.

- the whole of the Military District set aside will only contain about 1% fit for cultivation;
- the land is low and wet with many marshes;
- many watery, muddy marshes, in which a person could sink 6 to 18 inches;
- the balance of the land is so bad that there would not be more than one acre out of a hundred, if there would be one out of a thousand, that would admit to cultivation.

Surveyor General Tiffin then asked Meigs to advise President James Madison to stop all work on the survey and pay for the work that had been completed (White 1996). In response, Michigan Territorial Governor Lewis Cass wrote a letter in May, 1816, to GLO Commissioner Meigs to try to get the situation changed. In response, the surveys resumed in July of 1816, from the Military District's eastern boundary (the western boundaries of Livonia, Farmington Hills and Romulus) to Lake St. Clair and Lake Erie, excluding the private claims (Fig. 28.2).

Although Tiffin's letter to the President stopped the surveys for only a few months, its impact was felt for many years. For example, the two-million acres (809,000 hectares) that had originally been set aside in Michigan as Military District lands were never allocated to soldiers. Instead, these allocations were transferred to the Missouri Territory. Some observers feel that the removal of the Military District from Michigan actually may have reduced the activities of land speculators in the early days of settlement. Michigan also gained a reputation as a place of swampy and low quality land. Pioneer settlers tended to avoid the interior areas of the state, instead choosing land near the shores of the Great Lakes, or along the major river valleys. These circumstances intertwined to slow the general settlement of the state (Chapter 27).

The USPLS in Michigan

The USPLS is based upon the demarcation of a base line (X-axis) and a meridian (Y-axis), intersecting at right angles. This intersection is known as "the initial point" for referencing future township locations. A deputy surveyor would then lay out rectangularly shaped townships at six-mile intervals to the east, west, north and south of the initial point (Fig. 28.3). Townships (or Towns or Tiers) (T) would be measured north (N) or south (S) from the base line. Ranges(R) would be measured east (E) or west (W) of the meridian. Contracts would then be let to further subdivide the townships into 36, one square mile (259 hectare) parcels, called sections.

The Michigan Meridian

Deputy Surveyors Benjamin Hough, Alexander Holmes and their crews surveyed the Michigan Meridian north, from Fort Defiance, Ohio, in October of 1815. They stopped at a location 4 km north of the city of Hudson, and there they established the SW corner of the Military District. Hough then began to survey the southern boundary of the Military District, surveying the exterior lines of T6S, R1E. Thus, Rollin Township, Lenawee County, was the first USPLS township to be surveyed in Michigan Territory.

The Michigan Meridian/Indian territory boundary line was continued north, until Holmes encountered the Portage River (Sec. 7, T2S, R1E), 4.4 km north of present day Interstate Hwy. 94, or about 4.4 km south of the proposed initial point with the base line. The river was very deep, 40 m wide, and had a strong current. He then went east, north and west, around the township, and brought the meridian line down from the north, to the river. The meridian was later continued north, and an initial point was set for the base line on October, 1815 (Berry 1990). At least 12 other deputy surveyors continued the meridian northward, until it reached the Straits of Mackinac in 1840. Deputy Surveyor William A. Burt, assisted by John Mullet, surveyed the line across the water, using trigonometric techniques. Burt completed the meridian to the banks of St. Mary's River on August 25, 1840 (Jamison 1958). Although the original meridian was surveyed north from Fort Defiance, Ohio, the Michigan Meridian actually begins at the east-west trending Fulton Line (1805 Michigan Territory Line;

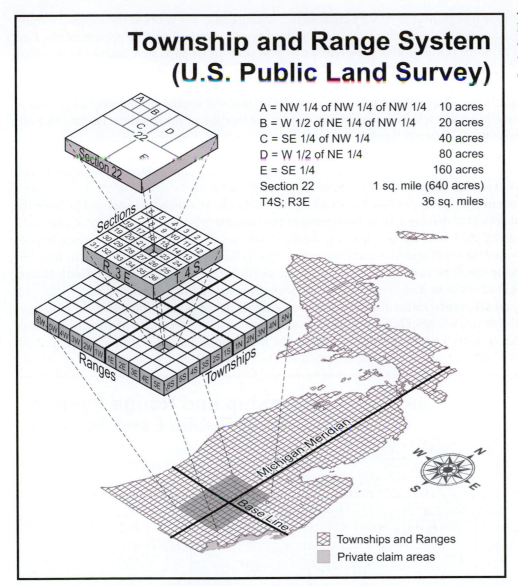

FIGURE 28.3 Examples of how the USPLS system works, for some property descriptions in Michigan.

Fig. 1.3). This unmarked location is 10.0 km south of the present day OH/MI border, in Fulton County, Ohio. The Michigan Meridian extends north from there for about 542 km, at or near longitude 84° 21' 36" W. It now forms the boundaries between the counties of Lenawee and Hillsdale, Clinton and Shiawassee, Gratiot and Saginaw, Roscommon and Ogemaw, Crawford and Oscoda, and Otsego and Montmorency. It also serves as the line of reference for several Ohio townships in Fulton, Wood and Lucas Counties, or the former "Toledo Strip" (Chapter 1).

■ The Base Line

The Michigan base line, which extends from Lake St. Clair across to Lake Michigan for about 278 kms, is actually composed of two distinct segments. The original plan was to run the base line from Lake St. Clair (eight miles, 12.9 kms) north of Detroit (currently Eight Mile Road) west, to intersect the Michigan Meridian. Due to bad weather conditions and uncertainty with the Native American population, however, this plan was never implemented. A subsequent plan to extend the base line east, from the initial point on the meridian, was also not completed.

Measurement of the east base line proved to be very challenging, because of many lakes in the rough, swampy, interlobate topography (Plates 8, 11). In all, five different deputy surveyors worked on this portion of the base line between 1815 and 1824. Some portions were surveyed east to west while other parts were laid out west to east. The survey field notes on the base line begin November 14, 1815, at the corners of R6 and 7E, 6.4 km east of Whitmore Lake (Dixboro Road). Alexander Holmes surveyed the base line eastward for 44 km, stopping just west of present day Woodward Avenue, quitting on November 18, 1815, due to the ice and wet conditions; he went to Detroit to recuperate. Deputy Surveyor Joseph Fletcher was assigned to run the last portion of the base line. He started at the west boundary of R9E (present day Haggerty Road), overlapping a portion of the line run by Holmes, crossed over some private claims, and finally reached the shore of Lake St. Clair at present day Grosse Pointe Shores on September 26, 1816 (White 1996). Because of deficiencies in measurement of this 122 km segment, Deputy Surveyor Joseph Wampler was contracted to resurvey the entire line in 1824.

The survey of the western portion of the base line (west of the Michigan Meridian) was delayed because the Native Americans had not yet ceded that land. With the signing of the Chicago Treaty in 1821 (Fig. 26.2), however, surveying this 156 km western portion of the base line was started in January of 1824 by Joseph Wampler. Deputy Surveyor John Mullet surveyed the middle portion and Deputy Surveyor William Brookfield completed the base line on May 24, 1827, when he reached the Lake Michigan shore at the north boundary of present day South Haven. The base line, at or near 42° 25' 28"N latitude, serves as the boundary between several counties (Plate 2).

The presence of two initial points, rather than the customary single initial point, where the two base lines meet the Michigan Meridian, makes Michigan unique. The east base line intersects the Michigan Meridian north of the west base line, creating a jog that that shows up on the Ingham and Jackson County line (Fig. 28.4).

FIGURE 28.4   The jog in the Michigan Meridian and base line.

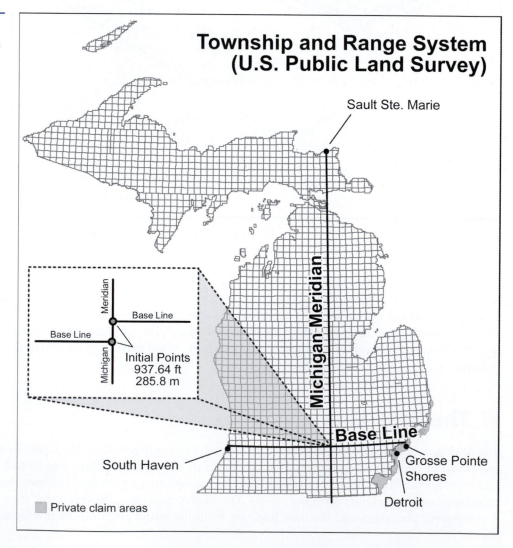

FIGURE 28.5 Monuments at Michigan's (A) north and (B) south initial points, set in 1824 and 1815, respectively. Photos by A. Schultz and B. Thomas.

Benjamin Hough is believed to have set the first initial point on the meridian in 1815. An 1824 resurvey of the east base line by Wampler led to the setting of the second initial point, 285.8 m north of the first initial point (White 1996). The jog does not affect the identification of property, because the south initial point references land to the west of the meridian and the north initial point references the land to the east of the meridian. Each of these initial points is now well marked by a large concrete platform (Fig. 28.5). The State of Michigan owns the ~35 hectares of land that surround the initial points. Although a plan once existed to create a Meridian-Baseline State Park, to recognize the importance of these two monuments, the plan has been indefinitely suspended.

USPLS descriptions

The major goal of the US Public Land Survey System was to define and describe the locations of land parcels, so that they could be accurately located on the ground (Fig. 28.3). USPLS property descriptions can be thought of as addresses for a land parcel, much like a house address. For example, the southern and eastern boundaries of T19N, R15W (Sheridan Township) is uniquely located 108 miles north of the base line and 84 miles west of the Michigan Meridian, in Mason County. It is the 19th Township north of the base line, and the 15th Township west of the Michigan Meridian.

Each township is further divided into 36 sections, each of which is approximately one mile on a side, and approximately 640 acres (259 hectares) in area. The Land Act of 1796 established the section numbering system, so that section number one would be in the NE corner of each township, proceeding west to the NW corner—section number six (Johnson 1976; Fig. 28.3). The sequence continues until concluding with number 36 in the SE corner of the township. Each section can further be subdivided into half sections (320 acres, 129 hectares) and quarter sections (160 acres, 65 hectares). Each half and quarter section can be further divided into parcels of 80, 40 and 10 acres (Fig. 28.3).

The legal description of a particular land parcel is written with the smallest parcel listed first. For example the NW¼ of Section 14, T19N, R15W, would be a quarter section (160-acre) parcel located in Sheridan Township of Mason County. No other parcel of land in the entire state of Michigan has that same legal description. As the size of the land parcels gets smaller, the length and complexity of the legal descriptions increases, so that accuracy is maintained. Lots in urban and suburban subdivisions are also tied to the USPLS. A typical urban parcel may be written as Lot 227, Holly Park, it being a part of the SW¼ of section 19, T4N, R2W.

This system of land description, which may seem daunting at first, is very logical and systematic in locating parcels of land. All land transactions in Michigan, except those in the private claim areas, are referenced to the base line and Michigan Meridian (Fig. 28.6).

Convergence and correction

Because of the curvature of the earth's surface, surveying N-S parallel lines for any distance will result in their subsequent convergence. For example, at 42°N latitude, the northern boundary of a township would be ~13 m shorter than the southern boundary (Moffit and Bouchard 1965). To minimize this problem, correction lines were

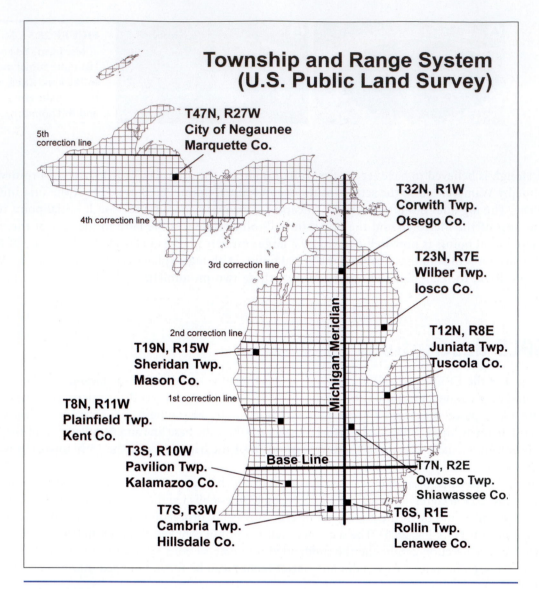

FIGURE 28.6   The US Public Land Survey System in Michigan, showing selected townships mentioned in the text, and correction lines.

set up at intervals of 60 miles (96.5 km), or every 10 townships (Fig. 28.6). Michigan is unique in this regard because, in most states surveyed later, the correction lines are only 24 miles (4 townships) apart. The presence of convergence can readily be seen along the east side of the Michigan Meridian, starting at the 3rd Township north of the base line, and progressing northerly from there. Here, sections 6, 7, 18, 19, 30 and 31 are greatly reduced in size, and are sometimes even missing (Fig. 28.7). Along the 2nd correction line between Manistee and Mason Counties, the section and range lines are also slightly offset (Fig. 28.8), due to convergence issues.

Surveyors were instructed to begin the survey of the interior section lines in the SE corner of each township, allowing all the errors of measurement due to convergence to accumulate along the northern and western boundaries of each township. Therefore sections 1–6 along the north line of a township, and sections 7, 18, 19, 30 and 31 along the western side of a township, are usually larger or smaller, respectively, than the prescribed 640 acres. They are referred to as fractional sections. Because the survey lines were run using a magnetic compass, the variance between true north and magnetic north, which in Michigan is 2–8°, had to be accurately calculated, and also introduced some potential error into the surveys.

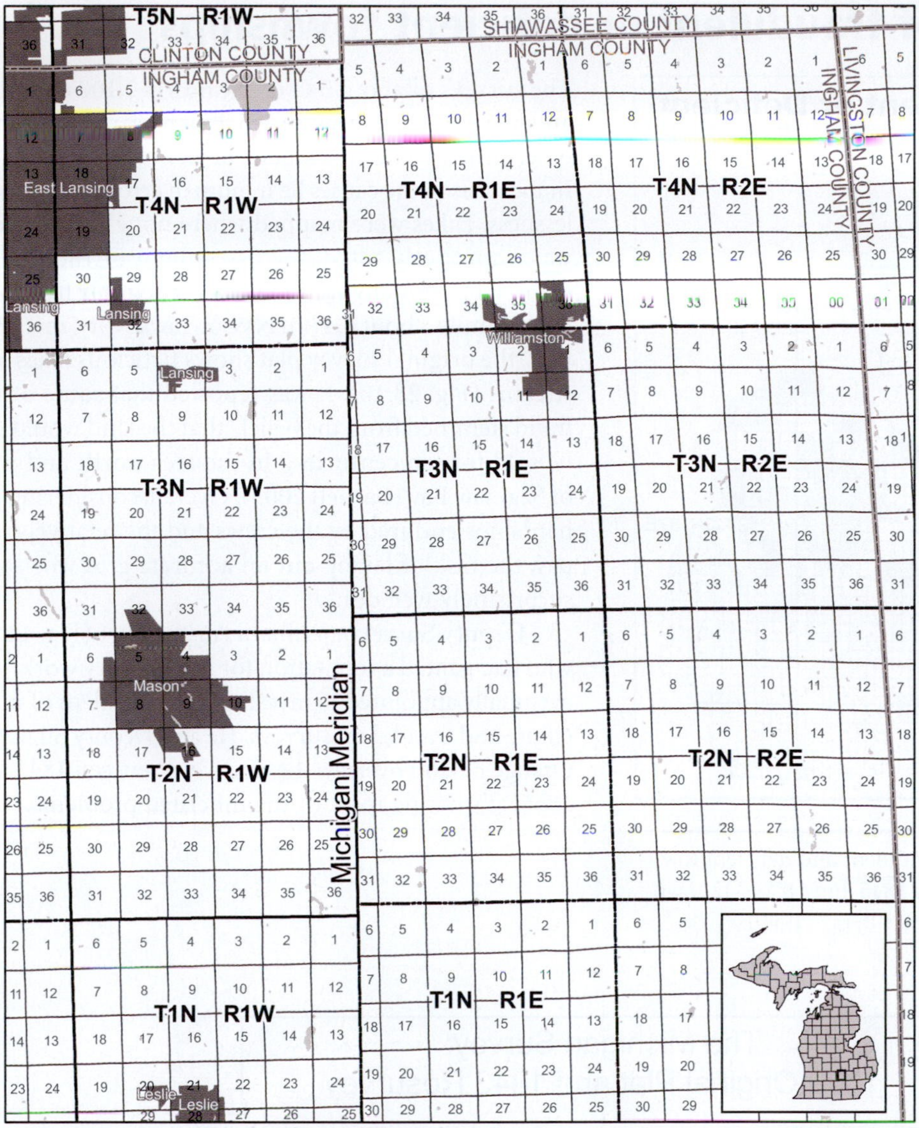

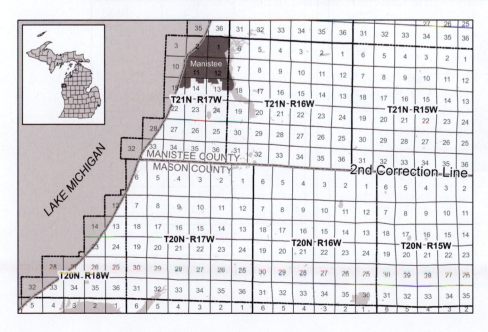

FIGURE 28.7
Convergence along the Michigan Meridian. Several sections are absent or greatly reduced in size along the east side of the Michigan Meridian, in Ingham County.

FIGURE 28.8 Offsets of range lines, along the 2nd correction line between Mason and Manistee Counties. The sections south of the correction line are larger than the prescribed 640 acres in size, because they occur along the northern boundary of a township.

■ Re-surveys of fraudulent or deficient townships

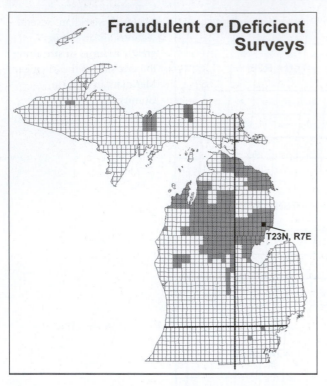

The surveys of about 342 of the nearly 2,100 complete and partial townships in Michigan were eventually determined to be fraudulent or deficient (Fig. 28.9). In most cases, the causes lie in human error and/or carelessness. Lakes were mapped where none existed, land was improperly rated, the assessment of the timber incorrect, and many section lines were simply fictitious. For example, about 6.4 km NW of Tawas City, in T23N, R7E, the original survey plat shows ficticious lakes and streams (Fig. 28.10). It was reported that some of the fraud stemmed from the belief "that the land would not be sold for ten centuries," in the area north and west of Saginaw Bay (Barnett 2003). Overall, considering the hardships endured by the crews and the relatively low pay, the task of laying out an accurate grid work was surprisingly well done.

Deputy Surveyor William Austin Burt (Fig. 11.1), who had gained a reputation for high quality work, was eventually appointed to investigate the problem of inaccurate and fraudulent surveys. He and Deputy Surveyor Orange Risdon oversaw the resurveys between 1845 and 1856, alleviating most of the inherited problems.

FIGURE 28.9 Locations of fraudulent and deficient township surveys. As a result, between 1845 and 1856, 342 townships needed to be resurveyed. After Berry (1990).

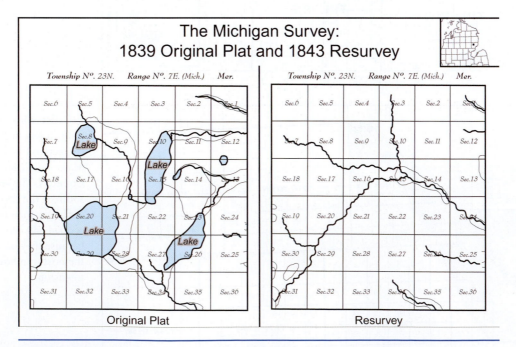

FIGURE 28.10 Color reproduction of an original fraudulent plat, and the resurvey plat, of T23N, R7E. Source: MSPS Foundation.

Surveyors' field notes

The deputy surveyors wrote detailed field notes of their observations along each township and section line. These notes, accompanied by a plat (map) of each township, were sent to the Surveyor General's Office for archiving. Today, these notes and maps represent tremendous sources of information about the landscapes that were observed as the surveys progressed across Michigan. The field notes also represent a history of the surveyors' activities in the field, as they located the survey lines and described certain physical and cultural features.

A typical survey crew included the deputy surveyor, his assistant, two chainmen, two axe men and sometimes one or two packers. Using a magnetic compass, a 66-foot (20 meter) long Gunter chain and a field note book (Fig. 28.11) they would walk along each section line in their contract area. To complete a survey of all the section lines in a township could take from 14 to 20 days. Initially, the deputy surveyor was to keep a record of the compass variation from magnetic north, the distance and direction between section corners, the type of natural vegetation, topographic features, rivers and lakes and rate the soil. As the surveys progressed, a more extensive list of notable features was developed (Moffit and Bouchard 1965). The surveyor's notebook and a sketch map are the official record of the lands surveyed by the GLO. To read from these notebooks, or their transcribed form, allows a person to visualize the state as it was during this era. Each surveyor had their own particular method of fulfilling the requirements. Some provided only the bare minimum of information, while others provided great detail. Copies of the field notes are available for viewing, free of charge, on microfiche at the State of Michigan Archives, Lansing.

Of particular interest are the tidbits and personal viewpoints that the deputy surveyors included in the notes. For example, an exasperated deputy surveyor wrote that the "land miserable not fit for even wolves to inhabit." This description was written in November of 1823, of a part of T7N, R2E, located about eight km NW of Owosso. In the same township, he noted a healthy White Oak tree that was 50 links (10 m) in diameter. In May of 1825, while working near a lake in T7S, R3W, a deputy surveyor encountered a large bear and her cubs. He set fire to the grass and weeds and chased the mother away, so they could get the cubs for supper (Caldwell 2001). This lake, located in Hillsdale County, is today named Cub Lake. Near the eastern boundary of section 25, T12N, R8E, about 9.7 km NE of Vassar, the soil is described as being "a rich black and chocolate colored sand and gravelly loam." The notes also indicate an "Indian trail E&W" on the line between sections 10 and 11 of the same township (Survey Notes, 6560). Below is an account along a section line in T3S, R10W, east of Portage in Kalamazoo County, written by Robert Clark Jr., in December, 1826 (Fig. 28.12).

North	Between sections 2 and 3	
24.00 chains	Leave swamp	
40.00 chains	¼ section post	
	White Oak	13 links diameter, at N62W, 39 links
	White Oak	16 links diameter, at N75E, 14_ links
42.97 chains	White Oak	16 links diameter
44.00 chains	Marsh	
53.00 chains	Leave marsh	
61.50 chains	Marsh	
67.00 chains	Leave marsh	
75 50 chains	Marsh	
81.25 chains	Leave marsh	
81.60 chains	Intersect North boundary	133 links east of stake
	Yellow oak	10 links diameter, S63_W, 56 links
	Yellow oak	10 links diameter, N44E, 60 links
	Upland rolling, barren, thin soil	
	Timber Oak	Undergrowth vines etc.
	December 27	Very cold, 3 men disabled by frozen feet

(Note: 1 chain = 66 feet; 80 chains = 1 mile; 100 links = 1 chain; 1 link = 7.92 inches.)

FIGURE 28.11 A Gunter chain, field notebook and magnetic compass—equipment commonly used by the GLO Deputy Surveyors. Courtesy of Museum of Surveying, Lansing, MI. Photo by M. Thomas.

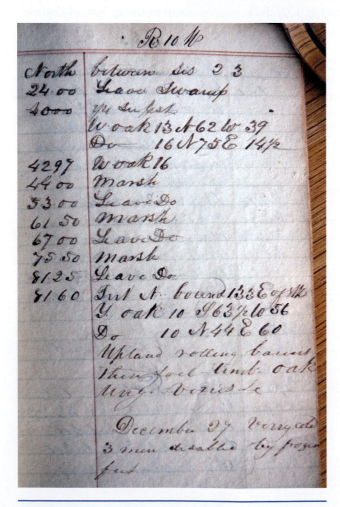

FIGURE 28.12 Field notes written by D.S. Robert Clark Jr., in December, 1826. Courtesy of the Archives of Michigan, Lansing, MI. Photo by M. Thomas.

Clark died in 1837, while surveying a township line just north of Grand Rapids in T8N, R11W (Caldwell 2001). On June 17, 1850, deputy surveyor William Burt (son of William Austin Burt) described a pine tree that was 8 inches (20 cm) in diameter on the line between sections 15 and 16, T32N, R1W (Survey Notes, 6563). Located about 17.7 km east of Vanderbilt, this red pine tree is presently about 76 cm in diameter.

Near present day Negaunee, Deputy Surveyor William A. Burt made a very important discovery on September 19, 1844. As he and his crew were surveying along the east side of Section 1, T47N, R27W, just south of Teal Lake, he noticed that the compass needle was behaving erratically. It was here that iron ore deposits were first found in Michigan (Burt 1994; Chapter 11). Shortly thereafter, geologic data, e.g., elevations and rock types, were also added to list of information required in the survey notes. This addition was largely due to the presence of the new State Geologist Douglas Houghton (Fig. 2.1), who worked with Burt on the surveys for a time in the western part of the Upper Peninsula. Burt and Houghton produced very detailed survey notes and township plats. It was during these surveys, in the fall of 1844, that Douglas Houghton drowned in Lake Superior, cutting short his promising career (Burt 1994).

FIGURE 28.13 The solar compass, invented by William Austin Burt to compensate for metallic interference in the iron ore-bearing rocks of the Upper Peninsula (Chapter 11). It was very accurate when used during the daylight hours. Courtesy of Museum of Surveying, Lansing, MI. Photo by M. Thomas.

■ William Austin Burt and the solar compass

William Austin Burt (Fig. 11.1), a native of Macomb County, found that, while surveying land that contained iron ore, magnetic compasses were useless. He proceeded to work on an attachment that would overcome this problem, and eventually invented a solar compass that was patented in 1836 (Fig. 28.13). Burt used this invention to create very high quality surveys, especially in the Upper Peninsula. However, it was not until 1841 that it was officially approved by the GLO. His solar compass gained widespread use and was subsequently copied by others (Burt 1985).

■ Legacy of the Public Land Survey system

The impacts of the GLO surveys are present on the Michigan landscape in several ways. The 66 foot long Gunter chain also played a major role, because the early rights-of-way were 33 feet on each side of the centerline of most rural roads. In towns and cities, the Gunter chain was used to create lot lines. As a result, many of these early lots were 33 feet by 132 feet, or 66 feet by 132 feet on a side.

The survey also influenced the political geography of Michigan. In the vast majority of cases, county boundaries follow the survey township lines, reinforcing the grid pattern. Michigan's 1,242 political townships are also based upon survey lines. Near rapidly expanding urban areas are Charter Townships, such as Meridian Charter Township in Ingham County or Shelby Charter Township in Macomb County, whereas in more rural areas General Law Townships are more common, e.g., Sheridan Township in Mason County. In each case, these townships function as important units of local government. In very sparsely populated areas, one or more survey townships were often combined to create a single General Law Township, e.g., Forsyth Township in Marquette County is composed of five survey townships. McMillan Township, in Luce County, has a land area of 1533 km², making it approximately equal to 16 survey townships and rendering it the largest township in Michigan. In southeastern Michigan, the boundaries of cities such as Livonia, Warren, Farmington Hills, Sterling Heights and Romulus are based upon a single USPLS township. Finally, as a provision of the Ordinance of 1785, the money generated from sale of Section 16 in each township throughout the state went into a fund to support public education. Even today, section 16 is often referred to as the "School Section" and often an old, one-room schoolhouse can still be seen there, or nearby.

The map of Michigan also shows the survey's legacy in the locations and names of streets and roads. In rural areas, fields and roads follow rectangular patterns, usually paralleling sections lines. Eight Mile Road and many other "mile" road names are a result of roads built on the rights-of-way along section lines. The predominant E-W or N-S orientation of roads results from their having been built along the survey grid lines (although in areas where the private claim surveys (long lots) exist, many roads and streets are laid out perpendicular to major rivers). Woodward Avenue and many other streets in Detroit and the Grosse Pointe area are referenced to the Detroit River. Kelly Road, on the east side of Detroit, functions as the dividing line between the private claims surveys and the

FIGURE 28.14   A monument cover and new monument section corner cap, typical of roadway intersections in Michigan. Photos by M. Thomas and J. Thomas.

USPLS. In Monroe County, roads such as Ida Maybee and Baldwin are based upon long lots referenced to the River Raisin (see FOCUS BOX on page 432). In St Ignace, the streets and property lines also show a distinct long lot orientation, left over from the French occupation of the land around the Straits of Mackinac.

Lakes such as Burt, Mullet, Higgins, Houghton, Hubbard and Wampler honor some of the GLO Deputy Surveyors. Hubbard Hall, the tallest building on the campus of Michigan State University, is named after Bela Hubbard, a GLO Deputy Surveyor. Names such as Meridian Road, Townline Road, Base Line Road, Quarterline Road, School Section Lake, Baseline Middle School and Lake Six further reinforce the presence of the survey legacy on the landscape.

The survey also had another type of impact on most of the inland lakes of Michigan. When the survey lines encountered lakes, the deputy surveyors were to make a judgment as to whether or not the lake was to be "meandered." The process of meandering called for measuring around the perimeter of a lake in a series of short straight lines, creating subdivisions known as government lots inside of the affected section or sections. At first, lakes that were judged to be more than 10 km in circumference were to be meandered. Later, the regulations changed the size to 25 acres (10 hectares; Berry 1990). Lakes that have been meandered are generally considered public water and the adjacent landowners do not control the water surface. Lakes that are not meandered are usually considered private property; the owner pays taxes on the land under and surrounding the lake, and thereby controls access to the water.

The Land Act of 1796 established the principle that, "The original surveys are without error, in that the distances and courses recited in the field notes and noted on the plat are the 'true distances,' regardless of what the modern surveyor re-measures with modern equipment" (Robillard et al. 2006). It also stipulated that after all corners, posts and distances were certified by the GLO, they could never be changed. Because of their importance to modern property lines, the State of Michigan passed Public Act 345 in 1990 to re-monument all sections corners and quarter posts. An eight-inch diameter metal monument cover marks section corners at road intersections (Fig. 28.14A); beneath the cover rests the actual section corner marker (Fig. 28.14B).

Conclusions

In the years between 1815 and 1854, the Deputy Surveyors of the GLO surveyed, and hence, transformed, the state of Michigan forever. Using a compass to show direction and the Gunter Chain to measure distances, the surveyors walked along each section and township line in the state, recording measurements and observations in small notebooks. This difficult task, undertaken in all kinds of weather and while enduring uncalculable hardships, measured the land and divided it into townships and sections. Their work impacts our lives every day; the road patterns, real estate transactions and place names of today are a reminder of the importance of the US Public Land Survey in Michigan.

Literature Cited

Barnett, L. 2003. Getting Southern Michigan into line. Michigan History 87(Jan–Feb):20–27.

Berry, R.M. 1990. Special Instructions to Deputy Surveyors in Michigan 1808–1854. Michigan Museum of Surveying. Lansing, MI.

Burt, J.S. 1994. Boys Look Around and See What You Can Find. Michigan History 78(Nov–Dec):10–15

Burt, J.S. 1985. They Left Their Mark. Landmark Enterprises, Rancho Cordova, CA.

Caldwell, N.C. 2001. Surveyors of the Public Lands in Michigan 1808–2000. Data Reproductions Corporation, Auburn Hills, MI.

Jamison, K. 1958. The Survey of the Public Lands in Michigan. Michigan History 42(Mar–Apr):197–214.

Johnson, H.B. 1976. Order Upon the Land. Oxford University Press, London.

Linklater, A. 2002. Measuring America: How an Untamed Wilderness Shaped the United States and Fulfilled the Promise of Democracy. Walker, New York.

Moffitt, F.H. and H. Bouchard. 1965. Surveying. International Textbook Company, New York.

Robillard, W.G., Wilson, D.A. and C.M. Brown. 2006. Evidence and procedure for boundary location. Wiley and Sons, New York.

Transcripts of Survey Notes. T12N; R8E. DNR. RG 89–74. Vol. 67. 6560.

Transcripts of Survey Notes. T32N; R1W. DNR. RG 89–74. Vol. 73. 6563.

White, C.A. 1996. Initial Points of the Rectangular Survey System. The Publishing House, Westminster, CO.

Further Readings

Barnett, L. 1982. U.P. Surveyors. Michigan History 66(Sep/Oct):24–31.

Brown, A.S. 1990. Mr. Tiffin's surveyors come to Michigan. Michigan History 74(Sep/Oct):32–36.

Cumming, J. 1986 Michigan for Sale. Michigan History 79(Nov/Dec):12–15.

Jacobson, D. 1988. The Michigan Meridian and base line: A teaching formulation for secondary school. Journal of Geography 87:131–140.

Pearce, M.W. 2004. The holes in the grid: Reservation surveys in Lower Michigan. Michigan Historical Review 30:135–166.

White, C.A. 1982 A History of the Rectangular Survey System. US Government Printing Office, Washington, DC.

29

Land-Use and Land-Cover

Bill Welsh, Daniel Brown and Joe Messina

■ Introduction

Land-use (LU) is defined as the human activity taking place on the land and the (usually multiple) ways in which human society or individuals interact with a given piece of land. *Land-cover* (LC) is defined as the biological and physical (biophysical) characteristics of the land that affect the functioning of its hydrological (water), ecological (life) and meteorological (atmosphere) processes (Table 29.1; Fig. 29.1; Plate 13). In this chapter, we describe Michigan's patterns of land-use and land-cover (LULC), and discuss (1) how they have changed over the past two centuries, (2) what factors have influenced those patterns and changes and (3) how geographers study them. Although one study may focus more on the biophysical aspects of the landscape, and another on the human, the study of LULC falls squarely within the geographic tradition of studying the interactions between humans and the environment. Geographers seek to understand the spatial patterns of human activity and how human activity interacts with,

FIGURE 29.1 Land-cover in the NW Lower Peninsula, in 2001. Source: State of Michigan (2005).

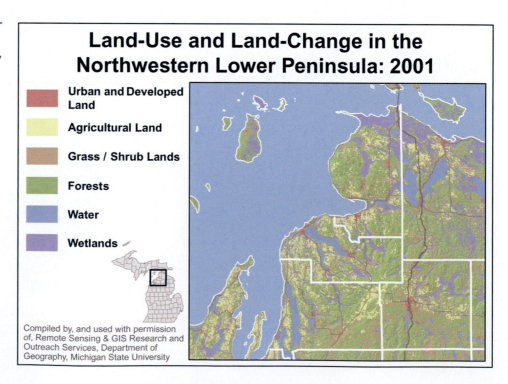

Land-Use and Land-Change in the Northwestern Lower Peninsula: 2001

- Urban and Developed Land
- Agricultural Land
- Grass / Shrub Lands
- Forests
- Water
- Wetlands

Compiled by, and used with permission of, Remote Sensing & GIS Research and Outreach Services, Department of Geography, Michigan State University

TABLE 29.1   Comparisons of the concepts of land-use and land-cover[1]

	Example 1	Example 2	Example 3
Land-Use	City park	Central business district	Agriculture
Land-Cover	Woodlands and lawns	Rooftops and paved surfaces	Cropland

1. *Land-use* implies human intention with regard to *Land-cover*, which refers to the biological and physical properties of the land surface. Geographers and other scientists often must assign land-use classifications when drafting a map. In contrast, measurements of the surface properties of the land-cover can be obtained using instruments such as remote sensing devices.

i.e., is affected by and affects, spatial patterns of natural resources and ecosystem functions. The study of these patterns is aided by the availability of remote sensing aircraft and satellites, and by geographic information systems (GIS), computerized tools for managing, visualizing and analyzing spatial patterns and processes. We describe these geospatial technologies in more detail below.

■ Geospatial technologies used to study LULC

Michigan has a long history of LULC mapping, but most of the older survey methods have long since been abandoned as too costly and time consuming. For example, historic LULC maps (ca. 1800) of Michigan are available from the Michigan Center for Geographic Information (Fig 29.2). More recently, post 1977, data on LULC patterns have been estimated using modern mapping techniques. The term *estimated* is used on purpose, because, in spite of the best scientific efforts and most sophisticated technologies, maps are never completely accurate (Monmonier 1991, Space Imaging Solutions 2001). In this section, we provide an overview of the modern technologies that make the measurement and monitoring of land-use and land-cover status/change possible, and introduce the wide range of national, state, regional and local mapping programs.

The map as model of reality

A map is a scale model of reality, an abstraction that represents only selected features. Maps are, therefore, simplifications of what we see. They are useful because they are abstract models of reality. LULC maps reduce the complexity of the real world, thereby allowing us to identify and understand patterns that are otherwise difficult or impossible to detect (Fig. 29.1). Although a map is a model of a selected geographic reality, scientists involved in LULC analyses extend and expand the concept of the model by constructing and utilizing specialized computer programs that attempt to account for the various factors that produce landscape changes, and allow for the simulation of geographic processes and patterns.

Modern geospatial technologies have been developed and implemented to a considerable degree in the past two decades, and are now widely used. Consider Google Earth™, which allows anyone with a computer and internet access to easily create detailed 3D images/maps of practically anywhere on Earth. This innovation is based on the same technologies that allow geographers and other scientists to map, monitor, model and otherwise study land-use and land-cover change. When you use Google Earth™ to draw a map, a mosaic of remotely-sensed images is displayed (draped) over a 3D elevation (altitude) model, along with overlays of map symbols representing geographic features, such as road networks and points for landmarks. All of these map data are geo-referenced; that is, they are imprinted with a geographic coordinate referencing system, e.g., latitude-longitude.

Geographic information systems

Most things that geographers study, including LULC, have a spatial or geographic dimension. Traditionally, *paper* maps have been used to compile, display and analyze spatial data. But by *digitally* encoding the map features in a geographic information system (GIS), however, we can adjust spatial scales and make complex measurements

FIGURE 29.2 Land-cover of Ingham County in 1800, compared to MIRIS 1978 land-cover. Source: Michigan Center of Geographic Information, Lansing, MI.

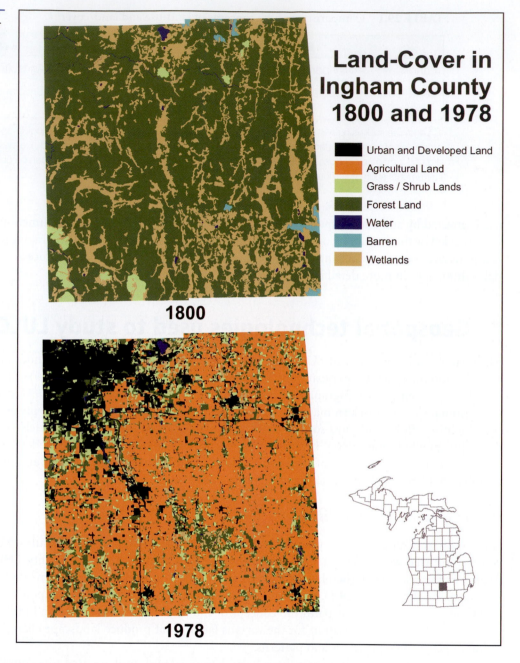

of variables much more easily and accurately. A GIS is a computer software and hardware system designed to capture, store, manipulate, analyze, visualize, display and output spatial (map) data and information. The most important and defining characteristic of a GIS is the use of spatial or geographic coordinate data as a unifying variable and concept. Mapped features stored in a GIS database can be encoded as points, lines and/or polygons, or as cells (also called pixels). It is the common spatial coordinate system for all variables in a GIS that allows us to iteratively recombine, re-scale, analyze and display the data, in order to produce more powerful information (which is not the same as data!).

Acquisition of LULC imagery and data

Given the importance of understanding and quantifying LULC for economic and environmental management purposes, the State of Michigan mandates the re-mapping of the state every five years. Likewise, a variety of aerial photography-based mapping programs have been implemented by the US Government, most commonly by the US Geological Survey. Traditional, film-emulsion-based, aerial photography is becoming less common, due to the maturation of digital remote sensing systems. Digital sensors can be mounted on either aircraft or spacecraft, i.e., satellite, platforms. In general, sensors onboard aircraft provide the greatest level of spatial detail of the landscape, as well as allowing the most flexibility in terms of timing of image acquisition. Satellite-based sensors, e.g., Landsat, generally provide less spatial detail but can image (view) a much greater area. Extensive use has been made of Landsat imagery in Michigan, such as by the Integrated Forest Monitoring Assessment and Prescription (IFMAP) project (Space Imaging Solutions 2001). Michigan State University is the home of Landsat.org, a clearinghouse where Landsat imagery are archived and disseminated. Aerial photography, and now aircraft-based, digital frame cameras, continue to play major roles in mapping and monitoring LULC change in Michigan (see FOCUS BOX below). Lastly, during the summer of 2005, a new set of aerial photography for the entire state of Michigan was collected, using an airborne digital color infrared scanner at one-meter spatial resolution (Jenson 2007).

Remote sensing in LULC mapping and monitoring

Remote sensing is a method of measuring something without being in direct contact with the target being investigated; it involves the detection and recording of electromagnetic radiation (EMR) emitted from, or reflected off, that object. An example of a remote sensing device is human vision, which detects visible light reflected off the various surfaces. The characteristics of the EMR absorbed, reflected or emitted by a surface often provide tell-tale information about the biophysical nature of the material, and can allow us to discriminate one type of surface from another.

A remote sensing system consists of sensors, which measure and record the EMR coming off the surfaces being monitored, and the platform, which carries the sensors. A remote sensing system records images, and may be either analogue (traditional film cameras) or digital. Remote sensing is a critical technology for LULC research. Remotely sensed images can capture the state of the LC of an area in a synoptic ("all-at-once") manner, with the data then converted to a map. By repeatedly imaging the landscape over time, we can create a time-series of land-use/land-cover maps. This, in turn, allows us to study change and predict the future state of the landscape, typically by using spatial models. Without remote sensing, the scientific study of LULC would be impractical to impossible.

FOCUS BOX: National LULC mapping programs

A number of national mapping programs exist, providing valuable data for students and researchers interested in LULC change and monitoring (Jensen 2007). The National High Altitude Photography (NHAP) and National Aerial Photography Program (NAPP) are fundamental sources of moderate resolution (approximately 1:50,000) black and white or color IR imagery. NHAP and NAPP data are used to compile and update US Geological Survey (USGS) topographic maps. Digital Orthophotograph quadrangles (DOQs) are produced from NAPP photography by the USGS, and are commonly used by Google Earth™. Prior to the recent NAPP data collection effort, the previous Michigan statewide data collection occurred in 1998–99, for color infrared DOQs. The US Department of Agriculture Photography program provides another useful source of imagery for LULC change analyses, and is commonly seen as the base image in county-scale soil surveys. Archival imagery from various sources, public and private, are very useful for image time-series development, although the geographic and temporal coverage can vary greatly. The EROS Data Center (EDC), located in Sioux Falls, South Dakota, serves as a geographic data repository for the National Aeronautics and Space Administration (NASA), USGS and other federal government agencies. The Earth Science Information Center (ESIC), operated by the USGS, is another centralized source for maps, images and other archival data. The Aerial Photography Summary Record System (APSRS), maintained by the USGS, also provides a centralized database. In short, there is no lack of data!

■ The history of LULC mapping in Michigan

Michigan has a long history in the development, use and distribution of geographic information. The largest effort was a project of the Department of Natural Resources (MDNR), called Michigan Resource Information System (MiRIS) (Fig. 29.2). MiRIS was created in 1979 by Public Act No. 204, which is currently embodied in Part 609, Resource Inventory, of the Natural Resource and Environmental Protection Act, Act 451 of the Public Acts of 1994. The program was part of the Michigan Resource Inventory Program, which also produces geographic data sets detailing political boundaries, soils, water well maps and oil/gas wells (Swanson 2003).

In April of 2002, the State of Michigan established the Michigan Center for Geographic Information (MiCGI), within the Michigan Department of Information Technology. Since that time, the State has invested more than $15 million in coordinated GIS data production, maintenance and standards. Support continues to grow, not only at the state level but also through the establishment of many partnerships with local communities and the higher education system (Swanson 2003). One important project of the MiCGI is called the Michigan Geographic Framework. Its primary function is to provide a statewide base map, which stores reference information for the geographic analyses. Specifically, this base map consists of features and attributes in the current TIGER/Line Files, base map features in the MDNR MiRIS Files and an enhanced linear referencing system built from the Michigan Accident Location Index (MALI). The Geographic Framework serves as a common reference for state projects, e.g., the new official 2007 State Road Map available from the Michigan Department of Transportation.

Classification schemes

In order to model and better understand changing environments, we must (1) describe the main system components and their interactions, and (2) define and describe basic LULC classes. In the Michigan context, there are seven broad classes of land-use and land-cover: the built environment, agriculture, forest, other vegetation, wetland, inland lake and barren. These classes were part of the Michigan base (1980), and of MiRIS. Table 29.2 provides an edited example of the official hierarchical Michigan Land Use/Land Cover Classification Scheme (2000). The LULC scheme used by Michigan is a hierarchical structure, in which each class has more detailed and less frequently occurring classes nested within. It is adaptable to various and multiple levels of detail. Each specific class in Table 29.2 has a corresponding description and a set of class-membership criteria. As an example, a description of the "Barren land" class of Table 29.2, is found in Table 29.3.

■ Historical perspectives on LULC in Michigan

An understanding of current patterns of land-use and land-cover requires a consideration of historical and prehistorical processes (Chapters 25, 27). The presence of high-quality timber in Michigan resulted in a rush to clear the land, initially of pine and then of hardwood trees, that was nearly complete by 1920 (Williams 1989). Lumber barons presided over the nation's largest timber producing state in the late 1800s, and white pine was the species of choice in the northern Lower Peninsula. At times, forest fires, e.g., the "Great Thumb Fire" of 1881, ravaged the area, burning tens of thousands of hectares, including one that burned from the west to east coast of the Lower Peninsula (Sodders 1999). Over a span of ~50 years, the Michigan timber industry fell from first in the nation in lumber production to a position nearer the bottom of the pack; the landscape was nearly denuded of forest. Even so, the lumber barons helped to concentrate wealth and build the state, and thus preceded the auto barons (Chapters 31, 40).

Patterns of soils, together with the persistence of strong climatic gradients, affect the spatial patterns of agricultural productivity in Michigan (Chapters 19, 20, 36–39). The forested, western half of the Upper Peninsula, starting at about Munising, is underlain by the Precambrian rocks of the Superior Uplands (Plates 5, 8; Chapter 3). An ecological transition zone, aligned approximately with Saginaw Bay, separates the mixed coniferous/deciduous forests of the north from the dominantly deciduous forests to the south (Plate 15; Chapters 7, 21). Savannah grasslands ("oak openings") in the far southern portion of the state are outliers of the Great Plains/tallgrass prairies, and were favored by settlers, as these lands were easy to clear for agriculture (Chapter 27). Many of these areas are, today, in agricultural and urban land-uses. The dominance of certain field crops in the south, e.g., corn along the borders with Indiana and Ohio, and sugar beets in the Saginaw lowlands, the abundance of fruit crops along and

TABLE 29.2 An example of a Michigan land-use/land-cover classification scheme, for urban and built up land[1]

1	Urban and built up			
11	Residential			
	112	Multi-family, low-rise		
		1121	Apartment	
			11211	High density
12	Commercial, services and institutions			
	121	Primary/Central Business District (CBD)		
	122	Shopping centers, malls, retail centers		
	126	Institutional		
		1263	Health	
			12631	Hospitals
				12631 General, acute
13	Industrial			
		131	Primary metal production (milling, smelting, forging)	
		1311	Blast furnaces and steel mill	
14	Transportation, communication and utilities			
2	Agriculture			
21	Cropland			
	211	Row crops		
		2111	Corn	
3	Grass and shrub lands			
31	Grasses and forbs			
	311	Upland grasses and forbs		
		3111	Bluegrasses predominate	
32	Shrubs			
33	Pine or oak openings (prairie)			
	331	Hardwood		
	331	Coniferous		
4	Forest land			
41	Broadleaved forests			
	411	Northern hardwoods		
		4117	Basswood predominates	
42	Coniferous forest			
5	Water			
51	Streams and waterways			
6	Wetlands			
7	Barren			

1: The entire Land-use/Land-cover classification scheme developed for Michigan is too large to fully portray here. It is a hierarchical classification system that is similar to other schemes developed by others in the United States and elsewhere. Source: Michigan LULC Classification System 2000 (2001)

TABLE 29.3   LULC definitions for Barren land[1]

7 BARREN
 	
      Barren land (non-vegetated) is land of limited ability to support life and has little or no vegetation. Land temporarily barren owing to man's activities is included in one of the other land-use categories. Agricultural land temporarily without vegetation because of tillage practices is still classified as agricultural land. Sites for urban development stripped of cover before construction begins should be classified as urban and built-up (196 Under Construction). Areas of extractive and industrial land have waste and tailings dumps and exhausted sources of material supply are often evident.
           71 Salt flats (not applicable to Michigan)
           72 Beaches and riverbanks
      Beaches are the sloping accumulations of sand and gravel along shorelines. The beach category is not used if there is vegetative cover or another land-use.
                721 Sand beach
                Aggregate smaller than 2-mm in diameter along a shoreline area.
                722 Gravel beach
                Aggregate larger than 2-mm in diameter along a shoreline area, varying from fine gravel to cobbles.
                723 Riverbanks
                Areas of exposed sand created by erosion along streambanks.
                729 Other
           73 Sand dunes / exposed bluff
      Sand other than beaches is composed primarily of dunes and accumulations of sand of eolian origin.
                731 Sand dunes
                A hill, mound or ridge of wind-blown sand in a primarily unvegetated condition.
                739 Other
           74 Bare exposed rock
      The bare exposed rock category includes areas of bedrock exposure, scarps, talus, slides, volcanic material and other accumulations of rock without vegetative cover.
                741 Rock knobs
                Rock formations resembling miniature mountains which are randomly exposed along the earth's surface.
                742 Escarpments
                A steep to perpendicular rock cliff along the side of a ridge or mountain.
                743 Shoreline rock outcrop
                Areas of shoreline consisting of exposed bedrock at the surface of the earth.
                744 Riverbank
                Areas of exposed rock created by erosion along streambanks.
                749 Other

1. Each class in a nested, hierarchical system, like this one, has a class description. Notice that the level 1 and 2 classes have descriptions. For general classes, formal descriptions are required. The level 3 classes, in the example here, have no additional descriptive text; the name alone is sufficient to distinguish any single class from any other. Source: Michigan LULC Classification System 2000 (2001).

near Lake Michigan (Chapter 38), and the relatively low level of agricultural production in the north, all are explained by human adaptations to the existing physical environment. The significant presence of public lands within the state, especially in the northern Lower and Upper Peninsulas, is the result of failed attempts to bring marginal lands under production. The combination of poor agricultural lands and the economic depression and droughts of the 1930s, led a significant number of landowners to forfeit the titles to their land because of their inability to pay taxes. These lands are primarily managed now as National and State Forests, Parks, Wildlife Refuges and Recreation Areas (Chapters 35, 41).

Similarly, the presence of the Great Lakes as a ready transportation system, together with the abundance of economically important minerals like iron and copper, shaped the industrial history of the state (Chapters 11, 12, 30), which, in turn, influenced early patterns of settlement and urban growth (Chapter 27). The general geographic configuration of the Upper Midwest's natural resources, in relation to the Great Lakes and population centers, creates a situation where the transportation of materials from the Lake Superior, Lake Michigan and Lake Huron drainage basins (an area rich in natural resources) must involve the Detroit River. These fortunate geographic site and situation characteristics helped make Detroit the most important manufacturing, economic, social and population hub in Michigan, with its own distinctive landscape patterns and history (Poremba 2002, Spreen and Holoway 2005). The position of Detroit on the Detroit River, which served as an important shipping route from the iron- and copper-bearing regions of Wisconsin and the Upper Peninsula to the important 19th century population centers of the east, secured its importance as one of the most important industrial cities of the early 20th century. The Detroit metropolitan region contains by far the highest concentration of people and economic activity, and hence urban and developed land, in the state (Chapter 33).

Land-use is equally affected by early and recent history, in the way human society has interacted with the land in Michigan. The patterns of agricultural settlement were strongly influenced by the US Public Land Survey System (Chapter 28), which created a rectilinear grid structure to the shapes of agricultural fields that persists to this day.

Some of the early settlements that developed around the mining (in the north) and automotive industries (in the south) have declined dramatically since the early 20th century, as a result of the diminished demand for, and/or depletion of, these resources. For example, the city of Calumet, in Houghton County, experienced a tremendous population surge during the "copper rush" of the late 1800s, reaching a population, together with surrounding towns, of about 60,000 in 1900. By 2000, the town's population has since declined to <900.

Contemporary LULC patterns and trends

The contemporary land-use/land-cover of Michigan (Plate 13) is, in many ways, a reflection of the socio-economic patterns shown on Plate 16, as well as the history of the state, built upon the pre-existing natural resources patterns. The comparatively remote and sparsely-populated Upper Peninsula contains one of the largest expanses of wilderness east of the Mississippi, and is still an important region for natural resource extraction and tourism. Agricultural patterns correspond largely to climate and soils, particularly the predominance fertile Alfisols, Inceptisols and Mollisols in the southern Lower Peninsula. Along with sandy Entisols, acidic, and often wet, Spodosols and Histosols dominate the landscape north of about Clare County (Plate 12), and as a result, agriculture is less frequent there. The deciduous forests and prairies of the southern Lower Peninsula today support the state's largest concentration of agricultural land and people. Michigan is on the northern and eastern margins of the Corn Belt, and the large amounts of corn harvested in southern tiers of counties (Fig. 36.4) reflect this fact. In addition to natural factors, agricultural patterns are also related to population patterns, especially in the case of higher value truck crops and dairy.

The changing nature of the global and national economies, together with an aging population, are also important to this story. Residential settlement patterns are decreasingly dependent on either the natural environment (as in agricultural settlement) or existing urban infrastructure (as in manufacturing and service industries). As elsewhere in the eastern US, broad areas of Michigan are being settled at relatively low densities (Chapter 32; Brown et al. 2005). These sprawling settlement patterns combine with the growth in recreation-related development (including that associated with boating, hunting, fishing and winter activities) to produce widespread development in rural areas, which, while normally low density, can be quite dense on the shores of the inland lakes in northern Lower Michigan. Many of these new developments are replacing agriculturally productive lands in the south, and are resulting in increasingly fragmented ownership patterns, especially in the forested north (Brown et al. 2000). The combination of declines in agricultural land and increases in low-density settlement has led to a significant increase in forest cover across the state (Fig. 41.1). These patterns can be seen in many areas in the northern Lower Peninsula, and in the south, where agricultural fields are being converted to exurban and suburban settlements that include significant amounts of tree cover. Because they are interspersed with residential developments, these forests do not serve the same ecological niches, e.g., as wildlife habitat, that the original forests did. Additionally, urban and suburban development in southeastern Michigan has resulted in significant increases in impervious surfaces, e.g., roofs, streets, driveways, etc., which increase runoff and reduce groundwater recharge.

The increasingly dispersed settlement patterns in Michigan also raise important challenges for state and local governments, as they struggle to provide important urban services, e.g., transportation, sewer, electricity and water. Second homes in Northern Lower Michigan are often retirement destinations (Chapters 35, 41), but they strain the health-care infrastructure, as the population becomes increasingly elderly and increasingly permanent (as opposed to seasonal; Stewart 1994).

■ Modeling LULC in the past, present and future_____

Theoretical considerations

In order to understand the processes by which LULC have changed, and to develop some predictive ability for LULC change in the future, geographers have developed computer simulation models that incorporate both biophysical and social processes. The predictions of land-use changes that these models present are important for planning purposes, so as to achieve specific environmental and/or social goals.

LULC change is a complex process affected by many social and ecological processes. Redman et al. (2000) defined the following interactions as the specific activities that link the human or social and ecological or environmental elements of the ecosystem: (1) Land-use decisions, (2) Land-cover status and changes, (3) Production, (4) Consumption and (5) Disposal. Models arising from non-geographic disciplines often treat the various and diverse elements of social and biophysical systems as distinct, without recognizing the inextricable linkages between these systems. Conversely, spatially relevant LULC change models explicitly link—through feedback mechanisms—social and biophysical systems. Characterizing an ecosystem requires not only the recognition of these factors, but also a comprehensive integrative perspective on what motivates these activities. To integrate the social, behavioral and economic aspects of human ecosystems, Redman et al. (2000) proposed this list of social patterns and processes that directly or indirectly influence LULC systems: (1) Demography, (2) Technology, (3) Economy, (4) Political and social institutions, (5) Culturally determined attitudes, beliefs, and behavior and (6) Information and its flow. It should be immediately clear that certain elements found on the social patterns and processes list would be difficult to describe, let alone model. For example, culture and information are difficult to integrate with more familiar demographic and economic factors. Further, geographers would argue that in a human system, all choices are not equally available to everyone; choices are limited by economic circumstances and preconceived notions (history), as well as the physical environment. In Michigan specifically, but also broadly applicable, we can ask three LULC questions: (1) How have ecological processes influenced the emergent social patterns and processes? (2) How have social patterns and processes influenced the use and management of resources? (3) How are these interactions changing, and how do these changes impact Michigan?

LULC change models can be categorized by subject matter, modeling techniques, or application. The US Department of Agriculture's Forest Services Group categorizes models using these criteria: (1) Does the model identify and assess the likely effects of changes in ecosystem structure and function on human communities and society? (2) Does it evaluate potential policy options for both rural and urban environments? (3) Does it evaluate potential impacts of both rural and urban management activities?

Agarwal et al. (2002) used the analytical framework of Veldkamp and Fresco (1996, 254), and for the remainder of this chapter, so will we, where land-use "is determined by the interaction in space and time of biophysical factors (constraints) such as soils, climate, topography, etc., and human factors like population, technology, economic conditions, etc."

As has become obvious, LULC change is a complex process, affected by many social and ecological processes. Even more problematic, the processes vary from place to place—in essence, geography matters. Thus, to guide the development of LULC change models that are more inclusive of diverse social patterns and processes, scientists are (forced for both technical and theoretical reasons) to focus on those factors that they believe most influence any given place, knowing not all drivers are equally important over time, space and across different scales.

Social and ecological processes operate at different scales. Unfortunately, generic statements of scale miss the complexity of the topic. There are multiple facets to scale. When considering models, the issue of scale expands to include space and time. The spatial scale of models includes factors of resolution (or grain) and extent. Spatial resolution is the smallest geographic unit of analysis for the model. Grain is the term we use when applying spatial resolution to models. Extent describes the total geographic area to which the model is applied. We might model a single county, region or the state. Time (or temporal resolution) is the period of observation, printed on a paper map or in the modeling world, a combination of both time step and duration. Time step is the smallest temporal unit of analysis for change to occur for a specific process in a model. In land-use change models, an iteration is often a time step, e.g., a day, month or year. Duration is the length of time that the model is applied. The Michigan Land Resource Project (Public Sector Consultants 2001) models were run for a duration of 60 years (Michigan Land Use Leadership Council 2003).

Clearly, when building models, especially those trying to integrate people with the environment, we are faced with the issue of managing those decisions that a planner or individual might make with the limitations of the environment. As modelers, we are obligated to create tools to allow just such integrations. The modeling community has agreed upon some basic definitions. For example, an agent refers to the human actor or actors in the model who make decisions, with an individual human being the smallest single agent. Large agents, e.g., households, state and local governments, are also frequently modeled, and can also be embedded within land-use and land-cover models. The domain usually refers to the social organization structures built in the model.

A second important and distinct attribute of human-environmental models is the approach used to address the complexity of time, space and human decisions found in real-world situations (Argarwal et al. 2002). Spatial complexity represents the extent to which a model is spatially explicit. There are two broad types of spatially explicit models: spatially representative and spatially interactive. A model that is spatially representative can incorporate, produce or display data, but cannot model topological relationships and interactions among geographic features. In these cases, the value of each cell might change or remain the same from one point in time to another, but the logic that makes the change is not dependent on neighboring cells. Alternatively, a spatially interactive model is one that explicitly defines spatial relationships and interactions over time. Most existing LULC models employ a range of statistical or econometric tools with both raster and vector approaches. Frequently these models are aspatial and use aggregated or clumped data. LULC models might use mechanistic or deterministic GIS simulations, combining layers of spatial information. Dynamic models including individual and multi-agent systems are emerging tools for LULC simulation and projection.

LULC projections for Michigan

The "Land Transformation Model" (LTM) simulates future LULC change, based on recent or historical LULC patterns (Pijanowski 2006). The model uses the Michigan Framework and MiRIS data to predict LULC in Michigan in 2030 (Fig. 29.3, Table 29.4). All LULC projections rely on one important assumption—that the process of change will

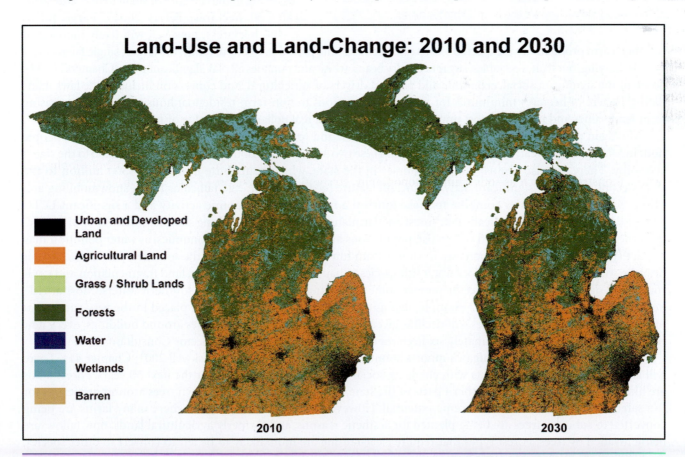

FIGURE 29.3 Examples of the LTM output for Michigan, for the years 2010 and 2030. Source: Dr. Bryan Pijanowski, ILWIMI LTM Data Portal. http://ltm.agriculture.purdue.edu/ilwimi

TABLE 29.4   LULC predictions for 2000 and 2030, based on the LTM model[1]

LULC Class	2000 km²	2030 km²	Change in area (km²)
Commercial	1447.8	4308.2	2860.4
Residential	2188.0	7904.8	5716.8
Other Urban	4562.7	4562.7	0
Agriculture—non row crops	22045.4	19881.3	−2164.1
Agriculture—row crops	16347.8	14961.3	−1386.5
Deciduous Upland	38032.3	39068.7	1036.4
Coniferous Upland	10603.5	10994.0	390.5
Mixed Deciduous	11647.2	11122.4	−524.8
Open Water	3616.5	3513.8	−102.7
Barren	205.1	176.3	−28.9
Wetland— Nonwooded	16113.2	13000.3	−3112.8
Wetland—Wooded	23312.4	20628.1	−2684.4

1: The classes shown here are aggregated from the full set.

continue without major divergence. Obviously, this assumption becomes ever more problematic, as we model further into the future. Thus, although it is possible to project LULC far into the future, e.g., 100 years or more, the likelihood of it being a correct prediction becomes increasingly unlikely.

Through 2030, the LTM predicts that the built environment, mainly by suburbanization around larger cities but also in the northern vacation areas in the state, will increase in total area. Coupled with this increase in the built environment will be a decline in the total area currently designated as agriculture, forest and other types. Most of this increase in built up land will occur in areas that have historically been in agriculture. Agriculture currently ranks as the second largest industry in the state, with almost 100,000 associated jobs (Ferris 2001). Most, about 80%, of Michigan's agricultural lands are in the southern part of the state, and it is in these areas that most of the transition from agriculture to suburban will occur (Chapter 32). The number of farms in Michigan is expected to decline from 42,000 in 2000 to 24,000 in 2040 with most of the loss being in the category of small to mid-size farms (20–200 hectares; Ferris 2001). Large farms (>400 hectares), however, will likely increase in number. Farm productivity is expected to increase over this time period as well. Currently, the largest single farm enterprise is dairying, but fruit, vegetables, sugar beets, dry beans, wheat and potatoes all play significant roles (Chapters 36–39). Some of the significant social, economic and political drivers of agricultural land conversion include state laws mandating 10 acre (4 hectare) minimums for property conversions to non-farm residential housing, rapidly increasing farm land values and probably most importantly, the decline in real dollars of the value of farm produce.

Michigan presents great opportunities for recreation and tourism (Chapter 35). Almost one million people hunt in Michigan each year; almost two million fish. These two activities contribute in excess of $800 million to the state's economy. There are also almost 800 golf courses in the state, which contribute more than $500 million to the state's economy. Other significant activities include nature (eco-) tourism, e.g., fall color tours, snowmobiling and skiing. All of these activities combine to make tourism a fundamental economic activity and a significant LULC change driver. Golf courses typically take forest and farmland for conversion. Fishing should remain a popular activity, although with some increased risk to fish populations and associated fishing economics, as water pollution may impact rivers and lakes due to increases in runoff from impervious surfaces. Also, the southern part of the state is near the southern limit of several cool water fish species (Chapter 23). Global warming, land fragmentation and environmental degradation may reduce or remove some cool-water species from these southern waters. Most at risk, however, is hunting. It is likely, for example, that as cottages and other buildings are placed in the very rural areas of the state, hunting opportunities will decline, given state laws regarding safety zones around buildings; every new rural structure removes approximately six hectares of land from hunting (Public Sector Consultants 2001).

The forest industry in Michigan supports about 150,000 jobs (Moore and Rockwell 2001; Chapter 41). There will also be direct forestry impacts with changing social and physical processes over the next 30 years. Forest lands are likely to be reduced in the northern parts of the state, as people settle and cut down trees around properties for fire safety, and to maximize their scenic potential. However, in southern Michigan, where many farms are being converted to suburbs, trees are being planted for aesthetic reasons, and formerly agricultural lands, now fallow, are being invaded by trees. Forest types that require clear-cutting are more likely to be left to convert to other species. By 2030, we are likely to see some homogenization in Michigan forests, with fewer areas of short-lived tree species and possibly less overall forest diversity. Finally, a relatively new and significant biological factor will impact much of Michigan's tree cover—the *emerald ash borer*, an insect accidentally introduced to the state from tropical southeastern Asia via wooden pallets used in shipping. This exotic pest has, at present, no natural predators, and the native ash (*Fraxinus* spp.) tree species have no natural defenses against it. Even though strict laws have been enacted to control the spread of this insect, it is likely that ash trees in Michigan face an endangered future. The emerald ash borer, like the gypsy moth before it, is an example of the type of environmental shock that is difficult, if not impossible, to predict using most LULC simulation models.

Conclusions

LULC change is a complex process that is affected by many social and ecological processes. The multidisciplinary nature of the study of LULC change is widely recognized in both the social and natural sciences, yet the institutional powers of the disciplines limit the ability to build teams capable of developing such models. The State of Michigan, through its various governmental units, is trying to track these changes and build policies to manage and mitigate LULC change impacts. Spatial data, combined with the efforts of social and physical scientists, policy makers and modelers, will allow us to better predict and manage Michigan's future, enhancing both the economic strength and environmental sustainability of the state.

The patterns of LULC in Michigan have changed markedly over time. In this chapter we examined the factors that have influenced those patterns and changes and how and why geographers study them. Aided by remote sensing aircraft and satellites, and by GIS, geographers have concluded that, under relatively stable natural conditions, particularly climate, and with minimal human interference, LULC patterns can remain stable for long periods. However, changes in climate patterns or intensification of human activities can lead to significant changes, from local to regional scales, and often over relatively short time periods. Michigan's LULC has in fact experienced many such changes due to human activities, from the massive deforestation of the late 1800's to the urban/suburban sprawl that has epitomized the 1970–2005 period. Whereas forest cover has been restored over much of the state, urban sprawl continues. Global climate change now appears to have the potential to alter the growing conditions throughout Michigan and beyond, which makes it likely even more changes are in store (Environmental Protection Agency 1997; Chapter 19). Whatever the future might hold for Michigan's LULC mosaic, we are now paying attention to it, and hopefully, we will be able to better manage and adapt to any changes that might occur.

Literature Cited

Agarwal, C., Green, G.M., Grove J.M., Evans, T.P. and C.M. Schweik. 2002. A Review and Assessment of Land-Use Change Models: Dynamics of Space, Time, and Human Choice. General Technical Report NE-297. US Department of Agriculture, US Forest Service, Northeastern Research Station, Indiana University Center for the Study of Institutions, Population, and Environmental Change.

Brown D.G., Johnson, K.M., Loveland, T.R. and D.M. Theobald. 2005. Rural land-use trends in the conterminous United States, 1950–2000. Ecological Applications 15:1851–1863.

Brown, D.G., Pijanowski, B.C. and J.D. Duh. 2000. Modeling the relationships between land-use and land-cover on private lands in the upper Midwest, USA. Journal of Environmental Management 59:247–263.

Environmental Protection Agency. 1997. Climate Change and Michigan. EPA 230-F-97-008v.

Ferris, J. 2001. Economic Implications of Projected Land Use Patterns for Agriculture in Michigan. In: D. Levy (ed), Michigan Land Resource Project. http://www.publicsectorconsultants.com/Documents/lbilu/forestry.pdf (last accessed January 7, 2008).

Jensen, J.R. 2007. Remote Sensing of the Environment: An Earth Resource Perspective. Prentice-Hall, Upper Saddle River, NJ.

Michigan Land Use/Land Cover Classification Scheme—2000. 2001. http://www.rsgis.msu.edu/pdf/lclu/Michigan_LC_LU_Classification_System_2000.pdf (last accessed December 24, 2007).

Michigan Land Use Leadership Council. 2003. Michigan's Land, Michigan's Future: Final Report of the Michigan Land Use Leadership Council. Report prepared for Governor Jennifer Granholm and the Michigan Legislature. 90 pp.

Monmonier, M. 1991. How to Lie With Maps. University of Chicago Press, Chicago, IL.

Moore, M.D. and H.W. Rockwell. 2001. Economic Implications of Projected Land Use Patterns for the Forest Industry in Michigan. In: D. Levy (ed), Michigan Land Resource Project http://www.publicsectorconsultants.com/Documents/lbilu/forestry.pdf (last accessed January 7, 2008).

Pijanowski, B. 2006. The Land Transformation Model (LTM). http://ltm.agriculture.purdue.edu/default_ltm.htm (software).

Poremba, D.L. 2002. Detroit: City of Industry. Arcadia Press, Chicago, IL.

Public Sector Consultants. 2001. Michigan Land Resource Project. http://www.publicsectorconsultants.com/Documents/lbilu/index.htm (last accessed 24 December, 2007).

Redman, C., Grove, J. M. and L. Kuby. 2000. Toward a unified understanding of human ecosystems: integrating social sciences into long-term ecological research. White Paper of the Social Science Commission. National Science Foundation, Long Term Ecological Research Network, Washington, DC. http://intranet.lternet.edu/archives/documents/Publications/sosciwhtppr/ (last accessed 25 Feb 2006).

Sodders, B. 1999. Michigan on Fire 2. Thunder Bay Press, Holt, MI.

Space Imaging Solutions. 2001. Integrated Forest Monitoring Assessment and Prescription (IFMAP): Review of Remote Sensing Technologies for the IFMAP Project, 2nd Revision. Prepared for the State of Michigan, Michigan Department of Natural Resources, Lansing.

Spreen, J.F. and D. Holloway. 2005. Who Killed Detroit: Other Cities Beware. iUniverse Publishers, New York.

State of Michigan. 2005. Center for Geographic Information, Michigan Geographic Data Library. http://www.mcgi.state.mi.us/mgdl/?rel=ext&action=sext (Last accessed April, 2008.)

Stewart, S. I. 1994. The Seasonal Home Location Decision Process: Toward a Dynamic Model. Ph.D. Dissertation. Department of Parks and Recreation Resources, Michigan State University, East Lansing.

Swanson, E. 2003. Geographic Information System (GIS) Information Enhanced Land Use. Michigan Center for Geographic Information, Department of Information Technology. http://www.michiganlanduse.org/resources/councilresources/GIS _LU_Planning.pdf (last accessed 26 January 2008).

Veldkamp, A., and L.O. Fresco. 1996. CLUE: a conceptual model to study the conversion of land use and its effects. Ecological Modelling 85:253–270.

Williams, M. 1989. Americans and Their Forests. Cambridge University Press, Cambridge, UK.

Further Readings

Avery, T.E. and G.L. Berlin. 1992. Fundamentals of Remote Sensing and Airphoto Interpretation. Macmillan and Company, New York.

Brown, D.G. 2003. Land use and forest cover on private parcels in the upper Midwest USA, 1970 to 1990. Landscape Ecology 18:777–790.

Gewin, V. 2004. Mapping opportunities. Nature 427:376–377.

Jensen, J.R. 2005. Introductory Digital Image Processing: A Remote Sensing Perspective. Prentice-Hall, Upper Saddle River, NJ.

Lillesand, T.M. and R.W. Kiefer. 2000. Remote Sensing and Image Interpretation. John Wiley and Sons, New York.

Mauldin, T.E., Plantinga, A J. and R.J. Alig. 1999. Land Use in the Lake States Region: An Analysis of Past Trends and Projections of Future Changes. Research Paper PNW-RP-519, US Department of Agriculture, US Forest Service, Pacific Northwest Research Station. 24 pp.

Orr, B. 1997. Land use change on Michigan's Lake Superior shoreline: Integrating land tenure and land cover type data. Journal of Great Lakes Research 23:328–338.

Rindfuss, R.R., Walsh, S.J., Turner, B.L., Fox, J. and V. Mishra. 2004. Developing a science of land change: Challenges and methodological issues. Proceedings of the National Academy of Sciences of the United States of America 101:13976–13981.

Whitney, G.G. 1987. An ecological history of the Great Lakes forest of Michigan. Journal of Ecology 73:667–684.

30

Iron and Steel

Kevin Patrick

■ Michigan and the American steel industry

The American steel industry has been favored by its Great Lakes location since the late 19th century, because the lakes allow for the easy assemblage of the iron ore, coal and limestone needed to manufacture iron and steel at lake shore sites, which in themselves also have ready access to North American markets. This expansive inland sea sits between the continent's best sources of iron ore, on the Canadian Shield to the north, and its largest deposits of high grade bituminous coal, within the Appalachian Mountains and the Central Lowlands to the south. Rich, pure sources of limestone are also plentiful along the shores of the central Great Lakes. Sprawling manufacturing sites, where iron ore is smelted, converted into steel and sent to end-users like the auto industry, have laid the economic foundation for the Great Lakes' megalopolis. This loose expanse of metropolitan areas stretches along the southern shores of the Great Lakes from Buffalo, through Cleveland and Detroit to Chicago and Milwaukee.

Virtually surrounded by the Great Lakes, Michigan holds a central position within North America's geography of iron and steel. Although Michigan's Upper Peninsula iron ore mines now produce only a fraction of what they once did, and its Lower Peninsula coal mines have long since shut down, the state accounts for 80% of the limestone shipped on the Great Lakes, and has two huge, integrated steel mills operating in the Detroit suburbs of Dearborn and Ecorse.

Great Lakes' steel plants are vertically integrated, to include everything from primary metal smelting on the upstream end, through steel making, to the fabrication of final products on the downstream end. The process starts at the blast furnace, where coke is burned to smelt pig iron from pelletized ore (with the assistance of a limestone flux). The flux draws impurities into a molten slag, which rises above the denser iron and is poured off. Temperatures in the furnaces are increased through blasts of hot gases, which are captured at the top of the furnace by down-combers and circulated back through adjacent stoves, where it is reheated for the next blast (Hayes 2005). A coke plant is commonly found at or near the mill site. Coke is made by roasting coal in an oxygen-deprived oven, to produce a blast furnace fuel that burns hotter and can support the weight of larger batches of iron. While still molten, pig iron is transported to a basic oxygen furnace (BOF), where pure oxygen is lanced in to burn off more impurities, reduce the carbon content and convert the metal into steel. Beyond the hot end of the mill, the traditional integrated plant has a large number of fabricating shops that manufacture a wide variety of steel products—from plate and sheet steel, to structural beams, tubes and wire. Currently, most molten steel goes directly from ladle to continuous caster, which makes steel slabs that are then rolled into sheets.

The resilience of North America's Great Lakes-oriented steel industry is illustrated by its description in J. Russell Smith's (1926) book, *Human Geography*, which closely matches that of more recent books about the geography of the US and Canada (Paterson 1989, Birdsall and Florin 1992, Hudson 2002). Such books trace how bulk freighters

FIGURE 30.1 Coal arrives by rail at the lakeshore outside of Mittal Steel's East Chicago Works. Photo by K. Patrick.

move iron ore south, from ports at the western end of Lake Superior, to steel mills on the southern shores of the Great Lakes, to which coal has been railed from mines in Appalachia (Fig. 30.1). There has been some variance to these general flow patterns, however. For example, coal and limestone get backhauled up the lakes to the Algoma Steel mill at Sault Ste. Marie, Ontario, and before it closed in 1979, to the US Steel mill at Duluth. Since the 1950s, iron ore has also come from the Quebec-Labrador border, where it is railed south to St. Lawrence River and then boated up to Great Lakes steel mills.

Even deep-seated structural changes in the global steel industry have not loosened these linkages. When mid-20th century steel manufacturing expanded toward the Atlantic and Pacific coasts, in response to foreign ore supplies and markets, high demand protected the Great Lakes steel industry. Some 30 years later, when cheaper steel imports forced drastic cuts in domestic production, these peripheral mills took the bulk of the hit, and the industry—albeit much smaller—re-concentrated itself around the Great Lakes.

Historical geography of steel manufacturing

The geography of the American iron and steel industry is an intriguing topic. The industry has shifted westward over time, from the Atlantic seaboard to Pennsylvania and finally to the Great Lakes—all in response to expanding markets and new sources of raw materials and fuel. Although the earliest iron furnace in North America went into blast on Virginia's Falling Creek in 1621, the industry's pre-Revolutionary focus was centered in southern New England, New Jersey and eastern Pennsylvania (Swank 1892). Pig iron was made by smelting local iron ores in charcoal furnaces.

The early iron and steel industry in Pennsylvania

The iron and steel industry became firmly seated in Pennsylvania, with the 19th century adoption of coal as a blast furnace fuel. The transition initially favored the use of hard coal, or anthracite, found in abundance in the folded Appalachian Mountains of northeastern Pennsylvania. The new fuel was used in a hot-blast furnace invented in 1828 (Eggert 1994). Anthracite surpassed charcoal as a blast furnace fuel in 1855, and was then eclipsed by coke, made from bituminous coal, in 1875. This caused the industry to re-center in southwestern Pennsylvania, where the Pittsburgh seam of the Connellsville coal field became the largest single source of the nation's best metallurgical coal. The Appalachian

Highlands also contained significant, but scattered, deposits of iron ore, especially in Pennsylvania's Juniata Valley, and at Cornwall, east of Harrisburg. Although important during the iron industry's early years, Appalachian deposits were later dwarfed and superseded by the big ore discoveries in the Lake Superior upland (Chapter 11).

Requiring extensive forests for raw materials, charcoal furnaces tended to be isolated from each other. Coal and coke furnaces, on the other hand, could be concentrated at urban locations, with their resulting transportation and market advantages. The shift in furnace fuel—from charcoal to anthracite to bituminous coke—also resulted in an increase in the size of iron-making establishments, thereby facilitating their transition from rural plantations out in the woods to urban industrial complexes. At the same time, technological advances led to the development of large scale steel production as a major addendum to the iron industry. This happened in the wake of two patents given Sir Henry Bessemer in 1856 for a converter (the Bessemer Converter), in which air was blasted under high pressure through a batch of molten iron. The process removed carbon and silica from the iron in a spectacular shower of sparks, and in so doing converted the iron into steel.

These innovations all came together on the outskirts of Pittsburgh in 1875, when Andrew Carnegie completed the Edgar Thomson Works—the nation's first integrated mill. This mill combined large scale iron-making blast furnaces with steel-making Bessemer converters and rolling mills, to manufacture a host of products, the chief of which was steel rails (Muller 2006). By 1880, Pennsylvania was manufacturing >3.6 million tons of iron and steel annually—half the nation's production. Pennsylvania's iron and steel output at this time was almost four times that of Ohio, the nation's second largest producer, with nearly three times the labor force (US Bureau of the Census 1880, 740; Fig. 30.2).

The early iron and steel industry in Michigan

While Pennsylvania was climbing to the center of the iron and steel universe, Michigan was still on the frontier. Michigan had 15 charcoal furnaces in blast as early as 1840, producing 601 tons of pig iron. All of them were located in the southern Lower Peninsula, using local bog ore, a low grade iron ore found in swamps. Wayne County actually led the state at this time with five furnaces, followed by Calhoun and Washtenaw Counties with two each. By 1859, Branch County had two bog ore furnaces; Kalamazoo County had one. All three were abandoned by 1880.

Michigan's early iron industry changed significantly after William Austin Burt's 1844 discovery of iron ore at the east end of Teal Lake in the Marquette Range (Brooks 1873; Chapter 11). This discovery was within one of Upper Peninsula Michigan's three iron ranges, part of the high grade Superior Upland iron ore field, which extended across northern Wisconsin and around the western end of Lake Superior into northeastern Minnesota (Fig. 11.2). The Jackson Mining Company arrived in Marquette County within a year to extract ore from Iron Mountain. About 130 kgs of ore were taken back to Jackson, Michigan, and smelted successfully in 1846, yielding the first bar of Lake Superior iron ore.

Several bloomery forges were built on Lake Superior after 1848. Bloomery forges were small-scale operations, where ore was heated to a semi-molten state and then pounded into a bloom—or bar—of iron. The quality of the

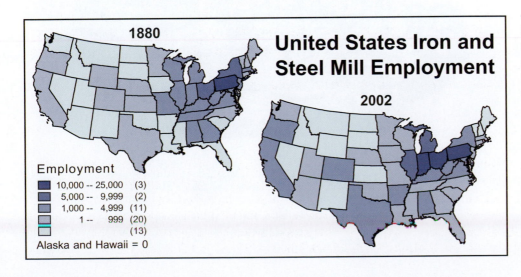

FIGURE 30.2 Iron and steel mill employment by state, in 1880 and 2002. Source: US Bureau of the Census (1880, 2002).

iron ore used in the bloomeries was excellent, but the Upper Peninsula was just too remote from any major market for these enterprises to be profitable. Lake Superior ores were also initially disadvantaged by its physical geography. Lake Superior sits about six meters higher than Lakes Michigan and Huron, enough of a barrier to prevent large boats from passing between Lake Superior and the lower lakes (Fig. 14.5). The vertical drop occurs in a set of rapids known as the Sault of the St. Marys River, today known as Sault Ste. Marie. In response to the 1840s copper boom in the Keweenaw Peninsula, a small fleet of boats was laboriously dragged across the St. Marys portage, and into Lake Superior. Upon return from the Keweenaw, the copper-laden boats had to be emptied above the Soo, the ore dragged across the portage in carts, and then reloaded into boats on the downstream side. Few commodities would be able to bear these break bulk costs, causing Lake Superior's treasure trove of metallic ores to be economically unobtainable—until the opening of the St. Marys Canal and its associated Soo Locks in 1855.

By 1880, Michigan ranked 8th nationally in iron and steel production, having manufactured 142,716 tons, by using 28 blast furnaces. All but one were fueled with charcoal. With its abundance of forested land, Michigan was the nation's largest producer of charcoal pig iron at that time.

The Sharon Iron Company of Sharon, Pennsylvania, bought the Jackson Mine (Fig. 11.4) in 1850, and soon shipped its first load of ore to Erie, Pennsylvania, where it was transferred to Sharpsville via the Ohio and Erie Canal, to become the first Lake Superior ore ever smelted in a coal-fired furnace. The operation proved profitable, and set the precedent for joining Superior iron ore with Appalachian bituminous coal, which would soon become the primary fuel source for the iron and steel industry.

Iron ore soon became a regular cargo for freighters leaving Lake Superior. In 1856, the Eureka Furnace opened at Wyandotte on the Detroit River, to smelt Superior ore, followed a year later by the Detroit Furnace (Fig. 30.3). In 1864, the Kelly Pneumatic Process Company built an experimental 2.5 ton converter at Wyandotte, to produce steel for a nearby rolling mill. This was the first Bessemer steel produced in the US. The pig iron made and used at all of these Lower Peninsula sites came from charcoal furnaces.

Because the Soo Locks were now open, investors from the south were encouraged to put charcoal blast furnaces in the Upper Peninsula iron fields, beginning with the Pioneer Furnace built at Negaunee in 1858, followed by a second furnace at this site the next year. Other furnaces followed, including one that opened at Duluth, Minnesota,

FIGURE 30.3   One of several iron-making firms operating in the Detroit area just before the Civil War, Wyandotte's Eureka Iron Company became the first mill to experiment with Bessemer steel. Source: Bacon Memorial District Library, 45 Vinewood, Wyandotte, MI.

in 1880, to use iron ore shipped from Marquette. Although the iron ranges north of Duluth, including the famed Mesabi, had even more high quality ore than did the Upper Peninsula's iron ranges, the first shipments from there would not occur until 1892. The long ore hauls and remote location consigned the Duluth furnace to bankruptcy within its first year.

Ultimately, the Upper Peninsula's charcoal furnaces were not much more successful than the previous bloomery forges. In addition to their distance to market, fuel prices increased over time, as more land was timbered off, decreasing the supply of charcoal. Of the 23 Upper Peninsula iron furnaces that opened after 1858, only 13 were still in blast 22 years later. By contrast, all 15 iron furnaces using Lake Superior ore that opened in southern Michigan, over the same time period, were still in operation by 1880 (US Bureau of the Census 1880, 109). The sheer size and quality of the Superior Upland ore fields would exert a profound influence on the location of iron and steel mills during the industry's subsequent drive to achieve economies of scale, drawing the industry to the shores of the Great Lakes. At the same time, the Superior Upland's remote location would ensure that most mill sites would remain on the southern shores of the lakes, closer to the Appalachian coal fields and the steel markets of the larger region.

By the 1870s, the Marquette Range was turning out over a million tons of ore annually, and additional strikes had been discovered in the Menominee Range to the south (Fig. 11.2). In 1877, the Chicago and Northwestern Railroad arrived in the Menominee Range, from Escanaba. Two years later, eight mines shipped 200,000 tons of ore, and, by 1882, Menominee Range production had topped one million tons. The iron mines of the Gogebic Range, on the Michigan-Wisconsin border, came on line during the 1880s, and the Minnesota Iron Ranges in the 1890s (Fig. 30.4).

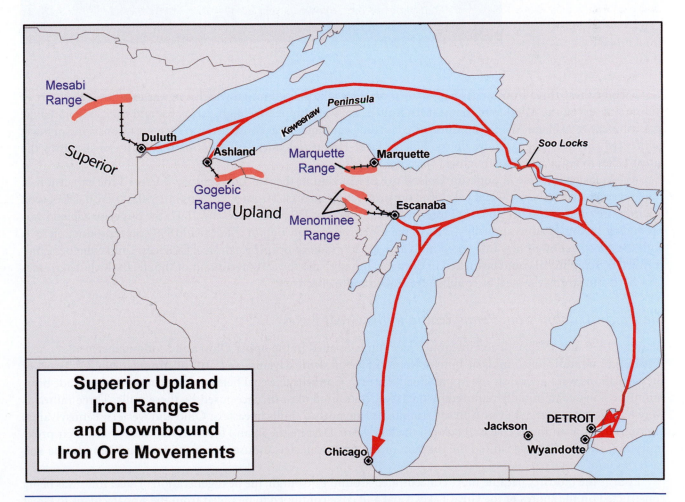

FIGURE 30.4   Opened in 1855, the Soo Locks were the critical piece of infrastructure needed to bring Upper Peninsula iron ore to the steel mill sites on the southern shores of the Great Lakes. Escanaba is the only ore port that can operate without the locks. Photo by K. Patrick.

FIGURE 30.5 Patented by Ohioan George Hulett in 1898, the Hulett unloader became the standard machinery used to remove iron ore from Great Lakes freighters, until made obsolete by the relatively recent adoption of self-unloading freighters. Approximately 75 of these unloaders were built, to work nearly every major ore dock on the Great Lakes. These are the only two left standing, used by the Chicago Coke Works to unload coal barges on the Calumet River in Illinois. Photo by K. Patrick.

Each of these three iron ranges had its own primary lake port, through which ore was exported. The Port of Marquette served the Marquette Range. Menominee ore was shipped through Escanaba, and the Gogebic Range was tributary to Ashland, Wisconsin. Specialized loading equipment was constructed at each port, consisting of huge, reinforced concrete and steel ore docks. Equally large Hulett unloaders stood along the southern shores of the Great Lakes to empty the lake freighters (Fig. 30.5).

An explosive increase in Superior Upland ore production in the late 19th century mirrored the expansion of the American steel industry. Great Lakes iron ore production increased from 5,700 tons in 1850, a mere 0.4% of total US iron ore production, to 9,003,725 tons in 1890, or 56% of US production. By 1897, the Superior Upland was producing 12,469,368 tons annually—70% of the American iron ore output (Mansfield 1899). Steel production rose, with the construction of new integrated mills and the adoption of open-hearth steel furnaces. Unlike the Bessemer converters, scrap metal could be melted in the open-hearths, and the carbon content of the steel, which determines how hard and strong the steel is, could be controlled more effectively.

Steel industry shift from Pennsylvania to the Great Lakes

Between 1875 and 1925, a dozen integrated steel mills opened in the upper Ohio and Monongahela valleys near Pittsburgh, in addition to mills at Johnstown and Sharon, Pennsylvania, and around Youngstown, Ohio. All of these locations were in or near the Appalachian Plateau's Connellsville coal field, which produced high grade bituminous coking coal, initially required by the large, coke-fired blast furnaces used by these mills. Three railroads were built to transport Superior iron ore from Lake Erie ports to mills in eastern Ohio and western Pennsylvania, and to return bituminous coal and coke to the lakeshore. Despite the inland locations of these mills, their proximity to Connellsville coal shifted the fulcrum of the American steel industry to southwestern Pennsylvania and eastern Ohio.

Even as the industry became more concentrated around Pittsburgh, the next generation of steel mills was being constructed on the shores of the Great Lakes. Coal and coke continued to be railed from the Appalachians to Great Lakes mill sites—mills that had the advantage of avoiding the cost of transporting Great Lakes iron ore to inland locations. In addition, advances in blast furnace technology allowed lower quality bituminous coals to be used, freeing the steel industry from the Connellsville coal field.

The steel industry achieved unprecedented scale economies with the formation of the United States Steel Corporation in 1901. The world's largest steel conglomerate was formed when Andrew Carnegie sold Carnegie Steel to the New York investment house of J.P. Morgan, who merged it with several other metal manufacturing firms. Five years later, US Steel began constructing the planet's largest integrated mill on the shores of Lake Michigan at Gary, Indiana. The mill was built around a manmade harbor, at which Superior iron ore was removed from bulk freighters into any one of twelve blast furnaces that fed pig iron into 56 open-hearth furnaces (Cotter 1921). As massive as the Gary Works was, US Steel also operated Chicago's South Works, which it had inherited from the original merger with Federal Steel. At a location between these two plants, two more were constructed on an artificial peninsula at Indiana Harbor. Inland Steel opened a mill there in 1901, followed by Mark Manufacturing in 1916 (Cutler 1995). The Mark Manufacturing mill was bought by Youngstown Sheet and Tube (later merged into LTV Steel) in 1923, and both Indiana Harbor mills became part of Mittal's East Chicago Works in 2005. Three other integrated mills would be built along the banks of the Calumet River on Chicago's South Side before the start of World War II.

The same fury to build integrated steel mills swept along the shores of Lake Erie. Soon after its founding, US Steel acquired the Johnson Steel mill that had been operating at Loraine, Ohio since 1894, and reconstructed it into the world's largest tube works. In Cleveland, Otis Steel opened a new integrated mill on the banks of the Cuyahoga River in 1914, simultaneous to the construction of the Corrigan McKinney steel mill on the opposite bank.

On the Detroit River, Michigan's largest city was experiencing its greatest period of growth, largely due to the rapid expansion of the auto industry and its upstream steel suppliers. Whereas auto plants were scattered at trackside locations throughout the metropolis, steel manufacturers were bound to ore docks with access to the Detroit River. Detroit's harbor for heavy industry was created in 1888, when the River Rouge Improvement Company deepened and straightened the short channel from Dearborn to the Detroit River. The channel cut through a River Rouge meander, forming an artificial mouth at the Detroit River, and isolating a piece of land that came to be called Zug Island, after its former owner. In 1901, the Detroit Iron Works erected two blast furnaces on Zug Island. The plant expanded and was eventually linked to open-hearth furnaces and fabricating mills that stretched south, along the Detroit River and into neighboring Ecorse. Known as Great Lakes Steel, the company was merged with M.A. Hanna and Weirton Steel in 1929 to create National Steel.

Michigan steel and the auto industry

In 1917, Henry Ford teamed up with industrial architect Albert Kahn to build an integrated steel mill and auto assembly complex of titanic proportions at the navigational head of the River Rouge, in Dearborn. Raw materials entered at one end of the River Rouge Plant, and automobiles literally drove out the other (Cabadas 2004; Fig. 30.6).

The first steel Model T body was produced at River Rouge in 1919. In 1927, the entire assembly line was transferred from Ford's Highland Park plant, where the Model T had first been produced in 1908, to River Rouge. Economies of scale dropped the per unit price for automobiles to such a level as to make them affordable to the masses. This coupling of mass production with mass consumption became an American standard for much of the 20th century. It is known as "Fordist production," because of the precedent set at River Rouge (Chapter 31).

Over the years, the River Rouge plant turned out Ford Model T's, Model A's, Fairlanes, Falcons, Thunderbirds, Mustangs and Mercuries. Steel was needed not only by the Ford production complex, but also for the Chevrolets, Pontiacs, Oldsmobiles, Buicks and Cadillacs produced elsewhere in Detroit, especially during the postwar economic boom. It was then that steel manufacturer Donald B. McLouth, after encouragement from General Motors executives, decided to build a new integrated steel mill along the Detroit River, at Trenton. In business since 1935, McLouth had purchased four war surplus electric furnaces from the US government in 1949, and was using them to make steel from recycled scrap. Three quarters of his production went to the auto industry. After the war, American mills were running at full capacity, and scrap and pig iron were in short supply, forcing McLouth to produce his own pig iron, just to stay in business.

The Trenton mill's two blast furnaces came on line in 1953. A year later, they were feeding pig iron to three 60-ton Linz-Donawitz furnaces, a 1949 technological innovation developed in Austria. These were the first basic oxygen furnaces (BOFs) built in the United States, coincidentally located near Wyandotte, where the country's first Bessemer steel was produced. Thus, the American adoption of two of the four major steel-making innovations

FIGURE 30.6 The 1000-foot "super freighter" American Integrity makes its way to and eventually through the Soo Locks, probably down to the steel mills of the lower Great Lakes. With a capacity of 78,850 tons, boats like these are an important cog in the iron and steel industry of Great Lakes region, which has also long been intimately linked to the automobile manufacturing industry in Michigan. Photo by R. Schaetzl.

(the other two being open-hearth and electric arc furnaces) is credited to Wayne County (American Society of Mechanical Engineers (ASME) 1985). The basic oxygen process, which converts pig iron to steel by injecting pure oxygen into the molten iron, revolutionized the industry. Open hearth furnaces accounted for 90% of the steel made in 1955. By 2000, 60% of America's steel would come from basic oxygen furnaces, and 30% from electric arc furnaces.

By the end of World War II, most of the high grade Superior ore was gone. As early as 1910, US Steel had built a beneficiation plant in Minnesota's iron ranges to concentrate the low quality ore before shipment. By the postwar era, the Superior iron ranges would have ceased to be significant, had it not been for pioneering research done in enriching low grade iron ore. Known as "taconite," this low grade ore had previously been uneconomical to mine. This changed with beneficiating, in which the ore was crushed, concentrated to increase its iron content, rolled into pellets and baked to harden them for shipment. The resultant iron ore pellets became the new raw material for the blast furnaces (Fig. 11.8). At the mine site pelletizing plants, the ore is first pulverized to powder size. Then, by a density separation technique in a thick liquid, the heavier iron minerals are allowed to settle out, while the lighter, waste (mainly silicate) minerals are skimmed off. The resulting iron ore concentrate is then mixed with clay and pulverized limestone (a fluxing agent), and shaped into pellets that are heat-hardened for shipment. This process increases the iron content of the ore from 25–30% to about 65–70%—high enough for efficient blast furnace smelting. Forming the ore concentrate into pellets makes handling the ore, in all phases of the process and at all locations along the line, simply easier than handling a powder would be. Recent improvements to the Soo Locks have also allowed larger ships to transport more ore at lower costs during the limited warm weather shipping season (Fig. 30.2).

FOCUS BOX: Great Lakes' ore freighters

The 1943 opening of the 800-foot (244 m) MacArthur Lock, at the Soo Locks in Sault Ste. Marie, ushered in an era of long ore boats, exceeding 700 feet (213 m). This era included the infamous *Edmund Fitzgerald,* a 729-foot (222 m) behemoth freighter built at River Rouge in 1957–58—the largest boat on the lakes. She was constructed of the same iron ore that she would be transporting, from the same mines, to the same steel mills of her birth—for the next 17 years. When the *Edmund Fitzgerald* went down in a Lake Superior gale on November 10, 1975 (see FOCUS BOX, Chapter 19) she was carrying 26,116 tons of iron ore pellets (484 tons shy of a full load), bound for National Steel's Zug Island blast furnaces.

If afloat today, however, the Edmund Fitzgerald would actually be one of the smaller lake boats! Between 1964 and 1969, the Soo's Poe Lock was rebuilt to a length of 1,200 feet (366 m), a width of 110 feet (34 m), and a

depth of 32 feet (9.7 m), accommodating the next generation of boats—the twelve "thousand-footers" that now rule the lakes (Fig. 30.6). The largest boat on the Great Lakes is now the 1,013.5-foot (309 m) long, *Paul R. Tregurtha,* with a capacity of 71,250 tons. By comparison, that means the *Tregurtha* can haul slightly more than two and a half *Fitzgerald*s.

The Great Lakes' freight *Edmund Fitzgerald,* seen here, is unloading a cargo of iron ore at the Great Lakes steel mill, on Zug Island. This is the last known photograph of the vessel—before its fateful sinking in 1975. Source: Marine Historical Society of Detroit, Robert T. Pocotte, Treasurer Department, 606 Laurel Ave. Port Clinton, OH.

■ Michigan's modern, integrated steel mills

The steel industry's high degree of geographic concentration around the Great Lakes is evident in the 2002 US Economic Census, which reported 119,349 people working in America's iron and steel mills and ferroalloy manufacturing plants (sector 33111 in the US Census North American Industrial Classification Code). The five highest ranked states in this sector accounted for 68% of this total; all of them are Great Lakes states (Fig. 30.7). Indiana led the nation in iron and steel mill employment with 23,314 laborers; most of this employment is concentrated in Lake and Porter Counties, both of which front Lake Michigan. This was followed by Pennsylvania with 20,885, and then Ohio with 20,493. Michigan ranked 4th, with 7,478 iron and steel workers, just ahead of Illinois (6,480; Table 30.1). More than a quarter of the nation's iron and steel mill laborers are in Chicago, Detroit and Cleveland (Fig. 30.7).

The degree of employment concentration is even greater within the state of Michigan. The smelting of ore into molten pig iron, to make steel, is virtually nonexistent outside of the Detroit metropolitan area, which employs

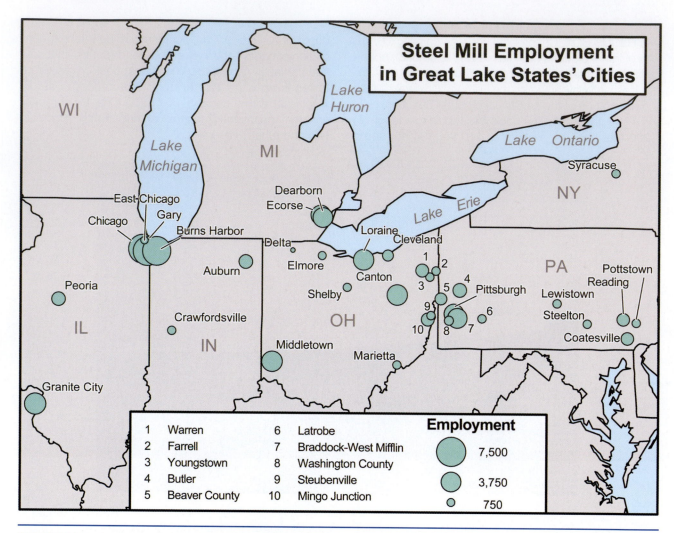

FIGURE 30.7   Locations of the iron and steel mill employees in the eight states that border the Great Lakes. Source: US Bureau of the Census (2002).

TABLE 30.1   Steel mill employment by state, 2002

State	Steel mill employment
Indiana	23,314
Pennsylvania	20,885
Ohio	20,493
Michigan	7,478
Illinois	6,480
Texas	4,990
West Virginia	4,645
Alabama	4,466
Maryland	4,773
South Carolina	2,718

Source: US Bureau of the Census (2002).

nearly all of the state's steel mill workers. And most of these workers are employed at two giant plants located within sight of each other along the banks of the River Rouge (Fig. 30.8). The Great Lakes works sprawls south, from the mouth of the River Rouge to Ecorse. Part of US Steel's 2003 acquisition of National Steel, the mill includes the blast furnace complex on Zug Island. Just upstream, Rouge Steel operates the mill at Ford's famous River Rouge assembly plant (Fig. 30.9).

The steel industry demonstrates the characteristics of economic agglomeration—the tendency for firms to cluster spatially, to realize an advantage. Clustering creates the threshold level of job opportunity needed to maintain a skilled labor pool, and the minimum market required to provide specialized services or equipment. It also facilitates more efficient communication between production steps, and reduces transportation costs.

FIGURE 30.8 As depicted by this map, Michigan's three integrated steel mills all operate in Wayne County, with direct access to the Great Lakes for raw material inputs. Rouge Steel and the Great Lakes Works continue to make steel, but the last division of the old McLouth Works closed in 2003.

FIGURE 30.9 A portion of Ford's massive River Rouge assembly plant, in Dearborn. Photo by K. Patrick.

The "least cost location," as defined by classic economic geography, still applies today (Weber 1929). Iron ore, coal, limestone, steel slabs and rolls of sheet steel are heavy, bulky and costly to move, especially relative to their value. Gathering these materials at lakeside production sites, therefore, eliminates break bulk transfer costs that would be incurred if plants were located farther inland. Lakeside mill locations are also central to the North American market for steel, most of it being rolled steel for the automobile industry (Fig. 30.10).

FIGURE 30.10 Coils of rolled steel, like the one memorialized here at the Great Lakes Works, are the primary end product of Great Lakes' steel mills. Most of this steel is used by the auto industry. Photo by K. Patrick.

Minimills

Today, Texas is the 6th largest employer of steel workers, and yet it has none of the advantages of the Great Lakes. It does, however, have access to a huge market—enough to stimulate the demand for recycled steel produced in minimills.

Ever since the restructuring of the 1970s and 1980s, the steel industry has made a decided shift toward minimills, which melt scrap steel in electric arc furnaces before fabricating it (Crandall 1981). Minimills avoid the direct, chemical reduction of iron ore, and are therefore freed of the locational constraints demanded by blast furnace inputs. With scrap metal and electricity as the major inputs, minimill locations have typically been more market-oriented, i.e., located near or in large cities, and thus, less influenced by the location of raw materials (Hall 1997).

Nucor Corporation began building and acquiring minimills to make bar and sheet steel in 1972. It is now the second largest domestic steel producer, after US Steel, having produced 18.4 million metric tons of steel in 2006, compared to US Steel's 19.3 million tons. Global steel manufacturer Mittal, which owns several plants in the US, produced 63 million metric tons of steel worldwide in 2006 (International Iron and Steel Institute 2006). Significantly, Nucor owns 33 steel making or fabricating facilities across the country, and not a single blast furnace. Twenty-three of its plants are in the South or West; only nine are in the Great Lakes region, and none are lakeside. This is in opposition to older, integrated steel mills, which favor Great Lakes' locations.

Steel production figures mirror employment, illustrating that approximately 2/3 of American steel is manufactured in Great Lakes' states; in 1910, that figure was 90% (D'Costa 1993). Some of the decrease resulted from the rise of Birmingham, Alabama, as a steel making center, and the mid-century expansion of mills in Baltimore, Texas, Utah and California. Most of the relative loss, however, is due to the more recent rise of minimills at non-Great Lakes' locations.

The competitive nature of the global steel industry has forced the integrated mills to be as efficient as minimills. Payrolls have been slashed, thousands laid off, and entire divisions abandoned, while new technologies have allowed more steel to be produced with fewer people. The improved efficiencies are not necessarily reflected in the landscape, however. Surplus mill buildings—rusting hulks—tower over weedy yards and parking lots. Even where redundant buildings have been razed, the expansive emptiness that remains bespeaks of a cataclysmic collapse. Technological advances have brought productivity back to the steel industry, but the lost jobs are gone for good.

Recent restructuring of Michigan's steel industry

The recent economic restructuring of the steel industry has initiated a major reorganization of Michigan's mills. In 1981, Ford formed the Rouge Steel Company to run its steel making facility. After building a BOF and continuous castor, Ford sold the company in 1989. National Steel continued to expand into the 1970s, building a finishing mill at Burns Harbor, Indiana in 1961, and acquiring a second integrated mill at Granite City, Illinois in 1971. The 1980s were a different story, however—characterized by a global glut of steel that idled 50% of National's capacity. By 1984, National had sold off its Weirton Steel Division to its employees, and was jointly owned by NKK Incorporated, Japan's second largest steel maker. NKK owned 53% of National at the time of its 2003 sale to US Steel. The three blast furnaces on Zug Island were rebuilt between 1986 and 1993. The blast furnace fuel at Zug Island comes from an 85-oven coke plant, built on site in 1992. The molten pig iron is sent to a BOF that made its first metal in 1970, and the resulting molten steel is poured into two continuous castors that came on line in 1977. The castors produce slabs of steel that are rolled to specification, then galvanized and annealed, before shipment to the customer, predominantly but not exclusively, the auto industry (Fig. 30.11).

Even with its pioneering basic oxygen furnaces, McLouth Steel declared bankruptcy in 1981, and was sold to its employees in 1988. The United Steelworkers of America managed the plant through a $25 million blast furnace rebuild, and a second bankruptcy in 1995. The mill was purchased out of bankruptcy a year later, and reorganized as the Detroit Steel Corporation. Despite these efforts, the blast furnaces were never again re-fired. Detroit Steel purchased the steel it needed for its rolling mills in nearby Gibraltar, until these, too, were shut down in 2003. The blast furnace row in Trenton was demolished in 2004, and since then, a mixed-used development proposed for the site has been shelved, largely due to the cost of environmental remediation (Thurtell 2004).

The mines and mills of Michigan are part of a globally sensitive, national assembly line of iron and steel that has experienced significant contraction over the last 25 years. Iron mining has ceased on the Menominee and Gogebic ranges. Ore continues to flow, however, through the Marquette and Escanaba ore docks, from Cleveland-Cliffs' Tilden and Empire mines on the Marquette Range. On the downstream end, Detroit's declining population has dropped its rank from 4th largest US city in 1970, to 10th in 2000, but its furnaces still furnish steel to auto assembly plants in the Midwest and Canada. Owned since 2004 by the Russian corporation, Severstal North America (Howes 2006), Rouge Steel is the key supplier to a revitalized Ford Rouge Center, which includes the new Dearborn Truck Plant.

FIGURE 30.11 The blast furnace row depicted here in 2005 is part of the famed River Rouge steel mill—now owned by Severstal North America. Photo by K. Patrick.

Employing 6,000, the Ford Rouge Center still holds its position as one of America's great industrial complexes, but the work force reflects the effects of long term de-industrialization and global competition, being a mere fraction of the 100,000 people who worked there in 1930.

Conclusions

Michigan's geography holds a central position in the American steel industry. Michigan is not the place of early industry dominance, like Pennsylvania, nor the location of the nation's greatest concentration of production, like northwestern Indiana. Rather, Michigan lies between these two extremes, but it shares the same legacy. Stretching from the iron rich hills of the western Upper Peninsula to the blast furnaces of the Lower Lakes' cities, the geography of Michigan, like no other state, encompasses all the production stages of an iron and steel economy. Fabulous wealth was realized in the expansion of Michigan iron mines, steel mills and auto assembly plants; more recently, the state has suffered a reversal of fortunes in those same industries.

Ford Motor, National Steel, US Steel and even McLouth Steel, once represented the epitome of American industrial stability. The rise of globalization and the increased ability to transfer capital on a planetary scale has undermined the footings of American industry, sidestepped the power of labor unions, and made local, state and to a degree, even national governments less relevant. In the shakedown, McLouth Steel has become a fading memory. Once the world's largest corporation, US Steel is now second in steel production to transnational Mittal, and Ford, beleaguered by foreign imports, buys River Rouge steel from Russian conglomerate, Severstal. Although suffering the fallout of de-industrialization, the existence of these multi-national corporations is proof that Michigan, too, is part of the global economy, and will continue to face the economic challenges that that entails.

Literature Cited

American Society of Mechanical Engineers. 1985. Oxygen Process Steel-Making Vessel, Trenton, Michigan. A National Historic Mechanical Engineering Record, Landmark Designation Report.

Birdsall, S.S. and J. Florin. 1992. Regional Landscapes of the United States and Canada. John Wiley and Sons, New York.

Brooks, T.B. 1873. Geologic Survey of Michigan, Upper Peninsula, 1869–1873. Michigan Board of Geological Survey pp. 236–237.

Cabadas, J. 2004. River Rouge: Ford's Industrial Colossus. MotorBooks/MBI, Osceola, WI.

Cotter, A. 1921. United States Steel: A Corporation with a Soul. Doubleday, Page and Company, Garden City, NY.

Crandall, R.W. 1981. The U.S. steel industry in recurrent crisis: Policy options in a competitive world. The Brookings Institute, Washington, DC. pp. 6–7.

Cutler, I. 1995. The Calumet Industrial Complex of Chicago and Northwest Indiana. In: M. P. Cozen (ed), Geographic Excursions in the Chicago Region. Association of American Geographers, Washington, DC. pp. 83–84.

D'Costa, A.P. 1993. State Sponsored Internationalization: Restructuring and Development of the Steel Industry. In: Noponen, H., Graham, J. and A.R. Markusen (eds), Trading Industries/Trading Regions. Guilford Press, New York. pp. 94–95.

Eggert, G.G. 1994. The Iron Industry in Pennsylvania. Pennsylvania Historical Association, Harrisburg, PA.

Hall, C.G.L. 1997. Steel Phoenix: The Fall and Rise of the U.S. Steel Industry. St. Martin's Press, New York.

Hayes, B. 2005. Infrastructure: A Field Guide to the Industrial Landscape. W.W. Norton and Company, New York.

Howes, D. 2006. Russians revive Rouge Steel. The Detroit News (April 9).

Hudson, J. 2002. Across This Land: A Regional Geography of the United States and Canada. Johns Hopkins University Press, Baltimore, MD.

International Iron and Steel Institute. 2006, May 19. World Steel in Figures. International Iron and Steel Institute, Brussels, Belgium.

Mansfield, J.B. (ed) 1899. The History of the Great Lakes, Volume I. J.H. Beers and Company, Chicago, IL. Transcribed and posted to www.halinet.on.ca/greatlakes/documents/hgl, Halton Hills, 2003.

Muller, E.K. 2006. The Steel Valley. In: J.L. Scarpaci and K.J. Patrick (eds), Pittsburgh and the Appalachians: Cultural and Natural Resources in a Postindustrial Age. University of Pittsburgh Press, Pittsburgh, PA. pp. 39–40.

Paterson, J.H. 1989. North America. Oxford University Press, Oxford, UK.

Smith, J.R. 1926. Human Geography. John Winston Company, London, UK.

Swank, J.M. 1892. History of the Manufacture of Iron in All Ages, and Particularly in the United States From Colonial Times to 1891. American Iron and Steel Association, Philadelphia, PA.

Thurtell, J. 2004. Once-mighty mill is scrapped. Detroit Free Press (October 21).

US Bureau of the Census. 1880. Tenth Census of the United States, Volume II, Statistics of Manufactures. United States Census Bureau, Washington, DC.

US Bureau of the Census. 2002. Economic Census Industry Series Reports, Manufacturing. Retrieved 12/16/2007, from http://www.census.gov/econ/census02/guide/INDRPT31.HTM

Weber, M. 1929. Theory of the Location of Industries. University of Chicago Press, Chicago, IL.

Further Readings

Ahlbrandt, R.S., Giarratani, F. and R.J. Fruehan. 1996. The Renaissance of American Steel: Lessons for Managers in Competitive Industries. Oxford University Press, Oxford, UK.

Bryan, F.R. 2003. Rouge: Pictured in its Prime. Wayne State University Press, Detroit, MI.

Hoerr, J.P. 1988. And the Wolf Finally Came: The Decline of the American Steel Industry. University of Pittsburgh Press, Pittsburgh, PA.

Rosentretter, R. 1994. Forging America's Future: 150 Years of Michigan Iron. Michigan History 78 (Nov–Dec). 72 pp.

Teaford, J.C. 1993. Cities of the Heartland: The Rise and Fall of the Industrial Midwest. Indiana University Press, Bloomington, IN.

31

The Auto Industry and the Manufacturing Sector

A. J. Jacobs

■ Introduction

Due to its geographic location in the Great Lakes Region, its abundant natural resources and the skills of its work-force, Michigan has been an industrial powerhouse for more than a century (Chapter 30). However, since the 1950s, a series of local and global factors have led to a decline in its industrial base. This chapter reviews the historical trends, related to manufacturing development in Michigan. Due to its prominence in the state, the primary focus is on the beginnings, rise and the recent decline of the US auto industry in Michigan.

■ Initial developments in Michigan's manufacturing sector

Although the necessary initial conditions for industrialization have always existed, i.e., the vast waterways of the Great Lakes, and the Upper Peninsula's ample supply of lumber and mineral resources, it was not until the late 1830s that manufacturing truly began to flourish in Michigan (Chapter 27). The state's first chief exports were food products, primarily flowing from the flour mills of Detroit (Green 1965). However, within close proximity to these mills were numerous small shops, specializing in the production and repair of mill machinery.

Copper and iron discoveries in the Upper Peninsula (Chapters 11, 12) and the completion of the locks on the St. Marys River at Sault Ste. Marie, in 1855, induced even more industrial activity in Detroit. The locks connected Lake Superior to Lake Huron, and with their completion, ships heading east to other manufacturing centers began to dock more frequently in Detroit's harbors (Green 1965). By the 1860s, in addition to food products, Detroit mills were producing steel, metal castings and ships. As Jacobs (1969, 123–124) wrote:

> "Detroit shipyards were among the first in the world to build steamships . . . as the export work of the shipyards grew, the yards supported a growing collection of engine manufactures and parts' makers, as well as suppliers of other fittings and materials for ships. By the 1860s, marine engines themselves were a major Detroit export . . . While the engine business was growing, it was supporting a growing collection of its own suppliers: shops that made parts and tools, others that supplied copper alloys, made from local ores, to shops where brass valves and to bits of engine brightwork were manufactured. The refineries . . . became so successful that between about 1860 and 1880 copper was Detroit's largest export."

Before its demise (Chapter 12), the copper industry had helped spawn a diverse industrial economy. In Detroit, the iron, steel, marine engine and railroad car and wheel industries formed the city's industrial core (Thomas 1992). Detroit, along with Flint, also was a hotbed for the carriage wagon industry. In addition, the city had countless export firms producing, among other things, paints, lubricating systems, tools and leather for upholstery (Jacobs 1969). It was this combination of industries that created the environment necessary for the development of Michigan's most important manufactured product, the automobile.

■ The auto industry grows and matures: 1889–1953 _____

Without discounting the importance of other industries, for roughly 100 years Michigan's economic and industrial fate has rested on its automobile industry. According to Hurley (1959, 1), the development of the auto industry in Detroit and Michigan was a classic case of "how historical accident and socio-economic factors combine to determine industrial sites." Hurley (1959, 4) stated that the following elements were "locational factors of great moment" for Detroit: the area (1) was equidistant between both coasts and therefore advantageously situated for shipment of parts to regional assembly plants in any part of the nation, (2) was in close proximity to the rail and water transport facilities of the Midwest, (3) was in close proximity to the iron ore resources of the Lake Superior region . . . , the steel centers of Chicago-Gary, Pittsburgh and Cleveland, and the rubber supplies of Akron, (4) contained pools of skilled and semi-skilled labor, and (5) had clusters of basic suppliers.

Detroit's first successful automobile assembly company was Oldsmobile, launched by Ransom E. Olds in 1889. Olds looked to the city's bustling marine and metalworking industries for many of his parts. For new car transmissions, he contracted with the marine engine maker Henry Leland; in 1902, Leland founded his own auto firm, Cadillac. To produce engines, Olds hired the second-generation machinists, the Dodge Brothers (Green 1965). The thriving horse carriage sector in Flint helped spawn yet another important auto firm, Buick, in 1899. Within ten years, Buick was the largest automaker in America (Chandler 1977, 1990).

Since 1904, Michigan's automotive industry has ranked 1st in the nation in the total value of auto products. By 1914, when Michigan had 320,611 people engaged in manufacturing, almost 121,000 of them were located in Detroit, the city that would become the automobile capital of the world. In that year, the state's 67,538 auto workers were contributing 62.9% of the nation's total value of automobile related products (US Department of Commerce 1918).

Several factors were vital to the continued rapid growth of Michigan's auto industry in the early 20th century. In 1908, Oldsmobile, Buick and Cadillac were among 20 auto firms that had been formed in, or that had shifted their operations to, Detroit (Green 1965). In that same year, Oldsmobile merged with Buick to form General Motors (GM). Over the next ten years, GM gained control of a number of other firms, including the Oakland Motor Car Company, based in Pontiac, i.e., its Pontiac division, Cadillac and Chevrolet (Chandler 1977). With GM's purchase of these firms, its factories began to expand north and west from Detroit, into Oakland County, Flint and Lansing. Chiefly as a result of GM's success with its Buick, Chevrolet, A.C. Spark Plug and Fisher Body Plants, Flint mushroomed from a town of 8,930 in 1890, to a city of 156,492 residents in 1930 (Thomas 2005, Firey 1946, 8–9, Michigan Society of Planning Officials 1995).

GM's Buick Division also spawned a second member of the US auto industry's Big Three—Chrysler. This event occurred in 1925, when former Buick Division manager, Walter Chrysler, resurrected the bankrupted Maxwell Motors and incorporated it as Chrysler Motor Company (Levin 1995). By 1928, he had acquired the Hamtramck and Detroit plants of the late Dodge Brothers, including the rights to build Dodge Brothers and Plymouth vehicles (Chandler 1990, Levin 1995).

It was Henry Leland's former chief engineer, Henry Ford, who truly sparked the emergence of Michigan's auto industry. In 1903, Ford founded the third member of the Big Three—the Ford Motor Company. In the beginning, Ford built his business through Detroit area connections. He bought all the items he needed to assemble his first car from suppliers in the city, e.g., transmissions and engines from the Dodge Brothers (Jacobs 1969). After a disagreement with Ford over the price of their parts, in 1914, the Dodge Brothers decided to build their own automobile plant in nearby Hamtramck. The opening of the Dodge Main Plant attracted thousands of Polish laborers to the village, pushing its population from 3,589 in 1910, to 46,615 in 1920 (City of Hamtramck 1997).

Although the Dodge Brothers eventually sold out to Chrysler, it was Ford's 1913 implementation of the world's first moving assembly line at his Highland Park Plant that proved to be the most significant catalyst behind Detroit's (and Michigan's) industrial growth. This process, which would dictate how most factory goods were manufactured for the next 75 years, made it possible to mass produce automobiles. Only two years after its installation, Ford had already produced its one-millionth Model T automobile (Garreau 1988). As Thomas (1992, 24–26) wrote:

"By 1910, the auto age had affected every facet of Detroit, transforming and increasing its population and revolutionizing its cultural and political character. Automobile production, and the magic and myth of Henry Ford attracted workers from other industrial areas, both in and outside the state. Yugoslavs, Finns, and Lithuanians who had worked in the copper mines and lumber camps of Michigan's Upper Peninsula, flocked to Detroit in pursuit of higher wages in the auto industry. Ukrainians and other Slavic Russians left the ... coal mines of New York and Pennsylvania ... for Detroit's auto factories. Sicilians, Poles, Bulgarians and Macedonians all were drawn into Detroit's boom industry ... By 1915, Henry Ford's promise of $5.00 a day [had also drawn] a large influx of Black laborers from the South to Detroit ... In 1900, Detroit was the 13th largest city in the nation ... By 1920 it [had] soared to 4th."

By 1921, the Ford Motor Company accounted for 55.7% of the passenger cars produced in the United States (Chandler 1990, 205). Henry Ford was spending much of his profits on the expansion of his new "Industrial Colossus," the Rouge Plant, which opened in Dearborn in 1919 (Nevins and Hill 1957). Within five years of its construction, "The Rouge" had its own steel mill, equipped with blast furnaces and foundries, supplying most of the iron, brass, steel and bronze castings used in Ford factories (Nevins and Hill 1957; Fig. 30.11). In doing so, over time, Ford slowly weaned away from its Detroit suppliers, integrating the production of parts, accessories and replacement parts into his own facilities (Chandler 1990). As a result, by 1929, the Rouge Plant had become an industrial city of its own, employing almost 100,000 hourly workers (Nevins and Hill 1957). These efforts were complemented by Ford Motor's building of scores of residential districts just west and north of the Rouge, to house the plant's factory workers. While this was no Detroit boom, the City of Fordson (now part of Dearborn), represented the beginning of the suburbanization of both the Ford Motor Company and its workers.

Ford further fueled the decentralization of manufacturing and housing in Metro Detroit in the early 1940s with the construction of its Willow Run Plant in Washtenaw County. At its peak in 1943, Willow Run employed over 42,000 people, many traveling to and from work along a Ford-built expressway (now Interstate Hwy 94) (Kidder 1995). Willow Run's main purpose however, during this period, was to supplement America's efforts in World War II, the state's final, pre-1950s industrial catalyst. WWII led to numerous government contracts for the Big Three automakers, for airplanes, tanks and other ordnance. Jobs in these sectors attracted hundreds of thousands of new residents to Michigan.

■ Michigan's auto industry disperses and downsizes: 1953 to 2005

In response to military orders for the Korean War, and booming demand for housing and goods by World War II veterans, manufacturing employment peaked in Michigan in 1953, at 1,261,871 (US Department of Commerce 1956, Jacobs 1999). Manufacturing jobs represented 59.2% of all private employment in the state in 1953, another post-war high (Fig. 31.1). The largest manufacturing sector in the state was Transportation Equipment Manufacturing with 505,490 jobs, and of these, 454,894 were in Motor Vehicles and Parts Manufacturing. Michigan's share of national Transportation Equipment employment was 25.9% in 1953, and its share of US jobs in Motor Vehicle and Parts Manufacturing was an astonishing 51.1% (Table 31.1). Unfortunately, both represented post-war peaks.

Geographically, almost 52% of the state's manufacturing employment, and just more than 57% of its Transportation Equipment jobs, in 1953, were located in Wayne County (Tables 31.2, 31.3). Moreover, just over 60% of its Motor Vehicles and Parts Manufacturing employment was located there. Another 30% of the workers in the latter two categories worked in five nearby counties: Genesee, Ingham, Macomb, Oakland and Washtenaw (Tables 31.2, 31.3).

After the Korean War, military production was scaled back, and the automakers began to disperse their production nationally and internationally, in an effort to be nearer to expanding consumer and supplier markets. Due to a decline in the supply of iron ore in the Lake Superior Region during the 1950s, the major US steelmakers closed many of their steel mills in the Great Lakes region and relocated them to foreign locales, e.g., Venezuela, where resources were more plentiful. This triggered relocations of auto-related suppliers, seeking to cut their transport costs by being closer to producers. Changes in foreign tariffs, foreign government regulations, automation and technological advancements in transportation and communication, all helped to quicken the pace of decentralization (Hurley 1959). As a result, both total and manufacturing employment in Michigan declined to 1.88 million and 922,029 jobs, respectively, in 1962 (Fig. 31.1). These figures represented drops of almost 250,000 in total jobs and 340,000 in industrial employment from 1953. The same was true for Transportation Equipment and Motor Vehicles and Parts employment, which contracted by roughly 225,000 and 282,000 jobs, respectively between 1953 and 1962 (US Department of

FIGURE 31.1   Temporal changes in manufacturing employment in the US and Michigan, 1953–2005. Source: US Census, County Business Patterns 1953–2005.

Commerce 1964; Table 31.1). As a result, by 1962, Michigan's shares of US Transportation Equipment and Motor Vehicles and Parts manufacturing employment had fallen to 18.2% and 40.4%, respectively (Table 31.3).

By the 1963 model year, the Big Three were producing 2.65 million vehicles annually in Michigan—about 322,000 more than in the 1957 model year. Nonetheless, the state's share of US vehicle production had fallen from 32.1% in 1957, to 30.7% in 1963 (Table 31.4). Still, at that time, Metro Detroit had plants located in numerous communities: Dearborn, Detroit, Hamtramck, Highland Park, and Wayne in Wayne County, Warren in Macomb County, Ypsilanti city and Ypsilanti Township in Washtenaw County, and Pontiac and Wixom in Oakland County (Ward's Communications 1958, 1964). In addition, Flint (Genesee County) and Lansing (Ingham County) were centers of car and truck production. The Big Three also had numerous parts plants in Detroit, Dearborn, Livonia and Trenton,

TABLE 31.1   Transportation Equipment and Motor Vehicle and Parts Manufacturing employment in Michigan and the US, in 1953, 1969, 1988 and 2005

Year	Transportation Equipment Employment			Motor Vehicle and Parts Employment		
	US	Michigan	% of US	US	Michigan	% of US
1953	1,953,054	505,490	25.9%	890,258	454,894	51.1%
1962	1,541,618	279,846	18.2%	651,019	262,876	40.4%
1969	2,020,619	368,753	18.3%	867,967	347,515	40.0%
1988	1,847,865	230,203	12.5%	739,044	215,695	29.2%
2005[1]	1,636,111	198,228	12.1%	983,174	189,622	19.3%

Sources: US Department of Commerce (1956, 1964, 1990, 2007).
1. Similar to prior years, this total includes Motor Home Manufacturing, but not Travel Trailers and Campers Manufacturing employment.

in Wayne County, in Genesee, Bay and Saginaw Counties, and in the state's western industrial center—Grand Rapids (Ward's Communications 1956, 1964).

Economic growth in the US, coupled with the Vietnam War, spurred a rebound in automobile production during the 1960s. By 1969, Michigan had approximately 1.2 million manufacturing jobs, with 368,753 jobs in Transportation Equipment, and 347,515 in Motor Vehicles and Parts Manufacturing (Table 31.2). In that year, Manufacturing represented 47.0% of all private employment in the state (US Department of Commerce 1971). Additionally, the state's share of US Transportation Equipment employment had risen to 18.3%; however, its proportion of Motor Vehicles and Parts employment had fallen to 40.0%. Michigan's share of US automotive production jobs has declined ever since (US Department of Commerce 1974).

Geographically, by 1969, the percentage of Michigan's overall Manufacturing and Transportation Equipment employment located in Wayne County had fallen to 35.0% and 36.4%, respectively—a decline of 17% and 22%, respectively, from 1953 (Tables 31.2, 31.3). Federal urban and industrial policies, beginning in the 1950s, as well as land assembly and price issues, had helped spur these moves. For example, the National Industrial Dispersion Program of 1951 promoted the decentralization of the auto industry, through its offering of accelerated tax amortization on capital machinery, as part of the US Defense Department's plan to encourage new plant construction outside of potential Soviet nuclear target zones. Reacting to this, complementary metal and machinery industries also clustered around these new factories (Hurley 1959, Hill 1984, Darden et al. 1987, Thomas 1990; Chapter 32). The Federal Housing Administration's Loan Program, and the National Highway Act of 1956, also helped make suburban areas much more accessible to industrial workers (Darden et al. 1987, Thomas 1997). Finally, the inability to assemble land in Detroit, its high land cost per unit area relative to the suburbs, and federal and state subsidies for local water and sewer extensions, prompted manufacturers to shift their employment away from the city center to suburban greenfields in Oakland, Macomb and Washtenaw Counties (Jacobs 2003, 2004; Chapters 32, 33).

In the two decades following 1969, the auto industry and related manufacturing continued their flight away from the Detroit and Wayne County, to the suburbs and, in some cases, out of the state altogether. Indeed, between 1969 and 1986, while manufacturing employment in Wayne County contracted by 192,576 (45.8%), it rose by 14.2% in Macomb County, by 16.4% in Oakland County and by 8.6% in Washtenaw County (US Department of Commerce 1971, 1988; Table 31.2). Wayne County also lost 80,206 (59.8%) of its Transportation Equipment employment jobs during this period (Table 31.3). On the whole, Michigan's Transportation Equipment employment declined by 108,678 (29.5%) between 1969 and 1986. In comparison, similar data for the US as a whole show a contraction of only 4,086 jobs (0.2%) in this sector. As a result, in 1986, Michigan's share of US Transportation Equipment jobs had fallen to only 12.9% (Table 31.1). Moreover, although Motor Vehicles and Parts employment in Michigan contracted by 131,819 (37.9%) between 1969 and 1988, it declined in this sector by only 128,923 jobs (14.9%) in the US as a whole (Table 31.1). Therefore, by 1988, the state's proportion of US Motor Vehicles and Parts manufacturing employment had dropped to 29.2%. Concurrently, at 3.32 million cars and trucks, Michigan's share of

TABLE 31.2   Manufacturing employment in Michigan's major auto-manufacturing counties, from 1953–2005

	Michigan	Total for six counties	Six counties (% of state)	Genesee County	Ingham County	Macomb County	Oakland County	Washtenaw County	Wayne County	Wayne (% of MI mfg)
1953	1,261,871	887,495	70.3	71,254	34,457	36,011	59,100	31,097	655,576	52.0
1962	922,029	593,427	64.4	64,027	25,953	57,714	61,295	25,473	358,965	39.0
1969	1,198,536	779,346	65.0	84,775	38,023	94,857	103,930	37,225	420,536	35.1
1986	995,798	594,199	59.7	63,629	32,859	108,981	120,329	40,441	227,960	22.9
2005	635,234	277,948	43.8	19,362	15,253	66,632	62,589	17,075	97,037	15.3
Change										
1953–1962	−339,842	−294,068		−7,227	−8,504	21,703	2,195	−5,624	−296,611	
1962–1969	276,507	185,919		20,748	12,070	37,143	42,635	11,752	61,571	
1969–1986	−202,738	−185,147		−21,146	−5,164	14,124	16,399	3,216	−192,576	
1986–2005	−360,564	−316,161		−44,267	−17,606	−42,259	−57,740	−23,566	−130,923	
1953–2005	−626,637	−609,547		−51,892	−19,204	30,621	3,489	−14,022	−558,539	
1969–2005	−563,302	501,398		−65,413	−22,770	−28,225	−41,341	−21,150	−323,499	
Percent Change										
1953–1962	−26.9%	−33.1%		−10.1%	−24.7%	60.3%	3.7%	−18.1%	−45.2%	
1962–1969	30.0%	31.3%		32.4%	46.5%	64.4%	69.6%	46.1%	17.2%	
1969–1986	−16.9%	−23.8%		−24.9%	−13.6%	14.24%	16.39%	8.6%	−45.8%	
1986–2005	−36.2%	−53.2%		−69.6%	−53.6%	−38.9%	−48.0%	−57.8%	−57.4%	
1953–2003	−49.7%	−68.7%		−72.8%	−55.7%	85.0%	5.9%	−45.1%	−85.2%	
1969–2005	−47.0%	−64.3%		−77.2%	−59.9%	−29.8%	−39.8%	−54.1%	−76.9%	

Sources: US Department of Commerce (1956, 2007)

TABLE 31.3   Transportation Equipment employment in Michigan's major auto-manufacturing counties, from 1953–2005

	Michigan	Total for six counties	Six counties (% of state)	Genesee County	Ingham County	Macomb County	Oakland County	Washtenaw County	Wayne County	Wayne (% of MI mfg)
1953	505,490	441,149	87.3	61,068	24,612	17,255	32,711	17,178	288,325	57.0
1962	279,846	240,518	86.0	49,788	18,607	16,939	31,677	10,420	113,087	40.4
1969	368,753	318,543	86.4	69,555	28,614	23,522	47,001	15,628	134,223	36.4
1986	260,075	213,748	82.2	51,159	25,159	22,578	41,968	18,867	54,017	28.6
2005	198,228	119,780	60.4	12,800	9,041	27,743	19,532	4,906	45,758	23.1
Change										
1953–1962	−225,644	−200,631		−11,280	−6,005	−3162	−1,034	−6,758	−175,238	
1962–1969	88,907	78,025		19,767	10,007	6,583	15,324	5,208	21,136	
1969–1986	−108,678	−104,795		−18,396	−3,455	−944	−5,033	3,239	−80,206	
1986–2005	−61,847	−93,968		−38,359	−16,118	5,165	−22,436	−13,961	−8,259	
1953–2005	−307,262	321,369		−48,268	−15,571	10,488	−13,179	−12,272	−242,567	
1969–2005	−170,525	−198,763		−56,755	−19,573	4,221	−27,469	−10,722	−88,465	
Percent Change										
1953–1962	−44.6%	−45.5%		−18.5%	−24.4%	−1.8%	−3.2%	−39.3%	−60.8%	
1962–1969	31.8%	32.4%		39.7%	53.8%	38.9%	48.4%	50.0%	18.7%	
1969–1986	−29.5%	−32.9%		−26.5%	−12.1%	−4.0%	−10.7%	20.7%	−59.8%	
1986–2005	−23.8%	−44.0%		−75.0%	−64.1%	22.9%	−53.5%	−74.0%	−15.3%	
1953–2005	−60.8%	−72.9%		−79.0%	−63.3%	60.8%	−40.3%	−71.4%	−84.1%	
1969–2005	−46.2%	−62.4%		−81.6%	−68.4%	17.9%	−58.4%	−68.6%	−65.9%	

Sources: US Department of Commerce (1956, 2007).

US vehicle production had fallen to 30.0% in 1988, down from 3.42 million and 32.9%, respectively, in 1969 (Ward's Communications 1970, 1989; Table 31.4).

After 1986, manufacturing and auto-related employment, as well as production, continued to decline in Michigan. Only 2.52 million vehicles were produced in the state in 2005 (Table 31.4), accounting for just 21.0% of all vehicles produced in the US in that year. In addition, by 2005, Michigan jobs in Transportation Equipment manufacturing had fallen to 198,228, with just 189,622 in Motor Vehicles and Parts manufacturing (Table 31.1). These totals represented just 12.1% and 19.3% of US employment in these sectors in that year; the latter figure was almost 21 percentage points less than in 1969.

The impacts of Michigan's post-1969 manufacturing decline were felt unevenly across the state, especially within the Detroit metropolitan area. Between 1969 and 2005, private employment, statewide, grew by 1.24 million jobs, or 58.8% (Table 31.5). Suburban Detroit counties of Macomb, Oakland and Washtenaw saw their employment grow

TABLE 31.4   Michigan and US Vehicle Production, from 1957–2005[1]

	Michigan Cars	% of US Cars	Michigan Trucks	% of US Trucks	Michigan Vehicles	% of US Vehicles
1957	2,151,200	34.7	179,554	17.1	2,330,754	32.1
1963	2,432,589	33.2	264,781	18.2	2,697,370	30.7
1969	2,886,885	347	533,136	27.4	3,420,021	32.9
1988	2,498,017	35.8	818,363	20.0	3,316,380	30.0
2003	1,528,101	33.9	1,255,738	16.6	2,783,839	23.0

Sources: Wards (1958, 1964, 1989, 2004)

1. Ward's reports production by state, for cars by model year. For trucks, it reports totals by state by calendar year.

TABLE 31.5   Private employment change in Michigan counties with 100,000 or more jobs, 1969–2005[1]

	1969	2005	Change 1969–2005	% change 1969–2005
Michigan	2,552,050	3,796,876	1,244,826	48.8
Detroit-Ann Arbor-Flint CMSA				
Genesee County	146,272	135,722	−10,550	−7.2
Macomb County	154,825	305,634	150,809	97.4
Oakland County	239,950	720,201	480,251	200.2
Washtenaw County	69,997	151,721	81,724	116.8
Wayne County	956,334	669,498	−286,836	−30.0
Detroit City, Wayne County[2]	631,405	304,254	−306,521	−50.2
Other Counties				
Ingham County	86,200	127,577	41,377	48.0
Kalamazoo County	62,804	109,046	46,242	73.6
Kent County	143,032	322,959	179,927	125.8
Ottawa County	29,474	104,804	75,330	255.6

Sources: SEMCOG (1980, 2006); 1969 and 2005 County Business Patterns.

1. Employment is by place of work and does not include government employees.

2. Detroit City data are for 2002.

by 96.4% or more during this period, and the western, out-state, counties of Kalamazoo, Kent and Ottawa grew by between 73.6% and 255.6%. However, manufacturing jobs in the urban core counties of Wayne and Genesee declined; Detroit alone lost 306,521 jobs after 1969. Conversely, Oakland County added 480,251 jobs.

Population trends were similar. For example, due to Detroit's population decline of 562,792, Wayne County's population contracted by 22.8% between 1970 and 2000. In contrast, Macomb, Oakland and Washtenaw Counties experienced population increases of more than 25%. Finally, as a result of the decline of Michigan's auto centers, income inequality by place has increased significantly within the Detroit metropolitan area since 1969 (Jacobs 2003, 2004).

■ Recent trends in Michigan's manufacturing sector

For more than 100 years, manufacturing, especially the auto industry, has been the lifeblood of Michigan's economy. In 2005, the state had 14,033 manufacturing establishments, employing 635,234 people and providing $31.6 billion in annual wages and salaries (US Department of Commerce 2007). Manufacturing jobs accounted for 16.7% of the state's 3,796,876 people in private employment in 2003 (Fig. 31.1). Although Michigan has a much higher percentage of its employment in manufacturing than does the nation (11.8%), its 2005 data were dramatically lower than in 1953, when 59.2% of the state's private employment was employed in manufacturing, as compared with 43.4% nationally (US Department of Commerce 1956, 2007).

Michigan's largest industrial sector has remained Transportation Equipment Manufacturing, with 198,228 jobs in 2005 (Table 31.6). Of this, 189,622 jobs were in Motor Vehicles and Parts Manufacturing, accounting for 19.3% of the US employment in that sub-sector (Table 31.1). After Transportation Equipment, the state's next largest industries were Fabricated Metals (87,391 jobs) and Machinery Manufacturing (76,387). Both of these have served as complementary sectors to automobile production.

Geographically, led by Wayne County, 15 of Michigan's 83 counties had 10,000 or more in manufacturing employ-

ment in 2005 (Table 31.7; Fig 31.2). In that year, southeastern Michigan counties accounted for 74.9% of the state's industrial employment, of which 51.7% was concentrated in Wayne, Oakland, Macomb, Kent and Ottawa Counties. Among the top six counties, the largest industrial sector, in 2005, in all but Kent County, was Transportation Equipment. This also was the case in 12 of the state's 15 counties with more than 10,000 in manufacturing employment (Table 31.7). Nonetheless, despite declines, the Detroit and Flint metro areas remain the heart and soul of Michigan's Motor Vehicle and Parts production. Metropolitan Detroit counties, and Kent County, were the state's centers of Fabricated Metals and Machinery Manufacturing.

Other major industries in the state include plastics (Kent and Macomb Counties), chemicals (Midland County, home to Dow Chemical), furniture (Kent and Ottawa), and food (Calhoun County's Battle Creek is home to cereal maker Kellogg's, and was formerly the home to Post Cereals, now part of Kraftco Inc.). In sum, while the automobile industry has been the primary engine of Michigan's economy since at least the early 1900s, historically, auto production has not been the only driving force behind the state's industrial growth, and continued diversification appears to be a part of Michigan's manufacturing future.

FIGURE 31.2   The major manufacturing counties in Michigan. Source: US Department of Commerce, Bureau of Census (1953–2005).

TABLE 31.6   Michigan manufacturing sectors with more than 10,000 employees, in 2005

	Total Manufacturing Employment	635,234
Industry code	**Industry description**	**Employees**
311	Food manufacturing	28,162
321	Wood product manufacturing	12,006
322	Paper manufacturing	13,933
323	Printing and related support activities	18,793
325	Chemical manufacturing	27,791
326	Plastics and rubber products manufacturing	55,270
	3261 Plastics product manufacturing	49,866
327	Nonmetallic mineral product manufacturing[1]	14,502
331	Primary metal manufacturing	27,784
	3315 Ferrous and non-ferrous foundries	14,600
332	Fabricated metal product manufacturing	87,391
	3327 Machine shops; turned product; and screw, nut and bolt manufacturing	29,577
	3328 Coating, engraving, heat treating, and allied activities	14,794
	3329 Other fabricated metal product manufacturing	14,076
333	Machinery manufacturing	76,387
	3335 Metalworking machinery manufacturing	35,788
	3339 Other general purpose machinery manufacturing	18,761
334	Computer and electronic product manufacturing	15,956
335	Electrical equipment, appliance, and component manufacturing	11,578
336	Transportation equipment manufacturing	198,228
	3361 Motor vehicle manufacturing	39,576
	33611 Automobile and light duty motor vehicle manufacturing	38,808
	336111 Automobile manufacturing	17,392
	336112 Light truck and utility vehicle manufacturing	21,416
	3363 Motor vehicle parts manufacturing	148,532
	33631 Motor vehicle gasoline engine and engine parts manufacturing	20,880
	33635 Motor vehicle transmission and power train parts manufacturing	19,789
	33636 Motor vehicle seating and interior trim manufacturing	15,360
	33637 Motor vehicle metal stamping	43,431
	33639 Other motor vehicle parts manufacturing	43,431
337	Furniture and related product manufacturing	23,640
339	Miscellaneous manufacturing	15,383

Source: US Department of Commerce (2007)

1. Includes clay and ceramics, glass, cement and concrete, and lime and gypsum product manufacturing

TABLE 31.7   Michigan counties with >10,000 persons employed in manufacturing, in 2005

County	Manufacturing employment	Code	Largest manufacturing sector(s)	Employees
Wayne	97,037	336	Transportation equipment	45,758
		332	Fabricated metal products	10,969
		333	Machinery	9,946
Macomb	66,632	336	Transportation equipment	27,743
		332	Fabricated metal products	11,648
		333	Machinery	11.092
Kent	64,015	333	Machinery	9,798
		326	Plastics and rubber products	7,887
		337	Furniture and related products	7,087
Oakland	62,589	336	Transportation equipment	19,532
		333	Machinery	12,744
		332	Fabricated metal products	10.249
Ottawa	38,439	336	Transportation equipment	11,282
		337	Furniture and related products	5,365
Genesee	19,362	336	Transportation equipment	12,800
Kalamazoo	17,604	325	Chemicals	3,769
Washtenaw	17,075	336	Transportation equipment	4,906
Ingham	15,253	336	Transportation equipment	9,041
Allegan	14,666	336	Transportation equipment	3,068
Muskegon	14,333	331	Primary metals	3,861
Saginaw	14,072	336	Transportation equipment	X
Calhoun	12,518	336	Transportation equipment	4,590
Berrien	12,083	336	Transportation equipment	1,993
Jackson	10,118	336	Transportation equipment	2,463
Total for these 15 counties: 475,796 (74.9%) of Michigan's manufacturing employment				

Source: US Department of Commerce (2007)

X: Exact figure not reported by the source, but in this category there is a range of 5,000–9,999 employees.

■ Conclusions

Mirroring national trends, only 17.5% of Michigan's private employment was in manufacturing in 2005—a drop of 42.5% from 1953. Nonetheless, manufacturing remains an important sector of Michigan's economy. In 2003, the State was home to 17 Big Three car and truck assembly plants, and one motor home plant (Ward's Communications 2004). This total included the factories of Chrysler Corporation, of which the US Equity firm Cerberus recently purchased an 80% share of from its former parent DaimlerChrysler. Michigan also houses factories of several US and foreign auto supplier firms, as well as the offices and research and development facilities of automotive firms headquartered in more than 20 countries. Despite losing almost 85% of its manufacturing employment since 1953, with the World Headquarters of GM in Detroit, and Ford in Dearborn, auto assembly plants Detroit, Dearborn, Flat Rock, Hamtramck and Wayne, and engine and supplier facilities in Livonia, Plymouth, Redford, Romulus, Trenton and Woodhaven, Wayne County remains the heart of Michigan's manufacturing engine.

Since 1953, as the US auto industry has reacted to local and global factors, it has also become economically restructured and more efficient and more globally focused. It has shifted much of its factory work out of Detroit, first to its suburbs, then to the Sunbelt states and finally to foreign countries (Jacobs 2003, 2004). Shifting factory locations, combined with improvements in productivity, has resulted in significant declines in manufacturing and auto industry employment in the state in recent times. For example, between 1953 and 2005 the number of manufacturing jobs in Michigan was effectively cut in half from 1.26 million to 635,234 (US Department of Commerce 1956, 2007; Fig. 31.1). As such, the state's decline during this period was far more severe than the nation's contraction in that same sector. Similar trends can be cited for employment within the various other manufacturing sectors. It is important to emphasize that most of these declines occurred after 1969, after which Michigan's share of US motor vehicles produced fell dramatically.

In closing, although the manufacturing sector has declined dramatically in the state over the past 50 years, Michigan's economic and industrial success continues to depend heavily on the fate of its automobile industry. Moreover, in spite of its pitfalls, Michigan has remained the center of the US auto production.

Literature Cited

Chandler, A. 1977. The Visible Hand: The Managerial Revolution in American Business. Harvard University Press, Cambridge, MA.

Chandler, A. 1990. Scale and Scope: The Dynamics of Industrial Capitalism. Harvard University Press, Cambridge, MA.

Darden, J., Hill, R.C., Thomas, J. and R. Thomas. 1987. Race and Uneven Development. Temple University Press, Philadelphia, PA.

Firey, W. 1946. Social Aspects to Land Use Planning in the Country-City Fringe: The Case of Flint, Michigan. Michigan State College, Agricultural Experiment Station, Special Bulletin 339. East Lansing, MI.

Green, C.M. 1965. American Cities in the Growth of the Nation. Harper and Row, New York.

Hamtramck, City of. 1997. In: Hamtramck, A City Within a City. City of Hamtramck (MI), Office of Economic Development, and Hamtramck Chamber of Commerce.

Hill, R.C. 1984. Economic Crisis and Political Response in the Motor City. In: L. Sawers and W. K. Tabb (eds), Sunbelt/Snowbelt: Urban Development and Regional Restructuring. Oxford University Press, New York. pp. 313–338.

Hurley, N. 1959. The automotive industry: A study in industrial location. Land Economics 35:1–14.

Jacobs, A.J. 1999. Intergovernmental Relations and Uneven Development in the Detroit (U.S.) and Nagoya (Japan) Auto Regions. Ph.D. dissertation. Michigan State University, East Lansing, MI.

Jacobs, A.J. 2003. Embedded autonomy and uneven metropolitan development: A comparison of the Detroit and Nagoya auto regions, 1969–2000. Urban Studies 40:335–360.

Jacobs, A.J. 2004. Inter-local relations and divergent growth: The Detroit and Tokai auto regions, 1969 to 1996. Journal of Urban Affairs 26:479–504.

Jacobs, J. 1969. The Economy of Cities. Random House, New York.

Kidder, W.B. 1995. Willow Run: Colossus of American Industry, Home of Henry Ford's B-24 'Liberator'= Bomber. KFT, Lansing, MI.

Levin D. 1995. Behind the Wheel at Chrysler: The Iacocca Legacy. Harcourt Brace and Company, New York.

Michigan Society of Planning Officials. 1995. Jobs and the Built Environment Trends. Working Paper, Michigan's Trend Future. Michigan Society of Planning Officials, Rochester, MI.

Nevins, E. and F.E. Hill. 1957. Ford: Expansion and Challenge, 1915–1933. Charles Scribner's Sons, New York.

Thomas, L. 2005. Flint timeline. http://www.flinthistory.com/history/timeline.shtml (Accessed October 25, 2005).

Thomas, J.M. 1990. Planning and industrial decline: Lessons from postwar Detroit. Journal of the American Planning Association 56:297–310.

Thomas, J.M. 1997. Redevelopment and Race: Planning a Finer City in Postwar Detroit. Johns Hopkins University Press, Baltimore, MD.

Thomas, R.W. 1992. Life for Us Is What We Make It: Building Black Community in Detroit, 1915–1945. Indiana University Press, Bloomington, IN.

US Department of Commerce, Bureau of Census. 1918. Census of Manufactures, 1914. Government Printing Office. Washington, DC.

US Department of Commerce, Bureau of Census. 1953, 1956, 1971, 1988, 2005, 2007. County Business Patterns 1953. Government Printing Office. Washington, DC.

Ward's Communications. 1956, 1958, 1964, 1970, 1989. Ward's Automotive Yearbook, 1956. Ward's Communications, Detroit, MI.

Further Readings

Bluestone, B. and B. Harrison. 1982. The Deindustrialization of America: Plant Closings, Community Abandonment, and the Dismantling of Basic Industry. Basic Books, New York.

Dicken, P. 2007. Global Shift: Mapping the Changing Contours of the World Economy. Guilford Press, New York.

Harrison, B. and B. Bluestone. 1988. The Great U-Turn: Corporate Restructuring and the Polarizing of America. Basic Books, New York.

Hill, R.C. 1989. Divisions of Labor in Global Manufacturing: The Case of the Automobile Industry. In: A. MacEwan and W. Tabb (eds), Instability and Change in the World Economy. Monthly Review Press, New York. pp. 166–186.

Jacobs, A.J. 2005. The Manufacturing City. In: R. Caves (ed), The Encyclopedia of the City. Routledge, New York. p. 304.

Maynard, M. 2003. The End of Detroit: How the Big Three Lost their Grip on the American Car Market. Currency/Doubleday Press, New York.

Rosentretter, R. 1996. Michigan Made: 100 Years of the Automobile. Michigan History 80 (Mar–Apr). 96 pp.

Womack, J., Jones, D. and D. Roos. 1991. The Machine that Changed the World. HarperPerennial, New York.

32   Urban Settlements: Suburbanization and the Future

Igor Vojnovic

Urban decentralization in America

Currently, half of the US population lives in suburbs, with the remainder split between urban and rural areas (US Census Bureau 2000). These developments are a concrete demographic and physical settlement pattern, reflecting a new spatial arrangement that began to shape the US urban landscape in the second half of the 20th century. In fact, since the 1970s, the majority of the population living in US metropolitan areas has lived in suburbs (US Congress 1995). Similar decentralization trends were also occurring among businesses, as they began following residents out of the city, or vice versa. For example, in 1970 25% of the office stock in metropolitan areas was located in suburbs, but by 1993, this figure had increased to 53% (US Congress 1995).

One of the defining elements of US cities over the last century has been urban decentralization and dispersion (Ewing 1997). Some people refer to this development pattern as "urban sprawl," but since sprawl has no clearly agreed upon definition or measure, the terms urban decentralization and low density suburbanization will, instead, be used in this chapter to describe this development typology. Urban decentralization was in part facilitated by new consumption practices in the real estate market, with an increasing amount of land used in the production of commercial and residential developments (Figs. 32.1, 32.2). This was particularly evident in the second half of the 20th century, as homes and lots became larger, streets became wider and new developments began to scatter and leapfrog each other. By the 1960s, urban analysts were becoming increasingly troubled by the newly emerging development patterns. As indicated by Boyce (1963, 242),

> "Urbanized areas in the United States used twice as much land in 1960 as in 1950. Yet, during the same period, population increased by only 38%. . . . Average density of urbanized areas has decreased from 5,410 persons per square mile in 1950 to only 3,759 persons per square mile in 1960, a decrease in density of 31%."

In the more recent context, overall land consumption trends continue to be as significant. For instance, between 1982 and 1992, while urban land in the US increased by >25%, the population increased by only 11% (Pendall 1999). Within the context of these wider, national patterns in urban development, questions emerge about the nature of urban decentralization in Michigan. This chapter will assess the variables that shaped Michigan's cities over the last century, exploring the unique built environment characteristics that facilitated large-scale urban decentralization. I will also explore the economic, environmental and social consequences of inefficient suburbanization in Michigan, and reflect on policies that might mitigate the premature development of natural and agricultural lands.

FIGURE 32.1   Early 1900 commercial and retail development in Detroit (A), vs that of present-day Michigan (B). In the new, land-extensive commercial and retail developments, a single store might have acres of land are devoted solely to parking.

FIGURE 32.2   Upscale residential homes in (A) early 1900 Detroit, vs (B) a post World War II bungalow in modern-day Michigan.

Drivers of suburbanization

During the 20th century, the decentralization of cities was facilitated by series of technological, social and economic factors. Some of these factors included (1) rapid population growth, (2) declines in real energy costs, (3) increases in incomes, (4) crime and violence in cities, (5) homeownership preferences for single-family, detached homes, (6) social and racial tensions and (7) the abundance of relatively cheap, rural land. It was, however, the introduction of the private automobile and the transport truck that enabled the rapid movement of people and goods throughout a wider geographic area, that was particularly important in facilitating suburbanization.

Suburbanization was also encouraged through public policy, with the goal of facilitating the outward, as opposed to the upward, growth of cities. The advocacy for urban decentralization was in reaction to the extreme densities and the development disorder of early 20th century industrial cities. Policies in the US that were introduced to facilitate decentralization included (1) public investment and subsidization of suburban infrastructure, e.g., roads, water and sewage networks, (2) public investment preferences for private over public transportation, and (3) Federal Housing Administration (FHA) mortgage guarantees that favored new housing purchases in the suburbs (Vojnovic 1999, 2000a, 2006).

Suburbanization in Michigan

Regionally, Michigan has not only been keeping pace with the US urban decentralization trends, it has been leading them. Orfield and Luce (2003, 4) noted that "Despite slow population growth in most areas, sprawling development in Michigan's regions is consuming more and more open space. From 1970 to 2000, the amount of developed land increased as much as 10 times faster than population." Similarly, the State of Michigan's Land Use Leadership Council (2003) indicated that the average urban population density in the state has declined from 1.5 persons/hectare in the early 1980s, to 1.1 persons/hectare by the late 1990s. US Census Bureau (2000) data show that, as of 2000, over 60% of Michigan's population lived in suburbs.

Michigan's 10 million people reside on a little less than 150,000 km². Metropolitan areas are still the economic, social and cultural focus of the state, with four out of every five Michiganders living in the metro regions of Detroit, Grand Rapids, Lansing, Kalamazoo, Flint, Saginaw and Traverse City. However, the decentralization of residents and businesses out of the older city centers has placed the inner-cities—and the older, inner-suburbs—under considerable strain. The Detroit region provides a good example of the population exodus into the suburbs, between the years 1960 and 2000 (Fig. 32.3).

Urban decentralization is not only characterized by the movement of people and businesses out of the city-centers, it has also taken with it the property tax base. In the year 2000, per capita property assessment in Detroit averaged only $7,573, with the city losing $147,128,606 in taxable assessment between the years 1990 and 2000 (SEMCOG 2003a). In contrast, the Detroit suburb of Bloomfield Hills maintained a per capita taxable value of $165,794 in 2000, with an increase in taxable value of $88,066,682 during the 1990s (Table 32.1). These decentralization patterns, and resulting fiscal discrepancies, are occurring throughout the state. Michigan's central cities maintain a property tax-base that is only 44% of the regional average.

Figure 32.4 illustrates the land-to-population growth ratios for several Michigan municipalities for 1960–1990. The figure illustrates the scale of natural and agricultural land consumption, and how the rate of growth in built-land exceeds that of population growth. When the rate of growth of urban land use exceeds that of population, urban land densities decrease. In addition, throughout much of the state, these low-density development patterns are not only continuing, but are increasing in number. In

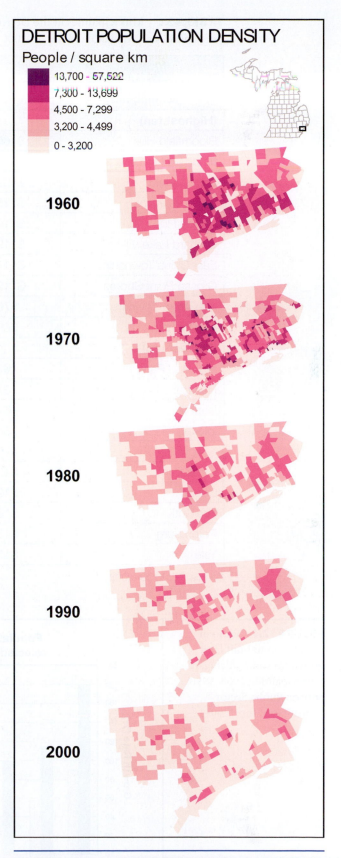

FIGURE 32.3 Detroit population densities, in 1960, 1980, and 2000. Source: US Census Bureau (1960, 1980, 2000).

TABLE 32.1   Municipalities in the Detroit region with the highest and lowest per capita assessed taxable values, in 2000

Municipality	Taxable value per capita, 2000	Change in taxable value, 1990–2000 (inflation-adjusted)
(Highest ten)		
Bloomfield Hills	$165,794	$88,066,682
Bingham Farms	$160,905	–$5,370,033
Lake Angelus	$132,393	$13,613,645
China Township	$128,835	–$211,070,756
Barton Hills	$119,187	$6,051,530
Orchard Lake Village	$119,049	$76,505,575
East China Township	$114,057	$2,637,179
Grosse Point Shores	$112,935	$640,509
Ann Arbor Township	$70,420	$64,531,029
Birmingham	$66,535	$170,392,931
(Lowest ten)		
Highland Park	$7,012	–$160,893,645
Hamtramck	$7,346	$20,497,092
Detroit	$7,573	–$147,128,602
Inkster	$8,401	–$2,258,755
New Haven	$10,875	$13,786,984
Hazel Park	$12,175	$18,616,127
Capac	$12,988	$5,299,744
Ypsilanti	$13,130	$8,689,726
Petersburg	$13,588	$4,278,398
Yale	$13,743	$8,798,688

Source: SEMCOG (2003).

FIGURE 32.4   Ratio of population to built land growth in some Michigan municipalities, 1960–1990. Source: Public Sector Consultants, Inc. (2001).

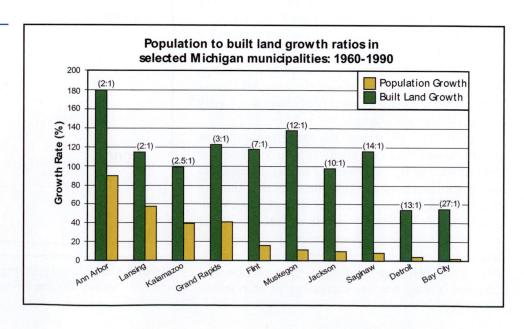

southeastern Michigan, for example, while the average urban density of the region was 1.15 housing units per hectare in 1990, new developments built between 1990 and 2000 averaged only 0.5 housing units per hectare (SEMCOG 2003b). Skole et al. (2002) illustrated the long-term consequences of maintaining these existing urban development patterns; Table 32.2 shows projected changes in land use through the year 2040, revealing the expected scale of conversion of natural and agricultural lands to urban uses (Chapter 29). Corresponding to these land-use changes, Figure 32.5 shows how these increases in built space are expected to be distributed throughout Michigan.

TABLE 32.2   Projected change in land use in Michigan, 1980–2040

Land-use category	Area in 1980 (hectares × 1000)	Area in 2020 (hectares × 1000)	Area in 2040 (hectares × 1000)	Percent change 1980–2040
Urban and built	929.5	1627.2	2552.4	+175%
Agriculture	4435.8	4111.6	3682.2	−17%
Forest	7371.0	7137.0	6827.1	−8%
Wetland	728.4	711.0	688.0	−6%
Other open space	1173.6	1051.0	888.7	−24%

After Skole et al. (2002).

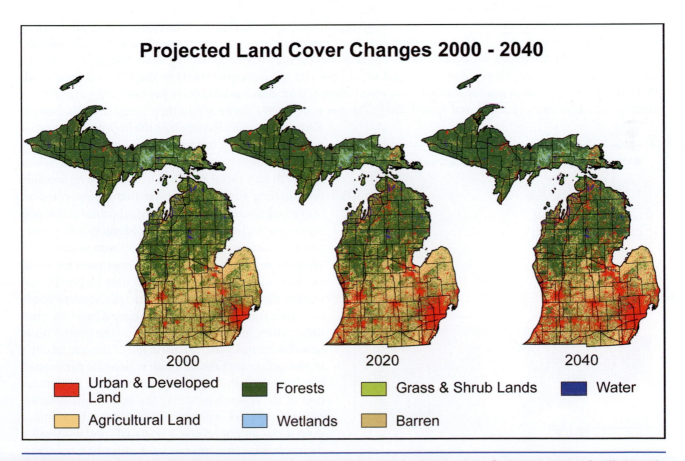

FIGURE 32.5   Expected distribution of land-cover changes and urbanized land conversions, from 2000–2040. After Skole et al. (2002).

Designing American suburbs: Promoting exclusivity and segregation

In the context of 20th century urban decentralization, suburbanization was also characterized by the separation of urban land uses and the adoption of the discontinuous road system. In reaction to the disorderly development of early industrial cities, planners began advocating single use zoning, which separated residential, commercial and industrial uses within cities, thereby decreasing the proximity of out of home activities to one's place of residence. Put another way, in pre-automobile developments, retail and commerce were integrated into residential neighborhoods (the corner store, restaurant or barber shop), whereas in the modern suburb, retail and commercial activities are concentrated in strip malls at the intersection of arterial roads, oftentimes far from one's home. Single use zoning, therefore, forces residents to travel increasing distances, as they move from their home to, and between, surrounding commercial destinations.

The other characteristic of modern suburbs that has led to increased distances between urban activities is the discontinuous road system—curvilinear streets, cul-de-sacs and loop street patterns. In the 18th century, Italian suburban villas began utilizing discontinuous roads as a defensible design strategy to maintain privacy and exclusivity, by closing themselves to outsiders. Similarly, in today's context, discontinuous roads enable suburban neighborhoods to close themselves to unwanted visitors; motorists recognize that they cannot turn into unknown local roads, as they have no way of knowing where the streets in these neighborhoods lead (Vojnovic 2006a; Fig. 32.6).

In general, all of these elements of modern suburbs (low-density decentralization, single-use zoning and discontinuous and curvilinear roads) are employed as defensible strategies, designed to ensure privacy and increase the distance between suburban residents and the land-use activities that they consider threatening. This conclusion leads to an important recognition within the discourse of suburbanization: the role of social tension—both class and racial—in shaping the urban built environment.

Residential location, based on socio-economic status, ethnicity and race, has been recognized since the work of Burgess (1924) and Park et al. (1925), who identified the concentration of upper income groups in preferred suburban locations. In Michigan, socioeconomic status is an important variable in driving decentralization, particularly because the state contains some of the richest and poorest urban census tracts in the US (Sommers et al. 1998). In addition, research has shown that, even more relevant than class, racial tension has been critical in decentralizing Michigan cities (Darden and Kamel 2000). Darden et al. (1987) illustrated in their seminal work, *Detroit: Race and Uneven Development*, the importance of racial tension in driving urban decentralization and segregation, a suburbanization process known as "white flight." In fact, racial and class tensions are responsible for initiating an economic cycle that is considered an important variable in accelerating suburbanization and inner-city decline (Chapter 33). Municipal fragmentation encourages upper-income taxpayers to move into suburbs, in part to avoid paying higher taxes for social services in the city. Since upper-income earners do not require social assistance, they generally want to minimize their contribution to this municipal function, even though they may earn their living in the central business district and make extensive use of the central city's infrastructure. As a result, urban regions are partitioned into exclusive suburbs, which maintain the concentration of the region's property tax-base, while deteriorating inner-cities experience fiscal distress. In addition, inner-cities do not receive a financial contribution for their infrastructure upkeep from suburban residents, despite the fact that many suburban residents earn their incomes in central cities (Vojnovic 2000b). This type

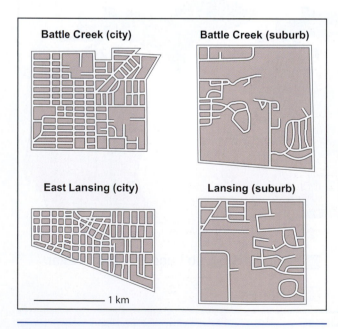

FIGURE 32.6   Street networks in selected city and suburban Michigan municipalities. After Vojnovic (2006a).

of inefficient suburbanization begins a devastating cycle for inner-cities. Since property taxes are determined by the assessed value of property and the tax rates, as upper-income earners leave the city and take their property assessment base to the suburbs, tax rates in the city are raised to compensate for the lost assessment. The higher urban tax rates, in turn, encourage other residents and businesses to move to the suburbs. The net property assessment value in the city again declines, and even higher rates are required to maintain basic public services, reinitiating the cycle and accelerating the decline of the central city (Vojnovic 2000b).

The nature of class and racial patterns that emerge from these suburbanization processes, although frequently discussed within the Detroit regional context, are evident in urban regions across Michigan. Tables 32.3 and 32.4 reveal minority and household income distributions between the largest Michigan cities and their counties, illustrating both minority and lower income concentrations in the cities. In many of these regions, the distinction between cities and

TABLE 32.3   Minority population in Michigan's urban counties, in 2005

	Minorities in city (%)	Minorities in county (%)	City vs county (ratioed % difference)
Ann Arbor	25.5	23.4	9.0
Battle Creek	25.3	15.5	63.2
Detroit	88.9	48.3	84.1
Flint	60.7	24.2	150.8
Grand Rapids	32.5	18.0	80.6
Kalamazoo	27.7	15.9	74.2
Lansing	32.6	20.0	63.0
Muskegon	39.4	18.4	114.1
Pontiac	67.8	20.0	239.0
Saginaw	53.0	25.1	111.2
Traverse City	4.0	3.6	11.1
Warren	15.4	11.0	40.0
Wyoming	21.5	18.0	19.4
Mean	59.4	27.0	120.0

Source: Michigan Higher Education Land Policy Consortium (2007).

TABLE 32.4   Median household income in Michigan's urban counties, in 2005

	Median city income ($)	Median county income ($)	City income (as % of county)
Ann Arbor	45,798	53,495	85.6
Battle Creek	35,491	40,223	88.2
Detroit	28,069	40,881	68.7
Flint	25,972	42,473	61.1
Grand Rapids	38,229	46,456	82.3
Kalamazoo	31,152	44,166	70.5
Lansing	34,367	42,502	80.9
Muskegon	27,929	41,911	66.6
Pontiac	27,802	64,022	43.4
Saginaw	26,485	39,957	66.3
Traverse City	37,330	47,572	78.5
Warren	44,855	53,321	84.1
Wyoming	42,729	46,456	92.0
Mean	32,397	48,280	67.1

Source: Michigan Higher Education Land Policy Consortium (2007).

the surrounding suburbs is, in fact, understated, as the wealthy population in many of these centers continues to push further out into surrounding counties, and as a result are not captured in this comparison.

Of the many implications associated with ongoing decentralization, the most serious is eventual urban irrelevancy. For example, in the case of the city of Flint and its region, the ongoing urban decline, decentralization and associated economic stress have produced some of the most severe urban pressures in the state. The city's devastating economic decline received international prominence in Michael Moore's film *Roger and Me*. Among larger Michigan cities, Flint maintains the lowest median household income (Table 32.4). The ongoing loss of population and businesses has also placed the city under considerable fiscal stress. Between 2002 and 2004, Flint went into receivership, after not being able to pay mounting state debts. While the population of Flint and Genesee Counties declined between 1970 and 2000, the amount of land devoted to urban uses increased by more than 70%. Due to urban decentralization, the local population is now developing stronger functional ties to the Detroit region than to the Flint area, as evident in the number of Genesee County residents that work outside of the Flint region. During the 1990's, for example, the number of Genesee County residents commuting to Oakland County increased by 134%, while the number of local commutes to work within Genesee County decreased by 6% (Orfield and Luce 2003). Simply put, the ongoing urban decentralization and decline in the region is making the central city of Flint increasing irrelevant.

■ Costs of excessive suburbanization

Research on various aspects of urban decentralization has illustrated the negative environmental, economic and social costs associated with low-density suburbanization.

Environmental costs

The most evident environmental cost of low density suburbanization is associated with the inefficient, or premature, consumption of natural and agricultural lands. Using southeastern Michigan as an example, if new developments averaged 1.15 housing units per hectare (the mean density per unit area for the year 1990), as opposed to the current densities of 0.5 housing units per hectare, new developments since 1990 would have used approximately 56% less land. These types of development decisions can produce considerable differences in land consumption over time, as evident in a comparison of the cities of Chicago and Houston, the third and fourth largest US cities. Although Houston uses over 1606 km^2 of land to house about 1.95 million people, Chicago uses only 606 km^2—almost one-third less land—to house 2.89 million people (Vojnovic 2003a, 2003b).

In addition to land consumption, low-density developments increase the spatial separation of daily activities, e.g., work, shopping, entertainment, which, in turn, leads to increased travel, energy use, pollutant emissions and urban infrastructure needs. Table 32.5 compares international urban densities, contrasting population concentrations in both metro and city boundaries, along with a set of indicators that are influenced by variations in urban density. Because of lower densities, a Detroit resident will travel, annually, an average of twice the distance of a European urban resident, and three times the distance of an Asian urban resident. In the process, the Detroit resident will consume more than three times the amount of gasoline when compared to an average European urban resident, and nearly nine times that of an Asian resident. The increased gasoline consumption will also generate corresponding increases in annual per capita pollutant emissions; a typical Detroit citizen emits 4,518 kg of CO_2 annually from their gasoline consumption, whereas the annual CO_2 emission of a resident of London is only 1,704 kg (and only 760 kg for a Hong Kong resident).

Economic costs

Since the 1950s, studies have shown that low density developments have higher infrastructure costs than developments built at higher densities (Wheaton and Schussheim 1955, Clawson 1962, Boyce 1963). A 1997 SEMCOG study of alternative development patterns in Michigan illustrated this relationship (Table 32.6). The study showed that, if new developments promoted more compact building configurations, compared to existing development standards in the state, by 2020 there would be a total of 3,304 hectares of land saved, and an annual savings in infrastructure

TABLE 32.5 Global comparison of metropolitan and inner-area densities and urban activities and functions

City	Population density (people/ha)		Gasoline use per capita	CO₂ emissions per capita	Annual travel in private cars (passenger km per capita)	Annual travel in public transportation (km per capita)	Road supply (meters per capita)	CBD parking spaces (per 1000 CBD jobs)
	Metropolitan density	Inner-area density[1]	Private transportation (MJ)	Total transportation (kg)				
USA Mean	**14.2**	**35.6**	**55,807**	**4,683**	**16,045**	**474**	**6.9**	**468**
Sacramento	12.7	19.4	65,351	5,524	19,239	117	8.8	777
Houston	9.5	18.4	63,800	5,193	19,004	215	11.7	612
San Diego	13.1	32.1	61,004	4,846	18,757	259	5.5	688
Phoenix	10.5	16.4	59,832	4,654	15,903	124	9.6	906
San Francisco	16.0	59.8	58,493	5,122	16,229	899	4.6	137
Portland	11.7	23.7	57,699	5,094	14,665	286	10.6	403
Denver	12.8	16.3	56,132	4,961	13,515	199	7.6	606
Los Angeles	23.9	28.7	55,246	4,476	16,686	352	3.8	520
Detroit	*12.8*	*28.6*	*54,817*	*4,518*	*15,846*	*171*	*6.0*	*706*
Boston	12.0	43.1	50,617	4,238	17,373	627	6.7	285
Washington	13.7	38.1	49,593	4,403	16,214	774	5.2	253
Chicago	16.6	47.3	46,498	4,069	14,096	805	5.2	128
New York	19.2	91.5	46,409	3,779	11,062	1,334	4.6	60
CANADA Mean	**28.5**	**43.6**	**30,893**	**2,764**	**9,290**	**998**	**4.7**	**408**
Calgary	20.8	22.7	35,684	3,393	11,078	775	4.9	522
Winnipeg	21.3	41.2	32,018	2,834	9,620	635	4.2	546
Edmonton	29.9	26.8	31,848	3,172	10,028	728	4.8	593
Vancouver	20.8	41.5	31,544	2,673	12,541	871	5.1	443
Toronto	41.5	60.0	30,746	2,434	7,027	2,173	2.6	176
Montreal	33.8	64.1	27,706	2,418	6,502	952	4.5	347
Ottawa	31.3	49.2	26,705	2,423	8,236	850	7.1	230

(Continued)

TABLE 32.5 (continued)

City	Population density (people/ha)		Gasoline use per capita	CO₂ emissions per capita	Annual travel in private cars (passenger km per capita)	Annual travel in public transportation (km per capita)	Road supply (meters per capita)	CBD parking spaces (per 1000 CBD jobs)
	Metropolitan density	Inner-area density¹	Private transportation (MJ)	Total transportation (kg)				
EUROPE Mean	**49.9**	**86.9**	**17,218**	**1,887**	**6,601**	**1,895**	**2.4**	**230**
Frankfurt	46.6	61.0	24,779	2,813	8,309	1,149	2.0	246
Brussels	74.9	91.0	21,080	2,114	6,809	1,428	2.1	314
Hamburg	39.8	85.7	20,344	2,680	7,592	1,375	2.6	177
Zurich	47.1	73.5	19,947	1,764	7,692	2,459	4.0	137
Stockholm	53.1	91.7	18,362	1,994	6,261	2,351	2.2	193
Vienna	68.3	128.6	14,990	1,505	5,272	2,430	1.8	186
Copenhagen	28.6	53.9	14,609	1,544	7,749	1,607	4.6	223
Paris	46.1	96.7	14,269	1,723	4,842	2,121	0.9	199
Munich	53.6	106.9	14,224	1,441	5,925	2,463	1.8	266
Amsterdam	48.8	89.3	13,915	1,475	6,522	1,061	2.6	354
London	42.3	78.1	12,884	1,704	5,644	2,405	2.0	?
ASIA Mean	**161.9**	**291.2**	**6,311**	**944**	**2,772**	**2,587**	**1.1**	**144**
Kuala Lumpur	58.7	68.8	11,643	1,424	6,299	1,577	1.5	297
Singapore	86.8	124.2	11,383	1,317	3,169	2,775	1.1	164
Tokyo	71.0	132.1	8,015	1,397	3,175	5,501	3.9	43
Bangkok	149.3	288.6	7,742	1,304	4,634	2,313	0.6	397
Seoul	244.8	298.8	5,293	705	2,464	2,890	0.8	49
Jakarta	170.8	266.7	4,787	653	1,546	1,323	0.5	?
Manila	198.0	372.4	2,896	529	1,281	2,568	0.6	27
Surabaya	176.9	265.1	2,633	404	1,568	555	0.3	?
Hong Kong	300.5	803.9	2,406	760	813	3,784	0.3	33

¹ Refers to the pre-World War II city area, developed mostly before the emergence of automobile-dependent lifestyles.
After Kenworthy and Laube (1999) and Newman and Kenworthy (1999).

TABLE 32.6   Annual impacts of current *vs.* compact growth in Michigan, in 2020

Community	Current growth			Compact growth			Cost differences ($)	Land saved (hectares)
	Added costs ($)	Added revenues ($)	Cost revenue impact ($)	Added costs ($)	Added revenues ($)	Cost revenue impact ($)		
Southeastern Michigan municipalities								
Harrison	1,542,388	861,076	−681,312	1,490,966	820,540	−670,426	10,886	61.5
Macomb	5,091,515	4,379,449	−712,067	4,053,520	3,969,190	−84,330	627,737	(27)
Bedford	996,846	1,134,165	137,319	965,328	1,121,665	156,337	19,018	41
Novi	14,769,424	11,766,829	−3,002,594	14,653,446	11,807,116	−2,846,331	156,264	288
Pittsfield	3,719,980	7,490,948	3,770,967	3,734,848	7,514,031	3,779,183	8,216	209
Canton	9,275,327	5,419,323	−3,856,004	7,924,363	4,942,195	−2,982,168	873,836	737
Grand Rapids / Muskegon region								
Kentwood	3,572,526	1,998,102	−1,574,424	3,390,741	1,962,729	−1,428,012	146,413	231
Allendale	912,787	1,113,150	200,363	845,180	1,058,339	213,159	12,796	397
Montague	339,440	330,129	−9,311	327,076	309,401	−17,675	−8,364	15
Muskegon	1,632,708	2,505,778	873,070	1,585,668	2,409,922	824,254	−48,816	20
Traverse City region								
Bear Creek	221,193	274,641	53,448	215,853	271,439	55,586	2,139	35
Petoskey	452,279	161,444	−290,835	430,191	153,176	277,015	13,819	4
Resort	271,442	119,814	−151,628	265,515	121,504	144,011	7,617	108
Garfield	1,925,993	1,998,648	72,655	1,776,888	1,925,961	149,073	76,418	688
Communities in other regions								
Portage	6,006,245	6,086,134	79,889	5,611,165	5,603,079	−8,086	−87,975	196
Hartford	82,057	79,616	−2,441	81,236	77,675	−3,561	−1,120	2
Meridian	1,920,088	1,582,411	−337,677	1,843,368	1,509,790	−333,578	4,099	253
M. Pleasant	2,697,763	3,740,532	1,042,769	2,548,033	3,575,147	1,027,113	−15,656	45
Totals	55,430,002	51,042,190	−4,387,812	51,743,387	49,152,900	−2,590,487	1,797,326	3,304

After SEMCOG (1997).

maintenance of approximately $1.8 million. The SEMCOG findings are consistent with the data presented in Table 32.5. Because of the increased use of land and greater automobile dependence, Detroit requires considerably greater per capita automobile-complementary infrastructure, as evident in road supply and parking spaces, when compared to its higher-density counterparts, leading to higher costs in infrastructure provision, if similar infrastructure standards are maintained.

In general, the greater the unit area needed to house a population, the greater the per capita infrastructure requirements, meaning that higher per capita infrastructure costs will be needed to build at, and maintain, lower density developments. Research continues to show that lower urban densities result in higher infrastructure costs and greater inefficiencies in service delivery than higher density developments (Ewing 1997, Vojnovic 1999, 2000a). Also, the increased demand for urban infrastructure associated with lower densities, results in the greater use of materials and energy for their construction and maintenance. Developing more compact and resource efficient cities, therefore, is both an environmentally and economically strategic management direction.

Greater distances and higher levels of automobile dependence in lower density cities also translates into high personal costs of automobile ownership. Kay (1997) noted that the average American spends approximately $6500 each year on owning and operating a car, ~25% of their annual income. If an effective public transit system is available, and automobile dependence was discouraged, households would be able to put more money toward alternative, and perhaps more socially beneficial, uses. For low-income households that do not own property, a $6500 increase in annual household income would make the purchase of a house a wiser investment than a car.

Social costs

Research has shown that there are numerous social benefits that can be realized with greater urban compactness. If less land is used for housing, dwellings can be more affordable. It has been demonstrated, however, that municipalities actively restrict compact developments through zoning, because they want to limit the availability of affordable housing, and thus, homebuyers, in that market segment (Vojnovic 2000a, Vojnovic et al. 2006). Indeed, many municipalities generally maintain a preference for expensive housing, characterized by large homes on large lots.

Other processes, associated with inefficient decentralization, also illustrate the ties between efficiency and equity. Low density developments are supported, in large part, by infrastructure subsidies that reduce the costs of suburban homeownership, making inefficient and costly, low density developments, more affordable. These subsidies, however, disproportionately favor upper-income groups living in low density suburbs (Vojnovic 2000a).

Another social concern associated with inefficient decentralization is mobility. While much of the US budget is directed to private over public transportation, there are large segments of the population, e.g., children, elderly and poor, that cannot drive, or that do not have access to an automobile. In fact, social isolation of the elderly is considered one of the top urban public health concerns in the US (Mullinc et al. 1996). Although many retirees are now moving into suburban communities that require greater automobile dependence, a more reasonable alternative would be to move into a traditional, pedestrian-oriented community, where people can walk to meet daily necessities, e.g., shopping and entertainment. This would encourage healthier lifestyles, by promoting moderate physical activity (walking), and also encourage automobile-independence, an important consideration, given that people walk for longer into their life than they drive (Vojnovic 2006a).

Another mobility issue, related to excessive decentralization, is the distancing of suburban job opportunities from inner-city residents, who are generally lower-income and ethnic minorities. With the decentralization of commercial activity in the latter 20th century, many employers have relocated to the suburbs. This increasing geographic separation between where the poor and minority populations live and where potential jobs are located is known as "spatial mismatch" (Chapter 33). In a cultural context that provides little financial support for public transit networks, inner-city populations become "trapped"—unless they can afford the costs of car ownership and operation. Many low-paying, suburban jobs also may not compensate for the added costs of the automobile commute.

With excessive suburbanization and inner-city decline, the locations of jobs is not the only accessibility issue faced by inner-city residents. With white flight, retail outlets began abandoning central cities, following upper-income earners into the suburbs. Studies of the Detroit metro area have shown that lower-income, central city neighborhoods, and particularly African-American neighborhoods, have fewer supermarkets than do upper-income, white suburbs (Zenk et al. 2005). The absence of competition then leads to higher prices in the smaller inner-city stores. For instance, a market-basket price survey by Bell and Burlin (1993) revealed that grocery prices were 41% higher in low income neighborhoods, when compared to prices for the same products in upper income areas. In addition, there are also important health dimensions to this spatial distribution, since it is more difficult to purchase fresh fruits and vegetables in the inner city. Zenk et al. (2005, 6) argued that "the limited availability of supermarkets in eastside Detroit and possibly other low-income communities and communities of color may adversely affect fruit and vegetable intake and consequently health, particularly among low-income women who may not be able to access supermarkets located outside their neighborhood."

◼ Development trends in Michigan

The supra-durable nature of urban form makes any change in the urban built environment a long-term process. It took Michigan cities more than half a century to evolve to their current condition, where suburbs dominate the urban landscape. Any policy initiatives intended to reverse this trend will take just as long, if not longer, to matriculate. To be sure, Michigan can realize significant environmental, economic and social benefits from encouraging more compact urban forms, but this will require the rebuilding and repopulating of its central cities. Most obviously, by pursuing greater compactness, Michigan municipalities can become more cost-effective and resource-efficient in delivering local services, reducing local taxes and making our cities more economically competitive.

Encouraging more compact communities does not mean pursuing densities such as seen in New York, Chicago or San Francisco. Although these urban densities may be appropriate for the city of Detroit, in mid-size Michigan municipalities the pursuit of even mid-density residential developments would generate considerable regional benefits. This change would allow for low and medium density, single family housing, but would also accommodate town centers with low-rise condominiums and row houses. Few Michigan municipalities allow for such robust housing choices, despite the fact that market dynamics illustrate that there is a strong demand for medium density developments with mixed building typologies, constructed around mixed-use town centers.

In Michigan's 2005 State of the State survey, residents were asked what type of urban environment they would like to live in (IPPSR 2005). Many (46%) responded that they would like to live in a downtown area or a neighborhood, with local stores (traditional neighborhood designs found throughout mid-density town centers), 29.3% wanted to live close to a regional shopping mall and only 5.6% indicated wanted to live next to a commercial strip. However, with over 60% of Michigan's population living in suburbs, and since commercial strips dominate the arterials of suburban developments, a large segment of the population finds themselves living adjacent to commercial strips, the least desired option.

These community preferences, however, are not only reflected in surveys. The few Michigan municipalities that exhibit built environments with vibrant, mid-density, town centers, e.g., Ann Arbor, Birmingham, East Lansing and Grand Rapids, maintain some of the highest real estate values in the state. It should also be added that many of the basic development characteristics that make these municipalities desirable, including mixed building typologies (combining single-family homes, rowhouses and condominiums), mixed land uses, pedestrian oriented developments along complex streetscapes, on-street parking and the use of trees, street furniture and public art along streets, are actually illegal in many Michigan municipalities!

◼ Implications for policy

Policy initiatives can facilitate inner-city revitalization and more compact urban forms. Perhaps most importantly, municipalities need to change their zoning ordinances to allow for higher densities and mixed land uses. Many municipalities still maintain zoning and design ordinances that were developed in reaction to the inefficiencies generated by the disorder and hyper-intensification of early industrial cities. Municipalities also need to focus on the development of urban regions with strong city centers, which has shown to be particularly successful in Michigan when undertaken collaboratively. The high degree of municipal fragmentation in Michigan produces high levels of inter-municipal competition for new developments. Inefficiencies are generated when suburban municipalities give incentives for new developments to move into their jurisdiction—adjacent to developed urban jurisdictions—with the inefficiencies caused by both the incentives and the associated decentralization (Vojnovic 2000b).

Grand Rapids can be used as a unique Michigan case study in this regard. During the 1980s, the Grand Rapids Metro area recognized that urban decentralization was not only leading to a decline of its regional center, but the competitiveness of the region. Therefore, in 1989, 29 member governments formed the Grand Valley Metro Council, with the goals of strengthening the economic competitiveness of the region by establishing strong town centers, increasing the compactness of developments surrounding the town centers and limiting urban decentralization (Vojnovic et al. 2006). The municipalities turned to regional cooperation, instead of inter-municipal competition, in fostering growth and rebuilding the regional core. Inter-municipal planning alliances were established for farmland preservation, land use, transportation, utilities and stormwater management. In 1999, these ideas were incorporated into a regional plan. Extensive investment was also directed to rebuilding downtown Grand Rapids, the region's core, with some $1 billion focused on downtown development. These initiatives have been successful in both stimulating inner-city revitalization and improving the economic competitiveness of the region. During the 1990s, the Grand Rapids region experienced the second largest regional population growth (16%) in Michigan. With total employment increasing by 32%, the region also experienced the fastest job growth in the state (Orfield and Luce 2003). The Grand Rapids region recognized that, in today's high-technology and specialized service economy, strong city centers and inter-municipal cooperation are necessary, if regions are to be economically competitive.

Similarly, in 2002, 14 Detroit area municipalities formed the Michigan Suburbs Alliance, in recognition that municipal fragmentation and excessive and inefficient competition between municipalities has been generating inefficient suburbanization and the decline in the competitiveness of the Detroit region. Currently consisting of 23 municipalities, the Michigan Suburbs Alliance views regional cooperation as critical in revitalizing Metro Detroit, and improving the economic competitiveness of the region.

Another important variable in limiting decentralization requires the reevaluation of the spatial nature of infrastructure investment. US policies, introduced to facilitate urban decentralization, have involved a series of initiatives, including public investment and subsidization of suburban infrastructure (roads, water and sewage networks), and public subsidization and investment preferences for private over public transportation. However, although these policies encouraged suburbanization as a means of addressing the disorder of early industrial cities, the policies were not dismantled when hyper-intensification was no longer a threat. This situation led to unique development patterns, evident in urban decentralization and dispersion. In fact, despite the ongoing existence of policies encouraging decentralization, current urban stresses in Michigan are caused by excessive suburbanization and inner-city decline, implying the necessity of the exact opposite policy direction - infrastructure investment in the urban core.

Understanding how public subsidies and market dynamics can be used to shape cities is an important consideration in this discussion, since it not only gives insight into a variable facilitating decentralization, but also provides a potential solution for rebuilding inner-cities and encouraging urban compactness. The subsidization of public infrastructure leads to its under-pricing, encouraging the increased consumption of this public good (Vojnovic 2000a). In addition, inefficiently subsidized urban infrastructure reduces serviced land prices, since the full infrastructure costs are not borne by homebuyers, enabling buyers to purchase a house with more serviced land than without the subsidy (Vojnovic 1999, 2000a). However, if the subsidy is too high, there will be an excessive use of serviced land in the construction of built-space, encouraging inefficient urban decentralization and dispersion.

FOCUS BOX: K-12 Education investment and inefficient suburbanization

The fragmented administrative organization of K-12 education in Michigan is a critical variable in driving suburbanization. Discrepancies in the quality of K-12 education throughout a metropolitan region affects housing demand and preferences for municipalities. Considerable differences can exist in the quality of educational provision in metropolitan areas, depending on municipal fiscal health. This fact is clearly evident in the Detroit region, where spending on education and quality of education is strongly dependent on location.

Expenditure differences on educational instruction in Metro Detroit, in 2003

Municipalities with highest expenditures	Instructional spending per pupil (annual $)	Municipalities with lowest expenditures	Instructional spending per pupil (annual $)
Bloomfield Hills	6,148	Clintondale	2,030
Southfield	5,518	Redford Union	2,444
Birmingham	5,271	New Haven	2,699
Grosse Pointe	4,973	Holly	2,907
Troy	4,963	Highland Park	3,054
Farmington	4,856	Detroit	3,100
Mt. Clemens	4,851	Southgate	3,120
Trenton	4,737	Pontiac	3,158
Dearborn	4,731	Hamtramck	3,171
West Bloomfield	4,704	Richmond	3,197

After Heath (2003).

K-12 education is one of the most important variables affecting housing demand and preference, for homebuyers with school age children. Thus, low quality education in fiscally distressed cities encourages families to move to wealthier suburbs that have more developed educational infrastructure, encouraging urban decentralization.

In fact, in 1993, partly as a response to what were then even greater funding inequities between school districts, Michigan voters approved Proposal A. After the passage of Public Act 145 of 1993, in an attempt to reduce different funding capacities between wealthier and poorer districts, a greater emphasis on school funding was placed on the state of Michigan itself. Overall, the gap between low and high spending school districts was reduced, but as evident in the table above, it was not eliminated. As noted by the Michigan Department of Treasury (2002), by 2002 the expenditure ratio of the top ten spending school districts to the lowest ten spending districts was reduced from 3:1 to 2:1. Differences in instructional funding continues to persist as school districts collect different amounts of state funding and confront different operating costs, which are generally higher in the older, declining urban schools.

Canada provides an alternative administrative structure (Vojnovic 2006b). Canada's educational system is centralized at the provincial level of government, the equivalent of the state. This centralized administrative structure is considered vital in maintaining both efficiency and equity in public education. The provinces maintain a more equitable distribution of funds across municipalities, minimizing differences between poor and rich cities. By minimizing fiscal discrepancies in educational funding, and by minimizing differences in educational quality, suburbanization pressures and associated stresses of inner-city decline are reduced.

Not all subsidies produce inefficient outcomes. Public goods, including urban infrastructure, are defined by market failures that lead to their under-provision, requiring subsidies to ensure optimal supply (Vojnovic 2000a). Introducing subsidies to under-price suburban infrastructure and encourage decentralization, in reaction to early 20th century hyper-intensification, did initially improve urban efficiency, reducing congestion within cities and reducing stresses caused by overcrowding. However, as in any case of over-medication, decentralization policies themselves began causing inefficiencies, when they were not timely ended. In fact, given the scale of urban decline and decentralization, what is now required is greater public infrastructure investment *within* cities.

The importance of concentrated infrastructure investment in urban areas is effectively illustrated with the economic restructuring experienced across the US, from the 1960s onwards. With the opening of international markets and the rise of the specialized services and high-tech economy, the US experienced a rapid deterioration in the competitive advantage of its older, traditional manufacturing centers. Cities such as New York, Chicago and Boston, and throughout the older Michigan industrial centers such as Detroit, Flint and Lansing, cities confronted plant closings and rapid urban decline, as capital investment, jobs and the tax base left their manufacturing cores. Between 1960 and 1978, for instance, the northeastern US lost more than 10% of its manufacturing jobs—619,000 factory positions (US Department of Housing and Urban Development 1980). Cities in the "rustbelt" experienced a rapid decline of their cores, as evident throughout traditional Michigan manufacturing centers (Chapter 31). In addition, President Reagan's deep cuts in federal expenditures to urban programs further exacerbated the condition of the older industrial cities. When the tax base left many of the older northern centers, the unemployed, minorities and lower income groups were left behind in the inner-cities, where high unemployment, poverty, crime and increasingly deteriorating urban infrastructures were concentrated. The resulting urban decline became, in itself, a driver of suburbanization, as both residents and businesses that could afford to leave the rapidly declining urban cores did so. While all of the older manufacturing centers experienced this process of urban decline throughout the 1970s and 1980s, some cities and states undertook initiatives, in the form of infrastructure investment and subsidies, to redevelop their cores. The success of such initiatives is evident in cities like New York and Boston. Like Detroit, they were experiencing significant urban decline, but they rebounded and recovered, once investment was directed to their urban cores. With appropriate public investment in their inner-cities, they were able to successfully stop the inner city decline and transition from a manufacturing to a high tech and specialized services economy. In Michigan, however, inner-city investment, in terms of infrastructure and urban development, was never realized to the scale that enabled such a transition.

Investment in educational infrastructure is particularly important within this context. The goal of educational infrastructure investment would be to increase the number and quality of post-secondary graduates, as well as to develop university-industry linkages. In the context of university-industry linkages in Detroit, academic programs establishing research and labor-supply links with the automobile industry are an obvious focus, particularly given that the decline of GM and Ford early in the 21st century has been partly attributed to their lack of investment in research. For instance, in 2004, while GM spent $7 billion on capital spending and research and development, Toyota spent $15.3 billion (Welch et al. 2005).

In Michigan, the authors of the *Lt. Governor's Commission on Higher Education and Economic Growth* (2004, 5–6) recently recognized the importance of education in driving regional development, noting that there is a

> "[S]trong correlation between the education level of a state's workforce and its economic vitality. States that educate and nurture creative talent—and that build and maintain the necessary K-12 and postsecondary educations systems—keep and attract people and investment and can capitalize on the multiplier effects that create new companies and jobs. Recent research shows that a 5% increase in the share of college-educated adults would boost overall economic growth by 2.5% over ten years, and the real wages of all Michigan residents by 5.5%."

In 2001, Michigan ranked 20th in per capita income and 47th in the proportion of its population aged 25–34 with a bachelor's or higher degrees. With regard to higher education specifically, Michigan's appropriations to higher education declined 8.1% between 2002 and 2007, putting it 46th nationally for changes in appropriation to higher education over that five year period (Center for Study of Education Policy 2007).

Universities have a dual role: training the local workforce and acting as centers for research and development. Well-known examples of university-industry linkages include Stanford University-Silicon Valley, MIT-Route 128, and UCLA-USC-Hollywood Cinema and Music. The importance of developed educational infrastructure, and urban infrastructure in general, was evident in the 2007 announcement by Volkswagen to move its headquarters from Auburn Hills, MI, to Herndon, VA. The president of Volkswagen of America said, in an interview with the Washington Post, that the move was the result of "Northern Virginia's high-quality schools, skilled workforce and proximity to the airport" (Goldfarb 2007, D01).

Post-secondary education also plays an important role in facilitating place-based development. The localized demand for services, generated by students, staff and faculty, causes expenditure concentrations in nearby areas. The impact of University of Michigan on Ann Arbor, or Michigan State University on East Lansing, illustrates this relationship.

Investments in intra-urban transportation networks, including rapid public transit, would improve the efficiency and the effectiveness of moving large numbers of people within cities, reduce transportation costs of moving both people and goods, and make cities more attractive to new investment. Various other urban infrastructure investments, including policing, communication networks and health services, would also facilitate urban revitalization, by not only concentrating investment and jobs in cities, but also by improving access to amenities. Increasing access to amenities has been critical in encouraging people to move back into the inner-cities, ensuring their revitalization, as is evident in Portland, Boston and New York.

Despite the extensive evidence on the importance of public infrastructure investment to drive local development and regional competitiveness, policies in Michigan continue to favor the suburbs. For instance, a tool that has considerable capacity to encourage reinvestment and revival of Michigan's central cities is the state's revenue sharing program. In FY1999–2000, 61.4% of state-generated revenue, a total of $14.4 billion, was transferred from state to local governments. Of this, $1.4 billion was in the form of unrestricted revenue sharing. In 1998, however, a formula used to distribute a significant portion of Michigan's unrestricted revenue sharing funds was amended to fiscally favor rapidly growing suburban communities, at the expense of the older, struggling central cities, thereby further encouraging urban decentralization (CRC 2000, Taylor and Weissert 2002).

■ Conclusions

This chapter examines the variables that have shaped Michigan's cities over the last century, with a particular focus on the unique built environment characteristics produced by large scale urban decentralization, i.e., urban sprawl. While the most obvious implications of excessive suburbanization are on the urban built environment, there are also environmental, social and economic costs associated with these development patterns, that ultimately reduce the welfare of Michigan residents and the economic performance of Michigan's cities—and the state itself.

During the 1980s, analysts and policymakers had argued that telecommuting, teleconferencing and e-shopping would lead to the dispersal of urban populations, reducing the importance of cities. Although this has been the general development direction in Michigan, the exact opposite has occurred in key global economic centers. Business and infrastructure *concentrations* began to occur in a number of urban regions, such as New York, London, Tokyo and Zurich, increasing their residential densities and the concentration of commercial activities in the urban cores (Sassen 2000, Friedmann 1986; Table 32.7). These urban regions have since emerged as global economic leaders, maintaining high concentrations of (1) foreign investment (2) intellectual talent, (3) cultural activities, arts, and entertainment, (4) higher education and research, (5) political power and (6) wealth in general.

At the national level, similar development and intensification patterns are evident. A number of urban regions, such as San Francisco, Boston and Washington DC, have made successful transitions to the high-tech and service economies. All of these cities are intensifying their urban core, associated with an increase in residential and commercial activities there. While during the 1970s these regions faced inefficient decentralization and a decline of their central cities, strategic efforts to reverse these development patterns were introduced, in recognition that excessive decentralization would mean the loss of regional economic competitiveness. Simply put, in the specialized services and high-technology economy, vibrant and dynamic central cities have become a key variable in ensuring regional economic well-being. It is easy to conclude that the ability of Michigan to regain its economic competitiveness will be closely dependent on its ability to develop strong urban cores and urban regions.

A number of arguments support the thesis that metropolitan areas with strong urban centers are the most economically competitive, maintaining high incomes and high property values. The first addresses the relationship between deteriorated cities and quality of education. Regions with excessive suburbanization and deteriorated central cities tend to have weak educational infrastructure, reducing the quality and productivity of workers and, therefore, regional competitiveness. Weak central cities also maintain comparatively low expenditures on infrastructure, reducing the operating efficiencies of retail, commerce and industry throughout the region. Third, regions with weak central cities and excessive suburbanization of commercial activity lose the advantages of agglomeration economies. Finally, and perhaps most importantly, long-term losses to the economic competitiveness of regions characterized by excessive decentralization and deteriorated inner-cities are associated with image, and this affects the entire metropolitan area. A poor metropolitan image increases risk perceptions among investors, leading to reductions in both business start-ups and plant expansions.

If Michigan is to be more competitive within the new global economy, greater effort needs to be directed to reducing excessive urban decentralization and rebuilding inner-cities and their infrastructure base. It is not only that compact cities are more efficient in their use of infrastructure and resources, but ultimately, the broader economic competitiveness of regions is dependent on ensuring strong urban cores.

TABLE 32.7 Intensity of land use within selected urban regions, in 1990

Cities	Central city density (CBD)		City density	
	Population (per hectare)	Jobs (per hectare)	Population (per hectare)	Jobs (per hectare)
Houston	17.9	303.3	18.4	21.6
Phoenix	16.6	89.7	16.4	31.1
Portland	34.0	371.0	23.7	23.5
Boston	71.2	297.7	43.1	34.1
Sacramento	26.6	117.1	19.4	12.7
Detroit	*16.5*	*256.9*	*28.6*	*10.9*
Denver	16.7	175.9	16.3	14.5
San Diego	27.2	128.0	32.1	19.6
Washington	27.3	688.5	38.1	45.1
San Francisco	111.1	744.3	59.8	48.3
Chicago	30.3	921.0	47.3	23.8
New York	226.6	989.1	91.5	52.4
Los Angeles	28.2	506.1	28.7	15.6
US mean	**50.0**	**429.9**	**35.6**	**27.2**
Calgary	33.6	290.9	22.7	23.8
Winnipeg	42.5	155.9	41.2	29.1
Edmonton	21.6	212.8	26.8	?
Vancouver	25.6	308.6	41.5	29.9
Toronto	51.1	927.0	60.0	44.3
Montreal	51.5	223.2	64.1	42.8
Ottawa	39.7	364.0	49.2	97.7
Canadian mean	**37.9**	**354.6**	**43.6**	**44.6**
Copenhagen	74.8	269.8	53.9	35.2
Hamburg	29.9	331.7	85.7	95.1
London	63.0	423.7	78.1	63.8
Paris	179.7	369.6	96.7	56.1
Frankfurt	65.5	498.9	61.0	93.6
Zurich	37.3	417.2	73.5	72.8
Amsterdam	93.2	98.0	89.3	43.1
Stockholm	101.4	262.3	91.7	126.4

(Continued)

TABLE 32.7   (continued)

Cities	Central city density (CBD)		City density	
	Population (per hectare)	Jobs (per hectare)	Population (per hectare)	Jobs (per hectare)
Munich	96.6	276.1	106.9	150.2
Vienna	60.4	378.4	128.6	110.4
Brussels	50.3	470.5	91.0	82.5
European mean	**77.5**	**345.1**	**86.9**	**84.5**
Kuala Lumpur	123.1	178.5	68.8	35.7
Singapore	82.8	386.2	124.2	132.9
Tokyo	63.2	546.8	132.1	108.3
Bangkok	324.6	132.2	288.6	119.5
Seoul	203.7	579.5	298.8	209.7
Jakarta	235.1	203.5	266.7	135.2
Manila	444.8	226.5	372.4	111.4
Surabaya	360.2	355.6	265.1	?
Hong Kong	113.8	1,712.6	803.9	775.1
Asian mean	**216.8**	**480.1**	**291.2**	**203.5**

After Newman and Kenworthy (1999).

Literature Cited

Bell, J. and B.M. Burlin. 1993. In urban areas: Many of the poor still pay more for food. Journal of Public Policy and Marketing 12:260–270.

Boyce, R.R. 1963. Myth versus reality in urban planning. Land Economics 39:241–251.

Burgess, E.W. 1924. The growth of the city: An introduction to a research project. Publications of the American Sociological Society 18:85–97.

Center for Study of Education Policy. 2007. Grapevine: An Annual Compilation of Data on State Tax Appropriations for the General Operation of Higher Education. Center for Study of Education Policy, Illinois State University, Normal, IL.

Commission on Higher Education and Economic Growth. 2004. Lt. Governor's Commission on Higher Education and Economic Growth. Final Report, State of Michigan, Lansing.

Clawson, M. 1962. Urban sprawl and speculation in suburban land. Land Economics 38:99–111.

CRC (Citizens Research Council of Michigan). 2000. Michigan's Unrestricted Revenue Sharing Program. Citizens Research Council of Michigan, Livonia, MI.

Darden, J.T. and S. Kamel. 2000. Black residential segregation in the city and suburbs of Detroit: Does socioeconomic status matter? Journal of Urban Affairs 22:1–13.

Darden, J.T., Hill, R., Thomas, J. and R. Thomas. 1987. Detroit: Race and Uneven Development. Temple University Press, Philadelphia, PA.

Ewing, R. 1997. Is Los Angeles-style sprawl desirable? Journal of the American Planning Association 63:107–126.

Friedmann, J. 1986. The world city hypothesis. Development and Change 17:69–84.

Goldfarb, Z. September 6 2007. Volkswagen Moving to Herndon. Washington Post D01.

Heath, B. May 25 2003. Michigan still shortchanges poor schools. The Detroit News. 1A.

IPPSR (Institute of Public Policy and Social Research). 2005. Michigan State of the State 39, Codebook. Institute of Public Policy and Social Research, Michigan State University, East Lansing.

Kay, J.H. 1997. Asphalt Nation: How the Automobile Took Over America, and How We Can Take it Back. Crown Publishers, Inc., New York.

Michigan Department of Treasury. 2002. School Finance Reform in Michigan Proposal A: A Retrospective. Michigan Department of Treasury, Lansing MI.

Michigan Land Use Leadership Council. 2003. Michigan's Land, Michigan's Future: Final Report of the Michigan Land Use Leadership Council. Michigan Land Use Leadership Council, Lansing, MI.

Mullinc, L.C., Elston, C.H. and S.M. Gutkowski. 1996. Social determinants of loneliness among older Americans. Genetic, Social, and General Psychology Monograms 122:453–473.

Orfield, M. and T. Luce. 2003. Michigan Metropatterns. Amergis, Minneapolis, MN.

Park, R.E., Burgess, E.W. and R.D. McKenzie. 1925. The City. University of Chicago Press, Chicago, IL.

Pendall, R. 1999. Do land use controls cause sprawl? Environment and Planning B 26:555–571.

Public Sector Consultants, Inc. 2001. Land Resource Project. Lansing, MI.

Sassen, S. 2000. Cities in a World Economy. Pine Forest Press, London, UK.

Skole, D., Batzli, S., Gage, S., Pijanowski, B., Chomentowski, W. and W. Rustem. 2002. Forecast Michigan: Tracking Change for Land Use Planning and Policymaking. Institute for Public Policy and Social Research and Urban Affairs Program, Michigan State University, East Lansing, MI.

Sommers, L., Mehretu, A. and B. Pigozzi. 1998. Rural Poverty and Socioeconomic Disparity in Michigan. In: L. Andersson and T. Blom (eds), Sustainability and Development: On the Future of Small Society in a Dynamic Economy. University of Karlstad Regional Science Research Unit, Karlstad, Sweden. pp. 269–277.

Southeast Michigan Council of Governments (SEMCOG). 2003a. Fiscal Capacity of Southeast Michigan Communities: Taxable Value and its Implications. SEMCOG, Detroit, MI.

SEMCOG. 2003b. Land Use Change in Southeast Michigan: Causes and Consequences. SEMCOG, Detroit, MI.

SEMCOG. 1997. Fiscal Impacts of Alternative Land Development Patterns in Michigan. SEMCOG, Detroit, MI.

Taylor, G. and C. Weissert. 2002. Are We Supporting Sprawl Through Aid to High-Growth Communities?: Revisting the 1998 State Revenue Sharing Formula Changes. In: D. Thornton and C. Wessert (eds), Urban Policy Choices for Michigan Leaders. Institute for Public Policy and Social Research and Urban Affairs Program, Michigan State University, East Lansing, MI.

US Census Bureau. 2000. Population Estimates of Metropolitan Areas, Metropolitan Areas Inside Central Cities, Metropolitan Areas Outside Central Cities, and Nonmetropolitan Areas by State (MA-99-6). Population Division, US Census Bureau, Washington, D.C.

US Congress. 1995. The technological reshaping of metropolitan America. Office of technology Assessment, Washington, DC.

US Department of Housing and Urban Development. 1980. 1980 President's National Urban Policy Report. US Government Printing Office, Washington, DC.

Vojnovic, I. 1999. The environmental costs of modernism. Cities 16:301–313.

Vojnovic, I. 2000a. Shaping metropolitan Toronto: A study of linear infrastructure subsidies. Environment and Planning B 27:197–230.

Vojnovic, I. 2000b. The transitional impacts of municipal consolidations. Journal of Urban Affairs 22:385–417.

Vojnovic, I. 2003a. Laissez-faire governance and the archetype laissez-faire city in the USA: Exploring Houston. Geografiska Annaler Series B 85:19–38.

Vojnovic, I. 2003b. Governance in Houston: Growth theories and urban pressures. Journal of Urban Affairs 25:589–624.

Vojnovic, I. 2006a. Building communities to promote physical activity: A multi-scale geographic analysis. Geografiska Annaler Series B 88:67–90.

Vojnovic, I. 2006b. Urban Infrastructures. In: T. Bunting and P. Filion (eds), Canadian Cities in Transition: Local Through Global Perspectives. Oxford University Press, New York. pp. 123–137.

Vojnovic, I., Jackson-Elmoore, C., Holtrop, J. and S. Bruch. 2006. The renewed interest in urban form and public health: Promoting increased physical activity in Michigan. Cities 23:1–17.

Welch, D., Beucke, D., Kerwin, K., Arndt, M., Hindo, B., Thornton, E., Kiley, D. and I. Rowley. 2005. Why GM's plan won't work. Business Week, May 9. p. 84.

Wheaton, W.L. and M.J. Schussheim. 1955. The Cost of Municipal Services in Residential Areas. US Department of Commerce, Washington, DC.

Zenk, S.N., Schulz, A.J., Hollis-Neely, T., Campbell, R.T., Holmes, N., Watkins, G., Nwankwo, R. and A. Odoms-Young. 2005. Fruit and vegetable intake in African Americans: Income and store characteristics. American Journal of Preventative Medicine 29:1–9.

Further Readings

Calthorpe, P. 1993. The Next American Metropolis: Ecology, Community, and the American Dream. Princeton Architectural Press, New York.

Hall, P. 2002. Cities of Tomorrow: An Intellectual History of Urban Planning and Design in the Twentieth Century. Blackwell Publishing, Oxford, UK.

Jackson, K.T. 1985. Crabgrass Frontier: The Suburbanization of the United States. Oxford University Press, Oxford, UK.

Rome, A.W. 1994. Building in the land: Toward and environmental history of residential development in American cities and suburbs, 1870–1990. Journal of Urban History 20:407–434.

Thomas, J. 1997. Redevelopment and Race: Planning a Finer City in Postwar Detroit. Johns Hopkins University Press, Baltimore, MD.

33 Race Matters in Metropolitan Detroit

Joe T. Darden

◼ Introduction

This chapter examines the significant role that race has played in creating and maintaining the social and spatial structure of metropolitan Detroit. Although race matters in all aspects of life, this chapter specifically examines how and why race matters in the employment and city/suburban residential patterns, as well as the social and economic characteristics of the various neighborhoods within the Detroit metropolitan area.

In this chapter, metropolitan Detroit is defined as consisting of Wayne, Oakland and Macomb Counties (Fig. 33.1). The core of the metropolitan area is the central city of Detroit, which is surrounded by several, smaller municipalities and suburbs. The three county area spans 5184 km², surrounding the city in all directions inland from the Detroit River-Lake St. Clair shoreline (Sinclair 1972).

◼ The significance of race: A conceptual framework

Race relations in Metropolitan Detroit are best understood within the theoretical framework of the white majority-nonwhite minority interactions in the workplace and home, and in the characteristics of the neighborhoods where these groups reside. The extent to which interaction between the white majority and nonwhite minorities occurs is governed by the ideology of white supremacy. Ideologies are characteristic features of any socially, spatially and politically organized area, including metropolitan Detroit, and are defined as systems of values that primarily reflect the interests of the majority group. In this context, the primary interest of the majority group in metropolitan Detroit has been to maintain racial inequality by setting racial minorities apart from the white majority. The degree to which the minorities are set apart is related to differences in phenotypical (skin color) and physical features, between the white majority and racial minorities, and to the size of the minority group. The greater the dissimilarity between the majority and minority groups, the greater the differences between them in terms of access to high status jobs, residential segregation and the social and economic characteristics of their neighborhoods (Marable 2000, Darden 2004). In other words, the nature of the interaction between the white majority and racial minority groups varies. Usually, those with lighter skin colors, i.e., Asians and Hispanics, are treated less harshly and receive less discrimination, compared to those with darker skin e.g., blacks (Gaus 1999).

Finally, the significance to which race matters is related to the size of the minority groups. Usually, the larger the size of the minority group, the greater the "threat" to the status of the majority, and the greater the resistance to equal employment, housing integration and equality of neighborhoods. Institutional discrimination is the primary mechanism by which racial inequality is sustained, and white majority-racial minority unequal status is maintained (Carmichael and Hamilton 1967). Through institutions, barriers may be constructed, hampering the economic, social and residential integration of minorities in the metropolitan area as a whole. Thus, minorities

508

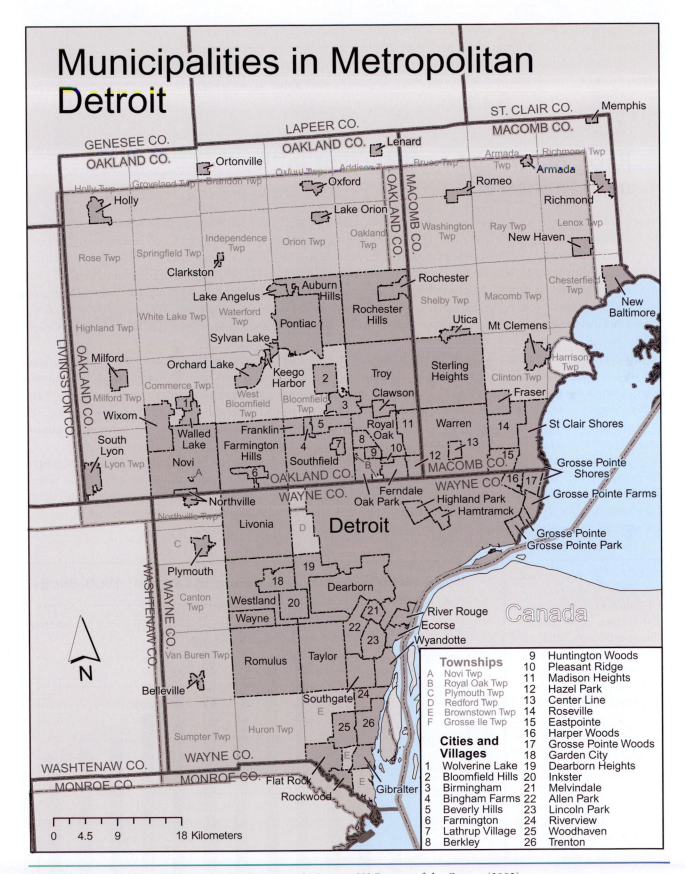

FIGURE 33.1 Municipalities in Metropolitan Detroit. Source: US Bureau of the Census (2002).

may be prevented from obtaining certain types of jobs (particularly high status ones) or housing in certain predominantly white neighborhoods (Farley et al. 2000).

Within US metropolitan areas, the size of racial minorities varies. In Metropolitan Detroit, the black population constitutes the largest and most distinctly different racial minority. Because it is between blacks and whites that race has mattered most in Metropolitan Detroit, this chapter will focus on the relationships between these two groups.

Race, place, and employment in the auto industry

Prior to 1950, Detroit was a thriving city. Investment in the city of Detroit had been great, generally associated with the auto industry (Chapter 31). As the auto industry grew, so did Detroit's population. Car factories were built next to railroad lines in open spaces not far from the city's available labor force. This available labor force included white immigrant groups (mostly from southern and eastern Europe), blacks (many from the southern US), and Mexicans (from the southwestern US and Mexico), as well as immigrants from the Middle East (mostly from Iraq and Lebanon). Most were recruited by Henry Ford to work in the automobile factories in Dearborn. Today, Arabs in Dearborn represent the largest concentration of Arabs anywhere in the United States (US Bureau of the Census 2007; Chapter 34).

Workers were not generally treated equally, however, in terms of job responsibilities; race played a significant role in determining job assignments. In 1940, almost all of the black workers in General Motors, Ford and Chrysler body plants were either employed in foundry work or in the lowest paid maintenance positions, as janitors and porters (Bailer 1944). By 1948, blacks had made some significant inroads into the auto industry, representing 20% of workers at Ford and 22% at Chrysler (Hill 1978). However, most black workers were still employed in foundry work (Thomas 1992).

Living in the city of Detroit—near the auto plants—had certain advantages. As long as these advantages existed, the population of Detroit continued to grow. The city reached its population peak in 1950, at 1.8 million people (Fig. 33.2). Population growth was clearly linked to investment in the auto industry. However, as new auto plants were built, farther from the city, residential development also spread. That residential development, as we shall see, was differential by race.

FIGURE 33.2 Measures of population change, black population vs all other, for Detroit, 1900–2006. Source: Gibson and Jung (2005); US Bureau of the Census. Population and Housing (1960–2000), US Bureau of the Census (2006).

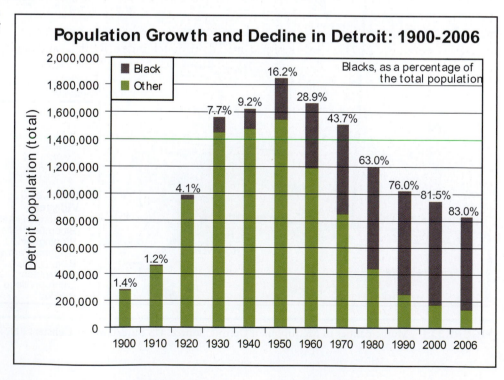

By the late 1940s, new auto plants were being built more frequently beyond the boundaries of the city of Detroit (Jacobs 1999). Between 1947 and 1955, for example, Ford, Chrysler and General Motors built 20 new plants in suburban Detroit (Darden et al. 1987), and suburban plant construction continued after 1950. The suburban pattern of auto investment at the expense of the city had a profound impact on its population; since its population peak in 1950, Detroit has experienced continued population decline.

■ Race mattered in the suburbanization of the auto industry and the population, 1960–2000

Just as population growth was related to investment in the city's auto industry, population decline was related to disinvestment in the city and a disproportionate investment in the suburbs (Fig. 33.2). With automation and decentralization of the automobile industry, the percentage of the work force employed in the Detroit's car factories dropped from 55% in 1950, to 44% in 1960, a loss of 97,000 jobs in a decade (Hill 1978). As automation in the auto industry increased, productivity per worker increased, but the number of workers decreased. Blacks were impacted most by this automation and spatial decentralization. Between 1955 to 1963, many plants did not hire a single black worker (Hill 1978). As a result, blacks who lived in the city found themselves residing in different locations than where most of the jobs were located.

Between 1958 and 1982, Detroit lost 187,000 jobs, mostly in manufacturing and retail sectors, where blacks were disproportionately concentrated (Darden et al. 1987, Darden 1989; Chapter 31). With jobs increasingly located in the suburbs, far from the blacks who resided in the city, the lack of equal access to jobs, particularly jobs in manufacturing, reduced the employment opportunities available to blacks. This spatial setup resulted in a wide gap in unemployment rates between the city of Detroit and the metropolitan area as a whole. This gap has continued; in 2006, when the City of Detroit had an unemployment rate of 22%, the rate in the metropolitan area as a whole was only 10.5% (US Bureau of the Census 2007).

Researchers have coined the term "spatial mismatch" to describe the situation that exists in the Detroit metropolitan area, where most blacks reside in the city, but most of the jobs are located in the suburbs. This concept was first introduced by Kain (1968), to explain the impact of the combined effects of residential segregation of blacks in the central city vs the locations of jobs in the suburbs. The impact of spatial mismatch was magnified in cities such as Detroit, where blacks faced both employer (Turner 1995) and housing discrimination (Farley et al. 2000). Table 33.1 shows the relationship between residential segregation, black suburbanization, black spatial mismatch and black/white income disparity. Compared to several similar metropolitan areas, blacks in metropolitan Detroit (1) are more residentially segregated, (2) are least represented in the suburbs (where most of the jobs are located) and (3) have a higher spatial mismatch index (Raphael and Stoll 2002). Blacks in metropolitan Detroit have lived for decades in different locations than did whites (Fig. 33.3A–C). Race matters in residential location.

TABLE 33.1   Relationship between residential segregation, black suburbanization, black spatial mismatch and black-white income inequality in metropolitan Detroit, in 2000

	Dissimilarity index	Blacks in suburbs (%)	Spatial mismatch index	Black/White income disparity[2]
Detroit	85.0	6.6	71.4	.599
Mean[1]	72.1	8.7	63.0	.576

1. Based on 18 Metropolitan areas.
2. A ratio of 1.00 = equality of income; a ratio <1.00 = inequality in favor of whites.
Sources: Logan (2000), Raphael and Stoll (2002), and http://mumford1.dyndus.org/cen2000/sepuneq/publicseparateune

FIGURE 33.3 Black population patterns in Metropolitan Detroit (Wayne, Macomb and Oakland Counties). Sources: US Department of Commerce (1972, 1983), US Bureau of the Census (1992, 2002).

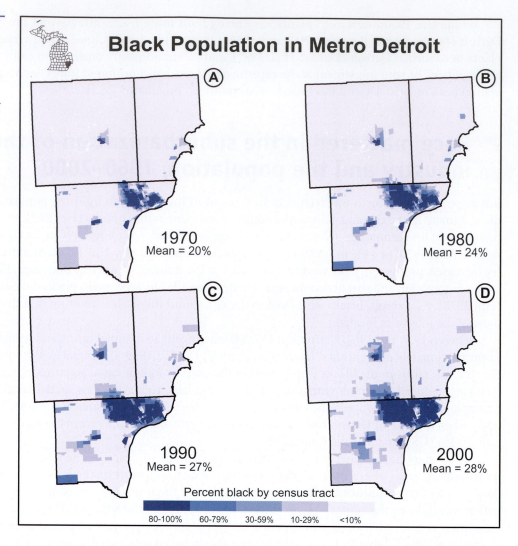

Race matters influencing city/suburban residential patterns

The Detroit metropolitan area has experienced slow growth since 2000. Of the 4,043,467 people that lived in the Detroit metropolitan area in 2000, 2.7 million (67.2%) were white, while 1.0 million (25%) were black. Of these, 96% of whites lived in the suburbs and only 4.3% resided in the city, as whites continued to move out to the suburbs. This migration pattern made an already predominantly black city even blacker (Fig. 33.3D). The total population of the City of Detroit declined from 1.0 million in 1990, to 951,270 in 2000; by 2006 the Detroit population had decreased even further, to 834,116. Detroit had also become 81.3% black in 2000, which was up from 75% in 1990 (US Bureau of the Census 2002). By 2006, Detroit had become 83% black, as the white population declined to 9.1%. Indeed, over the decade, Detroit lost 44.5% of its white population, while the decline of the black population was less than 1%. In 2006, 68% of all blacks in the metropolitan area lived in the City of Detroit, while only 2.6% of all whites resided there. Whites overwhelmingly reside in the suburbs. In fact, the suburbs are home to more than 50% of every racial minority group—except blacks. This pattern of uneven racial distribution over the metropolitan area has implications for socioeconomic inequality within the metropolitan area, creating a disadvantage outcome for the black population.

The Detroit metropolitan area's socioeconomic condition stands in sharp contrast to the city of Detroit. In 2006, households of the Detroit metropolitan area had a median income of $52,004, compared to $28,364 for households in the city of Detroit. Indeed, Detroit's 2006 median household income is listed among the ten lowest of all US cities (US Bureau of the Census 2007). While the poverty rate for the metropolitan area was only 9.4%, the City of Detroit had a poverty rate of 27.0%—2.9 times the rate of the metropolitan area as a whole. Finally, only 11.3% of Detroit residents 25 years and older have a bachelor's degree or higher, as compared to 26.3% of the residents in the metropolitan area.

These data all suggest that typical blacks and whites live separate and unequal lives in Metropolitan Detroit. To determine the actual extent to which the two groups live in separate neighborhoods, one can use the index of dissimilarity, which ascertains the degree of unevenness in the spatial distribution of two groups over subunits, in this case, census tracts. (For details on the computation of the index, see Darden and Tabachneck

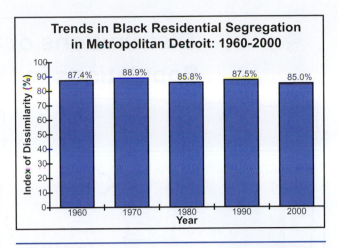

FIGURE 33.4   Temporal trends in black residential segregation in Metropolitan Detroit, 1960–2000. After Darden et al. (2007).

(1980).) Census tracts which have an average population of 4,000 can be used as surrogates for neighborhoods. If the two groups are evenly distributed, i.e., their proportions of the population are equal in the tracts, the index of dissimilarity would be zero, reflecting no residential segregation. If, on the other hand, the two groups do not share residential space, i.e., they live in completely different census tracts (neighborhoods), the index would be 100, reflecting complete residential segregation. Thus, as the index increases, so does the degree of racial residential segregation.

The index of dissimilarity for the Detroit metropolitan area in 2006 is 85; it has changed little since 1960 (Fig. 33.4). The index of dissimilarity for blacks vs whites is higher than the index for any other racial minority group in Metropolitan Detroit (Darden et al. 2007). Between Asians and Non-Hispanic whites in the Detroit metropolitan area, the index was only 53.4, and it was even lower between Non-Hispanics whites and Hispanics (48.3). According to the US Bureau of the Census (2002), Hispanics may be of any race. Moreover, the lowest indexes of dissimilarity were between Native Americans and whites (45.9), and mixed races and whites (45.0). These relatively low indexes (compared to the high black-white index) reflect a more even distribution of these population groups (Fig. 33.5). The non-black minority groups had a distribution that was more similar to the distribution of the white population (Figs. 33.5, 33.6). Of course, these minority groups were much smaller than the black population, and size does matter. The larger the racial minority group, the greater the perceived threat to the white majority group, because most whites want to maintain dominance (Darden 2003). Because Asians and Hispanics constitute <3% of the total Detroit metropolitan area population, mixed race populations comprise <2%, and Native Americans consist of <1%, the major racial tension, therefore, is between blacks and whites.

■ Central city vs suburban blacks and whites

Patterns of race and class segregation in the Detroit metropolitan area have evolved over time and did not occur by chance. The patterns were created by white real estate brokers, apartment managers and builders who controlled the housing market, and who had the capital to invest in economic development projects (Farley et al. 2000). They made decisions to exclude most blacks from purchasing or renting suburban housing, while allowing and even encouraging most whites to migrate there. At the same time, most white investors disinvested in the city and invested overwhelmingly in economic development and housing projects in the suburbs (Darden et al. 1987).

The exclusion of blacks from the suburbs also involved federal government policies. The Federal Housing Administration (FHA) insured mortgages that subsidized the growth of Detroit's suburbs. This program, however, primarily benefited white middle and working class residents, since the FHA adopted a racially segregationist policy and refused to insure properties that did not comply. White appraisers were told to look for physical

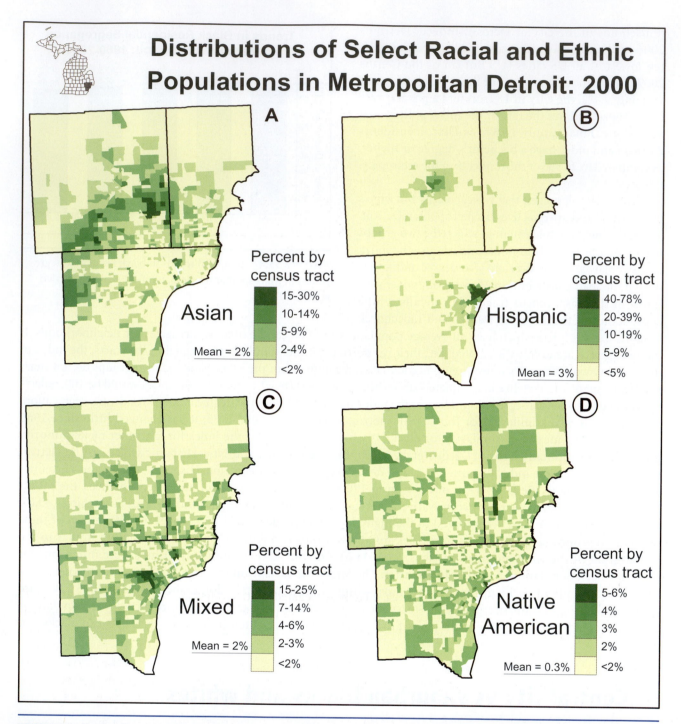

FIGURE 33.5 Patterns of occupation in Metropolitan Detroit, for four ethnic and racial groups, 2000. Source: US Bureau of the Census (2002). A. Asian population. B. Hispanic population. C. Mixed race population. D. Native American population.

barriers between the races, or find and honor racially restrictive covenants (Darden et al. 1987). Race was officially listed as a valid reason for rejecting a mortgage. As a result, most blacks were denied equal access to Detroit's growing suburbs. Between 1950 and 1980, at least 50 incorporated places were added to Detroit's metropolitan area. The population of these suburban places contained 737,007 whites but only 4,852 blacks (Darden et al. 1987). In the end, with the movement to the suburbs of the white population after 1950, the city of Detroit started to decline in total population (Fig. 33.2).

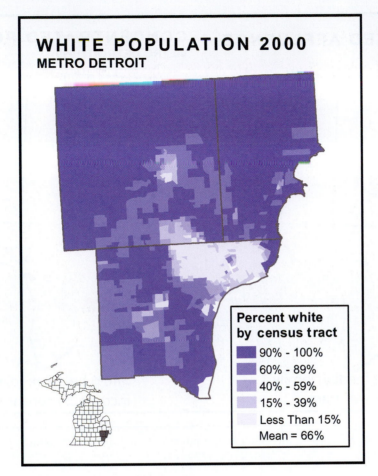

FIGURE 33.6 Distribution of the white population in Metropolitan Detroit, 2000. Source: US Bureau of the Census (2002).

Race and class segregation in metropolitan Detroit

As of 2000, metropolitan Detroit was the most racially segregated metropolitan area in the US (Darden et al. 2007). With such extreme racial residential segregation has come extreme class segregation. The stark inequality between poor blacks in the central city, and the more affluent whites in the suburbs, makes metropolitan Detroit unusual (Darden and Kamel 2000, Farley et al. 2000). As of 1999, all but three of the 48 concentrated poverty neighborhoods (census tracts where ≥40% of the population is poor) were located in the city of Detroit (Jargowsky 2003; Fig. 33.7B). On the other hand, all of the 11 concentrated affluent neighborhoods were located in Oakland County (Fig. 33.7A). Oakland County has a higher proportion of automotive executives, professional and other managerial and high level administrative workers than other Michigan counties. Auto executives and others have chosen to settle in such high, per-capita income municipalities as Bloomfield Hills, Birmingham and Huntington Woods. Detroit, on the other hand, has a higher proportion of poor than do the suburban municipalities. Indeed, Detroit was one of only ten US cities with a population >250,000 that had a median household income <$30,000 ($28,097) in 2007 (US Bureau of the Census 2008).

While the city of Detroit has been experiencing an economic decline related to globalization, auto industry disinvestment and economic restructuring (Chapters 31, 32), the Oakland County suburbs have remained comparatively prosperous. Indeed, Oakland County is one of the wealthiest counties in the US. Thus, population growth, social and spatial mobility, and economic development in Metropolitan Detroit are spatially uneven (Darden et al. 1987). Moreover, such unevenness is most visible by race, place and quality of life.

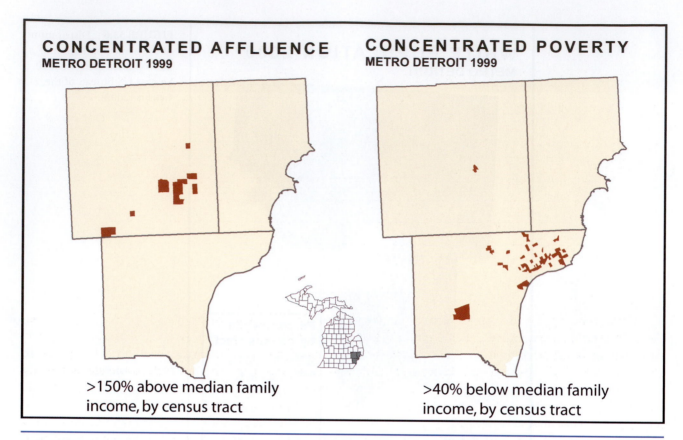

FIGURE 33.7   Concentrated (A) affluence in Metropolitan Detroit, in 1999 and (B) poverty. Source: US Bureau of the Census (2002).

■ Race and socioeconomic characteristics of neighborhoods

In Metropolitan Detroit and other metropolitan areas throughout the US, blacks tend to live in significantly poorer and lower quality neighborhoods than do whites (Bayer and McMillan 2005). The situation is made worse by the fact that, as Bayer and McMillan (2005) argued, there is a limited supply of black neighborhoods of high socioeconomic status in most metropolitan areas; neighborhood racial composition and neighborhood quality are explicitly bundled together. Sampson and Wilson (1995) showed that blacks of every socioeconomic status live in qualitatively different kinds of neighborhoods than do their white counterparts. Massey et al. (1987) found similar results for Philadelphia. High incomes do not buy blacks into neighborhoods with the same quality as those occupied by whites (Massey and Denton 1993). Thus, blacks, regardless of socioeconomic status, are impacted greatly by "neighborhood effects" that are often distinctly different from the neighborhood effects impacting whites.

Conceptually and theoretically, the quality of life of residents varies by the characteristics of the neighborhoods they reside in. Although some neighborhoods have characteristics that enhance residents' quality of life, others have characteristics that are detrimental or harmful. Emerging from this conceptual or theoretical framework is a body of literature on "neighborhood effects," the independent effect of a neighborhood, combined with its composite characteristics, on any number of outcomes (Oakes 2004). Geographers have studied the effect of neighborhood characteristics and racial inequality on home ownership, employment and education (Darden 2003, Darden et al. 1987). Sociologists have pointed to lack of role models in poor black neighborhoods (Wilson 1987). Black youth are especially impacted.

TABLE 33.2 Black-white residential segregation and neighborhood socioeconomic characteristics in metropolitan Detroit, in 2000[1]

Index of Socioeconomic Position (SEP)	Total white population (%)	Total black population (%)	Difference (%)
Very High SEP	26.6	4.4	−22.2
High SEP	27.9	3.8	−24.1
Middle SEP	26.0	7.8	−18.2
Low SEP	16.8	28.8	12.0
Very Low SEP	2.6	55.1	52.5
Total SEP	100	100	129.0

1. Index of Dissimilarity = ½ the absolute difference of 129.0 = 64.5
Source: Compiled by the author from data obtained from the US Bureau of the Census (2000).

There are a variety of theoretical views about the potential effects of neighborhoods on youths. The prevailing perspective is that neighborhoods that are socially and economically deprived have adverse causal effects on youth development, by exposing youth to violence and depriving them of positive role models, quality schools, health care and recreational facilities (Ellen and Turner 1997). Although the impact of neighborhood effects operates differently on adults, the literature generally agrees that neighborhoods matter (Ellen and Turner 1997). The well-being of families likewise varies across neighborhoods. Most poor neighborhoods have a limited availability of jobs, quality housing, grocery stores and other shopping facilities, putting them at a disadvantage, as compared to more affluent neighborhoods. Neighborhoods that are predominantly non-white usually have poorer quality and quantity of resources, compared to white neighborhoods. Thus, "neighborhood effects" studies are often conceptualized within the context of race and socioeconomic characteristics of places (Katz et al. 2001, Kling et al. 2004). Neighborhood effects are best captured by composite area, based numerical indexes.

One can capture the importance of neighborhood effects in metropolitan Detroit by examining certain socioeconomic variables. In this example, 2000 population and housing data are used. The socioeconomic variables are: (1) percentage of university degrees, (2) median family income, (3) percentage of managerial and professional status positions, (4) mean value of dwelling, (5) mean gross rent of dwelling, (6) percentage of home ownership, (7) percentage below poverty level, (8) unemployment rate and (9) vehicle ownership. These variables represent characteristics of area of residence, and are measured at the census tract level (Darden and Kamel 2000). Census tracts are surrogates for neighborhoods.

The results of an analysis of these variables shows that the spatial distribution of blacks and whites coincides with the characteristics of neighborhoods. The white population disproportionally resides in the neighborhoods with the highest socioeconomic position, or most advantageous neighborhoods, while the black population resides disproportionally in neighborhoods with the lowest socioeconomic position—the most disadvantaged neighborhoods. The results also reveal that only 4.4% of all blacks, compared to 26.6% of all whites, in Metropolitan Detroit reside in very high socioeconomic status neighborhoods (SEP). On the other hand, 55.1% of all blacks, as compared to only 2.6% of all whites, reside in very low SEP neighborhoods. Thus, one could conclude that racial residential segregation has unequal social and economic consequences, creating a geographic disadvantage for blacks. The index of dissimilarity between black-white residential segregation distribution and socioeconomic characteristics of neighborhoods in Detroit was 64.5 in 2000 (Table 33.2).

■ Conclusions

This chapter examines how and why race matters in Metropolitan Detroit. It focuses specifically on employment patterns in the growth and decline of the auto industry (Chapter 31), city/suburban residential patterns (Chapter 32) and the social and economic characteristics of neighborhoods. Race mattered in the assignment of the labor force to various jobs within the auto industry, which concentrated first in the city of Detroit and expanded to the suburbs over time. Blacks were disproportionately assigned to foundry work or the lowest paid maintenance positions. Then, as the auto industry and other jobs moved to the suburbs, race mattered in terms of which population groups were allowed to relocate into the various suburban neighborhoods, where new jobs were located. Whites were not only allowed to relocate, but were encouraged to do so by federal governmental programs. Blacks, on the other hand, were usually discouraged or prevented from moving into suburban neighborhoods. As a result, while white suburbanization occurred from 1950 to 2000, most blacks remained concentrated in the City of Detroit. And as the city became increasingly occupied by blacks, it also became poorer, due largely to disinvestment and a lack of employment opportunities in the city.

These trends all led to the sharp inequalities in the socioeconomic characteristics of neighborhoods within the Detroit area, as well as the high level of black residential segregation there, which has made metropolitan Detroit the most racially segregated metropolitan area in the US (Fig. 33.4). High racial residential segregation, combined with rigid class segregation, have resulted in unequal social and economic consequences, creating disadvantages for blacks. Thus, race matters in metropolitan Detroit.

Literature Cited

Bailer, L. 1944. The automobile unions and Negro labor. Political Science Quarterly 59:548–577.

Bayer, P. and R. McMillan. 2005. Racial sorting and neighborhood quality. National Bureau of Economic Research Working Paper Number W11813.

Carmichael, S. and C.V. Hamilton. 1967. Black Power. Vintage Press, New York.

Darden, J.T. 1989. Blacks and other racial minorities: The significance of color in inequality. Urban Geography 10:562–577.

Darden, J.T. 2003. Residential Segregation: The Causes and Social and Economic Consequences. In: C. Stokes and T. Melendez (eds), Racial Liberalism and the Politics of Urban America. Michigan State University Press, East Lansing. pp. 321–344.

Darden, J.T. 2004. The Significance of White Supremacy in the Canadian Metropolis of Toronto. The Edwin Mellen Press, Lewiston, NY.

Darden, J.T., Hill, R., Thomas, J. and R. Thomas. 1987. Detroit: Race and Uneven Development. Temple University Press, Philadelphia, PA.

Darden, J.T. and S.M. Kamel. 2000. Black residential segregation in the city and suburbs of Detroit: Does socioeconomic status matter? Journal of Urban Affairs 22:1–13.

Darden, J.T. and A. Tabachneck. 1980. Algorithm 8: Graphic and mathematical descriptions of inequality, dissimilarity, segregation, or concentration. Environment and Planning A 12:227–234.

Darden, J.T., Stokes, C. and R. Thomas (eds). 2007. The State of Black Michigan, 1967–2007. Michigan State University Press, East Lansing.

Ellen, I.G. and M.A. Turner. 1997. Does neighborhood matter? Assessing recent evidence. Housing Policy Debate 8:833–866.

Farley, R., Danzinger, S. and H. Holzer. 2000. Detroit Divided. Russell Sage Foundation, New York.

Gaus, H.J. 1999. The Possibility of a New Racial Hierarchy in the Twenty-First Century United States. In: M. Lamont (ed), Cultural Territories of Race: Black and White Boundaries. University of Chicago Press, Chicago, IL. pp. 371–380.

Hill, R.C. 1978. At the crossroads: The political economy of post-war Detroit. Urbanism Past and Present 6:1–21.

Jacobs, A.J. 1999. Intergovernmental relations and uneven development in the Detroit and Nagoya auto regions. Ph.D. Dissertation, Michigan State University, East Lansing.

Jargowsky, P.A. 2003. Stunning Progress, Hidden Problems: The Dramatic Decline of Concentrated Poverty in the 1990s. The Brookings Institution, Washington, DC.

Kain, J.F. 1968. Housing segregation, Negro employment and metropolitan decentralization. Quarterly Journal of Economics 82:175–197.

Katz, L.F., Kling, J.R. and J.B. Leibman. 2001. Moving to opportunity in Boston: Early results of a randomized mobility experiment. Quarterly Journal of Economics 116:607–654.

Kling, J., Liebman, J., Katz, L. and L. Sanbonmatsu. 2004. Moving to opportunity and tranquility: Neighborhood efforts on adult economic self-sufficiency and health from a randomized housing voucher experiment. John F. Kennedy School of Government Faculty, Working paper Series #RWP04-035. Cambridge, MA.

Marable, M. 2000. The Problematics of Ethnic Studies. In: M. Marable (ed), Dispatches from the Ebony Tower: Intellectuals Confront the African American Experience. Columbia University Press, New York. pp. 243–264.

Massey, D. and N. Denton. 1993. American Apartheid: Segregation and the Making of the Underclass. Harvard University Press, Cambridge, MA.

Massey, D., Condran, G.A. and N. Denton. 1987. The effect of residential segregation on black social and economic well-being. Social Forces 66:29–57.

Raphael, S. and M. Stoll. 2002. Moderate Progress in Narrowing Spatial Mismatch Between Blacks and Jobs in the 1990's. The Brookings Institute, Washington, DC.

Sampson, R.J. and W.J. Wilson. 1995. Toward a Theory of Race, Crime and Urban Inequality. In: J. Hagan and R.D. Peterson, Crime and Inequality. Stanford University Press, Palo Alto, CA. pp. 37–54.

Sinclair, R. 1972. The Face of Detroit. In: Swartz, R., Ball, J., Dohrs, F. and M. Ridd (eds), Metropolitan America: Geographic Perspectives and Teaching Strategies. National Council for Geographic Education, Oak Park, IL. pp. 1–59.

Thomas, R.W. 1992. Life for Us is What We Make It: Building a Black Community in Detroit, 1915–1945. University of Indiana Press, Bloomington, IN.

Turner, S.C. 1995. Race, space and skills in metropolitan Detroit: Explanations for growing wage and employment gaps between black and white workers. Ph.D. Dissertation, University of Michigan, Ann Arbor.

US Bureau of the Census. 1992. 1990 Census Summary File 3 (SF3). State of Michigan.

US Bureau of the Census. 1992. Population and Housing Summary File 3 (SF3). Michigan. Washington, DC.

US Bureau of the Census. 2002. 2000 Census Summary File 3 (SF3). State of Michigan.

US Bureau of the Census. 2006. American Community Survey 2005. US Government Printing Office, Washington, DC.

US Bureau of the Census. 2008. American Community Survey 2007. US Government Printing Office, Washington, DC.

US Department of Commerce. 1962. 1960 Census of Population and Housing: Census Tracts Detroit, Michigan Standard Metropolitan Statistical Area. PHC(1)-40. US Government Printing Office, Washington, DC.

US Department of Commerce. 1972. 1970 Census of Population and Housing: Census Tracts Detroit, Michigan Standard Metropolitan Statistical Area. PHC(1)-58. US Government Printing Office, Washington, DC.

US Department of Commerce. 1983. 1980 Census of Population and Housing: Census Tracts Detroit, Michigan Standard Metropolitan Statistical Area. PHC (1)-58. US Government Printing Office, Washington, DC.

Wilson, W.J. 1987. The Truly Disadvantaged: The Inner City, the Underclass, and Public Policy. University of Chicago Press, Chicago, IL.

Further Readings

Capeci, D. 1984. Race Relations in Wartime Detroit. Temple University Press, Philadelphia, PA.

Ewen, L.A. 1978. Corporate Power and the Urban Crisis in Detroit. Princeton University Press, Princeton, NJ.

Fine, S. 1989. Violence in the Model City: The Cavanaugh Administration, Race Relations and the Detroit Riot of 1967. University of Michigan Press, Ann Arbor.

Hendrickson, W.W. (ed). 1991. Detroit Perspectives: Crossroads and Turning Points. Wayne State University Press, Detroit, MI.

Meier, A. and E. Rudwick. 1979. Black Detroit and the Rise of the UAW. Oxford University Press, New York.

Rosentretter, R. 2000. Detroit at 300. Michigan History 84 (Nov–Dec). 97 pp.

Sands, G. 1981. Ghetto Development in Detroit. In: J.T. Darden (ed), The Ghetto: Readings with Interpretations. Kennikat Press, Port Washington, NY. pp. 89–107.

Sinclair, R. and B. Thompson. 1977. Metropolitan Detroit: An Anatomy of Social Change. Ballinger Publishing Company, Cambridge, MA.

Sugrue, T. 1996. The Origins of the Urban Crisis: Race and Inequality in Post War Detroit. Princeton University Press, Princeton, NJ.

Thomas, J. M. 1997. Redevelopment and Race: Planning a Finer City in Post-War Detroit. Johns Hopkins University Press, Baltimore, MD.

Demographic and Economic Characteristics

34

Richard Groop

Introduction

The term *population distribution* refers to the patterns of people and their settlements, as they are distributed across the landscape. These distributions can be measured as simply "where people are found" (Plate 17), or as *population density*—the intensity of population settlement—measured as the number of people per unit area (such as people per square km; Fig. 34.1). Both Plate 17 and Figure 34.1 illustrate some basic concepts about population patterns in general, as well as the actual population distribution in Michigan.

Michigan provides one of the best examples of the highly varied nature of population density across a state (Fig. 34.1). The northern part of the state represents some of the least populated territory in the eastern US, while southeastern Michigan is a very densely populated area. Census data show that the entire Upper Peninsula contains only a little over 3% of the state's population, while the southeastern urban corridor of Wayne, Oakland, Macomb, Genesee and Saginaw Counties has nearly 51% of Michiganders (Groop et al. 1984, US Census Bureau 2003a). Densities range from less than one person per km² in rural northern Michigan, to nearly 4,000 people per km² in many of Michigan's cities.

This uneven distribution results from several factors. In the early 1800s, migration into Michigan originated in the SE. Most immigrants traveled through the Great Lakes via boat, and began to disperse across the landscape from the Port of Detroit, to the north and west, seeking farming, lumbering and other extractive economic opportunities (Chapter 27). As this "flood" of people progressed northward, climate, soil fertility, terrain and other factors combined to dampen these opportunities, particularly in agriculture, and as a result, population density in many rural places leveled off or even declined, following initial settlement. With rising industrialization and accompanying urbanization in the early 1900s, the rural population to the north thinned even more, as cities in the south grew. Thus, the current

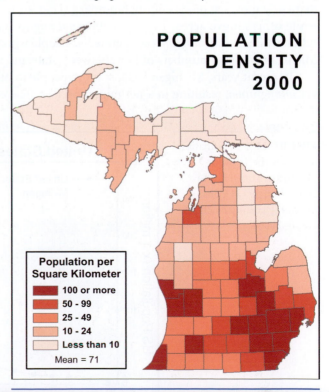

FIGURE 34.1 Population density in Michigan, in 2000. Source: US Census Bureau (2000).

population density pattern results from a complex combination of human settlement and economic activities, interacting with factors in the physical environment, for >200 years.

Population change and migration

Not only is Michigan's population highly varied in terms of location and density, it is also highly dynamic in terms of size. Since the early 1800s, around the time Michigan became a state, its population has grown continually, but at varying rates. Figure 34.2 compares the populations of the US and Michigan, showing that pre-1900s growth rates were generally similar for both the state and the nation. However, during the industrialization period of the earlier 1900s, Michigan's population grew at a faster rate than the rest of the country. That growth rate leveled off during the Great Depression, but again increased with rapid automotive manufacturing growth, during and following World War II. With the advent of de-industrialization in the US, particularly in Michigan, in the 1980s, the state's growth slowed considerably, fueled largely by emigration of people looking for jobs in the Sunbelt and elsewhere.

Changes in the size of Michigan's population have resulted from the interactions of three variables: (1) additions to the population resulting from births, (2) subtractions resulting from deaths and (3) additions and subtractions resulting from migration into and out of the state. In general, Michigan's birth rates have mirrored those of the nation. In the 1800s, high birth rates, associated with large families, predominated in a largely rural, agricultural economy. As industrialization increased, family size steadily declined, to the current (2006) crude birth rate of 13 births per 1000 population per year. In 2005, birth rates in Michigan were highest in the urban areas of southern Michigan and lowest in rural areas to the north (Fig. 34.3A). This pattern is largely the result of age differences across the state, not differences in fertility or family size. The same rationale applies to death rates (Fig. 34.3B)—higher death rates in the northern part of the state are age-related, not the result of more hazardous environments. In fact, when controlling for age, differences between birth and death rates across Michigan are negligible, implying that most population change in Michigan can be attributed to migration—the process of people moving some distance, to permanently change their residence. The US Census Bureau defines a migrant as someone who permanently moves across a county boundary (US Census Bureau 2003b), but some migrants move internationally, while others move across the street. *Internal migrants* are people who move within a country, usually between states, while *in-state migrants* are defined as people who move between cities, counties or townships within a state. Michigan has large numbers of both between-state and within-state migrants.

In recent years, Michigan has lost more people to other states via *emigration* than have migrated into the state via *immigration*, resulting in a net migration loss. Between 1995 and 2000, 559,568 people left Michigan for other

FIGURE 34.2 Population totals for the US and Michigan, from 1790 to 2000. Source: US Census Bureau. Decennial Census (1830–2000).

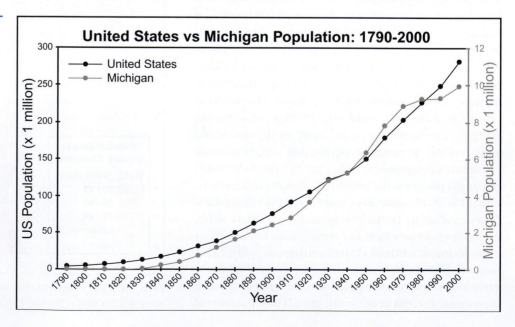

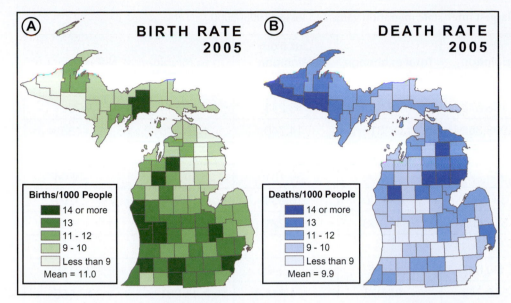

FIGURE 34.3 Maps of (A) birth rates and (B) death rates in Michigan, as of 2005, by county. Source: Michigan Department of Community Health (2004).

US destinations, while 467,638 people migrated to the state, resulting in a net loss of 91,930 people, or about 1% of our population (US Census Bureau 2003b). Figure 34.4 illustrates the states to which Michigan gained or lost population through migration, during a recent period of time. Perhaps most surprising is that nearly 4,000 more people left a struggling economy in California and moved to Michigan than did the reverse. Table 34.1 shows those states that have been impacted the most by migration to and from Michigan. Florida receives the most net migrants from Michigan, most of whom are retirees seeking a better climate. The same migration dynamic would apply to the other large net gainers from Michigan. Michigan gains the most people from Illinois—a few of them retirees, but the bulk moving for jobs and other economically related reasons. The same can be said for the other nearby industrial states. These migrants are part of what demographers refer to as "churning" migration, where large numbers of migrants in adjacent states trade locations, usually for job-related reasons. And typically, as Table 34.1 shows, the states with the highest numbers of emigrants from Michigan tend to be the states with the largest number of immigrants as well.

Internal migration in Michigan is best represented in Figure 34.5—a map of population change and, as such,

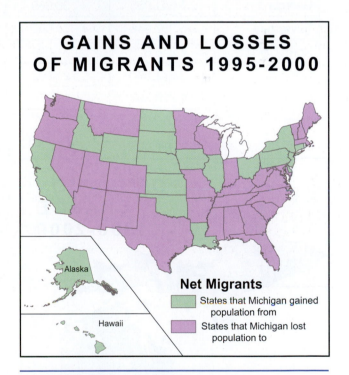

FIGURE 34.4 Map of the distribution of gains and losses of migrants, by state, to and from Michigan, from 1995 to 2000. Source: US Census Bureau (2003a).

includes births and deaths, as well as migration. Nonetheless, the growth and decline patterns illustrated in Figure 34.5 are primarily due to migration, and almost all are related to migration within the state. Although only the 1990 to 2000 period is shown, this time frame is characteristic of population change for the state over the past 50 years in general. Several major features of this distribution should be noted. First, most of Michigan's large cities either lost population or remained the same. Particularly noteworthy is Detroit, which declined in population from 1,849,568 in 1950 to 951,270 in 2000, almost a 50% decline (Chapter 33). Other larger Michigan cities have experienced similar, if smaller, declines, and almost all are due to out-migration to suburbs and the surrounding countryside (Chapter 32). Most of these out-migrants were people responding to negative factors such as crime and underemployment, associated with the city

TABLE 34.1   Michigan's largest inter-state migration gains and losses, 1995–2000

	Population	Total exchange	Out from Michigan	In to Michigan	Net migration
Gains From					
Illinois	11,193,674	78,387	35,243	43,144	+7901
New York	17,028,362	34,315	14,740	19,575	+4835
Ohio	10,479,383	91,005	43,371	47,634	+4263
California	30,008,971	76,206	36,151	40,055	+3904
Pennsylvania	11,390,307	24,560	10,634	13,926	+3292
New Jersey	7,544,503	12,103	5,221	6,882	+1661
Losses To					
Florida	14,390,997	113,742	74,949	38,793	−36,156
Arizona	4,569,742	36,075	24,814	11,261	−13,553
Georgia	7,351,055	36,059	23,945	12,114	−11,831
Tennessee	5,237,948	34,650	22,947	11,703	−11,244
North Carolina	7,316,828	31,099	19,810	11,289	−8521
Colorado	3,871,570	21,992	13,788	8,204	−5584
Nevada	1,778,508	11,270	7,867	3,403	−4464

Source: US Bureau of the Census (2003b).

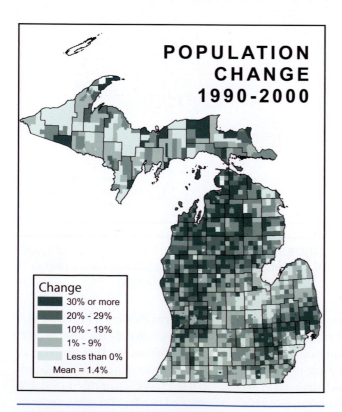

FIGURE 34.5   Map of population change in Michigan, from 1990 to 2000, by townships and incorporated places. Source: US Census Bureau. Decennial Census (1830–2000).

centers. Most were white, middle-income, wealthy families in younger and middle-age categories—in general, people who are most able to support themselves economically. They took with them not only their income and earning power, but their tax dollars as well. The same can be said for many other suburban areas in southeastern Michigan. Small towns and rural areas in counties such as Oakland, Macomb, Washtenaw and others, within commuting range of larger cities, experienced as much as 50% growth in the decade. Most of these migrants relocated for jobs, schools, and other amenities associated with suburban locations. The Grand Rapids area is an exception to the suburban growth pattern, experiencing rapid growth because of migration into the central city (Chapter 32), coupled with overall urban growth, all fueled by the locally prosperous economy. Third, a large area of the northern part of the peninsula, particularly in the NW, experienced rapid growth, mostly due to an influx of retirees seeking rural, scenic and recreational amenities "up north" (Chapter 35). Finally, the Upper Peninsula has had mixed growth and decline, associated with its highly localized economic booms or busts. Mine closings and openings, retirement opportunities, military base changes, fluctuations in the university climate, casino openings, and other local events either "pushed" migrants out, or attracted new population.

Demographic and ethnic characteristics

Demographers describe population using such metrics as infant mortality, ancestry, dependent population, age structure, family size, gender ratio and many others (Table 34.2). Three of these variables, birth rate, death rate and rate of growth or decline, have already been discussed. This section focuses on two others: age structure and ethnicity. Figure 34.6 illustrates the age-sex structure of Michigan, by showing the percentage of males and females in various age categories (cohorts). Very similar to the overall structure of the US, this "age-sex pyramid" is typical of stable populations, where a consistent number of children are added in each age cohort. This type of structure generally means that the population itself will grow very slowly; the pyramid will become more straight-sided as time goes on (Haupt and Kane 1978). "Baby boomers" are apparent in the pyramid as a mid-age bulge. As years pass, this bulge will continue upward into the older age categories, and help to exacerbate the retirement, health care and other socio-economic problems looming for Michigan and the US (Weeks 2005).

In terms of location, older and younger people are unevenly distributed in Michigan. As a percentage of the overall population, older residents are concentrated in the northern part of the state, while the southern areas,

TABLE 34.2 Demographic and ethnic comparisons for Michigan and the US

	Michigan	Percent/Rate	United States	Percent/Rate
Population (2000)	9,938,444		281,421,906	
Population (1990)	9,295,297		248,709,873	
Pop change (1990–2000)		1.4		3.3
Density[1]		67.6		30.7
Median age		35.5		35.3
Under 5 yrs	672,005	6.8	19,175,798	6.8
65 or older	1,219,018	12.3	34,991,753	12.4
Male	4,873,095	49.0	138,053,563	49.1
Female	5,065,349	51.0	143,368,343	50.9
White	7,966,053	80.2	211,460,626	75.1
Black or African-American	1,412,742	14.2	34,658,190	12.3
Am Indian or Alaskan	58,479	0.6	2,475,956	0.9
Asian	176,510	1.8	10,242,998	3.6
Hawaiian or Pacific Is	2,692	0.1	398,835	< 0.1
Other	129,552	1.3	15,359,073	5.5
Two or more races	192,416	1.9	6,826,228	2.4
White, non-Hispanic	8,133,283	78.6	216,930,975	69.1
Hispanic or Latino	323,877	3.3	35,305,818	12.5
Foreign born	523,589	5.3	31,107,889	11.1
Births (rate)[2]	130,850	13.0	4,093,000	13.8
Deaths (rate)[3]	86,306	8.6	2,434,000	8.3
Infant mortality[4]		8.0		6.8
Average family size		3.1		3.1

1: Persons per km^2
2: Births per 1000 population per year
3: Deaths per 1000 population per year
4: Deaths, age <1 year, per 1000 live births per year
Source: US Census Bureau (2003a)

FIGURE 34.6 Chart showing the age-sex structure in Michigan, as of 2000. This type of chart is commonly referred to as a population pyramid. Source: US Census Bureau (2000).

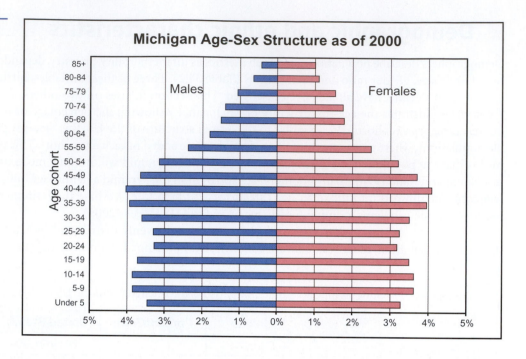

particularly urban and suburban places, have a much younger age structure (Fig. 34.7). As noted earlier, migration is the primary driver of the patterns shown in Figure 34.7. In the northern Lower Peninsula, in-migration of older people seeking retirement amenities has increased the median age considerably. In parts of the Upper Peninsula, the out-migration of younger people seeking better employment opportunities has also raised the median age. For example, the median age in the state of Michigan is 35.5 years, but in Roscommon County, which has had high levels of in-migration, the median age is 47.2. In Gogebic County, which has high levels of out-migration, the median age is 42.9. Such concentrations of older population can have both positive and negative economic effects.

The US Census Bureau (2003a) collects data on nine racial/ethnic groups, or combinations of two or more (Table 34.2). Percentages of these groups in Michigan differ noticeably from nationwide percentages in two categories.

1. The black population in Michigan is 14.2%, somewhat higher than the 12.3% for the US. This number is typical of industrial states in the Northeast and North-Central regions of the country, which served as destinations for southern black migrants during and following World War II (Chapter 33).

2. Michigan's Hispanic population is only 3.3%, as compared to 12.5% for the US. This is not surprising, since Michigan is quite distant from Mexico—a major source of Hispanic immigrants. California, Texas, Florida and other areas of the South and Southwest have been the primary destinations for Hispanic migrants in the last 50 years.

A map of minority and Hispanic populations (Fig. 34.8) shows that, in the southern part of the state, these populations are largely concentrated in a few locations, almost all of which are larger urban areas. Three notable exceptions to this pattern occur: (1) Lake County, in the west-central part of the Lower Peninsula, is home to a large percentage of blacks, resulting from historical settlement associated with an entertainment development in the rural Idlewild area, (2) High proportions of Native American populations occur in largely rural areas, particularly in the Upper Peninsula and (3) Some rural areas in the western Lower Peninsula have notable Hispanic concentrations, associated with migrant labor needs, in the fruit and vegetable operations of the area (Chapter 38). Beyond these exceptions, most minorities in Michigan tend to be located in urban areas. Indeed, most of the major cities of Michigan have sizeable minority populations (US Census Bureau 2003a; Table 34.3). These places account for 25% of Michigan's overall population, but have nearly 60% of its minorities and Hispanics. Detroit alone accounts for over 40% of the Michigan's minority and Hispanic population. As noted earlier, these concentrations have largely resulted from "white flight," as white and other non-minority populations move to nearby suburban destinations (Chapter 32). Those left behind in the central cities tend to be poorer minority populations, that are less able to economically support themselves and pay taxes, placing a strain on the city to provide services and amenities.

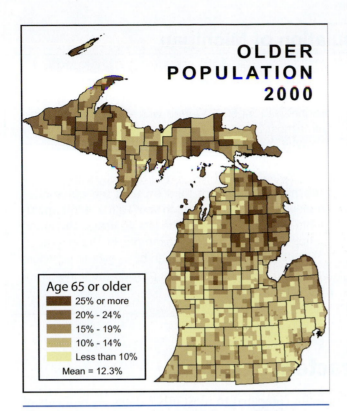

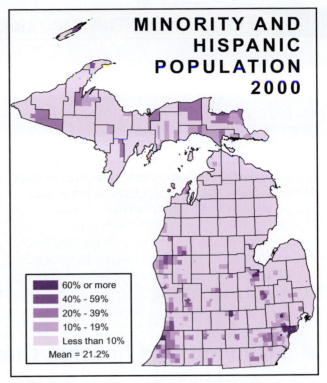

FIGURE 34.7   The distribution of older population in Michigan, as of 2000, by townships and incorporated places. Source: US Census Bureau (2000).

FIGURE 34.8   The distribution of minority and Hispanic peoples in Michigan, as of 2000, by townships and incorporated places. Source: US Census Bureau (2000).

TABLE 34.3   Minority and Hispanic populations in Michigan cities with >75,000 population

	Population	Minority and Hispanic Population	Percent of place	Cumulative percent of all Michigan minorities
Detroit	951,270	859,797	90.4	40.9
Grand Rapids	197,800	84,193	42.6	44.9
Warren	138,247	10,831	7.8	45.4
Flint	124,943	73,050	58.5	48.9
Sterling Heights	124,471	10,125	8.1	49.3
Lansing	119,128	47,773	40.1	51.6
Ann Arbor	114,024	29,207	25.6	53.0
Livonia	100,545	5,188	5.2	53.2
Dearborn	97,775	6,602	6.8	53.6
Clinton Twp	95,698	8,411	8.8	54.0
Westland	86,602	11,448	13.2	54.5
Farmington Hills	82,111	13,631	16.6	55.2
Troy	80,959	14,043	17.4	55.8
Southfield	78,296	46,483	59.4	58.0
Kalamazoo	77,145	23,406	30.3	59.1
Canton Twp	76,366	12,648	16.6	59.7
Michigan	9,938,444	2,103,852	21.2	

Source: US Census Bureau (2003a)

FOCUS BOX: The Arab population of Michigan

In 1990, Michigan had over 76,000 people of Arab ancestry, comprising nearly one percent of the total population. By 2000, that number had grown to over 115,000 (1.2%). The main ancestries represented were Lebanese (47%), Syrian (8%) and Egyptian (3%). This group represents the highest proportion of Arab-ancestry population in the US—a population segment that is also growing faster than any other ethnic minority in the state. Within Michigan, the Arab population is highly concentrated in Wayne County, which had over half of Michigan's Arab population, with 56,109 (2.7% of the county population). Within Wayne County, the Arab population is further concentrated in only a few communities. Dearborn has nearly 30,000 Arab-ancestry people, the highest pro-

portion (30%) of any place in the US (Chapter 33). Other concentrations include Detroit with >8,000, Sterling Heights with >4,500, Warren with ~3,500, and Livonia with almost 2,000.

Why the large concentrations of Arab people in Michigan? Although few Arab-speaking people arrived in the Detroit area at the end of the 1800s, the flow of Arab migrants did not take off until the automotive employment opportunities in the 1920s. More immigrants have settled here in the last 40 years. This immigration stream is a good example of the migration destination momentum that can build over time, where family and friend connections provide the impetus for the migration.

■ Economic and housing characteristics

Traditionally, Michigan has been relatively well-off economically, compared to most other states. As residents of one of the leading industrial states, people in Michigan have enjoyed higher wages, more home ownership, more disposable income and other positive economic indicators than more rural, less urbanized areas of the country. This trend is particularly true for the industrial growth years following World War II. In more recent decades, financial well-being and unemployment in Michigan have changed. With a heavy reliance on the success of the auto industry, Michigan's economy has experienced more drastic economic swings than has most of the rest of the nation (Chapter 31). Table 34.4 shows the relative standing of Michigan (as of 2000), compared to the US, on a series of economic measures. Note, first, that education levels in Michigan are higher than in the US in general, reflecting an investment in education at the state level, typical of most upper Midwest states, and Michigan's particularly strong support of education, dating back to the 1800s. Second, overall income levels are slightly higher than the rest of the country, which is also typical of the industrial states of the Midwest. Third, the proportion of employment (and income) dependent on manufacturing in Michigan is much higher than in most other parts of the US (Chapter 31). If the importance of manufacturing declines in coming years, as many economic predictions foresee, the relative wealth of the state may decline as well. Finally, housing values (and rents) are generally lower than the US average, again typical of Midwestern states.

The Census Bureau uses three general measures of income (US Census Bureau 2003a; Table 34.4): (1) *Per capita income* measures the annual income for each person >15 years of age, divided by the total population of a unit area, (2) *Family income* measures the total income of all family members >15 years of age, living together; and (3) *Household income* measures the total income of all people >15 years of age, living together, regardless of family relationship. Although these three measures describe different aspects of income, they do not vary significantly in their spatial distribution across Michigan (Fig. 34.9). Areas of higher income are found in southern Michigan in general, especially in the suburban areas of Detroit, Grand Rapids, Lansing and in other larger cities. Notice also the larger incomes associated with the Traverse City region and parts of the northwestern Lower Peninsula. Lower income areas are found in other parts of the northern Lower Peninsula, throughout most of the Upper Peninsula, and in Detroit. Most of this distribution can be explained by examining access to higher paying job opportunities in or near larger cities. However, low values of household income in Detroit, Flint, Lansing and other central cities suggest that race, education and other social variables also play a part in determining this pattern.

Income can also be broken down into different components, such as by source (wages, Social Security, dividends and others), all of which may have different geographic distributions. Most income in Michigan (78%) can be attributed to salaries and wages paid to employees, but an important component is *retirement income* (Fig. 34.10),

TABLE 34.4   Economic and housing comparisons: Michigan vs the US[1]

	Michigan	United States
Population	9,938,444	281,421,906
High school graduates (%)[2]	83.4	80.4
Per capita income ($)	28,900	30,033
Median family income ($)	53,457	50,046
Median household income ($)	46,929	42,873
Below poverty level (%)[2]	10.3	11.7
Retail employment (%)[3]	11.9	11.7
Manufacturing employment (%)[3]	16.5	11.2
Unemployment (%)[4]	7.3	6.0
Minority-owned firms (%)[5]	7.6	14.6
Mean travel time to work (mins)	24.1	25.5
Median house value ($)	115,600	119,600
Median monthly rent ($)	468	519
Homeowners (%)[6]	73.8	66.2
Homes built before 1950 (%)[6]	26.5	21.0
Mobile homes (%)[6]	6.5	7.6

1. Data are from 1999 or 2003.
2. Percent of total population.
3. Percent of all employment.

4. Percent of all workers aged ≥16, in the workforce.
5. Percent of all firms.
6. Percent of all homes.

Source: US Census Bureau (2003a).

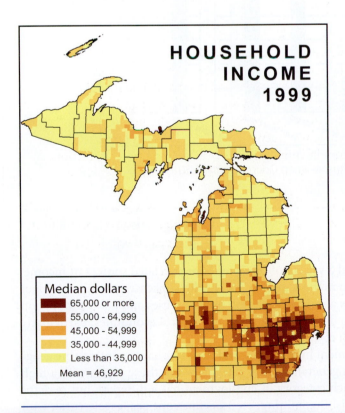

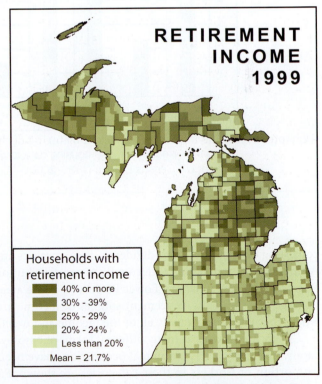

FIGURE 34.9   The distribution of household income in Michigan, as of 1999, by townships and incorporated places. Source: US Census Bureau (2000).

FIGURE 34.10   The distribution of retirement income in Michigan, as of 1999, by townships and incorporated places. Source: US Census Bureau (2000).

FOCUS BOX: A retirement county in northern Michigan

In the upper Great Lakes region, rural parts of Michigan, Wisconsin and Minnesota have become magnets for retirees seeking rural amenities, cheap land, recreational attractions and a "retreat" from urban environments (Chapter 5). "Retirement migration" has greatly altered the demographic and economic profile of these lightly-populated places. Roscommon County is a typical example. With a total population of just over 25,000, it has one of the highest proportions of older people in the country, almost twice the national average (see Figure below). Almost all of the Roscommon County populace is white, and a relatively high proportion own their own homes.

Vacant housing, usually seasonally-occupied, is common, indicating that many residents are "snow-birds" that migrate to Florida and other warmer climates during the winter. Most of the Roscommon County immigrants have retired from jobs in southern Michigan cities. Their retirement income, in the form of Social Security, retirement benefits and investment income, provides a steady flow of revenue to the area. In general, this combination of population growth and income flow has helped to sustain a relatively stable economic picture in Roscommon County, like it has in many other "retirement" counties in the upper Great Lakes.

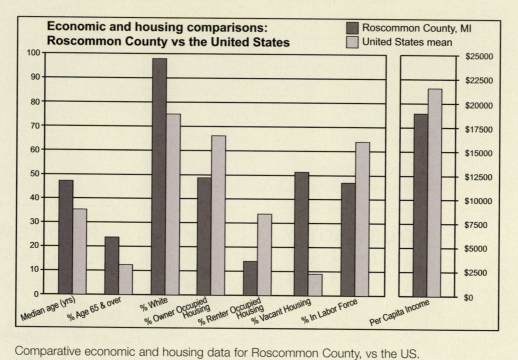

Comparative economic and housing data for Roscommon County, vs the US.
Source: US Census Bureau (1830–2000).

consisting of Social Security, dividends, rent, royalties and a variety of other retirement-related sources of income. As might be expected, this pattern reflects age distribution in the state (Fig. 34.7), with concentrations in the Upper Peninsula and the northern Lower Peninsula. These areas also have fewer job opportunities and a low proportion of wage income. Thus, retirement sources of income are usually very important to local economies, particularly where they contribute nearly all of the income and wealth to an area.

There are, of course, many different forms of employment in Michigan, and they, too, have an interesting geography. In Figure 34.11, individual occupations have been generalized into categories and those places with a high proportion of workers in these categories are shown. Each category of employment has a different, but perhaps predictable, distribution. Agricultural and extractive (fishing, mining, etc.) occupations are largely rural, with

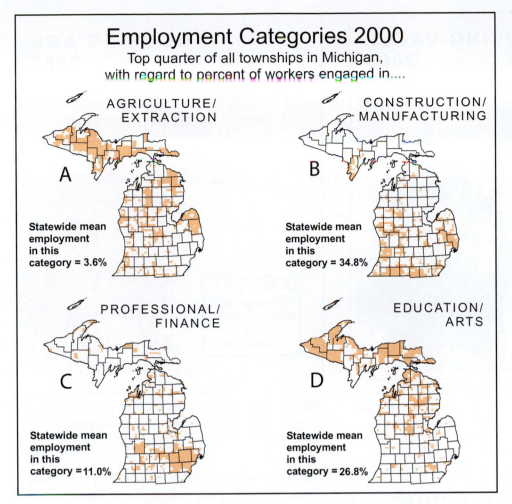

Employment Categories 2000
Top quarter of all townships in Michigan,
with regard to percent of workers engaged in....

AGRICULTURE/
EXTRACTION

A

Statewide mean
employment
in this
category = 3.6%

CONSTRUCTION/
MANUFACTURING

B

Statewide mean
employment
in this
category = 34.8%

PROFESSIONAL/
FINANCE

C

Statewide mean
employment
in this
category = 11.0%

EDUCATION/
ARTS

D

Statewide mean
employment
in this
category = 26.8%

FIGURE 34.11 Maps showing the top quarter of all townships and incorporated places in Michigan, with regard to percent of workers engaged in various employment sectors, as of 2000. Source: US Census Bureau (2000).

concentrations in the Upper Peninsula, the "thumb" region, and other agricultural areas in the Lower Peninsula (Fig. 34.11A). Relative amounts of construction and manufacturing employment (Fig. 34.11B) are *not* concentrated in the large urban counties in southern Michigan, because there are too many other competing employment opportunities. Rather, this category reaches high values in more rural areas, near urban centers. Professionals, e.g., doctors, lawyers and bankers (Fig. 34.11C), are concentrated in wealthier urban and suburban places in the Lower Peninsula. Lastly, education and arts employment shows higher values where there is little other competing employment (Fig. 34.11D).

The US Census Bureau collects a large number of variables on housing characteristics (US Census Bureau 2003a), ranging from age of the owner of the home to the number of bathrooms with plumbing fixtures. Almost all of these measures are geographically related to wealth—wealthier places have higher or more valuable housing characteristics, poorer areas have lower housing attributes. This relationship is apparent in Figure 34.12, which shows median housing values in Michigan. If compared to the map of income (Fig. 34.9), the patterns are almost identical. High housing values are found in suburban areas, near larger cities in the southern part of the state; the large central cities of Detroit, Flint, Grand Rapids, Lansing and others have significantly lower housing values than do the areas surrounding them. Lower housing values predominate in rural areas, particularly in the Upper Peninsula and the northern Lower Peninsula.

Interrelated with housing value are two other interesting housing distributions—housing age (Fig. 34.13) and mobile homes (Fig. 34.14). Older housing is found in almost all cities and villages and in rural areas that have not undergone significant in-migration of population in recent years, e.g., the "Thumb" area, agricultural areas along

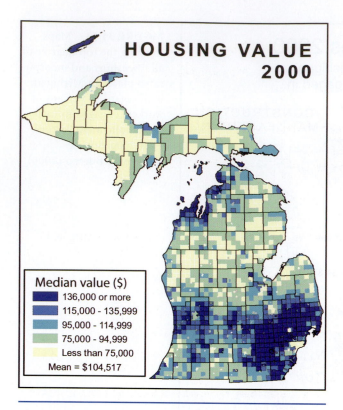

FIGURE 34.12 The distribution of median housing values in Michigan, as of 2000, by townships and incorporated places. Source: US Census Bureau (2000).

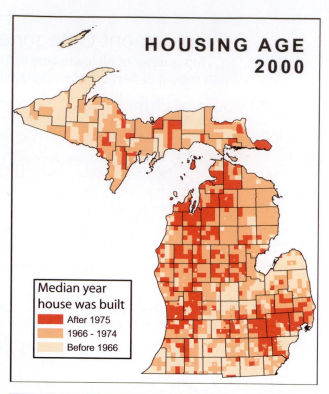

FIGURE 34.13 The distribution of the age of housing in Michigan, as of 2000, by townships and incorporated places. Source: US Census Bureau (2000).

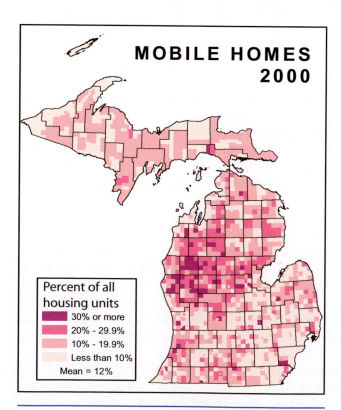

FIGURE 34.14 The distribution of mobile homes in Michigan, as of 2000, by townships and incorporated places. Source: US Census Bureau (2000).

the southern border, and the western Upper Peninsula. Newer housing, built roughly in the last 25 years, has been constructed in "urban sprawl" areas around larger cities, and in rural growth areas in the Lower Peninsula, where large proportions of immigrants have appeared in recent decades. Mobile homes tend to be concentrated in rural areas in the west-central Lower Peninsula, where they provide an inexpensive alternative to more permanent and costly housing. As before, both of these housing patterns are closely spatially related to income, wealth and migration.

■ Conclusions

Michigan's people, and the demographic and economic characteristics they possess, have highly varied, but predictable and explainable, geographic distributions. Therefore, they provide excellent fodder for many different kinds of geographic analyses. From population density to racial distribution, to measures of housing characteristics, Michigan has great variety in its cultural and economic landscapes. Although this is also true, to some extent for all other states, Michigan is particularly notable for the geographic diversity of its people, and their characteristics.

Literature Cited

Groop, R.E., Lipsey, J.M., Press, C., VerBurg, K., Medley, K. and L. Stein. 1984. Michigan Political Atlas. Michigan State University, Department of Geography, East Lansing.

Haupt, A. and T. Kane. 1978. Population Handbook. Population Reference Bureau, Washington, DC.

Michigan Department of Community Health. 2004. Michigan Residents Birth and Death Files 1900–2003. MCDH Division for Vital Records and Health Statistics, Lansing, MI.

US Census Bureau. 2003a. Census 2000: Population and Housing. Michigan Data CD ROM. Department of Commerce, Economics and Statistics Administration, Washington, DC.

US Census Bureau. 2003b. Census 2000: Population and Housing. Migration Data CD ROM. Department of Commerce, Economics and Statistics Administration, Washington, DC.

US Census Bureau Decennial Census. 1830–2000. U.S. and Michigan. Department of Commerce, Economics and Statistics Administration, Washington, DC.

Weeks, J.R. 2005. Population: An Introduction to Concepts and Issues. Wadsworth, Belmont, CA.

Further Readings

Darden, J.T., Stokes, C. and R.W. Thomas. 2007. The State of Black Michigan 1967–2007. Michigan State University Press, East Lansing.

Groop, R.E. and G.A. Manson. 1987. Nonemployment income and migration in Michigan. East Lakes Geographer 22:103–109.

Groop, R.E. 1999. Demographic and economic patterns in the Great Lakes region. In: W.W. Taylor and C. Paola Ferreri (eds), Great Lakes Fishery Policy and Management: A Binational Perspective. Michigan State University Press, East Lansing. pp. 73–92.

Manson, G.A. and R.E. Groop. 1992. Michigan state-to-state migration patterns, 1976–1988. Michigan Academician 24:443–451.

Manson, G.A. and R.E. Groop. 2000. Migration fields of Michigan counties in the 1990s. The Great Lakes Geographer 6:1–11.

Manson, G.A. and R.E. Groop. 2000. U.S. intercounty migration in the 1990s: People and income move down the urban hierarchy. The Professional Geographer 52:493–504.

35 Tourism and Recreation

Sarah Nicholls

■ Introduction

Tourism is widely recognized as one of the world's largest and fastest growing industries. In 2007, a record 903 million international tourism arrivals were documented worldwide, generating $856 billion in international tourism receipts. The US ranked third in international arrivals, welcoming 56.0 million international visitors (a global share of 6%), but first in receipts, receiving $96.7 billion (a share of 11%; United Nations World Tourism Organization 2008). These figures exclude domestic tourism, i.e., tourism by residents of a nation, *within* that nation's geographic boundaries, an activity that has been widely acknowledged to involve substantially larger volumes of tourists and receipts than international tourism activity (Jafari 2001). In this chapter, I explore and discuss tourism to, and recreation within, the state of Michigan.

The concept of tourism

The terms tourism and recreation are notoriously difficult to define and differentiate between, as has been discussed and debated in multiple different texts and industry publications, e.g., Williams (1998), Hall and Page (2001), Boniface and Cooper (2005). In this chapter, the term tourism is broadly defined to denote any temporary movement away from the usual place of home or work, for leisure, business or other, e.g., health or education, purposes, but without the expectation of monetary remuneration at the destination. Although tourism inherently involves travel—to, from and at the destination—not all travel can necessarily be defined as tourism. Although the temporal and spatial criteria used to distinguish tourism from other types of movement do vary, they typically include a minimum and/or maximum trip duration—often 24 hours and one year, respectively—and a minimum distance from the usual place of home or work, often somewhere between 81 and 161 km (50 and 100 miles) one-way.

Geographic perspectives on tourism

From a geographic perspective, tourism consists of three distinct components, which Leiper (1979) together labeled the "tourism system" (Fig. 35.1). The tourism journey begins and ends at the tourist's home—the tourist generating region—although the actual tourism experience takes place at the destination, or tourist receiving region. Origin and destination are linked by travel between the generating and receiving regions, which occurs along one or more transit routes.

The volumes and directions of tourist flows represent a form of spatial interaction between generating and destination regions, as tourists weigh a variety of push (demand) and pull (supply) factors in the home and potential destination regions, respectively. Examples of push factors include levels of disposable income and mobility, and the availability of leisure time, e.g., length of the working week, or vacation entitlement. Pull factors might include ease of access, e.g., distance or time required to reach the destination, number of flight connections and the quantity and quality of attractions, accommodations and other amenities. Some factors, such as climate, can serve as both push (from an unattractive climate) and pull (to an attractive climate) factors (Boniface and Cooper 2005).

Geographers often use gravity models to explain the movement of people, information, or goods between two points, based on each location's population and the distance between them. Specifically, it is assumed that larger places attract more people, information and goods than smaller places, and that the closer together two places are, the greater the attraction, or flow, between them. In the context of tourism, gravity models suggest that levels of inbound and outbound tourism increase with population, whereas they decline with increasing distance, due to the friction of distance between them (Boniface and Cooper 2005).

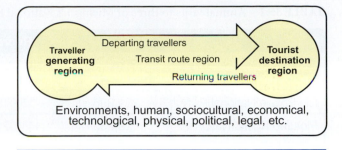

FIGURE 35.1   The tourism system. After Leiper (1979).

The concept of recreation

Recreation has no associated temporal or spatial restrictions. Rather, the term commonly refers to the activities engaged in, during one's leisure or free time. Recreational activities can be active/physical or passive, take place indoors or outdoors, and occur individually or within a group. Recreation does not necessarily require travel; it can occur in an individual's home or backyard.

This chapter focuses primarily on the types of recreational activity that typically require a public, outdoor setting. The typical tourist, therefore, especially if traveling for leisure rather than business, typically engages in multiple recreation experiences during their trip. The more specific definitions of tourism and recreation adopted by various organizations, and used as sources of statistics throughout the chapter, are noted where appropriate.

■ Michigan's tourism and recreation resources

Michigan supports one of the most impressive natural resource inventories of the US, and these resources, combined with the state's climate, provide the setting for a large and diverse range of year-round recreational opportunities. Michigan contains >11,000 inland lakes, 58,065 km (36,000 miles) of rivers and streams (including 1,613 km (1,000 miles) of blue ribbon trout streams), and 4,839 km (3,000 miles) of freshwater shoreline, more than any other state in the nation and second only to Alaska for total shoreline (Michigan Department of Natural Resources 2005). The state borders four of the five Great Lakes (Chapter 14; Plate 1); approximately 30% of this shoreline is publicly owned (Pogue and Lee 1999).

At the federal level, Michigan contains six of the 390 areas administered by the US National Park Service: Father Marquette National Memorial, Isle Royale National Park (Chapter 24), Keweenaw National Historic Park (Chapter 12), a portion of the North Country National Scenic Trail, Pictured Rocks National Lakeshore and Sleeping Bear Dunes National Lakeshore (Chapter 18). Recreation visits to the three national parks in Michigan equaled 1,591,808 in 2007, placing Michigan 33rd on the state list (National Park Service 2007; Table 35.1). Over 70% of these visits were to the most accessible of the three sites—Sleeping Bear Dunes National Lakeshore. Due primarily to its isolated position (it is accessible only by boat or float plane), Isle Royale typically receives some of the lowest numbers of annual recreation visits of all 58 US National Parks. Michigan also contains three national forests: the Hiawatha National Forest in the eastern Upper Peninsula, the Ottawa National Forest, in the western Upper Peninsula and the Huron-Manistee National Forest in the northern Lower Peninsula (Fig. 41.6). These forests cover over 1.1 million hectares and receive over eight million recreation visitor days yearly (US Department of Agriculture 2007; Chapter 41). Michigan is also home to three national wildlife refuges: Seney, Shiawassee and the Michigan Wetland Management District. Ten percent of the land in Michigan is owned and managed by the federal government (US Census Bureau 2005).

TABLE 35.1   Annual visits to three of Michigan's National Parks

Site	Size (hectares)	Recreation visits		Recreation visitor days	
		Visits in 2007	**Change since 2006 (%)**	**Visitor days in 2007**	**Change since 2006 (%)**
Isle Royale National Park	231,396	15,973	−6.4%	104,160	−1.2%
Pictured Rocks National Lakeshore	29,233	441,521	5.3%	194,145	8.4%
Sleeping Bear Dunes National Lakeshore	28,850	1,134,314	−6.5%	550,353	−1.7%
Michigan (total)	289,884	1,591,808	−3.5%	848,658	0.5%
United States (total)	34,217,030	275,581,547	1.1%	102,047,473	1.6%

Source: National Park Service (2007).

State-owned lands in Michigan—which total approximately 12% of the state's total land area—are managed by the Michigan Department of Natural Resources (MDNR). These lands include the 1.6 million hectare state forest system—the largest of any state in the nation—which contains more than 10,000 km (6,200 miles) of groomed snowmobile trails, 145 state forest campgrounds, 70 state wildlife areas, 97 state parks and recreation areas and 829 of the state's more than 1,300 public boating access sites. As a result of the size, number and distribution of these areas, a resident of, or visitor to, the state is never more than 10 km from a fishing spot, or one hour's drive from a state park or recreation area. Michigan's state parks and recreation areas receive approximately 22 million visitors annually (MDNR 2005, 2006). Given this abundance of natural resources, the high level of participation in outdoor recreation activities by both residents and visitors is not surprising. According to the MDNR (2006), Michigan ranks 8th in the nation for the number of licensed anglers, 3rd for numbers of licensed hunters and registered boats, and 1st in number of registered snowmobiles.

As a result of the state's rich industrial and agricultural past, Michigan also offers multiple opportunities for heritage tourism, a niche segment that first rose to prominence among tourism researchers and the tourism industry in the 1990s. It is now one of the most significant, and fastest growing, forms of leisure travel in the nation. Heritage tourism involves travel to sites that in some way represent or celebrate an area, community, or people's history, identity, or inheritance. It can occur at individual sites, in "heritage areas," and along "heritage routes," "corridors" and "trails" (Nicholls et al. 2004). For example, Keweenaw National Historical Park, in Calumet, celebrates that region's copper mining industry (Chapter 12), while the Michigan Iron Industry Museum in Negaunee focuses on the history and significance of the iron industry (Chapters 11, 30). Reflecting the historical and continued dominance of the auto industry in the state (Chapter 31), the MotorCities National Heritage Area, which encompasses 25,900 km² of central and southeastern Michigan, offers the largest concentration of auto-related sites, attractions and events in the world (MotorCities National Heritage Area 2005). The Michigan Department of Transportation's Heritage Route Program is designed to protect unique highway corridors throughout the state. Since its inception in 1993, the program has designated 14 heritage highways in three categories: four scenic, five historic and five recreational. These corridors include the entire length of US-12, from New Buffalo on the shores of Lake Michigan to downtown Detroit, M-22 in Leelanau County, and US-41 in Keweenaw County (Bessert 2006).

Michigan also boasts an abundance of agri-tourism attractions. The Michigan Department of Agriculture (MDA) maintains a list of over 255 farm markets, U-pick operations and agricultural tourism opportunities throughout the state (MDA 2006). Several regions have adopted the idea of developing and marketing agri-tourism routes or trails to local residents and tourists alike, e.g., the Southwest Michigan Wine Trail, which encompasses ten wineries and over 4,000 hectares of vineyards in the southwestern Lower Peninsula. Themed festivals and other events, focusing on distinct agricultural products of individual communities or larger regions, are also increasing in popularity, e.g., Traverse City's National Cherry Festival, Fairgrove's Michigan Bean Festival, the St. John's Mint Festival and the Leland Wine and Food Festival.

FOCUS BOX: Casinos in Michigan

As of 2006, Michigan was home to 20 casinos, 17 of which were operated by nine of the state's Indian tribes, and three commercially owned entities located in Detroit (Table 26.1). Casinos are an important component of Michigan's tourism, and the casino hotels in Detroit, licensed in 1999 and 2000, are seen by many as a crucial element of its downtown redevelopment. Benefits can include the creation of new jobs and income, as well as significant boosts to the local and state tax base—monies that can be used to further improve and revitalize local communities. Nevertheless, casinos are a controversial form of entertainment. Key concerns include addiction, increased crime, drug-related activity and prostitution, and the strain casinos and their patrons place on the local community and its physical infrastructure.

In Michigan, most of the revenue generated by casino activity accrues to the tribes. Since Indian tribes are sovereign nations, laws prohibiting casinos or otherwise regulating activities do not apply on Indian lands. However, states and tribes can choose to enter into agreements that give states some regulatory oversight over a tribe's casino operations, as has occurred in Michigan since 1993. These "gaming compacts," originally entered into with seven tribes, stipulated that 10% of gaming revenue be paid in the form of a tax, 8% for economic development (via the state Renaissance Fund) and 2% for local community improvements. However, this requirement was only to apply while tribes enjoyed the exclusive right to operate casinos in the state. Thus, since the ballot regarding commercially operated casinos passed in 1996, this tax has ceased to be levied (Public Sector Consultants 2002).

Overall, Michigan residents appear ambivalent regarding the relationship between casinos and tourism in the state. A 2006 survey revealed that, while over 70% of business owners surveyed somewhat or strongly oppose the opening of more casinos, nearly half think that state-sponsored tourism advertising and promotion should include mention of its existing casinos (Crain's Detroit Business 2006).

The natural and cultural amenities enjoyed by the state are supported by an extensive infrastructure, which provides the facilities necessary to service local and visitor, recreation and tourism activity. For example, the Michigan Lodging and Tourism Association (2008) represents over 500 hotels, motels, resorts and bed and breakfasts, comprising over 30,000 guest rooms throughout the state. According to the Michigan Association of Recreation Vehicles and Campgrounds (2005), over 1,200 licensed campgrounds, representing more than 80,000 campsites, are also available for overnight stays. More than 4,500 food service establishments are represented by the Michigan Restaurant Association (2006). Other opportunities include the more than 1,000 golf courses and 40 downhill ski resorts throughout the state, as well as the Michigan International Speedway, which hosts NASCAR and Indy Racing League series (Michigan Economic Development Corporation 2007). The role of casinos in the state is explored further in the FOCUS BOX above.

The travel and recreation activities engaged in by local residents, short-term visitors and seasonal home owners, generates large numbers of jobs and a substantial economic impact for the state. In 2004, for example, direct travel expenditures in Michigan totaled approximately $17.5 billion, of which 72% were accounted for by leisure travel. In addition, it is estimated that the Michigan travel industry supports at least 210,000 jobs (Holecek et al. 2006). Although the exact ranking varies, depending upon the source, tourism currently represents either the second or third largest industry in the state.

Tourism flows to, within and from Michigan

Despite the wealth of its natural attractions, Michigan, like most of the Midwest, is typically regarded more as a tourist-generating and transit zone than a tourism destination (Boniface and Cooper 2005). Michigan households made 11.9 million trips to destinations beyond the state boundary in 1995 (Holocek 2003). In the same year, Michigan received 8.4 million household trips from outside the state, a deficit of 3.5 million trips. In 1995, Michigan held a travel deficit with 37 states, and a surplus with only 11; this imbalance resulted in an outflow of over $1.5 billion. The preceding figures refer only to domestic travel, i.e., by US citizens within the US. When international travel is also included, the total deficit for 1995 exceeds $2.8 billion. These figures are based on data contained in the 1995 American Travel Survey,

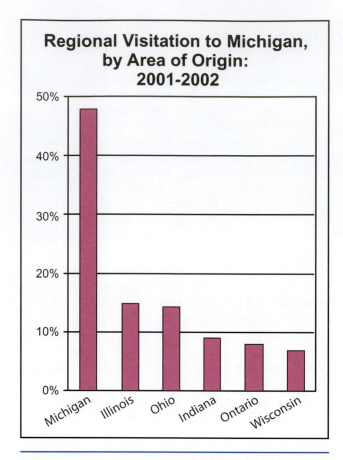

FIGURE 35.2 Distribution of regional visitation to Michigan, by area of origin, 2001–2002 Source: Nikoloff and Herbowicz (2003).

conducted by the Bureau of Transportation Statistics. Although the survey was initially intended to be conducted every five years, 1995 remains the most recent year for which data are currently available.

The majority of tourism that occurs in Michigan is of a regional nature. Most out-of-state visitors to Michigan—more than 48% in 1995 (US Department of Transportation 1997)—come from only three states: Indiana, Illinois, and Ohio. However, by far the largest proportion of tourism in the state is generated by Michigan residents. According to the 2001–2002 Michigan Travel Market Survey (Holecek et al. 2000), 48% of pleasure trips to or within Michigan were accounted for by Michigan residents, during 2001–2002, followed by visitors from Illinois (15%), Ohio (14%), Indiana (9%), Ontario (8%) and Wisconsin (7%) (Fig. 35.2).

Although the northern portions of the state are often perceived to be the primary tourism-receiving areas (Holecek 2003), analysis reveals that only two of the top ten most visited counties in the state in 2001–2002 were in the north (Fig. 35.3). (There is some seasonal variation, with the north gaining in popularity in the summer months.) Wayne County has, by far, the greatest share of annual visits received (12.5% in 2001–2002), with Grand Traverse County receiving the second largest proportion (5.6%). Despite the range and popularity of winter sports available in the state, the most popular season to visit Michigan remains the summer months; June, July and August accounted for 42% of all visitors in 2001–2002. Fall is typically the next most popular season, followed by spring and winter. The vast majority of visitors utilize a private car (rather than bus, RV, plane or boat) as their main form of transportation (91% in 2001–2002), and stay either in a hotel/motel (46%) or with friends and relatives (27%) (Nikoloff and Herbowicz 2003).

Besides the four major, inbound markets of Michigan, Illinois, Ohio and Indiana, the remaining domestic markets are diverse and account for very small proportions of total domestic inbound activity. In 2001, for example, while Michigan, Illinois, Ohio and Indiana together accounted for 72% of trips to Michigan, California provided 3% of visitors, and Texas, North Carolina, Florida, Wisconsin and New York provided another 2% each (D.K. Shifflet and Associates Ltd. 2003). And although the Great Lakes do serve as a major attraction for the state, they also limit access to it. For example, other states accommodate large numbers of auto-based visitors as they pass through them, to other, more distant destinations, if only for a night or two. However, the spatial configuration of Michigan, relative to the Great Lakes, discourages large volumes of "drive-through" traffic.

As an international destination, Michigan ranks 13th in the US (equal with Washington), receiving 1.8% of the 20.3 million overseas visitors to the US, in 2004. (These figures exclude visitors from Mexico and Canada.) For comparative purposes, the top three most visited states, together, received nearly 70% of all international visitors (New York, 26.7%; Florida, 21.8%; California, 20.7%; US Census Bureau 2005). International visitors to Michigan arrive primarily from Europe.

Reflecting its status as a regional destination, Travel Michigan, the state's official tourism agency, focuses its out-of-state marketing activities on three major markets: Chicago, Cleveland and Indianapolis. Travel Michigan also markets heavily within the state, in an attempt to encourage more Michiganders to stay in-state for their vacations and, thus, improve the balance of visitors and payments (Fig. 35.4). Fourteen Michigan "Welcome Centers," strategically located along major highways throughout the state, distribute complimentary brochures—representing >3000 different travel-related entities—and other industry publications to in-state and out-of-state visitors annually (Figs. 35.5, 35.6).

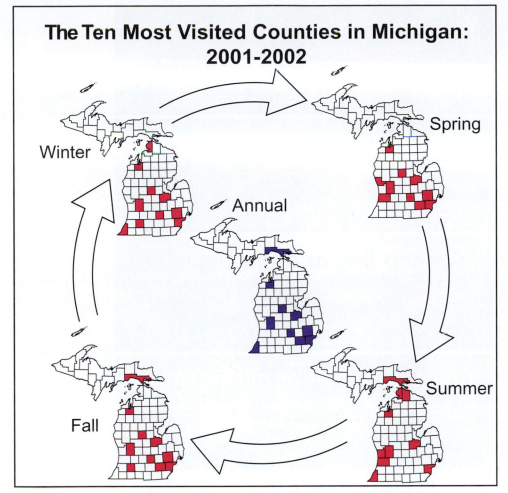

FIGURE 35.3 The ten most visited counties in Michigan, in 2001–2002, annual and by season. After Nikoloff and Herbowicz (2003).

Travel by Michigan residents is also dominated by regional, as opposed to long-distance, trips. Although estimates vary, approximately half of Michiganders' annual trips are typically to a destination within the state, leading to the description of Michigan as a "stay-at-home" state (Kakela et al. 2003). Out-of-state domestic trips are primarily to one of three states: Florida (predominantly in the winter months), Illinois and Ohio. International travel is dominated by trips to Canada—mainly to the bordering province of Ontario (Holecek 2003, Nikoloff and Herbowicz 2003).

Opportunities and challenges facing Michigan's recreation and tourism industries

The outdoor recreation and tourism industries in Michigan face a number of opportunities and challenges in the first half of the 21st century. These are discussed below.

Economic uncertainty

Rising unemployment, increasing health care and energy costs, and the continuing contraction of the auto industry (Chapter 31) are among many factors that combine to create an uncertain economic future for Michigan and the Midwest. Despite efforts to revitalize the state, including Governor Granholm's "Cool Cities" initiative (State of Michigan 2006), an approach that is heavily predicated on the existence of large numbers of high quality outdoor recreation and tourism opportunities in urban areas, it is likely that the foreseeable future will be dominated by a relatively cautious approach to disposable spending on recreation and tourism activities. Although stable or

FIGURE 35.4 Travel Michigan's "Pure Michigan" 2008 summer billboards. Source: Travel Michigan (2008).

FIGURE 35.5 Locations of Michigan's welcome centers. Source: Michigan Economic Development Corporation (2005). http://travel.michigan.org/industry/welcome_centers.asp

FIGURE 35.6 A "Welcome to Michigan" sign at a Michigan Welcome Center.

declining economic conditions might encourage more Michiganders to travel within the state, rather than to other US or international destinations, reducing the outflow of tourism spending from the state, it is likely that this gain will be offset by reduced visitation by non-residents. Nevertheless, it is important to note that Michigan tourism has grown steadily in recent times, by an average of about 4% per annum since the mid-1980s. Thus, the industry would certainly seem to deserve recognition as a key potential growth engine for the state, as Michigan continues to shifts its emphasis away from manufacturing (Fig. 31.1).

Image

Michigan does not enjoy as high a tourism profile as more popular tourist states such as New York, California, Arizona and Florida. In addition, outsiders' perceptions have, for the last several decades, been negatively impacted by their generally indifferent image of Detroit. However, in light of the new "Cool Cities" campaign, and the recent successful hosting of several high-profile sporting events, e.g., the Ryder Cup in 2004, the MLB All-Star Game in 2005, and the Super Bowl in 2006, this image may be improving. In 2006, Travel Michigan also unveiled its new, award-winning advertising campaign, entitled 'Pure Michigan,' which focuses on the state's natural assets, other attractions and world-class golfing opportunities.

Funding

Travel Michigan relies on state funding for its continued operation. Despite clear evidence to suggest that increased funding for the marketing of Michigan as a tourism destination would generate a substantial return to the state treasury, in the form of newly generated tax dollars (Longwoods International 2003), Michigan's state tourism office budget has dropped steadily from 7th in the nation to 31st from 1990 to 2005 (Holecek et al. 2006). The MDNR, in contrast, does not currently receive general tax monies, relying instead on user fees for funding. In 2004, the state park system received 25 million visitors (Love 2005); these visitors paid either a daily fee of $6–8 (resident-nonresident), or purchased an annual pass for $24–29. According to one estimate, the state park system is in need of more than $90 million in "critical repairs" over the next five years, raising controversial issues such as the increasing of fees, or the sale of "marginal" parks, in order to raise sufficient funding to maintain the remainder (Detroit News 2006).

Invasive species

The Great Lakes continue to be blighted by a variety of invasive species, which threaten the ecological integrity, fishing potential, and pristine image of this resource (Chapter 14). Some of the more important, current concerns include the zebra mussel, Eurasian watermilfoil, goby, ruffe and sea lamprey. On land, the emerald ash borer (EAB) was discovered in Michigan near Detroit in the summer of 2002, and already 8–10 million ash trees have died in Michigan, Ohio and Indiana as a result, most of them in southeastern Michigan (Chapter 29). The EAB outbreak has led to a quarantine on all ash products, including a prohibition on the movement of firewood, e.g., to second homes in northern Michigan (Michigan State University 2006).

Climate change

Evidence suggests that Michigan's climate may become substantially warmer over the coming decades (Sousounis and Albercook 2000; Chapter 19). Warmer temperatures do not bode well for Michigan's winter tourism industries, including downhill and cross-country skiing, snowmobiling and ice fishing. However, a longer summer season could benefit summer activity providers, e.g., golf courses and campgrounds. Research remains ongoing into the potential impacts of climate change for Michigan's outdoor recreation and tourism industries, e.g., the Pileus Project (2005).

House Bill 4803

In October 2005, Governor Granholm signed into effect House Bill 4803, which requires that, beginning with the 2006 school year, all Michigan schools begin their school year after Labor Day. It has been estimated that the addition of these (one or) two extra weeks to Michigan's summer tourism season may generate, annually, an additional $132 million in direct tourist expenditures, and $10 million in tax revenues, for the state (Holecek and Herbowicz 2006).

■ Conclusions

Michigan's outdoor recreation and tourism industries will undoubtedly face numerous challenges in the coming decades. Despite this, the natural resource base of the state remains one of the largest, most diverse and attractive in the nation, and participation in outdoor activities is likely to remain high. Similarly, Michigan should remain a popular regional tourism destination, attracting residents both from within the state as well as from surrounding states and Canadian provinces. In particular, as the notion of "niche tourism" continues to flourish (Novelli 2005), the increasing popularity of activities and events targeted at, and enjoyed by, more specific market segments, such as heritage, agricultural and casino tourism, offers considerable potential for further growth.

Literature Cited

Bessert, C.J. 2006. Michigan highways: Heritage routes. Available: http://www.michiganhighways.org/other/heritage.html (last accessed March 2006).

Boniface, B. and C. Cooper. 2005. Worldwide Destinations: The Geography of Travel and Tourism. Elsevier Butterworth-Heinemann, Burlington, MA.

Crain's Detroit Business. 2006. Crain's/Honigman tourism survey results. Available: http://www.crainsdetroit.com/apps/pbcs.dll/article?AID=/20060714/STATIC/60714005 (last accessed August 2006).

Detroit News. 2006, April 15. Michigan should prune unnecessary state parks: Government allows sprawling system to deteriorate.

D.K. Shifflet and Associates Ltd. 2003. Michigan 2001 travel summary. Falls Church, VA.

Holecek, D.F., Spencer, D.M., Williams, J.E. and T.I. Herbowicz. 2000. Status and Potential of Michigan Natural Resources: Michigan Travel Market Survey. Special Report 108. Michigan Agricultural Experiment Station, Michigan State University, East Lansing.

Holecek, D.F. 2003. Travel, tourism, and recreation in Michigan. In: Ballard, C.L., Courant, P.N., Drake, D.C., Fisher, R.C. and E.R. Gerber (eds), Michigan at the Millennium. Michigan State University Press, East Lansing, MI. pp. 455–473.

Holecek, D.F. and T. Herbowicz. 2006. 2006 Michigan Tourism Forecast. Michigan Lodging and Tourism Conference, Mount Pleasant, MI.

Holecek, D.F., Langone, L., Herbowicz, T. and C. Shih. 2006. 2006 Michigan Tourism: Past Performance and Future Expectations. Michigan Lodging and Tourism Conference, Mount Pleasant, MI.

Jafari, J. 2001. Retracing and mapping tourism's landscape of knowledge. Re Vista—Harvard Review of Latin America Winter 2001: Tourism in the Americas. Available: http://www.fas.harvard.edu/~drclas/publications/revista/Tourism/ jafari.html (last accessed December 2005).

Kakela, P., Haas, H., Holecek, D., Potter-Witter, K., Koelling, M., Fridgen, C., Winterstein, S., Garling, D. and J. Ferris. 2003. Status and Potential of Michigan Natural Resources: Michigan's Natural Resource Endowment. Michigan Agricultural Experiment Station, Special Report 117. Michigan State University, East Lansing.

Leiper, N. 1979. The Tourism System. Massey University Press, Palmerston North, New Zealand.

Longwoods International. 2003. Making the case for Michigan's tourism funding. Longwoods International, Toronto, Ontario.

Love, G. 2005. February 11. New panel to advise on financially strapped state parks. Available: http://cns.jrn.msu.edu/articles/2005_0211/STATEPARKS.HTML (last accessed August 2006).

Michigan Association of Recreation Vehicles and Campgrounds. 2005. Michigan RV statistics. Available: http://www.marvac.org/statistics.html (last accessed February 2007).

Michigan Department of Agriculture. 2006. Michigan farm market and u-pick directory. Available: http://www.mda.state.mi.us/market/u-pick/index.asp (last accessed August 2006).

Michigan Department of Natural Resources (MDNR). 2005. Michigan DNR at a glance. Available: http://www.michigan.gov/dnr/0,1607,7-153-10366-121638—,00.html (last accessed December 2005).

Michigan Department of Natural Resources (MDNR). 2006. Economic impact: Natural resources boost Michigan's economy. Available: http://www.michigan.gov/dnr/0,1607,7-153-38948-121641—,00.html (last accessed February 2007).

Michigan Economic Development Corporation. 2007. Welcome travelers. Available: http://www.michigan.org/travel/index.asp?m=0 (last accessed February 2007).

Michigan Lodging and Tourism Association. 2008. About MLTA. Available: http://www.michiganhotels.org/assoc/about.html (last accessed October 2008).

Michigan Restaurant Association. 2006. Welcome. Available: http://www.michiganrestaurant.org/ (last accessed February 2007).

Michigan State University. 2006. Emerald ash borer. Available: http://emeraldashborer.info/ (last accessed March 2006).

MotorCities National Heritage Area. 2005. About MotorCities: What is MotorCities National Heritage Area? Available: http://www.experienceeverythingautomotive.org/ (last accessed December 2005).

National Park Service, United States Department of Interior. 2007. 2007 Statistical Abstract. Public Use Statistics Office, National Park Service Social Science Program, Denver, CO.

Nicholls, S., Vogt, C. and S.H. Jun. 2004. Heeding the call for heritage tourism. Parks and Recreation 39:(9): 38–49.

Nikoloff, A. and T. Herbowicz. 2003. Michigan Tourism Market: 1996–1997 versus 2001–2002. Michigan Tourism Outlook Conference, Michigan State University, East Lansing.

Novelli, M. 2005. Niche Tourism: Contemporary Trends, Issues and Cases. Elsevier Butterworth-Heinemann, Burlington, MA.

Pileus Project. 2005. The Pileus project: Climate science for decision makers. Available: http://www.pileus.msu.edu/ (last accessed March 2006).

Pogue, P. and V. Lee. 1999. Providing public access to the shore: The role of coastal zone management programs. Coastal Management 27:219–237.

Public Sector Consultants. 2002. Casinos and other legal gambling. In: Michigan in Brief, 2002–03. 7th edition. Published by Public Sector Consultants, Inc., Lansing, MI. pp. 64–68.

Sousounis, P.J. and G.M. Albercook. 2000. Potential futures. In: P.J. Sousounis and J.M. Bisanz (eds). Preparing for a Changing Climate: The Potential Consequences of Climate Variability and Change - Great Lakes Overview. Atmospheric, Oceanic and Space Sciences Department, University of Michigan, Ann Arbor. pp. 19–24.

State of Michigan. 2006. Create Cool Cities. Available: http://www.michigan.gov/gov/0,1607,7-168-29544_29546 _29555—-,00.html (last accessed March 2006).

United Nations World Tourism Organization. 2008. Tourism Highlights. World Tourism Organization, Madrid, Spain.

US Census Bureau. 2005. Statistical abstract of the United States 2006. Statistical Compendia Branch, Administrative and Customer Services Division, US Census Bureau, Washington, DC.

US Department of Agriculture. 2007. Michigan National Forests. US Department of Agriculture, US Forest Service, Washington, DC.

US Department of Transportation. 1997. 1995 American Travel Survey. Bureau of Transportation Statistics, US Department of Transportation, Washington, DC.

Williams, S. 1998. Tourism Geography. Routledge, London.

Further Readings

Ashlee, L.R. 2005. Traveling Through Time: A Guide to Michigan's Historical Markers. University of Michigan Press, Ann Arbor.

Hall, C.M. and S.J. Page. 2002. The Geography of Tourism and Recreation: Environment, Place and Space. Routledge, London.

Powers, T. 1997. Michigan State and National Parks: A Complete Guide. Friede Publications, Davison, MI.

Wargin, K.-J. 1999. Michigan: The Spirit of the Land. Voyageur Press, Stillwater, MN.

Field Crops

36

Donald R. Christenson, Darryl D. Warncke,
Jacob E. McCarthy, David K. Beede,
Dale W. Rozeboom and Amanda G. Sollman

■ Introduction

Crop production in Michigan is diverse, because of soils, climate, markets and the development of expertise in production and marketing over many years. Michigan produces more than 100 different crops categorized as field, vegetable, fruit and floriculture/nursery (Michigan Agriculture Statistics 2004–2005). In this chapter, we discuss >25 different field crops, grouped as cereals, edible legumes, forage and root crops. Cereals produced are corn, wheat, oat and barley. Soybean and dry edible bean are edible legumes, whereas sugar beet and potato represent root crops. Forage crops include alfalfa, birdsfoot trefoil and several species of clover and grass, along with *Brassicas*. Canola, buckwheat and rye, among other crops, are produced in small amounts in Michigan, but are not specifically addressed in this chapter.

Corn and soybean are ranked number one and two in land area under production in the state, followed by hay (Table 36.1). More than 100,000 ha of wheat are also produced in the state.

Soils and their distribution are important aspects of the geography of crop production in Michigan. Field crops are produced across soils with vastly different textures (Fig. 20.1) and experience has shown that yield potential is somewhat unique for each textural class. Yield potentials for the major field crops grown on different soil textural classes, along with available moisture in the upper meter of soil, are given in Table 36.2. Available soil water has a significant effect on yield potential for all crops grown in Michigan, unless irrigated. Removal of excess water due to poor soil drainage characteristics is necessary for high crop yields (see FOCUS BOX on the following page).

TABLE 36.1 Hectares of production and mean annual yields for the major field crops grown in Michigan in 2004. Source: Michigan Agricultural Statistics (2005).

Crop	Hectares grown (2004)	Typical yield (metric tons/ hectare)
Corn (all)	885,650	
Corn for grain	777,350	8.4
Corn for silage	108,300	40.3
Soybean	809,700	2.6
Forages	445,300	
Alfalfa/alfalfa mixed	352,100	7.2
Other hay	93,200	–
Wheat	267,200	4.3
Dry edible bean	76,900	1.9
Sugar beet	66,800	47.3
Oat	4,250	2.4
Potato	18,600	37.0
Barley	4,850	2.7

TABLE 36.2   Yield potentials for various crops grown on well-drained soils of different textural classes, under excellent management and without irrigation, in southern Michigan[1]

Crop	Clay loam	Loam	Sandy loam	Loamy sand
Available water (cm water / 90 cm soil depth)	**15.5**	**15.5**	**10.9**	**8.4**
Corn (grain)	10.0	10.7	9.4	7.4
Winter wheat	5.0	5.4	4.0	2.7
Barley	3.5	4.3	3.0	2.7
Oat	3.2	3.6	2.7	1.7
Soybean	3.0	3.4	2.7	1.7
Dry edible bean	1.1	1.1	0.9	0.8
Alfalfa (five cuttings)	14.6	14.6	12.3	11.2
Sugar beet	52	54	42	—

1. Assumes a growing season >140 days. Yield potential is in metric tons/hectare. Yields for potato are not listed, as most production is irrigated. For grass hay and brassicas, yield relationships have not been established. Compiled from various sources.

FOCUS BOX: Subsurface soil drainage

Wet soils warm slowly and cannot support the weight of large farm machinery, making early tillage and seeding difficult. Additionally, excess soil water restricts the oxygen supply to roots, causing them to die. Internal drainage, used to remove excess soil water, is therefore necessary to optimize production. Across most of Michigan, drainage of soils involves the insertion of a perforated, subsurface tube, which does not allow the water table to rise any higher than the tube itself. Any groundwater entering the tube then can drain out, through the tube, into a drainage ditch at the edge of the field. In Michigan, the Saginaw Valley and Thumb regions, and many other small areas on organic soils, are the major areas where tile drainage is used, as these are the areas with the wettest soils (Fig. 20.9).

The first of these tube-like structures were made of kiln-fired clay, hence the name *clay drain tile*. By the end of the 19th century, the manufacturing process for making clay drain tile and the mechanization of their installation were beginning to be developed. By the middle of the 20th century, an industry had developed specifically to assist in the development of soil drainage technologies. In

This field, in the loam soils of the Saginaw Lowlands, has recently had plastic, subsurface drains installed by this large plow machine (A). The machine drags a large "shoe" into the soil, as it unrolls and places the plastic tile in, behind. Soil falls back into the vacated furrow, burying the tile. The grid-like pattern, made by the tile drains in the field, is shown in B. Photo by R. Schaetzl.

the last 40 years, perforated plastic pipe (still referred to as *tile*) has replaced clay tile. Plastic tile has many advantages over the hard, heavy, brittle, clay tile. Plastic tile is cheaper and easier to install. Rather than having to dig a trench, plastic tile is installed using a large plow that places the tile at the appropriate depth. Systems utilizing laser technology to control the depth of installation are common. Installation is much faster, and depth is more precisely controlled, using this system.

In the field, a herringbone arrangement is often used to layout the tile. These lateral tiles, usually 15 cm in diameter, drain into a common, and much larger, main line, which carries the water to a drainage ditch at the edge of the field. The spacing between the lateral lines is commonly 20–30 meters. The tile line is installed with a slope of about 1 cm/10 meters, to aid water flow. Tiles are installed at least 45 cm deep, to protect them from breaking during farming operations.

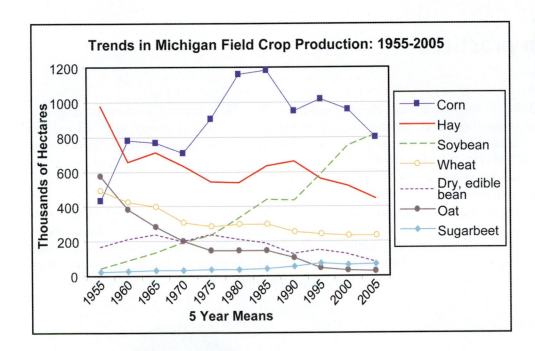

FIGURE 36.1 Running mean hectares of field crops produced in Michigan, for 1955–2005. Source: Michigan Agricultural Statistics.

Hectares of production of field crops have changed over the past 50 years (Fig. 36.1). Acreages of wheat, oat, dry bean and all classes of hay have declined. Oat and hay declined because of the replacement of horses by gasoline-powered tractors for farm work; horses required large amounts of these crops for sustenance. Dry bean and wheat production declined due to competition from other growing areas in the US, and because of lower demand in export markets. Conversely, production of corn, soybean and sugar beet has increased. In the case of corn, higher yielding hybrids with shorter growing season requirements have allowed Michigan farmers to grow more corn in northern and central Michigan. Higher corn prices, fueled by demand for ethanol, may cause corn production to expand even further in the future. Higher soybean demand, for food and industrial uses, along with the development of varieties better suited to Michigan's climate and soils, have contributed to its increased production. Soybean production now extends to the Mackinaw Straits, whereas prior to 1970, production did not extend further north than the Muskegon-Bay City line. Increased sugar beet production is attributed to better production practices and more efficient processing methods, allowing Michigan to remain competitive with other areas of production.

Why certain crops are produced in Michigan, while others are not

This issue is complex, encompassing market forces, advances in technology and trade policies. Over many years, and with the assistance of agri-business, governmental agencies and Michigan State University, growers have developed substantial crop production expertise. That know-how has been passed from generation to generation. Coupled with this is the development of essential infrastructure, including farm supply, product handling and processing, as well as marketing systems. Markets, political considerations, development of new technologies and lack of handling/processing facilities have limited production of some crops and the development of new industries.

Examples of crops once grown in Michigan, but no longer produced here, are numerous. Available markets have limited the expansion of potato production in Michigan. Malting barley was once produced in Michigan, but the closure of a company that processed the crop eliminated that market. Chicory was once grown in Michigan, but production ceased after World War II, due to trade policies favoring production in Europe. Flax for fiber was used to manufacture cushions for automobiles and furniture, but development of alternative materials eliminated the need for this product. Navy bean production in Michigan has declined, due to competition from other production areas, and poor consumer acceptance of beans in the diet. Expansion of canola production is limited by the lack of handling and processing facilities. In sum, there are a myriad of issues affecting crop production, the development of an industry, and the long-term viability of a particular industry.

■ Production practices

Tillage

Tillage practices have traditionally been divided into conventional and conservation systems. Conventional tillage systems utilize primary and secondary operations, resulting in less than 30% of the soil surface covered with crop residues when tillage is completed. Primary tillage is usually the initial, major soil manipulation operation. The moldboard plow is often used to *turn the soil over* (Fig. 36.2), but chisel and disk tools are also employed. Secondary tillage operations are separate and distinct, done for a specific reason, e.g., incorporation of fertilizer and chemicals, weed control or seedbed preparation. Field cultivators, harrows and disks are the usual tillage tools used (Robertson et al. 1979a, b).

In conservation tillage, >30% of the soil surface remains covered with crop residue, even after tillage is completed. No-till practices, where only a narrow strip is tilled for seed and fertilizer placement during the planting operation, while the remainder of the surface (and crop residues) is left unaltered, is the ultimate in conservation tillage. More intensive tillage may be done and still meet the goal of 30% of the soil surface covered with crop residues. Both disk and chisel types of tillage tools are used in conservation tillage operations.

FIGURE 36.2 An agricultural field in Saginaw County, on fine-textured soils, that has been recently tilled by moldboard plowing. Little or no crop residue remains on the surface. Farmers on the Saginaw Lake Plain must contend with these fine textured soils and gear their tillage operations accordingly. Generally these soils are plowed in the fall. Over-winter freezing and thawing reduces the size of the clods making the soil more malleable and easier to prepare for seeding in the spring. Photos by R. Schaetzl.

FIGURE 36.3 An example of a tillage tool used for primary, as well as secondary, tillage operations. The tines in the front break the crust and partially incorporate crop residues into the soil surface. The *rolling baskets* in the rear help smooth the surface, leaving a loose seed bed for planting.

Tillage practices have changed markedly over the past ten years. Tillage tools now available (Fig. 36.3) allow the soil to be prepared in a single pass. Referred to as *reduced tillage*, this form of tillage is intermediate between conventional and no-till. Crops can be seeded using newly developed planters, which work well in these systems.

Fertilization

Crops on all soils need supplemental nutrients for maximum production. Nitrogen (N), phosphorus (P) and potassium (K) are more widely needed, and therefore are used in larger quantities than other plant nutrients. Nutrients are expressed as N, P_2O_5 and K_2O for nitrogen, phosphate and potash, respectively. Quantities needed to replace the amount removed by each crop are given in Table 36.3. Other nutrients needed for specific crops are also noted. All of these, except Mg, are called micronutrients, because they are used in smaller quantities than are N, P or K. Through fertilizer and manure application, soil P concentrations in soils have increased, such that 70% of agricultural soils now contain adequate P for field crop production.

The amount of supplemental nutrients needed is best determined by utilizing soil-testing services (Warncke et al. 2004). Commercial fertilizers, soil amendments, animal manures, biosolids, by-product or refuse materials and legumes all may be used to supply additional nutrients. Special care needs to be exercised when using animal manure or biosolids, however, to insure that the correct amount of nutrients are applied. Several methods may be used to apply fertilizer. Broadcast application across the entire surface is a quick means of applying large quantities of nutrients. In band application, fertilizer is placed 5 cm to the side and 5 cm below the seed, during the seeding operation, thereby providing nutrients to the crop early in its growth, and directly in its root zone. Quantities applied are limited, however, due to the potential of reduction of seed germination, and seedling injury. Micronutrients may be applied with the banded fertilizer, or as a spray to the foliage after emergence (Vitosh et al. 1998). Sidedress and topdress applications involve applying additional N during the growing season. N may also be applied in the irrigation water, a practice called *fertigation*.

Pest control

"Pest" is a general term meant to include weeds, insects, nematodes, diseases and any other plant or animal invader that subjects crops to yield reduction. Control of weeds in crop production is vital for even modest yields. Several approaches may be used for weed control, including combinations of crop rotation, inter-row cultivation and chemical weed control. Weed control practices for corn, soybean, dry edible bean, potato and sugar beet are more intensive than those used for wheat, barley, oat and forage production.

Control methods for other pests include use of resistant varieties, crop rotation and biological and chemical control. Many diseases, nematodes and some insects are crop specific. However, insects such as wireworm (*Limonius* spp,), armyworm (*Spodoptera exigua* Hübner) and grasshopper (*Melanoplus* spp.), among others, may affect all crops. Infestations of such pests are sporadic and need to be controlled at the time of infestation (Jewett et al. 2005).

TABLE 36.3   Typical fertilization needed for field crops, under excellent management practices[1]

Crop and Crop Yield (metric tons/ha)	Nitrogen (kg/ha)	Phosphate[2] (P_2O_5) (kg/ha)	Potash[2] (K_2O) (kg/ha)	Other[3]
Corn (10.0)	200	55	40	Zn
Winter wheat (5.4)	100	50	30	Mn
Barley (3.8)	50	27	18	
Oat (2.7)	34	19	14	Mn, Mg
Soybean (2.4)	0	28	49	Mn
Dry edible bean (0.8)	45	22	29	Mn, Zn
Alfalfa (12.3)	0	72	275	B
Grass hay (6.7)	67	50	186	
Sugar beet (51.5)	100	30	37	B, Mn
Potato (44.8)	200	52	252	Mg

1. After Warncke et al. (2004).
2. Amount of phosphate and potash needed for maintenance, balancing crop removals.
3. Crop is responsive when supply from soil is limited.

■ Crop rotations

The sequence of crops grown from year to year on a particular field is referred to as the crop rotation. Growers in Michigan use many different rotations, which can be grouped into monoculture, cash crop and forage rotations.

Monoculture

Monoculture is a practice of growing the same crop year after year in the same field, i.e., no crop rotation is practiced. Generally, monoculture practices are seldom employed, because of higher incidence of problems, due to pests. However, there are some exceptions. Pastures (legume, grass, mixed species) for grazing livestock work well and are widely used as monocultures. Fields where alfalfa is grown most of the time, while not considered monoculture *per se*, are examples where the same crop is grown year after year. Continuous corn is most often used on livestock farms with limited land area and a high demand for corn silage and grain. In the past, there used to be more land area in continuous corn, but the amount has declined because of increased soybean production, and greater incidence of corn rootworm (*Diabrotica* spp.) (Levine Oloumi-Sadeghi 1991). This insect feeds on the roots of corn causing lodging of the stalks and decreased yield.

Cash crop

Cash crop farms generally do not have livestock, so there is no on-farm use for forages. Cash crop rotations usually include corn, soybean and/or wheat. These rotations are short in duration, usually 2 to 3 years in length, e.g., corn-soybean in a 2-year rotation, or corn-soybean-wheat in a 3-year rotation.

In areas where sugar beet and dry bean are produced as well, e.g., the Saginaw lowlands, these two crops are usually added to the cash crop rotation. Sugar beet commonly follows corn, but may also follow dry bean or soybean. The length of these rotations is longer, increasing the length of time between sugar beet crops, usually three or more years.

Forage rotations

When livestock is included in farming operations, the need for forages (as feed) leads to another type of rotation. In these rotations, corn may be followed by soybean, and then a forage crop (alfalfa) will be seeded. Wheat may also be included in these rotations. Alfalfa will be grown for five to seven years, and then followed by corn again. Oat and barley are substituted for corn in northern Michigan, where corn does not fare as well in the cool climate. Variations of this rotation may include dry bean and sugar beet. Most dry bean and sugar production, however, is in cash crop rotations.

■ Cereal crops

The four cereal grains (corn, wheat, barley and oat) are members of the grass (Poaceae) family. All are annuals, producing seed each year. Although the main goal is production of grain, whole corn plants are also harvested (chopped in the process) to make silage, which in turn is fed to animals (primarily dairy). Straw of the other three cereals may be removed for animal feed and bedding, or sold for cash.

Corn

Corn is Michigan's number one crop, both in hectares produced and cash receipts to the grower. Producing approximately one billion bushels of corn grain, Michigan accounts for approximately 2% of the total US production, ranking 14th among the states (Iowa is number one). Corn (*Zea mays* L.), often called maize outside the US, is a New World crop, found by 16th century European explorers. It probably originated in Mexico (Janick et al. 1969). However, by the 16th century, corn production extended from Chile in the south to the Great Lakes region in the north. Records indicate that American Indians selected and planted types of corn adapted to a wide range of conditions. Some have suggested this was the greatest crop selection endeavor in world history, and this effort has continued into the 21st century. Development of hybrid corn and other genetic modifications have resulted in improved yield, better quality, increased resistance to certain pests and adaptation to cooler climate.

Corn is grown in both tillage systems listed above, with ~20% as no till. Corn is sown in rows spaced 76 cm apart, at 60–80,000 seeds per hectare, between April 10 and May 15. Fertilizer listed in Table 36.3 may be broadcast prior to planting, or in a combination of broadcast and band. In many cases, most of the required N is side-dressed in early June. Corn for silage is harvested in September, whereas grain harvest occurs in October and November.

The length of time needed to produce mature corn is an important factor in determining where corn is produced. Yields of corn are usually greater for longer maturity corn hybrids. However, in the past 30 years, the yield potential of shorter maturity hybrids has been improved, thereby pushing corn production farther north in Michigan (Fig. 36.4). Greater production is centered on the finer textured soils, because of greater yield potential (Fig 20.1). Corn production on sandy soils in southwestern Michigan is enhanced by irrigation. Irrigation of medium and fine textured soils for corn production has been shown to be only marginally feasible economically, because the cost of most irrigation systems is not defrayed by the increase in yield (Christenson et al. 1992).

Corn for silage is utilized as livestock feed, as is corn for grain. Corn grain is also widely used outside of livestock feed. Corn is used in more than 3,700 products, with more being added each year. Primary products

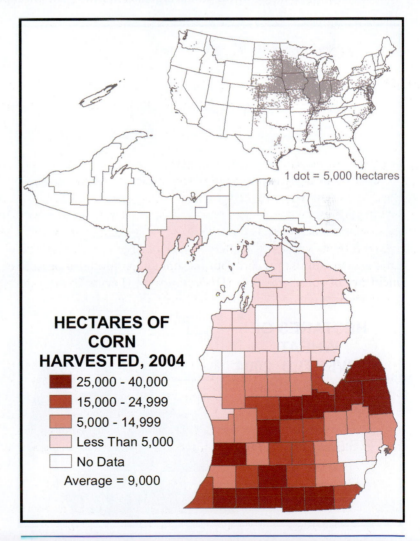

FIGURE 36.4 Distribution of corn production in Michigan, in 2004.
Source: Michigan Agricultural Statistics (2004–2005).

from corn grain are starch, dextrose, soluble and corn syrups. All four products are used in industrial applications, food products, pharmaceuticals and drugs and cosmetics. Corn is also used as a major feedstock for ethanol production.

Wheat

Wheat (*Triticum aestivum* L.), as currently grown, is a relative, modified by selection and plant breeding, of wheat grown in earlier times. It has been grown in the Fertile Crescent, from Egypt and Greece, east to Iran, for thousands of years (Martin and Leonard 1971). Two broad types of wheat are grown. Winter wheat is seeded in the fall, prior to harvest, while spring wheat is seeded in the spring of the harvest year. Several different classes of wheat are also grown worldwide, including hard red, soft, hard white and durum. Hard red wheat (grown in drier climates) is made into high-grade bread flour. Soft wheat yields flour useful for pastries and crackers. Flour from hard white wheat is also used for cereals and pastries. Durum wheat is used to make a product called semolina, that is used to make pasta. In addition to food, wheat is used in many industrial applications. Wheat starch is used in adhesives, cosmetic and pharmaceutical products, plastics, manufacture of paper and as a carrier of controlled release pesticides and flavors. Although wheat is an excellent animal feed, less than 10% is used for this purpose, because it is more valuable for human consumption.

Approximately 36 million bushels of wheat are produced in Michigan, giving it a ranking of 14th in the nation. Kansas is the number one wheat producing state. In Michigan, wheat production is predominantly in the southern half of the Lower Peninsula, and on finer textured soils (Fig. 36.5). Nearly all of the wheat grown in Michigan is soft winter wheat, of which 65% is red and 35% is white. Less than 5% of the wheat grown is used for seed, the remainder is processed for human consumption.

Winter wheat is seeded in September, usually following dry edible bean, soybean or another cereal (usually not corn) crop. The soil is often tilled lightly with a field cultivator prior to seeding, although some wheat is grown in no-till systems. Fertilizer, including 20 to 30 kg N/ha, is broadcast prior to planting (Table 36.3). The remainder of the N is applied as a top dress application in the spring. Manganese (Mn) is often applied as a foliar application, if deficiencies occur, in the spring.

Winter wheat is harvested in mid-July, using a combine, which cuts, threshes and separates the grain from the straw and other plant debris. The cleaned grain is collected in a bin before transferring it to storage or market.

Barley

An Old World cereal (Janick et al. 1969), barley (*Hordeum vulgare* L.) is grown on approximately 7,700 hectares in Michigan. Nearly 60% of barley production is in the Upper and northeastern Lower Peninsulas; the remainder is scat-

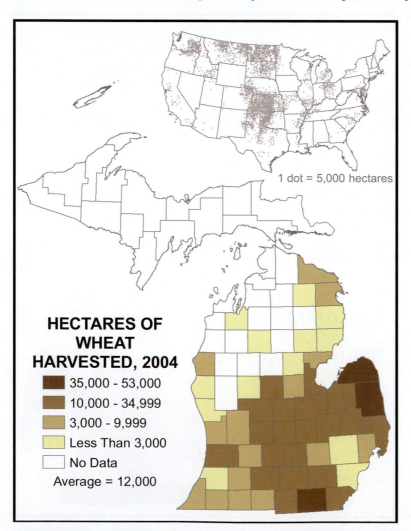

1 dot = 5,000 hectares

HECTARES OF WHEAT HARVESTED, 2004

- 35,000 - 53,000
- 10,000 - 34,999
- 3,000 - 9,999
- Less Than 3,000
- No Data

Average = 12,000

FIGURE 36.5 Distribution of wheat production in Michigan, in 2004. Source: Michigan Agricultural Statistics (2004–2005).

tered somewhat evenly over the rest of the state. Most of the barley produced in the US is grown in the Northern Great Plains. Michigan produces about one million bushels of barley annually, compared to 319 million for the nation. Although there are winter varieties of barley, Michigan produces only spring barley. As pointed out earlier, barley production for the malting industry ceased to be viable after the closure of a processing plant.

Barley is generally seeded in the spring on conventionally tilled soil. Most often, fertilizer is broadcast prior to seeding. Early planting allows the crop to compete with invading weeds. However, a broadleaf herbicide may be used for weed control, if weed pressure becomes too great. Harvest is usually in late August.

Michigan's barley crop is largely utilized for animal feed; nationally, about half is used for animal feed and 45% for malt production. Approximately 2% is used for human consumption, and the rest is produced for seed. Pearled (hulls removed) barley is used in soups and baby foods. Barley is also used in breakfast cereals, breads, cookies, crackers, and snack bars. However, since barley flour does not produce good quality bread, only small quantities of specialty products are made from this flour.

Oat

Oat (*Avena sativa* L.) is another Old World crop, having been grown in the same general area as wheat and barley. Even though land in oat production in Michigan fluctuates widely from year to year, it has been declining over the past 50 years (Fig 36.1). The distribution of production is fairly even across the state, as oat is a crop that grows well, even in the cool north (Fig. 36.6).

FIGURE 36.6 Close-up of some seed heads of almost mature oat plants. Photo by R. Schaetzl.

Like barley, oat is generally seeded in the early spring, on conventionally tilled soil, in rows 18 to 25 cm apart. Fertilizer is generally broadcast prior to seeding. Mn may be applied to the foliage when deficiency symptoms appear, most likely on soils with pH>6.5. Weed control relies on competition by the early sown oat, although some broad leaf herbicides are used. Harvesting occurs from mid-August through September, later the north. Some oat is used as a companion crop for under-seeded alfalfa. In this case the fertilizer may be applied with the seed at seeding.

There was much more oat produced in Michigan when horses were the prime source of power for farm field operations. Currently pleasure and racing horses are major consumers of oat produced in Michigan. It is also used as cooked and ready-to-eat breakfast cereals, as well as in a growing list of other types of food products. In addition, oat products are used in the cosmetic industry, as a replacement for talc. Oat consumption by humans has increased over the past 30 years, triggered by health-related attributes (Marshall and Sorrells 1992).

FOCUS BOX: Dairying in Michigan

For many people, the phrase "field crops" calls to mind corn, oats and wheat, and the human foods made from them. Although it is true that many of the crops Michigan farmers harvest become human food products, a substantial portion winds up not in cereal bowls, but on farms, where they are consumed by cattle—dairy cattle in particular. Dairy farming is a very important industry in Michigan, and dairy cows consume a great deal of the grains and forages we produce. In 2005, *all* field crops harvested in Michigan were valued at about $1.5 billion, while total cash receipts for dairy products, e.g., milk, cheese and ice cream, amounted to nearly $1 billion. In sum, milk production accounts for about two-thirds of Michigan's total animal agriculture revenue.

Michigan's unique topography and climate play a role in the distribution of dairies and dairy cows, the majority of which are located in the thumb region and southern half of the Lower Peninsula (see Figure on the next page). Tillable land, nutrient-rich, loamy soils, sufficient water supplies and temperate weather make these areas ideal for growing the field crops dairy cows require. Because transportation of field crops to out-of-state markets has always has been costly, in-state dairy production has thrived by converting these crops into milk, a valuable commodity, before transport.

In the past, there were more dairy farms and cows in Michigan; many of the areas in which people milked cows in the past are now urbanized. Today, dairy cows are concentrated on fewer, although much larger, farms. Although both the number of farms and cows has decreased, the average number of cows per herd has increased from 4 to 119, since 1910. This increase has resulted from dairy farmers' attempts to become more efficient, in a highly competitive marketplace. Even though there are fewer cows in Michigan today than in the past, total milk production has increased. In 1945, the average cow produced 2460 liters (650 gallons) of milk per year, while today's cows average 9880 liters (2610 gallons) per year.

The 20th century also saw changes in the destinations to which Michigan milk traveled for processing. In the past, most milk was handled and sold locally, by smaller creameries and dairies. Today, 90% of Michigan's farm milk is marketed by a handful of producer-owned milk cooperatives, which distribute milk across the state and nation. Similarly, while the majority of the forages and grains consumed by dairy cows in the past were grown locally, the demand for grains today may outstrip the local supply. The marketplace, however, makes the importation of grains and small amounts of forages from other states and Canada a viable alternative.

It is likely that the trends toward fewer farms with more cows, and more broadly distributed milk markets, will continue in the future, but several emerging factors also promise to shape the future of dairying in Michigan. For example, if demand for ethanol as a fuel alternative increases, so will the value of the crops used to make it. Some of these crops are staples in current dairy cow diets, and if their value increases, so will the cost of feed. Conversely, the process of converting crops to corn syrup for soft drinks (or ethanol for cars) results in co-products that can be a feed-source alternative for cows. How Michigan dairy farmers will react to the economic ramifications of these changes will be interesting to watch.

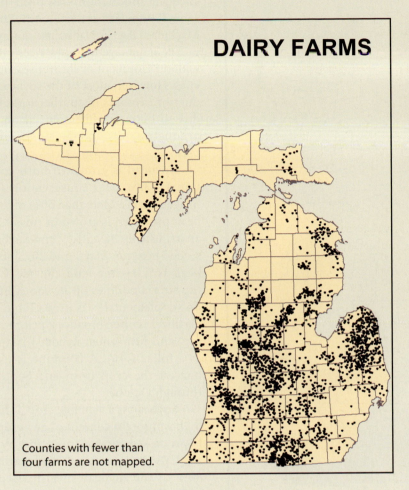

DAIRY FARMS

Distribution of dairy farms in Michigan, in 2002. Each dot represents one dairy farm, regardless of size or number of cows. In order to protect grower confidentiality, the location of each farm dot was randomly moved by up to 4.8 km. Source: USDA (2005).

Counties with fewer than four farms are not mapped.

■ Edible legumes

Edible legumes produced in Michigan include soybean (*Glycine max* L.) and dry edible beans (*Phaseolus vulgaris* L.). Soybean is an Old World crop originating in southeastern Asia. Although dry edible beans originated in both the Old and New World, most of the dry beans grown in Michigan are derived from genetic materials originating in Central and South America.

Soybean

Soybean is second to corn in land area under production in Michigan, as well as cash receipts for the grower. Illinois is the leading state in soybean production; Michigan ranks 11th. Even though Michigan produces >60 million bushels of soybean, it has only 2.4% of the national production. Over the past 40 years, the northern boundary for

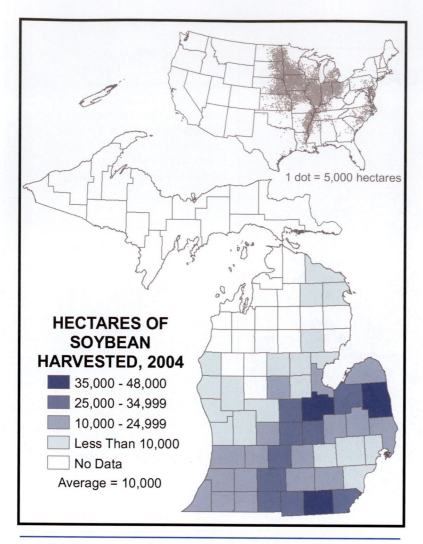

1 dot = 5,000 hectares

**HECTARES OF
SOYBEAN
HARVESTED, 2004**

- 35,000 - 48,000
- 25,000 - 34,999
- 10,000 - 24,999
- Less Than 10,000
- No Data

Average = 10,000

FIGURE 36.7   Distribution of soybean production in Michigan, in 2004.
Source: Michigan Agricultural Statistics (2004–2005).

soybean production has been pushed some 320 km farther north, to the Straits of Mackinac (Fig. 36.7), because of improvements in management practices, coupled with development of shorter season varieties. However, most of the soybean production remains in southern Michigan, due to better yield potential on more productive soils, and the longer growing season.

Soybean is grown in both conventional (60%) and conservation (40%) tillage systems. More than 50% of the soybean produced is grown in rows <76 cm apart, usually 38 and 19 cm. Soybean is seeded between May 1 and 20. Since soybean is a legume, and can *fix* N from the air via nodules on its roots, little or no supplemental N is used (Table 36.3). Fertilizer is often broadcast prior to seeding, and Mn (when needed) is applied as a foliar spray. A combine is used to harvest the crop from late September through October.

Soybean is a valuable crop. It has the highest protein content of any crop, and is processed for consumption by both animals and humans. Approximately 80% of the soybean meal is used as a major source of protein for the livestock industry. The remainder of the meal is processed into products for human consumption. Another notable product is soybean oil—used for food, cosmetic products and as a fuel for diesel engines. The oil is also used in building materials, candles, crayons, ink and insulation, among other products.

Dry edible bean

Several market (commercial) classes of dry edible bean are produced in Michigan. In order of hectares produced they are: black, navy, small red, pinto, dark and light red kidney and cranberry. Michigan growers produce approximately 143 thousand tons of dry edible beans annually, nearly 18% of the US production, and ranks second, to North Dakota (Michigan Agricultural Statistics 2004–2005). Michigan ranks first in the nation in production of black, cranberry, light red kidney, navy and small red beans, producing 69, 72, 26, 45 and 43% of US production, respectively. Michigan ranks third to Minnesota in the production of dark red kidney beans, producing 12% of the national output.

Dry bean production is concentrated on the productive soils of the Saginaw Valley, Thumb and central regions of Michigan, along with three counties of northeastern lower-Michigan (Fig. 36.8). Dry beans have been grown in Michigan since the 19th century, fostering the development of both expertise and infrastructure for their production, processing and marketing.

Even though conventional tillage is the most common method of soil preparation for dry bean production, the amount of dry beans under conservation tillage is increasing. Dry edible bean is usually seeded in rows 76 cm apart, although some growers solid-seed (rows 25 cm apart). Fertilization is similar to that used for soybean, except supplemental N is needed, since dry beans do not as efficiently fix N. Zinc may be included with the banded fertilizer, or applied to the foliage. Beans are sown around the first of June, and harvested in September. When the plants are mature (dry), the whole plant is lifted from the soil, using a knife or rod lifter, and placed in a windrow. The beans are later picked up by a combine and threshed. Often the beans are lifted in the morning and threshed in the afternoon. Significant losses may occur if the plants are allowed to become too dry, due to shattering of the seedpod. Bean breeders are developing new varieties with an upright growth habit for direct harvest.

Essentially no dry beans are used for animal feed, because heating is required to deactivate harmful enzymes, making their use economically unattractive. Most of the edible bean crop is exported. The portion that is consumed domestically is processed and canned for human consumption. Small quantities are cleaned, packaged and sold for direct consumption. Dry bean products are not used in industrial applications.

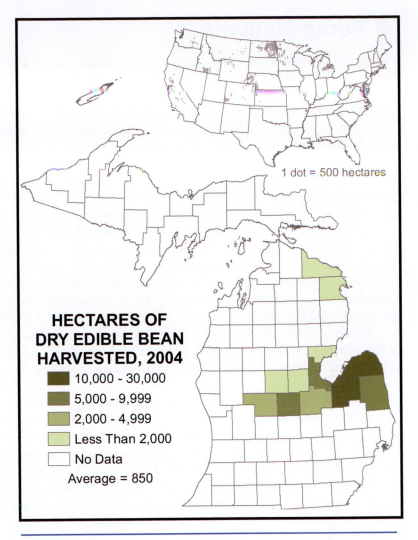

FIGURE 36.8   Distribution of dry edible bean production in Michigan, in 2004. Source: Michigan Agricultural Statistics (2004–2005).

Forage crops

Forage crops are consumed by animals (Janick et al. 1969). Legumes (Fabaceae family), grasses (Poaceae family) and brassicas (Brassicaceae family) represent the major forage crops grown. Legumes produced in Michigan include alfalfa (*Medicago sativa* L.), birdsfoot trefoil (*Lotus corniculatus* L.) and medium red, ladino, alsike, mammoth and white clovers (*Trifolium spp.*). Grasses used for forage include smooth bromegrass (*Bromus inermis* L.), orchard grass (*Dactylis glomerata* L.), reed canary grass (*Phalaris arundinacea* L.), timothy (*Phleum pratense* L.). perennial ryegrass (*Lolium perenne* L.), Italian ryegrass (*Lolium multiflorum* Lam) and tall fescue (*Festuca arundinacea* Shreb). Brassicas include forage turnips (*Brassica rapa* L. subsp. *rapa*), rape (*Brassica napus* L.) and kale (*Brassica olerocea* L). Corn grown for silage, and the straw from wheat, oat and barley, are also used as forage. Forage legumes, forage grasses and mixtures of these crops are collectively referred to as hay. Michigan produces about 2% of the total forages grown in the US, and ranks 17th among the states. Production is widely distributed across the state, with 52,600 ha in the Upper Peninsula, 87,000 in the northern Lower Peninsula, 137,600 in the central Lower Peninsula and 168,000 ha in the southern Lower Peninsula. Hay is produced across all soil texture classes. However, yields are lower on loamy sand and sand soils, due to droughty conditions.

■ **Forage legumes**

Alfalfa, also known as lucerne, is often referred to as the "queen" of forages. It is a high yielding, high protein crop. Being a deeply rooted perennial, it will thrive for a number of years under good management. It is an Old World crop, being reported by the Romans as a good crop for improving productivity of soils. In all likelihood it was grown prior to Roman times (Janick et al. 1969).

Alfalfa is produced statewide, on well-drained soils. Soil pH needs to be >6.5, either naturally or adjusted by lime application prior to planting (Christenson et al. 1988). Approximately 80% of the hay produced in Michigan is alfalfa, the remainder is other species, grown alone or in mixtures.

A common way to seed alfalfa is to clear seed (on tilled soil, without a companion crop), either in the spring or in August. Nearly 90% of the alfalfa in the Lower Peninsula, and 70% in the Upper Peninsula, is sown in this manner. Alfalfa is also sown in the spring with a companion crop, usually oat or barley. Winter wheat is not compatible as a companion crop for alfalfa, due to the late sowing date of the wheat. The cereal companion crop is harvested in year one, but the alfalfa will survive and produce forage in subsequent years. When clear seeded, the soil is prepared using a field cultivator. Fertilizer is broadcast prior to seeding. Boron, when needed, is often applied with this application. Fertilizer needs shown in Table 36.3 may be for the seeding year. Additional P and K will be needed in subsequent years, to replace crop removal. The most productive fields are treated with herbicide to suppress weed growth, although a vigorously growing alfalfa crop is also effective in reducing weed growth.

Alfalfa is harvested by cutting the whole plant. It may then be chopped and placed in a silo as haylage. More commonly it is allowed to dry and then baled, for transport and feeding elsewhere (Fig. 36.9). Under excellent management, alfalfa may be harvested five times per season in southern Michigan, decreasing to two cuttings further north.

Birdsfoot trefoil is grown on poorly drained sites, since alfalfa does not thrive in such conditions. Birdsfoot trefoil and also tolerates greater soil acidity than alfalfa (Janick et al. 1969). It is grown as a hay crop in the Upper Peninsula, but is used primarily as pasture in the Lower Peninsula. Fertilization is similar to alfalfa, but birdsfoot trefoil requires less K, since the amount of dry matter removed is less. Harvest is similar to alfalfa, except not as intensively, usually two or three times per year. About 5% of the acreage is grown for seed production.

Clovers are mainly utilized for pasture, and in mixtures with alfalfa and grasses as harvested forage. White clover is the most common. This plant is native to Michigan, volunteering on finer textured soils. It may also be

FIGURE 36.9   Alfalfa and other forages are cut, windrowed, allowed to dry and then baled, as shown in this field in Osceola County. Photo by R. Schaetzl.

seeded. Medium red clover is second in abundance, followed by ladino, alsike and mammoth. Clovers are excellent sources of protein, and are palatable to livestock. However, they generally yield less than alfalfa (smaller plants) and have shorter longevity, since the taproot rots away by the second year (Janick et al. 1969).

Forage grasses

Grass forages are not utilized to the same extent as legumes. Rather, they are grown in combination with alfalfa, as well as clear seeded. Fertilizer is broadcast before seeding, annually after that. Nearly 80% of the grass forage is used for grazing, while the rest is harvested for hay. Grass hay is fed to both horses and cattle. It is a preferred feed for a majority of horses, since the nutritive energy requirements of the animal is more closely met with grass than with legume hay.

Root crops

An underground portion of both sugar beet (*Beta vulgaris* L.) and potato (*Solani tuberosum* L.) are harvested. In the case of sugar beet, it is the root; for potato, an underground stem is harvested and eaten. Sugar beet is an Old World crop, grown as a leafy vegetable for thousands of years. Sweet variants were developed into the crop we now know as sugar beet (Draycott and Christenson 2003). Potato originated in the high Andes in South America, and was taken to Europe by explorers in the 16th century, and from there to the US.

Sugar beet

The sugar beet industry in Michigan had its beginning in 1839, when a pilot sugar plant (the second one in the US) was built at White Pigeon (Cass County). The venture failed, and no more beets were grown until the late 1880s, when Professor Robert Kedzie of Michigan State University imported some seed from Germany to use in demonstration trials. He promoted growing sugar beets in the state, earning the title of *Father of the Michigan Sugar Industry*.

Sugar beet is produced in fewer than 10 states. Michigan ranks 4th nationally, producing about 12% of the national total, behind Minnesota, the leading state. The importance of sugar beet to the Michigan economy is illustrated in that sugar beet represents about 10% of the total field crop cash receipts, but is grown on less than 3% of the land area in field crops.

Production of sugar beet is centered in the Saginaw Valley, Thumb and central county regions of Michigan (Fig. 36.10), due to the deep, productive soils there. While reproductively, sugar beet is a biennial, it is grown as

FOCUS BOX: The sugar beet industry

Sugar beet is the only field crop marketed through a contractual arrangement with a sugar company—a grower-owned cooperative. The first successful sugar beet factory was built in 1898, at Essexville, near Bay City. A total of 25 factories were eventually built in Michigan, between 1839 and 1920. As of 2006, only four processing plants were in operation, at Bay City, Sebewaing, Caro and Croswell. Michigan Sugar Company and Monitor Sugar Company have been the only two companies in operation in Michigan, since 1959. Growers contracting with Michigan Sugar Company purchased the company in 2002; those with Monitor Sugar followed suit in 2004. The two groups formed a farmer-owned cooperative now called Michigan Sugar Company.

The unique feature of sugar beet production is that the crop is sold solely on a contract basis, rather than on the open market, as are most other crops. For >100 years, sugar companies have contracted with growers to produce a predetermined number of hectares of the crop. Growers enter into a *Growers Agreement* in January of each year, to grow and deliver the beets produced for a given number of hectares. The number of hectares a grower may contract to grow is directly related to the number of shares owned in the cooperative. The grower is paid a price per ton of beets delivered to the factory, or to a reception area—typically a "flat pad" of concrete, at which they are moved into large heaps (see Figure on the next page). Payment to the grower is based on the price per ton, established by the cooperative, multiplied by the number of tons delivered. This price is determined after sale of the sugar, pulp and molasses.

Sugar beets being unloaded from a farmer's truck, at a receiving station near Caro. Beets are stored here, from harvest time until they are needed at the processing plant. These stations assist farmers, by reducing travel times to market (the processing plant). They also reduce the on-site storage needs of the processing plants. Photo by R. Schaetzl.

FIGURE 36.10

Distribution of sugar beet production in Michigan, in 2004. Source: Michigan Agricultural Statistics (2004–2005).

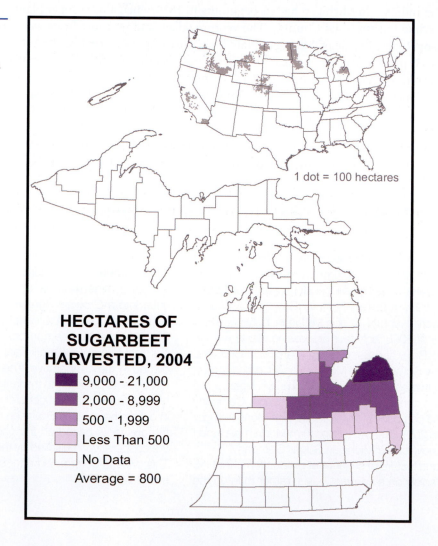

1 dot = 100 hectares

HECTARES OF SUGARBEET HARVESTED, 2004

- 9,000 - 21,000
- 2,000 - 8,999
- 500 - 1,999
- Less Than 500
- No Data

Average = 800

FIGURE 36.11 Sugar beet is usually seeded in rows 76 cm apart on conventionally tilled fields, such as these in Tuscola County. In this photo, the beets have been "topped"—stripped of their leaves—prior to digging and transport to market. Photo by R. Schaetzl.

an annual, seeded in the spring and harvested in the fall. Planting dates generally run from April 10 to May 10. Harvest occurs from late September to early November.

Sugar beet is generally seeded on conventionally tilled soil, in rows 76 cm apart, but some is seeded in rows 50 cm apart (Fig. 36.11). Some sugar beet is seeded utilizing conservation tillage. Fertilizer is most often applied in a band, including 30–50 kg N, plus all of the P and K. Mn and B may be included where needed. Additional N may be broadcast prior to planting, or side dressed early in June. Weeds are controlled using chemicals, inter-row cultivation, and in some cases, by hand removal. Blowing of soil on sandy ridges causes abrasion of young plants, resulting in damage to, or loss of, crop. To avoid this hazard, some growers plant rows of rye or other cereal grains in the inter-row space, to protect the young sugar beet plants. The cereal is removed by cultivation, or with herbicides, when the sugar beet plants have reached sufficient size to reduce the risk.

Harvest of sugar beet is a two-step process. First, the foliage is removed using a machine with rotating rubber flails. Next a harvester lifts the beets, removes soil from the root and elevates the roots into a truck for transport to the piling ground, or reception area (Fig. 36.11; see also the FOCUS BOX on page 559). The beets are stored in piles out of doors, until they can be processed. At the processing plant, the roots are washed, then sliced and the soluble components in the tissue removed with hot water. This solution is clarified to remove impurities, in a multi-step process. The thin juice, containing sucrose, is concentrated. The resultant white sugar is crystallized and packaged for retail sales, or shipped in bulk to bakeries. Sugar from sugar beet is not distinguishable for sugar produced from sugar cane. The by-products of this processing, beet pulp and molasses, are used for animal feed.

Potato

Potato production is widespread in Michigan; Montcalm and St. Joseph Counties have the most production (Fig. 36.12). Michigan ranks 10th in the nation, producing 620,000 tons annually, or 3% of the US output (Michigan Agricultural Statistics 2004–2005). Idaho ranks first. However, Michigan ranks first nationally in production of new-red potatoes. Nearly all of Michigan's potato production is on sandy soils, and the crop is always irrigated. Timing of irrigation is scheduled using a computer program developed at Michigan State University, thereby conserving the amount of water used and reducing leaching of nitrates and chemicals from the soil. Conventional tillage is most often used for potato production. Fertilizer may be applied in a band or broadcast prior to planting. Weed control is largely done by application of chemicals, supplemented with inter-row cultivation. Potato is seeded in early May. The *seed* is not a true seed, but rather a tuber, or piece of tuber. Harvesting of new potatoes for the fresh market begins in mid-July. Harvest for other uses begins in late August and continues into October. In the past, most of the new potatoes were red-skinned, but now both white- and red-skinned varieties are grown. About 70% of Michigan's potato crop is used for chips, while 25% are consumed fresh and 5% are grown for seed. Fresh potatoes may be processed and frozen, canned and/or dried.

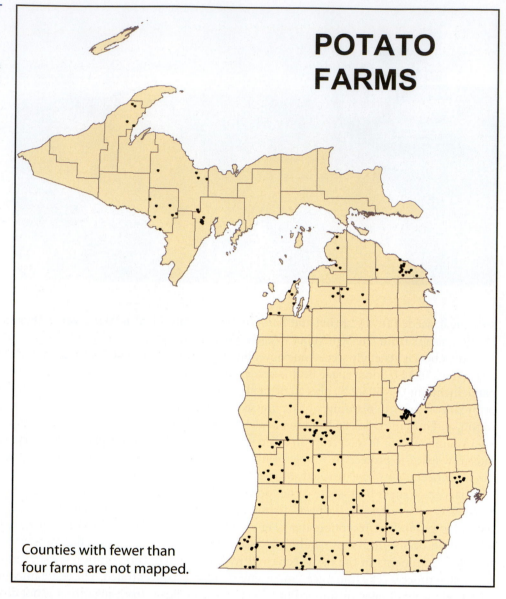

FIGURE 36.12
Distribution of potato producing farms in Michigan, in 2002. Each dot represents one operation, regardless of size or number of hectares in production. In order to protect grower confidentiality, the location of each farm dot was randomly moved by up to 4.8 km. Source: USDA (2005).

POTATO FARMS

Counties with fewer than four farms are not mapped.

FOCUS BOX: Pork production in Michigan

Pork production is important to the economy of Michigan, ranking 6th among agricultural commodities and accounting for approximately 4.6% of Michigan agriculture's $4.5 billion cash receipts (Michigan Agricultural Statistics 2007) and adding value to other commodities, through consumption of crops as feed, creating enhanced demand for foodstuffs. A typical swine diet is about 70% ground corn and 20% soybean meal. The success of pork production has gone hand-in-hand with that of crop production.

When "pork" is mentioned, many people think of the marketing slogan "Pork the Other White Meat," and the boneless pork chop. But other pork products are consumed by people every day, e.g., bacon, ham, pulled and barbequed pork, baby-back ribs and pork breakfast sausage. Indeed, worldwide, more pork is consumed by the average person than any other meat. Approximately 15% of the pork produced in Michigan and the US is exported to other countries.

Michigan's land and water resources and climate make crop and animal production possible throughout the state (see Figure on the next page). However, the majority of swine are raised in the southwestern and south-central regions of the state. In 2005, nearly 75% of Michigan's pigs were residing in the state's top 10 pork producing counties (see Table). The concentration of swine in these locations generally reflects the greater availability of lower-cost feeds, or greater crop yields at less expense and the greater availability of cropland upon which manure nutrients can be applied at agronomic rates, so that swine and crop production is done in an environmentally-responsible manner.

The 10 most densely populated hog and pig counties in Michigan, as of December, 2005

Rank	County	Inventory (head)
1	Cass	180,000
2	Allegan	160,000
3	Ottawa	72,000
4	Branch	65,000
5	Huron	62,000
6	Calhoun	56,000
7	Hillsdale	31,000
8	Gratiot	30,000
9	Van Buren	30,000
10	Kalamazoo	27,000

Source: Michigan Agricultural Statistics (2006).

Michigan's pork industry has changed dramatically over time. Previously characterized by many small farms with fewer pigs, to presently having fewer farms with larger number of animals (see Figure below), estimates today suggest that about 60% of all of Michigan's breeding swine are owned by only about 40 farmers. Viewed broadly, the change in farm numbers and farm size reflects the consumer's demand for a consistent, high quality, eating experience, each time they choose to eat pork, as well as the pork producer's effort to be efficient and profitable in a competitive global economy.

What develops next for the Michigan pork industry is of great interest to many. With the increased use of corn and soybeans for biofuel production, controlling feed costs will be a primary goal for swine producers. Farmers will have to be innovative in terms of feeding by-products, e.g., dried-distiller's grains. They will have to be innovative so that pork production will continue its long-standing, working relationship with crop production, in providing the citizens of Michigan with excellent quality food and a desirable quality of life.

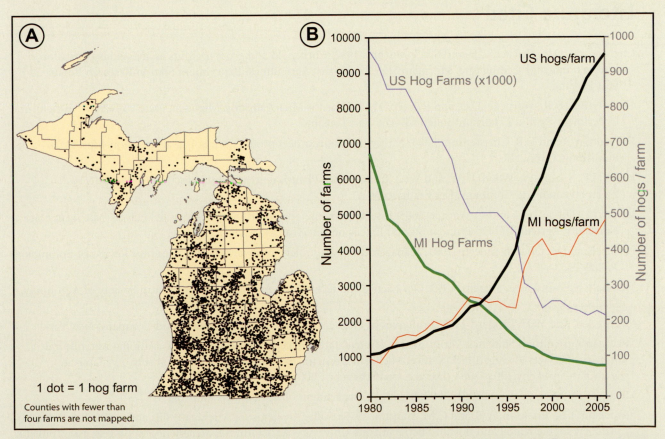

Hogs farms in Michigan over space and time. A. Distribution of hog-raising operations in Michigan, in 2002. Each dot represents one operation, regardless of size or number of hogs. In order to protect grower confidentiality, the location of each farm dot was randomly moved by up to 4.8 km. Source: USDA (2005). B. Number of hog farms and average hog inventory in the US and in Michigan. Source: Michigan Agricultural Statistics (1980–2007).

■ Conclusions

Michigan's agriculture has a major impact on the overall economy of the state, consistently ranking in the top three industries, along manufacturing and tourism. Field crops are part of a diverse system of production, accounting for approximately 30% of that economic impact. The efficiency of agriculture in the US contributes to a system where <20% of the consumer's disposable income is spent on food.

Growers across Michigan and the nation face continuing cost-price pressures in their operations. They incur increasing production costs and have no direct way of passing that cost on, since the purchaser of farm products largely establishes the price. In order to compete, many growers are using value-added products, to improve profitability. An example of this is the grower who produces ethanol from the corn raised on his farm. While this approach is not widespread, more growers are looking at ways to capture additional markets.

Many of the larger farms are incorporated as family corporations, where the owners are actively involved with day-to-day operations. Private consultants are employed to help with management of crop production. They offer advice on nutrient needs and pest control. They also provide in-season field scouting, to monitor the progress of the crop and provide advice on correcting problems as they arise.

A continuing challenge for field crop producers is to reduce movement of pesticides and fertilizer nutrients to off-target sites. New pesticide products with shorter residual times in the soil, along with the capability of low volume application, greatly aid in this process. Reduced tillage systems reduce movement of soil into surface waters, thereby greatly aiding in soil conservation and reducing environmental risks. In short, field crop production will continue to be a significant enterprise in the state of Michigan, supporting our excellent standard of living.

Literature Cited

Christenson, D.R., Bricker, C.E. and S.L.S. Murphy. 1992. Corn yield and gross margins as affected by irrigation, nitrogen rate and seeding rate. Michigan State University, Agricultural Experiment Station Research Report 525, East Lansing.

Christenson, D.R., Warncke, D.D. and R. Leep. 1988. Lime for Michigan soils. Michigan State University, Agricultural Experiment Station Extension Bulletin E-471, East Lansing.

Draycott, A.P. and D.R. Christenson. 2003. Nutrients for sugar beet production: Soil-plant relationships. CABI Publishing, Oxon, UK.

Janick, J.R. Schery, W., Woods, F.W. and V.W. Ruttan. 1969. Plant Science: An Introduction to World Crops. W. H. Freeman and Company, San Francisco, CA.

Jewett, M., DiFonzo, C. and C. Warner. 2005. Insect and nematode control in Michigan field crops. Michigan State University, Agricultural Experiment Station Extension Bulletin E-1582, East Lansing.

Levine, E. and H. Oloumi-Sadeghi. 1991. Management of diabroticite rootworms in corn. Annual Review of Entomology 36:229–255.

Marshall, H.G. and M.E. Sorrells. 1992. Oat science and technology. Agronomy 33. American Society of Agronomy, Madison, WI.

Martin, J.H. and W.H. Leonard 1971. Principles of Field Crop Production. Macmillan and Company, New York.

Michigan Agricultural Statistics. Various dates. United States Department of Agriculture, National Agricultural Statistics Service, Michigan Field Office, Michigan Department of Agriculture, East Lansing. Available at www.nass.usda.gov.2003–2004 (last accessed February, 2008).

Michigan Rotational Survey. 2001–2002. Michigan Department of Agriculture, Lansing, MI.

Robertson, L S., Erickson, A.E. and C.M. Hanson. 1979a. Tillage systems for Michigan soils and crops. Part I: Deep, primary, supplemental and no-till. Michigan State University, Agricultural Experiment Station Extension Bulletin E-1041, East Lansing.

Robertson, L.S., Erickson, A.E. and C.M. Hanson. 1979b. Tillage systems for Michigan soils and crops. Part II: Secondary tillage and cultivation. Michigan State University, Agricultural Experiment Station Extension Bulletin E-1042, East Lansing.

United States Department of Agriculture (USDA). 2005. 2002 Census of Agriculture. Agricultural Atlas of the United States. National Agricultural Statistics Service, Washington, DC.

Vitosh, M.L., Warncke, D.D. and R.E. Lucas. 1998. Secondary- and micro-nutrients. Michigan State University, Agricultural Experiment Station Extension Bulletin E-486, East Lansing.

Warncke, D., Dahl, J., Jacobs, L. and C. Laboski. 2004. Nutrient recommendations for field crops in Michigan. Michigan State University, Agricultural Experiment Station Extension Bulletin E-2904, East Lansing.

Further Readings

Acquaah, G. 2002. Principles of Crop Production: Theory, Techniques and Technology. Prentice Hall, Upper Saddle River, NJ.

Christenson, D.R., Bricker, C.E. and R.S. Gallagher. 1991. Crop yields as affected by cropping system and rotation. Michigan State University, Agricultural Experiment Station Research Report 516, East Lansing.

Copeland, L. and O. Hesterman. 1988. Seeding practices for Michigan field crops. Michigan State University, Agricultural Experiment Station Extension Bulletin E-2107, East Lansing.

Green, D.E., Wolley, D.G. and R.E. Mullen. 1981. Agronomy: Principles and Practices. Burgess International Group, Incorporated, Edina, MN.

Jacobs, L. and D. McCreary. 2003. Utilizing biosolids on agricultural land in Michigan. Michigan State University, Agricultural Experiment Station Extension Bulletin E-2781, East Lansing.

Metcalf, D.S. and D.M. Elkins 1980. Crop Production: Principles and Practices. Macmillan Publishing Company, New York.

Mutch, D. and S. Snapp. 2003. Cover crop choices for Michigan. Michigan State University, Agricultural Experiment Station Extension Bulletin E-2884, East Lansing.

Randall, C. 2002. Chemical treatment of agronomic seeds. Michigan State University, Agricultural Experiment Station Extension Bulletin E-2035, East Lansing.

Rector, N. 2003. Manure nutrient recycling. Michigan State University, Agricultural Experiment Station Extension Bulletin E-2826, East Lansing.

Robertson, L.S., Christenson, D.R., Smucker, A.J.M. and D.L. Mokma. 1978. Tillage systems. In: Robertson, L.S. and R.D. Frazier (eds), Dry Bean Production—Principles and Practices. Michigan State University, Agricultural Experiment Station Extension Bulletin E-994, East Lansing.

Smalley, S. and J. Sanchez. 2001. Integrated cropping systems for corn, sugar beet and dry bean rotations. Michigan State University, Agricultural Experiment Station Extension Bulletin E-2738, East Lansing.

Snapp, S.S. 2003. Managing manure in potato and vegetable systems. Michigan State University, Agricultural Experiment Station Extension Bulletin E-2893, East Lansing.

Snapp, S. and D. Smucker. 2002. Nitrogen management for Michigan potatoes. Michigan State University, Agricultural Experiment Station Extension Bulletin E-2779, East Lansing.

Thelen, K. 1999. How a corn plant develops. Michigan State University, Agricultural Experiment Station Extension Bulletin E-1933, East Lansing.

Thelen, K. 1999. How a soybean plant develops. Michigan State University, Agricultural Experiment Station Extension Bulletin E-1934, East Lansing.

37

Vegetable and Specialty Crops

D. D. Warncke and D. R. Christenson

Michigan farmers add diversity to the state's agricultural base by producing more than 40 vegetable crops (Table 37.1). Vegetables are produced on relatively small units (compared to field crops), accounting for about 7% of the total cash receipts received by Michigan farmers. Michigan ranks first nationally in production of processing cucumbers, accounting for 25% of the nations pickles, second in fresh carrot and celery, third in asparagus, fourth in processing carrot, fresh market cucumber, pumpkin, squash and processing tomatoes, while our snap bean production ranks fifth (Table 37.2). This chapter introduces and examines these vegetable crops, along with mint and sod (turfgrass), focusing on agronomic, geographic and economic issues of production.

In addition to classification by genus and species, vegetable crops may be grouped by their edible portions: root, tuber, bulb, stem, leaf, flower, fruit or seed. They may also be categorized by market class (fresh or processing), or as cool and warm season crops (Schroeder et al. 1995). Warm season members include snap bean, cucumber, eggplant, muskmelon, squash, peppers, tomato, sweet corn, sweet potato and watermelon; others in Table 37.1 are cool season crops (Maynard and Hochmuth 1997). The maximum temperature range for cool season crops is 24–29° C, while warm season crops grow well at 27–35° C.

◼ Centers of origin

The diet of early humans undoubtedly included wild fruits and vegetables. Most vegetables grown today do not resemble these wild species, however, having been improved through selection and plant breeding. Nearly all currently grown vegetable crops are not native to North America, but originated in one or more of six geographical centers around the world (Table 37.3).

◼ Distribution of production

Although Michigan grows a wide variety of vegetable crops (Table 37.1), some are produced in small quantities for specialty markets, fresh market use or for other urban markets, whereas others are grown in huge quantities for processing. Table 37.4 lists the principal vegetable crops grown in Michigan, i.e., those produced on more than 150 ha statewide (Michigan Rotational Survey 2001–02). Some are produced on both mineral and organic soils while others are grown predominately on one soil type (Table 37.4).

Small-seeded vegetable crops, such as carrot, onion and radish, establish and grow well on organic (muck) soils, because of good moisture supplies. Organic soils also warm rapidly in the spring, enhancing seed germination. However, timeliness of planting and harvest operations may be hampered by excess moisture. Good surface and

TABLE 37.1   The major vegetable crops, mint and sod grown in Michigan[1]

Crop	Genus and species
Asparagus	*Asparagus officinalis* L.
Bean, snap	*Phaseolus vulgaris* var. *vulgaris*
Beet, red	*Beta vulgaris* subsp. *Vulgaris*
Broccoli	*Brassica oleracea* var. *italica* Plenck
Brussels sprouts	*Brassica oleracea* var. *gemmifera* Zenker
Cabbage	*Brassica oleracea* L.
Carrot	*Daucus carota* var. *sativus* Hoffm.
Cauliflower	*Brassica oleracea* var. *botrytis* L.
Celery	*Apium graveolens* var. *dulce* (Mill.) Pers.
Chives	*Allium schoenoprasum* L.
Cilantro	*Coriandrum sativum* L.
Cucumber	*Cumcumis sativus* var. *sativus*
Dill	*Anethum graveolens* L.
Eggplant	*Solanum melongena* L.
Garlic	*Allium sativum* L.
Ginseng	*Panax ginseng* C. A. Mey
Greens—collard, kale, mustard, turnip	*Brassica* spp.
Leek	*Allium porrum* L.
Lettuce	*Lactuca sativa* var. *capitata* L.
Muskmelon	*Cucumis melo* var. *catalupensis* Naudin
Okra	*Abelmoschus escalentus* (L) Moench
Onion	*Allium cepa* L.
Parsley	*Petroselinum crispum* (Mill.) Nyman ex A.W. Hill
Parsnip	*Pastinaca sativa* subsp. *Sativa*
Pea, green	*Pisum sativum* L.
Pepper, bell, others	*Capsicum annuum* var. *annuum*
Pumpkin	*Curcubita pepo* L.
Radish	*Raphanus sativus* L
Rhubarb	*Rheum rhabarbarum* L.
Spinach	*Spinacia oleracea* L.
Squash	*Curcurbita pepo* L.
Sweet corn	*Zea mays* subsp. *Mays*
Sweet potato	*Ipomoea batatas* var. *batatas*
Swiss chard	*Beta vulgaris* subsp. *Vulgaris*
Tomato	*Lycopersicon esculentum* Mill.
Turnip	*Brassica rapa* subsp. *Rapa*
Watermelon	*Citrullus lanatus* var. *lanatus*
Watercress	*Nasturtium officinale* R. Br.
Mint, spear- and pepper-	*Mentha spicata* L. and *Mentha piperita* L.
Sod, bluegrass	*Poa pratensis* subsp. *Pratensis*

1. Source: Michigan Rotational Survey (2002).

TABLE 37.2   Michigan's national ranking for production of selected vegetable crops[1]

Crop	Rank	Percent of national production	Leading state
Cucumber (pickles)	1	27.9	Michigan
Carrot (fresh market)	2	4.8	California
Celery	2	6.2	California
Asparagus	3	15.5	California
Carrot (processing)	4	5.2	Washington
Cucumber (fresh market)	4	10.1	Florida
Pumpkin	4	10.4	Illinois
Squash (all)	4	14.6	California
Tomato (processing)	4	1.2	California
Snap bean	5	6.2	California

1. Source: Michigan Agricultural Statistics (2003–2004).

TABLE 37.3   Centers of origin of selected vegetable crops grown in Michigan[1]

Crop	Center of origin
Cabbage, cucumber, radish, onion	Chinese Center (Mountains of central and western China)
Cucumber, egg plant	India-Malaysian Center (Assam and Burma)
Carrot, onion, peas, spinach	Central Asiatic Center (India and Afghanistan)
Asparagus, beet, broccoli, cabbage, cauliflower, celery, lettuce, peas, rhubarb, turnip	Mediterranean Center
Corn Bean, pumpkin, sweet potato, peppers	Mexican and Central American Center
Bean, tomato, pumpkin, peppers	South American Centers (Peru, Ecuador, Bolivia)

1. After Schroeder et al. (1995).

subsurface drainage is, therefore, required on organic soils, because of their inherent poor internal drainage and high water table.

On mineral soils, vegetables are commonly grown on sandy loam and loamy sand soils, because of their inherent good drainage. However, because of their limited water holding capacity, irrigation is essential on these soils.

Major shifts in production in recent years include the movement of mint and carrot production from organic to mineral soils, and the abandonment of head lettuce production. There is also a trend for summer squash to be grown on organic soils. Over the last ~25 years, the number of hectares of vegetable production in Michigan has declined, due to competition from western states. Increasing energy and transportation costs, however, may favor increased vegetable production in Michigan in the future.

Several factors impact the location of vegetable production in Michigan. First, southern Michigan contains many hectares of suitable sandy and organic soils (Fig 20.1). Many immigrants of Dutch origin, knowledgeable in the production of vegetables on organic soils, settled in Michigan in the 19th century, producing celery, carrot, onion, potato and other vegetables on these soils. Second, the moderating climatic effects of Lakes Michigan, Huron and Erie makes more favorable the production of vegetables in the west central, southwestern, east central and southeastern parts of Michigan (Chapter 38). Some of these effects are crop-specific, as discussed below. Third, the proximity of markets in Detroit, Chicago and other major cities throughout the eastern US helped support vegetable production in southeastern and southwestern Michigan. Marketing systems soon developed in response to the need for a smooth flow of produce to the consumer. Fourth, to better use labor and infrastructure, frozen fruit processing plants expanded operations to process vegetables. For these reasons, the leading vegetable producing counties are predominately located in western and the southeastern Lower Peninsula (Fig. 37.1). Production of the principal vegetable crops ranges from over 14,000 ha for cucumbers, to only a few hundred ha for cauliflower and muskmelon (Fig. 37.2).

TABLE 37.4 General categories of soils on which vegetable crops, mint and sod are produced in Michigan, along with typical yield and optimal plant density

Crop	Soil type[1]	Yield Processing (tons/ha)	Yield Fresh (tons/ha)[2]	Plant density (number/ha)
Asparagus	Mineral	2.4	1.9	25,000
Beans, snap	Mineral	7.8	5.6	360,000
Cabbage	Mineral, some organic	53.8	35.8	40,000–45,000
Carrot	Mineral and organic	47.0	39.2	900,000–2,000,000
Cauliflower	Mineral	17.9	8.4	29,000–37,500
Celery	Organic	63.8	47.0	86,000
Corn, sweet	Mineral, some organic	—	6.7	43,000
Cucumber	Mineral	9.5	24.6	170,000–1,300,000
Muskmelon	Mineral	—	11.8	9,000–10,000
Onion, dry	Organic	30.2	—	200,000
Peas, green	Mineral	5.8	2.0	700,000
Peppers, bell	Mineral	—	29.5	37,500
Pumpkin	Mineral	13.4	—	6200
Radish	Organic	—	7.3	1,300,000
Squash, all	Mineral, some organic	32.4	18.1	10,000 (winter) 18,000 (summer)
Tomato	Mineral	76.2	23.5	12,500
Mint, oil	Organic shifting to mineral	56 (kg/ha)	—	—
Sod (turf grass)	Mineral and organic	—		—

1. Organic soils are Histosols, primarily muck (Chapter 20).

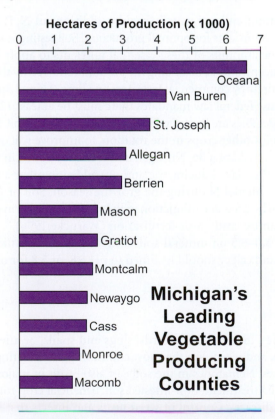

FIGURE 37.1 Hectares of vegetable production in the 12 leading counties in Michigan. Source: Michigan Rotational Survey (2001–2002).

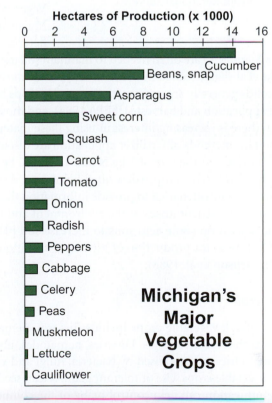

FIGURE 37.2 Hectares of principal vegetable crops grown in Michigan. Source: Michigan Rotational Survey (2001–2002).

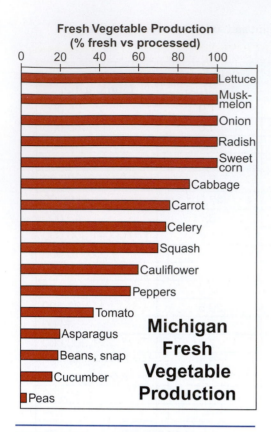

Fresh Vegetable Production
(% fresh vs processed)

Michigan Fresh Vegetable Production

FIGURE 37.3 Percentage of hectares of vegetable crops grown for fresh consumption. Source: Michigan Rotational Survey (2001–2002).

Approximately 55% of the hectares of all vegetables in Michigan are grown for processing. Annually, these values fluctuate, depending on processors' needs. Nearly all of the muskmelon, onion, radish and sweet corn are grown for the fresh market, whereas less than 25% of asparagus, snap beans, cucumber and peas are marketed fresh (Fig. 37.3). Presently, there is a trend toward greater consumption of fresh vegetables by consumers. Smaller farms tend to sell more fresh market produce, while larger units favor processing markets. Farms <10 hectares in size sell produce from 90% of their land as fresh market commodities, while farms larger than 100 hectares only sell produce from <40% of their land for the fresh market.

■ Production practices

Tillage

All vegetable crops, with the exception of asparagus, are grown using conventional tillage practices (see below). Crop residues left on the soil under conservation tillage practices (Chapter 36) are undesirable, because they serve as a source of inoculum for disease, and interfere with planting. Moldboard plows, therefore, are commonly utilized to turn the soil over, followed by secondary tillage, to prepare a fine seedbed and incorporate fertilizers and chemicals.

Fertilization

Vegetables, mint and sod usually require additions of N, P, K, Ca, Mg and micronutrients for optimal production. Soil testing is used to determine the amounts of these essential nutrients to apply (Table 37.5). P_2O_5 and K_2O are often needed to maintain soil test concentrations, balancing the amount removed by the crop (Warncke et al. 2004). Added nutrients are supplied almost entirely by commercial fertilizers and lime. Animal manures and biosolids generally are not used for vegetable crops because federal law mandates there must be at least 120 days between application and harvest (USEPA 1994), and most vegetables are harvested sooner than this time limit allows. However, there is increasing interest in using these materials for other crops in the rotation, to improve soil quality.

Common methods of fertilizer application are discussed in Chapter 36. Nitrogen and K may be added in trickle irrigation, usually at the rate of 1 kg N and 1.5 to 2.0 kg K_2O/ha/day, reducing the amount added in other applications. Several vegetable crops (described below) need supplemental N during the growing season. Soil or petiole nitrate analyses are often used to provide information that can be used in conjunction with known fertilization guidelines, to reduce nutrient losses to the environment and minimize costly over-fertilization (Warncke 1996).

Lime is used on some acid soils to increase soil pH to 6.0–6.5 on mineral soils and 5.3–5.5 on organic soils. Mineral soils used for production of asparagus, cauliflower and celery should be limed to pH 6.8, or 5.8 for organic soils (Christenson et al. 1988).

Pest control

Pests that attack vegetable crops include diseases, nematodes, insects, weeds, birds, slugs and snails, or any other biotic form that reduces yields. Diseases, nematodes, insects and weeds are the most common pests affecting crop production. Diseases are caused by bacteria, fungi and viruses. Nematodes in the soil can also result in major yield losses of vegetable crops. Use of tolerant plants, clean seed, seed treatment, non-infested soil, beneficial crop rotations and soil fumigation can help control many of the common diseases. Control of weed hosts and insects that spread disease, and the use of chemical fungicides and nematicides, are also practiced, singly or in combination (Schroeder et al. 1995, Bird et al. 2005). On-going research shows that some Brassica (mustard and other species) cover crops are

TABLE 37.5   Typical fertilization needs of vegetable crops and mint in Michigan[1]

Crop	Nitrogen (kg/ha)	Phosphate $(P_2O_5)^2$ (kg/ha)	Potash $(K_2O)^2$ (kg/ha)	Other nutrients[3]
Asparagus	56	9	22	
Beans, snap	45	11	74	Mn
Cabbage	157 M; 100 O[4]	45	228	
Carrot	134 M; 100 O	50	228 M; 190 O	B, Mn
Cauliflower	157	20	55	Mo
Celery	168	67	390	B, Mn, Ca
Cucumber	67	19	56	Mn
Lettuce	56	29	131	Mn
Muskmelon	112	15	85	Mn, Mg
Onion	157	72	134	Mn
Peas	45	15	33	
Peppers	112	19	75	
Pumpkin	80	16	91	Mn
Radish	22	3.5	25	B
Squash	90 M; 40 O	27	25	
Sweet Corn	134 M; 90 O	28	75	Mn. Zn
Tomato	90	22	28	B
Mint	112 M; 45 O	60	224	

1. After Warncke et al. (2004)
2. Amount to equal crop removal
3. When soil pH and soil test concentrations suggest
4. M = Mineral soils; O = Organic soils

effective in the control of some weeds, nematodes, and disease organisms (Daugovish et al. 2003). Insect pests can be managed using chemical and biological insecticides, avoiding infested areas, scheduling plantings to avoid greatest infestation, use of resistant or tolerant varieties and crop rotations. A variety of methods may be used to manage weed infestations. Among these are chemical herbicides (Zandstra 2005), crop rotation, avoiding infested areas and mechanical cultivation (Maynard and Hochmuth 2007).

Moisture management

Management of soil moisture is critical to yield and produce quality. Most of the vegetables grown on sandy soils, therefore, are irrigated. Two types of irrigation systems are used. The most visible is overhead sprinkler, configured either as solid set, big gun or center pivot systems (Fig. 37.4). Big gun systems utilize a single sprinkler head,

FIGURE 37.4   Center-pivot irrigation of pumpkins in the northern Lower Peninsula. Photo by R. Schaetzl.

spreading water in a circular pattern with a radius of 30–40 m; they are commonly used on cabbage, cucumber, peas, snap beans, sweet corn and mint. Trickle irrigation is increasing in use for production of fresh vegetables other than sweet corn and snap bean. It is often used in the production of fresh market tomato, vine crops such as pumpkin, pepper and some celery. In this system, water is delivered through a plastic tube placed next to the row, emitted through small holes, irrigating the soil adjacent to the plants. Advantages includes accurate water placement, lower water requirements and the option of continuing field operations during irrigation. Foliar diseases are less likely to occur, because the foliage remains dry. However, costs for maintenance, as well as labor for annual installation and removal, make these systems more costly than sprinkler systems (Ngouajio et al. 2007).

Planting/seeding practices

Large seeded crops such as bean, peas and sweet corn are usually seeded directly. Seeds for smaller seeded crops such as carrot, onion and radish are coated to form a pellet of uniform size, for ease of seeding. Precision seeding equipment places the seed at the desired depth and spacing within the row. Usually, seeding rates are higher than the target plant density, since not all of the seeds will germinate and there will be some seedling mortality. Plant densities for principal vegetable crops are given in Table 37.4.

Transplanting small plants of cabbage, muskmelon, summer squash, tomato and pepper directly to the field is the only way to ensure a good stand and economic return for these crops, since direct seeding may not produce favorable results, or may result in production that is too late in the season. Transplants started in the greenhouse have a 4–8 week advantage over direct seeded plants. Earlier harvests usually give the growers a more favorable price on the early market.

Transplanting is frequently done in conjunction with a system called plasticulture, where plastic mulch is used to cover the soil, after forming a raised bed (Ngouajio et al. 2007; Fig. 37.5). The mulch allows the soil to be fumigated, killing weeds, diseases and nematodes. Different colored plastics may be used to enhance soil warming, block light to inhibit weed growth, or increase light reflectance onto the plants, to enhance growth. Fertilizer may be applied before forming the raised bed, as the plastic reduces nutrient losses due to leaching.

In Michigan, if growers do not produce their own transplants, local suppliers often provide them on a contract basis. Some transplants are imported from outside of the state, but this is discouraged to prevent possible pest importation. Most of the transplants are produced in a containerized system, grown using sterile media, in plastic or polystyrene trays in a greenhouse. Each small compartment in the tray is seeded and a single plant is grown to an appropriate size before being transplanted into the field (Schroeder et al. 1995). Transplants are usually ready in 3–8 weeks.

FIGURE 37.5 Plastic mulch, laid down in preparation for planting of vegetable (probably melon) seedlings. Photo by R. Schaetzl.

Harvest and handling

Many fresh market vegetables are hand-harvested to minimize bruising. Hand harvest also permits multiple harvests of vegetables that produce over a long period, such as tomato, melon, peppers and summer squash. Labor requirements for hand harvesting are frequently met utilizing seasonal migrant workers. When harvested for the fresh market, the product needs to be cleaned, cooled and transported to the consumer in the shortest time possible. When produce is harvested for processing, similar care is exercised, although some slight damage or defects may be acceptable, especially if it is being used for juice, or a sliced/diced product. However, maintaining good quality in the harvesting, handling and transportation processes is still a desirable goal.

Most crops grown for processing (snap bean, peas, sweet corn, carrot, celery and cucumber) undergo a once-over, destructive, mechanical harvest. Determinate varieties of cucumbers, snap beans and peas are grown that give concentrated fruit set over a short time period, so as to maximize yield of produce of the same maturity.

■ Specific crops

In the following discussion, typical crop yields are given in Table 37.4. Reference will also be made to the agricultural districts of Michigan (Fig. 37.6), used by the Michigan Department of Agriculture for reporting agriculture statistics.

Asparagus

Michigan ranks 3rd in the US in the production of asparagus (Table 37.2) accounting for 15% of the total. California is the number one state in asparagus production.

After emergence from the crown, asparagus spears are susceptible to frost. Air temperatures warm more slowly near Lake Michigan, slowing emergence of spears and therefore reducing the risk of frost injury (Chapter 38). Consequently, 97% of the 6,300 ha of asparagus grown in Michigan are in the WC and SW districts (Figs. 37.6, 37.7B). Production in Mason, Oceana and Van Buren Counties accounts for 85% of the asparagus grown in Michigan. In addition to moderated climate, production is favored by sandy soils and proximity to processing plants. Since asparagus is harvested frequently (as many as 20–22 times a season), nearly all of it is grown on sandy soils, since the good drainage of these soils allows for timely and repeated harvesting. Less than 5% of the asparagus is irrigated.

Prior to planting asparagus, the soil should is limed to pH 6.8, to help reduce the incidence of disease, especially fusarium and crown rot. Asparagus is seeded in the spring in conventionally tilled fields. The plants are allowed to grow for up to two years, to produce crowns (rhizomes), which increase plant density in the row. These are then harvested and replanted. Phosphorus is frequently placed beneath the crowns to enhance growth. In turn, spears emerge from the crowns, which are harvested. However, in the first year after planting the crowns, the spears are not harvested, but are allowed to grow, producing fern (vegetative growth), which increases plant health and size of the crown. Even in the

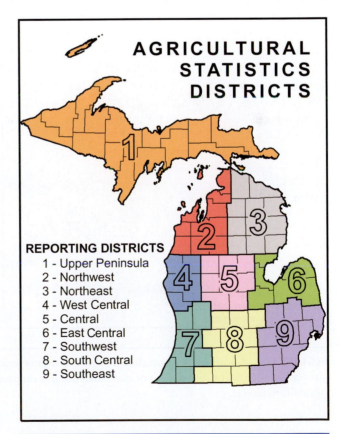

FIGURE 37.6 Michigan's Agricultural Statistics Reporting Districts. After Michigan Rotational Survey (2001–02).

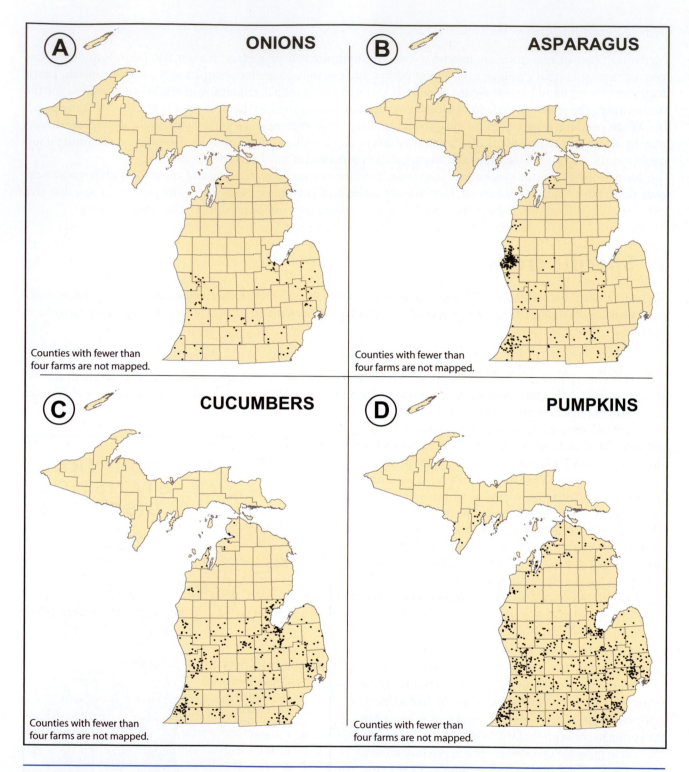

FIGURE 37.7 Locations of farms that grew one of four several specialty crops in Michigan, in 2000. In order to protect grower confidentiality, the location of each farm dot was randomly moved by up to 4.8 km. Source: USDA Census of Agriculture (2002).

second year, the number of pickings is limited, but in subsequent years, a full harvest of 20 to 22 pickings will be taken. A no-till system of management is used after establishment of the asparagus crop. Weeds are controlled with chemicals and mowing. Little or no inter-row cultivation is utilized so as to minimize injury to the plant roots and crowns. An established asparagus field may not need replanting for 15–20 years, and some plantings may last 30 years.

During May and June, asparagus spears, 20 to 25 cm in length, are hand-snapped every 2–3 days, washed, trimmed to a standard length and cooled. Only about 25% of the Michigan crop is sold as fresh market (Fig. 37.3), but this amount varies considerably depending on needs of processors. Recently, processors are using more imported asparagus, resulting in a larger amount of the Michigan crop being sold on the fresh market.

Snap bean

More than 90% of the snap beans in Michigan are grown on sandy soils in six counties in W and SW Michigan (Branch, Kalamazoo, Mason, Montcalm, Oceana and St. Joseph). Most of the production is under center pivot irrigation. The sandy soils allow for the timely harvest operations, for processing into baby food, frozen and canned products. Of the 6,700 ha of production, approximately 1,950 are produced for fresh market, primarily in SW and WC Michigan. Nearly all commercially grown snap bean is mechanically harvested, washed and graded, prior to packing for fresh market. Beans for processing are transported in bulk.

Cabbage

Of the 930 ha of cabbage grown in Michigan, 85% is grown for fresh market. Kent and Ottawa counties in the SW district, and Macomb, Monroe and Lenawee Counties in the SE, account for >75% of the production. Cabbage for processing is grown on three farms in western Michigan and is processed nearby.

Cabbage plants are transplanted in rows 76 cm apart, with plants spaced 35–45 cm apart. All harvesting is done by hand. For fresh market, the head is cut and placed on a conveyor belt, which moves it to a wagon for packing. Cabbage for processing is transported in bulk.

Carrot

Michigan produces approximately 80,000 tons of fresh carrots and 30,000 tons of carrots for processing, making it number two and four in the nation, respectively (Table 37.2). More than 60% of the 630 ha of carrot production for processing is grown in the WC district. Most are processed for baby food, juice and frozen products. About 70% of the 2,000 ha of fresh market carrots are produced in the WC and SE districts.

Only 30 years ago, 90% of Michigan's carrots were produced on organic soils in the WC and EC districts. A significant portion of this production has now shifted to sandy soils, made possible by improvements in deep tillage implements, and the use of raised beds to produce a loose, deep root zone. Utilization of center pivot irrigation systems on sandy soils also contributed to this shift.

When planting carrot, sufficient seed is used to give 900,000–2,000,000 plants per hectare (Table 37.4). Higher populations result in longer, smaller diameter roots used for cut and peel products. Mid-range populations are used to produce larger diameter roots for fresh market. Lower population fields are used for production of processing carrot, along with some grown for fresh market.

Carrots are harvested by machine, with a blade that runs under ground to loosen the soil and root, while a set of squeeze belts lift the plant by the top. The tops are then removed, and the roots conveyed into a truck for transport. The roots are washed and graded, prior to packing for fresh market. For some processing carrots, the tops are removed prior to digging. Dug carrots are conveyed on a link chain, which allows the soil to be separated.

Cauliflower

Michigan produces only 160 ha of cauliflower, divided among the EC, SW and SE districts, with some scattered elsewhere. All 60 ha grown for processing is in the SW district, with the remaining 100 ha grown for fresh market, and distributed as follows: 20 ha in EC, 30 in SW, 35 in SE and 25 in other districts.

Like cabbage, transplants are placed 35–45 cm apart in rows 76 cm apart. When head formation begins, the surrounding leaves may be tied over the head to keep it white. Newer varieties have upright leaves that shade the head, eliminating the need for tying. When the head reaches a desired size, it is cut by hand and packaged for market.

Celery

Michigan growers produce 50,000 tons of celery on about 770 ha, to rank second in celery production behind only California (Table 37.4). Approximately 75% of the celery is produced for the fresh market, centered in the WC and SW districts. Celery was produced on both east (SE district) and west sides of the state until about 10 years ago. Today, it is produced only on the west side, because these growers formed a marketing cooperative there, allowing them to remain competitive. The cooperative also operates a slicing and dicing plant, providing another outlet for celery.

Most celery producers grow their own transplants in greenhouses. It takes about eight weeks from seed, to produce a suitable size transplant. Celery is a shallow rooted crop with a high moisture requirement, so it is grown on organic soils and irrigated frequently (Fig. 37.8). It is usually transplanted in rows 76–80 cm apart, with plants spaced 15 cm apart. Planting is from early April until mid-July, providing a harvestable product from early July into October. April-planted celery is covered with a spun nylon fabric cloth (floating cover) to protect it from frost. The cover is removed when the danger of frost has passed.

Harvest begins around July 4 and continues into October. Celery is mechanically harvested by cutting the plant just below ground, while the tops are cut to about 38 cm. In a packing shed, celery stalks are trimmed and washed, prior to packing for fresh market or processing. Some celery is squeezed for juice or diced for use in soups and other food products.

Cucumber

Michigan is the top US producer of pickling cucumbers, producing about 160,000 tons on 12,500 ha (Table 37.4). Production is located near processing plants distributed across the Lower Peninsula (Fig. 37.7C). Cucumbers are grown primarily on well-drained sandy soils, allowing for timely mechanical harvest. However, some are produced on loams and clay loams. Pickling cucumbers are seeded in rows 30–40 cm apart, with seeds spaced 2.5–3.8 cm apart.

FIGURE 37.8 A mature celery plant, grown on organic soils (Histosols) in Barry County, with a field of celery in the background. Photo by R. Schaetzl.

Bees are very important for pollination of the flowers and setting fruit. Harvest is timed to maximize the number of fruit in sizes suitable for processing into pickles—usually 45–50 days after planting. Cucumbers are primarily mechanically harvested, in a once-over destructive process.

The SW and SE districts of Michigan produce most of the fresh market cucumber, but production is also scattered across the state (Fig. 37.7C). About 17% of all cucumber production in Michigan is fresh market. Hand-harvested pickling or slicing cucumbers are seeded 7.6–15 cm apart, in rows 76 cm wide. Hand-harvested cucumbers are picked up to ten times, for either pickling or fresh market consumption.

Muskmelon

There are approximately 250 ha of muskmelon produced in the state, primarily in the SE (43%), SW (25%) and the EC (20%) regions, with the remainder scattered across the state in small units of production. Nearly all melons are grown using plastic mulch and trickle irrigation (Fig. 37.5). Before laying the plastic, fertilizer is broadcast and incorporated into the soil. Plants are transplanted about 60 cm apart in rows 120 cm apart. Muskmelons are hand-picked when stems begin to loosen for the melon—a sign that it is ripe. Since melon fruits are set over a long period of time, multiple harvests must be made. Bees are very important for pollination of the flowers and setting of fruit.

The Howell area has created a niche market for the *Howell* melon, through advertising, promotion and careful quality control. However, there actually is no Howell variety. Rather, a number of varieties are grown and marketed as *Howell melons*.

Onion

Onion (dry bulb, yellow and red) is grown in Michigan on 1,660 ha, distributed over the WC (28%), SW (26%), SC (39%) and SE districts (5%). Nearly one-quarter is produced in Newaygo County. Onions are grown on organic soils, since they make good seedbed and contain excellent moisture supplying capacity (Figs. 37.7A, 37.9). In addition, most of the production is irrigated, to aid in seedling establishment and growth.

Onion is seeded in mid-April through early May. Some of the fertilizer is broadcast prior to seeding, with the remainder banded at planting. Onion bulbs are harvested after the tops have dried down—usually mid-August through mid-September. The bulbs are undercut to loosen the roots and allowed to cure for a few days before harvesting (Fig. 37.9). Michigan bulb onions are a type that can be stored in bulk and marketed through early March.

FIGURE 37.9 Mature, yellow, bulb onions drying in a field near Hastings, in Barry County. These onions have been grown on organic soils (Histosols). Photo by R. Schaetzl.

A small amount of green onions (bunch or scallions) are grown for the fresh market in Michigan. Green onions are seeded from early April through early July to extend the marketing season. They are hand harvested, gathered into bunches, trimmed, washed and cooled before being shipped to market. Commercial production is mainly on organic soils in the SC area.

Green peas

Nearly all green peas grown for processing in the state are produced in Montcalm County, on sandy soils and under center pivot irrigation. Peas are seeded 5.0–7.6 cm apart in rows about 18 cm apart. Generally, all fertilizer is broadcast prior to seeding. Production on well-drained sandy soils enables timely harvest, when the crop is at the most desirable size and tenderness. Peas are at this stage for only a period of one to two days, usually sometime in the last three weeks of June. Peas are mechanically harvested by stripping the pods from the plants. They are then separated from the pods by a threshing unit, conveyed into a holding tank on the harvester, and transferred to trucks for transport to the processor. Peas are processed into baby food, canned and into frozen products. Only about 20 ha of peas are produced for fresh market use.

Peppers

About half of the 1,150 ha of peppers produced in Michigan are green bell peppers for fresh market. These are produced in the WC, EC, SW and SE districts and marketed to nearby population centers. Other types include banana and hot peppers, of which 80% are grown for processing.

Most peppers are transplanted into a plasticulture system on raised beds, under trickle irrigation (Ngouajio et al. 2007). The raised bed is formed, and the plastic covering and trickle irrigation tube is laid in one operation. Peppers are hand harvested when they are of desirable size and firmness. Each field is harvested multiple times, every 7 to 14 days, from late July through September, or until the first frost.

Pumpkin

Pumpkin is produced statewide; however, the SW and SE districts account for over 60% of the production (Figs. 37.7D). The average Michigan pumpkin-growing farm produces approximately 4 ha of pumpkins. Most are marketed for decoration, as jack-o-lanterns at Halloween. Michigan ranks 4th in the nation in pumpkin production (Table 37.2).

Pumpkins are seeded during early to mid-June, with in-row seeds spaced about 0.8–1.5 m apart. Pumpkins are best harvested after they have turned completely orange. They are hand harvested and stored in a dry place to prevent spoilage (rotting).

Radish

Radishes are grown on organic soils, as they provide a good seedbed and abundant moisture (Fig. 37.10). Most of the production is located in the southern Lower Peninsula. A crop is ready to harvest in 25–35 days, so it can be grown before or after other vegetable crops such as celery, carrot, lettuce, squash or sweet corn. Growers do not generally seed radish sequentially, though, because of disease and nematode problems associated with the practice.

Radishes are seeded 2.5 cm apart in rows 30 cm apart. At harvest, radishes are loosened with an undercutting spade and lifted by the tops. The tops are then cut off and the radishes conveyed into a wagon or truck, to be transported for washing and packaging. A small amount of radishes are hand-harvested into bunches with the tops attached. The crop is marketed entirely as a fresh product.

Squash

Michigan growers produce about 2,800 ha of summer and winter (hard) squash. Summer squash includes zucchini and yellow types grown on 1,300 ha. Summer squash (320 ha) for processing is grown in the WC district, 80% of which is in Oceana County. Several processing plants are located in this area, where they process summer squash, primarily zucchini, into frozen (sliced and diced) products. Fresh market summer squash is produced in the WC,

FIGURE 37.10   Field of radishes being grown on organic soils (Histosols) near Hastings, in Barry County. Photo by R. Schaetzl.

SW and SE districts, with only 7% grown in other districts. Overall, Michigan ranks 4th nationally, producing almost 15% of the nation's crop (Table 37.2).

Winter squash, including acorn, buttercup, butternut, Hubbard and turban types, is grown on 1,500 ha statewide. About 30% of the winter squash is processed, and nearly all is grown in Mason, Newaygo and Oceana Counties. Fresh market, winter squash is primarily grown in the central, EC, SW and SE districts, with 20% grown elsewhere.

Generally, squash is seeded, although some is transplanted, especially summer squash for early harvest. Yellow and zucchini squash are often grown using plasticulture, and hand-harvested about every other day to keep fruit from over-sizing. Production lasts for 2–3 weeks, after which the field is disked under. Sequential plantings are made for season-long production. When winter squash fruit are mature, the vines begin to dry and the fruit are mechanically windrowed, picked up and conveyed into trucks for transport to the processor. Some types of hard squash are processed into baby food, *pumpkin* pie filling and frozen products. Acorn, buttercup and butternut squash are stored and sold for home consumption.

Sweet corn

Of the 4,250 ha of Michigan sweet corn, 44% is grown in the SE district, with the remainder scattered among the other reporting districts. Macomb and Oceana/Newaygo are the major sweet corn producing counties, both having >400 ha of production. All sweet corn is used for the fresh market.

In order to maintain a continuous supply, sequential seedings are made from late-April thru mid-July, and by using varieties with different maturity dates. Ears are mechanically or hand harvested, hand sorted and packed for marketing. Ears may also be hydro-cooled if they are to be shipped any distance.

Tomato

Michigan produces nearly 120,000 tons of processing tomatoes, for a ranking of 4th nationally (Table 37.2). Of the 2,100 ha of tomatoes in Michigan, ~65% is for processing, mainly in southern counties (Branch, Calhoun, St. Joseph, Lenawee and Monroe). Tomatoes produced in these counties are processed in Indiana and Ohio, primarily as canned whole or diced tomatoes, and as juice. Nearly two-thirds of the fresh tomatoes are produced in the SW district.

Berrien County is the leading county with ~375 ha. Fresh tomatoes are also produced in the EC, SW and SE districts. Roma (paste), cherry and grape tomatoes are produced in lesser quantities.

Most fresh market tomatoes are transplanted into raised bed plasticulture systems with trickle irrigation. With transplants being grown in small plugs of fertilized, artificial growth media, additional fertilizer is not necessary at transplanting. Plants are held upright by string, stretched between stakes. This practice improves quality, by keeping the fruit off the ground, and makes for easier picking. For machine-harvest, processing tomatoes, two rows of plants are transplanted on each raised bed.

The average Michigan producer of processing tomatoes grows nearly 100 ha of the crop, while fresh market producers average <10 ha. Processing tomatoes are all harvested by machine, while fresh market tomatoes are hand harvested.

Mint

There are nearly 1,100 ha of mint in Michigan, split about 60–40% spearmint-peppermint, grown mostly in Clinton County. In the mid-1900s, most of the mint in Michigan was grown on organic soils spread across 17 counties. Due to disease pressures and lack of organic soils for rotation, production has largely shifted to mineral soils.

Peppermint and spearmint grow well in Michigan, on organic and sandy loam soils. Mint is shallow rooted and has a high water requirement, so irrigation is essential, especially on mineral soils (Lacy et al. 1981). Mint is a vigorous, perennial plant, propagated from stolons (similar to rhizomes). Stolons are generally dug from nursery beds or from a clean, established field. Stolon pieces are mechanically dropped into a furrow, to form a near continuous row, and then are covered with about 8 cm of soil. Mint is usually planted in November or April. Once established, a mint field is usually maintained for harvest for up to five years without further planting, although stolons may be hand planted in thin spots to keep plant densities high.

Because mint grows in a row, for the first year it is referred to as "row mint." In the fall, row mint is plowed shallowly, no more than 15 cm. This redistributes the stolons and helps control pests. After the first year, mint is referred to as "meadow mint" (Fig. 37.11).

Usually mint is harvested once annually. The mint "hay" is cut and windrowed when the leaf oil content is highest, usually at early bloom, in late July or early August. After the hay is well wilted, usually about 24 hours later, it is chopped into specially constructed wagons containing perforated pipes in the bottom. A steam source is attached to the pipes and steam is forced through the chopped mint hay, volatilizing the mint oil. The oil-steam mixture is directed into a condensation chamber, through a large hood, clamped to the top of the wagon.

FIGURE 37.11 A close-up view of spearmint, in a field near St. Johns. Photo by R. Schaetzl.

FIGURE 37.12   A field of turfgrass (mainly bluegrass) in Ingham County. Most turf like this is grown on organic soils (Histosols). Photo by R. Schaetzl.

During condensation, water and mint oil are separated; the oil is collected for marketing. Mint oil is the main saleable product and can be stored for many years. Peppermint and spearmint oils are used as flavoring and essences in candies, chewing gum, toothpaste, medicines, pharmaceuticals, cosmetics and various food products. Use of mint oil in aromatherapy applications is an emerging market. None of the commercially produced mint is used in culinary preparations (leaves for flavoring or as garnish), as those needs are met by production on small "market garden" type units.

Sod

"Turfgrass" is the term used to refer to the crop in the field, but once cut, it is commonly called sod. Michigan sod (turfgrass) producers market approximately 2,000 ha per year (Turfgrass Survey 2002), produced on organic (70%) and mineral soils (30%) (Fig. 37.12). Production on mineral soils is on loamy sands, sandy loams and loams. All production is south of the Bay City-Muskegon line (Fig. 37.13), in the more populated region of the state. Wholesalers, including landscape companies, account for slightly more than 60% of sales by sod producers. Homeowners account for about 18%, with the remainder divided among golf courses, lawn service companies, public agencies and retailers.

Most Michigan-grown sod is a mixture of Kentucky bluegrass varieties. It is important to have a smooth, level surface for production, and thus the land is leveled prior

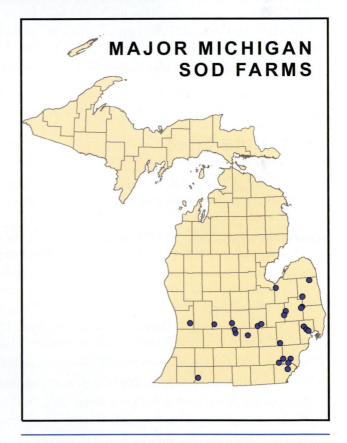

FIGURE 37.13   Distribution of sod production in Michigan. Source: www.michigansod.org

to seeding. Irrigation is essential for rapid establishment and development. Turfgrass is topdressed with 34–45 kg N/ha every 3 to 4 weeks, to enhance growth and keep it green. Sod is ready for harvest when root rhizomes are well netted together. An early spring seeding is often ready for harvest in the fall. Seedings made during the summer and fall will be ready the following year. Sod is cut in strips, rolled up and then unrolled as it is put in place. Cutting is done as thin as possible to minimize the amount of soil removed, likely 0.5–1.0 cm.

■ Conclusions

In Michigan, the numerous sandy and organic soils, and a climate moderated by the Great Lakes, both provide favorable environments for production of a wide variety of vegetable and specialty crops. The predominant vegetable growing areas in western Michigan are along Lake Michigan, and in southeastern Michigan, near Lakes Erie and St. Clair. Vegetable production is a significant player in Michigan agriculture, contributing 7% of the receipts received by Michigan farmers. Approximately 55% of the hectares of vegetables grown in Michigan are produced for processing. Produce sold as fresh market products can be found at roadside stands and "farmers markets," or is marketed directly to retail markets and through cooperative marketing arrangements. Markets in Detroit, Chicago and other major cities throughout the eastern US continue to play a role in the location of vegetable production in Michigan.

There have been some shifts in specialty crop production over the past 30 years. For example, production of head lettuce has essentially disappeared from Michigan. Celery is no longer produced on the eastern side of the state. Production of carrots and mint are shifting from organic to mineral soils. Processing tomato production has declined greatly, as tomato paste production has largely moved to California.

Specialty and vegetable crop growers face the same challenges as field crop producers: cost-price squeeze, protection of the environment and furnishing a high quality product to the consumer. Nonetheless, vegetable crop production will continue to play a major role in Michigan agriculture in the future.

Literature Cited

Bird, G., Bishop B., Grafius, E., Hausbeck, M., Jess, L. and W. Pett. 2005. 2006 insect, disease and nematode control for commercial vegetable crops. Michigan State University, Agricultural Experiment Station Extension Bulletin E-312, East Lansing.

Christenson, D.R., Warncke, D.D. and R. Leep. 1988. Lime for Michigan soils. Michigan State University, Agricultural Experiment Station Extension Bulletin E-471, East Lansing.

Daugovish, O., Downer, J. and O. Becker. 2003. Exploring biofumigational potential of mustards. Annual International Research Conference on Methyl Bromide Alternatives and Emissions Reductions, 2003: www.mbao.org (last accessed February, 2008).

Lacy, M.L., Stephens, C.T., Green, R.J., Jr. and A.C. York. 1981. Mint production in the Midwestern United States. North Central Regional Extension Publication 155. Michigan State University, East Lansing.

Maynard, D.N. and G.J. Hochmuth. 1997. Knott's Handbook for Vegetable Growers. John Wiley and Sons, New York.

Michigan Agricultural Statistics. 2003–2004. Michigan Department of Agriculture, Lansing, MI.

Michigan Rotational Survey, Turfgrass Survey 2002. Michigan Department of Agriculture, Lansing, MI.

Michigan Rotational Survey, Vegetable Inventory. 2001–2002. Michigan Department of Agriculture: Lansing, MI.

Ngouajio, M., Goldy, R., Zandstra, B. and D. Warncke. 2007. Plasticulture for Michigan vegetable production. Michigan State University Extension Bulletin E-2980, East Lansing.

Schroeder, C.B., Seagle, E.D., Felton, L.M., Ruter, J.M., Kelley, W.T. and G. Krewer. 1995. Introduction to Horticulture: Science and Technology. Interstate Publishers, Incorporated, Danville, IL.

USEPA. 1994. A plain English guide to the EPA Part 503 Biosolids Rule. EPA/832/R-93/003. United States Environmental Protection Agency, Washington, DC.

Warncke, D.D. 1996. Soil and plant tissue testing for nitrogen management in carrots. Communications in Soil Science and Plant Analysis 27:597–605.

Warncke, D., Dahl, J. and B. Zandstra. 2004. Nutrient recommendations for vegetable crops in Michigan. Michigan State University, Agricultural Experiment Station Extension Bulletin E-2934, East Lansing.

Zandstra, B. 2005. 2006 weed control guide for vegetable crops. Michigan State University, Agricultural Experiment Station Extension Bulletin E-433, East Lansing.

Further Readings

Acquaah, G. 1999. Horticulture Principles and Practices. Prentice Hall, Upper Saddle River, NJ.

Barnett, L. 1984. Mint in Michigan. Michigan History 68(Mar–Apr):16–20.

Calhoun, R. and D. Buhler. 2002. Broadleaf herbicides for commercial sod production. Michigan State University, Agricultural Experiment Station Extension Bulletin E-0001 TURF, East Lansing.

Davis, J.F. and R.L. Lucas. 1959. Organic soils: their formation, distribution, utilization and management. Michigan State University, Agricultural Experiment Station Special Publication 425. East Lansing.

Jeavons, J. 2002. How to Grow More Vegetables. Ten Speed Press, Berkeley, CA.

Lucas, R.L. 1982. Organic soils (Histosols): Formation, distribution, physical and chemical properties and management for crop production. Michigan State University, Agricultural Experiment Station Research Report 435. East Lansing.

Snapp, S.S. and D.R. Mutch. 2003. Cover crop choices for Michigan vegetables. Michigan State University, Agricultural Experiment Station Extension Bulletin E-2896, East Lansing.

Splittstoesser, W.E. 1979. Vegetable Growing Handbook. AVI Publishing Company, Westport, CT.

Vitosh, M.L., Warncke, D.D. and R.E. Lucas. 1994. Secondary and micronutrients for vegetables and field crops. Michigan State University, Agricultural Experiment Station Extension Bulletin E-486, East Lansing.

Zandstra, B. 1985. Peppers—Commercial vegetable recommendations. Michigan State University, Agricultural Experiment Station Extension Bulletin E-1591, East Lansing.

Zandstra, B. and T. Dudek. 1987. Celery—Commercial vegetable recommendations. Michigan State University, Agricultural Experiment Station Extension Bulletin E-1308, East Lansing.

Zandstra, B. and E. Grafius. 1986. Pumpkins, squash, gourds—Commercial vegetable recommendations. Michigan State University, Agricultural Experiment Station Extension Bulletin E-1953, East Lansing.

Zandstra, B. and E. Grafius. 1996. Onions—Commercial vegetable recommendations. Michigan State University, Agricultural Experiment Station Extension Bulletin E-1307, East Lansing.

Zandstra, B., Stevens, C. and E.J. Grafius. 1988.Commercial vegetable recommendations: Cole crops. Michigan State University, Agricultural Experiment Station Extension Bulletin E-1591, East Lansing.

Zandstra, B. and D. Warncke. 1986. Carrots—Commercial vegetable recommendations. Michigan State University, Agricultural Experiment Station Extension Bulletin E-1437, East Lansing.

Zandstra, B. and D. Warncke. 1989. Commercial vegetable recommendations Radish, rutabaga, turnip. Michigan State University, Agricultural Experiment Station Extension Bulletin E-2207, East Lansing.

38

The Fruit Industry

Jerome Hull and Eric Hanson

■ Introduction

Michigan is one of the nation's major fruit production areas. Only California, New York and Washington states have comparable fruit industries. Michigan's fruit production was valued at $173 million in 2005 (Table 38.1). Michigan produces about two-thirds of the nation's tart cherries, leads the country in blueberry production and raises about 8% of the nation's apples, 9% of the sweet cherries and 4% of the pears. In 2000, Michigan had 51,767 hectares of fruit on 2,377 commercial fruit farms, including grapes but not cranberries. The counties with the most acres of fruit, in order, were Van Buren, Berrien, Leelanau, Oceana and Kent (Fig. 38.1A). They contain 60% of the acreage of fruit in Michigan.

TABLE 38.1 Acreage and value of the major fruit crops grown in Michigan, and Michigan's national ranking in their production, in 2005[1]

	Total acreage (hectares)	Bearing acreage (hectares)	Farm value (million $)	National rank
Apples	17,200	16,390	$100.2	3rd
Tart cherries	12,950	11,050	47.9	1st
Blueberries	7,490	6,800	83.5	1st
Grapes	5,830	5,750	21.4	4th
Sweet cherries	3,640	3,320	16.7	4th
Peaches	2,300	2,020	6.8	5th
Strawberries	445	445	4.8	8th
Pears	364	324	0.8	5th
Plums	364	304	0.7	3rd
Brambles	223	na	na	na
Cranberries	105	na	na	na
Nectarines	40	na	na	na
Total tree fruit	36,870	33,400	173.1	
Total berries and grapes	14,090	13,000	109.7	
Total fruit	50,950	46,400	282.8	

1. Source: Michigan Department of Agriculture (2004a, b).

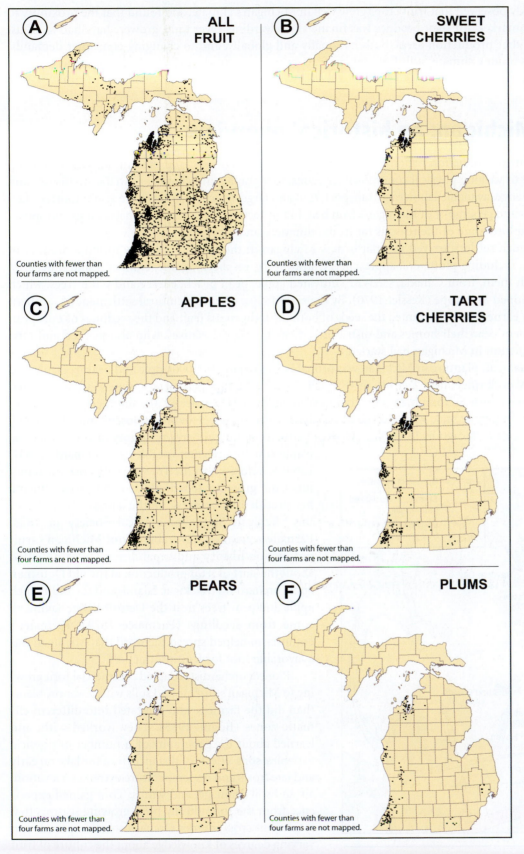

FIGURE 38.1
Locations of farms that grew fruit in Michigan, in 2002. In order to protect grower confidentiality, the location of each farm dot was randomly moved by up to 4.8 km. Source: USDA (2005).
A. All fruit. Includes any farm that sold fruit in 2002. B. Sweet cherries. C. Apples. D. Tart cherries. E. Pears. F. Plums.

Early settlers quickly observed that fruit crops grew well in Michigan's climate, and found that the proximity to large, relatively nearby markets for their produce was financially rewarding. Over time, growers have had to adjust to competition from other production areas, both nationally and globally, and to changing consumer demands. Nonetheless, the state's unique climate, soils favorable to fruit culture, and ready access to large consumer markets have enabled Michigan producers to consistently and competitively produce large, high quality fruit crops.

■ Fruit in Michigan: an historical overview

Michigan's distinctive fruit production region is a reflection of the efforts of past and present farmers to develop operations in response to varying physical conditions, e.g., soils, topography and climate, as well as to disease and insects. Cultural knowledge, available labor, easy transportation and large, nearby markets were also important factors in the development and geography of Michigan's fruit belt. In this section, we describe the beginnings and spread of the fruit belt, and explore some of the reasons for its development and location.

When the first French settlers arrived in what is now Michigan in the early 1700s, they found a number of wild, indigenous fruits, including plum, crabapple, cherry, strawberry, raspberry, grape, cranberry and blueberry. They also brought with them, from Canada, seeds of cultivated apple, pear, peach, cherry and plum trees, which had been initially developed in Europe (Kessler 1970). By the early 1820s, when agricultural settlement of southern Michigan had begun in earnest, settlers planted the seeds of both the indigenous fruit and the seedlings of European origin. They planted them near their homes and distributed them among the Natives, who also planted and nurtured them. Fruit production in Michigan had started.

The first commercial fruit planting in Michigan was probably an orchard of 2,000 apple and pear trees, planted by Governor William Woodbridge, near Detroit, in 1825 (Fig. 38.2). The first peach trees were seedlings planted ca. 1775 in Berrien County, near St. Joseph, by a fur trader, William Burnett (Kessler 1970). Shipment of fruit from Michigan began on a commercial scale with a cargo of peaches, grown by B.C. Hoyt in St. Joseph and shipped by boat from Benton Harbor to Chicago in 1839. Next, George Parmalee settled in Berrien County in 1845, where he planted the county's first sizeable peach orchard in 1847. Later, he relocated to the Traverse City area, introducing fruit growing techniques to that area. During his presidential address at the annual meeting of the Michigan State Pomological Society in 1874, Parmalee remarked favorably about Michigan's fruit production history and capabilities. He commented about the start of fruit production at the old Dousman apple orchard on Mackinac Island, and the old French apple and pear trees near the Detroit River, having all come from seedlings (Parmalee 1874). Parmalee's enthusiasm helped spread the word that Michigan was a favorable spot for fruit production.

Pioneer orchardists adapted commercial fruit growing to Michigan's climate and soils with fewer problems than did the farmers who migrated into different climatic zones (Bogue 1985). They worked with, and learned about the geography of, a number of physical variables: soils, effects of distance from the lake on early and late frosts and on temperature extremes, elevation, air and soil drainage, and winds. They gained experience from the sporadically poor growing seasons that resulted in crop failures. Orchardists also arrived with varying degrees of knowledge about the culture of fruit trees, bringing seeds to plant; soon they began buying trees of varieties familiar to them. Many pioneers did

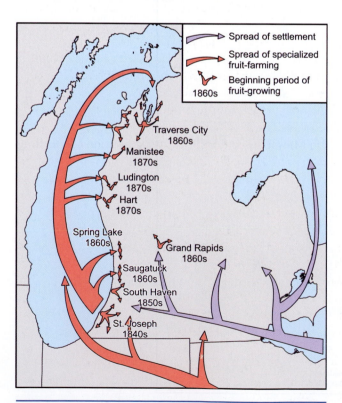

FIGURE 38.2   Spread of settlement and fruit farming in Michigan in the 1800s. After Olmstead (1951).

not fully understand for many years which fruit could be grown in Michigan, and where. Each pioneer was an experimenter, learning independently. This painful process of trial and error characterized the learning that occurred in the 19th and 20th centuries.

Very early in the settlement of southwestern Michigan, pioneer farmers recognized Lake Michigan's tempering influence on climate, and the positive effects such a climate could have on fruit production. Many had come from New England, where a family orchard was part of the general farm plan, and where the moderating influence of bodies of water on temperature and vegetation was conventional knowledge. They found in their new Michigan homes evidence of the suitability of the climate for fruit production, for some of the seedlings planted by fur traders and missionaries remained, as sizable and productive trees. By the 1830s and 1840s, orchards had sprung up from the apple and peach seeds that they had brought with them, especially near Lake Michigan (Fig. 38.2). By the end of the 1840s, it was common knowledge that farms near the lake had unusually good potential for fruit growing (Bogue 1985).

In 1866, Alexander Winchell, Professor of Geology at the University of Michigan and state geologist, presented a paper to the American Association for the Advancement of Science entitled, "The Fruitbearing Belt of Michigan." His isothermal (climatic) charts featured the climate of Lake Michigan's shoreline area, that would ultimately become a prolific, fruit-producing region. His data showed about a 4° F mean difference between Michigan and Wisconsin lakeshore temperatures in winter, a marked contrast in lowest temperatures, and a growing season 18 days longer at Grand Haven than at Milwaukee. When Winchell presented his charts and data at the annual meeting of the Michigan State Horticultural Society in Grand Rapids, he informed the fruit growers that Michigan's peninsular climate was easy to understand. It involved two fundamental factors: (1) the presence of a large body of water on its western boundary, combined with (2) the prevalence of westerly winds, making the east side of the lake comparatively warmer in winter and cooler in summer (Winchell 1880).

The choice of a good orchard site, quite aside from such consideration as markets and transportation, depended on shrewd, experienced judgment; it was also a gamble in a newly settled area. For example, Liberty Hyde Bailey, Jr., son of an eminent South Haven orchardist, grew up in the Lake Michigan fruit belt and defined rather precisely the peach growing region within it. He did this based on knowledge acquired by four decades of grower experimentation. In his Principles of Fruit Growing, Bailey (1897) noted that the limits of fruit-raising zones are exceedingly devious. Along Lake Michigan, the peach belt extended from 0.5–3.0 to 24–30 kms inland, depending on topography. Bailey observed that elevation, as expressed by distance above the lake, as well as distance from it, were the main determining factors for the location of the peach growing region. He also noted that, as a rule of thumb, frost immunity for fruit trees will not extend from a body of water beyond the crest of the elevation of land adjacent thereto, and not more than 60 m (200 ft) above that elevation, whichever occurs first.

Commercial fruit production in southwestern Michigan developed early, dating from the late 1840s, expanded significantly before 1857, and reached boom proportions before the close of the Civil War, in response to demand from large major urban markets, principally Chicago, but also Milwaukee and Detroit. Transportation connections from the fruit belt, by both rail and lake, were excellent, fostering production. The combination of the lake-tempering environment, along with good soils and various marketing advantages, combined to make specialization in fruit and vegetable production more profitable in the fruit belt, than in other areas.

The 1871 Chicago fire had an indirect but important influence in fostering commercial fruit production in Michigan. The fire created a sudden and urgent demand for lumber to replace the 17,450 buildings that were destroyed. Much of this lumber came from the forests of southern Michigan, freeing a considerable area for the planting of fruit trees. The Kalamazoo and South Haven Railroad was completed in 1870; the Chicago and Michigan Lake Shore Railroad followed, in 1871. Built mainly to carry lumber, they also provided an excellent means for the shipment of fruit (Kessler 1970).

The settlement of Michigan began in the south and extended northward (Chapter 27). The commercial fruit plantings tended to be near harbors, where perishable fruit could be delivered to lake steamers the same day that it was harvested, for shipment to Chicago, Milwaukee and other ports.

The northern Michigan fruit region, in and around Grand Traverse Bay (Fig. 38.1A), developed in the post-Civil War years, when lumbermen and the businessman and professionals serving them, plus one notable pioneer orchardist from southwestern Michigan (George Parmalee), planted commercial orchards to supply the needs of the lumber industry. As the lumbermen cut the timber, commercial fruit growing took on a new economic importance, growing substantially during and after the 1880s. Fruit production was being touted as an important wave of the future by worried lumbertown businessman, lumber companies, railroads and local companies owning cutover land. Excellent, available transportation, by rail and lake steamers, made distant urban markets available as additional outlets for fruit products. Some fruit went south, but much went directly west, via car ferries and rail. Much of the tart cherry crop, significant in this area beginning in the 1890s, went to newly established canneries (Bogue 1985). Thus, the favorable climate and large profits obtained from fruit sales encouraged rapid expansion of orchard plantings in western Michigan.

By the 1870s, however, orchardists began to realize that Michigan was not a utopia. Insects and diseases were becoming a menace. Particularly noteworthy were insects such as codling moth, curculio and oriental fruit moth. The curculio, apple borer and cherry borer were probably present in the native woodlands. However, diseases such as scab, blight and fruit rots, along with other insects, arrived with nursery stock imported from older, previously infested regions. The peach yellow virus was apparently brought to the St. Joseph area in nursery stock from New Jersey, in 1862. The only control for the virus was to remove all the infected trees.

■ The fruit belt

Michigan's fruit production occurs predominately in a location often referred to as the "fruit belt"—a strip of land about 24–40 km wide, on the west side of the state, in proximity to Lake Michigan (Fig. 38.1A). It extends from south of the Indiana border to the Straits of Mackinac, or from about 42°N latitude to about 46°N (Gourley 1923). The climate of this area is significantly influenced by Lake Michigan. Fruit production in this region does not occur, however, as a belt of uniform width, because it is also influenced by local topography and soils. The highest concentration of apple production is in the Grand Rapids area (Fig. 38.1C). Cherry production is concentrated in the Traverse City region (Fig. 38.1B, D), and peach and nectarine production is mainly in southwestern Michigan (Fig. 38.3).

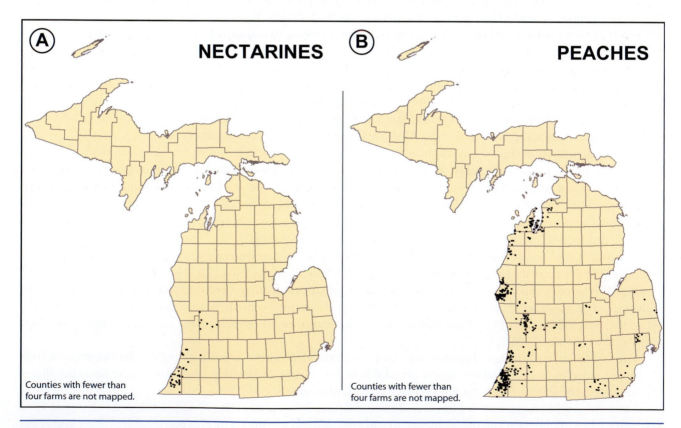

FIGURE 38.3   Locations of farms that grew (A) nectarines and (B) peaches in Michigan in 2002. In order to protect grower confidentiality, the location of each farm dot was randomly moved by up to 4.8 km. Source: USDA (2005).

Climate and fruit production

Climate is a major factor affecting the success or failure—and therefore the location—of fruit production in Michigan. Climatic hazards for fruit production are many; extremely low winter temperatures, late spring frosts, early fall frosts, hail, drought, wind and weather that favors diseases and insects are all problematic for fruit growers.

Precipitation and temperature are critical elements of climate for fruit production. Michigan benefits from a relatively uniform rainfall of about 7–8 cm per month—ample to maintain leaf and shoot development during the first part of the growing season, and uniform fruit development from bloom through harvest. Fruit is about 85% water; thus, available soil moisture is critical for fruit development, especially during the last few weeks prior to harvest, for most stone fruits and berries. During the winter season, abundant precipitation as snowfall provides an insulating layer over the soil surface. This prevents deep penetration of frost and ice into the soil, and protects root systems from freeze injury (Isard and Schaetzl 1998). As the snow cover melts on the unfrozen ground, it recharges the sandy soils of the fruit belt with moisture to sustain growth during the summer.

Michigan's fruit acreage, its location and wide expanse, are impacted by air temperatures, which influence plant growth and may damage buds and flowers during winter extremes and/or late spring frosts. The growing season is usually considered to be the period between the last killing frost in the spring and the first killing frost in the fall; it varies significantly across the state (Fig. 38.4). However, fruit plants usually do not function at temperatures <6° C, and thus the true "growing season" is slightly different from that of other crops. Cold winter temperatures, if they are too low or if they fluctuate widely, can also cause damage. Although extreme cold during the winter can cause winter injury to the tree, by killing branches and trunks, most winter injury is caused by cold snaps early or late in the dormant season, or by mid-winter thaws followed by rapid declines in temperature.

Plants initiate growth as soon as favorable temperatures occur in spring. Leaf buds open, producing new leaves and shoots. Flower buds, which began development the previous summer and fall, rapidly complete their development in spring, open and may develop into fruit. Fruit is harvested as it matures, and the plant's foliage will remain functional until leaf senescence in the fall, or until injured by fall frosts and freezes.

After leaf fall, the trees, having acquired winter hardiness, enter into both dormancy and a condition known as "rest," or endodormancy. Rest is the period during dormancy when growth of the above-ground portions of the tree cannot occur, even if temperatures become favorable. Rest is important for survival in cold climates, as it prevents growth during mid-winter warm spells and subsequent damage from periods of severe cold. Rest is "broken" or removed naturally by winter chilling. The period of chilling required varies with species and variety. Peaches require about 800–1,200 hours <7° C, cherries about 600–1,400 hours, and apples about 1,700 hours. In Michigan, for most temperate zone fruit plants, rest usually ends in January or February. Nonetheless, low temperatures, and hence, dormancy, can continue into March.

Tree roots are not as hardy as are the above-ground parts of the tree; they have been killed at temperatures ranging from −15 to −29° C. Small roots are more susceptible to injury than large ones. Soils cool more slowly than air, and some heat does rise from the subsoil, potentially limiting cold damage to the roots. However, continued cold periods, when the ground has time to freeze, can result in root injury. A heavy blanket of snow, or a cover crop during the winter, is often enough to protect the roots from injury.

Low air temperatures can cause damage to fruit trees at several different times and for different reasons. For example, cold temperatures in mid-winter can kill developing flower buds and, if cold enough, will even kill the trees. Also, during late fall, trees begin to acquire hardiness. As the tree enters the dormant season, the buds become progressively more resistant to, and tolerant of, low temperatures. Sudden exposure to freezing temperatures before these tissues acquire hardiness, however, can severely injure or kill the buds, or even the trees. Lastly, as trees approach bloom and during bloom, freezes can kill the flower buds.

Lake effect climate

Climatologists know that large bodies of water significantly influence (moderate) the climate of adjoining land areas. Lake Michigan is important in this regard—it moderates the climate, providing more desirable environmental conditions for fruit production in nearby areas. Michigan's climate, near Lake Michigan, is tempered by the prevailing winds passing over the lake, especially during the winter and spring months. This "lake effect" occurs because of

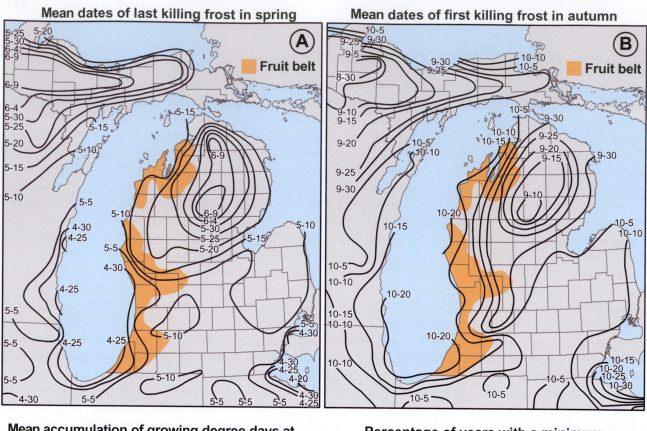

Mean dates of last killing frost in spring

Fruit belt

Mean dates of first killing frost in autumn

Fruit belt

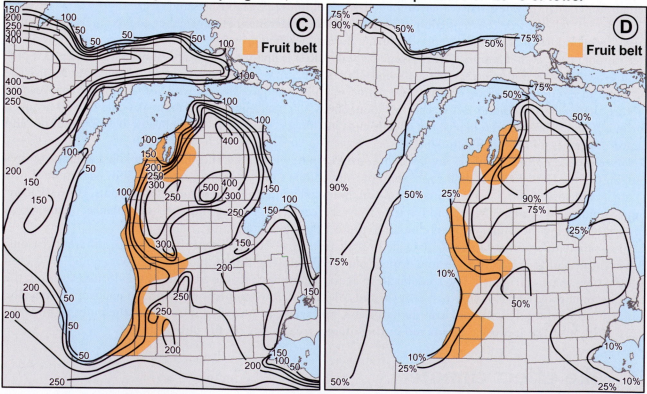

Mean accumulation of growing degree days at typical date of last killing frost in spring base, 5.8 C

Fruit belt

Percentage of years with a minimum temperature of -25° C or lower

Fruit belt

FIGURE 38.4 Climatic parameters pertinent to fruit production, for most of the state of Michigan. Period of record for these maps is probably 1910–1949. After Olmstead (1951). A. Mean dates of the last killing frost in spring. B. Mean dates of the first killing frost in fall. C. Mean number of growing degree days as of the last killing frost date in spring (base 5.8° C). D. Mean percentage of years that temperatures of −25.5°C or less are recorded.

the very high specific heat of water (Chapters 19, 39). To warm one gram of *water* 1°C requires more than four times as much heat as to warm the same amount (1 g) of *air* 1°C. And, in cooling 1°C, one g of water gives off more than four times as much heat as would be given off by one g of air (Chandler 1928). Thus, water warms up and cools down much more slowly than does air. And when each is near the freezing point at normal barometric pressures, one g of air occupies nearly 800 times as much volume as does a g of water. Thus, when the temperature of a given volume of water is lowered 1°, it gives off enough heat to raise 1° about 3000 times that volume of air (Chandler 1928)! For this reason, during even the coldest winters, the waters of Lake Michigan rarely get cold enough to freeze. Therefore, winds passing over it are warmed considerably in winter, and cooled in summer. This property is the famed "lake effect."

The areal extent of Lake Michigan is also important in regard to lake effect. The longer it takes an air mass to cross the water in winter, the more the air is warmed. Likewise, the greater the depth of a lake, the more total heat it can store. If Lake Michigan were just a broad expanse of shallow water, it would store less heat and would freeze over during a long, cold winter. But the deep lake stores sufficient heat to protect against severe midwinter cold, as well as impacting the timing of late spring and early autumn frosts.

The peach is the most tender tree fruit grown commercially in Michigan. Mid-winter temperatures of −24°C can kill peach flower buds and −25°C can even kill the tree. Figure 38.4D shows the percentage of years when such cold temperatures occur throughout Michigan. This distribution helps explain the concentration of Michigan's fruit production near the eastern coast of Lake Michigan, where the frequency of very low winter temperatures is much less than at sites farther inland (Fig. 38.1A, 38.3B). Lake Michigan seldom freezes over (Chapter 14); temperatures of its open waters in winter commonly are 3–5°C. During the winter, therefore, air masses that leave Wisconsin at temperatures slightly below freezing often arrive on the Michigan side at temperatures above (or near) freezing. Thus, flower buds are less apt to be killed and trees injured by very cold temperatures. Winter temperature data, therefore, can be used to predict the locations where fruit trees in Michigan are apt to be damaged (or not) during typical winters, e.g., Fig. 38.4D.

The cooling effect of the lake also delays bud activity in the fruit belt in the spring. Degree days—a measurement of accumulated heat—accumulate much slower near the lake, and thus trees begin growth and blossoming later in these locations (Fig. 38.4C). Thus, the trees and blossoms are less likely to be damaged by spring frosts, which occur later inland than in the fruit belt. Figure 38.4A shows the isothermal lines for the last killing frost for various Michigan localities, further explaining the location of the state's fruit belt. Early blossoming is one of the most common causes of a poor fruit crop—because these early blossoms often are damaged by a late freeze. It is not uncommon to have a spring frost in early June in Gaylord, while the last frost at Traverse City seldom arrives later than May 15. Fruit trees grown in Gaylord would not yield a successful crop in most years, for this reason.

In addition, late fall freezes are delayed near the lake, thus prolonging the growing season and enabling the trees to acquire more cold hardiness before the onset of winter. Figure 38.4B shows the first fall frosts in the fruit belt to not arrive as early as they do inland.

FOCUS BOX: The vagaries of weather in the fruit belt

The tempered climate of the fruit belt is not entirely free of the troublesome quirks of weather. Late frosts in spring, early fall freezes and extended warm periods in fall followed by sudden cold, hail, ice and sleet storms, excessive rain, wind storms and unusually cold winters can all result in varying degrees of crop loss, or even the loss of the entire orchard. Unusual or freakish weather occurs only occasionally, but that is too often for commercial growers.

Sometimes, severe cold develops in early spring, after a mild winter. Such was the case in March, 1890, when temperatures fell to −24° C in southwestern Michigan, killing practically all the peach buds. Another kind of cold that plagues Michigan fruit growers occurs in the fall when the wood of the fruit trees is still immature. One of the worst of such premature fall freezes occurred in October, 1906, when a temperature of −26° C was recorded at South Haven. Peaches were still being harvested and leaves were still on the trees; millions of trees died. A similar freeze was experienced on Thanksgiving Day, 1950. These periodic setbacks discouraged fruit growers, but during the mild years between calamities, the industry always seemed to recover and grow. Peaches are the exception; production never fully recovered from the fall freeze of 1906.

During the growing season, the lake also tends to keep the air warmer at night, when the temperature is falling, and lower in the daytime when temperature is rising. This reduction in the diurnal (daily) variation in air temperatures near the lake helps to avoid the retarding effect that very high temperatures (>30°C) have on photosynthesis.

In summary, air temperatures near Lake Michigan are warmer in the winter and cooler in the summer than in areas far from it. The eastern shore (lee side) of the lake experiences this climatic effect, while the western shore (Wisconsin, the windward side) is less impacted.

■ Effects of topography

A good "site" is a key factor to successful fruit production. In this context, site refers to a favorable location relative to the local topography. A determining factor for a good site centers on local microclimate and drainage of cold air, which can dramatically affect, or can even ruin, an orchard.

Elevation strongly influences air drainage, because cold air is denser and heavier than warm air, and therefore settles at ground level (on calm nights) and drains from topographically higher locations to lower elevations—cold "frost pockets" (Fig. 39.7). Thus, the elevation of a site—an orchard—above adjacent surrounding terrain, is very important. Most growers try to select a site for their orchard where cold air can drain or move to lower areas. For this reason, fields that slope, but are not too steep for efficient orchard operations, are usually most desirable. Obstructions on the slope below an orchard, such as a woodlot, can actually restrict air movement, and therefore growers try to remove them or cut swaths through them, to facilitate cold air drainage. Valleys and lowlands, from which cold air cannot drain away, are colder and therefore poor sites for fruit production. Level land is not objectionable, if frosts are not a problem or if the site is located within 3 km of a large body of deep water, so as to take advantage of the tempering effect of the water.

In summary, a good site should provide protection from damage caused by spring frosts and cold winters. It (1) provides acceptable drainage of cold air, by having an elevation higher than the surrounding fields, and (2) is more or less rolling, with gradual slopes for ready movement of orchard machinery, and yet not so steep as to facilitate runoff and soil erosion. Many ideal sites are on a relatively high, level or rolling upland, such as the tops of broad ridges or plains, bordering on lowlands.

Orchards on good sites have a lower chance of being damaged by a late spring frost than those on poor sites. Late spring frosts are particularly damaging to the crop, and of much concern to growers. As both floral and vegetative buds expand in spring, they progressively lose their ability to tolerate cold temperatures. Late spring frosts, occurring when floral buds are well advanced, can destroy many of the flowers and severely lower the eventual yield of the orchard. Lesser amounts of kill occur at warmer, better sites, which is why they are sought out as prime areas for fruit production.

■ Soils

Fruit trees and berry crops can thrive over a wide range of soil types, but the best orchard soils need proper drainage for good aeration and extensive root development. Deep, well-drained soils permit greater root penetration, resulting in increased production and longer-lived plants.

The soils in many successful Michigan orchards are predominately sandy loam in texture. These soils drain well after heavy rains and rapid snow melt, yet contain sufficient clay to remain moist through the growing season. Michigan's cool climate results in less summer evaporation than some other production areas, resulting in less moisture stress on the trees.

Cherry trees require less moisture than apple trees, and are therefore frequently grown on coarse textured (sandy) soils. Sweet and tart cherry trees are very sensitive to wet soils and cherry rootstocks vary in their degree of sensitivity. Mahaleb rootstock, used for tart cherries, is best suited to gravelly or sandy soils that are well drained, resulting in deep rooting. Sweet cherries, on Mazzard rootstock, perform well on loam or clay soils. Peach trees also require well-drained soils and perform best on coarser-textured soils, while apple, pear and plum trees perform satisfactorily on soils with greater clay contents, and even tolerate slightly poor soil drainage. However, good soil drainage is more important for fruit trees than for most annual crops.

Horticultural considerations and applications

Planting, pruning and training

Fruit trees are usually planted in early spring. Early planting allows for root growth before new leaves appear. Cool spring temperatures and spring rains favor early growth and establishment. Fall planting is possible, but carries more risks, as the trees may not be fully hardened for the approaching winter season, and thus may be more vulnerable to cold injury. Fall-planted trees usually begin growth as soon as temperatures rise in spring—often earlier than do nursery trees planted in the spring, thus making somewhat more growth during the first growing season.

Training (bending of branches) and pruning (removal of branches) are performed to influence the shape of the trees and to influence cropping and fruit quality (Fig. 38.5A). Training is a practice in which tree growth is directed into a desired shape and form. Its purpose is to shape the tree and develop a strong framework of scaffold branches, arranged and distributed to admit sunlight into the interior of the tree, in order to support profitable crops for the life of the tree. Training occurs during the early years, following planting, and in subsequent years in late winter/early spring. In high density plantings, training may continue for several years, often during the growing season.

Trees are usually pruned during the winter to control tree height, remove dead, diseased and broken branches, and reduce crowding and allow light to penetrate the canopy (Fig. 38.5B, C). In the colder regions of Michigan, pruning

FIGURE 38.5   Training, pruning and production of fruit. A. Training lateral branches of young apple trees into horizontal position, to promote flowering and fruiting at a young age. Photo by F. Dennis. B. Peach trees, recently pruned to open their centers and admit sunlight throughout the canopy. Pruning maintains vigorous shoots for fruit production. Photo by R. Schaetzl. C. Mechanical pruning with a double sickle bar mower. In the horizontal position, as shown here, the bar removes upward-growing limbs. The bar can be oriented vertically to trim the sides of the tree. Photo by F. Dennis. D. Peaches on shoots that grew the previous year. Trees are pruned to promote this type of growth and to remove crowding branches, so as to thin the crop and thereby increase the overall fruit size. Photo by R. Schaetzl.

of young trees is delayed until late winter, to avoid possible cold injury. Pruning helps maintain a balance between the vegetative and fruiting areas of the tree. Removal of older fruiting wood promotes the growth of new fruiting wood, which yields larger, higher quality fruit. Although removal of fruiting limbs reduces actual crop numbers, the fruit produced are larger and thus, more marketable (Fig. 38.5D). Pruning spreads the work load for the orchardist into a season when few other orchard activities compete for their time. Pruning peach and sweet cherry trees in mid-winter, however, may result in canker injury to the trees. Therefore, many orchardists delay this pruning until near bloom time, or after flowering, to reduce the risk of infection. Because peach trees have their best fruit on one-year-old shoots, the trees are pruned more heavily than other fruit trees. Sweet cherry trees require less pruning than other fruit trees.

Because ~95% of tart cherry trees are mechanically harvested, trees are also pruned to adapt them to mechanical shakers. Pendant lower limbs are removed, to provide the equipment operator a clear view of the trunk for attaching the trunk shaker. Thin, willowy, flexible branches are cut back, so that the fruit is borne on relatively stiff branches that better transmit the energy from the trunk shaker to the fruit, resulting in easier and more complete fruit removal. Some tart cherry trees are summer-hedged mechanically, cutting the sides of the trees with a double sickle bar, mounted vertically, to remove one-third to one-half of the current season's growth (Fig. 38.5C). This operation is performed 40–50 days after the petals have fallen from the flowers. The trees may be pruned by hand after completion of harvest, when labor is available. But care must be taken not to stimulate late shoot growth, which increases susceptibility to early fall freezing of tissues.

Summer pruning of large apple trees is sometimes performed in late summer (August), to remove part of the current season's shoot growth. This action removes some of the vegetation that may be shading the developing fruit. Improved exposure to sunlight also results in increased coloration of red varieties.

Insects—beneficial and otherwise

Temperature has a significant influence on flowering and fruit set. Bees, which facilitate pollenation, do not perform well at temperatures below 10°C. The germination of pollen grains and growth of the pollen tube in fertilized flowers is also significantly faster at 15°C than at 5°C, and is retarded above ~27°C. The period of time the ovule is receptive to fertilization and fruit set also varies with temperature. Low temperatures slow pollen tube growth, such that the ovule may no longer be viable when the tube reaches it.

Numerous insects and diseases attack fruit trees and the developing fruit. Pests have generally been controlled by applications of insecticides and fungicides. In the past, the time of pesticide application was often based on phenology—the stages of growth, e.g., bud development, leafing, flowering and fruit development. More recently, refined and improved models of the life histories of many insects and diseases have been developed. Equipment exists to more precisely monitor weather conditions (temperature, rainfall, humidity, duration of plant surface wetness, etc.). Equipment for trapping fungal disease spores also can help the grower predict the severity of potential infections. Entomologists use trapping techniques to trap harmful insects. They have also synthesized pheromones (sex lures) to assist with luring and monitoring of insect pests. Because insect development and activity are related primarily to temperature, degree-day models help determine when insecticide applications should be applied. Pheromones to disrupt insect mating are used to control several fruit insect pests.

Harvesting and marketing

Harvest time is always an important period in any fruit orchard. Below, we discuss harvest procedures, specific to each major fruit type.

Michigan orchardists raise many different apple varieties, which mature between late July and October. Depending on climate and season of the year, a variety may be harvested over a one- to three-week period, generally less during warmer weather that hastens ripening and fruit softening. The fruit are detached by hand and placed in a picking receptacle suspended from the picker's shoulders (Fig. 38.6A). The container holds one-half bushel of fruit, usually has metal sides, and has a canvas drop bottom that can be lowered to transfer the apples into a bushel crate or 20-bushel bulk bin (Fig. 38.6B). Bulk bins are handled with tractor forklifts. One-third of Michigan's apple crop is marketed fresh and about two-thirds are processed. Fruit not sold at harvest-time is placed in refrigerated storage for later marketing. Apples can be stored at 0° C for up to six months, depending on the variety and market demand. Alternatively, the fruit are placed in controlled atmosphere (CA) storage at harvest and stored up to 8–10 months for late season marketing. CA storage requires a gas-tight, refrigerated room in which the storage

FIGURE 38.6   Apple harvest images. A. A half-bushel, metal picking container with a canvas drop bottom. The container is suspended from the shoulders of the picker and, when full, lowered into position before the canvas bottom is opened, so as to avoid bruising. Photo by F. Dennis. B. Bulk bins, each containing 20 bushels of fruit. The bins are handled with forklift tractors. Photo by R. Schaetzl.

atmosphere is modified to increase the concentration of N and CO_2 gases, while at the same time reducing the level of oxygen. This lowers the rate of fruit respiration, retards softening and prolongs storage life. Michigan is the leading state for production of apple slices, both fresh and frozen, producing approximating 45% of the national market. Canning apples for applesauce is also a major market. One-third of our apples sold for processing are used for juice. Red Delicious, Golden Delicious, Jonathan, IdaRed, Rome, McIntosh, Empire and Northern Spy represent most of Michigan's apple crop (Table 38.2). Newer varieties that are likely to become increasingly popular include Gala, Fuji, Honeycrisp, Braeburn, Pink Lady (Cripps Pink), Pinata, Jazz and Sonya.

Peach harvest occurs from late July through September. Peaches are very perishable and must be handled carefully to avoid bruising. Not all fruit on the tree mature at the same time, so growers "spot" pick trees two to four times; at each harvest, only fruit that are firm, and have good color and size, are picked. Such fruit will withstand shipment to distant markets. Fruit for local sales are harvested when firm-ripe and ready to eat. The ripening process is greatly affected by temperature; fruit must be kept cool and handled quickly after harvest. Two-thirds of Michigan's peach crop (Fig. 38.5B) is marketed fresh to supermarket outlets or directly to consumers. The remainder of the crop is processed, with many of the clingstone peaches packed as a puree for baby food.

TABLE 38.2   The main apple varieties grown in Michigan

Apple Variety	Percent of total crop (2005)
Red Delicious	23.5
Golden Delicious	12.4
Jonathan	10.4
Ida Red	8.7
Rome	7.9
McIntosh	6.4
Empire	6.2
Northern Spy	5.4
Gala	4.4
Jonagold	2.5
Other	12.5

Nearly all tart cherries produced in Michigan are the Montmorency variety and are utilized in some processed form; seldom are they eaten fresh. The fruit mature 60–70 days after bloom, and are mechanically harvested. Trees are sprayed with ethephon (an ethylene-releasing compound) 7–14 days before anticipated harvest, to promote loosening of fruit from their stems. Temperatures within three days of application of ethephon markedly affect the chemical response. Higher temperatures increase the magnitude of response; lower temperatures reduce the response. Tart cherries are shaken from the tree by a trunk shaker attached (clamped) to the base of the tree (Fig. 38.7A). The shaker is mounted under a catching frame. The fruit may be collected on (1) two half inclined harvesters—one on either side of the tree, (2) a full wrap-around harvester, that wraps completely around and beneath the tree, or (3) a roll-out catching system, where the fabric catching surface lies on the ground and is stretched out underneath

FIGURE 38.7   Harvesting tart cherries. A trunk shaker (A). The fruit falls onto a canvas, which has been rolled under the tree. After shaking, the canvas is mechanically reeled back to a conveyor and the cherries are dumped into a receiving tank of cool water (B) for transport from to a processing plant. Photos by F. Dennis.

the tree after the shaker is clamped to it. After shaking the fruit from the tree onto the canvas, the canvas is reeled back to the edge of a conveyer by a power reel, and the fruit is dumped onto a conveyer. The conveyer deposits the harvested cherries into a tank of cooling water, to begin the cooling and firming process and to minimize scald (browning) damage (Fig. 38.7B). The fruit is soaked for 4–6 hours in cold, running water to cool it and increase firmness, so that mechanical pitting can proceed efficiently and accurately. Almost the entire Michigan tart cherry crop is sold for processing. The fruit are pitted and frozen, canned for pie filling, or individually quick frozen (IQF)—a rapid freezing of single cherries. IQF cherries can later be processed into such products as pies, pie filling, pastries, jams, jellies and juice, or dehydrated. Some fruit are dried as cherry "raisins" or used for juice.

Sweet cherries are susceptible to fruit cracking when rain occurs as the fruit ripens. Consequently, many sweet cherries produced in Michigan are harvested for brining, allowing them to be picked in a relatively immature state, before the fruit are vulnerable to cracking. Mechanical shakers harvest fruit for brining and for canning. Sweet cherries for fresh market are usually picked by hand to avoid bruising and marking, and then kept cool to minimize fruit softening, retain flavor and aid in rot control. Preharvest rains that can cause cracking of sweet cherries render them susceptible to fungal infection and rot. Therefore, only a small portion (2 to 3%) of Michigan's sweet cherry crop is sold to the fresh market. About 15% of the crop is frozen; a similar amount is canned. Two-thirds of Michigan's sweet cherry crop is picked in a relatively immature state and used for the brine market. Such fruit are mechanically harvested before they fully mature, to reduce the risk of cracking. The shaken fruit are stored in a $SO_2 + CaCl_2$ brine until they can be processed into cocktail (or maraschino), candied or glace cherries.

Pears are harvested in a manner similar to apples. The fruit is harvested in August and September, while it is still green and then ripened to eating quality after harvest. Bartlett pears—the major pear variety grown in Michigan—are well suited for both processing and fresh market. A high percentage of Michigan pears are sold for processing, mainly for baby food. Most sales of fresh pears from Michigan are through farm markets and specialized produce markets.

Plums are not a major commercial fruit crop in Michigan, often being raised to mainly diversify a grower's fruit production. About two-thirds of Michigan's plum crop is sold for processing into canned purple plums and baby food. However, the amount of the Michigan plum crop sold to the fresh market is increasing. A prune is an oval, purplish, European plum which, because of its higher sugar content, can be dried whole without fermentation at the pit. Prunes are produced mainly in California.

■ Distribution of fruit in Michigan

The location of Michigan's fruit belt is largely determined by the lake-effect climate, in conjunction with adequate soils and topography. Low temperature injury is probably the most important factor determining distribution of fruit crops in Michigan. Common types of damage are (1) mid winter kill of dormant flower buds, (2) death of cambium in twigs, branches and trunks, and (3) frost damage to flower and fruit during spring and fall. Both air drainage and water drainage need to be considered in selecting orchard sites.

The distribution of fruit *within* the fruit belt is driven by additional economic and physical factors. Some economic factors include proximity to major highways, population centers and markets, and fruit storage, packing and processing facilities. Important physical factors include terrain, e.g., the major ridges north of Grand Rapids that provide excellent cold air drainage, even though they are somewhat distant from Lake Michigan. Poorly-drained or otherwise wet soils are usually unsatisfactory for fruit production.

The peach is Michigan's most climatically tender, tree fruit crop. Peach trees are very susceptible to freeze injury damage from late fall and early winter cold spells. Thus, peaches are mainly grown in the warm areas of southwestern Lower Michigan (Fig. 38.3B). The frequency of extremely low winter temperatures primarily determines successful peach culture, because peach trees are often killed by mid-winter temperatures of −26° to −29°C; peach flower buds may be killed at −25°C. Michigan's safest regions for peach culture are those which rarely experience a minimum temperature of −24°C. In Michigan, the southwestern part of the state experiences such cold no more than seven times every 30 years (Fig. 38.4D). Berrien, Van Buren and Allegan Counties in southwestern Michigan are the major counties for production of freestone peaches for fresh market. Oceana and Mason Counties are important for clingstone peach production for processing, especially for baby food. The light textured soils in these regions also contribute to slowing of growth in late fall, and the acquisition of hardiness.

The nectarine is merely a peach with a recessive gene that results in fuzzless fruit. They are similar in appearance to peaches in tree growth and bearing habits, but the fruit is smooth and tends to be smaller. Nectarines are grown wherever peaches are produced (Fig. 38.3A), but require more management for control of pests, as they tend to be more susceptible to brown rot and curculio. California produces nearly all of the nation's nectarines, but as varieties adapted to Michigan's humid climate are developed, and that have more disease resistance and larger fruit size, local production will increase.

Tart cherry trees are generally more hardy than peach and sweet cherry trees, and have a longer rest period, requiring greater chilling to break winter rest. The flower buds are quite hardy in the winter, but very tender when bud swell begins in the spring; they can be killed at temperatures of only −2.5°C. These trees perform best on light textured soils and are very sensitive to poorly drained or wet soils. The period between bloom and harvest is about two months, another reason the crop is well adapted to the shorter growing season in the Traverse City area (Fig. 38.1D). About 40% of the state's acreage is in Leelanau (26%) and Grand Traverse (13%) Counties, and 25% is in Oceana County.

Sweet cherries are somewhat more hardy than peaches. Cherry wood and bark are susceptible to winter cold injury at temperatures of −26° to −29°C. Cherry trees blossom comparatively early; flower buds in bloom are subject to injury at temperatures of −1.5°C, while flower buds showing color may withstand temperatures 1–2°C lower than open buds. Thus, the distribution of sweet cherries is highly climatically controlled. Sweet cherries have a relatively short growing period from bloom to harvest and are well adapted to the short summers of the Traverse City area. Grand Traverse Bay provides excellent protection from deep winter cold and early spring frosts. The area's abundant snowfall also affords protection to the tree's root system, which is actually more susceptible to cold damage than the above ground part of the tree. Cherries develop good quality in this climate, which is too cool for peaches. Leelanau (47%) and Grand Traverse (21%) Counties contain more than two-thirds of the state's sweet cherry acreage (Fig. 38.1B).

Apples are the most extensively planted fruit crop in Michigan. They grow best on moderately light textured, fertile soils, on relatively high sites where spring frosts are not prevalent. However, the site and soil requirements for apple are not as exacting as for the stone fruits. Apple trees do not bloom as early as peach or cherry trees, and grow well on heavier soils than will stone fruits. Therefore, apples can be grown in inland areas, where lake effect moderation is not as pronounced (Fig. 38.1C). Most apple varieties also tolerate lower winter temperatures than most stone fruits. Kent County has more than 21% of Michigan's acreage; Berrien and Van Buren Counties each contain about 11% of Michigan's apple acreage.

Pears are more adaptable to climate and soil variations than are the stone fruits. The trees will tolerate winter temperatures of approximately −29° C without experiencing serious damage. Thus, pears have been raised in some locations in Allegan County not well suited for other fruit crops (Fig. 38.1E). Pear trees are also more tolerant of heavy and wetter soils than either apple or stone fruits.

Plum trees are winter hardy, but tend to bloom fairly early in the spring, mandating that they be grown within the lake effect fruit belt (Fig. 38.1F). Plum trees perform better on finer textured soils than do peach and cherry trees. Although plums are a major commercial crop for the Michigan fruit industry, they are a secondary, diversifying crop for most fruit growers who raise them. The primary plum variety grown is Stanley, which is sold for processing into canned purple plums and baby food, but in some years a considerable portion of the crop is sold for fresh market.

Blueberries

The highbush blueberry is native to North America. The US Department of Agriculture (USDA) began investigations in 1906 to determine the soil requirements of the blueberry, and initiated breeding and selection of varieties with large berry size. Dr. Stanley Johnston, Director of the Michigan Agricultural Experiment Station, made a small planting, at South Haven, of selections from the USDA, in 1923. This led to the first commercial blueberry planting in Michigan in 1928 near Grand Junction (Johnston 1938). Within 25 years, the Michigan blueberry industry had expanded to more than 1,600 hectares. By 2005, blueberry acreage was >7,500 hectares.

The highbush blueberry plant has exacting soil and climatic needs, requiring a mean growing season of 160 days. It is badly injured or killed by winter temperatures of –28° C or below. For this reason, most of Michigan's blueberry production occurs near Lake Michigan in the southwestern part of the state, in Van Buren, Allegan, Ottawa, Muskegon and Berrien Counties (Fig. 38.8), where such low wintertime temperatures are rare. The best sites for blueberries are large, flat, open areas, where air can move freely, reducing the chances for spring frost damage.

FIGURE 38.8 Locations of farms that grew blueberries in Michigan in 2000. In order to protect grower confidentiality, the location of each farm dot was randomly moved by up to 4.8 km. Source: USDA Census of Agriculture (2002).

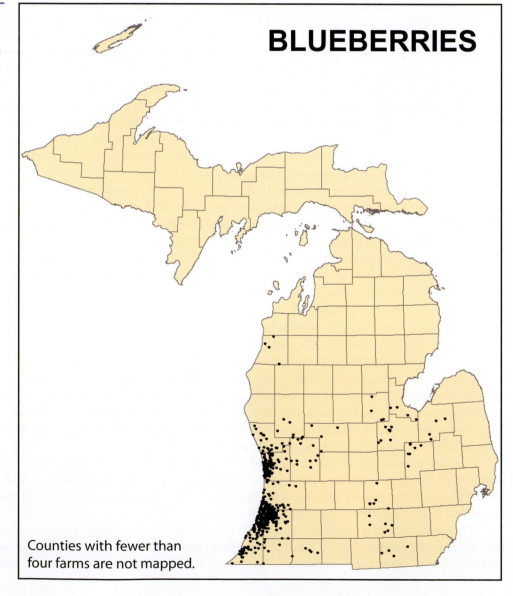

BLUEBERRIES

Counties with fewer than four farms are not mapped.

FIGURE 38.9 A mechanical blueberry harvester. The machine straddles the bushes and as they pass beneath, the berries are shaken from the canes and drop onto collecting plates positioned near the ground. The berries are then conveyed to bins at the rear of the machine. Photo by F. Dennis.

The blueberry requires an acidic soil, ranging from pH 4.0–5.1, and performs best on loose textured soils. Sandy, acidic soils with high organic matter contents are desired for blueberry production. Peat soils (Histosols) can be suitable, but they are usually found in low sites subject to frost and winter injury. Plants on peat also tend to grow late in the fall, and therefore are especially susceptible to injury from autumn cold snaps.

Blueberry plants require good drainage in the root zone, but also consistent water availability. The best soils are those where the water table remains between ~30–60 cm deep, typically within the somewhat poorly-drained class. Yet, good surface drainage is also very important since blueberry roots require good aeration. Most Michigan blueberries are irrigated (Michigan Department of Agriculture 2004a).

About one-third of Michigan's blueberry crop is sold to the fresh market and two-thirds is processed. Harvest occurs from July through September. Fields are harvested two to five times, depending on intended marketing. Over-the-row mechanical harvesters were developed in the early 1960s, in response to declining labor availability (Dale et al. 1994). Machine harvesting is most common (Fig. 38.9), although the field may be picked by hand for the first harvest, if the fruit is for fresh market. Plantings for processing are harvested fewer times, with a longer interval between harvests. Fields for the fresh market are harvested more frequently to avoid soft, overripe berries.

■ Strawberries

The strawberry was once one of the most important berry crops grown in Michigan, with about two-thirds of the crop sold to the fresh market. Plants can be grown on nearly any type of soil, containing a good supply of organic matter. However, the best yields are usually obtained on deep, fertile, well-drained loams with a high moisture-holding capacity. The site should be well drained, fairly level and without frost pockets.

Strawberries are extremely susceptible to late spring frost damage. Plants bloom during a two to three week period, and the first flowers are likely to be injured by late spring frosts. Sprinkler irrigation during frost can protect blossoms against temperatures as low as –7° C. Growers begin sprinkling when the temperature at plant level drops to 1° C, and continue irrigating until the temperature the following day rises to 1° C, and all ice has melted from the plants. Irrigating plants and flowers prevents frost damage because of heat of fusion, which is released as the water cools to the freezing point. Because of this heat of fusion, the temperature of a blossom, on which water is continually freezing, remains at or near 0° C, and the flower is not damaged.

Before World War II, US strawberry production was dominated by the southern states. In the late 1940s and early 1950s, the center of production shifted to the West Coast. California became the major production state, as a

FIGURE 38.10 Typical activities on a Michigan U-Pick strawberry farm. Photo by R. Schaetzl.

result of development of superior, highly-productive varieties adapted to California's climate. California now supplies the fresh market with strawberries for 8–9 months of the year—at the expense of Michigan and other production areas. Mexico has also become an important source of frozen strawberries. Michigan's strawberry production now is about 400 hectares, scattered throughout the state and located primarily near urban areas for local fresh markets and pick-your-own sales (Fig. 38.10). Only about 10% or less of Michigan's strawberry production is processed.

■ Conclusions

The history of fruit production in our state is long and rich. For decades, Michigan's farmers have taken full advantage of the favored microclimate, rolling topography and well-drained soils that exist in the fruit belt along, and inland from, Lake Michigan. As a result, we lead the nation in, or are a major player in the production of, many different kinds of fruits and berries. Given the continued benefits of the lake effect and topography that exist here, the future of the fruit industry in Michigan is promising.

Literature Cited

Bailey, L.H. 1897. Principles of Fruit Growing. MacMillan and Company, New York.

Bogue, M.B. 1985. The lake and the fruit: The making of three farm-type areas. Agricultural History Society, University of California, Davis.

Chandler, W.H. 1928. North American Orchards. Lea and Fobiger, Philadelphia, PA.

Dale, A., Hanson, E., Yarborough, D., McNicol, R., Stang, E., Brennan, R., Morris, J. and G. Hergert. 1994. Mechanical harvesting of berry crops. Horticultural Review 16:255–382.

Gourley, J.H. 1923. Text-book of Pomology. Macmillan and Company, New York.

Isard, S.A. and R.J. Schaetzl. 1998. Effects of winter weather conditions on soil freezing in southern Michigan. Physical Geography 19:71–94.

Johnston, S. 1938. The cultivation of the highbush blueberry. Michigan State College of Agriculture and Applied Science, Agricultural Experiment Station Special Bulletin 252.

Kessler, G.M. 1970. A history of fruit growing in Michigan. Proceedings of the Michigan State Horticultural Society. pp. 114–147.

Michigan Department. of Agriculture. 2004a. Michigan Rotational Survey Fruit Inventory. Michigan Agricultural Statistics Service, East Lansing, MI.

Michigan Department of Agriculture. 2004b. Noncitrus Fruits and Nuts. Michigan Agricultural Statistics Service, East Lansing, MI.

Olmstead, C.W. 1951. The pattern of orchards in Michigan. An historical-geographic study of the development of a pattern of land use. Ph.D. Dissertation, University of Michigan, Ann Arbor.

Parmalee, G. 1874. The past, present and future of Michigan pomology. Annual Report, Michigan State Pomological Society of Michigan. Lansing.

United States Department of Agriculture (USDA). 2005. 2002 Census of Agriculture. Agricultural Atlas of the United States. National Agricultural Statistics Service, Washington, DC.

Winchell, A. 1880. Annual report, Michigan State Horticultural Society. 19th annual meeting, Grand Rapids. pp. 155–163.

Further Readings

Anonymous. 2005. Michigan Fruit Management Guide. Michigan State University, Agricultural Experiment Station Extention Bulletin E-154. East Lansing.

Bald, F.C. 1954. Michigan in Four Centuries. Harper and Brothers, New York.

Bradford, F.C. and H.A. Cardinell. 1926. Eighty winters in Michigan orchards. Michigan State College, Agricultural Experiment Station Special Bulletin 149.

Childers, N.F., Morris, J.R. and G.S. Sibbett. 1995. Modern Fruit Science—Orchard and Small Fruit Management. Horticultural Publications, Gainesville, FL.

Childers, N.F. and W.B. Sherman. 1988. The Peach—World Cultivars to Marketing. Horticultural Publications, Gainesville, FL.

Dennis, F.G., Jr. and J.Hull, Jr. 2003. Deciduous tree fruit. HortScience 38:901–910.

Gardner, V.R., Bradford, F.C. and H.D. Hooker. 1922. The Fundamentals of Fruit Production. McGraw-Hill, New York.

Gardner, V.R., Bradford, F.C. and H.D. Hooker. 1927. Orcharding. McGraw-Hill, New York.

Gourley, J.H. and F.S. Howlett. 1941. Modern Fruit Production. McGraw-Hill, New York.

Hill, E.B., Riddell, F.T. and F.F. Elliot. 1930. Types of farming in Michigan. Michigan State University, Agricultural Experiment Station Special Bulletin 206.

Jones, A.L. and T.B. Sutton. 1996. Diseases of fruit trees in the east. Michigan State University, Agricultural Experiment Station Extension NCR 45.

O'Brien, M., Cargill, B.F. and R.B. Fridley. 1983. Principles and Practices for Harvesting and Handling Fruit and Nuts. AVI Publishing Company, Westport, CT.

Rom, R.C. and R.F. Carlson. 1987. Rootstocks for Fruit Crops. John Wiley and Sons, New York.

Rosentretter, R. 2006. Savoring the World's Finest Fruit. Michigan History 90 (May–Jun). 72 pp.

Ryago, K. 1988. Fruit Science: Its Science and Art. John Wiley and Sons, New York.

Sjulin, T.M. 2003. The North American small fruit industry 1903–2003. II. Contributions of public and private research in the past 25 years—and a view to the future. HortScience 38:960–967.

Tukey, H.B. 1964. Dwarfed Fruit Trees. MacMillan and Company, New York.

Upshall, W.H. 1976. History of Fruit Growing and Handling in the United States and Canada 1860–1976. American Pomological Society, Regatta Press, Kelowna, BC, Canada.

Webster, A.D. and N.E. Looney. 1969. Cherries: Crop Physiology, Production and Uses. CAB International, Wallingford, UK.

Westwood, M.N. 1993. Temperate-Zone Pomology, Physiology and Culture. Timber Press, Portland, OR.

39

Grape and Wine Production

Thomas J. Zabadal

■ Historical overview

Michigan is geographically blessed with excellent climate, topography and soils for grape production. The earliest recognition of the superb viticultural potential in Michigan can be attributed to French explorers, who found an abundance of wild grapes growing along a stream in southeastern Michigan, around 1796. They named this stream "Riviere aux Raisins," which translates to "River of Grapes." Its name today is River Raisin (Plate 11).

Shortly after Michigan's statehood in 1837, the first grapevines were planted in the southeastern corner of the state, near Monroe. These earliest plantings probably resulted from the expansion of grape production in neighboring Ohio, which at that time was the leading grape producing state. By 1859, the planting of vineyards had expanded to the Lake Michigan area, near Grand Haven and Spring Lake. The first grape planting in Grand Traverse County occurred in 1863.

Another important chapter in the state's grape history began in 1867, near Lawton, where A.B. Jones and D.C. Spicer planted Concord and Delaware grapes, issuing in the beginning of what would become a large juice grape industry in southwestern Michigan. However, in the 19th century, these early crops were packaged and sold only for the fresh market. The Lawton area, in the southwestern Lower Peninsula, soon became renowned for the growing and marketing of fresh-market grapes. The first crop in that area was sold in 1870 by A.B. Jones, for 12–15¢ per pound, for a total profit of $40 (Lawton Leader 1892). By the start of the 20th century, hundreds of carloads of table grapes were being shipped. The area prospered and the industry expanded. By 1869, about 800 hectares of vineyards had already been planted along the eastern shore of Lake Michigan.

Meanwhile, in southeastern Michigan, several wineries were operating near Monroe. By 1871, they had used more than 40 grape varieties for wine production, producing about 50,000 gallons (227,000 liters) of wine (Michigan State Pomological Society 1872). Amazingly, there were interspecific hybrids from at least three breeding programs in eastern North America growing in the state at that time. Nevertheless, Michigan wine production in the late 1800s was dominated by native American *Vitis labrusca* varieties, such as Isabella and Catawba.

The wine making technology of the day was poorly developed, so it is understandable that, in 1872, the Michigan Pomological Society (1872, 434) would report, "Grape growers may squeeze out the juice of the grape and ferment it and call the stuff wine; but it is not the wine of commerce, not the article that people esteem as wine." Despite these early struggles, Michigan's fledgling wine industry did survive, grow and prosper.

Two events dramatically changed the Michigan grape industry. The first was the discovery of a process to pasteurize grape juice by Dr. Thomas Welch in 1869. Exactly 50 years later, in 1919, his son, Dr. Charles Welch established a grape juice processing plant in Lawton, coinciding with growth of the prohibitionist movement (Fig. 39.1). The Welch's plant was not the first grape juice processing plant in Michigan, for at the start of the

FIGURE 39.1 This 1913 advertisement for Welch's grape juice illustrates the prohibitionist attitude that was developing during this era, and which led to the 18th Amendment of the US Constitution in 1919.

20th century, several small grape juice processing plants had emerged in the Lawton-Paw Paw area, because grape production at that time was exceeding fresh market demand. However, it would be the Welch plant in Lawton that would expand for almost a century, to become a dominant marketing component of Michigan's grape industry.

Secondly, all Michigan wineries were closed in 1919, with the beginning of Prohibition. Although no wineries operated in Michigan from 1920 to 1933, four wineries did establish themselves in nearby Windsor, Ontario. Products from those wineries would often mysteriously find their way into Michigan commerce. When Prohibition ended in 1933, 15 new wineries immediately established themselves in the Detroit area. One of these was the Meconi Winery, which had relocated from Windsor. This winery would eventually become St. Julian Wine Company—now the oldest and largest winery in Michigan.

By the mid-1930s, consumer preference was headed toward lighter, lower alcohol wines, rather than the heavier, fortified Michigan wines, which were made from the native American grapes of the time. The shipment of these types of wine from California to Michigan thus threatened the profitability of the Michigan wine industry. Therefore, in 1937, a 50¢ per gallon tax was placed on out-of-state wines, while Michigan wines remained taxed at only 4¢ per gallon. This form of protectionist taxation remained in existence for several decades. Nevertheless, even under this protectionism, Michigan consumer preference gradually evolved away from fortified, *Vitis labrusca*-based Michigan wines, such that, by 1961, only a handful of wineries were operating in Michigan. As a result, the market share of Michigan-produced wines had dropped from 80% of wine sales in the state, to less than 30% by 1975.

Michigan's wine industry might have faded away completely, but, starting in 1953, several events led to the recognition that Michigan possessed the geography to sustain premium wine grape production. This was the start of the renaissance era of the Michigan wine industry, because, for the first time, the Michigan wine industry was built on bonafide wine grape varieties, first the hybrids, and then *Vitis vinifera* varieties.

Contemporary wine production in Michigan

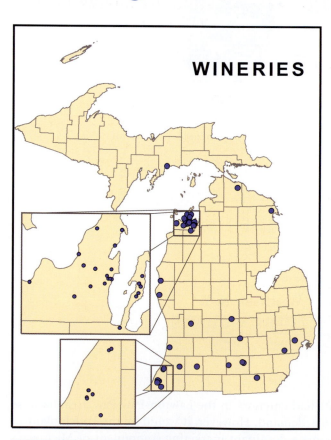

FIGURE 39.2   Locations of wineries in Michigan, in 2006. Source: Michigan Grape and Wine Industry Council.

The modern era of wine production in Michigan began in 1953, when the Bronte Winery near Paw Paw planted the first French-American hybrid vines in Michigan, of the variety *Baco noir*. The development of the wine industry in the Traverse City area began in 1965, when Bernard Rink planted vines on the Leelanau Peninsula. In 1970, Tabor Hill Winery in Buchanan became the first new Michigan winery in more than a quarter of a century, planting the first *Vitis vinifera* varieties in Michigan, including Chardonnay and White Riesling. In 1974, the Welch family began planting both hybrids and *Vitis vinifera* near Fennville, and in the same year Chateau Grand Traverse became the first winery on Old Mission Peninsula and the first to plant *Vitis vinifera* vines in that area. Bernard Rink's Boskydel Vineyards became the first bonded winery on Leelanau Peninsula in 1976, and over the next four years, Leelanau Wine Cellars, L. Mawby Vineyards and Good Harbor Vineyards opened their winery doors in that area.

Since then, there has been a steady influx of new Michigan wineries. Their locations follow closely the pattern of vineyard establishment, with concentrations in southwestern Michigan and the Traverse City area (Fig. 39.2). Several wineries have also opened along the eastern shoreline of Lake Michigan, and in the central and eastern portions of the Lower Peninsula (Fig. 39.2). As of 2006, there were more than 100 winery licenses and 46 fully functioning wineries in the state.

Michigan's physical environment and its effect on grape production

Grapes are a temperate climate crop, with worldwide production concentrated in the 30–50° latitude range (Gladstones 1992); their most successful culture is between 34° and 49° latitude (Winkler et al. 1974). Michigan's grape production is located from about 42–45° latitude (Fig. 39.3). Although *grapevines* can survive in a broad range of climatic conditions, most *grape varieties* which dominate worldwide wine production are best suited to a relatively narrow range of climatic and soil conditions.

The premium wine grapes are the so-called European varieties of the species *Vitis vinifera*. Dominant varieties in this category with recognizable names include: Cabernet Sauvignon, Cabernet franc, Merlot, Chardonnay, Riesling, Pinot noir and Pinot gris. A second category of wine grape varieties is the hybrids, which typically involve the *Vitis vinifera* species in combination with one or more other *Vitis* species. Variety names in this category include Seyval blanc, Vidal blanc, Vignoles, Chancellor, Chambourcin, Marechal Foch and Traminette. They may be used for varietal wines—named after the grape—or for various blends of generic label wines. Michigan has expanding acreages of grapes in both of these categories. In general, these wine grape varieties have more exacting vineyard site requirements than do the native American varieties.

With a few exceptions, wine grape varieties are less cold hardy than the native varieties. Thus, low temperature stress, caused by winter minimum temperatures in Michigan's climate, plays a major role in their culture. Some of the wine variety vines may be injured by winter temperatures as warm as −2° C (Howell 2000), making them unsuitable for production in Michigan. However, many premium wine grape varieties can tolerate winter minimum temperatures of −21° C, but even they become increasingly injured at temperatures between −23° and −26° C. By comparison, Concord, the principal juice grape variety (Fig. 39.4), often tolerates −26° C (Proebsting et al. 1980).

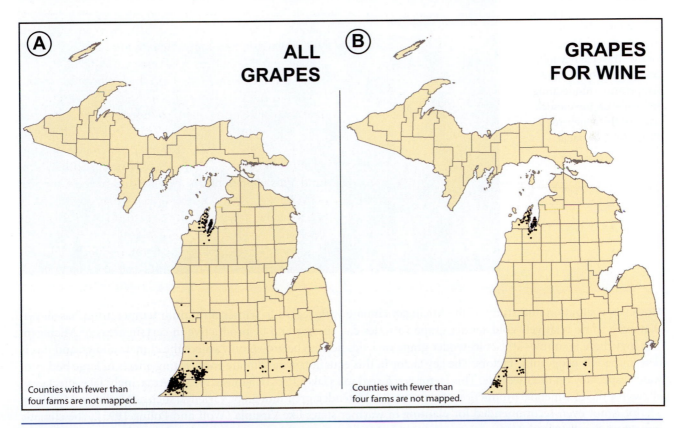

FIGURE 39.3   Locations of all (A) and wine grape (B) vineyards in Michigan, in 2002. This dot map shows the locations of all active vineyards of 2000, but in order to protect grower confidentiality, the location of each vineyard dot was randomly moved by up to 4.8 km. Source: USDA (2005).

FIGURE 39.4 Early shoot growth of Concord vines at the MSU Southwest Michigan Research and Extension Center, Benton Harbor. Photo by T. Zabadal.

FIGURE 39.5 A wine grape vineyard on the west side of Old Mission Peninsula. The West Grand Traverse Bay in the background has a large temperature-moderating influence on the mesoclimate of this vineyard. Photo by T. Zabadal.

However, evaluation and study of the Michigan climate with regard to winter minimum temperatures has shown that even some relatively cold-tender grape varieties can survive and be productive in certain areas of Michigan. The logic here is simple—the cold-tender grape varieties need to be grown only where the climate allows, and this is determined by geographic factors. The key factor in this equation is the climate-moderating effects of large bodies of water, especially on their lee side. This factor is referred to as lake effect (Chapters 19, 38). Amazingly, lake effect even allows for the commercial production of some very cold-tender, premium grape varieties, such as Merlot, in Michigan; Merlot is not even recommended for planting in warmer states like Virginia (Wolf and Poling 1995). The climatic impact on the distribution of grape production in Michigan cannot be overestimated, as it largely determines where (on a large scale) most varieties of grapes can be grown successfully (Fig. 39.3). On a smaller scale, topography is also a major controlling factor (Fig. 39.5). Chapter 38 discusses the intricacies of lake effect climate in Michigan, and its impact on *fruit* production; much of this discussion is applicable to *grape* production as well.

FIGURE 39.6 Overhead irrigation can be used to protect emerged grapevine shoots from sub-freezing temperatures. This Concord vineyard at the MSU Southwest Michigan Research and Extension Center, in Benton Harbor, produced a full crop. Photo by T. Zabadal.

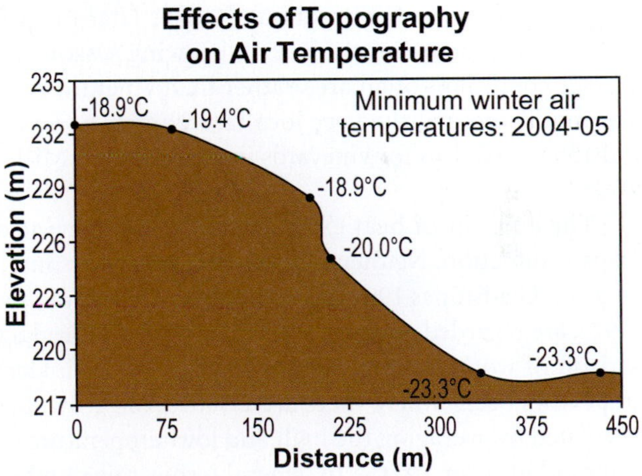

A second important climatic factor for grape production in Michigan is the length of the frost-free (growing) season (Fig. 38.4). As grapevines break bud in the spring, they lose their cold hardiness, such that temperatures even slightly below freezing (0° C) can cause extensive vine injury and crop failure (Proebsting et al. 1991; Fig. 39.6). Therefore, grapevines are often planted on hilly, sloping ground so that cold, heavy, dense air can flow downslope and away from the vineyard, reducing the risk of vine freeze injury (Figs. 39.5, 39.7). Risk of late spring frosts is greatest on cool, clear, calm nights, when the ability of denser, cooler air to flow downhill, i.e., uninhibited by wind, is at its maximum (Chapter 38). Sloping, rolling topography is common in the principal grape producing areas of Michigan (Figs. 39.5, 39.8). This same phenomenon is also important at the end of the growing season, when growers are often striving for fruit maturity. A freeze that destroys the functional leaf area on a vine brings an abrupt end to fruit maturation, because grapes are non-climacteric fruit, i.e., they will not continue to ripen on a vine without functional leaves, or when removed from the vine. Therefore, sloping topography, referred to by growers as "good sites," helps to delay fall freeze events for vines planted on the upper parts of those slopes, and is very important for the production of quality grapes.

Effects of Topography on Air Temperature

Minimum winter air temperatures: 2004–05

-18.9°C
-19.4°C
-18.9°C
-20.0°C
-23.3°C
-23.3°C

FIGURE 39.7 This diagram indicates the minimum winter air temperatures experienced on a hillside in southwestern Michigan, illustrating the importance of topography in determining the suitability of a site for a vineyard. These temperature differences occurred over a horizontal distance of 0.4 km and a difference in elevation of 14 meters. Source: unpublished data from T. Zabadal.

Although some viticulturists point to the need for a growing season of 210 days or more (Gladstones 1992), a minimum growing season length of about 165 days is usually adequate for many varieties of grapes in Michigan (Jordan et al. 1981). For late-ripening grape varieties, a growing season of about 180 days or more is necessary. In

FIGURE 39.8   This image of Terrace Hill Vineyards, in Berrien County, illustrates the point that vineyards on good sites are characterized by sloping ground, which reduces risks of low temperature injury in the fall, winter and spring. Photo by T. Zabadal.

southern Michigan, the frost-free period runs from about mid-April to early October. In the Traverse City area, the growing season begins about 10 days later in spring and ends about a week earlier in the fall. Generalized mapping of macroclimate data for growing season length, e.g., Figure 38.4, is misleading, because it reflects the average conditions of an area rather than vineyard sites on sloping land, which have longer-than-average growing seasons. Therefore, the very localized climate of a vineyard, i.e., its *mesoclimate*, will typically range 165 to 180 and 155 to 165 days for vineyards in southwestern Michigan, and those on the peninsulas near Traverse City, respectively.

The amount of heat experienced by a grapevine during the growing season is a third important factor for grape production. Neither long, cool growing seasons, nor very hot climates, are optimal for premium grape production (Gladstones 1992). Climates with warm but moderate temperatures, especially during ripening (Gladstones 1992), are regarded as optimal for quality grape production, and Michigan is blessed with such conditions. A comparison of worldwide grape growing regions (Winkler et al. 1974) indicates that the best climatic conditions for grapevines occur where there are 2,500–3,500 growing degree days (base 50° F) annually. A growing-degree-day is calculated by averaging the high and low temperature of the day and then subtracting from a base value (which for grapes is 50° F, or 10° C). In general terms, this number represents a physiologically important temperature range for growers. Growing-degree-day totals of 2,500–3,500 exist in several mesoclimate sites in the state. Somewhat cooler growing seasons may still be useful for grape production, however, as they can provide optimal conditions for a more narrowed list of premium grape varieties, as in the northern viticultural areas of Michigan.

Soil characteristics are also important to grape production. Because grapevines are not tolerant of water-logged soils, good internal drainage, as exemplified by natural soil drainage class data (Fig. 20.9) is the single most important soil characteristic for vineyards. Most Michigan vineyard soils are situated on well to excessively drained soils, containing at least 70% sand. Most of the sloping, higher-relief landscapes in the two main grape growing areas have rolling, sandy loam to loam soils that meet these criteria, having developed from sandy glacial drift of the Lake Michigan lobe of the last glacier (Chapter 17; Fig. 20.1).

Because of these site requirements for premium wine grape production, only a very small portion of the Michigan land mass is actually ideal for grape production (Fig. 39.3). In summary, the ideal site for grape production in Michigan would have well-drained soils, with a growing season of at least 180 days, and it would accumulate >3,000 growing degree days during that time. Within such mesoclimatic areas, sites on sloping land are also preferred.

The geography of grape production in Michigan

Michigan ranks 4th, nationally, in total grape acreage (Michigan Department of Agriculture 2003–2004). Michigan's vineyard acreage reached an all-time high of 17,800 ha (44,000 acres) in 1929, and then declined, due to reduced demand. Wine grape acreage has, however, grown steadily in recent decades (Table 39.1). By 1989, there were about 200 ha (494 acres) of wine grapes, with two-thirds of that being hybrids and one-third European varieties. Since 1990, wine grape acreage has tripled, to about 600 hectares. Today, Michigan vineyards cover about 5,800 hectares—more than the vineyard acreage of all other Midwestern states combined (Michigan Department of Agriculture 2003–2004).

Many sites in the state have ideal site conditions for grape production, but are farmed for other purposes, or are forested or otherwise developed. For example, Michigan has hundreds of hectares of peaches, which have similar site requirements to premium wine grapes. Therefore, it is easily conceivable that Michigan's current grape acreage could triple, if the economy demanded, and yet still only occupy <0.1% of Michigan's total land mass.

Michigan grape production is geographically concentrated in two areas (Fig. 39.3). Approximately 90% of the state's total vineyard acreage, i.e., about 5,250 hectares (12,970 acres), is in Berrien (Fig. 39.9), Van Buren, Cass and Kalamazoo Counties, and 5% of the state's total vineyards, i.e., about 300 hectares (741 acres), is in Leelanau and Grand Traverse Counties. Climatic data from other areas of the state, such as southeastern Michigan, indicate that acceptable to good conditions for commercial grape production exist there as well (Zabadal 1997). According to the USDA Census of Agriculture (2005), grape production for saleable products occurred in 50 out of the 83 counties in Michigan,

TABLE 39.1   Amounts of newly-planted wine grapes in Michigan for hybrids and Vitis vinifera, for various time periods

Time period	Hybrids (hectares)	Vitis vinifera (hectares)	Totals (hectares)
1972 or earlier	35	0	35
1973–1977	42	11	54
1978–1982	37	13	50
1983–1987	9	15	23
1988–1992	34	69	103
1993–1997	15	101	116
1998–2002	33	95	128
2003–2006	36	142	178
Totals	243	445	688

Source: Various USDA-NASS reports.

FIGURE 39.9   Aerial view of a large area of grape production in southern Berrien County. The contiguous vineyard blocks shown here are all involved in juice grape production. Photo by T. Zabadal.

in 2002. In addition to the six counties previously mentioned, two or more hectares of commercial vineyards were reported for Allegan, Antrim, Bay, Cheboygan, Ingham, Jackson, Monroe and Washtenaw Counties (Fig. 39.3). Some of these locations combine somewhat favorable geography for grape production, along with intensive vine management, to combat geographical limitations to grape production. "Viticultural exploration" is presently underway by pioneering individuals in many areas of both the Lower and Upper Peninsulas, and as far north as Chippewa County near Sault Ste. Marie!

■ Uses of grapes in Michigan

Contemporary Michigan grape production involves two distinct processing industries: juice and wine. Grape production for juice and related products is restricted to southwestern Michigan, and dominates Michigan viticulture with 5,250 hectares, or 90% of the state's total vineyard acreage. The juice grape industry utilizes two varieties, Concord (3,857 hectares in 2003) and Niagara (1,396 hectares in 2003).

Approximately 60% of Michigan's 600 hectares (1,482 acres) of wine grapes are planted to the European varieties, with the dominant varieties being Riesling (87 hectares), Chardonnay (77), Pinot noir (42), Pinot gris, Cabernet franc (Fig. 39.10) and Merlot. Hybrid varieties are planted on the remaining 40% of the wine grape acreage, with dominant varieties being Vidal blanc (42 hectares), Vignoles (38), Seyval blanc (32), Marechal Foch, De Chaunac and Chambourcin. There are about 300 hectares of wine grapes in the Traverse City area and 253 hectares of wine grapes in southwestern Michigan, with the remainder being dispersed across the state.

■ The culture and marketing of Michigan grapes

Michigan's juice and wine grape industries are distinctly different. Juice grape production has become increasingly concentrated on fewer and larger farms, with the largest operations exceeding 200 hectares (Fig. 39.9). A large percentage of juice grape acreage is situated on relatively flat ground, making it vulnerable to spring freeze episodes. Typically, wine grape vineyards are much smaller, in part because they are often nestled onto rolling hillsides, i.e., the "best sites" (Fig. 39.5).

FIGURE 39.10 These Cabernet franc grapevines, near Baroda, were part of the first commercial harvest of this variety in southwestern Michigan, in 1995. Photo by T. Zabadal.

The Concord and Niagara varieties typically begin to break bud about mid-April; wine grape varieties generally break bud somewhat later. In 2006, for example, about 75% of the juice grape crop in southwestern Michigan was lost to a spring freeze on April 26th. However, only 10–15% of the wine grape crop was lost, due to a combination of the superior sites with sloping ground on which these grapes are grown, and their somewhat later bud emergence. Historically, juice grape production in Michigan has suffered significant losses to spring freezes—about one out of every three years.

Juice grapes were picked manually until 1969, when the first mechanical harvest of grapes occurred (Fig. 39.11). Today, it is rare to find juice grapes picked manually. Fifteen years ago, no Michigan vineyards were pruned mechanically, but today 35–40% of the Michigan juice grape acreage is pruned in this manner. These changes resulted not only from a dwindling supply of labor, but also because of economic pressures and technological innovations. The production of wine grapes requires considerably more manual labor per hectare, for tasks like canopy management, crop adjustment and suckering, than does juice grape production (White 2005). Although much of the wine grape production in Michigan is currently mechanically harvested, almost half is still harvested by hand. Initial efforts on mechanical pruning of wine grapes began in 2006.

Record yields of Concord grapes in 2005 resulted in state average yields of more than 15 tonnes/hectare (7 tons/acre), with some yields exceeding 31 tonnes/hectare (14 tons/acre). Long term, average yields are about 11 tonnes/hectare (5 tons/acre). Yields on wine grapes are typically purposely limited to 4.5 to 9.0 tonnes/hectare (2–4 tons/acre) for the *Vitis vinifera* varieties, and 9.0–13.4 tonnes/hectare (4–6 tons/acre) for the hybrid varieties, to promote high quality fruit and wines.

Juice grape varieties are moderately susceptible to diseases, and typically require four to six pesticide sprayings per growing season. Vines that produce wine grapes are more challenging to manage than those for juice grapes, due to their increased susceptibility to both diseases and low winter temperatures. Wine grapes require 7–12 pesticide sprays per growing season, and even then, diseases like Botrytis bunch rot may be imperfectly controlled (Michigan Fruit Management Guide 2005).

Wine grape harvest dates range from about mid-September to the very end of October in southwestern Michigan, with about a two week delay in the Traverse City area. The Niagara variety is an early season variety by the standards of wine grape maturity; it ripens from early- to mid-September. The Concord variety ripens from late September to mid-October.

Michigan produces about 10% of the nation's production of Concord grapes (USDA 2004, 2006) and the pricing of this crop is heavily influenced by national and international supplies and demands for not only Concord and

FIGURE 39.11
Mechanized harvest of Concord grapes at the Grabemeyer Farm, near Sister Lakes. Photo by T. Zabadal.

Niagara, but also for juice produced from other grape varieties. In the best of times, Michigan juice grape prices have approached $300 per ton, but market pressures in 2005 reduced that price to about $160 per ton for most of the Michigan Concord grape tonnage. Pricing of wine grapes tends to be influenced more by local market conditions rather than regional or national supplies of grapes and wine. Prices for wine grapes range greatly, from about $400 to $1700 per ton, depending upon the type of grape and its local supply.

In Michigan, most areas receive about seven cm of precipitation per month, during the growing season. For this reason, irrigation of newly planted vineyards is often helpful, especially those on sandier sites, but the economic benefit of irrigating mature vineyards in Michigan is questionable. Even without irrigation, per-hectare vineyard establishment costs (wine grapes) can exceed $25,000 (White 2005). Annual production costs for wine grapes greatly exceed the approximate $2,500 per hectare needed to manage an acre of juice grapes.

The economics of the juice grape industry has been uncertain for many years. Were there to be a downsizing of that industry, no more than one-third of the Michigan juice grape acreage would be suitable for conversion to wine grapes. The Michigan wine grape industry, however, is likely to grow significantly in the years ahead, not only because of favorable climate and soils, but also because of the enormous opportunity for direct marketing of wines through tourism. Consumers of Michigan wines have an awareness of the price of other products, but that does not dominate their mindset when they buy wines. Many consumers highly value the opportunity and experience of purchasing premium wines directly from Michigan wineries. Currently the Michigan wine grape industry produces about 350,000 cases of wine per year, with a large percentage of that wine sold directly to consumers through tasting rooms at wineries and satellite locations. The future of Michigan wines is, indeed, bright.

Literature Cited

Gladstones, J. 1992. Viticulture and Environment. Winetitles, Adelaide, South Australia.

Jordan, T.D., Pool, R.M., Zabadal, T.J. and J.P. Tomkins. 1981. Cultural practices for commercial vineyards. Cornell University Miscellaneous Bulletin III, Ithaca, NY.

Michigan Fruit Management Guide. 2005. Michigan State University Extension Buletin E-154. East Lansing.

Michigan State Pomological Society. 1872. First Report. W.S. George and Company, State Printers and Binders, Lansing, MI.

Michigan Department of Agriculture. 2003–2004. Michigan Rotational Survey, Fruit Inventory. Michigan Agricultural Statistics, East Lansing, MI.

Proebsting, E.L., Ahmedullah, M. and V.P. Brummund. 1980. Seasonal changes in low temperature resistance of grape buds. American Journal of Enology Viticulture 31:329–336.

Proebsting, E.L., Brummund, V.P. and N.J. Clune. 1991. Critical temperatures for Concord grapes. Washington State University Extension Bulletin 1615. Pullman, WA.

United States Department of Agriculture. 2004. Noncitrus Fruits and Nuts. 2003 Summary. National Agricultural Statistics Service, Washington, DC.

United States Department of Agriculture (USDA). 2005. 2002 Census of Agriculture. Agricultural Atlas of the United States. National Agricultural Statistics Service, Washington, DC.

United States Department of Agriculture. 2006. Noncitrus Fruits and Nuts. 2005 Summary. National Agricultural Statistics Service, Washington, DC.

White, G.B. 2005. Cost of establishment and production of vinifera grapes in the Finger Lakes Region of New York—2004. Cornell University Cooperative Extension Bulletin EB 2005–06. Ithaca, NY.

Winkler, A.J., Cook, J.A., Kliewer, W.M. and L.A. Lider. 1974. General Viticulture. University of California Press, Berkeley, CA.

Wolf, T.K. and E.B. Poling. 1995. The Mid-Atlantic winegrape grower's guide. North Carolina State University, Cooperative Extension Service, Raleigh, NC.

Zabadal, T.J. 1997. Vineyard Establishment II, Planting and Early Care of Vineyards. Michigan State University Extension Bulletin E-2645. East Lansing.

Further Readings

Adams, L.D. 1978. The Wines of America. McGraw-Hill, New York.

Dami, I., Bordelon, B., Ferree, D.C., Brown, M., Ellis, M.A., Williams, R.N. and D. Doohan. 2005. Midwest Grape Production Guide. Ohio State University Extension Bulletin 919.

Hellman, E.W. (ed). 2003. Oregon Viticulture. Oregon State University Press, Corvallis.

Howell, G.S., Miller, D.P. and T.J. Zabadal. 1998. Wine grape varieties for Michigan. Michigan State University Extension Bulletin E-2643. East Lansing.

Isaacs, R., Schilder, A., Zabadal, T. and T. Weigle (eds). 2003. A pocket guide for grape IPM scouting in the north central and eastern U.S. Michigan State University Extension Bulletin E-2889. East Lansing.

Plocher, T. and B. Parke. 2001. Northern winework: growing grapes and making wine in cold climates. Northern Wine Work Incorporated, Stillwater, MN.

Zabadal, T.J., Howell, G.S. and D.P. Miller. 1997. Table grape varieties for Michigan. Michigan State University Extension Bulletin E-2642. East Lansing.

Zabadal, T.J. 1999. Pest control in small vineyards. Michigan State University Extension Bulletin E-2698. East Lansing.

Zabadal, T.J. 2002. Growing table grapes in a temperate climate. Michigan State UniversityExtension Bulletin E-2774. East Lansing.

Zabadal, T.J., Dami, I.E., Goffinet, M.C., Martinson, T.M. and M.L. Chien. 2007. Winter injury to grapevines and methods of protection. Michigan State University Extension Bulletin E-2930. East Lansing.

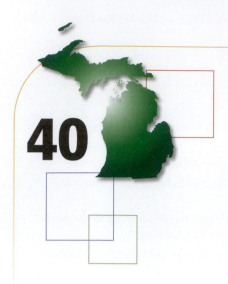

40

Forests and Forestry from an Historical Perspective

Donald I. Dickmann

■ Introduction

Forests are a defining feature of Michigan's geography. They are a renowned source of natural wealth and beauty, as well as an important engine of the state's economy. Traveling north through the Lower Peninsula and west across the Upper Peninsula, the landscape becomes increasingly forested (Fig. 40.1; Chapter 21). The most pronounced change occurs in the middle of the Lower Peninsula, where the southern, rural mosaic of fields and small forest patches rather abruptly changes to a landscape dominated by forests (Plates 13, 15). From that point northward and (when across the Straits of Mackinac) westward, the scene is dominated by trees. Chapters 21 and 29 discuss some of the reasons for this vegetative and land cover change. Not only are forests pervasive in the state, but they are wonderfully diverse. In fact, Michigan contains a greater diversity of forest vegetation types than any other state in the Midwest (Faber-Langendoen 2001).

Given the current forest richness, it is difficult to envision that Michigan once was a frigid, barren wasteland, devoid of trees or life of any kind, but it was (Chapter 7). At other times since then, vast tracts of the state that once were heavily forested were reduced to charred, unproductive stump land (see FOCUS BOX on page 623). In short, the forest history of Michigan is characterized by a recurring cycle of destruction and recovery—the theme of this chapter. The agents of both destruction and recovery have been natural and human, with humans playing a far greater role in recent times. To fully comprehend the forests of today, then, we must look back in time, to understand how they recovered from the periods of destruction.

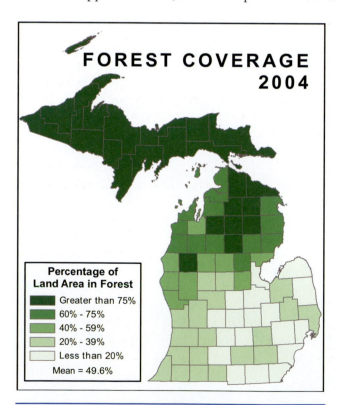

FIGURE 40.1 Percentage of land area in Michigan occupied by forests, by county, in 2004. Source: USDA Forest Service, Forest Inventory and Analysis, http://www.fia.fs.fed.us/ (last accessed March, 2008).

FIGURE 40.2 About 12,000 years ago, the spruce forests and bogs in southern Michigan would have looked something like this; however, the mastodons are missing. Photo by D. Dickmann

Origins of Michigan's forests

The ice sheets that covered Michigan during the Pleistocene Epoch (Chapters 6, 17) were both the destroyers and creators of forests. Whatever forests existed before or during lulls in the Ice Age were fully obliterated by the ice sheets. As the glaciers slowly ground their way across the landscape, everything beneath it, except the largest rocks and boulders, was pulverized. Yet, this incessant grinding formed the substrate on which the forests that we know today evolved (Chapter 20). When the last glacier finally began its slow retreat, about 18,000 years ago, it left behind moraines, till plains, drumlins, kames, eskers, outwash plains and lacustrine plains (Chapter 17), which were the parent materials for the soils that were to develop on them. From the standpoint of plant growth, these glacial sediments were a veritable diamond in the rough. But just as a diamond requires polishing to unlock its luster, so this raw substrate needed to be reworked and to evolve into the soils we see today.

The action of plants and animals, sun and rain, freezing and thawing, as well as subsequent transport by wind and water, soon transformed the glacial sediments into a medium hospitable to tree growth—soil (Chapter 20; Plate 12). As the glacier retreated northward, the moderating temperatures also allowed trees and other plants to colonize the post-glacial landscape (Chapter 7). The spruce, birch and tamarack migrants that formed Michigan's first Holocene forest 12,000 years ago (Davis 1981; Fig. 40.2) were the progenitors of the forests of today. As the soils continued to develop, under the increasing influence of early plant and animal colonizers, the remnant glacial landforms began to become habitats that could support the growing diversity of trees that were migrating into the state from refugia in the south (Fig. 7.5). Thus, over the course of millennia, the bareness became bountiful, and by about 4,000 years ago, the forests of Michigan began to roughly resemble those we see today (Kapp 1999; Chapter 7).

Forests at the time of Euro-American settlement

Paleo-Indian habitation of post-glacial Michigan began about 12,000 years ago, and native cultures prospered from that time onward (Shott and Wright 1999; Chapter 25). Native peoples had an intimate relationship with the land; virtually every plant and animal had a use or purpose. For them, trees like paper birch (canoes, shelter, containers, wrapping), white cedar (wood, medicine), sugar maple (maple syrup and sugar) and black ash (baskets and mats) were especially important (Densmore 1979). Although these pre-Columbian peoples developed an advanced civilization and enjoyed a standard of living that surpassed many contemporary Europeans (Mann 2005), there exist no quantitative data or descriptions of the forests they occupied, because these people had no written language.

That changed, however, when French and English settlement began early in the 17th century (Chapter 27). The Europeans were inveterate note takers and record keepers, and, although furs were their preoccupation, they also took notes on the forests proper. Regardless, it wasn't until the early 19th century that hard data on the forests of Michigan began to be recorded. The agents of record were the General Land Office (GLO) surveyors (Chapter 28). In addition to running township boundaries and section lines, GLO surveyors made notes about the land they traversed—the amount and condition of valuable timber, boundaries of burned and windfall areas, mineral deposits and navigable waterways. At every one-mile section corner, the species, diameter, distance and compass bearing of two to four "witness trees" were recorded; similar information was recorded for two witness trees at each quarter corner. The species, diameter and distance from a section corner of any trees that a section line intersected also were noted. This unparalleled record of early forest conditions is available in digital format, on microfiche, or in the original notebooks at the State Archives of Michigan, Lansing. Although this tree record must be interpreted correctly, it has nonetheless given us a unique picture of the forests of Michigan during the time when the GLO survey was being conducted, roughly from 1815 to 1860. In 1998, maps of the vegetation of the Lower and Upper Peninsulas of Michigan ca. 1800 were published, based largely on the GLO record (Comer and Albert 1998; Plate 15). These fascinating maps are a major historical accomplishment, documenting the state of Michigan's forests at a moment in the past. The maps are available in large format from the Michigan Natural Features Inventory, Lansing (http://web4.msue.msu.edu/mnfi/).

Because Michigan's virgin white pine forests were so impressive and would become the focus of logging late in the 19th century, they have taken on an aura of legend and myth (Reimann 1981). Some people have the impression that Michigan, particularly its northern reaches, was a sea of endless white pine. Indeed, many early loggers and land barons were certain that this vast resource was inexhaustible (Dempsey 2001). There certainly were large areas of virgin forest, that were dominated by big pines—both white and red—located in a diagonal, SW-NE swath across the northern Lower Peninsula, and in areas of sandy soil in the Upper Peninsula. But that is far from the full story; Michigan's 19th century forests were much more diverse than is commonly assumed (Chapter 21, Plate 15). Actually more land area *today* is classed as white pine-dominated than at ca. 1800 (Fig. 40.3), although the trees of today are much smaller, and more likely to occur in mixed stands. In those times, as now, hardwood (broadleaf)-dominated forests actually were pervasive across much of the state, and were the only kind of forests in much of the southern Lower Peninsula (Plate 15). White pine, however, was nonetheless present in many of these hardwood forests—sometimes in large amounts and in nearly pure groves. White pine also was mixed in with other conifers, including hemlock (Fig. 40.3). Vast areas, especially in the eastern Upper Peninsula, were conifer swamps, with spruce, cedar and tamarack the principal species, although white pine was also there (Chapter 21). In addition, about 2% of the state was prairie and 6% was open pine or oak savannas (barrens), with scattered or clumped trees. Altogether, this early forest was vast, magnificent and more diverse than is typically assumed. But, beginning in the mid-1800s, it met head on the exploitive mentality of the times, and its demise became a foregone conclusion.

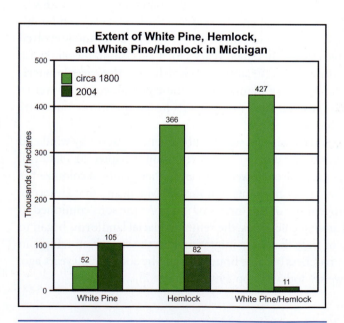

FIGURE 40.3   Area of white pine, hemlock and white pine/hemlock forest types, ca. 1800 and in 2004. Data from the Michigan Natural Features Inventory (1800) and the USDA Forest Service, Forest Inventory and Analysis (2004).

The era of plunder

Michigan became the 26th state in 1837; this event, and the opening of the Erie Canal in 1825, were the catalysts for a huge influx of settlers, looking for jobs, resources and land (Chapter 27). The mindset of these immigrants may seem at odds with our 21st century sensibilities, regarding land and forests, but it was very real to them. The forests that blanketed the new state were viewed as an obstacle to settlement, and therefore hindered the "civilizing" of the land; forests cannot be farmed and stood in the way of the development of roads and towns. But the forests also were an incredible economic resource, a veritable "green gold." Fortunes were there for the taking, if the prime timber was logged. Thus, for the people of that time, there was only one option: clear the forests and do it quickly. That option was exercised with a vengeance (Dempsey 2001).

The federal government owned most of the state and encouraged the "civilizing" of the new Michigan in several ways. Huge land grants were given to railroad, canal and road builders, to encourage them to extend their rights-of-ways into the wilderness. Individuals or companies could purchase land from government land offices for a mere $1.25 per acre—cheap even then. The Homestead Act of 1862 provided that anyone could obtain 160 acres (65 hectares) of land by paying a small fee, building a house with at least two windows, and staying on the land for at least five years. Civil War veterans were given benefit warrants that could be exchanged for land.

These programs led to a rush of land purchases and land speculation. But when large volumes of prime timber (Fig. 40.4) were located by surveyors—in those days, called "landlookers"—another practice became common; the timber was stolen. Thieves, many of them wealthy lumber barons, were rarely apprehended, seldom prosecuted, and generally accepted as part of the civilizing process. One of the most notorious of their schemes was the "round forty." An isolated 40-acre tract of land was purchased and all the timber on that tract was harvested. Then, all the timber surrounding it also was cut (Wells 1978). Finally, the whole cutover mess was abandoned, while the now worthless land reverted to state ownership via tax delinquency. Indeed, one of the best ways to determine when land during this era was logged is to examine tax records, which show the assessed value of the land plummeting immediately after the first wave of logging (Barrett 1998).

FIGURE 40.4 Michigan's virgin white pine timber was of exceptional quality. To 19th century lumber barons, it represented "green gold." Source: State Archives of Michigan.

FIGURE 40.5 During the 19th and early 20th century plunder of Michigan's virgin forest, rivers were major arteries of transport of pine logs from the woods to sawmills, via the major rivers of the state. Source: Maybee (1988), courtesy of the State Archives of Michigan.

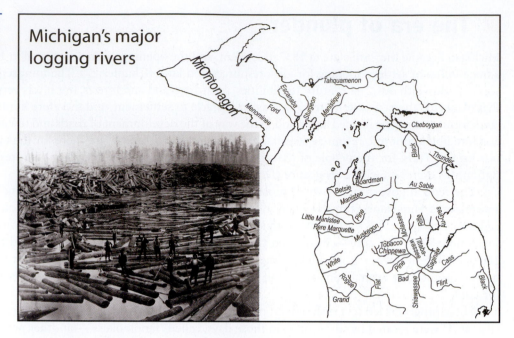

FIGURE 40.6 The introduction of bigwheels, in 1875, changed the yearly schedule of logging by allowing logs to be skidded out of the woods during the snow-free seasons. Source: State Archives of Michigan.

The great plunder roared into full gear in the greater Saginaw River valley (Fig. 40.5) in the 1850s, with the city of Saginaw and its many sawmills as its hub. Slightly later, Muskegon—like Saginaw, at the mouth of a major river system—became the epicenter of lumber production on the west side of the state. Early logging was confined to the winter months, and to areas within reach of rivers or streams, because logs could only be efficiently dragged out of the woods over snow and transported to sawmills by water. Many Michigan rivers—and the sawmill towns on their banks—became famous.

Later, two technical innovations, in the 1870s, triggered a dramatic increase in the scale of logging. In 1875, Silas Overpack of Manistee introduced "bigwheels," large, two-wheeled contraptions that enabled the front end of logs to be lifted off the ground, so they could be moved by horses or oxen (Fig. 40.6). Overpack's invention extended

FIGURE 40.7 Beginning in 1877, railroads opened up Michigan's interior forests to logging and settlement, but their locomotives set many wildfires. Source: State Archives of Michigan.

FIGURE 40.8 Shanty boys did the difficult, dangerous job of logging Michigan's virgin timber. Their camps were crude by today's standards, but met their basic needs. Source: State Archives of Michigan.

logging into the snow-free seasons, greatly increasing production. In 1877, narrow-gauge railroads began to push logging into the uplands, far away from major rivers (Fig. 40.7). Previously inaccessible tracts of timber then began to fall under the bite of the saw.

Logging was done by "shanty boys"—nicknamed after the crude lumber camp buildings where they lived (Fig. 40.8)—using double bit axes and cross-cut saws. Their work was difficult and dangerous, and earned them about a dollar a day. On the whole, shanty boys were a rough and tumble lot, renowned for their hard work as well as their carousing, drinking and fighting on days off in town (Holbrook 1956, Wells 1978). They also left behind a rich lode of folklore in songs and stories (Maybee 1988).

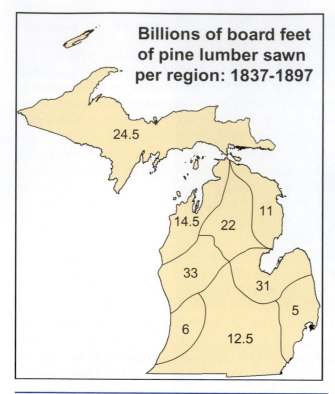

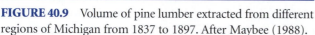

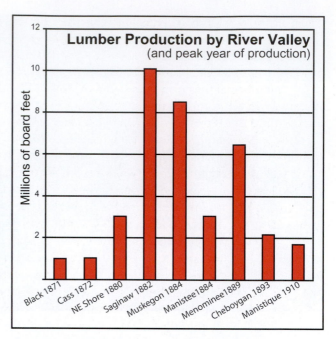

FIGURE 40.10   Volume of lumber sawn in Michigan's major river valleys, and their peak years of production. After Sommers (1977).

FIGURE 40.9   Volume of pine lumber extracted from different regions of Michigan from 1837 to 1897. After Maybee (1988).

Michigan's pine and hardwood lumber was shipped by schooners, steamers, barges and rail all over the country; it was renowned for its high quality. In the far northern Lower Peninsula and eastern Upper Peninsula, where limestone bedrock predominates (Plate 6), much hardwood also was cut, to make charcoal to fuel local iron smelters (Chapters 11, 30). The final tally of lumber produced by Michigan forests is staggering: 161 billion board feet of pine, plus 50 billion board feet of cedar, hemlock and hardwoods (Maybee 1988). If all the lumber from this era were stacked into a pile roughly 2 m wide by 2 m tall, it would circle the Earth 3¾ times! Indeed, Michigan led the nation in lumber production for 31 consecutive years: 1869–1899. Most of the pine had come from the northern Lower Peninsula (Fig. 40.9).

The lumbering boom did not last forever, even though many thought the timber was inexhaustible (Dempsey 2001). By the last decade of the 19th century, most of the prime pine timber in the Lower Peninsula had been cut (Fig. 40.10). The boom would continue, nonetheless, for a few more decades in the Upper Peninsula. But by 1920, however, it was all but over.

In the end, Michigan had been settled, but the environmental and long-term economic costs were staggering. Little was left of the magnificent Michigan forests, to fuel continued economic growth or for the succeeding generations to enjoy. But the plunder was only one element of catastrophe; what followed the logging was even worse.

■ The fiery aftermath

What remained after the logging was *slash*—a tangle of tree tops, branches, brush and unusable tree trunks. Not only was it unsightly, but, because it was highly combustible, it was also dangerous. And there were lots of ways to set it ablaze. Settlers purposely set slash on fire to clear the land for farming. Wood-burning locomotives, belching sparks and embers, also set many accidental fires (Fig. 40.7). People in those days, in general, were careless with fire. The results were fires, smoldering or blazing all over the landscape, and when weather conditions were right—drought, combined with low humidity, high temperature and strong winds—the fires would coalesce into a firestorm.

Thus, during and for many years following the plunder, Michigan experienced a series of horrendous wildfires, the likes of which no other state has ever experienced (Sodders 1997).

Michigan's fiery holocaust began on a dry day in October, 1871. The days that followed were the worst period of wildfire in American history. On October 7, Chicago burned—a fire that made national headlines. On that same day, a monumental firestorm roared into the town of Peshtigo, in northern Wisconsin, and leveled it. The infamous Peshtigo Fire, which also burned into Menominee County in northern Michigan, caused the greatest loss of life (1,300–1,500 dead) of any wildfire in US history (Holbrook 1944). Meanwhile several huge fires—in total consuming over one million hectares—burned in the Lower Peninsula, including the Thumb. Thousands were killed during those dreadful October days; many more were horribly maimed. The loss of property and animals was staggering. Like Peshtigo, many Michigan towns were wholly or partially obliterated. The stories told by survivors were hair-raising. They all described the eerie, stifling silence and darkness that preceded the fires, then the deafening roar as the flames swept in. Iron kettles melted in seconds. Hogs, turned loose to escape the fires, burned and melted into grease spots. Buildings suddenly exploded into flame. Tornado-like winds ripped trees out by their roots. People and animals caught by the flames had few ways to escape; only the very lucky survived.

People usually change their ways after catastrophes, and governments enact stringent laws to prevent a reoccurrence. Strangely, this did not happen. So, almost exactly 10 years later, another horrendous conflagration visited Michigan, this time in the Thumb. Preceded by a hot, dry summer, fires burning over the landscape came together in a wall of fire on September 4, 1881, and, driven by strong winds, roared to the NE. The infamous "Thumb Fire" (see FOCUS BOX on the following page), which lasted two days, was of unparalleled ferocity—extinguished only when it reached the shore of Lake Huron. Numerous towns were consumed, 282 people died, and over 400,000 hectares blackened. Two aspects of this fire's aftermath are particularly noteworthy. First, the American Red Cross, founded by Clara Barton and associates in Washington, DC, in May of 1881, contributed to the relief effort; this was the first disaster worked by this organization. In fact, were it not for the Thumb Fire, Barton's organization might have gone out of business. Second, Sergeant William O. Bailey of the US Signal Service, in Port Huron, accurately surveyed the burned area and produced a detailed report. The map of the extent of the fire in his report was the first of its kind (Bailey 1882; Fig. 40.11).

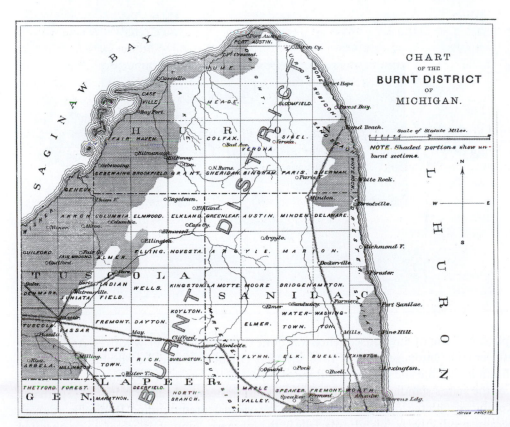

FIGURE 40.11 Sergeant William O. Bailey's (1882) map of the extent of the 1881 Thumb Fire.

FOCUS BOX: The Thumb fire of 1881—national news

The deadly conflagration that scorched Michigan's "Thumb" in 1871 received little attention in the national press, because it occurred concurrently with the horrendous Chicago and Peshtigo fires. The infamous Thumb Fire of 1881 was a different story; there was no competition. Sensationalist articles appeared in national newspapers, and in several issues the two most popular news magazines of the day—Harper's Weekly and Frank Leslie's Newspaper. Detailed lithographic drawings in these magazines depicted the destruction and mayhem produced by the fire (see figure below). Sodders (1997, 86) described the fire this way, "In some places it seems as though the scenes of Sodom and Gomorra were reenacted, and that the heavens rained fire. Survivors from the burned districts describe the scene as bordering on the supernatural. The fire did not move from building to building in the usual way, but while people were speculating as to the cause of the intense darkness, they were suddenly overwhelmed by a billow of fire that rushed upon them out of the darkness, and enveloped whole towns in the twinkling of an eye." Other survivors described the fire's ominous roar, the hurricane force winds and flames sweeping over stubble fields faster than a horse could run. The heat was intense; seven miles out in Lake Huron sailors could not bear to face it. Many of the victims disappeared amongst the ashes. Others died from asphyxiation or smoke inhalation, their bodies untouched by the flames. The toll exacted by this fire on many families can be felt by visiting the Hillside Cemetery near Argyle, in Sanilac County. There, shaded by a large black cherry tree planted by the man who buried them, lie the graves of a family wiped out by the fire. Mother, father, children, grandmother and niece, all perished when flames overran the Erhart farm. A memorial marker on the graves reads, "In memory of pioneer settlers, victims of the forest fire of September 5, 1881.

Emma Palmer, age 52   Neil Erhart, age 30
Mary Ann Erhart, age 24   Clare Howard, age 8
William Erhart, age 2   Clare Erhart, age 9 days"

The geography of today's Thumb provides little evidence of its fiery past. Forests mostly have been replaced by a mosaic of agricultural fields and small towns. Only a few memorials recall the disaster that in 1881 made headlines across the country.

The aftermath of the infamous Thumb Fire—the second to visit this part of Michigan in the space of 10 years—is vividly portrayed in this full-page illustration from the October 1, 1881 issue of Harper's Weekly.

Despite these catastrophes, nothing of any consequence was done to prevent further wildfires. And so they continued. Among the worst were the Ontonagon Fire of 1896, the Metz Fire of 1908 and the Ausable-Oscoda Fire of 1911, each causing significant loss of life and property. But the forests took the brunt of the damage. By the year 1926, 73 billion board feet of the state's standing timber had been laid to waste, nearly all of it by fire (Sparhawk and Brush 1929). That toll, combined with the logging, left only 7% of the original forest standing. Ironically, although some of the cleared forest became productive farmland, especially in the southern counties, much of it was unsuited

FOCUS BOX: Michigan's stump prairies—recovery short-circuited

The forested landscape of northern Michigan today gives little evidence that, a century ago, the region was mostly blackened, cutover stump land. Clearly, many areas have regrown into second- and third-growth forests. But a few tracts, usually those on dry, sandy soils, remain open and prairie like. They are characterized by scattered pine stumps, with a vegetative cover of bracken fern, grasses, lichen, prairie herbs, blueberries, small shrubs and a few trees. Why haven't these areas reforested?

A variety of explanations for the persistence of these "stump prairies" have been proposed: (1) hot logging era fires that "sterilized" the already nutrient-poor, sandy soils, (2) allelopathy (growth-inhibitors released by bracken fern and reindeer moss lichen), (3) frost-prone local climates caused by down-slope drainage of cold air, (4) the droughty nature of the sandy soils and (5) high populations of root-eating white grubs in the soil. While any one of these explanations might work for a particular stump prairie, none provides the smoking gun that works for all of them.

Professor of Geography Linda Barrett has developed a theory, however, that explains the origin of most, if not all, of Michigan's stump prairies (Barrett 1998). She first deduced that neither land ownership nor date of logging affected forest recovery patterns, and nearly all previously logged areas (stumped or recovered) appear to have burned. Barrett next examined the geographic patterns of presettlement vegetation from GLO notes. When the pre-logging upland forest had a large white pine component, stump prairie often remained, but where sugar maple, hemlock, beech, ash and other hardwoods were present among the pines, forest vegetation had re-established itself. She concluded that the stump prairie areas, where white pine existed in nearly pure stands, suffered particularly severe clear-cutting and fire, which destroyed nearly every tree, whereas in areas that today are forested, some seed trees and vegetative sprouts survived this first wave of logging. The contrast in apparent severity of logging practices between the two types of areas provides the answer to the stump prairie dilemma; white pine was so prized for lumber that, where present in pure stands, every tree was cut and the area later burned repeatedly. There simply were no seeds left to repopulate the area, and so the stump land persisted. Today, the only trees in many stump prairies are those whose seeds were brought in by birds—usually cherry.

Stump prairies remind us of what we, as humans, can carelessly do to a landscape. On the positive side, stump prairies are visually attractive and provide excellent blueberry picking. They also are excellent habitat for open-country wildlife, including the sharp-tailed grouse, which has become rare in the state.

The stump prairie of the Kingston Plains, in Alger County, as it existed in 2001. Slowly but surely, trees are encroaching at its edges. Photo by D. Dickman.

FIGURE 40.12 The plunder of Michigan's virgin timber and the wildfires that followed left a land that nobody wanted. Source: State Archives of Michigan.

for agriculture, and eventually abandoned. This vast area—some of it swampy but much of it sandy and too dry to farm—became the land nobody wanted (Titus 1945; Fig. 40.12). Its future was not promising.

■ Forestry is born, and the forests recover

During the early 20th century, vast areas of the state's once magnificent forests were brush land, maintained in that condition by repeated burning and neglect. Foresters knew that forests could not regenerate from the brush unless wildfires were brought under control, and that the best way to do this was to prevent them from starting. As early as 1888—when the first state forestry convention was held in Grand Rapids—efforts were made to educate the public about the dangers of wildfire, and to enact fire prevention legislation and ordinances. But these efforts came to nothing. Michigan's first comprehensive forest fire law was enacted years later—in 1903 (Act 249). It authorized the state to protect lands outside of state forest reserves, made township supervisors, mayors and village presidents ex-officio fire wardens, and authorized the payment of temporary fire wardens. Private timber owners also swung into action—the Northern Forest Protective Association was formed in 1910, in the Upper Peninsula, followed, in 1914, by the Northern Hardwood Manufacturers Association, in the Lower Peninsula. The responsibilities of both organizations were taken over by the state of Michigan, in 1917 (Mitchell and Robson 1950).

Meanwhile, forestry education in the state was beginning. Professors William Beal at Michigan Agricultural College (MAC, now Michigan State University) and Volney Spalding at the University of Michigan (UM) introduced forestry courses in the early 1880s (Fig. 40.13). Full forestry curricula at MAC and UM were offered by 1902 and 1903, respectively, and were among the first of their kind in the nation. A comparable curriculum was initiated in the Upper Peninsula at Michigan College of Mining and Technology (now Michigan Technological University), in 1936. This educational initiative produced a cadre of professionals, that could not only work to bring the fires under control, but begin to implement sustainable forestry practices. The recovery was beginning, and trained people were there to help it along.

FIGURE 40.13 Professors William J. Beal of Michigan Agricultural College and Volney M. Spaulding of the University of Michigan were pioneers in forestry education in the US. Photos courtesy of the Michigan State University Archives and Historical Collections, and the Bentley Historical Library, University of Michigan.

A third significant step towards the recovery of Michigan's forests involved bringing these "wastelands" into public ownership and management. The first state forest reserves were established on tax-reverted land in Roscommon and Crawford Counties, in 1903. Fire control was a major activity on these reserves; the quarter-mile grid of fire breaks established in those early days still is evident today as "two-track" roads. From that beginning, the current, dedicated state forest system—the largest in the country—was built (Botti and Moore 2006). In 1921, the Department of Conservation (now the Department of Natural Resources) was formed, to unite all conservation-related programs into one agency. With this reorganization, the expanding state forest system and its management became firmly established.

On the federal level, abandoned, derelict lands purchased from private individuals and the state formed Michigan's first national forests in 1909—the Michigan and the Marquette National Forests. Since then, these lands have been managed by the US Forest Service. These federal forests have grown and changed names, to become the Manistee and Huron National Forests in the Lower Peninsula, and the Hiawatha and Ottawa National Forests in the Upper Peninsula (Fig. 41.6). Today, Michigan has more land area in national forests than any state east of the Mississippi River.

Other noteworthy events also encouraged the recovery of Michigan's forests. The Forest Fire Experiment Station, near Roscommon, was formed in 1930, as a joint venture by the state and the US Forest Service, to improve fire-fighting techniques. It has become a world-renowned center for development of fire-fighting equipment. The Civilian Conservation Corps (CCC) is legendary nationwide, but its efforts in Michigan were particularly important (Salmond 1967). During the Great Depression, President Franklin Roosevelt's inspired government works program took unemployed young men off the streets and gave them paying jobs. They fought fires, planted trees and built necessary infrastructure, e.g., bridges, fire towers, firebreaks and housing. Their legacy of pine plantations and rustic buildings remains today. Smokey, the famous bear in blue jeans, came along in the midst of World War II, booming out his message: "Only YOU can prevent forest fires." One of the most successful advertising campaigns in history, Smokey still is going strong (www.smokeybear.com). His message, however, has changed slightly. Instead of warning against all forest fires, Smokey now only rails against *wildfires*. The distinction is important. We recognize today that many forests are adapted to periodic fires and need them for their health and vitality (Simard and Blank 1982, Cleland et al. 2004). Furthermore, unless these forests periodically burn under controlled conditions—called prescribed fires—fuels build up to dangerous levels, increasing the threat of catastrophic wildfires.

■ The forests of Michigan today

During any drive around the state, the view out the window gives evidence that the forests of Michigan today are well into their recovery (Fig. 40.14). Michigan's current 7.8 million hectares of forests are wonderfully diverse, and once again a significant economic engine for the state (Chapter 41). But besides being less mature, today's forests are distinctly different in other ways from the forests the GLO surveyors saw. Michigan's forests now cover just slightly more than half of the state, down from the 96% that was forested prior to Euro-American contact. Much of the original forest has given way to agricultural fields, mines, towns, subdivisions and human infrastructure. The lesson is clear: the real threat to today's forests is not wildfire or timber harvesting—forests recover from those—but human development (Chapter 29).

There are notable differences in the composition of contemporary forests, compared to their pre-1800 progenitors; the recovery is not an exact duplication. Savannas and barrens were the big losers. These open, park-like woodlands are intermediate between prairies and closed-canopy forests (Fig. 40.15), but today they occupy only a tiny fraction of their original area. Restoration efforts are underway to bring back some of these rare but appealing woodlands. But to fully keep them in their natural state, frequent prescribed fires are necessary—a practice not without danger in today's society.

Some species of trees also are less common than they once were. The big conifers, especially white pine and hemlock, did not fare well in most areas, during the recovery. Because white pine and hemlock (its tannin-rich bark was used for tanning leather) were so heavily harvested during the era of plunder, and because they were unable to reproduce in areas where repeated wildfires occurred, they are much less represented today than they once were (Fig. 40.3). Both are making a slow comeback, especially white pine. For example, many northern Lower Peninsula forests that are dominated by hardwoods in the upper canopy also have abundant white pine saplings and small trees in the understory. In time, the composition of these upland forests will be increasingly dominated by conifers. But for now,

FIGURE 40.14   A 75-year photo chronicle of forest recovery at a site in Cheboygan County. The 2001 photo is by L. Leefers; others are courtesy of the Michigan DNR.

FIGURE 40.15   Although savannas and barrens occupied ~890,000 hectares in Michigan, prior to Euro-American settlement, they are rare today. Shown here is an area of pine-oak barrens, typical of the dry, sandy soils of northern Michigan (Chapter 21). Photo by D. Dickmann.

the cool, moist western Upper Peninsula—especially Porcupine Mountains Wilderness State Park, near Ontonagon— is the best place to see white pine and hemlock in a condition approaching what they were in the early 1800s.

The big winners during forest recovery were the oaks and aspens, two types of trees well adapted to comeback after disturbances (Fig. 40.16). Oaks were common in southern Michigan's oak-hickory forests, and still are (Chapter 21). But prior to Euro-American settlement, oaks were uncommon as canopy trees on sandy soils in the northern Lower Peninsula. Rather, these areas were dominated by pines (Chapter 21). Today, however, >485,000 hectares of forests, dominated by oaks, grow in this region. Because oak wood is so valuable and acorns are such an important wildlife food, these forests provide prime timber and recreational opportunities. Thus, current forest management practices are aimed at sustaining the oaks, even though they are relative "newcomers."

Forests composed principally of quaking and bigtooth aspen also are much more common today than in the past (Fig. 40.16). Aspens are common invaders of disturbed sites, which have not been in short supply in Michigan. Once regarded by the timber industry as worthless, today more aspen timber is harvested annually than any other tree type (Cleland et al. 2001). Aspen forests also provide important habitat for deer, ruffed grouse, woodcock and many other wildlife species. Foresters love aspen, because after it is harvested (usually by clearcutting), dense stands of root sprouts (called suckers) spring up to renew the forest. Others with a more naturalistic viewpoint think differently. Even though there is less area classed as aspen today than in the 1930s, they think there's still too much. They argue that much of the aspen area should be allowed to naturally succeed to more long-lived, shade-tolerant forests, rich in maples, beech, yellow birch, balsam fir, spruce or white pine, a condition more reminiscent of the early 1800s.

Other types of forests are as well represented today as they were in the early 1800s, except the trees are not as large—after all, the recovery is <100 years old. Mesic hardwoods—also called northern hardwoods (Chapter 21)—is the most widely distributed forest type in the state today (Fig. 40.17). The northern parts of this forest—especially

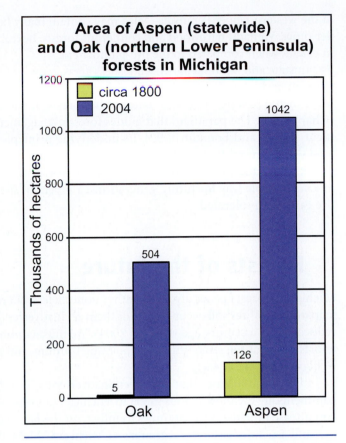

FIGURE 40.16 The land area of northern Lower Peninsula in oak, and state-wide aspen coverage, ca. 1800 and in 2004. Data from the Michigan Natural Features Inventory (1800) and the USDA Forest Service, Forest Inventory and Analysis (2004).

FIGURE 40.17 Mesic hardwood forests, usually dominated by sugar maple, are Michigan's most common forest type and can be found throughout the Upper and Lower Peninsulas. Photo by D. Dickmann

in the western Upper Peninsula—also may contain many hemlock and white pine, although not as much as in earlier times. Wetland hardwood and coniferous forests, boreal forests and jack pine-dominated forests also are similar in extent, when compared to the pre-plunder era.

In state and national parks, wilderness areas, nature preserves and other protected areas, forests will be allowed to grow, and—barring a natural disturbance—they may eventually reach the stature of the virgin forests of old. Most of the private, industrial and public forests of the state, however, are still harvested for timber products (Chapter 41). The paradigm that guides forest management on many of these lands is called ecosystem management (Kohm and Franklin 1997). Its underlying principle is that no one use, or small number of uses, of forest land should override all others, as was the case in the past. The intent is to maintain ecosystem integrity in an economically viable and socially responsible way. Today, we cherish forests and are intent on having them managed in a sustainable way for future generations; a repeat of the 19th and early 20th century era of plunder and wildfire cannot be tolerated.

Forests of the future

Michigan's forests generally are healthy; nonetheless, there are threats of human origin that put their future in jeopardy. Wildfires still occur—most of them set inadvertently or purposefully by humans—but their extent is much reduced from a century ago (Cleland 2004). We must continue to improve our wildfire prevention and suppression efforts, while at the same time implementing thinning and prescribed fires where necessary, to reduce the quantity of highly flammable fuels.

Insects and diseases that have been inadvertently introduced into the environment via trade goods from other continents are the most serious threat to Michigan's forests. Almost everyone knows about the devastation that Dutch elm disease inflicted, and continues to inflict, on the native elms. Recently, the European gypsy moth has defoliated oak and aspen forests over large areas in Michigan (McManus 1989). Fortunately, it is now beginning to act more like a native pest, with only occasional, localized outbreaks. The Chinese emerald ash borer (Fig. 40.18), which has killed millions of ash trees in Michigan, is one of the most recent introductions; it may turn out to be one of the worst (Cook and McCullough 2005). Larvae of the borer feed in the inner bark of trees, eventually girdling them. Although great effort has been made by state and federal authorities to eradicate it, this destructive insect is spreading throughout the state. Another pestilence is the beech bark disease (McCullough et al. 2005)—a fungus transmitted by an introduced insect, the beech bark scale. Large, heavily infected trees die standing, or break off in the wind. In parts of the eastern Upper Peninsula and in certain places along the shore of Lake Michigan, few large beech trees remain alive.

No one knows for sure what will be the eventual outcome of these pest invasions. The worst case is that some important tree species will be lost, as was the case with the blight that eliminated the magnificent American chestnut from the forests of the eastern US in the early 1900s. In a best case scenario, some forests will be disrupted, and some species will be diminished, but then they will recover, as they have before.

There is little doubt that the earth's climate is warming (Kolbert 2005). What does this warming portend for Michigan's forests? There are no definitive answers at this time, only educated speculations (McCarthy et al. 2001; Chapter 19). If Michigan's future climate is hotter during the summer, with more intense precipitation events, more stress will be placed on upland forests, favoring oaks and pines over maples, fir and spruces. Oaks and pines may come to dominate in forests where before they were less important, and their ranges may slowly expand northward. Hotter conditions will promote more fires—especially with ever more people to start them—and

FIGURE 40.18 The emerald ash borer, a recent invader from China, has killed millions of ash trees in southeastern Michigan. It poses a serious threat to ash forests across the state. Photos by D. Cappaert. A. A bark-boring larvae, typically ~1 mm in length. B. An adult, typically ~20 mm in length.

insect outbreaks, both of which are common forest disturbances. Trees adapted to disturbances, such as jack pine, aspen and paper birch, should benefit. A warmer climate may be accompanied by increased ozone in the lower atmosphere, creating additional stresses on forests (Dickson et al. 2000). The ecological response to these changes in the weather and atmosphere will be slow, and will occur over a long time, but the results may, nonetheless, be dramatic.

■ Conclusions

This chapter ends by restating its theme: destruction and recovery. The forests of Michigan have experienced this cycle over and over again. The most dramatic turn of this cycle in historic times—the 1800s plunder and the 1900s recovery—are well documented. Others are more subtle or obscured in the distant past. Michigan's forests face the same uncertain future that we humans do. Major and minor disturbances will occur again. But forests are wonderfully resilient, and they will recover, with help from foresters and land managers. Thus, future generations will enjoy the economic, recreational and spiritual prosperity that forests give, even though these forests might be different from those we experience and use today.

Literature Cited

Bailey, W.O. 1882. Report on the Michigan forest fires of 1881. Note no.1, US War Department Signal Service, Washington, DC.

Barrett, L.R. 1998. Origin and history of stump prairies in northern Michigan: forest composition and logging practices. Great Lakes Geographer 5:105–123.

Botti, W.B. and M.D. Moore. 2006. Michigan's State Forests: A Century of Stewardship. Michigan State University Press, East Lansing.

Cleland, D.T., Leefers, L.A. and D.I. Dickmann. 2001. Ecology and Management of Aspen: A Lake States perspective. In: Shepperd, W.B., Binkley, D., Bartos, D.L., Stohlgren, T.J. and L.G. Eskew (eds), Sustaining Aspen in Western Landscapes, Symposium Proceedings. USDA Forest Service, Rocky Mountain Research Station RMRS-P-18. pp 81–99.

Cleland, D.T., Crow, T.R., Saunders, S.C., Dickmann, D.I., Maclean, A.L., Jordan, J.K., Watson, R.L., Sloan, A.M. and K.D. Brosofske. 2004. Characterizing historical and modern fire regimes in Michigan (USA): a landscape ecosystem approach. Landscape Ecology 19:311–325.

Comer, P.J. and D.A. Albert. 1998. Vegetation of Michigan circa 1800 (2 maps). Michigan Natural Features Inventory, Lansing, MI.

Cook, W.E. and D.G. McCullough. 2005. Emerald ash borer and your woodland. Michigan State University Extension Bulletin E-2943, East Lansing.

Davis, M.B. 1981. Quaternary history and the stability of forest communities. In: West, D.C., Shugart, H.H. and D.B. Botkin (eds), Forest Succession: Concepts and Application. Springer-Verlag, New York. pp. 132–153.

Dempsey, D. 2001. Ruin and Recovery: Michigan's Rise as a Conservation Leader. University of Michigan Press, Ann Arbor.

Densmore, F. [1929] 1979. Chippewa Customs. Minnesota Historical Press, St. Paul (Reprint of Smithsonian Institution, Bureau of American Ethnology Bulletin 86).

Dickson, R.E., Lewin, K.F., Isebrands, J.G., Coleman, M.D., Heilman, W.E., Riemenschneider, D.E., Sober, J., Host, G.E., Zak, D.R., Hendrey, G.R., Pregitzer, K.S. and D.F. Karnosky. 2000. Forest atmosphere carbon transfer and storage (FACTS-II) The aspen free air CO_2 and O_3 enrichment (FACE) project: An overview. USDA Forest Service General Technical Report NC-214.

Faber-Langendoen, D. 2001 (ed). Plant Communities of the Midwest: Classification in an Ecological Context. Association for Biodiversity Information, Arlington, VA.

Holbrook, S. 1944. Burning an Empire. Macmillan and Company, New York.

Holbrook, S. 1956. Holy Old Mackinaw. Comstock, Sausalito, CA.

Kapp, R.O. 1999. Michigan Late Pleistocene, Holocene, and Presettlement Vegetation and Climate. In: J.R. Halsey (ed), Retrieving Michigan's Past: The Archaeology of the Great Lakes State. Cranbrook Institute of Science Bulletin 64. Bloomfield Hills, MI. pp. 31–58.

Kohm, K.A. and J.F. Franklin (eds). 1997. Creating a Forestry for the 21st Century: The Science of Ecosystem Management. Island Press, Washington, DC.

Kolbert, E. 2005. The climate of man—I. The New Yorker, April 25. pp. 56–71.

Mann, C.C. 2005. 1491: New Revelations of the Americas Before Columbus. Alfred A. Knopf, New York.

Maybee, R.H. 1988. Michigan's White Pine Era. Bureau of History, Michigan Department of State, Lansing.

McCarthy, J.J., Canziani, O.F., Leary, N.A., Dokken, D.J. and K.S. White (eds). 2001. Climate Change 2001: Impacts, Adaptation, and Vulnerability. Cambridge University Press, Cambridge, UK.

McCullough, D.G., Heyd, R.L. and J.G. O'Brien. 2005. Biology and management of beech bark disease. Michigan State University Extension Bulletin E-2746, East Lansing.

Mitchell, J.A. and D. Robson. 1950. Forest Fires and Forest Fire Control in Michigan. Michigan Department of Conservation, Lansing, MI.

Reimann, L.C. 1981. When Pine was King. Avery Color Studios, AuTrain, MI.

Salmond, J.A. 1967. The Civilian Conservation Corps, 1933–1942: A New Deal Case Study. Duke University Press, Durham, NC.

Shott, M.J. and H.T. Wright. 1999. The Paleo-Indians: Michigan's First People. In: J.R. Halsey (ed), Retrieving Michigan's Past: The Archaeology of the Great Lakes State. Cranbrook Institute of Science Bulletin 64. Bloomfield Hills, MI. pp. 59–70.

Simard, A.J. and R.W. Blank. 1982. Fire history of a Michigan jack pine forest. Michigan Academician 14:59–71.

Sodders, B. 1997. Michigan on Fire. Thunder Bay Press, Holt, MI.

Sparhawk, W.N. and W.D. Brush. 1929. The Economic Aspects of Forest Destruction in Northern Michigan. US Department of Agriculture Technical Bulletin 92. Washington, DC.

Titus, H. 1945. The Land Nobody Wanted: the Story of Michigan's Public Domain. Michigan State College, Agricultural Experiment Station Special Bulletin 332. East Lansing.

Wells, R.W. 1978. Daylight in the Swamp. Doubleday, Garden City, NJ.

Further Readings

Barnes, B.V. and W.H. Wagner, Jr. 2004. Michigan Trees. University of Michigan Press, Ann Arbor.

Barnes, B.V., Zak, D.R., Denton, S.R. and S.H. Spurr. 1998. Forest Ecology. John Wiley and Sons, New York.

Dickmann, D.I. 2004. Michigan Forest Communities: A Field Guide and Reference. Michigan State University Extension Bulletin E-3000: East Lansing, MI.

Dickmann, D.I. and L.A. Leefers. 2003. The Forests of Michigan. University of Michigan Press, Ann Arbor.

Karamanski, T.J. 1989. Deep Woods Frontier: A History of Logging in Northern Michigan. Wayne State University Press, Detroit, MI.

Micketti, G. 1981. The day Metz burned. Michigan History 65(Nov–Dec):12–16.

Smith, N.F. 1995. Trees of Michigan and the Upper Great Lakes. Thunder Bay Press, Lansing, MI.

41

Forests and Forestry from a Contemporary Perspective

Larry A. Leefers

■ Introduction

Most historical perspectives on Michigan's forests highlight the extensive logging in the 1800s and early 1900s, and the horrific fires that followed (Chapter 40). In the foreword to Sparhawk and Brush's (1929) bulletin on the forest destruction in northern Michigan, forester R.Y. Stuart wrote that, "Northern Michigan furnishes the most striking example of a region in which the destructive exploitation of vast forest wealth has almost run its course. Her virgin forests, which 50 years ago seemed inexhaustible and for several decades supported prosperous industries and communities, are practically gone. On millions of acres the ravages of fire have prevented the establishment of new forests, and the land has lain idle for years, a burden to its owners and to the community."

Fortunately, Michigan's lands are no longer idle! Our contemporary forests are once again playing important economic, social and ecological roles in society. The current focus is on sustaining these forests for their many functions and uses. Michigan's forests are expanding in area, increasing to 7.6 million hectares (19.3 million acres) in 2004 (Hansen and Brand 2006) or 53% of the state's land area. Total wood volume is also increasing (Fig. 41.1). Many of the depleted forest lands of the 1930s are now maturing and mature forests. Forest composition is also evolving, with a decline in pioneer species such as aspen and birch, and an increase in longer-lived maple-beech-birch, oak-hickory and oak-pine forest (Fig. 41.2).

Technically, forest lands are defined as being at least 1/6th covered by trees, or formerly covered and not currently developed for a nonforest use (Leatherberry and Spencer 1996). Therefore, although sparsely covered and recently harvested lands count as "forest," in actuality

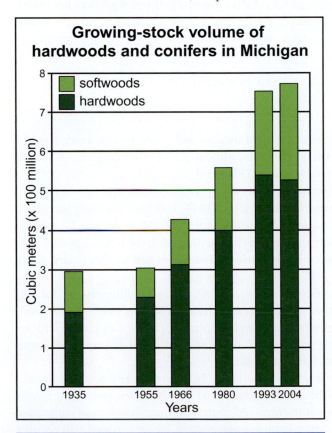

FIGURE 41.1 Growing-stock volume of hardwoods and conifers in Michigan, 1935–2004. Sources: Lake State Forest Experiment Station (1936), Findell et al. (1960), Chase et al. (1970), Raile and Smith (1983), Leatherberry and Spencer (1996) and Hansen and Brand (2006).

FIGURE 41.2 Area of timberland in Michigan, by forest type, 1935–2004. Sources: Lake State Forest Experiment Station (1936), Findell et al. (1960), Chase et al. (1970), Raile and Smith (1983), Leatherberry and Spencer (1996) and Hansen and Brand (2006).

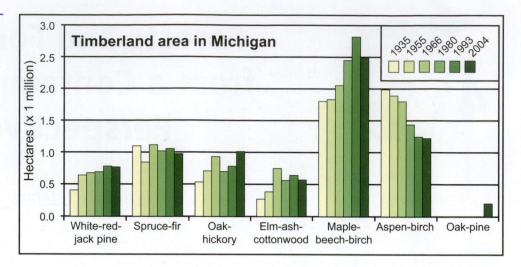

these lands account for <10% of all forest land. Most forest-related data are reported for timberlands—forest lands producing or capable of producing industrial wood crops. Lands withdrawn from timber utilization, e.g., wilderness areas and areas associated with urban and rural development, are also not counted as timberlands. About 97% of Michigan's forest lands are timberlands, indicating that the vast majority of Michigan's forests are biologically capable of producing timber.

A contemporary perspective on the forests of Michigan requires an understanding of forest owners and users, efforts for sustaining the forests, the role of the forests in economic well-being, and the challenges and opportunities facing them; those issues are the focus of this chapter. Forest uses and conditions were varied and dynamic in the early 20th century, they continue in the same vein in the early 21st century.

Forest owners and users

Diversity of flora and fauna typify Michigan's forests, as does diversity of owners and users. Private lands (owned by individuals, corporations and the forest products industry) comprise almost 2/3 of Michigan's timberlands (Fig. 41.3). State and federal lands are the next largest ownership classes (Plate 14).

Approximately 45% of the Michigan's timberlands are owned by individuals (Leatherberry and Spencer 1996). Leatherberry et al. (1998) estimated that there were 353,000 individual owners in 1994. This total has likely increased, due to parcelization—the splitting of larger land parcels into smaller ones (Chapter 29). Most owners have holdings of 0.4–3.5 hectares (1–9 acres). Private land owners have many reasons for owning land; the main expected benefit from owning forest land is aesthetic enjoyment, followed by recreation. Also important in this regard is the income derived from timber (Potter-Witter 2005).

Forests provide settings for many recreational opportunities—camping, hiking, skiing, wildlife viewing, fishing, off-road vehicle (ORV) riding, snowmobiling and many other nature-related activities (Nelson 1999). These activities provide a needed economic boost to many areas in northern Michigan (Chapter 35). Recreation-related infrastructure and related forest management provide jobs, often seasonal, for many residents. For example, Michigan has >900 public and private campgrounds, mostly in forested areas (Fig. 41.4).

Many Michiganders own a cabin, cottage or "camp" in northern Michigan. These are usually seasonal homes, and owners bring their families and friends (and money!) to the northwoods (Fig. 41.5). Their views regarding forests and natural resource management may differ from the views of the local residents, and their new homes contribute to an ongoing issue in Michigan—sprawl (Chapter 29). From a land-use perspective, larger forested parcels over time are subdivided into smaller, less forested or nonforested parcels. This process is termed "parcelization." One ecological concern regarding parcelization in forested areas is the potential effect on habitat—does it cause habitat fragmentation? And if so, which species are worse off due to parcelization and the resulting habitat fragmentation? This is an area of concerted study and will continue to be a contentious issue (Drzyzga 2000, Radeloff et al. 2005).

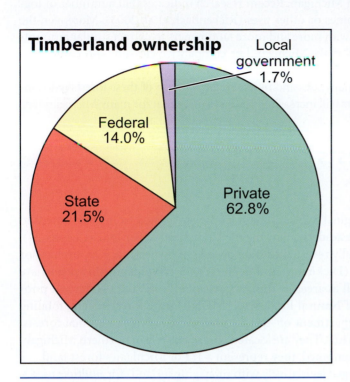

FIGURE 41.3   Ownership of Michigan's 7.4 million hectares (18.7 million acres) of timberland, in 1993. Source: Leatherberry and Spencer (1996).

FIGURE 41.4   Distribution of private and public campgrounds in Michigan, circa 1998. After Leefers and Vasievich (2001).

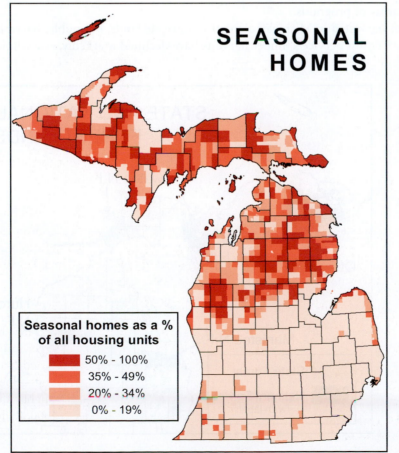

FIGURE 41.5   Seasonal homes as a percentage of total housing units, by minor civil division, in 2000, by townships and incorporated places. Source: US Census Bureau (2000, 2003).

Timber harvesting is a common activity in northern Michigan. Recent research indicates that a number of loggers are making *terminal harvests*—clearing land for homes or other uses (Rickenbach et al. 2003). Moreover, the trend toward smaller parcels will require loggers to work with more and more landowners to extract similar amounts of timber, thereby increasing their costs. This factor will make Michigan less competitive globally, and could contribute to the closure of some wood products mills.

Michigan's private forest lands provide a setting for many uses and users. Fragmentation of these forests will continue, and new conflicts will arise. Nonetheless, these forests will increasingly be a sylvan retreat for many Michiganders.

Sustaining Michigan's forests

Public forests

Michigan's public lands are an important legacy. The original public domain lands were passed from government to private ownership, i.e., purchased by speculators and homesteaders, following the Homestead Act of 1862 (Chapter 27). Many of the less agriculturally productive lands eventually reverted to state or federal ownership, via purchase or tax forfeiture, especially in the 1930s and early 1940s (Dickmann and Leefers 2003). Typical in this regard are sandy swamplands, and dry, sandy, barren areas, as well as areas of thin, rocky soils. Today, the two largest public forest landholdings are the Michigan Department of Natural Resources' (MDNR) state forest system, totaling 1.5 million hectares (3.8 million acres) and the US Department of Agriculture Forest Service's national forests, comprising >1.1 million hectares (2.8 million acres; Fig. 41.6). They are located almost entirely in northern Michigan, where forests dominate the landscape (Plates 13, 15). Combined, they represent ~1/3 of Michigan's forest land.

At the national level, the USDA Forest Service is charged legislatively with managing its lands for *multiple uses*— outdoor recreation, range, timber, water, wildlife and fish. "Range" is absent from Michigan's national forests, the Huron-Manistee, Hiawatha and Ottawa, but the other uses are significant. Although there is no state legislative mandate for multiple use, the philosophy is also applied to Michigan's state forests (Botti and Moore 2006). This mandate has been reinforced by recent legislation, requiring certification of sustainable forest management and annual appropriations for a wide array of programs.

The majority of timber harvested in Michigan comes from private lands, but public harvests are also important. In recent years, the US Forest Service's timber harvests have declined markedly, as a whole and in the state

FIGURE 41.6 Distribution of parcels of land in the state and national forests, in Michigan, ca. 2000. Source: Michigan Geographic Data Library (2007).

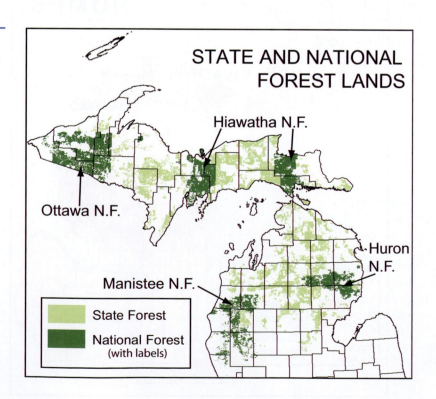

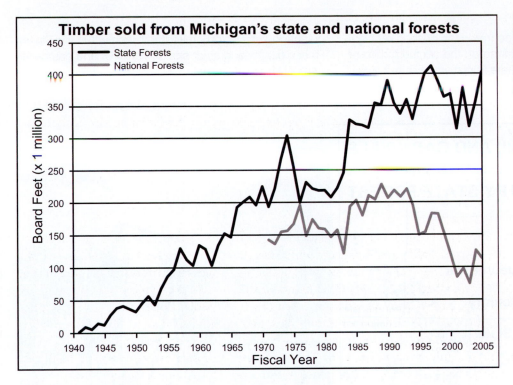

FIGURE 41.7 Timber sold from Michigan state forests (1941–2005) and national forests (1971–2005). Sources: MDNR and USDA Forest Service. Source: data compiled by the author, from USFS Cut and Sold Reports.

(Fig. 41.7). The initial decline in the early 1990s is often associated with the agency response to protection of the spotted owl in the Pacific Northwest, which led to dramatically lower harvests across the country. More recent declines are associated with reduced budgets and environmentalists' appeals of timber sales. Sales from state forests have increased in recent decades and have been maintained at a higher level, in line with the maturing of the forests, growth of wood product markets and legislative mandates. Most types of recreation and other uses of these forests also continue to expand.

Minerals management on public lands is balanced with the other multiple uses. In 2001, the MDNR reorganized and created a new unit, the Forest, Minerals, and Fire Management Division. Historically, minerals and forestry interests within the MDNR have not always been in agreement. This sometimes controversial relationship—oil and gas development vs recreational and ecological concerns—came to a head on state forest lands in the 1970s in the Pigeon River Country, at the nexus of Otsego-Montmorency-Cheboygan Counties (see FOCUS BOX below). In recent years, similar controversies have surfaced in Nordhouse Dunes Wilderness Area (Mason County), the Jordon River (Antrim County) and the Mason Tract (Crawford County). In all cases, the issue was whether subsurface minerals can be extracted by companies in areas receiving some level of special protection from public agencies.

FOCUS BOX: Pigeon River Country: elk vs oil and gas

In 1968, the MDNR accidentally sold oil and gas development leases for parts of the Pigeon River Country State Forest, north of Gaylord, and oil was soon (1970) discovered there. This event touched off more than a decade of heated debate over the appropriateness of oil and gas development in the Pigeon River Country, the heart of Michigan's elk herd. Most conservationists around the state were up in arms to protect the Pigeon River Country, its elk and the environment.

In 1975, the Michigan United Conservation Clubs' board approved "rigidly controlled oil and gas drilling," and lobbied to get the Kammer Recreational Land Trust Fund Act passed by the state legislature the following year. This act, modified to become the Natural Resources Trust Fund Act in 1985, provided an avenue to direct oil and gas royalties from state-owned mineral rights, for the purchase of additional public lands for resource protection and public outdoor recreation (Charles 1985). Oil companies, working with the MDNR, however, pushed development forward. Environmental groups sued to halt drilling. Three years later, in 1979, the Michigan Supreme Court agreed with the environmental groups, and halted drilling. Legislation that followed was based on a compromise pushed by conservation groups, to limit drilling on the southern third of the Pigeon River Country State Forest (see Figure below). The outcomes of this battle were a source of funding for purchasing state land, limited development in the Pigeon River Country, and strict standards for oil and gas development for the entire state—all part of the multiple-use balancing act so important to Michigan's future forests.

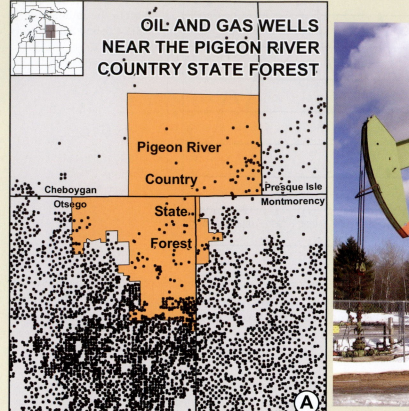

Oil and gas actvity in the Pigeon River Country. A. Map of oil and gas wells in and around the Pigeon River Country, NE of Gaylord. Source: Michigan Department of Natural Resources. B. An oil well operating in the Pigeon River Country. Photo by L. Leefers.

Other public forest uses have evolved as well, often with a focus on one dominant use. For example, we now have federal and state wilderness areas, wild and scenic rivers on federal lands, natural rivers on state lands and protected habitat for endangered species, such as the Kirtland's Warbler (see FOCUS BOX on the next page). And forests provide the backdrop for many of the 60 state game areas and other wildlife areas, concentrated in the southern Lower Peninsula. Federal wildlife refuges, notably the 37,485 hectare (95,212 acre) Seney National Wildlife Refuge (Schoolcraft County), are partially forested. Our 89 state parks and recreation areas are located in Michigan's forests. Examples of old growth forests can be found in Warren Woods (Berrien County), Hartwick Pines (Crawford County), Tahquamenon Falls (Luce and Chippewa Counties) and Porcupine Mountains (Ontonagon County) state parks. Michigan also has four units of the National Park System: Isle Royale National Park (Keweenaw County), Keweenaw National Historic Park (Keweenaw County), Pictured Rocks National Lakeshore (Alger County) and Sleeping Bear Dunes National Lakeshore (Leelanau County). Forests provide key elements of the natural settings in all of these. Gogebic County forests are the only other large public forest lands in Michigan; they cover over 14,173 hectares (36,000 acres). Financially, the county forest is self-supporting, due to timber sales; payments are made to local government in lieu of the private property taxes that are lost—the norm for all public lands. Like other public lands, recreational uses are a part of the mix in Gogebic County, too.

FOCUS BOX: Kirtland's warbler

Forests provide habitat for a wide range of plant and animal species. One notable species, the Kirtland's warbler (KW), is an example of a bird that has coevolved with a specific type of forest for millennia (see Figure below). The warbler's habitat is the dry, jack pine barrens, located mostly between Grayling and Lake Huron (Plate 15). Historically, wildfires swept through jack pine stands, consuming the trees, leaving ashes as fertilizer and opening their serotinous (heat-opened) cones (Chapter 21). Rains rejuvenated the forest by sprouting the prolific numbers of seeds dropped from the open cones. Succession to other forest types is precluded by fire or timber harvesting, which perpetuates the desired jack pine habitat.

The Kirtland's warbler is a ground nester that prefers young jack pine trees as its home (Chapter 22). As the trees mature, the lower branches die, eliminating the necessary nesting cover, and the bird moves on. The KW was listed as "endangered," under the federal Endangered Species Act of 1973 and the Michigan Endangered Species Act of 1974. For years, the population hovered around 200 singing males (females are difficult to count), but improved habitat conditions have contributed to a population exceeding 1000 singing males in recent years (see Figure below). Three important management practices have contributed to the increasing population: (1) controlling fire, (2) tree planting and (3) trapping and destroying Brown-headed cowbirds. The first two help assure that young jack pine habitat is created in an ongoing manner. The latter greatly reduces nest parasitism caused by the cowbird, which lays its eggs in KW nests. All three are essential for maintaining adequate habitat for this unique bird. Over 53,150 hectares (135,000 acres) are now being managed for warbler habitat by the MDNR, the USDA Forest Service and the US Department of the Interior's Fish and Wildlife Service (Huber et al. 2001).

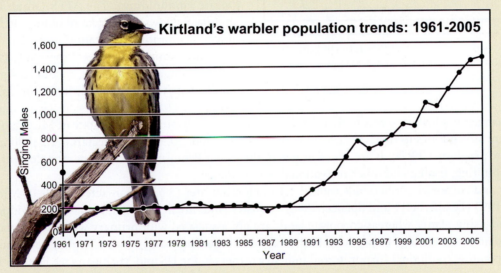

Counts of singing male, Kirtland's warblers, from the annual census in Michigan. Assuming each male has a mate, the total population would be twice the level presented. Source: USDA Forest Service. Photo by R. Austing.

Sustainability has been a central tenet of public forest management for decades. In recent years, a formal process for implementing sustainable forestry practices has evolved internationally, and in the US. This process is called forest certification—certifying that a forest is managed sustainably. Citizens want some assurance that forests, with their many uses and functions, can provide those benefits in perpetuity. The Michigan state forests were certified by the Sustainable Forestry Initiative (SFI) and the Forest Stewardship Council (FSC) in 2006. The former evolved from forest industry recommendations for sustainable forest management, and the latter came from an international, nongovernmental organization focused originally on environmental and social values associated with natural forests. These certifiers help insure that Michigan's state forests will be managed, using environmental, social and economic considerations. The MDNR makes management adjustments, if problems are noted, to meet

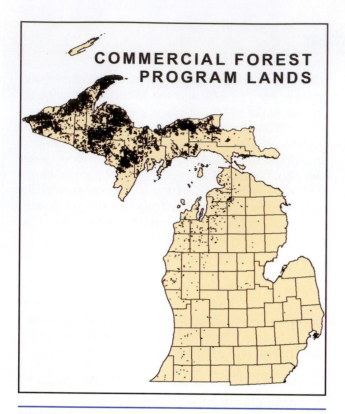

FIGURE 41.8   Commercial Forest Program lands in Michigan, in 2005. Source: MDNR, Forest, Mineral and Fire Management Division.

the standards developed by the SFI and FSC organizations. The USDA Forest Service completed a detailed planning process in 2006, which required extensive public participation and environmental analyses. In the end, the goal is sustainable management of Michigan's public forests, and the strongest guidelines ever developed are now being implemented in Michigan.

Private forests

Private forests, which are mostly owned by individuals, are managed for many purposes. Some owners focus on timber management; this is especially true for the >1,800 members of the Michigan Tree Farm System, which requires a forest management plan as a membership requirement. The plan is a stepping stone to sustainable forest management; it highlights how the forest property will be managed for multiple resources. In addition to SFI and FSC certification, there is also the American Tree Farm System (ATFS) Group Certification. SFI and FSC are most often applied to larger industry and corporate landholdings. The ATFS Group Certification approach allows smaller landholdings to be combined under a common certification umbrella.

The Commercial Forest Program (CFP) is the premier Michigan policy that encourages private forest landowners to manage their lands for timber production (Fig. 41.8). Landowners receive reduced property taxes, in exchange for allowing access to their lands for hunting and fishing, and the State of Michigan makes additional payments to counties to replace the lost tax revenues. In 2006, >0.9 million hectares (2.2 million acres) were enrolled in the program. CFP lands are concentrated in the Upper Peninsula. These lands complement public lands that provide hunting, fishing and other recreational opportunities.

Industry and corporate timberlands totaled 1.4 million hectares (3.6 million acres) (19% of Michigan's timberlands) in 1993 (Leatherberry and Spencer 1996). Industry lands are held by companies or individuals operating primary wood-using plants, whereas corporate lands are not associated with primary wood-using plants. Primary wood-using plants convert logs to products such as lumber, wood pulp and veneer. Timber investment organizations are supplanting traditional corporate and industry owners in the US and Michigan (see FOCUS BOX below).

FOCUS BOX: Changing corporate land strategies . . . From Mead to NewPage to Plum Creek

Pulp making first came to Escanaba in 1912, 45 years after Michigan's first paper mill was established in Kalamazoo. Water-powered grinders at the Escanaba Pulp and Paper Company's mill on the Escanaba River reduced wood to fiber-rich wood pulp. After being formed into sheets, the pulp was baled and shipped to nearby paper mills. The pulp mill consumed about 7000 cords of spruce and fir pulpwood per year. From the onset, George Mead was involved in mill investment and product marketing. By 1920, a paper mill was added, and

newsprint production was underway; the Escanaba Paper Company was born. In 1942, the Mead Corporation became the controlling owner, and the company became a Mead subsidiary. After a number of name changes and a recent merger, the company became MeadWestvaco. Then, following a 2005 sale, the ownership shifted to NewPage Corporation. The original plant and equipment have long since been replaced, and the 787 hectare (2000 acre) mill site now houses four immense paper machines with coated, premium quality paper as the main product. These machines use a whopping 1.6 million tons or 800,000 cords of wood annually—about 125 wood chip and pulpwood trucks per day!

Wood-using companies have different strategies for obtaining wood. They may purchase wood from public or private lands, and/or grow and harvest wood from their own lands. The latter was a significant part of the Mead legacy, but came to an end in 2005 when NewPage sold its 255,905 hectares (650,000 acres) to Plum Creek Timber Company, Inc. This move ended 60 years of company-based forest management. As others moved out of the timber business, Mead moved in—when it fit their plans. Over the 60 year span, they purchased forest land from Cleveland-Cliffs Iron Company, Cadillac Soo Lumber Company, Celotex Corporation, Royal Oak Charcoal Company, Sawyer Estates, US Steel Corporation, Copper Range Company, American Can Company, Nekoosa Papers, Ford Motor Company, Champion International and numerous individuals. When they purchased 34,252 hectares (87,000 acres) from the Ford River Timber Company (formerly Sawyer-Stoll Company) in 1975, they became the largest private landowner in the Upper Peninsula. Plum Creek, a timberland investment firm, will continue to supply wood to the mill, but the era of forest products companies owning timberlands is, indeed, coming to a close.

Michigan's forest products industry

Economic contributions and geographic distribution

The US Census Bureau uses the North American Industrial Classification System (NAICS) to categorize and gather data on firms across the country. For the forest products industry, there are three main categories of interest: wood products manufacturing, paper manufacturing and furniture and related product manufacturing. This varied set of manufacturers provides an important foundation for Michigan's economy. In 2004, >38,000 jobs were directly associated with 1,242 manufacturing firms in the forest products industry (Table 41.1). In 2002, the most recently reported year, the annual payroll was $1.5 billion, and the value of shipments was $8.5 billion. An additional 418 establishments with ~2,000 employees support this manufacturing base, via logging and other forestry activities (Table 41.2).

This industry is quite diverse and distributed across the state (Fig. 41.9). The MDNR maintains a database of firms and establishments in the forest products industry. In total they have data on 2,278 companies, including information on their raw material inputs, products and other salient attributes. The producers are typically loggers who harvest the trees and deliver logs or chips to manufacturers. Secondary manufacturers take the processed wood (lumber, veneer) from primary manufacturers, and use it in higher value-added products, e.g., furniture, molding and flooring.

TABLE 41.1 Forest products industry establishments, annual payroll and paid employees, in Michigan, in 2004

NAICS/ Manufacturers	Establishments	Annual payroll ($1000)	Paid employees
321	547	401,774	12,124
322	197	661,676	14,353
337	498	445,737	12,162
Total	1242	1,509,187	38,639

Note: NAICS 321 is Wood Products Manufacturing (traditional wood products such as lumber, plywood, veneer and wood flooring), NAICS 322 is Paper Manufacturing (pulp, paper and converted products such as paperboard, corrugated cardboard, tissue paper and disposable diapers), and NAICS 337 is Furniture and Related Product Manufacturing (wood-based furniture only, including household and commercial furniture and associated products such as cabinets and fixtures). Source: US Census Bureau (2006).

TABLE 41.2 Forestry establishments, annual payroll and paid employees, in Michigan, in 2004

Producers	Establishments	Annual payroll ($1000)	Paid employees
Forestry and logging	373	51,109	1872
Support activities for forestry	45	3,327	92
Total	418	54,436	1964

Source: US Census Bureau (2006).

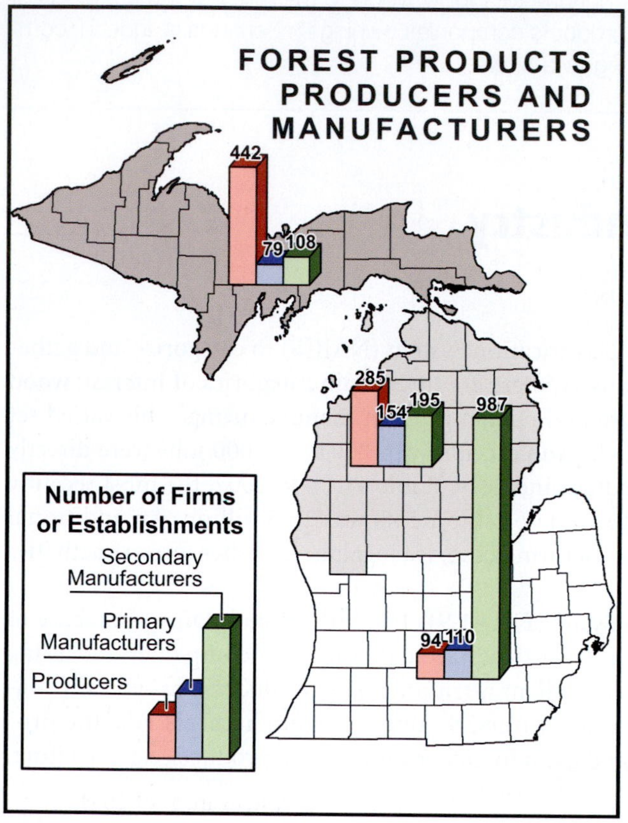

FIGURE 41.9 Forest products producers, primary manufacturers and secondary manufacturers, by regions in Michigan, in 2006. Source: MDNR (2007).

Michigan's citizens generally associate forests and forest products with the northern regions of the state. Indeed, wood product mills often provide the economic base for many northern rural communities. However, secondary manufacturers, which represent the largest number of firms, are actually concentrated in the southern Lower Peninsula (Fig. 41.9), closer to markets. Producers and primary manufacturers are more heavily skewed to the north, where forests are more plentiful. But even the primary manufacturers are well represented by a variety of different firms around the state (Fig. 41.10). The USDA Forest Service reports that the four largest uses of harvested roundwood are for pulpwood, sawlogs, composite products (particleboard, oriented strandboard, etc.) and fuelwood—all primary uses (Fig. 41.11). Although quite limited at this time, there is an expectation that more wood may be used for the production of biofuels in the near future.

Christmas trees and other non-timber forest products

Christmas trees represent another important type of firm and forest product in Michigan (Fig. 41.12). They are different in nature from the harvest of most forest crops, due to their holiday-only focus, rapid turnaround, and almost exclusive reliance on plantations. As of 2002, Michigan was the third leading Christmas tree producer in the country, after only Oregon and North Carolina, in terms of trees harvested. Both the total land area managed for Christmas trees, and the number of trees sold have, however, declined in recent years (USDA NASS and MDA 2005). In 2005, there were 16,535 hectares (42,000 acres) managed for Christmas tree production, by 780 operators. The sales value in 2004 was $41.5 million, with sales of 2.9 million trees, mostly to other states.

One-quarter of the Christmas tree operations in Michigan are "choose and cut only"; this provides opportunities for families to walk through fields and to select a tree for themselves. The second largest type of operator are "wholesale only," with more sales for local and export markets. Missuakee County is the leading county in terms of area, followed by Oceana, Wexford and Montcalm. Scotch pine (*Pinus sylvestris*) is the most commonly planted species, but Douglas-fir (*Pseudotsuga menziesii*), Fraser fir (*Abies fraseri*) and Colorado blue spruce (*Picea pungens*) are increasing in importance. This species shift is designed to position growers for success in increasingly competitive markets.

Forest products such as lumber, paper, furniture and Christmas trees are well known components of Michigan's economy. However, forests play another significant role, by providing non-timber forest products that enhance the

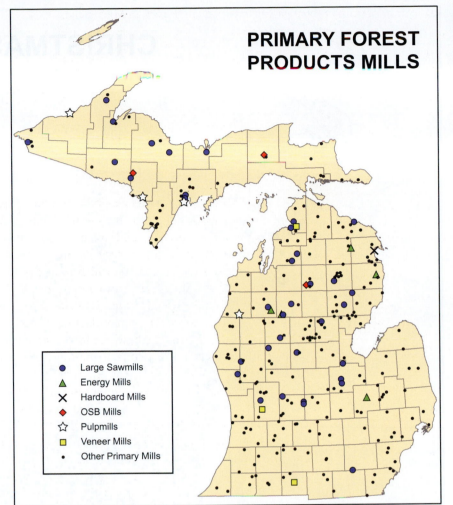

PRIMARY FOREST PRODUCTS MILLS

Legend:
- ● Large Sawmills
- ▲ Energy Mills
- ✕ Hardboard Mills
- ◆ OSB Mills
- ☆ Pulpmills
- ▯ Veneer Mills
- • Other Primary Mills

FIGURE 41.10 Location of primary forest products manufacturers in Michigan, in 2006. Source: MDNR (2007).

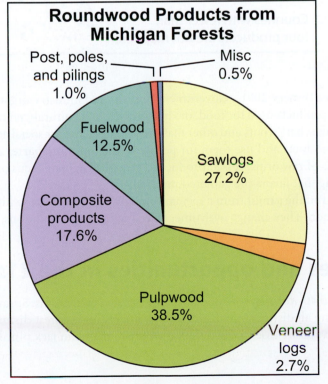

Roundwood Products from Michigan Forests

- Post, poles, and pilings 1.0%
- Misc 0.5%
- Fuelwood 12.5%
- Sawlogs 27.2%
- Composite products 17.6%
- Pulpwood 38.5%
- Veneer logs 2.7%

FIGURE 41.11 Percent of roundwood products by type of product, for Michigan, as of 2004. Source: USDA Forest Service (2007).

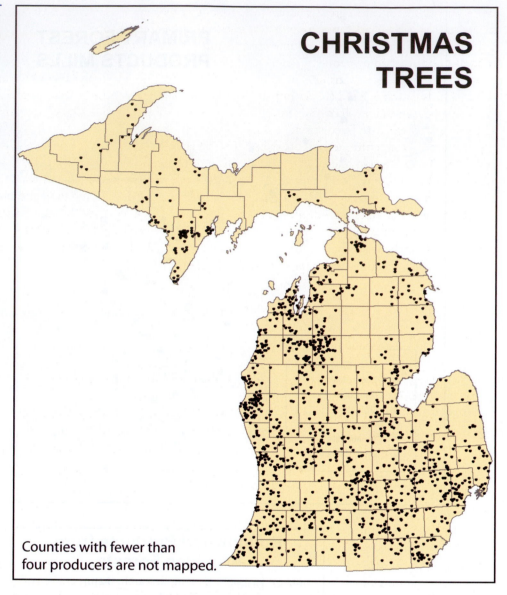

FIGURE 41.12 Locations of Christmas tree farms and plantations in Michigan in 2000. In order to protect grower confidentiality, the location of each farm dot was randomly moved by up to 4.8 km. Source: Michigan Agricultural Statistics (2003–2004).

livelihoods of many families (Emery 2001). Government bureaus and industry organizations tend not to monitor the myriad of forest-based products used for food, medicine, crafts and cultural/ceremonial purposes. Mushrooms, wild berries, maple syrup, nuts, bark, roots and other materials are gathered for social and economic purposes. People gather and harvest these products and use them for personal consumption, barter and gifts. They may also be a source of income from sales of raw or processed products. The gathering may focus on a specific location year after year, or an ecological setting that favors the gathered material.

Hence, forest products run the gamut from paper and energy produced by large high-tech mills, to berries hand-picked for home consumption. They change over time, reflecting resource conditions, social values and technology.

■ Disturbances and opportunities in the 21st century

As noted in Chapters 21 and 40, *disturbance* is the norm for forested ecosystems. Sprawl, wildfire, exotic insects and diseases, and global warming all disturb Michigan's forests. Interestingly, forest disturbance via harvesting is often desirable. For example, harvests are essential activities if we are to maintain jack pine habitat for Kirtland's Warbler and aspen habitat for ruffed grouse; both efforts provide needed raw materials for mills and, in turn, society. Harvesting creates more diverse landscapes, as long as it does not obliterate the forests, as was done in the 19th century.

Forest management, for its multiple uses, requires active habitat manipulation as well as thoughtful protection of areas not disturbed by people. In an economic sense, forest products mill closures reduce human disturbances, whereas new mills and expansions increase disturbances. In 2005 and early 2006, three major mills in the northern Lower Peninsula were closed (Paperloop 2005). These closures have economic impacts in terms of lost local jobs in the affected communities, economic losses due to lower prices for private timber owners, reduced revenue for public agencies and less early successional habitat formation.

Michigan's competitiveness in forest products will largely determine the prospective role of harvest-disturbances in the state. In addition to traditional markets, new products provide opportunities for the future. The renewed focus on a bio-based economy (Michigan State University 2006) may include directly burning wood as a fuel, converting biomass to ethanol, creating biochemicals and biomaterials, and developing food and pharmaceuticals. Composite materials with wood filler provide another potential market. Due to Michigan's long history of forest management, the biological resource for high-quality hardwood markets remains available. And there is an emerging market for carbon credits—the use of wood for carbon sequestration. Thus, ongoing and evolving ecological and economic forces ensure a continuing and important role for forests in Michigan.

Literature Cited

Botti, W.B. and M.D. Moore. 2006. Michigan's State Forests: A Century of Stewardship. Michigan State University Press, East Lansing.

Hansen, M.H. and G.J. Brand. 2006. Michigan's Forest Resources. Resource Bulletin NC-255. US Department of Agriculture, Forest Service, North Central Research Station: Paul, MN. 41 pp.

Charles, G. 1985. Pigeon River Country: The Big Wild. William Eerdman's Publishing Company, Grand Rapids, MI.

Chase, C.D., Pfeifer, R.E. and J.S Spencer, Jr. 1970. The growing timber resource of Michigan, 1966. Resource Bulletin NC-9. USDA Forest Service, North Central Forest Experiment Station, St. Paul, MN. 62 pp.

Dickmann, D.I. and L.A. Leefers. 2003. The Forests of Michigan. University of Michigan Press, Ann Arbor.

Drzyzga, S.A. 2000. Land ownership parcelization and forest fragmentation in three northern Michigan counties. M.S. thesis. Michigan State University, East Lansing.

Emery, M.R. 2001. Non-timber forest products and livelihoods in Michigan's Upper Peninsula. In: J. Zasada (ed), Forest Communities in the Third Millennium: Linking Research, Business and Policy Towards a Sustainable Non-Timber Forest Product Sector. GTR-NC-217. US Department of Agriculture, Forest Service, North Central Research Station, St. Paul, MN. pp. 23–30.

Findell, V.E., Pfeifer, R.E., Horn, A.G. and C.H. Tubbs. 1960. Michigan's forest resources. Station Paper 82. USDA Forest Service, Lake States Forest Experiment Station, University Farm, St. Paul. MN. 45 pp.

Hansen, M.H. and G.J. Brand. 2006. Michigan's forest resources in 2004. Resource Bulletin NC-255. US Department of Agriculture, Forest Service, North Central Research Station, St. Paul, MN. 41 pp.

Huber, P.W., Weinrich, J.A. and E.S. Carlson. 2001. Strategy for Kirtland's warbler habitat management. US Department of Agriculture, US Forest Service, and Michigan Department of Natural Resources. 31 pp.

Lake States Forest Experiment Station. 1936. Forest areas and timber volumes in Michigan. A Progress Report on the FOREST SURVEY OF THE LAKE STATES. Economic Notes No. 5. USDA Forest Service, Lake States Forest Experiment Station, University Farm, St. Paul, MN. 40 pp.

Leatherberry, E.C., Kingsley, N.P. and T.W. Birch. 1998. Private Timberland Owners of Michigan, 1994. Resource Bulletin NC-191. US Department of Agriculture, Forest Service, North Central Forest Experiment Station St. Paul, MN. 84 pp.

Leatherberry, E.C. and J.S. Spencer, Jr. 1996. Michigan Forest Statistics, 1993. Resource Bulletin NC-170. US Department of Agriculture, Forest Service, North Central Forest Experiment Station. St. Paul, MN. 144 pp.

Leefers, L.A. and J.M. Vasievich. 2001. An analysis of campground resources in the Lake States. In: Proceedings of the 5th Outdoor Recreation and Tourism Trends Symposium—Trends 2000: Shaping the Future. Department of Park, Recreation and Tourism Resources, Michigan State University, East Lansing. pp. 174–181.

Michigan Agricultural Statistics. 2003–2004. Michigan Department of Agriculture, Lansing, MI.

Michigan Department of Natural Resources. 2007. Michigan forest industry. http://www.dnr.state.mi.us/wood/quermain.asp (last accessed January, 2007.)

Michigan Geographic Data Library. 2007. GAP land stewardship. http://www.mcgi.state.mi.us/mgdl/ (last accessed January, 2007).

Michigan State University. 2006. Bioproducts for economic expansion: a strategy for Michigan's role in the new bioeconomy. Discussion draft prepared by Michigan State University, Lou Anna Simon, President, January 10, 2006. Michigan State University, Board of Trustees, East Lansing, MI. 10 pp.

Nelson, C.M. 1999. An assessment of Forest Management Division's recreation programs. Michigan Department of Natural Resources, Lansing, MI.

Paperloop. 2005. Moderation comes to Lake States pulpwood markets with mill closures and improved in-woods production. International Woodfiber Report 11:1, 4.

Potter-Witter, K. 2005. A cross-sectional analysis of Michigan nonindustrial private forest landowners. Northern Journal of Applied Forestry 22:132–138.

Radeloff, V.C., Hammer, R.B. and S.I. Stewart. 2005. Rural and suburban sprawl in the U.S. Midwest from 1940 to 2000 and its relationship to forest fragmentation. Conservation Biology 19:793–805.

Raile, G.K. and W.B. Smith. 1983. Michigan forest statistics, 1980. Resource Bulletin NC-67. US Department of Agriculture, Forest Service, North Central Forest Experiment Station, St. Paul, MN. 101 pp.

Sparhawk, W.M. and W.D. Brush. 1930. The economic aspects of forest destruction in northern Michigan. US Department of Agriculture Technical Bulletin 92. US Government Printing Office, Washington, DC. 120 pp.

US Census Bureau. 2000. Summary File 3 (SF3), 2000 Decennial Census. http://www.census.gov/Press-Release/www/2002/sumfile3.html (last accessed January, 2007).

US Census Bureau. 2003. Census 2000: Population and Housing. Michigan Data CD ROM. Department of Commerce, Economics and Statistics Administration, Washington, DC.

US Census Bureau. 2006. County Business Patterns 2004, Michigan. US Census Bureau, Washington, DC.

USDA Forest Service. 2007. Timber Products Output Mapmaker 1.0. http://ncrs2.fs.fed.us/4801/fiadb/rpa_tpo/wc_rpa_tpo.asp (last accessed January, 2007).

USDA National Agricultural Statistics Service (NASS) and Michigan Department of Agriculture (MDA). 2005. Nursery and Christmas tree inventory, 2004–2005. USDA National Agricultural Statistics Service and Michigan Department of Agriculture, Lansing, MI. 31 pp.

Further Readings

Dempsey, D. 2001. Ruin and Recovery: Michigan's Rise as a Conservation Leader. University of Michigan Press, Ann Arbor.

DuFresne, J. 2001. Best Hikes with Children Michigan Guide Book. The Mountaineer Books, Seattle, WA.

Flader, S.L. (ed). 1983. The Great Lakes Forest: an Environmental and Social History. University of Minnesota Press, Minneapolis.

Kates, J. 2001. Planning a Wilderness: Regenerating the Great Lakes Cutover Region. University of Minnesota Press, Minneapolis.

Sodders, B. 1999. Michigan on Fire 2. Thunder Bay Press, Holt, MI.

Appendix A

Oblique views of recognizable regions in Michigan

Joseph P. Hupy and Randall J. Schaetzl

These color, shaded relief, graphical representations of our state were constructed using ArcGIS desktop software, version 9.2 (© ESRI, Redlands, CA), with the ArcGIS 3D analyst extension, using 3D Scene to manipulate map views and design. The geographic data used to construct these maps were obtained from the Michigan Geographic Spatial Data Library, from the State of Michigan. The data follow the Michigan Georeference projection scheme, a.k.a. NAD1983 Hotine Oblique Mercator Azimuth Natural Origin. The Digital Elevation Model (DEM) data have National Elevation Data level II accuracy, with pixels that are approximately 30x30 meters apart.

A1. ISLE ROYALE. Isle Royale, the focus of Chapter 24, is a place like no other. The island is not only a National Park, but also an International Biosphere Reserve. The bedrock ridges that dominate here are the remnants of dozens of Precambrian-aged lava flows, which have subsequently been tilted into nearly vertical orientations and eroded by Pleistocene glaciers. The vast copper deposits here may never be mined.

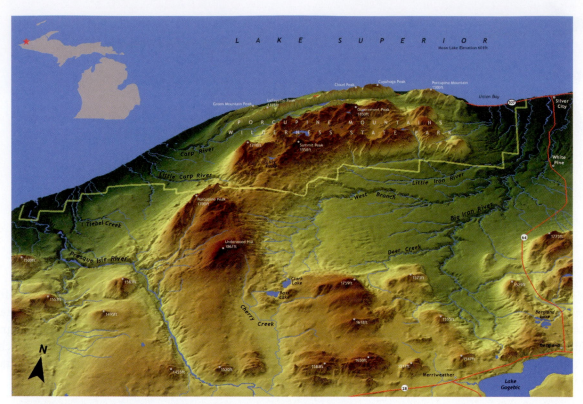

A2. THE PORCUPINE MOUNTAINS. One of the most picturesque places in all of Michigan, and yet seen by few, the Porcupine Mountains are home to two state parks and thousands of hectares of wilderness. The pristine Lake of the Clouds, set within the upland, is the gemstone of the region. The Porkies are a great place to get away from it all.

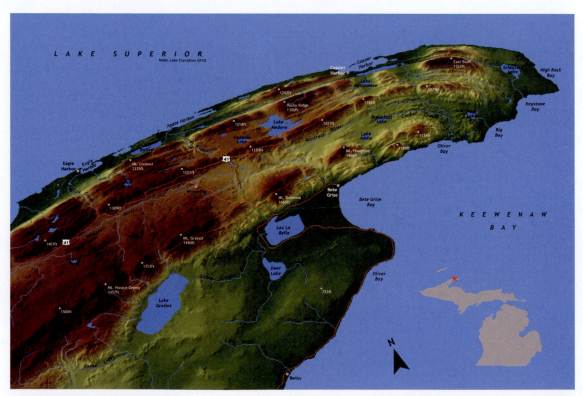

A3. THE KEWEENAW PENINSULA. The Keweenaw Peninsula and Isle Royale have similar geology, and hence the same sets of ridges are seen on both. Copper mining here was concentrated on the ridge tops, where the copper-rich bedrock was close to the surface (Chapter 12).

A4. THE PESHEKEE HIGHLANDS AND THE HURON MOUNTAINS. The Precambrian-aged, bedrock uplands to the west and north of Marquette are rich in minerals and offer excellent hiking and recreating opportunities. Bedrock knobs abound, as many parts of this area were scraped clean by the many ice sheets that invaded the region from the north. If visiting in winter, bring snowshoes!

A5. THE HURON MOUNTAINS. An especially remote and beautiful section of the Peshekee uplands—the Huron Mountains—are largely privately owned and thus difficult to access. With their deep, clear lakes, rounded bedrock knobs and immense trees, the Hurons are nearly as they were hundreds of years ago.

A6. THE MENOMINEE DRUMLIN FIELD. The Menominee drumlin field is composed of dozens of elongate hills known as drumlins. Each drumlin, about 1–2 km in length, was formed beneath the advancing glacier, and reflects the direction of ice flow. In Menominee County, these drumlins are cored with sandy loam drift, and typically separated by wide, flat expanses of cedar (*Thuja*) swamp.

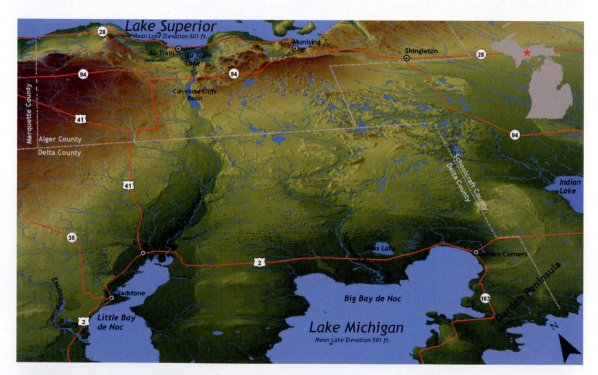

A7. THE AU TRAIN-WHITEFISH CHANNEL. About 11,900 years ago, when low outlets in the eastern Upper Peninsula were blocked by glacial ice, waters in the Lake Superior basin flowed across the low, central parts of the Upper Peninsula, carving out an immense river channel. A large delta, formed at the outlet of the channel, is today flooded and lies below the Lake Michigan surface. Today, only small streams sluggishly meander across the swamps of the Au Train-Whitefish channel.

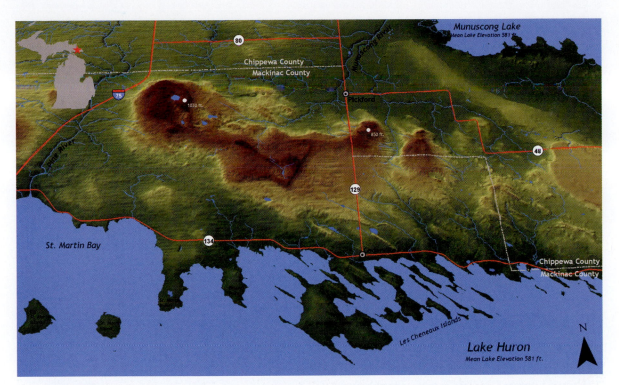

A8. THE LES CHENEAUX ISLANDS OF LAKE HURON AND THE MUNUSCONG ISLANDS OF GLACIAL LAKE ALGONQUIN. Beginning about 12,900 years ago, most of the Upper Peninsula was flooded by Glacial Lake Algonquin (Fig. 13.11). Only the highest bedrock uplands were flooded by this expansive lake. These islands, held up by the hard Niagara dolomite, are today known as the Munuscong Islands.

A9. THE PENINSULAS AND LINEAR LAKES OF THE NORTHWESTERN LOWER PENINSULA. The unmistakable linearity of the land and water in the northwestern Lower Peninsula is a hallmark of the area. Long, linear lakes and bays alternate with narrow, almost knife-crested peninsulas. Geologists have always known that this topography was created by glacial sculpting, but we now know that most of the erosional work here was done not by ice but by sub-glacial meltwater, forced through channels under tremendous pressure. These features are called tunnel channels, and few places on the Earth display them better than does this area.

A10. THE ANTRIM-CHARLEVOIX DRUMLIN FIELD. One of the most notable drumlin fields on Earth, the Antrim-Charlevoix field has a very high drumlin density—almost the entire landscape is drumlins. Across the field, their shapes change markedly, from long, thin, linear "flutes" on the west to more stubby, almost gumdrop-shaped hills on the east.

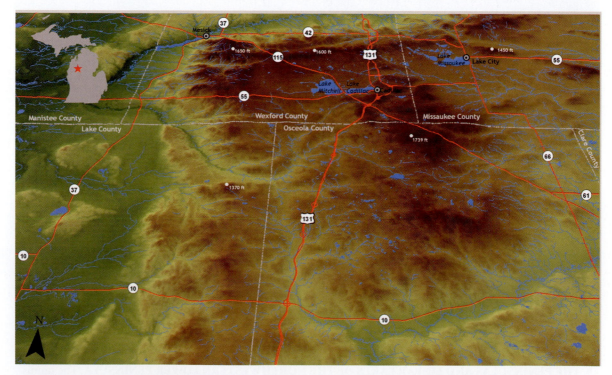

A11. THE CADILLAC INTERLOBATE HIGHLANDS. Lakes Mitchell and Cadillac sit in a broad swale, surrounded on all sides by high, sandy, hummocky uplands. These rolling hills were formed at the junction—or suture—between the Lake Michigan and Saginaw glacial lobes. Where two such lobes meet, tremendous thickness of glacial sediment can accumulate; just to the south of Cadillac these deposits exceed 300 meters—perhaps the thickest in North America.

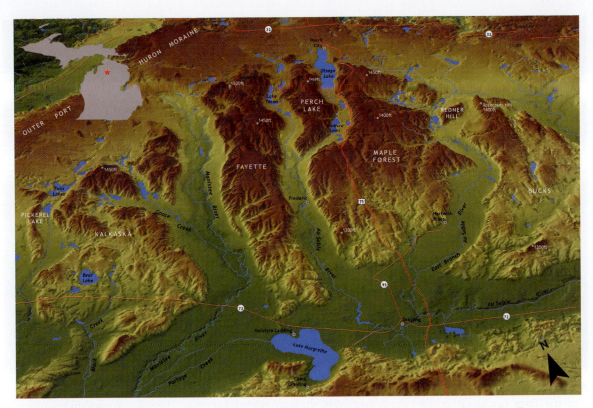

A12. THE GRAYLING FINGERS. These five, flat-topped ridges, separated by wide, flat-floored valleys, are known as the Grayling Fingers. They are composed of tens of meters of sand and gravel, deposited as the glacier that advanced into northern Michigan stalled at their northern margin, washing coarse-textured materials out in front. Later, during its retreat, the valleys were cut by meltwater.

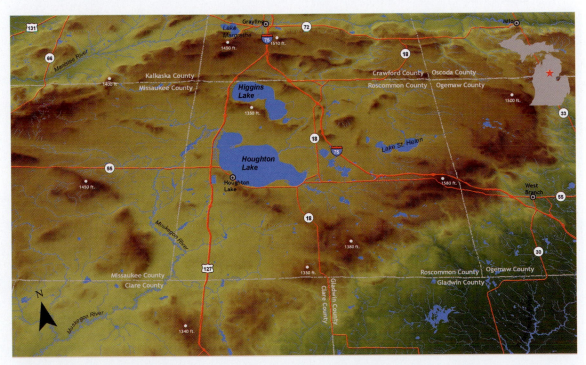

A13. THE HOUGHTON-HIGGINS LAKE FLATS. This high, sandy upland is surrounded by even higher and larger moraines of various kinds—the West Branch moraine on the SE, the Port Huron moraine on the north, and the Cadillac interlobate moraine on the west. Although not yet studied, it is likely that the intervening area was home to a large lake during deglaciation. The sandy lakebed sediments are, today, all dry, except for the shallow remnant of this former lake—Houghton Lake.

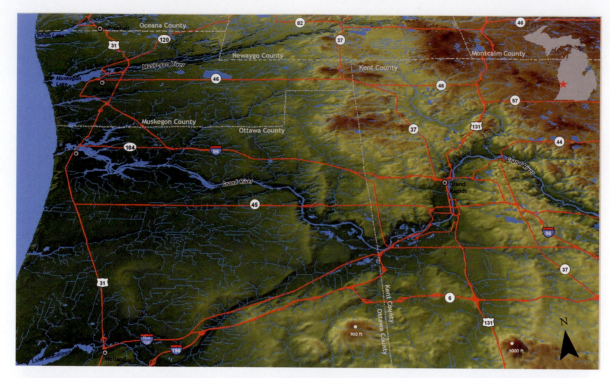

A14. THE LOWER GRAND RIVER VALLEY. The lower reaches of the Grand River is a classic example of an underfit steam, because its current size is dwarfed by the large valley it occupies. The valley is underfit because it once carried large amounts of water, draining from Glacial Lakes Saginaw and Maumee.

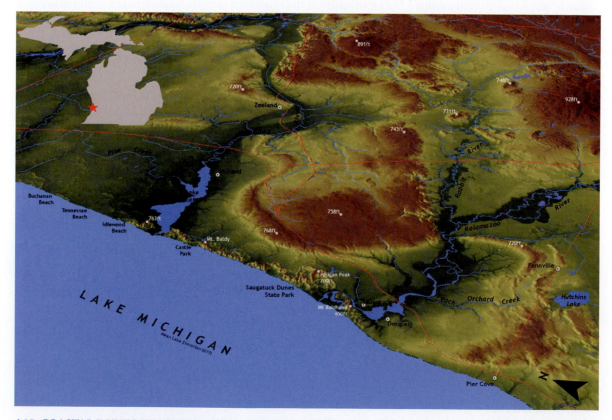

A15. COASTAL DUNES NEAR HOLLAND AND SAUGATUCK. Like many of Michigan's coastal dunes, the dunes near Holland are clustered near the shoreline. The sand source for these dunes is the beach, which helps explain their restricted distribution. Michigan's coastal dunes are some of the world's most impressive freshwater dunes.

A16. THE PORT HURON MORAINE AND TIP OF THE THUMB AREA. The Port Huron moraine is a prominent end moraine formed by a significant glacial readvance about15,200 years ago. Approaching from the north, where it abuts the flat landscape of the Saginaw Lake Plain, the ridge is truly an impressive feature. Meltwater from this advance spilled down the Cass River valley, filling it with sand.

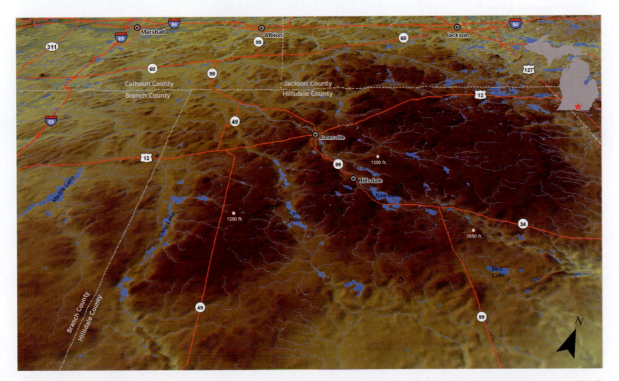

A17. THE IRISH HILLS. Perched atop the highest bedrock upland in the Lower Peninsula, formed by the Marshall Sandstone, the Irish Hills are a rolling, hilly region of forests and lakes. The elevation comes from the bedrock below, but the topography has its origins in its glacial history. This area was part of the SE Michigan Interlobate moraine (Plate 8B)—a region where many ice blocks became buried in sandy drift, only to later melt and form kettle lakes.

Appendix
B

Color Plates

PLATE 1

Legend:
- Interstate and Divided Highways
- U.S. Highways
- State Highways

1:3,950,029

0   30   60   120 Kilometers

KEWEENAW

MICHIGAN COUNTIES

N

ONTONAGON

HOUGHTON

BARAGA

GOGEBIC

MARQUETTE

IRON

ALGER

LUCE

DICKINSON

SCHOOLCRAFT

CHIPPEWA

MACKINAC

PLATE 2

DELTA

MENOMINEE

LEELANAU

EMMET

CHEBOYGAN

PRESQUE ISLE

CHARLEVOIX

ANTRIM

OTSEGO

MONTMORENCY

ALPENA

BENZIE

GRAND TRAVERSE

KALKASKA

CRAWFORD

OSCODA

ALCONA

MISSAUKEE

ROSCOMMON

OGEMAW

IOSCO

MANISTEE

WEXFORD

ARENAC

MASON

LAKE

OSCEOLA

CLARE

GLADWIN

HURON

BAY

OCEANA

NEWAYGO

MECOSTA

ISABELLA

MIDLAND

TUSCOLA

SANILAC

MUSKEGON

MONTCALM

GRATIOT

SAGINAW

KENT

SHIAWASSEE

GENESEE

LAPEER

ST. CLAIR

OTTAWA

IONIA

CLINTON

LIVINGSTON

OAKLAND

MACOMB

ALLEGAN

BARRY

EATON

INGHAM

VAN BUREN

KALAMAZOO

CALHOUN

JACKSON

WASHTENAW

WAYNE

MONROE

BERRIEN

CASS

ST. JOSEPH

BRANCH

HILLSDALE

LENAWEE

1:3,950,029

0   30   60   120 Kilometers

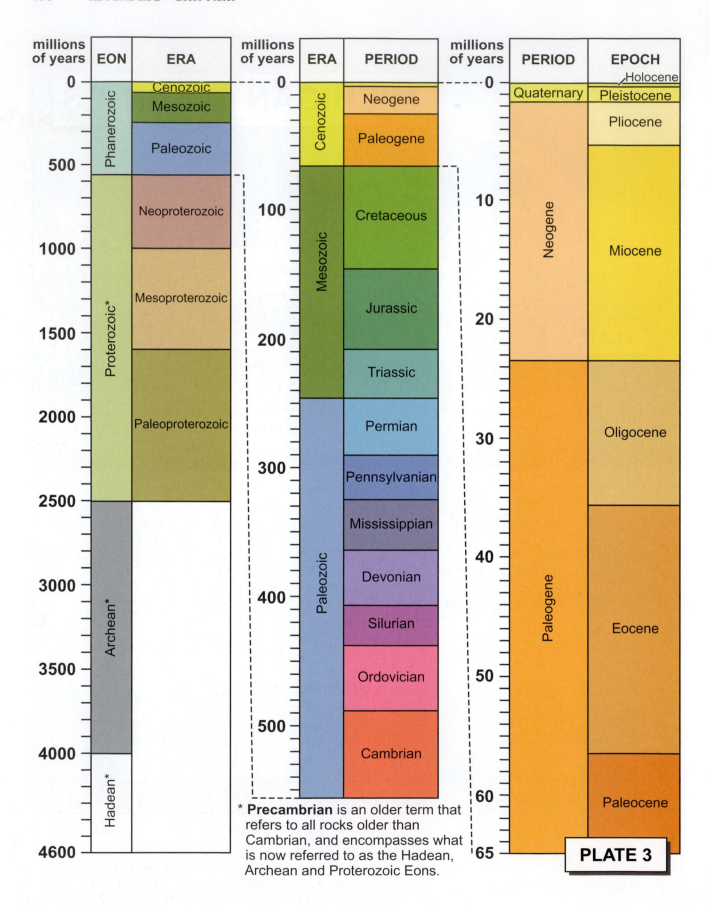

millions of years	EON	ERA
0	Phanerozoic	Cenozoic
		Mesozoic
500		Paleozoic
	Proterozoic*	Neoproterozoic
1000		Mesoproterozoic
1500		
		Paleoproterozoic
2000		
2500		
3000	Archean*	
3500		
4000		
	Hadean*	
4600		

millions of years	ERA	PERIOD
0	Cenozoic	Neogene
		Paleogene
100	Mesozoic	Cretaceous
		Jurassic
200		Triassic
	Paleozoic	Permian
300		Pennsylvanian
		Mississippian
400		Devonian
		Silurian
		Ordovician
500		Cambrian

* **Precambrian** is an older term that refers to all rocks older than Cambrian, and encompasses what is now referred to as the Hadean, Archean and Proterozoic Eons.

millions of years	PERIOD	EPOCH
0	Quaternary	Holocene
		Pleistocene
	Neogene	Pliocene
10		Miocene
20		
30	Paleogene	Oligocene
40		Eocene
50		
60		Paleocene
65		

PLATE 3

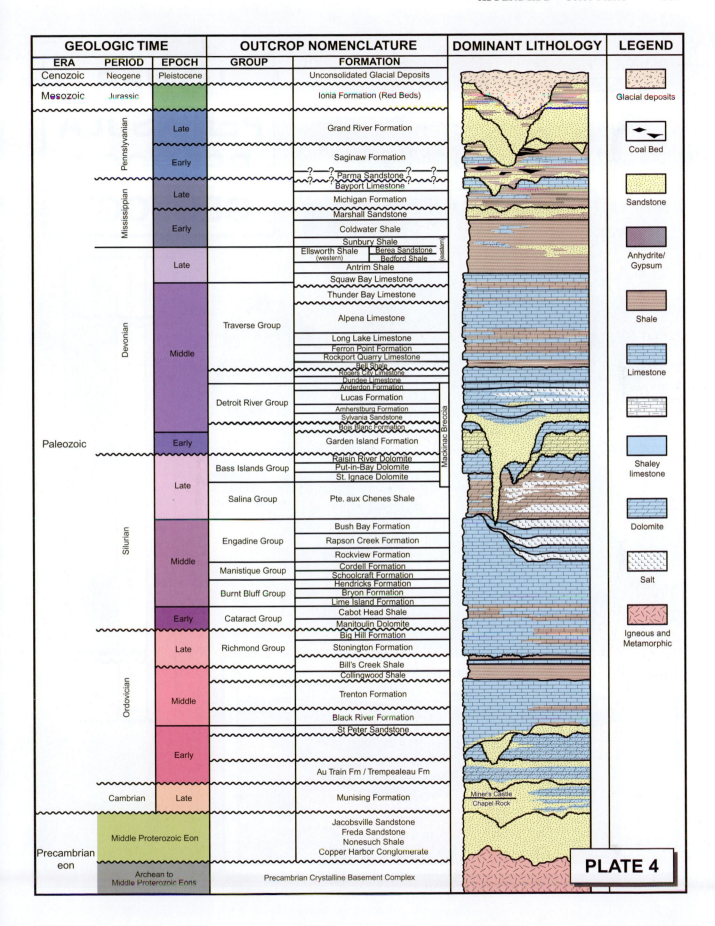

GEOLOGIC TIME			OUTCROP NOMENCLATURE		DOMINANT LITHOLOGY	LEGEND
ERA	PERIOD	EPOCH	GROUP	FORMATION		
Cenozoic	Neogene	Pleistocene		Unconsolidated Glacial Deposits		Glacial deposits
Mesozoic	Jurassic			Ionia Formation (Red Beds)		Coal Bed
Paleozoic	Pennsylvanian	Late		Grand River Formation		Sandstone
		Early		Saginaw Formation		
				? ? Parma Sandstone ? ?		
	Mississippian	Late		Bayport Limestone		Anhydrite/ Gypsum
				Michigan Formation		
				Marshall Sandstone		
		Early		Coldwater Shale		Shale
				Sunbury Shale		
	Devonian	Late		Ellsworth Shale (western) / Berea Sandstone (eastern) / Bedford Shale		Limestone
				Antrim Shale		
				Squaw Bay Limestone		
		Middle	Traverse Group	Thunder Bay Limestone		
				Alpena Limestone		Shaley limestone
				Long Lake Limestone		
				Ferron Point Formation		
				Rockport Quarry Limestone		Dolomite
				Bell Shale		
				Rogers City Limestone		
				Dundee Limestone		Salt
			Detroit River Group	Anderdon Formation		
				Lucas Formation		
				Amherstburg Formation		Igneous and Metamorphic
				Sylvania Sandstone		
				Bois Blanc Formation		
		Early		Garden Island Formation		
	Silurian	Late	Bass Islands Group	Raisin River Dolomite		
				Put-in-Bay Dolomite		
				St. Ignace Dolomite		
			Salina Group	Pte. aux Chenes Shale		
		Middle	Engadine Group	Bush Bay Formation		
				Rapson Creek Formation		
				Rockview Formation		
			Manistique Group	Cordell Formation		
				Schoolcraft Formation		
			Burnt Bluff Group	Hendricks Formation		
				Bryon Formation		
				Lime Island Formation		
		Early	Cataract Group	Cabot Head Shale		
				Manitoulin Dolomite		
	Ordovician	Late	Richmond Group	Big Hill Formation		
				Stonington Formation		
				Bill's Creek Shale		
		Middle		Collingwood Shale		
				Trenton Formation		
				Black River Formation		
		Early		St Peter Sandstone		
				Au Train Fm / Trempealeau Fm		
	Cambrian	Late		Munising Formation		
Precambrian eon	Middle Proterozoic Eon			Jacobsville Sandstone / Freda Sandstone / Nonesuch Shale / Copper Harbor Conglomerate		
	Archean to Middle Proterozoic Eons			Precambrian Crystalline Basement Complex		

Mackinac Breccia

Miner's Castle
Chapel Rock

PLATE 4

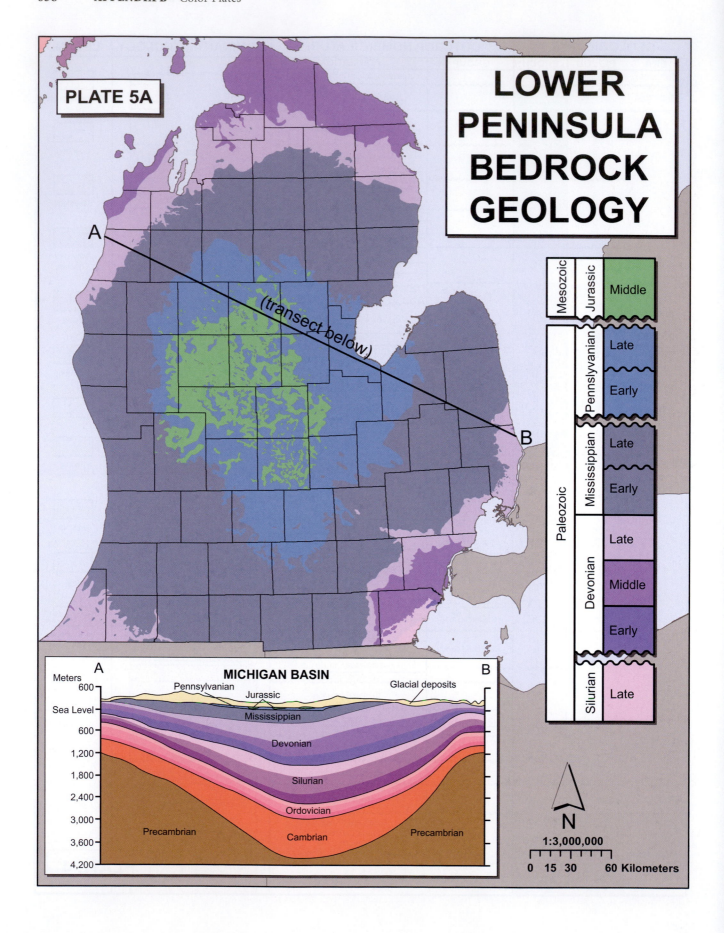

PLATE 5A

LOWER PENINSULA BEDROCK GEOLOGY

(transect below)

A

B

Mesozoic — Jurassic — Middle

Paleozoic
Pennslyvanian — Late / Early
Mississippian — Late / Early
Devonian — Late / Middle / Early
Silurian — Late

MICHIGAN BASIN

Meters
A   B
600   Pennsylvanian   Jurassic   Glacial deposits
Sea Level   Mississippian
600   Devonian
1,200
1,800   Silurian
2,400   Ordovician
3,000   Precambrian   Cambrian   Precambrian
3,600
4,200

N

1:3,000,000

0   15 30   60 Kilometers

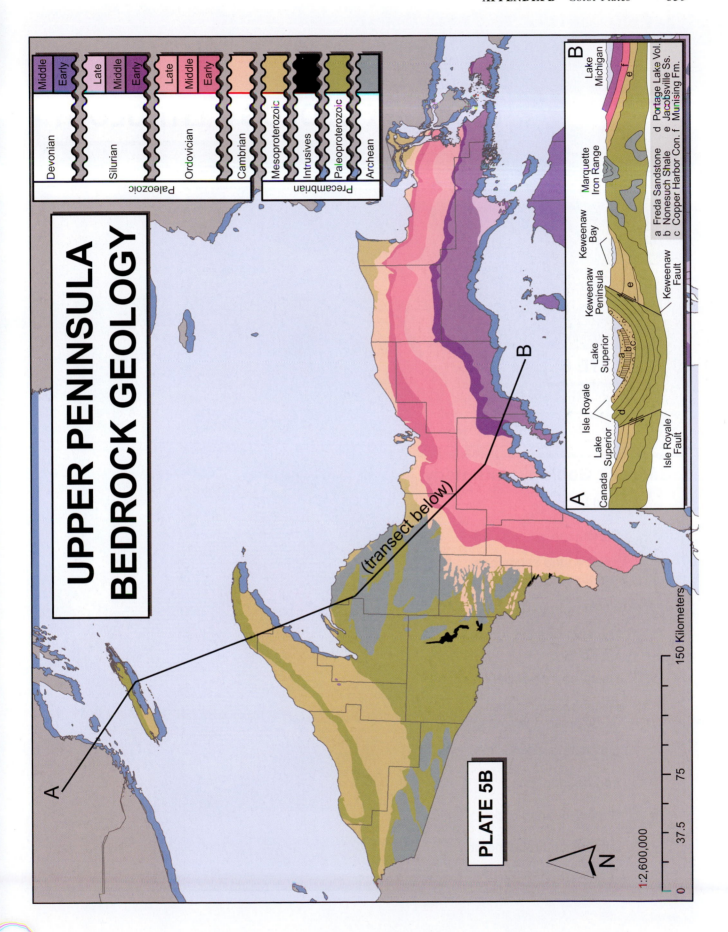

UPPER PENINSULA BEDROCK GEOLOGY

PLATE 5B

1:2,600,000

0   37.5   75   150 Kilometers

N

(transect below)

A

B

Legend

Paleozoic

Devonian — Middle, Early
Silurian — Late, Middle, Early
Ordovician — Late, Middle, Early
Cambrian

Precambrian

Mesoproterozoic
Intrusives
Paleoproterozoic
Archean

Cross-section A–B

Canada — Lake Superior — Isle Royale — Lake Superior — Keweenaw Peninsula — Keweenaw Bay — Marquette Iron Range — Lake Michigan

Isle Royale Fault — Keweenaw Fault

a Freda Sandstone
b Nonesuch Shale
c Copper Harbor Con.
d Portage Lake Vol.
e Jacobsville Ss.
f Munising Fm.

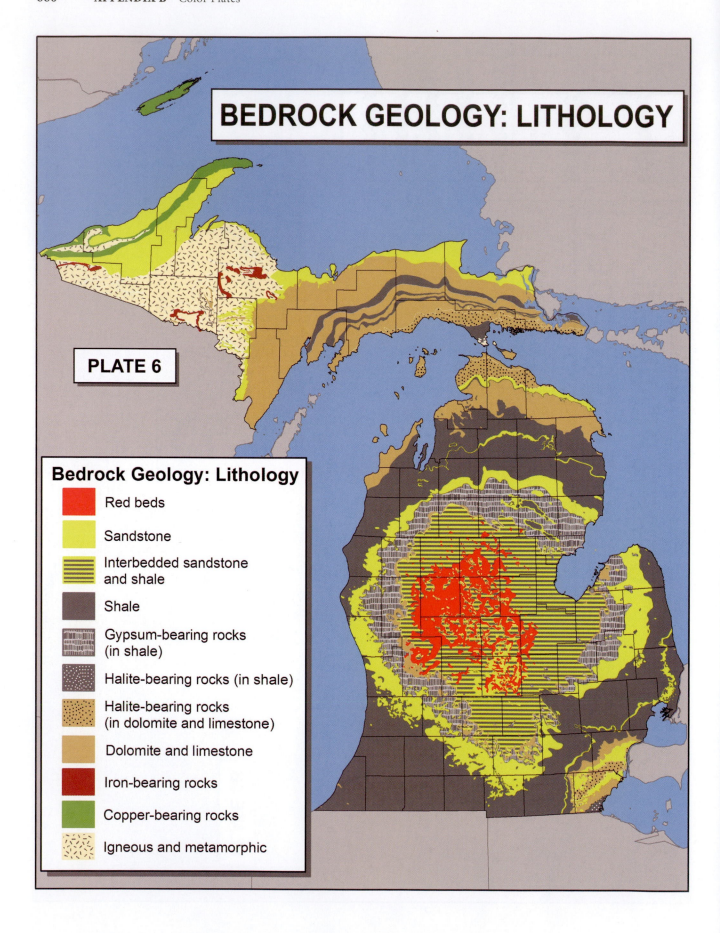

BEDROCK GEOLOGY: LITHOLOGY

PLATE 6

Bedrock Geology: Lithology

- Red beds
- Sandstone
- Interbedded sandstone and shale
- Shale
- Gypsum-bearing rocks (in shale)
- Halite-bearing rocks (in shale)
- Halite-bearing rocks (in dolomite and limestone)
- Dolomite and limestone
- Iron-bearing rocks
- Copper-bearing rocks
- Igneous and metamorphic

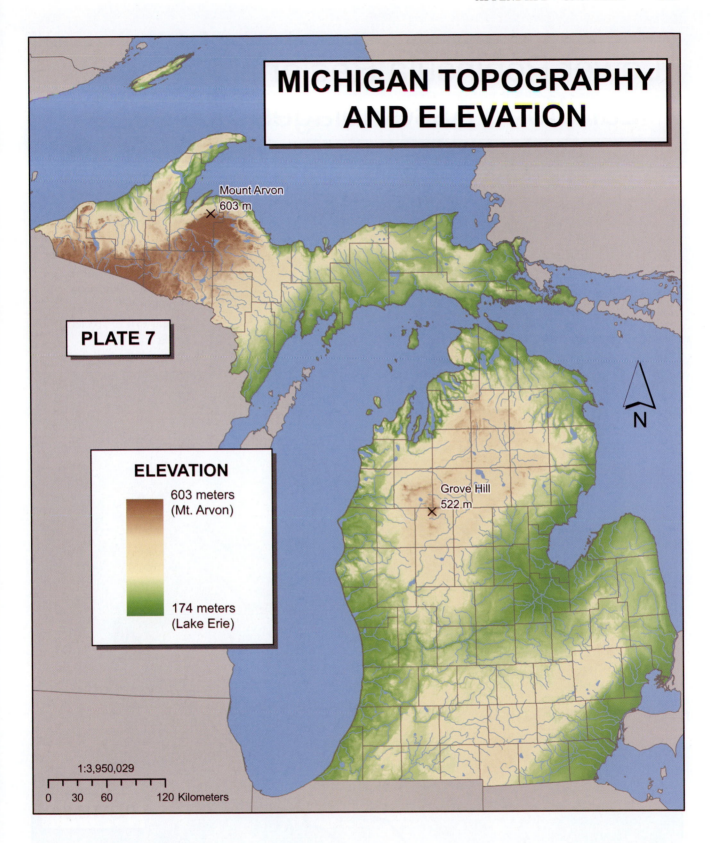

MICHIGAN TOPOGRAPHY AND ELEVATION

PLATE 7

Mount Arvon
603 m

Grove Hill
522 m

N

ELEVATION

603 meters
(Mt. Arvon)

174 meters
(Lake Erie)

1:3,950,029

0   30   60   120 Kilometers

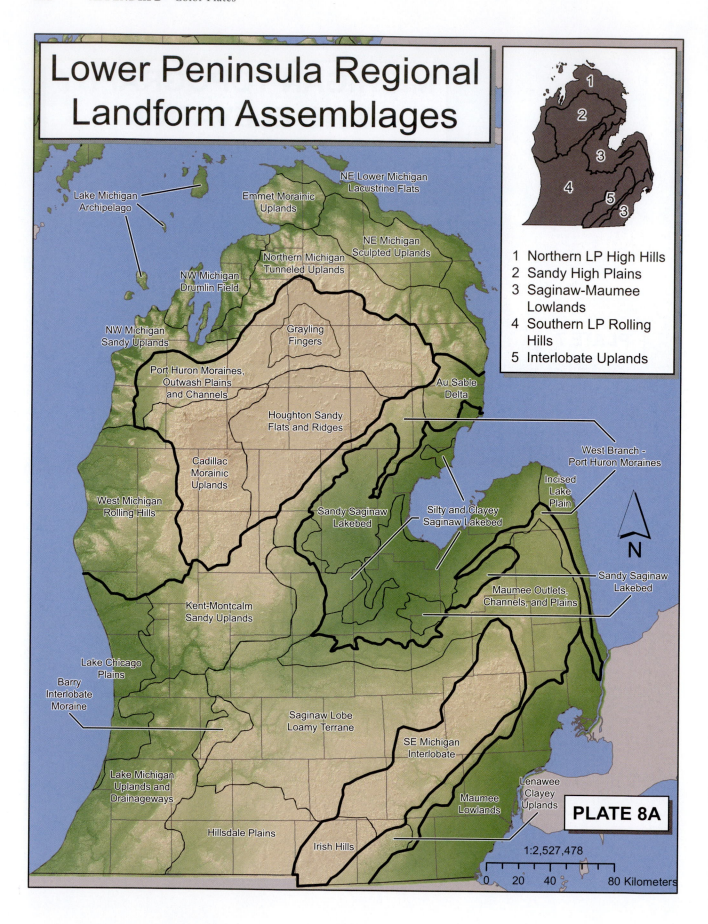

Lower Peninsula Regional Landform Assemblages

1 Northern LP High Hills
2 Sandy High Plains
3 Saginaw-Maumee Lowlands
4 Southern LP Rolling Hills
5 Interlobate Uplands

Lake Michigan Archipelago

NE Lower Michigan Lacustrine Flats

Emmet Morainic Uplands

NE Michigan Sculpted Uplands

Northern Michigan Tunneled Uplands

NW Michigan Drumlin Field

Grayling Fingers

NW Michigan Sandy Uplands

Port Huron Moraines, Outwash Plains and Channels

Au Sable Delta

Houghton Sandy Flats and Ridges

West Branch - Port Huron Moraines

Cadillac Morainic Uplands

Incised Lake Plain

West Michigan Rolling Hills

Sandy Saginaw Lakebed

Silty and Clayey Saginaw Lakebed

Sandy Saginaw Lakebed

Kent-Montcalm Sandy Uplands

Maumee Outlets, Channels, and Plains

Lake Chicago Plains

Barry Interlobate Moraine

Saginaw Lobe Loamy Terrane

SE Michigan Interlobate

Lenawee Clayey Uplands

Lake Michigan Uplands and Drainageways

Maumee Lowlands

PLATE 8A

Hillsdale Plains

Irish Hills

N

1:2,527,478

0   20   40   80 Kilometers

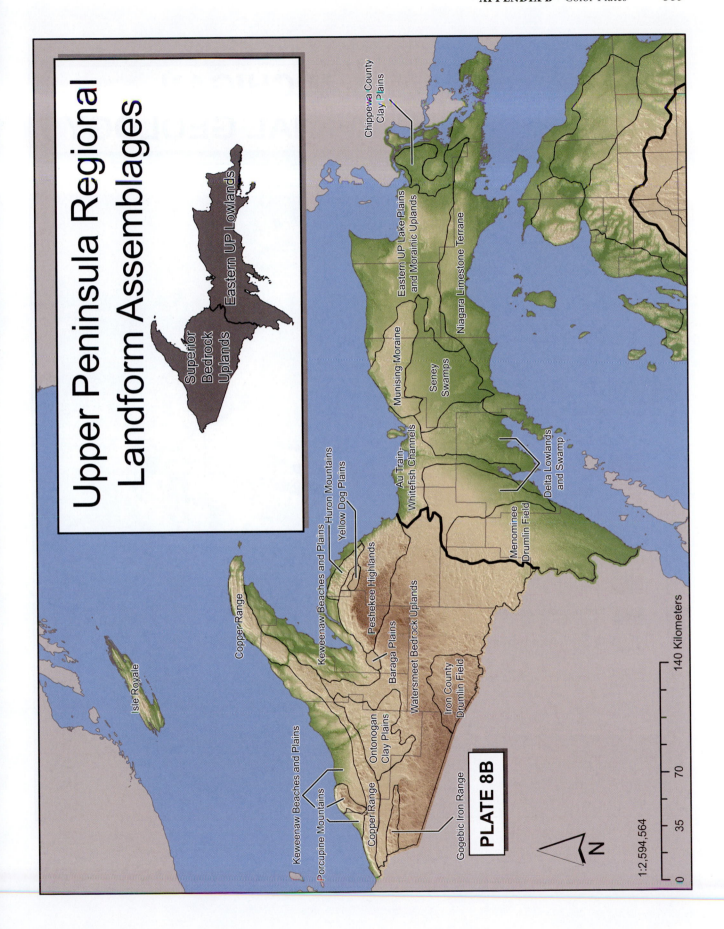

Upper Peninsula Regional Landform Assemblages

Superior Bedrock Uplands

Eastern UP Lowlands

Chippewa County Clay Plains

Eastern UP Lake Plains and Morainic Uplands

Niagara Limestone Terrane

Munising Moraine

Seney Swamps

Au Train-Whitefish Channels

Delta Lowlands and Swamp

Menominee Drumlin Field

Huron Mountains

Yellow Dog Plains

Keweenaw Beaches and Plains

Peshekee Highlands

Baraga Plains

Watersmeet Bedrock Uplands

Iron County Drumlin Field

Copper Range

Isle Royale

Keweenaw Beaches and Plains

Porcupine Mountains

Copper Range

Ontonogan Clay Plains

Gogebic Iron Range

PLATE 8B

1:2,594,564

0   35   70   140 Kilometers

N

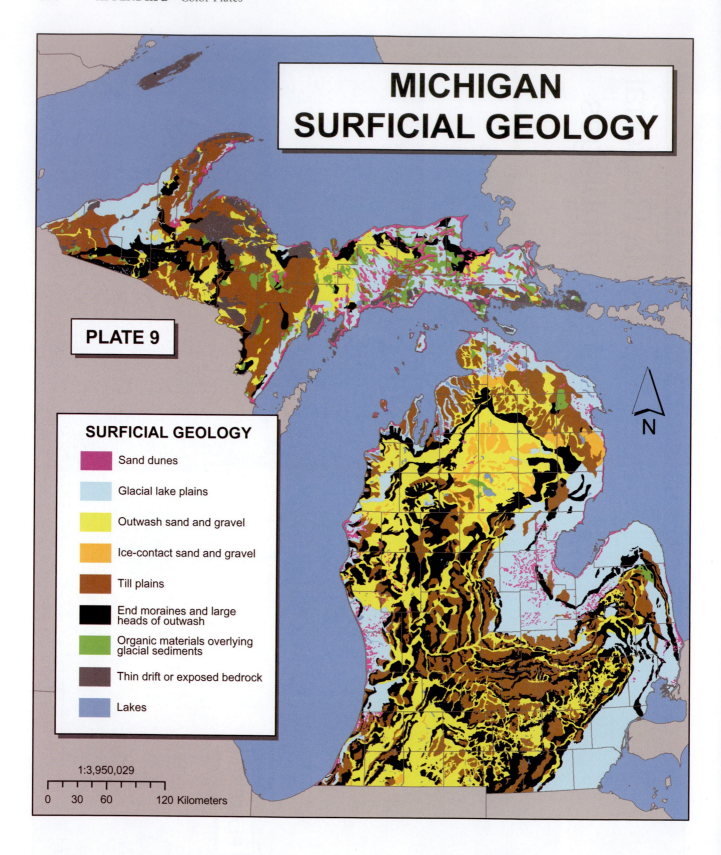

MICHIGAN SURFICIAL GEOLOGY

PLATE 9

N

SURFICIAL GEOLOGY

- Sand dunes
- Glacial lake plains
- Outwash sand and gravel
- Ice-contact sand and gravel
- Till plains
- End moraines and large heads of outwash
- Organic materials overlying glacial sediments
- Thin drift or exposed bedrock
- Lakes

1:3,950,029

0   30   60   120 Kilometers

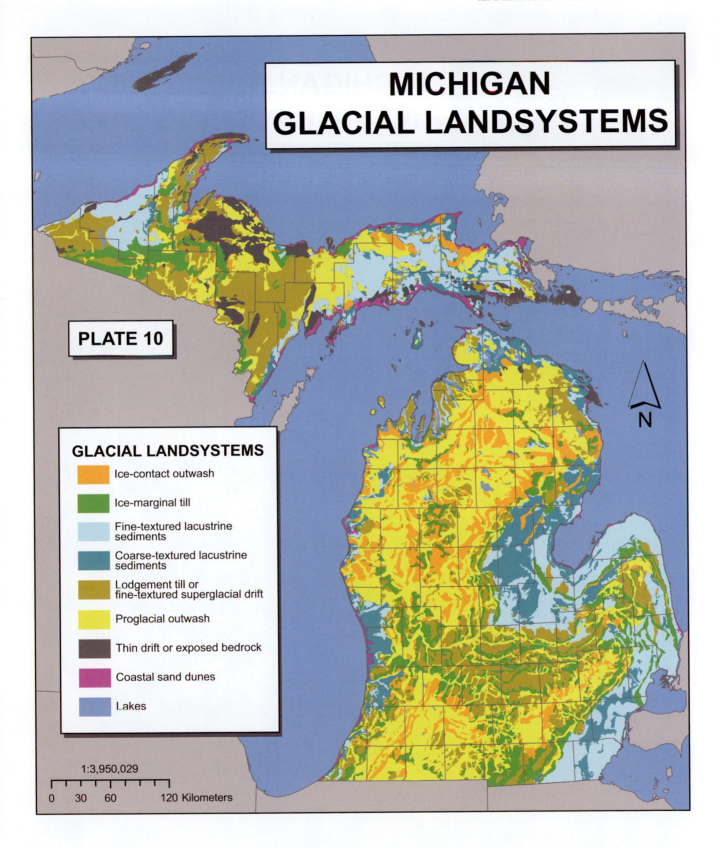

MICHIGAN GLACIAL LANDSYSTEMS

PLATE 10

GLACIAL LANDSYSTEMS

- Ice-contact outwash
- Ice-marginal till
- Fine-textured lacustrine sediments
- Coarse-textured lacustrine sediments
- Lodgement till or fine-textured superglacial drift
- Proglacial outwash
- Thin drift or exposed bedrock
- Coastal sand dunes
- Lakes

1:3,950,029

0 30 60   120 Kilometers

N

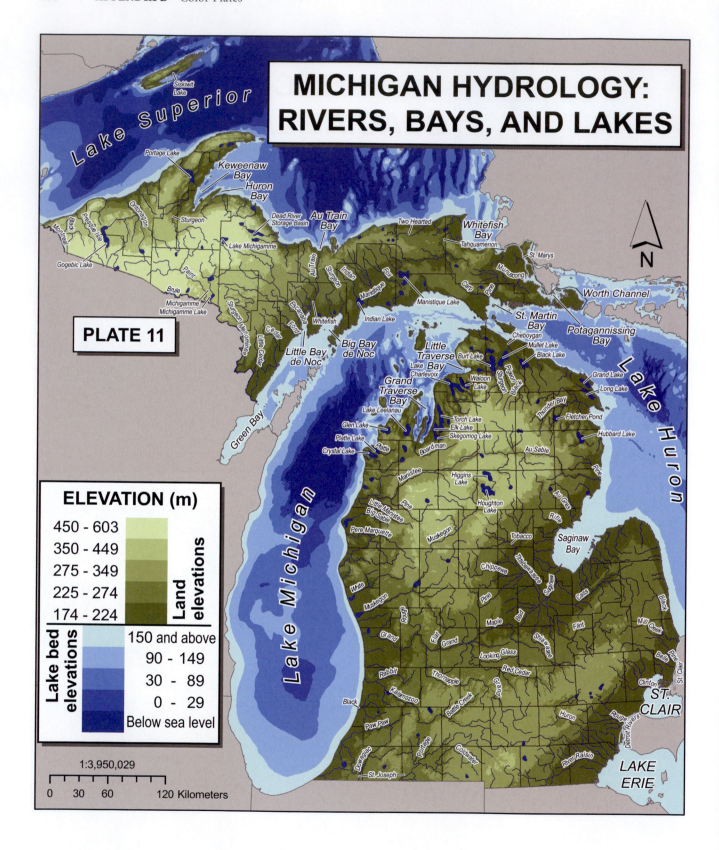

MICHIGAN HYDROLOGY: RIVERS, BAYS, AND LAKES

PLATE 11

ELEVATION (m)

450 - 603	
350 - 449	Land elevations
275 - 349	
225 - 274	
174 - 224	

Lake bed elevations

150 and above	
90 - 149	
30 - 89	
0 - 29	
Below sea level	

1:3,950,029

0   30   60   120 Kilometers

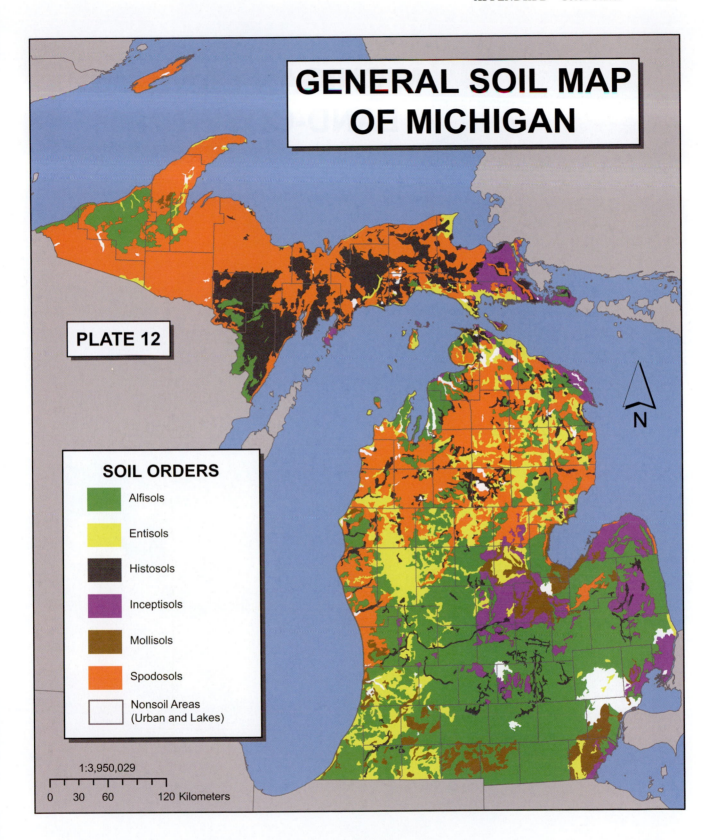

GENERAL SOIL MAP OF MICHIGAN

PLATE 12

SOIL ORDERS

- Alfisols
- Entisols
- Histosols
- Inceptisols
- Mollisols
- Spodosols
- Nonsoil Areas (Urban and Lakes)

N

1:3,950,029

0   30   60   120 Kilometers

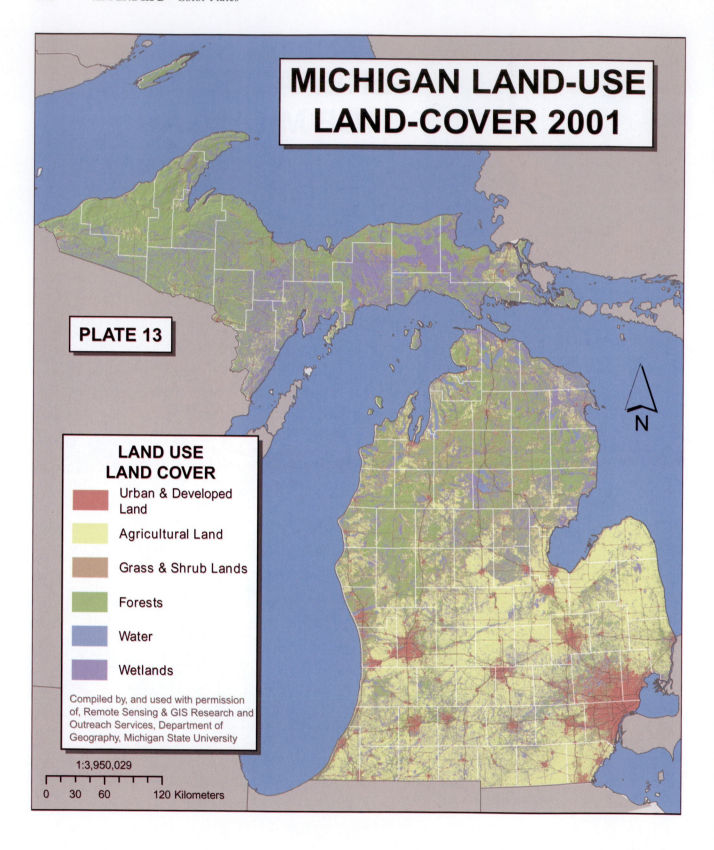

MICHIGAN LAND-USE LAND-COVER 2001

PLATE 13

LAND USE LAND COVER

- Urban & Developed Land
- Agricultural Land
- Grass & Shrub Lands
- Forests
- Water
- Wetlands

Compiled by, and used with permission of, Remote Sensing & GIS Research and Outreach Services, Department of Geography, Michigan State University

1:3,950,029

0   30   60   120 Kilometers

N

MICHIGAN PUBLIC LANDS

PLATE 14

Public Land Ownership

- National Forest
- National Parks, Lakeshore, and Wildlife Refuges
- State Forest
- Other State Lands

1:3,950,029

0   30   60   120 Kilometers

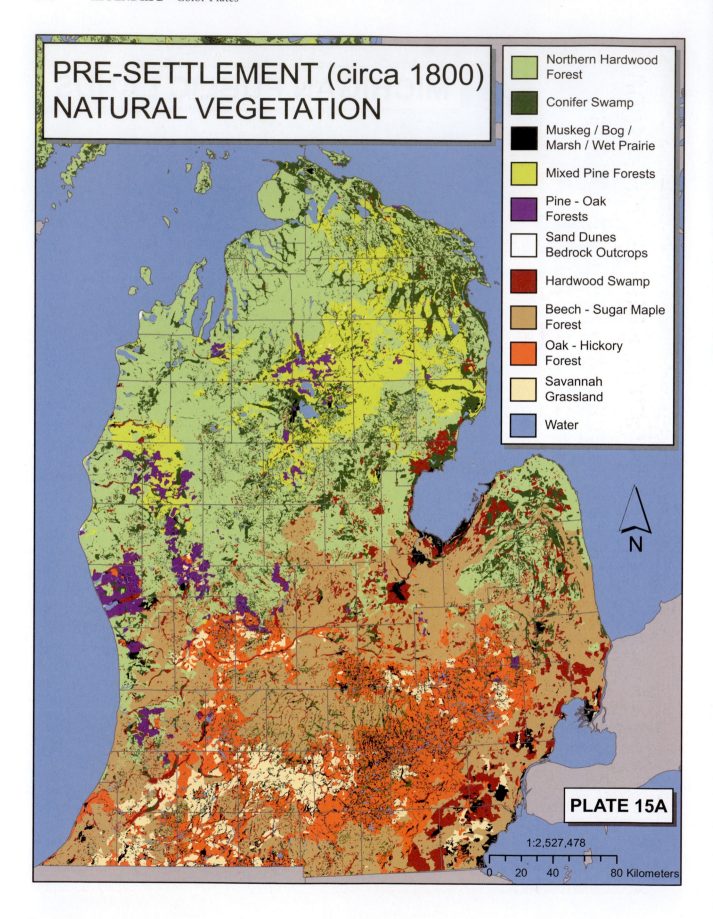

PRE-SETTLEMENT (circa 1800) NATURAL VEGETATION

Legend:
- Northern Hardwood Forest
- Conifer Swamp
- Muskeg / Bog / Marsh / Wet Prairie
- Mixed Pine Forests
- Pine - Oak Forests
- Sand Dunes Bedrock Outcrops
- Hardwood Swamp
- Beech - Sugar Maple Forest
- Oak - Hickory Forest
- Savannah Grassland
- Water

1:2,527,478

0   20   40   80 Kilometers

N

PLATE 15A

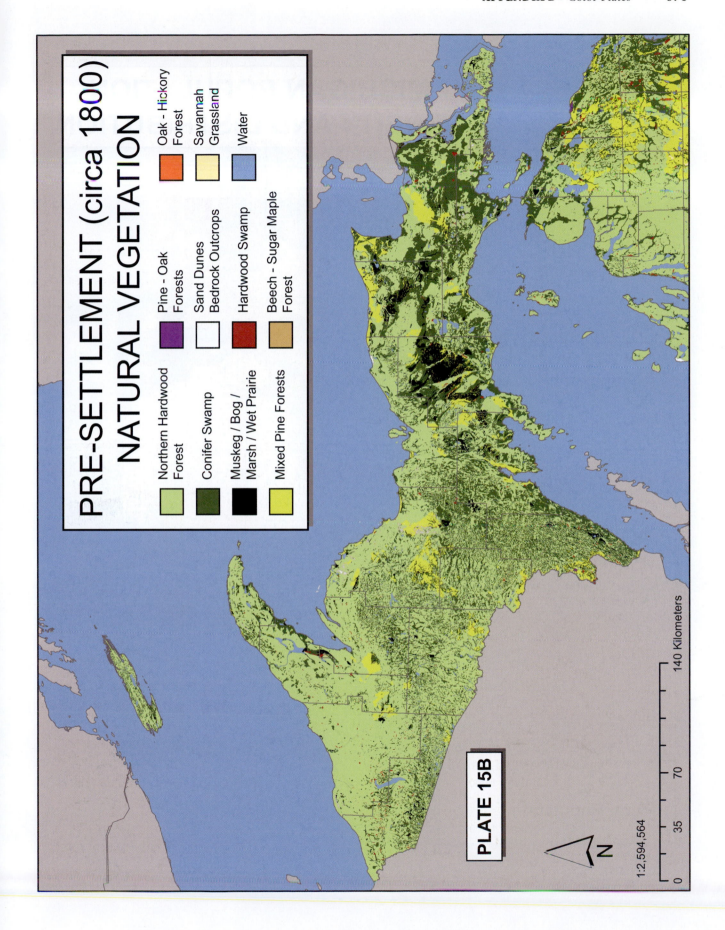

PRE-SETTLEMENT (circa 1800) NATURAL VEGETATION

Northern Hardwood Forest

Conifer Swamp

Muskeg / Bog / Marsh / Wet Prairie

Mixed Pine Forests

Pine - Oak Forests

Sand Dunes Bedrock Outcrops

Hardwood Swamp

Beech - Sugar Maple Forest

Oak - Hickory Forest

Savannah Grassland

Water

PLATE 15B

1:2,594,564

0   35   70   140 Kilometers

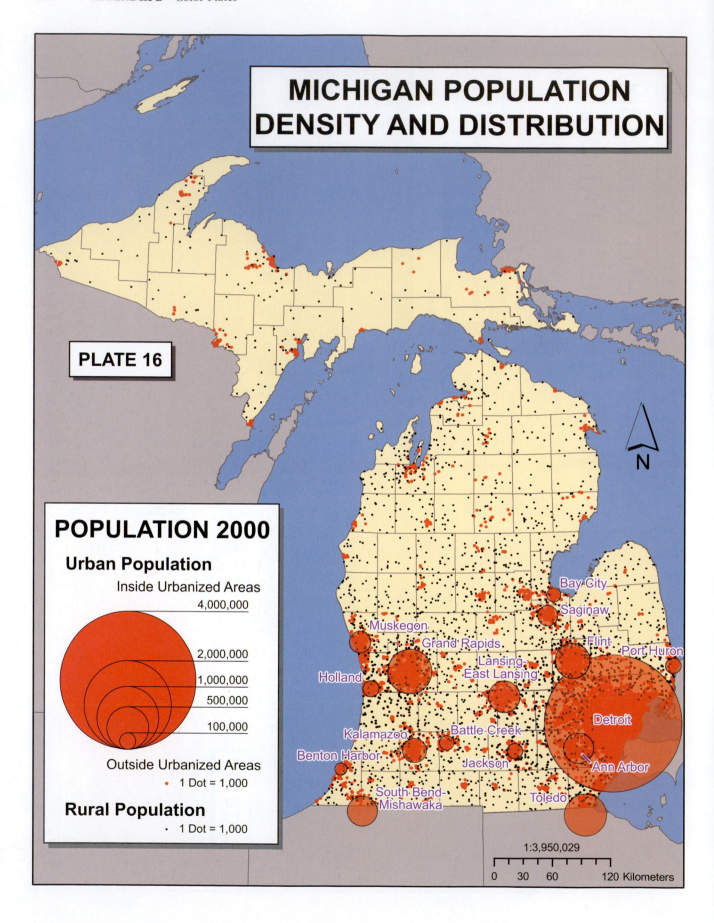

MICHIGAN POPULATION DENSITY AND DISTRIBUTION

PLATE 16

POPULATION 2000

Urban Population

Inside Urbanized Areas

4,000,000

2,000,000
1,000,000
500,000

100,000

Outside Urbanized Areas
• 1 Dot = 1,000

Rural Population
• 1 Dot = 1,000

Bay City
Saginaw
Muskegon
Grand Rapids
Flint
Port Huron
Lansing-
East Lansing
Holland
Detroit
Kalamazoo
Battle Creek
Benton Harbor
Jackson
Ann Arbor
South Bend-
Mishawaka
Toledo

1:3,950,029

0   30   60   120 Kilometers

N